America and the Sea:
A Maritime History

The American Maritime Library: Volume XV

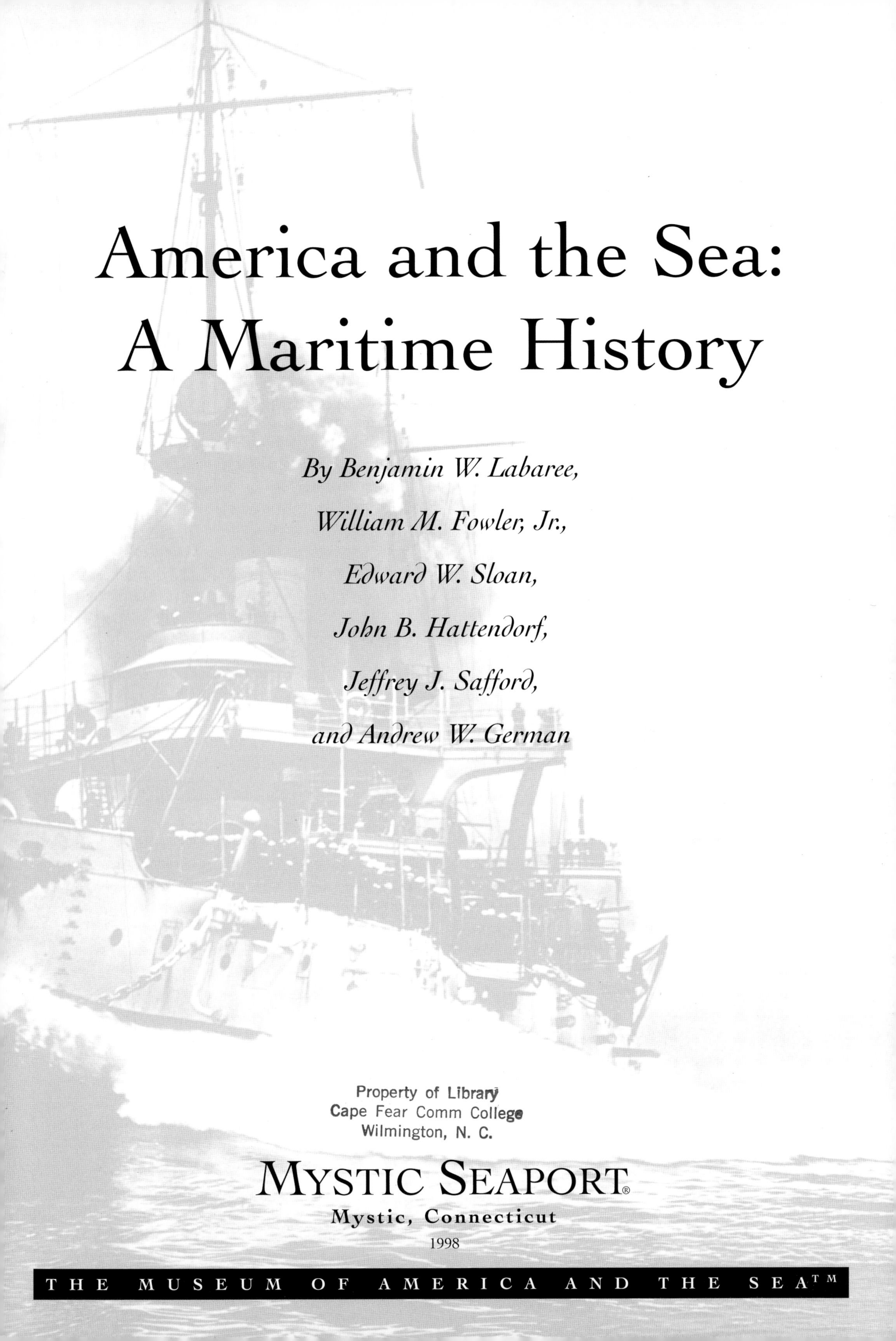

America and the Sea: A Maritime History

By Benjamin W. Labaree,

William M. Fowler, Jr.,

Edward W. Sloan,

John B. Hattendorf,

Jeffrey J. Safford,

and Andrew W. German

MYSTIC SEAPORT®

Mystic, Connecticut

1998

THE MUSEUM OF AMERICA AND THE SEA™

Mystic Seaport Museum, Inc., Mystic, CT 06355-0990
First edition
Second Printing
Printed in Hong Kong

Cataloging-in-Publication Data

America and the sea : a maritime history / by Benjamin W. Labaree ...
    [et al.]. – 1st ed. – Mystic, Conn. : Mystic Seaport Museum, 1998.
        p. : ill., maps ;   cm. – (American maritime library ; v. 15)
    Bibliography: p.
    Includes index.

    1. United States - History. 2. United States - History, Naval.
3. United States - Commerce - History. 4. Merchant marine - United
States - History. I. Labaree, Benjamin Woods, 1927-

E183.9.A43
ISBN 0-913372-81-1

Maps © Dennis O'Brien and Mystic Seaport Museum, Inc.

Book and jacket design by Trish Sinsigalli LaPointe, Old Mystic, Connecticut

Quotations from "Once by the Pacific" and "Neither Far Out Nor in Deep," by Robert Frost, from:
The Poetry of Robert Frost, edited by Edward Connery Lathem, Copyright 1936, 1956 by Robert Frost,
Copyright 1928, 1969 by Henry Holt and Company Inc., 1964 by Leslie Frost Ballantine.
Reprinted by permission of Henry Holt and Company, Inc.

Excerpt from "The Dry Salvages" in *Four Quartets*, copyright 1943 by T.S. Eliot and renewed 1971 by
Esme Valerie Eliot, reprinted by permission of Harcourt Brace & Company.

Excerpts from *The Edge of the Sea* by Rachel Carson. Copyright 1955 by Rachel Carson, renewed 1983
by Roger Christie. Reprinted by permission of Houghton Mifflin Company. All rights reserved.

Mystic Seaport gratefully acknowledges the Henry Luce Foundation as provider
of the financial support to make this publication possible.

Illustrations credited to M.S.M. are in the collections of Mystic Seaport.

Title-page illustration:
The USS *Connecticut* at full speed, 1906. Photograph by Enrique Muller. (M.S.M. 59.1275)

In Memory of Jerry Morris
Librarian, Publisher, Friend, and Inspiration for This Volume

Acknowledgments

Bringing to print a comprehensive study of a subject as broad as "America and the Sea" requires the support of many colleagues and friends, far too numerous to be individually cited here. In our selected bibliography we authors have acknowledged our debt to the work of more than 250 other historians, but the list of books and articles we consulted could easily have been doubled had space permitted. Some of these scholars read parts of our manuscript; others made suggestions that we have incorporated into our text. To them all we give our thanks.

We would particularly like to thank the many staff members at Mystic Seaport Museum who over the years have so greatly enhanced our teaching of maritime history at the Frank C. Munson Institute. We are also grateful to the museum's trustees, its director, and the other members of senior staff for their continuing support of the Institute, enabling us to offer our courses at the nation's leading maritime museum. We wish to express our appreciation to the museum's Publications Department and to the Henry R. Luce Foundation, whose generosity has made this book possible.

Most of all we as teaching scholars acknowledge our debt to the students who have taken our courses both at Mystic and at our home campuses. Without their interest, their research, and especially their persistent questioning, this book would never have been written.

We have dedicated this volume to the memory of a person whose entire professional life epitomized these contributions. Jerry Morris was one of the first students to enroll in the Munson Institute when it opened in 1955. During the next decade he played an important role in creating the G.W. Blunt White Library at Mystic Seaport Museum. Later, as head of that library, he assisted thousands of scholars, students and visitors in their research; and as head of the museum's Publications Department he enabled much of their scholarship to be put into print. During the last years of his life Jerry constantly reminded the authors of this book of the need for a comprehensive history of America and the sea, admonishing us "for heavens sake, put your heads together and write it!" We promised him we would do so, and we have at last fulfilled that promise—too late, alas, for those pithy comments of his that would have made it a better book.

Contents

Foreword   IX
Introduction   3

Part 1: Becoming America, to 1815   17

1   The Beginnings   18

2   The Rise of English America, 1660-1760   54

3   To American Independence   96

4   Maritime Dimensions of Revolution and Confederation   128

5   Maritime Affairs in the New Republic   164

6   Embargo and War   200

Part 2: The Expanding Nation, 1815-1865   235

7   Maritime Developments in an Age of Optimism   236

8   Maritime America in a Wider World   276

9   Modern Technology, Modern Warfare, and the Troubled Course of American Maritime and Naval Enterprise   322

Part 3: Rise to World Power, 1865-1939   363

10   The Sea and Post-Civil-War America   364

11   The Rise of Maritime Professionalism and Regulation   402

12   Expansion and Transformation of Maritime America   436

13   World War I   476

14   The Interwar Years   510

Part 4: World War II and After, 1939-   549

15   World War II   550

16   American Maritime and Naval Policy Since World War II   590

17   Americans Take to the Sea   628

Appendix: American Maritime Museums   662
Select Bibliography   664
Contributors   674
Index   676

Foreword

T IS DIFFICULT TO identify the moment of conception of this book. It could have been almost seventy years ago, when the museum that today is Mystic Seaport was founded. Perhaps it was almost fifty years ago, when Mystic Seaport recognized its role in university-level teaching and established the Frank C. Munson Institute. It might have been five years ago, when the Museum's staff and Trustees engaged in a strategic planning process and examined our role in the preservation of American maritime history. The book's beginnings may be found in all three of these events, and in many other moments in Mystic Seaport's development, which have collectively made it the extraordinary maritime museum and educational center it is on the eve of the new millennium.

The three founders of the Marine Historical Association, which has become Mystic Seaport, established the Museum on Christmas Day in 1929, motivated by their concern for the loss of artifacts and documents related to the maritime heritage of Mystic, Connecticut, and especially the Mystic River's shipbuilding traditions. The three founders had an even broader vision, which they expressed during the 1930s and which set the institution on the path toward its current role. They perceived that the maritime history of the nation was being lost or forgotten, and their objective was to see it preserved.

After the struggles of the Great Depression and World War II were passed, the Museum began to take on its present physical and intellectual shape. Exhibit galleries were created and historic ships were rescued, as were historic maritime structures that were threatened with destruction. In the years just after the war, the Museum established its library and its education department, key elements in fulfilling its broad educational mission. Within a few more years the Munson Institute, which would teach maritime history at the graduate level during the summer months, was established and began to attract the best scholars working in the field.

For almost fifty years the Institute's visiting faculty members have conveyed the American maritime story to scholars, college and high school teachers, graduate students, and museum professionals from around the country.

In the late 1980s, as part of its normal planning cycle, Mystic Seaport began a strategic planning process. We looked at our strengths and weaknesses and examined our internal structure and the environment in which the institution existed. Because of the physical dominance of our outdoor exhibits of buildings and ships representing nineteenth-century maritime New England, many perceived Mystic Seaport as a New England museum. We had, however, been functioning for decades under a statement of purpose that called for the much broader mission "to enhance man's knowledge and understanding of the sea's influence on American life."

From our planning work, we recognized that no museum in the country was telling the broad story of America and the sea, and that Mystic Seaport through its library, sponsored research, symposia, the Munson Institute, the Williams College-Mystic Seaport Maritime Studies Program, interpretive programs, exhibits, and publications was indeed accomplishing much of that goal. We established a revised mission to "create a broad public understanding of the relationship of America and the sea," and made it our goal to be, increasingly and substantially, the Museum of America and the Sea. The ideals of the Museum's founding, the involvement of leading scholars in our Munson Institute, and the new national focus of our mission, have brought about this book.

This book, in turn, is fundamental to much of the other business of accomplishing our mission, since all our projects and programs must be established on the foundation of solid scholarship. It was clear that no existing volume provided comprehensive coverage of the maritime history of the United States. It was also clear that it would be a difficult task for any one author to write such a book. The faculty members of the Museum's Munson Institute rose to the challenge and have masterfully covered this very complex subject in a way that can be easily comprehended. The work of Ben Labaree, Ted Sloan, Bill Fowler, Jeff Safford, and John Hattendorf reflects their years of scholarship

and experience as professors teaching the maritime history of the nation. Their writing has been complemented by the insightful editing of Mystic Seaport editor and researcher Andy German, who has also done a superb job as the book's picture editor. The book has also been enhanced by the specifically focused contributions of a number of other scholars whose work increases the depth and subtlety of the discussion.

In order to make this important publication available to as broad an audience as possible, we sought and received support from the Henry Luce Foundation. We were encouraged that this prestigious foundation would recognize both the need for this book and the caliber of those writing and preparing it for publication. While we initially set an earlier date for publication, it was realized that a better book would result if a bit more time was allowed. Once again, the Henry Luce Foundation saw the merits of this plan, and there is no doubt that the book is stronger because of this extra time and effort.

This volume is one of the initiatives undertaken by Mystic Seaport to fulfill its mission. Through its text, its vignettes, its illustrations, and its bibliography, it provides the public with a full and sophisticated understanding of the relationship of America and the sea. It is a book that will serve those conversant with our maritime history, those new to the subject, and those students approaching the topic as part of an academic program.

The founders of Mystic Seaport and of its Munson Institute would be proud of this achievement and appreciative of the work of the scholars who have created it. We hope that generations to come will benefit from *America and the Sea: A Maritime History*.

J. REVELL CARR
President, Mystic Seaport Museum, Inc.

America and the Sea:
A Maritime History

Introduction

"THE SEA IS ALL ABOUT US," wrote T.S. Eliot in "The Dry Salvages"; "the sea is the land's edge also." Comprising more than two-thirds of the earth's surface, the oceans separate the great continents from each other even as, paradoxically, they provide the means by which the world's peoples, cultures, and resources have mingled together. These two contrasting themes, the sea as barrier and the sea as highway, underlie all of maritime history.

Nowhere has this paradox had greater influence than in the history of America. Although a temporary land bridge across the Bering Sea enabled thousands of Asians to migrate into the two American continents thirty thousand or more years ago, these continents remained hidden from Europeans by the seemingly impassable Atlantic Ocean. Until early in the sixteenth century Europeans had continued to view the earth as a single landmass of three parts—Europe, Asia, and Africa—surrounded by a hostile sea. While adventuresome mariners like the Norse and later the Portuguese undertook voyages along the land's edge and to off-lying islands, no one dared set out to cross that barrier, for there was no reason to do so. None, that is, until Christopher Columbus determined that such a route would speed the way to the coast of Asia. It was in fact this Atlantic barrier that made America a truly "New" World to the people of what soon would be referred to as the "Old" World. Just how new and different America was, later generations of Europeans would realize when they attempted to rule their colonies across three thousands miles of ocean. At the same time, however, the Atlantic Ocean was the sea road by which Europeans— led by Columbus, the Cabots, Vespucci, and other mariners at the turn of the sixteenth century— first encountered, gradually explored, and

Detail of Washington Allston's Rising of a Thunderstorm at Sea. *(Everett Fund, Courtesy Museum of Fine Arts, Boston)*

eventually colonized the Americas over the next two centuries. Thus the barrier became a highway, enabling the resources and produce of the New World to enrich the nations of the Old, and affording a route over which some forty million Africans and Europeans traveled in the process of becoming Americans.

Spanning the three-thousand-mile gap between Europe and North America, the North Atlantic both separates and connects those two major landmasses, and therein lies the foundation of American maritime history. First revealed to European eyes by sea, explored and settled by sea, and for much of its five-hundred-year history sustained by sea as well, North America is the most maritime of the world's great continents. And yet, few historians have understood that fact, in part because they have taken a narrow view of the sea as a world apart from the land, a place of little consequence to people other than mariners, whose way of life kept them apart from the mainstream American experience of farm, factory, and family. Although drawn to it in increasing numbers for recreation, the public has an equally narrow perception of the sea as a place of danger, which seems to emphasize the extremes of piracy, marine disasters, and man-eating sharks.

America's maritime history is a complex creation. Its threads weave through the fabric of our nation's past and include both commerce and naval affairs, shipbuilding, the fisheries, mariners, the vessels they manned, and their unique culture. Women played active roles, sometimes at sea, more often ashore. Native Americans living near coastal areas depended on the sea; blacks and other ethnic minorities worked as crew members on board and along the waterfront. America's maritime world encompasses much that lies within "the land's edge": the bays, sounds, and waterways that link our coastal settlements; the seaports that stand as gateways to a continent; and the rivers, canals, and inland seas that have carried both people and waterborne commerce to and from the continent's vast interior. These waterways were as important in their own time as were the railroad networks of the nineteenth century and the highways of the twentieth, and they continue to provide a significant connection between land and sea.

The geographical situation of the United States makes it an island nation whose governmental policies toward military and naval activities, foreign affairs, and maritime industries have been strongly influenced by the oceans around it. Some of our greatest technological and scientific advances have been made in the ongoing effort to turn that oceanic barrier into a highway. The sea has enriched our language with nautical terms, and has inspired our writers and artists to some of their greatest work. It is the task of the maritime historian to demonstrate how the sea has served as the mediator between Americans and the rest of the world, binding us to our political friends, our cultural origins, our economic markets, and bringing to our shores that most precious of all cargoes—men, women, and children.

At critical times in our history the ocean has been more a moat than a highway. As Edmund Burke explained to a British Parliament trying to quell the rebellion rising in its American colonies in 1775: "Three thousand miles of ocean lie between you and them. No contrivance can prevent the effect of this distance in weakening government." Thomas Paine saw in this ocean barrier "strong and natural proof" that the authority of England over America "was never the design of Heaven." When George Washington advised against "entangling alliances" in his Farewell Address, he relied on the Atlantic barrier for enforcement, as did John Quincy Adams when warning European nations against further American colonization in the Monroe Doctrine. Both statesmen predicated their policies on the conviction that the Americas were fundamentally different from Europe. Cultural historians have marked the steady rise of this attitude of American "particularism," but few have noted the role of the sea as a cultural barrier against European influences that made this insularity possible. Thomas Paine suggested it when he wrote that "even the air of the Atlantic disagrees with the constitution of foreign vices. If they survive the voyage," he concluded, "they either expire on their arrival or linger away in an incurable consumption." And an Irish immigrant of the mid-nineteenth century was merely stating the matter another way when he took comfort in the belief that he had left behind the meddlesome leprechauns and other supernatural beings of the old country. "They're scared to pass the ocean," he confidently asserted. "It's too far!" Henry David Thoreau exulted in the observation that the Atlantic Ocean gave America "the opportunity to forget the Old World," while at the same time regarding the Pacific Ocean as "perhaps mankind's last chance before the Styx."

As Thoreau's observation suggests, Americans have long regarded the Pacific as a bridge to opportunity rather than a barrier against hostile forces. For one thing, Americans inherited from Europe the vision of a fabled East, rich beyond measure, whose resources were ripe for exploitation. As early as the 1790s American writers caught the spirit of Pacific expansion, as did Timothy Dwight when he predicted in his poem "Greenfield Hill" that the "starr'd ensign" of American commerce would soon "court Korean gales." Even as the East India companies of England, France, and the Netherlands fell by the way in the first half of the nineteenth century, American firms like Boston's Russell & Company made fortunes in the Asian trade. But Americans would carry more than commerce across the Pacific, Dwight believed. They would spread their vision of freedom.

> Then to new climes the bliss shall trace its way,
> And Tartar desarts hail the rising day.
> From the long torpor startled China wake;
> Her chains of misery rous'd Peruvia break.

In the first years after the purchase of Louisiana in 1803, many Americans valued the acquisition less for its land and other natural resources than as a pathway to the Pacific and thence to Asia. Jefferson's primary purpose in sending out the Lewis and Clark expedition was to find that route. Only when their overland trail proved impractical as a commercial highway did John Jacob Astor establish his fur-trading post at the mouth of the Columbia River by sea. Later, Senator Thomas Hart Benton would champion the idea that a transcontinental route to the Pacific, a "passage to India," as Walt Whitman later called it, would assure that "the American road to Asia will also become the European track to that region. . . . The European merchant as well as the American will fly across our continent on a straight line to China. The rich commerce of Asia will flow through our centre. And where has that commerce ever flowed without carrying wealth and dominion with it?"

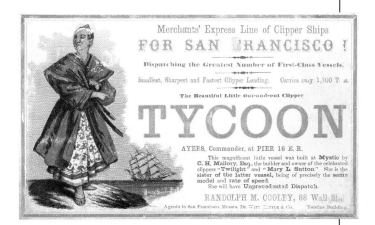

The name of the 1860 ship Tycoon, *meaning ruler or shogun in Pekingese and Japanese, symbolized the lure of Asia in the American maritime economy.* (G.W. Blunt White Library, Mystic Seaport)

Benton then listed, among other historic entrepôts of Asian trade, the cities of Alexandria, Constantinople, Venice, Lisbon, Amsterdam, and finally London. Control of trade with Asia would bring similar greatness to America, Benton predicted. By mid-century the image of "the China Trade" as a source of fabulous wealth for American enterprise became firmly fixed in the American imagination, where it has remained ever since. At the same time, Asian nations were too weak militarily to pose a serious threat to the United States, at least so we thought until our own expanding Pacific empire clashed with the rise of Japanese power in the twentieth century. Even so, the Pacific Ocean proved too vast for enemy forces to threaten the North American continent.

Meanwhile, behind its Atlantic barrier Americans used the waters along the coast to overcome obstructions to travel by land. The overland route between Boston and Philadelphia over deplorably rough roads required the crossing of no less than seven formidable rivers by ferry. No wonder young Benjamin Franklin preferred to make the journey by sea. By the time of the Revolution, packet sloops linked all of America's major ports from Falmouth in Maine, to Savannah in Georgia, carrying passengers, goods, and news on dependable schedules. Less glamorous perhaps than deep-sea voyaging, coastal commerce played an enormous role as the nation's economy reached the "take-off" point in the mid-1840s. By then merchant entrepreneurs had also developed extensive routes

Making her way up the Missouri River into Montana Territory, the steamboat Rosebud *navigates the 3,000-mile water route by which western settlers were linked to eastern commerce. David Barry photographed the* Rosebud *in 1886. (Courtesy Montana Historical Society, Helena)*

human beings who could not have reached America by any other means than by sea. "Give me your tired, your poor," read the unforgettable words of the poet Emma Lazarus on the base of New York Harbor's Statue of Liberty:

> Give me your tired, your poor,
> Your huddled masses yearning
>   to breathe free,
> The wretched refuse of your teeming shore,
> Send these, the homeless, tempest-tossed, to me.

Reaching America by sea was never easy; not in the age of sail and not even in the early decades of steam. One mid-nineteenth-century immigrant compared his Atlantic crossing unfavorably to the conditions he had suffered back in Ireland: "Supposin we war dyin of starvation [at home], it would still not be dyin like rotten sheep thrown into a pit, and the minit the breath is out of our bodies, flung into the sea to be eaten up by them horrid sharks."

Would-be immigrants passed through two challenging filters on the way to America. The first was psychological: the prospect of an eight- to twelve-week ocean passage must have dissuaded many a rural family from making the journey. The second filter was physical: the crossing itself exposed weakened travelers to disease, injury, and debilitating seasickness. After crossing to America by steam in 1840, Charles Dickens chose to return to England by sailing packet because he thought it would afford a more comfortable passage. And as late as 1879 Robert Louis Stevenson described the sounds coming from the steerage deck of his steamer during a North Atlantic storm thus: "the scarcely human noises of the sick joined in a kind of farmyard chorus. . . . I heard a man run wild with terror, beseeching his friend for encouragement. 'The ship is going down!' he cried with a thrill of agony. 'The ship is going down!'"

The nineteenth century saw so many spectacular inventions and technological advances revolutionizing the way ordinary Americans traveled on land that one can hardly blame historians for overlooking those developments that improved voyaging at sea. But reducing the Atlantic crossing from six weeks to six days in less than a century, while enhancing the comfort, safety, and regularity of the passage, was no mean feat. Ocean liners were the largest moveable objects

into the nation's interior by river and canal. Until the rapid development of railroads through the middle of the nineteenth century, coastal and inland waterways carried the greater portion of the nation's cargoes, whether measured by weight or by value. Waterways to America's heartland are still significant. Waterborne shipping still offers the cheapest rates per ton-mile of any method other than pipeline. The St. Lawrence River Seaway permits oceangoing vessels to carry cargoes far into the interior of the continent, except in the dead of winter. For almost two centuries Canada and the United States have preserved the Great Lakes for peaceful purposes—commerce, fishing, and recreation—a remarkable record among nations of the world.

In spite of the weight and value of the commodities entering or leaving our seaports, the most important "cargoes" have been the forty million

built by man. In point of technology they were also the most complex, especially considering they had to be designed and built to withstand physical conditions at sea rarely if ever encountered on land. But a vessel has always been more than just a product of technology. From the humblest coastal scow to the mightiest steamship, ships have been endowed with personalities, first and foremost by the rite of "christening" them with names. Secondly, mariners have always insisted that every vessel behaves differently—faster, or less sea-kindly, or more "crank"—than other vessels, even those of identical design. No sailor and few veteran passengers would ever doubt that ships are alive as surely as people are themselves.

Even as improvements in deep-sea navigation after the Civil War had begun to weaken the ocean's effectiveness as a cultural barrier, America's diplomats and military policy-makers continued to regard it as a protective moat. This was particularly true of the Atlantic, which allowed the United States to keep European affairs at arm's length. Not until late in the nineteenth century did naval authorities begin to modify their single-minded commitment to a strategy of coastal-defense and commerce-raiding and consider building a fleet capable of engaging enemy forces at sea. Even so, the nation was slow to adopt the idea of employing the navy as a means of "force projection," and then confined its use to the Caribbean and Pacific theaters rather than toward Europe. After our brief intervention in World War I we quickly reverted to reliance on the Atlantic as a buffer against European entanglements, even as we continued to expand our naval presence south and west.

No such reluctance impeded the efforts of American merchants to expand their commercial ties with European markets. The ink was hardly dry on the treaty that ended the War of Independence before American vessels cleared for British ports to reestablish commercial relations with the former "tyrant." Unencumbered by the niceties of diplomacy, merchants did business wherever they found the best terms, adjusting to changing political conditions far more rapidly than could the government. Matters that officials could not ignore, such as impressment, paper blockades, or illegal ship seizures, were written off by the pragmatic

Alfred Stieglitz's 1907 photograph, **The Steerage,** *has come to symbolize the immigrant experience at sea, though Stieglitz later recalled taking it on a passage from New York to Europe. This photogravure was published in* **Camera Work** *in 1911. (Courtesy Library of Congress)*

merchants as the costs of doing business. Only when those costs and the expense of marine insurance premiums rose to unacceptable heights did the American merchant turn to his government for protection. But by then national honor was at stake. As Henry Clay warned his fellow senators on the eve of the War of 1812, "if you wish to avoid foreign collision, you had better abandon the ocean—surrender all your commerce, give up all your prosperity. . . . Commerce engenders collision." He did not need to remind his listeners that the new nation was ill-prepared to survive collision with Britain's Royal Navy.

In some important ways America's maritime greatness reached a zenith on the eve of the Civil War. American-flag vessels carried most of our foreign commerce; our clippers marked a pinnacle in sailing-ship design; our whaling fleets reached every corner of the Pacific in search of their quarry; and profits from maritime enterprise became the nation's first significant domestic source of capital.

President Theodore Roosevelt welcomes the crew of the USS Connecticut *at the conclusion of the round-the-world voyage of the U.S. Navy's "Great White Fleet" in 1909, which announced U.S. intentions of being a world-class naval power. (Courtesy Naval Historical Center)*

Within a decade after the war, however, all of these accomplishments had small significance as our relationship with the sea began to change. While our nation's maritime trade continued to expand to extraordinary heights in volume and importance, by century's end foreign vessels carried 90 percent of our commerce, our wooden sailing vessels were giving way to steamships of iron and steel, and whale oil had lost out to petroleum. Only in the protected coastal trade

did American-flag vessels find a growing demand for their services. It would be a mistake, however, to conclude that the United States was no longer a maritime power by the end of the nineteenth century; rather, our relationship to the sea was undergoing major change.

As our deepwater merchant fleet continued its decline at the beginning of the twentieth century, the shift in America's maritime focus from mercantile to naval was already well underway. From an earlier emphasis on continental defense, American policy-makers steadily expanded their concept of sea power. During World War I the United States Navy added the role of protecting the sea-lanes of communication that connected us to our European associates. In the interwar years the navy's surface force finally achieved world-class status, and its submarine fleet acquired both the boats and tactics to interdict the sea-lanes of any enemy nation. Even so, as the United States entered World War II it faced an enormous task. As Winston Churchill noted in October 1942: "The whole power of the United States, to manifest itself in this war, depends on the power to move ships across the sea. Their mighty power is restricted; it is restricted by those very oceans which have protected them; the oceans which were their shield, have now become a bar, a prison house through which they are struggling to bring armies, fleets, and air forces to bear upon the great common problems we have to face."

Not until British and American naval surface and air power could wrest control of the North Atlantic from Germany's U-boat fleet was it possible for the United States to help turn the tide of battle in Europe. Most significantly, during the course of World War II the development of carrier task forces and amphibious warfare vessels gave the U. S. Navy the capacity to project American force against any coastal area. Finally, with the marriage of intercontinental ballistic missiles to atomic-powered submarines in the 1950s, the navy could deliver a devastating nuclear attack to almost any part of the world. One hundred years earlier the nation's maritime power was based on commerce. By the middle of the twentieth century, even as the American-flag deepwater fleet headed toward oblivion, the United States had become the strongest naval power the world had ever seen.

Besides the large trends of world commerce and naval policy, maritime history is about how people live and work at sea and along the land's edge. For more than two centuries after European settlement, most Americans lived in an agricultural economy that was based on the private ownership of land held by married men who tilled the soil alone, with assistance only from members of their immediate families and the occasional help of neighbors. Of course exceptions to this pattern

With spyglass in hand as a symbol of his authority, Captain John Bolles (1820-1871) poses for a photograph, ca. 1860. Bolles spent twenty years in command of New England whaleships. (M.S.M. 55.545)

abounded, particularly in cities and towns and throughout the tidewater regions of the South, but the model citizen for democratic America remained the independent farmer until well after the Civil War.

The maritime way of life has stood in sharp contrast to this individualism. Most vessels engaged in commerce or fishing have been owned by partnerships. Their cargoes consist of goods belonging to several merchants. The wharves and warehouses they use are owned by companies, or municipalities, and their insurance policies are issued by groups of investors. And most importantly, they are operated not by an individual but by a crew headed by that quintessential authority figure, the ship captain. On land a similar degree of power was wielded only by the plantation overseer, and not even he was legally permitted to execute a slave for disobedience, whereas a shipmaster could kill a mutinous sailor. By the very nature of his work the sailor was isolated from "normal" society for months on end, and when he came ashore, unless he had family

With a multi-racial crew hauling on her lines, the American neutral trading ship Abula *leaves the open sea behind and enters the harbor of Marseilles, France, in 1806. (M.S.M. 75.448; Claire White-Peterson photo)*

nearby, the authorities in most seaports effectively confined him to a waterfront district known as "Sailortown."

Furthermore, maritime enterprise takes place in the public domain—in harbors and on the open sea, not on private land—a circumstance that subjected merchants and shipowners to government regulations to a degree not experienced by landbound farmers or businessmen until the present century. Laws dictating which goods could be shipped where and at what cost in custom duties formed the basis of England's mercantilist policy, as did rules determining what vessels could operate within the empire. Similar laws were among the first to be adopted by the new federal government in 1789. Besides, navigation required the active participation of government: for protection by naval and diplomatic representatives; for the construction of lighthouses, jetties, and deepwater channels; for the control of unwelcome foreign competition wherever possible; and not infrequently for direct subsidies—first for the fisheries and

later for the maintenance of uncompetitive operations in the shipping business. Even if the term "free enterprise" exaggerates the degree of liberty found in our land-based economy, the government has played a far greater role in maritime enterprise than in the American business community at large, at least through most of our history. For all of these reasons and more, the maritime way of life varies enormously from what many historians consider the mainstream "American experience."

On the other hand, there is much about seafaring that beats to an American tempo. First and foremost, a voyage has a reason for being, a destination, both physically in the sense that a course is laid across a trackless sea toward another port, and philosophically in the sense of having a purpose: picking up or delivering a cargo, defeating an enemy, or gathering resources of the sea. In the spirit of American individualism, the mariner was free to follow his own course toward that destination, as Ishmael, in Herman Melville's *Moby-Dick*, exclaimed as he sailed toward Nantucket in the packet *Moss*: "how I spurned that turnpike earth! That common highway all over dented with the marks of slavish heels and hoofs and turned me to admire the magnanimity of the sea, which will permit no records." During the great age of sail, Americans also perceived that sea enterprise furthered the greater cause of national progress, a maritime equivalent perhaps of advancing the western frontier. Seafaring therefore fulfilled our custom of determining a thing's value by its usefulness.

A second thoroughly American aspect of a sea voyage was its inherent danger. The open sea remains the most hazardous place on earth into which humankind regularly ventures. For thousands of years inhabitants of the "land's edge" have endeavored to make a living from the sea while facing the dreadful risks of that workplace. For them the great expanse of open ocean has been a fact of daily existence; no one understands better than mariners the thin line that separates safety from disaster at sea. In "The Dry Salvages," Eliot conveyed this sense of unpredictable danger when he wrote of a "ragged rock in the restless waters" off Cape Ann, Massachusetts:

> On a halcyon day it is merely a monument,
> In navigable weather it is always a seamark
> To lay a course by: but in

the sombre season
Or the sudden fury, is what it always was.

When at sea mariners have constantly struggled to establish and maintain order amid conditions aptly considered to be utter chaos. The highest level of human control—rigid discipline, hierarchical command, and thoroughly maintained vessel and gear—may not be enough to survive overwhelming natural forces at sea. The transcendentalist philosopher Ralph Waldo Emerson suggested that a life spent working in such a hostile environment actually affected the character of mariners. "Who can guess how much firmness the sea-girt rock has taught the fisherman?" he asked in his essay "Nature." Nineteenth-century Americans admired risk-takers, especially those who risked their lives in the name of progress. That the mariner, like the frontiersman, faced death beyond the view of ordinary citizens added to his heroic stature in the American imagination. At the same time, however, it also reinforced the view that seafarers, like all heroes, were different from the rest of us.

Finally, sea voyaging played to the American fascination with space and distance, and particularly with speed in the effort to conquer these distances. On land, nature itself provided limits to the landscape in the form of rivers, lake shores, and particularly mountain ranges. And by the mid-nineteenth

"To Donald McKay Esq. builder of the Leviathan CLIPPER SHIP "GREAT REPUBLIC" This print is respectfully dedicated." Painted by J.E. Buttersworth, published by N. Currier, 1853. (M.S.M. 49.3186)

[11]

Rising of a Thunderstorm at Sea, by Washington Allston, 1804. (Everett Fund, Courtesy Museum of Fine Arts, Boston)

century, Americans for two hundred years or more had been building visible barriers of their own–fences, walls, the edges of clearings, lines of planted trees. By 1850 the frontier had reached that ultimate barrier, the Pacific Ocean. No wonder that the print of Donald McKay's magnificent clipper *Great Republic* should become one of Currier & Ives's most popular, for only with such vessels could Americans reach beyond that Pacific boundary. The stately portrait of the *Great Republic* encouraged landbound viewers to imagine what they could not see–that distant world beyond the horizon.

Maritime history should convey more than the profits of merchants, or the victories of admirals, or even the struggles of ordinary mariners. It should also embrace the sea itself, for all human activity takes place within the wider context of the natural world around us. Whether we live one mile or one thousand miles from the coast, the sea profoundly affects our daily lives. Rolling across thousands of miles of open ocean, the North Atlantic ground swell pounds against the coastline of North America, driven by winds that frequently reach gale force. Its relentless power has shaped coastlines from Maine to Florida, as the Pacific has done from Alaska to southern California. In "Once by the Pacific" Robert Frost observed that:

> The shattered water made a misty din,
> Great waves looked over others coming in.
> And thought of doing something
>   to the shore
> That water never did to land before.
>
> You could not tell, and yet it looked as if
> The shore was lucky in being
>   backed by cliff
> The cliff in being backed by continent. . . .

The ocean is a great engine that controls much of North America's climate, its currents affecting temperature and rainfall along our coasts, and its prevailing winds influencing climate conditions far into the continent's interior. Peoples of the Northwest can be sure of heavy rainfall from the Pacific, just as residents along the Gulf and Atlantic coasts can expect hurricanes spawned in the tropical latitudes of the mid-Atlantic. Even the continent's inland sea—the Great Lakes—affects the snowfall over several states. Unpredictable changes in the current along the South American coast—known as El Niño—alter climate patterns over much of North America at frequent intervals and inject a vexing element of uncertainty into the task of weather forecasting. Of great importance to mariners is the way in which prevailing winds and their associated currents affect conditions at sea. The best known of these "rivers in the sea," the Gulf Stream, was first publicized by the American genius Benjamin Franklin. It could reduce an eastbound passage across the Atlantic by as much as two weeks, or similarly impede a westbound passage. By the middle of the nineteenth century, when the American naval officer Matthew F. Maury issued his renowned sailing directions, ship captains knew precisely what course between any two ports the world over would take best advantage of prevailing winds and currents.

Central to the settlement patterns of this continent, and to the economies of tribe, colony, and nation, have been the marine resources found in the sea and in rivers and lakes. Coastal dwellers could harvest a bounty of protein from the shellfish that lived in the shallow bays and estuaries, a resource so rich that despite its poor soil the tiny island of Nantucket supported a Native American population of 2,500, equal to the density of western Europe at the time. Anadromous fish coming in from the sea to spawn in fresh waters each spring provided another supply of food. Europeans came seeking fish in the North Atlantic as well as riches on shore, establishing an industry that has operated for 500 years. And marine mammals, especially whales and seals, became prey to maritime entrepreneurs seeking oil for light and lubrication, and furs for human garments.

The gathering of these resources brought European and native cultures together— some-

For thousands of years before mariners brought them contact with European clothing and culture in the nineteenth century, Alaska natives depended upon the annual salmon runs for subsistence. Blending the two cultures on the bank of the Yukon River, hundreds of miles from the open sea, these Alaskans air-dry salmon caught as they returned from the ocean to spawn in the river of their birth. (M.S.M. 97.35.3)

times in cooperation but more often in conflict— and fostered the development of increasingly efficient, and deadly, techniques of harvesting. After more than two centuries of increasing slaughter, the hunt for whales by this nation died in the first quarter of the twentieth century, superseded by the hunt for petroleum, which became a maritime story with the move to offshore drilling after World War II. Since then, there has been increasing debate over the often mutually exclusive expectations of those seeking fish and those seeking oil at sea. And this conflict is all the more critical because the twentieth century has demonstrated the power of fishermen with modern technology to gather more fish than natural populations can reproduce.

At century's end the survival of the venerable relationship by which the sea has provided us sustenance and products of great value is more than ever dependent on our recognizing both our ability to despoil the sea and our need to conserve its resources. Until recently, the sea appeared too vast to be affected by our actions. To a lesser extent we have felt the same way about our large lakes and rivers.

Concern for the natural resources of the land began at least a century ago with John Muir's efforts to preserve the Sierra Nevada Mountains. Although Rachel Carson wrote about the delicate balance of life at "the edge of the sea" in the 1950s, not until the Santa Barbara oil-rig blowout of 1969 did the general public suddenly realize how we were damaging the marine environment.

Despite the abuse by humankind, the sea remains our planet's most extensive wilderness, an ever-changing combination of transcendent beauty, frightening power, and ultimate mystery. Like the wilderness, humans have increasingly tried to tame the edges of the sea for their own enjoyment. The shift from an emphasis on an agricultural economy in the United States created leisure time and the demand for a place to spend it. As in Europe, seaside recreation developed early in the nineteenth century as a healthful and pleasant diversion from urban life. Yachting was one

In his watercolor, Low Tide, Beachmont, *Maurice Prendergast captures the festive spirit of recreation that has become such a pervasive element of American waterside activity during the past century. (Courtesy Worcester Art Museum, Worcester, Massachusetts)*

way the wealthy found seaborne recreation and a form of competition that took on national significance after the *America* crossed the Atlantic and defeated a fleet of British yachts in 1851. Successfully defended against all comers until 1983, the America's Cup became the premier trophy in the sport of yacht racing.

The very technology that accelerated maritime commerce, steam railroads in the nineteenth century, and internal combustion automobiles in the twentieth, increased recreational access to the sea for nearly all levels of urban society. Whether engaged in the simplest childish pleasure at the seaside, or using equipment of the most advanced technology on or under the sea, or building a retreat at the water's edge, we each gain something from our experience there. Our continued national passion for the beach, and wide participation in water sports, ensure that today more Americans than ever have a relationship with the sea.

Beyond its commercial, diplomatic, providential, and recreational roles in American history, the sea has provided a powerful motif in art and literature. Artists from Washington Allston to Frederick Edwin Church, Thomas Eakins, and Winslow Homer tried to capture the sometimes placid, sometimes overpowering nature of the sea. The sea first appeared as a locale for American fiction in the first half of the nineteenth century in the writings of James Fenimore Cooper, Edgar Allen Poe, and of course Herman Melville. While other settings for popular novels, such as frontier, forest, and farm, began to lose their earlier popularity, the sea has remained one of the most enduring locations for literature and, with the rise of cinema in the twentieth century, for film as well.

Ultimately it is the mystery of the sea that so attracts us. Perhaps Frost best described how the eternal mystery of the sea captures the human imagination in these lines from his poem "Neither Far Out Nor in Deep."

> The people along the sand
> All turn and look one way.
> They turn their back on the land.
> They look at the sea all day.
>
> They cannot look out far.
> They cannot look in deep.
> But when was that ever a bar
> To any watch they keep?

It is the perpetual mystery of a frontier we cannot inhabit, leaving us always to wonder what lies beyond its horizon and beneath its surface, to feel overpowered by the unpredictability of its behavior, to ponder the ambivalence of our own feelings toward it, and to embrace the complex puzzle of its meaning in our own past.

Meditation by the Sea. *(M. and M. Karolik Collection of American Paintings, 1815-1865, Courtesy Museum of Fine Arts, Boston)*

Part 1
Becoming America, to 1815

Chapter 1

The Beginnings

The sea is all about us;
The sea is the land's edge also, the granite
Into which it reaches, the beaches where it tosses
Its hints of earlier and other creation:
The starfish, the hermit crab, the whale's backbone;
The pools where it offers to our curiosity
The more delicate algae and the sea anemone.
It tosses up our losses, the torn seine
The shattered lobsterpot, the broken oar
And the gear of foreign dead men.
The sea has many voices,
Many gods and many voices.

T.S. Eliot, "The Dry Salvages"

THESE LINES FROM THE PEN of the Anglo-American poet T.S. Eliot epitomize the eternal struggle between land and sea, never more dynamic than along the shores of Cape Ann, Massachusetts, where the North Atlantic groundswell pounds ashore with all the strength of its three-thousand-mile fetch. Along with the advance and retreat of glaciers and the rise of the ocean's level, this constant force has given us the present contours of the North American coastline, and the process continues.

The Atlantic shore is remarkably well endowed with bays, harbors, and other topographical features that have encouraged the inhabitants of this region to make use of the Atlantic Ocean and its resources. The retreating glaciers left behind more than a dozen major rivers and twice as many smaller ones. Flooded by a rising sea level, the banks of these rivers provided excellent places for seaports, and their waters abounded in marine life. Along the southern New England coast the glaciers' terminal moraine left a chain of islands from New York to Cape Cod as a barrier guarding a 200-mile stretch of protected water in its lee. The valley of the Hudson River, with its appended valleys, the Champlain to the north and the Mohawk to the west, offered settlers broad plains, rich soils, and a water route to markets. As the coastline turns south at the mouth of the Hudson, pounding seas and littoral currents have created barrier beaches and islands protecting inland waterways along the New Jersey coast, the eastern shore of Maryland and Virginia, the outer banks of the Carolinas, all the way down to the sea islands of Georgia and northern Florida. Behind this barrier a broad coastal plain runs along the Atlantic seaboard, where bays and sounds are bordered by thousands of square miles of relatively flat, arable land. By far the most significant have been

Detail of Coast Scene, Mount Desert, *by Frederic Edwin Church. (Courtesy Wadsworth Atheneum, bequest of Mrs. Clara Hinton Gould)*

Chesapeake Bay and the broad estuaries of the James, York, Rappahannock, and Potomac Rivers adjoining it. This region alone has proved capable of supporting a dense population because of its good soil and easy access to the sea. Tall pine and sturdy oak furnished ample timber for the domestic needs of farmers with enough left over for the construction of vessels required by maritime communities.

The entire peninsula of Florida lies within the coastal plain, and its southern tip supports the only coral reefs found within the continental United States. West from Florida the plain stretches along the edge of the Gulf of Mexico, giving way to the low-lying "pine hills" of present-day Alabama and Mississippi. Much of this region is accessible by south-flowing rivers such as the Apalachicola and the Mobile, each with a commodious estuary at its mouth. The Mississippi River provides a broad avenue to the sea, draining a 1,500-mile span of the continent, from the headwaters of the Ohio River on the Appalachian slope in the east to the Missouri River headwaters at the continental divide of the Rocky Mountains in the west. The wide, rich floodplain of the

In his 1863 painting Coast Scene, Mount Desert, *or* Sunrise off the Maine Coast, *artist Frederic Edwin Church captured the hopeful spirit of "Neptune's Nation" while accurately depicting the unrelenting power of the sea. (Courtesy Wadsworth Atheneum, bequest of Mrs. Clara Hinton Gould)*

Mississippi extends for hundreds of miles, terminating in the swampy bayous and delta. There, fresh water and nutrients pour into the Gulf to create a fertile nursery for marine life. To the west of the Mississippi delta another coastal plain nearly 300 miles in breadth stretches all the way to the Rio Grande river and beyond. Along much of this coastline, barrier islands protect bays and sounds from Tampa, Florida, to Laguna Madre, Texas. At the eastern end the soil of the coastal plain is of indifferent fertility, but further inland the crescent-shaped black belt around the southern end of the Appalachian Mountains is prime agricultural land. In the Mississippi River valley, annual flooding has for eons enriched the river valleys with topsoil washed downstream from the continent's interior. Timber continues to be a valuable resource throughout the eastern half of the plain, where longleaf yellow pine, cypress, and mixed hardwoods predominate. The climate of the entire region is dominated by the warm waters of the Gulf of Mexico, which has made it particularly suitable for the cultivation of short staple cotton and sugar.

In sharp contrast to the Atlantic and Gulf coasts, the Pacific shoreline of the North American continent is bordered by an almost continuous chain of mountains, stretching from the Coastal Range at the northern end to the Santa Ana and Laguna Ranges that run into the peninsula of Lower California. Along the upper half of the coast, these mountains intercept North Pacific weather fronts, and the rainfall nourishes great forests of conifers–firs, as well as the famous redwoods–that cover the mountain slopes down to the shoreline. The mountain barrier has only a few openings large enough to support a seaport with access into an interior hinterland. One is Juan da Fuca Strait, on the border between present-day Canada and the United States, which opens into the extensive inland waters of Puget Sound. Two hundred miles south, the Columbia River floods into the Pacific over a shallow bar, providing flatwater access into fertile country for 150 miles. Nearly six hundred miles to the south, one of the world's great natural harbors, San Francisco Bay, leads via the Sacramento River to the fertile interior valley of California and the mineral-rich Sierra Nevada Mountains beyond. And a further five hundred miles southward, just above the present-day Mexico–United States border, is San Diego Bay, formed by offshore gravel bars. In between these harbors lie at best an additional half-dozen smaller points of access. Another factor that limited maritime activity along the Pacific Coast to only a few seaports was the Cascade and Sierra Nevada Ranges, which prevented easy penetration into the interior.

North America's fourth coast (not counting the north shore of Canada) rims the interior Great Lakes. Formed by a succession of glacier advances and retreats, the Great Lakes filled a giant depression in the heartland of the continent. Through an interconnecting series of smaller lakes and rivers, with short portages in between, the Great Lakes provided not only a waterway into the continent's interior but also a through route from the Atlantic Ocean, via the St. Lawrence River or the Hudson and

Mohawk Rivers, all the way to the Mississippi River and thence to the Gulf of Mexico. The relatively flat and well-drained land between and around the Great Lakes once supported extensive forests and has excellent soil for farming. Until recently the waters of the lakes supported vast quantities of sturgeon, whitefish, and trout, and Atlantic salmon spawned in Lake Ontario.

So much for the land's edge. The waters that lie beyond these shores have their own unique characteristics as well. The effect of the earth's rotation, among other factors, drives the winds of the North Atlantic in a clockwise direction, and so the prevailing breeze along North America's eastern seaboard comes from the south and southwest. This wind in turn powers an immense flow of water–its various segments called the Florida Current, the Gulf Stream, and the North Atlantic Drift–from the Gulf of Mexico through the Straits of Florida, past the Carolina capes, and thence northeasterly across the North Atlantic. In mid-ocean the current begins to divide, the lesser branch running north around the British Isles and then northeast along the Scandinavian coast. The larger stream sets southeasterly toward the Bay of Biscay, swings south along the coast of the Iberian peninsula, and finally turns west back across the Atlantic as the North Equatorial Current to complete the circle. This immense "river in the ocean," as Matthew F. Maury called it, and the prevailing winds that power it across thousands of miles, affects almost every natural and human activity taking place in the bowl we call the North Atlantic Ocean.

Similar forces drive the powerful North Pacific Current into the Gulf of Alaska, where it turns south, as the California Current, to flow down along the west coast of the continent before swinging west above the equator to complete the circuit. On this coast, the prevailing winds blow from the northeast.

The Gulf of Mexico has a different action. Oceanographers see it as a large loop in the current that flows from the Caribbean Sea and through the straits of Yucatan on its way to become the Gulf Stream.

The continental shelf–that broad plateau that extends beneath the sea for more than one hundred miles eastward and southward from the North American mainland–was part of the main-

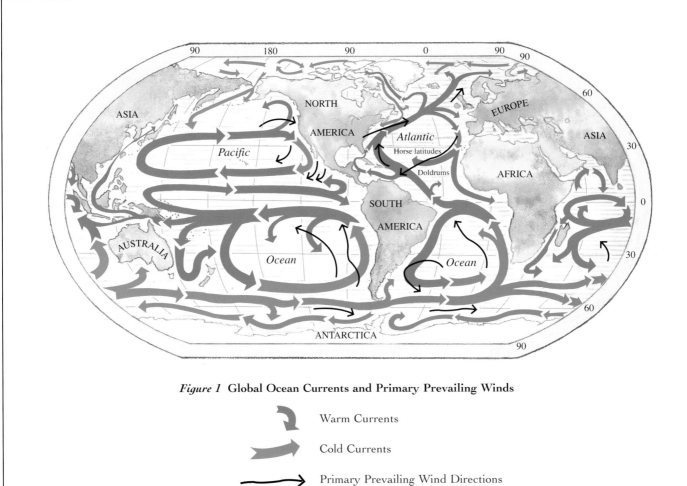

Figure 1 **Global Ocean Currents and Primary Prevailing Winds**

Warm Currents

Cold Currents

Primary Prevailing Wind Directions

(Dennis O'Brien map)

land's coastal plain until submerged by the rising sea about twelve thousand years ago with the melting of the last glacier. Except in its several submarine canyons, the shelf floor is shallow enough to support photosynthesizing vegetation, an important foundation for the region's marine food chain, especially on the undersea plateaus off New England and the Canadian Maritime Provinces, where the warm currents of the Gulf Stream meet nutrient-rich waters from the north. For thousands of years these 75,000 square miles of coastal waters supported immense populations of cod, haddock, and other groundfish. And for five centuries, from about 1450 to 1950, these stocks sustained themselves while feeding increasing multitudes of Europeans and Americans and providing a livelihood for thousands of fishermen from both continents. Along the protected waters of the Atlantic Coast, from Narragansett Bay and Long Island Sound south into Delaware and Chesapeake Bays and on into Albemarle and Pamlico Sounds, shallow inlets served as ideal spawning grounds for a wide range of shellfish: quahogs, clams, mussels, scallops, crabs, lobsters, and–where the water was sufficiently brackish–succulent oysters. Each spring, sturgeon, shad, alewives, Atlantic salmon, and other species of anadromous fish strove to regain the upriver streams of their own hatching in order to lay and fertilize eggs for the next generation, while vast schools of mackerel and menhaden traveled north along the coast. Perch, bass, bluefish, eels, and other edible species abounded in nearby coastal waters. The Gulf of Mexico lies entirely on the continental shelf, and its waters abound in shrimp, snapper, and sponge, while far beneath its floor carbon deposits in the form of petroleum signal its previous status as dry land. The Pacific Coast's narrow continental shelf, in some places less than fifty miles in width, denies the region the generous groundfish stocks that have supported generations of Atlantic and Gulf Coast fishermen. On the Pacific Coast, great schools of herring-like "sardines" often swarmed the California coast, while vast streams of several varieties of salmon fought their way upstream to spawn in every river along the 2,000-mile coastline from northern California to the Bering Sea. And, as in the Atlantic, marine mammals, including seals and several species of whales, roamed the coast in their migrations.

It was not only this abundance that most keenly impressed the European mariners who gazed upon the North American continent for the first time, but also the beauty of the land before them. "Coming ashore we stood awhile like men ravished at the beauty and delicacy of this sweet soil; for besides divers clear lakes of fresh water, whereof we saw no end; meadows very large and full of green grass; even the most woody places do grow so distinct and apart, one tree from another, upon green grassy ground, somewhat higher than the plains," wrote John Brereton in 1602 of the view from a hilltop overlooking Buzzards Bay, Massachusetts. Brereton concluded that the scene seemed,"as if Nature would show herself above her power, artificial."

The First
American Mariners

The North American continent was neither vacant nor virginal in the sixteenth and seventeenth centuries as increasing numbers of Europeans explored and then settled along its eastern and Gulf coasts. The continent's first discoverers and inhabitants, referred to here interchangeably as Native Americans or Indians, had come on foot, across the land bridge connecting Siberia and Alaska some 30,000 years ago. Most of these migrants moved southward into present-day Central America and beyond into South America itself. Others remained in the western portion of North America, but by about 10,000 B.C. some groups had reached the East Coast, close behind the retreating glacier. But unlike the Mayans, Aztecs, and Incas further south, and the Burial Mound cultures around the Ohio and Mississippi Rivers, the eastern woodland aborigines retained their Stone Age culture. At the time of European colonization, well more than 100,000 Indians—mostly of the Algonkian family, but also Iroquois to the north and Muskhogean to the south—lived along the eastern seaboard from present-day Canada to Florida,

with the greatest concentration in the region from Massachusetts to the Carolinas.

Although they were primarily woodland dwellers dependent on hunting and gathering and the cultivation of small plots of land, many tribes moved to the coast during the late spring and summer months to exploit the abundant marine resources. The methods used by Maine's Penobscot Indians typify those of other Algonkian tribes all along the eastern seaboard. In the spring they speared or netted runs of anadromous fish. From the bays and estuaries that indented the coastal plain they trapped fish in woven weirs and nets and speared eels and other species. At night they used torches to attract their prey to the surface. The women even dove for lobsters and fished for cod and bass with hook and line. Everyone joined in to gather large quantities of clams, oysters, and scallops, leaving behind the immense mounds of shells that fascinate today's professional and amateur archaeologists. The Narragansetts specialized in the art of fashioning the beads called wampum from periwinkle and quahog shells, the latter producing the more desirable dark purple or black variety. At first strings of wampum were woven together to make belts, necklaces, and other decorative items, but gradually wampum gained value as a medium of exchange, or currency, both by Native Americans of the northeast and by European colonists, who often used it in the fur trade with tribes of the interior.

To extend their range when mainland resources grew scarce, Indians paddled their birchbark or dugout canoes to off-lying islands and set up summer fishing camps. They dried or smoked most of their catch to preserve it for consumption during the hard winter months. In most years, fortunately, spring runs of anadromous fish came just as their winter stores of fish, corn, venison, and other staples were giving out. Seafood constituted about 10 percent of the Indians' diet, roughly comparable to the percentages from mammal and bird game hunting. So rich were the resources in the waters around Nantucket, for instance, that the historian Daniel Vickers has estimated the island supported a population of about 2,500 Native Americans at the time of European contact, a density much greater than that of the mainland and equal to many Old World communities of the time. Indians were apparently aware of the fertilizing qualities of

The Fishing of New England's Inhabitants

In this trade they be very expert, being experienced in the knowledge of all baits, fitting sundry baits for several fishes and diverse seasons; being not ignorant likewise of the removal of fishes, knowing when to fish rivers and when at rocks, when in bays and when at seas. Since the English came they be furnished with English hooks and lines; before they made them of their own hemp more curiously wrought of stronger materials than ours, hooked with bone hooks, but laziness drives them to buy more than profit or commendations win them to make of their own. They make likewise very strong sturgeon nets with which they catch sturgeons of twelve, fourteen, and sixteen, some eighteen foot long in the daytime. In the night time

they betake them to their birchen canoes, in which they carry a forty-fathom line with a sharp, bearded dart fastened at the end thereof. Then lighting a blazing torch made of birchen rinds, they weave it to and again by their canoe side, which the sturgeon, much delighted with, comes to them tumbling and playing, turning up his white belly, into which they thrust their lance, his back being inpenetrable. Which done, they haul to the shore their struggling prize. . . . In summer they seldom fish any where but in salt; in winter in the fresh water and ponds. . . .

The bass is one of the best fishes in the country, and though men are soon wearied with other fish, yet are they never with bass; it is a deli-

Like these natives of Florida, American Indians frequently smoked fish and other meats for preservation, thereby extending the availability of seasonal foods. Drawn by Jacques Le Moyne de Morgues and engraved by Theodor de Bry as Plate XXIV in America, *Part II (1591). (Courtesy New York Public Library)*

cate, fine, fat, fast fish, having a bone in his head which contains a saucerful of marrow, sweet and good, pleasant to the palate and wholesome to the stomach. When there be a great store of them, we only eat the heads and salt up the bodies for winter, which exceeds ling or haberdine. Of these fishes some be three and some four foot long, some bigger, some lesser. At some tides a man may catch a dozen or twenty of these in three hours. The way to catch them is with hook and line; the fisherman taking a great cod-line, to which he fasteneth a piece of lobster and throws it into the sea, the fish biting at it he pulls her to him and knocks her on the head with a stick. . . .

Lobsters be in plenty in most places, very large ones, some being twenty pound in weight. These are taken at a low water amongst the rocks. They are very good fish, the small ones being the best; their plenty makes them little esteemed and seldom eaten. The Indians get many of them every day for to bait their hooks withal and to eat when they can get no bass. The oysters be great ones in form of a shoehorn; some be a foot long. These breed on certain banks that are bare every spring-tide. This fish without the shell is so big that it must admit of a division before you can well get it into your mouth. The periwig is a kind of fish that lieth in the ooze like a head of air, which being touched conveys itself leaving nothing to be seen but a small round hole. . . .in some places of the country there be clams as big as a penny white loaf, which are great dainties amongst the natives and would be in good esteem amongst the English were it not for better fish. . . .

In the summer these Indian women, when lobsters be in their plenty and prime, dry them to keep for winter, erecting scaffolds in the hot sunshine, making fires like-

wise underneath them, by whose smoke the flies are expelled, till the substance remain hard and dry. In this manner they dry bass and other fishes without salt, cutting them very thin to dry suddenly before the flies spoil them or the rain moist them, having a special care to hang them in their smoky houses in the night and dankish weather.

William Wood, *New Englands Prospect: A true, lively, and experimentall description of that part of America, commonly called New England. . .*(London, 1634).

In his 1585 watercolor, **The manner of their fishing,** *John White depicted a fishing dugout canoe near the Roanoke settlement. In the background, two natives fish with spears, while a brush fish weir collects a bounty of passing fish at left. White illustrated a variety of species, from hammerhead shark to horseshoe crabs and shellfish, indicating the diversity of marine life consumed and otherwise used by the Native Americans. (Courtesy The British Museum, London)*

leaders among these people were the umealiq, the owners and commanders of the whaleboats.

Farther south, from the islands of the Alaskan panhandle to the coast south of the Columbia River, the Japan Current brought warm water and a moist, temperate climate. On the islands and narrow coastline of this region lived many tribes with similar cultures but from three different language groups. Abundant resources permitted these tribes to develop the world's most complex nonagricultural social structure and a settled living pattern oriented to the sea. The mountainous coastline was thickly forested with fir and cedar, which provided planks and beams for large communal houses, great trunks that could be hollowed into different types of specialized dugout canoes, and posts that could be carved into elaborate "totem poles" that denoted a family's lineage.

For all of these peoples, fishing was a full-time occupation. Families with status owned prime locations along the rivers and streams, where they would net or harpoon salmon swimming upstream to spawn in spring, summer, and fall. Salmon, halibut, cod, herring, and dogfish were caught with both hooks and nets from canoes in open water, and sea mammals were hunted with harpoons from canoes.

Canoes linked tribal lineages through both trade and war. Trade served to maintain tribal relationships, while ongoing feuds between lineages were maintained by raiding parties in sixty-foot war canoes that could carry as many as sixty warriors, who plundered and enslaved rival villages. The status conferred by wealth in these cultures was reflected in the potlatch feast, in which a family distributed great quantities of food and nonutilitarian objects.

Long before European contact, the different cultures had perfected characteristic watercraft types. In the northeast, central, and northwest regions

With the elders at the place of honor in the stern of their walrus-skin-covered umiaks, these Eskimos of Alaska's Kotzebue Sound, near the Arctic Circle, display signals of friendship. Eskimos depended on their skin boats for whaling, fishing, and trading along the desolate Arctic coast. Despite the scarcity of resources in this region, these Eskimos have painted their umiaks and wear decorative labrets of stone or whale ivory in perforations in their lips. Drawn by William Smyth. (Frederick W. Beechey, Narrative of a Voyage to the Pacific and Beering's Strait...in the Years 1825, 26, 27, 28, 2 vols. (London, 1831), 1: opp. 343)

fish–Squanto explained the technique to the Pilgrims at Plymouth–but "fishing" a cornfield with menhaden required enormous effort and was rarely necessary anyway because of other conservation practices. In 1585-86, from the ill-fated colony of Roanoke on Albemarle Sound, Thomas Harriot recorded the various species of marine life and described the Indians' method of fishing. Accompanied by the drawings of John White sketched in the same year, these reports give us our first reliable glimpse of North America's inshore marine resources.

Before European contact, the most completely maritime cultures on the continent lived on the Northwest Coast. In the far north, on the barren coast of Alaska, the Eskimos resorted to the sea for most of their needs, relying on seals, whales, and walrus for food, clothing, and building materials. Even their watercraft were built of sealskins. With a society organized around families, the most influential

bark canoes took different forms according to tribal custom. Along the Missouri River, skin "bull boats" were used in place of wooden craft, while Arctic Eskimos built their open umiaks and covered kayaks of sealskin. Dugout canoes from hollowed tree trunks took many forms, from the relatively plain ones of the Northeast through the cedar pirogues of the lower Mississippi region, to the spread and highly decorated cedar dugouts of the Pacific Northwest.

Before as well as after European contact, trade networks linked inland cultures with coastal groups. People of the Hopewell culture, centered in the Ohio River valley from approximately 300 to 1000 A.D., participated in an elaborate trade network that reached to Florida and the Gulf coast. As a result of these connections, materials such as conch shells and shark teeth are represented among the impressive body of decorative and utilitarian objects produced by the Hopewell people. In more recent periods, dentalium and abalone shells from the West Coast were traded to tribes of the Great Plains and Rocky Mountains, among whom they were popular for ornamentation and other uses.

The world's most complex nonagricultural societies were found on the Northwest Coast of North America. **Cheslakee's Village on Johnston's Straits** *depicts a Salish community, set on terraces between the forest and a tidal inlet. With its highly decorated houses bearing family crests, and numerous finely shaped dugout canoes for fishing, trading, and warfare, this settlement is representative of hundreds of communities along a thousand-mile stretch of coast from present-day Oregon to Alaska. (George Vancouver,* A Voyage of Discovery to the North Pacific Ocean...in the Years 1790...1795, *2 vols. (London, 1798), Vol. 2)*

Europe Rediscovers America

The Norse experience in America is by no means a historically isolated event. For one thing, Norse motives for expansion included many factors common to later overseas settlement by Europeans–population growth at

home, the search for security from oppression, a sense of adventure, and greed–for resources or just for plunder. Furthermore, the Norse established a pattern of maritime expansion duplicated by other Europeans in the centuries to follow. First came *discovery*, usually accidental, by remarkable navigators–although not so remarkable that they always went where they meant to go or knew where they were when they got there. Then came *exploration*, carried out in systematic fashion with a record that others could follow on their way to the new lands. Next was *settlement*, marginal at first, and heavily reliant on the Old World for many decades thereafter. Finally, came *development* of the New World's resources, a process that depended on old-world capital and markets.

Just as the Norse had discovered the New World by sea at the end of the tenth century, so other Europeans would rediscover it by sea at the end of the fifteenth and go on to explore it by sea throughout the sixteenth century. Even as the Norse settlements in Greenland were dying out, other European mariners were

From coast to coast, Native Americans created dugout canoes, although their sizes and forms depended on local timber resources and cultural traditions. Using both fire and stone or shell adzes to fell and hollow the logs, natives built dugouts up to eighty feet in length. The most elaborate examples were carved by the peoples on the Northwest Coast, who hollowed cedars to a thin shell, steamed and shaped them to a wider, more seaworthy form, and decorated them with carved and painted bow and stern attachments. This view of dugout construction in Virginia was engraved by Theodor de Bry after a watercolor by John White and published as Plate XII in America, Part I *(1590). (Courtesy Library of Congress)*

embarking on Atlantic voyages of their own. Enough tales of Atlantic ventures have been handed down in the folk traditions of the Irish, Welsh, Bretons, Basques, Portuguese, and even the German fishermen of Lubeck, to command our attention, but no firm archaeological or documentary evidence has yet been found to establish the authenticity of these traditions. We can be fairly certain that as the fifteenth century came to a close, and within a few years after the last Norse Greenlanders disappeared, fishermen of these and other countries had found the cod banks that lie off Newfoundland and were making seasonal trips to bring this rich resource back to European markets. It is likely that on one of these ventures Basque fishermen rediscovered Newfoundland, for that island was at first called "Baccaloas" by Sebastian Cabot in 1509 because, he claimed, the Indians called codfish by that Basque word. Until further light is shed on these earlier voyages, however, credit for the rediscovery of the North American mainland must go to John Cabot and his son Sebastian, Genoese navigators who had moved to Bristol, England, some years before. Backed by fellow townsmen and endorsed by King Henry VII, the Cabots sailed due west in search of a passage to Asia in 1497, just as Christopher Columbus had done much further south five years before under the flag of Spain. Like Columbus, Cabot also thought he had found Cathay, but in his report to King Henry he chose to emphasize what he considered to be the valuable attributes of the land he had encountered, probably Cape Breton or Nova Scotia, though possibly Newfoundland. It was covered with dense forests that could provide timber for shipbuilding, he reported, and offshore were codfish so numerous that his crew could catch them simply by lowering buckets overboard.

At first no one doubted that the lands encountered by Columbus, the Cabots, Amerigo Vespucci, Gaspar and Miguel Corte Real, and other mariners of the first decade of rediscovery (1492-1502) were exactly what they had been searching for—Asia. After all, according to the accepted cosmography of the time it could be nothing else, for Europeans believed that the earth had but one landmass comprising three parts—Europe on the west, Africa to the south, and Asia on the east—surrounded by a single ocean sea. The symmetry and symbolism of this tripartite design gave it special meaning to the Christians of medieval Europe. Convincing them that they had discovered a previously unknown continent would have been almost as difficult as persuading someone today that Earth possesses a second moon hidden from view by the visible moon. The analogy is useful because America was similarly hidden away by three thousand miles of tempestuous

Atlantic Ocean and therefore did not exist in the minds of Europeans. The handful of mariners who saw America first had no intellectual context by which to identify it other than as the backside of Asia. Then gradually the concept of a separate continent began to circulate, Vespucci himself coining the phrase "new world" in 1504. Three years later Martin Waldsemuller of Lorraine became the first cartographer to incorporate the idea on a map, but even so he confined his representation of America as a separate continent to a small corner embellishment. In the first decades of the sixteenth century the ocean sea that had kept the American continent hidden from Europeans now became the means by which European mariners explored it. No wonder they called it the "new world" and endowed it with qualities they believed were wanting in their "old world." In writing of his new mistress 150 years later, John Donne found the image of America still fresh:

> O my America! my new-found-land
> My kingdom, safeliest when with one man
>   manned,
> My mine of precious stones, my empery
> How blest I am in thus discovering thee!

Finally convinced that the landmass encountered by his father and himself was not a part of Asia, but still determined to reach that continent by sailing west, Sebastian Cabot undertook to search for a northwest passage around America in 1509. But after sailing as far north as perhaps the entrance to Hudson Strait, he was driven back by arctic conditions. Upon his return to England he learned that the new king, Henry VIII, was more interested in expanding the Royal Navy than in further exploration. Not until the reign of Elizabeth did English explorers return to the search for a northwest passage. Then, between 1576 and 1615 Martin Frobisher, John Davis, Henry Hudson, and William Baffin sailed in succession into the icy northern latitudes, leaving their names on various geographical features and strengthening English claims to this desolate area, but failing to find the coveted route to Asia.

Meanwhile, several thousands of miles further south, the lands discovered by Columbus in the course of his four voyages led to the founding of New Spain. Additional discoveries by Ponce de León (Florida, 1512-13), Alvarez Pineda (Louisiana and Texas, 1519), Hernando de Soto

The Norse Settlements in North America

In the year 982 A.D. Erik the Red, exiled for three years from Iceland for murder, sailed with a small band of his fellow Norsemen for a land rumored to lie several days to the west. Finding and passing around its southern tip, he and his followers made camp at the head of a long fjord. During the next three years Erik explored far to the north, finding numerous places suitable for habitation. Upon his return to Iceland, Erik named his new country Greenland, in part because of its open pastures, in part to attract colonists. In trouble again in 986, Erik organized several hundred Icelanders and headed off to establish permanent settlements in Greenland. Fifteen of his twenty-five vessels survived the crossing, and the majority of his followers chose

the area around Eriksfjord, near the present-day town of Julianehab. The others pushed northwesterly up the coast to the regions around the modern towns of Frederikshab and Godthaab. Later that year Bjarni Herjolfson, another Icelander, attempted to follow his father, who had accompanied Erik to the new land. Bjarni and his crew were blown off course by a North Atlantic storm, and after several weeks they encountered a low-lying stretch of wooded land. Knowing this could not be the mountainous and tree-less coast of Greenland, Bjarni shaped his course to the north, twice encountering still other land that also did not fit Greenland's description. After changing course to the east, he eventually sailed into his father's settlement at what is

In 1869 artist William Bradford photographed the well-preserved ruins of the Norse Hvalsey church in the East Settlement in southwest Greenland. For several hundred years a Norse economy based on raising livestock survived on these shores, at the end of a tenuous sea connection with the Norse of Iceland and Norway. (M.S.M. 54.1459)

today called Herjolfsness. Just where along the North American mainland Bjarni had made his landfall is uncertain; most probably it was along the coast of Newfoundland.

One of Erik the Red's sons, Leif, had heard of Bjarni's voyage while growing up in Greenland, and when he reached adulthood in A.D. 1000 or 1001 he determined to explore the lands Bjarni had encountered fourteen years before. He bought or borrowed the older man's knorr and set off with a small crew to retrace his route. They first encountered a coastline of flat stones, which they called Helluland, next a heavily forested land (Markland), and then two days later landed at a place with extensive meadows. This region they called Vinland, ostensibly because of the discovery of wild grapes, although a variant spelling of the word also meant "meadowland." They built shelters for the winter, and the next spring they returned to Greenland by the same route with a cargo of grapes and timber. A couple of years later Leif's brother, Thorvald, decided to explore further. He and his company wintered in Leif's Vinland huts and over the next two years ranged along the neighboring coast. During one such venture, Thorvald was killed in a fight that the Norsemen had provoked with some natives they encountered. A few years after that, around 1009, Thorfinn Karlsevni, Erik's son-in-law, organized a large expedition to Vinland, carried out extensive explorations, fought a close battle with the natives, and returned to Greenland. The sagas record just one more expedition to Vinland, perhaps around 1020, during which a quarrel ended in one faction exterminating the other. In 1960 the Norwegian archaeologists Helge Ingstad and Anne Stine discovered at L'Anse aux Meadows, on the northern tip of Newfoundland, what is in all likelihood Leif's campsite, used off and on for perhaps

two decades by other Norsemen.

Meanwhile, the Norse settlements in Greenland gradually expanded. Population eventually increased to 3,000 or more, and the settlers established a self-governing republic along lines they had known in Iceland. Greenlanders lived a subsistence life, raising livestock like sheep, cattle, and goats that could graze through the mild winters of the time. They scoured the shoreline for driftwood, fished in the fjords, hunted up north for polar bear, walrus, seals, caribou, and seabirds, and shipped the furs and skins (as well as polar bear cubs) back to Europe. Trading vessels provided a regular connection with the port of Bergen in Norway, as well as with Iceland. The Greenlanders also made regular visits to Markland to obtain fresh timber supplies. Christianity had taken root shortly after the colony began through Erik's wife, Sigfrid, and in 1126 Rome appointed the first of a succession of bishops, for whom the Norse built a cathedral at Gardar (now Igaliko).

But Greenlanders never quite gained economic self-sufficiency. They needed grain, ironware, cloth goods, and timber from home. Always dependent on the sea-link to Norway, life in Greenland continued through three entire centuries, with only a few changes. In 1261 Greenland lost its independence, along with Iceland and other northern islands, to Norway, but the tide did not really begin to turn against it until the Black Death—bubonic plague—devastated Norway in the middle of the fourteenth

century. Greenlanders were now cut off from their market and source of supplies, left to fend almost entirely for themselves in a climate that was becoming steadily colder. The regular run between Bergen and Greenland—the so-called "Greenland knorr"—continued until 1370 or so, and at least intermittent contact with Norway must have continued for at least another fifty years. By 1485, give or take a decade or so—five hundred years after Erik the Red's first colonization—the Norse settlements in Greenland disappeared, in all likelihood absorbed by the steady encroachment of Inuit culture from the north.

When writing about European colonization of America, most historians do not include the Norse settlements at Greenland, refusing to recognize what scientists have known for almost a century: geologically, Greenland is as much a part of North America as Canada or New England. With few exceptions they are quick to dismiss it as "a dead end," in the words of Samuel Eliot Morison, meaning that it did not lead to "us." But the Norse settlements *are* an important part of American maritime history for, unlike the aboriginal Americans, the Norse arrived by sea, explored their new home by sea, and depended on the sea as the vital link with their European motherland. Only when that sea-link failed did their settlements also fail.

Theodor de Bry's image of Columbus's landing on Hispaniola reflects the Spanish vision of the New World, a place of riches that would be freely offered by the native peoples, who would at the same time be willing converts to Christianity. But the Spanish quickly resorted to conquest to subdue the native peoples of the Caribbean and Central America, imposed Christianity on the survivors, and relied on African slaves to labor in the gold and silver mines and on the agricultural plantations of its New World colonies. Engraving from America. *(Courtesy Library of Congress)*

(Mississippi River, 1541) and Francisco de Coronado (inland Texas, 1540-42), enabled Spain to expand its claims into lands north of the Gulf of Mexico. By mid-century New Spain embraced a vast territory extending from New Mexico, Texas, and Florida on the north all the way to the River Plate on the south and including the major islands of the Caribbean Sea. The Spanish monarchy administered this region through a governmental structure firmly under its own control and strongly supported by both Church and army. Only France among other European nations would maintain such close governmental control of its colonial possessions. Spain never wavered from its ultimate goal: to extract as much wealth as possible from its New World possessions—directly in the form of gold and silver bullion where possible, indirectly

through the cultivation of crops like sugar, cocoa, cotton, and other tropical produce where necessary. Twice each year the Spaniards dispatched the fabled Manila galleon from Acapulco with silver bullion bound across the Pacific to the Philippine Islands, claimed by Spain upon their discovery by Ferdinando Magellan in 1521. On its return passage the galleon found the favorable westerlies at the latitude of Japan and then sailed down the California coast with the current to Mexico, bringing back rich cargoes of silk goods. Spain's Atlantic trade was also highly regulated. A fleet of vessels sailed from Spain to the Caribbean each spring and returned home the following winter. Spanish naval vessels protected the *flota*, as it was called, from the warships and privateers of European rivals as well as from the pirates who infested the Caribbean and

Bahamian waters. Fortified harbors at Cartegena on the Spanish Main and Havana on the island of Cuba gave further shelter to the fleet. In 1565 Spain had also established a settlement in Florida at St. Augustine to protect the strategic Straits of Florida, through which its plate fleet sailed on its passage home late each winter. Except for the Portuguese colony of Brazil, Spain held a monopoly of European-held lands in the New World until the beginning of the seventeenth century. Thereafter, Dutch, English, French, and finally American empire-builders made successive inroads into Spain's New World territories, which finally led to its expulsion at the end of the nineteenth century.

For nearly a century after the Cabots' first voyage, only a few European navigators explored the North American coastline south of Newfoundland, but fishermen from many nations flocked to the new grounds. Dried or salted fish could be kept throughout the year and provided an important source of protein for Europe's rising population. It was particularly a welcome substitute during the days (more than 150 each year) when Catholics were expected to abstain from eating meat. Some historians have even suggested that in the mid-1500s English monarchs increased the number of Anglican fast days to accommodate the large landings of cod. By century's end the northern fishery employed thousands of men from almost all of England's and the continent's Atlantic ports and some along the North Sea as well. The vessels went out in the early spring and fished for five months or so, most of them in the "green fishery" (also called the "wet fishery") in which the vessel anchored on the shallow banks in the open sea, and the

English fishermen characteristically processed their codfish on shore rather than packing them in brine on board ship as French and Spanish fishermen did. The fisherman at left displays the protective garb and the single baited hook used in the codfishery. At upper right, fishermen fish from barrels along the vessel's rail, each man handling several lines at a time. Ashore, the codfish are taken into a processing house, where they are headed, gutted, split open, washed, and salted. A final air drying on outdoor "flakes" (bottom) prepares the dehydrated fish for shipment to England. In a separate operation, the cod livers are placed in a press (left) to separate the oil for use in tanning leather. Engraving from Herman Moll's map of North America, published in his atlas, ca. 1715. (Courtesy British Library, London)

Giovanni da Verrazano (ca. 1480-1528), a Florentine mariner, made several notable voyages of exploration in the service of King Francis I of France. His 1524 voyage was the first recorded passage up the East Coast of North America, from Cape Hatteras into New York Bay, and on to Nova Scotia and beyond. Verrazano was killed in an encounter with Caribbean natives in 1528. Drawn by G. Zocchi and engraved by F. Allegrini, 1767. (Courtesy Library of Congress)

crew fished over the rail, or from small open boats called shallops brought along for the purpose. The fish were hauled aboard, soaked in brine for a day or so, and then pressed and stowed below for the trip home. With luck a vessel in the green fishery might make two trips in a season. The "dry fishery," on the other hand, was conducted from seasonal camps established mostly along the shores of Newfoundland and Cape Breton Island. The first captain into a particular cove each year served as "port admiral" to settle disputes. Each day the men put out in small boats and brought their catch back to camp, where it was split, salted, and set out to dry on racks of green boughs called "flakes." To avoid the harsh North American winters, fishing vessels returned by autumn to their European ports. There, dried fish brought a higher price than the salted variety because it could keep much longer and was in great demand as a provision for soldiers and sailors. Vessels in the banks industry comprised a wide range of types, from North Sea herring busses to ketches, and ranged

in size from 30 to 180 tons, with the typical vessel averaging 120 tons or so with a crew of 20 to 30 men. By the last decades of the sixteenth century, more than 300 vessels fished for cod each season in North American waters. Most were French, but Spanish, Portuguese, and later English and Dutch fishermen were also involved.

In addition to cod, some crews fished for salmon and mackerel, while still others discovered the value of marine mammals like walruses and seals for oil, ivory, tusks, and skins. Basque whalemen pursued bowhead and right whales in the waters around Newfoundland and the Gulf of St. Lawrence, but particularly in the Strait of Belle Isle during the autumn migration. In some years the men tried out more than one

Francis Drake (ca. 1540-1596) is best known for his victory over the Spanish Armada in 1588, but by then he had already made the first English circumnavigation of the world, 1577-80, during which he claimed the west coast of North America for England. In 1585, sailing as a privateer, in command of private armed vessels licensed to attack Spanish shipping, Drake sacked Spanish ports around the Caribbean, destroyed the Spanish post at St. Augustine, Florida, and rescued the failing Roanoke colony in Carolina. Knighted for his maritime successes against the Spanish, Drake died at sea in 1596 while conducting yet another raid on Spanish Caribbean ports. (Courtesy John Carter Brown Library, Brown University)

million gallons of "train oil" at stations along the north shore, sending it home to provide fuel for Europe's lamps, a basis for soap, and a lubricant. Because it was considered a fish, the whale's oil was also acceptable as a cooking fat during Lent. When opportunity presented itself, fishermen came ashore to trade their knives and other iron-ware with the natives for deerskins and the furs of beaver, marten, otter, fox, and other mammals of the region. Some vessels even brought a pin-nace for this specific purpose. Long before their compatriots considered establishing permanent settlements on the North American continent, thousands of Europeans "commuted" to the New World each season to work the fishing banks.

Continuing Exploration of North America

Meanwhile, additional intrepid naviga-tors undertook voyages of discovery for other European nations. Among the most notable were two Portuguese brothers, Gaspar and Miguel Corte Real, both of whom were lost at sea in the period 1500-02 while exploring the North American coastline from Labrador south to Newfoundland and perhaps beyond. In 1524 French interests sponsored a voyage by the Florentine navigator Giovanni da Verrazano to search for the northwest passage.

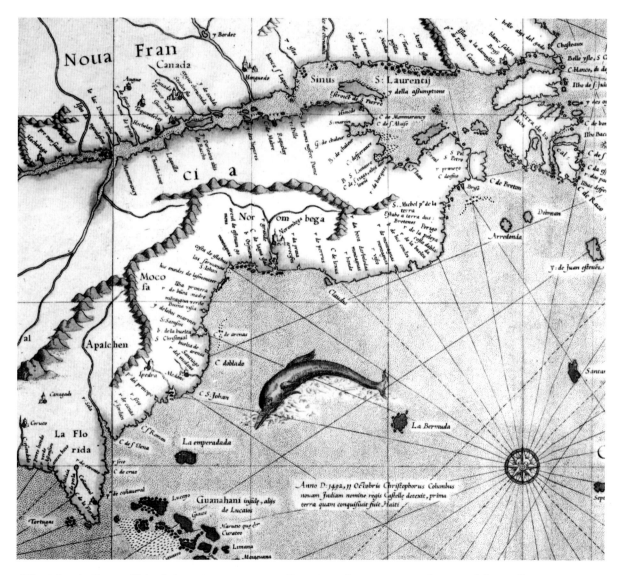

The Atlantic Coast of North America as it appeared on Gerard Mercator's 1569 map of the world. Mercator's projection for the first time produced a chart on which compass courses were accurate in any direction, although it distorted landmasses distant from the equator. By the end of the seventeenth century mariners trusted the Mercator projection enough to begin using it for navigation, making ocean travel far more predictable and easy to plot. (Courtesy Maritiem Museum Prins Hendrik, Rotterdam)

Making his landfall near Cape Hatteras, Verrazano coasted north and east all the way to Nova Scotia and perhaps beyond, discovering and mapping New York Bay, Block Island, and Narragansett Bay before heading back to France. The following year a Portuguese mariner, Estevan Gomes, charted the waters north of Cape Cod for his Spanish sponsors, but neither France nor Spain advanced claims to these territories. When France sent Jacques Cartier to explore the American coast further north for the elusive passage in 1534, however, the sturdy mariner from St. Malo discovered the gulf and river named for St. Lawrence and claimed the surrounding shores for France. In the year following, Cartier returned to sail up the great river as far as the rapids just upstream from an Indian village he renamed Montreal. He and his companions spent a difficult winter on the shores of the St. Lawrence River before returning to France. A few years later Cartier tried to establish a settlement at present-day Quebec, but conditions proved too difficult and the venture failed. Cartier's efforts nevertheless gave to the French a strong claim to a sizable part of the North American continent, which they would vigorously follow up, but not until the beginning of the seventeenth century.

England also postponed further American exploration for seventy-five years after the initial voyages of the Cabots. Then, in 1577, Francis Drake was sent out to the Pacific. After harassing unsuspecting settlements along the western coasts of Spanish America and capturing considerable quantities of booty, he sailed north to find a safe place for careening his ship, *Golden Hind*, in a bay north of the present-day harbor of San Francisco, whose entrance he failed to see. Drake claimed California for England, naming it "New Albion," and then set off in search of his primary quarry, the Manila galleon. Unsuccessful in that venture, he continued around the world, returning to England in 1580 to complete the first circumnavigation of the world since Magellan's fleet sixty years before. The booty he had captured was worth nearly £500,000. California had in fact been discovered in 1542 by the Spanish navigator Juan Rodgriquez Cabrillo, who had sailed along the coast as far north as Cape Mendocino but also missed the opening to San Francisco Bay; so well disguised was its entrance that the bay's eventual discovery in 1769 came not from the sea

at all but by an overland expedition. In part because of Drake's incursions, Spain continued intermittent exploration of the California coast throughout the sixteenth century, but not discovering anything considered of value, it made no effort to settle the area. A century later, the threat of Russian expansion down the Pacific coast from Alaska would prompt Spanish settlement, and they would establish their first California mission at San Diego in 1769. Others quickly followed at Monterey and Los Angeles, where a prosperous cattle industry would soon produce hides and tallow for export.

In the 1580s two other Elizabethan adventurers, Sir Humphrey Gilbert and Sir Walter Raleigh, attempted to found settlements at the extreme ends of England's claims along the Atlantic coast of North America–Gilbert's in Newfoundland and Raleigh's in what is now North Carolina. Neither undertaking succeeded, however, and for some of the same reasons that had ultimately brought down the Norse settlements in Greenland only a century before: harsh climate conditions, hostile natives, and insufficient support from home. But English interest in overseas expansion nevertheless quickened in the last decades of the sixteenth century, in part because of the writings of Richard Hakluyt, author of the *Discourse of Western Planting* (1584) and *The Principal Navigations of the English Nation* (1589), which touted the advantages of establishing settlements in North America. In this respect, among others, the English empire would differ dramatically from that of Spain. Hakluyt believed the colonial trade that would follow the founding of overseas settlements would greatly strengthen England's ability to thwart the growing power of Spain. The colonies could supply raw materials like timber and naval stores for the expanding fleet and would become markets for the nation's wool cloth and other products. Gilbert wrote of another advantage mentioned by Hakluyt: "We might settle there such needy people of our countrey which now trouble the common wealth and who through want here at home ar inforced to commit outragious offences. . . . "

With the new century came further efforts to colonize the North American continent. After making a landfall in southern Maine in the spring of 1602, Bartholomew Gosnold explored the New England coast as far as Cuttyhunk Island off the southern Massachusetts coast, where he

NOVA BRITANNIA:

OFFERING MOST
Excellent fruites by Planting in
VIRGINIA.

Exciting all such as be well affected
to further the same.

LONDON
Printed for SAMVEL MACHAM, and are to be sold at
his Shop in Pauls Church-yard, at the
Signe of the Bul-head.
1609.

The Promotional Pamphlet

First the voyage is not long nor tedious, six weeks at ease will send us thither, whereas six months suffice not to some other places, where we trade. . . .When we come to the coast, there is continual depth enough, with good bottom for anchor hold, and the land is faire to fall with all, full of excellent good harbours; the world afords no better for ships of all burdens, many pleasant islands great and small affronting the coast: two goodly rivers are discovered winding far into the maine, the one in the north part of the land by our western colonies, knights and gentlement of Excester, Plymouth and others; the other in the south part thereof by our colony of London, upon which river, being both broad, deep, and pleasant, abounding with store of fish, our colony have begun to fortify themselves, and have built a towne, and named it (in honor of our King) James towne, fourscore miles within land, upon the north side of the river (as is London upon the River of Thames) from whence we have discovered the same River, one hundred miles further into the main land, in the searching whereof, they were so ravished with the admirable sweetness of the stream, and with the pleasant land trending along on either side, that their joy exceeded and with great admiration they praised God.

There are valleys and plains streaming with sweet springs, like veins in a natural body; there are hills and mountains making a sensible proffer of hidden treasure, never yet searched; the land is full of minerals, plenty of woods (the wants of England) there are growing goodly okes and elms, beech and birch, spruce, walnut, cedar and fir trees in great abundance, the soil is strong and lustry of its own nature, and sends out naturally fruitful vines running upon trees and shrubs; it yields also rosin, tur-

pentine, pitch and tar, sassafras, mulberry trees and silk-worms, many skins and rich furs, many sweet woods and dyers' woods, and other costly dyes; plenty of sturgeon, timber for shipping, mast, plank, and deal, soap ashes, caviar, and what else we know not yet, because our days are young. But of this that I have said, if bare nature be so amiable in its naked kind, what may we hope, when art and nature both shall join, and strive together, to give best content to man and beast?

Robert Johnson, *Nova Britannia: offering most excellent fruites by planting in Virginia* (London, 1609)

Robert Johnson's **Nova Britannia,** *with its glowing accounts of North America, included an engraving of a typical ship-rigged vessel of the period. (Courtesy Library of Congress)*

built a temporary outpost. The next year Martin Pring set up a similar trading post along Cape Cod Bay, and in 1605 George Waymouth spent several weeks exploring the St. George River in Maine. Two years later, Ferdinando Gorges and George Popham attempted to found a settlement near the mouth of the Kennebec River, but after surviving the winter they returned home the following spring using the pinnace *Virginia of Sagadahoc*, which was the first vessel built in English America. The information brought back by these expeditions was sometimes heavily edited to create a falsely optimistic impression of the New World in order to encourage others to invest either their money or their lives in the continuing effort to establish English colonies on the far side of the tumultuous Atlantic. Thus Arthur Barlowe, the chronicler of the ill-fated Roanoke colony, in 1585 wrote of "such plenty. . .that I think in all the world the like abundance is not to be found," and John Brereton, who accompanied Bartholomew Gosnold's expedition to southeastern New England, proclaimed the sandy soil there "the most plentiful, sweet, fruitful, and wholesome of all the world." Even the native inhabitants took on paradisiacal attributes, being in Barlowe's words "the most gentle, loving, and faithful [people], void of all guile and treason. . . such as live after the manner of the golden age." After cruising along the New England coast from Virginia in 1616, Captain John Smith proclaimed that "of all the four parts of the world I have yet seen, not inhabited, I would rather live here than anywhere."

As these English efforts were going forward, Spain, France, and The Netherlands advanced their own claims to parts of the North American continent. Throughout much of the seventeenth century, England would be at war with one or another of these rivals. Because the Spanish outpost at St. Augustine, established in 1565, posed a threat to the English settlement at Roanoke, Drake descended upon the town 1586 and destroyed everything his fleet could not cart away. Although Spain subsequently rebuilt St. Augustine, it was never again a serious threat to the English.

At the other end of North America's lengthy coast the French nobleman Sieur de Monts, accompanied by Samuel de Champlain, began exploring and mapping the coast of New

England in 1604. They too made serious attempts to establish an outpost along these shores, first on an island in the St. Croix River and then in 1605 across the Bay of Fundy on the coast of Acadia (Nova Scotia) at Port Royal (now Annapolis). Champlain explored the entire New England coast as far south as Cape Cod, which he named Cape Blanc because of its white sandy beaches. The settlement at Port Royal hung on until 1613, when the English destroyed it, but by that time Champlain had already determined to make the St. Lawrence valley the focal point of New France. In 1608 he chose the site where the river narrows to found the fortress and city of Quebec. Despite this shift inland, however, French fishing interests based in Nova Scotia and Cape Breton would continue to challenge English hegemony in northeastern waters for another 150 years until finally quashed in the wars of the mid-eighteenth century.

The English had also to contend with another important rival when in 1609 the Dutch East India Company hired an English mariner, Henry Hudson, ostensibly to look for a passage to China via the waters north of Russia. After encountering ice, however, Hudson turned back and proceeded to cross the Atlantic instead, and after looking into Chesapeake and Delaware Bays he entered New York Bay and sailed up the river that bears his name. Verrazano's discovery of New York Bay in 1524 had never been followed up by his French sponsors so the Dutch laid claim to the best natural harbor on the entire Atlantic coast. After a Dutch trading post was established near present-day Albany in 1614, New Netherland remained in their hands for another half-century. England was, therefore, not without serious rivals on the eve of its first colonization of North America.

The Crossing

As the Europeans explored North America by sea at the beginning of the seventeenth century, so too did they finally manage to establish and maintain their first permanent settlements by sea. The death of Queen Elizabeth in 1603 brought the first Stuart king, James I, to the throne, along with a willingness to make peace with Spain and get on with the colonization of American lands claimed by England. Royal charters granted extensive territories to companies of investors who hoped to reap a profit from New World resources–ideally gold and silver, but at least the timber, furs, and fish that seemed so abundant. But to develop these resources they needed more than land and money; they needed laborers. Decades of economic turmoil had created a generation of what one historian has called "vexed and troubled Englishmen." Young yeomen, artisans and tradesmen, as well as laborers and the unemployed, saw in America an opportunity to find work and perhaps acquire the land that would give them independence and security unattainable at home. Most of the first colonists were single men, but a few brought wives, and a number of single women joined the migration as members of family households. Some immigrants could pay their own way, but many voluntarily signed contracts called indentures to work four years or more in exchange for their passage. Further thousands came involuntarily: criminals sent to America as an alternative punishment to hanging, prisoners of war, and Africans kidnapped from their native land and sold to European slave traders.

The search for religious asylum was yet another motivation for emigration from the Old World to the New. Persecution of Protestants under both Catholic monarchs, James I and his son Charles I, drove thousands of English Calvinists to America, where they founded communities modeled on their own strict beliefs. The Stuarts were glad to see them go, and they made generous grants of land to groups of both separatists (Pilgrims) and reformers (Puritans). Later, English Catholics, French Huguenots, German Lutherans, and Jews from the Iberian peninsula, among others, joined the migration to the New World. Most Protestants enjoyed the freedom of religion they had sought for themselves, while denying it for others like Quakers, Catholics, and Jews.

Whatever his or her previous status, every migrant coming to America shared one experience in common–the challenge of an ocean crossing. The vessels were small, rarely more than 100 feet in overall length or 200 tons burden, and usually much smaller, often crowded with one hundred or more passengers and crew. The *Mayflower* was typical: 90 feet long and 180 tons burden, according to the replica designed by the historian-architect William Baker and on exhibit

at Plymouth today. A direct course across the Atlantic meant bucking constant headwinds and unfavorable currents, so many shipmasters chose the southerly route instead, where the northeast trade winds brought them to a landfall in the West Indies, whence they sailed up the coast to their destination.

By either route the typical crossing lasted two months at least, and passages taking twice as long were not unheard of. Food and water supplies usually ran low, scurvy, small pox, and other illnesses often broke out, and passengers commonly suffered injuries incurred during storms. For some of the weak or elderly passengers a long bout of seasickness could well bring death from dehydration or the inability to hold down nourishment. Others perished from disease or later from prolonged weakening of body or spirit, and occasionally a vessel simply disappeared with all on board, the victim of storm, fire, or some undisclosed condition of unseaworthiness. The possibility of attack by enemy privateers during the frequent wars of the seventeenth and eighteenth centuries, or by pirates at any time, were other dangers faced by all vessels making transatlantic passages. A tearful ten-year-old explained to his uncle why he had been so scared during a ferocious Atlantic storm. "I know if I had died at land, I would have gone to Heaven," he sobbed, "but the thing that vexes me is, if I go to the bottom of this terrible sea, God will never be able to get me up; the fishes will eat me and I am done forever."

So traumatic was the Atlantic crossing, both in anticipation and experience, that only a few migrants considered returning to their homeland, even when they encountered extreme hardships in the New World. In this sense, crossing the Atlantic marked both a symbolic and actual commitment to a life in the New World. This was especially true for English Puritans, whose ministers frequently referred to the crossing as a test of faith, often attributing a successful landfall to God's favorable opinion of their endeavor. The Reverend Thomas Shepard recalled that in the middle of a storm he thought that "if ever the Lord did bring me to shore again I should live like one come and risen from the dead." John Winthrop was only the first among many who equated the Puritan crossing of the Atlantic with that of the Hebrews' flight across the Red Sea. In both cases a body of water prevented the

The Crossing:
Myth & Reality

The Myth:

Whoever shall put to sea in a stout and well-conditioned ship, having an honest master and loving seamen, shall not need to fear, but he shall find as good content at sea as at land. It is too common with many to fear the sea more than they need, and all such as put to sea confesses it to be less tedious than they either feared or expected. A ship at sea may well be compared to a cradle rocked by a careful mother's hand, which though it be moved up and down it is not in danger of falling. So a ship may often be rocked too and again upon the troublesome sea, yet seldom doth it sink or overturn because it is kept by that careful hand of Providence by which it is rocked. It was never known yet that any ship in that voyage was cast away, or that ever fell into the enemy's hand.

For the health of passengers, it hath been observed that of six hundred souls not above three or four have died at sea. It is probable in such a company more might have died either by sickness or casualties if they had stayed at home. For women, I see not but that they do as well as men, and young children as well as either, having their healths as well at sea as at land. Many likewise which have come with such foul bodies to sea as did make their days uncomfortable at land have been so purged and

clarified at sea that they have been more healthful for after-times, their weak appetites being turned to good stomachs, not only desiring but likewise digesting such victuals as the sea affords.

William Wood, *New Englands Prospect: A true, lively, and experimentall description of that part of America, commonly called New England...*(London, 1634).

The Reality:

We ran a Southerly course from the Tropicke of Cancer, where having the Sun within six or seven degrees right over our head in July, we bore away West; so that by the fervent heat and loomes breezes, many of our men fell sicke of the Calenture, and out of two ships was throwne over-boord thirtie two persons. The Viceadmirall was said to have the plague in her; but in the Blessing we had not any sicke, albeit we had twenty women and children.

Upon Saint James day, being about one hundred and fiftie leagues distant from the West Indies, in crossing the Gulfe of Bahoma, there hapned a most terrible and vehement storme, which was a taile of the West Indian Horacano; this tempest seperated all our Fleet one from another, and it was so violent that men could scarce stand upon the Deckes, neither could any man heare another speake, being thus divided, every man steered his owne course, and as it fell out about five or sixe dayes after the storme ceased (which endure fortie foure houres in extremitie) the Lion first, and after the Falcon and the Unitie, got sight of our Shippe, and so we lay a way directly for Virginia, finding neither current nor winde opposite, as some have reported, to the great charge of our Counsell and Adventurers. The Unity was sore distressed when she came up with us, for of seventy land men, she had not ten sound, and all her Sea men were downe, but onley the Master and his Boy, with one poore sailer, but we relieved them, and we foure consorting, fell into the Kings River haply the eleventh of August. In the Unity were borne two children at Sea, but both died, being both Boyes.

"A Letter of M. Gabriel Archer touching the voyage of the Fleet of Ships, which arrived at Virginia,...1609," Samuel Purchas, *Hakluytus Posthumus or Purchas His Pilgrimes* (London, 1625)

Three thousand miles of ocean separated Europe and North America, and even the increasingly sophisticated three-masted ships of the seventeenth century were easily overwhelmed by North Atlantic storms. This view of the "vast and furious ocean," engraved by Wenceslaus Hollar, 1665, suggests how much of an ordeal a transatlantic passage could be. (Courtesy The Huntington Library, San Marino, California)

refugees' enemies from pursuit. Even for the many settlers who had no strong religious convictions, the mere breadth and strength of the ocean barred a return to the Old World, no matter how disappointing life in the New World proved to be. Few of the migrants had ever encountered sailors before and were not used to being sassed by such as the "proud and very profane young man, one of the seamen [on board the *Mayflower*], of lusty, able body, which made him the more haughty. He would always be condemning the poor people in their sickness, and cursing them daily with grievous execrations. . . . "

The First English Settlements

In late December 1606, an expedition of three vessels left the Thames River en route to America, carrying just over 100 men in the employ of the Virginia Company with the intent of founding a permanent settlement on the shores of Chesapeake Bay. One of the captains, Bartholomew Gosnold, had already explored the New England coast, and quite possibly Christopher Newport, the overall commander, was also familiar with the continent. In any event, the fleet was off Cape Henry in late April 1607 and soon after established their outpost of Jamestown on a marshy island sixty miles inland on the banks of the river they named the James River. But within eight months half of the settlers had died, and the rest managed to hang on only because Newport returned in January 1608 with much-needed supplies and new recruits. Under the leadership of Captain John Smith, the settlers used pinnaces and other small craft to trade with local Indians for corn throughout the protected waterways of Chesapeake Bay, which Smith explored as far north as its head in 1608.

Disease, dissension, and discouragement gradually sapped the community's strength, however, and despite hundreds of new colonists, only sixty inhabitants remained in the spring of 1610. When a relief expedition arrived in May, the survivors piled aboard the four vessels and headed down the James with the intention of sailing for home. At the mouth of the river, however, they encountered the new governor arriving with yet more reinforcements, and the erstwhile refugees rather

sheepishly turned back. Encouraged by reports that Virginia could supply marketable quantities of timber products, pot and pearl ash, and furs, the company continued to send still further fleets with livestock, provisions, and more than five hundred additional men and women. For many years to come, Virginia would remain utterly dependent on its maritime connection with the mother country for survival. In light of the hardships faced by these early seventeenth-century settlers, perhaps the Norse achievement 600 years before gains new significance.

Dismissed from his position at Jamestown, Captain John Smith returned home to England, but in 1614 he came back to America to explore the coast between Cape Cod and the Penobscot River, a region which he named New England. His chart, published in 1616, provided valuable information to those who would follow. Even so, when Christopher Jones made a landfall in November 1620, at Cape Cod, rather than northern Virginia as intended, no contemporary chart could guide him through the dangerous shoals that blocked the way further south. Thus the band of 102 Pilgrims he had on board established their New World sanctuary at Plymouth instead. As in Jamestown, half the original settlers died during the first winter, but the survivors were more successful at fishing and trading with the peaceful natives of the area. Additional settlers arrived on board the *Fortune* the following autumn, and a cargo of clapboards and furs was immediately sent home in her. Although Plymouth colony received almost no support from home, it managed to subsist on trade with Indians and colonists in other settlements, while supplementing its agricultural production with fishing.

Meanwhile, a scattering of fishermen, fortune-seekers, dissidents from Plymouth, and others began to settle in places northward along the Massachusetts shore. The most significant was the outpost established by the Dorchester Adventurers at Cape Ann in 1623, close to the present site of Gloucester. But they soon discovered that their fishermen could not farm and the farmers would not fish, and so the enterprise collapsed.

Out of its ashes, through a complex series of mergers, grants, and new charters, the Massachusetts Bay Company eventually emerged. In 1629 a group of Puritans under the leadership of John Winthrop took control of the company. The Puritans were eager to escape the restrictions imposed by Charles I and Archbishop William Laud by finding a place where they could establish a church and community in conformity with their own beliefs. New England seemed ideal, and in 1629 they sent out five vessels with nearly three hundred co-religionists and others to settle at what now is Salem. In the following year another seven hundred Puritans arrived, along with Winthrop himself on board his flagship *Arbella*, and still more came later that fall.

One of Winthrop's first decisions was to move the principal place of settlement twenty miles south to the Shawmut peninsula, soon renamed Boston, which proved to be a much better site than Salem for what would become a major seaport. By 1640, when the Puritan migration ended, more than twenty thousand men, women, and children had crossed the Atlantic to seek religious sanctuary, economic opportunity, or both, in the score or more settlements that now comprised the colony of Massachusetts Bay.

Most of these early communities lay within the reach of tidewater, and for good reason. Rivers such as the Charles and the Merrimack, and other protected waterways like Plum Island Sound and Boston Harbor, offered relatively safe means of communication between settlements and thereby enhanced their ability to give and receive supplies or military aid when needed. Then too, rivers and sounds provided rich resources of fish, waterfowl, clams, saltmarsh hay, and even seaweed to the nearby residents. Only the pressure of increasing population forced habitation to move way from the shores of Massachusetts Bay. Even then, except for the Connecticut River valley towns, new settlements remained within a day's travel of the coast until mid-century or later.

Geographically, Boston was well favored to become a leading seaport. Its outer harbor was described by the historian William Wood as "safe, spacious, and deep, free from such cockling seas

Although a flotilla of eighty Calusa war canoes dissuaded Ponce de León from landing on the Florida coast in 1513, Native Americans were rarely able to prevail against Europeans armed with cannons and firearms. Both sides resorted to shows of force, ritual slayings, and kidnappings to press their interests. In Virginia in 1613, the English kidnapped Pocahontas to gain the return of captured Englishmen. After a truce (shown here) to demonstrate that Pocahontas was unharmed, peace was concluded the following year with the marriage of Pocahontas to John Rolfe, the first European cultivator of tobacco. Farther north, however, when the Pequots killed several English coastal traders in the 1630s, the English retaliated and nearly wiped out the entire tribe. Engraving by Theodor de Bry, America, Part X (1618), Plate VIII. (Courtesy Library of Congress)

as run upon the coast of Ireland and in the channels of England." With a seventeenth-century man's concern for defense, he also observed that it had "but one common and safe entrance, and that not very broad, . . . but being once within, there is room for the anchorage of five hundred ships." Boston was nearly at the center of New England's first coastal settlements that ranged in a wide hyperbolic arc from Newbury and Ipswich, forty miles to the north, to Plymouth and Duxbury, about the same distance to the south. These communities, even more than nearby inland towns like Concord, Sudbury, and Dedham, became Boston's first hinterland. Locally built shallops and pinnaces brought in fish, produce, and firewood to the port even as Bostonians began to look far beyond their immediate environs for

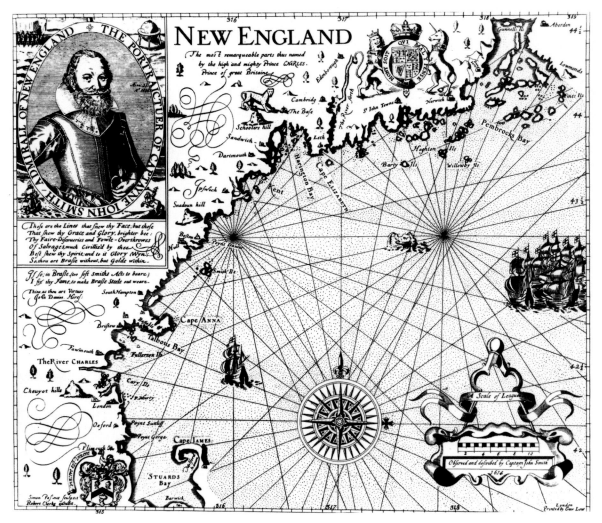

John Smith's map of New England, published in London in 1614, included a portrait of Smith, self-styled "Admiral of New England," who explored the coast in 1614. Prince Charles selected names for "the most remarqueable parts." Designated even before permanent English settlement, Plymouth, the Charles River, and Cape Ann have retained their names ever since. John Smith (1580-1631) claimed to have had many adventures as a soldier, privateer, and slave in the Mediterranean before joining the Virginia expedition of 1607. Under Smith's leadership, the settlement survived after its disastrous beginnings. Smith established cordial relations with the natives and explored the extent of Chesapeake Bay before injury led to his departure for England in 1610. After his 1614 voyage to New England, he worked to promote settlement and fishing in that region, but he never again returned to America. (M.S.M. 66.253)

commercial opportunities, arranging to trade fish and liquor with the Chesapeake for corn and tobacco and with Niew Amsterdam for sugar, furs, and sheep. The Bay Colony's first deep-sea vessel, the *Blessing of the Bay*, was built at Medford in 1631 and immediately set off on a trading voyage to Dutch-held Long Island. Within a decade Boston-built vessels were sailing to the West Indies with fish, timber, and other New England produce and returning with sugar, molasses, and rum. Transatlantic trade involved reexporting these same West Indian products, along with fish, ship timber and masts, and other naval stores–pitch, rosin, and turpentine. Returning vessels brought cloth, hardware, and other manufactured articles from European and English ports. Elsewhere along the New England coast smaller communities like Portsmouth, New Hampshire, Newport, Rhode Island, and New Haven Colony (which later merged with Connecticut) began to develop their own maritime commerce by mid-century, but none came close to challenging the hegemony of Boston.

Meanwhile, in Chesapeake Bay, the colony of Virginia had at last overcome its initial difficulties. In 1614 a crop of tobacco first developed by planter John Rolfe was sent to London for marketing. The development of this cash crop, combined with a policy that enabled individuals to acquire small parcels of land, within a decade revolutionized the economy of Virginia. Planters built their own wharves along the rivers and streams of the bay, where vessels arrived with imports from England and departed with cargoes of tobacco. English merchants controlled the trade from their offices in London, Bristol, and later Glasgow, marketing the tobacco manufactured in various forms throughout Europe and purchasing on account the goods ordered by their planter customers. For this reason, the lower Chesapeake developed no merchant class of its own and, until the emergence of Norfolk late in the eighteenth century, no seaports either. By the end of the 1630s, Virginia was annually exporting more than one million pounds of tobacco worth perhaps £5,000, figures that would increase tenfold over the next thirty years. Tobacco culture required labor, and vessels outbound from England brought altogether a thousand or more indentured servants each year. After working off terms of service that ranged from four to seven years, many of these immigrants acquired land for tobacco plantations of their own.

Fort nieuw Amsterdam op de Manhatans

Although New York Bay was discovered for France by Verrazano, the Dutch Nieuw Netherland Company claimed it in 1614 on the strength of Henry Hudson's 1609 voyage up the river that bears his name. Dutch settlers arrived on Manhattan Island in 1624, establishing a fort and trading for furs with the natives of the Hudson River valley. Native-American dugout canoes and Dutch ocean shipping and coastal craft mix off the growing community of Nieuw Amsterdam, ca. 1627, in this reverse-image engraving, t'Fort nieuw Amsterdam op de Manhatans, *published in Joost Hartgers,* Beschrivinghe van Virginia, Nieuw Nederlandt, Nieuw Engelandt *(Amsterdam, 1651). (Courtesy Miriam and Ira D. Wallach Division of Art, Prints and Photographs, The New York Public Library, Astor, Lenox and Tilden Foundations)*

After weathering a long winter crossing, two small vessels named *Ark* and *Dove* entered Chesapeake Bay in March 1634 with about 150 passengers on board. Their destination was land at the head of the bay granted by Charles I to George Calvert, Lord Baltimore, who named his feudal domain Maryland, in honor of the Queen. Although the Calverts intended to establish a refuge for English Catholics, they welcomed settlers of other faiths as well. Protestants centered their commercial activities near the mouth of the Patuxent river at a site later named Annapolis, the Catholic townspeople remaining at the earlier site of St. Mary's. Following the example of neighboring Virginia, however, and taking advantage of the rich soil, Marylanders planted their land in tobacco, corn, and other grains. Soon estates along the northern banks of the Potomac river and throughout the eastern shore were producing crops for export.

Between the English colonies of New England on the north and along Chesapeake Bay to the south, the Dutch West India Company undertook to exploit its claim to the Hudson River valley and beyond. The trading post 150 miles up the Hudson River was supported by the establishment of a fort and the entrepôt settlement of Nieuw Amsterdam on the tip of Manhattan Island in New York Bay. First settled in 1624 by a small band of Walloons and French Huguenots, Nieuw Amsterdam had several advantages over its English rivals. For one thing it possessed the best natural harbor along the eastern seaboard; for another its location, bought from the Native Americans in 1626, was flanked on either side by extensive protected waterways, Long Island Sound to the east and Raritan Bay to the west. Most important, the site commanded the entrance to the Hudson River, one of the best

Anxious to trade with the Native Americans for furs, the English and Dutch exchanged trinkets and a wide variety of European goods, including knives and ultimately firearms. In this view of impromptu commerce, natives in dugout canoes trade furs for beads, knives, and hats. Such trade, particularly in weapons, changed the balance of power among native tribes, as did European diseases such as measles, which were unwittingly spread by such cultural contact. Engraving by Theodor de Bry, America, Part XIII *(1634), Plate V. (Courtesy New York Public Library)*

routes into the interior of the North American continent. By mid-century the Dutch were sending 35,000 beaver pelts home to Amsterdam each year. To the east, Nieuw Netherland and New England interests clashed in the Connecticut River valley, where both groups had established trading outposts to tap the vast resources of beaver, mink, and otter furs, but by mid-century the English had taken over this region from the Dutch by sheer force of numbers.

The Dutch also expanded their commercial interests southward in 1619, bringing the first cargo of slaves from Africa to sell to the English colonists along Chesapeake Bay, and carrying their tobacco and other produce to European markets. In 1653 the Dutch overran the tiny settlement that Sweden had established at Fort Christiana (now Wilmington) on the banks of the Delaware River fifteen years before. Niew Amsterdam also established trade with the Dutch West India Company's colony at Guiana on the coast of South America, shipping fish, pork, beef, flour, and biscuit in exchange for sugar. Niew Amsterdam grew to rival Boston as a seaport with a population of 2,500 by mid-century. But increasing numbers of English settlers continued to encroach on Dutch-claimed territory in Connecticut, on Long Island, and along the Delaware. In the 1660s England's restoration government under Charles II adopted an aggressive colonial policy and in 1664 sent a fleet that successfully wrested Niew Amsterdam from the Dutch without firing a shot.

At mid-century the coastal regions lying south of Virginia remained virtually uninhabited by European colonists, despite successive efforts made by England, France, and Spain ever since the "lost colony" at Roanoke in 1585-88. Then, in 1663 Charles II granted the land, already known as Carolina from an earlier undertaking, to a new group of proprietors. Several abortive attempts by experienced settlers from other colonies led finally in 1670 to a group from Barbados founding the town of Charles Town, where, as the old saying goes, "the Ashley and Cooper Rivers join to form the Atlantic Ocean." Carolina developed slowly in its early years, the planters trying various crops like sugar, cotton, and tobacco, with indifferent results. Despite these discouraging beginnings, Charles Town had already become the center for the continental American slave trade. With the development of rice as a staple crop early in the next century, southern Carolina was well on its way to wealth.

After the settlement of Carolina, the last territory accessible from the Atlantic that was not yet occupied by English settlers lay between the colonies of New York and Maryland west of the Delaware River. The settlements founded as New Sweden nestled along the lower banks of that river, and upstream a group of English Quakers had purchased what became known as West Jersey in 1675. One of the trustees of that settlement was William Penn. In 1681, as repayment for the loan Penn's father had made years before, King Charles II granted the son all of the unoccupied land west of the Delaware River to colonize, demanding only that the new colony be named Pennsylvania in honor of the grantee's father. Penn proved to have an ideal combination of qualities as leader of the new colony. He negotiated with Native Americans for title to the land; he encouraged Quakers and others to settle with his policy of religious and cultural freedom; and he planned his colony as a series of regular townships, at the heart of which lay Philadelphia, "the city of brotherly love."

Situated on the neck of land between the Delaware and Schuylkill Rivers, Philadelphia became one of colonial America's major seaports within a few decades after its founding in 1683.

New England Fisheries

The Puritans who came to New England with John Winthrop knew that one of the region's most promising resources was the fishery. Yet most of them were farmers with no experience whatever as mariners. Besides, almost all of them had families, whereas fishing off the North American coast had been conducted almost entirely by companies of men living in remote camps alongshore or on offshore islands like Monhegan or Richmond. No amount of cajoling by Salem's Reverend Hugh Peter or encouragement from Governor Winthrop and the General Court could convert landsmen into fishermen. Puritan leaders turned instead to experienced men from Dorset and Cornwall, hired as servants. As further incentives, managers allowed members of their "boat-gangs" shares of the catch, and towns offered them grants of land for houselots, but the industry still struggled. Like most Englishmen, they chafed at the restrictions of a servant's life, while on the other hand community leaders viewed the drunken, raucous lifestyles of many fishermen with alarm.

The outbreak of civil war in England gave New England's fishermen their first break, as West Country fishermen gradually withdrew from American waters. With lessening competition from home, the value of New England's catch doubled by 1645 to £10,000, and was sent to markets in Spain, Portugal, and the Wine Islands in English ships. A few years later Winthrop discovered that West Indian planters had so concentrated their efforts on producing sugar that they needed outside sources of inexpensive foodstuffs for their slaves. Fish from New England filled the bill, and a pattern of exports soon evolved that dominated the industry for more than a century: "merchantable" fish of high quality went to Catholic Europe, while the less desirable "refuse" fish was sold at two-thirds the price in the West Indies.

As markets expanded, so too did the number of men willing to try their hand at a new undertaking. Villages north of Boston, especially

Marblehead, Salem, and Gloucester, which had ready access to the Gulf of Maine, enjoyed the boom, but so too did Ipswich, Newbury, and the smaller hamlets along the coast of Maine. By 1675, upwards of 400 vessels with at least one thousand men on board set out each year from this region alone. The towns of Plymouth Colony, including those on Cape Cod, contributed to New England's catch, which soon totaled some 60,000 quintals (a quintal being a long hundredweight, or 112 pounds). The typical arrangement involved a London merchant, with whom a colonist such as Salem's William Browne agreed to deliver an agreed-upon amount of "merchantable dry cod fish." Browne in turn contracted with companies of local fishermen to sell him their catch, advancing them provisions and equipment for the voyage, and giving each man a share of the profits.

As soon as they dared in late winter, when the cod first came inshore, and again in late summer when the fish returned, each company sent out its shallop with three or four men on board. Once anchored on the desired bank, the men fished two or three lines each with a couple of hooks baited with mackerel or herring. At the end of the day the boats returned to their shoreside station, where they set themselves up as a disassembly line, as it were, to gut, split, and salt down each fish. Then the shoreman took over, setting the fish on flakes to dry and carefully tending them while his companions returned the next day to the fishing grounds. Sometimes coasters called at the station during the season to bring more supplies and take part of the catch back to Boston or Salem.

Going to sea was always a dangerous occupation, and fishing entailed the greatest dangers of all. Not only were the vessels small, but because they could only make money while on the grounds, the crews tended to push their luck even as the weather turned foul. Then too, the shallow banks themselves produced a sharp chop difficult for small vessels to handle. For all these reasons mortality rates among New England's fishermen reached extraordinary heights. During the thirty-year period between 1645 and 1675 more than half of Essex County's mariners whose deaths were recorded in the courts died at sea, according to Daniel Vickers, the leading authority on the subject of early New England fisheries. Less than half of New England's seventeenth-century fishermen owned

John Roads, Fisherman of Marblehead

Through most of the colonial period, Marblehead, Massachusetts, was the greatest fishing port in America. By the middle of the eighteenth century, when visitors first recorded their impressions of the town, it was crowded and jumbled, busy but poor. A hundred years before, however, Marblehead had been a very different place–hardly a town at all. Fishermen first settled there in 1630 because they judged it convenient for their business. With a tolerable harbor ringed by a rocky shoreline suitable for drying fish, Marblehead was at once close to the better fishing grounds of Massachusetts Bay and less than an hour by boat from a source of provisioning in Salem. As a town, however, it was no more than collection of cabins, each surrounded by an acre or two of cleared ground running down to the shore where sheds for splitting fish were built out on piles over the water. There were no churches, no schools, no stores, no taverns, and little in the way of organized family life.

Into this frontier fishing settlement sometime in the mid-1650s sailed a young Englishman named John Roads. Where originally he came from in the old country is anyone's guess, though the fact that he was in his twenties and already an accomplished fisherman meant that he had almost certainly spent some time working in Newfoundland. He had married in England some years before–to a woman named Joan, who may have arrived with him but more probably joined him in Marblehead some years later once he had established himself there. The couple had at least two children, though daughter Sarah and son John must have been quite young when their father first came to Marblehead.

Neither John Roads nor any of his fishing neighbors moved to New England with the intention of settling there. They stumbled upon the place in the course of trying to make a living in a maritime industry that was spread across the North Atlantic. But why did they stay? Why would somebody choose to abandon their home in England to settle in this primitive community on Massachusetts' rugged North Shore? Spending the warmer months of the year working the cod-rich banks and inshore waters of the northwest Atlantic was one thing; emigrating permanently to the far fringes of European civilization was quite another. The prospects for fishermen based in the mother country during the 1650s were hardly bad enough as to force them into such a move. Indeed, fish prices were healthy, and the fleet that fished at Newfoundland was recovering by then from the chaos of the Civil War years. If England had not been an easy place to earn a living in recent years, there was at least at home the security of familiar surroundings and kinfolk to lend support when times got hard. New England held out the attraction of inexpensive land, but for a fisherman who made his living on the unenclosable sea, this was not a huge advantage. Indeed, the risks of earning a living in a commercial venture on the outmost fringe of Europe's North Atlantic economy were considerable. The problem of sending one's catch to market several thousand miles away, the difficulty in keeping oneself supplied with gear and provisions, the lack of alternative paying employment should the fishery fail, and the knowledge that should anything go wrong one might be stranded beyond the reach of family help, combined to dissuade most seventeenth-century English fishermen from ever emigrating to the New World.

In 1650, however, New England had one thing to offer resident fishermen–the fact that it was already a settled colony. Many of the supplies needed to carry on the fishery anywhere in North America had to be imported from Europe: hooks and lines, canvas sailcloth, many items of marine hardware, and most importantly salt. Some things that fishermen needed, especially food and drink for themselves, could be found in quantity in the New World–but only at one spot close to the cod-fishing grounds and that was in Massachusetts Bay. Between Cape Cod and Labrador, the only places where quantities of bread, beer, meat, and vegetables could be obtained fresh at reasonable prices were Boston, Salem, and the lesser seaports of the Bay Colony. Just as important to commercial fishermen, moreover, was the presence of a merchant community–something that Massachusetts also possessed from an early date. Fishermen have usually found their business easier to accomplish when they dwell close to their sources of credit, and in the North America of 1650, this could only happen in New England.

Soon after his arrival in Marblehead, therefore, John Roads made the acquaintance of George Corwin in Salem. Corwin had moved to the area during the Great Migration twenty years before and was now one of the most prosperous fish merchants on Massachusetts' North Shore. His business consisted chiefly in outfitting companies of independent fishermen with the necessaries for their voyages, buying their fish as it was brought in and cured, then arranging for the export of this dried cod to Southern Europe and the West Indies. Corwin's store was extraordinarily well-stocked with all the things that a fisherman and his family would need. From salt, bait, hooks, lines, and splitting knives to barrelled meat,

indian corn, brandy, almonds, cloth, lace, and children's shoes, the range of consumables was probably as wide as one could obtain anywhere on the continent at this time.

Furthermore, like every merchant in town, he offered his regular fishing customers large quantities of credit free of interest. There was a catch in this, of course. Corwin expected those favored in this way to remain loyal clients; fishermen could not regularly take their business to other merchants and expect him to tolerate much in the way of arrears. But for those who were prepared to live within the rules of financial patronage–that is, to relinquish the right to bargain freely with any of Corwin's merchant competitors–Corwin was willing to advance considerable quantities of goods, both for the prosecution of the fishery and for the maintenance of a household.

It was on credit advanced by Corwin in 1659 that John Roads acquired a boat of his own. It was only a small shallop, half-decked at most, and fewer than twenty feet from stem to stern, but the cost of purchasing and outfitting it for his first season fishing ran to more than £100 sterling, and this initial expenditure landed the fisherman in a cycle of indebtedness from which, as far as the records extend, he never emerged. Every year without fail thereafter, Roads or his wife rowed across the bay to Corwin's wharf to purchase necessities, and at the end of each season Roads delivered his fish to

pay the bill. In December, when the fishing year was over, the merchant patron and his client fisherman went over their accounts together and conducted a reckoning. Some years Roads managed to pare down a little of this debt; in other years he lost ground; but never did he manage to reduce the sum below £60 sterling.

If at home Roads was Corwin's client, however, at sea he was his own man. Every spring he formed a partnership with two or three other fishermen, and after obtaining their outfit from Corwin they sailed "to the eastward" towards Monhegan and the other fishing grounds along the coast of Maine. There they picked a sheltered harbor well provided with timber as their fishing station for the season. For several weeks Roads and his partners busied themselves preparing their camp or "room" for the fishing to come. By the shore they constructed a stage, where the cod could be split, cleaned, and salted; and on the beach they built a set of rough tables called "flakes" upon which the fish could be dried.

When the cod struck in, everyone's energies turned to the fishing itself. Each day that dawned favorably Roads and his mates rowed or sailed out to the grounds before sunup, heaved out their stone anchor or "killick," and settled down to work. Each fisherman tended a pair of lines–several fathoms in length, weighted with heavy leads and baited with clams, capelin, or mackerel—and spent the better part of every day in the constant, taxing labor of paying out line and hauling in cod. Late in the afternoon they returned to shore to dress their catch, then ate and turned in knowing they would have to rise at first light on the morrow. Nowhere on the coast did the season last very long, and the pressure to make the most of it caused everyone to push themselves through long days and short nights to the physical limits of their endurance. There would be plenty of time to relax when the cod departed, but only if the fish drying on the flakes was ample enough to pay back their outfitting costs and leave them something.

Sometimes Roads would carry his own fish back to Massachusetts; on other occasion he would have it freighted there while he remained in Maine to work. With the onset of winter, however, he usually came home and spent the colder months with his family. By the 1660s, the Roads household numbered at least six, and by 1665, if not before, they had a house of their own. What this dwelling or the belongings that filled it looked like we can only imagine, but if it resembled those of their Marblehead neighbors it was probably com-

posed of a single room and spartan in its furnishings. Likely they owned a table with a few chairs, a couple of beds with feather or silkgrass mattresses; probably they ate from wooden bowls and drank from pewter cups; their garden furnished them with some vegetables and a spot to keep chickens or a pig; and Joan fashioned their clothes from woolen or linen cloth. By comparison to most seafaring people elsewhere around the North Atlantic rim in the seventeenth century, this family was well-situated. With a house and garden for Joan to improve, a fishing boat that John with his sons could operate as their own, and ample supplies of firewood, fish, and wildfowl, the Roads family may not have been prosperous but were well beyond worrying about mere survival.

None of this would have been possible without credit, and this is what makes the story of John Roads important. In a frontier environment where labor and capital were both scarce, merchants and fishermen both saw an advantage to the sort of tight interdependence for which debt or credit was the financial expression. Those with capital to invest seldom wanted to bear the costs and risks of employing people directly; what they needed was a reliable source of fish, and credit gave them a lever that could ensure steady delivery from the fishermen themselves. For their part, fishermen worried most about dependable provisioning. Living in such a remote spot—far from alternative sources of employment—they wanted to be sure that in a bad season they would not be cut off; pledging themselves "to the company store" limited their freedom but guaranteed that they could make it through the worst of times.

The economic development of early America everywhere was a project of independent operators financed by merchant capital. Southern planters cleared land and raised crops with the help of indentured servants and slaves purchased on credit. Northern yeomen financed their westward march of land clearance and farm construction with borrowed money. The whaling industry in New England recruited its first labor force from amongst indebted Native Americans. Credit was at once, for John Roads and many other working Americans of his day, both a carrot and a stick—a source of opportunity and a tool of labor discipline.

Daniel Vickers

At this small seasonal fishing station on the Newfoundland coast, fishermen in a shallop land their daily catch of cod. Like fishing stations from New England to Newfoundland, it includes a "stage" or covered wharf on which the fish are processed, several "flakes," or racks for air-drying the salted cod, and rude quarters to shelter the fishermen during their six or seven months of work. Duhamel du Monceau, Traite des Pesches, Part II (Paris, 1772), Plate XVIII. (Courtesy Peabody Essex Museum, Salem, Massachusetts)

Native to Southeast Asia, the sugarcane was domesticated about ten thousand years ago. It had been brought to the Mediterranean region by 700 A.D. and was then taken from North Africa to Spain by the Muslims. Sugar production on slave-labor plantations was established on the Atlantic Islands in the 1400s, and brought from the Canary Islands to the Caribbean on Columbus's second voyage, in 1493. Between 1625 and 1650, the Dutch, English, and French established sugar as the primary economic product of their Caribbean islands, leading to their growing dependence on North American colonies for live-stock and foodstuff. This engraving by Theodor de Bry shows the labor-intensive nature of sugar production, with field hands to plant, tend, and cut the cane; others to strip and grind the canes in the sugar mill; and still others to boil the cane juice and finally crystalize the sugar and separate the liquid molasses. The introduction of sugarcane and the plantation system of agriculture to South America and the Caribbean islands was central to the establishment of an Atlantic economy. By 1505 Europeans had begun to ship enslaved Africans to the Americas, and during the course of 350 years of New World slavery more than six million Africans were brought to labor in the sugar industry. (Courtesy Library of Congress)

shares in their own boats and fewer still had sufficient capital for the purchase of salt, food, and other provisions necessary for outfitting a voyage. The price they paid for the advancement of these items from their merchants was high, however, because they gave up the opportunity to sell their catch to the highest bidder. Research done by Vickers shows that annual earnings for the typical fisherman of Essex County averaged about £20 in the seventeenth century, and the value of their estates at death averaged only £81 (Massachusetts currency) compared to £281 for the county as a whole. Worse still, because they depended on capital advances for the next season's fishing, they almost always owed their merchant money. Not only did they die at an earlier age than farmers, but instead of having acres of improved farm lands to leave behind, fishermen often left their widows and children deeply in debt. Thus, the next generation in a fisherman's family had to start all over again. When Salem fisherman Arthur Kibbins died in 1685 in his fifties, his merchant-creditor William Browne laid a claim of £77 against the estate's £106. After selling her house and furnishings at auction the widow Kibbins and her children had a mere £20 as legacy from her husband's lifetime of labor.

The West Indies

Because of their importance as trading partners with England's continental colonies in North America, we cannot leave this chapter without a brief account of the West Indies possessions of the various European nations. Until the seventeenth century the Caribbean was virtually a Spanish lake and, as such, remained off limits to the trading vessels of Spain's imperial rivals. But beginning with English settlement of St. Christopher in 1624, and quickly followed by that of Barbuda (1625), and Barbados (1627), Spain was no longer alone. Almost immediately the new English colonies were joined by other settlements founded by both France (a share of St. Christopher, 1627; Guadeloupe and Martinique, 1635) and The Netherlands (St. Eustatius and Tobago, 1632; Curaçao, 1634).

The first planters grew mostly tobacco and a little cotton, but by mid-century these and other islands became major producers of sugar. The system of sugar production had first been imported from the Canary Islands to Spanish Hispaniola and from Madeira to Portuguese Brazil, where the Dutch had established a foothold at Pernambuco in 1636. From there the Dutch introduced the industry into their Caribbean islands, and the British and French islands quickly adopted the plantation system of sugar production as well. In addition to producing the crystallized Muscovado and clayed sugars in great demand by Europeans, the process also yielded two important by-products, molasses and rum. So great was Europe's demand for sugar that planters soon dedicated all of their capital and land to its cultivation, while relying on outsiders for necessities like food, clothing, and even timber and livestock. Exporting a valuable product like sugar and importing processed goods from England and the empire earned Barbados recognition at home as "the brightest jewel in His Majesty's crown."

Until about 1660 the Dutch were the most aggressive traders in the Caribbean world. They held a foothold among the Portuguese in Brazil for a time, hung onto Guiana on the northeast corner of South America, and took Curaçao from the Spaniards. Their vessels were everywhere, bringing slaves to the New World, carrying back sugar, tobacco, or whatever else they could purchase for sale in Amsterdam or exchange elsewhere in the Atlantic world. Not surprisingly, Dutch commercial success led to retaliatory action by their principal rival, England. First, the Commonwealth Parliament under Oliver Cromwell enacted navigation laws in 1650-51 to exclude Dutch trade within the English empire. Then, after the first of three wars between the rivals broke out in the year following, the English navy won a series of battles that by 1674 resulted in its complete domination of the world's oceans for the next 250 years.

Neptune's Nation

From their uncertain beginnings in the first decades of the seventeenth century, the European colonies scattered along the eastern seaboard of North America were still groping toward a degree of security by 1660. Although some 80,000 immigrants had crossed the North Atlantic Ocean to the mainland colonies since 1607, such was the rate of mortality in the early years that the population still totaled only 75,000, concentrated almost entirely in Virginia, Maryland, and New England. Among them were fewer than 3,000 black slaves. New Jersey and Pennsylvania were not yet organized colonies; nor were Georgia and the Carolinas, except for a few planters along the shores of Albemarle Sound. Similarly, the New England coast north of New Hampshire was only sparsely populated. With few exceptions, settlers lived within a day's journey of tidewater, and the colonies continued to depend on their connections by sea with each other, with the West Indies, and particularly with England. Such were the modest beginnings of what would become over the course of four centuries one of history's most extraordinary episodes, the migration of some forty million people to the mainland of North America. Almost all of these men, women, and children, blacks and whites alike, came by ship. At the end of its first half-century, English America stood poised on the threshold of explosive growth: in population, economic power, cultural maturity, and political self-government. The very possibility of these later developments depended on the maritime discovery, exploration, and settlement that had taken place in the century and a half between 1492 and 1660. By the nature of its birth and early development, the nation that declared its independence in 1776 could truly be called "Neptune's nation."

CHAPTER 2

The Rise of English America

1660-1760

THE SUCCESS OF WHAT historians used to call the "old British empire" can be attributed to a number of factors. First, its American colonies ran through forty degrees of latitude, from the tropical islands of Trinidad, Barbados, Jamaica, and other possessions in the Caribbean to the subarctic lands around Hudson Bay. Its American possessions thus provided a wide variety of goods, few of which competed with the produce of Great Britain itself. Second, unlike the French and Spaniards, the English actively encouraged the settlement of their American dominions by giving colonists free land and extensive political rights. Third, although like other mercantilist powers the Britons valued their overseas possessions primarily as providers of raw materials, they realized far better than did their rivals that those colonies could also become significant markets for the mother country's manufactures. They also permitted colonial settlers to participate in trade within the empire, not only with the mother country but with other English possessions in America and with the colonies of foreign nations as well.

A survey of British dominions in North America in the period 1660-1760 illustrates the remarkable variety of their natural resources. From the Hudson Bay Company post in the subarctic regions Great Britain tapped the rich fur resources of the North American interior by trading with Native American tribes. At the continent's northeast corner, the island of Newfoundland gave access to the world's most abundant fishing grounds, the Grand Banks, as did the islands of Cape Breton and Nova Scotia, taken from the French by 1713. Until the end of the Seven Years' War in 1763, however, France controlled most of the northeast's interior regions, and in any case both British and French possessions there were sparsely populated, which made

Detail of the landing of British forces off Louisbourg. (Courtesy Beverly R. Robinson Collection, U.S. Naval Academy Museum)

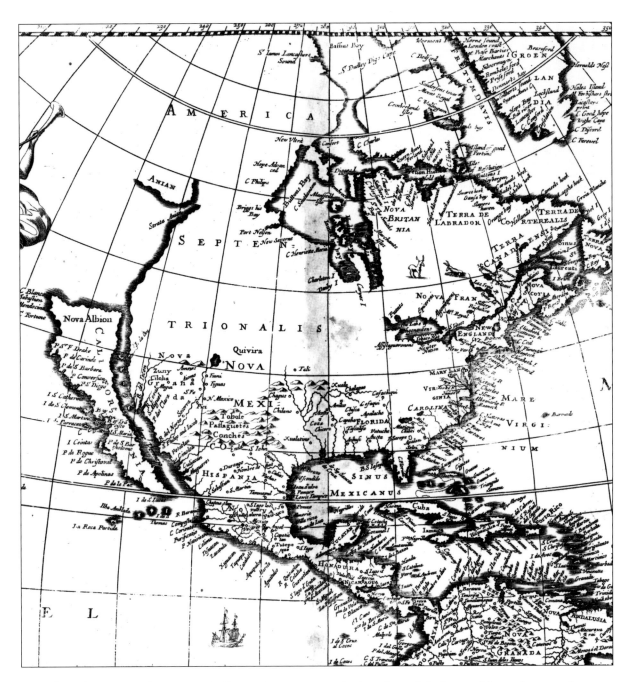

By the mid-seventeenth century, the dimensions of North America were more clearly understood by Europeans, although California–Drake's Nova Albion–was thought possibly to be an island, and the Great Lakes and Mississippi River had not yet been explored. Detail of a map of the Americas in John Ogilby, America *(London, 1671). (G.W. Blunt White Library, Mystic Seaport)*

the exploitation of other resources like timber difficult to achieve.

To the south and west lay the province of New England, densely populated by New World stan-

dards, where fish, fur, and forest became the basis for the region's expanding maritime trade. Here, too, the role of the sea as connector was most readily apparent. Settlers required vessels to reach the fishing banks offshore. Shipbuilders needed timber with which to build those vessels as well as ships to carry the fish, the furs, and forest products to markets in other colonies and overseas. The glaciation that had provided New England with many small harbors had also created numerous rivers that impeded land transportation along the coastal plain, although they did afford access to the interior. Coupled with the poor soil and challenging climate, these facts encouraged numerous enterprising New Englanders to turn to the sea for a living. Most of the settlers remained subsistence farmers through the colonial period, but some of the farms, especially along the eastern seaboard where grazing was good, produced surplus live-stock, meat products, and vegetables for market.

The Middle Colonies–New York (formerly New Netherland), New Jersey, Pennsylvania, and Delaware–depended at first on furs for a marketable commodity. But here both climate and topography encouraged agricultural enterprise. An abundant labor force of indentured servants soon turned the broad fertile valleys of the Hudson, Delaware, and Susquehanna Rivers into productive fields of wheat, corn, and other grains. A lively coastal trade quickly developed, built around the shipment of flour and other grain produce from these so-called "bread colonies." Shellfishing in New York and Delaware Bays provided another source of food. The region's topography did not provide so many natural harbors as in New England, with the important exceptions of New York and Philadelphia, both of which had excellent access into the interior. Until the early eighteenth century much of the region's commerce was carried in vessels from the mother country or the other colonies, but then both New York and Philadelphia grew rapidly as major seaports.

Nature most favored the British colonies located along the shores of Chesapeake Bay and the Carolina coasts. Excellent soil, relatively flat terrain well drained by numerous creeks and rivers, and above all a moderate climate and lengthy growing season made them particularly well suited for agriculture. Almost from their founding the Southern colonies imported African slaves for labor and exported valuable market crops, especially tobacco from the Chesapeake and North Carolina, indigo and rice from South Carolina, and, in the eighteenth century, sea island cotton from Georgia.

Meanwhile, two of the principal contenders for New World wealth–Spain and the Netherlands–lost ground to France and Great Britain. By 1674 the latter nation had driven the Dutch from the North American mainland altogether, but the Dutch managed to retain St. Eustatius and their other sugar islands in the Caribbean Sea. The Dutch wisely declared "Statia" a free port, where goods from all over the Atlantic rim could be bought, sold, or

exchanged. On the coast of South America the sugar production of Dutch Guiana doubled in the first half of the eighteenth century, and Netherlanders continued to profit from the slave trade. Spain began to lose possessions around the edges of its vast holdings as early as 1634, when the Dutch seized Curaçao. Then in 1655 the English captured Jamaica and fifteen years later gained Spanish acquiescence to its occupation of the Bahama Islands. Nor could Spain drive out the British lumbermen in Belize on the Yucatan Peninsula, who were cutting and shipping log-wood, a highly prized source of textile dye.

Spanish control in the Caribbean was most strongly contested by the buccaneers, a loose confederation of pirates, rovers, and Hispaniola cattle drovers, who established their main head-quarters at Port Royal, Jamaica, and the island of Tortuga off Hispaniola. Both England and France encouraged the buccaneers in their unde-clared war on Spain and benefited from Spanish preoccupation in defending ships and ports from buccaneer raids. England began to suppress the buccaneers in 1670 as it concluded a treaty agreement with Spain, but French buccaneers continued to operate for another decade, helping France take over the western third of Hispaniola, which became Saint Domingue, now Haiti. Thereafter, the buccaneers lost their political role and were considered outright pirates, and they in turn raided ships of any nation in the Caribbean and off the African and American coasts. It finally took the British Royal Navy and several highly publicized hangings in the first decades of the eighteenth century to rid the coast of such notorious freebooters as Charles Vane and Edward Teach–the infamous "Blackbeard"–both of whom frequented North Carolina. The case of Captain William Kidd, who began his career as an honorable privateer, licensed to raid enemy shipping, and died in a hangman's noose, condemned as a pirate, demonstrates the shifting line that distinguished piracy from legal raiding.

In the first half of the seventeenth century France had established control of the St. Lawrence River gateway to the interior of the North American continent from Montreal, its commercial center at the head of deepwater navi-gation. During the next fifty years or so it gradu-ally expanded its dominion inland by establishing trading posts throughout the Great Lakes region, especially at the portages that linked one body of

From the 1650s to the 1720s, buccaneers and pirates inhabited the contested regions of the Atlantic and Caribbean. Buccaneers were tacitly accepted as allies by the English and French in their wars against Spain. Pirates had no national allegiance, plundering the commerce of all nations, although on occasion they were tolerated by colonial officials, such as in New York and North Carolina, because of the hard currency they used to pay for supplies and refreshments. Pirate crews were usually loosely affiliated groups organized around one captain who established the group's rules of conduct. Notable among these usually all-male societies were the female pirates Anne Bonny (left) and Mary Read. Anne Bonny was the illegitimate daughter of an Irish attorney who moved to Charleston, South Carolina, and became a prominent merchant. Although she might have led a prosperous life in Charleston, Anne married wandering James Bonny who took her to the pirate center of New Providence in the Bahamas. There she became involved with the pardoned pirate "Calico Jack" Rackam. When he returned to piracy Anne accompanied him, fighting alongside the crew. Also in the crew was Mary Read, an Englishwoman who had already served as a sailor and a soldier in Europe while disguised as a man. Mary married a fellow soldier, but after his death returned to sea, was captured by Rackam, and joined his crew. Off Jamaica in 1720, when a British Royal Navy force surprised Rackam and captured his ship, Anne Bonny and Mary Read were the only pirates to resist. All of the pirates were sentenced to death, but the court spared Anne Bonny and Mary Read because they were pregnant. Engraving from Charles Johnson, A General History of the Robberies and Murders of the Most Notorious Pyrates *(London, 1724). (Courtesy Rare Books and Manuscripts Division, The New York Public Library, Astor, Lenox and Tilden Foundations)*

water with its neighbor. In 1673 came the first of two significant discoveries. New France's greatest governor, Count de Frontenac, appointed the Jesuit priest Jacques Marquette and fellow explorer Louis Jolliet to find the great western river. With the help of friendly American Indians the two pioneered a route from the shores of Lake Superior via a series of portages along the Fox and Wisconsin Rivers to the mighty Mississippi, which they followed downstream to the mouth of the Arkansas River, where they learned that Spaniards occupied the lower river. On their return trip they discovered yet another route, via the Illinois River, that brought them to the shores of Lake Michigan.

Nine years later Robert Cavelier, Sieur de La Salle, and a small party set out via the Illinois River to explore the entire lower Mississippi River and drive a

René-Robert Cavelier, Sieur de La Salle (1643-1687) of Rouen, France, came to Canada in 1666. After reaching an understanding with the Iroquois, he began to explore the territory west of Montreal, and met Louis Jolliet who had explored parts of the Mississippi River. In 1679 La Salle began an expedition to explore the Great Lakes and the Mississippi himself, despite Iroquois resistance to further European incursions inland. Just upstream from Niagara Falls, he built the Griffon, *the first European vessel on the Lakes. Although the landscape and vegetation are fanciful, this is an otherwise accurate depiction of the construction, with La Salle, Father Louis Hennepin, and shipwright Moise Hillaret conferring in the foreground while Iroquois warriors threaten them, and the blacksmith wards off an attacking Indian at left. Launched in 1679, the* Griffon *carried La Salle and his party to the shores of Lake Michigan, but was lost on the return. Despite formidable hardships, La Salle built a similar vessel on the Illinois River and in 1682 sailed down the Mississippi to its mouth, claiming the territory for France under the name Louisiana, then canoed back upstream. La Salle returned by sea in 1686 to settle on the Mississippi, but missed its mouth and wound up on the Trinity River in Texas, where he was killed by mutinous members of his party. Engraving from Louis Hennepin,* Nouvelle Découverte d'un tres grand Pays situé dans l'Amerique *(Utrecht, 1697). (Courtesy John Carter Brown Library, Brown University)*

French wedge between Spanish Texas and Florida. Reaching its mouth in April 1682, they claimed the entire Mississippi River valley for King Louis XIV, naming it Louisiana in his honor. Five years later La Salle died in an abortive attempt to establish a settlement at the river's mouth. The French persisted, however, and in 1718 a private company founded New Orleans between the river and Lake Pontchartrain. To avoid the tricky channels of the lower delta, the French opened an inshore route via the lake to connect New Orleans with two other French ports, Biloxi and Mobile, which they had established a decade earlier. France now firmly controlled both ends of the continent's two most important networks of waterways. From Montreal at the head of navigation on the St. Lawrence River to New Orleans at the mouth of the Mississippi River stretched a water route more than two thousand miles in length that gave access by other rivers to the great interior basin of North America.

Pierre le Moyne, Sieur d'Iberville, established a post at Biloxi Bay in 1699 as the first European settlement on the Gulf Coast. To populate its southern colony, France sent convicts to Biloxi and nearby Mobile. The development of the colony was slow until John Law proposed granting lands to wealthy individuals who would send a set number of colonists to occupy them. German and Swiss settlers and African slaves were all introduced to the area under this scheme, and the French government sent several ships with indigent "casket girls" to marry settlers. This engraving depicts the land concession of John Law at Biloxi in 1720, with settlers beginning the process of building a community, clearing ground for agriculture, and building vessels for trade, transportation, and fishing. After New Orleans became the capital of the colony of Louisiana in 1725, Biloxi became a backwater for more than a century until, in the later nineteenth century, it emerged as an important resort and fishing port on the Mississippi coast. (Courtesy Edward E. Ayer Collection, The Newberry Library, Chicago)

A System of Empire

No doubt some of the impetus for the strengthening of Great Britain's commerce in the seventeenth century came from traditional mercantilists. Eager to rationalize England's colonization of America according to their belief that nations had to compete for a finite amount of world trade, they argued for the founding of colonies as sources of raw materials and then monopolizing trade with those entities. In their view the total wealth of all modern nations was, except for the addition of bullion from the New World, a fairly stable sum. While most Englishmen did not share the theoretical assumptions of the mercantilists, the self-interested landed gentry, merchants, and manufacturers realized the practical value to themselves of strengthening the nation's economy by constructing a self-sufficient empire. Expanded trade would mean larger revenues from custom duties, and a reduction of reliance on the land tax. Increased importation of raw materials from the colonies would not only meet the needs of manufacturers and other consumers, but also provide a surplus that English merchants could profitably reexport to other markets. The British took the idea one step further. If its colonies were well populated with English peoples, and they became sufficiently prosperous to purchase English manufactures, the mother country would then be less dependent on foreign markets, and the empire would become truly self-sufficient. To a remarkable degree this is precisely what happened within the British empire during the course of the one hundred years between 1660 and 1760. Yet another benefit of encouraging maritime commerce accrued to England in this period. As an island nation it depended on the Royal Navy as its first line of defense. But the navy in turn required a pool of trained seamen that only an expanding merchant marine could provide. Pragmatic self-interest more than the dictates of abstract theory explain the evolution of a "colonial system." That practical seaman Sir Walter Raleigh perhaps put it best in the late sixteenth century when he wrote that "whosoever commands the sea, commands the trade; whosoever commands the trade of the world, commands the riches of the world, and consequently the world itself."

At the heart of the system was a series of acts of trade, popularly known as the Navigation Acts, which together established the rules for commercial operations within the empire. Concerned about the growing Dutch role in trade with England's colonies, Cromwell's Parliament enacted several of these measures in the 1650s. The Stuart monarchy considered the Commonwealth illegal, however, and when restored to power in 1660 it adopted its own version of commercial legislation. Three basic principles were established. First, all trade within the empire was reserved for British or colonial vessels. As defined by the Navigation Act of 1660, such vessels had to be built and owned in England or America, and their masters and three-fourths of their crews were to be English or American as well. The Act of 1660 also contained the second principle: that particularly valuable produce of the colonies could only be exported to the mother country. At first these so-called enumerated articles included only sugar, tobacco, and indigo, but others would be added later. The third principle, as established by the Navigation Act of 1663, gave British manufacturers a monopoly of the American market by requiring that with a few exceptions European goods (mostly manufactured goods like textiles or hardware) could be exported to the colonies only through England, where of course Dutch or French cloth, for instance, was subject to a prohibitive tariff.

Over the next one hundred years Parliament fine-tuned the system with additional legislation. Acts of 1673 and 1696 closed several loopholes and provided a tighter structure of enforcement. To protect an important home industry, the Wool Act of 1699 prohibited American colonists from exporting wool products. The Hat Act (1732) and Iron Acts (1750 and 1757) added further products to this list. In 1733 the British West Indian planter interest persuaded Parliament to impose heavy duties on rum, sugar, and molasses

Captain Thomas Smith was a mariner and artist who came to Boston from Bermuda about 1650. When he painted his self-portrait, ca. 1680, he included a naval battle in the background, suggesting his seagoing career in a turbulent era. As a good Puritan worn out by a life at sea he included a death's head and verses celebrating his spiritual faith: "Why why should I the World be minding/therein a World of Evils Finding./Then Farwell World: Farwell thy Jarres/thy joies. thy Toies thy Wiles thy Warrs/Truth Sounds Retreat: I am not sorye./ The Eternall Drawes to him my heart/ By Faith (which can thy Force Subvert)/ To Croune me (after Grace) with Glory." (Courtesy Worcester Art Museum, Worcester, Massachusetts)

imported into the North American colonies from the foreign West Indies. Because of enforcement difficulties, however, the legislation failed to prohibit this traffic. Throughout the eighteenth century the list of enumerated articles continued to expand. In 1705 rice, molasses, and naval stores (raw materials such as pitch, turpentine, and mast timber used in shipbuilding) joined the roll, as did beaver skins and furs in 1721. The Sugar Act of 1764 added hides and skins as well as pot and pearl ashes to the list. At the same time, however, Parliament also instituted a bounty system to encourage the production of certain scarce commodities. The 1705 Act provided bounties for naval stores, and later the cultivation of indigo would be encouraged as well.

Running the empire was never an easy nor a particularly efficient undertaking. Various ministries struggled with the problem throughout the

With their importance in European commerce, Jews had come to the Portuguese colonies in the New World by the 1580s, to Dutch possessions, to England in the 1650s, New York in 1654, and to Barbados, Jamaica, and tolerant colonies like Rhode Island soon after. The Sephardic Jews of western Europe established businesses in the Caribbean and North America through families such as the Lopezes of Newport, Rhode Island. The Ashkenazi of eastern Europe also established themselves in America and the Caribbean through families such as the Franks and Levys of New York. Moses Levy (ca. 1665-1728) came to New York about 1695 and by the time of his death was one of the city's wealthiest merchants. His trading network included both Jewish and Christian merchants in North America, the Caribbean, and Europe. When he had his portrait painted, he included his pet dog and a representation of a merchant brig and sloop. (Courtesy Museum of the City of New York)

eighteenth century. As Edmund Burke explained in his address to Parliament, "On Conciliation with America," in 1775: "three thousand miles of ocean lie between you and them. No contrivance can prevent the effect of this distance in weakening government. Seas roll and months pass between the order [from Britain] and the execution [in America]." For most of this period a committee of the Privy Council, called the Board of Trade, handled the appointment of governors

and other colonial officials and saw to it that Parliamentary legislation was compatible with crown policy. But the two secretaries of state also had their fingers in the colonial pie, as did the treasury department's Board of Customs, whose commissioners and other officers in the colonial seaports wielded considerable authority. Colonial merchants accused of violating the laws were brought before vice-admiralty courts, whose appointed judges rendered verdicts without the interference of troublesome juries comprising the accused's peers. And, finally, the Royal Navy had an important voice in colonial affairs since it provided the ultimate power of enforcement.

Although the purpose of England's colonial empire was to strengthen the mother country, the colonies themselves had something to gain as well. First and foremost, in an era when war on land and sea was a common occurrence, the protective arm of the Royal Navy was invaluable. Indeed, the colonies had neither the wealth nor the manpower to protect their own commerce and seaports, even if allowed to do so. Secondly, English merchants regularly extended credit to American planters and men of trade, albeit at a price. Without access to such capital, however, the colonial economy and population would have grown at a much slower pace. Third, the mother country and its Caribbean colonies comprised an ever-expanding market for the produce of the continental colonies. In some cases it was a protected market as well. English merchants could import tobacco only from the colonies, for instance, and only vessels constructed in English or colonial shipyards could be registered under the British flag. The sale of American-built vessels to the mother country was worth perhaps £100,000 annually by 1770, but these transactions rarely showed up in the official statistics of colonial trade. Yet another advantage was that American shipowners could participate in the carrying trade within the world's most prosperous empire on an equal footing with British-owned vessels. The bounties received by Americans for producing naval stores and indigo provided yet another source of profit. By the eve of the Revolution total payments of these subsidies amounted to £1,600,000.

The question of whether the Acts of Trade imposed a hardship on the American colonies has been argued by historians for decades. Textbook writers used to emphasize the negative effects of imperial regulations on the American colonial economy, some going so far as to consider the Navigation Acts a major cause of the American Revolution. While recognizing that the system had disadvantages for Americans, recent historians have disproved the charge that they were oppressive. True enough, there were drawbacks, especially to Southern producers of enumerated articles like tobacco, which could only be sent to the mother country, and rice. Likewise, colonial consumers of imported produce like tea and pepper paid a premium for shipment through England, and English merchants undoubtedly made the most of their advantage by charging more for their own goods. Yet, until the British amended the objectives of their colonial policy in the 1760s to include the raising of a revenue, few colonists complained about the old system of regulations. If indeed they thought they were paying a price for membership in the British Empire, they must have thought it a good bargain.

Patterns of Commerce

A variety of trading patterns became well established by the turn of the eighteenth century. Among the most important were New England vessels carrying fish and lumber products, provisions, and livestock to the West Indies and returning with molasses, rum, and sugar. New Englanders also carried fish and provisions to Southern plantation colonies, where they picked up cargoes of tobacco, indigo, and rice destined for England. Other vessels took masts, ship timber, pitch, and turpentine, along with rum and furs, directly from New England to the old country. There these cargoes helped pay for the vast quantities of British manufactured articles in such demand back home, particularly textiles, household goods, and hardware. In 1670, for instance, the forty-five-ton Boston ketch *Recovery* took a cargo of rum, wine, beer, sugar, fish-oil, and salt to Virginia, exchanging it for tobacco, peas, and pork, which she carried on to Barbados. There she swapped her Virginia goods for sugar, which she took back to the Chesapeake to use in purchasing a full cargo of tobacco. The *Recovery* took the tobacco to London, selling it for assorted manufactured articles and bills of exchange. She then sailed around to Liverpool for more English goods before clearing for home by way of the Azores, where she filled out her cargo with wines. Vessels from the Middle Colonies brought wheat, flour, and other grain products to the South and West Indies, where they too picked up plantation goods to take to England. Vessels from both New England and the Middle Colonies carried their own produce to the Iberian peninsula and the Atlantic islands in exchange for raisins, currants, wine, and salt. The plantation colonies of the Chesapeake and Carolinas carried relatively little of their own produce to market, but they did invest in voyages

Tobacco wharves, not seaports, were the focus of maritime commerce in the Chesapeake region. At this Virginia tobacco warehouse, gentlemen sample the tobacco crop while a cooper seals the tobacco casks and a clerk records their weight. African slaves perform the labor, whether serving refreshments to the plantation owner, moving casks, or handling the boat to transport the casks to the tobacco ship waiting at anchor in the river. Although little of it passed through American seaports, tobacco was the most important colonial export through much of the eighteenth century. Detail from Joshua Fry and Peter Jefferson, A Map of the Most Inhabited Part of Virginia... *(1775 edition). (Courtesy The Mariners' Museum, Newport News, Virginia)*

Colonial Ships and Shipbuilding

The vessels that brought Europeans to America in the seventeenth century ranged in size and rig from the 50-ton pinnace *Dove* to the 300-ton *Ark*, both of which brought the first settlers to Maryland in 1634. In between was a wide variety of vessels: sloops and ketches, brigantines, snows, and barks. To complicate matters, some of these terms originally referred to the hull of a vessel, others to the rig. Furthermore, the meaning of several terms changed when carried forward into the nineteenth century. A seventeenth-century *ship*, for instance, had squaresails on fore- and mainmasts and a fore-and-aft lateen on the mizzen. By the beginning of the nineteenth century, however, such a rig was called a *bark*, and the term ship-rigged meant a vessel with squaresails on all three masts. On the other hand, in the earlier period the term *bark* described a hull form rather than a rig. Some were ship-rigged, others had only two masts, although in all cases a bark was square-rigged. Only later did the term come to refer to a vessel with squaresails on fore-and mainmasts and a gaff-rigged mizzen.

In the early period a *ketch* was a two-masted vessel, best described as a ship with no foremast that set a square sail on the main mast and a lateen on the mizzen, Later, however, the term applied to fore-and-aft rigged vessels with main and mizzen. In both eras ketches were commonly used for offshore fishing and coastal trading voyages. Even a *pinnace*, usually though of as a single-decked lightly constructed vessel used in coastal waters, might carry two or even three square-rigged masts in the seventeenth century, although most were sloop-rigged, like the *Virginia of Sagadahoc*. The *sloop*, on the other hand, remained little changed throughout the colonial period, having a decked hull and a single gaff mainsail, a jib (or two), and often square topsail. The *shallop* was an open boat suitable for use in protected waters and inshore fishing. In the early eighteenth century the *schooner*, a new kind of vessel descended from Dutch and English forebears, appeared on this side of the Atlantic. Fore-and-aft rigged except for topsails, the schooner quickly gained popularity for its cheap construction and maneuverability.

Because most of the first settlers came from agricultural backgrounds they knew nothing about ship construction, and so their respective sponsors–the Virginia, Plymouth, and Massachusetts Bay colonies–sent shipwrights along to build the vessels needed for fishing, coastal trading, and Atlantic crossings. Many of the first builders, like other skilled artisans, were attracted to the New World by the promise of free land. At first almost any convenient spot along a shore that gently sloped to the water served as a building site. Within a few years particular areas became established as shipbuilding centers, among them Newbury, Salem, and Boston in Massachusetts Bay, New London, Connecticut, and the colony of New Haven. Until the beginning of the eighteenth century the colonies to the west and south of New England

launched only a few vessels, mostly for use in local waters. Then shipwrights began to appear at New York and Philadelphia, spurred in part by the demand for vessels during Queen Anne's War, and by 1720 the industry was well established there. Not until mid-century, however, did the Chesapeake and Carolina colonies begin to build significant numbers of vessels.

Reliable figures concerning the volume of colonial shipbuilding are hard to come by, but in his *Shipbuilding in Colonial America*, Joseph Goldenberg shows that more than half of the 1,680 colonial-built vessels listed in *Lloyd's Register of Shipping* for 1776 came from New England yards. Massachusetts alone accounted for well over 25 percent of the total, with Pennsylvania a distant second at less than 15

percent. Because only owners of larger vessels registered them with Lloyd's, however, hundreds of sloops and schooners are not included. Another record, covering the years 1768 through 1773 and copied from British records by the Harvard historian Jared Sparks, indicates that colonial shipyards built an annual average of 115 "top-sails" and 285 "schooners" during that period. (Whether this means that sloops were omitted is unclear). The Sparks figures show that almost three-fourths of these vessels were New-England built, with Massachusetts accounting for more than a third of the American total.

Modeled on its English counterpart, the colonial shipyard was owned and operated by a master shipwright, who had generally learned his trade through an apprenticeship. First customer and builder discussed the type of vessel required, sloop or schooner for the coastal and West Indies trades, brig, brigantine, or occasionally a full-

rigged ship for Atlantic crossings. Once they had agreed on dimensions, finish, and other specifications, along with the price per ton, the parties signed a contract, and the master shipwright drafted plans for his workers to follow.

Under the accepted rule-of-thumb approach to shipbuilding in the period, hulls had broad, buoyant bows and narrow sterns. A simple plan showing the hull form at a few sites along the keel was sufficient; shipwrights knew by experience how to complete the hull when given an indication of its proposed shape. The builder selected the timber from his yard, most likely white oak for keel, stem and sternpost, and frames; hackmatack for knees; and oak or pine for planks and decking. In addition to the work of shipwrights, construction of the vessel's hull required the skills of joiners and caulkers, along with smiths, who did the ironwork. If the contract called for painting or other

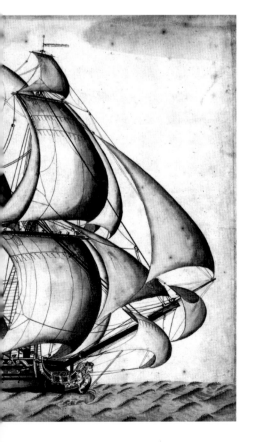

Built at Philadelphia in 1707, during Queen Anne's War, the twenty-gun merchant ship Cleavland *carried a crew of fifty to battle French and Spanish ships on the Atlantic. The* Cleavland *represents a number of developments in ship rig since the mid-seventeenth century. On all three masts she carries small topgallant sails above the large topsails, and between the masts she sets triangular staysails. Her square courses and topsails have reef points so they can be partially furled in strong winds, and studdingsails are set beside the fore and main topsails to increase the sail area in light winds. Although she still carries a square spritsail below the bowsprit, the* Cleavland *is a very modern ship for she has newly developed triangular jibs between foremast and bowsprit. On the mizzen mast at the stern she has the traditional lateen-rigged fore- and aft mizzen sail, which will be replaced by the gaff-rigged spanker on ships built a few decades later. The ship's wheel was another development of the period represented by the* Cleavland, *but we can't see whether she has a wheel or traditional tiller to control the rudder. (Courtesy Lancashire Records Office, United Kingdom)*

fancy finish work, those artisans now came aboard. To protect the vessel from marine growths and ship worms, the bottom was commonly coated with a mixture of pitch and lime, although late in the colonial period more effective (and expensive) copper sheathing was introduced. Smaller vessels might be almost completely fitted out for sea on the ways. In many cases, however, the hull was launched unfinished and then warped alongside the mastyard to receive its spars. There, blockmakers, riggers, sailmakers, and other artisans completed the outfitting, the master shipwright turned the vessel over to the owner, and it was ready for sea.

In many ways shipbuilding represents America's first manufacturing industry, if by that term we mean the process by which an entrepreneur brings raw materials to a site he owns, there to be transformed into a finished product by skilled wage earners under his employ. Missing from the

operation, of course, were aspects we identify with the later factory system: significant capital investment; structures that house machinery; and the mass production of identical goods for the market. In contrast, colonial shipyards usually built vessels one at a time and only to order, with capital investment limited to the cost of the site itself, perhaps a few storage sheds, and ship timber "sticked" for seasoning. The customer made a down payment and additional payments at specified points during construction to cover expenses, and sometimes provided various materials like iron or paint. The master shipwright did not even supply his workers' tools; they came (and went) with the men he hired, giving these ship carpenters bargaining power and mobility that would not be achieved by factory laborers until late in the nineteenth century.

The market for colonial-built vessels expanded rapidly in the eighteenth century, from fishermen and coastal traders to

merchants with extensive trading routes to the West Indies and across the Atlantic to Great Britain and southern Europe. During the increasingly frequent wars, venturesome shipowners ordered fast vessels for privateering, and very occasionally one or another colonial legislature called for the construction of a sloop-of-war or other vessel to be armed for defense. Not surprisingly, most customers ordered their vessels from nearby yards, but by the eve of the Revolution some areas had developed a wide reputation for sound construction. Two such in Massachusetts were Newbury, at the mouth of the Merrimack River, and the North River, back of Scituate. Even if the original purchaser had been a neighbor, he might easily sell his vessel at a profit in one of the other colonies, particularly in the Carolinas, where New-England-built vessels accounted for more than 20 percent of the vessels registered in the period 1760-75. Great Britain comprised another important market.

One historian has estimated that by the eve of the Revolution Americans sold to the mother country at least 18,000 tons of vessels worth at least £140,000 per year, which would rank ships just behind fish as the fifth most valuable export. Independence meant the complete loss of this market because under the Navigation Acts American-built vessels would no longer qualify for British registry.

The varieties of colonial shipping are illustrated in this view of the Grays Inn Creek shipyard near Rock Hall, Maryland, ca. 1760. At left are several large tobacco ships; two brigs (the one at left is actually a form of brig rig called a snow) and a Bermuda-model sloop are at center; at right are a sloop and two schooners. This overmantel painting was located in Spencer Hall, home of the shipbuilding Spencer family. (Courtesy Maryland Historical Society)

Ready for launch in the New England shipbuilding center of Boston, the partially rigged fishing snow Diligence rests on the stocks. Built in 1739, this full-bodied, sharp-sterned vessel was intended to carry New England salt cod to Bilbao or other European ports that, in times of peace, purchased as much as 22,000,000 pounds of New England fish annually. Reflecting the vagaries of Atlantic trade in the days of empire, the Diligence was launched for trade with Spain just as rivals Spain and Great Britain began to fight one another in the War of Jenkins's Ear. Mariner Ashley Bowen of Marblehead painted this watercolor in his journal. (Courtesy Marblehead Historical Society; Mark Sexton photo)

to Africa for slaves, paid for in gold, silver, firearms, and rum, among other commodities.

The tobacco trade between the Chesapeake colonies and the mother country dominated American commerce through much of the colonial period, just as the cotton trade would do in the nineteenth century. After a slow start, tobacco production expanded rapidly in the last quarter of the seventeenth century, reaching 30 million pounds by its end and employing more than 150 vessels, mostly British-owned. Import duties on tobacco brought the mother country sizable revenues, and the commodity proved to be important for reexport, earning valuable foreign credits. To complete the circle, the Chesapeake colonies became Great Britain's best customers, in some years around the turn of the century importing nearly £200,000 worth of goods from the mother country. No wonder that the British merchants trading to Virginia comprised one of England's most powerful lobbying groups. In the period 1675-1725, more than 250 merchants in London supported efforts to influence the government's tobacco trade policies, greatly exceeding the numbers lobbying on behalf of trade with all other mainland colonies combined.

While the patterns of North Atlantic trade were in one sense "geometric," and are often characterized as triangular in nature, they were just as often of the "out and back" variety. Prevailing winds, vessel sizes and rigs, and the kinds and amounts of cargo all determined the patterns by which goods moved. In his search for "returns"–goods that he could sell in England or Europe–a Philadelphia shipowner for instance would likely use several smaller sloop- or schooner-rigged vessels to trade with the numerous West Indies islands, and order them to bring their cargoes of sugar and molasses back home. Not until sufficient quantities had accumulated in his warehouse would he load one of his larger square-riggers, which were more suitable for the North Atlantic run to England. Because the goods carried to England were bulky raw materials, and the return cargoes finished goods, American vessels returning from the mother country almost always had extra space on board, often used for the transportation of indentured servants.

Much has been made by some authors of smug-gling and other illegalities in American colonial commerce. Of course merchants in all the colonies occasionally violated the Navigation Acts if they thought the chance of detection was remote. Smuggling has always been a problem for any nation that limits or taxes the importation of certain goods for whatever purpose. England, for instance, depended on the revenue collected by duties levied on a multitude of commodities. Bands of smugglers made a handsome living along the English Channel by running in goods from France and Holland. For them, smuggling was a business, and they did not hesitate to kill revenue officers if intercepted. In contrast, few Americans made a profession of smuggling and none went quite so far as deliberate murder. Illicit goods that did reach America came for the most part in vessels owned by men whose businesses were predominantly legal, respected merchants like the Whartons of Philadelphia and the Hancocks of Boston. The most common violations involved the importation of manufactured articles and East India goods, particularly textiles, gin, and tea through Amsterdam and other European ports. After passage of the Molasses Act of 1733, New Englanders smuggled in a fair amount of molasses from the foreign West Indies, sometimes making a deal with the customs officer to pay a fraction of the duty (plus a generous bribe!). Another common violation involved trading with the French or Spanish West Indies during those frequent occasions when the mother country was at war with one, another, or both of these arch-rivals. Although some contraband trading went on at most ports, little evidence exists to suggest that it amounted to more than a small fraction of the total or that large fortunes were made through such illegal activities.

One of the most serious problems facing the colonial merchant was the chronic shortage of specie in America. The colonies minted little coinage of their own, and the unfavorable balance of trade with Great Britain drained away what little English currency came their way. The most common silver coin was in fact the Spanish piece of eight and its later successor, the Spanish milled dollar. Gold coins in circulation were Portuguese *johannes* and Spanish *pistoles*. The shortage of metallic currency forced colonists to rely on other means of exchange. Known as "country pay," commodities like tobacco, rice, and wheat were legal tender in many colonies, but of course their values fluctuated wildly. Merchants and other businessmen used bills of exchange as a kind of currency. A planter in Virginia might purchase a cargo of New England fish for his slaves with a bill of exchange drawn on the Glasgow merchant who had bought his recent crop of tobacco. The New Englander could then use the same bill to purchase a cargo of cloth from a merchant in Bristol, although its face value might be subject to discount if the solvency of its issuer were doubted. However useful to merchants, bills of exchange were never intended to circulate through the public at large, and the shortage of currency continued to restrict business enterprise. Following the precedent set by Massachusetts Bay during King William's War in 1690, most colonies turned to the issuance of paper money as a solution to the problem. Pennsylvania's currency was unique among the colonies for its relative stability, the rapid depreciation of currency issued by other colonies only adding to the uncertainties facing American merchants. In 1740 Massachusetts entrepreneurs established a private bank that issued paper currency secured by land, but Parliament intervened the next year to abolish it. Then in 1751 Parliament severely limited the issuance of paper money by the New England governments and in 1764 banned all the colonies from using such currency as legal tender. Credit was itself still another problem. Merchants customarily extended credit to each other and to shopkeepers, who in turn sold goods on credit when necessary. Planters in the Southern colonies and merchants everywhere also lent money at interest whenever the expectation of repayment was good, and numerous artisans and small manufacturers got their start this way. But farmers had a more difficult time obtaining credit for the purchase of land, livestock, or other improvements.

Not surprisingly, Great Britain received the largest share of American colonial exports, accounting for just over half of the total. Twenty-five percent went to the British West Indies, 20 percent to Southern Europe and the Atlantic islands, and the rest principally to Ireland and Africa. These figures do not include the very extensive coastal trade between continental colonies, however, nor an undetermined amount of traffic with the Spanish and French West Indies. One can only estimate how much colonial trade was carried in American-owned vessels: probably less than a third at the turn of the eigh-

teenth century, but perhaps as much as half by the eve of the Revolution. On the one hand, British shipowners dominated the valuable tobacco trade, but at the same time American merchants controlled the carriage of West Indies goods. The two peoples shared the traffic along other routes.

The Rise of Seaports

The most important social consequence of colonial American trade was the creation of seaports. By the eve of the American Revolution nineteen of the twenty largest towns on the continent were seaports. Of those nineteen, eleven were in New England, and three were in the Middle Colonies, including the two largest (Philadelphia and New York). Though less than 10 percent of the population lived in these ports, they had significance far beyond mere numbers. In economic terms seaport merchants, lawyers and other professionals, and shipmasters dominated their respective colonies by controlling exports, distributing imports, and accumulating and investing capital. This group, perhaps 25 percent of a colonial seaport's population, provided alternative employment opportunities to the region's youth, at the least as a common laborer or mariner. These unskilled workers constituted another 25 percent of the work force. The skilled artisans, constituting almost 50 percent of the population of a typical seaport, produced a remarkable variety of manufactured articles, from the smallest silver spoons to the largest full-rigged ships, newspapers, hats, wagon wheels—almost every item their customers could reasonably demand. These artisans comprised the backbone of an urban middle class, most of them prosperous enough to be important consumers. Politically, these nineteen largest seaports included nine of the colonial capitals, where contact with legislatures and royal officials opened the door to government appointments and military contracts.

Seaports were America's earliest cities, and as such were the first communities to confront urban problems like sanitation, water supply, public health, and crime, among others. The problem of the poor could not always be handled within individual families, as in agricultural towns, and sometimes became a major charge on the public purse. Culturally these urban centers

*Captain John Waddell (1714-1762), the son
of English and Scottish parents, was in New York
by the age of twenty-two. He began as a shipbuilder, then moved from ship ownership to a
career as a very successful merchant. Representing
the public spirit that distinguished colonial
seaports, Waddell was one of the original
subscribers for the New York Society Library.
In this portrait, by the fashionable English
artist John Wollaston, ca. 1750, he points to
New York on a globe of the world. (Collection of
The New-York Historical Society)*

*Anne Kirten Waddell (1716-1773) was a woman of
influence in colonial New York. Married to Captain
John Waddell in 1736, and the mother of seven
children, she was also an incorporator of the New
York Society Library and served as one of its
trustees. After her husband's death she carried on
his business, becoming one of the wealthiest women
in the Province of New York. English artist John
Wollaston painted Anne Waddell in the latest
English style of the day, confirming New York's
place as a cosmopolitan city of the British Empire.
(Collection of The New-York Historical Society)*

soon became far more sophisticated than interior
towns. Schools and colleges, libraries, concerts,
and theater enriched the lives of townspeople. All
of the English-language newspapers in America
on the eve of the Revolution were published in
seaports, for here was where printers could get
the "freshest advices" from other continental
colonies, the West Indies, England, and the
European continent. Far more than their country
cousins, seaport dwellers had the opportunity to
know what was going on in the rest of the
Atlantic world.

Through most of the period 1690-1760,
Boston and Philadelphia vied for leader-
ship among American ports, with New
York a distant third, followed by Newport,
Rhode Island, and Charleston, South Carolina.

Partly because of its early start relative to its
later rivals, Boston remained colonial America's
predominant seaport until the middle of the eighteenth century. Unlike most other ports, Boston's
hinterland consisted not so much of interior agricultural communities (New England's soil was
mediocre at best) but of other coastal towns
active in the fisheries, for which Boston became
the *entrepôt*. Boston's commerce in 1753 shows an
interesting spread of destinations. More than half
of the year's nearly five hundred clearances were
coastwise: 87 to Nova Scotia, 76 to the Carolinas
and 40 each to Delaware and Chesapeake Bays.
Of the deep-water voyages, 154 cleared for the
West Indies, 42 for the British Isles (mostly
London), 20 to European ports, and 4 to Africa
or the wine islands of the Azores and Madeira.
These maritime activities required vessels, and

Boston was an early and persistent leader in ship-building throughout and long after the colonial period. After the middle of the eighteenth century, Boston's disadvantages made it vulnerable to rivals both near and far. While no single other New England port could challenge it as a regional entrepôt, together they drew off the area's meager agricultural resources and prevented Boston from keeping pace with the rest of New England's growth. One such port was New Haven, Connecticut, which specialized in the West Indies trade. Outward cargoes included horses, cattle, sheep, hogs, cheese, lumber, and assorted other farm produce like Wethersfield's famed onions. New London sent occasional cargoes of rum and lumber to the Barbary states in the Mediterranean for mules (which they carried back to the West Indies) and bills of exchange.

Philadelphia, founded a half-century after Boston, was in contrast to its New England rival endowed with a productive agricultural hinterland, which lay in the 100-mile swath between the Delaware and Susquehanna Rivers, and whose access to markets the port virtually monopolized. Good soil and a kindly climate favored the production of wheat, which in turn encouraged the establishment of flour mills and bakeries in the metropolis. Its early waterfront was dominated by the wharf of Samuel Carpenter, a wealthy Quaker merchant who arrived from Barbados in 1684. In time Carpenter operated ten warehouses, a lime kiln, and a crane. By 1730 or so the port was recovering from the depression Benjamin Franklin had remarked upon when he arrived seven years earlier. The West Indies served as a ready market for Pennsylvania's breadstuffs, and because wheat blast and other diseases impeded the cultivation of grains in New England, Philadelphia could send flour to the north as well. In the last years before the Revolution, as Europe's population expanded, Philadelphia also shipped flour to England and the continent. With prosperity came economic independence from New England. Shipyards along the Schuylkill and Delaware Rivers now built their own vessels, although one customer complained that "our ship carpenters

Established 100 miles up the Delaware River in 1681 as a Quaker city by William Penn, Philadelphia flourished as an entrepôt in the eighteenth century, shipping out flour and grain and taking in European and West Indian products along with an increasing flow of Scottish, Irish, and German immigrants. By 1700 the population of Philadelphia exceeded that of New York, and by 1750 it had surpassed that of Boston, making Philadelphia the largest city in America. By the time of the American Revolution, with a population of 25,000, Philadelphia was the second largest city in the British Empire. (Courtesy Historical Society of Pennsylvania)

A Description of New York and the Hudson River, 1755

After having passed the Barr & come from sea within the Hook & under the pleasant feel of still Water, the Eye is delighted with the View of a most noble bay. On the left are the rocky & high woodlands of the Navesink wild & Picturesque, constrasted by the settlements & cultivated land of Long Island on the right. The Farms on Staten Island & the very Peculiar View of the Narrows meet your Eye upon the Ships bow, the bay & harbour of Amboy lyeing right before you. These pleasing & thus varied Objects form the sides of this Noble Bay. As you advance through the Narrows the eye expands its view again into a still more pleasing second bay, a kind of Amphitheatre, to appearance Circular, of about 12 Miles Diameter. This being constantly covered with Boats Sloops & every kind of Shipping passing & repassing through it & across it in all directions seems all alive with bustle & buisness [sic]. As you advance you see in the center of the Background on the Point of an Island the City of New York having the opening of Hudson or North River with the high lands of Bergen & New-Jersey on the right of it & opening of the Harbour & Quays in the East River bounded by the bluff points of Red Hook & Yellow Hook &

the Heights of Brook line [Brooklyn] on the left of it. This populous & well built Town with the Fort in front with the many steeples of its Churches the Turret of the Stadthouse & [Ex]Change dispersed amidst its buildings & the multitude of Shipping with which it is thronged perpetually makes a very striking appearance & altogether as fine & as pleasing a View as I ever saw. . . .

There are four Principal Streets as nearly parallel to each other as the uneaveness of the ground will permitt, all the cross streets the less & secondary streets are at right angles with these & in general run from shore to shore across the narrow point whereon the town stands....The number of Houses & Buildings in the year 1753 were as follows:

Public Buildings	*25*
Dwelling Houses	*1991*
Store-houses	*207*
Stables	*150*
Distilling houses	*10*
Sugar Houses	*2*
Brew houses	*4*
Rope Walks	*4*
Total	*2393*

The Inhabitants of the City extending through out the Island were about 15,000. The average of the Rent of the Buildings were estimated

at £25 per Ann. To give some idea of the manner in which their Houses were furnished I here insert from the speculative estimate made for me by the Vendue-Master extracts of the averages of the value of the Plate and furniture of the First, Middling and lower Class of Householders. He averaged the first at £700, The second at £200, The third he sudivided into two Classes & averaged the value of the furniture of the first of these at £40 the second at £20.

This pleasant City standing in a most charming situation, & enjoying the most delicious Climate in the world was inhabited by an hospitable cheerfull social people living by their extensive fortune Landed & Commercial & from the plenty & cheapness of every article of living better & more hospitably without parades than I ever saw any people in the old world live. . . .

The North or Hudsons river, at the opening of which into the bay this City stands, is of the most perfect navigation; is seldom frozen up in winter which the Delaware on which Philadelphia stands generally is, as also often the harbour of Boston. This North river carries from New-York to Kinderhook which is about 20 miles below Albany pretty uniformly 7 fathom water except

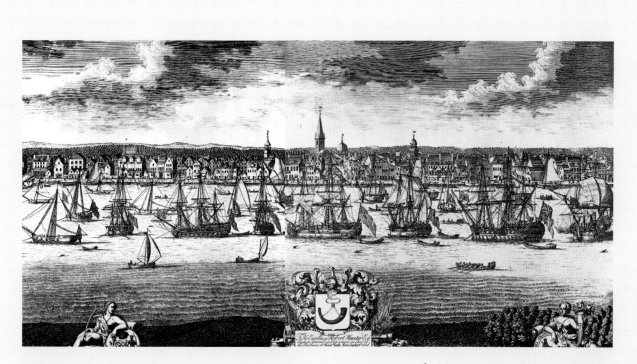

where it passes through the Highlands there its depth is from 15 to 30 fathom. From Kinderhook to the overslough (a barr of shallows) the depth is from 7 to 12 feet. After you are over the shallows of the overslough it deepens somewhat again up to Albany. The Navigation from New York to Albany was intirely carried on in a kind of Sloop of about 60 tons called a Yacht. The Dutch Schippers of Albany are the Chief Navigator. They had in 1754 twenty three of these Vessels in constant emply. From the Commodiousness & Cleanliness of these Vessels one enjoys the most agreeable passage that can be wished. These Yachts brought down the Produce of Albany County Wheat Flour Pease. The Produce of the Indian Trade &c to Newe York & their Back carriage was all sorts of european Goods & Produce Rum Sugar Salt & every article of manufacture both for the use of the Inhabitants and for the Indian Trade. . . . While all the Rivers from thence southwestward, are navigable with Sea Vessels in the Lower Flats only, this opens Communications with the Inland Parts of the Continent, of the utmost Importance to the British Interest. . . .

from T[homas] Pownall, M.P. *A Topographical Description of the Dominions of The United States of America* (London, 1776).

Even in 1717 New York still showed evidence of its Dutch heritage. Dutch buildings with their stepped gables still line the waterfront of lower Manhattan (in the left-hand view), and the "Dutch Church" steeple rises nearby. At far left is the crane for hoisting heavy cargo. Slips along the quay lead to covered market spaces. Several oceangoing sloops, a brig, and two merchant ships lie at anchor in the East River; all are armed, for peace in the Atlantic has not brought an end to piracy. The smaller unarmed sloops are coastal vessels, trading up the Hudson River or to the hinterlands of New Jersey, Long Island, and Connecticut.

Farther uptown (in the right-hand view) English buildings line the waterfront. North of the steeple of the "English Church," and the city hall cupola on Wall Street, stands the "French Church," attesting to New York's international flavor as a seaport. The roofed pavilion at the water's edge at the intersection of Wall and Water Streets is the Exchange, where merchants meet to conduct business. At far right a British warship under sail salutes the anchored Royal Navy station ship assigned to maintain a naval presence in New York. At left a merchant ship lies at anchor while another passes astern, either coming to anchor or leaving port with her anchor at the cathead and two tenders under tow. Details from William Burgis's A South Prospect of ye Flourishing City of New York, 1717. *(Courtesy Print Collection, Miriam and Ira D. Wallach Division of Art, Prints and Photographs, The New York Public Library, Astor, Lenox and Tilden Foundations)*

never season a stick." And Philadelphia's merchants maintained their own network of mercantile correspondents throughout the Atlantic world. In part because of its tradition of tolerance, Pennsylvania continued to receive large numbers of immigrants through the port of Philadelphia. In 1743 alone, twenty-two ships brought 7,000 Germans to settle in what was called "the best poor man's country," and the year following saw the arrival of 4,000 more.

Of North America's many coastal towns, New York was the most favored by nature to become a major seaport, as the nineteenth century would make abundantly clear. But in the period 1660-1760 New York lost its initial lead over Philadelphia in part because the population of its immediate hinterland grew at a slower pace and therefore produced far less wheat and other surplus grains for market. At the same time, New York's fur trade, a staple of the seventeenth century, could not keep pace with that of New France. Nor was New York able to establish a prosperous shipbuilding industry at this time. Yet the port at the mouth of the Hudson maintained a strong commercial tie directly with the mother country, primarily by shopping around the American perimeter of the Atlantic world for goods like sugar, flaxseed, logwood, rice, and naval stores to market in the British Isles. It helped that the British government found New York ideally situated as a base for its own military and naval activities in North America. Not only did its merchants receive European news sooner than its rivals, but also government contracts abounded, especially during wartime.

One more colonial American *entrepôt* rose to prosperity during the first half of the eighteenth century. Through an intricate network of protected waterways, Charleston (spelled Charles Town through much of the period) established a nearly monopolistic control over an enormously productive region that ranged along the Sea Islands of South Carolina and Georgia and far into the interior of both colonies (until Savannah began to challenge from the south for Georgia's custom). Its first exports were products of the forest—deerskins and furs, along with tar, pitch, and other so-called "naval stores" to England. Rice was introduced late in the seventeenth century, probably from Madagascar, and within a few decades became, with indigo, one of the region's principal exports. The latter was so valuable as a dye in England's growing textile industry that its production earned a bounty from the mother country. Although originally an enumerated article, rice could be shipped to continental ports south of Cape Finisterre after 1735 and by the eve of the Revolution ranked third in value (after tobacco, and flour and breadstuffs) among exports from the mainland colonies. Indigo ranked fifth behind dried fish. Unlike the larger seaports to the north, however, most of Charleston's commerce was carried in British-owned vessels. In fact the nature of the "Carolina trade" favored its control in every respect by British merchants rather than by those of Charleston.

Well might we ask with other colonial historians why the tobacco trade, America's single most valuable export, did not give rise to any major seaport in the Chesapeake region during the colonial period or for many years thereafter. The traditional explanation—that the region's many rivers and creeks made possible the shipment of tobacco directly from plantation to market—does not entirely satisfy Jacob Price, the preeminent scholar of the tobacco trade. He believes that because the tobacco trade was so complex, and the margins of profit so narrow, few Americans dared enter the business in competition with British merchants, who had dominated the business since its inception in the seventeenth century. Without the need for an indigenous community of merchants in America to run its commerce, Chesapeake Bay offered no reason for a major commercial center. Besides, the region offered attractive alternatives for the would-be entrepreneur: land speculation, shipbuilding, iron-making, or, toward the end of the period, the marketing of wheat, corn, naval stores, and other alternatives to tobacco.

Many of the institutions and structures that came to characterize seaports in the nineteenth century made their first appearance more than a century earlier. The art of building wharves, in part a legacy from the mother country, provided scores of berths for deepwater vessels along the waterfront of every seaport. By 1710 Boston alone had seventy-eight wharves, the most impressive of which, Long Wharf, reached out 800 feet from the shoreline. Fortunately, no American port had a tidal range in excess of ten feet, so that wet

This view of the Brooklyn, New York, ferry landing suggests the waterfront development in colonial American ports. Here, farmers, travelers, and townspeople mix outside the ferry house. Nearby is a pen to hold cattle for market. A wooden crib wharf filled with stone—a common colonial design—serves the flat-bottom scow ferry equipped with a sailing rig, which is loaded with oxen. A variety of small craft lie near the wharf, some of them tenders to vessels at anchor, some perhaps livery boats to carry passengers and goods around the harbor. The sloop under sail at right is an early American yacht, or recreational craft, the Fancy *belonging to Colonel Morris. Along the Manhattan shore can be seen several of the New York shipyards. Detail from William Burgis's* A South Prospect of ye Flourishing City of New York, *1717. (Courtesy Print Collection, Miriam and Ira D. Wallach Division of Art, Prints and Photographs, The New York Public Library, Astor, Lenox and Tilden Foundations)*

docks were not necessary. Capital came from merchants acting in company or as individuals. Shipowners also erected piers or other devices to mark obstructions and shoals that impeded navigation, but major harbor improvements, such as dredging and jetty construction, were beyond the means of private citizens and had to await federal government assistance. The first lighthouse in America was built in 1716 on what is now Little Brewster Island at the entrance to Boston Harbor. Other seaports boasted pairs of range lights to guide mariners through the channel to the waterfront. Some American sea captains owned a few English charts of the waters they regularly sailed, but the "Coast Pilot" was still in the future, and most mariners had to rely on "local knowledge" to keep them out of trouble. Without a lifesaving service, however, shipwrecked mariners were on their own, although at the very end of our period merchants in some localities had begun to provide shelters along exposed shores. At no time in our history was the business of going to sea more risky than in the eighteenth century.

Boston Light was the first American lighthouse. After Boston merchants petitioned the colonial legislature for a beacon in 1713, a committee proposed locating a lighthouse on Little Brewster Island, one of the harbor's outermost islands. The Massachusetts General Court appropriated funds for construction of a stone tower in 1715, and the light was first lit in September of 1716. Three years later a cannon was placed at the light to serve as a fog signal. The light's costs were covered by dues imposed on shipping in the port. Boston Light was damaged by fire in 1751 and blown up by British forces in 1776. The vessel in the foreground is a British naval sloop. Engraving by William Burgis, 1723. (Courtesy The Mariners' Museum, Newport News, Virginia)

A Century of Conflict

Despite their separation from the Old World by 3,000 miles of ocean, the English colonies in America became involved in each of the mother country's numerous wars in the one hundred years between 1663 and 1763. The reason was clear enough to the European nations vying for national economic security in those years: control of North America's resources were worth fighting for. To wrest a colony or island from one's enemy not only deprived a rival of valuable resources, but also added those riches to one's own coffers. Largely because of its growing sea power, Great Britain became increasingly adept at this zero-sum game until, by 1763, it had driven both the Dutch and the French completely out of North American waters, except for two small islands off Newfoundland. With the restoration of Charles II

to the throne, England opened an all-out offensive against Dutch commercial activities on both sides of the Atlantic. One weapon was the Navigation Act of 1660, whose exclusion of foreign vessels from the British empire was aimed at the ubiquitous Dutch trading vessels infesting England's American colonies. Another weapon was the Royal Navy, which launched a successful assault on New Netherland in 1664. Though briefly recaptured by the Dutch a decade later, New York—as the colony was renamed—became one of England's most valuable prizes of war. In the long run, England and the Netherlands had much in common: the Protestant religion for one, and for several decades after 1688 a shared monarch with the ascension of William of Orange and his English Queen Mary. In addition, a number of English mercantile houses set up branches in Amsterdam to strengthen commercial ties between the two countries. Relations between

Hazards of Seafaring in the Eighteenth Century

The Cabin-door burst open and I was overwhelmed with an immense wave, which brook my chair from its moorings, floated everything in the Cabin, and I found myself swimming amongst joint-stools, chests, Tables, and all the various furniture of our parlour. . . .It Blows harder and harder, the shrouds make a terrible rattling, it is a horrid sound. Oh Lord! here comes the Captain, who tells us the deadlights must be put up. I know the meaning of the word and yet it makes me shudder. He says, he expects a hard gale, I suppose he means this, a soft word for a hard storm. . . .The carpenter came in to put up the dead Lights, and a more dreary operation cannot be conceived; my heart, at that moment, seemed to bid farewell to sun, Moon and Stars. But I now know one god commands at Sea and at Land, whose omnipotence is extended over every element, I praise him for his Mercys past, and humbly hope for more. . . .

The storm roared over and around us, the Candle cast a melancholy gleam across the Cabin, which we now considered as our tomb. . . . the melancholy sound of the Sailors pulling with united strength at the ropes, the rattling of the sails and every thing joined to render the fearful scene more frightful. . . .

It was now about fifty hours the wind had been very high, tho' not dangerous. The sailors, however, began to complain heavily of their hard duty; besides, many things about the Vessel were beginning to give way: the ropes particularly, (which were not originally good,) were rendered so slight by the constant rain, that they every moment snapt in the working, by which means the Ship underwent such sudden and violent evolutions, that we were often thrown off our seats. This forced us to ly abed nor were we even safe there from its effects.

The rains continued, and the winds seemed to gain new strength from a circumstance that, in general, calms them. The sailors' hands were torn to piece by pulling at the wet ropes. Their stock of Jackets were all wete, nor was there a possibility of getting them dried, as the Steerage was quite full of the emigrants and hard loading; a piece of inhumanity, that I do not believe even Avarice ever equalled in any other owner. However our honest Johns did their best to keep a good heart, and weather out the gale. And when the wind would permit us to hear them, we were still serenaded with true love-garlands, and histories of faithful sailors and kind-hearted lasses. But on the fourth evening of the gale (as it was now termed) the whole elements

seemed at war: horror, ruin and confusion raged thro' our unfortunate wooden kingdom, and made the stoutest heart despair of safety.

Just after the midnight watch was set, it began to blow in such a manner, as made all that had gone before seem only a summer breeze. All hands, (a fearful sound) were now called; not only the Crew, but every man who could assist in this dreadful emergency. Every body was on deck, but my young friend and myself, who sat up in bed, patiently waiting that fate, we sincerely believed unavoidable. The waves poured into the state-room, like a deluge, often wetting our bed-cloths, as they burst over the half door. The Vessel which was one moment mounted to the clouds and whirled on the pointed wave, descended with such violence, as made her tremble for half a minute with the shock, and it appears to me wonderful how her planks stuck together, considering how heavy she was loaded. Nine hogsheads of water which were lashed on the deck gave way, and broke from their Moorings, and falling backwards and forwards over our heads, at last went over board with a dreadful noise. Our hen-coops with all our poultry soon followed, as did the Cabhouse or kitchen, and with it all our cooking-utensils, together with a barrel of fine pickled

Sea voyaging remained an extremely hazardous undertaking through the eighteenth century. Tropical hurricanes, North Atlantic gales, and coastal rocks and shoals all took their toll of the small colonial vessels that swarmed the Atlantic. "This Shews the Schooner Baltick in distress in 6 fathoms of water on Nantucket Sholes with every thing wash'd of the Decks & Two men Drouned," reads the legend on this watercolor, ca. 1766. (Courtesy Peabody Essex Museum, Salem, Massachusetts; photo by Mark Sexton)

tongues and above a dozen hams. We heard our sails fluttering into rags. The helm no longer was able to command the Vessel, tho' four men were lashed to it, to steer her. We were therefore resigned to the mercy of the winds and waves. At last we heard our fore maine mast [sic] split from top to bottom, a sound that might have appaled more experienced Mariners, but we heard all in Silence. . . .

Were you a sailor, I need only tell you our ship broached to. . . .The ship gave such a sudden and violent heel over, as broke every thing from their moorings, and in a moment the great Sea-chests, the boys' bed, my brother's cott, Miss Rutherford's Harpsicord, with tables, chairs, joint-stools, pewter plates, etc. etc. together with Fanny, Jack and myself, were tumbling heels over head to the side the Vessel had laid down on. It is impossible to describe the horror of our situation. The candle was instantly extinguished, and all this going on in the dark, without the least idea of what produced it, or what was to be its end. . . .To complete the horror of the scene, the sea poured in on us, over my brother's head, who held fast the ladder tho' almost drowned, while we were floated by a perfect deluge. . . .

Nothing can save a ship in this situation, but cutting away her masts, and the time necessary for this generally proves fatal to her, but our masts were so shattered by the late storm, that they went over by the Board of themselves, and the Vessel instantly recovered. This second motion, however, was as severely felt in the Cabin as the first, and as unaccountable, for we were shoved with equal Violence to the other side, and were overwhelmed by a second deluge of Sea waste. At last however it in some degree settled, and, thank God, no further mischief has happened, than my forehead cut, Jack's leg a little bruised, and the last of our poultry, a poor duck, squeezed as flat as a pancake.

Evangeline Walker Andrews, ed. *Journal of a Lady of Quality: Being the Narrative of a Journey from Scotland to the West Indies, North Carolina, and Portugal, in the years 1774 to 1776* (New Haven: Yale University Press, 1923)

England and France were another matter. The predictable enmity between Europe's leading Protestant and Catholic powers was exacerbated as far as the English were concerned by the ambitions of Louis XIV. The North American possessions of the two countries came into contact at numerous points of friction. On the one hand, English posts at Hudson Bay and northern New York threatened French fur-trading interests; on the other, French settlements at Acadia (Nova Scotia to the English) were a constant thorn in the side of New England fishing and commercial activities. In the Caribbean the two powers held numerous islands of strategic and economic value. In 1689 the Dutch and English joined forces in the War of the League of Augsburg to block French efforts to overrun the Netherlands. In its American counterpart, called King William's War, an amphibious expedition of colonials led by Maine native William Phips captured the French outpost at Port Royal, Nova Scotia, only to see it retaken soon after. Privateers of each belligerent raided the shipping of its enemy, and Indians allied to New France launched effective attacks against English frontier settlements, but the war ended in 1699 with little significant change.

Less than three years later the War of Spanish Succession (known in America as Queen Anne's War), broke out in Europe, soon followed by hostilities in North America, the Caribbean, and the waters in between. Now the English colonies at the southern end of the continent were vulnerable to attack from Spanish and French interests in both Florida and Louisiana, but the Carolinians succeeded in blunting the attacks of their rivals. New Englanders once again captured Port Royal, this time for keeps, and the Royal Navy gained mastery of the Caribbean. After more than a decade of struggle, the Treaty of Utrecht (1713) marked a turning of the tide in favor of Great Britain in the battle for North America. France was forced to give up Nova Scotia and recognize England's claims to Hudson Bay and Newfoundland. If American fishermen thought they were rid of the French, however, they were wrong. Within two years of peace France constructed fortress Louisbourg on Cape Breton Island to protect its fishermen, who had retained rights to the banks off Newfoundland. To New Englanders, Louisbourg became a symbol of a hostile presence in their midst, made real during

Cornelis Steenwyck (d. 1684) bridged the transition from Dutch to English rule in Nieuw Amsterdam. Born in the Netherlands, he came to Nieuw Amsterdam before 1651 and established himself as a merchant, engaging in trade to the Caribbean, Virginia, and Africa. Steenwyck frequently held city office, and in 1664 he acted as one of the Dutch commissioners in the settlement of English and Dutch claims to Nieuw Amsterdam. Under English rule he remained a trusted figure, twice serving as mayor of New York. When artist Jan Van Gootten painted his portrait in Holland, ca. 1668, he included a view of Nieuw Amsterdam. (Collection of The New-York Historical Society)

wartime when it harbored French privateers that preyed on Yankee shipping.

Peace continued between the major European nations for the next twenty-five years, until 1739, when the so-called War of Jenkins's Ear broke out between Spain and England over maritime rivalries. The war started badly for the colonists. Georgia's founder, James Oglethorpe, attacked Spanish Florida in hope of expanding his new colony, but without success. Later in the war three thousand Americans joined a British expedition against Cartagena, the Spanish stronghold on the Caribbean coast of South America, two-thirds of

The Two
William Pepperrells:
From Fisherman to Baronet

LT. GEN. SIR WM. PEPPERRELL, Bart.
The Victor of Louisbourg A.D. 1745.

Surely the most successful of New England fishermen was William Pepperrell, the elder. He came from Devonshire in the late 1670s as an apprentice aboard an English fishing vessel. When his term expired, he decided to stay on in New England, residing first at the Isles of Shoals off the New Hampshire coast. There he continued as a fisherman, drying his catch on the islands and taking it into Portsmouth for market. He soon moved to the mainland, where he settled in Kittery, on the harbor of Portsmouth, New Hampshire, but actually in the district of Maine, then a part of the colony of Massachusetts Bay. Pepperrell gradually expanded his fishing fleet, entered the Newfoundland trade, and married well. He also operated a shipyard, first as an adjunct to his fisheries activities and then as a business in its own right. His vessels carried fish to the Southern colonies, throughout the West Indies, and directly to Spain and Portugal. Sometimes selling both vessel and cargo, at every corner he turned a profit, much of which he reinvested in the construction of additional vessels and cargoes. He owned seven at the beginning of the eighteenth century, doubled that number by 1715, and a decade later had a fleet of thirty vessels and an interest in many more. At the same time he expanded both wholesale and retail business activities throughout the Piscataqua region, selling English goods he had imported himself as well as those he had bought from Boston merchants like Jonathan Belcher.

By the 1720s William Pepperrell, the younger, who was born in 1696, had grown to manhood and joined his father in partnership. Fish continued to be the mainstay of their business, but now they began to invest some of their profits in extensive tracts of timberland in southern Maine and entered the lucrative business of cutting and exporting masts and ship timber, mostly to the West Indies but occasionally to England for the Royal Navy. Of course the value of the Pepperrell lands rapidly increased as settlers moved north and east from Massachusetts. Young William Pepperrell spent much of his time in Boston, where he cut quite a figure in social circles. He married into the Sewall family, was commissioned colonel of the militia for the District of Maine, and at the age of thirty-one was appointed to the governor's council of Massachusetts Bay, a position he held until his death thirty-two years later. His successful leadership of the New England forces that captured the French fortress at Louisbourg in 1745 earned him a baronetcy from King George II, the first colonial American so honored. William Pepperrell, the son of a fisherman, had become Sir William Pepperrell. His Kittery home boasted fine woodwork, a large collection of portraits, and a splendid library that included works of literature, law, political philosophy, and of course navigation. His estate boasted gardens, orchards, and an extensive deer park. His coach was drawn by six white horses, and his barge was rowed

through the waters of the river and bay by half a dozen African slaves attired in black livery. Pepperrell died in 1759 at the age of sixty-three, but his mansion overlooking Portsmouth harbor from Kittery Point still stands.

William Pepperrell, Jr., merchant, became Lieutenant General Sir William Pepperrell, Bart., as a result of the successful siege of Louisbourg in 1745. Pepperrell (1696-1759) took over his father's flourishing business at Kittery, operating as many as thirty-five vessels in trade to Newfoundland, the Middle Atlantic colonies, the Caribbean, Spain, and Portugal. He served the Colony of Massachusetts as a local judge, a member of the governor's council, and as a diplomat in negotiations with Native Americans before being named general of New England troops in King George's War. After his knighthood, Pepperrell visited England, the place his father had left as an apprentice fisherman seventy-five years earlier. John Smibert painted Pepperrell's portrait with the siege of Louisbourg in the background. (Courtesy Peabody Essex Museum, Salem, Massachusetts; photo by Mark Sexton)

The British colonies viewed the French stronghold at Louisbourg on Cape Breton Island as a great threat to British control of the North Atlantic and to the fisheries pursued off that coast. With the outbreak of King George's War, a combined Royal Navy and colonial militia force arrived off Louisbourg in the spring of 1745. Under cover of a naval bombardment, the New England forces landed and laid siege to the fortress, forcing its surrender after forty days. This engraving commemorated Commodore Warren, General Pepperrell, and "the New England Men who bravely offer'd their service and went as private Soldiers, in this hazardous but very glorious Enterprize." Only three years later, Louisbourg was handed back to the French during peace negotiations. (Courtesy Beverly R. Robinson Collection, U.S. Naval Academy Museum)

whom succumbed to battle wounds or yellow fever in the disastrous campaign. But when France joined the fray in 1744 it became the War of the Austrian Succession (King George's War), and New Englanders saw their chance. Under the Massachusetts merchant William Pepperrell, they organized an expedition to capture Louisbourg. Brilliant tactics and a bit of good luck during a lightning campaign crowned the Yankee effort with success, and the dreaded French fortress fell in 1745. To the Yankees' disgust, British diplomats gave it back at the peace table in 1748 in exchange for Madras, the province in India that the French had captured. News of this deal prompted Thomas Hancock, a leading New England merchant and uncle of the more famous John, to remark that he hoped that the decision "may be for the good of the nation, tho' I don't think it will prove so to this country." This distinction between country and nation, between one's geographical home and national

allegiance, presented Americans with a cruel dilemma. For most people, East Anglians, for instance, their "country" was physically a part of their "nation." For Americans the two were separated by three thousand miles of tempestuous ocean.

The final confrontation between France and England came shortly after mid-century. Opening first in the American backcountry as the French and Indian War, the struggle expanded in 1756 to become the Seven Years' War with campaigns in Europe, Asia, and the Caribbean. After two years of failures, English fortunes began to turn under the leadership of William Pitt. In America a British amphibious force recaptured Louisbourg, though suffering much higher losses than had the New Englanders twelve years before. This time Great Britain dismantled the fortress and in the peace that followed retained the island of Cape Breton.

The capstone of Pitt's military policy was a two-pronged invasion of New France that led to the fall of Quebec in September 1759. When the Royal Navy defeated a French fleet with reinforcements and Montreal was captured, the conquest of Canada was complete. By the peace of Paris in 1763, France surrendered several sugar islands in the Caribbean and all of its North American possessions, save the islands of St. Pierre and Miquelon. In the previous year it had turned over to Spain its vast interior domain of Louisiana as enticement to join in the war against Great Britain.

To bring France to the peace table, Great Britain had to return one or another captured territory. The choice came down to the tiny sugar island of Guadeloupe or all of Quebec. To the traditional mercantilist the produce of the former island was far more valuable than the nearly barren stretches of Canada, and besides, some British observers feared that with the removal of the French from North America the English colonies might grow less dependent on protection from the mother country. Benjamin Franklin, among many others, argued persuasively that Canada was the more valuable to the Empire, however, and in the end England decided to retain it, in part as a long-term economic investment, but also, perhaps, because of a new sense of imperial grandeur. In the end, perhaps Governor Thomas Hutchinson was right when he wrote in the midst of the Revolution: "I am now convinced that if [Canada] had remained to the French none of the spirit of opposition to the mother country would have yet appeared. . . ." Although driven off the continent, France would get its revenge in 1781 when its fleet won the decisive battle off the Capes of the Chesapeake that sealed the fate of General Cornwallis at Yorktown.

The Colonial Wars at Sea

The long series of wars with France and Spain gave American shipowners the opportunity to profit in numerous ways, carrying provisions for the British army, importing war materiel such as gunpowder for colonial militia units, and sending out private armed vessels under letters-of-marque. This last role can be traced back to twelfth-century Italy, when rulers began to issue permits allowing subjects to seek reprisal for vessels seized at sea. In time of war, private armed vessels augmented national navies, although their actions differed from piracy only in the official sanction bestowed by a "letter-of-marque and reprisal." Strictly speaking, a letter-of-marque vessel was a merchant vessel undertaking normal trading voyages but armed for self-defense and authorized to seize enemy vessels if the opportunity arose. Crew members earned regular wages but they also shared in prize money if any captures were made. Privateers, on the other hand, were really private warships, authorized by a similar letter-of-marque but intended solely to cruise in search of prizes. They carried no cargo, were generally faster and more heavily armed than merchant vessels, and were manned by larger crews needed for seizing enemy vessels and bringing them into port. In either case, since the sixteenth century British law had stipulated that privateering cases would be adjudicated in admiralty courts, and privateers were required to post a bond to insure that they did not overstep the boundary between privateering and piracy.

Because of the greater risks involved, individual investors held only a fractional interest in any one privateer, but the adventuresome might own shares in several vessels. Like the owners, crew members signed on for shares of the prize money, dividing half the total proceeds by an agreed-upon formula. Success for an ordinary seaman might bring a year's wages in one short cruise; failure meant at worst, death by gunfire or drowning; at best, years of incarceration in a naval hulk until exchanged at war's end. The owners divided their share of prize vessels and cargoes according to their fractional ownership; yet they suffered only monetarily if their vessels were captured or sunk by the enemy. Privateering was legal only during wartime and operated under government regulations, but British officials had difficulty holding Americans to strict account when the colonists were losing their own merchant vessels by the score to French, Spanish, and Dutch privateers and warships.

During King George's War (1744-48) Americans armed more than one hundred privateers, more than half of which set out from New York. In the first weeks of hostilities French privateers out of Louisbourg seized thirty-six colonial vessels, mostly from Massachusetts, before the colonists knew they were at war. The Yankees got even by

The Boston letter-of-marque ship Bethel, *armed with fourteen guns, was on a trading voyage in the Mediterranean when she took a prize in 1748. Then, off the Azores, she encountered the twenty-six-gun Spanish merchant ship* Jesus, Maria and Joseph, *bound from the Caribbean with a valuable cargo including 171,000 Spanish pieces of eight. By a ruse, Captain Isaac Freeman of the* Bethel *convinced the Spanish captain he was outmanned and outgunned, and the* Bethel *arrived in St. John's, Newfoundland, with one of the wealthiest prizes of the war. This painting, which is one of the earliest American ship portraits, shows the* Bethel *in two perspectives getting under sail. (Courtesy Massachusetts Historical Society, Boston, and Peabody Essex Museum, Salem, Massachusetts)*

joining in on the capture of Louisbourg the year following. The Seven Years' War (1756-63) gave Americans even greater opportunity to invest in privateering. Massachusetts authorized the arming of more than 300 privately owned vessels and New York a further seventy-five, owned by twice that number of investors. They captured 400 prizes, worth more than £2,000,000. Both English and American privateers profited from the Admiralty's "Rule of 1756," which prohibited neutral vessels engaging in wartime trades from which they were excluded in peacetime. (It was just this sort of policy decision that prompted one historian to quip that "Britannia waives the rules.") Thus, a Dutch vessel trading with a

French or Spanish colony was fair game. Abuses inevitably resulted, however, and to mollify protests from the Netherlands, Great Britain imposed stricter regulations on both English and American privateers with considerable success. Privateering had other ramifications. For one thing, the demand for extra mariners diverted manpower from regular commerce and the fisheries and, for those who remained, drove up their wages by 28 percent during the Seven Years' War. Orders for specially designed private war vessels gave added business to shipyards, sail lofts, and mast-makers all along the coast, and of course the inhabitants of seaports enjoyed the opportunity of purchasing captured goods at auction. Some investors made fortunes, others lost them, and as always the ordinary seaman put his life on the line.

Massachusetts was one of several colonies that commissioned its own armed vessels to protect its merchant and fishing vessels during wartime. In the earlier wars at the turn of the century the colony sent out two vessels, each named *Province Galley*. During King George's War the General Court commissioned the snow *Prince of Orange*, the sloop *Massachusetts*, and the ship *Massachusetts-Frigate*. At the outbreak of the Seven Years' War Massachusetts voted that "Two suitable Vessells be provided at the Charge of this Government, the one for the Protection of our Coasters from the Southward, and another for the Protection of the Fishery, and other inward Bound Vessels." The snow *Prince of Wales* began service in the spring of 1757 and the 20-gun ship *King George* shortly thereafter. The latter vessel was commanded by Benjamin Hallowell, Jr., later to earn notoriety as one of the Commissioners of Customs at Boston on the eve of the Revolution. The warship served throughout the war, protecting Massachusetts commerce, capturing half a dozen prizes, and participating in several amphibious operations with the Royal Navy, including the recapture of St. John's, Newfoundland, in 1762.

The men who served in privateers and the public naval vessels of the colonies did so as volunteers. But during the course of the Anglo-French wars many other American seamen were impressed into the Royal Navy by desperate commanders stationed along the American coast. In order to gain support among the colonists during Queen Anne's War, Parliament had proclaimed that "no mariner or other person . . . in any part of America" could be impressed. Although from time to time British judges argued that the act had expired with the Treaty of Utrecht in 1713, Parliament did not specifically repeal it until 1775. The situation was sufficiently murky to deter impressment during peacetime for the most part, but when war broke out, many British commanders on the American station sent press gangs ashore or seized sailors off passing merchant vessels. HMS *Shirley* took nearly 100 men from Boston during King George's War, and a major sweep through New York's waterfront netted 800 seamen during one night in 1757, although half of

them were subsequently released.

Both merchants and seamen protested the practice, the former through appeals to government complaining about the harm done to their commerce, the latter more directly in the streets in defense of their liberties. What came to be known as the Knowles Riot in November 1747 resulted from a press carried out in Boston by Commodore Charles Knowles from his flagship, HMS *Lark*. A mob of sailors and waterfront workers, black and white together and numbering in the thousands, took some of the ship's officers hostage, attacked the sheriff, and forced Governor William Shirley to seek refuge at Castle William. When the mob seized a tender belonging to one of his vessels and burned it in front of the governor's house, Knowles threatened to bombard the town. The riot continued for three days before peace was restored by the release of the impressed Americans. Only then did Boston town meeting express its "abhorrence of such illegal criminal proceedings," referring to the riot, not the press gangs. But one young supporter of the sailors' cause, Samuel Adams, Jr., noted the effectiveness of the waterfront mob as a means of defending the common rights of man, and he would not forget the lesson.

The Fisheries and Whaling

The structure of New England's fishing industry changed radically in the half-century between 1675 and about 1725. Fishermen of the eighteenth century shipped out on larger vessels than their forebears, two-masted schooners and ketches capable of sailing far offshore and remaining on the grounds for weeks on end if necessary. Abandoning the Gulf of Maine to the declining number of smaller shallops, the big schooners headed north and east, to the grounds along the "eastern shore" of Nova Scotia, to St. Pierre Bank south of Newfoundland, and even as far as the Grand Banks. Offshore fishing required a change in the method of curing the catch. No longer did the vessel run into a coastal station every few days, where a shoreman dried the fish on flakes. Now it was split and salted on deck and then stowed away in the capacious hold below. Not until filled to capacity would the vessel return directly to its home port, where the fish was then set out to dry on flakes along the waterfront. This change meant more efficient use of both vessel and crew and gradually increasing catches. From 60,000 quintals in 1675, the fishermen of Massachusetts brought in trips totaling more than 200,000 quintals annually in the 1730s.

But as is so often the case in the fishing industry, prices for cod steadily declined through the same period, precipitating another change. Increasing numbers of inshore fishermen went broke, unable to pay their steadily increasing debt to merchant-creditors. One by one the merchants collected what debts they could, cut their losses, and shifted their capital investments from bankrolling fishermen to building and owning the vessels themselves. By the eve of the Revolution only a few skippers held shares in the vessels they sailed, and almost no other crew members did. The men were paid by a percentage of the catch, the crew dividing five-eighths of its value and the remaining three-eighths going to the vessel-owner. Each offshore fisherman hauled in almost twice the catch of his inshore predecessor, offsetting the fall in prices, and allowing him to keep a little ahead of a rising cost of living. Most young fishermen could now marry, in contrast to the past, and fishing villages like Marblehead "became notorious for their hordes of children," in the words of Daniel Vickers. On the other hand the offshore industry entailed harder work, harsher conditions, and greater dangers than its inshore counterpart. In one five-year period Essex County ports lost more than forty vessels and nearly three hundred men to late winter storms. For all these reasons offshore fishing was a young man's work, and by the eve of the Revolution few men over the age of thirty still went out to the banks. Unfortunately, they had limited opportunities for employment ashore and no land to farm, even if they knew how. Proper folks blamed the poverty they saw in Marblehead on the character of its inhabitants. "They have so little knowledge of moral life," wrote Salem's minister, the Reverend William Bentley, "that they are as profane, intemperate, and ungoverned as any people on the Continent." "They were savage in their nature and education," wrote a traveler from Connecticut, "and very poor in general. . . . One can hardly ride thro' the Town without being accosted [by beggars] by one half of the old women and children in it."

Meanwhile, competition from the fleets of other countries continued apace. Indeed, in the 1740s fishing for cod on the Grand Banks still attracted upwards of one thousand French fishing vessels, which, with crews totaling more than 20,000 men, took home more than one million quintals each season. In contrast, at mid-century the New England cod fishery employed about half as many vessels with smaller crews, bringing in one-fourth as many fish. Two hundred smaller vessels fished inshore, and about one hundred additional boats were engaged in mackerel fishing each season. In the 1760s almost all of New England's fishermen set out from Massachusetts ports, half of them from Marblehead and Gloucester and the rest from towns scattered along the coast from Nantucket and Cape Cod to Maine. Nearly half of the annual catch, which now totaled altogether perhaps 400,000 quintals, went to European ports, a slightly lesser amount to the West Indies, and the balance to the Southern plantation colonies. In the last years before the Revolution, New England's fishing industry continued to grow. Testifying before Parliament in March 1775 against the bill to exclude New Englanders from the codfisheries, Boston merchant Stephen Higginson estimated that the region's 700 cod schooners provided work for 10,000 men, including both the fishermen and those who processed the fish ashore and carried it to market.

Whaling by colonial Americans probably began along the shores of Long Island in the 1640s, when residents of Southampton first tried out the oil from drift whales stranded on their beaches. Cape Codders followed suit, and then the residents of Nantucket. Not content with waiting for whales to drift in, the men rowed out to kill humpback and right whales seen spouting nearby and towed their carcasses back so that the blubber could be tried out, or rendered into oil, in pots set up on the beach. Because of its offshore location, Nantucket soon became a leading center of the whaling industry. Within three years the island was sending out six sloops on month-long cruises, employing many Native Americans as crew members, and by 1730 its fleet had expanded to 25 vessels. Other coastal towns took up the industry, and soon the shore fishery died out altogether. By then New Englanders had begun to ship small quantities of whale oil to England for market.

In the 1750s two innovations revolutionized the

In 1853, artist William Allen Wall painted this interpretation of the early days of whaling in New Bedford (then Dartmouth), ca. 1763. The sloop at center represents the typical colonial whaling vessel, and at right is one of the shoreside tryworks for rendering oil, which were replaced by shipboard tryworks about this time. The men at right mince blubber for the try-pots and ladle the rendered oil into casks set up by the cooper standing at center. At left is Joseph Russell, the Quaker merchant who established whaling at Dartmouth, speaking with his African slave. An American Indian is depicted selling moccasins, although the local natives frequently served as mariners and whalemen. Wall's vision of the origins of the city's economic mainstay was highly regarded by New Bedford's whaling merchants of the 1850s, whose business it celebrated. (Used with permission of the Board of Trustees of the New Bedford Free Public Library)

whaling industry. The first was the successful installation of try-pots on board whaling vessels, freeing their masters from the necessity of returning to port with casks of blubber for trying out on shore. Longer, more profitable voyages followed as a matter of course. The second breakthrough came with the development of a method that made possible the full use of the sperm whale, first taken in 1712 by Nantucket whaleman Christopher Hussey. The head cavity of this species contained oil of the highest quality, along with a waxy substance called spermaceti, which once separated could be manufactured into candles. Nantucket soon dominated the sperm-whale fishery, its eighty-five vessels in the so-called southern fishery accounting for two-thirds of all the sperm oil landed by Americans in the years just before the Revolution. The towns of Dartmouth (now New Bedford), Wellfleet, and

Boston concentrated on the northern fishery, where right whales were sought not only for their oil but also for baleen (the flexible plates of keratin that non-toothed whales use to strain their food from seawater, called "whalebone" by whalemen) useful for its flexibility. New England whalemen ranged as far north as Davis Strait off Greenland and south as far as the coast of Africa and very occasionally to the Falkland Islands. By the 1770s the two branches together employed nearly two hundred vessels and more than 4,000 seamen, several hundred of whom were Native Americans.

Sloops of fifty to one hundred tons burden comprised the bulk of the whaling fleet, although brigantines and topsail schooners gained favor for the more distant grounds. Crews remained small, a dozen or so for the shorter voyages, no more than eighteen for the southern fishery. Depending on its size, each vessel carried two or three whaleboats. From using ordinary ships' boats earlier in the century, whalemen now developed small craft specifically designed for the purpose: about twenty-five feet in length, double-ended, and manned by a crew of six, rather than just five as earlier. This larger boat made possible its use as a drogue, so that once the quarry was ironed, the crew made the harpoon line fast and was towed by the rapidly tiring whale in what would later be romanticized as a "Nantucket sleighride."

The oil was usually sent to Boston for export to England, but occasionally Nantucket's merchants shipped a cargo directly to London. The business of making candles from spermaceti centered in Newport, Rhode Island, where the works were owned by Jewish merchants who had emigrated from Portugal. Because of their quality, the candles commanded a high price among merchants along the Atlantic seaboard as well as planters throughout the South and in the Caribbean. Because they were colonial manufactures, however, they could not be exported to England. Nevertheless, oil, bone, and other whale products became New England's most valuable export to the mother country, earning its merchants desperately needed sterling credits that amounted to more than £250,000 annually by the eve of the American Revolution.

The Slave Trade

Slavery was a characteristic of most European settlements in the New World. Europeans in the Americas engaged almost exclusively in extractive enterprises such as mining, trapping, fishing, timber harvesting, and plantation farming, all of which were labor-intensive to a degree not found in Europe at the time. The French and Dutch in North America successfully developed a fur trade by exploiting Native Americans to catch and process beaver pelts, but Spanish attempts to force Native Americans to work in their gold and silver mines ultimately failed. In the mid-sixteenth century Spanish and Portuguese settlements turned for their labor supply to Africa, where the Portuguese had already laid a foundation for the Atlantic slave trade. British sugar planters adopted the idea for their West Indian plantations early

in the seventeenth century. Through the eighteenth century, these plantations, which both grew sugarcane and processed its derivative products, were the largest and most complex manufacturing plants in the Atlantic world.

Although a Dutch warship brought nineteen Africans to Jamestown in 1619, the English mainland colonies did not turn to slave labor until much later in the seventeenth century. For one thing, as we have already seen, harsh conditions at home encouraged considerable numbers of English laborers and convicts to come to America as indentured servants seeking a fresh start. For another, space was relatively cheap on vessels heading west across the Atlantic to pick up a bulky cargo of tobacco or other raw materials. Until well after mid-century the plantations of the Chesapeake relied on white laborers who worked for a term of years before earning their "freedom dues," a small grant of money, perhaps, or clothing and tools, and rarely, a plot of land. White servants who ran away were hard to find, however, and improving conditions at home reduced the supply of English laborers needed to replace those whose indentures had expired.

Some historians have suggested that the first Africans came as servants rather than slaves, but all agree that by the 1670s or so perpetual slavery had become firmly entrenched as the basis of the labor system in the plantation colonies of English America. Thereafter, the Black population increased from less than 3,000 in 1660 to about 28,000 by the end of the seventeenth century, almost entirely the result of importations averaging about 500 slaves per year. During the eighteenth century these numbers increased dramatically in response to an almost insatiable demand for labor throughout the southern colonies. The establishment of rice and indigo plantations in the newly founded colony of South Carolina expanded the market, and Charleston became a major center for the slave trade. By the middle of the century, slave traders brought Blacks into South Carolina at the rate of 3,000 or more each year, and still the demand continued. Even so, these figures do not begin to measure the vast extent of the Atlantic slave trade. Historians have estimated that before the legal commerce was finally abolished in the early nineteenth century, between eight and ten million Africans were forcibly taken from their homelands and sold throughout the

The Middle Passage
Two Perspectives on the Slave Trade

The African view:

Broteer Furro was born at Dukandarra, Guinea, about 1729, the son of a prince. At about the age of six, during a tribal war, his father was killed and he was captured. He later recalled his introduction into slavery.

The invaders then pinioned the prisoners of all ages and sexes indiscriminately, took their flocks and all their effects, and moved on their way towards the sea. . . . Having come to the next tribe, the enemy laid siege and immediately took men, women, children, flocks, and all their valuable effects. They then went on to the next district, which was contiguous to the sea, called in Africa, Anamaboo. The enemies' provisions were then almost spent, as well as their strength. The inhabitants, knowing what conduct they had pursued, and what were their present intentions, improved the favorable opportunity, attacked them, and took enemy, prisoners, flocks and all their effects. I was then taken a second time. All of us then put into the castle and kept for market. On a certain time, I and other prisoners were put on board a canoe, under our master, and rowed away to a vessel belonging to Rhode Island, commanded by Captain Collingwood, and the mate, Thomas Mumford. While we were going to the vessel, our master told us to appear to the best possible advantage for sale. I was bought on board by one Robertson Mumford, a steward of said vessel, for four gallons of rum and a piece of calico, and called VENTURE on account of his having purchased me with his own private venture. Thus I came by my name. All the slaves that were bought for that vessel's cargo were two hundred and sixty.

After all the business was ended on the coast of Africa, the ship sailed from thence to Barbadoes. After an ordinary passage, except great mortality by the small pox, which broke out on board, we arrived at the island of Barbadoes; but when we reached it, there were found, out of the two hundred and sixty that sailed from Africa, not more than two hundred alive. These were all sold, except myself and three more, to the planters there.

The vessel then sailed for Rhode Island, and arrived there after a comfortable passage.

Venture Smith, *A Narrative of the Life and Adventures of Venture, A Native of Africa* (New London, 1798)

Olaudah Equiano was born at Essaka, Benin (now eastern Nigeria), in 1745, the son of an Igbo embrenche or chief. When he was eleven, Equiano and his sister were kidnapped and sold into slavery in Africa. Soon they were sold again and separated. Eventually Equiano was taken to the coast.

The first object that saluted my eyes when I arrived on the coast was the sea, and a slave ship, which was then riding at anchor, and waiting for its cargo. These filled me with astonishment, that was soon converted into terror, which I am yet at a loss to describe, and much more the then feelings of my mind when I was carried on board. I was immediately handled and tossed up to see if I was sound, by some of the crew; and I was now persuaded that I had got into a world of bad spirits, and that they were going to kill me. Their complexions too, differing so much from ours, their long hair, and the language they spoke, which was very different from any I had ever heard, united to confirm me in this belief.

Soon after this the blacks who brought me on board went off, and left me abandoned to despair. I now saw myself deprived of all chance of returning to my native country, or even the least glimpse of gaining the shore, which I now considered as friendly; and I even

wished for my former slavery, in preference to my present situation, which was filled with horrors of every kind, still heightened by my ignorance of what I was to undergo. I was not long suffered to indulge my grief. I was soon put down under the decks, and there I received such a salutation in my nostrils as I had never experienced in my life: so that, with the loathsomeness of the stench, and with my crying together, I became so sick and low that I was not able to eat, nor had I the least desire to taste any thing. I now wished for the last friend, death, to relieve me; but soon, to my grief, two of the white men offered me eatables; and, on my refusing to eat, one of them held me fast by the hands, and laid me across, I think, the windlass, and tied my feet, while the other flogged me severely. I had never experienced any thing of this kind before, and although, not being used to the water, I naturally feared that element the first time I saw it, yet nevertheless, could I have got over the nettings, I would have jumped over the side, but I could not; and besides the crew used to watch us very closely,

who were not chained down to the decks, lest we should leap into the water. . . . In a little time after, amongst the poor chained men, I found some of my own nation, which in a small degree gave ease to my mind. I inquired of these what was to be done with us. They gave me to understand we were to be carried to these white people's country to work for them. I was then a little revived, and thought if it were no worse than working, my situation was not so desperate. But still I feared I should be put to death, the white people looked and acted, as I thought, in so savage a manner; for I had never seen among any people such instances of brutal cruelty. . . .

While we stayed on the coast I was mostly on deck; and one day, to my great astonishment, I saw one of these vessels coming in with the sails up. As soon as the whites saw it, they gave a great shout, at which we were amazed; and the more so as the vessel appeared larger by approaching nearer. At last she came to an anchor in my sight, and when the anchor was let go, and my countrymen who

saw it, were lost in astonishment to observe the vessel stop, and were now convinced it was done by magic. . . . At last, when the ship, in which we were, had got in all her cargo, they made ready with many fearful noises, and we were all put under deck, so that we could not see how they managed the vessel.

But this disappointment was the least of my grief. The stench of the hold, while we were on the coast, was so intolerably loathsome, that it was dangerous to remain there for any time, and some of us had been permitted to stay on the deck for the fresh air; but now that the whole ship's cargo were confined together, it became absolutely pestilential. The closeness of the place, and the heat of the climate, added to the number in the ship, being so crowded that each had scarcely room to turn himself, almost suffocated us. This produced copious perspiration, so that the air soon became unfit for respiration, from a variety of loathsome smells, and brought on a sickness among the slaves, of which many died, thus falling victims to the improvident avarice, as I may call it, of their purchasers. This deplorable situation was again aggravated by the galling of the chains, now become insupportable; and the filth of necessary tubs, into which the children often fell, and were almost suffocated. The shrieks of the women, and the groans of the dying, rendered it a scene of horror almost inconceivable, . . . and I began to hope that death would soon put an end to my miseries. . . .

One day, when we had a smooth sea and moderate wind, two of my wearied countrymen, who were chained together, (I was near them at the time) preferring death to such a life of misery, somehow made through the nettings and jumped into the sea: immediately another quite dejected fellow, who on account of his illness was suffered to be out of irons also followed their example; and I believe many more would very soon have done the same, if they had not been prevented by the ship's crew, who were instantly alarmed. . . . two of the wretches were drowned; but they got the other, and afterward flogged him unmercifully, for thus attempting to prefer death to slavery. . .

At last we came in sight of the island of Barbadoes, at which the whites on board gave a great shout, and made many signs of joy to us. We did not know what to think of this, but as the vessel drew nearer we plainly saw the harbour,

and other ships of different kinds and sizes; and we soon anchored amongst them off Bridge Town. Many merchants and planters now came on board, though it was in the evening. They put us in separate parcels, and examined us attentively. They also made us jump, and pointed to the land, signifying we were to go there. We thought by this we should be beaten by these ugly men, as they appeared to us; and when soon after we were all put down under the deck again, there was much dread and trembling among us, and nothing but bitter cries to be heard all the night from these apprehensions, insomuch that at last the white people got some old slaves from the land to pacify us. They told us we were not to be eaten, but to work, and were soon to go on land, where we should see many of our country people. This report eased us much; and, sure enough, soon after we landed, there came to us Africans of all languages.

We were conducted immediately to the merchant's yard, where we were all pent up together like so many sheep in a fold, without regard to sex or age. . .

We were not many days in the merchants' custody before we were sold after the usual manner, which is this:–On a signal given, such as the beat of a drum, the buyers rush at once into the yard where the slaves are confined, and make choice of that parcel they

The European nations established trading posts along the West African coast, from Senegambia in the north to Angola in the south. Here on the Gold Coast (now Ghana) were the Dutch fort at Elmina, and the British outposts of Cape Coast Castle and Fort Royal at Manfrow. Further east, on the "slave coast" in the Bight of Benin near the Niger River, Whydah and Anamaboe also served as loading points for slaves for the British Empire. At these slave-trading posts, as Africans captured in war or stolen by slave traders were interned for market, families were further separated and ethnic groups were mixed. In this view, canoes ferry slaves out to slave ships anchored offshore. It might take months to assemble a full cargo of these unwilling immigrants, about 4 percent of whom would end their voyage of despair in North America. Engraving from Jean Barbot, **A Description of the Coasts of North and South-Guinea** *(London, 1746). (G.W. Blunt White Library, Mystic Seaport)*

like best. The noise and clamor with which this is attended, and the eagerness visible in the countenances of the buyers, serve not a little to increase the apprehensions of the terrified Africans, who may well be supposed to consider them the ministers of that destruction to which they think themselves devoted. In this manner, without scruple, are relations and friends separated, most of them never to see each other again. . . .

This ambrotype, ca. 1865, depicts the fort at Elmina on the Gold Coast. Established by the Portuguese in 1482 and captured by the Dutch in 1637, Elmina was an important entrepôt for the trade in African gold and slaves for more than three centuries. Although most of the surrounding buildings in this photograph date to the nineteenth century, the fort, the open roadstead with ships anchored offshore, and the beach with many African canoes reflect the period when tens of thousands of slaves began their "middle passage" to the New World here. (M.S.M. 80.22.4)

I stayed in this island for a few days; I believe it could not be above a fortnight; when I and some few more slaves, who from very much fretting were not saleable among the rest, were shipped off in a sloop for North America.

Olaudah Equiano, *The Interesting Narrative of the Life of Olaudah Equiano, or Gustavus Vassa, the African* (1789; reprint, Leeds, 1814)

The merchant's view:
Henry Laurens of Charleston,

South Carolina, to Robert and John Thompson and Co., Owners of the *Africa, Lancaster,* 5th July 1755

Gentn, . . .The Sale of Slaves having continued with us much the same as we advised you last, that is: have hitherto sold mighty well, all the Vessells arriv'd with us this Year are two sloops from Gambia who between them brought about 110 Slaves which avarag'd something above £30 Sterling, a Snow from the Bight with 170 which has lain Quarentine for 5 or 6 Weeks having the small Pox to be sold next Week, a ship from Angola to our selves brought 243 very pretty Slaves on the general, these we sold on the 24th Ulto, a few of the finest Men at £290 many at £280, & very few under £270. This Cargo tho the Women were but midling avarages £33.17/ Sterling. Had we had double the Number on that day we had more than Purchasers enough for them and not one sold for longer Credit than the month of January. 'tis owing to our success last Year in Indigo and a very good prospect we have the present that People buy with this Spirit. . . .

Quoted in Philip M. Hamer, ed. *The Papers of Henry Laurens*, 12 vols. (Columbia: University of South Carolina Press for South Carolina Historical Society, 1968), 1:288-89.

A Description of the Slave Trade of Newport, Rhode Island, 1764

Formerly the negroes upon the coast were supplied with large quantities of French brandies; but in the year 1723, some merchants in this colony first introduced the use of rum there, which, from small beginnings, soon increased to the consumption of several thousand hogsheads yearly; by which the French are deprived of the sale of an equal quantity of brandy; and as the demand for rum is annually increasing upon the coast, there is the greatest reason to think that in a few years, if this trade be not discouraged, the sale of French brandies there will be entirely destroyed. This little colony, only, for more than thirty years past, have annually sent about eighteen sail of vessels to the coast, which have carried about eighteen hundred hogsheads of rum, together with a small quantity of provisions and some other articles, which have been sold for slaves, gold dust, elephants teeth, camwood, etc. The slaves have been sold in the English islands in Carolina and Virginia, for bills of exchange, and the other articles have been sent to Europe; by this trade alone remittances have been made from this colony to Great Britain, to the value of about £40,000 yearly. . . .

Quoted in Elizabeth Donnan, ed., *Documents Illustrative of the History of the Slave Trade to America*, 4 vols. (Washington, D.C.: Carnegie Institution, 1932), 3:203-204.

Americas. Brazil's mines and plantations consumed almost 40 percent of this number and New Spain somewhat more than 15 percent. The West Indian possessions of Great Britain and other European nations accounted for another 40 percent, the remaining 5 percent (or 500,000 people) coming directly to the British colonies on the mainland. Occasionally, planters there also bought "seasoned" slaves from the West Indies.

The most dehumanizing aspect of the slave trade was how willingly its participants and their associates considered their fellow beings as objects of commerce. The importation of Blacks from Africa became part of a complex network of transatlantic trading patterns involving numerous exchanges of commodities. Nothing illustrates this reality better than the voyage of the brigantine *Sanderson*, belonging to the Rhode Island merchant William Johnston. Leaving Newport in March 1752, Captain David Lindsay took a cargo of lumber, barrel staves, and horses to the Caribbean, returning home with molasses and cocoa. The molasses was distilled into rum, which Lindsay then took to Anamaboe, West Africa, in February 1753. At the time of his arrival a single hogshead of rum that cost about £11 in Newport could buy one slave in Africa worth £30 back in America. Lindsay was able to take on board a cargo of fifty-seven slaves altogether, losing only one in the ten-week "middle passage" across the Atlantic to Barbados. There he sold most of his Blacks, taking his proceeds in a cargo of rum, sugar, and bills of exchange, which he brought back to Newport. Allowing for all expenses, the voyage probably netted Johnston a profit of more than £500.

The inhuman dimensions of the trade were graphically demonstrated in the voyage of the Rhode Island brig *Sally*, under command of Captain Esek Hopkins, in 1764-65. It took Hopkins nine months to purchase 196 Africans with rum, textiles, and other goods, obtaining them a few at a time from a local slave-trading chief. Stolen from their communities and confined in the hot, stinking hold, the Africans had begun to die from disease and suicide even before Hopkins left the Guinea coast. When his crew fell ill at sea, Hopkins let a few Africans on deck to help sail the vessel, and they freed their companions and tried to revolt. Like most slave uprisings, this one failed, and many were killed as the crew fired into the hold. By the time the *Sally* reached the West Indies, where the market was reported to be bet-

ter for slaves than in Charleston, eighty-eight Africans had been lost, and the voyage was a financial disaster.

Despite the human cost, one British mercantilist claimed that the slave trade was the "spring and parent whence the others flow," and the twentieth-century historian Eric Williams has argued that profits from this trade made possible British entry into the industrial age. While most other historians have rejected such close linkage, many recognize Williams's more general proposition that the plantation trade did contribute to "that accumulation of capital in England which financed the Industrial Revolution."

It is easy to assign primary responsibility for the American slave trade to the southern planters who demanded cheap labor, and to the northern and southern merchants who trafficked in human misery, but the institution was integral to the entire Atlantic economic system. Chieftains along the African coast kidnaped members of rival tribes and sold them for western goods like rum, gunpowder, and bar iron; Yankee traders carried the produce of New England—fish, boards, livestock—to plantation owners and marketed the sugar and molasses produced by slave labor; and northern farmers and fishermen derived income from the sale of produce and fish to the plantation islands and eagerly consumed the sweet and intoxicating products of slave labor. Ultimately, the whole system depended on racial attitudes deeply intertwined in seventeenth- and eighteenth-century European conceptions of humankind, and on individuals who were unable or unwilling to see the injustices in that outlook, and who could point to Biblical precedents for the endurance of slavery.

The Importance of Maritime Enterprise

No historian seriously doubts what an important contribution maritime commerce made to the development of the American colonies. Its economic consequences extended through much of the continent, illustrating the principle that the sea connects all places. In New England, maritime commerce provided an extended market for fish and timber, the former industry employing 4,000 fishermen and an equal number of shoreside processors. It also employed thousands of mariners in more than a score of seaports and stimulated the shipbuilding industry, which constructed nearly 500 vessels annually by the 1770s. Farmers living within a day or two of the coast could export their meager surplus produce and find wintertime employment making shingles, clapboards, hoops, and staves for shipment to the West Indies. Equally important, overseas trade created the opportunity for shipowners, merchants, and shipbuilders to begin the process of accumulating capital needed for expansion and innovation.

Further south the impact on American agriculture had greater consequences. Maritime commerce encouraged farmers of the Middle Colonies to grow crops like corn and wheat for market and prompted expansion into the fertile interior river valleys. It also stimulated the creation of the big flour mills around Philadelphia that became America's first factories and in the process gave hundreds of artisans the opportunity to become manufacturers. Vessels returning to the Middle Colonies brought thousands of immigrants, making this area the fastest growing in British America. The economies of the Chesapeake and Carolina colonies depended more heavily on overseas commerce than those of any other region of mainland America. Concentration on the culture of tobacco, rice, and indigo, in turn, led to the development of a planter class and created a perceived need for cheap slave labor. Intensive agriculture exhausted the soil of the tidewater regions by the mid-eighteenth century and encouraged migration into the interior in search of virgin lands.

"Overseas commerce did not merely make colonial life comfortable; it made it possible," conclude John McCusker and Russell Menard in their definitive book, *The Economy of British America, 1607-1789*. Without foreign trade, the colonists could not have earned the credits required to import necessaries. Equally important, it was the promise of prosperity that attracted most settlers to America. Without an expectation of improving their lives, many immigrants would not have come. In addition to the exportation of commodities like tobacco, rice, fish, breadstuffs, and so forth (which economists call "visibles" because they are

reported in governmental statistics), the colonial economy also relied on "invisibles." The term includes transactions that were not recorded, such as charges for freight, commissions, and insurance earned in the carrying trade, which some historians consider second in importance only to tobacco as a source of credit for the colonists. Colonial-built ships sold abroad constituted another such "invisible," worth nearly £150,000 on the eve of the Revolution. Yet another source of colonial income came from British military expenditures in America–estimated at some £400,000 per year by the 1770s. By then, McCusker and Menard conclude, the visible and invisible aspects of maritime trade together accounted for nearly 20 percent of the colonists' per capita income. Merchants were, for the most part, the only colonial American entrepreneurs able to accumulate any appreciable amount of liquid capital. Farmers had most of their wealth tied up in land, and southern planters had heavy investments in slaves as well, both of which were relatively inelastic commitments.

Beyond these economic factors, maritime commerce directly affected the everyday life of many Americans. For those who lived along the eastern seaboard the development of coastal trade routes greatly increased their mobility. Travel by land was nowhere easy in the eighteenth century, but it was particularly difficult along the Atlantic seaboard because of the scores of rivers, some as wide as the Hudson, which had to be crossed en route. Coastal vessels provided a service that was at once more comfortable, safer, and cheaper than travel by land. These vessels brought publications from other colonies and distributed European news from whichever American port had received it first from overseas. In the end one cannot measure the importance to ordinary seaboard inhabitants of this connection to American coastal communities beyond their immediate neighbors, and we can only surmise that it strengthened American nationalism when the crisis with the mother country approached. At the same time deep-water commerce linked all of the colonies to the greater Atlantic world.

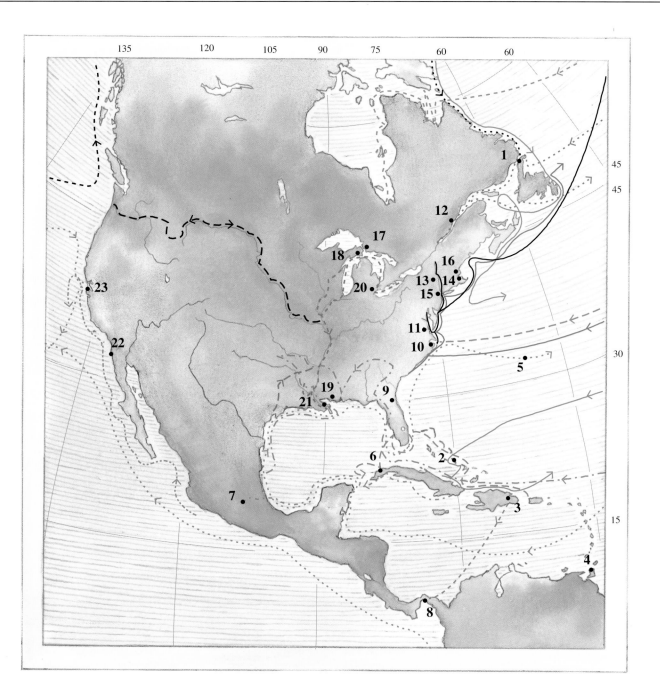

Figure 2 **The Maritime Exploration and Settlement of North America**

Voyages of Exploration

Misc.
- - - - - Norse: Leif Eriksson,
ca AD 1000
————— Dutch: Hudson, 1609
– – – – Russians: Bering and
Chirikof, 1741
— — — Americans: Lewis & Clark,
1804-6

Spanish
————— Columbus, 1492
· · · · · Vespucci, 1497-8
–·–·– Balboa, 1513
–··–··– De Leon, 1513
– – – – Cortez, 1518-21
— — — De Soto, 1539-43
——— Cabrillo, 1542-3

English
————— John Cabot, 1498
· · · · · Drake, 1577-80
– – – – Raleigh, 1585
– – – – Hudson, 1610

French
————— Verrazano, 1524
· · · · · Cartier, 1535
– – – – Marquette and Jolliet, 1673
— — — La Salle, 1685

Settlement Dates
1. L'anse aux Meadows,
ca AD 1000
2. San Salvador, 1492
3. Santo Domingo, 1496
4. Trinidad, 1498
5. Bermuda, 1515

6. Havana, 1515
7. Mexico City, 1519
8. Panama, 1519
9. St. Augustine, 1565
10. Roanoke, 1587
11. Jamestown, 1607
12. Quebec, 1608
13. Albany (Ft. Orange), 1614
14. Plimoth (Plymouth), 1620
15. New York City
(New Amsterdam), 1625
16. Boston, 1630
17. Sault Ste. Marie, 1668
18. St. Ignace, 1671
19. Biloxi, 1699
20. Detroit, 1701
21. New Orleans, 1718
22. San Diego, 1769
23. San Francisco, 1776

(Dennis O'Brien map)

CHAPTER 3

To American Independence

AT THE conclusion of the Seven Years' War in 1763, Great Britain stood unchallenged as the most powerful nation in the world. Neither Spain nor France could singly or even together match its strength. While the most evident manifestation of British power was the Royal Navy, its source was less obvious: the intricate web of economic relationships that comprised the British empire. At home a diversified agricultural system produced increasing quantities of almost all basic commodities throughout the eighteenth century, stimulated by growing markets in the cities of the realm. Burgeoning industries, encouraged by wartime government expenditure, provided work for an expanding population which reached 7.5 million by 1763, three times that of the American colonies. At the center of this economy stood the Bank of England, furnishing a reliable currency, moderating inflation, and, albeit crudely, maintaining an atmosphere that encouraged the investment of foreign and domestic capital in the country's infant industrial sector. Over all reigned the popular House of Hanover with its succession of Georges, although real political power had long since shifted to the House of Commons, where an unchallenged Whig majority comprising landed gentry and their allies ruled supreme. Administrative affairs were the special business of a growing bureaucracy of specialists, most of whom remained in their posts no matter which political faction controlled the Ministry.

Overseas, British power and influence reached from the territorial claims of the East India Company on the Indian subcontinent around the ports of Bombay, Madras, and Calcutta, and into the interior regions of Bengal, to its numerous colonies on and around the North American continent. In between, Britain controlled the mid-

Detail of "Sea Captains Carousing in Surinam," by John Greenwood. (Courtesy The Saint Louis Art Museum. Purchase.)

Atlantic island of Bermuda, the strategic straits of Gibraltar, the Mediterranean island of Minorca, and the former French West African colony of Senegal. At the end of the Seven Years' War no one doubted that the most valuable jewels in the imperial crown were Great Britain's possessions in the New World, although, as we have seen, the Guadeloupe v. Canada debate revealed a disagreement over which of them was of greater worth. In the Caribbean lay four principal groups of British islands. Clockwise from the Bahamas to the north one moved southeast (and against the prevailing winds) first to the Leeward group of Nevis, Antigua, and St. Kitts, then on in the same direction to the easternmost Windward island of Barbados. In between were the recently acquired islands of the Grenadines as well as the former "neutral islands" of Dominica, St. Vincent, and Tobago. At the westernmost corner lay the most valuable of all British possessions in the region, the island of Jamaica. All of these islands produced sugar and its by-products, molasses and rum, in great quantities, along with lesser amounts of cotton, cocoa, and dyestuffs. To a much lesser extent these possessions also comprised a market for goods of the mother country, and of course the carrying of these cargoes employed many tons of British-flag shipping. The sugar in turn found a willing market not only at home but as a reexport to the European Continent. The cost of administering these dependencies and protecting them against the French and Spanish, however, was a constant concern to the officials in Whitehall, for none of these islands had the slightest ability to govern or defend itself.

In 1763 the Treaty of Paris brought vast new territories, albeit sparsely populated, to the British empire's possessions on the North American mainland. South of Georgia, East and West Florida were acquired from Spain and France respectively. Near the end of the serpentine coastline that stretched northeast for some 1,800 miles, France also surrendered its remaining Acadian possessions, the most important of which was Cape Breton Island, with its fortress at Louisbourg, now lying in ruins after its most recent capture by British forces. Along the St. Lawrence River valley the French province of Quebec, with about 80,000 French-speaking *habitants*, had also fallen to Great Britain, as did that part of Louisiana that lay east of the Mississippi. Except for New Orleans itself, only the fishing islands of St. Pierre and Miquelon off the Newfoundland coast now remained of France's once vast American empire.

As could be predicted by the arguments in the Canada v. Guadeloupe debate, the spoils of war added few assets to the British empire in America that promised immediate economic dividends. And although the removal of both France and Spain from the mainland east of the Mississippi reduced the ability of those two nations to attack the English colonies, such a marked shift in the balance of power just as surely provided ample incentive for Gallic revenge, as had happened time and again for nearly a century. The obsession of successive British ministries with the possibility that its continental colonies might fall under the sway of France became an important factor in the approaching crisis between America and the mother country.

Immigration

Because of the extensive maritime commerce connecting North America to the Old World, Europeans wishing to find new beginnings in the English colonies could do so with relative ease. Vessels heading to mainland North America for bulk produce like tobacco, sugar, or rice had plenty of space in the 'tween decks for paying passengers. An immigrant who could not afford the price of a passage could become a "redemptioner" by agreeing to let the shipowner sell his labor to a colonist willing to pay whatever balance remained. The usual term of service was four years, an expensive agreement even for those immigrants who owed the entire cost of transportation. Profit margin for merchants engaged in servant trade varied throughout the century. The most reliable figures suggest costs ranging from £4 to £10 per servant and selling prices that ranged from £6 to almost £30, with most sales between £10 and £15. Net profits on a single shipment of immigrants commonly exceeded £500. Emigration from England proper fell off in the middle decades of the century but increased markedly from the other parts of the British Isles, particularly Scotland and Ulster. Along with Germans from the Palatinate and elsewhere who sought religious freedom or economic opportunity,

THE SHIP St HELENA GEO ARTHUR (Comm^d)

The 240-ton ship St. Helena represents the large transatlantic freighters that carried bulky commodities, such as tobacco, from the colonies to England, returning with manufactured goods and often with immigrants. Built at Beaufort, South Carolina, in 1766, the St. Helena traded between the Carolinas and Bristol, England. Launched in a time of peace on the Atlantic, she carried no armament. English shipmaster and marine artist Nicholas Pocock depicted her under full sail for a downwind passage from America to England, displaying a modern eighteenth-century rig. Forward, she has two square spritsails below the bowsprit and three triangular jibs above. Both the fore- and mainmast have the relatively new, light-weather sail called the royal set above (in ascending order) the course, topsail, and topgallant. Three fore-and-aft staysails are set between each mast, and with the wind aft a square driver sail has been set from the gaff of the fore-and-aft mizzen. To increase the area of the square sails, light studdingsails are set on the windward side of the fore course and fore and main topsails and topgallants. Bands of reef points on most of the square sails allow them to be reduced in area as the wind increases. Painted by an experienced shipmaster, this view demonstrates the increasing sophistication of square-rigged ships in the eighteenth century. (Courtesy the Science Museum, London)

they flocked to the New World, almost exclusively to New York and Pennsylvania. In the fifty years between 1717 and 1776 at least 65,000 Germans arrived at Philadelphia, and probably as many Scots landed at New York in the same period.

Conditions on board immigrant ships were horrendous even in good weather, which was relatively rare because departures were often in January or February so that the servants would arrive just before spring planting, when the market for labor in America was at its height. The average passage from time of embarkation lasted eight to ten weeks in the mid-eighteenth century, during much of which time the passengers were confined to the narrow spaces of the 'tween decks, for it was often too dangerous for them to remain topside. Wooden benches served as bunks, and each passenger was allotted a space no more than five feet long and two feet wide. With headroom rarely more than five feet, and the hatch open only during fair weather, the air below decks quickly became intolerable. But toleration was the servants' only option in bad

weather, when they were confined below, sick and terrified, in their rolling and pitching prison. On board the eighty-ton brig *Jamaica Packet*, sailing from Scotland to North Carolina via the West Indies in 1774-75, a cabin passenger described in her journal the food available for the company of Highlander emigrants on board.

It is hardly possible to believe that human nature could be so depraved, as to treat fellow creatures in such a manner for a little sordid gain. They have only for a grown person per week, one pound neck beef, or spoilt port, two pounds oatmeal, with a small quantity of bisket, not only mouldy, but absolutely crumbled down with damp, wet and rottenness. The half is only allowed a child, so that if they had not potatoes, it is impos they could live out the Voyage. They have no drink, but a very small proportion of brakish bad water. As our owner to save our expence, took the water for his ship from a pit well

in his own back yard, tho' fine springs were at a very little distance, even this scanty allowance is grudged them. . . .

As a result of this great movement of people across the Atlantic, and of natural increase in the New World, the thirteen British colonies that became the United States comprised a diverse population on the eve of the American Revolution. Of an estimated total of 2,500,000 inhabitants, only half were actually of English stock. The inclusion of some 350,000 Scots, Ulster-Irish, Welsh, and Irish colonists– largely in the Middle Atlantic colonies–brought the English-speaking share closer to two-thirds. Blacks were the next largest ethnic group, at least as many as 500,000, with the highest concentration from Maryland south, followed by nearly 200,000 German-speaking Europeans, mostly in Pennsylvania. As the French traveler, Hector St. Jean de Crèvecoeur, asked rhetorically:

What then is the American, this new man? . . . He is an American who leaving behind him all his ancient prejudices and manners, receives new ones from the new mode of life he has embraced, the new government he obeys, and the new rank he holds. He becomes an American by being received in the broad lap of our great *Alma Mater*. Here individuals of all nations are melted into a new race of men, whose labours and posterity will one day cause great changes in the world. . . This is an American.

American Commerce on the Eve of Revolution

It was a commonplace in the eighteenth century to consider the continental American colonies in four rather distinct groups. First came the three southernmost colonies, Georgia on the south and the two Carolinas. Politically and socially less mature than the plantation colonies further north, this region had nevertheless a similar economy, based on African slave

English artist Thomas Leitch painted this view of the Charleston waterfront from Shute's Folly island at the mouth of the Cooper River in 1774. The steeple of St. Michael's English (Episcopal) Church rises at center. To its right is the imposing facade of the new Exchange building at the public landing. Between 1750 and 1770 Charleston's population grew from 6,000 to 12,000, about 50 percent of whom were black. By the 1770s the port received about 450 vessels a year, 40 percent in trade with the British Isles, 20 percent in the Caribbean trade, and 10 percent each in trade to the northern colonies and to southern Europe. (Courtesy the Museum of Early Southern Decorative Arts)

The Women of Nantucket

As the sea excursions are often very long, their wives in their absence are necessarily obliged to transact business, to settle accounts, and in short, to rule and provide for their families. These circumstances being often repeated give women the abilities as well as a taste for that kind of superintendency to which, by their prudence and good management they seem to be in general very equal. This employment ripens their judgment, and justly entitles them to a rank superior to that of other wives; and this is the principal reason why those of Nantucket. . . are so fond of society, so affable, and so conversant with the affairs of the world. The men at their return, weary with the fatigues of the sea, full of confidence and love, cheerfully give their consent to every transaction that has happened during their absence, and all is joy and peace. "Wife, thee hast done well," is the general approbation they receive for their application and industry. What would the men do without the agency of these faithful mates...?

The richest person now in the island owes all his present prosperity and success to the ingenuity of his wife this is a known fact which is well recorded; for while he was performing his first cruises, she traded with pins and needles, and kept a school. Afterward she purchased more considerable articles, which she sold with so much judgment, that she laid the foundation of a system of business, that she has ever since prosecuted with equal dexterity and success. She wrote to London, formed connections, and in short became the only ostensible instrument of that house, both at home and abroad. Who is he in this country, and who is a citizen of Nantucket or Boston, who does not know *Aunt Kesiah*? I must tell you that she is the wife of Mr C[offi]n, a very respectable man, who, well pleased with all her schemes, trusts to her judgment, and relies on her sagacity with so entire a confidence as to be altogether passive to the concerns of his family. They have the best country seat on the island, at Quayes, where they live with hospitality and in perfect union. He seems to be altogether the contemplative man.

To this dexterity in managing the husband's business whilst he is absent, the Nantucket wives unite a great deal of industry. They spin, or cause to be spun in their houses abundance of wool and flax; and would be for ever disgraced and looked upon as idlers if all the family were not clad in good, neat, and sufficient homespun cloth. *First Days* [Sundays] are the only seasons when it is lawful for both sexes to exhibit some garments of english manufacture; even these are of the most moderate price, and of the gravest colors; there is no kind of difference in their dress, and they are all clad alike and resemble in that respect the members of one family. . . .

Michel Guillaume St. Jean de Crèvecoeur, *Letters from an American Farmer; Describing Certain Provincial Situations, Manners, and Customs, Not Generally Known* (London, 1782)

Eliza Mitchell Myrick (1790-1864), shown in the painting above, was young enough to be Kesiah Coffin's granddaughter, but her life was also shaped by Nantucket's dependence on the sea. The daughter of a merchant in the China trade, and the wife of whaling master George Myrick, Jr., she faced uncommon responsibilities during her husband's extended absences. In this portrait, ca. 1815, her stylish trappings of wealth do not soften her expression of determination. (Courtesy the Nantucket Historical Association)

labor and dedicated to the production of crops valuable to the mother country. In the case of the Carolinas, rice, indigo, and naval stores (pitch, rosin, and turpentine) comprised the majority of exports. Since the founding of Georgia in 1732, the cultivation of sea island cotton along the coast offered additional profits. The region had but two seaports of any consequence: Savannah, Georgia, and "Charles Town" (Charleston), South Carolina. The latter harbored not only the commerce of its own colony, but also much of the trade generated by both Georgia and North Carolina. In addition, Charleston controlled the slave trade of the southern colonies. In the period 1769-72 this region exported annually nearly £400,000 in produce to Great Britain and consumed imports worth nearly the same.

Among the continental colonies, Virginia and Maryland provided the mother country with the largest share of exports, in excess of £800,000 a year, and bought nearly as much in return. Here tobacco ruled supreme, constituting three-fourths of the region's agricultural production. More than one-third of all Americans, black and white, lived in these two colonies, most of them within a few miles of the Chesapeake and its many tributaries. No seaport was necessary here, for the planter could load his tobacco at his own wharf, and British factors rather than American merchants still controlled the trade. Although Annapolis carried on a lively coastal commerce with other colonies and Norfolk grew slowly into a port of some significance by the eve of the American Revolution, the greatness of maritime Baltimore near the head of Chesapeake Bay was still in the future.

Two of the four so-called middle colonies, Pennsylvania and New York, were among the commercially most important of all continental American provinces. (The other two, Delaware and New Jersey, in contrast, were among the least significant). In Pennsylvania settlers from all parts of the British Isles and the Continent grew wheat and other grains, raised livestock, and hunted deer and other animals for their skins. The mother country had little interest in these commodities, however, and like the other northern colonies, Pennsylvania had to look elsewhere for markets. Its most valuable product was biscuit flour, ground in the large mills along the banks of the Schuylkill and other tributaries of the Delaware River on the outskirts of Philadelphia, America's largest city and seaport. Pennsylvania ranked fourth in population among the continental colonies, a fact reflected in its annual importation of British goods worth some £350,000. New York exported even less than Pennsylvania did to the mother country, but despite a smaller population it managed to import even more in return, some of which was undoubtedly distributed through coastal trade to New Jersey and Connecticut towns. The province was not yet able to capitalize on its superb geographical advantages, however, and the harbor was still several decades away from becoming America's preeminent seaport.

To the north and east lay the four New England colonies, whose inhabitants have been referred to by one historian as "the Dutch of England's empire." The south-facing settlements of Connecticut and Rhode Island were inexorably drawn toward New York through the protected waterway of Long Island and Block Island Sounds. Over Massachusetts and New Hampshire the port of Boston held sway. Massachusetts ranked second to Virginia in population at the end of the Seven Years' War, but a stagnant economy and little free land slowed the growth rate to a trickle. Its greatest wealth came from the sea, directly as the produce of nearby fishing banks, indirectly through shipbuilding, small coastal trading ventures, and in transatlantic freighting runs. The cornerstone of New England's maritime commerce remained its connection with the West Indies. Together these four colonies continued to dominate the maritime activities of the American continent. Yet because the region still produced little of direct value to Great Britain, New England had a bad reputation in the mother country. In the decade following the Peace of Paris, that reputation would grow far worse.

American trade in the twelve-year period between the end of the Seven Years' War and the beginning of the American Revolution expanded rapidly. The extensive records that have survived, especially for the years 1768-72, show a complex series of relationships tying the American colonies to each other and to the mother country. The most valuable exports from the North American continental colonies were, in order, tobacco, bread and

flour, fish, and rice. It is interesting that each of these exports originated from a different region. Together they accounted for almost two-thirds of all exports by value, followed by wheat and other grains, timber products, livestock products, whale oil, and indigo of secondary importance. More than half of these exports went to the mother country, with southern Europe and the West Indies accounting for almost all of the balance. Although records of the goods imported into the continental colonies are not so detailed, we know that high on the list were textiles of all sorts, hardware, wrought iron, brass and copper, glassware and earthenware, crockery, other metals, and other manufactured products such as paint, glass, and paper.

The most tangible evidence of commercial economic activity lay in the growth of the colonial seaports. In the fifteen years between 1760 and

John Greenwood's charmingly irreverent painting of shipmasters carousing in Surinam, ca. 1758, has long been thought to represent Newport, Rhode Island, captains in the Dutch sugar-producing region around Demerara. Gambling, smoking, and drinking copious quantities of rum punch, these captains unwind far from home. The captain at the far side of the gaming table, in a blue coat with red facings, is generally believed to represent Esek Hopkins, merchant shipmaster, privateer, slave trader, and future captain in the Continental Navy. ("Sea Captains Carousing in Surinam," by John Greenwood. Courtesy The Saint Louis Art Museum. Purchase.)

cleared and entered at New York. As busy as they were, these five ports still accounted for less than half the total maritime activity of the thirteen continental colonies. Smaller ports from Portsmouth, New Hampshire, to Savannah, Georgia, also benefited from commercial expansion. In fact, on the eve of the Revolution nineteen of colonial America's twenty largest communities were seaports. (The only inland "interloper" was Lancaster, Pennsylvania.)

Unfortunately, we cannot know for certain how much of this overall maritime activity was carried out by American-owned vessels. Figures do show that vessels owned in Great Britain accounted for slightly more than half the tonnage clearing colonial ports for the mother country. Colonial shipping comprised about 25 percent, and vessels belonging to British merchants temporarily resident in the colonies about 20 percent. As might be expected, British shipping was most heavily involved in the carrying trade with the Chesapeake and lower south, while American-owned vessels dominated the commerce of New England, New York, and Pennsylvania with the mother country. But trade with Great Britain accounted for only 28 percent of the continental colonies' total commerce. The West Indies and coastal trades were both slightly larger (about 30 percent each), and on these routes American-owned vessels had a virtual monopoly.

1775, population in the five leading ports of Boston, Newport, New York, Philadelphia, and Charleston increased by an aggregate 42 percent, with Philadelphia leading the five with a 68-percent expansion. In the year 1772, the last year before the Revolution for which reliable figures have survived, there were more than 3,000 vessel-entries at America's five busiest ports, and not surprisingly about the same number of clearances. About 50 percent of the origins and destinations were from and to other continental American ports (including Canada), with the West Indies representing 30 percent of the voyages, and Great Britain and Ireland about 10 percent. The balance involved passages to or from southern Europe, the Wine Islands, and Africa. Boston and Philadelphia were virtually tied as the continent's two busiest ports, the former seeing a larger number of vessels, but the latter slightly greater tonnage. Charleston held third place in tonnage, although more vessels

In the same years, commerce with its American colonies had grown steadily in importance for the mother country. On the eve of the Revolution this trade employed annually nearly 500 British vessels and 18,000 seamen. Except for its own coasting trade, no other aspect of British maritime commerce utilized so many resources. The value of this trade has been variously estimated by both contemporary observers and later historians. In his address "On Conciliation with America," delivered to Parliament in March 1775, Edmund Burke stated that British exports to North America and the West Indies had increased more than tenfold from £569,930 in 1704 to £5,155,734 in 1772. But Burke's figures included all of Britain's American possessions, not just the continent. An estimate of between £2.5 and £3.0 million annually to the American mainland colonies would seem likely for the years just before the outbreak of war. The colonies

The Colonial Sailor and his World

For reasons not easily understood by sailors, seafaring has often been viewed by landsmen as a romantic way of life. The popular image of "Jolly Jack Tar" as a carefree, childlike person, suggested that he was free to have fun in ways that family men were not supposed to consider. While working conditions for the modern merchant mariner are indeed comfortable, and his wages exceed those for many comparable jobs on land, these developments are relatively recent. During the age of sail, and through most of the age of steam as well, the job of sailoring had little to commend it. For one thing, work took the sailor away from the social, sexual, and psychological support that home, no matter how humble, provided the landsman. Second, the sailor was part of a hierarchical work force, bound by law to obey the will of his captain, no matter how oppressive. Disobedience or refusal to work brought harsh punishment, including close confinement or a severe beating. Except for slaves, no landsman faced such conditions. The sailor could not choose the men with whom he worked and lived, where he was going, or when (and if) he would return. Next to the fisherman, and of course the slave, Jack Tar earned the lowest wages of any American worker. Evidence in the estates of Boston's

mariners in the period 1685-1715 suggests they earned between £12 and £15 sterling a year. By mid-century peacetime wages had doubled, but so too had the cost of living.

In the seventeenth and eighteenth centuries most colonial mariners worked on small vessels: forty- to sixty-footers if engaged in the coastal or West Indies trade, sixty- to ninety-footers if undertaking transatlantic voyages. The smaller sloops and schooners required a crew of only three or four men in addition to the captain and mate, with the least experienced sailor employed as cook, while the larger, square-rigged vessels called for a second mate, a cook, and eight to twelve mariners. For much of the typical voyage the workday was not much longer than many shoreside jobs, nominally twelve hours. However, in order to operate the vessel round the clock, a crew was normally divided into two "watches," which worked alternating four-hour watch periods (with two two-hour "dog watches" from four to eight P.M. to alternate the cycle each day). Frequently the daylight watches below were usurped by ship's work, and in stormy weather, when the watch below was turned out to help shorten sail or man the pumps if necessary, there were barely enough men to do the job.

Going to sea was generally the most dangerous work a man could do in the age of sail. Shipwreck, accidental injury, falling overboard, or disease–each took its toll of victims. Wartime added the prospect of battle wounds, sinking, or capture and incarceration in a fetid prison hulk. During the latter half of the eighteenth century, in the seafaring town of Beverly, half of the mariners died in their twenties or thirties, while less than 10 percent of the farmers died that early. Crew lists verify that sailoring was a young person's work, too strenuous for most men by the time they reached the age of forty (if they survived that long), unless they had come up "through the hawsehole" to the rank of shipmaster. A sailor sometimes spent weeks ashore between voyages, unpaid of course, while living in cheap boardinghouses along the waterfront, unless fortunate enough to be in his own home port while looking for another berth. If his ship were to be delayed for any length of time in a foreign port, some tight-fisted owners instructed their captains to discharge the "people," as the crew was called. Thereafter the men had to fend for themselves, and when ready to sail the captain scurried around "sailortown" to find his old crew or other sailors to take their places. Occasionally the owner decided to sell the ves-

sel in a foreign port; then both officers and sailors had to arrange their own means of getting home by finding another berth.

Given these circumstances we can only wonder why anyone would go to sea as a common seaman. Surely there is some truth in Samuel Eliot Morison's oft-quoted dictum that many Yankee sailors first went to sea as "adventure-seeking boys." Faced with the prospect of struggling with New England's indifferent soil for the rest of his life, a farmer's son might well be tempted to run off to sea, at least for a time. One measure of the perceived strength of

Brook Watson was a fourteen-year-old sailor aboard a Boston vessel when he lost his leg to a shark in the harbor at Havana, Cuba, in 1749. Almost thirty years later Watson, the future lord mayor of London, commissioned expatriate American artist John Singleton Copley to commemorate the incident. Although Watson's shipmates are unknown, Copley depicted a representative mix in typical sailor garb. As befits a colonial vessel, they are mostly young men, and one of the ten is black. Beyond its representation of a historical event, Copley's 1778 painting can be interpreted in many ways, but certainly one thing it depicts is the cohesion of a seafaring crew in the face of the great hazards of the sea, personified by the exaggerated head of the shark. Watson and the Shark *is considered to be the first formal marine painting by an American artist. (Gift of Mrs. George von Lengerke Meyer, Courtesy the Museum of Fine Arts, Boston)*

The sailor was an essential figure in colonial American commerce, as suggested by this eighteenth-century tobacco advertising card showing a planter (right), slave, and sailor (left). Like the sugar economy that produced the rum for this sailor's cup of punch, the tobacco economy depended upon a few hundred planters who provided the capital, thousands of plantation slaves who provided the labor, and perhaps 4,000 sailors who conveyed the product to market. With his baggy trousers and neckerchief, the sailor is shown at leisure, holding his pipe of tobacco and cup of punch, reinforcing the popular image of the sailor as a distinctive, carefree figure outside the bounds of conventional society. (Courtesy Heal Collection, Department of Prints & Drawings, The British Library, London)

this temptation is the myriad of warnings against it from "wiser heads." Thus Cotton Mather expressed the hope in 1700 that "the *Enchantments* of the sea may not have too strong and quick a force upon some to make them rashly leave *Good Callings*." Josiah Franklin dissuaded his famous son from running away to sea, and Ben, in turn, had to bring his own son back from a privateer about to leave Philadelphia during King George's War.

There were negative reasons for shipping out as well. Young apprentices, unhappy with the terms of their indentures, might also find escape in the fo'c'sle of an outward-bound vessel. Still others might be fleeing tyrannical fathers, determined creditors, persistent court officers, or demanding wives or sweethearts. And certainly men went to sea because they could find no alternative means of employment. Some were Indians, free blacks, slaves hired out by their masters, or "old country" British sailors without opportunities in American ports.

The calculations of historian Ira Dye that, on average, American seamen of the late eighteenth century spent only seven years at sea before returning to land ("swallowing the anchor," they would have said), tells us that for most sailors going to sea constituted only a small part of their life's work.

Picking up from where the historian Jesse Lemisch left off in the 1960s with his seminal essay "Jack Tar in the Streets," several scholars of the 1980s and 1990s have turned their attention to the condition of America's seamen. Some have argued that sailors in the colonial period formed a distinct underclass, even a proletariat, although that description seems more fitting for British than for

American seamen. There the former sailor might find work as a longshoreman loading and unloading vessels, or in a ropewalk or sail loft or shipyard, where his previous experience would be useful. Along with the port's active mariners, these former seamen might well have constituted an urban working class in the larger seaports like Boston, New York, or Philadelphia, but there is little evidence to show that they thought of themselves in those terms. In the smaller ports mariners were more likely to have family ties, making their position in the community somewhat more secure. Those mariners who were qualified to vote in town affairs—perhaps as many as one out of three—made no effort to form a majority with the far more numerous artisans against the political leadership of the community's merchants, shipmasters, lawyers. The habit of deference died slowly along the Atlantic seaboard of North America.

That being said, the latter half of the eighteenth century provides numerous examples of mariners and artisans as well expressing their views on public affairs more directly. In addition to violent demonstrations against impressment gangs, the working people of American seaports took to the streets to protest changes in British colonial policy after the Seven Years' War that they felt affected their welfare. The riot against the Stamp Act that swept through New York City at the end of October 1765 involved several hundred seamen. General Thomas Gage, who witnessed the event, later reported that "the Sailors, who are the only People who may be properly Stiled Mob, are intirely at the Command of the Merchants who employ them." But New York's mariners had their own concern: that the requirement of stamped clearances would curtail the port's commerce, and their jobs. When a box of stamps arrived at Philadelphia for use by customs officials, "a Rabble of Boys, Sailors, and Negroes &c." required the box's return to the vessel on which it came. Similar incidents disrupted enforcement of the Stamp Act from New England to the Carolinas. The threat of continued violence in American ports helped convince members of Parliament to rescind the Stamp Act the following year.

But the violence continued nevertheless. On the Delaware, sailors ganged up on customs officials attempting to curtail the age-old custom sailors had of bringing in a few undeclared goods for their own profit. In January 1770 sailors attacked British soldiers who held off-duty jobs in New York's Golden Hill section, depriving the mariners of that work. More famous was the Boston Massacre of March 1770, involving a gang described by John Adams as "a motley rabble saucy boys, negroes and molattoes, Irish teagues and out landish jack tarrs." They had joined in a running fight between workers and British soldiers who had taken part-time work at a ropewalk. When the cornered soldiers opened fire, five men were killed, including the mulatto seaman Crispus Attucks. By far the most consequential episode of anti-British action in a colonial seaport was the Boston Tea Party of December 1773. While the Tea Act directly affected commerce–the duty on tea, the disruption of established trade practices, and the threat to smugglers– the showdown at Griffin's Wharf drew protestors from far beyond the waterfront community of sailors and other maritime workers. Mariners had many reasons for opposing authoritarian officialdom, and they contributed mightily to the protest movement that led to the final breach between Great Britain and America, but they were not alone in this struggle, nor even at its forefront in many colonies, as some historians have insisted. The road to independence had many travelers, sailors among the most determined, if not always in the van.

The 45-ton Massachusetts schooner Baltick, *built at Newbury in 1763, is typical of thousands of American colonial vessels in the coastal and Caribbean trades. Like the* Baltick, *many of these vessels carried square sails for downwind sailing. The* Baltick's *very deep square fore course has a removable foot called a bonnet. Like the multiple bands of reef points visible on her sails, this feature allowed the sail area to be reduced. "This shows the Schooner Baltick Coming out of St. Eustatia ye 16th of Nov. 1765" reads the caption of this watercolor by an unidentified artist. (Courtesy Peabody Essex Museum, Salem, Massachusetts)*

received more than half of England's exports of textile manufactures, and about the same of its wrought metal, iron nails, and chinaware.

The value of goods exported from the thirteen continental colonies directly to the mother country for those years amounted to no more than half that figure, or roughly £1,375,000. Some of the difference was made up in earnings from the "invisibles" noted earlier: the carrying trade, the sale of colonial-built vessels, and bills of exchange earned for the most part by New York and Pennsylvania merchants trading with the Wine Islands and European ports south of Cape Finisterre. Only by including British governmental and defense expenditures in America as a credit does the balance sheet draw more even, but many colonial merchants and planters remained in debt to their British correspondents.

The Impending Crisis

American colonists shared a sense of triumph, and of relief, at the conclusion of peace with France in 1763. Proud to be members of the world's most powerful empire, they recognized that their ties with the mother country had brought them prosperity as well as protection. At the same time, however, they were increasingly conscious of no longer being, strictly speaking, Englishmen. For one thing, about 50 percent were of different ethnic backgrounds–African, Scots, German, Welsh, Irish, and scatterings of French, Dutch, Swedes, and Spaniards. More subtly, the distinction between "nation" and "country" first made by Thomas Hancock in 1748 had gained further recognition during the French and Indian War. The phrase "British Americans" to describe the colonists gained popularity in part because it implied the feasibility of dual allegiances, one national, the other provincial. Except during wartime, Great Britain had paid little attention to its American colonies. Likewise, only those American colonists who lived along the Atlantic coast, most particularly in a dozen or so seaports, were likely to notice any signs of their connection with Great Britain.

Yet, as we have seen in the foregoing chapters, the ocean that separated colonies from mother country also provided the only connection between them. Maritime communities within the British empire on each side of the Atlantic had long since established strong commercial bonds with their counterparts on the others. As the system of mercantilism intended, the colonists depended on the mother country for markets as well as for manufactured goods. What was not expected, however, was that the mother country would one day become equally dependent on its colonies. Nevertheless, by the 1760s that day had arrived. The American colonies (including the West Indies) were now Britain's principal suppliers of imports and, more important, were the leading purchasers of its goods, surpassing Northern Europe. Under ideal circumstances this mutual dependence served to tie the empire together. But the 1760s were not the best of times for British imperialists, and the trade that had once served as an economic bond suddenly became a political weapon.

Without seaports, there would probably have been no American Revolution, at least not in the closing decades of the eighteenth century. This is not, as many history textbooks have commonly suggested, because of the Navigation Acts themselves. People in the seaports did not protest against the mercantile system as such until the very eve of independence. Rather, it is because the new British policy introduced after the close of the Seven Years' War to raise revenue from the American colonies struck first and foremost in seaports. The weight of the Sugar Act (1764) and Stamp Act (1765) bore heaviest on maritime communities, as did the Townshend Act of 1767 and the Tea Act of 1773. Tangible symbols of British power abounded in the seaports. Here the governors, customhouses, admiralty courts, and troop garrisons provided targets for the resentments, real or imagined, of the inhabitants ("the mob" if you were a loyalist; "the people" if

you were a patriot). Here, too, could be found the means for mass communication: newspapers and broadsides, meeting places, and ready access to news from "outside"–other seaports, other colonies, other lands. Urban artisans enjoyed a more flexible work schedule than their country cousins, who were often tied to the farm by the care of livestock through most of the working day, unable to attend protest meetings and rallies, and in most cases living at a distance from village centers.

In the first months of peace the British government turned to the long-postponed project of overhauling the system of colonial administration, especially its commercial aspects. Widespread evasion of the molasses duty, ineffectual law enforcement through colonial courts, and confused direction of policy from London were among the conditions that begged for improvement. Had the project stopped at reformation the Americans might have found the changes more palatable. But the new British ministry under Lord Grenville had a further goal in mind. Britain's national debt had doubled during the war with France, and the decision to retain Canada gave the army vast new regions to garrison. The press of colonial population westward required a British presence to keep the peace between Indians and Whites. Almost all Britons agreed that the colonists should contribute to the cost of their own defense and supported the enactment of two new laws, the Plantation Act of 1764 and the Stamp Act of 1765. To help combat smuggling, the first law revised downward the duties charged on sugar and molasses imported into the colonies from the foreign West Indies with the expectation that, in the words of its preamble, "a revenue be raised for defraying the expenses of defending, protecting, and securing" the colonies. Called the Sugar Act in America, the 1764 Plantation Act also included a number of measures designed to strengthen the enforcement of the navigation acts, including the establishment of a vice-admiralty court in Halifax, where suspected smugglers might be required to defend themselves against the accusations of a strengthened force of customs officials.

When the text of the Sugar Act reached the colonies, one legislature after another lodged strong protests with the mother country. Rhode Island based its objections on commercial expediency, complaining that the new taxes would stifle its colony's molasses and rum trades and deny its workers the ability to purchase British manufactures. After echoing Rhode Island's commercial objections, New York's assembly shifted the argument to a matter of principle. While conceding that Parliament had the right to regulate the Empire's commerce, even to the point of favoring the welfare of the mother country over its colonies, the New Yorkers denied Parliament the right to impose "involuntary taxes" on those colonies. Virginia's House of Burgesses cited what it considered a fundamental principle of the British constitution, "that the people are not subject to any taxes but such as are laid on them by their own consent, or by those who are legally appointed to represent them." Altogether eight colonial legislatures petitioned Parliament to rescind or modify the Sugar Act and to withdraw the impending Stamp Act from further consideration. The Philadelphia merchant Samuel Rhodes took a more practical course when he informed his English trading partners that unless Parliament changed its mind about the new legislation, "I fear that all our trade with you must come to an end."

The Stamp Act of 1765 extended to America a pattern of excise taxes that Britons had borne for many years. Legal documents of all sorts, including ships' clearances and bonds, were subject to new duties, as were pamphlets and newspapers. Because almost every seaport had both courthouses and newspapers, the shock of the Stamp Act bore most heavily on the maritime communities, whose inhabitants were already sensitive to the presence of British authority. Seaports also had large numbers of longshoremen, day-laborers, and mariners, many from other ports, colonies, and countries, young men without local family attachment. Given sufficient inspiration, leadership and courage (moral or liquid) this crowd of people could easily become a mob.

When the text of the Stamp Act reached America in the spring of 1765, widespread protests broke out, not only because of the law itself but because colonists learned that Parliament had refused even to receive American petitions. One conservative New York jurist, who remained a loyalist, lamented to a British friend that "this single stroke has lost

Great Britain the affection of her colonies." While Virginia's Patrick Henry and other legislators took the podium to condemn the new legislation on the principle of "no taxation without representation," the heat of political opposition (and, perhaps, of the summer months as well) brought more violent protestors onto the streets of America's seaports. In Boston a mob ransacked the homes of several officials who had agreed to cooperate with the new law, including that of Lieutenant Governor Thomas Hutchinson. The mob stole everything it could lay its hands on, including plate, portraits, clothing, and £900 sterling in money. In a final act of mindless defiance the rioters scattered or destroyed Hutchinson's books and papers, some of which he had been collecting for his *History of Massachusetts Bay*. Violence also broke out in Newport, New York, and Annapolis, Maryland, among other seaports, before reasonable men and women, whatever their political beliefs, managed to restore order. By 1 November 1765, when the Stamp Act was to take effect, only one solitary official could be found in the thirteen continental American colonies willing to carry out the law, and he soon abandoned the effort.

Customs and other officials charged with the hapless task of enforcing the new provisions of the Sugar Act were subjected to a rising tide of violence. On one occasion the colonial fort commanding Newport Harbor opened fire on the Royal Navy schooner *St. John* as it attempted to seize a suspected smuggler. In New York the captain of the British sloop-of-war *Hawke* was jailed for an allegedly improper seizure. Americans believed that naval captains were prohibited by law from impressing American sailors, but sometimes they did it anyway. The arrival of the frigate *Maidstone* at Newport in June 1765 scattered local vessels like chickens running before a fox. When the search officers picked up a few unfortunate sailors from an unsuspecting vessel just entering the harbor, the populace was so furious it seized the warship's boat and burned it on the town common. In Charleston, South Carolina, the British ensign received "the highest insults" from the crew of a vessel being searched by the warship *Sardoine*, its captain reported. While no British official was actually killed in the line of duty, it was not for want of effort on the part of American mobs. Besides, murder was not necessary. As one customs officer who was seriously beaten by a mob in Philadelphia later testified, "I have had a constant pain in my breast ever since, besides a kind of inward fever, which hangs about me, no appetite to my victuals, and spirits very much depressed. I could not think of tarrying among a set of people," he concluded, "whose greatest pleasure would be to have an opportunity of burying me."

Meanwhile, the merchants of several ports came up with their own means of protest: a boycott of English goods. By September 1765 a number of individual merchants had already canceled their orders for spring goods from London until repeal of the unwanted act. A block of two hundred New York merchants made a similar pledge, as did importers in many other seaports. Cynics might note that languishing trade conditions made such cutbacks good business sense, but the primary motivation for the boycott was political. By refusing to import goods from the mother country, American merchants hoped that their British counterparts would exert pressure on Parliament to repeal the Sugar and Stamp Acts. Repeal did come in the spring of 1766, before the boycott took full effect, but mainly as the result of internal British politics rather than colonial pressure. The really important consequence, however, was that American merchants *thought* their nascent boycott was responsible, and they would return to "playing the commerce card" as a weapon again and again. The mother country would also use commerce, first as a means of raising further revenues in America and later as a means of punishing recalcitrant colonists.

In 1767 the continuing need for income from America prompted a new British ministry to adopt the Townshend Act, which charged duties on the importation of commodities such as paper, glass, painters' colors, and tea into the colonies. No one needed a crystal ball to predict the reaction to this thinly disguised effort to use the power of regulation to raise a revenue. By the spring of 1768 tensions along the Boston waterfront needed only a spark to set off an explosion. Seizure of John Hancock's sloop *Liberty* for suspected smuggling provided that spark, and another riot broke out in early June. Before the night was over, the customs collector and his son narrowly escaped serious injury and with other officials were forced to seek asylum aboard the British frigate *Romney*. The *Liberty* affair turned

out badly for the Crown, whose prosecutors were forced to drop the case, but not before Hancock had gained a popular reputation throughout America. News of the *Liberty* riot prompted British officials to send troops to Boston, greatly increasing tensions there. Meanwhile, a series of articles by John Dickinson, titled "Letters from a Farmer in Pennsylvania," appeared in newspapers in all the leading seaports. Dickinson reminded his readers that the Townshend duties were simply another effort to tax Americans without their consent and hinted that a repetition of nonimportation might bring another repeal. Distrust between the merchants of Boston, New York, and Philadelphia delayed that action until the spring of 1769. Meanwhile, ordinary citizens joined a grass-roots effort against the consumption of various imported goods, but soon the movement focused on tea. Not only was tea subject to one of the Townshend duties, but it was a luxury that came to symbolize English rather than American culture.

Merchants committees in the major seaports struggled to enforce their nonimportation agreements, dependent as they were only on public opinion. Outright defiance by Boston's loyalist merchants was widely publicized in other ports, much to the embarrassment of leaders there, and leaks elsewhere revived intercolonial rivalries. Nevertheless, total imports from England, which had averaged about £2,000,000 in each of the years 1767 and 1768 before the boycott, fell by a third to £1,320,000 in 1769. Collection of duties under the Townshend Act fell even more sharply, from £13,302 in 1768 to £2,727 two years later. When Parliament voted in the spring of 1770 to repeal all Townshend duties save that on tea, most merchants decided they had won another significant victory, and their protest movement was curtailed. Once again America's maritime community had used a commercial boycott to bring about a desired political end. But Parliament's insistence on retaining the tea duty as a symbol of its right to tax the colonists was fraught with foreboding.

On the very day that Parliament repealed most of the Townshend duties, 5 March 1770, three thousand miles away in Boston the need to garrison British troops brought about the tragic massacre that was triggered by young sailors and laborers taunting some of the Redcoats. When panic-stricken soldiers opened fire, men began to fall, mortally wounded, onto the icy street in front of the customhouse. Although most of the soldiers were acquitted of manslaughter with the help of the Boston patriot-lawyer, John Adams, the confrontation was one more step in the seemingly inexorable slide toward open rebellion in America's seaports. One immediate consequence was the British colonel's decision to withdraw his troops to Castle William on an island in Boston Harbor. This concession gave town, province, and continent a chance to settle their nerves a bit, but three years later, when the troops were needed once again to keep the peace, they would not be immediately available.

The Boston Tea Party

For the most part the period 1770-73 brought a return to normal conditions throughout maritime America. Trade with the mother country grew at a dizzying pace. Altogether the continental colonies purchased more than £9,000,000 worth of British goods, up from £5,400,000 during the previous three-year period and almost double the annual rate of the 1760s. Whatever their political views, Boston's merchants did not hesitate to order quantities of goods from the mother country, including over 500,000 pounds of English tea, on which they paid more than £6,000 sterling in duties. Future loyalists and patriots alike profited from the sale of tea. The only reason the merchants of New York and Philadelphia did not do likewise was because they could smuggle far greater quantities of Dutch tea in from Amsterdam. Further south in the Chesapeake and the Carolinas, shipments of tobacco, rice, and indigo to Great Britain reached record levels, enabling the Southerners to remain good consumers of English goods. To be sure, customs officials were still at serious risk for doing their job, as collector John Hatton discovered when he boarded a vessel unloading its contraband cargo into small boats halfway up the Delaware River. Hatton was severely beaten and then jailed for allegedly wounding one of his assailants! In June 1772 a far worse episode occurred in Rhode Island's Narragansett Bay involving the naval schooner *Gaspee*, whose conscientious commander, Lieutenant Thomas

Dudingston, was thoroughly hated for his literal enforcement of every conceivable customs regulation. When his vessel had the misfortune to run aground on a falling tide while in pursuit of a suspected smuggler, local patriots got their revenge. Under the leadership of Providence merchant John Brown, eight boatloads of men waited till nightfall, then boarded the hapless vessel. Dudingston suffered a painful gunshot wound, and HMS *Gaspee* was unceremoniously burned to the water's edge. When Admiral John Montagu arrived in Newport some weeks later to investigate the episode, the local battery refused to salute his flagship. With a straight face the governor explained that budgetary constraints limited salutes to certain holidays only! Despite these and other provocations, moderates on both sides of the Atlantic seemed to prevail in their efforts to keep the peace between the mother country and its fractious colonies. Barring any new crisis, it seemed likely that they would continue to do so.

And then, through an almost incredible series of ill-fated decisions, came the catalyst that would ultimately precipitate revolution in America. The first mistake, already noted, was Lord North's determination to retain the Townshend duty on tea as the symbol of British authority in America. Better for Britain had he chosen glass or painters' colors, neither of which was a major consumer item. The second mistake came with the decision, made in the spring of 1773, to allow the East India Company to export some of its surplus tea directly to American consignees in four major ports–Charleston, Philadelphia, New York, and Boston–bypassing the usual channel through British wholesale merchants to American importers and retailers. By excluding ordinary merchants on both sides of the Atlantic from the profitable tea trade, this arrangement tossed a plum to a small number of favorites, mostly loyalists, who were chosen as consignees. Not so incidentally, the East India Company would probably have undersold smugglers of Dutch tea at both Philadelphia and New York. North committed a third error when he rejected a suggestion to exempt the Company's special tea shipments from the duty. "I tell the Noble Lord now," curmudgeonly William Dowdeswell predicted, "if he don't take off the duty they won't take the tea." But North believed otherwise, misled perhaps by the knowledge that

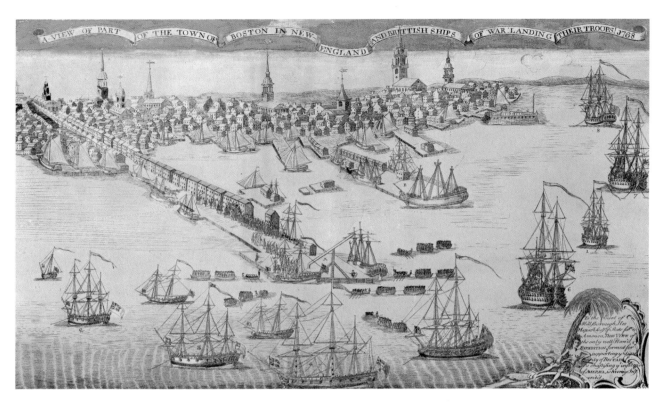

Paul Revere engraved this view of the Boston waterfront to commemorate the occupation of Boston by British troops in the fall of 1768 in response to rioting over the seizure of John Hancock's sloop Liberty. *In the foreground is the British fleet from Halifax, landing troops on Long Wharf. The large wharf to the right of Long Wharf is Hancock's Wharf, where the* Liberty *was lying when she was seized on the charge of smuggling wine from Madeira. Long Wharf, built in 1710, was a half-mile avenue that linked Boston with the prosperity of the British Empire. At the head of Long Wharf is the low tower of the State House, seat of the colonial government. Just to the right of the wharf, the large building with cupola and dormers is Fanueil Hall, built as a market building with meeting hall by wealthy French Huguenot merchant Peter Fanueil in 1742 and frequently used for political meetings. (Courtesy Winterthur Museum)*

plenty of dutied tea had entered America in the last three years.

All through the autumn of 1773 tensions mounted in the four ports destined to receive East India Company tea. Arguments against the scheme took several forms. First, both in both timing and importance was the contention that Parliament planned these shipments of cheap tea as bait to tempt Americans into recognizing its right to tax the colonies. The second charge argued that the real goal of the scheme was to grant the East India Company a monopoly of all American import trade, not just in tea. As the opposition grew at Boston, New York, and Philadelphia, threats of bodily harm persuaded most of the consignees to resign their commissions. The vessels were to be turned back before they came up to the wharves to unload their cargoes. In neither New York nor Philadelphia did the governor make any

effort to interfere with what was clearly the popular will. The situation at Boston, however, was rather different.

On Sunday, 28 November 1773, the bluff-bowed ship *Dartmouth* worked its way into Boston Harbor, nine weeks from London, with a cargo of 114 chests of East India Company tea on board. As their counterparts at New York and Philadelphia were to do, Boston's patriots insisted that the tea be returned forthwith to England, but Governor Thomas Hutchinson had other ideas. In the first place, his sons were among the consignees. in the 1760s the young Hutchinsons and the Clarkes had held out against the nonimportation agreements for months and were responsible for importing most of the dutied tea that had entered Boston since 1767. Now they were determined not to surrender to popular demands that they resign like the consignees at New York. At the same time, Hutchinson was

A routine dispute between a Boston ropemaker and a British soldier led to a violent confrontation forever after called the Boston Massacre. On the evening of 5 March 1770, several days after the dispute, a young man harangued the British sentry in front of the customhouse. Fire alarm bells brought a crowd into the street, including a group of sailors and waterfront workers. A squad of soldiers arrived to disperse the crowd, but gunfire broke out when Crispus Attucks, a sailor of black, white, and American-Indian descent, threatened the soldiers. Attucks, sailor James Caldwell, and ropemaker Sam Gray were killed, and two other laborers died of their wounds. The Boston Massacre both increased the British perception of Boston as an unruly seaport and increased the colonial perception of the ruthless imposition of British authority in the colonies. Paul Revere copied this engraving from a sketch by John Pelham, half-brother of artist John Singleton Copley. (Courtesy Boston Athenaeum)

itching for a showdown with the patriot forces who had tormented him for years. With British troops close at hand at Castle William and Admiral Montagu's warships anchored in the harbor, he was determined to see that the tea was landed and the duty paid. For their part, the patriots were still smarting under the criticism that they had "permitted" so much dutied tea to enter Boston in previous years and were equally determined that the tea consigned to Boston be sent back to England. They knew that in twenty days the customs officials would be free to seize the tea for its unpaid duties if it had not been landed. Once ashore, the patriots feared, the tea would find its way into the marketplace, and Boston would once again be disgraced.

Mass meetings on 29 and 30 November drew more than 5,000 inhabitants of Boston and surrounding towns to Old South Church, demonstrating how widespread the interest was in the affairs of a major seaport like Boston. Demands were made that the consignees resign and the tea be returned, but to no avail. "Let us take our axes and Chissels and split the Boxes and throw their Contents into the Harbor and then we shall have Tea enough without paying any Duty," cried a spectator. The consignees had taken refuge at Castle William, and the vessel could not carry its cargo back without Governor Hutchinson's approval, which he had no reason to grant. Meanwhile, two more vessels came in with more tea, and news reached Boston that the consignees at both New York and Philadelphia had resigned. "You failed us [before] in the importation of tea," taunted the merchants in those ports. Frustration mounted daily, most of it directed at Hutchinson, who had himself retreated to his country estate in Milton.

O n 16 December, the last day before the twenty-day period expired, yet another mass meeting at Old South sent a last-minute appeal to Hutchinson asking that the vessels be allowed to return the tea to England. The emissary returned to Old South with the governor's refusal in late afternoon, which elicited "hideous Yelling...as of an Hundred People, some imitating the Powaws of Indians and others the whistle of a Boatswain." In the minds of the patriots, the time had come for action. In one of the most famous episodes in American history, hundreds of citizens rushed down through the streets of Boston to the waterfront, amid cries of "Boston Harbor a teapot tonight!" "Hurrah for Griffin's Wharf!" Out of the crowd came fifty or sixty men, some of them crudely disguised as American Indians, who climbed aboard the *Dartmouth*, *Beaver*, and *Eleanor*, hoisted more than three hundred chests of tea out of the holds, and dumped their contents into the dock. Within three hours,

Despite the heightened tensions between the American colonies and the British Parliament, commerce went on in the prescribed manner. When the owners of the Boston brigantine Lydia *planned a whaling cruise to the African coast in 1772 they secured a Mediterranean pass from the Admiralty to shield the vessel from molestation by corsairs from the Barbary states of North Africa. (G.W. Blunt White Library, Mystic Seaport)*

tea worth about £10,000 was destroyed in Boston Harbor. "This is the most magnificent movement of all," wrote John Adams the next day. "This destruction of the tea is so bold, so daring, so firm, intrepid & inflexible, and it must have so important consequences and so lasting," he concluded, "that I cannot but consider it as an Epocha in history." John Adams was right as usual.

The Bostonians Pay the Excise-man, or Tarring & Feathering, *epitomizes the British perception of rebellious Boston by 1774. The Liberty Tree representing the demise of the Stamp Act (right rear), the Boston Tea Party (left rear), and the tarring and feathering of customs officer John Malcom early in 1774, are combined in one cartoon lamenting the challenge to royal authority in the thirteen colonies. With his baggy breeches and short, tight jacket, the nearest figure may represent a sailor, an occupational group commonly viewed as either rebellious or revolutionary, depending on one's perspective. Mezzotint printed for R. Sayer and J. Bennett, London, 1774. (Courtesy Winterthur Museum)*

The Final Break

What made the Boston Tea Party the catalyst that precipitated the American Revolution was not simply the act itself but, even more significantly, the British government's reaction to it. Overshadowing a decade of arguments in both England and America about customs officials, the right of taxation, the threat of monopoly, control of western lands, and the establishment of the Anglican Church, was a simple, unambiguous fact: A British company had sent a valuable cargo to a colonial port only to see it destroyed by a mob. If the mother country could no longer safely export its goods to its colonies, the ministry concluded, the very foundation of the empire was at risk. Throughout the winter and early spring, while Parliament considered how to respond to Boston's act of violence, duties tea once more became the symbol of British tyranny. When a private shipment arrived at Boston in March 1774, it too ended up in the harbor. Anti-tea mania spread down the Atlantic seaboard like a smallpox epidemic, infecting students at Princeton, patriots at Annapolis, and the women of Edenton, North Carolina, among many others. "I love Great Britain and rever the King," wrote a Philadelphian to his English friend. "But it is my duty to hand down Freedom to my posterity, compatible of Englishmen. Therefore," he concluded, "no tea duty, nor any unconstitutional tax whatever."

Now it was Great Britain's turn to play the commerce card. In the most vindictive of four measures that became known as the Coercive Acts, Parliament closed the Port of Boston to all commerce, coastal as well as foreign, until the town compensated the East India Company for its losses, brought the culprits to justice, and guaranteed future good behavior of the town's inhabitants. In the battle between England and America, maritime commerce—the very bond that had held the empire together for nearly two hundred years—now became the primary medium through which each side attacked the other. Closing a port punished everyone in it, not just the perpetrators of the crime: housewives, shipowners, caulkers, shopkeepers, mariners, ropewalk workers, children. And it punished as well the thousands of people who lived in Boston's hinterland: farmers, artisans, and par-

ticularly the storekeepers who brought produce of the countryside into the port and returned to Concord or Hingham or Lynn with stock for their stores. When Admiral Samuel Graves took over the North Atlantic station at Boston, he enforced every provision of the Port Act. Coastal vessels with food and firewood were forced to unload outside the district and send their cargoes overland in wagons soon dubbed "Lord North's coasters" by Yankee wits. Watercraft operating within the harbor were harassed at every opportunity. Other measures comprising the Coercive Acts moved the seat of government to Salem, altered the charter of Massachusetts Bay, and made changes in the administration of justice. But it was the Port Act that caught the attention and sympathy of the entire continent, even moderates who had condemned the Tea Party itself. As George Washington wrote just after Virginia's House of Burgesses voted a day of fasting, humiliation, and prayer, for the first of June, "The Cause of Boston, the despotic measures in respect to it I mean, now is and ever will be considered as the cause of America (not that we approve their conduct in destroying the Tea)."

Support for the once-despised port of Boston came pouring in from every quarter—cash from more prosperous communities, wheat, foodstuffs, and livestock from farming towns and individuals alike. At last, people on the grassroots level could do something about what the people of Windham, Connecticut, labeled "the cruel and unmanly attacks by the British Parliament on the loyal and patriotic town of Boston." When a sloop laden with provisions arrived from Cape Fear, North Carolina, in July, Boston's committee thanked the southerners for their "tender sympathy and brotherly kindness." Tiny Brooklyn, Connecticut, sent 125 sheep with the hope that Boston "may be enabled to stand firm, if possible in the glorious cause." Short of life itself a farmer or artisan could give no more precious gift than the fruit of his land and labor. And with the gift came a commitment to what was considered the cause of freedom.

The reaction to the Coercive Acts united the colonies as never before. Delegates from various constituencies representing twelve colonies convened the first Continental Congress at Philadelphia in September 1774. There they

Boston had reigned as the preeminent American seaport from the 1630s to the 1750s. Surpassed in population by Philadelphia and New York around 1760, Boston remained a close second to Philadelphia in annual shipping tonnage by 1770. Although Boston had a small hinterland with scant surplus produce to fill their ships, Boston merchants engaged in trade throughout the Atlantic world, and a large percentage of the city's 17,000 residents had maritime occupations. Normally bustling Boston Harbor became very quiet in 1774 as a result of the Coercive Acts passed to close the port until payment was made for the tea destroyed in the Boston Tea Party. Surrounding colonies rallied to support Boston by land, but the port remained the domain of the British Royal Navy, with very little commercial traffic, until 1776. Engraving by Joseph Des Barres, The Atlantic Neptune *(London, 1779). (G.W. Blunt White Library, Mystic Seaport)*

played their own commerce card, immediately banning all imports from the British Isles and prohibiting exports to Great Britain after 10 September 1775 unless the Coercive Acts were rescinded by then. In their determination to force the repeal of the Coercive Acts, it is not surprising that patriot leaders turned once more to an economic boycott. But the resolves of 1774 were different. Instead of relying on voluntary nonimportation agreements among the mer-

chants of the several seaports, as earlier boycotts had done, the Congress drew up articles of agreement signed by almost all of the delegates on behalf of their colonies. In addition to binding the colonial governments to enforcing the boycotts on imports and exports, the Continental Association prohibited the importation of slaves and of tea from whatever country. It also called for a general posture of austerity throughout the colonies, discouraging "every species of extrava-

The Continental Association, 1774

We his Majesty's most loyal subjects, the delegates of the several colonies. . . to obtain redress of these grievances, which threaten destruction of the lives, liberty, and property of His Majesty's subjects in North america, we are of opinion that a non-importation, non-consumption, and non-exportation agreement, faithfully adhered to, will prove the most speedy, effectual, and peaceable measure; and therefore we do, for ourselves, and the inhabitants of the several colonies whom we represent, firmly agree and associate, under the sacred ties of virtue, honour, and love of country, as follows:

1. That, from and after the first day of December next, we will not import into British america from Great Britain or Ireland, any goods, wares, or merchandize whatsoever, or from any other place, any such goods, wares or merchandise as shall have been exported from Great Britain or Ireland; nor will we after that day import any East-India tea from any part of the world; nor any molasses, syrups, paneles, coffee, or pimento from the British plantations or from Dominica; nor wines from Madeira or the Western Islands; nor foreign indigo.

2. We will neither import nor purchase any slave imported after the first day of December next; after which time we will wholly discontinue the slave trade. . . .

3. . . . from this day, we will not purchase or use any tea, imported on account of the East India Company. . . . and after the first day of March next, we will not purchase or use any East India tea whatever; nor will we. . . purchase or use any of those goods, wares, or merchandise we have agreed not to import . . . .

4. The earnest desire we have not to injure our fellow-subjects in Great Britain, Ireland, or the West Indies, induces us to suspend a non-exportation, until the tenth day of September 1775; at which time, if the said Acts and parts of the Acts of the British Parliament herinafter mentioned are not repealed, we will not directly or indirectly export any merchandise or commodity whatsoever to Great Britain, Ireland, or the West Indies, except rice to Europe. . . .

11. That a committee be chosen in every county, city, and town, by those who are qualified to vote for representatives in the legislature, whose business it shall be attentively to observe the conduct of all persons touching this association; and when it shall be made to appear, to the satisfaction of a majority of any such committee, that any person within the limits of their appointment has violated this association, that such majority do forthwith cause the truth of the case to be published in the gazette; to the end, that all such foes to the rights of British-America may be publicly known, and universally condemned as the enemies of american liberty; and thenceforth we respectively will break off all dealings with him or her. . . .

14. And we do further agree and resolve, that we will have no trade, commerce, dealings or intercourse whatsoever with any colony or province in North america, which shall not accede to, or which shall hereafter violate this association, but will hold them as unworthy of the rights of freemen, and as inimical to the liberties of their country.

And we do solemnly bind ourselves and our constituents, under the ties aforesaid, to adhere to this Association until the Acts of Parliament complained of are repealed. And we do recommend it to the provincial conventions and to the committees in the respective colonies to establish such farther regulations as they may think proper, for carrying into execution this association.

A View of New York from the N...

gance and dissipation" including horse racing, gaming, plays and "other expensive diversions and entertainment," and promoted agriculture, manufactures, and American self-sufficiency in general. The Association called upon each county or town to elect a local committee to enforce its terms. Not surprisingly, actual compliance ranged from vigorous in New England and the Chesapeake colonies to mixed in New York and virtually nonexistent in Georgia. Even so, from a loose series of voluntary nonimportation agreements the colonial protest movement had advanced to the establishment of extralegal quasi-governmental bodies.

Despite the petitions of various groups of English merchants seeking a restoration of peace and harmony with the colonies, Parliament took a firm stand against the actions of the Continental Congress. In an effort to drive a wedge between the colonies it enacted the New England Restraining Act in March 1775, limiting the commerce of the four northernmost colonies to the British Isles (and British West Indies) and barring them from fishing on the banks of Newfoundland, an important cornerstone of

months, Parliament authorized the seizure of all American vessels found engaged in any form of commerce "as if the same were the ships and effects of open enemies," which by that time of course they were. As a logical response to this Prohibitory Act the Continental Congress voted in April 1776 to throw open the ports of America to the vessels of all nations, confirming in principle what had already happened in fact–American commercial independence.

The bridge of commerce that had once bound England and America together through a system that benefited each partner had become the battleground between them. Each party was convinced that denial of these benefits to the other would force a modification of its opponent's political position. In the event, both sides were wrong, and when that bridge collapsed, Great Britain's Atlantic empire fell with it. The fact that so great an ocean as the Atlantic separated the two lands only heightened the separation and exacerbated the misunderstandings between them. Meanwhile, as American coastal commerce increased in the decade before the Revolution, important lines of communication grew with it. The exchange of colonial newspapers, published almost exclusively in the seaports, contributed to the expanding awareness of similarities between the inhabitants of the various colonies and their shared differences from the mother country. From being a geographical expression, "America" took on cultural and political meanings as well, and coastal commerce played an important role in that development.

Few Englishmen had ever seen America, and fewer still of the colonists with British roots had visited the mother country. Not many of the people living in the American colonies on the eve of the Revolution had themselves emi-

New England's maritime commerce. The ink had hardly dried on this bill before Parliament extended its terms to all the other colonies save New York, North Carolina, and Georgia, where loyalists continued to resist compliance with the Continental Association. Parliament had thus made good on Lord North's earlier boast to Governor Hutchinson, now a refugee in England, that if the colonies refused to trade with the mother country "Great Britain would take care they should trade no where else." In December 1775, after British and American forces had been at war on land and sea for eight

Even as Americans discovered an increasing sense of unity among their colonies, the presence of Britain's Royal Navy reminded them that they were still a part of the British Empire. Here a British frigate lies off the Battery in New York, while small craft pass along the Hudson River waterfront at left. "A View of New York from the North West," engraving by Joseph Des Barres, **The Atlantic Neptune** *(London, 1779). (G.W. Blunt White Library, Mystic Seaport)*

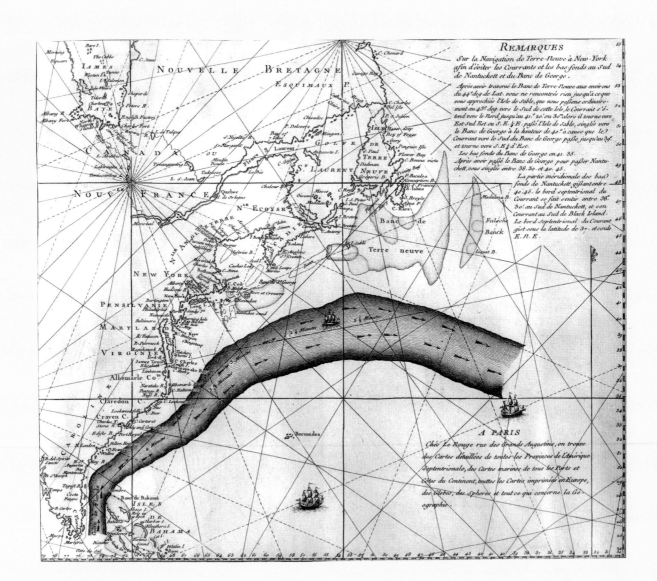

Benjamin Franklin
Describes the Gulf Stream

Vessels are sometimes retarded, and sometimes forwarded in their voyages, by currents at sea, which are often not perceived. About the year 1769 or 70, there was an application made by the board of customs at Boston, to the lords of the treasury in London, complaining that the packets between Falmouth and New-York, were generally a fort-night longer in their passages, than merchant ships from London to Rhode-Island, and proposing that for the future they should be ordered to Rhode-Island instead of New York. Being then concerned in the management of the American post office, I happened to be consulted on the occasion; and it appeared strange to me that there should be such a difference between the two places, scarce a day's run asunder, especially when the merchant ships are generally deeper laden, and more weakly manned than the packets, and had from London the whole length of the channel to run down before they left the land of England, while the packets had only to go from Falmouth, I could not but think the fact misunderstood or misrepresented. There happened then to be in London, a Nantucket sea-captain of my acquaintance, to whom I communicated the affair. He told me he believed the fact might be true; but that the difference was owing to this, that the Rhode Island captains were acquainted with the gulf stream, which those of English packets were not. We are well acquainted with that stream, says he, because our persuit of whales, which keep near the sides of it, but are not to be met with in it, we run down along the sides, and frequently cross it to change our side; and in crossing it have sometimes met and spoke with those packets, who were in the middle of it, and stemming it. We have informed them that they were stemming a current, that was against them to the value of three miles an hour; and advised them to cross it and get out of it; but they were too wise to be counselled by simple American fishermen. When the winds are but light, he added, they are carried back by the current more than they are forwarded by the wind; and if the wind be good, the subtraction of 70 miles in a day from their course is of some importance. I then observed that it was a pity no notice was taken of this current upon the charts, and requested him to mark it out for me, which he readily complied with, adding directions for avoiding it in sailing from Europe to North-America. I procured it to be engraved by order from the general post-office, on the old chart of the Atlantic, at Mount and Page's, Tower-hill, and copies were sent down to

Falmouth for the captains of the packets, who slighted it however, but since printed in France, of which edition hereto annex a copy. . . .

Having since crossed this stream several times in passing between America and Europe, I have been attentive to sundry circumstances relating to it, by which it is interspersed, I find that it is always warmer than the sea on each side of it, and that it does not sparkle in the night....The thermometer may be an useful instrument to a navigator, since currents coming from the northward into the southern seas, will probably be found colder than the water of those seas, as the currents from the southern seas into the northern are found warmer. . . .

The conclusion from these remarks is, that a vessel from Europe to North-America may shorten her passage by avoiding to stem the stream, in which the thermometer will be very useful; and a vessel from America to Europe may do the same by the same means of keeping in it. It may often happened accidently, that voyages have been shortened by these circumstances. It is now well to have the command of them.

Transactions of the American Philosophical Society 2 (1786): 314-17.

Benjamin Franklin's chart of the Gulf Stream, based on the observations of Nantucket whalemen, advanced the possibilities of scientific navigation on the Atlantic. This French version of the chart reflects the greater acceptance of Franklin's work in France than in England. (Courtesy Peabody Essex Museum, Salem, Massachusetts)

grated from the British Isles. Englishmen and Americans most familiar with the other side of the Atlantic were with few exceptions among those moderates searching for a compromise to the imperial crisis. They had good reason to believe that the colonies were not strong enough to survive as independent states in the war-torn world of the eighteenth century and feared that, without the protection of Great Britain, they would be quickly gobbled up by France or Spain. Then these lands and people, which had once contributed to British strength, would enhance the power of Great Britain's mortal enemies, and the balance would be irretrievably upset.

The major reason that so many Americans showed reluctance to repudiate their place in the British empire was their knowledge that the benefits of that system to Americans had far outweighed its costs. In an era when the naval powers of the world were at war more than half the time, the American colonists were protected by the world's most powerful navy, for which they paid nothing and in which they rarely had to serve. They had a share in the empire's lucrative carrying trade. They enjoyed a protected market for their plantation goods, even receiving bounties for some; they could sell their vessels to British shipowners; they were extended vast sums of money on credit; and they had access to British capital with which to expand their own enterprises. Under mercantilism the American colonies prospered beyond anyone's wildest expectations. Prosperity meant sophisticated urban centers, well-educated merchants and planters, literate artisans and farmers.

On the eve of the American Revolution the colonists enjoyed a greater level of prosperity than that of their forebears (or, for that matter, of their immediate descendants as well) and certainly greater than that enjoyed by most other peoples of the Atlantic world. The best attempts to quantify this growth, by McCusker and Menard, estimate that the real per capita income of continental Americans more than doubled in the period 1650-1774 in constant figures. Because of the extraordinary growth in population through the period, colonial America's gross "national" product increased at the annual rate of 3.5 percent between 1650 and 1775. Over that same period economic growth in the mother country was only 0.5 percent per year. The per-

capita growth rate for white Americans is even more remarkable considering that the total population on which these figures are calculated included half a million African Americans, few of whom had any personal wealth to enjoy. Because the price commanded by American produce increased relative to the cost of British goods in the years just before the Revolution, the colonial standard of living rose accordingly. The historian Marc Egnal has pointed out one example to demonstrate the result: in 1740, 100 bushels of wheat bought 150 yards of British woolen cloth; twenty years later, the same amount of wheat could purchase 250 yards.

At the same time, colonial American trade had become valuable to the British as well, particularly in providing access to a rapidly expanding market, as colonial America's population expanded more than eightfold in the first three-quarters of the eighteenth century. Therefore, when Americans disrupted that trade through nonimportation agreements, British leaders were alarmed. They feared that Americans intended political independence, which was not true until 1776. The British could not afford to lose America, not only because its trade was essential to them, but also because they could not risk the possibility that the colonies would fall into the hands of the French, or at least under French influence, and thereby enrich an arch-rival at Great Britain's expense. Not oppression, but prosperity, was the consequence of colonial American trade: prosperity for Great Britain that it could not risk losing; prosperity for America that led it to resent political bullying from the mother country. The result, given American conditions, was a self-fulfilling prophecy: American political independence. But, as Lord Sheffield predicted in 1782, so advantageous was the bond of commerce between the two countries that they would remain each other's best trading partners for more than a century after the end of the American Revolution.

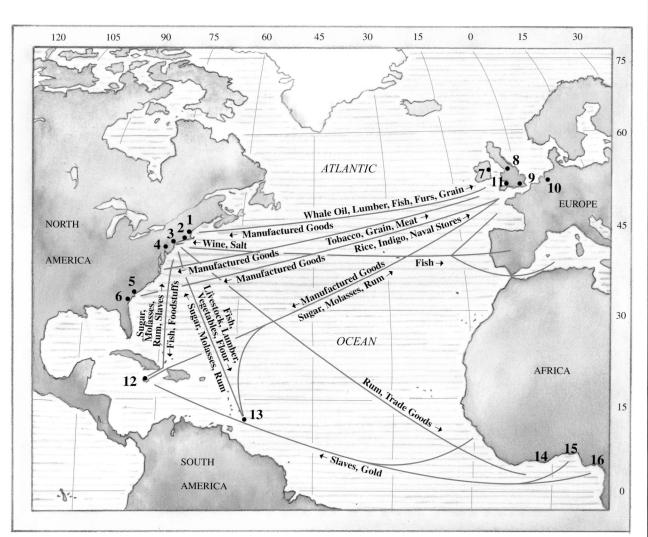

Figure 3 **Eighteenth-Century Atlantic Ocean Trade Routes**

——————— Trade Routes

1. Boston
2. Newport
3. New York City
4. Philadelphia
5. Charleston
6. Savannah
7. Dublin
8. Liverpool
9. London
10. Amsterdam

11. Bristol
12. Jamaica
13. Barbados
14. Gold Coast
15. Bight of Benin
16. Bight of Biafra

(Dennis O'Brien map)

CHAPTER 4

Maritime Dimensions of Revolution and Confederation

HAT BEGAN AS A mission to confiscate colonial munitions ended as the first day of an eight-year war. When the British Regulars crossed the Charles River and marched inland toward Lexington on that morning of 19 April 1775 they knew the colonists were alarmed, just as they had been at Salem bridge in February. But this time the colonial militiamen on Lexington Green, and at Concord's North Bridge, shot back, compelling the troops to retreat to the safety of Boston. And this time the militia remained under arms, gathering around Boston to besiege His Majesty's troops.

King George III's stubborn refusal to accommodate American grievances, and now the bloodshed in Massachusetts, demanded the convening of a Second Continental Congress. On 10 May 1775 the Congress assembled in Philadelphia. Among the first items of business was a request by the Massachusetts Provincial Congress that the delegates in Philadelphia "adopt" the New England militia force confronting Boston and make it a Continental army.

Not everyone in the Continental Congress was enthusiastic. Indeed, representing thirteen separate colonies spread along 1,500 miles of coastline, with a wide range of economic interests and allegiances to the Crown, Congress was, as John Adams suggested, "like a large fleet sailing under convoy. The fleetest sailers must wait for the dullest and slowest." As one of the strongest proponents for outright independence, Adams was one of the "fleetest sailers." Many others in Congress still sought reconciliation, hoping to persuade by force what Parliament had not accepted by supplication.

Nonetheless, enough delegates agreed to pass a resolution creating the Continental Army. On 15 June Congress appointed George Washington, a Virginia delegate to Congress and a tobacco

Detail of fire-ship attack on the Hudson River, by Dominic Serres. (M.S.M. 49.804; Claire White-Peterson photo)

planter with considerable military experience during the Seven Years' War, to lead the army. On the afternoon of 3 July under the shade of a great elm tree on the common at Cambridge, Massachusetts, Washington took formal command of what were now the first units of the Continental Army.

The fights at Lexington and Concord, the siege of Boston, and the appointment of Washington as commander in chief of the Continental Army had shaken the colonies to their very core. Royal authority began to collapse as royal governors took flight and provincial assemblies took control. Those people loyal to the crown–Loyalists or Tories–found themselves isolated and vulnerable. Their only choice was to flee to the closest place where they might take refuge behind the arms of the King. In Massachusetts, for example, more than 1,000 Loyalists fled to Boston. Those Tories who remained behind, beyond the protection of the King's arms, were often summoned before local committees where they were interrogated and humiliated. They would be safe only as long as they were silent.

In the ports, too, radicals drove the Tories to ground. While General Gage and his troops could protect the King's friends in Boston, elsewhere along the coast they were not so fortunate. For a dozen years American merchants and mariners had been struggling with the uncertainty and violence brought on by British trade policies.

Sailors, in particular, had been hard hit by the decline in trade over the previous years. Indeed, they had been among the first to take to the streets to defy King and Parliament. And even New England fishermen, who spent so much of their time at sea, hauling cod out of the cold and stormy North Atlantic, found themselves thrown out of work by the New England Restraining Act of March 1775, which prohibited American fishermen from the Grand Banks. The rush of events energized them and made them more aware of their growing identity as Americans.

Merchants too were drawn along. A dozen years of rising defiance in the ports had done much to weaken conservative elements, giving groups such as the Sons of Liberty increasing credibility. Like the men who manned their ships, shipowners had been hard hit by the tumult brought on by the taxes and other unpopular acts decreed by the King's ministers. The extreme measures taken by Lord North against Boston sounded a tocsin in coastal communities. Most hoped that recent events would demonstrate to London that Americans would defend their rights, and thereafter compromise and reconciliation would be forthcoming. That, of course, was the hope in the Congress. In the meantime, however, preparations for war continued, focused on Boston.

As Washington surveyed his tactical situation he found comfort on the land side. His army, albeit weak in organization and experience, was vastly superior in numbers to the besieged British. The Regulars might probe at the American lines but they could never break through. On the water side, however, affairs were less agreeable.

Every day from the tops of hills overlooking Boston, American sentries could see the British men of war riding at anchor in the harbor. Bristling with guns, these ships guaranteed the British control of the waters surrounding the town. That control allowed free and uninterrupted entry to a stream of vessels bringing supplies to the trapped enemy. So confident was the Royal Navy of its control that it permitted these heavily laden merchantmen to sail from England unarmed and unescorted. Seeing an opportunity to fill his own depleted stores with British supplies, Washington decided to intercept the British vessels.

With advice from Colonel John Glover, a Marblehead merchant who had risen from shoemaker to fish vendor, Washington chartered the colonel's schooner *Hannah* and instructed her master to intercept inbound British ships. On 5 September the *Hannah* sailed on her first cruise. The next day she captured the supply vessel *Unity*, laden with naval stores and provisions. Encouraged by the *Hannah's* success, Washington chartered other vessels to cruise off Boston. Over the next several months Washington commissioned eleven vessels. This aggressive little squadron took fifty-five enemy prizes.

The success of Washington's squadron off New England encouraged Congress to venture even bolder moves at sea. As early as August 1775 the delegates from Rhode Island had urged the creation of a Continental navy. However, not until the success of Washington's commerce raiders did the idea of a navy gain currency in Congress.

On 13 October 1775, Congress authorized the fitting-out of two vessels to carry ten guns each and cruise for three months against British ships. Three members of the Congress—Silas Deane, a well-connected lawyer and merchant from Connecticut; former Royal Navy purser and Charleston merchant Christopher Gadsden of South Carolina; and seafaring merchant John Langdon of New Hampshire—were appointed the Naval Committee to oversee the work. By this act the American navy was born.

Creating a Continental Navy

Samuel Chase of Maryland called launching the Continental Navy "the maddest idea in the World." Other Southern delegates murmured agreement. They complained that the plan was designed to benefit northern interests, for it was in that region that vessels would be fitted-out and manned, and it was to northern ports that prizes would be taken for sale. Southern concern was not without foundation. While working on the committee, Silas Deane wrote to a friend in New London, Connecticut, pointing out to him how admirably situated the town was to receive an American fleet and how "worth while it would be for New London to labor to obtain the advantages of such a Collection of Navigation expending their Money there."

Four days after their appointment the committee members made their report to Congress. Boldly, they greatly exceeded their charge and asked the body to authorize ten ships. That was far beyond Congress's means; nonetheless, they agreed to fit out four ships, twice the original number. To share the added burden of administering this growing fleet, four men were added to the Naval Committee: John Adams of Massachusetts; merchant politician Stephen Hopkins of Rhode Island; merchant Joseph Hewes of North Carolina; and gentleman legislator Richard Henry Lee of Virginia.

As lobbyists for their cause, the Naval Committee was particularly effective. Thanks to the cajoling of fellow delegates, the four warships originally authorized soon grew to eight. More

Joseph Hewes (1730-1779), the son of New Jersey Quakers, became a successful Philadelphia merchant before moving to North Carolina, ca. 1760. Prospering in both business and politics there, he was elected to represent North Carolina in the Continental Congress, 1774-77. A strong proponent of colonial liberty, he was at last persuaded to support outright American independence, and he played a prominent role in Congress. As an active member of the Naval Committee and chairman of the Marine Committee, Hewes was, in practice, the first civilian head of the navy of the United States. Among his contributions was the nomination of John Paul Jones as an officer in the Continental Navy. Hewes returned to Congress in 1779 and literally worked himself to death in the cause of American independence. This miniature portrait of Hewes was painted by Charles Willson Peale in 1776. (Courtesy U.S. Naval Academy Museum)

ships meant more captains, and the committee turned its attention to finding commanders. In a clear case of nepotism, Esek Hopkins (brother to Stephen on the Naval Committee) was appointed commander in chief of the navy. Esek's son, John B. Hopkins, was given command of the *Cabot.* Commodore Abraham Whipple of the Rhode Island State Navy became captain of the *Columbus,* and Silas Deane's brother-in-law, Dudley Saltonstall, ended up commanding the *Alfred.* The only outsider among these friends and relatives was the Pennsylvania captain Nicholas Biddle, who took charge of the *Andrew Doria.* Family connections aside, all of these men were experienced commanders, and some, like Esek Hopkins, had been successful privateersmen during the Seven Years' War.

In Congress, southern delegates looked askance at this Yankee fleet. To allay their fears the Naval Committee decided that Hopkins's first assignment would be to sail south along the coasts of

Virginia, the Carolinas, and Georgia to rid those waters of the British raiders that had been harassing towns near the shore.

By mid-February 1776 Hopkins was ready to sail. His fleet of eight warships–*Cabot, Columbus, Andrew Doria, Alfred, Hornet, Providence, Fly*, and *Wasp*–rendezvoused in the lower Delaware River. Hopkins was instructed to head for Chesapeake Bay where Virginia's former royal governor, John Murray, fourth Earl of Dunmore, had organized a small squadron and was prowling the tidewater area. After dispensing with Dunmore, Hopkins was expected to lay a course along the southern coast, sweeping those waters, then turn north to end the cruise in Narragansett Bay.

Esek Hopkins was hardly a model officer. Irascible, obstinate, and lacking political sensibilities, Hopkins made a foolish decision. Instead of following orders he departed the Chesapeake, abandoned the southern colonies, and set a course directly for Nassau in the Bahamas, which he was informed was lightly defended and promised to be an easy prize.

Hopkins's intelligence was correct. On 3 March 1776 he landed a force of 300 Continental Marines under Captain Samuel Nicholas. With covering fire from the *Providence* and *Wasp* Nicholas's marines easily captured Forts Nassau and Montagu, and took control of New Providence Island. This was the first time American marines went ashore in an amphibious operation. Hopkins took the forts' cannons and ammunition to supply the continental army, and on 17 March the squadron departed the Bahamas and headed for Rhode Island.

Off Point Judith, near the entrance to Narragansett Bay, the Americans encountered the British frigate *Glasgow*. Despite his overwhelming superiority, Hopkins failed to take the *Glasgow* in an embarrassing display of American naval ineptitude.

The failure to follow orders, the botched affair with the *Glasgow*, and Hopkins's general disdain for Congress threw the new navy into a whirlwind of controversy. Hopkins and several of his captains were summoned to Congress to explain their actions. Although he would not be formally dismissed from the service until 1778,

Hopkins was finished as a commander. Yet, the fact that an American fleet had actually gotten to sea and succeeded in attacking the British sent some members of Congress–particularly those from New England–into euphoric notions about what an even larger and better-led fleet might accomplish.

During the previous December, while Hopkins was still fitting out in the Delaware, Congress had created the Marine Committee, a successor to the Naval Committee. Political considerations required that the committee be composed of thirteen members, one from each state. The committee soon prepared a report calling for the construction of thirteen frigates: five of thirty-two guns, five of twenty-eight guns, and three of twenty-four guns. To gain support throughout Congress, construction was distributed amongst key colonies. Four vessels were to be built in Pennsylvania, two each in Massachusetts, New York, and Rhode Island, and one each in New Hampshire, Connecticut, and Maryland.

The act authorizing the building of thirteen frigates was pure hubris. At a time when Congress could barely afford to buy uniforms for Washington's army they were committing millions of dollars to naval construction. Given the scant resources at its disposal, the Continental Congress was attempting to build a preposterous structure on a pitiful foundation. It was neither the first nor last time that the Congress would act with such wild disregard of reality. Although Congress authorized many additional ships during the war, only seven of the original thirteen were even completed, and all were lost during the war.

The Problem of Trade

The issue of trade was one that had troubled the Continental Congress for some time. Trading in the mercantilist world of the eighteenth century was never free. No one knew this better than the American colonists. For nearly two centuries they had benefited–despite some restrictions–from being part of an empire firmly committed to the principle and practice of mercantilism. However, the Revolution created a new set of circumstances that forced the Congress to varied responses.

By the rules of the Association, adopted on 20 October 1774, Congress was pledged neither to trade with Great Britain nor to consume products from that country, effectively breaking the bond of mercantilism that had bound the colonies to the mother country. Nonintercourse and nonconsumption were intended first as a measure to punish the British, but by the summer of 1775, as the Congress moved to organize and equip an army, this policy had become an obstacle that prevented the importation of arms from abroad. On 15 July 1775 Congress forced the first crack in the wall of trade, resolving that vessels bringing in weapons and powder could bring out produce of the same value.

Most members of Congress agreed to the importation of materiel for defense; all agreed, however, that the colonists remained subjects of the King, and open defiance of his laws was not a welcome course. As the months wore on, however, the inexorable drift away from King and Parliament pushed Congress to consider more radical measures. What the colonies needed most was precisely what no mercantilist power could ever accept: free trade. Although they had prospered under the mercantilist system, the colonies quickly turned on their heritage and claimed the right of free trade.

Parliament made its own contribution towards pushing Congress in a more radical direction, passing the Prohibitory Act on 15 December 1775. By this measure, the colonies were removed from the protection of British arms and law, trade with them was prohibited to British merchants, and colonial vessels were subject to seizure as lawful prizes. This unnecessarily harsh measure did much to undermine the position of moderates within Congress, who had been urging caution in the hope of generating a moderate response from London.

Parliament's stiff measures hardened American hearts, and on 23 March 1776 Congress took the countermeasure of authorizing the issuance of letters of marque to privateers sailing against British commercial vessels. Some members of Congress still held back from fear, in the words of John Adams, that new measures might be interpreted as "a bold step to independence." Notwithstanding the tremulous members, on 6 April 1776 Congress opened American ports to all nations save Great Britain.

This was indeed a bold step to independence; so too was the decision on 12 June to appoint John Dickinson, Benjamin Franklin, John Adams, Benjamin Harrison, and Robert Morris a committee to prepare a plan of treaties to be proposed to foreign powers. On 7 September, two months after Congress declared independence, the committee's report was adopted by Congress. Embodied in the plan was the new nation's policy on neutral trade.

Congress laid down four principles that, with little alteration, would govern American policy towards wartime trade for several generations. These were the principles of a nation dependent upon, yet defenseless on, the sea.

The first principle asserted that if either the American states or an ally became involved in war and the other remained neutral, it was the right of the neutral to trade with enemies of the belligerent, not only to and from enemy ports but also between ports of the enemy. The second principle articulated the doctrine that "free ships make free goods"; that is, if a ship is neutral then its cargo is exempt from seizure unless it is specifically enumerated as contraband. The third principle laid down a very precise and narrow definition for contraband: arms, munitions, and horses. Finally, Congress agreed that neutral goods found in enemy ships could be seized.

Having opened American ports, declared independence, and set forth principles of neutral commerce, the American Congress had every intention of pursuing trade. As early as 1775, French vessels from Nantes arrived secretly in the rebellious colonies carrying arms and munitions. In return American vessels brought skins, tobacco, and barrel staves to Nantes. Since France was technically at peace with England, and commerce with the belligerent colonies would violate that peace, these exchanges were shrouded in a complex net of clandestine arrangements for several years. That veil was broken in 1778 when France and the Continental Congress entered into a "Treaty of Amity and Commerce."

Ironically, the treaty of 1778 actually harmed trade between the colonies and France. News of the alliance ruptured the already tenuous peace between France and England, giving the Royal Navy opportunity to lay a blockade on French ports. American trade with Nantes, for example, fell by more than 90 percent.

In addition to trade with France, Americans also made efforts to establish relations with the Netherlands and Spain, both countries with a long history of animosity towards Great Britain. Spain, while fighting against Great Britain, never formally agreed to a treaty relationship with the Continental Congress. The Netherlands, on the other hand, did sign a commercial treaty in 1782.

Despite these efforts, however, American trade with Europe suffered disastrously. The most desired American product, tobacco, rose tenfold in price, a clear indication of its scarcity. Tobacco's scarcity reflected not only the difficulty of eluding the British blockade, on both sides of the Atlantic, but also a precipitous decline in production itself. As a result of enemy raids and general wartime dislocation, American tobacco production fell by nearly 70 percent during the Revolution.

Despite their previous allegiance to the empire, American merchants had become accustomed to trading with England's competitors on the French, Dutch, and Spanish islands throughout the Caribbean. With the coming of war, it was natural to turn to these same islands for trade.

By far the most important of these destinations was the Dutch island of St. Eustatius. Captured by the Dutch from Spain in 1632, St. Eustatius, or Statia, was located only eight miles northwest of British St. Kitts. Unlike that agricultural island, Statia thrived as an international entrepôt. Here, goods from around the world were vended without restrictions, whether they arrived on the busy waterfront

Portsmouth, New Hampshire, established near the mouth of the Piscataqua River in 1630, began to flourish as a seaport after 1730, and particularly after it became the capital of the new royal colony of New Hampshire in 1741. As New Hampshire's principal port, Portsmouth specialized in shipping fish and in supplying white pine timber for Royal Navy masts. In the decades before the Revolution it developed many of the institutions of prosperous American seaports, including a newspaper. Protected by fortifications at the mouth of the Piscataqua, Portsmouth became an important trading, privateering, and naval shipbuilding and outfitting center during the war. In this view from the north side of the Piscataqua, a ship sails downstream past "Strawberry Banke," site of the original settlement. Aquatint engraving by Joseph Des Barres, **The Atlantic Neptune** *(London, 1779). (G.W. Blunt White Library, Mystic Seaport)*

legally or were smuggled. Protected by their claim of neutrality, the commercially opportunistic Dutch authorities allowed a thriving trade during the Revolution. Luxury goods as well as war materiel from Europe were deposited on the island and then transshipped to American ports. And in an incident the British could not forget, Fort Orange on Statia formally acknowledged the American flag with a military salute to the brig-of-war *Andrew Doria* on 16 November 1776. This "first salute" was a symbolic recognition of the American nation that did not sit well with Great Britain.

When the Dutch joined the war against Great Britain the happy arrangements on Statia came to an abrupt end. In January 1781 Admiral George Rodney, commanding the West Indies station, learned that the Netherlands and England were at war. Driven as much by cupidity as strategy, in February 1781 Rodney descended on the island and with slight difficulty

seized it. It was the richest capture of the war. Rodney seized dozens of vessels and cargoes worth millions, several of them British smugglers engaged in trade with the enemy.

Americans also traded with the Spanish colony of Cuba. Until Spain's entry into the war in 1780, Cuba was another neutral haven in the Caribbean. Baltimore and Philadelphia merchants were particularly involved in shipping foodstuffs to Havana and bringing back salt and wine that had come to Cuba from Spain.

While Cuba and St. Eustatius garnered the bulk of clandestine trade in the islands, American ships visited other places as well. The French islands of Guadeloupe and Martinique were popular stops, as were the Spanish ports on Hispaniola. Located just 600 miles east of the Carolinas, Bermuda also became a participant in American trade. Although Congress forbade trade with Great Britain and her possessions, it made an exception in the case of this island, and a considerable amount of smuggling took place there, with American produce being exchanged for British goods.

Nevertheless, the swarm of small American trading vessels was increasingly diminished by the wide-ranging British Royal Navy. The fall of St. Eustatius, a tightening coastal blockade, and

The Dutch West Indian island of St. Eustatius was known as the "Golden Rock" for its role as the foremost Caribbean entrepôt of the eighteenth century. Between 1763 and 1781, Statia enjoyed its greatest period of prosperity, despite a devastating hurricane in 1772. As suggested in this rather crude engraving, the island has peaks at either end, with an open roadstead for shipping on the sheltered western side of the island. By the 1770s warehouses full of products from around the world lined a mile of beach below the town. As many as 3,000 ships called there each year during the American Revolution, when Statia became a major American source for arms and gunpowder. Fort Orange (#1, on the bluff at right center) offered the first foreign salute to an American vessel on 16 November 1776. When Great Britain declared war on the Netherlands, Statia was the first target, and in February 1781 a British fleet captured the island and ended its lucrative contribution to American independence. Engraving by I. Ottavicini, after N. Matraini. (Courtesy The Mariners' Museum, Newport News, Virginia)

American privateers frequently found the risks greater than the rewards. On the evening of 29 May 1782, the sixteen-gun Boston privateer ship Jack, *commanded by John Ropes, was cruising for prizes near Halifax, Nova Scotia, when the twelve-gun HM brig* Observer *engaged her in battle. During a three-hour fight Captain Ropes was killed, and the* Jack *finally surrendered with more than one-third of her crew killed or wounded. This engraving by Robert Dodd was published in London in 1784. (Courtesy Beverly R. Robinson Collection, U.S. Naval Academy Museum)*

Royal Navy victories against French and Spanish forces spelled trouble for American trade. By 1782 marine insurance rates, which before the war had been running at 5 percent, had risen to 50 percent and higher. Shipbuilding was at a near standstill, and exports had fallen to a small fraction of prewar levels.

The War at Sea: Privateers

Shipowners did not always confine themselves to trading. American merchants and mariners had been heavily engaged in privateering during the wars with France, so they moved easily into conducting a similar guerre de course against their former country. Rhode Island began to commission privateers as early as June of 1775, and on 23 March 1776 the Continental Congress authorized privateering. Several weeks later, Congress approved a set of regulations gov-

erning the conduct of American privateers according to the "usages and Customs of the Nations," and continued British practice of requiring the posting of a performance bond upon receipt of a letter-of-marque and of adjudicating cases in admiralty courts.

Because both Congress and the individual states issued letters of marque and reprisal, it is difficult to determine precisely how many privateers were commissioned during the war. A rough estimate based on the incomplete records of the time suggests that approximately two thousand American privateering vessels sailed during the Revolution. Recorded commissions for 1,491 privateers represent the following breakdown:

1775-76	136 vessels	1360 guns
1777	73 vessels	730 guns
1778	115 vessels	1150 guns
1779	167 vessels	2505 guns
1780	228 vessels	3420 guns
1781	449 vessels	6735 guns
1782	323 vessels	4845 guns

Voyage of the Privateer *Revenge*, 1777

Roughly 2,000 American privateers sailed during the American Revolution. An example was the eighty-ton, ten-gun, sloop-rigged vessel *Revenge*, owned in southeastern Connecticut and sailing from the port of Stonington. The *Revenge* was a relatively successful privateer, making numerous cruises between October 1776 and September 1779 and taking at least nineteen prizes.

As indicated by the articles of agreement signed by Captain Joseph Conkling and his crew of about fifty men in January 1777, a privateering voyage was viewed as a cooperative risk-taking venture, like a fishing or whaling voyage. The owners agreed to provide a sound and thoroughly outfitted vessel, and the crew agreed to provide labor and skill within specified rules of conduct and for a specified length of time. Both parties agreed to a proportional return—half to the owners and half to be divided among the crew—of whatever proceeds were awarded by prize court ajudication of enemy vessels captured during the voyage. The crew was encouraged to bravery and risk by provisions awarding extra shares for the most deserving men and offering extra compensation for specified disabling injuries. Here are the *Revenge* Articles:

Made between the owners of the armed Sloop, called the Revenge, of Eighty Tons: fitted from Stonington in the State of Connecticut, of the one part: and the Commander, Officers and men, of the other part: Witnesseth, that the said Owners shall fitt said vessel for the Seas in a War like manner. And provide her with Cannon, Swivils, Small Arms, Cutlasses, Sufficient Ammunition, and Provisions; with a Box of Medicines and every other necessary at their own Expence, for a Cruize against the Enemies of the Thirteen United States of America; and against Such as Shall in a Piratical or hostile manner, infest, invade or ann[o]y these States; Disturb, or molest them in the peaceable Enjoyment of their just rights and Liberties; and against all such as shall aid or assist the said Enemies. In special, to Seize all British property on the Seas; and that the said owners Shall have one half of all prizes, Effects & things: which may be taken. And the Commander, Officers and men the other half. As follows, The Captn Shall have Seven Shares. The first and Second Lieutnt, master & Doctor, four shares each. Two

Masters Boatswains, Gunner and Quarter master Marine Carpenters Two Shares each. Prize masters Two & half shares each. All Lesser Officer not more than one & half shares. Privates one share. Boys half share. All Interprizes at Sea, or on Shore: Shall be Solely Directed by the Captain. There shall be five Dead Shares, to be given to the most Deserving men to be adjudged by the Committee.–If any one in any Engagement, Shall Lose a Leg or an Arm, He shall have Three hundred dollars, out of the whole Effects taken. If any one of the Company shall Mutiny, or raise any Disturbance on board, Game, or Steal, or Imbezzel on or of any prize, whither at Sea or in port. Disobey his Officer; prove a Coward, Desert his Quarters, absent himself, without Leave of his Superior Officer for the Term of Twelve Hours, exercise any Cruelty: or inhumanity in Cold Blood: he shall forfeit his whole share, or shares to the Company And more over be Liable to Such Corporal punishment as the Committee shall think fit to inflict. The Committee shall Consist of the Chief Commanding Officer first and Second Leutnt and Master. The Capt shall have full power to misplace such officers as he shall think proper.–Lastly the said Commander, officers and men here by Enter ourselves on the Cruise for the Term of Four Months if the Cruize Shall Last so Long; or untill Sooner Dischardge.

Journal kept by John Palmer, Marine

As suggested by these entries from the phonetically spelled journal of marine officer John Palmer, the *Revenge* left Stonington in January 1777 and cruised to the south. When the vessel crossed the tropic of Cancer the crew performed the ceremony later used for crossings of the equator in which novice sailors were ritually shaved and sworn in as experienced seamen. The *Revenge* spent several weeks refitting at the French West Indian island of Guadeloupe, where the crew became discontent for lack of pay. After hunting enemy vessels among the islands north of Guadeloupe, the *Revenge* headed back to New England, landing at what is now New Bedford, Massachusetts, exactly four months from the date of her departure.

Left Stonington January the 22 Day–and at 8 am Waide anchor in the harbour and Stood out to See Coarse S with the Wind NW Cleare and Coald and at 8 Pm maide for a Sail to the Estarde but Soone Lost Site of them so Ends these 24 howers. . . .

Friday the 24 Day of January this morning

Reignny and Squally and a Large See a going and We a Lying two under a Trisle all this Twenty fore howers most all hands See Sick on Board and Dull Times–So Ends these 24 howers. . . .

Wednesday the 5 Day of february this Morning Clear with a Lite Brease and our corse ENE and at 2 Pm all handsWas Called to Exercise Everyone to his Quarters [battle stations] and at 4 Pm We Was all Desmist So Ends these 24 howers. . . .

Monday the 10 Day of february this morning Clear and all most Calm We Went to Work to take Cloath out of our mainsail–and at 9 am We made a sail to the Easterd of us and all hands Was called to man the oars and at 1 Pm We Got our mainsail Dun and then Sprung up a brease of Wind and We Set our mainsail and foresail and Jibb and fliing Jibb and Topsail and Topgallantsail and at 2 Pm We handid our Topgallant sail and Shee was a standing for us and Shee firde two guns to the Luard [as a signal] for a friend But We Return No Answer and at 3 Pm we came up with her we Being to the Luard of her We fird a shot at hur & Shee Returnd another and then We Dischargd a Broad Side and Shee gave us two for it–Shee fird about 30 guns at us–and we about 20 Before we Past one another–and Shee fird one Shot through foresail and one through our Jibb and

three through our Topsail and Several Shot huld us but how many we hit her with I Cant Say–We Was a Standing to the Easterd and She Was a Standing to the Westerd–Shee Was A Ship Mounted 14 guns as Near as We Could tell–We hove about and Stood Back for hur But there came up a Squall of wind and Reign which Partid us for this Knight Very Wind and Reignny and a Large See a going So Ends these 24 howers. . . .

Thursday the 13 Day of february this morning our course S and at 7 am We maid a Sail Which prooved to Be the Same Ship–this Day we Crossed Tropic Line and We had full imploy A Shaving the hands and Swairing them So Ends these 24 howers. . . .

Saterday the 1 Day of March this morning Clear and at 6 am See a Sail all hands Was Call to make sail We Set out mainsail and Square Sail and Studdindsail and Jibb and fliing Jibb and Topsail and Water Sail and Wringtail our Course SW and the wind to the Northerd a Smart Brease a going 6 or 7 knots Set our Topgallan We Drawd hur Very fast and at 1 Pm See hur of on the Decks and at 4 Pm Shee hove two and Hawld up her Coarses in order for Battle and at 5 Pm We in Musket Shot of hur and Quick found hur Superior force to us–We gibed and She Wore Round–and give Chaice to us–and fird Several Shot at us and the thirde Shot Shee firde Shee fird away one of our Lanyards and Struck our Starbord bow gun and carde a Way the upper Parte of our Porte Sill— We made all sail for to git Cleare of hur and stood Cource SbW—Till 10 Pm and then We hawld our wind and Stood Cource SE till 11 Pm and then hove two under foresail and So Ends these 24 howers. . . .

Sunday the 16 Day of March a Lite brease and Very Pleasant and at Sunrise We Spoake With [a] Sail and Shee Was a Schooner from Halifax Bound to Domineco Laden with fish and Lumber and We fetched the Capt and maite all hands Except one on Board of us and mr King and mr foster and three of our hands Went on Board and took the charge of hur and at 12 a clock We Both got under Way Stood Cource WNW With a Smart Brease With the Wind at East and all hands in good Spearits We in Company With the Schooner all this afternoon till night—Took hur in the Latd By Observation 16..4 Daye out 54 So Ends these 24 howers. . . .

[At Pointe-à-Pitre, Guadeloupe]
Wednesday the 2 Day of April this morning I took five men With me and Went after Water and at 11 am Returnd on Board With my Water—Simeon Williams Was Very Sick all this Day—and at 7 Pm We Was ordered to heave up Drop further a Sturn and all

hands Wrefusd to till they was allowd Some money for their Shears—the Leutn fish give his Word that We Should have some money Before We Saild and then We hove up and Dropt further a sturn and then come to anchor So Ends these 24 houers—all hands mad on Board & in Confusion this Night. . . .

Wednesday the 9 Day of April this morning Before Day which Was my Watch on Deack I heard Sombody hallow as tho they Was a Drownding a hallowing for Sargt Dening Which We Went and took him up and it Prooved to be Irish Daniel he had Stoling Some things and Went to Rhun a Way We took him up and Beroat him on Board and Put him in Irons and Set a Sentry over him—and at 1 Pm he Was Whipt Nineteen Lashes with the Cat of Ninetails on his Naked hide—and at 11 am We hove up and com to Sail and Stood out inorder for to go the Cruze this after Noon a beating up the Island See Several Sail this after Noon So Ends these 24 houers. . . .

Monday the 21 Day of April this morning We made an Island Colled Sant bartins and two Small Sail Cloast in with the Land We hove about and Stood from them for to Decoy them and thene they hove about & stood after us and at 9 am one of them came up in gun Shot from us We giv Chace to hur and kept fireing on hur Several Broad Sides But We Could Not

Cotch hur Nor fire a Way hur masts So We Chized hur till 2 Pm then hove about and Stood Cource NNW So Ends these 24 howers. . . .

Wednesday the 14 Day of May these 24 howers Coms in Coald and Reighny We a Lying two and at 8 We got under Way stood cource SW and at 10 am Made a Sail a Way to the Luard We made Sail inorder for to Speak hur and at 9 Pm Near a Nof to throug a S[h]ot We giv hur a gun and Shee hove two and We Sent our Barge on Board of hur and Shee Was from Domineco bound to halifax laden with Rhum &c hur Name Was the Venture it all most calm We hove about stood Cource W and the Schooner With us mr havins and mr Parker took the charge of hur and We kept Company all this Night a Lite Brease of Wind So Ends these 24 howers. . . .

Thursday the 22 Day of May this morning a Lite Brease and at 6 am We made Bedford and at 8 am struck a ground and theare Lay till 3 Pm then got aflot and com to Sail and Run up against the town and com to anchor and at 6 Pm Several of us Went ashoar to Drink Som Wine and at 10 Pm We Returnd on Board So Ends these 24 howers
So Ends Four Months

John Palmer Papers, Collection 53, volume 5, G.W. Blunt White Library

Even though the majority of the two thousand or so privateers may well have been poorly armed and inexpertly manned and commanded, they managed to inflict considerable damage on British trade. The principal British marine insurance house, Lloyd's of London, estimated that 3,100 merchant vessels had been snatched by these American rascals. Nine hundred of these unfortunate victims were either recaptured or ransomed, leaving a net loss of 2,200 British merchant ships for a total financial loss of approximately four million pounds.

In the early days of the war most of the American privateers were converted merchant sloops and schooners, small and lightly armed. Although they managed to take a fair number of prizes, especially in the West Indies, they did so at a great cost to themselves, since they were easy prey for Royal Navy patrols. Gradually, as these vessels were eliminated, larger, more heavily armed privateers were constructed to take their place. Commanded by men such as John Foster Williams, Silas Talbot, Joshua Barney, and Jonathan Haraden, these privateers left a mark on British commerce and American history. Romantic tales of high adventure and dramatic sea battles have left a larger-than-life image of these captains.

Privateersmen were motivated by patriotism and profit, not necessarily in that order. The purpose of the voyage was to take prizes and bring them to port for sale. When a prize arrived in port the first task was to libel her, that is, present the vessel and an account of her capture to a local court or admiralty court which might then determine whether or not the vessel was a "good prize." In most instances the judgment went in favor of the privateersmen, although on occasion the case could be complicated when the nationality or ownership of the prize was uncertain. Once libeled, however, the prize and her cargo could go up for auction.

Merchants in ports to which prizes were sent did well. Charleston, South Carolina, was the favorite port of destination for American privateers operating in the lucrative cruising grounds of the West Indies. New England ports, particularly those north of Cape Cod, also benefited. Boston, for example, after the evacuation of British forces in March 1776, became a busy port for both privateers and the Continental Navy.

Fortunes could be made by astute merchants who invested in privateers and then handled the sales of captured vessels and cargo. The combination of profit and patriotism even attracted investors from beyond the seacoast with capital to venture, and on occasion French investors helped finance American privateers. Privateering provided a considerable boost to local economies and often supplied much-needed commodities, albeit at inflated prices, to local markets.

Not everyone appreciated the role of privateers. Men engaged in privateering often sailed close to the legal wind. The very nature of the business was likely to draw individuals not overly concerned with the niceties of law, international or domestic. More than one neutral trader found herself under the guns of an American privateer who ignored her status and then brought her into a "friendly" court where profits outranked justice. In some instances privateersmen recaptured an American vessel and failed to recognize the original owner's claim. Admiralty courts in both the states and the Continental Congress were kept busy adjudicating prize cases brought to them by careless privateersmen.

Aside from the legal and diplomatic nuisances that privateersmen generated there were other reasons to criticize their activities. Privateers were in direct competition with the Continental and state navies. Given the poverty of the states and Congress it was a competition their navies could never win. The story repeated itself again and again at Boston, Providence, Philadelphia, Charleston, any port where privateers and public warships were fitting out and recruiting men. Whoever could pay the most would get the cannon, ballast, provisions, cable, anchors etc. Which ship could offer the promise of the richest prizes at the least risk would have no trouble filling her forecastle. It was a contest privateers always won. Their owners could afford to pay the best price, and when it came to enticing men aboard they could again outbid the public. Not only did privateers offer to share all the proceeds of a voyage with the crew (public warships had to yield a significant portion to the state or congress) but they also provided greater promise of a fat return at less risk. Vessels of the state and Continental navies were, in the words of John Paul Jones, intended to go "in harm's way." Their mission was to find and destroy the enemy. Privateers on the other hand set their courses strictly on profit. They had no desire to meet with any enemy unless the victim was inferior and rich. They avoided all other peril.

Privateering probably helped Americans more than it hurt the British. While the loss of more than 2,000 vessels over the course of the war might seem startling, in point of fact it was quite manageable. The rates at Lloyd's, the main barometer of risks at sea, rose—but not enough to appreciably harm trade. There was little point in worrying about American trade since the Revolution had itself ended the trade. Nor is there any evidence that the Admiralty ever felt the need to divert ships to defend against privateers in numbers sufficient enough to weaken British interests elsewhere.

Evidence suggests that American privateers did not inflict great harm on the British; yet they did bring great help to America. Captured cargoes provided an important source of both civilian and military goods at a time when such resources were in short supply. Furthermore, without the activities of privateers America's major towns, all of which were seaports, would have fallen into dreadful depression.

Lastly, it should be noted that privateers, like the Continental Navy, kept the revolutionaries in touch with Europe. Despite the myriad of problems that followed in their wake each time they entered a neutral port, American privateers were a visible reminder that the American Revolution was an enduring crusade being fought by a people determined to triumph.

The War at Sea: State Navies

Even as Congress planned its Continental Navy, most of the constituent states established their own state navies. Beginning with Rhode Island, nearly all of the thirteen rebellious colonies commissioned warships. On 15 June 1775, Rhode Island Governor Nicholas Cooke ordered Abraham Whipple to take command of the sloop *Katy* and proceed down Narragansett Bay "to encounter expulse expel and resist by Force of Arms, as well by Land and Sea, and also to kill, Slay and Destroy, by all fitting Ways Enterprizes

and Means, whatsoever, all and every such Person and Persons, as Shall attempt or enterprize the Destruction, Invasion Detriment or Annoyance of the Inhabitants of this Colony or Plantation."

In August 1775, Massachusetts took two vessels into state service, and over the course of the war her fleet would number at least fifteen warships. Several of the Massachusetts Navy vessels were commanded by men who later gained fame as privateers, including John Foster Williams, and Captain Jonathan Haraden of the Massachusetts vessel *Tyrannicide*. Connecticut built several row galleys to defend her coastline and, along with a fleet of armed whaleboats, to conduct raids on Loyalist targets across Long Island Sound. The threat of British control of the Delaware River led Pennsylvania to create the largest state navy, numbering at least fifty vessels ranging from small guard boats and row galleys to full-rigged ships, in order to defend the river. Virginia and Maryland, concerned primarily with defending the shores of Chesapeake Bay, launched a variety of small sailing and row vessels. Further southward, North Carolina commissioned a few gunboats to keep Ocracoke Inlet open for commerce, and Georgia manned small vessels to patrol her intricate network of coastal waterways.

For the most part vessels in the state navies never sailed off soundings. Their mission was to remain close to home and defend local interests. Chief among their tasks was to act as a check on Loyalists who might be tempted to harass trade. In that goal they were fairly successful. However, when they were confronted by the Royal Navy they invariably came off considerably worse for the encounter.

The War at Sea: Strategies of a Coastal Conflict

While the state navies provided a coastal defense screen, the states also looked to the Continental Navy to protect their coasts and commerce. But even in its best hours the Continental Navy could not effectively defend the American coast. The navy did manage, with the help of state and privateering forces, to restrain and hinder Loyalist

raiders, and they even dissuaded a few British vessels from ranging too close to shore; nevertheless, whenever the Royal Navy decided to attack in force, as at New York in 1776, Philadelphia in 1777, or Charleston in 1780, its superior numbers and firepower overwhelmed American naval resistance.

Another defensive assignment for the navy was convoy duty. Frequently this meant escorting merchant ships far enough out to sea so that they were out of reach of blockading squadrons. On occasion, naval vessels themselves acted as cargo and dispatch carriers to and from France or the West Indies. On several occasions they ferried American diplomats to their posts overseas and returned them home, as when Captain Lambert Wickes carried Benjamin Franklin to France aboard the *Reprisal* in the fall of 1776. In this regard the Continental Navy provided an important link to the outside world.

Defending a coastline of several thousand miles, acting as the good shepherd for flocks of merchantmen, and ferrying cargo, letters, and diplomats were important jobs that the Continental Navy fulfilled reasonably well. However, such practical service did not suit the more energetic and strategically minded congressmen and naval officers. They understood that a navy is an offen-

After the British invasion force entered New York Bay in July 1776, HMS Phoenix and Rose and the support schooner Tryal were sent up the Hudson River to cut off the supply route to the Continental Army in New York. Without a naval force to challenge British ships on the Hudson, General Washington resorted to fire ships to drive the enemy frigates downriver. On 16 August 1776 several fire ships and armed row galleys attacked HMS Phoenix (left), Rose (right), and Tryal (far right). This and a later fire-ship attack were repelled with little damage, and the Royal Navy retained control of the lower Hudson until British forces left New York in 1783. Dominic Serres painted this view in 1777, based on a sketch by Sir James Wallace, commander of HMS Experiment. (M.S.M. 49.804; Claire White-Peterson photo)

sive weapon by its very nature, and they were determined to use it offensively.

In American waters the navy's first offensive action, the expedition to Nassau, had brought mixed results. However, in 1776 cruises by the *Andrew Doria* under Nicholas Biddle and the *Providence* with Captain John Paul Jones proved very successful in taking a number of enemy prizes in the waters between Bermuda and Newfoundland. Such successes were attributable both to the verve of the captains in command and to the slow reaction of the Royal Navy in moving to defend trade.

Although the Royal Navy could muster at least 800 ships, since the end of the Seven Years' War in 1763 it actually had declined in size and effectiveness. Like most British officials, the Lords of the Admiralty had underestimated the determination of the Americans and their ability to carry on a revolution. As Congress had warned the British people in July 1775, "We can retire beyond the reach of your navy, and without any sensible diminution of the necessities of life, enjoy a luxury, which from that period you will want–the luxury of being free." Even at sea, the rebellious Americans showed their aggressive determination. The capture of supply vessels in Massachusetts Bay and the fall of Nassau were lessons.

Early in 1776 British forces abandoned Boston. Still believing that a bold, decisive strike might subdue the rebellious spirit of the colonies, the ministry decided on an invasion of New York, both by sea and overland from Canada. The British fleet arrived in New York Bay in July of 1776, and the Regular troops drove Washington's Continental Army north of Manhattan Island with relative ease.

The one significant event in the futile Continental resistance to the occupation of New York was the introduction of the submarine for undersea warfare. In 1775, David Bushnell, an inventive Yale graduate from Saybrook, Connecticut, had devised a barrel-like one-man vessel. Powered by a hand-cranked propellor, Bushnell's *Turtle* was designed to submerge, approach an anchored enemy warship, and screw an explosive torpedo with clockwork detonator to its bottom. After trials in Boston Harbor, Bushnell brought the *Turtle* to New York to attack the assembled British fleet in the summer of 1776. This primitive submarine performed well, but the protective copper sheathing on British warship bottoms foiled the operator's attempts to attach the torpedo. Bushnell would try again in 1777 against the British fleet in the Delaware River, but he never succeeded in sinking a British vessel, despite the ability of his *Turtle* to operate underwater.

The defeated Continental Army moved north to the Highlands, retaining control of most of the Hudson River. However, British forces held New York City as a strategic naval base until the end of the war. But in the process they alienated the port's Loyalists, who had been among the strongest supporters of the Crown in America. The privations and restrictions of living under occupation converted many Loyalists to silent rebels.

At the same time as the capture of New York City, one of the most important naval engagements of the American Revolution took place two hundred miles north on Lake Champlain, the long, narrow body of water that reaches a hundred miles into New York from the Canadian border south of Montreal. This had been a military pathway during the Seven Years' War, and in the spring of 1776 General Guy Carleton, commanding British forces in Canada, was preparing to use it again. To coordinate with the invasion of New York and a push up the Hudson River, he planned an invasion down Lake Champlain to the Hudson. Control of the lake was essential, so Carleton set to building a squadron at St. Johns, near the northern end of the lake.

To challenge the British, General Benedict Arnold (a former Connecticut shipmaster and the same officer who would later betray the American cause) was dispatched to Fort Ticonderoga, at the southern end of the lake. Under his direction a variety of small vessels were built at Skenesborough, including several oar-powered gundalows.

By late August 1776 both the British and American squadrons were on the lake. Arnold had approximately fifteen vessels, one sloop, two schooners, three galleys, one cutter, and eight gundalows. Carleton's force was considerably larger and better armed. Because of his proximity to the St. Lawrence River, he had been able to disassemble, then bring overland and reassemble, several powerful vessels including the three-masted sloop of war *Inflexible* armed with eighteen twelve-pounders.

On 23 September Arnold took his squadron to an anchorage on the west shore of the lake at Valcour Island. On 11 October Carleton's fleet, under the command of Captain Thomas Pringle, hove into sight. After a ferocious engagement Arnold ordered his men to withdraw. The British pursued, mauling the Americans. Just when Pringle thought he had the Americans trapped Arnold made a brilliant escape in the night. The British continued the pursuit, and by the end of the day on 13 October the Americans had been completely defeated and their fleet sunk.

Although Arnold was forced to retreat, his stand at Valcour Island may well have saved the American Revolution. Had Arnold not contested Carleton for control of the lake, the British commander could have moved rapidly south, taken Fort Ticonderoga, and been in Albany before winter. Had that been the case the British would have effectively severed New England from the rest of the states. By delaying Carleton's advance, Arnold gained a year for the Americans, and when the British army under General John Burgoyne advanced again in 1777 it would suffer a stunning defeat at Saratoga, ending the effort to divide New England from the rest of the states along the Hudson River-Lake Champlain line.

As it became clearer that the Americans were not about to lay down their arms in the face of British might, the ministry sought to isolate and gradually strangle resistance. The Admiralty dispatched vessels to establish a blockade of the American coast in 1776, and it organized convoys to protect British merchantmen on the high seas. The blockade was never entirely successful in sealing the coast, and some Continental captains, such as Abraham Whipple, continued to take prizes as the war progressed. Nevertheless, cruises close to home proved increasingly dangerous for Continental ships, as they faced the dual danger of escaping to sea and then trying to run the gauntlet and return home at voyage's end.

Late in 1776, a British fleet appeared off the Rhode Island coast, and before the end of the year Newport had fallen and the American refuge of Narragansett Bay lay under British naval control. Six months later a British amphibious force sailed up Chesapeake Bay and disembarked to attack Philadelphia by land, while a naval force subdued the Delaware River fortifications. By October 1777 British forces occupied the American capital while continuing to hold the other principal seaports of New York and Newport.

In 1778 Admiralty strategy turned to a series of amphibious raids on the New England coast. By far the worst defeat of the war for the Continental Navy took place in Penobscot Bay, about 150 miles northeast of Boston midway along the coast of Maine. Although the region was remote, in 1779 it attracted British attention as a possible Loyalist refuge, as a base from which to secure timber supplies for the Royal Navy at Halifax, and as a location from which they might harass the rest of the New England coast. In mid-June Captain Henry Mowatt and General Francis McLean arrived from Nova Scotia with a combined force to occupy

Bagaduce, a small peninsula jutting into the bay.

In Boston the news of the British move into mid-coast Maine created alarm. The danger was too great and too close to be ignored. The Massachusetts General Court instructed the state Board of War to prepare an expedition to dislodge the enemy. As part of the effort the State asked for help from the Continental Navy.

To assist Massachusetts, Congress ordered Captain Dudley Saltonstall of the frigate *Warren* to join the expedition, along with the Continental sloop *Providence* and the fast brig *Diligent*. These three Continental warships were joined by two vessels from the Massachusetts State Navy, *Active* and *Tyrannicide*, the New Hampshire state navy vessel *Hampden*, and at least 16 privateers. Also along were several transports carrying militia under the command of General Solomon Lovell.

On 25 July the American fleet dropped anchor off Bagaduce, but the American captains did little more than argue and delay for three weeks. Finally, as they prepared to attack on the morning of 13 August, lookouts aloft spotted several sail tacking into the bay. It was Admiral Sir George Collier with a relief squadron out of New York.

Unaccustomed to facing the guns of His Majesty's men of war, the American privateers-men attempted to run, followed by the state and Continental ships. Within a few hours the shores of Penobscot Bay were littered with American ships deliberately run aground and destroyed so that their crews could scurry away overland. The entire American fleet of warships, privateers, and transports was lost. Not until 7 December 1941 would the American navy experience a loss as great as that suffered in Penobscot Bay.

The disaster down east was the greatest and last attempt by the Continental Navy to do anything by way of naval squadrons. The defeat made a shambles of an already weakened navy.

"A View of the New England Arm'd Vessels in Valcure Bay on Lake Champlain, 11 October 1776," by C. Randle, depicts General Benedict Arnold's fifteen-vessel flotilla anchored at Valcour Island to intercept the British invasion force as it moved south on the lake. Arnold's fleet included the schooner Royal Savage *(center), the sloop* Enterprise *(right), and eleven gunboats. During a two-day running fight, Arnold's fleet was destroyed. However, by delaying the British invasion through the fall of 1776, Arnold's freshwater navy foiled the British strategic effort to sever the ties between New England and the rest of the United States. (Courtesy National Archives of Canada, Ottawa, C13202)*

When Admiral Sir George Collier's squadron sailed up Penobscot Bay in August of 1779, it trapped an American fleet of more than forty vessels, composed of Continental warships, vessels from the Massachusetts and New Hampshire state navies, at least sixteen privateers, and twenty transports. The Americans had been preparing to attack a British outpost at Bagaduce. However, outgunned, unwilling to fight, and unable to escape the British relief squadron, the American force scattered, and all of the vessels were lost in this naval disaster. This engraving of the action at Bagaduce, after a painting by Des Barres, was published in the Naval Chronicle, *1814. (M.S.M. 61.711)*

Since the southern colonies produced goods not found elsewhere in the empire, they had always been valued over the middle and northern colonies. In addition, it was widely believed in London that these colonies were a resource of Tory strength. Consequently, in 1778 the ministry decided to focus on the south. Philadelphia and Newport were abandoned so that forces could concentrate southward. In December 1778, a British amphibious force captured the port of Savannah, Georgia, and the next year drove off a combined American army and French navy expedition attempting to recapture it. The next British target was Charleston, South Carolina.

Late in 1779, anticipating the attack on Charleston, Congress dispatched nearly all that was left of the Continental Navy–the three frigates *Boston, Providence,* and *Queen of France* and the sloop *Ranger*–to the city to help in its defense. After a long siege, the city fell on 12 May 1780. In the defeat, the *Queen of France* was scuttled and the remaining ships were captured. The defeat at Charleston just about finished the Continental Navy in American waters. Indeed, without the entry of France into the war, the expansion of

the naval conflict to the Caribbean and European waters, and the arrival of a French fleet under the Comte de Grasse in American waters in 1781, the British fleet would have sailed the American coast with impunity.

The War at Sea: The Continental Navy in European Waters

Still smarting from defeat in the Seven Years' War, the French saw the strategic value of helping the Americans smite the British. For the first two years of the Revolution the French held back from any official alliance. Nonetheless, in a variety of clandestine ways they provided assistance to the rebels. One such way was to offer safe haven to Continental ships. The *Reprisal,* Captain Lambert Wickes, was the first Continental vessel to arrive in European waters. On 24 October 1776 Congress dispatched the *Reprisal* to carry the American

Vessels of the Continental Navy performed a variety of duties, from engaging Royal Navy warships to raiding British commerce, carrying diplomats and dispatches, and even transporting military supplies. The Continental Navy brigantine Lexington *began her American service as the* Wild Duck *when she was purchased at St. Eustatius for the Maryland Committee of Safety. After arriving at Philadelphia with a cargo of gunpowder in March 1776 she was bought, renamed, and refitted with fourteen guns for Continental Navy service. After several successful cruises off the American coast, the* Lexington *made a voyage to the Caribbean for a cargo of military supplies. On her return, in December 1776, she was captured by HMS* Pearl. *However, the* Lexington's *crew, secured below decks, talked the prize crew into freeing them in exchange for rum, then recaptured the vessel. In February 1777 the* Lexington *departed for France and joined the Continental brigs* Reprisal *and* Dolphin *for a successful raid on British shipping around Ireland. The Royal Navy chased the Continental brigs into French ports, where they remained until France—still neutral and under diplomatic pressure from Britain—expelled them in September 1777. The* Lexington *lay becalmed off Ushant when the Royal Navy cutter* Alert *(right) attacked her on 19 September. With her rigging badly damaged and her powder supply exhausted, the* Lexington *(left) surrendered. Painting by Thomas Whitcombe. (Courtesy Peabody Essex Museum, Salem, Massachusetts)*

Commissioners, Benjamin Franklin, Silas Deane, and Arthur Lee to France. After completing that mission Wickes took his vessel on a cruise off the coasts of France and Spain, capturing several prizes and sending them into French ports. The British authorities howled in protest while the French evaded the issue of proper neutral behavior. In the months to follow, violations of neutral behavior by the French became even more egregious as more Continental ships poked into European waters to torment British trade and to use French ports as havens for themselves and their prizes.

American naval activities in Europe and French connivance contributed mightily to the growing breach between England and France. After the victory at Saratoga in the fall of 1777 demonstrated American capacity to achieve independence, the French Court at Versailles decided to ally formally with the rebellious colonists. On 6 February 1778 the treaty was signed. Eight days later in Quiberon Bay the Continental sloop of war *Ranger* under the command of Captain John Paul Jones exchanged an official salute to the flag with the *Robuste*, flagship of the French Admiral Lamotte-Piquet.

Jones's arrival in France, coincident with the alliance, offered new opportunities for the Continental Navy. No longer would Continental captains have to navigate through a diplomatic maze trying to explain their belligerent presence in a neutral country. Under these new

John Paul Jones

"I profess myself a Citizen of the World," wrote the man known as America's greatest naval hero of the American Revolution. He was born in 1747 and christened John Paul, the son of an estate gardener in Kirkbean, on the west coast of Scotland. As one of a large family of children with few prospects for advancement at home, John Paul went to sea at age thirteen as an apprentice mariner. Coming from such humble origins, and sailing from a relatively small outport of the British Empire, he left little evidence of his early career, much of which has been reconstructed from scattered references in his later correspondence.

For three years seaman John Paul made annual voyages from Whitehaven, Scotland, to the British West Indies and Virginia (where his brother had a tailoring business in the port of Fredericksburg), on a Scottish brig carrying English goods out and American products home—sugar to Virginia, and tobacco to England. By the age of seventeen he was third mate of a slave ship, spending several years in this service, although he considered it an "abominable trade." In 1768 he was traveling home from the Caribbean as passenger in a brig when the officers died of disease. Because he knew how to navigate, John Paul took command, arrived safely, and earned himself a perma-

Captain John Paul Jones (1747-1792), an accurate mezzotint depiction by J.M. Moreau le jeune, engraved in Paris in 1780. (Courtesy Library of Congress)

nent captain's berth at age twenty-one.

Captain John Paul was extremely competent as a navigator, sailor, and supercargo in charge of buying and selling cargo, but he was also extremely temperamental. On his second voyage he flogged the ship's carpenter for some offense and later had to defend himself in court. In 1772 he moved up to command of a London ship in the transatlantic trade, and on his second voyage, in 1773, he had a lethal run-in with his crew at Tobago. When the crew demanded advance pay, Jones refused; then he killed their leader when that sailor threatened him. Warned by friends on the island that he

would not get a fair trial, Captain Paul fled and arrived in Virginia as "John Jones."

"Jones" hoped to retire ashore in "calm contemplation and Poetic ease" in America, but he could find neither the woman nor the Virginia estate to fulfill this plan. With the outbreak of war in 1775, Jones went to Philadelphia and offered his services to the Continental Navy, now calling himself John Paul Jones. Joseph Hewes, the partner of a Scottish acquaintance of Jones, was a member of the Continental Congress and the Marine Committee. In December 1775 Hewes secured an appointment for Jones as lieutenant aboard the Continental ship *Alfred*. Like Hewes and many other Americans at this stage, Jones had no desire for American independence. Fighting for "Liberty" in the colonies he accepted a subordinate officer's rank; consequently, after the Declaration of Independence he would find himself junior to many less competent officers in the navy's seniority list.

Jones demonstrated his competence during the expedition against New Providence, but he also demonstrated his penchant for criticizing his superiors—often accurately, but never tactfully. In May 1776 he was given command of the sloop *Providence* and successfully raided British commerce off the American coast. That fall he took command of a small squadron with the *Alfred* as his flagship. Thinking strategically, if unrealistically, Jones proposed capturing the Island of St. Helena in the South Atlantic and intercepting the British East India merchant ships there to inflict real economic hardship on Great Britain. Instead, Congress ordered him on a raid against Nova Scotia commerce, which he conducted with skill. "I admire the spirited conduct of little Jones," wrote Robert Morris of the Marine Committee, and Jones made a spirited effort to obtain command of one of the new American frigates under construction.

But in June 1777 Congress ordered him to take command of the new sloop of war *Ranger*, being completed in Portsmouth, New Hampshire. Jones struggled to find a crew, and finally sailed for France in November. There, he tried to obtain a larger vessel even as he made great changes to the *Ranger*'s rig and arrangements in his tireless efforts to perfect the performance of every ship and crew he commanded.

"When an Enemy thinks a design against them is improbable, they can always be surprised and attacked with advantage," wrote Jones as he prepared to sail in the *Ranger* to carry the war into British home waters. After raiding Whitehaven, Scotland–the first foreign incursion on British soil in 110 years–Jones attempted to take an earl hostage in order to compel release of

American naval prisoners of war. After crossing to Ireland and capturing HMS *Drake* in an hour-long battle, Jones returned to France in May 1778. He was received with a mixture of acclaim for his daring and controversy over his crew's largely unwarranted complaints about his treatment of them and their lack of pay.

Jones then spent a terribly frustrating nine months seeking a new command. The American minister in France, Benjamin Franklin, helped and cautioned him by turns, but politics and Jones's irascible nature worked against him, even though his abilities were sorely missed at sea in this dark period for the Continental Navy. As he searched for a vessel in France, Jones wrote, "I wish to have no Connection with any Ship that does not sail *fast*, for I intend *to go in harm's way. . . .*" He also looked to the future, proposing, "When the Enemies land force is once conquered and expelled the Continent, our [Navy] will rise as if by Enchantment, and become, within the memory of Persons now living, the wonder and Envy of the World. . . ."

After a great deal of negotiation with the French, in 1779 Jones was given use of the *Duc de Duras*, an old French East Indiaman. In honor of his friend Benjamin Franklin (author of *Poor Richard's Almanac*), who had been very helpful in getting the *Duc*, Jones renamed his vessel *Bonhomme Richard*. Jones championed a land-sea inva-

sion of Liverpool led by General Lafayette and himself, but that plan fell through. Jones was then slated to lead a diversionary raid while French and Spanish fleets defeated the British fleet to open the way for an invasion.

In August 1779 Jones set out in the *Bonhomme Richard*, accompanied by several French ships, to raid English waters. Even as he departed, the combined French-Spanish operation was falling apart due to disease in the French fleet.

Jones took prizes and attempted to capture Leith, Scotland, in retaliation for British raids on American seaports. Driven off by bad weather, he soon encountered a convoy of naval stores, bound from the Baltic to England, under the protection of HMS *Serapis*.

The *Bonhomme Richard* and *Serapis* maneuvered slowly to gain an advantage in the light winds. When several of his guns exploded, Jones realized that he could only win by grappling and boarding the more heavily armed *Serapis*. The *Serapis* tried to stand off and win with cannon fire, but Jones succeeded in closing with the *Serapis* and fighting rail-to-rail for three hours into the night.

In the midst of the battle Captain Richard Pearson of the *Serapis* called over to Jones, "Sir, Do you strike?" Jones is reputed to have delivered the immortal reply, "I have not yet begun to fight." Although British can-

Paul Jones Shooting a Sailor who had attempted to strike his Colours in an Engagement, from the Original Picture by John Collet, in the possession of Carrington Bowles, *represents the English impression of Jones as a piratical renegade. In reality, Jones always dressed in a formal naval uniform, and he never shot a sailor–although he did level a cowardly gunner with a thrown pistol during the battle with HMS* Serapis. *Despite the facts, circulation of such exaggerated images colored popular opinion about Captain John Paul Jones for more than a century. (Courtesy The Mariners' Museum, Newport News, Virginia)*

non shot gutted the *Richard*, and both crews had to stop firing for a time to extinguish fires, Jones's inflexible will prevailed, even when some of his crew were ready to give up. Nearly half the crew on each ship was killed or wounded, but American sharpshooters cleared the British deck, and an American hand grenade caused such an explosion that a short time later it was Pearson, not Jones, who struck his colors in surrender.

The badly damaged *Bonhomme Richard* sank a few days later, so Jones arrived in the Netherlands as commander of the *Serapis*, not returning to France until the new year. When he arrived he was already famed throughout Europe as Paul Jones, a great hero in France, a great villain in England. Enjoying the acclaim, he began to call himself Paul Jones and cut a gay figure in the salons and theaters of Paris.

But Jones was wed to naval service. Despite numerous affairs in America and France with women who considered him "the most agreeable sea-wolf one could wish to meet with," he never married. Although he was as irresistible to women as they were to him, he never formed a warm bond with any of his crews. He was an uncommonly solicitous officer when it came to the health and compensation of his crews. Nevertheless, he was almost universally detested by those who served under him. Midshipman Fanning of the *Bonhomme Richard* described Jones as "passionate to the highest degree one minute, and the next ready to make a reconciliation." Lieutenant Lunt, a valuable officer who made several voyages with Jones, wrote, "I would Sooner Go in a Warlike Ship with Capt Jones than any Man Ever I Saw if I Could be treated with Respect, But I Never Have Been." Abigail Adams described Jones as "small of stature, well proportioned, soft in his speech, easy in his address, polite in his manners, vastly civil, understands all the etiquette of a lady's toilette as perfectly as he does the mast, sails and rigging of his ship. Under all this appearance of softness he is bold, enterprising, ambitious and active." Her husband, John Adams, like many men, reacted to Jones's undisguised ambition. Adams described him as "the most ambitious and intriguing officer in the American Navy. Jones has Art, and Secrecy, and aspires very high. . . . Eccentricities and Irregularities are to be expected from him–they are in his Character, they are visible in his Eyes. His voice is soft and still and small, his eye has keeness and Wildness and softness in it." To Jones's misfortune, his peerless talents and vision for the navy were never fully realized because of the figure he cut among his subordinates, his peers, and the men who conferred power.

Jones returned to America in 1781, in command of the sloop of war *Ariel*, laden with supplies for Washington's army. Although his command was sailing more as transport than warship, Jones did try to defeat a more heavily armed British privateer, which surrendered and then sailed away before the Americans could board it. This was Jones's last action of the American Revolution.

Political intrigue still followed Jones; yet Congress gave him command of the United States' first ship of the line, the *America*, then under construction at Portsmouth. Jones strained to get the ship completed, only to have Congress vote in 1782 to give the ship to France in compensation for a French ship sunk in Boston Harbor. He made his last cruise of the war as a guest on a French ship in fleet maneuvers in the Caribbean. More than his adopted country, France recognized his military talents and in 1782 decorated him with l'Ordre du Mérite Militaire, which accorded him the right, thereafter, to call himself Chevalier Paul Jones.

In 1783 Jones obtained a commission to travel to France to collect the prize money still due American naval crews. Completing that assignment in 1785, he met John Ledyard, who proposed an expedition to the Northwest Coast of North America to collect sea-otter pelts for the Asian market. Jones agreed, hoping to open trade with Japan, but financial and political considerations quashed the venture.

Jones returned to New York

in 1787 to defend the prize claims and to seek the rank of admiral, which was not forthcoming. Yet he continued to make far-sighted recommendations for a U.S. Navy and for a proper training system for its officers. He returned to Europe to settle a controversy over American prizes sent into Danish ports during the war, and in 1788 was offered a commission in the Russian Navy to fight the Turks in the Black Sea. As Kontradmiral Pavel Ivanovich Jones he spent four months of "vexation" trying to break the Turkish blockade of the Liman (mouth) of the Dnieper River. With his professional efforts thwarted by unreliable subordinates and an unclear chain of command, Jones had only partial success, though demonstrating again his bravery and boldness. Hoping to be named to another important post in the Russian Navy, Jones settled in St. Petersburg, where he advised Catherine the Great on improvements to the Russian Navy and encouraged Russia to recognize the United States. Jones's Russian career ended in 1789, when he was falsely charged with rape.

Jones returned to France in 1789, and for two years he lived a hollow existence. Thomas Carlyle described him: "In faded naval uniform, Paul Jones lingers visible here; like a wine-skin from which the wine is drawn. Like the ghost of himself!" He schemed unsuccessfully to find a command worthy of his skills, and he proposed ways of saving American sea-

men enslaved by the Algerians. The American Congress agreed to name him American consul to Algeria, but the appointment came too late. On 18 July 1792 Captain John Paul Jones succumbed to kidney infection, jaundice, and pneumonia at the age of forty-five.

The French gave Jones a proper funeral, but he was buried in an unmarked grave in Paris. Only long after his death was he recognized as the most capable and distinguished naval hero of the American Revolution, in many ways the spiritual father of the U.S. Navy. Finally, in 1905, his body was exhumed, examined, and transported with highest honors to his adopted land, where he was reinterred in a monumental tomb in the crypt of the chapel at the U.S. Naval Academy in Annapolis, Maryland.

conditions they might now expect enhanced and open assistance from the arsenals of their ally. These welcome developments set the stage for the most famous, if not most important, chapter in the history of the Continental Navy—the cruises of John Paul Jones in command of *Ranger* and *Bonhomme Richard*.

On 10 April 1778 the eighteen-gun Continental sloop-of-war *Ranger* departed Brest, France, and headed north to cruise the Irish Sea. Although Jones managed to take several prizes, he desired above all else to strike an even more dramatic blow at the British and do what no enemy had done in more than 100 years: land on English soil.

Jones's target was Whitehaven, Scotland, on the Solway Firth, a port near his birthplace, which he had sailed out of as a boy. Shortly before midnight on 22 April Jones led a party of forty men into the harbor. As the alarm went up, Jones and his men managed to set fire to a few ships before with-drawing. Although they accomplished very little in the way of actual damage, the mere fact that an enemy had stepped on English soil humiliated the Royal Navy and caused an uproar in Parliament.

Jones set a course across the Irish Sea for Belfast lough, where he planned to engage HMS *Drake*. With great stealth Jones brought *Ranger* into the lough. The British captain hesitated, allowing Jones to approach within close range before revealing his true identity and letting loose with a broadside. In an hour the *Ranger* had shattered and defeated HMS *Drake* within the waters of a British port.

Upon his return to France from the Irish Sea, Jones was feted as a hero. Saluted in the salons of Paris, he spent his time ashore lobbying the American commissioners and the French Marine for a larger ship. It took months to accomplish, but finally in February 1779, thanks to French largesse, Jones took command of an old East Indiaman, *Duc de Duras*, which in honor of his patron Benjamin Franklin he rechristened *Bonhomme Richard*.

It took six months to complete the refitting of the *Bonhomme Richard*, but finally on 14 August, in company with six other French and American vessels, she sailed from Isle de Croix, heading up along the rugged west coast of Ireland.

Gradually the squadron diminished in size as captains decided to go off on their own. Jones continued across the top of Scotland and in company with his remaining consorts, the *Alliance, Pallas,* and *Vengeance,* bore south along the east coast of England. His attempt to capture and ransom Leith, Scotland, in retaliation for British assaults on American ports, was only prevented by a windshift.

Some miles off the Yorkshire coast Jones interrogated a local fisherman and learned that the Baltic fleet was due soon. On 23 September, about three in the afternoon, a cry came from aloft that several sail were coming down from the northeast on a heading bringing them towards the Americans. It was the Baltic fleet, forty-one merchantmen on their way home to England with a valuable cargo of naval stores for the Royal Navy.

Jones's appearance was not a surprise to the convoy commander, Captain Richard Pearson of the frigate *Serapis*. Both he and Captain Thomas Piercy, commander of the other escort vessel, HMS *Countess of Scarborough*, had been warned that the Americans were in the area. Pearson signaled his convoy to run for cover while the *Serapis* and *Countess* cleared for battle.

As the two enemies closed, Jones understood that he was at the disadvantage. The *Serapis* was newer, faster, and better armed. Pearson's best tactic was to range close and batter the *Richard* to pieces. Jones's only hope was to grapple, board, and fight it out hand to hand. In this deadly ballet, Jones and Pearson showed themselves to be able seamen. The *Serapis* tried to "cross the T," that is, cut across her bow or stern and fire unopposed to sweep the deck from end to end. She almost succeeded, but a slight error of the helmsman brought her too close and her bowsprit tangled with the *Richard*'s mizzen. Momentum swung the two vessels close enough so that Jones's crew could heave their grappling hooks. The two vessels were locked together.

For more than two hours the *Richard* and *Serapis* fought with cannon and small arms, shattering both vessels and littering their decks with wounded and dead men numbering nearly half of each crew. Meanwhile, the *Vengeance* kept away at a safe distance and never engaged a British vessel, while

Off Flamborough Head on the evening of 25 September 1779, the Bonhomme Richard *and HMS* Serapis *fought a classic ship-to-ship duel for more than three hours. In this slightly inaccurate painting by Lieutenant William Elliott of the Royal Navy, ca. 1780, the* Richard *is shown crossing the bow of the* Serapis, *at which point the ships became entangled and locked side by side. The* Serapis *then dropped anchor and the battle continued for two more hours. In this view the* Serapis *has lost her mainmast, although that actually occurred at the very end of the battle and caused Captain Pearson to surrender. In the background the British convoy flees to safety while the French frigate* La Pallas *defeats HMS* Countess of Scarborough. *At right the American frigate* Alliance, *commanded by the unstable Captain Pierre Landais, appears to rake the* Serapis's *stern, whereas in reality the* Alliance's *few broadsides did more damage to the* Richard *than the* Serapis. *(Courtesy U.S. Naval Academy Museum)*

the *Pallas* was fully engaged with the *Countess of Scarborough.* The one vessel of Jones's squadron to approach was the *Alliance,* under command of French Captain Pierre Landais. Either a fool or a scoundrel, Landais circled the *Richard* and *Serapis,* firing into the former, and then hauled away.

During the battle Captain Pearson reportedly called across to ask if Jones was prepared to strike his colors in surrender, to which Jones retorted "I have not yet begun to fight." Although the *Richard* was slowly sinking under him, Jones continued the battle, and at last Pearson relented and lowered the colors on the nearly dismasted *Serapis*. Not long after the *Countess* lowered her flag as well.

Jones ordered the squadron to sail for the Continent. Along the way the *Bonhomme Richard,* damaged beyond salvage despite her victory, was abandoned and slipped beneath the waves at eleven in the morning of 25 September 1779.

Jones's triumph was celebrated in France and America, while the British portrayed Jones as a pirate and honored Captain Pearson as a hero for sacrificing his ship to save the Baltic fleet. Indeed, although it was a rare feat of pluck and courage in an otherwise mediocre American performance at sea during the war, the victory of the *Bonhomme Richard* over HMS *Serapis* came ultimately to represent the entire American naval effort in the popular imagination. It was also

John Paul Jones's last significant action as an American captain. Returning to America in command of a ship laden with military supplies, he was promoted to command a new ship of the line under construction in Portsmouth, New Hampshire, and did not return to sea before the war's end.

The Navy and Independence

Aside from a few spectacular victories, the real story of the Continental Navy is that it did not much affect the outcome of the war. While it may well be true that the American Revolution was decided at sea, it was decided by the great fleets of Britain, France, and Spain. In engagements in the waters of the West Indies, as well as Europe and the Indian Ocean, these nations struggled over control of the routes of commerce. The strain on Great Britain to defend her worldwide empire was enormous. In the end her leaders decided that the expense was simply too great.

In the waters of the West Indies as well as Europe and the Indian Ocean the fleets of these nations fought for control of the seas. For the cause of American independence, however, the most important battle took place off the Virginia Capes.

Following the capture of Charleston, General Charles Cornwallis had been left in command of the British army in the south with instructions to consolidate control over South Carolina and Georgia. Instead of remaining in the area Cornwallis decided to invade Virginia. By late June he had marched his army into the Old Dominion and taken up a position at Yorktown, a port on the York River near Williamsburg, which presumably could be supported by the British fleet from New York.

Cornwallis's situation was serious. American and French forces moved to trap him with his back to the sea. His only hope of reinforcement or escape was the British fleet at New York. In the meantime, through an extraordinary turn of good luck, the French fleet under the command of the Comte de Grasse arrived off the Chesapeake.

Naval action continued long after the British surrender at Yorktown. In April 1782 Philadelphia merchants sent a convoy down the Delaware River under the protection of the letter-of-marque ship Hyder Ally, commanded by the twenty-two-year-old privateer and naval officer Joshua Barney. Off Cape May on 18 April, the flotilla was approached by HMS Quebec and the sloop of war General Monk, formerly the American privateer General Washington. Captain Barney sent the convoy back upriver to safety (background). In maneuvering to fight, the armed American ship General Greene ran ashore on Cape May (right) and the brig Charming Sally grounded on a shoal (left center). While the Quebec maneuvered around this shoal (left) the General Monk ran down on the Hyder Ally (center). Overmatched by the British ship, Barney let the British captain hear him give intentionally misleading orders to the helmsman so the British ship unwittingly fouled its bowsprit in the American rigging, locking it in position to be raked repeatedly by American broadsides. In a twenty-six-minute battle, the Hyder Ally defeated and captured the General Monk. Barney commissioned Louis Phillipe Crepin to paint this view of the action in 1802. (Courtesy U.S. Naval Academy Museum)

Initially, the French fleet provided logistical support by transporting parts of Washington's army down Chesapeake Bay to beseige Cornwallis. Then, on 5 September, after several days of maneuvering, the French and British fleets met off the Virginia Capes. Although unable to achieve a decisive victory, de Grasse inflicted enough damage on the British to force them to withdraw. Cornwallis's situation was hopeless. While the French and British struggled offshore, Washington moved his Continental troops and a large number of French soldiers into positions around Cornwallis. After a prolonged siege, on 19 October 1781 the British laid down their arms.

The surrender at Yorktown was a devastating blow to the British. "Oh, God! It is all over," lamented Lord North. Although the British still held Charleston and New York, the rest of America was under rebel control. Faced with the prospect of a long war in America and the continuing challenge of fighting the French and Spanish in other regions of the world, the ministry opted to open peace negotiations early in 1782.

The Confederation Years

Peace negotiations in France continued for most of 1782. Adams, Franklin, and John Jay represented the American states. In initial discussions Franklin attempted to talk the British representatives into giving up Canada. When Jay joined the discussion and pressed for British acceptance of American independence, Canada became nonnegotiable. Adams forced the fishery issue, gaining liberty for American fishermen to fish along the coast of British Newfoundland and even to land on uninhabited shores there to salt their fish. Britain also agreed to give up the western frontier south of Canada, including its military posts. However, to force the payment of American debts to British merchants incurred before the war–a condition of peace agreed to but long evaded by the Americans–the British would retain control of those western posts until 1795.

By the terms of the Treaty of Paris, agreed to by the negotiators on 30 November 1782 and ratified by Congress on 19 April 1783, the United States became a free and independent nation. Its territory was actually far larger than the settled portions of the former colonies, stretching from the boundary with Canada on the north to the 31st parallel (about fifty miles inland from the Gulf of Mexico) in the south, and from the Atlantic Ocean to the Mississippi River. As part of the international peace settlement, Spain received Florida.

No one was more pleased at the good news from Paris than American merchants and shipowners. After eight years of war they looked forward to a return to peace. For the most part the Revolution had not brought on a radical upheaval of classes, and so in each of the ports the families that had been doing business before the Revolution were still in place after independence. Where Tory families had left–half of the total number of Loyalists came from New York alone–it was often the case that their property had been taken up by equally well-to-do and established supporters of the Revolution.

On the other hand, in the countinghouses and taverns of America's towns, particularly those on the coast, some were cautiously reflecting on the cost of independence. No longer were Americans part of the British Empire. No longer could shipbuilders expect to sell their ships to British owners, nor could planters receive bounties for growing indigo and naval stores. No longer could American merchants expect favored treatment and access to all the goods of the world through their old trading partners in London or Liverpool. And no longer could seafarers hide behind the wooden walls of the Royal Navy. In every way, Americans would have to fend for themselves in a world that rarely wished them well.

The former colonies had learned to work together, however contentiously, through the Continental Congress. And most of the former colonies had created new state constitutions during the war to transfer power from the King and Parliament to elected local officials. But Congress itself had not resolved a unified structure for America. The Articles of Confederation, drafted in 1776 and finally ratified in 1781, retained the sovereignty of the states, including the right of taxation and the regulation of trade, permitting Congress only the exclusive right to regulate foreign affairs, initiate war and peace, establish measurement standards, negotiate with the American Indians, and establish a postal service. The Articles provided for a Congress in which each state had a single vote; they created a weak president—essentially his only duty was to preside over Congress; and they did not provide for a separate judiciary. Strongly resistant to taxes and trade regulations imposed from outside, and even to a national currency, the states specifically eliminated such responsibilities from Congress, retaining all important fiscal and commercial matters under the jurisdiction of the individual states.

Just how well the new nation of confederated states would fare in a hostile environment depended in good measure upon the degree of unity at home. From a maritime point of view the Articles were particularly troublesome. With the exception of negotiating treaties, regulation of trade was left in the hands of the states. Each state could enact its own tariff regulations, and many did just that, even levying tariffs against the products of neighboring states. Instead of providing a single national voice speaking for trade and commerce, the Articles of Confederation accommodated thirteen competing voices. It soon became apparent that the nation was in a weak and vulnerable position.

Great Britain moved quickly to punish the new nation by placing high tariffs on American goods, including whale oil. Trade with the British West Indies, once the most important maritime business out of New England, was prohibited. John Adams accused the British ministry of trying to ruin "our carrying trade" by "annihilating all our Navigation and Seamen."

Almost as soon as the Treaty of Paris was signed, Congress's erstwhile ally France, and her neighbor Spain, began to revert to their mercantilist ways as well. France would not allow American vessels to carry French Caribbean sugar to France, and placed severe restrictions on the importation of American flour. Spain behaved with even more self-interest, prohibiting American direct trade with Cuba, Puerto Rico, and Hispaniola.

Cut off or restricted in their old trades, Americans were forced to seek new markets, such as in the Mediterranean. Here too they found obstacles, including the Barbary corsairs. The first inkling of trouble arrived in October 1785, when the Massachusetts *Centinel* announced that the Boston schooner *Maria,* carrying salted codfish to Portugal

in exchange for salt and wine, had been taken off Cape St. Vincent by an Algerian corsair. The *Maria*'s fate was a signal of more severe distress: Algiers had declared war on the United States.

For generations Algiers and her North African neighbors, Tunis, Tripoli, and Morocco had dispatched their sleek xebecs to prowl the western Mediterranean and adjacent Atlantic in search of merchant prey. The Barbary states, a name taken from the Berber tribes that inhabited the area, were nominal vassals of the Sultan of Turkey, but in fact they operated independently. They viewed the waters near their homes as their private preserve, and those wishing to sail through had either to fight or pay tribute.

The latter was the preferred response. Since the first half of the seventeenth century, paying tribute had been British policy. As long as the American colonies flew the Union Jack, they had been covered under the empire's umbrella insurance policy. Shortly after the end of the Revolution, however, a new British minister, Charles Loggie, arrived in Algiers and announced to the bey that vessels hailing from the United States no longer enjoyed the protection of Great Britain. At nearly the same time that Loggie was inviting the bey's unwanted attention towards American vessels, another development portended peril for the new nation's commerce.

For several years Algiers and Spain had been at war. The principal effect of this belligerency was a Spanish blockade of the Straits of Gibraltar. Peace opened that gate, and the *Maria* was among the first American merchant vessels captured by the Algerines, now let loose in the Atlantic.

Americans were anxious. Like their compatriots in Boston, merchants in New York, Baltimore, and Philadelphia also had sent vessels into the Mediterranean. Keen to trade for wine and other southern European commodities, these men saw the Barbary corsairs as a threat to a valuable trade. A few vessels escaped by hoisting British colors in place of the Stars and Stripes, but that successful ruse only emphasized the weakness of the American position on the high seas. Indeed, the last ship of the Continental Navy had been sold in 1785 so, despite provisions for a navy in the Articles of Confederation, the new nation had no naval force with which to oppose the Barbary pirates.

While American traders struggled to find new markets in Europe, suffered under restrictions in the West Indies, and endured the insults of the Barbary corsairs, there was at least one bright spot in the new nation's commercial galaxy: China. British trade with India and China was a monopoly of the East India Company and had been forbidden to the American colonists. American merchants, however, were well aware of the American fondness for tea and desire for the status implied by possessing Chinese silks and porcelain. Now free to trade directly with China, the only question was what products the notably isolationist Chinese would accept in exchange. In the winter of 1783-84 the Boston sloop *Harriet* sailed with a cargo of ginseng, a medicinal root used by the Chinese. When she arrived at the Cape of Good Hope, agents of the East India Company purchased her cargo to prevent her from continuing on to Canton, where trade with China was conducted. Although she never reached China, the *Harriet* was the first American vessel to engage in trade to Asia.

While the *Harriet*'s voyage attracted the interest of the waterfront, the published reports of Captain James Cook were even more intriguing. Prior to the Revolution, Cook had ventured twice into the Pacific and Antarctic, sailing under orders from the Admiralty. In 1776 he departed on his third voyage into those regions. The American minister to France, Benjamin Franklin, provided Captain Cook with a letter of safe passage to protect him from molestation by American warships or privateers. Cook's third voyage turned out to be his last. He was killed by natives in the Hawaiian Islands in 1779.

Sailing with Cook was John Ledyard, a young American adventurer from Groton, Connecticut. In 1783, three years after the completion of the voyage, Ledyard returned home to Connecticut and published *A Journal of Captain Cook's Last Voyage*. Among the most popular parts of Ledyard's book were the sections describing Cook's explorations of Nootka Sound, on the Northwest Coast. According to Ledyard, the natives in this region were anxious to trade sea-otter pelts for inexpensive European trade goods. The pelts could then be carried to Canton, where they were in great demand as trim for the silk coats of the mandarin elite.

Ledyard attempted to persuade Robert Morris and a group of New York and Boston investors to join him in venturing to the Northwest Coast to obtain sea-otter pelts and carry them to Canton in exchange for tea and silk. However, while the investors agreed with Ledyard on the promise of trade with China, they did not share his enthusiasm for a voyage to the Northwest Coast, believing the distances and risks were too great. They engaged the Philadelphia ship *Empress of China*, and she sailed from New York on 22 February 1784 on a direct route around the Cape of Good Hope, reaching Canton on 30 August. She returned to New York in May 1785 with a profitable cargo of tea and silks as the harbinger of a new trade. Almost immediately, the wealthy merchant Elias Haskett Derby of Salem, Massachusetts, who had made a fortune financing privateers during the Revolution, sent out the ship *Grand Turk*, establishing Salem's role in the China trade. Other ports followed, and during the first decade of the trade an average of ten American ships a year made their way halfway around the globe to Canton.

Outward-bound goods remained a puzzle. The Chinese had no interest in American foodstuffs or other common products. Chinese merchants were willing to accept gold and silver, but American merchants had little hard currency to trade. In light of Ledyard's rapturous descriptions of sea-otter pelts and their demand in China, a group of Boston merchants fitted out the ship *Columbia Rediviva* and sloop *Lady Washington* for a voyage to China via the Northwest Coast.

Commanded by Captain Robert Gray, the *Lady Washington* reached the coast first, in August 1788, and began a tentative trade with the coastal tribes, interspersed with violence, discovering that copper and firearms were the most desired commodities on the coast. Farther north, the Americans discovered British adventurers under the Portuguese flag already engaged in trade, and both of these expeditions were trespassing in territory claimed by Spain. Captain John Kendrick's *Columbia* rendezvoused with the *Lady Washington* in Nootka Sound on Vancouver Island, and the party spent the winter ashore. The following spring, in the Queen Charlotte Islands, the Americans at last secured a full cargo of sea-otter pelts, and when a Spanish naval vessel arrived to investigate the

After a 188-day passage, the Empress of China *became the first American vessel to complete the 18,000-mile journey to China. One of thirty-four foreign vessels to call at Canton in 1784, the* Empress of China *carried lead, lumber, cotton cloth, ginseng, and silver specie to exchange for tea, silks, and porcelain. During the ship's four-month stay in China, the ship's carpenter, John Morgan, purchased several pieces of porcelain, including this punch bowl decorated with a Chinese impression of a Swedish ship. Morgan died during the passage home, but his pieces of the first Chinaware imported directly into the U.S. were delivered to his family in Groton, Connecticut. (M.S.M. 38.77)*

activity on the coast Kendrick claimed his vessels were on a voyage of exploration.

At the end of July 1789, Captain Gray set off for China in the *Columbia* while Kendrick remained on the Northwest Coast in the *Lady Washington*. Gray stopped first at the island of Hawaii, about which British and Hawaiian mariners had informed him while on the Northwest Coast. At Kealakekua Bay, where Captain Cook had been killed ten years earlier, the *Columbia* made the first visit by an American vessel to the Hawaiian Islands. After taking on provisions and visiting all of the major islands, Gray continued to China, carrying along Attoo and Kalehua, two Hawaiians who would be the first of their people to see Boston. Gray reached Canton and exchanged 1,215 pelts for $21,400, half of which he had to use to refit the *Columbia*. With a modest cargo of tea, and freight consigned to two rivals of her Boston owners, the *Columbia* left China in February 1790 and proceeded home via the Cape of Good Hope, thereby becoming the first American vessel to circumnavigate the globe. Although her voyage took nearly three years and was a financial loss, Captain Gray persuaded the *Columbia*'s owners to undertake a second voyage, and this time Gray would come upon the mouth of the great western river that he named Columbia in honor of his vessel. In the meantime, the *Lady Washington* had also gone on to China and then back to the Northwest Coast. During the return passage she stopped on the Japanese coast,

attempting unsuccessfully to establish a commercial relationship in this first visit of an American vessel to Japan.

The voyages of the *Columbia* and *Lady Washington* established an American commercial presence in regions of the Pacific that would have great future significance. Initially, however, the voyages marked the opening of a trade between Boston and the peoples of the Northwest Coast that endured for several generations despite cultural conflict and the near extermination of the sea otter. These and succeeding voyages displayed the extremes of determination and resourcefulness that firmly established the American merchant marine as a force on the oceans of the world.

But in spite of optimistic prospects in the China trade, American merchants in the late 1780s were pessimistic about the state of the new nation's sea commerce. In particular they were concerned that the problems facing them were issues that could only be solved by firm government action. To whom should they turn? The Articles of Confederation offered little hope. In the midst of their troubles merchants welcomed news that a movement was afoot to provide the new nation with a stronger government more favorable to their interests.

Yankee Mariners and Early Contact in the Pacific

Confrontation between Yankee traders and the natives of the Northwest Coast punctuated cooperative exchanges as the two cultures worked out their relationships. While trading with friendly natives in the Queen Charlotte Islands in 1792, Captain Gray and the crew of the ship Columbia were confronted by twenty war canoes from a clan they had skirmished with earlier. Gray warned them off with the ship's cannon, then killed two of the leaders who refused to back down. Drawing by George Davidson. (OrHi 49264, Courtesy Oregon Historical Society)

On 27 August 1797, the ship *Neptune* from New Haven, Connecticut, crossing the Pacific on a sealing voyage, made the Island of "Attoi" in the Hawaiian Archipelago. As evening fell the *Neptune* ran in for shore, and the next morning a canoe came off towards the ship, carrying Hawaiians bearing island foodstuffs to trade. As it came alongside, the *Neptune*'s supercargo, Ebenezer Townsend, hailed the canoe, asking "Who are you?" He had not really expected to be understood, but Townsend was astonished to hear one of the Hawaiians reply, "I am General Washington."

This exchange suggests how dramatically and unpredictably contact with Yankee mariners was beginning to rearrange Hawaii and the Pacific. "General Washington," it transpired, had shipped on an earlier Yankee vessel during a voyage to trade for furs along the Northwest Coast of America. His experience had given him a new name, and a new sense of himself and his place in the world. This was becoming more common by the time the *Neptune* reached Hawaii, less than a decade since the first American vessel called there. On island archipelagos like the Marquesas and Hawaii, along the coastlines of Patagonia and northwestern North America, on the edges of the ancient metropolitan civilizations of East Asia; indeed, all across the Pacific, Yankee mariners in pursuit of new enterprise skirmished, had sex, recruited hands, jumped ship and settled, and even began to ferry missionaries, consuls, and diplomats.

Above all, they traded. At nearly every port of call, markets sprang up and an array of new goods began making their way into the material lives and folkways of Pacific peoples. The ships shed parts of their cargoes and pieces of themselves as they went, and acquired parts and pieces of the peoples among whom they moved. Take the *Jefferson*, a Boston fur- and China-trader that plied the Pacific in the early 1790s. At the Marquesas the Yankees bartered with nails and bits of iron hoop for breadfruit and other island foodstuffs (and meanwhile lost glass lamps, a compass, and other loose parts of the ship to theft). At Hawaii the Yankees swapped more iron pieces and tools, as well as muskets and powder, for sweet potatoes and hogs.

But it was along the Northwest Coast of North America that the *Jefferson's* hold opened most widely. The ship cruised along the coastline for several trading seasons, from May 1793 to August 1794, seeking sea-otter pelts to carry to market in Canton, China. In the course of this business the *Jefferson* off-loaded a rich stock of goods. Among the Nootkans on Vancouver Island the Yankees traded iron towes (chisel heads), copper sheets (as well as copper hats and pans), cloth, muskets, powder, iron swords and collars (forged onboard by the blacksmith), great coats, jackets, and trousers. As they moved north to the Queen Charlotte Islands, where Haida traders offered an especially rich supply of sea-otter pelts, the men of the *Jefferson* found they had overstocked on iron tools and pieces, and soon exhausted

their other trading stock. For a time they stayed in business by trading leather war armor made of elk hides ("clemmons," acquired in trade with Native Americans further down the coast), supplemented by clothing cut from spare sailcloth and wooden trunks manufactured by the ship's carpenter. And then, as Haida traders continued to bring more canoeloads of sea-otter skins, Captain Roberts and his crew began to strip the vessel of whatever they could do without, whatever they could sell. "Every thing that could be spaired on board were purchass'd up by the natives with the greatest Evidity," James Magee recorded in his journal; the Indians "seemed in want of Every thing they got thire Eye on." In trade the Haida obtained the ship's longboat, jolly boat, spare sails and rope, sea line, rockets, fishing seines, "old Clothes of the Captn." and his trunk, the ship's tablecloth and sheets, oil skins and clothing from the lockers of the officers and crew, the main cabin lookingglass and much of the ship's crockery. By the time it left the Queen Charlotte Islands, no small part of the *Jefferson* itself was sinking into the material, social, and spiritual lives of the Haida.

At the same time, trading with natives drew the Yankees, at least temporarily,

semi-wittingly, into native patterns of society and culture. After trading with the *Jefferson* for a month, the powerful Haida "cheef" Cumeah approached the captain for help raising a totem pole—a "sepulture of a daughter of Cumeah's," the ship's journal recorded. As the captain complied, sending crew members ashore with tackles and several spare topmasts to use as sheers, he entered a train of ritual events that carried him to the core of Haida folkways. The next day Cumeah's family invited the ship's officers to a celebratory feast, where Cumeah "adressed his Cheeffs & people. . . urging the propriety of thire making such acknowledgement to [Captain] Roberts for his service & assistance in setting up the monument as they saw fit, & by which they would shew they considered him as thire frend, & by whose frendship they might hope to create mutel advantages &c. or in words to that affect." The captain promised to paint the totem, and Haida clan leaders sent him back to his ship with ceremonial gifts of several more skins to add to the hold. The affair climaxed several weeks later when the *Jefferson's* officers were invited back to shore for a second ceremony in which an elaborate distribution of presents

Although it dates from several decades after initial contact, this argilite carving represents the Haida perception of the "Boston men" who came among them to trade. (M.S.M. 45.891)

commemorated the erection of the totem and the incision of several young women for labrets (discs worn by high-ranking Haida women in their lips). Roberts and company were impressed with the solemnity of the proceeding, but they only vaguely sensed its meanings; what the Yankees were participating in was a potlatch, a complex ceremony in which Northwest Native Americans articulated, or validated, or negotiated the finely calibrated rankings that undergirded their societies.

The protocols of trade on voyages like the *Jefferson*'s (at least, before they reached Canton, which had a very strict trading protocol) were often improvised. In order to do business with each other, Yankee and native had to piece together workable components of trade: sign languages and pidgin trading vocabularies, interpreters and brokers, prices and exchange rates, and procedures for giving and receiving. The Yankees commonly found themselves negotiating on the natives' terms, which they only dimly understood. Local chiefs, who controlled access to most furs, demanded ceremonial gifts before opening trade with a vessel. Trade at a particular anchorage tended to start slowly, as the Indians examined the Yankees' offerings, retreated to shore, returned, often went back and forth for several visits, testing the market, waiting for the Yankees to put favorable rates of exchange on the table. In this waiting period, the natives held a good deal of leverage, for if they did not like the goods or prices offered, they

could always hold their furs for the next vessel to come along. Once actual trading commenced, the Northwest Indians proved to be sharp, skillful traders, who haggled stubbornly, applied their leverage shrewdly, avidly exacted maximum profit–so stubbornly, so shrewdly, so avidly, in fact, that they drove Yankee ship captains and supercargoes to distraction. "The people of these isles in general possess a truly mercantile spirit," Joseph Ingraham remarked after several days of trading while the brigantine *Hope* was anchored off Washington's Island in the Queen Charlotte group, "for they will not part with a single skin til they have exerted their utmost to obtain the best price for it."

The structure of the fur trade along the Northwest Coast warns against making easy generalizations about early Yankee-native contacts in the Pacific. Native Americans like the Haida and the Nootkans managed to take fur traders like the *Jefferson* on largely their own terms. These first Yankee mariners of the 1790s came well in advance of later, more intrusive settlers, missionaries, and conquerers. From the first, contact with Americans and Europeans did carry pernicious, destructive consequences: exposure to new diseases like smallpox and venereal disease, for example, and in the case of native North Americans, overhunting of local fur animal populations. And by definition, Yankee-native trade drew previously isolated peoples into a commercial network of exchange and influence that expanded

across the globe. But contact, especially early contact, created new opportunities as well, and in many cases indigenous peoples (and people) responded resourcefully, resiliently.

The next stage of the *Jefferson*'s voyage was especially revealing in this regard. From the Northwest Coast, the ship sailed to Hawaii, where the Yankees stopped over for reprovisioning. Lying directly athwart developing sea-lanes, the Hawaiian islands were receiving the full brunt of contact. Captain James Cook's third voyage of exploration had revealed the islands to Europeans and Americans in 1778. By the time the *Jefferson* made Hawaii less than twenty years later, Yankee merchantmen crossing the Pacific were regularly stopping at the islands, islanders were starting to ship out on Yankee and British vessels in substantial numbers, and Yankee and European mariners were, in smaller numbers, beginning to settle on the islands. With all of these exchanges, these border meetings and crossings, intercultural give-and-take accelerated rapidly. When the men aboard the *Jefferson* opened trade, they found a ready market for iron tools, as well as a strong demand for muskets, swivel cannon, and powder–armaments fueling heated military expansion and a campaign of conquest by Kamehameha, *ali'i*, or king, of the "Big Island." On the Hawaiian side, business negotiations were handled by two western mariners, John Young and Isaac Davis, whom Kamehameha had drawn into his retinue to administer relations with visiting ships, to train his army in musket and cannon tactics, and to oversee a modest but growing fleet of royal schooners and brigs.

But the Hawaiians' striking capacity of assimilation, for advantageously adapting to contact, manifested itself most fully when the *Jefferson* ran up on a reef about fifteen leagues off Maui. Over the next several weeks, the Hawaiians offered invaluable assistance to the beleaguered Yankees. Canoes came off from shore bearing teams of islanders to man pumps, dive to inspect the hull, and shift the hold to work the vessel off the rocks—a highly organized relief operation administered not only by the officers of the *Jefferson*, but also by local Hawaiian leaders as well as a polyglot cadre of foreigners who had settled on the islands. As the ship's log recorded, "Besides our own company, we were assisted by Messrs. Howel, Davis, Evans, Boyd, Cox, Dinsdale (a lone American, the rest are Europeans), Kelly, Baptist (an Italian), and Hoppo (a Chinese)." And meanwhile, one of Kamehameha's schooners arrived and hovered alongside the ship, receiving her cargo. James Magee observed from on board the *Jefferson*: "she was navigated altogether by natives & Commanded by Capt Caheira, & no man could entertain a higher idea of this important station, than himself, by the many airs that he had been taught to assume, on account of his rank, as first commander of the Kings schooner, & of which his display was highly diverting in many respects." The Yankees' condescension

Kamehameha I (ca. 1749-1819), warrior nephew of the monarch of the "big island" of Hawaii, became the unifying figure of the Hawaiian Archipelago. Until his emergence as a leader in the 1780s, the islands had been home to individual kingdoms constantly at war. Using European and American weapons, vessels, and the expertise of expatriate mariners to augment his own army, Kamehameha subdued the competing rulers of the other islands between 1782 and 1815. While remaining true to Hawaiian culture and religion, King Kamehameha had a passion for European and American vessels, clothing, and material goods, and he established a lucrative Hawaiian economy based on trade with visiting vessels. This aquatint of Kamehameha dressed in European clothing, ca. 1816, was published in Otto von Kotzebue's A Voyage of Discovery, *vol. 1 (London, 1821). (G.W. Blunt White Library, Mystic Seaport; Claire White-Peterson photo)*

notwithstanding, the Hawaiians here were clearly, actively incorporating western technologies into indigenous island life, taking contact into their own hands, molding and fitting its offerings into distinctively Hawaiian forms.

So the rescue and refitting of the *Jefferson* becomes an intriguing, revealing look at Hawaii in transition. Already the islands were becoming a major maritime crossroads and a rich intermingling of peoples and cultures. The *Jefferson* itself carried on this process of cross-pollination, entering on its lists and bearing away "Moses Montcalm & William Collett for the remainder of the voyage, Hoppo the Chinese for Macao, Sam, a young chief, nephew to Tahoomoto, & 10 other natives, young lads, also engag'd to visit America with us." So the ship bore off with new "General Washingtons," agents of change who would be even more revolutionary than their namesake.

Hawaiian adaptation to these new circumstances was uneven, sometimes brutal, jarring. But contact was not simply unilateral victimization; it took on more organic forms of assimilation and adaptation. Hawaii, it is worth noting, would manage to retain its sovereignty for more than one hundred years after the *Jefferson* sailed away, skillfully playing one would-be imperial conquerer off against another, even as tightening commercial and diplomatic ties drew the islands further into the orbit of the United States.

Fred Dalzell

CHAPTER 5

Maritime Affairs in the New Republic

HE CRY FOR A STRONGER central government echoed inland, and soon a variety of voices were heard urging reform. Early in the fall of 1786 representatives from Virginia and Maryland met at Annapolis to discuss issues concerning state borders. The success of that meeting encouraged some of the participants to plan a greater meeting of representatives from all the states at Philadelphia during the upcoming spring. In the winter, as the invitation went out for the Philadelphia meeting, alarming news arrived from western Massachusetts. Disgruntled and dispossessed farmers were closing courts and threatening lawful authority. Marching behind a former captain in the Continental Army, Daniel Shays, these insurgents struck fear into the propertied classes of the east who saw in them the twin evils of anarchy and chaos.

Loyal militia easily scattered the Shaysites, but fears that the "Little Rebellion" had raised were not so easily erased. Indeed, while events in Massachusetts were more dramatic, rumors of restiveness elsewhere prompted many to doubt that the weak Confederation government could manage the affairs of a nation. Thus, the meeting planned for Philadelphia might turn into an opportunity not simply to reform the old government, but in fact to fashion a new one.

At the outset the men convening in the Pennsylvania State House knew that they had a dual task. Somehow they had to shape a new government strong enough to deal with the national issues that thus far had befuddled the Confederation. Equally important, this new government could not be so powerful as to threaten the liberties of its citizens. Balancing these dual and often contradictory goals was the supreme challenge of the Philadelphia meeting.

Detail of the corner of Wall and Water Streets, New York, by Francis Guy. (Collection of The New-York Historical Society, 1907.32)

For sixteen long, hot weeks delegates debated the nature of power and its proper distribution within society and government. Among the central issues debated was the question of commerce. The experience of the Confederation persuaded nearly all present that the central government ought to control interstate and foreign trade. To what degree such power ought to be exercised, however, was a matter of dispute.

In the South, for example, where the economy was dependent upon the export of staple crops to Europe, planters feared that New England shipowners would use the federal government to get control of the carrying trade and thus give great advantage to Yankees. Charles Cotesworth Pinckney of South Carolina offered a measure to subvert such a likelihood. He suggested that two-thirds approval be required for any act regulating commerce. Recognizing that such a high threshold would likely cause paralysis, Northern delegates offered a compromise. After debate, the Constitutional Convention agreed that the new government would be prohibited from levying export taxes and that it could not interfere with the slave trade for a period of twenty years. By these provisions the South's staple export trade was protected and, for a time at least, Southern planters would be able to augment their slave labor force.

By comparison to the commercial powers exercised by the highly centralized European governments, the United States Constitution left much to be desired. In addition to explicitly denying the federal government the right to collect export taxes, the Constitution required that international treaties, one of the most important vehicles for defining national commercial policy, be approved by a two-thirds vote in the Senate, in which all states were represented equally. Despite these restrictions, the Constitution did give an important array of authority to the new government, best summed up in Article One, Section 8: "The Congress shall have the power To lay and collect Taxes, Duties, Imposts and Excises. . . but all Duties, Imposts and Excises shall be uniform throughout the United States; . . . To regulate Commerce with foreign Nations, and among the several States; . . . To define and punish Piracies and Felonies committed on the high Seas, and Offenses against the Law of Nations; To declare War, grant Letters of Marque and Reprisal, and make Rules concerning Captures on Land and Water; . . . To provide and maintain a Navy. . . ." And Section 9 specifically forbade discrimination in commerce and duties between states, and prohibited individual states from creating their own navies or entering into foreign treaties. These broad powers, used wisely, could make the federal government a vital friend to maritime interests.

In September 1787 the Constitution was reported out of the Convention and forwarded to the states for approval. In each state a special convention met to consider ratification. Debates were heated, and often centered on commercial issues. In Delaware, for example, the day was carried by delegates from New Castle County who saw great advantages from a national commercial union that would allow them free access to markets in adjacent Pennsylvania. Advocates for ratification expressed similar sentiments in other states while also pointing out the obvious benefits of a single commercial policy when dealing with foreign powers.

Those who favored ratification, and the federal government that it would create, came to be called Federalists. At the risk of oversimplifying, it is apparent that the Federalists shared certain characteristics–for instance, a strong sense of nationalism. They disdained the Confederation as a weak expression of nationalism, and they yearned for a stronger union. They tended to be men of property who lived near or in commercial centers, which were predominantly seaports. Indeed, supporters of the Constitution were often creditors to both the state and Confederation governments. They had a vested interest in creating a government powerful enough to live up to its financial obligations.

With greater resources of money and support than the opponents of the Constitution, the Federalists were able organize an effective campaign for ratification. In New York City a series of essays written under the pseudonym "Publius" appeared. Actually prepared by Alexander Hamilton, John Jay, and James Madison, these essays, collectively referred to as *The Federalist Papers*, were widely reprinted throughout America. Among other things they argued that the powers over commerce, foreign relations, and taxation provided to the federal government in the Constitution would create a strong and prosperous nation.

Not the least of the advantages the Federalists had over their opponents, whose negative position gained them the name Anti-Federalists, was that they included America's two greatest heroes, George Washington and Benjamin Franklin, both of whom had sat in the Constitutional Convention. Indeed, Washington had presided over the meeting.

Delaware was the first state to ratify (7 December 1787). It took several months for the other states to vote, but with New Hampshire's approval on 21 June 1788 the necessary two-thirds of the states had assented, and by November 1788 twelve states had ratified. Rhode Island remained a holdout. Despite the commercial interests of the ports of Newport and Providence, the state was under the control of agricultural interests who strongly opposed national taxation and had instituted a highly inflated paper-money economy to alleviate the great debt load borne by Rhode Island farmers. Rhode Islanders had thoughts of remaining an independent nation, the equivalent of the Netherlands in America, but under the threat of economic pressure from the United States, Rhode Island would finally ratify the Constitution in May 1790.

It was not simply the propertied Federalists who saw their future in the Constitution. When New York City celebrated the state's ratification of the Constitution with a parade in the summer of 1788, various artisan groups marched to show their support. The city's shipwrights marched under the verse: "Our Merchants may venture to ship without fear/ For Pilots of skill shall the Hamilton steer/ The federal ship will our commerce revive/ and merchants and ship wrights and joiners shall thrive. . . ."

In March 1789 members of the first United States Congress assembled in New York City. On 23 April President-elect Washington boarded a large, elaborate barge at Elizabethtown Point, New Jersey, for a ceremonial crossing of New York Harbor. Rowed by thirteen New York Harbor pilots, and accompanied by highly decorated barges and coastal sloops, complete with vocal and instrumental music, Washington crossed to New York and came ashore at Wall Street. A week later he took the oath of office as president, and the new federal government went to work.

Regulating the Republic's Maritime Trades

First on the agenda of the new government was the issue of national revenue and trade regulation. The first tariff legislation, enacted on 4 July 1789, set up a discriminatory schedule that encouraged American shipping by discounting the tariffs on all foreign goods by 10 percent if they were imported in American vessels. Congress also enacted legislation aimed more specifically at protecting and encouraging the American merchant marine. The Tonnage Act of 20 July 1789 established standard tonnage duties for vessels entering American ports. Those built and registered in the United States paid six cents per ton; those built in the United States but registered under a foreign flag paid thirty cents per ton; and foreign-built and foreign-owned ships paid fifty cents per ton. Foreign-built but American-owned vessels were eligible for registry, but only if they had been registered by 29 May 1789; thereafter any foreign-built vessel, regardless of ownership, was not eligible.

As an outgrowth of practice in the British Empire, and among the several states of the Confederation, Congress enacted provisions for documenting the nationality of the country's vessels. An act of September 1789, superseded by acts in December 1792 and February 1793, set up a system for licensing, enrolling, or registering American merchant vessels, depending on their size and employment. To determine size, or tonnage, a measurement formula was used to approximate the volume of the hull, expressed in tons. Small coasting and fishing vessels of between five and twenty tons measure were issued a yearly license. Vessels of over twenty tons that were employed in coasting, fishing, or whaling were enrolled, and then issued either a coasting or a fishing license. All vessels over 20 tons that were engaged in foreign trade were required to be registered.

In the coastwise trade the Congress did not, as was demanded by some, grant exclusive carrying rights to American vessels. It did, however, do the next best thing by requiring that foreign vessels pay tonnage duties each time they entered port, while American vessels only needed to pay

The elegant brick Tontine Coffee House was built on the corner of New York's Wall and Water Streets in 1792 to accommodate the daily gathering of New York merchants "on exchange." To facilitate business, merchants were required to gather here at a prescribed time to transact, or exchange, business between them. Outside in Wall Street, the maritime commerce of the city overflows the waterfront, and merchants, shopkeepers, women, laborers, and sailors intermingle. A few wooden dwellings, converted into shops, still survive from old New York, but modern brick townhouses and commercial blocks predominate on the reclaimed land between this corner and waterfront South Street in the distance. Oil painting by Francis Guy, ca. 1797. (Collection of The New-York Historical Society, 1907.32)

their duties annually. In effect, the law achieved the goal of exclusive carrying rights (sometimes referred to as cabotage) for American vessels.

Congress also enacted duties heavily weighted in favor of supporting the infant trade to China. A duty of twenty cents per pound was levied on hyson teas arriving at American ports in American bottoms. If the tea came via Europe but still in an American ship, then the duty increased to twenty-six cents per pound. If, however, the tea arrived in a foreign vessel, whether directly or indirectly from China, then the duty leaped to forty-five cents per pound.

The Tariff Act and two additional acts in the summer of 1789 established a national Customs Service to collect duties, and divided the nation into customs districts for that purpose. All entering and clearing vessels, even if they were trading to small, remote ports, were required to stop at the customhouse in the main port of entry for the district to enter or clear their papers before proceeding. Again following British and Confederation practice, each customs district was headed by a collector, who supervised a number of subordinates, depending on the size of the district. They might include a "naval officer" (a civilian deputy collector who handled paperwork), inspectors (known as tidewaiters and landwaiters), surveyors (who measured vessels), weighers, gaugers (who measured the volume of barrels and casks), and other functionaries. After 1791 the customs district might include a bonded warehouse, where merchants could deposit foreign goods pending their reexport. As long as the goods remained in the warehouse, no duties were owed.

Customs officers were among the first, and most numerous, of federal employees. In a combination of political patronage and local expediency, the position of collector usually went to a prominent revolutionary figure and Constitutional supporter, such as Generals Benjamin Lincoln in Boston and Jedediah Huntington in New London, Connecticut. The collector, in turn, could name political or business associates to ancillary positions, which made him a highly influential figure within the maritime community.

During the Republic's first decade, the Customs Service provided nearly 90 percent of the entire federal revenue. Yet, as the King's government had learned to its woe a generation earlier, the Customs Service quickly found that collecting revenue was not always an easy task, even when the collector had strong local influence. Simply because the new government was their own, it did not necessarily follow that American merchants were any more willing to pay duties to President Washington's government than they had been to that of King George III. If the collectors were to collect revenue they needed an enforcement agency to compel the recalcitrant and apprehend transgressors.

On 22 April 1790 Secretary of the Treasury Alexander Hamilton presented to Congress a

"Report on Defects in the Existing Laws of Revenue." Hamilton called for a Revenue Cutter Service with boats assigned along the coast: "two, for the coasts of Massachusetts and New Hampshire; one for Long Island Sound; one for New York; one for the Bay of Delaware; two for the Chesapeake (these of course to ply along the neighboring coasts); one for North Carolina; one for South Carolina; and one for Georgia." After some debate, on 4 August Congress approved Hamilton's request, giving birth to the Revenue Cutter Service. Hamilton's cutters were small, swift vessels, usually schooner-rigged. These lightly armed vessels undertook a variety of missions, including patrolling for smugglers, charting harbors, and aiding distressed vessels.

Through these measures Congress set the Republic's maritime policy. It was a policy by which the federal government took direct responsibility for encouraging the growth and prosperity of the nation's maritime interests, and used the duties levied on the importation and exportation of goods to finance the operation of the federal government and to pay down the national debt inherited from the Confederation. Nonetheless, while Congress's benevolent hand offered protection for the American merchant

David Gelston (1744-1828) served as collector of customs for the port of New York from 1801 to 1820. Born on Long Island, Gelston was a merchant in the port of New York, a member of the New York Assembly, the New York Constitutional Convention, the federal Congress of 1789, and the New York State Senate. He gained judicial experience as a surrogate judge for New York County, 1787-1801. Unlike the initial customs collector appointees, Gelston was a Republican, being named to the post by President Thomas Jefferson. Reportedly, a fellow New York merchant deferred to Gelston for the office because Gelston had been "unfortunate" in business and needed a position. As collector, Gelston was faithful and zealous in pursuing the interests of the Treasury Department during the difficult times of neutral trade, embargo, and war. John Wesley Jarvis painted Gelston's portrait, ca. 1810. (Collection of The New-York Historical Society, New York City)

Off the dramatic stone arch called Hole in the Wall, on the island of Abaco in the Bahamas, a British revenue schooner waylays an American trading brig. From 1783 to 1831, American vessels were restricted from trading with their customary partners in the British West Indies. Some American vessels resorted to smuggling their produce into British islands, risking seizure by British revenue vessels; others traded with the French islands, risking seizure by British warships or privateers during the Napoleonic Wars. In either case, the traditional ways of American maritime commerce in the Caribbean changed greatly once the U.S. became an independent nation. This image was published in the British Naval Chronicle *in 1803. (G.W. Blunt White Library, Mystic Seaport)*

marine, and consequent benefit to the nation, it did not guarantee success. That burden was left to owners and captains. To these men fell the task of reinvigorating old trades and exploring new ones.

No nation was more important to the development of America's overseas trade than Great Britain. While the Revolution had secured political independence, and the Constitution had created a new government in America, neither had altered the basic economics of the Atlantic world: the United States was an exporter of agricultural products and an importer of manufactured goods. In that regard the new nation's economy was still most compatible with that of its former master. At the same time, the United States promised to be a fierce competitor to Great Britain for, like the former mother country, the U.S. had a substantial merchant marine ready to compete in the carrying trades.

British interests were most vulnerable in the West Indies. American foodstuffs delivered in American vessels had long sustained the planters and their slaves in the British islands of Barbados, Antigua, St. Kitts, and Jamaica, as well as the many French islands. If permitted, these same shippers, now operating under the American flag, would tighten their hold on island trade and effectively shut the British merchant marine out of this important commerce. The West Indies trade was essential to the growth and health of the British merchant fleet, which had more capital, men, and ships invested in this business than in any other trade within the British Empire. Understanding the potential for disaster, Parliament had closed the islands to American vessels immediately after the war. American shipowners suffered, but so too did the British planters, who now had to pay premium prices for foodstuffs delivered from British

Canada and from Ireland. High prices were an incentive to smuggling from the United States.

If one of the costs of independence was loss of trade to the British islands, a benefit was opportunity to trade with non-British islands. By 1790, America's total trade with the West Indies was greater than it had been before the Revolution. Slightly more than one-third of all American exports–chiefly foodstuffs–went to the islands, and although trade with the British islands was illegal, and therefore no official records exist, it seems likely that a considerable amount of illegal trade was conducted.

While island trade was a variation on an old theme, American trade with the European mainland offered new opportunities. Both the Netherlands and France had been allies in the Revolution, and so it was natural that American

merchants would turn to them for markets. Tobacco exports from the Chesapeake region found a ready market in northern Europe. In southern Europe–Spain, Portugal, and the Mediterranean ports–to which some limited trade had been permitted in colonial days, merchants now looked to expand business.

Despite the emergence of new markets in the islands and Europe, Great Britain continued to be America's chief trading partner. Merchants in Boston, New York, Philadelphia, and elsewhere were accustomed to dealing with British houses. They understood one another's commercial needs and habits, and British manufactured goods suited American tastes and were cheap.

Postwar adjustments notwithstanding, by 1790 America's seaborne trade was greater than it had been at any time in history. Exports were still

Coming into the harbor at Naples in 1797, the brightly painted sixty-seven-foot Boston schooner Samuel *shows the American flag in the Mediterranean. Built at Wethersfield, Connecticut, in 1795, the* Samuel *represents the small New England vessels that headed out to establish commercial relations with all corners of the world in the decades after the Revolution. For downwind sailing during ocean passages, fore-and-aft-rigged schooners like the* Samuel *had square topsails. This gouache painting is attributed to Michele Felice Cornè. (Courtesy Peabody Essex Museum, Salem Massachusetts; photo by Mark Sexton)*

almost entirely composed of agricultural products, but a slight shift was discernible. Tobacco, rice, indigo, and naval stores—long among the most valuable exports—had slipped behind grain, beef, and pork. The former had come mainly from the South, while the latter group were Middle Atlantic products. This trend, and the opening of trade to the European mainland, had important implications for the development of maritime trade. At the end of the first year of the American Republic the federal government produced the first set of reliable figures quantifying the nation's trade. They showed that approximately one-third of American exports went to the West Indian islands, another third to Great Britain, and slightly less than a third to the European continent. The remainder of the new nation's foreign trade was tied to the far distant, but profitable, routes to Africa, the Indian Ocean, and China, where exotic products such as cinnamon, pepper, and tea were purchased and brought home.

America's maritime growth supported a number of industries. Shipbuilding, for example, benefited not only from increased trade but from the protective measures of Congress as well. The tax advantages accruing to domestically built vessels made American ownership of foreign-built vessels a practical impossibility. In addition, American-built vessels were generally cheaper than foreign vessels. Thanks to a plentiful and inexpensive supply of high-quality oak and pine timber, construction costs in domestic yards were sometimes 50 percent below costs in British and European yards. Although New England continued to be the major producer of ships, other regions participated as well. Philadelphia, the principal American port, had long been a center for shipbuilding. New York, with its geographic advantages, was clearly on the rise; and Baltimore, with a rapidly expanding trade, was also showing signs of strength. South of the Chesapeake, shipbuilding remained a minor industry.

Because of the small-scale, localized character of the majority of American maritime commerce, American shipyards tended to launch small vessels. Most common were fore-and-aft rigged, single-masted sloops and two-masted schooners of 40 to 80 feet in length and 40 to 120 measurement tons. Larger ports and more distant trades required larger vessels, commonly square-rigged, two-masted

brigs and three-masted ships of 60 to 120 feet in length and 120 to 300 measurement tons.

Scarce capital and unpredictable demand for new vessels meant that the majority of American shipyards operated on a very small scale and irregular schedules. Typically, an experienced master builder contracted with a prospective owner to build a vessel of stated dimensions. On his own property or perhaps at a leased waterfront site, he then assembled the necessary timber and a small crew of journeymen, an apprentice or two, and perhaps a couple of free black or slave laborers. Only in the busiest urban shipyards did shipwrights practice specialization of function. In most yards, all engaged in the sawing and hewing of timber, the framing, planking, and decking of the hull, and the finishing of the rudimentary accommodations. A frequent exception was the skill of caulking—sealing the hull with hemp fibers driven into the seams between planks. Caulkers might be independent contractors, as might be the riggers and pump and block makers who completed the vessel. Usually within less than six months, the 40-to-120-foot vessel would be ready for launch.

The inventory of shipbuilding timber in the yards was kept to a bare minimum. Indeed, American builders were known for using unseasoned timber, since they could not afford to let stock sit in the yard in anticipation of the next contract. Consequently, Lloyd's of London, in setting vessel insurance rates, gave American-built ships a first-class rating for only six years, compared to thirteen years for London-built vessels. However, ships built in the south with extremely durable live oak frames and yellow pine planking, though more expensive than northern vessels, were rated first-class for twelve years.

Like shipbuilders, shipowners faced economic challenges. A few unusually successful shipowners, like Elias Hasket Derby and William Grey of Salem, might own their vessels outright, but most American vessels were owned jointly by groups of investors. Each vessel was a new and separate venture calling for a new organization of capital. Shares were offered in even units ranging from 1/2 to 1/64. Such an awkward system generally was incapable of amassing large amounts of capital, but the capital was so widely distributed that the loss of a vessel was not likely to ruin an individual investor.

With flag flying and a celebratory crowd on board, the hull of the brig Reaper *is prepared for launch at the Thatcher Magoun shipyard in Medford, Massachusetts. Shipwrights spread tallow on the launching ways and prepare to cut the blocks, permitting the vessel to slide. At left, under the staging ramp "brow" at the bow, is the shipyard steambox, used to steam oak planks to make them pliable for installation. Captain Isaac Hinckley labeled this watercolor in his journal, "An attempt to shew the Brig Reaper, as she appear'd on the stocks, at Medford,—but it is past my art, therefore I leave it." After her launch in 1809, the 284-ton* Reaper *made three successful voyages to India. (Coll. 184, G.W. Blunt White Library, Mystic Seaport; Claire White-Peterson photo)*

Small vessels, cheaply built and efficiently manned, characterized the infant American merchant marine. With lower operating costs than their European competitors, shipowners in New England, New York, Philadelphia, and elsewhere could offer foreign shippers low freight rates, a fact not lost on the Europeans, who moved quickly to erect legal barriers against these enterprising Americans. Nonetheless, earnings from the American carrying trade were considerable and helped offset the chronic imbalance of imports over exports.

The problem of organizing maritime capital was not confined to shipbuilding. Insurance underwriters felt the pinch as growing trade made increased demands on their services. Marine insurance had been written in

America since at least 1721, when John Copson opened "An Office of Publick Assurances. . . at His House in the High Street" in Philadelphia. Others followed in New York, Newport, and Boston. Each conducted business in the tradition and style of Lloyd's of London, the principal British marine insurer. Every voyage was a separate undertaking. A shipowner would visit the underwriters' rendezvous, frequently an office or public house, and ask that a policy be laid on the table describing his vessel and venture. Those who wished could then examine the offer and decide whether or not they would underwrite their names and for what amount.

As the new Republic's trade grew, and as Lloyd's deliberately discriminated against insuring American vessels, the need for a more regular method of insurance grew. In November 1792 a group of Philadelphia merchants met and organized the first marine insurance company in America. On 10 December they received their charter from the State of Pennsylvania and opened their offices as the Insurance Company of North America with a capital fund of $600,000.

Philadelphia's example was followed in other ports, and within a decade virtually every port had at least one local marine insurance office. These companies provided an important service to the maritime community, and they also served as collectors and organizers of capital, which could then be reinvested, usually in banks. Profits generated from marine insurance provided a financial engine to drive other ventures, including an infant textile industry.

From the earliest days of settlement, Americans had understood the benefits of banding together in mutual support. Churches, libraries, schools, fire companies, and a host of other organizations had long brought citizens together in voluntary associations. In the face of challenges to seaward this same spirit united people in associations to help one another. Among the first in America to assume responsibility for aiding mariners were a group of Boston captains who on 1 June 1742 assembled at the Sun Tavern to form "a loving and friendly Society called the Fellowship Club," organized "to promote the Interest of each other in all Things in their Power, . . . as well as to relieve such Members of this Society, who by Misfortunes and Losses shall become proper Objects, according to the ability of the Box."

The "Box" was a leather-bound container placed on the table at meetings. As they returned from voyages, members were expected to contribute to the "Box" so that those in distress might receive help. Boston's example was followed by shipmasters in New York, Newburyport, Portsmouth, and Salem.

Marine societies were one way by which sea-minded communities banded together to help one another. Another way was in the erection of navigational aids, principally lighthouses. From the days of earliest settlement, beacon fires had been kept at harbor entrances, not so much for the purpose of safe navigation but rather to be lit as a warning of the approach of an enemy. Varieties

of other navigational aids, crude buoys, and day markers were also used, but it was not until 1716 that the first American lighthouse was constructed outside Boston Harbor. Other ports followed until by the time of the first Congress, at least ten lights were lit along the coast from Portsmouth, New Hampshire, south to Tybee Island, Georgia, each maintained by local authorities. Under the new federal government, lighthouses and other navigational aids came under federal rather than state jurisdiction. On 7 August 1789 Congress enacted legislation placing these facilities in the Treasury Department, reporting to the Commissioner of Revenue. In practice, the local collector of customs became responsible for overseeing lights in his district.

Buoying channels, manning lighthouses, collecting duties, and chasing smugglers were all efforts to promote trade and derive revenue from it, which properly belonged to the federal government. The new government undertook them readily and performed them well. In the related area of lifesaving, however, the Republic's government was content to leave affairs in the hands of private associations.

Associations devoted to lifesaving coalesced around the discovery that certain methods of resuscitation could revive people who appeared dead from drowning. The first such organization was formed in Amsterdam in 1767. The idea spread quickly to England, where the Royal Humane Society was established in 1774. By 1780 a society was active in Philadelphia, followed shortly thereafter in 1784 by the Humane Society of the Commonwealth of Massachusetts in Boston.

These societies dedicated to reviving the drowned naturally focused their efforts in the shipwreck-prone areas near the well-traveled approaches to ports. Since most shipwrecks took place in foul weather, and often in winter, sailors lucky enough to reach shore often died of exposure. Aware of the seamen's travail because of their concern with drowning, humane societies on both sides of the Atlantic turned their attention to helping victims of shipwreck. In 1787 the Massachusetts society built three huts on exposed beaches near Boston and south towards Plymouth. Stocked with food and blankets, these refuges saved the lives of countless storm victims.

Mishaps by mariners were often the result of

Cap Cook Cast a Way on Cape Cod 1802

Disaster at sea remained a constant threat, despite more seaworthy ships and efforts to improve the lot of survivors or families of deceased mariners. And even with the establishment of lighthouses and other aids to navigation, coastal shipwrecks remained common. In this painting, Michele Felice Cornè depicted the last moments of the ship Ulysses as a northeast storm drives her into the breakers on the Cape Cod shore in February 1802. With two masts overboard, the sailors take to the foremast rigging. (Courtesy Peabody Essex Museum, Salem, Massachusetts; Mark Sexton photo)

faulty navigation. Unable to determine their correct position at sea, captains might well drive their vessels on shore or sail into dangerous waters that could otherwise have been avoided. Even those voyages completed safely were often unnecessarily long because masters did not have the information to enable them to plot the best course.

In the earliest days of the American merchant marine great reliance was placed upon British authorities for navigational tables and charts, particularly *The New Practical Navigator* by J.H. Moore. With American shipping expanding at

such a rapid rate, however, two enterprising and able men recognized the need for comparable American publications.

In 1796 Edmund M. Blunt of Newburyport, Massachusetts, published the *American Coast Pilot*. Blunt's *Coast Pilot* was the first set of sailing directions to encompass the entire East Coast. Three years later he decided to publish an American version of Moore's work. Appreciating that certain errors had crept into Moore's tables, Blunt asked twenty-six-year-old Salem mariner Nathaniel Bowditch to correct the tables. Bowditch, a self-taught mathematician and astronomer, made

Edmund March Blunt and Nathaniel Bowditch

As they ventured forth to carry American commerce to all points of the compass, the new nation's shipmasters faced the essential puzzle of finding their way at sea. Without visible landmarks to guide them, mariners practiced both the art of celestial navigation on the open sea and the art of piloting in coastal waters. To determine his position beyond the sight of land, the mariner used celestial navigation to calculate both the ship's latitude–distance north or south of the equator–and the longitude–distance east or west of the prime meridian, which by general convention in the English-speaking world was taken as the longitude of Greenwich, England.

Celestial navigation was based on the accumulated knowledge of precisely where in the sky the sun, the moon, and a large number of stars and planets would be seen from day to day, which was published annually after 1766 in the *Nautical Almanac*, by order of the British Admiralty. The process required, first, an accurate measuring device to determine the angle of elevation between the heavenly body and the earth's horizon, or the angle between two heavenly bodies. The crude astrolabe and backstaff of the fifteenth and sixteenth centuries were replaced by the more accurate Davis quadrant, invented in 1586. The even more accurate octant, or Hadley's quadrant, was invented in 1731 by both John Hadley in England and

Octants and sextants are triangular in shape, with an arc marked with a scale of degrees as the base (the arc of an octant is one-eighth of a circle; that of a sextant one-sixth). The movable index arm has an index mirror at the top. The left leg of the frame has a fixed glass, half of which is mirrored, through which the navigator can see the horizon and the reflection from the index mirror at the same time. The mariner catches the image of the heavenly body in the index mirror and moves the index arm until the reflection aligns with the horizon on the horizon glass and mirror. He then notes the angle of elevation indicated by the position of the index arm on the arc. The same method can be used to align two heavenly bodies and measure the angle between them. This octant was built by John Greenwood of Providence, Rhode Island, in 1793. (M.S.M. 33.127; Mary Anne Stets photo)

Thomas Godfrey in Philadelphia, and by the nineteenth century they were largely superseded by the sextant (invented about 1757). Many of these instruments were imported from Europe, but American instrument makers in the principal seaports also produced these devices for local mariners.

To determine latitude, the navigator used an octant or sextant to take a noon sight of the sun, measuring the angle of the sun above the horizon at its zenith to determine distance north or south of the equator.

The determination of longitude was far more difficult. Indeed, American captains frequently sailed to the Caribbean without calculating longitude at all. It was sufficient to sail south to the appropriate latitude, then head west with the prevailing winds until encountering the islands. However, calculation of longitude was critical for more distant voyaging. To determine longitude the navigator measured the angles for two celestial bodies. Then he turned to a book of mathematical tables, such as James H. Moore's *Practical Navigator* (first published in London in 1772), the *Nautical Almanac* giving the positions as seen at Greenwich, and a precise determination of his local time to make his calculations.

Until John Harrison perfected an accurate seagoing timepiece between 1731 and 1759, the mariner could not get a precise reading of time at sea. But Harrison's chronometer was unaffected by tempera-ture, humidity, or the motion of a ship on the sea, varying by mere seconds over the course of many months. Harrison's successors built compact, affordable chronometers that gave competent shipmasters the ability to determine longitude. The chronometer carried the time of a reference point—usually Greenwich, England—to sea.

Between sights, the mariner used dead reckoning to estimate his position each hour, based on compass direction and speed through the water as measured by a log line.

Once the mariner arrived "on soundings," in water shallow enough to measure with a lead line, he began to pilot his vessel. Increasingly accurate charts recorded depths and bottom characteristics, both of which could be sampled with a lead line and compared to the chart. Landmarks were also noted on charts, and landfalls and sailing directions into harbor were described in pilot guides, such as John Seller's *The English Pilot*, first published in 1671.

Two of the most influential contributors to American navigation were contemporaries from the seacoast north of Boston. Edmund March Blunt was born at Portsmouth, New Hampshire, in 1770 and entered business as a publisher and bookseller at Newburyport, Massachusetts, in 1793. In this prosperous port at the mouth of the Merrimack River, Blunt published a newspaper and operated a lending library before taking up an expanding business in nautical instruments and books. In 1796 Blunt published Captain Lawrence Furlong's *American Coast Pilot*, a compilation of sailing instructions for entering safely into ports on the American coast from Maine to the Mississippi River.

Nathaniel Bowditch, the son of a shipmaster turned cooper, was born at Salem, Massachusetts, in 1773. Leaving school at age ten, Bowditch worked in his father's cooperage and then became apprenticed to a ship chandler. Despite his limited schooling, Bowditch read constantly, teaching himself algebra, geometry, trigonometry, French, and Latin, as well as studying astronomy and other branches of science.

In 1795 Bowditch went to sea as clerk aboard the ship *Henry*, bound for the Isle of Bourbon in the Indian Ocean. In 1796 he returned to sea on board Elias Hasket Derby's ship *Astrea* for an attempt to open direct trade with the Philippines, serving as supercargo in charge of commercial exchanges. During the voyage, Bowditch checked and corrected the navigational tables contained in Moore's 1793 *New Practical Navigator*. This was the standard source by which British and American shipmasters worked out their calculations, but Bowditch and his brother William discovered thousands of errors. In 1799 Blunt published the first American edition of Moore, with Bowditch's corrections, and a second edition with further corrections the following year.

Because of the scope of the

Edmund March Blunt (1770-1862), in an oil painting by an unidentified artist, ca. 1815. (M.S.M. 67.84)

---

corrections, Blunt suggested that Bowditch write an entirely new navigation text. During his 1799-1800 voyage, again as supercargo of the *Astrea*, Bowditch prepared his text. Blunt had it ready for publication in 1801, but having sold rights for an English edition he waited until 1802 to issue it at the same time as the English publication of the work. Bowditch's *New American Practical Navigator* almost immediately became the standard navigation text for American and many European shipmasters. Bowditch's work on practical navigation was considered so significant that he was elected a Fellow of the American Academy of Arts and Sciences in 1799 and was awarded an honorary Master of Arts degree by Harvard University in 1802.

Bowditch made one more voyage, 1802-03, and then was appointed president of the Essex Fire and Marine Insurance Company, which benefited from his nautical and mathematical skills for twenty years. For the last fifteen years of his life, until his death in 1838, Bowditch was actuary of the Massachusetts Hospital Life Insurance Company. Yet he found time to pursue his passion for languages, mathematics, and astronomy, charting the waters around Salem, publishing translations of French scientific works, and writing on astronomy. His *New American Practical Navigator* went through ten editions during his lifetime, and the work remains in print, now in its seventy-fifth edition.

Nathaniel Bowditch (1773-1838), detail from a painting by Charles Osgood, 1835. (Courtesy Peabody Essex Museum, Salem, Massachusetts)

Edmund March Blunt's publishing business flourished on the success of the *American Coast Pilot* and *New American Practical Navigator*. In 1797 he produced a chart of Georges Bank, off the Massachusetts coast, and in 1806 published Bowditch's Salem chart. He then expanded his chart business, although a fit of temper over the production of a chart, during which Blunt threw a skillet at his engraver, earned him unwanted attention when the engraver published a caricature and crockery illustration of Blunt in the act of throwing. After an unsuccessful libel suit, and following a fire in Salem that destroyed a portion of his stock, Blunt moved to New York in 1811.

There, at his store, the Sign of the Quadrant, he continued to produce and sell nautical books and charts, making it the center for American navigational publishing. He obtained a license to publish an American version of the *Nautical Almanac* in 1811, updated his other works frequently, and produced other practical books on seamanship. In 1816, Blunt began to sponsor coast surveys on which to base his charts. His son George William Blunt became his principal surveyor, and in 1833 would become the First Assistant in the U.S. Coast Survey, which provided the data for U.S. government charts.

Edmund March Blunt retired from his nautical publishing business in 1833, although he lived on in retirement and died in 1862 at age ninety-two. Just as his collaborator Nathaniel Bowditch produced a legacy that survives to this day in the *American Practical Navigator*, Blunt's *Coast Pilot* remains in print in its thirty-second edition, now published by the National Oceanographic and Atmospheric Administration as the *United States Coast Pilot*. Between them, Blunt and Bowditch produced the basic technical works that have informed American navigators for nearly two hundred years.

the corrections, and in 1799 Blunt published *The New Practical Navigator*. The book was an immediate success. More additions and corrections were made so that by the time of the third edition (1802) it was published under its own title *The New American Practical Navigator*. Universally accepted by American shipmasters as the authority on navigation, *The New American Practical Navigator* became popularly referred to as the "Bowditch"; indeed, the book was so dominant in the field that the term "Bowditch" was often used to describe almost any book of navigational charts and tables. Even in an age of satellite navigation, Bowditch remains a standard and is still in print.

Perhaps no American maritime enterprises suffered more from the Revolution than fishing and whaling. Not only did His Majesty's Navy and privateers drive American fishermen and whalers from the sea, but as a result of the war both lost their most important markets. Fishermen lost lucrative markets for their salt fish in the British West Indies, and whalers were confronted with exorbitant duties on their products in England after 1783.

New England was hard hit. During the peace negotiations ending the Revolution, John Adams, a staunch New Englander, had done all that he could to protect his region's interests. Late in 1782, after he had fended off a French scheme to deny Americans the right of fishing off Newfoundland, along with the apparent willingness of Congress to accept such a harmful measure, he wrote to his friend Elbridge Gerry in Marblehead "Thanks be to God that our Tom Cod are safe in spite of the malice of enemies, the finesse of allies, and the mistakes of Congress." Unfortunately, Adams succeeded only in part. He argued that Americans ought to have the "right" to fish in Canadian waters. In the end the treaty acknowledged the "liberty" of Americans to fish those waters. The change was more than semantic. For more than two hundred years Americans and Canadians have argued over fishing rights.

Political and diplomatic enemies abroad were only part of the problem for American cod fishermen, who numbered about 3,287, sailing in 539 vessels, during the late 1780s. The experience of Marblehead, Massachusetts, fishermen indicated that a vessel might earn a bit more than $450 a year on expenses of $416. This slim margin, which in years like 1789 might become an actual

deficit, kept fishermen on the edge of financial ruin. Then, in July 1789, Congress imposed duties on molasses, rum, fish hooks, lead, cordage, salt, and a variety of other commodities important to the fishermen. Caught between declining markets and rising costs, the New England fishermen howled in protest. Congress heard them, lowered the molasses duty, and, to encourage and protect the trade, offered a bounty of five cents per quintal (112 pounds) of dried fish and an equal amount for every barrel of pickled fish sent abroad, with a duty of fifty cents per quintal and seventy-five cents per barrel on fish imports. In 1792, the second Congress would simplify matters a bit and offer a direct subsidy to fishermen based on the tonnage of their vessels. This bounty system, which in 1792 could pay as much as $170 per vessel, was an investment in New England's codfishery that lasted until shortly after the Civil War.

Congress's attention helped. In the two decades between 1790 and 1810, the tonnage of the Massachusetts fishing fleet grew from about 20,000 tons to 69,000 tons, or about 1,100 fishing vessels. Half of them headed north around Cape Breton Island into the Bay of Chaleur and off the Labrador coast to fish for cod. Distances were so great to those grounds that only one trip per year was possible. The remainder of the fleet went to the closer Nova Scotia coast and the Grand Banks of Newfoundland, where as many as three trips per year could be made. Cleaned, salted, and stowed below, the cod was brought home to New England to be packed and shipped off. Catholic markets in Southern Europe received the first-quality fish, while the less perfect "refuse" fish was sent to feed slaves in the West Indies.

Whaling too suffered the pangs of separation from Great Britain. Concentrated for the most part in the ports of Massachusetts, particularly on the islands of Nantucket and Martha's Vineyard, the industry declined precipitously in the postwar years. Not only was the British market effectively closed by the high tariff of 1783, imposed by Parliament to foster the British whaling industry, but the habits of consumers changed as well. Wartime shortages of whale oil had turned Americans toward tallow candles, resulting in a steep decline in demand for whale products. To offset this decline and encourage recovery, in 1784 the State of Massachusetts offered bounties of five

After the Revolution, New England fishermen returned to their accustomed grounds off Nova Scotia and Newfoundland, in the Gulf of St. Lawrence, and offshore on the Grand Bank of Newfoundland. In this detail from a portrait of the ship America, *a New England fishing schooner lies at anchor on the busy Grand Bank (right), with others on the horizon. The ship* America *is hove to while the crew catches fish for provisions, and a French brig sails in the distance. During voyages that lasted weeks or even months, the fishermen made a meager living pulling codfish from the sea bottom with their baited hooks, then splitting and salting the fish for preservation. This painting is attributed to Michele Felice Cornè, ca. 1803. (Courtesy Peabody Essex Museum, Salem, Massachusetts; Mark Sexton photo)*

pounds per ton on white spermaceti oil, sixty shillings per ton on brown or yellow sperm oil, and forty shillings per ton on whale oil. Ironically, the bounties accomplished just what the state had wanted. They increased the supply of whale products. Unfortunately, they did not create a concomitant increase in the market for whale products. Oversupply resulted in falling prices.

By 1790 some recovery in the industry was at hand. Domestic consumers began to turn away from tallow and return to whale products. At the same time, as the keeper

of lighthouses, the Treasury Department decided to rely on whale oil for illumination, a measure that both encouraged the industry and increased the quality and brilliance of lighthouse illumination. Abroad too there were positive signs. While the British market remained inaccessible, new markets on the Continent, especially France, opened up.

These signs of modest recovery coincided with the opening of new whaling grounds in the Pacific. The *Amelia* of London was the first whaler to venture around Cape Horn and enter the Pacific Ocean, which would prove to be the richest sperm whale grounds in the world. Shortly after the *Amelia* returned in 1790, Americans headed for the Pacific. The *American Hero* of Hudson, New York, rolled down and around the Horn into the Pacific and returned a year later with 2,000 barrels of sperm oil. The rush to the Pacific whale harvest was on and, although a New York vessel led the American hunt into the Pacific, men from Nantucket soon came to dominate the grounds.

Alas, the opening of the Pacific grounds, which increased the supply of sperm oil, came as Europe entered the chaos of the French Revolution. The outbreak of war disrupted markets. Long voyages and a heavy investment in special equipment made it difficult for whalemen to adjust quickly to changes in the market. An abrupt contraction of the fleet came about as both Great Britain and France, in the course of warring against one another, seized American vessels, including whalers.

Despite the situation overseas, the domestic market for whale products grew sufficiently to support a modestly growing business. Nantucket held its lead and, by 1807, 120 whaleships sailed from the port to hunt leviathan as far away as Brazil, the Indian and Pacific Oceans, and Australia.

As old trades and business relationships reemerged so too did old enemies. Since the mid-1780s the Barbary corsairs had generally ignored American ships that ventured to Southern Europe. In part this was a result of an ongoing war with the Portuguese, who effectively blockaded the Straits of Gibraltar, preventing the corsairs from sailing into the Atlantic. Unfortunately for the United States, Portugal and Algiers concluded a treaty early in the fall of 1793, and within days Algerine xebecs were preying on American trade.

News of the Algerine captures moved Congress and the president to establish a navy, as authorized by the Constitution, but not without considerable debate. Several members from Southern states spoke in opposition. They were fearful that by building a navy the nation would be tempted to entwine itself in foreign adventures. Others saw in the plan an attempt on the part of the Northern states to grab profitable public shipbuilding contracts. Opposition notwithstanding,

on 27 March 1794 Congress authorized the construction of six frigates, three of forty-four guns and three of thirty-six guns. To appease their opponents, the pro-navy members agreed that construction on the ships would halt if peace were secured with Algiers.

With plans drawn by the well-known Philadelphia naval architect Joshua Humphreys, aided by skilled draftsmen Josiah Fox and Thomas Doughty, builders at the ports of Portsmouth, New Hampshire, Boston, New York, Philadelphia, Baltimore, and Gosport (near Norfolk), Virginia, got underway. It took considerable time to organize construction and assemble materials. Amidst this effort came news that peace had indeed been secured with Algiers on 5 September 1795. In accordance with the act of 27 March, President Washington ordered construction halted. At the same time, however, he also asked Congress to authorize the completion of three of the six frigates. On 20 April Congress agreed and permitted the completion of frigates at Boston (*Constitution*), Philadelphia (*United States*), and Baltimore (*Constellation*).

Washington's desire to complete at least three of the frigates was in part a reaction to a series of distressing events overseas. Although under Washington's administration the nation was politically stable and the economy improving, there were ominous signs of trouble. Not the least of these was the outbreak of war between France and Great Britain, an event that promised to upset the tenuous stability of the Atlantic world. In December 1793, Secretary of State Thomas Jefferson summed up his observations on the unsettling state of maritime commerce.

> First in Europe–
> Our bread stuff is at most times under prohibitory duties in England, and considerable duties on re-exportation from Spain to her colonies.
> Our tobaccos are heavily dutied in England, Sweden, France and prohibited in Spain and Portugal.
> Our rice is heavily dutied in England and Sweden and prohibited in Portugal.
> Our fish and salted provisions are prohibited in England and under prohibitory duties in France.
> Our whale oils are prohibited in England and Portugal.

And our vessels are denied naturalization in England, and of late, in France.

Second in the West Indies–
All intercourse is prohibited with the possessions of Spain and Portugal.
Our salted provisions and fish are prohibited by England.
Our salted pork and breadstuff (except maize) are received under temporary laws only in the dominions of France, and our salted fish pays there a weighty duty.

Third. In the article of navigation–
Our own carriage of our own tobacco is heavily dutied in Sweden, and lately in France.
We can carry no article, not of our own production, to the British ports in Europe. Nor even our own produce to her American possessions.

Noting Jefferson's "just apprehensions," Washington dispatched John Jay, Chief Justice of the Supreme Court, to negotiate a treaty with Great Britain in April 1794. Jay's instructions fell into four categories. He was first to negotiate an end to the "vexations, spoliations, captures etc" that had resulted from British seizure of American vessels and seamen since the outbreak of the war with France. Second, he was to insist that the British live up to the provisions of the Treaty of 1783, and in particular that they evacuate the western American posts that they still held. Third, the issue of debts owed by both sides needed to be concluded. Finally, Jay was instructed to secure a reopening of the West Indies trade.

Jay succeeded in extracting a treaty out of the British, but it fell far short of American expectations. The British did consent to abandon the western posts that they had been holding since the end of the Revolution, but on other points they were far less conciliatory. In the matter of the West Indies they would only allow vessels of seventy tons or less to trade–a restriction that might permit the majority of American vessels sailing from United States ports to carry produce to the islands–but which effectively eliminated any opportunity for a West Indies-to-Europe carrying trade in larger American vessels. Furthermore, American vessels could only carry American products to the

islands, and any island products going out in American bottoms could only be shipped to an American port and could not be reexported. These were humiliating conditions.

Jay's Treaty touched off a storm of opposition in the United States. Maritime interests in particular were not happy with the restrictions. But however merchants might sputter and fume, they were left with little choice except to support the treaty dictated by the new nation's most important trading partner. Indeed, were the treaty rejected, economic hardship would befall not only the merchants but the entire nation. Nearly 90 percent of the federal government's income was derived from tariffs. Any disruption in trade would bring a precipitous decline in revenue. On 24 June 1795, with a notable lack of enthusiasm but a deep sense of realism, the Senate ratified the treaty.

Quasi-War with France

If Jay's Treaty did little to reconcile America to Great Britain, it certainly helped to divide France from her former ally. The revolutionary government in Paris viewed the apparent rapprochement between England and the United States as a betrayal of the Treaty of 1778. Hence, they determined upon retaliation and turned a sour face across the Atlantic, launching themselves on a course to harass American commerce.

American vulnerability to French annoyance was most acute in the West Indies. With a studied casualness the government in Paris tolerated the seizure of American vessels by both French national warships and French privateers on the grounds that the vessels in question were engaged in illegal trade with France's enemies. In December 1796, when the American minister Charles Cotesworth Pinckney arrived in Paris to discuss the rising crisis the government refused to receive him.

Relations between the United States and France deteriorated rapidly. On 4 March 1797 the new president, John Adams, took the oath of office. Only two days before the French had issued a decree permitting attacks against American vessels, sending marine insurance rates from

William Birch and Son labeled this engraving of the frigate Philadelphia *under construction "Preparation for WAR to defend Commerce." The man standing at left center may represent Joshua Humphreys, the Philadelphia shipbuilder who received the commission to design the six U.S. Navy frigates authorized in 1794, or Josiah Fox, who collaborated on the final designs and also designed the* Philadelphia. *Underwritten by the citizens of Philadelphia in response to the Quasi-War with France, the* Philadelphia *was one of several naval vessels built by private subscription rather than public expenditure and presented to the U.S. Navy. This twenty-eight-gun frigate was built in the city's Southwark neighborhood in 1798-99 and commissioned in 1800. After capturing several French prizes in the Caribbean before the end of the Quasi-War, the* Philadelphia *made a year-long Mediterranean cruise in 1801. Two years later she returned to the Mediterranean to fight in the war with Tripoli. On 31 October 1803 the* Philadelphia *ran aground off Tripoli and was captured by the Tripolitans, only to be destroyed in a daring raid led by Lieutenant Stephen Decatur, Jr., in February 1804. (Courtesy Free Library of Philadelphia)*

their normal 6 percent for West Indies voyages to more than 30 percent. On 14 March, President Adams learned that Pinckney had been rebuffed. That same day he sought advice from his cabinet and summoned a special session of Congress before which he laid out the details of the French crisis. Still seeking an amicable solution, Adams, with the consent of Congress, sent three special commissioners to Paris: Charles Cotesworth Pinckney, John Marshall, and Elbridge Gerry.

Pinckney, Marshall, and Gerry found a cool reception in Paris. Amid the shifting power structure of revolutionary Paris, the Americans were first shunned and then insulted by veiled threats and demands for bribes. After weeks of frustration they reported to the president.

On 19 March 1798, Adams forwarded a message to Congress alluding to dispatches he had received from his envoys. He reported, "I per-

During the war with France, the frigate Constitution *patrolled the coast of Hispaniola to intercept commerce with the French colony of Saint Domingue. In May of 1800, Captain Silas Talbot of the* Constitution *learned that the French-owned ship* Sandwich *was loading coffee at Puerto Plata, in the former Spanish colony of Hispaniola. Although Spain had ceded the territory to France in 1795, Puerto Plata remained under Spanish control and was, therefore, neutral territory. Risking diplomatic censure, Talbot sent Lieutenant Isaac Hull to capture the* Sandwich. *Hull commandeered the American sloop* Sally, *which was engaged in smuggling, loaded her with ninety sailors and marines, and came alongside the* Sandwich *on a peaceful Sunday. In this view, the Americans storm aboard the* Sandwich *while a boatload of U.S. Marines heads ashore to spike the cannon in the fort overlooking the harbor. In a bloodless action, both the* Sandwich *and* Sally *were brought out of Puerto Plata as prizes, only to be surrendered to Spain as reparations for the breach of Spanish neutrality. Michele Felice Cornè painted this view of the action. (Courtesy Boston Athenaeum)*

ceive no ground of expectation that the objects of their mission can be accomplished on terms compatible with the safety, the honor, or the essential interests of the nation." On 2 April the House requested to see the dispatches. Adams sent them over the following day, knowing full well they would stun the members. The letters revealed that certain French agents, referred to only as X, Y, and Z, had approached the American envoys and told them bluntly that only by public apology on the part of President Adams and the payment of a large bribe would relations be restored. Although members initially pledged to keep the papers confidential, the House of Representatives reversed itself and voted to publish the dispatches.

Congressional and public action was predictable. One Federalist newspaper noted angrily, "To be lukewarm after reading the horrid scenes is to be criminal–and the man who does not warmly reprobate the conduct of the French must have a soul black enough to be *fit* for *treasons stratagems* and *spoils.*"

Determined to defend the Republic, Congress instructed the president to fit the three frigates *Constitution, Constellation,* and *United States* for sea. Three weeks later they enacted a law "to provide an additional armament for the further protection of the trade of the United States; and for other purposes." It authorized the president to build, purchase, or hire "a number of vessels, not exceeding twelve, nor carrying more than twenty-two guns each to be armed, fitted out, and manned under his direction." On 30 April 1798, Congress created the Department of the Navy at cabinet rank. Benjamin Stoddert of Maryland became the first secretary. Congress then authorized the president to direct American armed vessels to "seize, take, and bring into any port of the United States" any armed vessel found "hovering" along the American coast and to retake any American vessel that might have been captured. Thus began the Quasi-War with France.

Neither the United States nor France had much to gain from this war. Nonetheless, for the next two years these former allies contended with one another. With some minor exceptions virtually all of the action took place at sea in the West Indies, where Stoddert divided his forces into two squadrons. One kept station near the French islands of Guadeloupe and Martinique and the other near Hispaniola. The former's principal mission was to keep watch for French warships and privateers that might sortie from those islands, while the latter patrolled the waters off Hispaniola, convoying the stream of American merchant vessels bound to the islands.

Although nominally French, Hispaniola was in chaos. Inspired by the rhetoric of the French Revolution–"Liberty, Equality and Fraternity"–slaves on the island had struck for freedom. Led by the remarkable Toussaint L'Ouverture, black armies were struggling to gain freedom and independence for the island. American merchants had been quick to take advantage of the island's condition, and were busily involved in the coffee and sugar trades. To continue this lucrative business, however, they needed protection against a swarm of privateers and pirates that had been let loose in the confusion.

In this, its first effort to defend the new Republic, the U.S. Navy acquitted itself well. Altogether fifty-four vessels served. They captured eighty-five French ships, including the frigates *Le Berceau* and *L'Insurgente,* at a cost of only one American warship, the schooner *Retaliation.* In addition, the government granted nearly 400 privateering commissions. For the most part, however, these were of little use since the British navy had seen to it that there were few French merchantmen to be taken.

Neither President Adams nor the French government desired or intended that this war should become a major event. Deeply engaged in their struggle with Great Britain, the French had little interest in taking on another adversary. As for the Americans, while the war was popular in some quarters, that popularity ran thin as taxes were levied to support the effort. No one understood the need for peace better than John Adams.

As early as October 1799, against the advice of his cabinet, Adams had sent a delegation to negotiate a peace. By the spring of 1800 the discussions were in a stalemate, but in July the French changed their terms. The Americans were able to reach an agreement, and on 1 October 1800 a convention was signed. It took more than a year to work out the myriad diplomatic details, but at the end of 1800 Stoddert instructed his commanders to "treat the armed vessels of France, public or private, exactly as you find they treat our trading vessels." With the French menace eliminated, American shipowners could renew their lucrative business in the West Indies without fear of French interference.

While the Quasi-War temporarily disrupted American trade with the West Indies, it had no effect in other parts of the world. From 1797 to 1800, American registered tonnage increased by 15 percent, and freight earnings increased as well. A world at war was a boon to American shipowners. Thanks to the Royal Navy, which had nearly swept the seas clear of other merchant carriers, the United States had become the preeminent neutral nation in shipping.

America's merchant marine thrived by taking up the carrying trade of others even as American exports burgeoned. Eli Whitney's invention of the cotton gin in 1793 quickly made it possible for the American South to harvest and process cotton in quantities never before imagined. Between 1793 and 1800 cotton exports went from less than a half million pounds to nearly twenty million pounds. Newly opened and mechanized English textile mills provided an enormous market for American cotton.

The first bag of American cotton arrived in Liverpool in January 1785 direct from Charleston, South Carolina. The second bag, however, came via New York on board the ship *Tonquin.* Within four years the port of New York became the principal exporter of cotton, surpassing all the Southern ports as well as its chief rival, Philadelphia. Herein were the beginnings of the "Cotton Triangle," by which Southern cotton went to overseas markets via New York, and return cargoes of manufactured goods found their way back to the South via the same route. New York's initial advantage in this trade would yield great benefits to the port in the years to come.

The expanding cotton economy increased the demand for slave labor. Virginia had prohibited

James Forten, Sailmaker

When wealthy African-American sailmaker James Forten died in March 1842 he was eulogized in reform circles as a champion of causes ranging from abolition to women's rights. However, although committed to an agenda he hoped would bring about America's moral rebirth, Forten saw himself primarily as "a man of business," someone intimately connected with the commercial life of one of the nation's premier ports. And that was how many of Philadelphia's white merchants saw him. They had bought sails from him, borrowed money from him, made loans to him, traded real estate with him, mulled over the state of the market with him, and gossiped about him. Now they joined with abolitionists and reformers to pay a final tribute to a remarkable man who had had a foot in both camps.

James Forten was born in Philadelphia on 2 September, 1766. In a city where most of the 1,400 black residents were slaves, he was freeborn. His father, Thomas, had himself been born free, but Thomas's father—James's grandfather—was an African slave. James's mother, Margaret, had probably spent her early years in bondage.

Thomas Forten was a jour-neyman sailmaker in Robert Bridges's loft, and the loft became school, playroom, and workplace for James. He earned his first few pennies sweeping the floor, salvaging scraps of twine and canvas, and melting beeswax and shaping it into handy-sized pieces for the journeymen to wax their thread with. And as soon as James could handle a palm and a needle, his father began teaching him how to sew a sail.

In 1773 Thomas died. Margaret struggled to support the family, and for two years managed to send James to the Quakers' "African School." Eventually, though, he had to go out to work. He found a job cleaning and clerking for a grocer. It was not what his parents had hoped for, but with tensions between Britain and her American colonies disrupting trade, job prospects were limited.

The war brought new opportunities. Robert Bridges was one of many businessmen who combined patriotism with profit. He owned shares in six privateers, and Forten, now into his teens, may have worked in his loft, helping to make or repair their sails.

In 1781 James Forten signed on to serve on the privateer *Royal Louis*. Young, strong, and handy with a needle and palm, he was the sort of recruit Captain Stephen Decatur, Sr., could use. But why would Forten risk his life for the American cause? After all, most leading Patriots shied away from discussing racial equality. Despite all the evidence to the contrary, though, he believed an American victory would lead to profound social changes. On a more practical level, privateering offered the chance to make money.

His first voyage was a great success, but his second ended abruptly when his ship was captured. Forten and the rest of the crew found themselves in irons aboard HMS *Amphion*, bound for the prison-hulks in New York Harbor. That was bad enough, but Forten had heard that the British sold black prisoners as slaves. A curious twist of fate saved him from enslavement. The *Amphion*'s captain, John Bazely, had his young son, Henry, on board. Bored and idle, the boy was constantly in trouble. He needed a companion, and Bazely spotted fifteen-year-old James Forten. Impressed by his "honest and open countenance," he assigned him to keep Henry out of mischief.

As the *Amphion* neared New York and Bazely made ready to discharge his prisoners, Henry begged him to spare his new friend. Bazely sent for Forten and made him an extraordinary offer. Would he come to England and be educated with Henry? To the amazement of father and son, Forten refused, insisting: "I have been taken prisoner for the liberties of my country, and never will prove a traitor." Bazely had no choice but to send him to a prison-ship, although he did give orders that he be treated the same as the white prisoners. Forten spent seven months on the infamous *Jersey*, battling hunger and disease. In 1782 he was exchanged and returned home to find his family had given him up for dead.

Once the war ended, Forten ventured off to sea again. When his ship reached London, he asked to be discharged. While it is tempting to imagine him visiting the Bazelys, there is no evidence to suggest he did. He probably found work in a sail loft, for the war had left many British dockyards short of skilled workers.

In 1785 he was back home in Philadelphia working as an apprentice in Robert Bridges's loft. Within a year he was the foreman, with Bridges quelling a minor rebellion to keep him in that position. In the normal course of events he would have remained as foreman, employed by Bridges, and then by whichever son or son-in-law inherited the business. However, that was not

Bridges's intention. He had become a sailmaker because his merchant father had died young and his guardians had bound him out to learn a trade. He wanted better for his own sons. They would become merchants. As for his daughters, they would marry merchants, not artisans. His designated successor in the sail-loft was his foreman.

As foreman of the Bridges loft James Forten mastered the technological aspects of his craft. He also learned how to deal with captains and shipowners–white men who looked askance at Bridges's choice of a successor. Then there was the vexed issue of

This watercolor attributed to African-American artist Robert Douglass, Jr., is believed to depict James Forten (1766-1842). (Courtesy Leon Gardiner Collection, The Historical Society of Pennsylvania)

interacting with white workingmen. When Bridges retired, his apprentices "all, with one consent, agreed to take [Forten] as their new master." But the journeymen were worried. Would Forten succeed? Would they be paid regularly? Robert Bridges came to the rescue with moral and financial support, and there was no exodus of journeymen.

Forten never forgot Bridges's decision to stand by him. Nor did he forget his early labor troubles. Once secure as owner of the loft, he integrated the workforce. He brought his relatives into the business, hiring his three nephews, his niece's husband, and his father-in-law. Eventually his sons began learning his trade. But Forten wanted to do more than ensure the prosperity of his family. He often lamented the fact that there were so few chances for young black men to learn skilled trades. "If a man of color has children, it is almost impossible for him to get a trade for them, as the journeymen and apprentices generally refuse to work with them, even if the master is willing, which is seldom the case," he wrote.

If too few white masters would train black men, then black masters must make a commitment to do so. Forten's loft produced two generations of African-American sailmakers. Some eventually established their own businesses. Two went to California, two to Haiti, and another to Liberia. Two more bought the loft from Forten's heirs. At no point did Forten consider dismissing his white workers. He kept those who had worked for Bridges and hired more. Deeply committed to the idea of integration, he wanted a workforce in which black men and white men worked harmoniously together.

So much for Forten's workers, but what about his clients? He retained Robert Bridges's customers and gained new ones. He had the advantage of beginning in business as Philadelphians were entering the China trade. They needed to fit out their vessels with the finest quality sails for the long voyage to Asia and back. If Forten produced the best sails, then that fact outweighed all other considerations. His loft was on the premises of the powerful mercantile firm of Willing & Francis. The partners gave him many commissions. Near neighbors were merchants Louis Clapier and Stephen Girard, and Forten received orders from them. Another valued customer was Patrick Hayes, nephew of Commodore John Barry. Hayes had interests in the China trade and in commerce with Cuba. He was a Warden of the Port of Philadelphia, and his son, who commanded several of his vessels, was married to Commodore William Bainbridge's daughter. In an association that lasted well over a decade, Forten supplied sails and sailmaker's gear, did repairs, redesigned sail plans, and even made a cover for Hayes's piano.

Forten learned early in his career the wisdom of diversifying investments. He used profits from his loft to buy real estate. Some properties he sold, and others he rented out. With his earnings he acquired bonds, mortgages, bank stock, and shares in various companies. And he made loans.

For more than forty years Forten was an active participant in a complex network of credit arrangements. His transactions almost always involved men he knew as customers or as neighbors, either at South Wharves, where his loft was located, or on Lombard Street, where he lived. These men borrowed from him; they also loaned money to him. It depended on many variables whether at any given time one was a debtor or a creditor.

But buying and selling, borrowing and lending–these transactions only constitute a part of the equation. What did the predominantly white business community think of Forten? He had his close friends, like merchants William Deas and Thomas Ash, and Captain Daniel Brewton, a fellow prisoner from the *Jersey*. Then there were hundreds of acquaintances, like Charles Perry, who carried word of Forten's entrepreneurial success to Cuba. The likes of Perry never quite knew what to make of Forten. They certainly gossiped about him. In 1831, when Harriet Forten married the son of an Anglo-Scottish cotton merchant and his mulatto mistress, word went around that Forten had made "some sacrifice of his fortune" to buy "a whiter species" of husband for his daughter. It made a good story except for a few crucial facts. Light-skinned Robert Purvis, who could have "passed" as white, chose to identify himself as a man of color; he was an outspoken abolitionist; and he was richer than Forten.

For James Forten the inescapable fact was that, try

as he might to be a member of the merchant fraternity–"a gentleman of the pave"–who happened to be of African descent, he was, to all but a handful of men in the business community, a man of color first. They saved his letters because, as one observed, it was a novelty to have a letter from "a Negro gentleman." Merchant Samuel Breck, who admired Forten for his respectability, paid him a backhanded compliment. He was "a black gentleman. . . [who] by his urbane manners, manly and correct deportment, deserves the epithet I have used, [in spite of] his black face." As an abolitionist editor observed, to "white men in Philadelphia. . . [i]t would have seemed a sort of sacrilege to despise him, and they made him an exception to his race."

It was this contradiction that puzzled an English visitor to Philadelphia in the spring of 1842. He was greatly impressed by the throngs of black and white, rich and poor, who followed James Forten's coffin to St. Thomas's African Episcopal Church:

> I was rejoicing that his colour had proved no impediment to his rising in the world, and that he had been allowed so much

In this view of Philadelphia's Arch Street Ferry Landing, small coastal trading sloops and large ocean sailing ships line the waterfront. Here, near the wharf and warehouse of leading merchant Stephen Girard, travelers coming and going on the ferry to New Jersey, agricultural produce of the surrounding region, and exotic products of ports from China, Europe, and the Caribbean share space on the busy wharves. One of the longshoremen handling cargo at lower left appears to be depicted as black, which is appropriate for Philadelphia, where African Americans made up almost 20 percent of the maritime labor force at this time. William Birch & Son published this engraving in 1800. (Courtesy Library of Congress)

> fair play as to succeed in over-topping the majority of his white competitors, when I learnt. . . that, not long before his death, he had been especially mortified, because two of his sons had been refused a hearing at a public meeting where they wished to speak on some subject connected with trade.

The realization that he and his children could advance so far and no farther in an America that sanctioned slavery and racial barriers in commerce and society, motivated Forten to devote much of his wealth, built on maritime opportunity, and his time to the abolition of slavery and the promotion of social reform. But that is the other half of James Forten's story, and beyond the scope of this brief sketch.

further importation of African slaves in 1778, and economic depression in the former tobacco colonies kept the demand for slaves low there as well. But further south, demand increased as cotton culture spread through the 1790s. Provisions worked out during the Constitutional Convention left slavery and the slave trade essentially unhampered for twenty years–until 1 January 1808. With the expansion of cotton, those twenty years saw the largest importation of African slaves of any twenty-year period in American history. Savannah, Georgia, became the leading slave port in the 1790s, but in 1804 South Carolina would reopen its ports to slavers to replenish the labor force on the state's rice and cotton plantations. From 1804 to 1808 Charleston was the leading port, receiving nearly 10,000 Africans annually. Between 1783 and 1808 the total number of slaves brought into the U.S. approached 100,000, or almost 20 percent of the Africans brought over since 1619. While the trade would legally end on the first day of 1808, the new and expanding emphasis on cotton production would encourage the smuggling of slaves for decades to come.

Cotton was not the only American export finding overseas demand. The disruptions of wartime meant that foodstuffs, grains, and meat fetched premium prices in European markets. New farmland opened along the Mohawk River in New York and elsewhere produced increasing supplies of agricultural produce to meet this demand. New York City, Philadelphia, and Baltimore, each having the advantage of access to rich farmland via navigable rivers, enjoyed increased activity as a result of agricultural exports.

That America should be blessed by Europe's distress did not always sit well abroad, particularly in London. Having gone to the trouble of isolating French and Spanish colonies in the Americas from their mother countries, the British were understandably angry at Americans who now, under the claim of neutrality, were carrying on the very trades they had worked to destroy. American shipowners took a very generous view of the rights of neutrals and argued that they were operating fully within the realm of international law. The British, on the other hand, had a very different view. They also had the world's most powerful navy.

On 4 March 1801, Thomas Jefferson took the oath of office as third president of the United States. In his inaugural address the new president spoke of America "engaged in commerce with nations who feel power and forget right." Jefferson, who had once served as American minister in Paris, understood well the nature of America's maritime difficulty. Ironically, however, Jefferson's first challenge abroad came not from the British but from an old adversary–the Barbary corsairs.

War With Tripoli

Pasha Yusuf Karamanli of Tripoli was unhappy that the expected tribute from the United States had not arrived, and the American consul in Tripoli, James Cathcart, seemed unable to provide acceptable reasons for the delay. On the afternoon of 14 May 1801, Tripoli declared war on the United States in their time-honored way–the pasha sent a delegation to the American consulate where they proceeded to chop down the flagpole. Within days, Tripolitan corsairs were prowling for American victims. Cathcart reported that "their mode of attack is first to fire a Broadside, and then to set up a great shout in order to intimidate their enemy, they then board you if you let them, with as Many men as they can, armed with Pistols, large and small knives and probably a few with Blunderbusses; if you beat them off once they seldom risque a second encounter, and three well directed broadsides will ensure you a complete Victory."

Even before he learned of the declaration of war, Jefferson had settled on sending a naval squadron to the Mediterranean. On 20 May 1801 he ordered Commodore Richard Dale with the frigates *President*, *Philadelphia*, and *Essex*, and the schooner *Enterprise*, to sail for the Mediterranean. In August the *Enterprise* had the first action with the Tripolitans when she captured the *Tripoli* off the coast of Malta. Despite the *Enterprise*'s small success, Dale's mission was a failure. With only four ships, and only one with a draft shallow enough to allow her to sail close to shore, Dale found it impossible to hold a blockade against Tripoli. In September he abandoned the blockade, and early in 1802 he returned home.

Dale's successor, Commodore Richard V. Morris, arrived with a stronger force; however, he had no more success than Dale in bringing the Tripolitans to terms. Indeed, Morris's failures were even more egregious than Dale's. He returned to the United States in the spring of 1803 to be censured by a court of inquiry for "inactive and dilatory conduct."

Jefferson's poor luck with naval commanders for the Mediterranean finally turned with the appointment of Edward Preble, a captain who was as hard and sharp as the Maine coast from which he came. Born in 1761 at Falmouth (later Portland), Maine, Preble first went to sea in 1778 as a seaman aboard the privateer *Hope*. Two years later he was serving in the Massachusetts State Navy as an acting midshipman on the frigate *Protector*, commanded by John Foster Williams. In the postwar years he turned to the merchant service and within a short time was commanding vessels on coastal and transatlantic routes. But the routine of mercantile voyaging was not to his liking, and as soon as Congress founded the U.S. Navy Preble was at the door seeking a commission. However, not until 1798, with the onset of the Quasi-War, did he get his appointment. Preble acquitted himself well, and his obvious talents won him promotion to captain in 1799. With the rank came a greater command–the frigate *Essex*, subscribed by the citizens of Essex County, Massachusetts, and given to the U.S. Navy that year–which he had the honor of commanding when she became the first American warship to double the Cape of Good Hope and show the flag in the Indian Ocean.

On 14 August 1803 Preble got underway. In addition to the *Constitution*, Preble's squadron consisted of the frigate *Philadelphia*, sloops *Argus* and *Siren*, and schooners *Nautilus*, *Vixen* and *Enterprise*. When the fleet arrived at Gibraltar a month later, Preble found that Tripoli was still actively at war against the United States; Tunis had expelled the American consul; and Morocco was making belligerent threats. Only Algiers showed good will toward the United States. Preble concluded that force was the only answer.

True to his commander's aggressive example, Captain William Bainbridge of the *Philadelphia* pursued a Tripolitan vessel toward Tripoli harbor. Running before the wind with cannons firing and an enemy about to be taken, all on board the frigate were drawn into the excitement. Bainbridge knew the waters were shallow; indeed, he had three leadsmen heaving from the chains and calling out the depth. When his quarry escaped, Bainbridge brought the *Philadelphia* around and was beating back into open water when he suddenly felt his ship shudder and grind to a stop. She was hard aground on a sloping ledge. Frantic attempts to lighten and refloat the vessel failed, and soon the Tripolitans had overwhelmed the helpless frigate. For the next nineteen months and three days the *Philadelphia*'s 307 crew members were prisoners in Tripoli. The frigate herself, however, was destined for a different fate.

Almost as soon as Preble learned that the *Philadelphia* was in the hands of the enemy he made plans to destroy her. On the evening of 16 February 1804, Lieutenant Stephen Decatur took the sloop *Intrepid* into Tripoli harbor disguised as a local vessel. With a Sicilian pilot on deck, Decatur and eighty American volunteers lay below as the *Intrepid* sailed quietly toward the *Philadelphia*. As they came alongside, the Americans rushed on deck, heaved grappling hooks, and swarmed onto the *Philadelphia*'s spar deck. Caught unawares, the Tripolitans either surrendered or jumped over the side. Within minutes, Decatur's men had set their incendiaries and ignited the ship. From shore the pasha of Tripoli could only watch as his prize frigate was engulfed in flames.

Having humbled the Tripolitans and regained American honor–renowned British Admiral Horatio Nelson reportedly referred to Decatur's triumph as "the most bold and daring act of the age"–Preble returned to the business of protecting trade and blockading Tripoli.

During the next ten months, Preble bombarded Tripoli five times. His energy and bravery against the corsairs made him a national hero. In September 1804, Samuel Barron replaced him as commodore, and in the spring of 1805, thanks in great measure to Preble's actions, the Tripolitans signed a peace treaty with the United States by which they agreed to release American hostages and refrain from molesting American trade. In return the United States agreed to pay the pasha $60,000.

Louisiana

Jefferson's policy of diplomacy backed by force worked well in the Mediterranean, where it secured important commercial advantages for American trade. On the Mississippi River the challenge was even greater. By 1800 nearly one million Americans were living in the area between the Appalachians and the Mississippi River. The lure of cheap land, and in some cases free land for veterans of the Revolution, had drawn these people west to farm the rich soil of the Ohio and Mississippi valleys. As settlement increased, new states entered the union: Kentucky in 1792, Tennessee in 1796, and Ohio in 1803. As western farmers prospered they looked for ways to get their produce to markets in the eastern United States as well as overseas. Land transportation across the Appalachians was expensive and difficult, and so they floated their crops down the river system to the port of New Orleans.

Founded in 1718 by the French as part of their grand scheme for a North American empire, New Orleans stood guardian over the most important route into the interior of the American continent. The Seven Years' War had ended French dreams for a North American empire, and as part of the final settlement of that war France had given the territory of Louisiana, including New Orleans, to Spain. In 1795 the American minister to Spain, Thomas Pinckney, negotiated a treaty by which Spain guaranteed free navigation on the Mississippi and granted the right of deposit for American goods at New Orleans.

Americans were generally content with the agreement with Spain. As a weak and declining power in the Western Hemisphere, Spain posed no threat to the expanding United States, and New Orleans appeared destined, eventually, to fall into American hands. Contentment turned into near panic when, shortly after his inauguration, President Jefferson learned that under heavy pressure from the Emperor Napoleon, Spain had ceded Louisiana back to France.

Napoleon's plans were always grand in scale. In 1802 he had signed a peace with England, the treaty of Amiens. Neither he nor the British believed that this was anything more than an interlude in their war for the control of Europe; nonetheless, Napoleon took the opportunity to begin his plan for the reestablishment of the French empire in the Western Hemisphere. His plan of empire was centered on Hispaniola, then the richest island in the Caribbean, which had been in a state of revolt for ten years. Although

Captain Edward Preble (1761-1807), went to sea aboard an American privateer at age sixteen and survived internment on the British prison hulk Jersey *after his capture aboard the Massachusetts Navy frigate* Protector *in 1781. Preble finished the war in naval service, then commanded merchant vessels in the Atlantic trade for fifteen years before applying for a commission in the new U.S. Navy in 1798. As commander of the frigate* Essex, *Captain Preble was the first to take an American naval vessel into the Indian Ocean. Having contracted malaria during the voyage, Preble submitted his resignation in 1802, but was put on sick leave and then given command of a Mediterranean squadron to operate against Tripoli in 1803. His success was crucial to the development of the U.S. Navy. Preble was widely known for his quick and violent temper, but his Mediterranean squadron provided essential training for "Preble's boys": William Bainbridge, Stephen Decatur, Isaac Hull, James Lawrence, Thomas Macdonough, David Porter, and several others who admired him greatly and would demonstrate their promise during the War of 1812. Preble did not live to see their naval success. When superseded by a senior officer in the Mediterranean late in 1804, Preble resigned, dying three years later as a result of tuberculosis and the stomach ulcers from which he suffered for much of his life. Rembrandt Peale painted this oil portrait of Preble, holding a chart of Tripoli, in 1805. (Courtesy U.S. Naval Academy Museum)*

In 1801 the Pasha of Tripoli declared war on the United States to demand annual tribute for permitting American merchant ships to sail the Mediterranean. The U.S. Navy had limited success in combatting the Tripolitans until Captain Preble took command of the squadron in 1803. Although the frigate Philadelphia *ran aground and was captured, along with her crew of 300, the squadron maintained a blockade of Tripoli and destroyed the captured* Philadelphia. *Then, on 3 August 1804, the USS* Constitution *(right center) led the squadron, including several Sicilian gunboats, into the harbor to force the return of American prisoners. In hand-to-hand combat as well as long-range cannon fire, the squadron captured Tripolitan gunboats and merchant vessels, and bombarded the pasha's palace. Subsequent assaults and the ongoing blockade finally brought an end to the Tripolitan war in 1805 with an exchange of prisoners, ransom for the American captives, and free passage for American merchant ships in the Mediterranean. Michele Felice Corné completed this oil painting of the 3 August action in 1805. (Courtesy U.S. Naval Academy Museum)*

rich in sugar and coffee, the island needed a reliable source of timber and foodstuffs. Louisiana could supply these needs and so the two might be joined–Hispaniola supported by Louisiana.

Alarmed by the consequences of such a Napoleonic foothold, Jefferson informed Robert R. Livingston, the American minister in Paris, of his concern about "New Orleans, through which the produce of three-eighths of our territory must pass to market. France placing herself in that door, assumes to us the attitude of defiance. The day that France takes possession of New Orleans [we will be forced to] marry ourselves to the British fleet and nation."

To forestall such a calamity Jefferson instructed Livingston to open negotiations for the purchase of New Orleans. The president authorized him to offer up to two million dollars. At the same time, he sent his friend James Monroe to assist Livingston. Monroe arrived in Paris on 12 April 1803. Two days later the French Foreign Minister Talleyrand stunned Monroe and

Livingston by offering to sell them all of Louisiana including New Orleans. Talleyrand, of course, was operating at the direction of Napoleon, whose scheme for a new American empire was rapidly becoming impossible.

Under Toussaint L'Ouverture, the people of Hispaniola continued their rebellion against French domination. Thirty thousand troops sent to the island by Napoleon had been decimated by Toussaint's forces and by mosquito-borne yellow fever. With little prospect of subduing Hispaniola, the French now found Louisiana to be more of an expense than a strategic territory. With war threatening again in Europe and a treasury in need of replenishment, Napoleon decided that the best course was to rid himself of his American adventure and sell out to the United States.

Even though the offer exceeded the price allowed in their instructions, Livingston and Monroe wisely decided to take up Talleyrand's offer.

On 30 April 1803 the United States bought the Louisiana Territory for fifteen million dollars. New Orleans, the Mississippi River, and western trade were securely in U.S. hands.

Hazards of Neutral Trade

As expected, the peace between England and France ended in May 1803. Continental nations watched helplessly as the Royal Navy swept their merchant fleets off the seas. In this vacuum American neutral shipping blossomed once again. To carry goods from foreign possessions to Europe, Americans relied upon an internationally accepted legal doctrine known as the "broken voyage." American shipowners maintained that by landing foreign cargo in the United States, they ended or "broke" their voyage. Theoretically they entered and paid duties on the goods, but customs regulations provided drawbacks, or refunds, on duties paid for goods later reexported. When they reexported cargo it qualified as American, and was therefore considered neutral goods. In practice this meant that sugar picked up by an American vessel in the French islands became "American" after it was landed in Salem, and it remained so even if it was reexported to a French port. If stopped by

and to handle this volume the nation's registered tonnage increased by 20 percent.

As long as the United States remained unaligned in the European war, American merchants and mariners could benefit from neutral trade with both England and France. But, if allowed to continue, the legal fiction of the "broken voyage" would defeat the whole purpose of the British blockade against France and her allies. It was just such a concern that dominated the Admiralty court room in Nassau on a July day in 1805.

The case involved the ship *Essex* of Salem. According to Admiralty documents, she was stopped at sea by the Royal Navy and found to be "wholly laden with goods the produce of Spain, bound to a Spanish colony, having previously called in at a port on the continent of America, where the cargo was unladen, and there almost immediately reshipped." Being "reshipped" of course was the legal fiction the *Essex*'s Captain Joseph Orne hoped would save him from condemnation, as it had so many before him. However, with the war in Europe raging and American carriers so flagrantly carrying enemy cargo, the British High Court of Admiralty took a different tack and condemned the *Essex*.

With this precedent established, American merchants could no longer hide behind the charade of the "broken voyage," and America's overseas

a British cruiser, the ship's captain need only produce his manifest and customs documents listing the cargo as an American–neutral–product to avoid capture as contraband. Although the precise volume of this trade is difficult to determine, customs figures indicate that, between 1802 and 1804, more than one-quarter of import duties were paid back as drawbacks when imported goods were reexported. More than one-third of the tea, almost half the imported indigo and sugar, three-quarters of the coffee, five-sixths of the pepper, and seven-eighths of the cotton imported in 1801-03 was reexported. By 1807, the $59,643,558 in reexports exceeded the value of American-produced exports by $11,000,000,

"Under My Wings Every Thing Prospers" reads the optimistic banner over Boqueto de Woiserie's "View of New Orleans taken from the Plantation of Marigny, November, 1803." Established in 1718, ninety miles upriver from the mouth of the Mississippi, New Orleans grew slowly as a French and then Spanish colonial outpost. The cupolas mark St. Louis Cathedral and the Casa Capitular–"Cabildo"–the government building where Louisiana was transferred from Spanish to French rule in November 1803 and from France to the U.S. a few weeks later. A number of American vessels line the levee, already beginning the carrying trade in Midwest and Southern produce that would make New Orleans the second largest American port within fifty years. (1932.18, Courtesy Chicago Historical Society)

trade entered a very difficult period. Britain proclaimed a blockade of French ports in 1806, and Napoleon in turn issued the Berlin Decree, which prohibited British ships from European ports. The British Orders in Council of 1807 required that any ship headed for a French port first stop at a British port, pay duty on the cargo, and obtain a license. Napoleon's Milan Decree announced that any ship with a British license would be considered a British ship and seized. Between 1803 and 1807, the British navy seized more than 500 American neutral traders, and France took another 300. Speaking of the two warring nations and their retaliatory efforts against American neutral traders, President Jefferson said, "The one is a den of robbers, the other of pirates."

While Americans were harassed by both the British and the French, the Royal Navy had a greater capacity to deliver harm than did the enfeebled French forces at sea, particularly after Lord Nelson's victory over the heart of the French fleet at the Battle of Trafalgar in October 1805. Nowhere was this more apparent than in the matter of impressing seamen.

Seafaring was a dangerous business, but perhaps no more so than going west to face the hardships and rigors of life on the frontier. It was safer to stay home and work on a farm or learn a trade, but that lacked the excitement of going to sea. Americans went to sea for the same reasons men had gone to sea for generations–profit and adventure.

Most American vessels were relatively small and so their crews were not large. It would have been highly unusual to find an American vessel with more than twenty men, and many sailed with less than ten. Sailors of the period were young, a few as young as thirteen, most in their early twenties, and few older than thirty. In some ports, including New York, Philadelphia, and Providence, Rhode Island, 17-20 percent were African Americans. In a port like New London, Connecticut, perhaps 6 percent were blacks, and another 3 percent were Native Americans. In these smaller ports most of the seamen were relatively local and homogeneous, but a few English, Irish, Portuguese, or West Indian men might be found in a New England crew. The "hands" lived forward in the triangular world of the forecastle,

below decks at the bow. It was the officers' privilege to live aft in the larger, lighter, more private, and more comfortable accommodations at the stern, near the steering gear. The foc's'le was crowded with rude bunks and with the sea chests in which sailors stored their clothing and personal effects. When not on watch this was the seaman's world. Richard Cleveland, a foremast hand who rose to captain wrote, "the forecastle was home to the sailor at sea, where he tried to sleep between watches and manfully downed his often vermin-infested hardtack, dried peas, and salt meat. Off duty seamen played cards, made music, and, if ambitious, studied navigation from their 'Bowditch.'"

Cleveland's recollections may be a bit romantic; nonetheless, it is true that the life of American merchant seamen–who numbered almost 20,000 by 1806– was considerably easier than that of their counterparts in naval service, either British or American. In a 1790 "Act for the Government and Regulation of Seamen," Congress had formalized the seaman's work contract, known as the shipping articles, had specified the obligations of seamen, and had set minimum standards for food and medicine on overseas voyages. With the exception of voyages to the East Indies and China, as well as whaling, trips were measured in weeks, not months. The food, prepared in a simple galley or camboose on deck and eaten out of a common wooden kid in the foc's'le, might be unpalatable, but wages were relatively good. Obedience to the captain and officers was expected to be instant and unquestioning, but discipline rarely involved the harsh brutality common in naval service, and the expanding merchant marine offered opportunities for rapid advancement to those who learned navigation. The advantages of signing aboard an American merchantman were often enough to encourage deserters from the Royal Navy to seek a berth in that service. This exodus did not go unnoticed by the Admiralty as the demands of war forced them to increase impressment.

Impressment was a rough-and-ready version of selective service. In wartime, the Royal Navy had a nearly insatiable appetite for men. Volunteers might be expected to furnish some portion of this need, but they could never supply it completely. In either wartime or peacetime, service in His Majesty's fleet did not offer many attractions. Harsh discipline, low pay, long

Departing from Le Havre, France, the Philadelphia ship Maysville *gives little indication that she was built and launched 1,000 miles from the sea. As settlement spread into the Ohio River Valley in the 1790s, Kentucky (admitted to statehood in 1792) and Ohio (which became a state in 1803) developed agricultural economies far removed from their markets on the Atlantic coast. The rudimentary roads over the Appalachian Mountains made transportation of grain and other produce arduous and expensive. Once the U.S. obtained control of the lower Mississippi River through the Louisiana Purchase, a convenient water route from the Ohio River to Atlantic ports became available. Most river trade was carried downstream in flatboats for transshipment in seagoing vessels at New Orleans. However, between 1800 and 1810, at least thirty-five seagoing vessels were built in Kentucky and Ohio. The 180-ton full-rigged ship* Maysville *was one of these, built of local white oak and white pine and launched at Maysville in Macon County, Kentucky, in 1804. Loaded with a cargo of local grain and produce, the* Maysville *would have negotiated the rapids at Louisville and traveled 1,000 miles down the Ohio and Mississippi before setting to sea to reach her home port of Philadelphia. She then entered a typical career as an Atlantic trader, calling at ports in the Caribbean, British Isles, Spain, Russia, and South America during the ensuing fifteen years. Alexander Montardier painted this view of the* Maysville, *ca. 1815. (M.S.M. 93.95.5; Claire White-Peterson photo)*

periods away from home, and the ever-present specter of death or injury from combat, disease, or accident helped keep seamen away from the navy in droves. The same conditions of service enticed those already on board to desert, a practice that in the Napoleonic Wars had reached near epidemic proportions. The only way for the service to maintain itself was by the age-old but detested custom of impressment. There was no quicker way to empty a waterfront tavern or brothel than the cry "Press gang!" Nor was there anything to make a sailor more nervous at sea than to have his vessel ordered to heave to and prepare to receive a press gang from one of His Majesty's vessels. Had the British confined this onerous practice to their own shores and ships it would have been bad enough, but the need for men and the well-known fact that many British deserters were serving aboard American merchant vessels

legislation provided for the issuance of Seamen's Protection Certificates. These were documents issued by customs officials or consular officials abroad to American seamen. The certificate gave a physical description of the bearer and certified that he was an American citizen. If the seaman were stopped by an English officer, the certificate was intended to provide evidence that he was an American citizen, and therefore not to be impressed. Unfortunately, the certificates were forged easily and soon a considerable market in forged documents emerged. This gave British officials a convenient excuse to ignore them entirely.

The Philadelphia armed merchant ship South Carolina *crosses tacks with a British frigate in this 1805 portrait by Antoine Roux of Marseilles. Built at Philadelphia in 1800, the* South Carolina *was actively engaged as a neutral trader with both English and French ports. In April 1805 she returned to Philadelphia from Liverpool, departing six weeks later for Marseilles. In 1806 she made a voyage to Calcutta, demonstrating the wide-ranging trading patterns maintained by American merchants. (M.S.M. 67.208; Louis S. Martel photo)*

caused officers of the Royal Navy to feel justified in stopping and searching American ships, and removing men they considered to be British subjects, even though they might be aboard an American vessel.

Estimates of the actual number of Americans impressed vary. In the decade between 1792 and 1802, probably 2,400 men were conscripted off American ships. In the following ten years, because of the rising intensity of the Napoleonic conflict, the number nearly tripled. How many of these men were, in fact, British citizens or deserters is again impossible to estimate; however, by their own actions the Admiralty in the period 1802-12 did release one-third of those taken, thereby admitting to having wrongfully taken them in the first place.

Since British authorities asserted that they impressed only seamen who were British subjects, in May 1796 Congress passed "An Act for the Protection and Relief of American Seamen." This

As long as the British confined their impressment activities to merchant vessels, taking a few expendable seamen, the issue remained a chronic but endurable burden. Occasionally, though, the Royal Navy overstepped itself. In April 1806 HMS *Leander* sought to waylay an American sloop just outside New York Harbor. Word that a British shot had accidentally killed the American helmsman brought a strong public outcry against Great Britain. A year later, the Royal Navy went even further, precipitating a crisis that brought howls of anger from Americans and nearly precipitated the war with England that was soon to come.

Shortly after dawn on 22 June 1807, the United States frigate *Chesapeake*, under the command of Captain Samuel Barron, got underway from Norfolk, Virginia, bound to her new station with the Mediterranean squadron. As she came down past Lynn Haven Bay, Barron noticed the British vessels *Melampus* and *Bellona* at anchor, "their Colours flying and their appearance friendly." Further on, at Cape Henry, the *Chesapeake*'s lookout reported that one of the two ships of the line on station was making sail and standing out to sea, following after Barron. It was HMS *Leopard*.

By four in the afternoon the *Leopard* had run down to the *Chesapeake* and was rounding up on her starboard quarter, all the time keeping the weather gauge. Barron watched, but with his frigate still fresh from refitting, and with stores littering the decks, he was thoroughly unprepared to fight.

It was common knowledge in Norfolk and elsewhere that British deserters were serving in the

American navy. In the case of the *Chesapeake*, the knowledge was quite precise; three deserters were aboard from the *Melampus*. The *Leopard's* captain was determined to have them back.

At a signal from the *Leopard*, the *Chesapeake* hove to and received a British party under the command of Lieutenant John Meade. The lieutenant asked Barron to muster his crew for inspection. After some discussion Barron refused the request and Meade returned to his ship. A few moments later the *Leopard* fired several warning shots across the *Chesapeake's* bow and then ranged alongside at point-blank distance and fired a broadside. Within fifteen minutes the *Leopard* poured three broadsides into the American. To stop the carnage Barron ordered the flag struck.

The British refused the *Chesapeake's* surrender, but they did come aboard and removed the three sailors in question, plus a fourth. For her part the *Chesapeake* had four men killed, eight wounded seriously, and ten wounded slightly, including Barron himself. In a sorry condition the American frigate limped home.

Thomas Jefferson was profoundly disturbed by the *Chesapeake* affair. He feared that unless America took decisive action the nation would be ineluctably drawn into war. The *Essex* decision and now the *Leopard* outrage were ominous signs of British hostility towards the United States. Yet, in a cruel twist of irony, the very events that troubled Jefferson so greatly were only lightly felt by American shipping interests who ought by right to have been more outraged than a Virginia planter serving as president.

Notwithstanding Britain's belligerent behavior on the high seas, American shipowners were doing very nicely. By 1807 American foreign trade was at an all-time high. Even if an estimated two out of nine neutral traders were condemned by one belligerent or another, Massachusetts merchant George Cabot claimed that a successful voyage by just one vessel out of three was sufficient to make a comfortable profit. Freight earnings were soaring, and ships were being launched in ever-increasing numbers. Seaport towns from Maine to Georgia were flourishing. British harassment, however insulting to national honor, was not particularly damaging to maritime profits. As president, Jefferson was more concerned with honor than profits.

Some would have preferred to assert American honor by force. That was not Jefferson's choice. While the Barbary powers might be cowed by the U.S. Navy, the fleet was small, and in the face of the might of the Royal Navy it was virtually impotent. Nothing could be gained from force. Other measures were available, some of which hearkened back to the days of the Revolution. In 1807, to keep America out of war and to punish those who insisted on violating her neutral rights, President Jefferson proclaimed a trade embargo.

In an oft-repeated scenario, a shot from HMS Leander forces an American sloop to heave to off Sandy Hook, 28 April 1806. This example of the flagrant British practice of waylaying American ships at sea and impressing any crew members suspected of being British citizens was unique only in that it occurred just off the entrance to New York Bay, and that the American helmsman, John Pierce, was killed by an all-too-accurate shot. John J. Barralet engraved this view to stir public outrage over the incident. (Courtesy Library of Congress)

CHAPTER 6

Embargo and War

NEVER SEEN AS A particular friend to maritime commerce, Thomas Jefferson was now reviled as the seaman's foe with his embargo. In imposing the embargo, Jefferson was harkening back to the decade before the Revolution, when Virginia and Massachusetts led the colonies in refusing to import British goods until king and Parliament acknowledged their rights. Those were the days of the Stamp Act, nonimportation, Committees of Inspection, Sons of Liberty; a time, in Jefferson's mind at least, when Americans rallied to defend their liberties with idealism and determination. Jefferson's remembrance, like that of most participants in historic events, was layered with a veneer of romanticism. Jefferson hoped to energize that same spirit against the same enemy a generation later, apparently forgetting that peaceful protests, petitions, and economic action did not sway king and Parliament. In the end what worked was war.

Jefferson also mistakenly believed that his fellow citizens would support his noble and peaceful effort to persuade the British to respect American rights. Here too, perhaps, he idealized the days of the Revolution, and envisioned patriots rallying to support his embargo. In truth, even during the revolutionary days, when American liberties were clearly at risk, many Americans expressed less than enthusiastic support for nonimportation and boycotts. With persuasion and intimidation, the Sons of Liberty, Committees of Inspection, and other groups had kept the wavering and recalcitrant together in the face of a threat made real through the image of an evil king and the presence of British force.

Unlike the 1760s, the 1790s had been boom years for American trade. Between 1790 and 1807 American trade (imports and exports) had increased more than five-fold. In 1792 over 90

Detail of engagement between USS Chesapeake *and HMS* Shannon. *(M.S.M.64.692; Mary Anne Stets photo)*

percent of the imports into the United States arrived in American bottoms, and in the decade before 1807 American shipyards doubled their output while total tonnage sailing under the American flag more than tripled. Prosperity at sea was reflected in seaport development. Boston, New York, Philadelphia, and Baltimore all grew rapidly. Between 1790 and 1810 the percentage of Americans living in urban centers (almost all seaports) rose from 5 to 7.3 percent. The nation's five largest cities all were seaports: New York, Philadelphia, Boston, Baltimore, and New Orleans, which had a population of nearly 10,000 French creoles and slaves at the time of the Louisiana Purchase.

Wealthy merchants in every coastal town gave evidence of their prosperity by building elegant homes lavishly furnished. America's architectural style was at last emerging from the staid Georgian manner imported from Great Britain–with its emphasis on symmetry, form, and order–to a more expressive and elegant aesthetic, named appropriately enough the Federal style.

In Boston, Charles Bulfinch took commissions from wealthy merchants to provide plans for homes to be built in his fashionable style. In Salem, Samuel McIntire created a large number of homes in the Federal style, including one for Salem's richest merchant, Elias Hasket Derby. Built between Essex Street and the waterfront, Derby's home and grounds occupied an entire block. Merchants in New York, Philadelphia, Baltimore, and even in smaller ports such as Annapolis, also built monuments to their success.

New York was also the American center for the development of an entirely new form of marine transportation, the steam-powered vessel. Although John Fitch on the Delaware and James Rumsey on the Potomac had operated small steamboats as early as 1786, New York led in steamboat development. Since 1798 Robert R. Livingston, in collaboration with his brother-in-law Colonel John Stevens, both old Revolutionary patriots, had held a monopoly on steam navigation in New York. Stevens's petitions to Congress to protect his steam-engine designs had led to the establishment of the U.S. patent laws, and work-

The Crowninshield family's India Wharf, built on the waterfront of Salem, Massachusetts, in 1802, represents an advanced wharf complex of the time. Constructed of timber cribbing filled with stone and paved over, the wharf reaches several hundred feet across the harbor's mud flats to provide deep-water access for large ships. The undifferentiated surface can accommodate goods stored in barrels, extra spars, anchors, and ships' boats, teamsters with their horse-drawn drays, merchants in their horse-drawn chaises, and strollers on foot. Several warehouses hold the international assortment of goods that flowed into Salem and were either reexported as part of the nation's neutral trade with Europe or dealt out to shopkeepers in Salem's hinterland. At the inner end, a one-story shipsmith shop, with smoking chimney, produces marine ironwork. In front of the neighboring warehouse, barrels of goods are weighed, and nearby several pumpmakers bore a log to produce a ship's bilge pump. Representing the breadth of Salem's world trade, the ship-rigged vessels lying at the wharf include the America, *which conducted Crowninshield's pepper trade with the Dutch colonies in Indonesia and the coffee trade with Arabia; the* Fame, *which Crowninshield used in the China trade; the* Prudent, *which was captured by the British near India in 1806; and the* Belisarius, *which traded to Mediterranean ports. George Ropes painted this scene in 1806. (Courtesy Peabody Essex Museum, Salem, Massachusetts)*

ing with early engine-builder Nicholas Roosevelt he had launched the first screw-propelled vessel, *Little Julianna*, in 1804. By then, Livingston had departed as minister to France, where he negotiated the purchase of Louisiana. In France, Livingston met expatriate American artist and civil engineer Robert Fulton, an expert on canal design and submarine warfare. Working for

Livingston, Fulton designed a prototype steamboat in France, ordered a British steam engine, and returned with it to New York in 1806. Fulton launched his *North River Steam Boat* in 1807 and traveled up the Hudson River to Albany, inaugurating practical steam transportation in the U.S. Under the terms of Livingston's monopoly, Fulton controlled steam navigation in New York waters,

Robert Fulton (1765-1815) is best known for putting a steamboat into successful commercial operation on the Hudson River, but this was just one of his technological achievements. Born near Lancaster, Pennsylvania, Fulton demonstrated his inventive nature at an early age, reportedly building a paddle-wheel boat during his teens. At seventeen he went to Philadelphia to become an artist, and in 1786 traveled to London where a family friend, the artist Benjamin West, was painting. Fulton became involved with the development of canal transportation in England, devising a system for building cast-iron aqueducts, inventing a dredging machine, and designing an inclined-plane railway for getting canal boats over abrupt heights, some of which would be applied to canal design in the U.S. after his death. Fulton experimented with steam propulsion, rope-making machines, and other mechanical inventions, but the Napoleonic Wars at sea turned his attention to submarine warfare. A strong proponent of the freedom of the seas, he traveled to France to work out his designs for submarine mines and self-propelled torpedoes. There he also built a "diving boat," the submarine Nautilus. *Fulton did not prove the efficacy of submarine warfare to either the French or the British, but his discussion with the American minister to France, Robert R. Livingston, in 1802 led to an agreement to build a steam vessel for use on the Hudson River, to fulfill Livingston's monopoly on the development of steam-powered vessels in New York. Fulton built a prototype in France, then ordered an engine in England while he pursued his submarine plans. In 1806 Fulton returned to the U.S. with a British Watt steam engine and launched his steamboat in 1807. While it was neither the first nor the most innovative design, Fulton's* North River Steam Boat *demonstrated the commercial potential for steam-powered vessels in the U.S. when it entered regular service on the 150-mile run between New York and Albany on the Hudson River. Although he was largely engaged in expanding commercial steamboat service in New York, Fulton continued his experiments in submarine warfare, and during the War of 1812 he designed the first steam-powered warship,* Demologos *or* Fulton the First, *which was launched after its designer's death in 1815. While Fulton's designation as "father of the steamboat" is not actually correct, his demonstration of the commercial and naval potential of steam power, and his practical developments in canal building and underwater warfare, made him the most influential marine engineer in the new republic. This portrait of Robert Fulton was painted by, or copied from, Elizabeth Emmet. (Collection of The New-York Historical Society)*

and when Stevens launched his own steamboat, *Phoenix*, in New Jersey in 1807, he was restricted from crossing into New York waters. In 1809 Stevens took the *Phoenix* from New York Bay, down the coast of New Jersey, and up the Delaware to Philadelphia, making the first ocean passage ever made by a steam-powered vessel. In 1811, Fulton and Roosevelt collaborated to build the steamboat *New Orleans* on the Ohio River at Pittsburgh, Pennsylvania. After a successful thirteen-day passage down the Ohio and Mississippi, she entered service at New Orleans, introducing the power of steam on the great western river system. Although the first decade of the nineteenth century ended with just a handful of American steamboats in operation, the potential importance of steam power to the nation's internal commerce was immediately evident.

While commerce produced wealth and elegance in the new nation's seaports, it also brought problems. Although colonial governments had enacted measures to regulate waterfronts, for the most part the rules had been slight and laxly enforced. Rapid development after the Revolution, however, brought a

Colonel John Stevens's steamboat Phoenix *became the world's first steam-powered vessel to make an ocean passage when she traveled from New York Bay to the Delaware River in June 1809. Designed by Stevens with an American-built engine (Fulton's steamboat had a British-built engine), and launched at Hoboken, New Jersey, in 1808, the 110-foot vessel was prohibited from crossing into New York waters by the terms of the monopoly on New York steamboat operation awarded to Livingston and Fulton. With limited opportunities on the New Jersey side, Stevens decided to send the vessel around to the Delaware to operate from Philadelphia. With storms and mechanical difficulties the 250-mile trip took eleven days, although just six days were spent underway. The* Phoenix *served on the Delaware River between Philadelphia and Trenton through the War of 1812 and then seems to have been abandoned. In 1810 she was altered and given a new engine, resulting in the configuration depicted in this painting by an unidentified artist. (Courtesy The Mariners' Museum, Newport News, Virginia)*

new urgency to the need for public control, management and planning. In New York City, for example, the demand for new wharves had private individuals, as well as city authorities, rushing to buy, fill, repair, and build new facilities along the shore. All this resulted in a ragged and uneven waterfront awkward and unsafe to approach from shoreside and in some places hazardous for approaching vessels.

In 1789 the "Outer Streets and Wharves Act" gave city authorities the power to plan and control waterfront development. Streets were laid out, including South Street along the East River and West Street parallel to the Hudson River, on a straight line, plans were laid to fill in watery spaces between wharves landward of the new streets, and the length of wharves was limited. By these measures New York City shaped its port. Albeit more slowly, and on a smaller scale, other American ports followed, each community recognizing that regulation of the port was in the best interests of commerce.

Having made their own lives comfortable, some merchants directed their new wealth to charitable, educational, and medical institutions. In Providence, Rhode Island, the Brown family gave generously to a variety of causes, including a college renamed in their honor. Boston benefited from the generosity of China merchant Thomas Handasyd Perkins, for whom a school for the blind was named. In New York, merchant John Pintard helped organize the New-York Historical Society, and in Philadelphia Stephen Girard supported a number of causes, including a school for poor white orphan boys. In all of America's seaports, churches, schools, hospitals, and libraries felt the benevolent hand of merchants who had done well in the republic's first two decades. "Europe's distress was America's blessing." Neutrality had made many Americans rich.

First among the ports made prosperous was New York. In November 1807 the British traveler John Lambert wrote a paean to what he saw in Manhattan: "The port was filled with shipping and the wharves were crowded with commodities of every description. Bales of cotton, wool, and merchandise; barrels of pot-ash, rice, flour, and salt provisions; hogsheads of sugar, chests of tea, puncheons of rum, and pipes of wine; boxes, cases, packs and packages of all sizes and denominations, were strewed upon the wharves and landing places, or upon the decks of the shipping. All was noise and bustle. The carters were driving in every direction; and the sailors and labourers upon the wharves, and on board the vessels, were moving their ponderous burthens from place to place."

One thing had not changed since the Revolution, however; Great Britain was still the republic's most important trading partner. In 1807, 65 percent of American exports went to British ports. This general maritime prosperity, and the nation's continuing dependence on Great Britain, would run afoul of Jefferson's embargo.

While shipowners and merchants were inconvenienced by the violation of their neutral rights and the impressment of American seamen, these were small issues compared to the larger question of profits. During the Revolutionary years, people of the seaports had supported action against Great Britain, but now American merchants felt strongly that their sympathies and profits were linked to England.

Notwithstanding howls of protest from coastal communities, the Embargo Act passed the Senate (18 December 1807) and the House (21 December 1807). Support for the measure was strongest in the West and the South, whose representatives were influenced by strong feelings of nationalism and outrage at British actions, and saw the measure as a blow to be struck on behalf of the country's honor. Representatives from maritime regions saw the measure otherwise. Senator Timothy Pickering of Massachusetts called it a "nefarious act" and called upon the states to resist "the usurpations of the central government." One wag wrote:

America needs no wooden walls
No ships where billows swell;
Her march is like the terrapin's,
Her home is in her shell.

The embargo became law on 22 December 1807.

According to its provisions, all seaborne commerce with foreign nations was prohibited. Coastwise shipping between American ports could continue, but shipowners had to post a bond double the value of the cargo to guarantee that they would not stray abroad. Finally, although foreign vessels might enter with cargo, they could not take American goods on board for export.

Time was of the essence. There could be no grace period; the embargo was effective immediately. The game now was to get the news to customs officers before ships could rush to sea. Dispatch riders fanned out from Washington with orders for the customs collectors to shut down foreign trade.

No official means of communication has ever beaten an informal rumor network, and as the government dispatch riders dismounted in the ports they were greeted with a frenzy of activity. The news they brought was not news at all. John Lambert described a particularly dramatic scene in New York: "On a sudden the streets were full of merchants, ship-owners, ship-captains, supercargoes, and sailors hurrying toward the waterfront. Astonished at this unusual commotion, men of all sorts followed and by eight o'clock the wharves were crowded with spectators, cheering the little fleet of half-laden ships which, with all sail spread, was beating down the harbor. None of them had clearances. Many were half manned. Few had more than part of a cargo. One which had just come in, rather than be embargoed, went off without breaking bulk. . . the captains made crews of the first seamen they met, and, with a few hurried instructions from the owners, pushed into the stream."

Since the very beginning of the republic the federal government had derived the major portion of its income from duties levied on trade. Alexander Hamilton and his Federalist allies had combined fiscal acumen with political intuition to craft a system that gave the new republic's government its financial life blood. It had not been easy. After all, barely two decades earlier the British Empire had come apart on this very issue–the taxation of trade.

Hamilton had deftly avoided the pitfalls of his royal predecessors. His scheme was the work of men legitimately representative of the people, not some distant government across the sea. But even more important, it was a revenue system that offered rewards for those who obeyed it. It gave protection for shipowners, encouraged the American merchant marine, and even provided some small protection for "infant industries." This was Hamilton's grand design. While brilliant, it might not have worked quite so well if the war in Europe had not offered such a lucrative role to American trades. As the single most prosperous sector of the new nation's economy, maritime trade could well afford to pay its duties.

A revenue system imposed by the consent of the governed upon a prosperous industry that could afford to pay, and enforced by revenue officers who were known to be reasonable–all this spelled success. Jefferson's embargo plunged the system into chaos. American exports had totaled $108,000,000 in 1807; a year later they were just $22,000,000, and in the same period imports fell from $145,000,000 to $58,000,000.

Now idle were ports that weeks before had bustled with trade, whose harbors had been crowded with vessels, and whose warehouses had been stuffed with both agricultural produce ready for shipment overseas and newly arrived manufactured goods awaiting distribution inland. Vessels lay unattended, and seamen, shipwrights, warehousemen, and others thrown out of work by the embargo gathered in taverns and elsewhere to lament their plight and curse the president. In countinghouses and fashionable parlors the conversations were more polite, but the hatred for Jefferson was no less. In the spring of 1809 John Lambert described a New York waterfront quite different from the one he had witnessed a few months before:

> The coffee house slip, the wharves and quays along South Street, presented no longer the bustle and activity that had prevailed there five months before. The port, indeed, was full of shipping; but they were dismantled and laid up. Their decks were cleared, their hatches fastened down, and scarcely a sailor was to be found on board. Not a box, bale, cask, barrel or package, was to be seen upon the wharves. Many of the counting houses were shut up, or advertised to be let, and the few solitary merchants, clerks, porters, and labourers, that were to be seen, were walking about with their hands in their pockets ... a few coasting sloops, and schooners, which were clearing out for some ports in the United States, were all that remained of that immense business which was carried on a few months before . . . In fact, everything presented a melancholy appearance. The streets near the waterside were almost deserted, grass had begun to grow upon the wharves.

With their ships idle and their profits sinking, it is not surprising that owners and captains quickly found ways to avoid the embargo and defy Jefferson. At both ends of the coast, in Georgia and Maine, an unusual amount of new activity began to be seen. The little port of St. Mary's, Georgia, for example, suddenly saw a huge influx of rice and cotton. Right on the border with Spanish Florida, it was well situated for smuggling these cargoes, either aboard British vessels that slipped across the border or American vessels ostensibly carrying the rice and cotton to another American port, which actually stopped at Amelia Island, Florida, to transfer the cargo onto a British vessel bound for Liverpool.

At the other end of the coast the situation was equally distressing. From Machias on the New Brunswick border came surprising news that the flour trade was booming. Ships from Boston and other ports to the south were sailing into this port and depositing thousands of barrels of flour on the local wharves. Why? The simple answer was that most of this flour was being sent across the border to New Brunswick in defiance of the embargo.

While it was most egregious in places close to for-

Mrs. Forbes's Ordeal:
A Voyage to France in 1811

Margaret Perkins was born in 1773, the last child of a small-time Boston merchant who died when she was an infant, leaving her mother to carry on as a shopkeeper in that port. After the Revolution, Margaret's older brothers, Thomas H. and James, prospered in trade with Europe and China, as did her brother-in-law Russell Sturgis. Known for her "impulsive and vehement" temperament, Margaret Perkins married Ralph Bennet Forbes, who was as unsuccessful at business as his brothers-in-law were successful. Eventually Ralph Forbes left his family living in genteel poverty in Massachusetts while he went to France to seek his fortune. In January 1811 Margaret

Perkins Forbes and their sons, eight-year-old Thomas and six-year-old Robert Bennet, sailed to join him, taking passage on the Perkins schooner *Midas*, laden with 200,000 pounds of salt cod. Their trip soon became an ordeal, which Margaret Forbes described to her sister in the following letter.

On Thursday the 17th of January, 1811, I embarked for Marseilles, and ran off the coast with every prospect of a good passage; but our hopes were soon blasted. Shortly after clearing the capes it became almost calm; every rope was covered with ice; the wind soon came out ahead, and the prospect seemed gloomy indeed. The same

state of things continued until the Wednesday following, when a violent tempest arose, lasting until Saturday morning. We were hove-to in the gulf for forty-eight hours, the wind blowing almost a hurricane, so that we found it difficult to keep in our berths. Many articles were washed off of our deck; among these the quarter boards, the bulwarks, and part of the rails were carried away, also the jib-boom and the camboose house, two casks of water, a small anchor;

Margaret Perkins Forbes (1773-1856). (Courtesy Robert Bennet Forbes House, Milton, Massachusetts)

sails were split, the boat stoven, the tiller broken, and the skylight over the cabin was thrown off and broken, much water found its way into the cabins; all the fowls, and two pigs were drowned. We had constant rains and head seas, and were most of the time under water. . . . accidents occurred. Bennet was quite ill, but had crawled into the cabin to get some air, and if possible some food. We had not been able to light a fire for some days; but on this morning, with much trouble, the kettle had been boiled. Bennet was sitting directly under the skylight, when it was washed off, and he was thrown to the deck clinging to a pot of hot chocolate, and drenched completely through.

Tom and myself had suffered much during the night, and had not risen; the noise was loud and excited much alarm; our stateroom door was open, and as Tom slept in the lower berth he was entirely enveloped in water. The captain and all hands were on deck; the man at the helm was hurled violently over the side of the schooner, but held on and was saved.

From the dreadful crash, and the apparent alarm of the captain and seamen, I imagined we had not much chance of escape. How I was supported through all this, God only knows. I instantly dressed myself, and put the children into my bed with dry clothes,

and waited the coming of the captain with feelings I am unable to describe. When he came I inquired if there was any immediate danger. His reply did not silence my fears; he said he could not positively say, but would give me timely notice. Shortly after a sailor came calling for an axe; I inquired eagerly as to our situation. He said, "Bad enough," and he could not predict the consequences of shipping such another sea. When he left I found myself fainting. To make any one hear was impracticable. An effort must be made; and with great difficulty I reached the companion-way, and the air restored me to a sense of our unhappy situation. However, the Almighty was near, and saved us from perishing; the storm suddenly ceased, the thunder and lightning disappeared, and the sun came out with splendor. The waves, however, continued to rear and to toss us about dreadfully until Sunday, when it became calm and serene. . .

Unfavorable winds continued until the 5th of February, when there came a gale in our favor, and the wind raged with unusual violence until the 10th. The vessel plunged so that it seemed doubtful if she would ever rise again; the helmsman with great difficulty kept his station, while we were scudding as fast as she could go. I suffered more than during the first gale, as I knew that having suffered so much there was less chance of escape to our

frail craft. . . .The "Midas" is said to be a remarkably good seaboat, or we should never have weathered the storms.

February 20. Thirty-one days out. . . .We have been under water most of the time; not a sailor has had the comfort of a dry shirt or a dry bed since we left home; the cabin and my stateroom have been so wet as to compel me to bail out the water constantly. Many days we lived in darkness, or only seeing by the light of a dim lamp. The boys behave better than their mother; for the first fortnight they were very seasick, but are now quite well and seem to enjoy themselves. At night I am often obliged to have them in my bunk, theirs being wet. I was sick only three weeks; my principal trouble has been faintness and nervous headache. . . .

March 6. Fifty days out. It is raining and a thick mist obscures everything; we are only thirty miles from our destination, and expect to be there by three o'clock this afternoon.

Seven o'clock. Three large frigates bearing down on us. I am trying to prepare my mind for new trials; fortunately the elasticity of my mind and feelings bid me hope (almost against probability) that we may yet escape. The Almighty arm which has been our shield through storms and tempest may yet avert this treatening evil.

Eight o'clock. A shot has just come whistling over our deck. All is lost, and our destiny is as melancholy as was predicted; still I feel that I have fortitude enough to bear up under this new disappointment. No exertion shall be wanting to obtain our release. I know that God will aid me in a virtuous cause.

A boat from the nearest frigate has just reached us. You can scarcely imagine any sight more grand than these ships. It is raining and the sea runs high; the elements seem to be at war with each other, and the scene is well suited to my feelings. Adieu!

March 18. On board of his Britannic majesty's ship, the "Blossom," Captain W. Stewart. On the sixth I left you in much agitation as to the result of our capture. . . . The Lieutenant who came in the boat descended into the cabin where the children and I sat; he was shocked at our condition, and expressed his regret at being obliged to perform a duty so much in opposition to his feelings. He asked for the log-book, and said he was ordered to search the vessel and examine the papers. I offered him my letters and my passport, which he kindly rejected. He treated us with the utmost delicacy, and said that we should probably be ordered to Gibraltar. To abandon the hope of meeting my husband was impossible, and I told the lieutenant I must see the

commanding officer. . . . After a search of an hour they were convinced that we had only fish on board. The lieutenant said we should be allowed to proceed; a signal from the "Resistance," was to tell us to go, when most unexpectedly another from the "Apollo" was to detain us. This determined me to make a personal application. I went on board, saw the captain, stated my situation and begged that we might be permitted to proceed. I used every argument to induce him to comply, but in vain. He acknowledged that we were not worth sending in, but added that it was no longer in his power to decide; it was in opposition to his wishes, but as the signal to detain us had been made by the senior officer he had no authority. He said we must go either to Gibraltar or Minorca. I objected to the former, as much further from my destination than the other. He wrote two letters ordering us to Minorca to await the decision of Admiral Sir Charles Cotton, who was at Port Mahan, Minorca.

After three weeks aboard HMS *Blossom* mother and sons were landed near Marseilles, where the French kept them in quarantine for three more weeks. After the family was reunited, the boys were enrolled in a French school while their parents toured the Mediterranean for a year and a half. Their return to the U.S. in 1813, in the midst of the War of 1812, was as harrowing as the passage to

Europe, for they were twice chased down and captured by British warships.

Ralph Forbes never did find success as a merchant. He died in 1824, having spent his last years as an invalid. But the Forbes children prospered. The youngest, John Murray, who was born in France, would make a fortune in China and then invest in American railroads. Both Thomas and Robert B. Forbes received China-trade appointments from their uncle, Thomas H. Perkins. Thomas remained in Canton as a business agent until he drowned in an accident in 1829. Robert began as a sailor, advancing to mate and master after a few voyages. He then made a fortune in China managing an opium depot, returned to Boston to marry, and lost his money during the Panic of 1837. He recouped his wealth during another sojourn in China as a partner in Russell & Company, 1838-40. Returning to Boston, he became a prominent figure in that port, devising improvements in sailing-ship rigs and lifesaving equipment, promoting iron steamship designs, and encouraging benevolence to sailors. In 1848 he commanded a ship laden with provisions for famine victims in Ireland. When he died in 1889, he was buried under the inscription, "He tried to do his duty." Among his first actions as a wealthy man had been to build his mother a large and stylish home in Milton, Massachusetts, in which she lived out her days in comfort.

Robert Bennet Forbes, *Personal Reminiscences* (Boston: Little, Brown, 1882)

eign ports, smuggling went on elsewhere as well. In remote coves and harbors all along the coast, vessels quietly loaded cargo out of sight of inquiring revenue officers. Long Island Sound, the outer part of Cape Cod, and Nantucket were favorite places for clandestine dealings.

In other settings shipowners and captains connived with sympathetic local customs officers. Having cleared for an American port, vessels often encountered storms and distress that "forced" them into the closest, albeit foreign, port hundreds of miles from their original destination. Unusually credulous customs officers suspended disbelief and rarely imposed penalties on these unlucky mariners.

Charged with enforcing the embargo, the Revenue Cutter Service was in despair. In his drive for government economy Jefferson had reduced the number of cutters. It was impossible for those few left to enforce the law. To assist the beleaguered cutters, on 25 April 1808 the president authorized the U.S. Navy to begin patrolling against smugglers.

Jefferson's embargo was an embarrassing sieve. Neither revenue cutters nor naval gunboats could seal the coast. Indeed, in some places, particularly New England, their presence incited resistance. In January 1809 the people of Newburyport practically mobbed a cutter that had seized an illegal cargo of fish. After watching the ineffectiveness of gunboats, a somber Secretary of the Treasury Albert Gallatin wrote to Jefferson that this was all that could be done, "and, of course, we must remain satisfied with the result, whatever it may be."

Even Jefferson understood that the results were not good. A government unable to enforce unpopular laws could only suffer a loss of face. In the meantime, while the embargo struck particularly hard at people on the coast it hurt those inland as well. By 1808 the price of wheat, one of the chief western exports, had fallen by nearly 50 percent, striking a painful blow at western farmers.

Understanding the failure of the embargo, Jefferson signed the Non-Intercourse Act (1 March 1809) three days before he left office (to be succeeded by his friend and neighbor James Madison). Nonintercourse was at best only a slight modification of policy. It repealed the embargo on all trade except that with England and France, stipulating that, if either of these nations should agree to respect American neutral rights, trade would be reopened with that nation and continue to be closed with the other. As a policy, nonintercourse made even less sense than embargo. For revenue officers it made life more complicated, while for those wishing to flaunt the law it made life easier since it provided a plethora of legal trading opportunities behind which they might hide illegal activities.

Preparations for War

Adding to the Non-Intercourse Act's sour image was the national embarrassment it caused. David Erskine, the British minister to the United States, on his own accord gave assurances to Madison that his government would agree to the terms of the act. Taking Erskine at his word, Madison issued a proclamation reopening trade with Great Britain while continuing to deny the privilege to the French. Unfortunately, Erskine had acted without consulting London. As soon as the cabinet learned of their minister's presumptuous action they disavowed him, leaving an unhappy Madison to reciprocate by revoking his own proclamation. It was an untidy business.

Nonintercourse proved as ineffectual as the embargo, and in May an increasingly restive Congress passed Macon's Bill Number Two, sponsored by Nathaniel Macon, a representative from North Carolina and chairman of the Committee on Foreign Affairs. This was another variation on a tired theme. The bill authorized the president to open trade with all, including the French and English, but if either of them agreed to respect American rights then trade with the other might be suspended. Macon's bill also banned warships of either Britain or France from entering American ports.

Macon's bill found as little favor with the maritime community as had its predecessors. In the eyes of shipowners, Congress was waging a futile economic war at their expense. Given a choice between national honor and profits, the men of the seacoast were inclined to pocket the latter in favor of the former.

People not blessed by the high freight profits of neutral trade were less inclined to tolerate national indignities. The same British government that insulted the American flag at sea also behaved badly in the West. It was an open secret that agents of the king were selling guns to the western tribes and warning the Native Americans to be wary of the Americans moving west and stealing their land. Such warnings were taken to heart, and war cries could be heard from the lands of the Choctaw and Cherokee in the South, north to Tecumseh's Shawnee tribe around the Great Lakes, and the Sauk and Fox to the west.

Westerners detested the British for what they were doing on land and at sea. Exacting punishment against the king was a popular notion west of the Appalachians, particularly if it might come in the form of land. Gradually in the West arose a cry for Canada, while in the South others coveted Florida.

Politics laced with anger, frustration, and nationalism produces a volatile mix. Such was the result of the congressional elections of 1810. As new members took their seats it became clear that Congress was to be dominated by "War Hawks." Young men for the most part, and often identified with the frontier, they demanded that the national honor be satisfied. Henry Clay of Kentucky, only thirty-four years old and in his first term in the House, was elected Speaker. He and another new addition to the chamber, John C. Calhoun of South Carolina, were strident champions of the American Republic.

Neutral rights, impressment, Native Americans, and expansion were drawing the nation into war. British intransigence stirred the Congress into an ugly mood. President Madison, hardly a War Hawk, found himself unable to control events in a world drifting towards conflict. In May 1811 the U.S. Navy enlivened the crisis when the American frigate *President* attacked the British sloop-of-war *Little Belt* off Cape Henry, Virginia. The *President's* captain, John Rodgers, expressed regrets at having failed to properly identify HMS *Little Belt*. It was small comfort to the battered British crew, but great comfort for Americans who remembered the sad fate of the *Chesapeake*. Both President Madison and the secretary of the navy commended Rodgers for his action.

Through the latter part of 1811 Madison continued to seek reconciliation. It was impossible. When the young British Minister Augustus John Foster, a neophyte diplomat, asked the American government for reparations for the damage done to the *Little Belt* he was rebuffed. The minister was informed that the United States had no intention of discussing this point until the British made reparations for the *Chesapeake*. In the meantime, British cruisers carried on impressing American seamen as muskets and rum continued to find their way through Canada to hostile Native Americans in the West.

When Congress assembled in November, Madison informed them of events and asked that they put the nation in a state of readiness. He urged them to enlarge the army, strengthen the navy, and prepare coastal defenses. At the same time he held out hope for peace, a goal that might only be achieved by a change of heart in London–an unlikely prospect. Nonetheless, in December Madison despatched Master Commandant James Lawrence, in command of the sloop-of-war *Hornet*, to England. Lawrence carried important letters urging the ministry to consider carefully their position and insisting that the American government was determined to defend its interests even to war.

Hearing nothing from London, Madison sent a confidential message to Congress on 1 April 1812 recommending an immediate embargo on all trade. Congress wasted no time agreeing, and on 4 April they declared an immediate ninety-day embargo. Unlike Jefferson's embargo, Madison's embargo appeared to be a traditional warning of war, intended to prevent merchant ships from getting to sea and to allow those at sea time to get home to avoid capture. Not surprisingly, as in 1807, in every American seaport merchants sought to venture one last voyage before customs officers could seal the harbor.

In Norfolk, Captain Elijah Cobb brought his vessel alongside the customhouse wharf on Saturday afternoon only to be told that unless he cleared from the port by noon Monday he would be held by the embargo. As quickly as he could he rounded up longshoremen, off-loaded his cargo, and hurriedly loaded flour destined for Portugal. He cast off Monday morning at ten, satisfied that he had beaten the deadline. The customs officers were not so agreeable. At noon Cobb was away from the wharf and underway, but he was still technically within the customs district. He looked aft to find the collector's barge bearing down on him. Thankfully, a fair breeze came up and Cobb had the pleasure of waving goodbye.

Elijah Cobb's experience was more dramatic than most, but not unique. Quick departures at unusual hours became common. So too did the outcry from the ports. Everyone understood that this embargo, unlike the one in 1807, was not a policy intended to persuade the British. This was a policy to prepare for war.

The merchants of Providence, Rhode Island, were typical in their response. In a meeting held on 7 April, they resolved that, because of the embargo, "the peace, prosperity and happiness of these United States are in great jeopardy." These merchants rightly pointed out that trade with Great Britain was "of more importance, to the United States, than with the world besides."

Debate raged as petitions and resolutions similar to that from Providence flooded into Washington. Frustrated at British refusal to negotiate, Madison still held some hope that the *Hornet* might return with encouraging news. On 22 May, Lawrence delivered the long-awaited despatches. The news was not good. The British Foreign Minister, Lord Castlereagh, refused to alter policy.

Seeing no other choice, on 1 June 1812 Madison asked Congress to declare war. In his terse and somber message he told them: "We behold, in fine, on the side of Great Britain, a state of war against the United States; and on the side of the United States, a state of peace towards Great Britain."

Madison's message upset many in the House and Senate. After furious and sometimes bitter debate, the House voted seventy-nine to forty-nine in favor of war. It was even closer in the Senate–seventeen to thirteen. The core of opposition, mostly Federalist, rested in the Northeast. Republican strength from the South and West carried the vote. On 18 June, Madison signed the declaration of war; Great Britain's counter declaration did not come until January 1813.

"Fir Built Frigates" on the Offensive

American military aims were twofold. First, along the Great Lakes American army and militia forces, soon to be supported by a naval contingent on Lakes Ontario and Erie, were poised to threaten Upper Canada, between Montreal and Detroit. By capturing territory in the British colony of Canada, the U.S. hoped possibly to extend its boundaries above Lake Erie and certainly to gain a bargaining position in peace negotiations. Initial American success in the capture of Detroit and the invasion of Upper Canada were reversed when Tecumseh aligned with the British, and the Americans were driven back, even losing the outpost at Michilimackinac between Lakes Huron and Michigan. Thereafter, the balance of power on the lakes rested on the opposing naval forces under construction there.

At sea, American naval strategy called for three three-ship squadrons to operate in the Atlantic: that of Commodore Rodgers in the North Atlantic, that of Commodore Stephen Decatur in the eastern Atlantic off the Azores, and that of Commodore William Bainbridge in the South Atlantic. In these regions the squadrons were well-positioned to challenge British warships as well as raiding Britain's transatlantic and Asian traders. The latter was of particular interest to American naval seamen who, like privateers, shared in the prize money generated by the sale of captured merchant cargoes.

With the declaration of war, shipowners who had scurried to get their vessels to sea were now faced with the problem of getting their flocks home. Fortunately, the declaration of war had caught the British unprepared. Beset with the continuing war against Napoleon on the Continent, the ministry had not fully reckoned with the possibility of war in North America. Even so, they were not inclined to worry about an American threat at sea. And why should they? In the face of His Majesty's 640 commissioned ships–including 124 ships of the line and 116 frigates–27,800 cannon, and 151,572 seamen, the Americans could sortie with just 17 ships, 442 cannon, and 5,025 seamen. Even the best of those, the three forty-four-gun frigates *Constitution, President,* and *United States,* were rudely dismissed as "a few fir built frigates with stripes of bunting, manned by sons of bitches and outlaws."

Hubris can be dangerous. From August to December 1812, the Americans and their "fir-built frigates" managed to humiliate the British in a series of battles that sent the Royal Navy and the British public reeling. Since the beginning of

With the declaration of war in June 1812, the U.S. Navy's three large frigates went on the offensive against the Royal Navy and British shipping. On 19 August 1812 the frigate Constitution *began to chase a distant sail, which proved to be a British frigate. As Captain Isaac Hull reported: "At 3/4 past 3 the chace backed her Maintopsail, and lay by on the Starboard tack; I immediately ordered the light sails taken in, and the Royal Yards sent down, took two reefs in the topsails, hauled up the foresail, and mainsail and see all clear for action, after all was clear the Ship was ordered to be kept away for the Enemy, on hearing of which the Gallant crew gave three cheers, and requested to be laid close alongside the chace." In this view, Michele Felice Cornè depicted the moments before the battle, as the* Constitution *bore down on the enemy frigate* Guerrière *and more than fifty seamen aloft made the sails ready for action. Within a short time the* Constitution's *guns had shot away the* Guerrière's *mizzenmast—"Huzza, my boys, we've made a brig of her," cheered Hull, who split his breeches in his excitement. Some of the* Guerrière's *eighteen-pound shot bounced off the* Constitution's *sides, earning her the nickname "Old Ironsides." An hour after the first American broadside, the completely dismasted* Guerrière *was "a perfect Wreck," with 101 casualties, and Captain Dacres had no choice but to surrender. (Courtesy New Haven Colony Historical Society)*

the Napoleonic Wars in 1793, the Royal Navy had fought 200 single-ship engagements, losing only five and each to a superior enemy. In only a few months the minuscule American navy would nearly match a record that had taken Britannia's enemies twenty years to accomplish.

Isaac Hull, commander of the *Constitution*, forged an early link in this chain of victories. Without waiting for orders from Washington that organized the American naval squadrons, he departed Boston on 2 August, intending to cruise against enemy shipping off Nova Scotia. After taking several prizes on 19 August, in latitude 40° 20' and longitude 55° west, the *Constitution* engaged HMS *Guerrière*.

For more than two hours the two ships fired into one another, until the *Guerrière* was dismasted and surrendered. In the midst of the battle an American seaman is reputed to have seen British cannonballs bouncing off his ship's sides. Astounded at her strength he cried out, "Huzzah, her sides are made of iron." Forevermore the *Constitution* would be affectionately known as "Old Ironsides."

Hull's victory was celebrated everywhere, even in Federalist Boston. His example helped charge other officers with an aggressive spirit. Next to fall heir to a hero's mantle was Master Commandant Jacob Jones, commander of the sloop-of-war *Wasp*.

The *Wasp* was sailing to join her squadron in the sea-lanes connecting London and the West Indies when, on 18 October, she encountered a homeward-bound convoy of six merchantmen escorted by HMS *Frolic*. In a savage and quick battle, the *Wasp* captured the *Frolic*, but was then captured in turn by HMS *Poictiers*, a seventy-four-gun ship of the line. Surrender or not, in the mind of the American public Jacob Jones was a hero who had bravely fought against overwhelming odds.

Eight years after his heroics at Tripoli, Captain Stephen Decatur was also anxious to earn his laurels in this war. Decatur commanded one of the three U.S. Navy squadrons combing the Atlantic for British merchant vessels. Aboard the forty-four-gun frigate *United States*, he was sailing a course 500 miles south of the Azores, hoping to spy some rich British merchantmen lumbering home from the East Indies. On Sunday morning, 25 October, the lookout called to the deck that a sail could be seen off the starboard bow. As the *United States* closed, Decatur could make out that the ship was no fat merchant vessel but HMS *Macedonian*, a thirty-eight-gun frigate. Outmaneuvering the *Macedonian*, the *United States* quickly dismasted and captured her. The American navy had taken yet another of His Majesty's frigates.

The final scene of the first act of the naval War of 1812 took place off Brazil with the *Constitution* again the victor, this time under the command of William Bainbridge, who commanded the third

Captain Isaac Hull (1773-1843) was born in Derby, Connecticut, and began his seafaring career in New England vessels trading to the Caribbean. At age twenty-one he took command of a Rhode Island brig carrying flaxseed to Ireland, thereafter returning to the Caribbean trade, carrying livestock out of Norwich, Connecticut. After losing two vessels to French privateers, he was commissioned fourth lieutenant aboard the new frigate Constitution *and joined the ship in 1798. His bold action in capturing a French ship at Puerta Plata in 1800 earned him a reputation for bravery and competence, as did his actions as commander of a naval brig during the war with Tripoli. Hull was promoted to captain in 1806, supervising gunboat construction and handling other shore duties before taking command of the* Constitution *in 1810. An extremely able seaman, Hull used creative sailing tactics to save the* Constitution *from capture by a British squadron early in the War of 1812. In August 1812 his destruction of HMS* Guerrière, *with little damage to the* Constitution *or her crew, was celebrated nationwide as the first American victory at sea. Hull spent the rest of the war in command of the Boston and Portsmouth Navy Yards. As commodore, Hull returned to sea in the 1820s, commanding the Pacific Station and operating along the coast of revolutionary Peru and Chile. After commanding the Washington Navy Yard he made a two-year tour as commander of the Mediterranean Station and retired from sea upon his return in 1841, fifty-seven years after his first voyage as a boy. John Wesley Jarvis painted this portrait of Captain Hull on the deck of the* Constitution *to commemorate his victory over the* Guerrière. *(Courtesy Art Commission of the City of New York)*

Commanding the forty-four-gun frigate United States, *the vessel in which he first went to sea as a midshipman, Captain Stephen Decatur encountered the forty-nine-gun British frigate* Macedonian *in mid-Atlantic on 25 October 1812. Decatur moved to the attack, and for an hour and a half the frigates exchanged broadsides. The twenty-four-pound cannonballs fired with great accuracy and speed by the* United States *brought down the topmasts and smashed the eighteen-pound cannon of the* Macedonian, *killing and wounding more than 100 of the 301 British sailors. With just twelve casualties on the* United States, *Decatur then broke off the action to make minor repairs before returning to threaten the British frigate into surrender. Decatur had the* Macedonian *jury-rigged and escorted her to New London, Connecticut, in December, setting off a nationwide celebration for the second American victory over a British frigate. Benjamin Tanner's 1816 engraving of the action was based on a painting by Thomas Birch. (M.S.M. 61.37; Gene Myers photo)*

American squadron. Four days after Christmas 1812, the *Constitution* came within sight of two vessels. Suspecting they were British, Bainbridge took the wind and headed offshore hoping to draw at least one of the vessels after him. One followed, and by early afternoon she was close enough to identify as the British frigate *Java*. Again the *Constitution*'s cannon fire devastated an opponent's rigging, and not long after an American sharpshooter mortally wounded the British captain, the *Java* surrendered.

In just five months the United States Navy had defeated the British warships *Guerrière, Frolic, Macedonian,* and *Java.* The Admiralty offices were in an uproar, facing criticism from the press and demands for action from Parliament.

In America the reaction was unbridled joy. Hull, Bainbridge, Decatur, and Jones were feted and toasted as heroes, and the *Constitution* acquired the renown she still enjoys. Everywhere, newspapers and broadsides heralded the victories of the navy, but along with this upwelling of patriotism came a troubling note. Many of the same people who were quick to toast Captain Hull were equally eager to condemn President Madison and "his" war. For the most part, those who looked to the sea for their livelihood still viewed the war as an unmitigated disaster.

During the glorious naval fall of 1812, while American frigates were humbling British frigates, American merchants were also dealing with the British but on far different terms. At the borders with Florida and Canada, as well as in upstate New York and on Lake Champlain, trade with the British flourished. Such behavior was hardly surprising, for these people had from the first opposed a war hurtful to their business. While illegal and unpatriotic, their behavior was consistent. For years these citizens had successfully defied the government's embargo and nonintercourse policies. Now they were defying its war. In the face of such defiance Secretary of the Navy Paul Hamilton issued stern orders to his captains: "The palpable and criminal intercourse, held with the enemy's forces, blockading and invading the waters and shores of the United States, is, in a Military view, an offense of so deep a dye, as to call for the vigilant interposition of all the Naval Officers of the United States." Concerned about the actions of "foreigners, under the specious garb of friendly flags, who convoy provisions, water, and succors of all kinds, (ostensibly destined for friendly ports, in the face, too, of a declared and rigorous blockade) direct to the fleets and stations of the enemy, with constant intelligence of our Naval and Military force and preparation," as well as the treachery of "profligate citizens, who, in vessels ostensibly navigating our own waters, from port to port, under cover of night, or other circumstances favouring their turpitude, find means to convey succours, or intelligence to the enemy, and elude the penalty of the law," Secretary Hamilton ordered his captains to add policing to their belligerent duties. Thereafter, naval commanding officers would be expected to "stop and detain, all vessels, or craft, whatsoever, proceeding or apparently intending to proceed, towards the enemy's vessels, within the waters, or hovering about the harbours of the United States; or towards any station, occupied by the enemy, within the jurisdiction of the United States."

Despite the vehemence and emotion of the secretary's order the situation was confused, and neither London nor Washington was entirely consistent in its policies. Before the advent of modern communications a declaration of war took time to become known, particularly for ships at sea and in foreign ports. The British navy base at Halifax, Nova Scotia, for example, was not aware that the war had begun for nearly a week after the American declaration, and the Admiralty in London was unaware for nearly a month. These delays worked to the advantage of American shipping.

The British had not taken seriously a threat of war with the United States, so their cruisers in the western Atlantic were following their normal peacetime routine. The commander at Halifax, Admiral Herbert Sawyer, was in a difficult situation. In recent months, in order to meet obligations in other parts of the world, the Admiralty had reduced the number of ships under his command. In a move designed to prevent any untoward incidents with Americans, Sawyer had been instructed not to allow his vessels to sail any closer than fifteen leagues (approximately fifty miles) from the coast. Those instructions served the purposes of diplomacy but were ill designed for war. Five months after war broke out, Sawyer was ordered to blockade American ports, but with so few ships and limited intelligence the task was impossible. Although ships took station off the mouths of the Delaware River and Chesapeake Bay early in 1813, and the blockade was extended to American ports from the Mississippi River to Long Island Sound, it was a very porous screen, and when bad weather drove the blockading vessels offshore American vessels could run for sea.

Sawyer's inability to close American ports had been made distressingly apparent to his superiors when they started to lose their frigates to the free-ranging American ships like the *Constitution* and *United States*. Ironically, the same ineffective blockade that brought embarrassment to the Royal Navy actually brought help to the larger British war effort.

President Madison's announcement of the embargo in April had set off a riot of speculation in the American flour market. Since the early 1790s the price of American flour had been rising steadily. Production in the rich farm areas north and west of Philadelphia, as well as in New York's Hudson and Mohawk valleys, had enjoyed considerable gains. By 1811-12 a good portion of these exports were bound for the port of Lisbon, destined eventually for the Duke of Wellington's British troops fighting in the peninsula campaign.

On the day news of the April embargo arrived in Portugal, Lisbon harbor was crowded with American shipping, their holds still dusty with the residue of their flour cargoes. For captains and supercargoes it was a perilous situation. Only the most naive among them entertained the thought that war would not come. The most cautious in the fleet decided to lay up their vessels right where they were and await developments. Others

USS *Constitution*

It was no accident that the *Constitution* and her sister forty-four-gun frigates were so successful in their actions against British frigates. The British Royal Navy emphasized ponderous ships of the line of sixty-four guns and more, and had emphasized fleet tactics against comparable French ships of the line. The smaller and faster British frigates were designed for reconnaissance, commerce raiding and blockade duty, and for diplomatic and dispatch missions. They were typically about 150 feet long, operated with a crew of about 300 men, and were armed with between twenty-eight and forty-four guns that fired eighteen-pound shot.

The United States had no ships of the line. However, the forty-four-gun frigates on which the U.S. Navy relied fell between British frigates and ships of the line in size and fire-power, and often mounted more than their nominal forty-four guns. The 204-foot *Constitution* carried as many as 440 men, and was armed with a potent combination of cannon totaling fifty-five guns. On her gun deck (below the upper, or spar, deck) she had fifteen long twenty-four pounders on each side. A long twenty-four-pound cannon was about nine feet in length, weighed almost 5,000 pounds, and could fire a twenty-four-pound solid shot more than a mile and a half. Its "point-blank" (unelevated) range was about 1,000 feet. When fired at close range, a twenty-four-pound shot could

penetrate two and a half feet of ship timber.

On the spar deck–the upper deck–the *Constitution* carried an eighteen-pound bow "chaser" firing forward, and twelve "carronades" on either side. First produced at the Caron foundry in England in the 1770s, a carronade was a short cannon that sacrificed range for weight of projectile. A thirty-two pound carronade weighed the same as an eighteen-pound long gun, and it could send a thirty-two-pound solid shot about half a mile. When fired at close range a carronade would do extensive damage to a wooden ship.

With five or six men to operate each cannon, more than 250 of the *Constitution*'s crew worked the guns. With block and tackle they drew the guns inboard to ram powder and shot down the muzzles, then ran them out with muzzles extending through the gunports, aligned them roughly for aim, and fired them by igniting powder in the touch hole at the breech. A skilled gun crew, perhaps assisted by their counterparts on the other side of the ship, could get off about one shot a minute.

The most destructive method of firing was the broadside, when all of the guns on a side fired at once, hurling 750 pounds of iron at the opposing ship. Or the guns might be fired individually or in groups. This was especially devastating when a ship

"crossed the T" of an opponent, passing across its bow or stern to rake the length of its deck with shot. When raking an enemy ship the guns might be loaded with grape shot or canister, both of which were clusters of small shot designed to separate and sweep the deck, killing or wounding all in their path. Gunners used the roll of their ship to advantage. To dismast an opponent they fired as the ship rolled up, elevating their guns. American gunners frequently fired on the down roll, striking their opponent's hull near the waterline.

Of course the *Constitution* could not fight with guns alone. Even in the midst of battle, her sailors had to tend her sails to maneuver around the enemy. To operate such a large, heavily sparred ship, with a main masthead 189 feet high, a main yard 95 feet across, and thirty-seven sails, a forty-four-gun frigate required 140 able-bodied seamen experienced in all aspects of ship work. Another 172 less-skilled ordinary seamen and boys provided additional manpower in place of expertise. The crew included a complement of U.S. Marines to lead boarding parties and to act as sharpshooters, firing down on the enemy deck from the large platforms on the masts called tops.

British officers originally believed the big American frigates were too large to sail well and too heavily armed to fight efficiently. However, the

Constitution and her sisters proved their speed and maneuverability, and demonstrated that their gunners could handle a twenty-four-pound cannon as well as a British crew could handle its lighter eighteen-pounders. And the Americans were aggressive, actively seeking combat with British frigates. As a response, British tactics changed. In 1813 British frigate captains were instructed to sail in squadrons of at least two ships in order to even the odds against the American forty-fours.

The operation of a U.S. frigate during battle in the War of 1812 is suggested by the following extract from Commodore Bainbridge's Journal on board the *Constitution*.

At 3:05 P.M., after an hour of maneuvering and exchanging broadsides, the Java's *bowsprit fouls the* Constitution's *mizzen rigging. British boarders run up the bowsprit to attack the* Constitution's *crew just as the* Java's *foremast falls, leaving the British ship unmanageable. Aquatint engraving by Nicholas Pocock, from a sketch by Lieutenant Buchanan of HMS* Java. *(M.S.M. 64.693)*

Tuesday 29th December 1812

At 9 AM, discovered two Strange Sails on the weather bow, at 10. AM. discovered the strange sails to be Ships, one of them stood in for the land, and the other steered off shore in a direction towards us. At 10.45. We tacked ship [changing course by bringing the bow through the wind] to the Nd & Wd and stood for the sail standing towards us,–At 11 tacked to the Sd & Ed haul'd up the mainsail and took in the Royals. At 11.30 AM made the private signal for the day, which was not answered, & then set the mainsail and royals to draw the strange sail off from the neutral Coast [of Brazil].
Wednesday 30th

December 1812, (Nautical Time) Commences with Clear weather and moderate breezes from E.N.E. Hoisted our Ensign and Pendant. At 15 minutes past meridian, The ship hoisted her colours, and English Ensign,–having a signal flying at her Main Red-Yellow-Red At 1.26 being sufficiently from the land, and finding the ship to be an English Frigate, took in the Main Sail and Royals, tacked Ship and stood for the enemy

At 1.50. P.M, The Enemy bore down with an intention of rakeing us, which we avoided by wearing [changing course by turning away and bringing the stern through the wind].
At 2, P.M, the enemy being within half a mile, of us,

and to wind ward, & having hawled down his colours to dip his Gafft, and not hoisting them again except an Union Jack at the Mizen Mast head, (we having hoisted on board the *Constitution* an American Jack forward Broad Pendant at Main, American Ensign at Mizen Top Gallant Mast head and at the end of The Gafft) induced me to give orders to the officer of the 3rd Division to fire one Gun ahead of the enemy to make him show his Colours, which being done brought on a fire from us of the whole broadside, on which he hoisted an English Ensign at the Peak, and another in his weather Main Rigging, besides his Pendant and then immediately returned our fire, which brought on a general action with round and grape.

The enemy Kept at a much greater distance than I wished, but Could not bring him to closer action without exposing ourselves to several rakes.— Considerable Manoeuvers were made by both Vessels to rake and avoid being raked.

The following Minutes Were Taken during the Action.

At 2.10. P.M, Commenced The Action within good grape and Canister distance. The enemy to windward (but much farther than wished).

At 2.30. P.M, our wheel was shot entirely away

At 2.40. determined to close with the Enemy, notwithstanding her rakeing, set the Fore sail and Luff'd up close to him.

At 2.50, The Enemies Jib boom got foul of our Mizen Rigging

At 3   The Head of the enemies Bowsprit & Jib boom shot away by us

At 3.5 Shot away the enemies foremast by the board

At 3.15 Shot away The enemies Main Top mast just above the Cap

At 3.40 Shot away Gafft and Spanker boom

At 3.55 Shot his mizen

At 4:35, after firing several raking broadsides that leave the Java with only her mainsail dangling from a broken yard, the Constitution sails out of range to make repairs. Aquatint engraving by Nicholas Pocock, from a sketch by Lieutenant Buchanan of HMS Java. (M.S.M. 64.694)

At 5:25 the Constitution crosses the Java's bow, prepared to fire a raking broadside. With one jury-rigged jib set, the Java cannot maneuver to return fire, so she surrenders. Aquatint engraving by Nicholas Pocock, from a sketch by Lieutenant Buchanan of HMS Java. (M.S.M. 64.695)

mast nearly by the board

At 4.5 Having silenced the fire of the enemy completely and his colours in main Rigging being [down] Supposed he had Struck,

Then hawl'd about the Courses to shoot ahead to repair our rigging, which was extremely cut, leaving the enemy a complete wreck, soon after discovered that The enemies flag was still flying hove too to repair Some of our damages.

At 4.20. The Enemies Main Mast went by the board.
At 4.50 [Wore] ship and stood for the Enemy

At 5.25 Got very close to the enemy in a very [effective] *rakeing* position, athwart his bows & was at the very instance of rakeing him, when he most prudently Struck his Flag.

Had the Enemy Suffered the broadside to have raked him previously to strikeing, his additional loss must have been *extremely* great laying like a log upon the water, perfectly unmanageable, I could have continued rakeing him without being exposed to more than two of his Guns, (if even Them)

After The Enemy had struck, wore Ship and reefed the Top Sails, hoisted out one of the only two remaining boats we had left out of 8 & sent Lieut [George] Parker 1st of the *Constitution* on board to take possession of her, which was done about 6. P.M, The Action continued from the commencement to the end of the Fire, 1 H 55 m our sails and Rigging were shot very much, and some of our spars injured–had 9 men Killed and 26 wounded. At 7 PM. The boat returned from the Prize with Lieut. [Henry D.] Chads the 1st

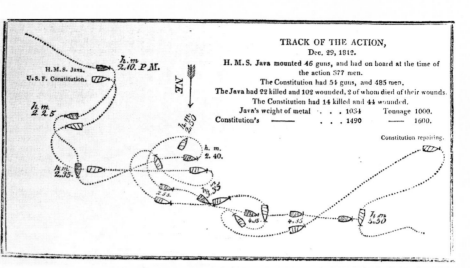

TRACK OF THE ACTION,
Dec. 29, 1812.
H. M. S. Java mounted 46 guns, and had on board at the time of the action 377 men.
The Constitution had 54 guns, and 485 men.
The Java had 22 killed and 102 wounded, 2 of whom died of their wounds.
The Constitution had 14 killed and 44 wounded.
Java's weight of metal . . . 1034   Tonnage 1000.
Constitution's ——— . . . 1490   ——— 1600.
Constitution repairing.

of the enemies Frigate (which I then learnt was the *Java* rated 38–had 49 Guns mounted–). . . . –Capt [Henry] Lambert of the *Java* was too dangerously wounded to be removed immediately.

The Cutter returned on board the Prize for Prisoners, and brought Capt [John] Marshall, Master & Commander of The British Navy, who was passenger on board, as also Several other Naval officers destined for ships in the East Indies. The *Java* had her whole number complete and nearly an hundred supernumeraries. The number she had on board at the commencement of the Action. The officers have not candour to say; from the different papers we collected, such as a muster book, Watch List and Quarter Bills, she must have had upwards of 400 souls, she had one more man stationed at each of her Guns on both Decks than what we had The Enemy had 83 wounded & 57 Kill'd.

The *Java* was an important ship fitted out in the com-

pleatest manner to [carry out] the Lieut. Genl & dispatches. She had Copper &c. on board for a 74 building at Bombay, and, I suspect a great many other valuables, but every thing was blown up, except the officers baggage when we set her on fire on the 1st of January 1813 at 3 P.M. Nautical Time.

RG45, CL, 1813, Vol. 1, No. 8 1/2, National Archives, Washington, D.C.

Ship-to-ship actions required commanders skilled at maneuvering their vessels and able seamen ready to handle sails and make repairs in the heat of battle. This plot of the action between the **Constitution** *and* **Java** *shows how the ships used the northeast wind to maneuver around one another until the* **Java's** *foremast fell and she could no longer maneuver. This diagram was published in the* **British** **Naval Chronicle** *in 1813.*

decided to up anchor, get to sea as quickly as possible, and head for home, hoping that they made it before war broke out and the Royal Navy began hovering off their home ports. It was a gamble.

For most the gamble paid off. No more than forty American merchant vessels were taken by British patrols during the summer of 1812. About half of the captures were vessels bound home from the Iberian peninsula or the Mediterranean.

The British considered trade with the Iberian peninsula too profitable and important to allow war to interfere. Preoccupied with the Continental war against Napoleon, the British were vexed by the nuisance of an American war and the interruption of essential trade. American vessels arriving home with salt and wine also brought information that the British ministry was willing to grant licenses to American ships carrying foodstuffs for Wellington's army. If stopped on the high seas by one of His Majesty's warships this license was a guarantee against capture. Issued over the signature of Viscount Sidmouth, these licenses were referred to as Sidmouths. Some were legal–that is issued by proper authority of His Majesty's government–while some were forgeries bought on what fast became an open market in spurious documents. At the moment when the Republic's navy was trading broadsides with His Majesty's navy, American merchantmen were scurrying to supply the enemy's army.

The British accepted such behavior as normal– British woolen manufacturers were known to sell uniforms to Napoleon's quartermasters, for example. Unlike the London government, the administration in Washington did not officially condone such action, although it made few efforts to disrupt it. From his hilltop perch in Charlottesville, former president Jefferson, architect of embargo, wrote: "If she [the Peninsula army] is to be fed at all events, why may we not have the benefit of it as well as others?... Besides, if we could, by starving the English armies, oblige them to withdraw from the peninsula, it would be to send them here; and I think we had better feed them there for pay, than feed and fight them here for nothing. A truth, too, not to be lost sight of is, that no country can pay war taxes if you suppress all their resources. To keep the war popular, we must open the markets. As long as good prices can be had, the people will support the war cheerfully."

Hundreds of tons of American grain, mostly from the ports of New York, Baltimore, and Philadelphia, were unloaded at Lisbon and elsewhere on the Iberian peninsula, then carted away to feed Wellington's hungry army. In the first half of 1813 alone, 165 American vessels cleared customs at Lisbon. Gradually, as Wellington rolled the French army back and British quartermasters found other supplies of grain more readily and cheaply available in Europe, the American trade declined. No longer dependent upon American flour, the British government could afford stricter measures against the United States, and by the fall of 1813 the Admiralty was ready to send additional ships to the western Atlantic. By winter 1813 the blockade had tightened on the Middle Atlantic and Southern coasts. Along New England shores, however, it was still a bit relaxed. Influenced by spies, New England newspapers, and the smuggling that took place at the Canadian border, the British had good reason to believe that with proper inducements New Englanders might hinder the American effort and actually aid the British. Anxious to encourage such sympathies, the Royal Navy tolerated commerce between Canada and New England, particularly in the Gulf of Maine. In September 1813 this illicit trade took on a violent and tragic dimension.

Early in 1813 the American naval brig *Enterprise* had been transferred from New Orleans to the East Coast. In late summer, under the command of Lieutenant William Burrows, she was cruising out of Portland in the Gulf of Maine on the lookout for British privateers as well as American vessels involved in illegal trade. Also in the area was His Majesty's brig *Boxer*, commanded by Captain Samuel Blyth.

On the afternoon of 5 September, while cruising just to the north of Portland, Burrows heard cannon fire coming from the direction of Seguin Island at the mouth of the Kennebec River. It was the *Boxer*, chasing an American merchantman, or so it was meant to appear. A more likely explanation is that Blyth was playing a part in a drama much performed along the coast. An American vessel on an illegal voyage from further east would arrange to be "chased" by a British warship so as to give the appearance of a narrow escape from capture and thus not be suspected of collusion with the enemy.

The *Enterprise* was not part of the plan; closing quickly, she engaged the *Boxer*. There was little tactical maneuver in the battle; victory went to the superior gunnery of the *Enterprise*. Both commanders were killed, and in an elaborate ceremony they were laid to rest side by side in a Portland cemetery.

Elsewhere along the coast, illegal trade was conducted under less dramatic circumstances. At Amelia Island, Florida, for example, the same sort of clandestine trade that had evaded the embargo continued in wartime. Southern products found their way easily through a tangled coastal waterway onto the island, where Spanish authorities were neither inclined nor capable of enforcing the law.

In the Gulf of Mexico a particularly lively trade was being carried on in the Mississippi River delta south of New Orleans. Captain John Shaw, in command of the naval station at New Orleans, had been having the devil of a time patrolling the waters below the city to control pirates and smugglers. With too few vessels and men, he found his job impossible. In the fall of 1812 he beseeched the secretary of the navy for 200 able-bodied seamen and six fast schooners to patrol the region. "Our whole coast Westwardly of the Balize (the main opening of the Mississippi), is at this moment, infested with pirates and smugglers, who appear to have arrayed themselves, with a determination of opposing the laws of our country by force; and of setting at defiance, all the means afforded us of punishing them," he wrote.

A Private War

To some, like the notorious Jean Lafitte and the others trading in the bayous of Louisiana, or the lowlands of Amelia Island, the war was an inconvenience to be avoided. Smuggling and illicit trade was their enterprise. Others, however, saw legal profit in the conflict through the traditional method of privateering.

"The trumpets of one victory drown the muffled drums of a thousand defeats," wrote Herman Melville, and never was this observation more apt. With their regular trade closed to them, and ignoring the potential for danger, losses, and

death, shipowners envisioned lucrative employment for their vessels in capturing valuable British merchant vessels. Sailors tossed on the beach by the war were eager to sign aboard in the hopes of great riches as they shared in the sale of prizes. Departing Norfolk, Virginia, in July 1812, the privateer *George Washington*, "with the stars and stripes floating in the breeze, was saluted with a tremendous cheering from the shore," wrote seaman George Little.

Not long after leaving Norfolk, the *George Washington* visited Baltimore at the other end of Chesapeake Bay. Here too, enthusiasm for the war and profit prevailed. "When we arrived in Baltimore, I found the most active preparations were in progress to prosecute the war" wrote Little. "A number of privateers were fitting out; and everywhere the American flag might be seen flying, denoting the places of rendezvous; in a word, the most intense excitement prevailed throughout the city."

Baltimore's "intense excitement" led that town to send to sea more privateers than any other port in America. Baltimore outfitted and despatched at least 130 vessels during the war. The schooner *Amelia* was typical of the sleek schooners and sloops dropping down Chesapeake Bay from Baltimore. At the end of the first cruise her captain, Charles A. Adams, brought his schooner into New York with eighty prisoners, having captured one million dollars worth of prizes. Her last cruise, which ended in April 1815, saw her take nearly 2,300 tons of enemy shipping and 112 prisoners. Armed with only six guns, her success was due to her sailing qualities and the skill of her officers and men.

The *Amelia* and her sisters were carrying on a tradition for their home port. In the years before the war, Baltimore builders had earned a special reputation for building speedy vessels, the so called Baltimore clippers. Probably growing out of a broader Chesapeake Bay pilot schooner model, these schooner-rigged vessels were exceptionally fast and maneuverable, although rather unstable. With tall, strongly raking masts, low freeboard, a wide deck–well suited for handling cannon in a small vessel–Chesapeake schooners were easily recognized.

It is more than coincidental that in the years after the war Baltimore enjoyed a reputation for con-

The fourteen-gun Philadelphia privateer brig Rattlesnake *(left) and the fifteen-gun New York privateer schooner* Scourge *(center) combined to capture twenty-two prizes in a single season when they attacked the grain fleet returning to Great Britain from Russia in 1813. In this view by British marine artist and former navy officer Thomas Buttersworth, the two privateers subdue the British ship* Brutus *in the North Sea. (Courtesy South Street Seaport Museum, New York)*

---

tinuing to build swift craft, many of which were destined for the illegal slave trade and privateering in the Latin American revolutions. And the adventurous and crafty men who sailed them were often veteran privateersmen.

New York City was a close second to Baltimore, sending forth fifty-five privateers. Despite a close blockade off Sandy Hook, numerous New Yorkers managed to elude British patrols and get to sea.

W. B. Dobson, captain of the schooner *Young Teaser*, was among the boldest of the New York captains. Cruising off Nova Scotia, Dobson was chased by the British privateer *Sir John Sherbrooke*. Caught between his pursuer and the shore, Dobson decided to make a run for Halifax. He entered the harbor flying the Union Jack over the Stars and Stripes, the common signal to indicate a vessel had been captured. The ruse worked. The sentries took the *Young Teaser* to be a prize and Dobson sailed right under the guns of

the harbor's forts and then out again, disappearing over the horizon.

Two days after sailing out of Halifax, Dobson sent a message into the town, with "audacious impudence" declaring "all Halifax in a state of blockade." He went on to challenge the commander of HMS *Le Hague*, riding at anchor in the harbor, to come out and fight *Young Teaser*. With the enemy fast overtaking him, Dobson scurried for a shallow bay where *Le Hague*'s deep draft would not permit her to enter. *Le Hague* kept watch, but Dobson managed to slip out to sea. However, *Le Hague* again overtook *Teaser*, and as she approached the American schooner blew apart in a violent explosion, which could only have been caused by an accident in the magazine. Thirty of the *Teaser*'s crew of thirty-seven were killed. Dobson survived, was later exchanged, and resumed his privateering career out of New York before the war ended.

With their long seafaring and sea-fighting traditions, and despite pro-British sympathies, New Englanders were also quick to turn to privateering. Late in July 1812, a committee of merchants in Salem, Massachusetts, reported to Secretary of the Navy Hamilton that, "Eight privateers, carrying about 400 men, were added and Equipped within ten days after the declaration of War was received." By the end of the war, Salem had sent at least forty privateers to sea.

Salem, as well as her larger neighbor Boston, which sent thirty-five privateers to sea, enjoyed the advantage of the loose blockade early in the war. As a result, Salem's best year for privateering was 1813. In that year alone, receipts from sale of prizes amounted to nearly $700,000. Thereafter, the tightened blockade made privateering more difficult.

While Baltimore, New York, and the New England ports launched the majority of American privateers, Southern ports also preyed on British shipping.

Altogether, about thirty-six privateers sailed from Norfolk and ports south. The Virginia port was home to six, among which perhaps the most successful was the schooner *Roger*. Between early 1814 and the end of the war she took seven prizes, including a vessel laden with a valuable cargo of sugar and rum bound to England, and the packet *Windsor Castle* bound out from Falmouth to Halifax.

Safely ensconced up the Cape Fear River, where British ships could not venture, Wilmington, North Carolina, sent out the privateers *Hawk*, *Lovely Lass*, and *Snap Dragon*. The last named had most of the luck, taking ten prizes, including the brig *Ann* with more than a half million dollars of dry goods stowed below. Ironically, these British manufactures were bound for an American port where they were to be smuggled in for sale.

Charleston was the most active privateering port in the South, commissioning at least thirteen vessels. While ports north of the Chesapeake con-

The letter-of-marque schooner Patapsco *of Baltimore was commissioned in 1812 and made trading voyages between Baltimore, the Caribbean, and France during the war. Equipped with six guns and a crew of forty, she was also prepared to capture British merchant vessels she encountered on the high seas, and she was credited with taking several prizes. On 21 September 1814 the* Patapsco *ran afoul of an eighteen-gun British brig off the Canary Islands, but escaped after receiving three broadsides from the Royal Navy vessel, as depicted in this painting by an unidentified artist. (Courtesy Maryland Historical Society)*

The Boston letter-of-marque brigantine Rambler *cruised all the way to China in 1814, taking several British vessels with valuable cargoes in Asian waters. Armed with twenty-two guns, she was a formidable opponent. During her visit, a Chinese artist depicted her in two positions, getting under sail and tacking out of the Pearl River. During her return passage, with a valuable cargo of Chinese goods, the* Rambler *took another British prize near South Africa, arriving home in 1815, well after the end of the war. (Courtesy Peabody Essex Museum, Salem, Massachusetts)*

centrated on attacking trade in the Gulf of Maine and off the Grand Banks, Southern ports aimed at the West Indies trade. Although the number of captured vessels brought into Charleston may not have compared to the numbers arriving in New York, Boston, and Salem, they normally carried rich cargoes of coffee, sugar, and rum.

Of all the Charleston privateers, the most famous was the schooner *Saucy Jack,* named for her daring commander, J.P. Chazel. Her low black hull with a white sheer stripe gave her a sleek and threatening appearance. Among the most successful of all American privateers, the *Saucy Jack* hunted the waters around the island of Hispaniola, managing to cull out six ships, six brigs, nine schooners, and two sloops from the British merchant marine. On her fourth voyage, in the spring of 1814, she grabbed her richest prize, the ship *Pelham,* ultimately by boarding with heavy casualties. This capture was reported to the

secretary of the navy, as "another honorable specimen of the bravery and good conduct of American seamen."

Charleston's success was not mirrored in the South's other two key ports, Savannah and New Orleans. The *Saucy Jack* alone took more enemy vessels than all the privateers of Savannah and New Orleans combined.

Despite the glamour of the business, the romance of the chase, and the great wealth occasionally gained, the reality was grim. At least 1,500 privateering commissions were issued during the war. Some privateersmen never got to sea. Many sailed off and never found a single prize; others found the enemy, only to be captured or killed. Only a few like the *Saucy Jack* triumphed, but their stories, though exceptional, enthralled the public, found their way into the romantic literature of the period, and remain today a vibrant— if mythological—part of the American past.

America on the Defensive

Privateers pricking at the British merchant marine and "fir built Frigates" besting the Royal Navy; these are the abiding images of the War of 1812. Most of these scenes were painted in the first year of the war–1812–the *annus mirabilis*. Intoxicated by victories, in January 1813 Congress voted to construct two seventy-four-gun ships of the line and six more frigates. None of these vessels would be ready for sea by war's end.

Also in 1813, Captain David Porter took the thirty-six-gun frigate *Essex* around Cape Horn, making her the first American naval vessel to enter the Pacific Ocean. Porter had been ordered to join Bainbridge's squadron, but missing the rendezvous he headed off for a successful raid on the British whaling fleet in the Pacific. With his prizes he refitted the *Essex* in the Marquesas, and in early 1814 entered the neutral port of Valparaiso, where he was blockaded by the British frigates *Phoebe* and *Cherub*. Damaged in a squall as she attempted to run to safety, the *Essex* fought it out under a flag proclaming "Free Trade and Sailors' Rights," eventually succumbing to the combined fire of the *Phoebe* and *Cherub*. Nevertheless, she had projected American naval force into the Pacific to challenge the British there.

Along the Atlantic coast the British blockade tightened during 1813. When the American frigate *Chesapeake* escaped from Boston she was intercepted by HMS *Shannon* and defeated in a fifteen-minute battle, although her mortally wounded captain, James Lawrence, exhorted his crew "Don't Give Up the Ship." Most of the other American frigates were trapped in port, awaiting a chance to slip through the blockade and return to sea.

The mood along the nation's waterfronts gradually turned grim. As the war dragged on, crowds no longer gathered to celebrate victory, and there were fewer victories to celebrate. As trade plummeted, small knots of men sat idly on pierheads grumbling about lack of work. The true cost of the war had been masked initially by the

---

Captain Samuel C. Reid (1783-1861) was the son of a British naval officer who was captured during the Revolution and converted to the patriot cause. Born at Norwich, Connecticut, Samuel Reid first went to sea at age eleven, spending six months in prison after his ship was captured by a French privateer. After serving as a naval midshipman, Reid returned to the merchant marine, commanding the brig Merchant *at age twenty. During the War of 1812 Reid took command of the New York privateer brig* General Armstrong, *which captured twenty-four British prizes. In September 1814 the* General Armstrong *reached Fayal in the Azores just as a British naval squadron arrived, en route to join the British expedition against New Orleans. Despite the neutral status of the Portuguese Azores, the British commander was determined to capture the American privateer. The* General Armstrong *drove off two assaults by boat and one by a brig of war before Reid scuttled his vessel to avoid capture. The British suffered several hundred casualties, compared to less than ten American killed and wounded, and the action was credited with delaying the departure of the British squadron long enough to alter the timing of the invasion of New Orleans. By the time British forces arrived on the Mississippi, General Andrew Jackson had organized a defensive force that saved the region from occupation. Samuel Reid became a celebrity, both for his heroic defense of the* General Armstrong *and for his inadvertent disruption of British naval plans. For many years after the war he served as harbormaster for the port of New York, where he professionalized the harbor pilot service and obtained the establishment of a lightship off New York Bay to improve navigation. Reid devised a system of flag signaling at sea and a mechanical telegraph for land communication, and he also proposed the standard design of the American flag with just thirteen stripes. John Wesley Jarvis painted this portrait of Reid in 1815 to commemorate his action at Fayal. (Courtesy Minneapolis Institute of Arts, the William Hood Dunwoody Fund)*

The War of 1812 brought a U.S. Naval force into the South Pacific when Captain David Porter took the frigate Essex *around Cape Horn in February 1813 and raided the British whaling fleet off South America. After capturing eleven British whaleships and sending home $100,000 worth of whale oil, Porter took the* Essex, Essex Jr. *(a British whaler refitted as an American sloop of war), and four prize vessels west to the Marquesas. Arriving in October 1813, the Americans were warmly welcomed and spent seven weeks at Nuku Hiva, overhauling the* Essex *with the help of native labor. Porter was much impressed with the Nuku Hivans and their culture, and his crew was delighted by the sexual freedom there. The local chieftain persuaded Porter to assist in defeating his enemies on the island, and on 19 November 1813 Porter claimed the island for the United States, calling it Madison's Island and renaming Taiohae Bay Massachusetts Bay. In this engraving, after a sketch by Porter, the unrigged* Essex *(center) and her prizes lie below Fort Madison, while American sentries guard the native village Porter called Madisonville. Porter intended Nuku Hiva to become a permanent American outpost in the Pacific, but soon after he departed on 13 December the occupying force left, and President Madison never acted on Porter's claim of annexation. Engraving published in David Porter,* Journal of a Cruise *(Philadelphia, 1815). (G.W. Blunt White Library, Mystic Seaport; Judy Beisler photo)*

large number of vessels at sea, and by British willingness to tolerate certain trades. As the vessels came home, and as the enemy tightened the blockade, the bills for war came due. Foreign trade was down 30 percent in 1813 and more than 80 percent by the following year.

Decline in trade dealt a heavy blow to federal revenue. Thanks to war expenses, government expenditures quadrupled between 1812 and 1815. Revenues, on the other hand, were falling far behind as a result of the embargo and then the war. With the whole economy under strain, the government was reluctant to impose additional taxes. As expenses climbed and revenues fell, the government borrowed heavily. By 1815 the permanent debt had nearly tripled. It was a cruel irony, not lost on the government's opponents, that Jeffersonians, who had never been particularly fond of trade or public debt, but were willing nonetheless to support the government from revenue derived from trade, had now killed trade and run up huge debts.

No one in the maritime world needed to be reminded of the nation's condition. Shipbuilding,

and all the smaller industry it supported, was at a virtual halt. Some men who had worked in the navy yards at Boston, New York, and Philadelphia were sent inland to the Great Lakes and Lake Champlain with the talented immigrant shipbuilder Henry Eckford to build the naval fleets on fresh water. But only a few went, and for the most part the caulkers, riggers, sailmakers, and carpenters who remained behind were idled. Unemployed workers, silent ship yards, vessels swinging at anchor in quiet harbors, and empty warehouses all stood as uncomfortable reminders of the pain of war.

Amidst the distress caused by the war, there were small signs of change. Although ships sat idle and seamen remained stranded, the capital that had once financed their business was still available for other purposes. Merchants with profits made either before the war, or perhaps in privateering, were looking for new investment opportunity away from the sea.

Chief among new directions for capital was textile manufacturing. Having pioneered the industry in the last decades of the eighteenth century, British manufacturers had done all that they could

In one of the few American naval losses during the first year of the War of 1812, HMS Shannon *defeated the thirty-six-gun frigate* Chesapeake *off Boston on 1 June 1813. Launched at Norfolk, Virginia, in 1799, the* Chesapeake *served in both the Quasi-War with France and the war with Tripoli, and then was laid up in 1803. When she returned to service and departed Norfolk in 1807, she was waylaid by HMS* Leopard, *whose captain demanded to search for Royal Navy deserters among the* Chesapeake's *crew. Commodore James Barron refused, then surrendered when the* Leopard *fired into the unready* Chesapeake. *After repairs the* Chesapeake *cruised the New England coast under command of Captain Stephen Decatur, enforcing the embargo. With the beginning of war in 1812, the* Chesapeake *was armed with forty-two guns and sent to patrol the South Atlantic, capturing British merchant vessels. After refitting at Boston in May 1813, she ventured out under Captain James Lawrence and met HMS* Shannon, *a thirty-eight-gun frigate whose Captain Broke had challenged the* Chesapeake *to fight. Lawrence had not received the challenge, but he was ready to engage despite his untrained crew. Flying a banner proclaiming "Free Trade and Sailors' Rights," the* Chesapeake *closed with the* Shannon, *which opened fire about 6:00 P.M. at a range of fifty yards. As the* Chesapeake *forged ahead, Lawrence tried to luff the sails and slow the vessel to remain in the favored windward position. But when shots damaged her rigging the* Chesapeake *lost steerage and exposed her stern to the* Shannon, *which raked her until the* Chesapeake *drifted alongside. Lawrence was mortally wounded by musket fire as British boarders swarmed aboard the* Chesapeake, *and Captain Broke was severely wounded as well. After just fifteen minutes of battle the Americans surrendered, despite Lawrence's exhortation: "Don't give up the ship!" The* Chesapeake *lost 141 men killed or wounded, while British casualties totaled 77. Great Britain cheered the* Shannon's *victory, and the* Chesapeake *spent the next seven years as HMS* Chesapeake *in the Royal Navy. This oil painting of the beginning of the action is attributed to British marine artist John Christian Schetky. (M.S.M. 64.692; Mary Anne Stets photo)*

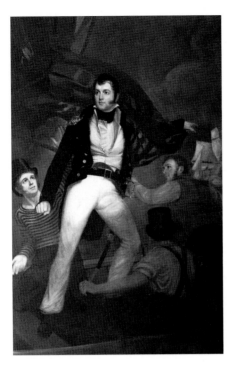

Oliver Hazard Perry (1785-1819) of Rhode Island entered the U.S. Navy in 1799 as a fourteen-year-old midshipman on a ship commanded by his father. After service in the Caribbean against the French and in the Mediterranean during the war with Tripoli, he was promoted to lieutenant and assigned to oversee construction of a gunboat flotilla in New England, enforcing the embargo. Dissatisfied with gunboat service, he sought a more active position as the War of 1812 began. With the rank of master commandant, he joined Commodore Isaac Chauncey's command on the Great Lakes and was assigned to build a fleet at Erie, Pennsylvania. His fleet was ready in August 1813, and at that point the British fleet withdrew westward to the Detroit River, allowing Perry to get his vessels across the shallow sandbar at Erie by removing their cannon. Perry established his base at Put-in Bay in Ohio's Lake Erie islands, and on 9 September 1813 set out with his ten vessels to meet the advancing British fleet of six vessels. Aboard the brig Lawrence, *with a battle flag inscribed with Captain Lawrence's exhortation, "Don't Give Up the Ship," Perry engaged the British flagship. After almost three hours the* Lawrence *was a wreck, so Perry transferred to the* Niagara, *which joined the action and quickly defeated the British flagship. The entire British fleet then surrendered, leaving the U.S. in control of Lake Erie. Perry then provided naval support to the U.S. Army as it invaded upper Canada. Highly acclaimed for his victory, Perry was promoted to captain, recalled to the Atlantic, and given command of a frigate, but he could not get to sea because of the British blockade. After the war, Perry commanded a frigate in the Mediterranean, quarreling with his marine officer and later engaging him in a duel. In 1819 he was sent to South America on a diplomatic mission and died of yellow fever during the return voyage. In this heroic painting completed by John Wesley Jarvis in 1815, Perry holds his battle flag while being rowed from the* Lawrence *to the* Niagara. *(Courtesy Art Commission of the City of New York)*

to hold the technology secret. But that was impossible. In 1798 Samuel Slater had brought the technology to America and, with the financial backing of Moses Brown, set up America's first water-powered cotton mill in Rhode Island. The capital investment for mills was considerable, however, and as long as the flood tide of neutral trade was swelling maritime profits, capital flowed in that direction rather than to textiles. In 1805 U.S. textile mills had barely 5,000 spindles. As neutral trade became less attractive, the number of mills rose. Between 1808 and 1812, 36 new cotton mills opened in New England, which had an abundance of falling water for power and many potential factory laborers as agricultural opportunities declined there. In the same period an even larger number of woolen mills began operation. More spectacular was the growth caused by the war. By 1816, more than 100,000 spindles were in use.

On the Great Lakes, naval action intensified in 1813. Commodore Isaac Chauncey commanded the American naval forces on the lakes. At his post at Sackett's Harbor New York, on the east shore of Lake Ontario, Chauncey constructed a fleet of small warships to oppose the British fleet under construction across the lake. These two fleets raided the opposing coasts but never engaged in direct conflict. Instead, to control the lake both sides raced to launch 100-gun ships of the line, neither of which would be launched before the war ended.

Chauncey also commanded the fleet of nine vessels being constructed on Lake Erie at Erie, Pennsylvania. Master Commandant Oliver Hazard Perry was in direct command of this fleet. When Perry complained to Chauncey that sixty men sent to join his command were "a motley set, blacks, Soldiers and boys," Chauncey replied, "I have yet to learn that the Colour of the skin, or cut and trimmings of the coat, can affect a mans qualifications or usefullness—I have nearly 50 Blacks on board of this Ship and many of them are amongst my best men, and those people you call Soldiers have been to

Sea from 2 to 17 years. . . ." Perry soon learned of the quality of his 600 men, nearly 25 percent of whom were black. In his flagship brig *Lawrence*, with its "Don't Give Up the Ship" pennant, Perry led his fleet against a similar British fleet near Put-in-Bay in September 1813. When the *Lawrence* was disabled, with casualties well over 50 percent, Perry transferred to the *Niagara* and resumed the attack, later issuing his famous report, "We have met the enemy; they are ours. . . ."

Perry then used his fleet for an amphibious operation, ferrying American forces across the lake for another invasion. The army force was turned back, but not before Tecumseh was killed, ending the possibility of a unified Indian nation in the west.

Seeking Peace

The British proposed peace negotiations in November 1813, and Congress agreed in January 1814. When the peace commissioners met at Ghent, Belgium, both sides proposed unacceptable terms. The British claimed northern territory and demanded that the U.S. set off a sovereign American Indian nation in the west and give up its fishing rights off Newfoundland. The U.S. defended its fishing rights and freedom of the seas and made counterdemands for territory.

With Napoleon defeated and exiled in the spring of 1814 to the island of Elba, Great Britain could concentrate on the war with America. In April the blockade of the U.S. coast was extended to New England, and in September British forces from Halifax occupied Castine, Maine, and strategic points on the eastern Maine coast. Elsewhere, the British planned a three-pronged assault to bring America to the peace table and possibly gain some territorial concessions. In the north, an army and fleet from Canada was organized to descend Lake Champlain into New York. Far to the south, a force in Jamaica was prepared to sail up the Mississippi and capture New Orleans. And on the East Coast another amphibious invasion force was ordered to enter Chesapeake Bay and raid Washington, D.C., and Baltimore.

In August 1814 a combined British force moved up the Chesapeake. They managed to drive the government out of Washington and burn the

White House and the Capitol, but the defenses of Baltimore, anchored at Fort McHenry, proved too tough. After a bombardment that inspired Francis Scott Key to write "The Star Spangled Banner," the British finally withdrew from the Chesapeake in September.

Similar results came from Lake Champlain in September, when a naval squadron under Master Commandant Thomas Macdonough, waiting at anchor in Plattsburgh Bay, turned back the British invasion force. This otherwise minor naval victory was a turning point in the war, for thereafter Great Britain gave up its territorial demands in the peace negotiations.

At heart, neither side saw any merit in carrying on the war. Having been engaged in near-constant conflict since 1793, the people of Great Britain were drained emotionally and fiscally. When approached to go to America and take command against the Americans, Arthur Wellesley, Duke of Wellington, the hero of the Peninsula, responded that he would do so only on condition that the ministry give him men and material enough to control the northern lakes. The ministry had little enthusiasm for such an expensive undertaking.

American enthusiasm had waned as well. While the Republic had thus far proven it could survive against the British onslaught, it was clear to all that survival did not mean victory. The situation was, at best, a stalemate. The war would end because no one had an interest in prolonging it. British and American diplomats signed the treaty on Christmas Eve 1814.

But fighting continued until the news reached around the world by sea. At New Orleans in January 1815, General Andrew Jackson and a force of frontiersmen, African Americans, American Indians, and Jean Lafitte's pirates sent the third British invasion force reeling back down the Mississippi. To the north, on a stormy January night, Captain Stephen Decatur took the frigate *President* out of New York to evade the British blockade, only to run aground and then run up against the thirty-eight-gun HMS *Endymion*. The *President* defeated the *Endymion* in a single-ship action, but as other blockading vessels approached the damaged *President*, Decatur was compelled to surrender. Although he had lost the only forty-four-gun American frigate to be captured, for his brave

In a plan similar to General Burgoyne's attempt to isolate New England by invading up Lake Champlain thirty-eight years earlier, a British invasion force prepared to move south on Lake Champlain in 1814. In 1776, Benedict Arnold commanded a fleet to resist the invasion; this time, Master Commandant Thomas Macdonough led a fleet of fourteen vessels, with the flagship Saratoga mounting twenty-six guns. Defending the American post at Plattsburgh, on the New York shore, Macdonough anchored his fleet in Plattsburgh Bay to sweep the approaches. On 11 September 1814, as land forces fought in Plattsburgh (right), HMS Confidence, a thirty-six-gun frigate, led sixteen British vessels into the bay to destroy the American fleet. During a two-and-a-half-hour fight, the anchored Saratoga (right center) fought until her starboard battery was demolished, then sprung around on her anchor lines to bring her port guns to bear. Assisted by the American gunboats (right), which were rigged like Mediterranean galleys, she finally battered HMS Confidence (left center) into surrender. Two other British vessels also struck their colors, leaving a brig (right) and gunboats to flee under fire from the anchored American vessels. This combined land and lake victory by American forces stalled the British advance and ultimately persuaded British peace negotiators to give up territorial claims in America and sign a treaty on Christmas Eve. Benjamin Tanner published this engraving, after a painting by H. Reinagle, in 1816. (M.S.M. 61.39)

---

efforts Decatur was treated to a hero's welcome on his return. Still later, the *Constitution* defeated the British frigate *Cyane* and sloop-of-war *Levant* off Madeira in February 1815, and the U.S. sloop-of-war *Peacock* would fire the last shots of the war on 30 June, when she attacked a British merchant brig in the Sunda Strait, south of China.

The war ended just as New Englanders engaged in one final gasp of protest. Between 15 December 1814 and 5 January 1815, representatives from all the New England states met at Hartford, Connecticut. Delegates condemned the president's declaration of a war against the nation's principal economic partner, which was being largely pursued in the West in an apparent attempt to acquire territory, and which was requiring the New England states to defend their own coastlines and protect U.S. Navy installations at state expense. The Convention proposed a series of amendments to the Constitution to strengthen states' rights. Although not part of the official report, there was at the meeting the slight

hint of secession. Ironically, the convention's report reached Washington almost simultaneously with the good news from Ghent and New Orleans. The Hartford Convention simply highlighted New England's unpatriotic behavior and helped plunge the Federalist Party into deeper public disfavor.

Peace resolved the overt concerns of the Hartford Convention, but the incompatibility of sectional interests and federal policy would become an increasingly divisive issue for half a century. New Englanders had suggested Constitutional amendments to maintain the region's interests as the sectional balance tipped away from the seacoast. Forty-five years later, Southern states would resort to outright secession when federal policy seemed to favor Northern commercial interests.

Status Quo Ante Bellum was the principle agreed to in Ghent; that is, matters as they were before the war. A war that had ostensibly been launched because of maritime issues was settled without any mention of maritime issues. Neutral rights were not addressed, nor was there any mention of impressment. As far as the treaty was concerned, the British, at least from their point of view, were free to behave in the same ways that had caused the war. While that was the agreement of diplomats, reality was somewhat different.

Both sides understood that with the end of war in Europe, issues of neutral rights and impressment were moot. The Royal Navy had no further cause to harass American vessels. Impressment ceased because the need for sailors evaporated with the laying up of the Royal Navy fleet at the end of the wars against France and the United States. All agreed there was no need to allow these past differences, now essentially settled, to trouble future relations. Merchants and shipowners on both sides of the Atlantic were anxious to return to the good old days of vigorous trade between the two countries, to say nothing of new trade possibilities opening up in other parts of the world. Through the window of 1815, America's maritime world looked bright indeed.

In its first four decades the American Republic had fought four wars: two against Great Britain, one against France, and another against Tripoli. Of these four, three–the Barbary War, Quasi War, and War of 1812–were fought over matters of foreign trade, and in them the U.S. Navy distinguished itself. Each of these wars was rooted in the fact that the United States was a nation dependent upon the sea.

The War of 1812 had not only established the permanence of the American Republic, it had also secured the new nation's control of the vast area west of the Appalachians and into the Mississippi Valley. Americans were restive to move west, till the soil, and harvest crops on these fertile lands. Yet even as settlers moved west they could not turn their back on the sea, for the overriding lesson of the Republic's first four decades was that the well-being of the nation depended upon access to markets via ocean routes. Settlers in the West and seafarers in the East were tied to one another. They depended upon the sea as their link to a wider world.

Captain Stephen Decatur (1779-1820) of Philadelphia, the son of a Revolutionary War privateer captain, entered the U.S. Navy at nineteen, despite his mother's desire that he seek a career on land. After service aboard the frigate United States *in the Quasi-War with France, Decatur commanded a schooner in the war with Tripoli and proposed a raid to destroy the captured American frigate* Philadelphia. *Using a captured Tripolitan vessel and a Maltese pilot to approach the unsuspecting Tripolitan defenders, Decatur led eighty Americans who boarded the* Philadelphia, *set her afire, and escaped safely. For this action, which British Admiral Lord Horatio Nelson called "the most bold and daring act of the age," Decatur was promoted to captain at age twenty-four. On another occasion Decatur led a boarding party to capture a gunboat, then attacked another vessel to avenge the death of his brother, barely avoiding death himself. During his career, Decatur further demonstrated his impetuous bravery by engaging in several duels. Returning to America in 1805, Decatur commanded naval forces in Chesapeake Bay and on the southern coast. In 1808 he served on the court martial that suspended Captain James Barron for surrendering the frigate* Chesapeake *to HMS* Leopard, *incurring Barron's ongoing resentment. As captain of the* United States, *Decatur made two cruises in 1812,*

capturing HMS Macedonian *in October. After his return to the U.S., Decatur was blockaded at New London, Connecticut, in 1813 and New York in 1814. He finally took to sea in command of the frigate* President *during a gale in January 1815, but a British squadron intercepted and captured the* President *after she defeated HMS* Endymion. *A court of inquiry exonerated Decatur of blame for the loss of the* President, *and he was soon off to the Mediterranean to force concessions from the Barbary port of Algiers. Decatur clearly stated his position in a toast: "Our country! In her intercourse with foreign nations may she always be in the right; but our country, right or wrong." Decatur was appointed to the Board of Navy Commissioners late in 1815 and was still so engaged in March 1820 when Captain James Barron challenged him to a duel for opposing Barron's return to service. In this affair of honor Captain Stephen Decatur fell mortally wounded, to be mourned by his former crews and fellow officers alike. Rembrandt Peale painted Decatur's portrait, ca. 1815. (Collection of The New-York Historical Society)*

Part 2

The Expanding Nation, 1815-1865

CHAPTER 7

Maritime Developments in an Age of Optimism

LL OF AMERICA'S major centers of population in 1815 were located on the water. All but one, the rapidly growing Ohio River port of Cincinnati, were Atlantic seaports. Of the nearly eight and one-half million people inhabiting the United States, some 85 percent were located along the Atlantic Coast, with about half the nation's total population in New England and the Middle Atlantic states.

Travel and transportation in the United States had barely changed from the relatively primitive conditions of earlier centuries. Roads were few and in poor shape, often becoming impassable during the winter or after major storms at any time of the year. Americans depended on the waters for food as well as transportation, so that coastal and deep-sea fishing, ranging from the northern regions off Newfoundland and New England down the coast to Chesapeake Bay and southern waters, was essential in supporting the rapidly growing American population.

To be sure, the great majority of Americans worked on the land, and many of these exemplified the self-sufficient Jeffersonian yeoman farmer ideal. Moreover, an increasing portion of the population worked in industries not directly related to seafaring or waterborne commerce. Yet while the main wealth of the country was generated by agricultural output of staple (market-oriented) goods, the maritime element was still vital.

With the severe limitations of land transportation, most agricultural products came from regions in proximity to the seacoast or to navigable rivers that linked these agricultural areas and their inhabitants to the seacoast and its major commu-

---

Detail of the Detroit waterfront, painted by William James Bennett, 1836. (Photograph © The Detroit Institute of Arts, Gift of the Fred Sanders Company in memory of its founder, Fred Sanders)

nities. In 1820 only 7.2 percent of the population lived in cities with more than 2,500 inhabitants, and only 5 percent in those with more than 5,000. By 1820 the largest city in the nation was New York, which over the previous ten years had grown from 96,400 to 123,700 inhabitants. Twelfth in size among American population centers was the only major inland river port, Cincinnati, whose population of 9,600 in 1820 was nearly four times what it had been just ten years before.

On the basis of total national product and distribution of population, the United States in the immediate postwar era still was overwhelmingly agricultural. Yet the focus of national economic investment and activity remained what it had been in the Colonial and Revolutionary periods: maritime. Commerce and trade was essentially waterborne, whether on the high seas or the many rivers and bays indenting the seacoast. Seaport merchant capitalists continued to direct the course of the nation's economic development and powerfully influence the content and direction of political agendas, whether on the national or state and local levels.

Immediately following the end of formal hostilities with Great Britain, once again it was business as usual, as the postwar years saw significant American growth in commerce and trade with her former enemy. Great Britain, as before, was the major market for American agricultural products. Moving across the Atlantic Ocean from the United States to Great Britain came an increasing flow of both raw materials and processed goods. Cotton, the major export product, came from South Carolina and Georgia, and increasingly from the Gulf region where the new producing areas of the deep South and newly acquired Southwest produced a phenomenal boom in raw cotton destined for both foreign and domestic textile factories. Wheat, from the newly-opened Midwestern region, joined Chesapeake and Kentucky-grown tobacco (the great Middle Atlantic and Southern export product of the colonial era) as especially important exports during the first decade of the postwar era. Naval stores (tar, resin, and turpentine), along with high-quality ship timber, were important North Carolina products for export. From both Southern states and those of the Mississippi River region came lumber, and in later decades there were cargoes of lead that had been mined in Illinois and shipped down the Mississippi to New Orleans. Processed goods from the American Midwest, notably beef and such pork products as hams, lard, and bacon, joined such important New England products as potash and leather goods for the British market. Among other important processed or manufactured goods in America's transatlantic export trade were flour, which came from both the Chesapeake Bay region and interior states; and candles, especially fine spermaceti candles from the New England whaling centers.

All of this variety of export goods traveled by sail, with the great bulk of these goods being carried in large wooden square-rigged cargo vessels, usually three-masted ships or two-masted brigs, primarily from the major American centers of commerce and navigation. These were the northeastern American ports of Boston, New York, Philadelphia, and Baltimore; the South Atlantic ports of Charleston and Savannah; and the Gulf ports of Mobile and New Orleans.

The return cargoes from Great Britain and from both northern European continental and Mediterranean seaports were even more varied and valuable. Industrial manufactures–textiles, iron, and specialty steel products–came from such continental ports as Antwerp, Bremen, Hamburg, Havre, and Rotterdam, and from the main British ports of Liverpool and London. Processed goods, notably wines, brandies, and other alcoholic beverages, came directly from France, Spain, Portugal, and Madeira, or through the British port of London. And the vital raw material salt came from Spain.

Transition to a National Market Economy

During America's first true quarter century of economic and political independence, the nation successfully met the challenges of sustained economic growth at the same time the population was rapidly increasing and pushing westward. The maritime industries were in the vanguard of this growth, for trade was the engine of economic progress, and central to the demands of trade was transportation by water.

Alexis De Tocqueville on the Maritime Greatness of the United States

No other nation in the world possesses vaster, deeper, or more secure ports for commerce than the Americans.

The inhabitants of the United States form a great civilized nation, placed by fortune in the midst of wildernesses, twelve hundred leagues from the main heart of civilization. Hence America stands in daily need of Europe. In time, no doubt, the Americans will come themselves to grow or to manufacture most of the things they need, but the two continents will never be able to live entirely independently of each other. There are too many natural links between their needs, ideas, habits, and mores.

The Union grows some things that have become necessary to us and that our soil entirely refuses to provide or can grow only at great expense. The Americans consume only a very small part of these products; they sell us the rest.

Consequently Europe is the market for America, as America is the market for Europe. And sea trade is as necessary to the inhabitants of the United States to bring their raw materials to our harbors as to bring our manufactures to them.

The United States would either provide a great deal of business to other maritime nations, if they were to give up trade themselves, as up till now the Spaniards in Mexico have done, or must become one of the leading maritime powers of the world; that alternative is inevitable.

At all times the Anglo-Americans have shown a decided taste for the sea. Independence, by breaking their commercial links with England, gave a new and powerful stimulus to their maritime genius. Since that time the number of the Union's ships has grown at almost as quick a rate as the number of its inhabitants. Today it is the Americans themselves who carry to their shores nine tenths of the products of Europe. It is the Americans too who carry three quarters of the exports of the New World to European consumers.

American ships fill the docks of Le Havre and Liverpool, while the number of English and French vessels in New York harbor is comparatively small.

Thus American commerce cannot only face competition on its own ground, but can even compete to advantage with foreigners on their own.
The European navigator is prudent about venturing out to sea; he only does so when the weather is suitable; if any unexpected accident happens, he returns to port; at night he furls some of his sails; and when the whitening billows indicate the approach of land, he checks his course and takes an observation of the sun.

The American, neglecting such precautions, braves these dangers; he sets sail while the storm is still rumbling; by night as well as by day he spreads full sails to the wind; he repairs storm damage as he goes; and when at last he draws near the end of his voyage, he flies toward the coast as if he could already see the port.

The American is often shipwrecked, but no other sailor crosses the sea as fast as he. Doing what others do but in less time, he can do it at less expense. . . .

An American navigator leaves Boston to go and buy tea in China. He arrives at Canton, stays a few days there, and comes back. In less than two years he has gone around the whole globe, and only once has he seen land. Throughout a voyage of eight or ten months he has drunk brackish water and eaten salted meat; he has striven continually against the sea, disease, and boredom; but on his return he can sell tea a farthing cheaper than an English merchant can: he has attained his aim.

I cannot express my thoughts better than by saying that the Americans put something heroic into their way of trading.

The universal movement prevailing in the United States, the frequent reversals of fortune, and the unexpected shifts in public and private wealth all unite to keep the mind in a sort of feverish agitation which wonderfully disposes it toward every type of exertion and keeps it, so to say, above the common level of humanity. For an American the whole of life is treated like a game of chance, a time of revolution, or the day of a battle.

These same causes working simultaneously on every individual finally give an irresistible impulse to the national character. Choose any American at random, and he should be a man of burning desires, enterprising, adventurous, and, above all, an innovator. The same bent affects all he does; it plays a part in his politics, his religious doctrines, his theories of social economy, and his domestic occupations; he carries it with him into the depths of the backwoods as well as into the city's business. This same spirit applied to maritime commerce makes the American cross the sea faster and sell his goods cheaper than any other trader in the whole world.

As long as American sailors keep these intellectual advantages and the practical superiority derived from them, they will not only continue to pro-vide for the needs of producers and consumers in their own country, but they will increasingly tend to become, like the English, the commercial agents of other nations. . . .

England is now the natural commercial center for all neighboring nations; the American Union is destined to fill the same role in the other hemisphere. So every nation that comes to birth or grows up in the New World does so, in a sense, for the benefit of the Anglo-Americans.

Should the Union be dissolved, the trade of the states forming it would no doubt for a time be checked in its growth, but less than is generally supposed. It is clear that whatever may happen, the trading states will remain united. They all are both contiguous and share the same opinions, interests, and mores, and they are capable of forming a very great maritime power. Even if the South of the Union did become independent of the North, it still could not manage without it. I have said that the South is not a land of commerce, and there is nothing at present to indicate that it will become so. Therefore a long while ahead the Americans of the southern states will be obliged to rely on foreigners to export their produce and to bring them the things they need. Of all possible intermediaries, their northern neighbors are most certainly those able to serve them most cheaply. So they will serve them, for low cost is the supreme law of trade. There is no sovereign will or national prejudice that can fight for long against cheapness. . . .

Reason suggests and experience proves that there is no lasting commercial greatness unless it can, at need, combine with military power. . . .

I am convinced that dismemberment of the Union, far from reducing American naval strength, would have a strong tendency to increase it. At present the trading states are linked to others that do not trade and that therefore are often reluctant to increase a maritime power from which they benefit only indirectly.

But if all the trading states of the Union were combined in one coherent nation, then for them trade would become a national interest of the first importance; they would then be disposed to make great sacrifices to protect their ships, and there would be nothing to stop their following their inclinations in this respect.

I think that nations, like men, in their youth almost always give indications of the main features of their destiny. Seeing how energetically the Anglo-Americans trade, their natural advantages, and their success, I cannot help believing that one day they will become the leading naval power on the globe. They are born to rule the seas, as the Romans were to conquer the world.

Democracy in America. George Lawrence, trans., J.P. Mayer, ed. (1835, 1840; reprint, Garden City, New York: Anchor Books, Doubleday & Company, 1969), 400-07, *passim*.

The maritime trades flourished in seaports large and small during the first half of the nineteenth century. In this view of the Gloucester, Massachusetts, waterfront, in the 1840s, shipwrights frame a small vessel, probably a fishing schooner like the two silhouetted against the salt cod packing houses on Fort Point. Although fishing was Gloucester's principal industry, a topsail schooner loaded with lumber, a trading brig, and a bark also lie in the harbor, representing the port's maritime ties to a larger world. Fitz Hugh Lane painted this view of "The Fort and Ten Pound Island" in 1848. (Courtesy The Newark Museum/Art Resource, NY)

By 1840 different sections of the new nation had developed in sharply contrasting ways. Sectional differences led to complex patterns of trade in both international and interregional markets. During this early national period, America's major geographical regions had become increasingly specialized in production. The South focused on cotton as a primary commodity, although tobacco, rice, and sugar were also grown commercially for market. These Southern plantation-grown agricultural products moved primarily as exports directly to foreign customers, but a significant and growing amount of these commodities was shipped to northern American markets for both export and domestic use. The Northeast remained engaged in shipping and commerce, along with the ancillary enterprises to support these activities: shipbuilding, insurance, and financial services. In addition, northern producers continued their concentration on fishing, whaling, and small-scale agriculture.

Perhaps the most remarkable example of regional specialization that depended entirely on American shipping was New England's ice trade, initiated by the ingenious and irrepressible Boston entrepreneur Frederic Tudor, America's "Ice King." In 1805 Tudor began his ambitious project to ship to the tropics a cargo of ice, carefully insulated within sawdust, that had been harvested from such small New England freshwater sources as Walden Pond and Fresh Pond, near his home in Cambridge, Massachusetts. It took many years for Tudor to establish his business on a profitable basis, but with the assistance of Nathaniel J. Wyeth, also from Cambridge, Tudor finally developed the ice trade into a major export business for Massachusetts. By the 1840s his ice was sold worldwide, with customers in Persia, India, the East Indies, China, Australia, and Central and South America. As he watched Tudor's Irish-immigrant laborers cut ice on Walden Pond, Henry David Thoreau observed, "Thus it appears that the sweltering inhabitants of Charleston and New Orleans, of Madras and Bombay and Calcutta, drink at my well."

Northeastern factories by 1840 had become more competitive with manufacturers in Great Britain, taking Southern cotton and turning it into cotton textiles and ready-made clothing, taking hides from California and South America and turning them into shoes, boots, and other leather goods, and taking local and Middle Atlantic iron and turning it into machinery. New England vessels carried these goods both south and west to domestic consumers. The interior regions, especially around the Great Lakes and in the Mississippi River system, produced raw and processed agricultural materials, such as wheat, corn, and livestock, which traveled to eastern markets by waterway. Cotton production boomed in the Deep South region along the Gulf of Mexico and, like the Midwestern raw material producers, Southerners consumed the goods manufactured in the Northeast or imported into northern seaports. As the economic historian Douglass North has pointed out, this regional specialization and interregional trade stimulated national economic growth and a general shift to a market economy in the United States.

This pattern of regional specialization required each area to be dependent on trade, and relied on the capability to ship large volumes of goods at a reasonable cost. Commercial agricultural products, such as cotton, wheat, and corn, were bulky cargoes, as were the valuable products of the forests. In the half century following 1815, timbers for masts, lumber, tar, pitch, turpentine, and hemp remained essential for both maritime and land-based construction industries, and firewood still was the primary fuel for heating most buildings. A vigorous competition, involving coastal trade in sail, steamships on the rivers and the Great Lakes, barges on the canals, and the emerging rail links, made possible the emergence of a transportation network capable of enabling such spectacular national growth. Thus, in the antebellum period maritime activity provided the crucial linkages needed for the market economy. However, regional specialization also created significant social, economic, cultural, and political differences; and these differences soon placed severe strains on national unity.

Even more than in previous decades, the North possessed a number of cities that were important and thriving maritime and commercial centers. Throughout the 1815-60 period these cities, whose leadership came largely from the mercan-

tile class, would continue to grow through the expansion of both commercial activity and industrialization. With the exception of New Orleans, the South failed to experience comparable urban growth. Charleston, Savannah, and Mobile served as major seacoast centers for the export of cotton, but they were not hubs of significant economic activity and growth at all comparable to the major seaports of New England and the Middle Atlantic regions.

The plantation economy, which brought prosperity to the South through the ever-increasing demand for cotton, rested on slavery; and slavery, together with the extensive lands that relied on slavery for their production, comprised a major area of Southern capital investment as well as a system of social and labor control. The rising cost of slaves and rapidly enlarging scope of production meant that while cotton-growers increased their income, the small farmers making up the majority of the white population did not, but instead continued to engage in subsistence farming. The resultant uneven distribution of income limited the ability of the South, as a whole, to purchase goods even as the new Northern manufactures became available.

In the central states and those of the "Old Northwest," around the Great Lakes, income was more evenly distributed, as family farms geared agricultural production to markets. Both foreign and domestic demand for wheat, corn, and other grains surged, and the repeal of the British Corn laws in 1846, along with the Irish famine of the 1840s, opened more international markets for American agricultural products as well as lumber and minerals from western mines.

The 1840s witnessed the annexation of Texas; the acquisition of the huge southwest territory of New Mexico, Arizona, and California as a result of the war with Mexico; and the addition of the territory of Oregon. There now existed a continental United States with its long Pacific seacoast. During the later 1840s and well into the 1850s, a sudden and substantial increase in shipping capacity, the extension of transportation access to the hinterlands, and the generally favorable costs of shipping facilitated the integration of these immense new territories in the national market economy.

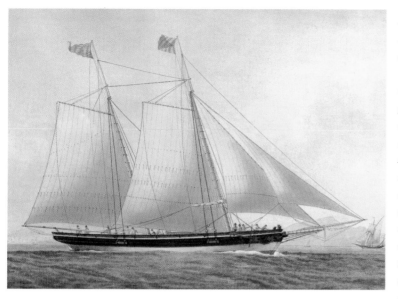

Among the regional sailing vessel types used for coastal trade was a breed of fast, shallow-draft schooners developed around Chesapeake Bay. An extreme version established a reputation for great speed in privateer service during the War of 1812 and influenced the design of vessels for a number of illicit trades, including the African slave trade and the Asian opium trade. A later form of Chesapeake schooner shared the wide, shallow hull and raked masts, but with more conservative proportions. Built in 1818, the Young Brutus represents the postwar model, which was handy in working up Chesapeake Bay creeks, speedy in delivering small cargoes along the coast, and seaworthy enough to make occasional transatlantic passages. Frederic Roux painted the Young Brutus in the Mediterranean, ca. 1825. With several bands of reef points on her jib, foresail, and mainsail, and removable bonnets on the the foot of the jib and foresail, the Young Brutus is prepared to sail in the lightest winds or remain secure in gale conditions. A square topsail, furled and lowered on its yard, aids in downwind sailing. The black sailors on her foredeck represent the important role of African Americans as mariners during the first third of the nineteenth century. (Courtesy Chesapeake Bay Maritime Museum, St. Michaels, Maryland)

The 113-foot bark Fanny, launched at Mystic, Connecticut, in 1849, spent more than ten years in the coastal trade. She was built for Charles Mallory, a sailmaker who had expanded his fortune through investments in whaleships in the 1840s. As Mallory's first cargo vessel, the Fanny ran in the E.D. Hurlbut & Company packet line from New York to Mobile, and later in Eagle & Hazard's Eagle Line on the same route. Originally a mariner from Connecticut, Hurlbut had established his line in 1825, as Gulf cotton shipments increased, and by 1846 operated thirteen vessels, with one sailing every ten days. The Fanny represents changes in American sailing-ship design since the 1820s, with her elongated hull and relatively sharp bow, a tall rig, and a deckhouse "forecastle" for crew quarters rather than the older below-deck fo'c'sle. Rigged as a bark, with no square sails on her mizzenmast, the Fanny is easier to maneuver through the changeable coastal winds than a full-rigged ship would be. Nevertheless, she carries a tall square-rig, with a skysail on the main and with studdingsails set alongside the square sails, fore-and-aft staysails between the masts, and a "ringtail" behind the fore-and-aft spanker at her stern, to increase the sail area in light winds. Like many ships designed to carry cotton, the Fanny has an extended quarterdeck, or "roof," extending forward to the mainmast, under which she could accommodate passengers or a larger cargo of cotton bales. This 1850 portrait is attributed to J. Hansen. (M.S.M. 37.105)

The 150-mile stretch of the Hudson River between New York and Albany was an essential link in the maritime economy of New York, particularly after the completion of the Erie Canal. A distinctive form of wide, shallow-draft sloop with large sail area developed on the Hudson in the eighteenth century to carry passengers and freight. Refined in the nineteenth century, these sloops (like the one at far right and in the distance here) survived through mid-century despite competition from two-masted Hudson River schooners with similar hull form (examples of which are seen here right and left), and especially from steamboats. Robert Fulton found economic success for the steamboat on this route, and increasingly large and fast steamers plied the river through the nineteenth century. Coming upriver in this view is the Mary Powell, *a 288-foot side-wheeler capable of carrying several hundred passengers upstream at a speed of twenty-two knots. Albumen photograph ca. 1865. (M.S.M. 85.113.5)*

The Maritime Foundation for National Economic Growth

The survival, let alone the growth, of the new American nation after 1815 depended to a great degree on the ability of its various and widespread regions to become well-integrated, economically as well as politically. To achieve such a harmonious integration of disparate interests, systems of transportation and communication had to be developed to permit the regions to interact freely and productively with one another. Americans met this challenge in the half century preceding the Civil War by developing passenger and freight shipping lines to move goods up and down the Atlantic coast, from the Gulf of Mexico, and eventually to the Pacific coast.

They also constructed a series of canals that contributed to interregional and even foreign trade by extending the reach of navigable rivers and moving large quantities of freight slowly but cheaply over distances by barge. At the same time, steam-powered vessels permitted traffic to move up as well as down the network of great rivers. Americans continued to explore new possibilities for trade while initiating other technological improvements.

The costs of meeting the challenge were high; to meet them satisfactorily required a combination of individual and group entrepreneurial initiatives, a huge application of private investment capital, legislative action on various levels of government, and an extraordinary expenditure of public funds.

Despite Americans' active efforts to extend their commercial reach throughout the world, their nation's trade along its Atlantic coastline continued throughout the period as the most active area of America's waterborne enterprise. As more of the nation's agriculture became commercial, the prosperity of the United States was even more dependent upon the ability of farmers to get their products to markets. The long colonial experience in Atlantic coastal and foreign maritime operations meant that the seaports, with their wharves, warehouses, rigging lofts, ropewalks, cooperages, blacksmith shops, and other essential ingredients for maritime activity, were already in place, as were the seamen, shipbuilders, merchants, and others engaged in maritime commerce and navigation.

Of fundamental importance was the absence of foreign competition for the coastal trade of the United States. An essential element in the growth of the country after 1815, the coastal trade was limited by law to American-flag shipping by the Navigation Act of 1817, a landmark piece of Congressional legislation, which prohibited foreign vessels from engaging in trade between one American port and another. This policy of "cabotage" was no departure from previous practice; even earlier, preferential federal legislation to support the nation's maritime industries had been put in place, beginning with the Tonnage Act of 1789. The 1789 Tonnage Act was not exceptional for its time, but reflected the current (and generally traditional) mercantilist-based practice of maritime nations of protecting their maritime industries and developing their merchant marine through such preferential or even exclusionary provisions. While the 1789 Tonnage Act had only placed discriminatory tariffs on foreign-flag vessels in coastal service, the 1817 Navigation Act formally excluded foreign-flag vessels from trading between American ports.

With the protective umbrella provided by the 1817 Act, America's coastal trade thus flourished during the decades preceding the Civil War. The ease of entry for American sailing vessels, coupled with the enforced absence of low-cost foreign competition in this trade, continued to attract new entrants to coastal shipping, so that by 1820 the coastwise fleet exceeded in size America's large and expanding foreign trade fleet. With no government restrictions or controls on their activity, shipowners enjoyed great flexibility in being able to shift their vessels freely from one branch of shipping enterprise to another, in order to take advantage of the constantly changing supply and demand for America's large variety of commodities.

This favorable protected business environment also encouraged the organization of the far more expensive coastal steamship services that played a prominent part in America's coastwise trade from the early 1820s on. However, this was by no means a laissez-faire arena for American shipping entrepreneurs. Legislation and court decisions on both state and federal levels were crucial in shaping the development of these domestic steamer services as well as the nature of competition of such enterprise.

The unusually heavy start-up costs for steamship service produced demands from operators for protection of their "infant industry" from competition. They sought special preference, even exclusive rights, from the state legislatures that customarily granted charters to these companies. However, it immediately became apparent that an individual state's grant of monopoly rights was often at odds with comparable grants from other states, let alone the business interests of competing operators in other states. The New York-chartered Fulton-Livingston steamboat enterprise enjoyed monopoly rights on New York waters for nearly a decade after the end of the War of 1812. However, it had to contend with Connecticut steamboat operators in providing service on Long Island Sound. Not only was there a bitter struggle over freight rates, but at one point the competing interests induced their respective state legislatures to forbid out-of-state steamboat lines from operating in a state's home waters. Such potentially disastrous restrictions on interstate travel were avoided by the United States Supreme Court's landmark decision, *Gibbons v. Ogden*, which basically clarified (if not entirely resolved) the troubling issue of state rights in the area of interstate commerce.

The Court's *Gibbons v. Ogden* decision of 1824 struck down a New York State grant of monopoly right to the Fulton-Livingston interests, who had granted Aaron Ogden a license to operate steamboat service in the waters surrounding New York Port. A rival group, led by Thomas Gibbons and Cornelius Vanderbilt, defied the New York State grant of exclusivity by running a competing line in the same waters, which touched on New Jersey as well as New York shores. The Supreme Court's decision, guided by Chief Justice John Marshall, insisted on the primacy of federal government powers over any state powers as they might affect the conduct of interstate commerce. This decision greatly aided the coastwise trade of the United States by effectively prohibiting any state or states from the sort of restrictive control that had so impeded open competition among New York and Connecticut coastal shipping interests, as well as those of New York and New Jersey.

The federal government also retained responsibility for many of the coastal and river improvements that facilitated commerce. The federal commissioner of revenue remained in charge of the nation's lighthouses until they were turned over to the fifth auditor of the U.S. Treasury in 1820. This was a busy period for lighthouse development as navigation increased all along the coasts. Lighthouse construction began on the Great Lakes in 1819 and along the dangerous Florida Keys and the Gulf coast in the 1820s. The first lightship was commissioned in 1820 on Chesapeake Bay, followed by a lightship off Sandy Hook at the entrance to New York Bay in 1823 and one at Diamond Shoals off Cape Hatteras, North Carolina, in 1824.

Although the fifth auditor was more concerned with economy than with the safe and efficient expansion of the lighthouse service, a number of technical developments took place. After considerable delay, the Fresnel lighthouse lens, with its prismatic structure to focus light, was introduced in America in 1840 at the Navesink Light on the highlands above the entrance to New York Bay. By the 1850s the Fresnel lens was the standard for significant U.S. lighthouses. In 1850, the British screw-pile lighthouse design was introduced in the U.S. at Brandywine Shoal on Delaware Bay. With cast-iron legs that were screwed into soft bottom, this design permitted the establishment of fixed light stations on submerged shoals or on the low sand islands of the Florida Keys, which were frequently inundated during hurricanes.

By 1852 mariners were guided by 331 lighthouses and 42 lightships on the American coasts. But management of the system was considered so insufficient that responsibility was vested in the new Lighthouse Board, made up of representatives of the U.S. Navy, the Topographical Engineers, the Army Corps of Engineers, the U.S. Coast Survey, and a number of prominent scientists. With a more scientific approach, the Lighthouse Board took steps to upgrade the general condition and operation of the lights, and to experiment with alternative fuels to replace the increasingly expensive sperm whale oil that had been burned in lighthouse lamps since the eighteenth century. Perhaps the greatest engineering achievement of the Lighthouse Board before the Civil War was

the construction of a stone lighthouse on the submerged Minots Ledge in Massachusetts Bay near Boston Harbor. Similar to Scotland's Inchcape Rock Light, this was the first American lighthouse built on a wave-swept location in the open sea.

Meanwhile, the U.S. Coast Survey, established in 1807 but only briefly active before 1830, was reinstituted in 1832 to survey and chart the nation's coasts and harbors. Superintended by the Swiss scientist Ferdinand Hassler, and then by Benjamin Franklin's grandson, the army-trained engineer Alexander D. Bache, when it was reorganized in 1843, the Coast Survey relied on the survey abilities of First Assistant Edmund Blunt (son of the chart and coast-pilot publisher) and his colleagues. The Coast Survey was extended to the West Coast in 1851.

Other maritime engineering works were overseen by the U.S. Army's Topographical Engineers and Corps of Engineers. Coastal masonry fortifications were designed and begun to defend important harbors from Maine to the Mississippi River, including Fort Sumter in Charleston Harbor. The brilliant engineering officer, Robert E. Lee, was involved in this work for several decades. In 1837, while stationed in St. Louis, Lee turned his attention to the hydrodynamic problem of shoal formation in the Mississippi River, which threatened to hamper river commerce at St. Louis. Lee designed a jetty to constrict the river and scour the shoals. Farther down the Mississippi, levees built by private and state initiatives had provided relative security from flooding to lands along the river, but shoaling in the delta hampered the increasingly large ships engaged in the cotton trade from New Orleans. During the 1850s, Congress sponsored a large-scale study to determine solutions to the flooding and navigational problems of the nation's principal waterway.

Canals: Vital Webs of Internal Trade

Before the introduction of railroads, canals provided a particularly effective way to meet the need of moving large amounts of goods and peo-

Monomoy Light was established in 1823 on the end of a long sandspit at the southeast corner of Cape Cod, Massachusetts, to help guide mariners through the shoals on the busy coastal route that passed between Cape Cod and Nantucket Island. The light was rebuilt as a cast-iron tower with external bracing in 1849, and eight years later, as part of the improvements undertaken by the Lighthouse Board, the tower was refitted with a Fresnel lens, giving it eleven miles of visibility. The chicken coops at left and the wash hanging out to dry suggest the self-sufficiency required of the lighthouse keeper and his family at this remote location. Photograph by Masury, ca. 1865. (M.S.M. 79.148.20)

ple in the early decades of the 1800s. Yet construction of canals required the mobilization of unusually large amounts of investment capital. Because of their recognition of the public interest in creating the infrastructure for economic growth, state and local governments were willing to invest public funds, although the American experience with canal-building prior to this period had met with very limited success. Nevertheless, the combination of public and private capital, increasingly sophisticated engineering techniques, and a rapidly expanding immigrant labor force made canal-building a practical undertaking by 1820.

Of critical importance to the immediate postwar

era of American canal building was the leadership of New Yorker DeWitt Clinton, who called for a canal to connect the Hudson River with Lake Erie. After approval by the New York State Legislature in 1817, construction quickly got under way. The Erie Canal was built in short sections by the letting of local contracts; upon completion each section would be opened to local traffic, so that the first section, from Utica to Rome, began operating in1819. By the time of official completion on 26 October 1825, local boat traffic was already making considerable use of the Erie Canal.

The completion of the Erie Canal made a great economic impact. Freight rates for the 364-mile

The Erie Canal was financed by the State of New York, which collected tolls to maintain the waterway. Tolls were assessed on the weight of freight carried by the canal boats. At five locations along the canal, the state operated hydraulic weigh locks, like the one shown here at Rochester. With the lock doors closed and the lock drained, the boat rested on a scale large enough to record its weight. At the beginning of the season, each canal boat was weighed empty. When it came to a weigh lock during each trip on the canal, the boat was weighed loaded and the weight of the cargo was computed and a toll was levied. (M.S.M. 95.138.1)

trip from the Lake Erie port of Buffalo to Albany, near the head of the Hudson River, dropped to an astonishing extent–from $100 per ton to $10 per ton. In five years, tolls exceed $1 million a year, with the volume of shipments increasing in both directions. The canal, as part of a vital water network of communication and trade, facilitated the transportation of grain from western lands to the East Coast for domestic consumption and, in the later decades, for export. The importance of the Erie Canal for grain shipment is indicated by the proportion of grain transported; in 1854, 83 percent of the nation's shipment of grain went by this route. Use of the Erie Canal for passenger travel stimulated the flow of migration to undeveloped western land. Only three days after the canal's opening, the first boatload of immigrants reached Buffalo. In a year, over a thousand immigrants a day were making the trip from New York City up the Hudson River to Albany, and then by canal to Buffalo.

Pennsylvania shortly followed New York in building a canal system, with the Main Line Canal, the first of its States Works projects, opening fully in 1834. Construction across the Allegheny Mountains posed far greater problems than had the Erie Canal with its water-level route through northern New York State. To cross the Appalachian Mountains, the Pennsylvania project required a series of inclined planes, on which canal boats were hoisted on rails, that made the system unusually expensive. However, in the early period, the amount of cargo carried and the revenues so generated contributed importantly to trade between Philadelphia and the Ohio River basin, thus providing another vital link between the interior and the seaboard. Subsidiary canals were subsequently constructed in Pennsylvania as local communities pressured the state legislature for extension of canals as a path to local prosperity. In eastern Pennsylvania, the Schuylkill Canal and others were built specifically to carry anthracite coal from the mines to Philadelphia.

Other areas took up canal building in order to provide alternative modes of shipping as well as to lower transportation costs. New England had several canals, including the Farmington; that ambitious project was built north from New Haven toward Canada, but it only reached into Massachusetts before being supplanted by a railroad line in the 1840s. In Maryland, the Chesapeake & Ohio Canal was chartered in 1824, in order to provide a waterway west along the Potomac River. This canal was intended to link Washington, D.C. and Pittsburgh, but rugged terrain and competition from the Baltimore & Ohio Railroad were too much to handle, and the project never reached its goal. Farther south, the James River & Kanawha Company extended the canal begun in the 1780s in Richmond, Virginia, with the support of George Washington; it also failed to pierce the Appalachians and never became a conduit for western goods. On the other side of the mountains, farmers and merchants of the western lands in the Ohio and northern Mississippi River basins sought eastern markets as an alternative to New Orleans. Canals built in Indiana, Illinois, Michigan, and Ohio brought the desired economic growth as well as population increase in the 1835 to 1840 period.

For a variety of reasons, including shortage of funds, many of these efforts were not successful in creating economic efficiencies, but they did contribute to financial speculation, particularly in state bond sales. This canal-building frenzy was part of a more general speculative boom, based on the shaky and unsystematic credit structure of local and state-chartered banks, that became a national political scandal. Accordingly, President Andrew Jackson in 1836 determined that only specie (coin) would be accepted in payment for federal land sales. Jackson's controversial Specie Circular touched off the Panic of 1837 and left newly inaugurated President Martin Van Buren with a serious economic downturn that he was unable to reverse or bring under control throughout his four years in office. The prolonged depression that followed was particularly severe and led to all but total cessation of canal building, as states, towns, and private firms all staggered into bankruptcy.

Notwithstanding the nation's economic turmoil after 1837, the Northeast by 1840 had created the nation's largest maritime transportation infrastructure, setting the stage for future economic growth. In that year America had over 3,000 miles of canals in operation, mostly in the Northeast. While no new canals of importance were built after 1840, and while many of the smaller systems of feeder canals had gone bankrupt and ceased operating during the depression, the major canals, particularly the Erie, would continue to carry as much freight as the expanding network of railroads until 1860.

Seaports and Commercial Specialization

Seaports, as in earlier decades, were the commercial centers for their region of the country and the adjacent hinterlands, although there was a general trend to distinctive specialization in response to their primary export and import cargoes. The organization of commerce in these mercantile and shipping centers changed substantially in the antebellum period, and to a considerable extent reflected the sectional and regional differences among major seaports. By the 1830s New York was clearly America's largest seaport city, followed in order

Although photographed nearly seventy-five years after the height of the canal era, this view from the towpath on the Chesapeake and Ohio Canal suggests the scale of operations. A typical ninety-two-foot freight boat leaves one of the canal's seventy-four locks. Through the trees is the stone house built by the canal company for the locktender. The boat has cabins fore and aft for the boatman and crew, and perhaps his family or an occasional passenger. The hatch amidships leads to the "stable" for the mules that tow the boat. Coal was the most common downstream freight on this canal, and a typical boat could carry 120 tons in the two cargo holds. Although it faced competition from the Baltimore & Ohio Railroad almost from the start, the Chesapeake and Ohio Canal flourished between 1828 and 1850, and it did not cease operations until 1924. Photo by Henry D. Fisher, ca. 1910. (M.S.M. 93.45.30)

by Philadelphia, Baltimore, Boston, New Orleans, and Charleston. The smaller seaports and tidewater ports played a key role in the coastal trade, as did those on the rivers along the eastern seaboard. These smaller maritime centers served as points of transshipment of goods to the major seaports for movement to other regions or abroad.

In the Northeast, New York was already leading in volume of trade and poised for its explosion of growth as the leading commercial and financial center, with its merchant houses engaged in the operation of coastal packet lines. Philadelphia, America's largest industrial city by 1830, experienced a slowdown in growth as a port in the early decades, since it had relied on flour and grain trade with the West Indies and Southern Europe, but it regained importance with the opening of the extensive Pennsylvania anthracite coalfields and the expansion of the interior trade by the state-promoted canal system.

Boston remained a major seaport although its hinterland had few rich farmlands to supply agricultural products to its market. In addition, alternative and more promising areas of capital investment, notably in textile manufacturing, drew funds out of shipping and merchant trading activities. However, Boston could draw from such emerging satellite ports as Portland, Maine, which sent lumber, lime, granite, fish, and firewood primarily by sail to Boston. The growth of manufacturing in these early decades permitted Boston to remain prominent in coastal trade.

A rapid increase in Southern raw cotton production and in the trade of this product resulted in a swelling volume of cotton bales shipped from Southern ports to Boston, while textiles and other manufactures made the return trip. Flour, coming in from interior states as well as up from the Middle Atlantic region, was in great demand for feeding the growing numbers of New England industrial workers. In their traditional role as shipping operators as well as commodity merchants, Boston firms initiated a number of coastal and transatlantic sailing packet services, but were slow to engage in steamship operations outside of their immediate region.

In 1830, a thriving steamship service opened between Portland, Maine, and Boston, as

This view of Baltimore Harbor in 1836 suggests the volume of trade that helped make Baltimore the nation's third largest city by 1860. At left is Federal Hill, with the inner harbor in the distance and the maritime enclave of Fells Point at far right. Gouache by Nicolino Calyo. (Courtesy The Baltimore Museum of Art: Purchased by the Women's Committee from funds derived from the 60th Anniversary Ball)

Mobile, Alabama, was the second leading Gulf cotton port after New Orleans. Established by the French in 1710, and taken by the U.S. in 1813, it became a thriving port city in the 1820s. Located forty miles from the Gulf on a broad but shallow bay, with steamboat access to cotton country on the Alabama and Tombigbee Rivers, the port flourished on the exchange of cotton for Northern and European manufactured goods. Between 1817 and 1860, 6,500,000,000 pounds of cotton left Mobile aboard ship. Lithograph by James Bennett, 1839. (Courtesy The Mariners' Museum, Newport News, Virginia)

Portland developed as a major regional port. Passengers from Boston initially sailed to Portland and then could change to smaller coastal steamers. Cargoes tended to move by sailing vessel, although after 1842 a growing volume came by rail. Due to the dangers of rounding Cape Cod, direct steamship service between Boston and New York did not begin until 1864. Before then, New England cargoes bound for New York moved by sailing vessel, or else by railroad to a point on Long Island Sound where they could be transferred to a steamer.

Starting in 1836, south-bound passengers from Boston could take the Boston and Providence Railroad to Providence, Rhode Island, and transfer to a steamer of the Boston and New York Transport Company for the trip to New York City. Soon the completion of the

Providence and Stonington Railroad would provide a means for travelers to continue to Stonington, Connecticut, by rail and then board a larger steamer for the trip to New York. In 1847, the completion of the Fall River Railroad from Boston encouraged the formation of the Fall River-New York Steamboat Line. As this route provided the fastest service between Boston and New York, it became the leading line and continued for nearly a century.

Baltimore, located near the head of Chesapeake Bay and close to the mouth of the Susquehanna River, flourished in the postwar period as its merchants took the lead in marketing the tobacco of Virginia and Maryland, fish and shellfish from the eastern shore, grain from western Maryland and Pennsylvania, and bituminous coal from

Faith, Sailortowns, and the Character of Seamen's Benevolence in Nineteenth-Century America

For much of the nineteenth century, the United States was a world leader in the effort to save the sailor. In the first half of the century, tens of thousands of sailors passed through American ports each year, spending a few days on shore to refresh themselves before returning to their nomadic existence at sea. Increasingly, these were rootless men, at once worldly and naive, with no ties to the communities they visited. Distinctive in dress and demeanor, heroic at sea yet clearly childlike ashore, and the victim of economic abuse in both worlds, the sailor appeared to social reformers as a figure in need of salvation.

Seamen's benevolence flourished around the rapidly expanding American merchant fleet for a number of reasons. Prominent among them were the American traditions of volunteering, spiritual zeal, and revivalism. Reform and benevolence also were a legacy of the social theory of the Age of Enlightenment, which held that the application of rational man's efforts could correct society's ills. The era of reform was also one of millennialist beliefs and apocalyptic

fears. With developments as far reaching as the American Revolution and the advent of industrialization and urbanization within just fifty years, the attendant social, political, and economic upheaval led to a widespread spiritual dislocation. The perception of a crumbling cosmos called for activism. Thus, a secular commitment to reform, which was deeply rooted in heartfelt Christian faith, experienced a widespread revival during the Second Great Awakening of the first third of the nineteenth century.

Americans of that era wedded rationality with the new, alluring perceptions of Romanticism which saw God as benevolent, nature as beneficent, and man as divine. Thus, it was incumbent upon nineteenth-century Americans to reform the social order, in order to allow God's plan for mankind to be fulfilled. Social reform in America took on the character of an evangelical crusade whose leaders were often members of the clergy. They sought to reform schools, drinking habits, prisons, the institution of slavery, the condition of female mill workers in the textile industry, the lot of the sailor, and

more. The combined moral fundamentalism and radical comprehensiveness made this period of reform unlike any other in the nation's history. All of these elements influenced the development of seamen's benevolence in the United States.

The world's first reform organization created specifically for sailors was the Boston Society for the Religious and Moral Improvement of Seamen, founded in 1812. By the early 1820s other local seamen's aid societies were scattered all along the eastern seaboard.

Although problems of safety and abuse of authority at sea were common, reformers focused much of their energy on the segment of the mariners' world visible to them, the waterfront section of America's seaports. In these "sailortowns" the seafarer was robbed of his money, his dignity, and possibly his hopes for eternal salvation. In sailortown, society appeared to be dysfunctional and unstable. For the members of the middle class who made up the reform societies, instability was perceived as a threat to both the body politic and spiritual wellness.

Many aspects of sailortown were seen to bedevil the mariners', and society's, moral welfare. Among the most obvious of these were saloons and dance halls. Whatever the quality of their entertainment and their liquor, the essential purpose of such establishments was to disengage the clientele from their cash as quickly as possible. Dance halls could be found in sailortowns the world over, all characterized by cheap liquor, loose women, and toughs at the door.

Streetwalkers also threatened the welfare of the sailor. Theirs was a world about which the middle class supposedly knew very little. Yet we can glimpse the decay that permeated New York City's sailortown in the 1850s through the journal of middle-aged attorney and seaman's protector Richard Henry Dana, Jr. He wrote of a stroll:

> Turned down Anthony St. to the Five Points. At almost every door were girls standing, and whispering loud to me as I passed, . . . The door of one house stood open, with laughter coming from the room. I walked in and there was an old harridan, with fat cheeks and a quick, sharp, devilish eye, standing at the door, and four girls, all young, and three of whom must have been once quite handsome . . . . There were obscene prints hanging about the walls to help excite the passions of the young who would drop into the house. . . . Some sailors came in swearing and calling for drink, and I slipped out.

Finding entertainment in such an environment could be expensive and dangerous for a sailor, but just locating a place to stay between voyages could be equally threatening. It was easy to find a waterfront boardinghouse that would provide meals and a bed for what seemed to be reasonable prices. In larger ports especially, foreign nationals ran boardinghouses that catered to seamen from their home country. But sailors' boardinghouses became infamous for their methods of running sailors into debt and sending them to sea in short order.

The crimping game, as it was known, lured the men to these houses with liquor and promises of pleasurable times. Once inside, they would be greeted cheerfully, but the goal was to bilk the men of their pay and run them into debt as quickly as possible. The boardinghouse master would then find them a ship for the next voyage. For this service, he would claim (depending on the size of the labor pool) one or two months' pay from the sailor's upcoming voyage. The payment of this "blood money" sent the mariner outward-bound with little more than a debt to show for his time ashore. Certainly, this web did not catch all sailors. Many avoided establishments of bad repute, and many others moved into and out of the seafaring labor force quickly. Yet the predatory "land-sharks" found many naive or indifferent sailors to exploit, and in some large seaports it was difficult for a sailor to sign aboard a ship except

through a boardinghouse master. The abduction of the naive George Staples may not be typical of the dangers of sailortown, but crimping, prostitution, alcohol, inflated prices for rooms, food, and equipage were all ills that haunted the seafarer ashore.

During January of 1874 the story of George F. Staples of Rome, New York, was published in the American Seamen's Friend Society's *Sailor's Magazine.* Staples, it was reported, had been virtually kidnapped by a "runner" who forced him to sign on the full-rigged ship *Baltic* for a passage to San Francisco. Before shipping out, the frightened young carpenter had been kept a prisoner in a boardinghouse directly across the street from the famed Sailor's Home run by the American Seaman's Friend Society. The plight of George Staples highlights the struggle between those who sought to profit from the sailor ashore and those who sought to protect him.

Reformers used a number of approaches to counter the exploitive strategies of land-sharks in seaport cities. These methods, combined with the comprehensive evangelical thrust of nineteenth-century reform, established the character of seamen's benevolence in the United States.

One of the first strategies employed to counteract the influence of sin in the sailor's world was to distribute copies of the Bible. Thousands upon thousands of pocket editions of the Gospel were given to seafarers by organizations like the American Bible Society and the American Tract Society.

Preaching on the streets was another rudimentary way to uplift the denizens of sailortown. The best-known and most charismatic of the ministers who sought to rouse spiritual fervor among seamen was Father Edward T. Taylor, whose style was commemorated by Herman Melville in the character of Father Mapple in *Moby-Dick*. A former sailor himself, Taylor had been an itinerant preacher before his appointment as minister of the Boston Seamen's Bethel in 1830.

In active seaports, friends in the community might put up sufficient capital to bring a waterfront ministry indoors. Perhaps one would rent a storefront or a sail loft in which to hold religious services until a more permanent site could be procured. Another of the strategies for meeting the sailor's needs in the way of a place of worship was to establish a bethel, or sailor's church, aboard a refurbished old hulk floating in the harbor. Or an agency might build a brand-new floating church to accomplish the same goal.

Many other seamen's bethels occupied traditional shoreside houses of worship. These churches varied in size from small chapels to large edifices that could seat hundreds of worshipers at a time, and they could be found around the globe. The first American church exclusively devoted to sailors was the First Mariners Church in New York City,

dedicated in 1820. The opening ceremonies of this church reflected the ecumenical character of the American seamen's friend movement. Attending the bethel's dedication were clergymen from the Presbyterian, Episcopal, Dutch Reformed, and Methodist churches. This nonsectarianism was a hallmark of the seamen's mission in America, and the lack of interdemoninational quibbling helped make the American seamen's mission movement a world leader. As churches sprang up in seaports throughout the United States, the character of the movement evolved even further as reformers sought to challenge the illicit traffickers of sailortown directly.

The reformers tried to meet the sailors' needs on several levels. If sailors lost self-determination and money to the crimping game, then Sailors' Homes could offer an alternative to the boardinghouse. In New York and several other American ports, separate sailors' homes were established for African-American sailors. The Coloured Seamen's Home in New York was run by William P. Powell, who first opened a temperance boardinghouse for black sailors at New Bedford in the 1830s. Powell combined the social reform issues of temperance and the abolition of slavery with his efforts on behalf of black sailors.

To counter the debauchery of sailortown dance halls and brothels, reformers offered wholesome pastimes in sailors' libraries and reading

rooms. If seamen had a difficult time keeping their money, then the missionaries created mariners' banks. Sailors were often fleeced by disreputable outfitters, so the benevolent societies opened clothing stores of their own. Shipping offices run by the reformers sprang up in the larger ports as well, thereby denying the crimps their monopoly on the job market.

The American Seamen's Friend Society copied the idea of English mission exemplar, George Charles Smith, and published the *Sailor's Magazine,* a monthly filled with information and uplifting articles, for well over a century. The distribution of loan libraries was another hallmark of the A.S.F.S., which sent thousands of boxed collections of morally uplifting books to sea, as did its sister organizations. There were many similar organizations with their reading rooms, bethels, and homes, but the A.S.F.S. became something of an umbrella organization that embraced many smaller groups. Eventually the Society established sites all around the world.

As was typical of the era, women rarely held positions of leadership in the seamen's benevolent movement, but their volunteerism was vital to the movement's success. Sarah Josepha Hale, editor of *Godey's Lady's Book*, was the exception that made the rule. Her female Seamen's Aid Society subscribed, funded, and administered the Mariner's Home in Boston's North End. She also helped many wives and daughters of common seamen, who frequently fell on hard times and might turn to prostitution to sustain themselves. Hale's Free School for the Daughters of Seamen taught young women to sew and then sold the well-made garments to sailors, who might otherwise be forced to purchase poor goods at inflated slop shop prices.

Another characteristic of the American seamen's benevolent movement was the gradual secularization of its approach. Although the Christian faith and its clergy continued to drive this reform effort, the message became less evangelical over time. This was in response to the general secularization of the world at large.

By catering to the sailor's practical and intellectual needs, as well as offering religious services, counseling. and emergency assistance, the seamen's friends maintained a waterfront presence for a century and a half. Battling against the pleasures of sailortown was a difficult and often thankless task, since many sailors did not want outsiders proselytizing or telling them how to spend their time ashore. But for others, the good works of the seamen's' missions offered a welcome relief from the abuse to which they were subjected.

Since the nineteenth century, tremendous changes in cargo handling, shipping patterns, ship design, and crew requirements have altered the sailor's shoreside routine. There is much less need for

Edward T. Taylor (1793-1871) of Richmond, Virginia, was orphaned at an early age and went to sea when he was seven. Converted to Methodism about 1810, he retired from the sea after the War of 1812, during which he was captured while serving on a privateer. Taylor traveled as a peddler and itinerant preacher until he learned to read; then studied for the ministry and became a Methodist clergyman in 1819. With the establishment of the Port Society of Boston, Taylor was chosen as minister of the Seamen's Bethel in 1830. During his forty years there he became one of the greatest American preachers of his era, and he won the implicit trust of sailors. Engraving from Gilbert Haven and Thomas Russell, **Father Taylor, the Sailor Preacher** *(Boston, 1872).*

sailors' homes and reading rooms. Consequently, many of the societies have closed their doors. Others, however, have adapted to changing

times and continue their work through telephone banks in the automated port facilities, dockside recreation halls, and legal advice in addition to spiritual guidance.

Today, the Gomorrah of the shellback's sailortown is gone, but those involved in seamen's' mission continue to address contemporary needs and beliefs, as their predecessors have done since the early years of the last century.

Glenn S. Gordinier

Pennsylvania. Baltimore became the leader in the production of flour, a significant product in coastal trade. The port benefited from the construction of two canals: the Chesapeake and Delaware Canal, which opened in 1829 to link the head of Chesapeake Bay with the Delaware River by cutting across the state of Delaware; and the Susquehanna and Tidewater Canal along the lower Susquehanna, which diverted considerable Pennsylvania produce to Baltimore rather than Philadelphia. While specialized Chesapeake Bay sailing vessels–small but fast sloops and schooners–continued to use

Baltimore as their port, the protected waters of the Bay prompted the early initiation of steamship operations. Steamer service began in 1813 between Baltimore and Frenchtown, with shore connections to Philadelphia. Baltimore's steamboat passenger and frieght service soon reached from Philadelphia (via the Chesapeake and Delaware Canal) to Norfolk, and subsequently extended to Washington and Richmond.

Of major Southern ports, Charleston, Savannah, and Mobile retained their status as cotton-exporting centers but did

pendence in 1836 and then as a newly enlarged and westward-developing United States emerged from the war with Mexico in 1848.

More than fifteen hundred miles upriver, the thriving port of Cincinnati, on the Ohio River, was becoming the nation's leading meat-packing center. Like the other river ports, Cincinnati had no wharves; rather, the paved slope of its waterfront permitted steamboats to land whatever the river level might be. From Cincinnati, steamboat lines ran upriver to the expanding iron and glass manufacturing port of Pittsburgh; downriver to Louisville, where the Louisville and Portland Canal opened in 1830 to circumvent the falls of the Ohio River; and all the way down the Ohio and Mississippi to New Orleans.

Near the confluence of the Missouri River with the Mississippi, St. Louis grew rapidly as the "gateway to the west." St. Louis thrived as a transfer point for goods traveling between east and west and north and south, handling western furs and later grain, produce from the upper Mississippi, and American and European manufactured goods destined for western consumers. St. Louis became a particular focus for German immigrants, who came into the country in great numbers from the 1830s through the 1850s. Many came via New Orleans and up the Mississippi, until St. Louis had 40,000 residents of German origin. In 1846, more than 2,000 steamboats called at St. Louis, and more than 200 steamboats were destroyed during the great fire on the St. Louis waterfront in 1849.

not expand into other growth areas. New Orleans, in contrast, not only grew as a major cotton port but also benefited from the adoption of steam engines for riverboats on the Mississippi and Ohio River systems; this meant that passengers and goods could be transported reasonably on schedule upriver as well as downstream. Although located ninety miles above the mouth of the Mississippi, New Orleans became the major American port on the Gulf of Mexico, acting as the entrepôt between sea and river travel. New Orleans was in a strategic position for expanding its commercial reach, first as Texas gained its inde-

A military outpost in the eighteenth century, and recaptured by American forces in 1813, Detroit, Michigan, had become one of the principal Great Lakes ports by the 1830s. The steamboat Walk-in-the-Water established service between Buffalo and Detroit in 1818, and this route brought many immigrant settlers to Detroit after the opening of the Erie Canal. During the 1830s and 1840s the Michigan Central Railroad established links between the port and interior Michigan, making it an entrepôt. William James Bennett painted this view of the Detroit waterfront, with several steamboats approaching, in 1836. (Photograph © The Detroit Institute of Arts, Gift of the Fred Sanders Company in memory of its founder, Fred Sanders)

By the 1850s, the St. Louis waterfront stretched for six miles, and well over one hundred steamboats could be found there on any day. As both a manufacturing and a transshipment center, St. Louis maintained commercial links in a web that extended south to Memphis and New Orleans, east to Cincinnati and Pittsburgh, north to Galena and St. Paul, and west to St. Joseph and Fort Benton. Anything from chairs to bags or casks of produce and boxes of manufactured goods passed across the St. Louis levee. Here, one boat prepares for the regular 200-mile packet service to Keokuk, Iowa, while the Federal Arch *(center) lays over between trips on the 1,300-mile run to Pittsburgh via Louisville. Such trade, and its location on the verge of the West, elevated St. Louis to the seventh largest American city by 1860. Daguerreotype by Thomas Easterly, 1853. (Courtesy Missouri Historical Society Photograph and Print Collection)*

The Erie Canal turned Buffalo, New York, into a major port on the Great Lakes. As the transshipment point for the increasing flow of western grain, Buffalo operated at a disadvantage until Joseph Dart opened the first grain elevator there in 1843. Two hundred and fifty miles west, where the waters of Lake Huron flowed through a strait into Lake Erie, the port of Detroit flourished on the site of an eighteenth-century French outpost. On the west shore of Lake Michigan, the town of Chicago was established in 1833 on the site of Fort Dearborn. The Illinois and Michigan Canal began the community's rise as a transshipment point on Lake Michigan. With the construction of railroads from Chicago into the agricultural hinterlands to the west, the port grew tremendously, from 4,000 people in 1840, to 30,000 in 1850, to more than 100,000 in 1860.

The Fishing Industries

As the oldest form of American maritime enterprise, and of central importance to the American colonial economy, fishing experienced vacillating fortunes in the decades after 1815. Ongoing disagreement over the rights of U.S. fishermen in Canadian waters since 1783 was addressed in 1818 when American and British negotiators agreed on American liberty to fish and process the catch on certain uninhabited stretches of the Labrador and Newfoundland coasts. A federal subsidy of two cents per pound of fish packed encouraged American codfishermen to exploit this liberty. The bounty system of federal support to the cod fishery, instituted in 1792 and repealed in 1807, had been renewed in 1813 and was increased in 1819. The annual federal bounties of $3.50 to $4.00 per gross ton, provided ostensibly to encourage a pool of fishermen who could be tapped for naval service, was a welcome support and political commitment to the New England maritime economy, whether or not the fisheries in fact served as the cradle of the American navy and merchant marine. In fact, the fishing fleet grew steadily in size, from 37,000 tons in 1815 to 163,000 by 1860. However, the accompanying registry laws for American fishing vessels put them increasingly at a disadvantage with lower-cost competitors from Canada and Europe. With the benefit of abundant and cheap sources of wood and duty-free iron, Nova Scotians could build their vessels for much less expense than their New England rivals from nearby Maine and Massachusetts. By 1835, the New England fisheries had lost much of their lucrative West Indian markets and in the European markets were slipping far behind their Canadian, English, and French competitors. The competition between Canadians and New Englanders over fishing "rights" or "liberties" to their common fishing grounds and to shore-side facilities for drying the catch was especially fierce, to the point where the U.S. Navy was obliged to provide a protective force in 1853, before a diplomatic resolution was achieved. The Canadian Reciprocity Treaty of 1854 awarded both sides fishing privileges in each other's waters and established duty-free importation of fish and agricultural produce across the border.

Gloucester, Massachusetts, was the great center for American fishing, although after mid-century the state of Maine led in total tonnage of fishing vessels. By the early 1830s fishermen were ranging further offshore, not just to the distant Grand Bank of Newfoundland, but also onto the dangerous but rich grounds of Georges Bank, east of Cape Cod. The New England fisheries paid a heavy price in lives for this increased activity; in 1846 a single storm brought a loss of twelve vessels from Marblehead fishing off George's Bank and a far larger fleet of Gloucestermen went down in the celebrated gale of 1851.

Fishing for cod and mackerel with hand-lines from the main vessel (usually a good-sized schooner) remained the New England fisherman's characteristic method until the latter 1850s. The mackerel fishery, which chased schools of surface-swimming mackerel along the coast in summer, had gotten a boost early in the century with the introduction of the shiny jig that served as a lure. In the 1850s, the huge purse seine net, with a drawline to purse the bottom around a school, was first adapted to mackerel fishing and increased the catch dramatically. Whether fresh or salted, the seasonal catch of mackerel was in high demand among consumers. The fleet of shallow-draft, broad-beamed, lofty-rigged "sharpshooter" and clipper schooners built to pursue mackerel incidentally increased the mortality rate of fishermen. When these vessels were put into service for offshore fishing, their characteristics of hull and rig made them prone to capsize.

The codfishery also underwent a change in the scale of the effort per individual during the 1850s and 1860s. In place of a few hooks dangled by each fisherman from the rail of the vessel, New England codfishermen adopted the European trawl line, a long line that lay on the bottom with many baited hooks attached at intervals. To set this gear, schooners began to carry flat-bottomed, nearly double-ended dories, which were launched from the fishing schooner on the fishing grounds each day, typically with a one or two-man crew. This method was nearly three times as productive as the old handline method of bottom fishing.

Beginning about 1850, the use of ice for preserving fresh fish became important by greatly extending the market area for fresh fish, in contrast to the salt cod that remained a product of foreign trade and a commodity for domestic consumption far from the sea. Nearby stocks of halibut, the largest species of flatfish, were nearly depleted in the late 1840s in the rush to supply northeast markets with fresh halibut. The market for fresh fish was sufficient in urban ports to harbor small local fleets to deliver seasonal catches of shad, salmon, bluefish, and other species, although cod and mackerel remained by far the most economically significant species.

Shellfish became increasingly important in the marketplace as well. New York Bay and Long Island Sound oysters were so popular that the natural supply was largely depleted, encouraging northern oystermen to ship oysters north from Chesapeake Bay. Connecticut oyster harvesters discovered they could actually transplant the

The Gale of 1862

The winter of 1861-62 was the quietest of the Civil War. By mid-February, the western theater was heating up, but General McClellan had still not launched his attack on Richmond, and in many parts of America the full reality of war had not yet struck home. Throughout the North, local matters were still foremost in people's minds, and in Gloucester, Massachusetts, the chief interest of most residents was still the fishery. During the previous quarter-century the town on Cape Ann had risen to become the greatest fishing port in America, and the business of the harbor never slackened now at any point in the year. In the spring and summer of 1861, hundreds of vessels had sailed north and east to the banks off Nova Scotia and Newfoundland or into the Gulf of St. Lawrence to set trawls for cod or to hook mackerel. These fisheries continued through the fall, but in the New Year the center of activity shifted to nearby Georges Bank, where fresh halibut could be landed for the Boston market and where vast schools of spawning codfish struck about the beginning of February. Georges had a bad reputation, being shallow and crossed with dangerous tidal currents. Local fishermen had only started to work this bank in earnest in the 1830s, and since then hardly a year had passed without at least one vessel being lost to the winter

storms. Still, the trips were short, and for men tough enough to endure the cold the money was good.

This particular winter had already been a grim one. Three schooners carrying twenty-eight men had been lost on New Year's Day returning from Newfoundland, and eight more had died at the end of January on Quoddy Head. Fishermen remarked that the pressures of fishing were fiercer than they had ever been. More vessels seemed to be chasing fewer fish; methods and gear had to be adapted constantly to compensate for this depletion; and the rise of the fresh fisheries meant that every skipper had constantly to balance the need to augment his haul against the rate of spoilage in his hold. The fishing schooner itself was now built for speed, with a wide, shallow hull, sharp lines, and a lofty rig to rush the catch to market, though vessels built for speed necessarily sacrificed safety. That a cycle of fisheries was now pursued the year round—even in the dead of winter on one of the most dangerous grounds in the northwest Atlantic—only underlined the growing competitiveness within the industry and the rising personal risk that fishermen confronted.

By February, however, the weather had turned mild on Georges, and by mid-month

almost a hundred vessels rode at their anchors about a half-mile apart from one another across the bank. From dawn until sundown, a thousand Gloucester fishermen stood to the rail—eight or ten to a vessel—throwing out and hauling in their lines in a wearisome struggle to fill their holds quickly and be home again. The Georges Bank cod fishery was quite traditional in its method. The schooners carried no dories and set no trawl lines, nor were any nets or seines employed. The basic technique of fishing from the rail with baited hooks, cleaning the catch on deck and packing it in salt below decks in the evening, and then ferrying it home every few weeks to be cured and dried on shore, had been practiced by New England fishermen for nearly two hundred years. The only thing really new about this fishery was the extraordinary risk with which it was attended. Indeed, fishermen were about as likely to survive three months on Georges during the 1860s as slaves had been to negotiate the Middle Passage alive at the beginning of the century.

At sundown on 23 February, just as the men were stowing away their gear, a mass of clouds rolled over the horizon and the sky suddenly darkened. As Georges Bank was plunged in inky blackness, the wind veered to the northeast, and it began to snow. Skippers checked their cables

and ordered the men to pay out as much as possible, knowing the key to surviving a gale on Georges was to hold one's mooring and avoid collision with other vessels in the closely packed fleet. Hatchets were placed forward near the windlass so the cables could be cut in an instant should a drifting vessel loom out of the darkness to windward. By midnight all the schooners in the fleet were pitching wildly in the sea and straining on their anchors, while their cordage shrieked in the wind. Every hour or two, a cable would part, consigning a vessel and its crew to the mercies of the storm. A fishermen recalled one such craft that he spotted in the first light of morning:

> The drifting vessel was coming directly for us; a moment more and the signal to cut must be given!

With the swiftness of a gull she passed by, so near that I could have leaped aboard, just clearing us. . .The hopeless terror-stricken faces of the crew we saw but a moment, as they went on to certain death. We watched the doomed craft as she sped on her course. She struck one of the fleet a short distance astern, and we saw the waters close over both vessels, almost instantly, and as we gazed, they both disappeared.

The storm continued all day, and by sundown on the twenty-fourth, fifteen schooners had disappeared. What exactly happened to them was a matter of some speculation. Some were known to be the victims of collision; others may have been knocked down by monster waves; still others were believed by fishermen to have drifted into shallow

In this painting, Fitz Hugh Lane depicted the conditions faced by Gloucester fishermen in the shoal waters of Georges Bank. With reefed mainsail set to keep their schooner's bow to the wind, fishermen use handlines to haul up codfish. At right a similar fishing schooner passes under reefed sails, negotiating the chop in the face of an ominous sky and rising seas. (Courtesy Cape Ann Historical Association, Gloucester, Massachusetts)

water and foundered there. But most of this was guesswork, for when vessels were lost on Georges in the winter there were seldom any survivors, and none of the 120 men who crewed those fifteen vessels lived to tell their tale.

Most of the fleet did manage to weather the storm somehow. Every vessel dragged some, and all of them yawed about in the terrible rollers that broke over the shoals of Georges Bank. On the night of the twenty-fourth, however, the winds moderated, and as the following morning was tolerable fishing weather the men got out their lines and returned to the business at hand. Most put in a week or more of fishing to complete their "trip" before turning their nose homeward and heading back to Cape Ann.

Although the Gale of 1862 was the single most deadly storm ever to strike the New England fishery, it was not the only one, and, indeed, the appalling mortality of the winter fishery was known to all. Trying to understand why men would agree to work under these conditions is a historical puzzle, but one that we can at least begin to answer because the crew lists of the schooners lost on Georges Bank that terrible winter day have survived. Combining them with other records, it is possible to reconstruct the social composition of a fishing fleet that in spite of the risks involved never failed for want of willing recruits.

As recently as the 1840s, the different fisheries that worked out of Gloucester still managed to crew most of their vessels with local men. Mainly they were Babsons, Parsons, Robinsons, Lufkins, Pools, and the like—descendants of those families who had constructed the town's fishery early in the eighteenth century. During the 1850s,

however, the social composition of the Gloucester fishing community began to shift noticeably, and nowhere was this more obvious than in the Georges fleet. Even by the most generous of estimates, fewer than one-quarter of those who drowned in the Gale of 1862 were native-born Gloucestermen; the rest were new arrivals from all around the North Atlantic rim.

The greatest number of these were Nova Scotians, Newfoundlanders, and "down-easters" from Maine. These regions had been connected to Massachusetts for a century or more, and just as young men from those parts were familiar with the sea-ports of New England, so Gloucester vessels were no strangers to the coastal villages these fishermen had left behind. The population of Maine and the provinces that would one day compose Atlantic Canada was growing rapidly in the middle decades of the nineteenth century, and the numbers of those competing for work meant that steady employment in any one trade was often hard to find. A judge in Nova Scotia who knew that the sons of his less prosperous neighbors had to follow a seasonal round of activities to get by termed them "all things by turns and nothing long." The circumstances of trying to earn a living in a world with long winters and marginally productive soil forced them into this dilemma, to which fishing out of Gloucester furnished an obvious solution.

This pattern was not confined

to the maritime Northeast. Indeed, virtually all those parts of Europe and North America that had not yet begun to industrialize were suffering in the middle of the nineteenth century, both from the growing pressure of population on the land and from the decline of rural manufacture. The poverty of rural Scandinavia, Ireland, the West of England, Southern Italy, and the Azores was approaching crisis proportions, and young people from all of these regions were beginning to contemplate temporary or even permanent emigration. Many of those familiar with fishing found their way to Gloucester; and the crew lists of the vessels that foundered on Georges in 1862 included young men from every one of these impoverished places.

In the days when Gloucester vessels were chiefly manned by native sons, the few who came to work in the local fishery had lived with local families, and to a large degree this tradition was still alive in the 1860s. Especially if fishermen came with their wives, they were likely to rent a couple of rooms in a local home or in a building that contained a small number of separate apartments. In 1860, Elijah Gardner from Nova Scotia lived with his sister Sarah (a seamstress), his wife Mary, and their two little girls in a rented house with another Nova Scotian family that had moved to Gloucester to follow the fishery. By this period, however, the number of immigrant fishermen had totally outstripped the town's supply of spare rooms, and to meet the demand for accommodation local developers threw up boardinghouses, and rented rooms for a few dollars a week to the fishermen ashore. Some of these were pleasant enough, while others were "dingy and tumbledown," but all of them were crowded with young men and inevitably rowdy. Frank Williams and his wife Mary had moved to Gloucester from the Azores during the 1850s, and by 1860 they were running a house that boarded thirteen countrymen–all in their twenties and early thirties and only one of them accompanied by a wife. Kennet Hanson from Sweden was another ex-fisherman who was now operating a boardinghouse where fellow Swedes could find familiar food and easy conversation. Not all such establishments were ethnically segregated in this manner, but as institutions where immigrants could find friendship, credit, and the personal connections that could ease their way into the local labor market, these boardinghouses served an important cultural function.

The Georges Bank fishery was the first in Gloucester to be dominated by outsiders. Those locally born men who still labored in the fisheries preferred easier voyages, especially mackereling in the summer, which was relatively pleasant work. Since a great many skippers were still Gloucester natives, and since they controlled the hiring process, it is no surprise that local men obtained the berths they preferred. The numerical importance of outsiders in the more dangerous Georges Bank fishery spoke to the difficulty those from outside the Yankee community encountered in breaking into the more attractive branches of the business. The winter fishery did provide them with a cash income every bit as lucrative as that of other fisheries, and cash itself was something that people who had grown up in village communities overseas had often not enjoyed. But the price that immigrant fishermen paid to obtain this income in terms of human suffering was disproportionately high.

The forces drawing fishermen to Gloucester persisted, however, and by the end of the century every one of Gloucester's different fisheries was manned predominantly by the foreign-born. Indeed, the town's waterfront had become an immigrant neighborhood. In 1850, only 27 percent of all those who lived in Gloucester and called themselves fishermen had been born outside of Massachusetts, and only 15 percent had been born outside the United States. By 1880–a mere thirty years later–72 percent of Gloucester fishermen had been born out-of-state, and a whole 63 percent were from abroad. And in 1910, by which time one would have expected the ranks of locally born fishermen to have been swelled by the sons of those immigrant fishermen who had survived their careers on Georges, 81 percent were now from outside Massachusetts, and 74 percent were foreign-born.

The Gale of 1862 affords a view of the social history of the American fisheries at a critical turning point. Until the middle of the nineteenth century, most commercial fishermen had been part of, or descended from, the First Great Migration–that wave of English colonists that settled this land during the seventeenth century. Since the middle of the nineteenth century, most American fishermen have been descended from the Second Great Migration–that which brought millions of Europeans and Asians to these shores in search of employment in an industrializing country. The Gale of 1862 struck Georges Bank and buried 120 unfortunate souls–chiefly newcomers–in the icy Atlantic just as the first crest of this second wave was breaking. Those arriving on this second wave, who survived that storm and dozens of others since, have constructed the American fishery of modern times.

Daniel Vickers

oysters into formerly productive waters, and even onto hard bottom that had never borne oysters before. And they discovered that they could lay down shells, called cultch, at spawning time to collect the set of juvenile oysters, then transplant them and grow them out for market. By the 1850s Connecticut was granting–later leasing–barren seabottom to individuals for oyster cultivation. This was the beginning of American aquaculture. The tremendously prolific oyster fishery on Chesapeake Bay received strong impetus when an oyster cannery was established at Baltimore in the 1850s.

Like oysters, lobsters remained of little consequence until they could be brought to market in bulk. Depleted early in southern New England and New York, they became a delicacy in urban centers even as they were subsistence food in Maine where they were so common. Connecticut mariners began to carry them to market live in wet-well vessels by the 1830s, about the time William Underwood's method of hermetically sealing food in jars and cans was applied to lobsters. Lobster canning proliferated throughout Maine in the 1840s, and the method was later applied to other seafood,

sands of fish at a time, and establishing factories to separate oil and flesh. Boiled, pressed, and dried, the flesh became "fish guano," a popular fertilizer. The menhaden oil boiled and pressed from the flesh was a significant component of paint, was used as a leather tanning oil, and was also used to adulterate whale oil. Similarly, other fish oils, such as cod liver oil for tanning, were important by-products of the fisheries throughout this period.

Continental Expansion and Steam on the Inland Waterways

By the later 1840s the United States had fully emerged, both economically and emotionally, from the long and severe depression following the Panic of 1837. In the full flood of national self-assertion, with spread-eagle confidence in its "manifest destiny," America proclaimed its capability to equal, if not to surpass, the wonders of the Old World. This was an era of youthful national vigor and boundless aspiration that promised endless possibilities and justified unlimited expansion–in particular, the seizure from Mexico of huge tracts of territory in the Southwest and along the West Coast, and an equally ambitious effort to combat British claims to the lands of the Pacific Northwest. Approaching mid-century, Americans proclaimed the virtues and special mission of the United States and its people in this era of such impressive national growth.

including oysters, clams, herring, and salmon.

And not least of importance was the use of fish for more humble purposes; until the 1830s, and especially before the critically important use of ice as a preservative, Maine lobsters commonly joined menhaden as a primary source of fertilizer. All along the East Coast, vast schools of oily, bony menhaden moved inshore in spring and summer, where they could be netted and plowed into the soil. In the 1830s a distinct menhaden fishery developed in southern New England, introducing purse seines to capture tens of thou-

The rapid development of the steamboat on the western rivers soon supplanted the flatboats and keelboats that had carried the bulk of downstream commerce in the first decades of settlement along the rivers. Yet the free spirit of the boatmen remained a feature of river life captured by George Caleb Bingham in his 1857 painting, "The Jolly Flatboatmen in Port." Note that while these boatmen dance–as children gather bits of spilled cargo and shippers check the tally–steamboats along the waterfront signal the end of the flatboatmen's way of life. (Courtesy The Saint Louis Art Museum. Purchase.)

The later 1840s witnessed technological achievement along with territorial expansion and economic development. Of critical importance to American maritime enterprise was the rapidly growing use of steam propulsion on both inland waterways and the high seas. Steam also played a major role in naval operations during the War with Mexico. Several decades of experience with steamboats on bays, lakes, and rivers now led to both an increase in American commerce and trade and a change in its methods of operation. Ready access to fuel and the ability to use fresh water in steam boilers contributed to the quick development of inland steamboats. In contrast, the saltwater oceans of the world posed serious problems for seagoing steam machinery, so that only in a more restricted manner and in a later period would oceangoing steamships begin to make their impact on commerce and transportation.

The continental expansion of the United States was, to a great degree, made possible by the great rivers and their tributaries. While some rivers were navigable and used by sailing craft, the shallow water, changing channels and currents, seasonal fluctuation in depth, and submerged hazards made river transport difficult. The great distances to be traveled on western rivers made the slow and difficult transport downstream by barge a trial for shippers and riverboatmen alike, and the keelboats and flatboats that floated down the Ohio to join the Mississippi and journey on to the port of New Orleans made a trip involving weeks. The possibilities of tremendous improvement appeared with the early development of the steam engine and its use on rivers. Robert Fulton's 1807 Hudson River venture demonstrated the possibility of new steamboat enterprises on other rivers. In 1811, the Fulton-Livingston enterprise sent the *New Orleans*, a 371-ton steamboat built in Pittsburgh, down the Ohio and Mississippi to New Orleans. However, this steamer remained in operation on the lower Mississippi and did not travel far upriver. In 1815 the steamboat *Enterprise* demonstrated the possibility of long upriver voyages by traveling from Monongahela, Pennsylvania, above Pittsburgh, down the Ohio and Mississippi to New Orleans and then returning. Two years later, seventeen steamboats were in operation on western rivers, with the number quickly rising to sixty-nine by 1820. The new technology reduced downstream freight rates by more than 60 per-cent and dropped upstream rates by 95 percent between 1815 and 1860.

After a steamboat reached St. Louis, Missouri, in 1817, the upper Mississippi, above the confluence of the Ohio, was opened to steamboat navigation. Above St. Louis, the first steamboats ventured up the Missouri River in 1819; one of them, the survey boat *Engineer*, was fitted with a large serpent head at the bow to frighten the Plains Indians through whose territory it passed. Regular service soon flourished on the Mississippi between St. Louis and New Orleans as well as between New Orleans and Louisville, Kentucky, at the falls of the Ohio River. A large fleet of steamboats also connected St. Louis with the important lead mines around Galena, Illinois, and Dubuque, Iowa. The Arkansas River was opened to navigation to Little Rock in 1822. Service on the Missouri developed more slowly, but with the growth of westward migration, steamboats delivered essential supplies at the trailheads and far into the west. By 1859, steamboats carried goods and passengers as far as Ft. Benton, Montana, 3,000 miles above St. Louis.

By the 1820s, more and more steamboats plied the waters of the western rivers, as well as the eastern rivers, bays, and sheltered coastal waters. In the East, steam machinery design reflected some attention to safety and fuel economy, while also taking into account the special problems encountered by coastwise vessels steaming on the open sea. Accordingly, the low-pressure reciprocating marine steam engine, operating at only a few pounds per square inch above atmospheric pressure, became the standard for driving large, relatively slow-turning side wheels.

Within twenty years of Fulton's introduction of steamboat service, the standard form of eastern steamboats had been established. Typically powered by a vertical single-cylinder engine that drove the side wheels by means of a "walking beam" mounted above the superstructure, the boats had very long, narrow, shallow hulls. Side extensions to the hull, called guards, protected the side wheels from damage and also provided additional deck space and a location for the steam boilers. Passenger accommodations were located in the superstructure of at least two decks, topped by a pilothouse. To equalize the great stresses on these long wooden hulls, steamboat builders took

Speeding down Long Island Sound, the steamer Connecticut *demonstrates the characteristics of coastal sidewheel steamboats in the northeast. The relatively narrow hull has lateral extensions, called guards, that enclose the sidewheels. The steam boilers on the guards feed steam to the single vertical engine cylinder. The vertical piston stroke is transmitted to the crank that turns the side wheels by means of the walking beam just forward of the stacks. Hog frame trusses and a set of vertical spars and tensioning cables equalize the stresses on the hull. The two decks provide staterooms and elegant dining facilities for several hundred passengers. Launched at New York in 1848, the 302-foot steamboat* Connecticut *ran on a number of busy Long Island Sound routes: New York to Hartford, New York to Norwich, and New York to Stonington. After government service during the Civil War, the* Connecticut *ran on the Hudson River, finishing her forty years of service as a Hudson River towboat. Painting by Jurgen F. Huge, 1848. (M.S.M. 38.246)*

lessons from bridge engineers and added a "hog frame" truss above the superstructure to stiffen the vessel. These coastal steamboats averaged nine years of service despite their stresses and the hazards of fire, collision, boiler explosion, and other perils of coastal and river navigation. The variety of hazards was suggested when the Long Island Sound steamer *Chancellor Livingston* sank the *Washington* in a collision in May 1831, with the loss of three people; when the boilers of the Sound steamer *New England* exploded in 1833, with the loss of fifteen passengers; and when the Sound steamer *Lexington*'s cargo of cotton caught fire in January 1840, and nearly one hundred people perished as the vessel sank.

In the West, however, engine design was radically different. On the shallow and protected, if treacherous, western rivers the steamboat machinery was designed to meet demands for low cost, light weight, great power, and ease of repair. Thus western steamboats used engines of high-pressure design that, by 1840, operated at steam pressures to 100 pounds per square inch. The long distances that many steamers traveled on the western rivers involved many hazards, such as the seasonal fluctuations of the shallower river beds, narrow and shifting channels, and sudden obstructions such as floating

trees and logs. To contend successfully with such problems, whether expected or not, western riverboatmen, such as the young Mark Twain, relied on engines that gave their boat greater maneuverability due to the combination of lightness and speed. Just as East Coast steam vessels early on had developed their long, narrow form and employed side-wheel propulsion, the western river steamboats took the form developed by Henry Shreve: a shallow and relatively wide hull with high superstructure and towering stacks. Power came from horizontal steam engines driving either side wheels or a wide stern wheel. The wheelhouse on top of the superstructure gave the pilot a high vantage point to judge river conditions. Movable gangways suspended at the bow allowed these boats to stop at undeveloped landings and wood-supply points anywhere along the riverbanks.

The high steam pressures came at a stiff price, and not just in dollars. Western steamboats compiled a disastrous safety record, especially in comparison with the eastern steamers. Between 1825 and 1850, 1,400 people were killed on western rivers as a result of steamboat explosions, which accounted for two-thirds of all casualties on western steamers. Passengers, however, were willing to face the hazards of such steamer

The 138-foot steamboat Tecumseh, *built at Cincinnati in 1826, represents the transition from eastern-style steamer to the characteristic western riverboat design that took place from the 1820s to the 1840s. Although the* Tecumseh *still has a relatively deep hull with bowsprit and figurehead like a contemporary eastern boat, her superstructure and layout represent the western prototype introduced by Henry Shreve a few years before. The steam boilers and their tall stacks, as well as a large supply of cordwood, are forward. The vessel has a main deck with cabins aft of the side wheels, and the so-called boiler deck with cabins and dining saloon above that. The high pilothouse stands on the hurricane deck, providing clear visibility. The prominent jackstaff on the bowsprit and flagstaff at the stern help the pilot take bearings while navigating the rivers. The* Tecumseh *is best known for making a then-record eight-day trip over the 1,350 miles from New Orleans to Louisville, at a time when a keelboat would require a hundred days to make the trip. Later steamboats would cut the* Tecumseh's *time in half, but even in the 1820s it was clear that steam was revolutionizing commerce on the western rivers. Photograph of a watercolor, taken by Carpenter ca. 1890. (Negative C4, © Mystic Seaport Museum, Inc., Rosenfeld Collection)*

travel because of the speedy transport offered. Not surprisingly, the operational life of western steamboats was considerably less than for eastern ones–two years in comparison with nine–and remarkably shorter than the twenty-year life of a sailing packet or the sixty-year operational life of a whaler.

The amount of investment required to build and operate a river steamer was relatively moderate, but the risks and the potential profit to investors and owners had to be weighed carefully. Virtually all investment in steamers was private. The large and relatively fast eastern steamboats could cost over $100,000, but the medium-tonnage steamboats of the western rivers could be built for as little as $20,000. Eastern steamers and those of the Great Lakes tended over time to be owned by corporations that ran their lines with many vessels on regular schedules. The different

conditions and circumstances in the West resulted in steamship ownership by one person or a small association of part-owners financed by local capital being more common. Individual steamboats operated as separate business ventures. To form a line of packets with regular schedules, the single owners of western steamboats tended to form a flexible agreement for operating their separate vessels as part of the line but only on an annual or seasonal basis.

Public funds were the primary source for deepening rivers, removing obstructions, and maintaining slack-water navigation. Aside from its significant court decisions, the federal government played a minor role at this point, especially in financing such projects. Funds came primarily from the states, as they either undertook the work directly or contracted with private companies to carry it out. States heavily invested their own funds in these private companies, as well as chartering them

Working Life on the Western Rivers Steamboats

The Pilot

Having assumed the pen name Mark Twain (two fathoms, or twelve feet to the steamboat leadsman and pilot), Samuel Clemens described in fictional form his training as a Mississippi River pilot. Although theoretically subordinate to the vessel's captain, the pilots had ultimate control of the vessel's navigation, steering according to their mental map of the river, their judgment of the local conditions signaled by the banks and shoals, and the depth soundings called out by the leadsmen. In *Life on the Mississippi*, Twain described how a pilot might approach a difficult stretch of river such as Plum Point, 100 miles below Cairo, Illinois:

"It was in the night, there, and I ran it the way one of the boys on the *Diana* told me; started out about fifty yards above the wood-pile on the false point, and held on the cabin under Plum Point till I raised the reef– quarter less twain [a quarter fathom less than two fathoms, or ten and a half feet]–then straightened up for the middle bar till I got well abreast the old one-limbed cotton-wood in the bend, then got my stern on the cotton-wood, and head on the low place above the point, and came through a-

booming–nine and a half."

"Pretty square crossing, an't it?"

"Yes, but the upper bar's working down fast."

Another pilot spoke up and said:

"I had better water than that, and ran it lower down; started out from false point–mark twain–raised the second reef abreast the big snag in the bend, and had a quarter less twain."

Twain's pilot told him:

"My boy, you've got to know the shape of the river perfectly. It is all there is left to steer by on a very dark night. Everything else is blotted out and gone. But mind you, it hasn't the same shape in the night that it has in the daytime."

"How on earth am I ever going to learn it, then?"

"How do you follow a hall at home in the dark? Because you know the shape of it. You can't see it."

"Do you mean to say that I've got to know all the million trifling variations of shape in the banks of this interminable river as well as I know the shape of the front hall at home?"

"On my honor, you've got to know them better than any man ever did know the shape of the halls in his own house. . . ."

"You see, this has got to be learned; there isn't any get-ting around it. . . . you only learn the shape of the river; and you learn it with such absolute certainty that you can always steer by the shape that's in your head, and never mind the one that's before your eyes."

Now it was an ancient river custom for two pilots to chat a bit when the watch changed. While the reliev-ing pilot put on his gloves and lit his cigar, his partner, the retiring pilot, would say something like this:

"I judge the upper bar is making down a little at Hale's Point; had quarter twain [two and a quarter fathoms, or thirteen and a half feet] with the lower lead and mark twain with the other."

"Yes, I thought it was mak-ing down a little, last trip. Meet any boats?"

"Met one abreast the head of 21, but she was away over hugging the bar, and I couldn't make her out entirely. I took her for the Sunny South– hadn't any skylights forward of the chimneys."

Mark Twain, *Life on the Mississippi* (1874)

The Fireman

The work of a fireman is as hard as any in the world; though he has only four hours in the day and four in the night to keep up the fires, yet the heat of the boilers, the exposure to the cutting cold night air when in deep perspiration, the quantity of brandy he drinks to prevent falling sick, the icy cold water poured into the burning throat, must, sooner or later, destroy the soundest and strongest constitution. How I, unaccustomed to such work, managed to stand it, has often surprised me.

In addition, there was the dangerous work of carrying wood, particularly in dark and wet nights. One has to carry logs four or five feet in length, six or seven at a time, down a steep, slippery bank, sometimes fifteen or twenty feet in height when the water is low, and then to cross a narrow, tottering plank frequently covered with ice, when a single false step would precipitate the unfortunate fireman into the deep stream, an accident which indeed happened to me another time on the Mississippi. It is altogether a miserable life, offering moreover a prospect of being blown up, no uncommon misfor-

tune, thanks to the rashness of American engineers.

Friedrich Gerstäcker, *Wild Sports in the Far West* (New York, 1854)

The Deck Hand

Dirtier and more toilsome work than this landing of the freight I have seldom seen. Heavy boxes, barrels of flour and whiskey had to be lifted and rolled up steep paths in soft sand to the summit of the bank. Often the paths were so narrow that but one man could get hold of the end of a barrel and lift it, while another hauled it from above, their feet sinking deep at every step. Imagine a gang of forty or fifty men engaged in landing boxes, casks, sacks of corn and salt, wagons, livestock, ploughs; hurrying, crowding, working in each other's way, sometimes slipping and falling, the lost barrel tumbling down upon those below; and the mate driving them with shouts and curses and kicks as if they were so many brutes.

John T. Trowbridge, *The Desolate South, 1865-1866* (New York, 1866)

Each steamer carried forty or more hands and "rousters." For them, the broken meat was piled into pans, all sorts in each pan, the broken bread and cake into other pans, and jellies and custards into still others—just three assortments, and this, with plenty of

boiled potatoes, constitutes the fare of the crew below decks. One minute after the cry of "Grub-pile!" one might witness the spectacle of forty men sitting on the bare deck, clawing into the various pans to get hold of the fragments of meat or cake which each man's taste particularly fancied.

George B. Merrick, *Old Times on the Upper Mississippi: The Recollections of a Steamboat Pilot from 1854 to 1863* (Cleveland, 1909)

This boat-life was harder than sea-faring, but the pay was better and the trips were short. The regular thing was to make two trips, and then lay up for a spree. It would be too hard upon a man, [a British sailor] thought, to pursue it regularly; two trips "on end" was as much as a man could stand. He must then take a "refreshment." Working this way for three weeks, and then refreshing about one, he did not think it was unhealthy, nor more so than ordinary seafaring.

Frederick Law Olmsted, *The Cotton Kingdom: A Traveller's Observations on Cotton and Slavery in the American Slave States* (New York, 1861)

for specific projects. The federal government, in contrast, made only a series of small grants for river improvements, totaling barely $6 million.

Federal government involvement, however, did accelerate sharply in 1838, with the attempt to regulate steam vessels carrying passengers, in response to concerns over the high accident rate of steamboats. As such explosions and other accidents persisted, Congress amended the 1838 legislation in 1852. The 1852 Act continued the inspection of steam-powered vessels and established standards for steam-engine construction. Perhaps most importantly, this act provided for the examination and licensing of the engineers who operated marine steam engines and of the pilots who navigated steam vessels, both at sea and on the rivers and lakes.

The Centrality of America's Inland Seas

The term "Great Lakes" hardly does justice to the more than 95,000 square miles that comprise those immense bodies of water located along the northern border of the United States. With their more than 8,100 miles of coastline shared by the United States and Canada, these five major areas of fresh water more properly should be considered as inland seas. Varying widely in area, depth, configuration, and elevation, the "Great Lakes" have been a significant part of American maritime enterprise for centuries, but during the nineteenth and twentieth centuries commerce and trade on the Lakes became vital to the economy of the United States.

Steam appeared on the Lakes shortly after the end of the War of 1812; the Canadians had a steamer on Lake Ontario in 1816, and the United States soon followed. Noteworthy among American steamers was the *Walk-in-the-Water*, built and launched on the Niagara River in 1818. To get the small steamer onto Lake Erie posed a problem; the river currents were too strong for the underpowered steam engine. But American ingenuity prevailed, the necessary auxiliary power supplied by twenty yoke of oxen—a "horned breeze," as one contemporary observed. The steamer thereafter operated successfully, carrying passengers and cargo on a nine-to ten-day round trip voyage

from Buffalo to Detroit, with stops along the way at Cleveland and Sandusky.

Essential to the growth of Great Lakes commerce and navigation was the executive agreement between Great Britain and the United States to demilitarize the Lakes. The Rush-Bagot Agreement, resulting from a formal exchange of notes during 1817, specified that neither country would keep any naval force in being on the Lakes, other than armed revenue cutters. This agreement, which has essentially remained in force to the present day, led the way to a more general policy of disarmament that eventually would result in an open frontier between Canada and the United States.

By the 1850s the Lakes enjoyed a boom in passenger transportation by steamer. Most passenger traffic moved between Buffalo and Detroit, through Lake Erie with its major port at Cleveland; although by the 1850s large and increasingly luxurious steamers, such as the 2,000-ton *Western World* (1854) with its 300 well-appointed staterooms, were traveling beyond Detroit to Lake Michigan and its major port of Chicago, by way of Lake Huron and the Straits of Mackinac. However, steam was still so expensive and inefficient that it was largely confined to the same kinds of passengers and small-bulk, high-paying cargoes that were characteristic of steam on the oceans. For bulk cargoes as well as packaged cargoes on the Great Lakes, this remained an era of sail well past mid-century. The largest number of sailing vessels was achieved during the late 1860s and early 1870s, with 1,855 barks, brigs, schooners, and smaller sailers aggregating 294,000 gross tons recorded for the year 1868; for the same year there were 634 steamers totaling 144,000 tons. Yet for the Great Lakes a new age was looming; beginning in the 1840s, the discovery and opening up of the great iron ranges in Minnesota and northern Wisconsin—above all, the fabled Mesabi range in 1875—heralded a basic transformation in both typical cargoes and vessel types. The decades after 1865 would introduce the "modern" era of raw material bulk cargoes and the highly specialized iron steamers designed to carry them.

Access by water to the iron ranges depended on building a canal and lock system that would connect Lake Huron to Lake Superior by way of the St. Mary's River. Between 1853 and 1855, under the direction of Connecticut-born Charles T. Harvey, this major engineering challenge was met, so that by mid-1855 Lakes traffic was open by way of the Sault Ste. Marie lock system–called the "Soo"–which would later become one of the economically and militarily most vital canals in the world.

America's Maritime Boom Years

While national growth in general may have been retarded by the economic downturn of the late 1830s and early 1840s, much of American maritime enterprise was thriving. Starting around 1830, shipping and many other types of American maritime activity enjoyed a long period of extraordinary growth in volume of business, with increased revenues and profits. This maritime "boom" era extended well past mid-century and in many ways marked the zenith of American maritime fortunes. By the early 1830s a huge increase in the volume of shipping– inland, coastal, and international– brought men and money in ever greater numbers into America's maritime centers, primarily those of the Northeast.

By the later 1840s the upsurge of national economic activity produced a bonanza for shipping, shipbuilding, and other maritime enterprise. Increased prices for grain and corn encouraged

The 190-foot steamboat Michigan, *launched at Detroit in 1847, provided regular service on the 750-mile route between Buffalo, Detroit, and Green Bay, Wisconsin, for seventeen years. Bulk cargoes continued to travel under sail on the Great Lakes through the first half of the nineteenth century, but steamers like the* Michigan *quickly came to dominate the passenger and high-value package trades. A side-wheel steamer with arched "hog frame" to equalize the stresses on the hull, and a walking beam atop the superstructure to transmit the vertical action of the engine piston to the crank driving the side wheels, the* Michigan *has much in common with East Coast steamboats. However, her octagonal pilothouse and the mast on which steadying sails could be set for open lake passages are characteristic of Great Lakes steamboats. Ambrotype, ca. 1855. (M.S.M. 95.115)*

In 1847 San Francisco was a village on a large bay occasionally visited by American whaleships. Two years later, more than 800 ships arrived in the first wave of gold-rush fortune hunters, clogging the waterfront with abandoned vessels. Within another few years it had evolved from a landing place to an active port and the principal West Coast entrepôt. This portion of a photographic panorama depicts the waterfront in 1853. The great crowd of ships at left obscures the growing waterfront development along Market Street. Since the great fire of May 1851, a substantial city constructed of brick has begun to take shape. Above it stands Telegraph Hill, with a semaphore station to signal the arrival of ships at the Golden Gate (beyond the hills). The ranks of anchored vessels include both abandoned gold-rush vessels and active merchant ships that carry on San Francisco's expanding trade with the East Coast, Europe, South America, and Asia. Daguerreotype by William Shew. (Courtesy Smithsonian Institution, NMAH/Transportation)

an extension of western farming. Much of the land available in Ohio, Indiana, and Illinois was naturally swampland and therefore had not been farmed. However, 1840 saw the introduction of pipe tiles imported from Scotland for drainage purposes, vastly increasing the available farmland. Fertilizer–initially the guano shipped from Peru and Chile–was now generally applied to increase the productivity of the soil. Opening the Kansas and Nebraska territories in 1854 further increased the farm acreage of the Midwest. New applications of technology, such as the McCormick reaper that was manufactured in Chicago from 1847 on, dramatically increased the production of wheat in the 1850s, just in time to sustain the export economy of the North during the war-disrupted era of the early 1860s.

Although railroad mileage was increasing rapidly through the late 1840s and into the 1850s, with a consequent surge of traffic towards the railroad system linking the eastern seaboard with the interior, the great preponderance of goods shipped within the United States still was carried by water.

The acquisition of the Oregon territory in 1846, and the end of the Mexican War in 1848, created an America of vast and largely unexploited lands that lured emigrants ever westward; but above all it was the discovery of gold in California that produced a sudden and overwhelming demand for ship passage from the eastern seaboard to the Pacific coast. This was especially dramatic in the case of San Francisco, a small coastal town that

With 80,000 "forty-niners" headed for California in 1849 alone—25,000 of them by sea—East Coast residents set aside routine and clamored for news of local adventurers in the goldfields. The quickest dispatch for news was by steamship mail, with letters and western newspapers abstracted in New York newspapers for distribution. In William Sidney Mount's 1850 painting, California News, a Long Island post office has become both the focal point for those seeking news and an information center for those wishing to depart for California themselves. (Courtesy The Museums at Stony Brook; Gift of Mr. and Mrs. Ward Melville, 1955)

suddenly was transformed into America's maritime center on the Pacific. Nearly forty thousand persons arrived in San Francisco aboard 805 ships during just nine months in 1849-50. Most were headed for the mountain goldfields, but enough settled in the port to make it the fourteenth largest American city by 1860. And while the first few years saw such a rush of passengers and goods to California that hundreds of ships were laid up in San Francisco Bay, the developing commerce of the port supported an increasing return trade with the East Coast by the mid-1850s.

Considering its remote location, 13,000 miles from New York by way of Cape Horn, San Francisco had regular steamship ties with the East Coast at a surprisingly early date. Soon after signing the peace treaty with Mexico, the United States government awarded steamship-line contracts to carry mail from the East Coast to California and Oregon. The contract to carry the mail from New York to Colon in Panama went to a New York City merchant, George Law; contracts to carry the mail from Panama to California and Oregon were awarded to another New York merchant, William Henry Aspinwall, whose business firm, Howland & Aspinwall, had extensive trading ties to China and on the west coast of South America. Because these routes from the East Coast to California originated and ended at American ports, the federal government, under the 1817 Navigation Act provisions, considered them part of the coastal trade and thus open only to American shippers, with the stipulation that steamships must be used for the mail carriage. The steamer California, the first of Howland & Aspinwall's Pacific Mail Line vessels, reached the West Coast just as the gold rush began. With this fortuitous timing, a regular and highly lucrative steam transportation system served San Francisco by way of the Isthmus of Panama, rapidly integrating the West Coast into the nation.

Despite economic uncertainty and the threat of disunion, the United States in 1860 reflected the vibrancy of its internal maritime commerce. Of the nation's fifteen largest cities, only two were not ports. New York, Philadelphia, Baltimore, and Boston remained the leading cities, but the river ports of New Orleans, Cincinnati, and St. Louis followed in succession, with the Great Lakes ports of Chicago and Buffalo close behind. Louisville on the Ohio River; Albany, where the Erie Canal met the Hudson River; San Francisco, which had grown from Mexican village to American seaport city in only a decade; and the old New England port of Providence maintained the primacy of waterborne connections in a list where only Newark, New Jersey, and Washington, D.C., did not rate as ports.

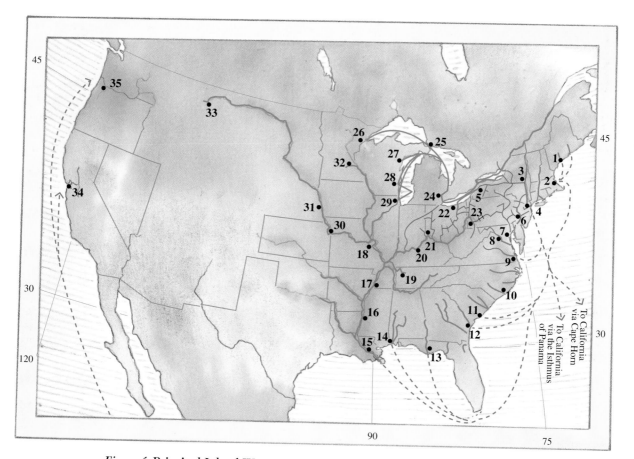

Figure 4 Principal Inland Waterways and Coastal Shipping Routes, 1825-1860

〜〜〜 Navigable Rivers, Lakes

〜〜 Canals

‒ ‒ ‒ Coastal and Ocean Routes

⚓ Railroad Connecting
Two Canals

1. Portland, ME
2. Boston
3. Albany
4. New York City
5. Buffalo
6. Philadelphia
7. Baltimore
8. Washington, DC
9. Norfolk
10. Wilmington, NC
11. Charleston
12. Savannah
13. Apalachicola
14. Mobile
15. New Orleans
16. Vicksburg
17. Memphis
18. St. Louis
19. Nashville
20. Louisville
21. Cincinnati
22. Cleveland
23. Pittsburgh
24. Detroit
25. Sault Ste. Marie
26. Duluth
27. Green Bay
28. Milwaukee
29. Chicago
30. Kansas City
31. Omaha
32. Minneapolis/St. Paul
33. Ft. Benton
34. San Francisco
35. Portland, OR

(Dennis O'Brien map)

CHAPTER 8

Maritime America In a Wider World

NEW YORK CITY'S
emergence as the undisputed leader of American
maritime activity became clear during the several
decades after 1815. Endowed with a location and
topography that, on balance, surpassed any of its
adjacent rivals (notably Boston, Philadelphia, and
Baltimore), New York also benefited from a group
of aggressive New England maritime entrepreneurs,
mainly from Massachusetts, Rhode Island, and
Connecticut, who came to New York in the postwar
years to find opportunities greater than their smaller
home ports could offer.

Notable among these New Englanders were such
Connecticut men as George Griswold and his brother, Nathaniel, from Old Lyme, who started as shipping brokers and flour exporters in Connecticut. By
1796 they had relocated to New York City, where
they shipped flour to the Caribbean islands in
exchange for sugar and rum. Soon, with their growing fleet of sailing vessels, they expanded into the
China trade, while also branching out into New
York City banking and real estate.

Other prominent New York-based New Englanders
were the Lows from Salem, Massachusetts (China
trade); the Howlands from Norwich, Connecticut
(Latin American trade); the Grinnells from New
Bedford, Massachusetts (shipowners); and three
Morgans from Connecticut; Junius (the father of
J.P. Morgan), a Hartford banker who expanded his
financial enterprises in New York; Edwin, a wholesale merchant and importer born in Massachusetts,
who came to New York via Hartford; and Charles,
from Killingworth, who became a New York ship
chandler, fruit importer, shipowner, and early steamship operator in the Gulf region. While still a youth,
Edward K. Collins journeyed from the small town
of Truro, far down on Cape Cod, Massachusetts, to
New York to start as a clerk in a mercantile house;
at the apex of his career in the 1850s he had become
both a leading merchant and the most celebrated
individual shipowner and operator in America.

Detail of the clipper ship David Crockett.
(M.S.M. 92.21.10; Mary Anne Stets photo)

Preserved Fish (1766-1846), the son of a blacksmith in Portsmouth, Rhode Island, rose to command of a whaleship before settling ashore as a whale oil merchant in New Bedford, Massachusetts. Like many ambitious southern New England merchants in the first decades of the nineteenth century, Fish moved to New York, entering a partnership with his cousin Joseph Grinnell of New Bedford in 1815. Their business expanded from commission sales of whale oil to encompass a wide variety of ocean trade. In 1822 Fish & Grinnell established the Swallowtail Line of Liverpool and London packets. Fish retired in 1829 and thereafter served as president of a New York bank. His firm, which became Grinnell, Minturn & Company, remained among the most prestigious operators of packets and clipper ships through the middle of the nineteenth century. When his portrait was painted, ca. 1830, Preserved Fish commemorated his seagoing career, being depicted holding a spyglass, with a whaling scene through the window. (Collection of The New-York Historical Society)

With their ambition, energy, expertise, and tenacity, these transplanted New Englanders were vital to the rapid growth of New York City. New York Port swiftly became America's major center for shipping, finance, and com-

merce, and one of the nation's most important locations for shipbuilding. Moreover, New York soon emerged as one of the world's greatest seaport cities and the western terminus for a large share of all transatlantic navigation and commerce.

By 1860 the port of New York was handling two-thirds of the total value of American imports and more than a third of all exports by value. The New England states collectively might build, own, and operate far more vessels than New York, and supply twice as many mariners and four times as many masters of vessels, yet all the seaports of New England together only imported 11 percent and exported 5 percent of the nation's foreign commerce in 1860.

New York in the decade after 1815 achieved its stature in part because it benefited from the immediate postwar flood of British and continental European goods into an eager American market. Seizing upon this opportunity, New York merchants instituted an auction system that would greatly facilitate the marketing of such European imports, and this novel sales method encouraged an even greater flow of imports into New York.

By 1817 a group of Quaker merchants in New York City had put together a fleet of four fast-sailing cargo vessels in order to introduce a coordinated, year-round service between New York and the major British port of Liverpool. Beginning operation in early January, 1818, their "Black Ball Line" of sailing ships operated as common carriers on a fixed schedule, with the then-remarkable commitment that each vessel would sail, weather permitting, on its scheduled date of departure whether fully loaded or not. Such an enticing promise to potential shippers and passengers was risky for the shipping operators, but it paid off. The Black Ball Line quickly established itself as a profitable carrier of low-bulk, high-value cargoes (such as perishable items, mail, official dispatches, and bullion) where time was at a premium. This predictability of sailing was equally appealing to well-to-do travelers, businessmen, and government officials desiring a relatively quick, comfortable passage across the Atlantic Ocean–and willing to pay a premium fare for such convenience and predictability.

The booming trade between England and the United States during the next decades encouraged the organization of other American transatlantic sailing packet lines, from both New York and her rival American seaport cities. By the later 1830s five New York-based lines were sending passengers and cargo on a three-to-four-week voyage just to the port of Liverpool. While New York continued to dominate the major sea route to Liverpool, liner service from New York also ran to London and such Continental ports as Le Havre, Amsterdam, Antwerp, and Bremen. American merchant groups in Boston, Philadelphia, and Baltimore each generated their own liner service across the Atlantic, but they did not approach the frequency of New York packet sailings or the elegance and speed of that service.

Throughout the year a comparable number of sailing packets departed Liverpool and other European seaports for what almost always was a considerably longer return voyage, since west-ward-bound sailing ships had to contend with the adverse prevailing winds that normally aided the eastward-bound vessels. As a consequence, the voyage to North America might, with luck, last no more than a month. All too often it was extended several more weeks, so that travel to America by sail—even in a luxuriously appointed sailing packet with elegant service and lavish food and wine—was often a frustratingly long and dreary experience.

The transatlantic sailing-packet business was distinctly American. From the outset Americans clearly were in control, so that American-built, American-registered packet vessels dominated the premium transatlantic trade for several decades, even into the early years of steam propulsion. But while these celebrated sailing packets carried the cream of the transatlantic trade, by far the greatest number of American cargo vessels plying the oceans were smaller, slower, and decidedly less glamorous. There were the "regular traders," which held to

As the port for Great Britain's principal manufacturing district, and the leading embarkation point for emigrants, Liverpool maintained a large volume of packet and regular trade with U.S. ports. Here, the Baltimore packet Franconia *departs Liverpool for the North Atlantic run, likely laden with British manufactured goods, and perhaps emigrants. This painting is attributed to Samuel Walters. (M.S.M. 33.2; Claire White-Peterson photo)*

While the elegant packet ships that operated on schedule attracted the most public attention, the bulk of American trade was carried by regular traders, which sailed on relatively regular routes, and by tramps, which sailed on whatever routes offered attractive freight rates. The eighty-seven-foot New York snow American, *built at Middletown, Connecticut, in 1816, carried on this form of Atlantic trade through the 1820s. For example, in December 1819 the* American *entered New York with 10,000 hides from Montevideo, South America, then cleared for Marseilles, where Ange-Joseph-Antoine Roux painted this portrait. In June 1820 she returned to New York by way of Tarragona, Spain, with wine, brandy, olives, rope, paper, aniseed, and specie. Another South American voyage followed, from which she returned in January 1821 with 140 tons of dried beef. The* American's *designation as a snow indicates that she is a two-masted, square-rigged brig with a separate spar just aft of the mainmast to which the fore-and-aft spanker is affixed. As the volume of trade expanded and became dominated by a few large ports, small oceangoing square-riggers like the* American *would become increasingly obsolete, except for specialized uses such as the coffee and fruit trades. (M.S.M. 53.4558; Claire White-Peterson photo)*

a much less firm schedule and usually made just two transatlantic trips a year between an American port and a designated foreign port, so as to avoid the worst of the winter season. Even more numerous were the "transients," or tramp ships, which had no schedule or fixed route but sailed worldwide from port to port with whatever cargoes were available at good freight rates.

Typical of such transient activity was the trading pattern directed by the New-York based merchant and shipowner Captain Israel Collins (father of Edward K. Collins), as managing operator of the 216-ton, Maine-built ship *Farmer* between 1821 and 1823.

He sent cargoes in that vessel (frequently commanded by his nephew, John Collins) to trade, successively, at Cadiz, Spain; New Orleans; Cork, Ireland; St. Ubes, Portugal; Tenerife; Amsterdam; Göteborg, Sweden; and Cork, Dublin, and Belfast, Ireland, before returning to New York. The vessel's cargoes ranged from salt, lemons, and wine to bundles and bars of iron, plow molds, wool, and coal.

Also critical to the success of New York was its coastal navigation and trade. During the early decades of the nineteenth century the larger seaports along the Atlantic and Gulf Coasts were absorbing and centralizing the coastwise busi-

With its broad bay and convenient water connections to the developing portions of the United States, and its strong economic connections with European ports, New York led all American seaports in foreign trade. In this painting by Thomas Birch, ca. 1830, a large packet ship passes Castle Williams on Governors Island on her way to a berth at one of the East River piers in the background. Harbor traffic includes a coastal top-sail schooner heading up the harbor, an oceangoing brig lying at anchor, a steamboat and a Hudson River sloop headed down the bay, and, at center, a pettiauger with a party of men and women on board, perhaps seeking recreation in what was normally a harbor workboat. (M.S.M. 65.55; Mary Anne Stets photo)

ness, so that smaller ports that had enjoyed vigorous local activity in the eighteenth and early nineteenth century tended to fall into the orbit of major seaports. New York soon dominated regional trade up Long Island Sound and as far east as Cape Cod, at the southern extreme of Boston's economic sphere of influence. Similarly, New York-based vessels increasingly took over trade along the New Jersey coast down towards the Delaware River and Chesapeake Bay, where Philadelphia and Baltimore were major centers of shipping.

New York by the 1820s had extended its coastwise reach into the Caribbean and Gulf Coast areas, so that a small but regularly scheduled sailing packet service began operation between New York and Veracruz, Mexico, in 1827. Far more important were the several New York sailing packet lines to New Orleans and Mobile, because along with cabin passengers these liners carried a significant volume of cotton back up the coast for

transshipment abroad as well as for domestic consumption in the New England textile mills. From New York these big coastal packets brought both domestic and foreign manufactures to Southern markets.

The celebrated opening of the Erie Canal in 1825 was another signal of New York Port's domination. Now bulk goods from the Great Lakes region and beyond could be shipped by barge through the water-level route from the lake port of Buffalo, New York, across to Albany near the head of the Hudson River, and then down to the river's mouth at New York City. And the traffic flowed both ways, so that access to America's interior was greatly enhanced, with New York City serving as the primary point of origin as well as terminus for passengers and cargo on this major east-west route.

Clearly, the Erie Canal was vital to New York City's economic growth, but it did not initiate, let alone single-handedly produce, New York's dominance; in fact, by 1825 New York already had achieved commercial leadership over its East Coast rivals. However, the Erie Canal was immensely valuable in providing an alternative route for Midwestern farm products that previously tended to move down the Ohio and Missouri Rivers into the Mississippi and thence to New Orleans. For several decades after its opening, until the railroads took over most of the long-haul bulk traffic and passenger business on the east-west route, the Erie Canal significantly redirected the flow of goods from the American interior; if anything, it was more important to national economic development than to the rise of New York Port.

Americans in the Pacific Ocean

The period after 1815 witnessed a flourishing of American maritime activity throughout the vast reaches of the Pacific Ocean. American sailing vessels both traded and exploited the resources of an area ranging from Alaska to Celebes, from the west coast of South America to the Chinese mainland, from California to the Southeast Asian region of the Malay Archipelago, and beyond. American sailors—whether on whalers or merchantmen— came to know Hawaii, Java, Sumatra, Borneo, the Philippines, Samoa, Fiji, and a profusion of

other large and small islands scattered across this immense body of salt water. By the mid-1850s even Japan, however reluctantly, was ending its centuries of self-imposed economic and political isolation in the face of American diplomatic, military, and commercial pressures.

Americans were not alone in this penetration of new markets. At times, as in the case of trade with the Empire of China, American traders followed the lead and profited from the economic and diplomatic initiatives of Great Britain. This was especially the case in gaining greater access to the Hong merchants at the one officially authorized point of access on the Chinese mainland: Canton. Great Britain's

decision in 1834 to end the British East India Company's monopoly of trading rights was soon followed by the British victory in the first "Opium War." The result, following the formal agreements made by the 1842 Treaty of Nanking, was to provide more general access by both British and foreign traders to the Chinese market at Canton as well as to several other mainland Chinese ports. Entering quickly on the heels of this British effort, the American President, John Tyler, in 1843 sent a New England lawyer and politician, Caleb Cushing, to arrange for trading rights and privileges similar to those extracted by the British. The 1844 Treaty of Wanghia between China and the United States satisfied that objective, and American trade continued to grow, reaching its maximum value in the early and mid-1850s and

Until the Treaty of Nanking in 1842, all legal trade with China was carried out at Canton, about seventy miles up the Pearl River. China trade vessels first stopped downriver at the Portuguese colony of Macao to obtain permission to trade. Then they proceeded upstream to Whampoa anchorage, thirteen miles below Canton, to discharge their cargo and wait for a cargo of tea, silks, porcelain, and other Chinese products. Because the Chinese sought to insulate themselves from the "foreign devils" who came to trade, American and European merchants in Canton were confined to a small neighborhood of warehouses with living quarters called factories or hongs, seen here ca. 1850. Trade with the foreigners was carried out by especially designated Hong Merchants, the best known of whom was the highly respected Houqua, perhaps the wealthiest man in the world in the 1830s. In this view, a variety of Chinese ceremonial and commercial craft, plus an American or English pleasure sloop (left center), pass the American and European factories. The hong system survived from 1782 through the 1830s. However, official Chinese resistance to opium as a commodity of trade (which debilitated the population and was subject to smuggling and piracy), at a time when few other commodities had commercial value in China, led to confrontation and ultimately Chinese concessions following defeat in the First Opium War. Thereafter, a number of "treaty ports," including Shanghai and especially Hong Kong, began to supersede the role of Canton in American trade with China. (M.S.M. 54.590; Mary Anne Stets photo)

encouraging the United States to broaden its commercial contact with China through the provisions of another formal set of agreements, the 1858 Treaty of Tientsin.

Throughout this period there persisted the problem of a trade imbalance between the United States and China. Chinese silks, fine chinaware, specialty cotton goods, and–above all–tea, were of far greater value than the American cargoes of furs (especially seal and sea otter), sandalwood, and ginseng that largely satisfied the demands of the Chinese market. The British, especially after 1842, could easily produce a positive balance of trade with China by flooding the Chinese market with opium. However, few Americans entered the opium trade, lucrative though it was, so the source of payment for Chinese products had to be found elsewhere. This was achieved by sending to China large sums of specie, in the form of silver that during these decades was flowing into the United States, largely from American trade with Mexico.

For a number of merchants along the American East Coast–especially in Massachusetts, Rhode Island, Connecticut, New York, and Philadelphia–the China trade generated substantial fortunes, and the furnishings of many merchants' homes were distinguished by a sumptuous array of elegant chinoiserie. Even more modest Chinese products found their place in American homes, as indicated by an April 1844 request by a New York merchant, William H. Aspinwall, to his agent in China, Samuel Comstock: "Would you send me two small 'sallad' bowls to match the larger piece of China herewith and four oval dishes on stands–also of same pattern two sets of 'antique' and odd shapes and two pots something of the shape of flower pots, also on stands, for ice cream–also three small sets of teacups and saucers 'for little girls four or five years old'. Being playthings they need be only shiny, not expensive."

The China trade increasingly called for sailing vessels of extraordinary speed. By the 1840s and continuing well into the 1850s American designers and shipbuilders responded with ships that could beat the swiftest British vessels on the long haul from Canton with tea for the major English markets, where the first vessel to arrive commanded premium prices for its cargo. Many

of the earliest American "clippers" were ships that initially served in the China trade, and after 1849 many other clipper ships regularly shifted back and forth between the East Coast-to-California route and the transpacific run out to China, and from there to either American or European destinations.

American interests in the Pacific also brought increasing attention to two promising areas for American trade and, finally, American control: Alaska and Hawaii. While American fur trading on the Pacific Northwest Coast had severely declined by the later 1830s, at the same time there was growing interest in "saving the Oregon Territory" from British control. Russian willingness back in 1824 to relinquish its claims to North America south of the 54° 40' line of latitude encouraged an expansion of American whaling in these northern waters, to the point where, by the 1850s, Americans from both East and West Coast ports were vigorously pursuing commerce and trade with Alaska. The 1867 Alaska purchase and the annexation of this territory to the United States would come as a predictable consequence not just of American expansionism, but also of several decades during which American domination of this region became firmly established.

Hawaii–known to Americans for many years as the Sandwich Islands–had served both as an important source of sandalwood for the China market and, after 1819, as a major stopover point for American whaling vessels. A particularly convenient location for raw materials, for supplies, for trans-shipping goods, for signing on (or discharging) sailors, and for leisurely interruptions of whaling voyages, Hawaii held such attraction that American interests–commercial, diplomatic, expansionistic, and even missionary–brought Hawaii firmly into the American orbit by mid-century. Efforts to annex Hawaii to the United States in 1854 were not successful; but, short of such formal control, it was clear–and stated repeatedly by presidential administrations of the 1840s and 1850s–that the United States, beyond any other world power, had a special interest in Hawaii and considered the islands as firmly within America's sphere of influence.

The Latin American Maritime Connection

After 1815 Latin American trade remained vital to the United States economy and to its merchant marine. Central to British North American maritime activity in the Colonial period, Latin American markets were of even greater concern after the infant United States found itself no longer favored in British or European imperial markets. The world's leading neutral trader during the stormy 1793-1815 era, the United States now sought to expand its participation in world trade and to break down European mercantilist barriers, especially those that restricted American trade in Central and South American markets. Jay's Treaty of 1794 had failed to open the lucrative British West Indian region to American traders, so in the immediate postwar months the United States Government moved to promote American maritime enterprise by forging economic connections in the Caribbean and in other world markets.

Much of this seafaring enterprise was to continue in the pattern of eighteenth-century trade, so that well into the nineteenth century, for example, Connecticut mariners persisted in their distinctive trade to the West Indies. Connecticut sailing vessels–primarily sloops and brigs–hailed from large and small ports on Long Island Sound and the Connecticut River. Their specialized cargo, which was central to the strong economic link that persisted between New England and the Caribbean region, was large live animals: horses, mules, sheep, and cattle.

In 1815 Congress passed a Navigation Act to encourage a general opening up of trade relationships and an easing of trade barriers on the basis of reciprocity between the United States and other major world trading powers. In the same year America signed a reciprocity treaty, or "commercial convention," with Great Britain, with the intent of expanding markets and encouraging unrestricted access, along with fair and open competition between the two nations. This treaty would soon produce a major benefit to American shipping interests in the transatlantic trade.

Yet the British West Indies were a troubling exception. They remained closed to American vessels of any substantial size, so that Americans were at a competitive disadvantage with their British and Canadian rivals. American exports of farm products, lumber, and fish to the British West Indies, and the return cargoes of sugar and molasses, remained severely limited at a time when Great Britain held a decided advantage in the transoceanic routes of trade. Large British cargo vessels could sail from ports in the United Kingdom to America with heavy bulk goods and manufactures; then from the United States to the British West Indies with agricultural products, lumber, horses, cattle, and fish; and back to Britain with sugar and molasses. Alternatively, these British vessels could sail from the West Indies to American South Atlantic or Gulf ports, from which they carried baled cotton and tobacco back to Europe. In any case, the larger American vessels were shut out of the British West Indian portion of the trade, so that they were at a severe disadvantage on the transatlantic leg of their trading journey. With their advantage in the West Indian market, rival British vessels could drive down transatlantic freight rates even to the point of operating at a loss, if necessary, and pick up their profits on the other legs of the trade.

The American solution to this trading problem was to employ a carrot-and-stick strategy, encouraging reciprocity while forcing the hand of the British by shutting British West Indian products out of the American market. Thus, from 1820 until 1830 both the United States and Great Britain engaged in adversarial diplomatic maneuvering in pursuit of their mutually incompatible objectives in world trade: the Americans pushed for free trade, the British for traditional mercantilist restrictions. Following the British decision in 1826 to close all of their colonial ports in the Western Hemisphere to American vessels, the presidential administration of John Quincy Adams responded the following year by shutting all American ports to British vessels carrying British colonial goods from anywhere in the Western Hemisphere.

This Anglo-American diplomatic impasse over trade, now a major national political issue, was overcome after the election of Andrew Jackson, who had promised during his 1828 presidential campaign to resolve the West Indian trade prob-

For countless centuries, seabirds have fed off the anchovies that flourish in the cold Humboldt Current along the west coast of South America. Their feces, deposited on rocky islands, accumulated to great depth in the arid climate of the region, representing a rich, but smelly, source of the nitrogen and phosphorus essential for agricultural fertilizer. When the properties of this material, called guano, were recognized in the 1830s, an international rush to exploit similar deposits on arid islands around the world began. In 1856, the U.S. Congress passed the Guano Act to empower American citizens to claim uninhabited guano islands, and American whalemen laid claim to a number of such islands they encountered in the South Pacific. But Peru had the richest guano reserves. Beginning in 1840, Peruvian companies, and then the government itself, mined and sold the guano to European and American merchants. The Chinchas—three volcanic peaks fifteen miles off the coast of Peru—were the principal Peruvian source, with deposits one hundred feet deep. As depicted here, ca. 1860, a fleet of American and European sailing vessels was in perpetual attendance, waiting to come alongside chutes by which the guano was loaded into their holds, or to receive the boatloads brought off in rough weather. The stench endured by the ships' crews was nothing compared with the conditions faced by the miners and trimmers—largely Chinese coolies and Pacific islanders—who worked as virtual slaves amid the searing dust. From the 1840s through the 1870s, this noxious but essential trade employed both burdensome merchant vessels and occasional clipper ships in search of a return cargo after making the run from New York to San Francisco. The vessel third from right in this photograph appears to have clipper dimensions. (M.S.M. 94.107.1.17)

lem. Accordingly, in 1830 the United States and Great Britain signed a reciprocity treaty that finally opened up the West Indian trade, even to the extent that American vessels could now carry British West Indian products not just to the United States but to anywhere in the world.

This seagoing commercial interchange with Central and South America soon became the second most important element in American foreign trade, especially after the Latin American revolutions of the early 1820s and the emergence of the large and economically important independent republics of Mexico, Brazil, Argentina, and Chile. The United States soon responded to both the political and business opportunities that resulted from the breakup of Spain's empire in the New World. While the American presidential administration of James Monroe, through the Monroe Doctrine of 1823, was proclaiming the new Latin American states' right of self-determination and freedom from European political intervention or future European colonization in the Western Hemisphere, American merchants and shipowners aggressively entered the Caribbean and South American markets now open to them.

An unusual yet significant element of United States trade with Latin America was that of guano, the bird droppings that provided a major source of vitally important fertilizer to support the increasing agricultural production in the United States for several decades around mid-century. The major deposit of guano was on the Chincha Islands off the Peruvian coast, and by the end of the 1840s huge quantities of Peruvian guano were moving around Cape Horn by sea to Baltimore, Norfolk, and New York, as well as across the Atlantic to the major ports of Great Britain and Continental Europe. The growth of this trade just with the port of Baltimore gives sufficient indication of its importance: 445 tons in 1844; 25,500 tons in 1852; and 54,134 tons in 1860.

Trade with newly independent Latin American countries could be immensely profitable, but it was very risky. In this respect, Mexico serves as a good example. The infamous pestilential climate of the Mexican Gulf coast, with its seasonal threat of "El Vomito" (yellow fever), was at least predictable; not so the constantly shifting political climate of the New Mexican Republic or the sudden appearance of Caribbean pirates. With American naval support, the problem of piracy quickly declined, and the political turmoil in Mexico at times even appeared to benefit American traders; between 1827 and 1837 there was an especially profitable business in shipping large amounts of specie (hard currency) out of Mexico, along with many political refugees. To Mexico came a variety of American agricultural products and manufactures. Machinery, ironware, furniture, and vehicles shared the cargo hold with linens, woolens, silks, building timber, medicines, leather goods, papers, marble, and livestock.

Together with its active penetration into these markets, United States trade with the surviving Spanish colonies of Cuba and Puerto Rico, with the British, French, and Dutch West Indian Islands, and with European colonial possessions in Central and South America expanded swiftly during this period and greatly strengthened America's intercontinental ties. Between 1825 and 1860 United States imports and exports with Latin America averaged 20 percent of the value of the nation's entire foreign trade.

Slaves and Freemen: African Americans in the Maritime World

Not all United States trade with Latin America was in agricultural produce; an important segment of this maritime activity was the slave trade. The legal importation of slaves into the United States had ended in 1808, but the illegal trade flourished, even after Congress in 1820 declared slave trading to be piratical, punishable by death. A lenient system of courts in the American South worked against prosecution of slave importers, and even in the North, despite common knowledge of the practice by a few shipmasters, the only execution for slave trading did not occur until 1862. Direct importation from Africa may have diminished, but with the expansion of the plantation system in the deep South slaves were shipped between states on the South Atlantic and Gulf coastwise routes. While there were sporadic efforts to eliminate slavery in the United States by means of emancipation and expatriation back to Africa of former slaves–notably the American Colonization Society's efforts during and after the 1820s–on balance the effort was futile.

The slave-based plantation economy in America was swiftly enlarging, and with such demand for slaves came a corresponding increase in illegal and undocumented importation of Africans, usually by way of Cuba, where the expanding plantation economy also fostered an illegal trade direct from Africa. Legally considered as a species of property, slaves had little if any protection from the vagaries of a market economy in which they were regularly bought, sold, and otherwise treated as things, not humans. Illustrative of this problem as well as of the emerging antislavery efforts in the Northern states was the *Amistad* affair.

The *Amistad* was a Spanish schooner on its way in 1839 from one Cuban port to another, carrying fifty-three Mende men and children, who previously had been captured, enslaved, and shipped from Africa to Cuba, and illegally registered as Cuban-born slaves by Spanish slave traders. Under their leader, Joseph Cinqué, the Africans seized control of the *Amistad* and attempted to return to their African homeland; instead, the Cubans they relied on for navigating the vessel sailed erratically, so that they finally made their

Joseph Cinqué, or Sengbe Pieh, was a Mende rice farmer captured in Africa and illegally imported into Cuba as a slave. He became a celebrity for American abolitionists when he led a revolt of illegally enslaved Africans on board the Cuban schooner Amistad *in 1839. After the vessel was intercepted off Long Island, New York, by an American revenue vessel, the legal case over salvage and property rights turned into both a diplomatic dispute on the rights of the U.S. to impose judgment on foreign property and a human rights issue on the status of Africans illegally sold into slavery. After an impassioned address by former President John Quincy Adams, the U.S. Supreme Court ruled in favor of Cinqué and his fellow captives, and they were eventually returned to Africa. Although it set no precedents for U.S. slavery, the* Amistad *case over maritime property rights helped focus the abolition movement within the U.S. Portrait by Nathaniel Jocelyn. (Courtesy New Haven Colony Historical Society)*

landfall at the eastern tip of Long Island. Here they were arrested by a United States revenue cutter, and finally ended up in New Haven, Connecticut, where they were imprisoned while the Federal District Court there considered the

charges against them—including piracy, theft of a vessel, and murder. Word of their plight swiftly spread throughout the Northeast, and a large, enthusiastic effort was launched to defend the Africans against the accusations of the Spanish colonial plantation owners, who sought restitution of both their human property and their ship. After a long and involved hearing, with former President John Quincy Adams speaking in their defense, the United States Supreme Court in 1841 decided in favor of Cinqué and his comrades, and ordered that they be shipped back to Africa as free people. Although the ruling had no bearing on slaves within the U.S., to this day the *Amistad* remains a powerful symbol of Africans' resistance to slavery and of American antislavery efforts in the face of a legal system—and a prevailing sentiment in the nation's capital—that implicitly condoned slavery and actively protected the property rights of slaveholders.

African Americans, whether born enslaved or free, were actively engaged in maritime enterprise throughout this era. Escaped slaves, such as Frederick Douglass, often made their way to such Northern seaports as New Bedford, Massachusetts, where they might find a generally hospitable reception and even employment. Indeed, Douglass made his escape from Baltimore to the North disguised as a sailor, because sailors had greater freedom of travel than any other black workers in the South. Douglass was perhaps more fortunate than most runaway slaves by possessing marketable skills that any maritime community would value; during his period as a slave in Baltimore, Douglass had become a skilled caulker while working in the shipyards.

Notable among free-born African Americans was the Philadelphia sailmaker, merchant, community leader, and antislavery activist James Forten. Another black freeman, the New Bedford blacksmith Lewis Temple, in 1848 contributed a major improvement to the whaling industry with his ingenious design of a harpoon toggle-head that, once penetrating a whale's body, would stay firmly fixed. On occasion, freemen owned and sailed their own vessels, even operating at times with an all-black crew. Perhaps best known of these mariners is that exceptional maritime entrepreneur, Paul Cuffe, of both African American and Native

American parentage, whose profitable career spanned the late-eighteenth and early-nineteenth centuries until his death in 1817. Yet these men were exceptional, even in the North, where most free blacks labored in service jobs or found occasional employment on the waterfront with little chance of economic advancement.

As before the War of 1812, a large number of African Americans found employment as sailors, although for those in both coasting and high-seas trades there always remained the danger of arrest when their vessel arrived at a Southern port. The notorious and intimidating South Carolina Negro Seamen Acts of 1821 were copied by Georgia, North Carolina, Florida, Alabama, and Louisiana–as well as Spanish Cuba–in an effort to prevent black sailors from communicating with slaves in Southern ports and encouraging slave revolts. These laws authorized seizure and imprisonment of any black seaman–slave or free–for the period that their vessel remained in port. The Negro Seamen Acts were eased in the 1850s to permit black sailors to remain on board their ships, or to come ashore with a passport, but until then thousands of African American seamen suffered imprisonment while in cotton ports. Many others abandoned seafaring, no longer finding in it economic equality and recognition based upon their skill, or a means of communicating with a larger African world on the shores of the Atlantic. As a consequence, the proportion of African American mariners aboard American ships, once as high as 15-20 percent in Northern seaports, began to decline by the 1850s, and where once they served as able seamen they were increasingly relegated to the service positions of cook and steward.

Many black seafarers went into the whaling industry, to join Native Americans–especially those from Gay Head on Martha's Vineyard and from Long Island, New York–as well as a great variety of seafarers from other parts of the globe, as Herman Melville so vividly portrays in *Moby-Dick*. Adding to this ethnic richness among American whaling crews were experienced African-Portuguese seamen from the Cape Verde Islands, off the African coast, who so often came to settle with their families in New England whaling ports.

The Global Outreach of American Whaling

Whaling in the 1815-60 period became a more distinctively American enterprise than ever before or since. American whalers roamed over the globe in pursuit of flexible baleen, which

Created as a provision of the 1796 Act for the Protection and Relief of American Seamen, and issued to sailors who could provide proof of U.S. citizenship, the seaman's protection certificate was intended to shield American sailors from impressment or other forms of abuse by other nations at sea. After the War of 1812, and indeed until 1940, the certificates served more as identification papers. For black sailors before the Civil War, they made an ironic proclamation of citizenship, although the bearer had few of the rights of citizenship when ashore. Nevertheless, a protection certificate was official evidence that could prevent a free black sailor from being kidnapped into slavery or, as in the case of Frederick Douglass, help a slave escape to freedom. This protection certificate declared the U.S. citizenship of John H. Roberts, a twenty-year-old African American mariner born in Boston, who sailed aboard Boston ships in the European and China trades. (Coll. 238, G.W. Blunt White Library, Mystic Seaport)

Although they played a vital role in the lower echelons of whaling, few Native American or African American whalemen were able to surmount prejudice and rise to command. One who did was Amos Haskins, of the Wampanoag tribe, whose whaling career extended from 1839 to his death at sea in 1861. In 1851 Haskins became master of the whaling bark Massasoit. *Daguerreotype, ca. 1850. (Courtesy Old Dartmouth Historical Society–New Bedford Whaling Museum)*

whalemen called whalebone; whale oil from a variety of species, especially the right and bowhead whales whose baleen they sought; and the more valuable oil and spermaceti from the toothed sperm whale. After first entering the Pacific Ocean in 1791, American whalers worked along the South American coast and the equator, opened grounds off Japan in 1819, moved into the Indian Ocean in 1828, brought the industry to the Northwest Coast of North America in 1835 and off Siberia in the 1840s, entered Davis Strait in the eastern Arctic in 1846, passed through the Bering Strait into the Arctic Ocean off Alaska in 1848, and followed the whales into Hudson Bay in 1862. Whether for baleen, oil from blubber, or spermaceti, the hunt for the "salt-sea Mastodon" expanded until the American whaling fleet achieved its greatest tonnage in 1846. By then there were more than 700 American vessels out of the world total of 900 whaleships. Although the prices for whale products hit their peak during and immediately after the Civil War, the largest value of whale products brought back to the United States was in 1854. Yet by the end of the 1850s, with the discovery of petroleum in Pennsylvania and then with the sub-

sequent development, by the early twentieth century, of spring steel, the need for whaling products greatly diminished. During the war years of the 1860s Confederate commerce raiders destroyed forty-six whaleships–many of them at the very end of the war–while many of the older vessels were loaded with stone early in the conflict and purposefully sunk in a Union attempt to block the Confederate harbors of Charleston and Savannah. Another thirty vessels would be destroyed in 1871, when much of the Arctic fleet was trapped in the ice off Alaska and abandoned.

For several decades after 1815, however, American whaling enterprise flourished. The Massachusetts whaling ports of New Bedford and Nantucket were the great centers of American whaling, but many other Northeastern ports were important, through building and fitting-out whaleships and in processing the cargoes of oil and baleen brought in from world-ranging cruises that might extend to three or four years–and even longer. While whaling expeditions went out from Atlantic ports all the way from Maine to New Jersey and Delaware, most whaling was centered in Southern New England. In this small area were such offshore whaling towns as Edgartown, on Martha's Vineyard; along with many large and small shoreside towns, including Salem, Provincetown, Gloucester, and Marblehead, Massachusetts; Warren and Newport, Rhode Island; New London, Mystic, and Stonington, Connecticut; and Sag Harbor and Cold Spring Harbor on Long Island.

Whaling, and the parallel enterprise of sealing, spread American seafarers all over the globe, and not just in the temperate and tropic regions. Sealing had first taken mariners far up the Pacific Northwest coast, even to Alaska; by the 1820s they had turned to the more promising grounds to the south of Cape Horn. Two intrepid Stonington, Connecticut, mariners, Edmund Fanning and the much younger Nathaniel Palmer, were particularly successful in this enterprise. Palmer, at age twenty, commanded the small sloop *Hero* on a voyage south of Cape Horn and the Shetland Islands, where he was the first to encounter the Antarctic Continent. This was just the first of Palmer's many celebrated exploits; in later years, as a leading ship designer and advocate of the "flat-floored" model for large cargo vessels, he was a noted cotton-packet commander on the New Orleans-to-New York run, and after that he was equally eminent as a

With much idle time during voyages that normally lasted for several years, whalemen created a characteristic artform called scrimshaw, which involved engraving or carving whale bone, baleen, and sperm whale teeth. On a piece of panbone—whale jawbone—an unidentified whaleman depicted several steps in the whaling operation. At right, two six-man whaleboats attack a whale spouting on the surface. In each boat the harpooner stands in the bow, ready to dart his "iron" (harpoon), which will attach the boat to the whale. The harpooner then exchanges places with the mate—standing at the stern with a long steering oar—who will lance the whale to kill it when the boat can be brought near. At left, a whale is "cut in" alongside the whaleship. Using long cutting spades, the officers have begun to remove the whale's insulating blubber in a continuous strip, which is hoisted on board, minced, and rendered into oil in a brick tryworks on deck. About fifty whales were sacrificed for each successful voyage of a whaleship. (M.S.M. 39.1962)

commander of transatlantic sailing packets to Liverpool. Then, in 1842, Palmer moved into the China trade where he commanded such famous clipper ships as *Houqua* and *Samuel Russell*.

Sealing—as Fanning had demonstrated back at the turn of the century with a $53,000 net profit for a single voyage—could be spectacularly rewarding. Whaling, with the possibility of several thousand dollars of oil or whalebone derived from a single whale, also could be highly profitable—at least for owners and captains. Often it was not; and after many months at sea, extending into years, a whaler with only a modest catch upon its eventual return to home port had little left over for the crew. Whalemen customarily signed aboard ship for an agreed-upon percentage of the net returns of the voyage, called a "lay," rather than receiving fixed monthly wages. With the interest charged for cash advances or for purchases from the ship's slop chest of clothing and personal items, most whaling crew members came away with far less than men working either on transoceanic merchant vessels or on coasters, let alone those who worked in industries on the land. By mid-century the whaling crewman could expect, on average, an income that was only half that available on a merchantman, and only a third of the average industrial worker's wage ashore.

Another drawback to a career in whaling was the delay in receiving one's pay, since for a whaleman it came only at the end of the voyage. For those who were married and with dependents there was an additional concern: what were the wife and children (or, sometimes, dependent parents) back at home to do in the meantime? Whaling agents, as representatives of the owners, might assist whaling families while the wage-earner was at sea, but all too often there was not enough money at the end of a protracted voyage to cover monetary advances dependents had received.

The uniquely long absences of whaling captains occasionally resulted in wives and children coming aboard for the voyage. As early as the mid-1820s women such as Polly Gardiner of Long Island had begun to accompany their husbands. Especially noteworthy was the well-recorded career of whaling wife and "sister sailor" Mary Brewster of Stonington, Connecticut. During two voyages from 1845 to 1851 she was influential in persuading a number of whaling captains to follow the example she had set in sailing with her husband on his long whaling cruises into the Pacific. In 1849 she became the first American woman to cross the Arctic Circle and sail in the Arctic Ocean. By 1853, a missionary in Hawaii estimated that one out of six whaling captains had his spouse, if not children as well, along for the entire period of the whaling cruise; the total number of these seagoing whaling wives eventually exceeded 400. The presence of these women produced mixed results, at best; sailors, leaning on time-honored superstition or on a more complex preference for a masculine world afloat, often bitterly resented any woman on board, let alone one who might divert the captain from his task or otherwise interfere with the primary business of whaling. Owners often agreed, but a few of them saw a beneficial result from wives being aboard; as whaling merchant Charles W. Morgan commented, these women brought "more decency and order" to a whaler. At times, a shipmaster's wife provided more than moral support; on a few occasions whaling wives helped to navigate and perform other shipboard duties customarily reserved to men.

Most wives and families, however, remained home while the men were at sea. The woman's lonely and frequently bitter burden of managing the household and raising children was even heavier when there was little if any money available; all too often this was the case, especially with whaling crewmen, whose savings at best were slim and whose prospective income was so indeterminate. To a lesser degree, this was also the plight of any family dependent on the earnings of a seafarer, even if he were engaged in brief coastwise voyages and could expect a regular monthly wage. As the nineteenth century progressed, a growing number of American men left the sea for steadier and more profitable employment ashore, and fewer American-born boys went to sea at all. Increasingly, the crews of whalers, fishing vessels, merchantmen, and warships were foreign-born and often unskilled men, either forced or willing to take the lower and less dependable income that seafaring promised.

The Onrush of Steam and the Revolution in World Communications

By the 1840s vessels powered by steam had appeared everywhere, carrying freight and passengers on the major rivers and bays, on the Great Lakes, and along all of the nation's coastline. Steam tugboats and ferryboats busily thrashed about the waters of seacoast and inland ports. Wherever the use of sail was sufficiently undependable; whenever a reasonably tight

Nathaniel B. Palmer (1799-1877) epitomized the indomitable American mariner of the first half of the nineteenth century. Palmer joined the fishing fleet of his native Stonington, Connecticut, at age fourteen, rising to command a fishing vessel at eighteen. In 1819 he sailed as second mate of a brig engaged in sealing off the Falkland and South Shetland Islands. Returning to these waters in 1820, in command of a forty-seven-foot sloop, Palmer encountered a rugged shore in ice-choked waters, which proved to be the continent of Antarctica. Palmer's discovery of the previously unknown continent was documented in 1822 when that portion of Antarctica was named Palmer Land. After another voyage of Antarctic exploration in the seal fishery, Palmer commanded vessels in trade with a number of South American countries during their wars of liberation from Spain. Palmer made two more sealing voyages, 1829-33, then turned to the expanding coastal and North Atlantic packet trade, becoming the senior captain of Edward Knight Collins's Dramatic Line. In 1843 he turned to the China trade, designing as well as commanding several of the fast, early China clippers, including the ships Houqua *(1844),* Samuel Russell *(1847),* Oriental *(1849), and* N.B. Palmer *(1851). Frequently accompanied at sea by his wife, Eliza Babcock Palmer, Captain Palmer remained an active mariner until 1850. Thereafter, he served as a director of the Fall River steamboat line and competed in New York Yacht Club races. This daguerreotype, ca. 1845, is believed to depict Palmer posed before a globe turned to show Palmer Land, the Antarctic peninsula he discovered in 1820. (M.S.M. 96.7)*

Sailing Between a Rock and a Hard Place

Navigating Manhood in the 1800s

In 1867, an American sailor named Edward Mitchell entered into his journal a short poem he had written about a shipmaster's wife. "She walks the deck with majestic grace," he noted, "With her cherry picker nose all over her face." Mitchell's little rhyme was a singularly unflattering comment about a seafaring woman, but it was echoed–in less creative ways–by many other sailors. Sailor Edward Kirwin complained that the "Capt[s] woman sick and I wished she would dye." Another sailor described a seafaring wife as a "disgusting woman," and a third argued that the woman aboard his ship was a "source of trouble." Mariners working at the height of American deepwater sail in the middle years of the nineteenth century seemed to concur that a sailing woman was a disturbing oxymoron. "It is no place for a woman," said one mariner, "aboard a . . . ship."

The sentiments of these nine-teenth-century sailors bear investigating, for they provide insights into how the world's largest spatial domains–the oceans–have come to be claimed and inhabited by men almost exclusively. Such an investigation presumes that social divisions of global space are not immutable or natural, but are human

formulations that vary across time and cultures.

Mariners who voyaged on deep-sea ships at the height of merchant sail and in the heyday of American whaling traveled in the company of their own sex for months, sometimes years at a time. Sailors' diaries and correspon-dence indicate that many of these (mostly young) mariners hoped that the voyage would, among other things, condition and strengthen "manly" attributes, and that voyage earnings would ease them into financial independence and into the male role of family provider.

The American deepwater ship was dominated by men, but it was also inhabited by images of women. Shipboard culture was replete with references to women, and shipboard space was coded "female" in distinc-tive ways. But although "women" were present in shipboard culture, their appearances were sharply circumscribed, and their limited presence gives some indication of how these American men viewed gender and power.

Among the many things to which deepwater sailors assigned gendered meaning was the biggest object in their lives: the vessel itself. The

ship was a "she" of course. Sometimes she was a domesti-cated woman. One sailor saw in his sailing vessel "a true emblem of the fair sex when hurrying through the labors of a washing day." Other seamen saw the ship as a female body, clothed with sails, which they might engage, repeatedly, in disrobing. The ship was further sexualized in the way they might "ride" her as she plunged through the sea. And mariners regularly discussed the ship's "anatomy." She had, for instance, a "bottom," which, according to one seaman, might "be so full of barnacles that it takes nearly a gale o' wind to set her going." On the other hand her bottom might be particularly plump. A merchant sailor on a ship called the *Taskar* complained in verse that "The Taskar is the thing to Roll/ O ee roll & go/ Her bottom's round as any bowl! /O ho roll & go!"

Sailors thus animated the ship with "womanly" qualities– both sexual and domestic–and then celebrated their ability to command both of her person-ae. In a more explicit way the ship's figurehead was both a female object of domesticity– sometimes she was a model of Victorian virtue–or a semi-nude woman of "primitive" origins. This wooden woman, who was thrust forward at the bow of a ship, exemplified

Officers on deepwater ships had a similar sort of ritual. On Saturday nights, shipmasters and mates sometimes set aside time for a toast to "sweethearts and wives." Raising a glass of rum, or on temperance ships, cold water, these mariners acknowledged the women they had left behind them. As one officer noted in his diary, "One hour each week we'll snatch from care/ As through the world we roam/ And think of dear ones far away/ And all the joys from home."

The limiting of homeward thoughts in this sea song is telling. Women, either real or represented, had a restricted place on shipboard. Occasionally, however, women—and their sea-captain husbands—did not respect the proprieties of the seafaring spheres. A growing number of sea captains' wives in the middle and late 1800s went aboard ship with their husbands on global voyages.

conflicting views of the seafaring female. She headed the ship, and faced down the tempestuous seas firsthand, but she was immobilized from the waist down. Like the fish-tailed mermaids who figured strongly in sailor lore, these women had distinctly compromised mobility.

Sailors surrounded themselves with "females" not only in their ships but in their personal spaces as well. Men who lived before the mast on whaling and merchant vessels lived communally, in the public space of the forecastle. Each seaman had his own private domain of a sea chest,

however, and within this, a space that connoted "woman." This included the sailor's ditty box, which contained a variety of domestic items and often a packet of letters. On Sundays, men before the mast recognized, in ritual, this material and this space. In what was called a "Sailor's Pleasure," seamen literally opened their lives to the memories and presence of women at home. During this time they organized or overhauled their ditty boxes, sorting out such utensils such as needles, buttons, thimbles, perhaps looking over a Bible, and gazing at daguerreotypes and letters.

While many of these women seem to have kept to themselves in the officers' quarters, others walked the decks, watched men at work, and occasionally conversed with members of the crew. As we have seen, these women sometimes elicited caustic commentary from sailors. One whaleman summed up his and other mariners' feelings about sailing with a woman when he complained that it was "hell afloat."

Sailors before the mast offered various reasons why they felt that women were intrusive. Females aboard ship interfered, first of all, with male solidarity afloat. Then they seemed to expand the privilege and presence of the captain. (Some captains' wives had special quarters built either above or below decks.) Women who scrutinized sailors' work in the ship also seemed to violate the men's sense of privacy. Finally, women seemed to interfere with male rites of passage.

Youths who set out from shore when they were in their late teens hoped to return to shore as "men." At sea they enhanced "masculine" attributes like courage and daring, and in port practiced drinking and sexual conquest. Many sailors hoped to sail home, too, with the means to provide for a wife and a family. Historians have shown that the seafaring voyage served as a means to manly independence for black men and white men alike. Through at least the 1830s, African-American sailors were able to enjoy a relative degree of fraternity and economic liberty at sea, based not on their skin color but on their abilities as sailors.

The presence of a woman at sea, just as youths were busy trying to differentiate themselves from things "female" and learning to assert their power in a patriarchal order, was thus suspect. There were a few young sailors who appreciated the attentions of a captain's wife, like cabin boys or genteel young men, but most mariners wished women away. One whaleman described the happy future day when he might see the captain's wife and her family "in the heart of Cape Cod burried up to their necks In sand."

The boundaries established or sought by seamen for women may also be related to mariners' concerns about women ashore generally. One of the great ironies of the seafaring voyage as a rite of passage into power and independence was that during the time that boys were becoming men at sea—which was a considerable four to five years in the whaling industry—women were not sitting idly at home. As historians have recently pointed out with regard to the whale fishery, women actively sustained the industry with their domestic efforts and their hard labor. The image of the passive female at home corresponded with prevailing ideals of "proper" womanhood, but it often hid the active contributions and decisions that women made. Sailors at sea were well aware of how women were at home, and their intense efforts at empowering themselves physically, financially, and emotionally, as well as their concern at sea to limit women's presence, may in part reflect their worries about women's influence and power.

The sailor's recognition of women's agency and leverage was especially well expressed when it came to the subject of courtship and sexual constancy. Victorian purity was a dim hope for mariners who felt that women at home were not only capable of expressing their sexual and romantic needs, but were even impatient to do so. "I have been listening," said Mate Marshall Keith, "to hear the captain tell how untrue women were to their husbands while they were away."

Whalemen learned of female infidelity from shipboard gossip, in meetings at sea called "gams," and from letters sent by relatives and friends at home. Shore-bound brothers of sailors, perhaps not surprisingly, readily offered unsettling information. In 1845, Charles Babcock wrote to his whaling brother Henry that his sweetheart Sarah had found another companion, and that he might well have expected such: "In my opinion the best of girls would not remain true in the absence of 2 years of a lover, mark my word they are faithless things unless you are with them everyday."

A recurrent nightmare for anxious sailors was the homecoming in which, more often than not, the sweetheart or wife turned away from the newly arrived sailor and gave him the cold shoulder, or

James F. Smith (1831-1904) accompanied his father and mother on the 1838 voyage of the New London, Connecticut, whaleship Chelsea to Desolation Island in the Indian Ocean. He was depicted by artist Isaac Sheffield, at about age ten, wearing a penguin-skin coat brought back from the voyage while the Chelsea "cuts in" a whale in the background. Smith later became a whaleman himself, rising to command before switching to coastal steamboat operation (Courtesy Lyman Allyn Art Museum, New London, Connecticut)

asked him to sleep on the couch, or had disappeared with another man. Sailors reinforced their insecurities by sharing with each other stories of infidelity, and they recorded their own sad experiences in their journals. One sailor

wrote hopeful poetry to "Miss Mary," his love at home: "To find thee true, would well repay / The toils and sorrows I have known / If fortune smiles, I'll claim thy Hand / My Beautiful My own." But when he arrived home in New York, Miss Mary had found another suitor. "Fortune did smile," wrote this exasperated mariner, "and I got Home and found her darn her married. Woman, woman, verily thou art the Devil!!"

Brothers at home recommended that mariners live with women to keep them true. Sailors may have found a related solution closer to hand. Ashore in foreign ports, for instance, whalemen solved the problems of constancy by marrying prostitutes temporarily and by purchasing loyalty along with sex. "All our young men what had got married since our arrival here, got divorced by mutual consent," reported a whaleman, "and their late spouses with all their children and donnage either went on shore or on board of some other ships to obtain new employement."

While there are certainly many reasons sailors married seaport women, one of them was the desire for commitment. The truism that a sea-

man had a wife in every port usually serves as a comment on married sailors' inconstancy. It must also refer, though, to single sailors' desire for allegiance. "You see," remarked one sailor, "We can hire the girls. . . to remember us that is more than the girls at home will do." One whaling veteran cautioned his brother against seafaring on the grounds that women ashore did not sit dutifully or patiently at home. His advice to his brother was to "stick fast to old terre firma. Find a good woman," he urged, and "cage her up."

The nineteenth-century sailing voyage, then, was an experience in paradox. It promised a sailor everything that a "man" might want: mobility, social experience, independence from domesticity, and economic reward. Women were warned not to interfere with this formative experience, and those who did appear at sea were, both in representation and reality, put in their place. But in part because men were at sea for so long, women at home pushed at the boundaries of proper, dependent womanhood and acted with a degree of freedom, autonomy, and authority. Mariners thus found themselves sailing between the Scylla and Charybdis of enhancing both women's power and their own.

Margaret Creighton

schedule demanded reliable departures and arrivals; whenever speed of delivery was a paramount consideration; whenever people had the money and willingness to pay for such special and expensive service, waterborne steam vessels increasingly appeared to provide the needed service.

However, the use of steam power for long-distance oceanic transportation lagged well behind developments in inland and coastal steam. In 1819 the auxiliary American side-wheel steamer *Savannah*, under the command of Captain Moses Rogers, had voyaged from the United States to Europe and back, but most of the trip had been under sail; in any event, crossing the Atlantic entirely by steam power was widely believed an impossibility–until 23 April 1838, when the British steamships *Sirius* and *Great Western* arrived within hours of each other at New York, after successful passages by steam all the way from the British coast. Thereafter, steam would seriously challenge sail in the mid-century transatlantic packet service.

As a part of their service in foreign and interregional trade, those sailing vessels operating as packets had for many decades carried on communication functions, particularly the transport of mail, business documents, government documents, currency, and important business and government officials. With the feasibility now confirmed by steam-powered vessels of far more regular transatlantic scheduling, if not greater speed as well, governments moved to support with public funds the construction and operation of oceangoing steamships. In 1839, the British government awarded Canadian-born Samuel Cunard and his British associates an Atlantic mail contract that provided an ample annual subsidy to support a steam liner service from Liverpool to Halifax, Nova Scotia, and thence to Boston. Such government subsidies for transoceanic mail service made profitable transatlantic steamship operations at last a reasonable possibility, although during the 1840s, of the several British and American attempts to inaugurate steam liner services between Britain and the United States, only the Cunard Line was able to survive.

The United States responded to the British use of subsidy when Congress passed legislation in

1845 that authorized the postmaster general to make contracts for transporting oceanic mail with American carriers. The initial transatlantic contract went to the newly established Ocean Steam Navigation Company for transportation between New York and Bremen, Germany. With two side-wheel steamers, the *Washington*, soon followed by the *Hermann*, the company began transatlantic service in 1847, with faster crossings, especially on the westbound passage in the face of prevailing winds, than the competing sailing packet lines.

At the same time, Edward Knight Collins, a successful New York operator of sailing packets, lobbied for Congressional subsidy for the creation of a steamship line that would directly challenge Cunard. Collins proposed to build and operate a transatlantic mail steamship line between the major ports of New York and Liverpool, in direct competition with the now well-established Cunard Line of British mail steamers.

A Cape Cod native who had become a leading New York City merchant, shipowner, and shipping operator, Collins over the previous decades had built a considerable fortune and a stellar reputation in American maritime enterprise. Beginning 1827 with a sailing packet service between New York and Veracruz, Mexico, Collins had moved on by the early 1830s to manage the major cotton-packet sailing line between New Orleans and New York. Then, in late 1836 he inaugurated his remarkably successful "Dramatic Line" of sailing packets between New York and Liverpool. By the mid-1840s he determined to sell off all of his interests in sail and, with the substantial financial assistance of the eminent Brown Brothers banking firm, create the largest, fastest, and most luxurious steamships in the world.

Surmounting initial opposition and delays, Collins finally received Congressional approval of a large subsidy. By late 1850, Collins finally had his four nearly identical wooden, side-wheel steamers *Atlantic, Arctic, Baltic,* and *Pacific* operating on the transatlantic run. These elegant and uncommonly fast 280-foot vessels attracted immense publicity and diverted an impressively large number of first-class passengers and equally high-paying cargo from the Cunard Line, setting transatlantic speed records in the process.

New England Whalemen's Wives and the Sentimentalization of Seafaring, 1820-1870

On 21 May 1853, Eliza Brock set sail from Nantucket on the ship *Lexington*, bound round Cape Horn on a Pacific whaling voyage. She was the captain's wife, and the only woman on board. In the back of the journal she kept at sea, Eliza carefully copied out the following unattributed poem:

The Sailor's Wife

Thou o'er the world, and I at home—
But one may linger, the other may roam,
Yet our hearts will flee o'er the sounding sea
Mine to thy bosom, and thine to me.

Thy lot is the toil of a roving life,
Chances and changes, sorrow and strife,
Yet is mine more drear to linger here
In a ceaseless, changeless war with fear.

I watch the sky by the stars' pale light,
Till the day dawn breaketh on gloomy night,
And the wind's low tone hath a dreary moan
That comes to my heart as I weep alone.

During much of her husband's twenty-year career as a whaling captain, Nancy Chapman Bolles remained at home with family and friends. However, she made at least one voyage, 1850-53, leaving home with two children and returning with four. "I have been as contented here with my family as I should have been at home," she assured her sister in a letter written partway through the voyage. Photograph, ca. 1860. (M.S.M. 55.546)

The poem explains in some measure why Eliza chose to join her husband at sea and, as with all of the captain's wives who went, voluntarily take on the loneliness, confinement, and discomfort as the only woman on board ship on an arduous whaling voyage lasting three years or more. But Eliza Brock's copying of "The Sailor's Wife" also illustrates the extent to which new ideas about marriage and women's roles had begun to affect the way New England mariners' wives—those few at sea and the many more on land—understood themselves and their world.

In "The Sailor's Wife," the manly sailor's occupation takes him roaming over the world in an active life full of chances, changes, and strife. In explicit contrast is the setting and role of his wife: she is at home, fearful and alone, passively waiting, watching, and weeping. The set of oppositions is relieved only by the brief and ineffectual mention of the tie that binds them together–their hearts, fleeing over the sounding sea–in other words, an exclusive romantic relationship that somehow survives prolonged and repeated separations. There is no reference to children, family, home, community, or work; in fact, there is no reference to social or economic context at all.

"The Sailor's Wife" renders, in maritime terms, the nineteenth-century notion of "separate spheres" for women and men, that geographic metaphor by which Victorians divided up their conceptual universe into such polar oppositions as public vs. private, work vs. home, head vs. heart, active vs. passive, male vs. female. Indeed, with its focus on the isolated romantic relationship, "The Sailor's Wife" represents a highly sentimental vision of seafaring. One of many perspectives on seafaring current in the nineteenth century, this sort of "sentimentalization" affected a number of ways in which land-based society and seamen interacted, from shaping paternalism within maritime industries to the agendas of maritime reformers. For maritime women, sentimentalization represented an ideal that played down female activity

and women's contributions to their communities, emphasizing instead women's emotional role and their experience of deprivation and loss. As their letters, diaries, and other records testify, New England whalemen's wives took these ideas to heart–and often to great personal cost.

As part of the sweeping economic and social changes that transformed America in the nineteenth century, New England's deep-sea industries expanded rapidly and restructured after the War of 1812. Integral to these changes was the conceptual polarization of gender roles into separate spheres for men and women. When work–or, more precisely, the kind of labor that was valued as "work"–was removed from the home, men went with it into the public world of business and politics. Women remained behind within an increasingly isolated domesticity, with their labor no longer defined as "work," and their most important tasks being the nurture and emotional support of their families. At the same time, marriage was redefined as less a functional partnership and more a strictly emotional, even spiritual, union. The bond between husbands and wives was the crucial link that held the spheres, and society, together. So the theory went, anyway.

This intellectual realignment occurred within the whaling communities of New England, too, despite the fact that the gender division of labor remained what it had traditionally been: men went to sea and women stayed on land

(except for those few captain's wives like Eliza Brock). Yet, despite the poem's implications, or the theory of separate spheres, most maritime women did not simply wait and weep alone. Rather than any passive isolation, the lives of whalemen's wives were characterized by extensive community interaction, flexible household arrangements, and hard work, which enabled them to survive the seamen's absences and sustain family and community ashore.

Like all whalemen, the career mariners were generally paid in a lump sum at the end of their voyages. In the interim, their wives had to find other ways to support their families. A few women requested cash advances from their husbands' employers; many others worked for wages. Women in urban centers earned the money they needed by turning most often to traditional female work. Records document instances of women doing laundry, preparing food, selling milk, spinning, weaving, sewing, nursing, keeping boarders, keeping inns, taverns, and shops, teaching school, and even making small-scale investments. Centre Street, part of the business district in Nantucket, even came to be known as "Petticoat Row" for its female shopkeepers. (Plenty of women in port communities participated in other, less licit income-raising activities, but the women connected to the career whalemen appear to have remained well within the bounds of respectability.) In rural areas, some women typically kept family farms going with their own labor and that of their children, other relatives, neighbors, and hired help. Whether in town or on the farm, wives carefully managed family budgets and stepped in for absent husbands when necessary, settling debts, handling property, paying taxes, buying insurance.

And, of course, they cared for their children. But this was not always easy in what was a virtual single-parent situation. In 1850, Betsey King wrote to her husband, then at sea, that their youngest daughter was "a real little chatterbox." The harried mother confessed, "I get along very well when the other two are at school but when they come home it seems sometimes as though I should go crazy." She added, "It is a task to bring up three children. . . I feel the responsibility more and more every day."

Caroline Gifford ran the family farm in Dartmouth, Massachusetts, for some twenty-five years after her marriage in 1849, while her husband Charles commanded one whaleship after another on Pacific voyages. Despite her years of experience, Caroline did not find her responsibilities easy. In 1866, she reported proudly to Charles of their infant son, "he is the smartest & hansomest boy that I ever see." Two years later, though, she was evidently having some problems with her older son, then nine; she warned Charles, "I think Norman begins to need the care of a judicious man." Adding to Caroline's woes were unreliable hired hands and her acri-

monious relationship with her husband's brother, with whom she shared farm equipment. Caroline wrote Charles bitterly, "if I have got to work any harder I had rather go the Alms house." In her next letter, she complained, "I call it a trial to bring up a family mostly without any Father to help manage."

To "help manage," whalemen's wives had to turn instead to extensive networks of relatives, neighbors, and friends. Childbirth and care for the young, the sick, and the elderly were times for cooperative female work, as women's labor shifted from household to household in response to need. Such shared work brought women in and out of each other's homes on a daily basis or on visits lasting days or weeks. In fact, mariners' wives seem nearly as mobile and constantly in motion as their seafaring men were out at sea. Libby Spooner of New Bedford spent months on end in extended visits to various relatives and connections throughout the region. In a letter she teased her absent husband Caleb: "I have got to roveing so much are you not afraid you will not be able to keep me at home when you wish? Well you need not fear, the more I knock about the more anxious I am to settle down quietly somewhere."

Whalemen's families expanded and contracted with the demographic rhythms of the whale fishery as well as the more common rhythms of birth, marriage, and death. The Spooner family into which Libby married demonstrated just how malleable

whaling households could be. Libby's husband Caleb and both of his brothers, Gideon and Shubael, went whaling, and all three eventually made captain. Gideon married in 1835 and seems to have brought his wife Elizabeth into his parents' home. In 1839, a Spooner sister, Sophia, married another whaling captain, George Clark, who also joined the Spooner household when he was ashore. Elizabeth, Sophia, and the two Spooner sisters who remained unmarried evidently all lived together, caring for their children as well as the aging Spooner parents, while their men went whaling. Such flexible and cooperative interaction wove together the whaling communities, enabling women to sustain and renew life under the extreme stresses of the fishery.

But, with the sentimentalization of seafaring, the substance of women's labor was obscured in the emphasis placed on its emotional association. Samuel Braley, far off in the Indian Ocean in 1850, hesitated to wear the socks his wife Mary Ann had knit for him: "It seems sacralage: how much I prize evry thing that is the work of thy dear hands." And, when Samuel learned that Mary Ann was about to give birth to their first child, he wrote, "Oh that I could be with thee to comfort thee in thy coming tryals. . . I never knew how much I loved thee till now when thou art about to suffer for me."

With the sentimentalization of seafaring, the major role for maritime women like Mary Ann was indeed to suffer for their men: in a line coined by English poet Charles Kingsley, "men must work and women must weep." As Sylvia Leonard of New Bedford wrote to her husband, John, in 1856, "William Crowell sailed two weeks ago and left his beautiful wife to mourn for him. Ah I can sympathize with her deeply." In July 1838, the evangelical publication, the *Sailor's Magazine and Naval Journal*, reprinted a newspaper report titled "Perils of the Sea," which listed both the number of Cape Cod seamen lost during the year 1837 (78), and the number of seamen's widows then living on the Cape: 914! After speculating on the "violent and terrible" forms of death at sea, the author meditated at length on the misery of the "bleeding heart" of "the mother, the wife, the sister" left at home, thereby linking the dangers men confronted on the ocean with women's sufferings at home, and stressing the notion of men's activity and women's passivity.

Other evidence suggests, though, that women suffered not so much for the men as for themselves. Contrary to the new ideal, few maritime women retreated into passivity. Many even actively exerted pressure to keep their men at home. Sweethearts and young wives typically urged their mates to forego seafaring on romantic grounds. Sarah Pierce told Captain Elijah Chisole in 1852, "I want you dearest. . . to make your mind up that you will never leave me again to go to sea, for I never could be happy with you at sea and I at home far from you that I love."

Elisabeth Taber wrote dramatically, "Dear Husband I hope that thare will be a day that you will not have to plough the raging Ocion for your living, I will do all that I can to prevent it. . . I do hope that we may never be sepperated agane in this World." She continued with some morbid speculation on whether he might at that very moment be sick, or dying, or even dead, and she added emphatically, "I do not want that you should follow the sea for your living."

For women married longer, whose cares mounted with every additional child and year of their husbands' absences, the new cultural emphasis on their deprivation and loss perhaps predictably shaded over into antagonism and even, on occasion, outright hostility. "We can scarcely conceive a situation more wretched than that of the wife of an active sailor," noted an author in the *Sailor's Magazine* in 1838. "The anxiety which her husband subjects her to, will prey upon and finally destroy the finest constitution. Every wind that blows is a source of fear; every rain that falls causes sorrow; every cloud that rises is big with the fate of her nearest friend. These feelings, which tug at the heart-strings, are honourable to the nature of women, but noble and generous as they are, they are poisonous to her existence, and sink too deeply into the breast to be eradicated." Marriage to a sailor, then, could prove hazardous to your health.

The author went on to assign blame: "Those who make long

voyages pass but a small part of their time with their families; a few months at home, answer for years at sea, and they finally drop away, before they have hardly bestowed a thought upon death; or without, in many instances, leaving a competency for his family; and she who has borne up against trouble in her early life has to struggle with poverty in its decline."

These are hostile words, and they seem to have expressed a resentment felt by many maritime women. Myra Weeks, who noted that "I have to write with one hand and rock the cradle with the other," told her husband William, "I hope you will be blest with a short and prosperous voyage and then make up your mind to stay at home the remainder of your days. . . I think it is rather lonesome to be shut up here day after day with 3 little children to take care of. I should be glad to know how you would like [it]. . . I think that thare may be some way to get a living without your always being away from your family and friends."

Caroline Gifford wrote Charles, "I am in hopes if you live to perform this voyage that you will not have to go to sea again unless," she added pointedly, "you can enjoy yourself better than on the land." On one of Caroline's later letters, their daughter Eleanor penned an ambivalent postscript, "it seems a long time for a man to be away from his folks 3 or 4 years at a time I send my love to you and hope you will prosper. . . for it seems as though you ought to stay at home a while

and not be on the water all your days."

Rather than support and reinforcement for the enterprise, then, some women demonstrated a rather subversive view of seafaring, or at least of seafarers. Libby Spooner told Caleb, "Nehemiah talks of moving back to the farm I think he best wait till spring but he is a *sailor* and consequently very *uneasy*. I know something about it, they never stay set down in one place till they get so stiff and old they cannot get out of it."

Captain William Loring Taber was stung when his wife Susan doubted his attachment to her. "You wrote you wish you could think that this was the last time we should be seperated," he recorded in one letter home, "you know that many have said so before, [but] that Agents give successful captains such induce-

ments that they cannot resist them, and you will not insure one of my ambition against their temptation." But the captain insisted, "I think a married man's place is at home with his family, and if he can stay, he ought to." And his word was good; after his return a year later, he gave up commanding ships and managed them from shore instead. Many more mariners, though, continued to ply the sea as long as they were able, despite their sometimes fervent protests that *this* voyage would be their last.

The Victorian sentimentalized interpretation of seafaring represented a convergence of maritime and nonmaritime cultures, as prevailing ideas about men's and women's proper roles and relationships were imposed on maritime experience. But, while it brought land and sea closer along conceptual shores, sentimentalization introduced new tensions and deepened divisions between women and men within the maritime community. Neither the concept of separate spheres nor the ideal of a transcendent love made the whalemen's absences any easier for their wives. Indeed, sentimentalization only sharpened the unhappiness of

repeated conjugal separations. With evident personal feeling, Libby Spooner told Caleb about his brother's wife: "Lizzie write me a long letter full of troble down-spirited enough, she feel Shube's [Shubael's] departure deeply. . . Cornelia Winslow [another mariner's wife] is with her now, t[w]o lonely ones togather, but tis our lot God help us." She concluded sadly, "O the life of a sailor & sailors wife, how frought with sorrow and heartpangs."

Lisa Norling

Mary Brewster (1822-1878) of Stonington, Connecticut, spent just five months with her whaling-captain husband during their first four years of marriage. She then accompanied him to sea for two voyages, 1845-51, circling the globe and becoming the first American woman to pass through the Bering Strait and enter the Arctic Ocean. In her journal of the voyages, preserved at Mystic Seaport, she noted: "I am far more happy here than when I was at home though it appeared to some I knew no sorrow then. Alas they could not see my feelings nor will they ever know of the many bitter hours I have experienced. . . . Here I am happy in the society of one who loves me for myself alone." This daguerreotype by J. Gurnsey was taken ca. 1854. (M.S.M. 48.1146)

The 230-foot steamships Washington *(right) and* Hermann, *launched at New York in 1847, were the first practical American transatlantic steamships. With modified sailing rigs to supplement the 470-horsepower, single-cylinder engines, they could travel at nine and a half knots, which was slower than the Cunard liners. Designed to comply with the mail subsidy provisions of the Postal Act of 1845, they operated successfully between New York, Southampton, England, and Bremen, Germany, until the U.S. Mail contract expired in 1858. Uneconomical without a subsidy, the two ships were sold to West Coast owners and ended their days in the Pacific. The* Washington *was broken up in 1864 and the* Hermann *was wrecked off Japan in 1869. They are depicted in New York Bay in this oil painting by James E. Buttersworth. (M.S.M. 38.561; Mary Anne Stets photo)*

In 1851 the *Baltic* took the "blue riband" for the fastest transatlantic passage with a crossing of nine days, eighteen hours from New York, then lowered her own record by five hours the next year. Yet, despite a large initial federal government subsidy, which then was more than doubled in 1852, the Collins Line never paid a cent in dividends, and appeared to be losing money steadily year after year. The tragic loss of the *Arctic* in late 1854 and the subsequent disappearance at sea of the *Pacific* early in 1856 were too much for the line to handle, especially in the face of increasing political attack from many sides.

With the Collins Line at the center of the storm, the issue of mail subsidies had became the subject of increasingly bitter Congressional debates based on sectional concerns, political differences, and economic rivalries. In 1857, just as the new and even larger *Adriatic* joined the Collins Line, Congress pulled back on its heavy financial support and the line soon ceased operating. By early in the next year, as the nation struggled back from the Panic of 1857, the Collins Line declared bankruptcy, and the three remaining steamers were sold at auction. E.K. Collins's

The Different Worlds of Steam and Sail: Impressions of Richard Henry Dana, Jr.

Under Sail:

31 July 1836–Notwithstanding all that has been said about the beauty of a ship under full sail, there are very few who have ever seen a ship, literally, under all her sail. A ship coming in or going out of port, with her ordinary sails, and perhaps two or three studding-sails, is commonly said to be under full sail; but a ship never has all her sail upon her, except when she has a light, steady breeze, very nearly, but not quite, dead aft, and so regular that it can be trusted, and is likely to last for some time. Then, with all her sails, light and heavy, and studding-sails, on each side, alow and aloft, she is the most glorious moving object in the world. Such a sight, very few, even some who have been at sea a good deal, have ever beheld; for from the deck of your own vessel you cannot see her, as you would a separate object.

One night, while we were in these tropics, I went out to the end of the flying-jib-boom, upon some duty, and, having finished it, turned round, and lay over the boom for a half an hour, admiring the beauty of the sight before me. Being so far out from the deck, I could look at the ship, as at a separate vessel;—and, there, rose up from the water, supported only by the small black hull, a pyramid of canvass, spreading out far beyond the hull, and towering up almost, as it seemed in the indistinct night air, to the clouds. The sea was as still as an inland lake; the light trade-wind was gently and steadily breathing from astern; the dark blue sky was studded with the tropical stars; there was not a sound but the rippling of the water under the stem; and the sails were spread out, wide and high;—the two lower studding-sails stretching out on each side, twenty or thirty feet beyond the deck; the top-mast studding-sails, like wings to the top-sails; the top-gallant studding-sails spreading fearlessly out above them; still higher, the two royal studding-sails, looking like two kites flying from the same string; and, highest of all, the little sky-sail, the apex of the pyramid, seeming actually to touch the stars, and to be out of reach of human hand. So quiet, too, was the sea, and so steady the breeze, that if these sails had been sculptured marble, they could not have been more motionless. Not a ripple upon the surface of the canvass; not even a quivering of the extreme edges of the sail–so perfectly were they distended by the breeze. I was so lost in the sight, that I forgot the presence of the man who came out with me, until he said, (for he, too, rough old man-of-war's-man as he was, had been gazing at the show,) half to himself, still looking at the marble sails–"How quietly they do their work!"

Richard Henry Dana, Jr., *Two Years Before the Mast* (New York, Harper & Brothers,1840), chapter 33.

Under Steam:

Saturday. Aug. 23rd.[1856]–Set sail from Liverpool, this afternoon, in the new and splendid [Cunard Line] steamer *Persia*, which has just crossed in eight days and twenty three hours. She has over two hundred cabin passengers. . . .

Sunday, Aug. 24th. Service read by the Capt.–Judkins–who reads extremely well. Few clergymen read as well. Fully attended. We are off the South coast of Ireland. Made signal for a boat, and set ashore two Irishmen, who had stowed themselves away at Liverpool, to get free passage to America. They were wretched looking Paddies–and although this proceeding made "*Two freemen* less, America, to thee", we were glad to be rid of them. At night, took our last view of Europe, which was Cape Clear, in Ireland.

Tuesday, Sep. 2nd. This is the tenth day of our passage, and we expect to reach New York tonight, or early tomorrow morning. The first three days of the passage were very disagreeable, with a heavy, broad sea, and the ship pitching a great deal. Most of the passengers are sea-sick. Monday and Tuesday, there were sixty who did not leave their berths, and Wednesday there were forty. Thursday was calm and pleasant, and Capt. Judkins went below, and talked to the passengers, and succeeded in getting them all out of their berths. I have been in high condition, enjoying the bad weather and heavy sea. Once, for a few minutes, I felt a little sick, after a long dinner in a close room, but it passed off immediately; and generally I enjoy a heavy sea, and pitching ship. Perhaps there is a little pride generated by the contrast, as one rolls through the passage-ways, in rough wet clothes, with a cheerful face, redolent of outer air, among the wretched helpless creatures below. There have been two or three good days, but the other days have been foggy and rainy. It is often clear at night. We have four instruments on board, and have music after dinner, for a couple of hours, and since it has cleared off, and become smoother, we have dancing, chiefly by the children, of whom there are a great many on board, none of them sea-sick, and all in the wildest

good spirits. They have been the life of the company.

By leave of the officers, I went below, to see the great works of fire and steam, that moved this vast bulk, and its freights through the water. Here is a world unknown to the common passengers. Hundreds cross the ocean in these boats, and know nothing and see nothing of the power that moves them. As all the machinery is under deck, it can be seen only by those who visit it, below. Except the chimneys and the paddle wheels, the passenger sees nothing but what the decks and cabins of a sailing ship might disclose. He talks of the winds and speed, and watches the sails, and the unimportant manoeuvres of the deck, while all the time, down in the abysses of the hull, is working, with ceaseless energy, day and night, day and night, the enormous, complex machinery,—these huge boilers are steaming, and forty fires, fed at forty iron doors, opened and closed ever and anon to be replenished, are keeping up a body of flame, hundreds of cubic feet in measurement, supplied with coal at the rate of nearly one hundred tons a day;—and all this bulk of flame, of steam, of water at boiling heat, enclosed within the walls of a vessel, with hundreds of human beings, alone on the great ocean! It is a great spectacle, to be sure; but, so far from exciting my admiration, as a triumph of science, and skill, it seems to me a reproach to the science of the age that this must be. Such a bulk of imprisoned fire, an imprisoned power of steam suffi-

cient to destroy the ship and all it contains, requiring a cargo of so many hundreds of tons of coal, for a single Atlantic passage;—all this, with its perils, and its huge size, to transport men and women over the water, when the immense latent power of electricity and galvanism is known,—this is rather a discredit than an honor to our century.

In these deep and unknown regions, down by the keelson of the ship, led to by stories of winding stairs, in the glare of the opening and closing furnace doors, live and toil a body of grim, blackened, and oily men, stokers or machinists, coal-carriers, fire-feeders, and machine tenders, who know as little of the upper ship, as the upper ship knows of them. When down among them, on the brick and iron floors between the walls of brick and iron, amid the sights and sounds of their work and care, I lost all sense of being at sea, or even on ship-board, and for aught that I could hear or see, might have been in the subterranean recesses of a steam factory in Staffordshire.

The Journal of Richard Henry Dana, Jr., Vol. II, Robert F. Lucid, ed. (Cambridge, Massachusetts: Harvard University Press, 1968), 816-17.

maritime career had ended in disaster, and Great Britain now was virtually without any rival for transatlantic steam services.

By the 1840s and 1850s the use of steam to expedite the North Atlantic crossing and the ability of American steamers—notably those of the Collins Line—to compete with their British counterparts in setting new speed records on the transatlantic run might be widely celebrated, yet this was only part of the irresistible maritime search for ever-greater speed. Of all the American achievements in the maritime world, none was so spectacular or so caught the American popular imagination—then and since—as the famed Yankee clipper ships.

The Clipper Ship Era and America's Short-Lived Zenith of Wooden Shipbuilding

The clipper ship has become legendary as a unique American contribution to the glory of seafaring under sail. In fact, "clipper ship" is a difficult term to define, since many more vessels aspired to the designation than actually met the unwritten criteria of length, sharpness of bow, fineness of line, and excessive height of masts and spread of sails that distinguished clipper ships from other large ocean sailing ships. Historians generally agree that about 350 American vessels built between 1833 and 1858 qualify as clipper ships, although elements of the design predated 1833 and were further refined after 1858. In addition, other nations made important contributions to this distinctive vessel type, and the unquestioned world supremacy of the "Yankee" clipper lasted only for two decades or so. During that era, stretching roughly from the early 1840s to the 1860s, some spectacular vessels came into being, some spectacular performances were recorded, and some spectacular profits were made from the celebrated efforts of such hard-driving clipper-ship captains as Josiah P. Cressy, Nathaniel B. Palmer, and Robert H. Waterman.

The celebrated designers and builders of these glamorous vessels—such as Boston's Donald McKay and New York's William H. Webb—were as much artists as craftsmen; such clippers as

Rainbow, Sea Witch, Flying Cloud, Sovereign of the Seas, Red Jacket, Romance of the Seas, and *Lightning* were the product of intuitive genius as well as precise measurement and mathematical calculation. For a brief time, especially after the 1848 discovery of gold in California, such vessels commanded premium rates for passengers and cargo in the three- to four-month, 13,000-mile passage around Cape Horn to San Francisco. Two clippers—*Flying Cloud* in 1851 and 1854, and *Andrew Jackson* in 1859—made the run in eighty-nine days, a record that was not broken by a sail-powered vessel until the 1990s. Besides serving the California boom, some clippers were intended for the China trade,

The 280-foot, wooden-hulled side-wheel steamers Atlantic, Pacific, Arctic, *and* Baltic *established new standards for transatlantic service between New York and Liverpool when the Collins Line was launched in 1850. After four years of safe operation, tragedy struck the Collins Line with the loss of the* Arctic *on 27 September 1854. Bound for New York, she collided with the French iron steamer* Vesta *in a fog off Cape Race, Newfoundland. When the crew discovered that the Arctic's hull was pierced below the waterline, panic broke out. The Arctic sank about five hours after the collision, taking down all but some of the male passengers and most of the crew, who had escaped with the lifeboats. More than 300 men, women, and children drowned, including Collins's wife, daughter, and son. This catastrophe, plus the disappearance of the* Pacific *two years later and the rising costs of operation, doomed the Collins Line. It ceased operations in 1858. Lithograph published by N. Currier in 1854, drawn by J.E. Buttersworth, from Charles Parsons's interpretation of an eyewitness sketch by passenger James Smith. (Courtesy The Mariners' Museum, Newport News, Virginia)*

The extreme clipper Seaman's Bride, *built at Baltimore, was one of fifty-four American clipper ships launched in 1851. At 150 feet she was considerably shorter than many contemporary clippers, but she had especially sharp lines and was one of very few clippers to set moon sails—the highest square sails—on all three masts. This daguerreotype depicts the* Seaman's Bride *ready for launch. The two men on deck may be her builders, Richard and Edward Bell. The photograph documents both the sharp lines that made this vessel a clipper ship, and the fine workmanship and decoration that went into these celebrity vessels. On her first voyage, the* Seaman's Bride *circled the world—New York-San Francisco-Shanghai-New York; then she made two more San Francisco voyages before she was sold at Hamburg, Germany, in 1855. By that time, small extreme clippers had been rendered obsolete by the medium clippers, which combined speed with greater cargo capacity. (Courtesy Maryland Historical Society)*

others to serve as packets on the transatlantic run from New York to Liverpool, still others for trade in the Indian Ocean or out to Australia; and for a few year their profits were as huge as their towering masts. If they hit just the right market conditions for their cargo some clippers could pay off their entire cost of construction and outfitting with the proceeds of a single voyage. However, these clippers were built for speed, not cargo capacity. Their immense spread of canvas and exquisitely fine lines were impressive; so was the cost of operating these vessels. Characteristically ship-rigged, with three unusually tall masts and comparably large spars—a clipper required a large crew, spare masts and yards, and extra suits of sails. This translated into very high operating costs in carrying the small volume of revenue-producing cargo.

So long as freight rates remained so extraordinarily high, all was well for the clippers. But then the bottom fell out by the mid-1850s; California freight rates dropped swiftly—from $60 a ton in 1850 to $28 a ton in 1854, and down to $10 a ton in 1857—so that soon only the ships with less extreme lines and more cargo capacity, the "medium" clippers, still could sail profitably.

Notable among these medium clippers was the *David Crockett*, a 1,679-ton ship built in Mystic, Connecticut, that was one of 120 clippers launched in the year 1853. In early November of that year, when she was loading her first cargo in New York, she was only one of twelve new clipper ships that all were making their first voyage from that single port. Before her career was over in 1883, the *David Crockett* had sailed on the Liverpool-New York run, from Liverpool to Bombay and return, and then for many years on the New York-San Francisco run. Never the fastest clipper in service, she still made respectable times and, more importantly, never lost or damaged her cargo and never cost her insurance underwriters a penny in her thirty years of service. When at last she was laid up (and finally converted into a coal barge) the *David Crockett*, which cost $93,000 to build and outfit, had earned well over half a million dollars net of all expenses.

Orders for new vessels, especially those for the California trade, flooded into shipyards up and down the northeastern coast for several years after 1849. In particular, the shipyards of New York and Boston, which excelled in the design and construction of large wooden sailing vessels, were pushed to their productive capacity. Between 1850 and 1855, American shipyards launched 161 California clippers. Yet by 1855 the demand for California clippers had declined markedly as the much shorter route across the Isthmus of Panama became the preferable way to travel to America's Pacific Coast. Steamship lines from Eastern ports to the Caribbean coast of the Isthmus and then from the Pacific side up to California quickly developed, especially with the opening of New York shipping merchant William H. Aspinwall's Panama Railroad across the Isthmus. As freight rates to California began to fall rapidly, the extreme California clippers, with their small cargo capacity, became less desirable. Some of these ships were bought or chartered by the British and French governments at the time of the Crimean War in 1854, and were reduced to use as military transports. Many clippers were sold abroad; some were lost at sea or laid up; but most ended up carrying prosaic cargoes, in a pathetic shadow of their former glory. One such clipper was the famed *Sea Witch*, reduced to carrying coolies from China to the Chincha Islands off the coast of Peru, to mine the guano that served as fertilizer for American farms.

While the American clippers justifiably became world-renowned, they represented only one aspect of American achievement in wooden shipbuilding and design during the early- and mid-nineteenth century period. In 1855 alone, American shipyards were busy building 381 ships and 126 brigs for ocean trade. American wooden vessels of this era were generally the best in the world, constructed at lower cost and higher quality than anywhere else by exceptionally skilled American shipwrights who, like the vessel designers, were true craftsmen. As yet there was little apparent reason to be diverted from such enterprise, since wood for ship construction in sufficient amount and quality was still available, although the timbers increasingly came from areas more distant from the shipbuilding centers of New York and Boston. Superbly designed New York- and Boston-built American sailing packets—the workhorses of the transatlantic trade—became ever larger, more elegant in their accommodations, and even faster than before; some could rival the clippers in speed and even outrun the transatlantic steam liners on rare occasion. New England shipbuilders relied heavily on Southern timber: live oak from coastal swamps, yellow pine from the middle South, and white oak from the upper South. "Live oakers" might be sent south to cut their valuable framing wood, and gangs of workers in Virginia might actually shape white oak framing timber in the local forests, and then ship it north to be assembled into ship ribs for New England-built vessels.

In the immediate prewar era much of American shipbuilding still took place in the Northeast. New York and Boston remained major centers of shipbuilding, and many of the largest and most respected yards, both for sail and steam, were located here. After 1830, the yards building the larger ships tended to become more permanent, ongoing operations. Vessel size kept increasing for those craft designed to serve as passenger freighters requiring the capability of sustained speed on well-traveled routes or on routes of great distance, such as the China trade. The bulk carriers engaged in the cotton trade, both coasting vessels and foreign traders, were designed to maximize cargo space, yet they were often as large, elegant, and speedy as all but a handful of the celebrated clippers. The smaller brigs and schooners designed for employment in the coastal trade and for transporting perishables were often built in smaller, less permanent yards scattered about a number of the smaller seaports, as well as in Boston, New York, and other major maritime centers.

American design found expression in more than working vessels, since a lively interest in pleasure boating and yacht racing was very much a part of America's maritime centers throughout this period. Competitive rowing was growing out of spirited matches between professional watermen, and in the 1850s would become the first intercollegiate sport when crews from Harvard and Yale met in 1852. Sailing races in extreme versions of working watercraft were also becoming popular diversions in such ports as Philadelphia and New York. The Detroit Boat Club is often considered the first U.S. yacht club, but the better-known New York Yacht Club, which was founded in 1844, led the way in the racing of large yachts in America. Largely confined to a wealthy elite in such major ports as Boston and New York, yachting

nonetheless inspired some of the most brilliant American shipbuilders and designers and produced some remarkably fast and beautiful sailing vessels. Among the best of American wooden-ship designers was George Steers, who produced designs for a wide range of superlative vessels and, before his untimely death in 1856, displayed his versatility by designing the huge and exceptionally fast wooden-hulled steamship *Adriatic* for the Collins Line. With a commission from members of the New York Yacht Club, Steers designed the sailing yacht *America*, which was sent to Great Britain to represent American shipbuilding prowess at the Great Exhibition of 1851. She defeated the Royal Yacht Squadron so decisively in a much-publicized regatta that the trophy she

The 215-foot medium clipper ship David Crockett, *launched at Mystic, Connecticut, in 1853, proved the economic potential of the medium clipper design. Though named for the popular nineteenth-century folk hero, the vessel did not initially follow his spirit westward; rather, she served as a North Atlantic packet and made a run to Aden and India before entering the California trade in 1857. Although suffering her share of damage on the rough Cape Horn run, and losing one captain washed overboard in a storm, the* David Crockett *made twenty-five profitable California voyages between 1857 and 1883. By 1876 she had earned a net profit of half a million dollars, or more than four times her $93,000 original cost. Although her fastest run to San Francisco was two weeks off the record clipper passage, she could carry more than 2,000 tons of wheat in the California grain trade and thus remained in service far longer than many of her contemporaries. Even after being retired from the California trade, the* Crockett *was put in service on the Atlantic, and ended her days as a coal barge. Her forty-year career was double the typical life of a wooden ship in such arduous service. James E. Buttersworth painted the* David Crockett, *ca. 1860, depicting her with a balanced rig to ride out heavy weather rather than the clouds of sail that usually characterize a clipper ship. (M.S.M. 92.21.10; Mary Anne Stets photo)*

won became the prize for the world's premier yachting competition, the *America*'s Cup races.

John W. Griffiths (1809-1882) was the most influential American naval architect of the nineteenth century. The son of a New York shipwright, Griffiths was trained as a ship carpenter before becoming a draftsman at the navy yard in Portsmouth, Virginia, and at the Smith & Dimon yard in New York. Griffiths led the move away from "rule of thumb" design to a scientific approach based on calculations and hydrodynamic theories. In 1836 he first published articles on naval architecture, and the lecture series on design principles that he delivered in the 1840s is considered the first public discussion of shipbuilding theory in America. Griffiths' designs for the early clipper ships **Rainbow** *and* **Sea Witch** *helped establish the general form of the clipper ship, and his steamship design theories were incorporated in the impressive Collins liners. Griffiths also introduced and patented a number of technical improvements in ship construction. To disseminate his ideas he published three books on naval architecture, and he edited two journals to promote discussion of shipbuilding design and practice. Unlike his contemporaries Donald McKay and Isaac Webb, Griffiths never owned a shipyard, but his theoretical accomplishments were the equal of those better-known designer-builders. This daguerreotype of Griffiths dates to the 1850s. (Courtesy Smithsonian Institution, NMAH/Transportation)*

The Darkening of America's Maritime Horizon

The economic expansion in the United States produced a steady and large demand for ships, especially from 1843 to 1855. In this period, American shipyards built 2,656 merchantmen to carry on its foreign and coastal trade. Moreover, with the repeal of the British Navigation Laws in 1849, American ships now could be used by British shippers. British manufacturers were seeking new markets for goods throughout the world to keep pace with their production, and consequently needed vessels for transportation to countries all over the world. The superiority of American wooden vessels and their relatively competitive cost made them attractive to British shippers–to the chagrin of Canadian as well as British shipbuilders who previously had enjoyed their own protected market.

But the superior quality of American's wooden vessels, and their undeniable success in satisfying the needs of both domestic and foreign shipping firms, was not entirely beneficial for the American maritime industries in the long run. The very success of these wooden sailing vessels diverted Americans' attention from building steamships for deep-sea trade and from exploring the possibilities of the newer shipbuilding technologies in iron. While Britain and the other leading European countries began to build "composite" vessels–wooden sailing ships with extensive iron frames and bracing–or even sailing vessels with hulls entirely of iron during the decade between 1847 and 1857, the United States did not. Instead, American wooden shipbuilding for the antebellum decades reached its peak in the 1850s, both in numbers and in the size of the vessels. Because of its emphasis on the production of high-quality wooden vessels, the American shipbuilding industry remained a highly competitive one with new yards opening to meet the high demand of the peak decade. Rather than realizing the economies of scale being developed in those European yards begin-

Herman Melville Describes the Emigrant Passage

We were all now very busy in getting things ready for sea. The cargo had been already stowed in the hold by the stevedores and lumpers from shore; but it became the crew's business to clear away the *between-decks*, extending from the cabin bulkhead to the forecastle, for the reception of about five hundred emigrants, some of whose boxes were already littering the decks.

To provide for their wants, a far larger supply of water was needed than upon the outward-bound passage. Accordingly, besides the usual number of casks on deck, rows of immense tierces were lashed amid-ships, all along the *between-decks*, forming a sort of aisle on each side, furnishing access to four rows of bunks,–three tiers, one above another,–against the ship's sides; two tiers being placed over the tierces of water in the middle. These bunks were rapidly knocked together with coarse planks. They looked more like dog-kennels than any thing else; especially as the place was so gloomy and dark; no light coming down except through the fore and after hatchways, both of which were covered with little houses called "*booby-hatches*." Upon the main-hatches, which were well calked and covered over with heavy tarpaulins, the "*passengers'-galley*" was solidly lashed down.

This *galley* was a large open stove, or iron range–made expressly for emigrant ships, wholly unprotected from the weather, and where alone the emigrants are permitted to cook their food while at sea. . . .

The wind was fair; the weather mild; the sea most smooth; and the poor emigrants were in high spirits at so auspicious a beginning of their voyage. They were reclining all over the decks, talking of soon seeing America, and relating how the agent had told them, that twenty days would be an uncommonly long voyage.

Here it must be mentioned, that owing to the great number of ships sailing to the Yankee ports from Liverpool, the competition among them in obtaining emigrant passengers, who as a cargo are much more remunerative than crates and bales, is exceedingly great; so much so, that some of the agents they employ, do not scruple to deceive the poor applicants for passage, with all manner of fables concerning the short space of time, in which their ships make the run across the ocean.

This often induces the emigrants to provide a much smaller stock of provisions than they otherwise would; the effect of which sometimes proves to be in the last degree lamentable; as will be seen further on. And though benevolent societies have been long organized in Liverpool, for the purpose of keeping offices, where the emigrants can obtain reliable information and advice, concerning their best mode of embarkation, and other matters interesting to them; and though the English authorities have imposed a law, providing that every captain of an emigrant ship bound for any port of America shall see to it, that each passenger is provided with rations of food for sixty days; yet, all this has not deterred mercenary shipmasters and unprincipled agents from practicing the grossest deception; nor exempted the emigrants themselves from the very sufferings intended to be averted.

No sooner had we fairly gained the expanse of the Irish Sea, and, one by one, lost sight of our thousand consorts, than the weather changed into the most miserably cold, wet, and cheerless days and nights imaginable. The wind was tempestuous, and dead in our teeth; and the hearts of the emigrants fell. Nearly all of them had now hied below, to escape the uncomfortable and perilous decks: and from the two "*booby-hatches*" came the steady hum of a subterranean wailing and weeping. That irresistible wrestler, sea-sickness, had overthrown the stoutest of their number, and the women and children were embracing and sobbing of all the agonies of the poor emigrant's first storm at sea.

Bad enough is it at such times with ladies and gentlemen in the cabin, who have nice little state-rooms; and plenty of privacy; and stewards to run for them at a word, and put pillows under their heads, and tenderly inquire how they are getting along, and mix them a possett: and even then, in the abandonment of this soul and body subduing malady, such ladies and gentlemen will often give up life itself as unendurable, and put up the most pressing petitions for a speedy annihilation; all of which, however, only arises from their intense anxiety to preserve their valuable lives.

How, then, with the friendless emigrants, stowed away like bales of cotton, and packed like slaves in a slave-ship; confined in a place that, during storm time, must be closed against both light and air; who can do no cooking, nor warm so much as a cup of water; for the drenching seas would instantly flood their fire in their exposed galley on deck?. . .

We had not been at sea one week, when to hold your head down the fore hatchway was like holding it down a suddenly opened cess-pool. . . .

I have made some mention of the "Galley," or great stove for the steerage passengers, which was planted over the main hatches. . . .

At making the fire, the emigrants take turns; as it is often very disagreeable work, owing to the pitching of the ship, and the heaving of the spray over the uncovered "galley." Whenever I had the morning watch, from four to eight, I was sure to see some poor fellow crawling up from below about daybreak, and go to groping over the deck after bits of rope-yarn or tarred canvas, for kindling-stuff. And no sooner would the fire be fairly made, than up came the old women, and men, and children; each armed with an iron pot or saucepan; and invariably a great tumult ensued, as to whose turn to cook came next; sometimes the more quarrelsome would fight, and upset each other's pots and pans.

Many similar scenes occurred every day; nor did a single day pass, but scores of the poor people got no chance whatever to do their cooking.

This was bad enough; but it was a still more miserable thing, to set these poor emigrants wrangling and fighting together for the want of the most ordinary accommodations. But thus it is, that the very hardships to which such beings are subjected, instead of uniting them, only tends, by imbittering their tempers, to set them against each other; and thus they themselves drive the strongest rivet into the chain, by which their social superiors hold them subject. . . .

Many of them at last went aft to the mate, saying that they had nothing to eat, their provisions were expended, and they must be supplied from the ship's stores, or starve.

This was told to the captain, who was obliged to issue a ukase from the cabin, that every steerage passenger, whose destitution was demonstrable, should be given one sea-biscuit and two potatoes a day; a sort of substitute for a muffin and a brace of poached eggs.

But this scanty ration was quite insufficient to satisfy their hunger hardly enough to satisfy the necessities of a healthy adult. The consequences was, that all day long, and all through the night, scores of the emigrants went about the decks, seeking what they might devour. They plundered the chicken-coop; and disguising the fowls, cooked them at the public galley. They made inroads upon the pig-pen in the boat, and carried off a promising young shoat: *him* they devoured raw, not venturing to make an incognito of his carcass; they prowled about the cook's caboose, till he threatened them with a ladle of scalding water; they way-laid the steward on his regular excursions from the cook to the cabin; they hung round the forecastle, to rob the bread-barge; they beset the sailors, like beggars in the streets, craving a mouthful in the name of the Church.

At length, to such excesses were they driven, that the Grand Russian, Captain Riga, issued another ukase, and to this effect: Whatsoever emigrant is found guilty of stealing, the same shall be tied into the rigging and flogged. . . .

We had been outside of Cape Clear upward of twenty days, still harassed by head-winds, though with pleasant weather upon the whole, when we were visited by a succession of rain storms, which lasted the greater part of a week.

During this interval, the emigrants were obliged to remain below; but this was nothing strange to some of them; who, not recovering, while at sea, from their first attack of sea-sickness, seldom or never made their appearance on deck, during the entire passage. . . .

Nevertheless, it was, beyond question, this noisome confinement in so close, unventilated, and crowded a den: joined to the deprivation of sufficient food, from which many were suffering; which helped by their personal uncleanliness, brought on a malignant fever.

The first report was, that two persons were affected. No sooner was it known, than the mate promptly repaired to the medicine-chest in the cabin: and with the remedies deemed suitable, descended into the steerage. But the medicines proved of no avail; the invalids rapidly grew worse; and two more of the emigrants became infected. . . .

The sight that greeted us, upon entering, was wretched indeed. It was like entering a crowded jail. From the rows of rude bunks, hundreds of meager, begrimed faces were turned upon us; while seated upon the chests, were scores of unshaven men, smoking tea-leaves, and creating a suffocating vapor. But this vapor was better than the native air of the place, which from almost unbelievable causes,

was foetid in the extreme. In every corner, the females were huddled together, weeping and lamenting; children were asking bread from their mothers, who had none to give; and old men, seated upon the floor, were leaning back against the heads of the water-casks, with closed eyes and fetching their breath with a gasp. . . .

About four o'clock that morning, the first four died. . . .

On land, a pestilence is fearful enough; but there, many can flee from an infected city; whereas, in a ship, you are locked and bolted in the very hospital itself. Nor is there any possibility of escape from it; and in so small and crowded a place, no precaution can effectually guard against contagion. . . .

On the second day, seven died. . . ; on the third, four; on the fourth, six, of whom one was the Greenland sailor, and another, a woman in the cabin, whose death, however, was afterward supposed to have been purely induced by her fears. These last deaths brought the panic to its height; and sailors, officers, cabin-passengers, and emigrants—all looked upon each other like lepers. . . .

And still, beneath a gray, gloomy sky, the doomed craft beat on; now on this tack, now on that; battling against hostile blasts, and drenched in rain and spray; scarcely making an inch of progress toward her port.

On the sixth morning, the weather merged into a gale, to which we stripped our ship to

a storm-stay-sail. In ten hours' time, the waves ran in mountains; and the Highlander rose and fell like some vast buoy on the water. Shrieks and lamentations were driven to leeward, and drowned in the roar of the wind among the cordage; while we gave to the gale the blackened bodies of five more of the dead.

But as the dying departed, the places of two of them were filled in the rolls of humanity, by the birth of two infants, whom the plague, panic, and gale had hurried into the world before their time. The first cry of one of these infants, was almost simultaneous with the splash of its father's body in the sea. Thus we come and we go. But, surrounded by death, both mothers and babes survived.

At midnight, the wind went down; leaving a long, rolling sea; and, for the first time in a week, a clear, starry sky. . . . By afternoon of the next day this heavy sea subsided; and we bore down on the waves, with all our canvas set; stun'-sails alow and aloft and our best steersman at the helm; the captain himself at his elbow;—bowing along, with a fair, cheering breeze over the taffrail.

The decks were cleared, and swabbed bone-dry; and then, all the emigrants who were not invalids, poured themselves out on deck, snuffing the delightful air, spreading their damp bedding in the sun, and regaining themselves with the generous charity of the captain, who of late had seen fit to increase their allowance of food. A detachment of them now joined a band of the crew, who proceeding into the steerage, with buckets and brooms, gave it a thorough cleansing, sending on deck, I know not how many buckets-ful of defilements. It was more like cleaning out a sta-ble, than a retreat for men and women. This day we buried three; the next day one, and then the pestilence left us, with seven convales-cent; who, placed near the opening of the hatchway, soon rallied under the skillful treat-ment, and even tender care of the mate. . . .

Our days were now fair and mild, and though the wind abated, yet we still ran our course over a pleasant sea. The steerage-passengers—at least by far the greater num-ber—wore a still, subdued aspect, though a little cheered by the genial air, and the hopeful thought of soon reaching their port. But those who had lost fathers, hus-bands, wives, or children, needed no crape, to reveal to others, who they were. Hard and bitter indeed was their lot; for with the poor and des-olate, grief is no indulgence of mere sentiment, however sin-cere, but a gnawing reality, that eats into their vital beings; they have no kind condolers, and bland physi-cians, and troops of sympa-thizing friends; and they must toil, though to-morrow be the burial, and their pall-bearers throw down the hammer to lift up the coffin.

How, then, with these emi-grants, who, three thousand miles from home, suddenly found themselves deprived of brothers and husbands, with

but a few pounds, or perhaps but a few shillings, to buy food in a strange land?. . .

The steerage was now as a bedlam; trunks and chests were locked and tied round with ropes; and a general washing and rinsing of faces and hands was beheld. While this was going on, forth came an order from the quarter-deck, for every bed, blanket, bolster, and bundle of straw in the steerage to be commit-ted to the deep.–A command that was received by the emi-grants with dismay, and then with wrath. But they were assured, that this was indis-pensable to the getting rid of an otherwise long detention of some weeks at the quarantine. They therefore reluctantly complied; and overboard went pallet and pillow. Following them, went old pots and pans, bottles and baskets. So, all around, the sea was strewn with stuffed bed-ticks, that limberly float-ed on the waves—couches for all mermaids who were not fastidious. Numberless things of this sort, tossed overboard from emigrant ships nearing the harbor of New York, drift in through the Narrows, and are deposited on the shores of Staten Island; along whose eastern beach I have often walked, and speculated upon the broken jugs, torn pillows, and dilapidated baskets at my feet.

A second order was now passed for the emigrants to muster their forces, and give the steerage a final, thorough cleaning with sand and water. And to this they were incited by the same warning which had induced them to make an

offering to Neptune of their bedding. The place was then fumigated, and dried with pans of coals from the galley; so that by evening, no stranger would have imag-ined, from her appearance, that the Highlander had made otherwise than a tidy and prosperous voyage. Thus some sea-captains take good heed that benevolent citizens shall not get a glimpse of the true condition of the steerage while at sea.

Herman Melville, *Redburn, His First Voyage* (New York, 1849).

ning to build iron ships, the American shipyards operated in a small-scale carpentry and hand-craft tradition. But eventually the rising cost and increasing scarcity of timber, and the increased cost of labor, began to add substantially to the cost of the wooden vessels. At the same time, improvements in iron and steel vessels made those ships increasingly competitive with American wooden vessels.

Nevertheless, the size of the American merchant marine increased steadily until, in 1861, it reached its peak of well over five and one-half million tons, with the coastal (or documented) fleet somewhat larger in size than the high-seas (or registered) American-flag fleet. Moreover, in 1861 the American deep-sea fishing fleet totaled 182,106 tons. Yet by the later 1850s, well before the outbreak of war, there were clear signs of trouble–both present and future–for America's maritime industries.

The Anglo-American Oceanic Connection

Overshadowing all other trading part-ners of the United States was Great Britain. The British market, by absorbing American exports and supplying its imports, was so important throughout the era that it dominated the American economy. A large portion of the American merchant marine–ships and seamen alike–was involved in this transat-lantic trade, and import duties from the trade (in this era before federal income taxes) were both large and essential in supplying a major portion of federal government revenue.

The primary categories of American imports throughout the 1815-60 period were textiles, "hardware" (iron products), and "wet goods" (wines, brandies, etc.). Great Britain was by far the major American supplier of the first two, and a significant transshipper of the third. Textiles were Britain's chief item of export; they also were America's most valuable item of importa-tion. Textiles from England's cotton factories of Lancaster and Birmingham would be shipped to the port of Liverpool on the Irish Sea; there they would be added to woolens, silk goods, and linens for the export market. Liverpool's other

main export to America was emigrants from Ireland, England, Scotland, Wales, and even the European continent.

Iron products from abroad, primarily from Britain, constituted 60 percent of total American iron consumption as late as 1850. Such "hard-ware" ranged from railroad iron, to pots and pans, to copper disks for American fabrication into cooking ware. Much of the wine and other wet goods might originate in the Mediterranean and Iberian regions, but a substantial amount of this cargo came to America by way of the Netherlands and Britain, especially through the port of London.

United States exports throughout the 1815-65 period were primarily made up of raw materials, and Great Britain provided by far the largest market for these goods. Above all, raw cotton shipments to Britain shaped America's foreign trade and the employment of its merchant marine. In the peri-od 1856-60, for example, cotton shipments made up 54 percent of the total value of American exports; next in importance was all American manufactures, at just 12 percent of the total. Other significant export products in that period were almost entirely raw materials: wheat and flour (especially following the repeal of the British Corn Laws in 1846) at 11 percent of the total value of exports; raw tobacco at 6 percent; pork and pork products at 4 percent; and corn, beef, and timber each at 2 percent.

Cotton emerged early as America's leading export product. By 1820 well over half of the yearly crop was being exported, and by the 1820s the figure was over 75 percent. Soon cotton would become so dominant that each year for several decades cotton represented over half the entire value of American exported goods. Great Britain was consistently taking over half the entire world's cotton product during this period, and thus continued as America's primary market, but France and the Low Countries also absorbed a substantial amount of this dominant American export crop.

Cotton exports were crucial to the growth of the American merchant marine. In 1852 the for-eign cotton trade of the United States employed 800,000 tons of American-flag shipping and some 40,000 men. The even faster-growing

Loading Cotton in Mobile

The Seaman's Impression in Story and Song

Our boat-sailing and fishing lasted nearly a month; when one day, returning on board from a race, a letter from the captain informed us that the ship was "taken-up."

"Where for?" was, of course, a question eagerly put.

"For Liverpool," was the answer, "and the cotton to come down next week."

All was now bustle and preparation. Numberless matters were to be attended to before the ship was really ready to take in cotton–the ballast was to be squared, *dunnage* prepared, the water-casks, provisions, and sails to be lugged on deck, out of the way of cargo, the nicely painted decks covered with planks, on which to roll cotton, topgallant and royal yards crossed, and tackles prepared for hoisting in our freight. We had scarcely gotten all things in proper trim, before a lighter-load of cotton came down, and with it a stevedore and several gangs of the *screw men*, whose business it is to load cotton-ships. Screwing cotton is a regular business, requiring, besides immense strength, considerable experience in the handling of bales and the management of the jack-screws.

Several other ships had "taken up" cargo at the same time we did, and the Bay soon began to wear an appearance of life–lighters and steamboats bringing down cotton, and the cheerful songs of the screw gangs resounding over the water, as the bales were driven tightly into the hold. Freights had suddenly risen, and the ships now loading were getting five eighths of a penny per pound. It was therefore an object to get into the ship as many pounds as she could be made to hold. The huge, unwieldy bales, brought to Mobile from the plantations up the country, are first compressed in the cotton presses, on shore, which at once diminishes their size by half, squeezing the soft fibre together, till a bale is as solid and almost as hard as a lump of iron. In this condition they are brought on board and stowed in the hold, where the stevedore makes a point of getting three bales into a space in which two could be barely put by hand. It is for this purpose the jack-screws are used. A ground tier is laid first; upon this, beginning aft and forward, two bales are placed with their inner corners projecting out, and joining, leaving a triangular space vacant within. A hickory post is now placed against the nearest beam, and with this for a fulcrum, the screw is applied to the two bales at the point where the corners join, and little by little they come together, are straightened up, and fill up the triangular space. So great is the force applied, that not infrequently the ship's decks are raised off the stanchions which support them, and the seams are torn violently asunder.

Five hands compose a *gang*, four to work the screws, and one to do the headwork–for no little shrewd management is necessary to work in the variously sized bales. When a lighter-load of cotton comes alongside, all hands turn to and hoist it in. It is piled on deck until wanted below. As soon as the lighter is empty, the gangs go down to the work of stowing it. Two bales being placed and the screws applied, the severe labor begins. The gang, with their shirts off, and handkerchiefs tied about their heads, take hold the handles of the screws, the foreman begins the song, and at the end of every two lines the worm of the screw is forced to make one revolution, thus gaining perhaps two inches. Singing, or *chanting*, as it is called, is an invariable accompaniment to working in cotton, and many of the screw-gangs have an endless collection of songs, rough and uncouth, both in words and melody, but answering well the purposes of making all pull together, and enlivening the heavy toil. The foreman is the *chanty-man*, who sings the song, the gang only joining in the chorus, which comes in at the end of every line, and at the end of which again comes the pull at the screw handles. One song generally suffices to bring home the screw, when a new set is got upon the bale, and a fresh song is commenced.

Charles Nordhoff, *The Merchant Vessel: a Sailor-Boy's Voyages to See the World* (New York, 1855).

This activity was described in one of the sailors' work songs, called chanteys, that proliferated during the nineteenth century. Like the cotton-stowing chanteys, or other songs used in gang labor, sea chanteys helped coordinate heavy, repetitive work, such as hoisting sail or raising the anchor. At least partially influenced by African call-and-response songs, chanteys were sung by one of the sailors, who acted as chanteyman, while the crew sang and hauled on the chorus. Some lyrics were relatively standard, but usually they were impromptu comments by the chanteyman referring to women, the work at hand, the condition of sailors, or even the ship's officers.

Roll the Cotton Down

Come rock and roll me over,
Roll the cotton down!
Let's get this damned job over.
Oh, roll the cotton down!

Was ye ever down in Mobile
   Bay,
Roll the cotton down!
Screwin' cotton by the day?
Oh, roll the cotton down!

Oh, a black man's pay is
   rather low,
Roll the cotton down!
To stow the cotton we must go.
Oh, roll the cotton down!

Oh, a white man's pay is
   rather high,

Roll the cotton down!
Rock and shake her is the cry.
Oh, roll the cotton down!

Oh, so early in the mornin',
   boys,
Roll the cotton down!
Oh, afore the day is dawnin',
   boys.
Oh, roll the cotton down!

Five dollars a day is a white
   man's pay,
Roll the cotton down!
So bring yer screws an' hooks
   this way.
Oh, roll the cotton down.

And bring yer sampson posts
   likewise,
Roll the cotton down!
Oh, bear a hand, get a curve
   on, boys.
Oh, roll the cotton down!

We'll floor her off from fore
   to aft,
Roll the cotton down!
There's five thousand bales for
   this 'ere craft.
Oh, roll the cotton down!

Lift her up an' carry her along,
Roll the cotton down!

Screw her down where she
   belongs.
Oh, roll the cotton down!

Oh, tier by tier we'll stow
   'em neat,
Roll the cotton down!
Until the job is made
   complete.
Oh, roll the cotton down!

Oh, Mobile Bay's no place for
   me,
Roll the cotton down!
I'll pack me bags an' go to sea.
Oh, roll the cotton down.

Stan Hugill, *Shanties from the Seven Seas* (U.S. edition, Mystic: Mystic Seaport Museum, 1994).

The significance of cotton to the maritime economy is suggested by this late-nineteenth-century view of the levee at New Orleans, where longshoremen rest amid the ranks of cotton bales brought downriver for shipment by sea. Keystone View Company photo. (M.S.M. 96.6.1)

domestic trade was equally important: 1,100,000 tons of shipping and 55,000 men were involved in the transportation of raw cotton from Southern ports to the textile mills of the North. It has been calculated that about 47 percent of the registered American fleet (American flag shipping in foreign trade) and 55 percent of the documented (coastal) American fleet was engaged in the cotton trade. American-flag vessels dominated the cotton export trade, with between 75 and 80 percent of the total export crop sailing in American vessels.

Based on cotton, both as raw material and as finished product, there soon emerged a trade pattern that became as politically contentious as it was economically vital to the nation. From Southern ports, with the Gulf ports of New Orleans and Mobile becoming increasingly dominant, baled raw cotton sailed for foreign markets over 4,500 miles away in Liverpool or Le Havre. From Britain and European ports, vessels then would sail towards America with manufactures (textiles, hardware) and emigrants—but not to the ports from which the raw cotton had originated. Instead, the transatlantic passage usually would end in a Northern port, such as Boston, Baltimore, Philadelphia, or (most important of all by far) New York. From these Northern ports, the final leg of the passage brought both imported and domestic manufactured goods and some cabin passengers down the coast some 700 or 800 miles to Charleston or Savannah, or around the tip of Florida into the Gulf of Mexico and then to New Orleans or Mobile, some 1,700 often dangerous and always difficult sea miles from New York. Yet all of the southern cotton was not shipped directly to Europe. Especially in the earlier decades, a substantial amount moved up the coast to New York, and from there was transshipped for a 3,200-mile voyage to Europe.

Northern seaports, notably New York, thus were cutting heavily into the direct line of commerce and navigation between Southern ports and their European markets. The extent of this Northern involvement was so great that both contemporaries and historians of a later era recognized that New York Port, in particular, had effectively "enslaved" the Southern economy and its cotton ports. Not only did Northerners direct the flow of shipping by owning and operating the vast majority of American vessels in the

trade; they also commanded the financing of the cotton trade, so that Southern producers and merchants saw themselves increasingly at the mercy of Northern "parasites." As an 1837 commercial convention in Charleston, South Carolina, proclaimed: "The South thus stands in the attitude of feeding from her own bosom a vast population of merchants, shipowners, capitalists [bankers and speculators], and others, who, without the claims of her progeny drink up the life-blood of her trade."

Southern merchants tried to free themselves from this Northern dominance, but to no avail. Especially after the major panics and subsequent depressions of 1837 and 1857, they argued for both the right and the need of the South, as the primary producer and source of national wealth, to assert its economic independence. But they failed to establish a viable direct trade between Southern ports and European markets, carried in ships owned and operated by Southerners. From their failure grew an increasing bitterness towards Northern traders and speculators, especially in New York City. These Yankees, many Southerners argued, were not true producers but only merciless leeches on the honest yeoman farmers of the South. Such growing frustration and outrage among Southern merchants and planters fueled the inflammatory rhetoric and political maneuvering that ultimately led to secession—an assertion of economic as well as political independence— and to civil war.

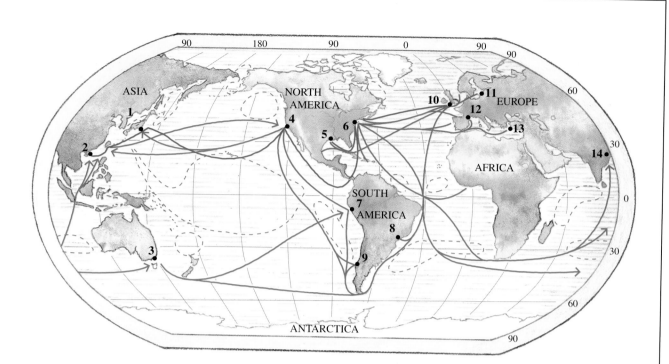

Figure 5 Nineteenth-Century World Trade Routes and Principal Seaports

World Trade Routes

——————— Clipper Ship Routes

——————— Steamship Routes

- - - - - Principal Whaling Grounds

Principal Commercial Cities

1. Tokyo
2. Canton/Hong Kong
3. Sydney
4. San Francisco
5. New Orleans
6. New York City
7. Lima/Callao
8. Rio de Janeiro
9. Valparaiso
10. Liverpool
11. St. Petersburg
12. Marseilles
13. Smyrna
14. Calcutta

(Dennis O'Brien map)

CHAPTER 9

Modern Technology, Modern Warfare, and the Troubled Course of American Maritime and Naval Enterprise

THE WAR THAT convulsed the United States between 1861 and 1865 looms large in the history of American maritime enterprise. Some historians have seen the American Civil War as totally decisive in its maritime impact, arguing that the ocean carrying trade of the United States was prostrated by war. As Robert Albion has stated, the steam-propelled commerce raiders of the Confederacy "dealt Yankee shipping such a deadly blow that it failed to recover until World War I, a half a century later." An internal conflict in its origins and much of its land-based military aspects, the war nonetheless produced worldwide disruption so far as maritime interests were concerned. No part of America's maritime industries was untouched by the war, and many of them were wholly transformed, temporarily or permanently: high-seas shipping, coastal transportation under sail and steam, shipbuilding in wood and iron, whaling and fishing, canal and river operations—all of these felt the impact of war.

Evidence to support the argument for such a distinctively war-produced transformation and setback to America's maritime fortunes is abundant, even to the point of creating the impression that *without* the war the latter half of the nineteenth century would have been both fundamentally different and vastly better for maritime America. For instance, in 1860 American vessels comprised

Detail of the CSS Nashville *burning the clipper ship* Harvey Birch. *(Courtesy Peabody Essex Museum, Salem, Massachusetts)*

more than 70 percent of all tonnage entering and clearing ports in the United States; by 1865 the figure had dropped to 46 percent. Of the total value of cargoes in American foreign trade, 66 percent traveled in American vessels just before the outbreak of war; by war's end the American participation had dropped to under 28 percent. Such a dramatic shift has led one historian to describe its result as "the greatest single decline in American maritime history." Moreover, the abrupt wartime loss of cargoes transported in American-flag vessels was not just a temporary dislocation; the decline would persist, with only brief periods of revival until, by century's end, less than 10 percent of the nation's foreign trade still traveled in American-flag vessels. Moreover, the United States Navy was essentially transformed by the war experience, and for the navy this fundamental change would be permanent, notwithstanding all the efforts in the postwar era to back away from the full implications of that war-impelled replacement of wood by iron and of sail by steam.

The impact of the war, then, is undeniable. What is not so clear, however, is how much change in the maritime industries and the navy was caused by the war, and how much of this change was simply accelerated by the war. Evidence to support the latter argument also is abundant; moreover, such evidence is convincing: in the "Golden Age" of maritime America there already were troubling developments that, war or not, indicated future difficulties for much of maritime America. These problems are clear enough in hindsight; but how aware were contemporaries of the situation? And—to the extent they were aware—what did, and could, they do to address these problems?

Naval Obligations and Efforts in the Prewar Decades

A formidable power in the era of fighting sail, the United States Navy in the peacetime decades after 1815 had grown smaller, older, and increasingly less effective relative to European navies. To be sure, its peacetime duties were many and quite varied.

Protecting and promoting commercial interests and serving in support of national diplomatic policy spread United States naval vessels throughout the world's sea-lanes. Bringing piracy under control, suppressing the slave trade, supporting the expansion of commercial and diplomatic relations, playing a major role in scientific research and exploration, contributing to significant improvements in navigation–all of these activities demanded an American naval presence and often a vital contribution. Yet the peacetime American navy required fewer warships and a smaller complement of seamen and officers, most of whom continued in sail–both by serving on sailing vessels and by holding on to the distinctive traditions of the sailing age.

Protecting American merchantmen from the Barbary States corsairs was a pressing postwar concern, so by the end of 1815 a squadron under Stephen Decatur's command, followed later by a squadron commanded by William Bainbridge, aggressively attacked pirate vessels and their strongholds, to the point where American merchantmen in the Mediterranean became relatively safe in their pursuit of trade. Caribbean pirates were a more difficult group to subdue, since they were less centralized and well-organized than the Barbary pirates. Between 1818 and 1825 Caribbean pirates' attacks on American shipping were severe enough to bring on a flurry of naval activity in the early 1820s, coming to its peak with Commodore David Porter's fleet of seventeen vessels sent to the West Indies in 1823. In command of the little 100-ton *Sea Gull*, a former Connecticut river steamer and the first steam war vessel to serve actively in the navy, Porter led a successful effort that effectively suppressed West Indian piracy by 1825. While piracy briefly reappeared in the Mediterranean in 1827, and periodically surfaced along the coast of China or in the Malay Straits throughout this era, American naval force usually was sufficient to protect the ever-expanding activities of America's fleet of merchant ships.

Suppressing the seaborne slave trade to the United States, in accord with provisions of the 1807 Congressional act formally abolishing the right of American citizens to participate in that trade, was another matter. Here, for domestic political as well as foreign diplomatic reasons, the United States Navy's presence at best was modest in the international effort, led primarily by

After the U.S. admitted Texas as a state in 1845, friction arose with Mexico over Texas claims to territory extending west to the Rio Grande. When Mexico refused to sell the territory and fighting broke out along the Rio Grande, the U.S. declared war on Mexico. U.S. Army and Navy forces secured the Mexican state of California by early 1847, while other forces prepared to invade Mexico itself. Under command of Captain Matthew Calbraith Perry, the twenty-seven vessels of the navy's Home Squadron converged off Veracruz, on the east coast of Mexico, in March 1847. On 9 March 1847 the squadron conducted the navy's first large-scale amphibious operation, landing General Winfield Scott's U.S. Army forces, as depicted here. Two weeks later the squadron bombarded the defenses of Veracruz and captured the port. The squadron also extended a blockade along the entire Mexican east coast while Scott's army, landed just 150 miles from the Mexican capital, defeated the Mexican defenders and captured Mexico City in September. Mexico surrendered, and a treaty was ratified the following year, by which California, New Mexico, and west Texas became U.S. territory. Although the artist has depicted the Home Squadron's ships as classic large sailing vessels, they actually included several of the navy's newest side-wheel and screw-propelled auxiliary steamships. Lithograph by N. Currier, 1847. (M.S.M. 53.3940)

Great Britain's Royal Navy, to put an end to this commerce in humans. Part of the United States Navy's difficulty was that while slavers were designated as pirates by an 1820 Congressional Act, the legacy of many decades of British warships stopping American vessels and impressing their seamen resulted in the United States refusing to permit the Royal Navy to stop suspected slavers when sailing under the American flag. Correspondingly, American naval vessels were limited to examining only U.S. flagged vessels among those that were suspected slavers. For several decades, following the organization in 1817 of the American Colonization Society, the navy's role in African waters was primarily that of aiding the Society's efforts to resolve the problem of

American slavery and the slave trade by resettling freed American slaves in the newly created country of Liberia on Africa's west coast. After the collapse of that always-controversial project, the navy maintained a presence with a small African Squadron, but any large-scale American naval effort to deal with the trade—whether cooperating with the British or not—was seriously hindered by Southern congressional opposition and pro-Southern sentiment that persisted in a number of presidential administrations up to the outbreak of the Civil War.

Postwar reduction of the American naval force on the Great Lakes and Lake Champlain was enabled by the provisions of the 1817 Rush-Bagot

Matthew Calbraith Perry (1794-1858), the younger brother of Oliver Hazard Perry, entered the U.S. Navy in 1809. He was aboard the USS President when she attacked HMS Little Belt in 1811, served under Commodore John Rodgers during the War of 1812, and after the war combined navy service off Africa and in the Mediterranean, with merchant ship command and duty at the New York Navy Yard. In 1835 Perry was appointed supervisor of construction of the the navy's first steam frigate, USS Fulton II, launched in 1837, becoming a strong proponent of naval steam power. Known as a strict disciplinarian, though solicitous of his crews' health, Perry found his career briefly set back by the Somers affair, when his brother-in-law, Alexander Slidell MacKenzie, hanged several supposed mutineers aboard that navy training brig. After a two-year assignment in command of the Africa Squadron, patrolling for slavers and maintaining relations between African coastal nations, Perry was placed in command of the Home Squadron during the War with Mexico. The Home Squadron, the largest fleet yet assembled by the U.S. Navy, blockaded the east coast of Mexico during the war. After his experience in these waters, Perry became a vocal advocate of a canal across the Isthmus of Panama. Following the war, Perry was named general superintendent of mail steamers to oversee the construction of the Collins Line and Pacific Mail steamships authorized in the Mail Subsidy Acts of 1845 and 1847. Perry tried to avoid the political debates over the costs of these vessels and their suitability for conversion to naval warships. He had developed a strong interest in the U.S. position in the Pacific, and particularly in the potential of Japan as a trading partner and a coaling station for steamships operating between the U.S. and China. As commodore of the East Asia Squadron, Perry led the navy's diplomatic expedition to Japan, 1852-54, negotiating the Treaty of Kanagawa in March 1854. He died in 1858, not long after publication of his comprehensive Narrative of the Expedition, and before the attainment of his goals: the opening of trade with Japan in 1859 and inauguration of a transpacific steamship line via Japan by Perry's old merchant associate, William H. Aspinwall, in 1867. Perry appreciated the pictorial sense of the Japanese but, as this Japanese portrait of Perry demonstrates, they viewed this unwelcome American visitor in their terms, just as Perry saw them through his own perspectives on western civilization and American destiny in the Pacific. (Courtesy Library of Congress)

Agreement between the United States and Great Britain, so there was increasingly little need on these inland waters for major warships, let alone a squadron such as Oliver Hazard Perry had so successfully commanded on Lake Erie back in 1813. It was on the high seas and also along America's Atlantic, Gulf, and Pacific coastlines where the navy continued to support several squadrons; these served primarily to meet the occasional needs of diplomacy, scientific research and exploration, and trade.

With the suppression of the Barbary corsairs and with piracy in the Caribbean reasonably under control after 1825, the use of the navy became largely one of routine cruises. The brief war with Mexico between 1846 and 1848 did, however, produce a flurry of naval activity and an opportunity to gain

considerable experience under wartime conditions with some of the navy's early steamers. A naval squadron including a number of steam-powered gunboats and frigates under the command of Commodore Matthew C. Perry was essential to the remarkable success of General Winfield Scott's major military amphibious operation on the Mexican Gulf Coast at Veracruz early in March 1847. On the West Coast, Commodore John Sloat's Pacific Squadron of sailing warships was under orders from Secretary of the Navy George Bancroft to take control of San Francisco, which duly occurred during a bewildering period when Sloat's successor, Commodore Robert Stockton, cooperated with Captain John C. Frémont's forces in subduing Mexican opposition along the central California coast. Subsequently, Stockton's squadron mounted an effective coastal blockade, cutting off supplies and munitions from

Mexican forces, but not before contending with vigorous native California uprisings. Stockton's forces, also with some difficulty, disputed with General Stephen Kearney, whose military successes in California were complicated no end by his ongoing struggle with Frémont for official American control of that Pacific Coast.

By mid-century the growing significance of machine technology for the navy was emphatically demonstrated by the achievement of Commodore Matthew C. Perry's steam-powered naval squadron of 1852-54, through bringing Japan to abandon its centuries-long practice of political isolation and of extreme restrictions on economic interchange with the rest of the world. With the acquisition of California, the United States, in this age of "manifest destiny," determined to expand its role as a major power in the Pacific Ocean. American interests in promoting and greatly expanding its Pacific trade beyond that with China, compounded by increasing conflicts with Japan's exclusionary policy, brought President Millard Fillmore's administration to the point of demanding a formal diplomatic resolution of these concerns. Perry's intimidating presence and considerable diplomatic skill combined in producing the March 1854 Treaty of Kanagawa, which provided for the long-sought protection of Americans in Japanese territory and an initial opening of Japanese ports to American shipping. Following up on Perry's initial achievement, the navy in 1855 sent its screw-propelled steamer *San Jacinto* on a long and productive journey, by way of South Africa, the Indian Ocean, and the Straits of Malacca, to Bangkok; here, Commissioner Townshend Harris joined the vessel for transportation to Hong Kong, China, and finally to Shimoda, Japan, where in late August, 1856, he began his duties as America's first consul general and minister to that country.

Steam Power and the Navy

Steam for the United States Navy had been introduced as early as 1814, with the launch of Robert Fulton's floating steam battery *Demologos*, but this vessel was an experiment that produced no immediate consequence. Despite the large number of civilian riverboats, tugs, and even small coastal steamships in service by the 1820s,

not until 1837 did the navy have its first major steamship, *Fulton II*. Thereafter, steam slowly and cautiously intruded into the naval service, with such early and fairly large seagoing steamers as the USS *Mississippi* and *Missouri*, both launched in 1841. The great expense for fuel and the chronic unreliability of marine steam machinery required full sail power for these early naval steamers. Advances in steam technology and metal fabrication would not produce the desired efficiencies and reliability for steam power until the final years of the nineteenth century, so that throughout the period from 1815 to 1865, and for many years afterwards, seagoing warships were customarily equipped with full sailing rig and a full crew of sailors capable of handling the vessel under sail power alone.

Perhaps the most novel of the early steamships was the *Princeton*, a wooden-hulled, screw-propelled warship designed and developed by the Swedish inventor John Ericsson, together with the navy's Commodore Robert F. Stockton, and launched in 1843. Reasonably economical in operation, if not especially fast, she in many ways represented a significant advance in naval technology. Unfortunately, the *Princeton* also was known as the warship on which a Stockton-designed experimental cannon exploded in 1844, killing several high government officials and invited dignitaries, including the American secretary of state and secretary of the navy; by sheer chance President John Tyler was below decks at the time, or he would likely have been still another celebrated casualty.

Men of sail had little enthusiasm for steam. Their attitudes toward naval steam were usually suspicious and derisory, if not actively hostile throughout the period from 1815 to 1865. That celebrated naval hero from the sailing era, Stephen Decatur, was quoted as glumly remarking: "Yes, it is the end of our business. Hereafter any man who can boil a tea-kettle will be as good as the best of us." During the Van Buren administration, Secretary of the Navy James Kirke Paulding complained to a friend that he was "steamed to death" by those who were pressuring him to convert the navy to steam. Acknowledging that he would be foolish to resist what by this time was an emerging majority sentiment in favor of steam power, Secretary Paulding conceded that "I am willing, therefore, to go with the wind, though I don't mean to carry full sail, and keep the steam enthusiasts quiet by

Late in 1851, the secretary of the navy authorized Captain Matthew C. Perry's proposed diplomatic expedition to Japan, to establish relations with the island empire that had resisted all but the most limited contact with Europeans. As commodore of the East Asia Squadron, Perry led eleven steam and sailing vessels to China, and then proceeded to Okinawa, and on to Edo (Tokyo) Bay. Arriving to confront the Japanese in July 1853, Perry delivered a letter from President Fillmore seeking peaceful relations, then departed with the understanding that he would return in the spring. During this unsettled period in Japanese history, officials of the empire sought to avoid contact. For his part, Perry returned to China by way of Okinawa, where he forced trade concessions and arrangements for a coaling station. In February 1854 Perry arrived back in Edo Bay, and by March nine American warships were anchored off Yokohama. On 8 March 1854, as shown here, Perry came ashore with an armed guard of 500 men to open negotiations with the Japanese. Although he hoped to obtain trade provisions similar to the Treaty of Wanghia that opened Chinese ports to trade, Perry settled for the Treaty of Kanagawa, which acknowledged the mutual peaceful interests of the two nations, opened two ports to American ships or shipwrecked sailors seeking refuge, authorized American purchase of coal in Japan, and arranged for a U.S. consul to reside in Japan. Signed on 31 March 1854, it marked the opening of diplomatic relations between the United States and Japan. After Perry's death, negotiations in 1858 opened Yokohama, Nagasaki, and Hakodate to American trade, beginning in 1859. Lithograph by expedition artist Peter B.W. Heine, published by Sarony & Co. (M.S.M. 63.350)

warily administering to the humor of the times; but," he concluded emphatically, "I will never consent to let our old ships perish, and transform our Navy into a fleet of sea monsters."

Naturally, proponents of steam dismissed such attitudes as pathetic whimperings of entrenched, if baffled, reactionaries, able only to express—in the words of naval engineer Benjamin Isherwood—"the mouldy prejudices

of an effete regime." Yet there were leaders of the sailing age, such as David Porter in commanding the little steamer *Sea Gull* in the Caribbean, who were involved directly, if at times uncertainly, with early steam power in the navy. Stephen Decatur, in fact, was actively engaged with steam power at its outset, through his connection with Robert Fulton's *Demologos*—whose first naval commander, moreover, was David Porter. The next generation of sailing officers, notably Matthew

Calbraith Perry, would make a more sustained and positive contribution to early naval steam. Perry supervised the construction and then became commander of the navy's first large seagoing steamer, *Fulton II*. In the later 1840s he supervised the construction of the Collins Line steamers in New York City, and in the early 1850s commanded the naval squadron of steamships that opened up Japan to American and European power and influence.

Early naval and maritime steam propulsion developments frequently were wracked by intense rivalries both within the government services (especially after the 1842 creation of the U.S. Navy's Engineer Corps) and among self-acknowledged civilian experts. The United States Treasury's Revenue Marine, even more than the navy, paid a heavy price; all too often "practical seamen" had to operate seriously flawed steamers that had resulted from the impractical and visionary enthusiasms of such self-promoting "authorities" in engineering. Similar to other areas of waterborne transportation in America, the navy contended with marine engineering that was still in its infancy, whether as a stage in technological development or as a profession.

The first commissioned naval engineers, such as Charles Haswell, Daniel Martin, and Benjamin Isherwood, were civilians both by background and by temperament. They clashed among themselves but even more with the traditional naval men of command, the officers of the line who had been born and bred in sail. There was heated public argument and political maneuvering between naval engineers, such as Benjamin Isherwood, and professional civilians, notably the Swedish inventor and engineer John Ericsson. And in this age when one could be a layman and still participate importantly in technological developments, there were the zealous amateurs. Noteworthy among them was the New York patent attorney

John Ericsson (1803-1889), the son of a Swedish mine owner, demonstrated a passionate talent for engineering projects even as a child. He was trained as a mechanical engineer and served as a topographical engineer in the Swedish Army before moving to London in 1826. There he did pioneering work on steam-engine improvements, began developing plans for a hot-air "caloric" engine, and perfected the concept of the screw propeller. After building successful propeller-driven vessels in Great Britain, Ericsson came to New York in 1839 to design a screw-propelled warship for the U.S. Navy. Several merchant vessels on the Great Lakes were built with Ericsson-pattern propellers before the USS Princeton *was launched in 1844. During the ship's trials, a gun designed by Captain Robert Stockton exploded, killing the secretary of state and secretary of the navy, for which Ericsson was unfairly blamed. Embittered, Ericsson returned to his caloric-engine project, although his prototype vessel, the* Ericsson *of 1851, was not a success. During the 1850s Ericsson also designed an armored warship with revolving turret, which he proposed to the French government. The vessel was not built, but when war broke out in America and the Navy Department sought designs to counter Confederate ironclad ships, businessman C.S. Bushnell presented Ericsson's ironclad concept. As one of three prototypes, the navy's Ironclad Board selected Ericsson's design. Under Ericsson's direction, the ship with its many entirely new features was designed and built in just 100 days and launched in January 1862 as the* Monitor. *The small ship proved itself against the much larger ironclad CSS* Virginia *in a battle that clearly marked the end of the wooden warship. After receiving the thanks of the U.S. Congress, Ericsson spent the rest of the war developing the fleet of Union monitors and designing other military improvements. Although he never perfected his caloric engine, and his 1870s plans for a naval torpedo boat were too advanced for the navy of the time, Ericsson's screw propeller and revolving gun turret have been basic elements of warship design for more than a century. A brilliant, temperamental designer and independent thinker, John Ericsson was among the most influential maritime figures of the nineteenth century. Photo by Charles Fredricks, 1861. (M.S.M. 97.155.3)*

Edward N. Dickerson, whose business and political influence permitted the translations of his technological visions into the actuality of engines, boilers, propellers–even entire steamships–all produced to prove his pet theories about steam technology, no matter how impractical or ill-informed they might be.

Thus, the reality of American technological development in maritime steam was not simply a matter of abstract theories and design problems, nor was it confined to the navy. It also involved personalities and institutions whose interplay embraced the navy, the engineering professions, the political establishment within and outside the service, and the economic and social environment–the "culture"–in which such development took place and to which that development had to accommodate.

By the 1840s several oceangoing steam warships were in the naval service, although these vessels, such as the *Mississippi* and the *Missouri*, were wooden-hulled paddle wheelers whose speed and old-fashioned armament was modest if not marginal for a warship, especially in light of European developments in naval technology. Screw propulsion for warships, promoted in the United States by John Ericsson, Commodore Stockton, and others, was slow to be accepted either in the U.S. Navy or in its merchant marine, notwithstanding dramatic demonstrations abroad of the wholly submerged screw's superiority over the cumbersome and exposed paddle wheel as an effective propelling mechanism for oceangoing vessels. In periods of economic austerity, especially after the Panic of 1837 and the long depression that ensued, Congressional and naval leaders largely agreed that capital ships–the modern equivalent of the old ships of the line–were not needed for a nation that saw itself removed from (indeed, superior to) the ongoing imperial, ideological, and dynastic conflicts that gripped European nations and occasionally brought them to open warfare. Europeans might forever be jockeying for positions of naval strength; the United States, many Americans urged, should not be drawn into their conflicts, so there was no need for a large and expensive American navy and naval establishment.

Consequently, when in the early 1840s tensions arose with Great Britain over the Canadian boundary and rival claims to the Oregon Territory, the American response was not to build up its navy in anticipation of any possible battle at sea against the world's most powerful naval force. Instead, Congress and the Navy Department joined to develop a program whereby the federal government would subsidize the construction and operation of civilian steamships that were designed to be easily and quickly converted to military use, even as full-fledged warships. Of the various oceangoing steamships and steamer lines so subsidized in the 1840s and 1850s, certainly the most impressive was the ill-fated steamship venture of Edward Knight Collins.

The failure of the Collins Line has been attributed to a variety of factors, not the least being the wildly inflated expectations of its promoter and his financial backers, if not their managerial ineptitude as well. Yet part of the problem was a result of the United States Navy's insistence that Collins's steamships be designed and constructed as commerce destroyers. An unarmored wooden-hulled paddle-wheeler certainly would be unsatisfactory for battling modern warships at sea, as many Congressmen realized and argued throughout this period. However, there still might be compelling justification for public support of such steamships if they were financed, built, owned, and operated primarily by civilians. These and other such government-subsidized steamships, as the "small-navy" proponents in and out of Congress insisted, would be an inexpensive way of assuring that America had the ability to respond to any naval or maritime aggression from abroad. American merchant steamships that could carry a few cannon and have the ability to run down any prey or outrun any predator appeared to be an attractive alternative to committing far more public funds in order to build steam-powered warships comparable to those beginning to appear abroad.

Thus, as a striking example of interaction between civilian and military sectors in peacetime, the U.S. Navy played an active part in supervising the design and construction of the Collins Line steamers. Such naval officers as Gustavus V. Fox (who later became assistant secretary of the Union Navy) were formally designated as naval representatives on the Collins liners once they went into service. The result of such active federal government participation was higher costs of construction and considerable delays as Collins sought to satisfy the stipulations of government inspectors, in exchange for the public funds that subsidized both construction and operation of his steamships. By the end of this era the outcome for American interests was dismal. There had been little if any real savings for the government, and the navy remained weak, underpowered, and inadequate for protecting American merchantmen and other American maritime enterprise on the high seas when confronted by a major foreign naval power. Collins, despite all he could do to make a profit (including a very secret revenue-sharing and price-fixing agreement with the Cunard Line) had failed in his ambitious venture. The United States had ended up once again dependent on the British for delivering the transatlantic mail. Steamship subsidies, both in theory and practice, were under heavy attack from many quarters by the end of the 1850s, in great measure because of the Collins Line experience.

Naval Authority and Individual Rights in an Era of Reform

The world of sail, both mercantile and naval, was authoritarian. It relied on a strict system of discipline, a sharply defined social structure aboard ship in which everyone was to know his place as well as his duties. The vessel's commander possessed absolute authority when at sea; harsh and arbitrary treatment of the men– whether rational or not–could be found on merchantmen as well as on warships. Richard Henry Dana, Jr., in his *Two Years Before the Mast* (1840) provided a memorable example of unbridled tyranny on the small brig *Pilgrim*, bound for California in 1835. The brig's commander, Frank Thompson, flogged a seaman not for disobedience or for shirking duty, but simply for questioning an order, for interfering in the captain's enjoyment of his absolute power. Dana recorded the captain's exultant cry: "'If you want to know what I flog you for, I'll tell you. It's because I like to do it! . . . It suits me! That's what I do it for!'" The culprit submitted to the flogging until the pain

became unendurable; then he cried out, "'O Jesus Christ! O Jesus Christ!'" To this, Dana tells us, the captain responded: "'Don't call on Jesus Christ! *He can't help you. Call on Frank Thompson!* He's the man! He can help you! Jesus Christ can't help you now!'"

Naval regulations specified, in general, how a warship commander might choose to exercise his authority and to some extent provided a system of limitations on that authority; yet arbitrary policy, irrational behavior, and brutality were common enough on American naval vessels. Herman Melville, writing from his own experience when sailing on an American frigate from Hawaii back to the United States, painted a grim picture of such a rigid, restrictive, and frequently irrational shipboard society in *White Jacket* (1850), his detailed and impassioned critique of life in the sailing navy of the late 1830s.

The United States Congress, to some extent influenced by the works of Dana and Melville, sought to remedy the more glaring abuses in the navy by abolishing in 1850 the centuries-old punishment of flogging and, in 1862, by eliminating the customary grog ration. Both of these efforts to alleviate the conditions of naval seamen reflected a more general American urge for social betterment, to the extent that this entire period from the 1820s well into the 1850s comprised a distinctive era of American reform. Thus, the specific efforts towards naval reform may be seen as part of the American crusade for temperance, if not outright prohibition, in using alcoholic beverages and for seeking other and presumably more salutary forms of discipline than corporal punishment.

Another aspect of naval reform addressed the training of career naval officers. The United States Navy traditionally had followed a practice of individual appointments as a midshipman largely through an unsystematic selection of candidates based on personal favoritism, family influence, and political patronage, similar to the practice in Europe. In the swiftly democratizing America of the early nineteenth century, a strong resistance to creating an entrenched professional and social elite within the navy had resulted in the failure to create a naval academy similar to the Army's West Point. However, the issue of naval officer training was unexpectedly and dra-

Like plantation slaves, U.S. Navy sailors were disciplined with the lash. Used for even minor infractions of shipboard regulations, flogging wounded, disfigured, and humiliated its victims. In his fictionalized account of naval life, based on his experiences and published as White Jacket *in 1850, Herman Melville wrote: "You see a human being, stripped like a slave; scourged worse than a hound. And for what? For things not essentially criminal, but only made so by arbitrary laws." Some navy officers claimed that only through fear of the cat 'o nine tails used for floggings could the undisciplined men who joined the navy be controlled. But in the spirit of humanitarian reform that moved temperance supporters and those who pressed for the abolition of slavery, Congress abolished flogging aboard navy ships in 1850. Twelve years later, in the spirit of temperance, Congress abolished a naval tradition far dearer to navy sailors: the grog ration. William H. Myers depicted this flogging aboard the USS* Cyane, *ca. 1842. With all hands on deck to witness punishment, the victim has his feet bound to a hatch grating and his hands tied to the rail where the crew's hammocks are stowed. (Courtesy Naval Historical Center, Washington, D.C.)*

matically resolved early in the 1840s with the infamous *Somers* affair, when an experiment in officer training at sea degenerated into charges of mutiny, summary executions, and political recriminations.

With the training cruise idea discredited, and with the advent of steam power in the navy requiring greater technical knowledge among officers, the United States Navy now could move forward in 1845 to establish a real naval academy, which Congress authorized for construction at Annapolis, Maryland. By the 1850s the academy evolved into a four-year academic program, and appointments were made by Congressional district, as at West Point.

Naval Science and Exploration Before the War

While the United States Navy in 1860 was not prepared for waging war on modern terms, individual naval personnel for several decades previous had been in the forefront of scientific and technological investigations. The ever-contentious and controversial Matthew Fontaine Maury, beginning in the 1840s, for many years drew on a vast array of logbooks and reports from vessels to make a contribution of world-wide importance. Justly recognized as "Pathfinder of the Seas," Maury,

The *Somers* Affair

The USS *Somers* was a notably fast sailing brig of war, chosen in early 1842 for an experiment designed to make more systematic and effective the training of young naval officer cadets. The *Somers* embarked on her extended training cruise under the command of the socially and politically well-connected Captain Alexander Slidell Mackenzie. Brother-in-law of Matthew C. Perry, Mackenzie was a seasoned career officer whose parallel career as an author had brought him favorable notice—and some measure of jealous resentment—within the service and without. His heavily sparred, 100-foot vessel was greatly overcrowded, with seventy-four teenage apprentice cadets added to the regular crew of forty-seven. The *Somers* crossed the Atlantic, carrying dispatches for the frigate *Vandalia* on patrol against slavers along the west African coast. Failing to find the frigate, Captain Mackenzie headed back across the Atlantic. During the passage, in late November 1842, Captain Mackenzie learned that for some mysterious reason a mutiny was about to take place. Confronting the three men whom he considered ringleaders of a plot to seize the brig and turn her into a pirate vessel, Captain Mackenzie quickly placed them in irons. Then, for several days he debated with himself and with his executive officer, Lieutenant Guert Gansevoort, about how to handle what looked like a growing crisis among the *Somers*'s young and largely inexperienced crew. Mackenzie's solution, faithfully seconded by Gansevoort and all the other officers, was to hang the culprits rather than run the risk of waiting for officially sanctioned courts martial ashore. Accordingly, on 2 December 1842 the three men were put to death and the *Somers* thereafter quietly completed the last few days of her cruise.

Mackenzie's preemptive act, however justified in his own eyes, drew a storm of criticism once the *Somers* reached New York City. Killing three men in peacetime for an act that, even if actually planned, had never taken place was controversial enough; that the instigator of the plot had been Midshipman Philip Spencer, the son of the current secretary of war and former New York senator, created an explosive situation. Endless and wildly opinionated newspaper reports fed an avid reading public, while maritime and naval experts divided sharply over the rights and wrongs of Mackenzie's act. R.H. Dana, Jr., the famed champion of seamen's rights, staunchly defended the *Somers*' captain, while James Fenimore Cooper, naval historian and literary giant, bitterly denounced him.

In due course, Mackenzie was exonerated by a naval board of inquiry and subsequently acquitted (although not "honorably" so) by a naval court martial. Thereafter he remained in the navy until his death during the War with Mexico, but both Mackenzie and the *Somers* would forever be tainted by the episode. And in 1891 Herman Melville (presumably with inside knowledge derived years earlier from his cousin, Guert Gansevoort) drew on Mackenzie's dilemmas as the *Somers*'s commander in the process of composing his final work, *Billy Budd*.

In response to public interest in the **Somers** *affair, N. Currier published this lithograph of the 100-foot brig under sail, with the bodies of two of the suspected mutineers hanging from the mainyard. After this tragic end to her maiden voyage, the* **Somers** *served in the Gulf of Mexico. In December 1846, while engaged in blockading the Mexican coast during the Mexican War, the* **Somers** *capsized and sank during a squall. Her commander, Lieutenant Raphael Semmes, survived to play a prominent role during the Civil War. (M.S.M. 83.89.13)*

through his meticulous studies of seasonal and regional winds, currents, temperatures, and barometric pressures throughout the world's oceans, produced accurate and detailed charts that resulted in great savings of time over long-distance voyages. Maury was able to chart the best areas for whaling and the best routes for sailing vessels at any given time of the year. His *Sailing Directions*, begun in 1848 as a modest pamphlet, swelled into a heavy tome within a few years and became the bible for seafarers. Use of his charts and data permitted a significant decrease in sailing time between New York and California—a savings, it has been estimated, of forty-seven days, and one that translated into millions of dollars annually in reduced transportation costs.

Other American naval officers also made important advances to scientific and technological knowledge. As a leading authority on navigation, Alexander Dallas Bache, from 1843 on, revived and expanded the work of the U.S. Coast and Geodetic Survey, authorized by Congress in 1807, which both produced accurate navigational charts and provided scientific training for a number of young American naval officers. A complementary contribution was that of Charles Henry Davis, through guiding the publication of the annual *Nautical Almanac*, so essential for celestial navigation calculations by mariners. John Mercer Brooke was an inventor and explorer of note, and would become chief of ordnance and hydrography for the Confederate States Navy. As major contributors to developments in naval ordnance, both Brooke and John Dahlgren led American efforts to replace the navy's smoothbore cannon, which fired spherical solid shot, with rifled cannon capable of firing conical explosive shells far more accurately and

Matthew F. Maury (1806-1873), a Virginian, demonstrated his mathematical abilities even before his appointment as a U.S. Navy midshipman in 1825. As sailing master of the USS Falmouth in 1831, he made a systematic study of sailing routes around Cape Horn and plotted a course that saved considerable time on the passage. A progressive and outspoken naval officer, Maury encouraged the development of naval steam power, more professional naval education, more accurate and powerful naval armaments, and more scientific navigation aboard naval vessels. After a leg injury, Maury was appointed superintendent of the navy's Depot of Charts and Instruments, which maintained and issued the chronometers, navigational instruments, and charts used on naval vessels. Intrigued by the possibility of identifying "paths" through the seas, Maury obtained navy approval in 1842 to develop a new type of chart from the data in navy logbooks filed at the depot. For five years Maury employed his staff in analyzing navy logbooks for navigational information and compiling it for publication in chart form. Between 1847 and 1860, Maury issued six series of wind and current charts. They included plots of the course information derived from logbooks, charts of Atlantic and Indian Ocean trade winds, pilot charts that analyzed wind direction frequency, Atlantic Ocean temperature charts, storm and rain charts, and charts of the world's whale populations for the use of whalemen. Within a few years, mariners found these charts so useful in speeding their passages that they willingly compiled and submitted abstract logs of their voyages to Maury's office for use in updating his charts. Maury published his theory of oceanography, The Physical Geography of the Sea, in 1855. Remaining loyal to his native state, Maury resigned from the U.S. Navy in April 1861. After working to develop electric "torpedoes" (undersea mines) for the Confederacy, Maury went to Europe on diplomatic business and was in Cuba at the war's end. He did not return to the U.S. until 1868, a few years before his death. His charts were reissued by the navy's Oceanographic Office in 1883, and they form the basis for the pilot charts issued today. This photograph of Lieutenant Maury was hung in the East India Marine Society of Salem, Massachusetts, upon his election as a member in 1859. He was expelled and it was removed from the wall two years later when he joined the Confederacy. (Courtesy Peabody Essex Museum, Salem, Massachusetts)

at a far greater distance. Such guns would shift naval tactics away from reliance on the many-gun broadside toward ships armed with fewer cannon per side, and usually one or more large, accurate pivoting guns on deck. Brooke's and Dahlgren's work would eventually result in the navy's adoption of modern, breech-loading cannon.

Part of the navy's role in connecting America with the wider world was in promoting exploration. Charles Wilkes, another controversial naval scientist, writer, and career officer, achieved distinction (and notoriety) by commanding the elaborate Great Exploring Expedition of 1838-42, in which a squadron of six sailing vessels ranged over the Pacific Ocean from Antarctica to Fiji and Hawaii, to the west coast of North America as far as Puget Sound. With the overt intention of furthering American commercial interests in the Pacific, the expedition collected flora and fauna, documented aspects of the native cultures, and concluded commercial treaties with a number of tribal groups.

As a relatively new field for systematic research, marine engineering began to move beyond the level of intuitive tinkering through the work of such career American naval engineers as Benjamin Isherwood. In the later 1850s and early 1860s Isherwood and several associates conducted a series of careful experiments on steam machinery and naval and civilian steam vessels. He then published the results of these exhaustively detailed investigations as important, if controversial, contributions to the ongoing debate about more economical uses of steam.

The navy also relied increasingly on modern technology for the more traditional assignments in support of diplomatic missions and foreign trade emissaries, notably assisting American trading efforts in Southeast Asia by helping to suppress the piracy that so frequently preyed on merchantmen. Either on special missions to foreign countries or as a part their normal duties while on cruise, American naval officers routinely examined scientific and technological developments abroad, so that the United States Navy, while relatively small in size, was deeply involved in both collecting and disseminating up-to-date information and techniques as America increasingly extended its

world-wide presence and employed its seagoing capabilities to enhance its connections abroad.

Navigating Civil War

Although sectional animosity had increased throughout the 1850s, the U.S. Navy was not prepared for secession and the possibility of war. In March 1861, the navy suddenly was in disarray. Many officers, such as John Brooke and Matthew Maury, had resigned their commissions and moved to join the newly-formed Confederate States Navy. The major naval base at Norfolk, Virginia, appeared to be so vulnerable to a Confederate takeover that the Union reluctantly abandoned the base, after destroying as much as possible of vessels and equipment. Among those naval vessels burned to the waterline and scuttled was the new wooden-hulled steam frigate *Merrimack*. From such straits the navy would rise to play a prominent role in the Union effort to reunite the nation. For its part, the Confederate States Navy would develop a strategy to promote Southern independence and access to the maritime world.

Confederate Naval Strategy and the Impact on Anglo-American Diplomacy

The eleven seceding states that ultimately formed the Confederate States of America had no navy and virtually no merchant marine, but they did claim 3,350 miles of Atlantic and Gulf coastlines, including nearly 200 navigable estuaries and bays and ten large seaports, as well as thousands of miles of navigable rivers. In light of the overwhelming Union advantage in steam warships assigned to blockade the Southern coast immediately after the war began, the Confederacy was faced with the pressing and perplexing issue of what to do in response that would be not just effective but possibly decisive in affecting the course of the war. There was no hope of creating a merchant marine essentially from scratch, nor was the building of a major high-seas Confederate naval fleet a possibility, and without such a naval

Charles Wilkes (1798-1877) had a long and controversial career as an officer in the U.S. Navy. The son of a New York businessman, Wilkes was well educated before going to sea at age seventeen and obtaining an appointment as a midshipman in the navy three years later. After cruises in the Mediterranean and Pacific, Wilkes was promoted to lieutenant in 1826, conducted coast survey work, and was named head of the Depot of Charts and Instruments in 1833. After further survey work, Lieutenant Wilkes was chosen to command the long-planned U.S. Exploring Expedition, 1838-42. Wilkes led his flotilla of six ships through the South Atlantic and around the Pacific, from Antarctica to the Northwest Coast, taking surveys, collecting specimens, and observing the potential for American commercial relations in the Pacific. This important peacetime naval operation established the U.S. as a contributor to world scientific endeavors, and it increased the nation's understanding of both naval and natural science. Although his scientific work was praised, Wilkes was court martialled and reprimanded for harsh treatment of his men. Between 1843 and 1861 Wilkes served ashore, preparing the published reports of the expedition, and was promoted to the rank of captain in 1855. Early in 1861, when the USS Merrimack was scuttled to avoid capture by the Confederacy before Wilkes could take command, he was assigned to bring the USS San Jacinto back from the African Station. Off Cuba, Wilkes heard that Confederate emissaries James Mason and John Slidell would leave Havana for Europe on the British mail steamer Trent. Using a liberal interpretation of the international law permitting seizure of wartime dispatches from a neutral vessel, Wilkes seized Mason and Slidell themselves. Initially hailed throughout the North for his bold action in thwarting Confederate diplomacy, he was soon after condemned for his zeal when British authorities protested and hinted at the possibility of war. Mason and Slidell were released, and Wilkes was placed in command of a river flotilla. Promoted to rear admiral and given command of a West India squadron, Wilkes violated local neutrality laws in his unsuccessful attempts to capture blockade runners, and he was placed on the retired list in June 1863. As a result of his ongoing dispute with the Navy Department, a court martial in 1864 found Wilkes guilty of insubordination, disobedience, and disrespect, and he was suspended from the navy for a year. Charles Wilkes was finally commissioned admiral on the retired list in 1866. Wilkes was photographed in Matthew Brady's studio. (M.S.M. 97.155.2)

force there was little chance of breaking the Union Navy's blockade and opening the sea-lanes to Confederate commerce and navigation. Yet there remained a reasonable prospect of disrupting the Union naval and maritime strategy, even to the point of forcing the war to a conclusion that would favor the Confederate States of America.

Named Confederate secretary of the navy shortly after the Confederacy established its government in February 1861, Stephen Mallory drew on his years of federal government naval supervision to provide the guiding spirit as well as the managing hand of the Confederate naval effort. The son of a

Connecticut shipmaster, Mallory had grown up in Key West, Florida, where the volume of salvage cases made him an expert on maritime law. As a U.S. senator during the 1850s Mallory had advocated naval reforms, and he brought a progressive outlook to naval matters, despite a distressing shortage of iron and other materials of war in the South. Aware of European experiments with armored vessels and with the ancient concept of the ram ship, Mallory in June 1861 inaugurated the Confederacy's emphasis on ironclad rams with the project to resurrect the hulk of the USS *Merrimack* as the CSS *Virginia*, sheathed with railroad iron and sporting an iron ram on her bow capable of sinking a warship. Mallory also encouraged the development of "torpedoes"–floating explosives more recently called mines–and of submarine warships as defensive measures in Southern harbors and rivers. Mallory pushed forward the construction or conversion of armored vessels to defend the western rivers as well. Indeed, the CSS *Manassas*, a converted tug with a turtle-like shell of iron commissioned at New Orleans in the summer of 1861, was the first armored vessel launched in the Americas.

Turning to a traditional American policy of improvisation and commerce raiding in wartime, the Confederacy first issued letters of marque to a small number of Confederate privateers–the last time such vessels were licensed in America–while building or purchasing a few powerful steam-propelled vessels to serve as commerce raiders. If successful, the thinking went, these warships would so seriously disrupt the Union's foreign trade that war would become too expensive to continue. By destroying enough Northern merchant vessels the Confederate commerce raiders could force a diversion of Union warships from their blockading duties in order to search for the Confederate cruisers on the high seas. This, in turn, would assist the blockade-running efforts of the Confederacy so that cotton could be carried to European markets and earn revenues sufficient to pay for the Confederate war effort. In addition, with the forced relaxation of Union blockading efforts, munitions and medicines could be carried back to Southern ports to relieve the increasingly short supply of these vital items in the beleaguered South. Such a logical strategy, however, was not so easily accomplished.

Confederate efforts to secure the South's survival as a separate nation depended on gaining favorable material and political support in Europe, especially by the British and French governments. Material support for the Confederate navy was sought in the form of British-built and largely British-manned warships; here, the Confederates had considerable success, although they failed to obtain armored seagoing ram steamships that could effectively break the Union blockade. During 1861, 90 percent of English and Confederate blockade runners successfully evaded capture, leading Southern diplomats to label the Union effort a "paper blockade." Since by European diplomatic convention–and by U.S. assertion during the period of neutral trade sixty years earlier–a blockade must be effective to

be legal, the South sought to discredit the effort in order to obtain British support in maintaining trade.

The most effective blockade runners were rakish iron-hulled side-wheel steamships similar to those used for British coastal service. Fast and hard to spot from the water, they congregated at Bermuda, Nassau, or Havana, then made a run for the coast, seeking to get into shallow water and then into port before being detected. It has been calculated that, along the Atlantic coast, blockade runners had an 84 percent success rate through the war. Perhaps the record belongs to the steamer *Syren*, which made thirty-three passages through the blockade; an average vessel made four. But the profits could be immense for just one trip. A vessel capable of carrying 1,000 bales of cotton could net $250,000 from a successful voyage. To prevent profiteering in luxury goods, the Confederacy eventually regulated the quantities of essential supplies that blockade runners were required to deliver, and some Confederate states, such as North Carolina, actually invested in blockade runners. While such daring efforts maintained a trickle of supplies for the Confederacy, the trade to Southern ports was minuscule compared to what it had been before the war.

Although British merchants were happy to profit by sending their vessels through the blockade, efforts to bring either the British or French governments into the war on the side of the Confederacy failed, as did the more likely possibility of gaining formal diplomatic recognition– and thus a measure of international legal standing–from these major European powers. Perhaps the closest Confederate agents came to influencing British policy was indirectly as a consequence of U.S. Navy action. In November 1861 the Confederate diplomats to Britain and France, James Mason and John Slidell, ran the blockade to take passage on a British mail steamer at Havana. Aboard the USS *San Jacinto*, Captain Charles Wilkes determined to capture the two Confederate agents, making a liberal interpretation of international maritime law to equate the men themselves with the diplomatic dispatches they were carrying. Since enemy dispatches could be seized from a neutral vessel in time of war, Wilkes intercepted the British steamer *Trent* and forcibly removed Mason and Slidell, unfortunately leaving their dispatches on board. Until the Lincoln administration backed down and

The CSS Atlanta *represents the preferred form for Confederate ironclad rams. Like the prototype CSS Virginia, the* Atlanta *was built on the hull of an existing vessel: the blockade-runner* Fingal, *built in Scotland in 1861. At Savannah in 1862, Confederate shipwrights cut down the* Fingal *to the waterline, retaining her bottom, engine, and propeller. They added a wide, low, armored deck with a ram at the bow to pierce the hull of an enemy ship. The ship's four rifled guns were housed in an iron-sheathed casemate with sloping sides to deflect cannon shot. A low armored pilothouse with slit windows sat at the forward end of the casemate. A crew of 145 men operated the 204-foot vessel. The* Atlanta *defended the mouth of the Savannah River until 17 June 1863, when she was captured by two ironclad U.S. monitors. Taken into the Union Navy as the USS* Atlanta, *the ship joined the blockade, serving on Virginia's James River as depicted in this photograph, probably dating from the summer of 1864. (Courtesy Massachusetts Commandery, Military Order of the Loyal Legion and the U.S. Army Military History Institute, Carlisle Barrack, Pennsylvania)*

freed Mason and Slidell, the British Parliament appeared ready to declare war over this flaunting of the sovereignty of a British vessel on the high seas. Thereafter, Confederate representatives in Europe had little diplomatic success, although they did purchase vessels, munitions, and supplies, especially through the efforts of the Georgian James D. Bulloch.

The Union effort to strangle the Confederacy by blockade and the Confederate effort to disrupt the Union economy by employing blockade runners and high-seas commerce destroyers produced an ironic departure from America's traditional insistence on freedom of the seas and the rights of neutral vessels to have access to the trade of

Great Britain's stance of neutrality at times was shaky, and the Confederacy drew considerable benefit from the informal backing it enjoyed in many quarters of the British government and economy, as Great Britain's major prewar supplier of raw materials. The most controversial British involvement in the war came from supplying the "big three" of the Confederate commerce destroyers: *Alabama*, *Florida*, and *Shenandoah*. Each one of these wooden-hulled, screw-propelled steam warships was built in England, released into Confederate hands over the protest of Union officials in London, and subsequently armed, equipped, and largely manned from English vessels. The *Alabama*, the most destructive of the lot, captured sixty-four U.S. merchant vessels between September 1862 and April 1864, haunting the sea-lanes as far east as Singapore before succumbing in a ship-to-ship duel with the USS *Kearsarge* off Cherbourg, France, in June 1864. After the war, and following an international arbitration established by treaty, the English in 1872 acknowledged their responsibility for such un-neutral actions by paying the United States $15,500,000 to settle the *Alabama* claims issue.

The Union's Naval Strength and Strategy

Prior to 1861 the United States Navy at best had made a grudging accommodation with steam power and had done scarcely anything about armoring its wooden warships with iron plates. There was little interest, as well, in building iron-hulled war vessels, so that the iron-hulled paddle-wheel steamer *Michigan*, built in 1842 for Great Lakes service, clearly stands apart from accepted shipbuilding policy. When the war formally commenced on 12 April 1861 with the Confederate firing upon the Union garrison at Fort Sumter, in the harbor of Charleston, South Carolina, the navy was small, dispersed, and distinguished by a great deal of sail and very little smoke. Of the ninety vessels officially on the books, only forty-two were in commission, and among these were just twenty-six steamers of all shapes, sizes, and degrees of effectiveness. In

belligerents in wartime. Indeed, since the federal government officially considered the South to be in a state of rebellion, and not a sovereign nation, Europeans pointed out that international law had no provisions for a nation to blockade its own coast. Thus, the Union found itself very much in the position of Great Britain during the American Revolution, while Great Britain, as neutral, took the position of promoting the rights of its merchant marine to trade with the Confederacy as well as with the Union. As the maritime historian Robert Albion has pointed out, in this situation of "reversed roles," "Federal judges condemned British vessels on the very same grounds that the High Court of Admiralty had used against Yankee neutrals in the past; and the British protests simply paraphrased Jefferson's and Madison's tirades against such 'piracy'."

Blockaders and Blockade Runners

Aboard the USS *Florida*, in the North Atlantic Blockading Squadron stationed off Cape Fear, North Carolina, in 1863, Charles A. Post noted in his diary:

> April 1st. Pretty stupid work this blockading. In one of her letters, mother hopes that I will not become enamored with this life of "adventure!!" If I had been in search of the millenium I could not have come to a better place! We never see an enemy, from morning to night. I told her she could get a fair idea of our "adventures" if she would go on the roof of the house, on a hot summer day, and talk to half a dozen hotel hallboys, who are generally far more intelligent and agreeable than the average "acting officer." Then descend to the attic and drink some tepid water, full of iron rust. Then go on the roof again and repeat this "adventurous process" at intervals, until she was tired out, and go to bed, with everything shut down tight, so as not to show a light."

Charles A. Post, "A Diary on the Blockade in 1863," *U.S. Naval Institute Proceedings* 44 (October 1918): 2346.

Noel W. Blakeman, with the august title of acting assistant paymaster, reminisced about his experience aboard the bark USS *Kingfisher*.

> Blockading was not a very attractive service, but although it was not "so easy as it looks," it was far less monotonous than was generally supposed. True, much of the time we were in a condition of masterly inactivity, but then . . . we were always in a warlike attitude; and then we were constantly watching and waiting . . . for "something to turn up," and whether that something proved to be the appearance of a blockade runner or a hostile demonstration from the enemy, we were always ready to fight or run, as prudence or necessity required. . . .
>
> Nevertheless, the pleasures of blockade service had to be experienced to be fully appreciated. There may have been an occasional spot of monotony here and there, but upon the average station the experience was as varied as it was exciting. An occasional skirmish on shore with an outlying picket of observation; a midnight alarm, which sometimes resulted in a beat to quarters merely to receive on board a boatload of contrabands seeking refuge under cover of darkness on the "Lincum" gunboat; frequent dashes after blockade runners that somehow or other so often managed to elude our grasp; a cutting-out expedition that often resulted in the gallant capture of a very hostile fishing-smack; the destruction of salt works that increased in number the more they were destroyed; and . . . "laying low" for the monthly visit of the beef boat, that brought our supplies of fresh meat, ice, blockade sherry, and our mail, made up a round of duty that could not be fairly termed monotonous. . . . If you want to find out what a man really is, go and spend a year with him on blockade and you will discover what kind of stuff he is made of as well as what kind of a fellow you are yourself.

A. Noel Blakeman, "Some Personal Reminiscences of the Naval Service," in A. Noel Blakeman, ed., *Personal Recollections of the War of the Rebellion*, 2nd. ser. (Boston, 1897)

Captain John Wilkinson of the *Robert E. Lee* ran the Union blockade off Wilmington, North Carolina, in 1863, and described one night's work:

> The *Lee* continued to make her regular trips either to Nassau or Bermuda, as

To maintain the blockade close inshore, and in the winding estuaries of the southern coast, the U.S. Navy commissioned numerous double-ended gunboats, including twenty-eight Sassacus-class vessels, the largest single class of U.S. Navy warships built before World War I. This is the earlier double-ended side-wheel steam gunboat Miami, launched at the Philadelphia Navy Yard in November 1861. Although Gustavus Fox called the 208-foot Miami "a great clumsy, ugly, eight knot boat," the vessel was extremely active during the war, participating in the attack on Forts Jackson and St. Philip that led to the capture of New Orleans, and proceeding up the Mississippi to attack Vicksburg in June and July 1862. Returning to the East Coast, the Miami served off Norfolk, Virginia, and then in North Carolina's Albemarle Sound, where she engaged the Confederate ironclad Albemarle in April 1864. The Miami finished the war on the James River guarding Union transports during the army's siege of Petersburg and blockading the Confederate naval squadron on the James. Approximately half the crew of 134 officers and men—at least eleven of them African Americans—have gathered on the foredeck for this photograph during their service on the James River in 1864. During the ship's service on Albemarle Sound, fully 28 percent of the crew was black. Because the vessel has a rudder at either end, she has a wheel on the foredeck. At the starboard (right) bow is a rifled Parrott gun firing eighty-pound shells, while two smoothbore Dahlgren guns are ready for action to port. The photographer has depicted the crew at their leisure: some play checkers on painted canvas checkerboards; two pose with banjo and drum at left center; two black sailors mend clothes at right; while an officer stands at the bow. Civil War navy service included a lot of such sitting around, but this crew has also had considerable experience under fire. (111B-129, courtesy National Archives)

The iron-hulled Confederate blockade runner A.D. Vance, *or* Advance, *was originally the Scottish packet steamer* Lord Clyde. *Partially owned by the State of North Carolina, and named for a prominent figure in the state, the speedy side-wheeler carried cotton and other Confederate produce out to Bermuda or Nassau and returned to Wilmington with military supplies for North Carolina troops as well as limited quantities of consumer goods. The A.D. Vance was particularly successful at running the Union blockade, making more than twenty voyages (forty passages) before her capture in September 1864. After her capture she was added to the Union blockading fleet under the name* Advance, *later* Frolic. *Flying the Confederate flag and displaying one of her efficient feathering paddle wheels, the A. D. Vance was photographed at Nassau, Bahamas, in 1863. (Courtesy Charles V. Perry and Naval Historical Center, Washington, D.C.)*

circumstances required, during the summer of 1863, carrying abroad cotton and naval stores, and bringing in "hardware," as munitions of war were then invoiced. Usually the time selected for sailing was during the "dark of the moon," but upon one occasion, a new pilot had been detailed for duty on board, who failed in many efforts to get the ship over the "rip," a shifting sand bar a mile or more inside the true bar. . . .

The tide serving at ten o'clock, we succeeded in crossing the rip at that hour, and as we passed over New Inlet bar, the moon rose in a cloudless sky. It was a calm night too, and the regular beat of our paddles through the smooth water sounded to our ears ominously loud. As we closely skirted the shore, the blockading vessels were plainly visible to us, some at anchor, some under way; and some of them so near that we saw, or fancied we saw, with our night glasses, the men on watch on their forecastles; but as we were inside of them all, and invisible against the background of the land, we passed beyond them undiscovered. The roar of the surf breaking upon the beach, prevented the noise of our paddles from being heard. . . .

Discovery of us by the fleet would probably have been fatal to us, but the risk was not really so great as it appeared; . . . the vigilance on board the blockading fleet was much relaxed during the moonlit nights. The vessels were sent to Beaufort to coal at these times. . . Captain Patterson then commanding the blockading fleet off the Cape Fear. . . . remarked. . . that he never undressed nor retired to bed, during the dark nights; but could enjoy those luxuries when the moon was shining. On this hint I acted.

John Wilkinson, *The Narrative of a Blockade-Runner* (New York, 1877)

As captain of the CSS Alabama, Raphael Semmes (1809-1877) personified the Confederacy's strategy of commerce raiding during the Civil War. A native of Maryland, commissioned as a midshipman in 1826, Semmes combined naval service with a law career in Cincinnati, Ohio, and Mobile, Alabama. After survey duty in the Gulf of Mexico and action during the Mexican War, as master of the brig Somers when she sank in a squall, Semmes commanded the mail steamship Illinois and was then assigned to inspect lighthouses. Resigning his commission when Alabama seceded from the Union, Semmes persuaded Confederate Secretary of the Navy Stephen Mallory to license privateers and to give him command of a navy commerce raider. As captain of the CSS Sumter, Semmes preyed on Union shipping in the Gulf of Mexico and Atlantic from July 1861 to January 1862. When Union warships blockaded the Sumter in the neutral port of Gibraltar, Semmes left the ship. In August 1862 he traveled to the Azores to take command of hull 290, which Confederate agent James Bulloch had secretly

ordered from the Laird shipyard in Liverpool. Christened the Alabama, the 220-foot vessel was armed in the Azores and manned with a largely British crew. Late in August, Semmes set out to hunt U.S. merchant ships, sinking whaleships near the Azores, fishing vessels off the Grand Banks, and merchant ships in the North Atlantic, Gulf of Mexico, and off Brazil. In the summer of 1863 Semmes took the Alabama east across the Indian Ocean, sinking a number of ships near Singapore before returning to the Atlantic and taking the ship's sixty-fourth and last prize, the bark Tycoon, in April 1864. Seeking a place to repair his ship, Semmes arrived at Cherbourg, France, early in June. On 19 June, he steamed out to give battle to the USS Kearsarge. The engagement lasted just forty-five minutes, as the Alabama's faulty gunpowder and poor aim did little damage to the Kearsarge, while the Kearsarge's more accurate firing sank the Alabama. Semmes was photographed, (above) beside the Alabama's large rifled Blakely pivot gun at Cape Town, South Africa, in August 1863. Aft near the ship's wheel is the executive officer, John McIntosh Kell, a Georgian who had served in the U.S. Navy through the Mexican War and on Perry's expedition to Japan, resigning to join the Confederate Navy when Georgia seceded from the Union. Both men escaped to England when the Alabama was sunk in June 1864. Semmes finished the war as commander of the Confederate fleet on the James River guarding Richmond. Raphael Semmes, whose ships had captured eighty-seven U.S. merchantmen, or nearly one-third of the total taken during the war, spent the rest of his life teaching, editing a newspaper, and writing about his service afloat. (Courtesy George Eastman House, Rochester, New York)

[343]

THE TROUBLED COURSE

comparison to the formidable naval forces of Great Britain and France, both of which were rapidly moving into the age of armored warships propelled by steam and carrying powerful cannon of the latest design, the Union Navy was unimpressive and obsolete, with just 1,200 officers and 7,500 seamen.

The Union Navy, inheriting the bulk of naval career officers as well as vessels of the prewar United States Navy, had a complex and contentious organization. The key position of secretary of the navy fell to Gideon Welles, a somewhat elderly and austere Connecticut Democrat-Unionist, who many years before had served briefly as a naval bureau chief in the Polk administration. Welles turned out to be far better than most of the Lincoln administration's proponents had expected; much of his success undoubtedly depended on the effective work of his assistant secretary, former naval officer Gustavus V. Fox, who had a knack for working with such younger, but quickly advancing, career naval officers as David Dixon Porter. Between them, Welles and Fox got the job done, while fending off congressional critics, civilian lobbyists, and political opponents within the president's cabinet. Welles's influence on the navy persisted beyond the end of the war, although his predilection for Native American tribes in naming all the vessels that suddenly flooded into the wartime naval list was often unappreciated by officers and seamen, let alone politicians from other parts of the nation.

The Union (or North) entered the war with immense advantages in both maritime and naval force. The prewar American merchant marine essentially was owned, financed, and operated by Northern merchants operating from Northern seaports. The South, with its overwhelming preoccupation on profitable agricultural production for both foreign and domestic markets, possessed little manufacturing capability of its own. Relying heavily on foreign or Northern domestic sources for industrial products, the South necessarily depended as well on both foreign and Northern vessels for transporting these imports. To a comparable extent the South also depended on such merchant fleets to carry its agricultural produce to foreign and domestic industrial centers.

Because the Confederate States of America had no navy to speak of in 1861, the Union Navy, with all of its limitations in size and effectiveness, nonetheless could operate against the Confederacy with little initial opposition. The Union naval strategy, as part of General Winfield Scott's "Anaconda Plan," was to strangle the Confederacy economically by blockading the South's Atlantic and Gulf coastlines and gaining control of the major inland waterway systems, notably that of the Mississippi River. While stifling Southern trade with the outside world, the North intended to trade freely and thus support its own war economy while shutting down that of the South.

After its shaky beginnings, the Union blockade became relatively effective in 1862. With almost 150 vessels on station at any one time, it created a clear, if porous screen along the coast. By the end of the war, almost 1,500 blockade runners had been captured or destroyed, although on average each had made four successful trips through the blockade before its loss. U.S. Navy sailors had an incentive for enduring this maddeningly routine duty. As in past wars, they shared in the profits realized from the sale of the captured vessel and cargo. Split fifty-fifty with the U.S. government, the ship's share of a prize vessel could still amount to hundreds of dollars for each seaman, not to mention profits of more than $100,000 for a handful of squadron commanders.

The Anaconda Plan also called for the seizure of Southern ports, and the sequence of invasions was planned to meet the navy's logistical needs. With existing bases only at Hampton Roads, opposite Norfolk, Virginia, and at Key West, Florida, the Union Navy required additional coaling and supply bases for its blockading steam warships, since with their inefficient engines they could carry only limited amounts of coal while cruising, and they burned that coal all too quickly when under full steam power. Early in the war, on 7 November 1861, a large joint expedition of Union forces, including seventy-seven vessels under the command of Flag Officer Samuel F. du Pont, seized the base of Port Royal, South Carolina, to serve as a vital naval depot at a midpoint on the Confederate Atlantic coastline. A similar amphibious effort on the North Carolina coast at Roanoke Island in February 1862 brought Albemarle Sound and much of coastal North Carolina under Union control. In the following month the Union occupation of Jacksonville, Florida, and du Pont's successful amphibious assault on the old smuggling center of Amelia Island, on the Florida coast near the Georgia border, closed down Confederate blockade running to a great extent.

The screw-propelled wooden sloop of war Hartford *represented the most modern U.S. Navy design when she was launched at the Boston Navy Yard in 1858. Armed with twenty-four guns and carrying a crew of 302, the* Hartford *served as the flagship of the East India Squadron until news of the Civil War reached Asia. Arriving in Philadelphia in December 1861, the* Hartford *became flagship for David G. Farragut, commander of the West Gulf Blockading Squadron. In April 1862 the* Hartford *was engaged in the capture of New Orleans, narrowly escaping destruction opposite Fort St. Philip when she ran aground and was struck by a fire raft. After leading the way up the Mississippi for the capture of Baton Rouge and Natchez, the* Hartford *made an unsuccessful attack on Vicksburg in June 1862. In March 1863 the ship ran through heavy fire from the Confederate batteries at Port Hudson, Louisiana, to operate against Vicksburg until its surrender in July 1863. A year later the* Hartford *served as flagship of the fleet of eighteen vessels that passed the Confederate forts and engaged the small Confederate fleet in Mobile Bay. Lashed in the* Hartford's *main rigging as the ship passed through the fire of Fort Morgan, Farragut urged the fleet through a minefield, drove off the Confederate gunboats, and brought his wooden ship into action against the ironclad* Tennessee. *The surrender of the* Tennessee *sealed Mobile as a Confederate port. Although she was a wooden ship engaging heavy rifled guns in shore fortifications and aboard ironclad vessels, the* Hartford *survived all of these actions, in part because Farragut armored her engine room with lengths of chain cable ranged along her topsides. After the war, the* Hartford *spent much of her time on duty in the Pacific. Rebuilt in the 1890s, the USS* Hartford *served as a training and station ship, and was finally dismantled in 1956. Shortly after the Battle of Mobile Bay, McPherson & Oliver of New Orleans took this photograph of the* Hartford's *starboard battery, with its large Dahlgren guns. Lieutenants Mundy and Adams, veterans of the battle, stand near the wheel. (M.S.M. 97.155.1)*

The Union recapture of Norfolk, Virginia, and of St. Augustine, Florida, further narrowed the effective area of Confederate activity, so that the major port of Savannah, Georgia, now was relatively isolated, especially with the capture of Fort Pulaski, at the mouth of the Savannah River, in April 1862. The important stretch of Carolina coastline from Charleston north to Wilmington, North Carolina, persisted as the most difficult area to bring under control. Charleston proved too strong to subdue, turning back a Union assault by nine ironclad warships in April 1863. Despite intensive shelling by besieging land and sea forces, especially in the summer of 1863, Charleston was not evacuated until it was threatened by General William T. Sherman's overland invasion in mid-February

Robert Smalls (1839-1915), son of a slave mother and white father, grew up in Beaufort, South Carolina. Sent to Charleston as a slave laborer at age twelve, Smalls began as a waiter, then became a stevedore, rigger, and sailor. By March 1861 he was wheelman—pilot—of the coastal steamboat Planter in Confederate service. In the early hours of 13 May 1862, Smalls got the Planter underway with his wife, children, and several other slaves on board. Passing through the Confederate defenses of Charleston, Smalls delivered the Planter to the Union blockading fleet, saying: "Good morning, sir! I've brought you some of the old United States guns, sir!" The entire crew received a reward for their "capture" of a Confederate vessel, the feat generated much attention in the Northern press, and Smalls was taken North as a spokesman for slaves seeking freedom. Despite the publicity, Smalls returned south as a pilot in service of his admirer, Commodore Samuel F. du Pont, commander of the South Atlantic Blockading Squadron. Smalls piloted the monitor Keokuk during the unsuccessful naval assault on Charleston in April 1863, and he also commanded the Planter in army service until after the fall of Charleston in February 1865. Returning to Beaufort after the war, he entered Reconstruction politics in South Carolina, serving in the state legislature and senate, 1868-75, and as U.S. Congressman, 1875-78 and 1880-88. In the 1890s he served as customs collector for the port of Beaufort and remained a Republican Party advisor during the era of increasingly stringent Jim Crow laws. As a skilled and vocal former slave, this one-time sailor embodied the promise of emancipation, spending much of his life to provide black South Carolinians "an equal chance in the battle of life." This tintype depicts Robert Smalls in May 1862. (Courtesy Massachusetts Commandery, Military Order of the Loyal Legion and the U.S. Army Military History Institute, Carlisle Barracks, Pennsylvania)

1865. Nevertheless, Union naval activity off Charleston effectively sealed off access to its harbor by blockade runners, leaving Wilmington, on the Cape Fear River, as the principal Confederate port on the Atlantic. Effectively defended by the Confederate guns at Fort Fisher until an amphibious assault by Union combined forces in mid-January 1865, this port, with a direct railroad to the seat of war in Virginia, was the terminus for hundreds of passages by blockade runners from Bermuda, Nassau, and even Nova Scotia. The Confederate surrender of Fort Fisher, forty-five months after the war began in Charleston Harbor, at long last completed the Union's strategic objectives in stifling Confederate commerce and navigation by its Anaconda Plan.

On the Gulf Coast, the fortified naval base and sur-

rounding waters at Pensacola, Florida, were preserved for the Union when a joint expedition landed there on 17 April 1861 to reinforce the garrison at Fort Pickens—no doubt to the intense relief and gratification of President Abraham Lincoln, who had stated: "I want that fort saved at all hazards." As a result, throughout the war Pensacola could support Union naval efforts against the largely Confederate-controlled coastline stretching from Florida to Texas, which welcomed blockade runners from Havana. The coast also provided a staging area for the April 1862 invasion of the Mississippi to pass the defending forts and capture the port of New Orleans. The Virginian David Glasgow Farragut commanded a flotilla of steam sloops of war (frigates were too deep to cross the Mississippi bars), steam gunboats, and schooners armed with mortars to lob explosive shells into the

The USS Cairo was one of the U.S. Navy's eight Cairo-class ironclad gunboats on the western rivers. Designed by naval architect Samuel Pook, and built by steamboat builder and entrepreneur James Eads at Carondelet, Missouri, and Mound City, Illinois, "Pook's turtles" combined the flat bottom, shallow draft, and stern wheel of a river steamboat with an armored casemate superstructure somewhat similar to those of Confederate ironclads. The 175-foot-long vessels were covered with two and a half inches of iron strapping, including the paddle-wheel housing aft and elevated pilothouse forward. Each ship required a crew of 251 to operate the engine and serve the thirteen heavy guns. Although the gunboats were commanded by navy officers, the crews included riverboatmen, soldiers, and civilians, and the gunboat flotilla operated under U.S. Army control. The Cairo was commissioned in January 1862, and proceeded up the Cumberland River to occupy Nashville, Tennessee, after the fall of Fort Donelson. The Cairo was then engaged at Plum Point Bend and Memphis as the Western Gunboat Flotilla descended the Mississippi. After the gunboat flotilla was transferred to navy control in October 1862, the Cairo joined the expedition to capture Vicksburg by way of the Yazoo River. On 12 December 1862 the Cairo struck a "torpedo" (submerged mine) and sank off Haines Bluff, Mississippi. Although the Cairo was sunk by a mine, these vessels were superior to all but a few Confederate warships on the rivers, and they provided essential service in the Union effort to control the Mississippi and its tributaries. One hundred years after sinking, the Cairo was partially salvaged and has been preserved as a museum at Vicksburg. (Courtesy Massachusetts Commandery, Military Order of the Loyal Legion and the U.S. Army Military History Institute, Carlisle Barracks, Pennsylvania)

forts. Although Forts Jackson and St. Philip, seventy-five miles below New Orleans, were modern masonry fortifications, Farragut's fleet was able to assault the forts and then run past them, scattering Confederate gunboats and compelling the surrender of New Orleans, the Confederacy's most important city, on 29 April 1862.

The Union's Anaconda strategy also depended on control of interior water routes–notably the Mississippi River–so that a major portion of the navy's strength was directed to that effort. President Abraham Lincoln in 1861 had declared, "The Mississippi is the Backbone of the Rebellion; it is the key to the whole situation." In its approach to war on the rivers, the Union merged army and navy functions. Although the vessels were manned by U.S. Navy crews, the command of inland operations was first lodged with the U.S. Army, in an effective collaboration between General U.S. Grant and Admiral Andrew H. Foote. East of the Mississippi, the Union capture during February 1862 of Fort Henry, on the Tennessee River, and

nearby Fort Donelson on the Cumberland River, was a promising start for the Union strategy, seriously breaching the northern Confederate line of defense and opening the way for Union occupation of the principal agricultural and industrial centers of Tennessee.

On the Mississippi itself, matters were very different. Notwithstanding the Union capture of New Orleans and the mouth of the Mississippi in April 1862, and its seizure of Island No. 10, the vital Confederate stronghold on the upper Mississippi, earlier in that same month, Confederate operations on the Mississippi and other rivers for some time remained a serious challenge to Union strategy. Confederate steamboats converted into rams made a surprise attack at Plum Point Bend in May, stalling the Union advance. To combat the Confederate rams on the river, northern engineer Charles Ellet had supervised the conversion of nine Union steamboats into rams. Supported by a new force of ironclad river gunboats, the rams went into action at Memphis on 6 June, and in a wild battle of maneuver and collision the Union fleet won, clearing the Mississippi of Confederate vessels for 300 miles above Vicksburg, Mississippi.

Following the capture of New Orleans, Farragut's oceangoing fleet ventured up the Mississippi, helping to secure Baton Rouge and then cooperating with the army and with Admiral David D. Porter's fleet of river gunboats in ongoing attempts to capture the Confederate strongholds on the bluffs at Port Hudson, Louisiana, and Vicksburg, Mississippi. Farragut's first run at Vicksburg in June 1862 failed. Thereafter, Porter's gunboat flotilla supported General Grant's investment of Vicksburg, which began with an unsuccessful attempt to dig a diversionary and reroute the Mississippi away from Vicksburg. Foiled by nature and by Confederate defenses from navigating the bayous to cut off Vicksburg by water, Porter's gunboats helped Grant's army run past Vicksburg in April 1863 and begin a successful invasion from the south. Meanwhile, Farragut's squadron, led by the sloop-of-war *Hartford*, provided artillery support for the siege of Port Hudson. The Union's naval efforts in the American West finally prevailed with the Confederate surrender of Vicksburg to General Grant on 4 July 1863, and the surrender of Port Hudson five days later. The Mississippi River now was entirely under Union control, and the Confederate states west of the Mississippi were effectively isolated from the rest. As President Abraham Lincoln wrote in appreciation, "The Father of Waters again goes unvexed to the sea. . . . Nor must Uncle Sam's web feet be forgotten. At all the watery margins they have been present. Not only on the deep sea, the broad bay, the rapid river, but also up the narrow, muddy bayou, and wherever the ground was a little damp, they have been and made their tracks."

Late in 1863 the Union launched an amphibious expedition along the Texas coast to seize its ports and assert U.S. control over Texas in case the French in Mexico had designs on this most western state of the Confederacy. The western half of the coast was occupied, but Galveston resisted capture. In the spring of 1864, as part of Union efforts to press the Confederacy on all sides, and to renew the invasion of Texas and open up the cotton-producing lands of west Louisiana to U.S. trade, General Nathaniel Banks and the navy's rising star, David Dixon Porter, commanded an ambitious joint military and naval expedition up the Red River toward

Shreveport. Banks and Porter became preoccupied with the seizure of cotton for their own benefit until the mission degenerated into a dismal failure and nearly a catastrophe. As the water level fell in the Red River, the navy's gunboats were frustrated by low water and snags to the point where they barely escaped being scuttled and abandoned. The rescue was due to the imaginative plan of the Union Army's Lieutenant Colonel Joseph Bailey, who proposed to dam up the Red River so that the higher water level would permit the gunboats to escape by successfully passing through a mile of dangerous rapids. With the aid of army troops the dam was built and by 13 May all of Admiral Porter's gunboats had passed over the rapids to safety. As a vastly relieved Porter wrote, "Words are inadequate to express the admiration I feel for the abilities of Lieutenant Colonel Bailey. This is without a doubt the best engineering feat ever performed. . . he has saved to the Union a valuable fleet, worth nearly $2,000,000."

In August 1864 Union naval forces in the Gulf turned to subdue the final large Confederate port on the Gulf coast, Mobile, Alabama. With a flotilla of wooden warships and ironclads, Admiral David Farragut ran past the fire of the defending forts to engage a Confederate fleet of ironclads and gunboats in Mobile Bay. When a torpedo (underwater mine) sank the leading ironclad, *Tecumseh*, Farragut, lashed in the *Hartford*'s rigging, reportedly ordered his executive officer: "Damn the torpedoes! Full speed ahead!" There followed a wild battle as ironclad and wooden warship alike exchanged broadsides and attempted to ram. Too deep to escape up Mobile Bay, and without enough fuel to run, the huge Confederate ironclad *Tennessee* was compelled to surrender. Despite heavy casualties, the U.S. Navy had closed Mobile's access to the sea, further limiting the Confederacy's commercial contact with the outside world. With the capture of Wilmington, North Carolina, in February 1865, described above, U.S. Navy control of the Southern coastline was virtually complete.

Naval Responses to the Demands of War

From a service with fewer than ten thousand men and one hundred vessels, the U.S. Navy grew quickly. Although there was still a need for expe-

The U.S. Navy's Bureau of Steam Engineering was largely responsible for the rapid and successful expansion of the U.S. Navy during the Civil War. Established as a separate entity within the Navy Department in 1862, the bureau's engineers, draftsmen, and clerks oversaw the design and construction of the steam engines for new navy vessels. Seated at center in this view of the bureau's staff is Chief Engineer Benjamin F. Isherwood (1822-1915). A draftsman in a New York railroad shop at age fourteen, Isherwood supervised the construction of lighthouse lenses before working at the Novelty Iron Works to gain experience in marine steam engine design. He then entered the U.S. Navy's new Engineer Corps in 1844, serving aboard the first propeller-driven warship, USS Princeton, and various other steam-powered vessels during the Mexican War and on the West Africa and Asia Stations. Throughout his service he studied the characteristics of every steam engine he had access to, publishing his Engineering Precedents *in 1859 and* Experimental Researches in Steam Engineering *in 1863 and 1865 to explain his theory of the effects of steam in a steam engine. He was appointed the navy's engineer-in-chief in 1861 and personally designed the engines for forty-six side-wheel steamers and seventy-nine propeller craft during the war. Although he was criticized for the heavy, simple design of his engines, Isherwood planned them to endure operation by unskilled engineers under the extremes of wartime conditions. By the end of the war the U.S. Navy fleet had grown from twenty-eight ships to nearly 600 steam vessels. Most of the naval vessels constructed during the war were designed for coastal blockade and river duty. Isherwood, however, advocated a navy that could also command the sea-lanes, and he helped design a class of commerce raiders for that purpose. His* Wampanoag, *launched in 1864 but not commissioned until 1867, was the fastest ship in the world, steaming at almost eighteen knots during her trials in 1868. Nevertheless, the ship was soon laid up as the postwar navy had reverted to traditional designs. After eight years Isherwood was relieved as engineer-in-chief, thereafter continuing his studies of engine and propeller design until retiring in 1884. During the remaining thirty years of his life he wrote many scientific articles while watching the U.S. Navy finally approach the modern overseas potential he had advocated decades earlier. (Courtesy Massachusetts Commandery, Military Order of the Loyal Legion and the U.S. Army Military History Institute, Carlisle Barracks, Pennsylvania)*

On 30 June 1864, eleven days after the Kearsarge sank the Alabama, French photographer Francois Rondin took this view of the Kearsarge officers on the quarterdeck. At left is the after eleven-inch Dahlgren pivot gun. One of that gun's crew had been mortally wounded by an exploding shell during the battle, but the ship's two Dahlgrens had been instrumental in sinking the Confederate raider. After forty-five minutes of firing as the ships traversed a corkscrew course a thousand yards apart, the Alabama had foundered from the effects of the Kearsarge's slow, steady firing. Although the Kearsarge relied on her engine to a large degree, she did carry a sailing rig, and her officers represented the division between the deck crew and the engine-room crew. Third from left is Captain John A. Winslow (1811-1873). A North Carolinian, Winslow had entered the navy in 1827, was commended for bravery during the Mexican War, and was serving on shore when the Civil War began. A staunch abolitionist and a particularly pious captain, Winslow commanded gunboats on the Mississippi before he was sent to command the Kearsarge in April 1863, after making derogatory remarks about the Lincoln administration. After defeating the Alabama, Winslow became a celebrity, and he commanded the Gulf Squadron and the Pacific fleet as an admiral before ill health caused him to retire in 1872. Chief Engineer William H. Cushman (far left) entered the navy in 1855 and was commissioned as chief engineer in October 1861, serving through the Kearsarge's 1862-64 cruise despite increasing disability from tuberculosis. The others represent the mix of regular navy officers and volunteer mariners who served in the expanded U.S. Navy during the Civil War. Had they not engaged and defeated the CSS Alabama after two fruitless years of patrol off southern Europe, this group would have had little to distinguish it from the navy's nearly 600 other vessel commands. (M.S.M. 90.65.1)

rienced seamen aboard the many vessels still equipped with sails, the many tasks attendant to operating a steam engine required large numbers as well, from unskilled coal heavers to experienced engineers. Enlistments of "landsmen"–the least skilled naval rating–increased dramatically. As an example, the new seven-gun sloop-of-war *Kearsarge*, commissioned at Portsmouth, New Hampshire, early in 1862, carried a crew of about 160, 25 percent of whom worked in the engine room (five engineers, nineteen firemen, and fifteen coal heavers). Deck and rigging duties were handled by 45 percent of the men (thirty-one able-bodied seamen, nineteen less experienced ordinary seamen, and twenty-one inexperienced landsmen), while the rest were officers, mates, gunners, cooks and stewards, boys, and a contingent of eleven Marines. While the army had age restrictions on volunteers, the navy accepted boys as young as fourteen and men in their fifties–the ages of the *Kearsarge* crew ranged from sixteen to fifty-four. Although their opportunities at sea had declined in the decades before the war began, African Americans entered the navy in large numbers, as they had in earlier wars. Northern blacks joined the navy to fight slavery long before they were permitted to join segregated regiments in the army in 1863, and male slaves who sought refuge at U.S. Navy bases on the southern coast also enlisted. At least 10 percent of U.S. Navy enlisted men during the war were of African descent.

In 1861 the immediate problem for the Union Navy was to find enough vessels to implement a blockade along the Confederacy's 3,350 miles of coastline, much of which was double because of the extensive natural intracoastal waterway along the Atlantic seaboard. Between the South Atlantic Coast and the Gulf Coast there were 189 harbors or navigable river outlets–and any one of these potentially could shelter a blockade runner. The navy thus worked frantically to build up a force of steamers, with the blockading mission uppermost in mind. Before the war was over the Union possessed a navy of over 600 steamers; of these, more than 400 had been purchased or leased, often at exorbitant prices. To get steamers onto station as quickly as possible, the Union extracted from the existing civilian steam fleet a great variety of vessels, ranging from yachts to ferryboats, from tugs to oceangoing steam liners. As in any war there was considerable profiteering, exemplified in this instance by the shrewd bargaining conducted by the

steamship magnate Marshall O. Roberts. Roberts, as Robert Albion relates, "bought the 1,750-ton *Empire City* at auction from his old company for $12,000, and, without counting his naval charters, received $833,000 for her services to the army alone." In addition, another of Roberts's steamers earned $414,000 in charters and then, as a result of President Lincoln's direct order, was sold to the army for $442,000.

The Union Navy, relying on its Bureau of Construction and Repair and on its newly created Bureau of Steam Engineering, designed and either built itself or contracted with private yards to build some 200 steamers of even greater variety than those purchased or leased. The first of these Navy Department steamers were the "ninety-day gunboats," produced in such a remarkably short time because the navy had recently designed such vessels for the Russian Navy. Then there were the "double-enders": fast side-wheel riverboats with rudders and pilothouses at both ends, so that the vessel could reverse direction without having to turn around in narrow channels. For high-seas service there were the large, wooden-hulled steam sloops of war; perhaps the best known of these by war's end was the 1,550-ton USS *Kearsarge*, commissioned early in 1862, which cruised off Europe in search of blockade runners and Confederate commerce raiders until meeting and defeating the famed Confederate steamship *Alabama* off Cherbourg, France, on 19 June 1864.

The possibility of Great Britain's intervention on the side of the Confederacy, and the likely consequence of the British Royal Navy being thrown into the maritime arena, brought the Union Navy Department in 1863 to design a special class of high-powered super-cruisers, displacing around 4,000 tons, that could pose a devastating commerce-raiding threat to the British merchant marine, very much as the Confederates were currently presenting to American merchant vessels. As matters turned out, this *Wampanoag* class of screw-propelled, wooden-hulled cruisers was not completed until 1867, but the British were sufficiently concerned to develop their own class of even larger, heavily-armed cruisers, intended to thwart this American challenge. The British had good reason to be apprehensive; on her speed trials in 1868, the *Wampanoag* achieved an extraordinary sustained speed at sea of nearly eighteen knots, a record that would stand for decades.

Although the European navies experimented with armored vessels for several years before 1861, the U.S. Navy did so only after the Confederate States Navy had made ironclad vessels a priority. Indeed, the first Union ironclads were designed and promoted by civilians, not by the Navy Department. Some were essentially conventional vessels sheathed in iron, while the most radical, the *Monitor*, was an entire departure from American warship design. Constructed of iron plates, with all but a few feet of the hull submerged, the *Monitor* appeared to be little more than an iron raft with a low pilothouse and a large iron turret on deck. Turned by the ship's steam engine, this rotating turret contained the ship's two large guns, protecting their gun crews even as it provided a virtually unrestricted field of fire no matter what direction the *Monitor* was traveling. Designed by the brilliant but difficult Swedish engineer John Ericsson, promoted and financed in part by a New Haven, Connecticut, grocer, Cornelius Bushnell, and built at New York's Continental Iron Works. Ericsson's *Monitor* was completed barely in time to be towed south to Hampton Roads, Virginia, in early March 1862, for her celebrated if inconclusive confrontation with the Confederate ironclad ram *Virginia*. The Confederates, supervised by John Brooke, had raised the sunken and burned *Merrimack*, cleaned up her machinery, erected a casemate of railroad iron on the old *Merrimack*'s wooden hull, and attached a ram to her bow. Rechristened *Virginia*, this hybrid ironclad steamer demolished two wooden-hulled Union warships by ramming and gunfire before the *Monitor* arrived on 9 March 1862 for the duel of the ironclads that ever since has been the most celebrated and debated naval encounter of the war. Which vessel "won" remains an open question; in any event, neither vessel surrendered. The *Virginia* retreated upriver, to be used again only briefly and with little consequence; and just as the year ended the *Monitor*, on her way south to join the Union Navy's blockading forces off Beaufort, South Carolina, sank off Cape Hatteras while under tow. Although neither vessel survived for long, they served as the prototypes for their nations' ironclads: turreted monitors in the North and casemate ram vessels in the South.

Many other ironclads served both Union and Confederate navies, with mixed results, during the war. The shallow-draft Union Navy's armored river gunboats were not heavily enough sheathed to withstand the fire of Confederate ironclads and river fortifications; nevertheless, they performed exceptional service in the river war. The Union's slow but heavily armed and armored ironclad casemate *New Ironsides* performed brilliantly in blockade duty off Charleston, South Carolina, in early April 1863, and later in the successful mid-January 1865 Union assault of the Confederate bastion of Fort Fisher, near Wilmington, North Carolina.

Early in the war the Union Navy designed and constructed double-turreted seagoing monitors that were far more seaworthy than Ericsson's original vessel. After the war was over the Boston-built, 3,300-ton *Monadnock* made a safe passage around Cape Horn to San Francisco (the U.S. Navy had already shipped a disassembled monitor to San Francisco to be rebuilt in order to defend that valuable port from Confederate activity). Early in May 1866 the large monitor *Miantonomah* made a successful transatlantic voyage, with Gustavus Fox on board. Frequently under tow to save burning coal—and, with her characteristically low freeboard, barely above the surface for most of her voyage—she crossed the North Atlantic to England, and then went on to the Russian port of Cronstadt before returning without mishap. Both of these voyages encouraged the navy to continue building monitor-type vessels until the end of the century.

Of the more than thirty ironclads that the Confederacy built or tried (and largely failed) to acquire abroad, the lightly armored *Manassas*, along with the unfinished ironclad *Louisiana*, saw considerable action before being destroyed by Union gunfire during the naval battle for New Orleans in April 1862. More impressive, if short-lived, was the fighting career of the Confederate ironclad ram *Arkansas* on the Yazoo and Mississippi Rivers in July 1862. After heavily damaging two Union gunboats on the Yazoo River, the *Arkansas* entered the Mississippi and heroically ran the gauntlet through Admiral Farragut's fleet near the key Confederate stronghold at Vicksburg. The ironclads *Palmetto State* and *Chicora* made a successful attack on the Union fleet at Charleston early in 1863, but they were not able to break the blockade. And the August 1864 Battle for Mobile Bay involved the formidable Confederate ironclad ram *Tennessee*, which seemed invincible until the Union fleet under Admiral Farragut's command finally put

Swedish-American inventor John Ericsson revolutionized the concept of the ironclad warship with his proposal for a raft-like vessel with a single rotating turret to point the ship's two guns in any direction. The Navy Department accepted his plan in October 1861, and the 172-foot vessel was launched at New York in January 1862. Named Monitor for the lesson she was expected to teach the Confederacy and Great Britain, the vessel was commissioned just a month later and within days was hurrying south to Hampton Roads, Virginia, where the Confederate ironclad ram Virginia was known to be nearing completion. The Monitor arrived on 8 March, hours after the Virginia had ventured forth and sunk the conventional wooden warships Cumberland and Congress. At dawn of 9 March the Virginia came out again, but this time the Monitor came forward to engage her. The two ironclads battled for four hours. The Virginia had to maneuver to bring her broadside guns to bear, or to attempt to ram the Monitor, while the Union vessel could fire from any position simply by rotating her steam-powered turret. Both ships suffered damage, and Captain Worden of the Monitor was injured, but neither crew could claim victory in the engagement. They did not meet in action again, and after the Virginia was destroyed as the Confederates evacuated Norfolk the Monitor moved up the James River in an unsuccessful attempt to capture the Confederate capital of Richmond by water. In this view, taken on the James River in the summer of 1862, almost half the Monitor's crew of just fifty-nine men gathers around a portable cookstove set up on the after deck. A lookout stands atop the turret, shaded by a removable awning. The turret is built up of eight layers of one-inch iron plates riveted together. On the right side, at waist level, can be seen a dent where it was struck by one of the Virginia's heavy shot. The two iron boxes on deck are stacks to improve the draft of the Monitor's boilers and keep seas from flooding the fire room. Living and working in such an iron vessel was hot in summer and cold in winter, but the combination of low freeboard and armored turret proved so effective against Confederate ironclads and shore fortifications that thirty-six single- and double-turret seagoing monitors were launched before the end of the war. The original Monitor, however, did not survive the year. On 31 December 1862, while under tow off Cape Hatteras, the Monitor foundered and sank, with the loss of four officers and twelve men. (Courtesy The Mariners' Museum, Newport News, Virginia)

her out of commission and forced a surrender. Perhaps the most primitive but prophetic vessel of them all for either combatant was the man-powered Confederate submarine *H.L. Hunley*. The Confederates had built other types of submersible vessels, as well as small semi-submersible steam torpedo boats called "Davids," but the *Hunley* won by far the most attention and fame by sinking the Union steam warship *Housatonic* with a spar torpedo off Charleston in mid-February 1864. However, the *Hunley* was as much a danger to her own crew as to an enemy; as one Confederate engineer noted, "She was very slow in turning, but would sink at a moment's notice–and sometimes without it." She had gone down twice on her trials, taking most of her crews (including her namesake and part owner) to their deaths. When the *Hunley* sank the *Housatonic*–thus becoming the first submarine ever to sink an enemy vessel in battle–she was too close to her victim, so this notoriously unstable vessel finished her brief career by sinking for the last time–again, with all of her crew.

Of the Confederate naval effort, by far the most effective results came from the steam-powered, wooden-hulled commerce raiders built in England, notably the *Alabama*, *Florida*, and *Shenandoah*. Under the command of Raphael Semmes, a complex former U.S. Navy officer and attorney whose wide-ranging intellectual powers meshed uneasily with his flamboyant, even obsessively zealous personality, the *Alabama* was the most successful by far of the Confederate raiders. Built on the River Mersey across from Liverpool and manned largely by British seamen, the *Alabama* throughout her world-ranging career was a source of dispute between the Union and British governments, not to be resolved until the post-war *Alabama* claims commission issued its decision. Semmes (condemned by Union sympathizers as nothing more than a pirate) fought his final battle of 19 June 1864 against a Mexican War shipmate, John Ancrum Winslow, whose own controversial naval career and his more immediate disappointments and frustrations in commanding the *Kearsarge* were erased by that vessel's decisive victory over the *Alabama* and her world-renowned commander.

The European-built *Florida*, previously commanded by John Newland Maffitt, maintained a threatening Confederate presence on the Atlantic

A Utilitarian View of the *Monitor*'s Fight

Plain be the phrase, yet apt the verse,
  More ponderous than nimble;
For since grimed War here laid aside
His Orient pomp, 'twould ill befit
    Overmuch to ply
  The rhyme's barbaric cymbal.

Hail to victory without the gaud
  Of glory; zeal that needs no fans
Of banners; plain mechanic power
Plied cogently in War now placed–
    Where War belongs–
  Among the trades and artisans.

Yet this was battle, and intense–
  Beyond the strife of fleets heroic;
Deadlier, closer, calm 'mid storm;
No passion; all went on by crank,
    Pivot, and screw,
  And calculations of caloric.

Needless to dwell; the story's known.
  The ringing of those plates on plates
Still ringeth round the world–
The clangor of that blacksmiths' fray.
    The anvil-din
  Resounds this message from the Fates:

War shall yet be, and to the end;
  But war-paint shows the streaks of
  weather;
War yet shall be, but warriors
Are now but operatives; War's made
    Less grand than Peace,
  And a singe runs through lace and feather.

Herman Melville

sea-lanes until October 1864, when the Union steam frigate *Wachusett* violated international law by capturing her in the neutral harbor of Bahia, Brazil. Under the command of James Waddell the Confederate *Shenandoah*, another commerce raider built in England and commissioned by the remarkably effective Confederate agent James D. Bulloch, was a formidable presence in Pacific waters. However, the luster of her final achievement, in destroying much of America's whaling fleet in the North Pacific, was dimmed by having occurred in late June 1865, well after the war was over.

The Impact of War on Maritime Industries

The Confederate efforts in commerce raiding were undeniably impressive. More than 110,000 tons of Northern shipping, made up of 150 foreign traders and 50 coasters, were captured or destroyed, and most of these vessels were the big ships and barks that had carried so much of American's prewar cargoes. Even more significant was the "flight from the flag" of so many more of these big American sailing vessels. In an attempt to avoid capture and confiscation, many such vessels transferred registry to a foreign flag and thus achieved neutral status in wartime. For every vessel taken by commerce raiders, eight others were indirectly lost to America's merchant marine by such transfer of registry—more than 1,600 vessels aggregating 774,000 tons. Those merchant ships remaining under the American flag paid a heavy price, not just by running the risk of capture but also, as belligerents, by having to pay sharply higher insurance rates on vessels and cargoes. Moreover, their competitive position already was endangered by foreign ships charging substantially lower freight rates.

The result of all this was that American vessels during wartime suffered some 25 percent higher shipping costs than those of their leading foreign competitors. For an American merchant shipowner the alternative was all too easy to embrace: seek safety *and* high profits by going under foreign-flag registry. By 1865, then, more than one-third of the entire prewar American foreign trade fleet no longer sailed under the American flag; and because of a 1797 law specifying that an American vessel sold to a foreign nation or registered under a foreign flag could not be repatriated, the loss of these vessels to America's merchant marine became permanent.

Prewar American foreign trade had relied heavily on the export of raw cotton. From more than 3.5 million bales in 1859, such exports dropped to ten thousand in 1861, and even less in subsequent war years. The fleet transporting this cotton, where American vessels had outnumbered foreign carriers by four to one, suffered a comparably precipitous decline. Such small amounts of cotton as did move abroad were part of the Confederacy's efforts to supply foreign customers, especially in Great Britain and France. Yet even here the amount of cotton shipped from the South was sharply curtailed by the Confederate government, in the mistaken belief that British manufacturing interests would become so desperate in the face of an extreme cotton shortage that they would force Great Britain to extend formal diplomatic recognition to the Confederacy—or even come into the war as a Confederate ally in order to regain their lost raw material supplies.

The even larger American coastal fleet that had transported Southern cotton to Northern textile mills suffered an immense loss of business, since the inter-regional Atlantic coastal trade of all varieties of raw materials and manufactured goods, along with passengers, now effectively ceased. Moreover, here again it was not just a matter of brief if traumatic disruption; instead, the war experience marked the end of the American cotton fleet, both foreign and coastal. Cotton exports abroad were slow to recover and did not regain the prewar volume until 1879. By that time British and Canadian vessels, both old wooden sailers and the newer iron-hulled, screw-propelled steamers, dominated the carrying of American cotton abroad, to the extent that American vessels never regained more than one-third of this trade.

Lessons Learned or Not Learned: The War's Maritime Heritage

As naval historians Harold and Margaret Sprout observed many years ago, the United States experience with modern naval warfare in the 1860s produced, at best, a mixed result. Of the lessons to be learned, some

were ignored and others were misunderstood, either totally or in part. Clearly, advances in the technologies of ship design and construction, materials, systems of propulsion, armor, weaponry, munitions, and communications all indicated that a modern navy could no longer be quickly and effectively improvised at will. The "minuteman tradition" that might have been appropriate for the age of fighting sail no longer applied.

Merchant vessels, however large and fast, no longer could be converted into efficient men of war. During the American Wars for Independence large sailing ships could be so employed, since many of them were as heavily

built, and could be as heavily gunned, as most sailing warships. But by the 1860s, now an age of maritime steam, even the former Collins Line vessels were able to serve only as troop transports; with their huge, exposed side wheels, their military use, even as unarmored commerce destroyers, was not realistic for the new age of heavily armed and armored iron, screw-propelled steam warships.

Steam had supplanted sail power; iron armor (whether over wooden frames and planking or over iron hulls) had replaced unprotected wooden walls for warships. Even the wooden-hulled *Kearsarge* had been partly (perhaps crucially) protected by improvised chain-cable armor when bat-

Commerce raiding, as a strategic policy for determining the outcome of war, was no more successful in the 1860s than it had been in the War of 1812. The Confederacy might have seriously disrupted Northern mercantile enterprise, but commerce raiding failed to dictate the war's final results. Instead, a truly effective maritime and naval strategy had to rely on successfully blockading the enemy's coastline. The British had demonstrated this to Americans all too clearly in 1814; the Union Navy appeared to confirm this principle in the early 1860s, even granted that many Confederate blockade runners had easily slipped through the Union net throughout the war. To make a blockade effective, as some American naval strategists were coming to realize, one also had to command the open seas. Control of the sea-lanes, and using squadrons or fleets of naval warships to implement this control, was a vital principle of naval strategy: so argued Benjamin Isherwood and John Lenthall (who, ironically, had designed and produced the *Wampanoag* class of super-powerful commerce raiders) in their formal,

---

Because of its comparatively limited resources, the Confederacy was more innovative than the North in its approach to naval technology, leading in the development of the ironclad, the ram vessel, and the "torpedo" (underwater mine). The Confederacy also built the first submarine to sink an enemy warship, the H.L. Hunley. Built at Mobile, Alabama, early in 1863, to plans by Hunley and others, the forty-foot vessel was fashioned from a four-foot-diameter steam boiler, with tapered ends, diving planes, and a hand-cranked propeller. Eight men cranked the propeller while one steered. The vessel was designed to navigate under an enemy warship, towing a torpedo that would explode on contact, but it was later outfitted with a spar torpedo at the bow, which could be driven into an enemy ship's keel and detonated by a trigger line. Brought to Charleston in August 1863, the Hunley *underwent tests, sinking on several occasions and drowning most of her crews, including Hunley himself. The* H.L. Hunley *finally succeeded in attacking a Union vessel, the USS* Housatonic, *on 17 February 1864. The explosion sank the* Housatonic, *but the submarine and its crew did not return from the historic mission. Conrad Wise Chapman painted the* H.L. Hunley *at Charleston in 1863. At the bow is the torpedo spar. (Courtesy The Museum of the Confederacy, Richmond, Virginia; Katherine Wetzel photo)*

tling the unarmored, wooden-hulled Confederate raider *Alabama*. As new and symbolically important as these two vessels were during the war, they already were obsolete in design and in the battle tactics they represented. The ever-increasing need for iron armor was a function of improved gunnery, since rifled cannon firing explosive shells now determined the outcome of battle. The British and French navies, in particular, had recognized these realities and begun to accept such technological innovations by the late 1850s; but would the United States Navy, from its own wartime experience as well as in light of what was occurring abroad, respond to these new imperatives?

The Wartime
Shipbuilding Boom at
Mystic, Connecticut

In the North the effects of the Civil War on shipbuilding and shipping could be not better exemplified than in the seacoast village of Mystic, located in southeastern Connecticut.

On the eve of the war the lingering effects of the economic depression of 1857 were still being felt by the shipbuilders and shipowners at Mystic. Prior to this economic downturn, Mystic's vessels had been heavily immersed in the business of carrying cotton on the coastwise routes as well as across the Atlantic. Mystic's shipbuilders and investors had many commercial contacts in such Southern ports as Galveston, New Orleans, Mobile, Apalachicola, and Key West.

Nevertheless, in April of 1861, when the flag was fired upon at Fort Sumter in Charleston Harbor, Mystic's residents were aroused to a fever pitch of patriotic indignation despite the obvious loss of the cotton markets.

It soon became apparent, however, that the war might bring alternative economic opportunities. "All our shipyards are hard at work. Whatever the effect of the war in other places, we believe it will prove a benefit to Mystic" wrote the editor of the local newspaper a few weeks after Fort Sumter. And, so it was; before the war's end nearly 5 percent of the North's total wartime production of steamships would be launched from

the four shipyards of this small port. Fifty-seven steamers, the largest output in New England, would be built between June of 1861 and June of 1865. In addition, seventeen sailing vessels were also constructed. Mystic's population of 2,800 nearly doubled as shipyard workers with their families arrived to find employment. The war work at Mystic drew the attention of a New London, Connecticut, observer who noted "the sound of workmen's axe and hammer and the merry seacraft hum, earnestly obeying the call of our beloved and imperiled government for war keels, with which to seal the blockade of rebel ports. I have nowhere found so busy a town of late."

The yards received contracts for several naval vessels. The most famous of the war steamers was the experimental ironclad *Galena*, launched early in 1862 by Maxson, Fish & Co., who upgraded their yard with a shiphouse to shelter construction and brought in more than 100 ironworkers to install the intricate iron armor on the wooden hull. The Charles Mallory & Sons yard built the government-model "ninety-day" gunboat *Owasco*, and two steam vessels Mallory built on speculation, the *Stars and Stripes* and *Varuna*, were purchased by Cornelius Bushnell, the financial backer of the *Monitor*, who sold them to the government as gunboats.

However, the shipbuilders at Mystic specialized in the construction of coastal steam vessels, both side-wheel steamers for sheltered waters and more seaworthy screw-propelled steamers with auxiliary sails. Both types were suitable for troop and supply transports, and forty-six of the fifty-seven steamers launched at Mystic during the war were leased or sold outright to the War Department, the Navy Department, or the Quartermaster Corps. These forgotten workhorse vessels, with names such as *Thorn*, *Idaho*, and *City Point*, were in constant service between Northern ports and Union supply centers in the South, as well as blockade rendezvous points on the Atlantic and Gulf coasts. Even the Greenman brothers, whose religious faith mixed abolitionism with pacifism, participated in this lucrative work.

Fourteen of the eighteen vessels they built during the war were chartered for naval or transport service. The Reliance Machine Company and the Mystic Iron Works were also busy manufacturing and installing engines and boilers for Mystic-built steamers as well as for vessels built elsewhere. Yet the boom was short-lived. From twenty-one vessels launched in 1864, the number declined to just six in each of the following two years, and wooden shipbuilding at Mystic would never regain its prominence in the local economy.

If shipbuilding activity brought short-term work and wealth, the war did have its downside for shipowners. Early in the conflict the Mystic-built clipper ship *Harvey Birch* was among the first of the American merchant marine to succumb to the activities of Confederate commerce raiders. Its capture and destruction off the New England coast by the Confederate steamer *Nashville* signaled hard times for shippers and owners in the North. Before the end of 1864 the Mystic-built ship *B.F. Hoxie* and the barks *Texana*, *Tycoon*, and *Lapwing* were destroyed in similar fashion by the *Alabama* and other raiders. These incidents, and many others, of the so-called "rebel piracy" sent insurance rates on American vessels skyrocketing. This in turn accelerated the move to sell American ships abroad during the war, including at least fifteen large Mystic-built sailing vessels, among them the famous clippers *Twilight* and *Andrew Jackson*. While a few large

sailing vessels would be built and owned in Mystic during the decade after peace returned to the seas in 1865, this "flight from the flag" symbolized the declining fortunes of Mystic shipowners and shipmasters, as well as their neighbor shipbuilders. The community would never regain the maritime heights it had attained during the "golden age" of the 1850s.

William N. Peterson

Launched at Mystic, Connecticut, in 1854, the clipper ship Harvey Birch *was built for the California trade, but also served in the cotton trade out of New Orleans and in North Atlantic trade before the Civil War. In November 1861 the* Harvey Birch *was returning to New York from Le Havre, France, when she was captured and burned by the Confederate commerce raider* Nashville. *The* Nashville, *a prewar passenger steamer on the New York-to-Charleston run, was appropriated for Confederate service after the fall of Fort Sumter. In October 1861 the* Nashville *ran the blockade and crossed the Atlantic as the first vessel to fly the Confederate flag in British waters. On her return to North Carolina she captured the* Harvey Birch *and another Northern vessel. Thereafter, the 215-foot side-wheel steamer became the blockade-runner* Thomas L. Wragg *and the Confederate privateer* Rattlesnake *before she was destroyed by Union forces in February 1863. Duncan McFarlane painted this scene in 1864. (Courtesy Peabody Essex Museum, Salem, Massachusetts; Mark Sexton photo)*

Launched at Cincinnati, Ohio, early in 1863, the 260-foot side-wheel steamboat Sultana *went into service on the Ohio and upper Mississippi Rivers, frequently carrying troops and military supplies. After the fall of the Confederate strongholds at Vicksburg and Port Hudson opened the Mississippi, she began commercial runs between St. Louis and New Orleans. With a crew of eighty, and forty passengers on board, the* Sultana *arrived at Vicksburg in April 1865 as former prisoners of war were being shipped north to be discharged. Although rated to carry 376 passengers, the* Sultana *took on board at least 1,964 paroled prisoners for the upriver trip. This photograph of the* Sultana *and her human cargo was taken by T.W. Bankes at Helena, Arkansas, on 26 April 1865. Less than a day later, just upriver from Memphis, the ship's boilers exploded. More than 1,700 were scalded, burned to death, or drowned in the conflagration. The loss remains the worst maritime disaster in U.S. history. (Courtesy Library of Congress)*

published report to Secretary Welles in 1862. But the time and circumstances for embracing such a departure from traditional American ideas about naval strategy were not right; this lesson in the fundamentals of sea power, as it soon became glaringly apparent, was one that the United States and its navy was unwilling to accept, either during the war or for several decades into the postwar era.

Yet the larger issue of the war's impact persists: Was the war so responsible for the undeniable postwar decline of America's maritime fortunes? Even before the war's outbreak there were visible signs of change, both within the United States and abroad, that would fundamentally alter the American maritime situation, war or no war. After 1865, having undergone the convulsions of such a major war, the United States undeniably was a different nation in many ways. What part would maritime enterprise, both civilian and naval, play in that postwar nation, and how great—or little—would such a maritime role be?

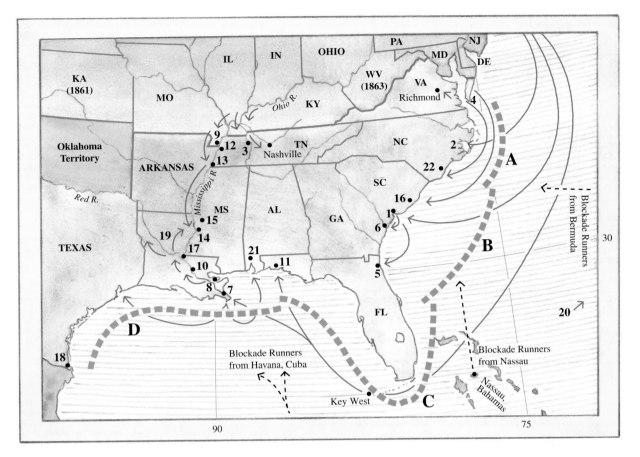

Figure 6 **Civil War Naval Actions and Blockades**

Movements

 Union Activity

━ ━ ━ ━ Union Blockading Squadrons

A North Atlantic Squadron
B South Atlantic Squadron
C East Gulf Squadron
D West Gulf Squadron

- - - - -> Confederate Activity

Union States

Confederate States

Principal Actions

1. Port Royal/Beaufort/Hilton Head, South Carolina, November 1861
2. Albemarle Sound, North Carolina, February 1862
3. Fort Henry/Fort Donelson, Tennessee, February 1862
4. Hampton Roads, Virginia, March 1862
5. Jacksonville, Florida, March 1862
6. Fort Pulaski, Georgia, April 1862
7. Forts Jackson and St. Philip, Louisiana, April 1862
8. New Orleans, Louisiana, April 1862
9. Island No. 10, Missouri, April 1862
10. Baton Rouge, Louisiana, May 1862
11. Pensacola, Florida, May 1862
12. Plum Point Bend/Ft. Pillow, Tennessee, May 1862
13. Memphis, Tennessee, June 1862
14. Vicksburg, Mississippi, June 1862-July 1863
15. Yazoo River, Mississippi, July 1862-March 1863
16. Charleston, South Carolina, April 1863-February 1865
17. Port Hudson, Louisiana, May-July 1863
18. Brownsville, Texas, November 1863
19. Red River, Louisiana, March-April 1864
20. *Kearsarge* vs. *Alabama*, Cherbourg, France, June 1864
21. Mobile Bay, Alabama, August 1864
22. Fort Fisher/Wilmington, North Carolina, January-February 1865

(Dennis O'Brien map)

Part 3

Rise to World Power, 1865-1939

CHAPTER 10

The Sea and Post-Civil-War America

W

HEN THE principal armies of the Confederate States of America surrendered in April 1865, effectively ending the Civil War, the Confederate flag still flew at sea. On 28 June 1865, the last active Confederate commerce raider, CSS *Shenandoah*, had her most successful single day, capturing eleven New England whalers in the Bering Strait. More than a month later, Captain Waddell of the *Shenandoah* hailed an English bark and received positive news that the war was over. With guns stowed, the ship rounded Cape Horn and traversed the Atlantic, arriving at Liverpool, England, in a passage of 123 days under sail. There, Waddell surrendered the *Shenandoah*, ending the existence of the Confederate States Navy. The fate of the Confederacy's last commerce raider illustrates several things about the maritime world in the aftermath of the American Civil War. It suggests the time delay typical in maritime affairs of that time; it highlights the reason behind the concern for the safety of merchant commerce that dominated the Civil War at sea and postwar

diplomatic and naval concerns; and it clearly shows that this was an era of British maritime ascendancy.

Consciously and unconsciously, Britain's maritime presence remained an important factor in American calculations throughout this period. Most of the time Americans silently dealt with it as an accepted reality; at other times it was a source of dispute. In his first State of the Union message to Congress in December 1865, President Andrew Johnson underscored the role that Britain had played in fitting out ships for the Confederacy and encouraging attacks on American commerce. "The consequences of this conduct were most disastrous to the States then in rebellion," Johnson declared, "increasing their desolation and misery by the prolongation of our

Detail of the Neptune *crossing the fishing banks, by John E.C. Peterson, 1866. (M.S.M. 58.626; Mary Anne Stets photo)*

civil contest. It had moreover, the effect, mostly, to drive the American flag from the sea, and to transfer much of our shipping and our commerce to the very power whose subjects had created the necessity for such a change." In the years that followed, this very point became the issue in a long diplomatic dispute between the United States and Britain.

The *Alabama* Claims

As Andrew Johnson made clear, the United States held Britain responsible for $2,125,000,000 worth of direct and indirect damages that the British-built CSS *Alabama*, *Florida*, and *Shenandoah* had wrought on U.S. shipping during the war. The prolonged diplomatic negotiations over this issue lasted until 1872. In the background, some American politicians loudly backed schemes to invade or otherwise incorporate Canada into the United States. Even before this, Canadians had sensed the danger of retaliation from the northern United States, further spurring the confederation movement to unify the provinces of British North America. The Johnson administration ended trade reciprocity in 1866, acquired Alaska from Russia in 1867, and failed to curb the raids on Canada by New York Irish immigrants who hoped to negotiate the independence of Ireland. Sentiment continued to grow in Canada for unified relations with Britain. In 1867, Parliament passed the British North America Act, joining Quebec, Ontario, Nova Scotia, and New Brunswick to create the Dominion of Canada. With the Dominion's further growth to include Manitoba and British Columbia in 1870-71, additional issues arose in maritime relations with the United States.

In trying to solve some of these postwar problems, Britain and the United States reached a compromise in the Treaty of Washington. Britain avoided a full apology for building and arming Confederate raiders, but expressed "in a friendly spirit, the regret felt by Her Majesty's Government for the escape, under whatever circumstances, of the *Alabama* and other vessels from British ports and the depredations committed by those vessels."

The treaty left several issues for arbitration at an international tribunal, and this was an important innovation in international affairs, reviving a procedure that had not been widely used since medieval times. A panel of representatives from Italy, Switzerland, and Brazil, meeting in Geneva, ruled that Britain should pay an indemnity of $15,500,000 to the United States for the direct damages, but gave no award for the larger sum claimed as indirect damages. The emperor of Germany, Kaiser Wilhelm I, was the final arbiter for establishing the maritime boundary between the American Washington Territory and Britain's Vancouver Island, while the treaty itself provided for a ten-year period of fishing and trade rights. This laid the basis for a continuing pattern of consultative arrangements to defuse potential crises. In addition, U.S. citizens gained the freedom of navigating the St. Lawrence River from the Great Lakes to the sea in exchange for freedom of British subjects to navigate several rivers in Alaska.

The settlement of the *Alabama* Claims was a significant achievement in U.S. diplomatic efforts involving maritime issues, but it did not affect the deterioration of American naval and mercantile strength. In contrast to the flourishing American maritime industries before the Civil War, the postwar years witnessed marked decline. In 1865 alone, the U.S. Navy reduced the number of ships on its register from 530 to 117 and the number of officers and men from 51,000 to 12,128.

Such a drop is typical for a navy in an immediate postwar period, but the nature of the U.S. merchant marine also changed. The fleet engaged in internal trade flourished, but on international routes American ships carried less and less of the nation's foreign trade, falling from 33 percent in 1865, to 16 percent in 1881, to 8.7 percent in 1910. By the eve of the First World War, only 2 percent of the world's deep-sea carriers flew the American flag.

Consequently, while the period between the Civil War and World War I has been variously called the "Gilded Age," the "Age of Excess," the "Age of Energy," and the "Age of Enterprise"–as it certainly was for American finance, heavy industry, and internal development–it was an age of profound change for the traditional American maritime industries. The maritime patterns that characterize this period are important reflections of national values and economic preoccupations in a time of intense internal development that became the basis for the nation's international prominence in the twentieth century.

The Period of Profound Peace, 1865-1897

In the decade immediately after the Civil War, American society changed rapidly. Wartime production had spurred economic growth in agriculture, industry, and transportation, and much of this growth continued after the war, spreading into the South during the economic reconstruction of the defeated Confederate states. Nearly five million acres of land in the West was transferred to settlers and corporations in that decade. During the war, the redirection of agricultural workers into military service had forced the remaining farmers to adopt labor-saving machinery, increasing the efficiency and scale of agricultural production. Railroads in the North and West increased by 4,000 miles of track, while production of iron rails doubled. Even before the war ended, charters were granted for the construction of a transcontinental railroad, which provided access to new agricultural land in the West and, after its completion in 1869, offered a convenient overland connection to the Pacific coast.

In the immediate postwar decade, the production of bituminous coal for steam generation and iron smelting was 50 percent greater than it had been in the prewar decade. Pig-iron production doubled, and the production of American steel began on an economical basis. All of these developments had an impact on the direction of the nation's maritime industries.

Postwar industrial development was encouraged by government policy. A few years earlier the 1862 Homestead law, the Morrill Land Grant Act (1862) for the benefit of agricultural and mechanical education, and the creation of a national banking system in 1863, had all contributed to fostering continued industrialization and the growth of American capitalism. Immediately after the Civil War, these expansive trends in the United States coincided with a crisis in European economic, agricultural, and industrial growth. As a result, a surge of European immigrants–averaging nearly 300,000 per year between 1865 and 1875–brought workers to an America that needed their skills and their sweat. The assimilation of these new people brought labor, ethnic, and social tensions, but this expansion of the work force began a long-term increase in jobs for those in transportation, communication, trade, and clerical occupations.

The stature of the American merchant marine is generally measured by the tonnage registered for foreign trade. This was clearly in decline after 1865; but internal tonnage was just as clearly on the rise. The nation's enrolled or coastal and internal tonnage had surpassed the registered tonnage as early as 1838. Even when the registered tonnage reached a peak of 2,500,000 tons in 1861, the enrolled tonnage was 150,000 tons greater. In 1866 there was a change in the formula for measuring tonnage in the U.S. This technical change in measurement resulted in reduced tonnage figures, but enrolled tonnage grew steadily until, in 1900, the nation's 4,286,000 enrolled tons were four times the total of registered tonnage. And although coastal and river vessels were increasingly powered by steam, it was not until 1894 that steam tonnage surpassed sail. Even in 1900, sailing vessels represented more than 46 percent of the American fleet. That year, 59 percent of the enrolled tonnage operated on saltwater coastal routes, 36 percent on the Great Lakes, and 5 percent on the western rivers.

To a large degree, the trades that occupied enrolled tonnage were based on natural resources being exploited in ever-greater quantities. The lumber trade, for example, kept a large fleet of schooners active on the East Coast, carrying soft pine timber south from Maine and hard pine timber north from Georgia and Florida. Lumber was in constant demand in the expanding cities for new housing and new factories.

The center of the American timber industry had moved steadily west from Maine to Pennsylvania and then to Michigan at mid-century. By the 1890s, Duluth, Minnesota, was the leading timber port, shipping lumber to the growing cities along the Great Lakes, and served by a fleet of increasingly larger wooden schooners built in Great Lakes shipyards.

On the West Coast, the timber resources of the Pacific Northwest were tapped even before the

The vast coastal forests of the Pacific Northwest began to be cut for the lumber trade as early as the 1850s. Here at Port Blakely, established on the west side of Washington's Puget Sound in 1863, workers load rough-sawn lumber aboard a fleet of European and American square-rigged ships. By the 1890s the sawmill at Port Blakely alone could produce nearly a million board feet of lumber per day, producing cargo for delivery to California, Australia, the East Coast, and Europe. Stereograph, ca. 1895. (M.S.M. 92.2.3)

Civil War with the tremendous expansion of San Francisco. By the 1870s, sawmill communities, such as Grey's Harbor on the Washington coast and Port Blakely on Puget Sound, were producing millions of board feet of Douglas-fir lumber. Schooners carried much of the output south to California. An international trade also developed, shipping lumber to Australia and Europe, mostly in foreign bottoms. The great redwood forests of northern California also contributed to the trade. But on this exposed coast, vessels frequently had to load at "dog holes"—slight indentations in the coastal bluffs—using a catenary wire to sling the cargo out to the anchored vessel. From about 1880, West Coast schooners began to add auxiliary steam propulsion. Known locally as "steam schooners," they were handy in the small rivers and shallow harbors that larger lumber carriers could not reach. In 1893, further changes came to this fleet when the Kerchoff-Cuzner Company of Los Angeles introduced oil for fuel in their small steam schooner *Pasadena*. After the discovery of oil at Petrolia, California, shipowners quickly

shifted to the new fuel. By 1911, less than a dozen steam schooners in California were still coal-fired.

Other construction materials carried by water included the lime, granite, and brownstone of New England. Lime kilns at Rockland, on Maine's Penobscot Bay, for example, produced quick lime for the production of plaster. A fleet of small coasting schooners carried the lime to Boston and New York. This was a dangerous trade, as these vessels faced a fiery end if the barreled lime got wet and produced spontaneous combustion. Quarries on islands in Penobscot Bay and on the Connecticut coast produced granite for street curbing and for fireproof and ornamental building construction. The quarries around Rockport on Cape Ann, Massachusetts, specialized in cutting granite paving blocks for city streets. Until the demand for granite declined in the twentieth century with the expansion of steel and concrete construction, "stone schooners" delivered their heavy cargoes to ports along the Atlantic seaboard.

Natural ice, cut on lakes in winter and stored in insulated warehouses, remained an important commodity through the second half of the nineteenth century. The Maine ice trade from the Kennebec and Penobscot Rivers grew rapidly after the Civil War, carried to market in wooden schooners. Just a decade before mechanical refrigeration began to replace natural ice, Benjamin Morse and his Knickerbocker Towing Company introduced large barges to the trade. His firm eventually merged all the natural-ice companies of the northeast coast into the American Ice Company in 1899.

If the nineteenth century was the age of steam, it was also the age of coal. The hard anthracite coal of northeast Pennsylvania began to be commercially important after an effective grate for burning it was developed in 1814. The shift from wood to coal to heat city buildings in the 1830s and 1840s increased the demand for coal transportation. Canals linked the coal region with both Philadelphia and Rondout Creek on the Hudson River, and schooners carried the coal to markets up and down the East Coast. In the post-Civil War period, this trade continued to expand.

In an early example of vertical integration, the Reading Railroad, which tapped the northeast-Pennsylvania coalfields and owned mines there,

The 126-foot steam schooner Phoenix *is securely moored at Mendocino, California, while cargo is delivered by means of a catenary wire. Launched at Alameda, California, in 1902, this typical Pacific Coast steam schooner, with a crew of thirteen, worked the "dog holes" of northern California, exchanging packaged goods for lumber. Despite the rugged shore and insufficient harbors, the sea remained the principal transportation route in this region until the advent of paved highways well into the twentieth century. (Courtesy Nannie Escola Photographic Collection, San Francisco Maritime National Historical Park)*

built a fleet of small iron-hulled steam-powered colliers to deliver anthracite from Philadelphia to New York and New England. The company also bought waterfront property in a number of ports and built coal docks to store its product for local distribution. The Reading also pioneered the use of schooner-rigged barges, towed singly or in strings, to deliver anthracite along the coast. Between 1879 and 1919, the Palmer shipyard in Noank, Connecticut, alone built more than 165 of these specialized barges.

The most important coal trade was in soft, bituminous coal from western Pennsylvania, Maryland, and West Virginia. Soft coal had supplanted wood for industrial steam generation well before the Civil War, and gas for urban lighting was a derivative of coal combustion. Both the Chesapeake and Ohio Canal and the Baltimore and Ohio Railroad were early links between western coalfields and tidewater ports in the 1840s.

In 1881 Collis P. Huntington's Chesapeake & Ohio Railroad reached Newport News, Virginia, to link the West Virginia coalfields to marine transportation. Two years later, the Norfolk & Western Railroad connected the Pocahontas coalfields to the port of Norfolk, across Hampton Roads from Newport News, and in 1909 H.H. Rogers's Virginian Railroad linked the Kanawha coalfield to Norfolk, where the Sewalls Point facility became the nation's largest coal dock, handling 36,000 tons a day.

The demand for coal increased as the nation adopted Thomas Edison's light bulb and electric-generating system in the 1880s. Although only 8 percent of the nation's homes were wired for electricity by 1907, these were largely in urban areas where there was heavy demand for electricity in businesses and factories. And a network of electric street railways and interurban lines developed throughout the northeast, all powered by electric plants that burned coal.

The 329-foot, six-masted schooner Wyoming *was the largest wooden vessel to carry cargo under sail. Launched at Bath, Maine, in 1909 as the last of ten six-masted coal schooners, the* Wyoming *spent fifteen years carrying coal from Hampton Roads, Virginia, to New England ports before she ran aground and was lost in 1924. The* Wyoming *was particularly fast and easy to handle for such a large ship, but even she could not match the reliable schedule kept by the new steam-powered colliers that drove the coal schooners out of business during the first quarter of the twentieth century. Henry D. Fisher photographed the* Wyoming *unloading at a coal-fired power plant in Boston in 1911. (M.S.M. 76.208.671A)*

To meet the rising demand for coal, the average size of a three-masted coal schooner grew from 500 to 920 gross tons (about 180 feet in length) during the 1870s. In 1879, the first of sixty-seven four-masters appeared. These schooners, averaging about 1,700 tons and 230 feet, were followed after 1889 by fifty-five five-masted schooners, averaging about 2,500 tons and 260 feet. The first six-master, the *George W. Wells*, was built in 1900 and, with a crew half the size of a steam collier's complement, could efficiently haul 5,000 tons of coal in a single passage. The *Wyoming*, largest of this type and, at 329 feet and 3,730 tons, the largest wooden ship to carry cargo, operated with a crew of only a dozen men.

In 1907 the New England Gas and Coke Company ordered the large steel steam colliers *Everett*, *Malden*, and *Melrose*. Although these vessels cost about twice as much as a comparable wooden schooner, and their crews were twice the size of a schooner crew, they made about four times as many voyages per year and on an annual basis were at least three times as efficient as a schooner. By the 1920s, steam colliers would supplant sailing schooners in the coal trade.

Perhaps the greatest volume of bulk cargo was handled on the Great Lakes. As early as the 1840s, copper and iron deposits had been discovered on the Upper Peninsula of Michigan, near the shores of Lake Superior. Attempts to smelt the ore at locations close to the mines–for example at Fayette, Michigan–failed due to problems in finding workers and marketing the finished iron. At first, ships took Minnesota ore cargoes to the eastern end of Lake Superior, where they were portaged overland around the falls on the St. Mary's River before continuing down Lake Huron and Lake Erie to ports close to the coalfields of Pennsylvania, such as Ashtabula and Cleveland in Ohio, and Erie in Pennsylvania.

In the years before the Civil War, these cargoes were relatively small, and the nation's iron pro-

The *Thomas W. Lawson*

Even after steamships had captured the market for passengers and fast freight, there was still a role for sailing ships in the coastal trades with low-value, bulk cargoes. In the 1870s, the growing demand for coal led to an increase in the size of coal-carrying vessels. At the time, the typical coal-carrier was a schooner with three masts of equal height, called a "tern." During that decade, the size of coal schooners grew from about 500 to 920 tons, and they were soon carrying steam "donkey" engines to help reduce crew numbers in handling the sails. By the turn of the century, four-, five-, and six-masted schooners had been introduced to carry large cargoes with crews as small as twelve men.

The largest schooner ever built, and the only seven-masted one, was the 395-foot, 11,000-ton *Thomas W. Lawson*. Designed by Bowdoin B. Crowninshield, the steel-hulled schooner was built at the Fore River Shipbuilding Company of Quincy, Massachusetts, in 1902 at the cost of $240,000. The *Lawson* had steam-powered steering gear, steam-heated quarters, and a double bottom to carry water ballast. The sails for the middle five masts were identical and could be interchanged. This efficient vessel could be handled by only sixteen men.

Sailing in the coal trade between Hampton Roads, Virginia, and Boston, the *Lawson* reportedly earned

$75,000 per year in freight. However, the ship proved to be difficult to handle and expensive to operate. Converted to an oil tanker in 1907, after only five years of service, the *Lawson* was wrecked on the Scilly Isles during an intense storm as she approached England on her first deep-water voyage.

The 395-foot, steel-hulled **Thomas W. Lawson,** *the only seven-masted schooner built. Nathaniel L. Stebbins photographed the* **Lawson** *in 1902. (M.S.M. 83.23.1)*

Saluted by fishermen in a skiff, the tug Champion *tows a string of Great Lakes schooners in the Detroit River. Although these schooners are taking advantage of steam power to pass through the constricted Detroit River on their way between Lake Huron and Lake Erie, they indicate a common practice in Lakes navigation from the 1870s through the 1890s of combining a steam freighter with one or more consort barges or schooners in tow. Seth Arco Whipple painted this watercolor, ca. 1880. (From the collections of Henry Ford Museum & Greenfield Village, Dearborn, Michigan)*

duction was centered in eastern Pennsylvania and New York. Even in the early years, however, some investors saw future opportunities in improving water access to the ore deposits around Lake Superior. Charles T. Harvey combined forces with a group of businessmen that included August Belmont, Erastus Corning, and John Murray Forbes, to invest in mineral lands and finance the construction of two 350-foot locks at Sault Ste. Marie, Michigan. These were completed in 1855 and were the first of the famous "Soo" Locks.

Iron mining on the Great Lakes expanded rapidly after the Civil War. In 1873, 1,750,000 tons of ore were shipped from the Marquette Range in Northern Michigan. At the same time, the Northwestern Railroad opened a new line from the Menominee Range to the Lake

Michigan port of Escanaba, providing an entirely new outlet. Having increased four-fold between 1865 and 1880, shipments of iron ore from the Lake Superior ports rose dramatically from 1,908,745 gross tons in 1880 to 10,429,037 tons in 1890, and to 46,318,747 tons in 1915. In 1884 the Vermilion Range opened an outlet to shipping at Two Harbors, Minnesota, and in 1885 the port of Ashland, Michigan, began to tap ore from the Gogebic Range. The largest source of all, Minnesota's Mesabi Range, was opened in 1891, and thereafter Duluth became the principal iron-shipping port.

The nation's insatiable demand for iron and steel produced a highly integrated rail and water transportation system to carry the ore by rail from the mines to loading facilities on the western shore of Lake Superior, by water through the locks at

Sault Ste. Marie to the Cleveland area, and again by rail to the mills and foundries close to the coal deposits near Pittsburgh, which quickly developed into the center of the nation's iron and steel industry. And with that industry's need for lime, ships began to carry limestone on the Great Lakes from newly opened quarries in Michigan.

Other centers for iron and steel developed on the Great Lakes. With Illinois coal as a resource, industrialists in Detroit and Chicago built iron and steel plants. For example, in 1906 J. Pierpont Morgan's U.S. Steel Corporation built a new steel mill at the southern end of Lake Michigan, where water and land transport met halfway between the Mesabi Iron Range and the source of coal in southern Illinois. U.S. Steel created a major steel mill and a city it named Gary, Indiana, in honor of its chairman of the board, Elbert H. Gary.

These dramatic developments on America's Inland Seas created specialized methods for handling cargoes as well as specialized types of ships. The first ore carriers were typical sailing craft of the time and about 700-800 tons in size. The first ship designed especially to carry iron ore, the *R.J. Hackett,* was launched at Cleveland in 1869. Setting the pattern for future Great Lakes ore-ship design, despite its wooden hull, the vessel was steam-powered, with the propulsion machinery aft to permit a continuous hold and with large hatches spaced twenty-four feet apart.

The new ore-ship design, the ever-increasing demand for iron from the northern Great Lakes ports, and the short navigation season encouraged the development of rapid cargo-handling methods. At first, ore ships were loaded with wheelbarrows and carts, but in 1872 the Lake Superior port of L'Anse, Michigan, introduced a loading complex of tipples, by which ore was dumped from railroad cars through chutes into ships' holds. Thereafter, ore ports featured these trestle-like railroad piers for loading.

Increasing efficiency in unloading ore ships was somewhat more difficult. In 1867 Cleveland dockmaster J. D. Bothwell reduced unloading time to a third by employing steam engines instead of horses to power the winches that lifted buckets of ore out of the holds. In 1892, dockmaster Alexander Brown developed an unloading system using a series of buckets running on a cable from the ship to the pier. Later, Brown developed a large bucket that hoisted five tons of ore at a time through the cargo hatches. In 1899, George H. Hulett improved on this with a clamshell bucket that held fifteen tons. Although it required enlarged hatches, and thus changed the design of ore carriers, the Hulett unloader was so efficient that it became the standard.

By the 1870s Great Lakes steamship design was distinctively different from ocean steamship design. The loose ore cargo demanded straight, hopper-like sides and flat bottoms; the loading and unloading equipment necessitated removal of all obstructions above and below decks; and the increasing demand for more cargo meant larger ships. The width of the Soo Locks, however, restricted beam, and the result was the long, narrow vessels characteristic of Great Lakes trades.

The relative cheapness of wooden ships made them attractive as ore carriers for many years, but larger hulls and weight of cargo demanded greater strength. The first iron-hulled ore carrier, *Onoko,* was not built until 1882; the first steel steamer, *Spokane,* was launched in 1886. In the first decade of the new century, steel vessels became more common as 297 ore freighters were launched in Great Lakes shipyards, which pioneered in the use of pneumatic riveting for steel ships. At the same time, ships became longer, reaching 600 feet with the *J. Pierpont Morgan* of 1906. The *Morgan* remained the largest ore carrier built on the Lakes until the 1930s.

The increasing length of ore ships had only one restriction: the size of the Soo Locks. The locks had to be made larger, and in 1881 the 515-foot Wetzel Lock opened with a seventeen-foot depth. A new 900-foot lock on the Canadian side of the river opened in 1895, followed a year later by the 800-foot Poe Lock on the American side, with a width of 100 feet and depth of 22 feet. The Soo Locks reached 1,350 feet in length with the Davis Lock of 1914 and the Sabin Lock of 1919.

Ore was not the only bulk commodity that traveled on the Great Lakes. Grain from Minnesota and the Dakotas was shipped from Chicago and other western ports through the Lakes to Buffalo and other rail terminals for delivery to the coast. The Great Lakes proved to be a barrier to the nation's expanding rail network until, in 1888, rail

Whaleback Steamships

One of the most radical ship designs of the late nineteenth century appeared on the Great Lakes: the whaleback. Innovation was not new for Great Lakes ships. The U.S. Navy's first iron-hulled ship, the USS *Michigan*, had been launched at Erie, Pennsylvania, in 1843, and she remained afloat on the Lakes for more than a century. Toward the end of the nineteenth century, a number of significant changes were taking place that allowed much larger vessels to use the Lakes. As cargoes shifted from lumber to grain to iron ore, Great Lakes shipping grew dramatically. In 1886, twenty-one steamships on the Lakes were larger than 1,500 net tons, and there were just six steel-hulled ships. Four years later, in 1890, 110 Lakes steamers exceeded 1,500 tons, and there were sixty-eight steel-hulled ships.

Conditions on the Lakes strongly influenced local ship design. Iron- and steel-hulled ships offered a great advantage. Their strong and durable hulls could withstand the rough cargo-loading methods used in the iron ore trade as well as deal with the short, steep seas on the Lakes. At the same time, the need to navigate rivers as well as ship-canals required ships that were long and narrow.

Among a wide range of successful innovations to meet these conditions, the whaleback design offered the most radical profile. Captain Alexander McDougall, who invented the whaleback, was a successful mariner and stevedore on the Great Lakes who had emigrated from Scotland to Canada as a child. McDougall patented the design of his distinctive whaleback model in 1881 and 1882, but he was not able to finance construction of one until 1888. The first whaleback launched was the 191-foot barge *101*. A number of larger, 253- and 276-foot-long barges followed, and in 1890 the first whaleback steam-powered freighter, the *Colgate Hoyt*, was launched at Duluth.

Both barges and steamers had a flat bottom, a flattened cylindrical shape, and conical bow and stern. The freighters had a rounded turret forward that housed deck winches. Aft, more rounded turrets supported the cabins, which housed machinery and crew. The pilothouse was located on top of the after cabin. With a low profile and extremely strong construction, whalebacks were especially stable and practical for operating in the strong winds and waves of the Great Lakes. Nevertheless, many people ridiculed their look, suggesting that they resembled floating cigars. With their distinctive cylindrical, blunt bow that looked like a snout, they were nicknamed "pig-boats."

After building his initial whaleback barge, McDougall solicited financing from John D. Rockefeller's associate, the banker and railroad developer Colgate Hoyt. He then chartered the American Steel Barge Company to construct the vessels, and in 1890 McDougall moved his yard to Superior, Wisconsin, where he was able to build his vessels for less than two-thirds the cost of a conventional Great Lakes iron steamship. In 1892, McDougall became involved in the railroad company that was connecting the new Mesabi Iron Range to Duluth in order to secure a monopoly on the line's shipment of iron ore for his whalebacks. Comparative tests on the 900-mile route from Duluth to Ashtabula suggested that a whaleback could be operated for slightly more than half the operational cost of a conventional steamer.

McDougall also saw opportunities for whalebacks on salt water. In 1891 he piloted the whaleback steamer *Charles W. Wetmore* down the St. Lawrence River rapids to the sea. She carried Canadian grain to Liverpool, and on her arrival an English newspaper reported, "As evidence of her steadiness at sea, when the hatches were taken off the foot prints and shovel marks of the grain trimmers were plainly visible in the cargo. The wheat had not shifted at all in the voyage, so steadily did the whaleback run."

Returning across the Atlantic to Philadelphia, the *Wetmore* was loaded with industrial equipment and made a passage around Cape Horn to Everett, Washington, where McDougall had established the Pacific Steel Barge Company to build whalebacks to carry bulk cargo on the Pacific. The new yard launched the *City of Everett* in 1894, and the ship delivered a cargo of grain to India before completing the first circumnavigation of the globe by an American steamship.

Inspired by the *Charles W. Wetmore*, British shipbuilders developed a modified whaleback design with conventional bow and stern called "turret" ships after the first of the type, the *Turret Court*.

The most famous of the whalebacks was the passenger ship *Christopher Columbus*, built in 1892 for the World's Columbian Exposition in Chicago. McDougall promised to build the vessel in just three months if Hoyt's associates would finance her. He produced the elegantly appointed vessel on time, and she carried nearly two million passengers during the 1893 exposition season. The *Christopher Columbus* went on to operate as a passenger steamer until she was scrapped in 1937, having carried more passengers than any other American vessel.

McDougall's energy and demonstrated ability made him a hero among proponents of an expanded American merchant marine. However, the financial Panic of 1893 curtailed McDougall's operations. Squeezed out of the management of the American Steel Barge Company when he could not pay for his stock option in the company, McDougall lost his patents. The company built a few more vessels, but enthusiasm for the type was waning. The last and largest whaleback, at 413 feet and 3,672 tons and designed with a conventional

McDougall's iron-hulled whaleback barge 130 lies at the grain elevators in Chicago, loading a cargo of wheat for delivery to Buffalo, New York. This barge was one of ten whalebacks built at McDougall's American Steel Barge shipyard at Superior, Wisconsin, in 1893 before the national economic panic halted operations and McDougall lost his financial stake in the company. Only a few whalebacks were built after 1893, and the once-promising design was superseded by conventional ships better suited to new ore-unloading equipment. Like many whalebacks, barge 130 migrated to salt water, carrying coal on the Atlantic Coast until being scrapped in Texas in 1924. (M.S.M. 94.87.1)

bow, was launched in 1898 with the appropriate name *Alexander McDougall*. In all, seventeen whaleback steamships and twenty-six whaleback barges had been built in the U.S. through McDougall's efforts.

Despite the fact that whalebacks were inexpensive and easy to build, few other shipbuilders were interested in the patented design. McDougall himself turned his energies elsewhere after losing control

of his patents. And the small cargo hatches of the whalebacks were unsuited to the the large bulk ore unloaders, such as the Hulett, which were being developed in the 1890s. By the end of the decade, these curious ships had been converted for other uses, such as grain shipping, or sent to the Atlantic to carry coal or oil. Only one survives, the *Meteor*, ex-*Frank Rockefeller*, preserved at Superior, Wisconsin.

Having made the 900-mile passage from Duluth, the ore-carrier J. Pierpont Morgan *has steam up as she lies alongside the new Hulett unloaders at Ashtabula, Ohio. Launched in 1906, the 600-foot* Morgan *was the largest ship on the Great Lakes for thirty years, easily carrying 14,000 tons of iron ore in her hold. The ship survived until 1979. First installed in 1899, the steam-powered Hulett unloader was a form of mobile steam shovel, mounted on a gantry crane bridging railroad tracks. The operator rode in a control booth directly above the clamshell bucket, descending into the hold to scoop up fifteen tons of ore, rising up, then rolling back to deposit the ore into railroad hopper cars for delivery to ironworks in Ohio and Pennsylvania. This gang of Hulett unloaders could hoist sixty tons at a time, greatly increasing the efficiency of ore-handling and increasing the size of ships that could be operated economically in the ore trade. (Courtesy Great Lakes Marine Historical Collection, Milwaukee Public Library)*

On a frosty day shortly before ice closes the Great Lakes to navigation, the 401-foot steel-hulled ore-carrier Queen City *and another steamer pass through the Poe Lock at Sault Ste. Marie on the St. Mary's River. The swirling water suggests that the 800-foot lock is filling as these vessels head back to the Lake Superior ore ports. Built at Cleveland in 1896, the* Queen City *spent almost fifty years shuttling iron ore on the Great Lakes. Detroit Publishing Company photo. (Courtesy Library of Congress)*

ferries were introduced to carry trainloads of grain across Lake Michigan.

Through the second half of the nineteenth century, the expanding railroads acted as both competitors and partners for marine transportation systems. Within the United States, the railroads linked natural resources in widely separated regions, at low freight costs and with minimum regulation. They created new centers of production in the process, and through connections to the coast they supplied foreign trade in deep-water shipping. Faster than canal travel, with lower passenger fares and freight charges, the railroads were also easier and cheaper to build and maintain than canals, and they could traverse more rugged territory. Between 1865 and 1900, American railroads superseded nearly 1,700 miles of commercial canals. In 1868, 96.1 percent of western grain shipments passed through canals. This figure dropped to less than 50 percent in 1880, and to a mere 12 percent in 1898.

Despite the decline of the inland canal system, coastal ship canals remained valuable in maritime trade. Important deep-water canals that opened at the beginning of the twentieth century include the the Cape Cod Ship Canal, proposed in the nineteenth century and opened in 1914 to bypass the hazardous coastal navigation around Cape Cod; the Houston Ship Canal, opened in 1914 to create a more sheltered port than nearby Galveston; and the Lake Washington Canal at Seattle, designed to gain closer access from the sea to the coal mines and begun in 1893, but not finished until the First World War.

The expansion of the nation's railroad network also boosted trade on the western rivers. Immediately after the Civil War, river trade flourished for both passengers and freight with the renewal of deep-water ship visits to New Orleans. Giant 300-foot side-wheel and stern-wheel riverboats four decks high were launched at the shipbuilding centers of Jeffersonville, Indiana, on the Ohio River, and around Pittsburgh. Liner service on the Mississippi between St. Louis and New Orleans remained significant for a decade after the war, but as passenger and high-value freight was diverted by new railroad construction, steamboats began to specialize in carrying bulk cargoes of cotton and cottonseed, and in linking river ports that lacked railroad connections. Freight lines and independent operators maintained service on a river network that stretched from the Alleghenies nearly to the Rockies: up the Tennessee as far as Chattanooga; up the Cumberland to Nashville; along the length of the Ohio from Pittsburgh and beyond; on the Wabash; on the upper Mississippi as far as St. Paul; and on the Missouri, Arkansas, and Red Rivers.

Steamboat traffic on the Missouri River served the mining region of Montana Territory and tapped the expanding agricultural region of the Dakota Territory, with St. Louis remaining the entrepôt for the Missouri River trades. However, competition from railroads began with the westward extension of tracks from Chicago in 1868, the completion of the transcontinental railroad in 1869, and construction of the Northern Pacific in the 1870s. Former steamboat agent James J. Hill

The port of Chicago looks as busy as any ocean port in this photograph of the Rush Street Bridge over the Chicago River, ca. 1869. Through this period, Chicago grew rapidly as an entrepôt, where lake transportation met the railroads that served the agricultural regions of the Great Plains, as well as the expanding steamboat connections to the Mississippi River by way of the Illinois River. Although the waterfront was destroyed during the great fire of 1871, Chicago's port facilities were rebuilt to serve the thriving grain and passenger trades, and were further expanded at the turn of the century to serve the increasing industrial development in the region. Stereograph by J. Carbutt. (Courtesy Chicago Historical Society)

brought the demise of profitable Missouri River trade with his Great Northern Railroad, which had crossed the Dakotas and tapped Montana by 1887. The shift from river to rail moved the focus of westward transportation from St. Louis to Chicago.

The coastal passenger and "package" trades also employed a sizable portion of the enrolled fleet. The Civil War had stopped the growth of land transportation in the South. Immediately after the war, reconstruction and the slow integration of the southern railroads provided a temporary advantage for coastal shipping.

Although railroad transportation cut into the proportion of freight carried by water after the Civil War, river steamboats continued to carry much bulk cargo, especially in regions not served by railroad lines. Here, the stern-wheel steamboat Geo. W. Wylly *stops at a small landing on the Flint River in southwestern Georgia to load a few bales of cotton. (M.S.M. 96.103.2)*

With relatively little rail competition, Northern shipping lines and tramp ships competed for North-South trade with such cotton ports as Charleston, New Orleans, and Galveston between 1865 and 1875. Much of the trade was seasonal, based on the agricultural cycle of the region.

New Orleans, for example, was served by three weekly steamship lines from New York by 1870. One relative latecomer to this trade, C.H. Mallory & Company, successfully entered the competition by laying up ships in the summer, making semiweekly rather than weekly sailings, and filling excess freight space with cargoes such as potatoes and hay on the run south and fruit and sugar on the return north. Increasingly, Mallory Line steamers on the New Orleans-New York route called at Havana or some other port on the northern leg of the voyage, adding several thousand dollars in value to the cargo.

C.H. Mallory & Company was an early entry in the postwar trade to Galveston, and was able to eliminate competition from tramp steamers, but the firm soon came into competition with the Morgan Line, which operated from New York to Houston. It was Charles Morgan's aim to dominate Gulf Coast trade, but the two lines reached an accommodation in 1878 that allowed the Morgan Line to control coastal trade with New Orleans and the Mallory Line to maintain its position on the Texas run. The railroad in Texas played a key role in balancing the competition between them. The two shipping lines—the nation's second- and third-largest—agreed that it would be ten cents cheaper to ship by the Mallory Line to Galveston than by the Morgan Line to Houston, and the Texas railroads agreed that it would cost ten cents more to carry goods from the wharves of Galveston than those of Houston. Morgan himself began to shift his investments out of steamships and into railroads.

By the 1880s, railroads competed directly with shipping lines to carry freight and passengers between the East Coast and Texas. An agreement in 1885 established rates that made shipping to Texas from the region east of Buffalo and Pittsburgh and north of the border between the Carolinas cheaper by water than by rail. This agreement assured the profitability of the Mallory Line's Galveston route, along with its subsidiary New York and Texas Steamship Company, from 1886 through the end of the century.

On a number of coastal routes on the East Coast, shipping goods by water remained cheaper even after rail transportation was well-established. On the coast of Maine and in Chesapeake Bay, steamboat lines continued to provide the most direct and efficient transportation well into the twentieth century. The geography of New York Bay also favored water transportation and acted as a barrier to efficient land transport until the

The 189-foot Far West *was built at Pittsburgh in 1870 for service on the Missouri River. She routinely carried cargo from St. Louis to Fort Benton, Montana, 3,000 miles upriver. In 1876, the* Far West *was serving as a transport for the U.S. Army on the Yellowstone River in Montana when Colonel George A. Custer and his command were killed at the Little Big Horn. Steaming 920 miles downriver in just fifty-four hours, the* Far West *delivered the news at Bismarck, Dakota Territory. The vessel was also used during negotiations with the Sioux. To operate on the extremely shallow and shifting Missouri, steamboats like the* Far West *were powered by sternwheels and fitted with "grasshopper" legs at the bow to lever the boat over shoals in the river. In 1883 the* Far West *struck a snag (submerged tree trunk) and sank in the Missouri near St. Charles. (Courtesy Montana Historical Society, Helena, Montana)*

1930s. For both passenger and freight carriage, the Hudson River and Long Island Sound were profitable routes for steamboats long after railroads offered parallel service. In 1883, the Fall River Line's *Pilgrim* was the first merchant vessel under the American flag to be lighted throughout with electricity, the first commercial vessel to have a double bottom, and the first to have her machinery spaces protected by fireproof, metal bulkheads.

Symbiosis and competition both led to amalgamation between steamship lines and railroads and to several potential monopolies. In 1892, the New York, New Haven and Hartford Railroad acquired the Providence and Stonington Steamship Line. In 1893, the same railroad leased the Old Colony Railroad, which controlled the Fall River Steamship Line. Over the next six years, the New Haven Railroad acquired more steamship lines until, by 1898, it controlled all the Long Island Sound lines east of New Haven. In 1901, Charles W. Morse expanded his holdings from the Kennebec River ice trade to attempt to control the steamboat lines along the East and Gulf Coasts through his Consolidated Steamship Company. The New Haven Railroad, under the direction of Charles Mellon and J.P. Morgan, attempted to compete through further acquisition. The overextended Consolidated Steamship Company failed during the economic panic of 1907, and the New Haven Railroad was required to divest its maritime holdings by provisions of the Panama Canal Act of 1912 that

With the shift from side-wheels to screw propulsion around the time of the Civil War, coastal steamships took the form seen here. The 306-foot iron-hulled steamship Colorado *was built in 1879 for the Mallory Line at the John Roach yard in Chester, Pennsylvania. Designed for both passengers and cargo, the ship was powered by a compound steam engine, with auxiliary sails, and could travel at twelve knots. The* Colorado *first ran in Roach's United States and Brazil Mail Steamship Line between New York and Rio de Janeiro, but when that service proved unprofitable, despite the mail subsidy to support it, the ship entered its intended service for the Mallory Line between New York and Galveston, Texas. The* Colorado *sank after a collision in 1896, but was salvaged and completed thirty-seven years of coastal service before being broken up in 1918. Painting by Alexander Charles Stuart, ca. 1880. (M.S.M. 43.799; Claire White-Peterson photo)*

prohibited railroads from owning competing shipping lines.

On the West Coast, the Pacific Mail Steamship Company—the nation's largest steamship line—used its new iron-hulled steamships on the run from San Francisco and San Diego to Panama City, where the Panama Railroad linked with the water route from Panama to New York. The company also opened transpacific service to Japan and China via Hawaii in 1867. In San Francisco Bay and on Puget Sound, small sailing freighters were superseded by steamboats. Vessels of the Oregon Steam Navigation Company dominated shipping on the Columbia and Willamette Rivers, tying settlements along the river with Portland. Locks at the Cascades on the Columbia River, built between 1878 and 1896, opened direct navigation as far as the upper falls at the Dalles. In 1879 the Oregon Steam Navigation Company was purchased by Henry Villard as an adjunct to his

Northern Pacific Railroad, which also operated the Oregon Railway and Navigation Company, whose coastal steamboats connected Portland and San Francisco. Regular steamship service to Alaska began with the Klondike gold rush of 1897. The Alaska Steamship Company, with its connections to the Guggenheims and the Kennecott Copper Company, emerged as the major ore carrier and the major commercial link to the lower states of the U.S.

Long before the annexation of Hawaii in 1898, strong American economic, maritime, and naval connections had been formed with the kingdom and the republic that succeeded it. By the Civil War, a number of American and foreign shipping firms had established themselves in Honolulu, capitalizing on the rapid development of San Francisco and on Hawaii's intermediate location on world trade routes. A treaty of commercial reciprocity with the United States in 1878, along with an agreement that Hawaii should not dispose of any territory to a third power, was a positive economic stimulus. Earlier in the 1860s, the war years had greatly increased sugar production in Hawaii, and sugar replaced service to the whaling industry as the islands' main economic strength. The trend to agriculture was bolstered by success with pineapple production after 1885, and with other tropical crops. The expansion of a plantation form of agriculture, together with a long-term decline in the native population, attracted emigrant labor. Chinese workers began to arrive in large numbers during the 1870s, followed by Portuguese laborers from the Azores and Madeira beginning in 1878, and by Japanese workers after 1885. While this was occurring, the California sugar magnate Claus Spreckels had taken control of the sugar industry on the island and established the Oceanic Steamship Company, which would become one of the main commercial links between Hawaii and American ports on the Pacific Coast. In addition, treaty provisions with the Republic of Hawaii permitted the U.S. Navy to establish a base at Pearl Harbor in 1887.

Foreign Trade

While the nation's protected coastal trade was expanding, transatlantic commerce remained the most important portion of foreign trade. Total exports from all U.S. coasts rose 400 percent from $279,000,000 in 1865 to $1,173,000,000 in 1897, while imports rose 300 percent from $343,000,000 to $1,071,000,000. Between 1900 and 1915, American exports continued to expand by 75 percent. This dramatic rise reflected the tremendous growth of the American economy and the increasing output of industry and agriculture. Underscoring the importance of maritime trade, U.S. customs receipts from foreign trade remained a substantial percentage of the federal government's resources, averaging more than 50 percent of the U.S. Treasury's income.

With a few exceptions, for half a century after the Civil War, ships flying the American flag took relatively little part in the dramatic growth of America's foreign commerce. American shippers remained relatively unsuccessful in competing with the British, German, French, and Dutch lines that dominated trade on the Atlantic. The transfer of labor inland accompanied the transfer of capital from seaborne to land-based enterprise. Despite the huge growth of the nation's economy after the Civil War, however, the amount of capital available for investment had its limits. A Congressional commerce committee understood well the implications for shipping when it reported: "Lacking sufficient capital of our own to improve our soil, develop our mines and manufactures, build our railroads, carry our government bonds, and own ships for our ocean-carrying trade, all at the same time, capital has sought those investments that would yield the largest returns."

In 1865, foreign vessels already had a slight edge, with 2,212,000 tons of cargo clearing American seaports under foreign flags, while U.S.-flag vessels carried 1,615,000 net tons. By 1898, the contrast was dramatic: American tonnage, at 3,231,000 tons, had not even doubled, while foreign net tonnage in America's foreign trade had grown nearly nine times to 18,661,000 tons. On the basis of cargo value, the participation of American-flag vessels dropped from 36 percent of total cargo values in 1870 to 10 percent in 1910.

After the Civil War, the old private single-ship companies common to every navigable stream on the Atlantic Coast rapidly disappeared. No longer could a small or moderate-size American sailing vessel earn its way as a tramp trader, carrying whatever cargo was offered to whatever port the goods were consigned. As ports around the world were linked by telegraphic communication, such as the transatlantic cable, shipping became both more routinized and more competitive, and the ownership of vessels now shifted to specialized shipping firms.

Large-scale U.S. investment in shipping continued after the Civil War, but without the American flag. American ownership of foreign-flag ships had begun with the sale of the controlling interest in a large proportion of the U.S. merchant fleet to European owners during the Civil War to secure their safety from Confederate raiders. After the war, the registry laws prevented these ships from returning to the U.S. flag. By 1901, the amount of U.S.-controlled foreign shipping reached 672,000 gross tons, close to the 880,000 gross tons of U.S.-flag shipping in foreign trade. In terms of steamships, however, American-owned foreign-flag vessels had already exceeded those sailing under the American flag by 1894. Small-scale

The 560-foot Inman liner City of Paris *was the height of transatlantic luxury and speed when she was launched at Glasgow, Scotland, in 1889. With accommodations for 540 passengers in first and second class and 725 in steerage, and powered by two triple-expansion steam engines, the ship made the crossing at twenty knots, winning the blue riband for transatlantic speed in 1889. In 1893, the Inman liners* City of Paris *and* City of New York *were transferred to American registry by Act of Congress to maintain the Inman Line's U.S. mail contract. As the* Paris *and* New York, *they became the first modern, large American-flag passenger ships. After duty as the USS* Yale *during the Spanish-American War, the* Paris *returned to passenger service until grounding in the English Channel. Refitted, she resumed service as the* Philadelphia *until 1918. The thirty-year-old vessel operated as the transport USS* Harrisburg *after America's entry into World War I, and was dismantled in the early 1920s. Note the arched skylight over the main saloon. Although the ship was powered by two reliable and efficient triple-expansion steam engines operating off three sets of steam boilers, she also carried an auxiliary sailing rig. As multiple reliable engines became the standard power source for ocean steamships, with little likelihood of engine failure leaving them dead in the water, auxiliary sailing rigs like this would disappear. The prolific Danish-born marine painter Antonio Jacobsen, who emigrated to New York in 1873, painted this portrait of the* City of Paris *in 1889.(M.S.M. 63.466; Mary Anne Stets photo)*

owners invested to obtain lower-priced vessels, while large firms used foreign investment to maintain their business in an otherwise unfavorable climate. Railroads and other large corporations found in foreign shipping a useful way to diversify, while some of the large capitalists found in ships a profitable place to invest surplus funds.

Among such firms were the Guion Line, started in 1866 by Williams and Guion, who owned the Black Star Line of sailing packets operating between New York and Liverpool. Formally named the Liverpool and Great Western Steamship Company, the Guion Line was largely American-owned, but it operated British-built ships flying the British flag under the command of American captains. The Guion Line operated successfully as a freight and emigrant line until 1875, when it attempted to move into the luxury-liner business. While its

steamships *Arizona*, *Alaska*, and *Oregon* were noted for fast transatlantic passages, the company could not sustain its ambitions and ultimately failed in 1894. The Atlantic Transport Line also operated American-owned vessels under the British flag. Established in 1882, it carried freight and cattle between Baltimore and London, and briefly operated a passenger service from New York.

In 1873, a group of businessmen from Philadelphia established the International Navigation Company to operate steamers with Belgian registry between Antwerp and Philadelphia as the Red Star Line. The company grew by acquiring the American Line in 1884 and the British-flag Inman Line in 1887. With a transatlantic mail contract, the firm obtained congressional approval to reregister its British-built *City of Paris* and *City of New York* as American vessels in 1892, providing that it contracted to build

Transatlantic trade remained essential to U.S. commerce, but even as John E.C. Peterson completed this painting of the Black Ball Line packet Neptune *in 1866, participation by American ships was waning. Despite American reliance on sail for ocean shipping, European steam vessels were dominating the North Atlantic trades, and sailing packets were virtually obsolete. Nevertheless, the Black Ball Line, which had initiated scheduled transatlantic packet service in 1817, survived until 1878. Launched by William H. Webb at New York in 1855, the 190-foot* Neptune *served in the Black Ball Line until stranding on Sable Island, off Nova Scotia, in 1876. The number of passengers at the rail suggests that the* Neptune *is bound for New York with immigrants on board. Around her, with their schooners anchored in the North Atlantic shipping lane in peril of collision, New England dory fishermen catch cod on the Grand Bank of Newfoundland. (M.S.M. 58.626; Mary Anne Stets photo)*

two steamships, the *St. Paul* and *St. Louis*, in American yards.

The International Mercantile Marine Corporation (IMM) was the most significant American foreign-flag venture, and the largest American-owned shipping business before World War I. Capitalized in 1902 by J.P. Morgan, the American financial genius who had formed U.S. Steel the previous year as the world's first billion-dollar corporation, IMM grew quickly to a massive 1,000,000 gross tons–greater in tonnage than the American deep-water merchant fleet or the entire French merchant marine. Considered one of the "boldest acts of enterprise in American business history," IMM combined several British and American steamship lines, including the Red Star, White Star, Atlantic Transport, Dominion, Leyland, and American Lines, as well as a majority interest in the Holland-America Line. Until the loss of the White Star liner *Titanic* in 1912, Morgan's International Mercantile Marine Corporation controlled nearly 20 percent of the North Atlantic liner trade.

Morgan's venture raised American expectations for the revival of the nation's maritime fortunes, but the new shipping corporation made several serious mistakes, relying on government subsidies that did not materialize, overcapitalizing, and paying too much for ships in the quest to control various lines. By 1914, IMM was bankrupt and in receivership. Although Morgan had demonstrated that American capital could be raised to finance a large shipping firm, he had also demonstrated that foreign-trade investments would not stimulate Americans to legislate aid for the nation's merchant marine.

Beyond the North Atlantic, where U.S. investment in foreign shipping supplanted American-flag shipping, American maritime enterprise was nowhere near as innovative as American industry on land. The effects of the opening of the Suez Canal in 1869 as a shortcut to Asia, which revolutionized British patterns of sea trade, illustrate the problems faced by the American maritime industry. The canal and the Red Sea were nearly impossible for sailing vessels to negotiate, so

Asian trade was increasingly dominated by British steamships. Had Americans possessed significant steamship capability, they might have engaged in the thriving world-wide tramping trades, but the slim profit margin in tramping required economies in ship-construction and operational costs that Americans could not hope to achieve. The parallel development of deep-sea ports to facilitate incoming rail-borne shipments of exports, as well as coal supplies for foreign shipping, also worked to favor those nations that operated larger, steam-powered vessels.

The relatively high wages paid to American sailors placed American ships at a competitive disadvantage with European vessels. Nevertheless, operators of American sailing ships often had difficulty finding qualified seamen, since wages and working conditions on deep-water ships were less desirable than those offered in coastal trades or construction jobs on shore. A few men, largely from Maine, still sought careers at sea and rose through the ranks to command, but seafaring could not compete with land-based occupations as a route to prosperity in the years between the Civil War and World War I.

Although U.S. dominance in the cotton trade to Europe declined markedly after the Civil War with cotton cargoes increasingly handled by British-flag sail and steam vessels, Americans continued to use their traditional resources in wood to advantage in carrying long-distance, low-value cargo. The wooden sailing ships that dominated America's deep-water merchant fleet were best suited for long-distance trades in bulk cargoes such as grain, coal, hides, jute, coffee, and wool, for which speed and on-time delivery were not vital. As an example, after entering the guano trade in 1865, William R. Grace developed a fleet of square-rigged carriers that remained active into the twentieth century, when the firm shifted to steamships.

On a smaller scale, sailing vessels pioneered the trade in Caribbean and Central American fruit—especially bananas—which became important commodities in the decades after the Civil War. S. Oteri and Company of New Orleans and Lorenzo Dow Baker of Cape Cod led their regions in developing an increasing fruit trade from the Central American republics and Caribbean islands such as Jamaica. By the 1880s these firms were replacing their sailing vessels with steam-powered fruit carriers. A number of the firms in the Northeast merged at the end of the century to establish the United Fruit Company and built a fleet of distinctive steamships—mostly launched from British shipyards.

The West Coast grain trade grew rapidly after the Civil War. From its beginnings in 1855, the export of California wheat reached a value of $1,750,000 in 1865. Within a year, it leaped to a value of $6,700,000, and it peaked in 1882 when 559 ships carried away more than a million tons of wheat and barley and almost a million barrels of flour. This lucrative trade was pioneered by the wooden, square-rigged "Down-Easters," mostly built in Maine. American cabotage regulations placed them at a competitive advantage with European vessels in this trade, for they made a passage from the East Coast to the West Coast with coal, iron, or manufactured goods before carrying grain to Europe and returning to the East Coast with European goods. However, the foreign trade in grain from San Francisco, Portland, and Puget Sound ports eventually went to iron ships under foreign flags. Although the large, fast, efficient "Down-Easters" represented the culmination of American wooden cargo-ship design, by the end of the century they were unable to compete with iron and steel ships, which had larger cargo capacities and lower insurance rates. While 224 of the 356 ships that loaded grain in California during 1880-81 were American, only 39 out of 273 such grain ships flew the American flag a decade later.

E. & A. Sewall in Bath, Maine, attempted to compete in 1890-92 by building four large wooden grain ships, including the four-masted bark *Roanoke*, one of the largest square-rigged wooden sailing ships built in the United States. Sewall turned to steel construction in 1894, with the 3,005-ton, four-masted ship *Dirigo*, but the builders had to import the steel from England at considerable cost and had to employ high-wage metal-trades shipwrights. The operators had expected to obtain a drawback on the import duty paid on the British steel, but the tariff acts limited the ship's use in the coastal trades, including the grain trade, to less than two months per year if the owners chose not to pay the full duty.

Captain Jordan Complains of His Crew

Launched in 1883, the "Down-Easter" *R.D. Rice* was the last square-rigged vessel built at Thomaston, Maine. The 252-foot ship was built and owned by Samuel Watts, who operated the largest single fleet of these wooden ocean carriers. Captain Newell B. Jordan of Thomaston, Watts's stepson, commanded the ship from 1883 to 1894. The *R.D. Rice* was a fast ship with a capacity of 3,350 tons of grain. "What's the matter with 291 miles in 24 hours in a Down East wood boat with her belly full of wheat?" Jordan wrote after the passage from San Francisco to Cork in the spring of 1889. Then, on 29 June 1889, he addressed Watts from the Isle of Wight with grave concern about the quality of seamen available for a ship like his.

Dear sir

I am sorry to say that I have hade to put in here to get some sailors as with the men I have got on board it is *impossible* for me to get the ship home. I left Antwerp at two oclock in the morning and, of course, my crew was mustterd in the night and it was not possible for me to tell That there was no sailors among them out of the twenty men I have got There is *only two* even at sea before and Thay are *boys* and not *one man* in the *lot* able to speak a word of *English* of course That would not matter if thay was only sailors I assure you I would take a good many chances before I would put my ship in but in This case There is no help for it. I have wired to Antwerp to stop all advances but am afrade it is to late so of course as in all cases where a Ship is concerned The ship has to suffer in all my short experience I never heard of a case of this kind if I only had four sailors I would come along but with only two boys and One of them at the wheel There is no one to lead The rest along I got sail on the ship and to get it in I and my two mates had to go aloft to make it fast with my Pilots at The wheal I have writting my *Stevedore Shipping Master American Consul* Baxter by name that I shall hold him responsible for this job but that is all it will amount two the ship has got to suffer I am only to Thankfull to get the ship in, as had I (of) had bad weather I must of lost my ship tomorrow is Sunday and I dont know as I can get any men I only Want Eight if I can get Eight men I can do but my god only two it is something teraible I never in my *life* new how helpless man is untill I found my self to sea in a big ship with two boy for a crew you will say why did you not stop at flushing but the wind was Easterley and I did not know realey what a crew I did have there is 14 of them That I could not drive over the sheerpole I rope ended Them and thay layed right down on deck and cried like children Thay could not get up aloft I got four of them up to the main top and I assure you I was glad when I got them on deck again as thay came very near to falling and then I would of got hung when i got home I am not very thin skined but the chances to take to get the ship home with This crowed is too large for me to take was it possible for me to proceed I must of lost my charter for I could not carry any sail I suppose this job will cost at least £100. and I feel very badley over it but what was I to do I new men was not pleanty in Antwerp and I was anchous to get to sea but I did think I had some sailor after paying a big price for them two

I expect to have to send to London for men.

I am yours respt
N. B. Jordan

At San Francisco's Green Street Wharf in the early 1890s, an American wooden "Down-Easter" (left) and several European iron and steel sailing vessels load cargo. "Down-Easters" remained competitive because they carried cargo on the protected route between the East and West Coasts. Portable steam-powered winches speed the handling of mixed cargo at the wharf. Perhaps the barrels at right contain salmon for delivery to Europe. (Courtesy O.V. Lange Photographic Collection, San Francisco Maritime National Historical Park)

In 1899-1902, the Sewalls used domestic steel in the construction of several large sailing ships. Among them were three vessels built for Standard Oil Company, *Astral, Acme,* and *Atlas.* The 332-foot, 3,381-ton *Atlas* was the largest square-rigged sailing ship built in the United States. To import petroleum, European shippers developed the steam-powered oil tanker in the 1880s. With sufficient domestic petroleum supplies in the U.S., the Standard Oil Company used its fleet of sailing ships to export case-oil (kerosene), which had become an important commodity in Asia.

These European-model steel sailing ships took advantage of cabotage restrictions and incorporated a coastal passage to compete. At the turn of the century, the cost of a ship in the United States was between 25 and 50 percent more than in the world's major shipyards in Britain and Germany. Yet, in terms of cargo carried in American ships, the gross-ton mileage ratio, as high as four to one in favor of sail over steam at the turn of the cen-

tury, continued to favor sailing vessels until World War I.

Besides the high cost of American-built ships, a subject to be discussed later in this chapter, the institution of high tariffs on imports worked to suppress American shipping. The Republican Party, which held the reins of power and had strong ties in industry and finance, was determined to nurture the nation's growing economy by establishing a protective policy. Many materials required for ship construction were placed on the protected lists. Of these, iron was probably the most critical for shipping. With the American iron industry centered away from the seacoast and with much of its production going into railroad expansion, relatively little marine iron and steel was produced in the U.S. in the late nineteenth century, and what little was produced was expensive. Because Congress enacted high tariffs on imported iron to protect domestic iron production, shipbuilders could not obtain cheaper imports from Europe.

British owners, by contrast, could purchase a British-built iron-hulled vessel for one-third the price of a similar vessel built in an American yard.

Consequently, American ship construction, carried out in a captive domestic market protected by tariffs and restricted registry, was sufficiently costly to discourage investment in the construction of oceangoing vessels. Despite arguments that the nation's rapidly growing economy demanded an integrated oceanic shipping system for the disposal of its agricultural and industrial surpluses, high tariffs on materials critical to the construction of ships remained fixed in the United States until 1914. The fact that freight rates actually declined in the late nineteenth century also served to negate the arguments of those who opposed high tariffs and who decried the loss of revenue paid out to foreign carriers. In the years 1874 to 1895, this amounted to $650 million. In addition, the decline in rates probably further stimulated American agricultural exports.

Despite resistance by free-trade advocates, protectionists in Congress experimented with subsidies for shipping. As part of an effort to stimulate U.S. trade to South America, President Benjamin Harrison's administration promoted the authorization of subsidies for steamships on these routes. Although intended to support mail contracts on fifty-three different routes, the subsidy was not attractive to the shipping industry, and the government only received eleven bids.

Unfortunately, those subsidies were applied for the most part to areas where they had the least chance of success: the lines on the North Atlantic that competed with British lines, and later with German lines. A policy combining free ships and selective subsidies for the improvement of operations, similar to those granted to American railroads, might have worked. Bounties to encourage new-vessel construction and greater vessel efficiency might also have succeeded, as they did in France. But efforts to apply these remedies were consistently defeated. In effect, U.S. policy supported the American shipbuilding industry and abandoned the shipowners and operators in foreign trade. Americans simply could not purchase, construct, or operate ships cheaply enough to compete successfully with foreign ships carrying America's foreign trade.

The U.S. Navy, 1865-1883

Despite the extensive use of ironclad warships during the Civil War, the navies of France and Britain, and not the United States, were in the forefront of the shift from wood to iron and from sail to steam, setting new standards for the world's navies. At first, other countries could neither afford to follow their lead nor thought it immediately necessary. America's ocean moat protected her from the conflicts of Europe, and the great breadth of the American continent, with its three long coasts, prevented any foreign naval power from making a serious attack.

But even as the nation's energies and resources were massively applied to internal development in the years between the Civil War and World War I, the United States remained, at its core, a trading nation, marketing its goods around the world by sea. To most of those Americans who thought about the subject after the Civil War (and the number could not have been large), the fundamental role of the U.S. Navy was to protect maritime commerce and to show the flag as a means of promoting trade and safeguarding American enterprise abroad. The Confederacy's aggressive *Alabama* had clearly proved that attacks on maritime commerce were dangerous and could have far-ranging economic effects. In the immediate post-Civil War period, Europe provided the strongest market for American goods, but the most attractive prospects for new markets were relatively undeveloped areas such as West Africa, the Indian Ocean region, and East Asia. There the U.S. Navy could still be a credible force by maintaining the dual advantage of sail and steam, and by launching warships of cheaper domestic wooden construction at a time when high-priced iron ships had to be purchased abroad.

In the first two decades after the Civil War, the U.S. Navy was a target of partisan politics. In the elections of 1868 and 1872, the political opponents of Presidents Johnson and Grant attacked the Navy Department for corruption and mismanagement as part of the Democratic Party's larger dispute with the Republicans over Reconstruction policy. Congress repeatedly cut the navy's appropriations, halting the plans that Secretary of the Navy Gideon Welles had laid to maintain a small but technologically efficient fleet with supporting navy yards. There was also a

foreign trade, and a dramatic example was the world cruise of the wooden, screw-propelled sloop-of-war *Ticonderoga*, which had been built during the Civil War and hunted Confederate commerce raiders. In 1878, under the command of Commodore Robert W. Shufeldt, the *Ticonderoga* began a two-year, round-the-world cruise, to expand existing trade relations and to establish new ones. Covering more than 36,000 miles, she bypassed European ports in search of new possibilities in Africa and Asia, calling at Monrovia, Cape Town, Aden, Bombay, Penang, Singapore, Manila, Hong Kong, Nagasaki, Pusan, and Honolulu, and making several commercial treaties en route that had long-range consequences.

The protected cruiser Chicago *was the last of the U.S. Navy's steel ABCD ships to be commissioned, entering service in 1889. The largest of these transitional vessels, the 325-foot* Chicago *carried a conventional bark rig to supplement her compound engines and twin screws on long passages. The heavily armed ship could attain a speed of fifteen knots and was operated by a crew of 409 officers and men. Since these vessels did not have heavily armored side plating, the term "protected" cruiser referred to the cambered watertight steel deck that protected the engines and ammunition magazines. In 1894, as flagship of the European Squadron, the* Chicago *was the last sea command of Captain Alfred Thayer Mahan. Superseded by more modern designs in the 1890s, the* Chicago *was rearmed and converted to a gunboat without a sailing rig. She remained in naval service through World War I and served as a barracks ship at Pearl Harbor before foundering at sea in 1936. (M.S.M. 97.86.9)*

Failing to establish diplomatic relations with Korea during this cruise, as Perry had with Japan some thirty-five years earlier, Admiral Shufeldt pursued this the following year when he was sent to help reorganize the Chinese Navy. Koreans had burned the American-owned merchant ship *General Sherman*, which ran aground in the Taedong River near Pyongyang in 1866, and in 1871 Korean forts on the Salee River above Inchon had exchanged fire with five American warships under Rear Admiral John Rodgers, who seized the forts and held them for a short period. Obtaining the appropriate diplomatic credentials in 1882, Shufeldt finally succeeded in obtaining Chinese encouragement for negotiating a treaty with Korea that could fulfill Shufeldt's plans for expanding American maritime commerce in Asia.

After his return to the U.S. in 1882-83, Shufeldt chaired the Naval Advisory Board to select a new design for American warships. During the *Virginius* affair in 1873, the navy had been slow and ineffective in an attempt to mobilize its forces. Later, both the Chilean naval victory over

continuing dispute among professional naval officers over rank and privilege for engineering specialists, and the result of this was a reduction in the number of active steam vessels. These developments produced the limited roles for the navy that many Americans preferred.

One of the roles that remained was promotion of

Peru early in the War of the Pacific in 1879, and France's interest in building a canal across the Isthmus of Panama in the same year, persuaded much of the American public that it was time to modernize the navy and improve coastal defenses. The sweeping Republican victory in 1880, giving that party control of both houses of Congress and the presidency, briefly opened an opportunity for naval modernization. Through the efforts of Secretaries of the Navy William H. Hunt (1881) and William E. Chandler (1881-84), the Naval Advisory Board recommended designs for three cruisers and a dispatch boat, all built from American-produced steel.

These vessels were the light cruisers *Atlanta* and *Boston*, the heavy cruiser *Chicago*, and the dispatch boat *Dolphin*. Known as the ABCD ships, these first vessels of the new American steel navy were light and fast, designed for commerce protection and to show the flag in such promising places as Asian and African waters. They were not designed to battle heavily armed European warships. The new American vessels were a compromise between tradition and modernity, carrying full sailing rigs in addition to their compound steam engines. The concept was clear, but the construction of these ships called for an industrial capacity the United States had not yet proved. No American mill had rolled steel for hull plates, and no American foundry was able to forge steel for the eight-inch guns and gun-mountings that the new ships were to have. In addition, the Naval Advisory Board asked for American standards in steel production that surpassed those of current foreign practice. Although the ships were completed successfully, the shipyard of John Roach, which had won the contract to build them, went bankrupt in the process of meeting these challenges.

The authorization for these new naval vessels and the associated call for high domestic industrial standards appealed to nationalistic impulses. With the Democratic Party's victory in the election of 1884, Democrats no longer needed to discredit Republican attempts to build up the navy. Members of Congress in both parties could see political value in encouraging construction of naval yards in their home districts, and such construction promised benefits for American labor, the promotion of technological development, and trade. From this confluence of interrelated interests, the U.S. Navy created a major link in an alliance between government and modern industry that President Dwight D. Eisenhower seventy years later rightly identified as the military-industrial complex.

Technological Development and the American Shipbuilding Industry

The government's ship-registration policy of 1852 required U.S.-flag merchant vessels to have been built in America or to have been rebuilt or repaired in an American shipyard to the extent of three-quarters of the original cost of construction abroad. In 1870, a Congressional Committee chaired by Congressman John Lynch of Maine secured the foundations of this policy by preventing the return of the former U.S.-flag vessels that had sought the protection of foreign registry during the Civil War. The committee's recommendations were designed to protect New England shipbuilders. Above all, the Lynch Committee wanted to prevent a free-trade policy in shipbuilding, claiming that foreign competition would undercut American shipbuilders, putting them out of business and endangering the nation's ability to construct its own naval vessels. When Congress failed to accept the full recommendations of the committee, the issue was decided on political rather than economic grounds.

After the Civil War, American shipbuilders anticipated a return to normalcy with an emphasis on wooden construction. By then ships were far larger; builders had to find timber supplies in other regions of the country; and such innovations as steam-powered band saws and planers, and the threaded auger, had reduced much of the hand labor in shipbuilding. Nevertheless, the overall process had changed little since the beginning of the century. It was not a healthy industry. Despite a brief flurry of orders for both sail- and steam-powered wooden vessels immediately after the war, many formerly prosperous shipbuilders soon found their yards idle. The New York shipyards, once leading producers of finely appointed packet ships, launched no large wooden vessels after 1869. At Mystic, Connecticut, only one square-rigged vessel was built after 1869, and in numerous other ports large-scale shipbuilding came to a close during the 1870s. Only in Maine, led by the shipbuilding center at Bath on the Kennebec River, did construction of large, square-rigged ships survive through the last quarter of the century, relying on cheap labor and to some degree on local timber supplies. While large coastal schooners for the coal trade became an increasing proportion of Maine's output, square-rigged "Down-Easters"–named for their origin in Maine–were built in considerable numbers through the mid-1880s. Frequently more than 200 feet long, and registered at 2,000 tons and more, these vessels combined reasonable speed with ample cargo capacity. Largely employed in the California grain trade, they survived competition from European vessels by making one protected coastal passage to deliver cargo from the East to the West Coast during each voyage.

One of the greatest challenges to America's maritime industries came from the British development of inexpensive iron-hulled sailing ships. Scotland, especially, produced well-built inexpensive iron ships that competed not only in terms of price but in freight rates as well. Iron was stronger, lighter, and more durable than wood, and iron ships were less prone to leakage. With reliably dry compartments for perishable goods such as grain, wool, nitrate (guano), jute, sugar, and coal, iron ships commanded lower insurance rates, creating a differential in freight rates that averaged between 8 and 15 percent less than the rates for wooden vessels in the 1880s. After 1863, when British shipbuilders introduced even lighter, stronger steel hulls, they further undercut the costs of wooden ships through their cheaper and more useful product. Many British-built ships (like the 1863-built *Star of India* still afloat in San Diego, or the 1886-built *Balclutha* presently moored in San Francisco) entered American foreign trade.

A major reason that iron and steel ships superseded wooden ships was a matter of ship design, not simply the fact that a wooden ship cost more to build and to maintain. As ships grew larger to accommodate increasing volumes of bulk cargo efficiently, shipbuilders determined that the maximum practical length for a wooden ship was about 300 feet. Beyond that, a wooden hull could not be built rigid enough to prevent leaking. While metal allowed the construction of longer

and larger ships, metal construction required new and specialized tools and techniques that were very different from the old tools and skills of wooden shipbuilding. A wooden ship had ribs built up from wooden segments, covered with inner and outer planking of wood caulked to be rigid and watertight, all reinforced with a massive keel structure and deck beams thoroughly braced with angled wooden "knees." In contrast, a metal ship was built up with bent angle-iron ribs set on a box keel, covered with a skin of iron or steel plates cut and bent to precise specifications and riveted together through pre-punched holes. The result was an extremely rigid, watertight hull with its cargo space uninterrupted by strengthening members. Metal hulls were subject to rust and to fouling by marine growths during long passages, but they were far more durable than wooden ships. This was especially true for steam vessels, whose engines were a source of constant vibrations.

American shipyards made little effort to compete with the Europeans in iron or steel sailing ships. In the United States, both John Roach's yard at Chester, Pennsylvania, and the American Shipbuilding Company on the Delaware tried to compete in 1883-84 by building large, square-rigged ships of iron, but they were not successful due to the comparatively high cost of their construction. The few that were built in the U.S., such as the Sewall fleet of efficient four-masted barks, launched at Bath, Maine, in the 1890s, were 33-40 percent more expensive than similar carriers built on the Clyde in Scotland. As freight rates began to fall dramatically at the end of the century, American-built ships became even less competitive, particularly when the French government began to compete in 1893 and gave substantial bounties to French-flag sailing vessels. This French initiative virtually forced the surviving American sailing ships out of the market.

One of the incentives for higher technology in world shipbuilding after the Civil War was the competition among steamships for the blue riband signifying the fastest passage across the Atlantic. This became an international competition that demonstrated a nation's excellence in ship design and shipyard production. By 1874 the largest liners crossing the Atlantic measured 5,000 tons and could travel at sixteen knots, reducing the length of the voyage to seven days. By 1881, liners of the blue-

On all coasts, American shipbuilders specialized in wooden construction well into the twentieth century. Here, at the W.A. Boole and Son Shipyard in Oakland, California, in 1902, a crowd celebrates the launch of the 221-foot barkentine Koko Head *for the transpacific trade. Although U.S. shipbuilders persisted in wooden construction, an iron ship was calculated to be one-third lighter and able to carry half again as much cargo weight as a wooden vessel. (Courtesy Annie M. Rolph Photographic Collection, San Francisco Maritime National Historical Park)*

riband class had reached 7,000 to 8,000 tons and, with efficient triple-expansion engines and boilers producing 100-pounds-per-inch steam pressure, could average twenty knots. With the British-built, 704-foot *Oceanic* of 1899, liners began to exceed the size of the 690-foot *Great Eastern,* built nearly half a century earlier. Not until the 535-foot transatlantic steamships *St. Louis* and *St. Paul* of 1895 and the 622-foot transpacific steamships *Minnesota* and *Dakota* of 1903 did U.S. shipyards produce anything comparable to European steamships. This was because U.S. yards had chosen not to compete. In 1870, only three of the thirty-six American liners engaged in foreign trade were iron-hulled, and they were small vessels used as West-Indian packets.

By the 1870s and 1880s, steam-powered ships represented a sophisticated technology that would quickly supplant sail in all trades. The standard for measuring efficiency was the number of pounds of coal required to produce one indicated horsepower hour. The compound (two-cylinder) reciprocating engine from the 1870s produced up to 60 percent savings in the cost of fuel to produce the indicated horsepower. Higher steam pressures in a compound reciprocating engine required improvements in the design and construction of boilers and engines, including the shift from salt water to fresh water in the condensation process. When combined with lighter and stronger iron and steel hulls, these technological changes in engines produced vessels with large cargo capacity and long range of operation that could compete successfully against sailing ships for low-value bulk cargoes, even though sailing ships were also increasing in size and efficiency during the final decades of the nineteenth century.

Yet, even modern steamships were still equipped with sails for auxiliary and emergency power into the 1890s, sometimes using both propulsion systems–"motor-sailing"–when the winds permitted.

In the mid-1880s, a further technological development hastened the end of the age of sail: the triple-expansion engine. In a triple-expansion engine, high-pressure steam expanded successively into three separate cylinders before being cooled and condensed back into water. The three cylinders were increasingly larger so that each stage of the expanding steam produced equal force on the piston. When first introduced for practical use in Britain in 1881, the triple-expansion engine used 125-pounds-per-square-inch steam. By using so much of the expansive force of this high-pressure steam, the triple-expansion engine was close to 25 percent more efficient than a compound engine operating in a similar ship. This efficiency meant both fuel economy and increased speed. The advantages of triple-expansion engines were so dramatic that they quickly superseded compound engines at sea.

In 1889 the Inman Line's new steel-hulled 560-foot transatlantic passenger liner *City of Paris* carried two of the most modern triple-expansion engines, as well as auxiliary sail. Built at Glasgow, she was brought into American registry in 1893, along with her sister ship, *City of New York*, to become the first modern American-flag passenger liners. Her boilers delivered 150-pound steam to the engines, which created a maximum 20,100 indicated horsepower. Crossing the Atlantic at a speed of twenty knots, she used just one pound of coal per indicated horsepower. Calculated out, that meant that she used thirteen tons per hour and a total of some 2,700 tons of coal during a six-day crossing. This was far less fuel than earlier steamships had used. In terms of their size, speed, and cargo capacity, the new steamships after 1885 could operate, on average, at a speed that allowed a steamer to make three times as many voyages as a sailing ship in the same period. The triple-expansion engine had pushed sailing vessels to the margins of commerce by the end of the century.

Although the triple-expansion steam engine became the standard marine engine, technological development continued. In 1884, the English inventor Charles A. Parsons introduced a reaction turbine, in which the rotor wheel was driven by a jet of steam striking its periphery. Shortly afterward, Swedish inventor Carl de Laval patented a turbine in which a jet of steam pushed turbine blades fitted on a wheel. The most dramatic moment in the rapid advance of the marine turbine came in 1897 when Parsons demonstrated his turbine-powered *Turbinia* at the international naval review held at Spithead to celebrate the sixtieth anniversary of Queen Victoria's coronation. Racing at an unprecedented thirty-four knots past the warships of a dozen nations, all of which were powered with triple-expansion engines, Parsons demonstrated a capacity for speed which no navy then possessed.

Many nations quickly adopted the turbine. At the naval review in 1914, all the major warships present had turbine engines. Yet the path between these two events was neither simple nor easy. Relatively light in weight, turbines were inherently efficient and were not limited in size. But a high-speed turbine could not be directly linked to a slow-turning propeller. A solution to the speed problem came about 1910 in the development of three different forms of transmission. In Germany, inventors produced a hydraulic speed-reducing couple that allowed the turbine to run at its higher optimum speed while the propeller could operate at its lower optimum speed. In Britain, the same result was achieved by developing a mechanical reduction gear between the turbine and the propeller shaft. American inventors, approaching the problem from a different angle, developed a system in which turbines drove electrical generators, which in turn ran electric motors attached to the propeller shaft. The mechanical reduction system became the most common form used.

The most successful American iron shipbuilding firms were located on the Delaware River: John Roach & Son in Chester, Pennsylvania; Harlan & Hollingsworth Company in Wilmington, Delaware; and William Cramp & Sons at Philadelphia. These yards were near, but not adjacent to, the center of the nation's expanding iron and steel industry. No country in the world could rival Britain, with her coal mines, iron foundries, and shipbuilding centers all close to the sea. The other growing industrial powers, Germany, France, and the United States, all had greater distances to transport materials over land for shipbuilding. Thus, competing freight on land was a major issue for shipbuilding.

In many respects, the development of the U.S. Navy was a key factor in the further development of the American shipbuilding industry in that age of new maritime technology that followed the Civil War. The navy's order for its first steel ships created a revolution in American shipbuilding. Up to the Civil War, the naval shipyards had constructed most warships, and even during the war those shipbuilders that had built warships were diversified enough in their customers not to depend to any great extent on government contracts. The very use of steel provided distinct advantages by saving costs in construction and in reducing the weight of a ship, but its use depended upon having available the heavy machinery and specialized tooling as well as the raw materials.

The shipyard of John Roach had been building iron ships since 1872, and was able to convert to steel construction. Roach won the contracts for all four of the ABCD ships, although competing yards protested, claiming collusion between Roach and the navy. The competing yards turned out to be lucky not to be chosen. Due to design complications, construction delays, and a faulty propeller shaft on the *Dolphin*, Roach declared bankruptcy, and the government seized the shipyard to complete the other three vessels.

Roach's misfortune underscored the difficulties for American yards in developing as competitive steel shipbuilders. The American yards that undertook this new work for the navy had to borrow funds to obtain specialized equipment from abroad. The Cramp Yard in Philadelphia spent $350,000 on new hydraulic and other equipment for forging and working steel, and the Union Iron Works in San Francisco made similar investments. These two yards became the principal producers of steel naval vessels until the turn of the century, when the Newport News Shipbuilding and Dry Dock Company in Virginia, the New York Shipbuilding and Bethlehem Steel yards on the Delaware River, the Bath Iron Works in Maine, and the Fore River yard in Quincy, Massachusetts, were established or reorganized to undertake naval construction. Despite naval contracts, American shipyards could not produce steel ships at a level that made them competitive in the world market. The shipyards that did well were those that acquired contracts from the U.S. Navy or were part of the specialized shipbuilding industry that grew up on the Great Lakes to construct large bulk carriers for the iron-ore and grain trades.

Fishing

Technology began to change other American maritime industries after the Civil War. Demand for fish landed fresh on ice had begun to expand in the 1850s, and would capture 90 percent of the fish market by the end of the century. The use of the longline trawl, with its many baited hooks for catching bottom-dwelling groundfish such as cod, had expanded through the Civil War to replace the less-efficient handline in the principal fisheries. But this form of fishing required that fishermen leave their vessel to set their lines from dories. These flat-bottom, nearly double-ended boats, developed for fishing from the beach, were easily adapted for use offshore. They were relatively seaworthy, could hold hundreds of pounds of fish, and could be stacked on the deck of the fishing schooner that served as "mother ship." With the use of the trawl line and the popularity of fresh fish, haddock joined cod as a leading species to be harvested by New England fishermen.

Net forms of fishing also expanded in scale and complexity, made economical by the development of net-making machines. The use of large fence-like fish traps, set alongshore to catch fish during their seasonal migrations, increased in the Northeast, on the Great Lakes, and in the Pacific Coast salmon fishery. Gill nets, set to snare unsuspecting fish at night, were also introduced in a number of shore and river fisheries. With the expansion of the menhaden and mackerel fisheries, the purse seine became the principal means of catching schools of fish on the surface. Set by one or a pair of boats to encircle a school of fish, the seine's bottom was pursed to form a bag capable of catching tens of thousands of fish at a time.

The efficiency of these net forms of fishing compelled shore fishermen in southeastern New England, who still used hook and line, to petition their state legislatures to ban fish traps. When the issue was referred to Washington, Congress established the U.S. Fish Commission in 1871 to investigate conditions in the fisheries. Under Spencer F. Baird, the commission studied American and European fishing technology, conducted scientific surveys of the marine environment around the nation, and set up hatcheries to propagate commercially important species.

Fishing-vessel technology also changed during this period. Steam power was introduced in the Connecticut oyster fleet and in the New England menhaden fishing vessels in the 1870s. The offshore fisheries remained under sail, but a more seaworthy hull form for the sailing schooners working in the dory trawl-line fisheries was introduced in the early 1880s after several decades of

losses among the fast but unstable schooners that had been developed in the 1850s. Rudyard Kipling's evocative novel *Captains Courageous* (1897) represents the Gloucester, Massachusetts, cod fishery during the 1880s, when several hundred schooners made Gloucester America's principal fishing port, with landings that approached 100,000,000 pounds a year.

There were signs of even greater changes to come. Boston emerged as a significant market for fresh fish in the 1880s and would exceed Gloucester in the quantity of fish landed during the first decade of the twentieth century. With the encouragement of the U.S. Fish Commission in the 1880s and 1890s, fishermen in

New England and on the West Coast began to experiment with the European method of dragging a conical-net beam trawl or otter trawl to sweep up groundfish. In 1905, Boston investors would finance the British-style steel-hulled steam trawler *Spray*, which successfully introduced this form of fishing in the U.S. Within twenty years it would supersede the dory-trawl form of bottom fishing that had prevailed since the Civil War. This form of fishing added flounder to the species commonly available in the marketplace, for otter trawls caught great quantities of these small flatfish that had not been caught with hook-and-line methods. Otter trawling also harvested large quantities of "scrod," a term coined in the 1890s for small cod or haddock of less than two pounds in weight.

As fish-catching methods became more productive, preservation and marketing efforts increased as well. The shift from salt to ice for preserving many sea fish for fresh consumption was aided by improvements in railroad transportation that allowed fresh fish to reach markets further inland. The development of mechanical freezing plants also increased the availability of "fresh" fish. The fisheries of Maine, with their dried and salted codfish, were particularly hard hit, losing their domestic market in the shift to fresh fish and their Caribbean and South American market to cheaper Canadian salt cod. To compete, salt-fish producers began processing their salt cod in boneless form or canned as codfish cakes, making the once-staple salt cod into a specialty food. Through the canning process, Maine herring found a wide market when packed as "sardines" in imitation of that European fish. Smoked fish, especially herring and haddock–"finnan haddie"–also found wider consumption through improved land transportation.

The geography of U.S. fishing also expanded after the Civil War. In 1866, American halibut fisherman first ventured as far as Greenland, and within a quarter-century some were working Icelandic waters to find that scarce fish. Menhaden fishing had expanded into Maine in the 1860s, but when the migratory menhaden disappeared from Maine waters for several years in the 1870s the industry shifted south. Captain Elijah Reed had observed menhaden in Chesapeake Bay, and in 1868 he set up operations on the site that would become Reedville, Virginia, the principal menhaden port through the first half of the twentieth century. The fishery also expanded to North Carolina at this time.

In the waters of Florida, sponge-gathering developed rapidly after 1884, when Greek immigrants arrived and introduced Mediterranean methods.

Resting at their oars, these mackerel fishermen give little indication of the intense labor involved in setting and hauling a purse seine. With increased demand for fresh mackerel, more fishermen engaged in this unpredictable seasonal fishery, earning either a large share or virtually nothing for their six months of work. Oil painting by Milton J. Burns, ca. 1880. (M.S.M. 75.291; Mary Anne Stets photo)

Winslow Homer, American Marine Artist

Winslow Homer is recognized today as America's greatest and most characteristically American painter of the nineteenth century. A contemporary of Degas, Manet, Monet, and Whistler, Homer created works that have continued to move and to engage viewers a century after they were painted. Like the others of his generation, he was particularly interested in capturing the life around him and in the relationships of natural daylight to color and form.

Known for his maritime subjects, he never limited himself to that theme. Born in Boston in 1836, Winslow Homer was an entirely self-taught artist. His first introduction to the field came as an apprentice to a lithographer and later as a free-lance illustrator for magazines. He first achieved recognition for his woodcut drawings in *Harper's Weekly* and other journals.

In 1859, Homer left Boston for New York City, in order to be closer to his publishers. Intending to go to Europe to study art seriously, he altered his plans at the beginning of the Civil War. The editors of *Harper's Weekly* commissioned him as a war artist, and he produced wood engravings and paintings that focused on the ordinary soldier and on camp life in the lull between battles, rather than the battle scenes of other combat artists of his day.

After the Civil War, Homer painted a variety of scenes from American domestic life showing women and children at work and at play. In the summers of 1873 and 1880, he visited Gloucester and began to work on his first maritime scenes in watercolor. Many of those from the 1873 visit shared his earlier approach to the scenes of country life that he had been painting, while those in 1880 expressed a romantic view of the sea. Then, in 1881, he went to England, where he spent two years in a village on the North Sea coast near Newcastle. While in northern England, he began to take a more serious approach to his painting. There, he painted a series of detailed studies of fisherwomen, carrying on the tedious work of bait collecting, net repairing, and fish cleaning in a way that expressed their heroic qualities as they toiled on the shores of a dangerous sea.

After returning from England in late 1882, Homer took up residence at Prout's Neck, Maine, where his family had often summered. He maintained his fascination with the sea, and in Maine his focus was on the Atlantic, although he did produce a series of watercolor scenes of hunting and fishing in the Adirondack Mountains.

In 1885, he painted a set of three works that captured the life of North Atlantic fishermen: *The Herring Net, Fog Warning*, and *Lost on the Grand Banks*. One reviewer commenting on the last of the three wrote: "It is not only powerfully dramatic in conception, but carried out with a serious almost grim intensity that adds to its significance." Such qualities were typical of his approach, eschewing a romantic view of the sea and seeking to express the sea as a great

natural force battling against mankind and the land.

Other paintings, such as his 1887 *Eight Bells*, his 1890 *Signal of Distress*, and his 1896 *The Lookout—All's Well*, captured moments of typical shipboard life—but he painted them in a manner that transcended the anecdotal moment they depicted and created dramatic images of mankind's life-and-death struggle with the sea.

With a similar approach, Homer addressed the theme of shipwreck and disaster. His most famous works on such subjects were the *Lifeline* of 1883, his graphic 1886 view of two men pulling unconscious women through the surf in *Undertow*, his 1896 study of lifeboats being readied on the beach in *The Wreck*, and the stormy, shark-filled waters surrounding the dismasted sloop and its Bahamian sailor in *The Gulf Stream* of 1899. Each

showed men and women struggling directly against the forces of the sea.

A third approach to his maritime work was a series of paintings of the sea itself. Typically, they show the sea crashing violently against the shore, as in his 1883 view of *Prout's Neck—Rocky Shore,* his *Sunlight on the Coast* of 1890, or his 1895 *Northeaster* and *Cannon Rock.*

To the general public, Winslow Homer became a kind of late-nineteenth-century Thoreau, who lived a solitary bachelor life in an isolated seaside studio, painting powerful images of an untamed sea. His work remains a complex and moving testimony of the relationship between America and the sea.

Winslow Homer's 1885 painting, Fog Warning, *depicts a doryman returning with a load of halibut as a fog bank approaches his schooner. Although the use of dories and trawl lines greatly increased the catch of groundfish, it separated fishermen from their vessels as much as 100 miles offshore. Homer may have responded to the image of a lone mariner calculating his chances against the elemental sea and fog. Yet, he also captured the reality of dory fishing, in which fishermen worked singly or in pairs far from their "mother ship" and all too often went astray. With these conditions, the mortality rate for offshore fishing was second only to that for hard-rock mining. (Courtesy Museum of Fine Arts, Boston, Otis Norcross Fund)*

In New England, the shift to fresh fish brought Boston into the forefront as America's largest fish market by 1910. Here on Boston's T Wharf in the winter of 1911, Henry D. Fisher photographed the schooner Elsie, *sheathed in salt-spray ice, with one of the new steam trawlers astern. Fresh fishing took place year-round to satisfy the demand for groundfish like the cod or haddock in the cart at right. (M.S.M. 76.208.639)*

By 1908, 622,000 pounds of sponge were harvested in Florida. Gulf oysters and eventually shrimp also began to reach wider markets with the establishment of canneries along the coast.

On the Pacific Coast, the salmon fishery grew dramatically after the Hume brothers from Maine perfected a cleaning and canning process for Pacific salmon in the mid-1860s. The Humes established operations on the Columbia River in 1866, and the fishery expanded into Puget Sound in 1877 and to Alaska in 1878, in each area competing with native fishermen. U.S. consumers were slow to adopt canned salmon, but the product found a ready market among English workmen and became an important commodity of trade between the West Coast and Great Britain. In this seasonal fishery, fishermen were usually employees of the canneries, using company boats and fishing gear to provide fish for specific canneries. Chinese fish cutters did much of the processing of the tens of millions of salmon until the development of a salmon-cutting machine in 1903. The Alaska fishery expanded rapidly through the 1880s, and the cannery owners established the Alaska Packers Association in 1893 to

manage competition. The association maintained a fleet of square-rigged sailing ships to carry their laborers north at the beginning of the season and return with canned fish for market at the end of the season. Outproduced by the Alaska packers, the canneries on the Columbia consolidated in 1897 into the Columbia River Packers Association to control labor costs and remain competitive. West-Coast fishermen also developed large-scale North Pacific cod and halibut fisheries, largely pursued in Alaskan waters.

Shellfishing also grew in the decades after the Civil War. The oyster fishery in Chesapeake Bay grew dramatically with American demand for a seafood that had been a delicacy in Europe and here was plentiful enough to become food for all classes. The Tidewater oyster fishery soon dominated the national market, with Baltimore packers canning more than ten million bushels in the 1870s. The "Oyster Wars"—conflicts between Maryland and Virginia oystermen, and between tongers and dredgers—were heavy and violent. In 1877, the Virginia and Maryland governments intervened and attempted to avoid further disputes by assigning the natural oyster beds to state control. Tension continued, however, as Maryland oystermen claimed that Virginia had banned them from the best beds. Fights broke out between the two groups of oystermen in 1895, and the issues were not resolved until the beds were over-harvested and became unproductive after 1910.

The oyster fishery also flourished in New York and southern New England. Connecticut oystermen had once imported stock from the Chesapeake to supplement the supply from the local natural beds. By the 1850s they had begun to "farm" oysters by leasing barren bottom and laying down juvenile oysters to grow to maturity. Later, they used mature oysters dredged from the natural beds to spawn and set a new crop on shells spread on their leased beds, making this the first full-fledged form of aquaculture in the U.S. As in the Chesapeake, Connecticut protected the natural oyster beds by prohibiting dredging there with powered vessels from the 1870s to the 1960s. Yet, by granting private control of portions of the bottom of Long Island Sound, Connecticut and its towns changed the concept of the sea bottom beyond the tide line as common property.

With the increasing popularity of New England lobsters, the fishery expanded in Maine, both for canning and for live delivery to market. The lobster fishery was among the earliest to be regulated for conservation. For example, in 1879 Maine imposed laws on the lobster fishery that included limiting the season from April through July. In 1883, Maine placed a nine-inch minimum limit on the size of lobsters, and in 1884 the other New England states joined in the conservation effort by banning the catch of egg-carrying female lobsters. As the demand for lobsters grew and the supply declined, Maine continued its pioneer efforts with more stringent rules, shortening the season even more in 1891 and increasing the minimum size in 1895 to ten and a half inches. About this time, both state and federal agencies began to experiment with methods of artificial propagation for lobsters.

Around the nation, the fisheries expanded and flourished after the Civil War as the nation's population expanded, especially with immigrants who had a taste for fish and shellfish, or religious reasons for consuming it, and found in seafood a staple protein they could afford.

As in many maritime industries, technological development and economies of scale favored an increasingly corporate approach to fishing in vessel ownership and in fish processing and marketing. And in many fisheries during the latter decades of the nineteenth century, fluctuations in the annual catch served as early warnings that fish resources were not unlimited, and that human efforts might someday challenge the survival of entire species.

Throughout the nineteenth century, many characteristic watercraft developed in specific fisheries or regions. Here, two fishermen haul a gill net near the mouth of the Columbia River in their Columbia River salmon boat. These double-ended sailing craft were developed for the California gill-net fishery in 1868 and then were adopted for use in the Columbia River and Bristol Bay, Alaska, salmon gill-net fisheries. In the distant background can be seen the piles for numerous fish traps, which were even more productive than gill nets in catching salmon. Photo by J.H. Bratt, 1895. (Courtesy Library of Congress)

The expansion of fish canning after the Civil War provided a new form of industrial work for women. From the lobster and herring canneries of Maine to the oyster canneries of Chesapeake Bay and the Gulf Coast, to the salmon and sardine canneries of the Pacific Coast, women and children found seasonal employment packing seafood. These women pause for the photographer at a sardine packing plant in Monterey, California, ca. 1900. (22-FFC-759, courtesy National Archives)

Whaling and Sealing

The American whaling fleet had begun to decline before the Civil War, and the fleet had been seriously damaged by Confederate commerce raiders during the war. After 1865, the increasing use of petroleum products for lighting and lubrication continued to diminish the market for whale products. Yet, even as the value of whale oil declined, the demand increased for baleen (the flexible strips in the mouths of nontoothed whales that strain krill from the water for food). Baleen, which whalemen called whalebone, was used to produce a variety of products, from corset stays to buggy whips. The distant Arctic whaling grounds became increasingly important in the hunt for baleen from right and bowhead whales. In 1871, the American whaling fleet suffered the single most serious loss in its history, when thirty-two ships were caught in unusual weather conditions off Point Belcher, Alaska, and crushed in the pack ice. Escaping in whaleboats, 1,219 whalemen and captains' families were brought to Honolulu in

whaleships that had avoided the pack ice. This disaster was only another in a long pattern of decline. The fleet dwindled from 174 active ships in 1880 to 36 in 1910, when the market for baleen collapsed. The last American whaleship using nineteenth-century methods sailed in 1927.

Seal-hunting, which increased after the Civil War, drove some vessels as far as Desolation Island at the bottom of the Indian Ocean to kill elephant seals for their oil and pelts, while other sealers hunted fur seals in Hudson Bay or on the islands in the vicinity of Cape Horn. After the acquisition of Alaska, American sealers ventured westward to the Pribilof Islands, where the U.S. government leased sealing rights to the Alaska Commercial Company, which took nearly two million skins between 1870 and 1890. Payments on the lease, at $55,000 per year and $2.65 per pelt, nearly equaled the purchase price of the entire territory. As the commercial value of sealskins rose, foreign sealers began to develop pelagic sealing in the open sea, outside the three-mile territorial limit. The seal herd was finally being so rapidly

Most species of seals were hunted for their pelts, but the elephant seal was hunted, like the whale, for its oil. After its discovery in 1853, Heard Island in the far south Indian Ocean was frequented by American sealers, who camped on its exposed beaches between the glaciers and butchered and rendered the huge sea elephants that bred there for several months each year. This naive painting depicts the process used by New London, Connecticut, sealers. (M.S.M. 39.1256; Mary Anne Stets photo)

depleted that the United States began to impose restrictions. In 1889, Congress unilaterally claimed dominion over the waters of the Bering Sea and attempted to close it to sealers who hunted with guns. In an exchange of diplomatic notes the following year, the U.S. secretary of state characterized pelagic sealing as "just short of piracy." In reply, the British foreign secretary warned the United States that Britain would hold the United States responsible for acts contrary to the established principles of international law and the freedom of the seas. The situation was complicated further when Russia seized American sealers who were endangering seal stocks in the open sea close to Russian territorial waters.

The United States attempted to impose further restrictions by closing 120-mile-diameter zones around all seal rookeries in the area, but this action brought further protest. In 1892 and in 1902, international tribunals denied the rights of a coastal state to impose conservation regulations on foreign vessels off its coast. Short of international agreement among the nations involved, the tribunal limited states to applying conservation measures only to vessels flying its own flag. The situation demonstrated the insufficiency of international law to deal with the wasteful exploitation of resources. In 1911, representatives of the United States, Great Britain, Russia, and Japan agreed to outlaw

pelagic sealing for fifteen years north of 30° north latitude, established a U.S. monopoly on the catch, and authorized an allocation of the sealing profits to be paid to Britain and Japan for withdrawing from sealing in the Bering Sea. This agreement remained in effect until 1940, but it only governed the exploitation of North Pacific seals by the four countries that had signed it.

The late nineteenth century was a dark age for many American maritime industries, especially for firms engaged in shipbuilding and overseas shipping. It was, nevertheless, an era of widespread maritime activity, innovation, and development. While the overseas fleets declined in the face of more economical foreign competition, coastal trades flourished and the size of coastal trading ships grew. The continuing expansion of waterborne traffic on America's rivers and on the Great Lakes was an integral part of Western expansion. The growth of American industry and agriculture in the heartland of the continent owed much to the availability of cheap water transport. The problems that arose for Americans in fishing, whaling, and sealing, in particular, raised early issues of conservation and made clear the need for rationalization of resources. In all areas, from the fisheries to naval affairs, the decades between the Civil War and World War I witnessed the rise of professionalism, bureaucracy, standardization, and regulation.

CHAPTER 11

The Rise of Maritime Professionalism and Regulation

THE LATE NINETEENTH
century was an era of professionalism, bureaucracy, standardization, and regulation in America. In the years after 1870, there was an enormous expansion in higher education. While universities and colleges became dynamic centers of research and education, government agencies also grew, became more specialized, and increasingly applied federal funds to scientific research as well as to regulate and to standardize aspects of national life.

These wider developments had their counterpart in the American maritime world, although with some significant differences. While maritime activity characteristically takes place in the public domain and, therefore, has always required more government regulation than activities ashore, the latter half of the nineteenth century saw a much greater increase in maritime bureaucracy, standardization, and regulation. Much of this was due to the impact of steam propulsion and metal ship construction, as well as the introduction of many new forms of maritime activities, but it extended into more traditional maritime areas as well.

Professionalizing the U.S. Navy

The first steps toward maritime professionalization began in the U.S. Navy. Just before the Civil War, officers instructing at the Naval Academy had begun to see a great need to develop textbooks and manuals for instruction in the new methods. Modeling their work on comparable British works, Lieutenants Foxhall Parker and Stephen B. Luce were the first to

Detail from Men of the Docks, *by George Bellows, 1912. (Courtesy Maier Museum of Art, Randolph-Macon Woman's College, Lynchburg, Virginia; Randolph-Macon Art Association purchase, 1920)*

publish such works for the U.S. Navy with their *Instruction for Naval Light Infantry* (1859, 1862) and *Seamanship* (1862). From its third revision in 1866, Luce's *Seamanship* became the leading textbook on the subject for both the navy and for the merchant marine in America. In 1901, it was succeeded by Austin M. Knight's *Modern Seamanship*, which was still in print in 1997 after its seventeenth substantive revision.

In the area of shipbuilding, Americans had tended to use their practical experience and empirical observation of ships at sea as they improved successive ships, rather than to use mathematical formulae in design. Despite efforts by John W. Griffiths, William H. Webb, and a few other theoretical designers, most prominent American ship designers in the mid-nineteenth century normally used half models rather than drawings to provide the shape of a hull, carving the half model to the designer's rule-of-thumb

Stephen B. Luce (1827-1917), a native of New York, received an appointment as a midshipman at age fourteen. After seven years of sea duty he attended the Naval Academy and was promoted to passed midshipman, serving in the Pacific, in coast-survey duty, and on station in the Gulf of Mexico through the 1850s. In 1860, Luce was appointed head of the department of seamanship at the Naval Academy's temporary location in Newport, Rhode Island, and there he compiled the material for his textbook, Seamanship, *published in 1862. After commanding a monitor and a gunboat during the last eighteen months of the war, Luce became commandant of midshipmen at the Naval Academy, 1865-69. Following this appointment, he combined service in the European Squadron and other posts at sea with efforts to promote naval and maritime education. Even before the Civil War, Luce had seen the need for educational reform in the navy. However, his first opportunity came through helping to draft a bill to establish a merchant marine academy on the lines of the land-grant colleges authorized by the Morrill Act of 1862. During 1874, Luce planned the program, wrote the textbook, and fitted out the sloop of war* St. Mary's *to serve as the New York State Maritime School. He then commanded naval schoolships in support of his aim to establish a naval apprentice program, which for the first time would provide formal training for enlisted personnel. Luce's concept would become the basis for naval instruction in the "new" steel navy after the 1880s. Luce then turned to the higher education of naval officers. While the Naval Academy taught midshipmen the basics of ship operation and command, Luce wished to teach them to think about the theory and practice of war. During service on a commission to review navy yards, Luce became acquainted with Secretary of the Navy Chandler, to whom he proposed the idea of a program that was established as the Naval War College in 1884. As first president of this new institution, situated in Newport, Rhode Island, Luce set up a curriculum that viewed naval theory as a science that could be discovered through individual study and discussion, and could be tested through war games and fleet maneuvers. Luce's belief that naval officers must comprehend the political and diplomatic implications of naval action was personified by his appointment of Captain Alfred T. Mahan as lecturer. Mahan's lectures were published in 1890 as* The Influence of Sea Power Upon History. *After its first session in September 1885, Luce returned to sea, and Mahan took over presidency of the Naval War College. As commander of the North Atlantic Squadron, Luce attempted to establish fleet exercises as the practical side of naval education. Retiring as rear admiral in 1889, Luce remained dedicated to the work of the Naval War College and to naval reform. As late as 1912 he was still involved in efforts to improve the administration of the U.S. Navy. For more than fifty years, Stephen B. Luce had been the strongest voice for professionalizing the U.S. Navy, an effort that enabled the service to take on an international role in the twentieth century. Photo by D. Bachrach, ca. 1866. (M.S.M. 97.12)*

Midshipmen at the U.S. Naval Academy man the fleet of cutters for boat drill. The Academy returned to its Annapolis home in 1865 after spending the Civil War in Newport, Rhode Island. Admiral David D. Porter superintended the Academy from 1865 to 1869, with Lieutenant Commander Luce and other able officers in teaching positions. Although it was sometimes called "Porter's Dancing Academy" for the formal social activities that he sponsored, the Academy improved training in all areas. Porter's innovative attempts to interest midshipmen in steam engineering failed during this period, but he established cordial relations with the U.S. Military Academy at West Point, and, like universities of the period, recognized athletic clubs among midshipmen. In many respects, however, the Naval Academy remained a small, tradition-bound institution through the 1880s, and did not change dramatically until the building program of 1898-1913. In the background of this photo, ca. 1868, are the USS Santee (left), a down-rigged sloop of war, probably the Marion, and the USS Constitution (right). Begun in 1820 but not launched until 1855, the Santee served as a navy schoolship from 1862 to 1912. The Constitution also served as a Naval Academy schoolship, from 1858 to 1871. Photo by D. Bachrach. (M.S.M. 51.892)

for hull form rather than the result of scientific experimentation. As the increasing use of iron and steel showed the need for more precise design in ships, the move toward a more disciplined training in naval architecture slowly increased. In 1869, Commander Richard Meade published his *A Treatise on Naval Architecture and Shipbuilding* for the Naval Academy's first course in this subject. Nearly a decade later, Naval Constructor Theodore Wilson followed with his Naval Academy textbook, *An Outline of Ship Building, Theoretical and Practical* (1878).

In 1873, the Navy Department took advantage of Captain Stephen B. Luce's long-standing interest in education, ordering him on an assignment to develop plans for a maritime

college with the city of New York's board of education. The same year, Luce laid out his plan to improve professional education in both the U.S. Navy and the merchant marine in a lecture, published in the very first issue of the journal issued by the navy's newly established professional society, the U.S. Naval Institute. The Naval Institute was a private organization, established by a small group of naval officers, including Luce, Foxhall Parker, and David Dixon Porter, that would serve as a vehicle to advance professional and scientific knowledge among naval officers. By providing and sustaining the means for officers to publish their thoughts on professional issues, the Naval Institute helped cultivate professional education and promote literary skills and constructive thought among officers, all of which soon led toward the formulation of broad maritime theory.

In June 1874, Congress incorporated many of Luce's ideas in the Marine School Act, extending the principles of the 1862 Land Grant Act to establish colleges for agricultural and mechanical arts to include nautical education. This new act authorized the navy to loan ships and to order officers for duty at public maritime schools. Luce personally laid out the plans and organization for this school. In 1875, the USS *St. Mary's* became the school ship for the New York Maritime School, the institution that later evolved into the State University of New York Maritime College at Fort Schuyler. In 1877, the Treasury Department's Revenue-Marine also established a two-year school of instruction at New Bedford, Massachusetts, on board its first training ships, the schooner *Dobbin* and bark *Chase*. This school was the precursor of the present-day U.S. Coast Guard Academy. In 1890, Pennsylvania established a maritime academy with the school ship USS *Saratoga* at Philadelphia, and Massachusetts set up the school ship USS *Enterprise* at Boston in 1891.

Luce also pressed for improvements in the navy's training for apprentice seamen. From 1877 to 1883, he commanded school ships for this purpose. In 1883, the navy acquired Coaster's Harbor Island at Newport, Rhode Island, and the work was transferred ashore as the embryo for a naval training system. Now the foremost leader in naval education and training, Luce next turned his attention to the top level of education with his plan for a graduate-level college to prepare naval officers for the highest levels of responsibility. Establishing the Naval War College in October 1884, Luce and a small group of officers in Newport began to examine history, political and military theory, international law, and foreign relations. While Luce recognized the importance of technological advances in the navy, he founded the Naval War College as "a place of original research on all questions relating to war and to statesmanship connected with war, or the prevention of war."

By 1890, the Naval War College had made important contributions as an early center in the United States for the study of international maritime law. Simultaneously, officers at the college developed the naval war game as a means to

analyze ways to strike a balance among the various forces affecting naval power: the goals of national policy and strategy, the limitations placed on military force by international law, and the accepted practice of nations along with the realities and characteristics of developing technology. In the public eye, however, these achievements were overshadowed by the publication of the lectures from the college's first history course: Alfred Thayer Mahan's *The Influence of Sea Power Upon History, 1660-1783*.

This educational innovation within the U.S. Navy paralleled some other organizational innovations that were evolving within the service. The Navy Department's Office of Naval Intelligence, established in 1882, collected and coordinated information on foreign maritime and naval powers that could be useful for naval planning, for professional naval study, and for use of the merchant marine. At the same time, the Navy Department's newly established Office of Library and Naval Records worked to establish a research library for naval and maritime affairs. The first major work of this office was to publish the documentary record of naval operations during the Civil War. The purpose of this multi-volume project was to encourage professional men to study "not only the first war in which naval operations on a great scale have been conducted since the introduction of steam, but it is the only war in which those modern appliances have been used which have revolutionized the art of naval warfare."

These three separate naval activities, the Naval War College, the Office of Naval Intelligence, and the Office of Library and Naval Records, were particularly associated with many reform-minded officers at the Naval War College, who led the movement toward the creation of a staff of naval officers in uniform who would give professional advice to the secretary of the navy, who since the formation of the U.S. Navy had retained in civilian hands the sole responsibility for officer assignments, strategy, and operations. Their intended functions—to write contingency plans, create operational doctrine, and direct the country's naval operations at sea—took more than thirty years to come to fruition. Eventually, after a number of intermediate steps, Congress established the Office of the Chief of Naval Operations within the Navy Department in 1915.

The professional organizations that grew within

Alfred Thayer Mahan, Naval Historian and Strategist

Rear Admiral Alfred Thayer Mahan was a prolific writer and the most prominent American naval historian and strategist of his time.

Mahan was born in September 1840 at the U.S. Military Academy in West Point, New York, the son of Dennis Hart Mahan, professor of military engineering and chairman of the West Point academic board. He named his son in honor of the boy's godfather, Colonel Sylvanus Thayer, former superintendent and a key figure in West Point's history. The elder Mahan was an important early student of the theory of warfare and, having studied in France, became the principal interpreter for the ideas of Baron de Jomini, the leading thinker on warfare writing in French.

Despite his father's attachments, the young Mahan joined the U.S. Navy in 1856 and graduated from the Naval Academy at Annapolis in 1859. He had a relatively routine career for a naval officer in this period. During the Civil War, he served on three different ships conducting blockade duties and was on the Naval Academy staff in 1862-63, serving under Lieutenant Commander Stephen B. Luce on board a training ship for midshipmen. After the war, he had the usual spells of shore duty at the principal navy yards in New York and Boston, alternating with sea duty. He served at sea on the Asiatic Station and then commanded the steamships *Wasp* and *Wachusett* in South American waters. The only thing slightly unusual about his naval career to this point was that he had published an article on naval education that had won an honorable mention in the Naval Institute's Prize Essay contest, and he had written a straightforward narrative history of Civil War naval operations in his first book, *Gulf and Inland Waters*.

The great change in Mahan's career came in 1884, when Commodore Stephen B. Luce invited him to come to the newly established Naval War College and serve as its first lecturer in naval history and tactics. He was Luce's second or third choice for the position. When the others were unavailable, Luce laid out precisely what he wanted from Mahan: lectures that linked the history of international relations with naval operations and the broad issues of military thought. At the same time, Luce wanted someone to do for naval science what Jomini had done for military science. Highly influenced by the academic approach and the focus of ideas at the Naval War College, Mahan eventually fulfilled both of Luce's objectives.

Leaving command of his ship in South America in 1885, Mahan had returned to his home in New York City, where he spent a full year as a newly-promoted captain studying naval history before he went on to take up his new teaching responsibilities. By the time Mahan arrived at the Naval War College in 1886, Rear Admiral Luce had just returned to command the North Atlantic Squadron, leaving Mahan to take up the administrative responsibilities as War College president as well as his lecturing.

In 1890, Mahan published his first series of Naval War College lectures under the title, *The Influence of Sea Power Upon History, 1660-1785*. Although he went on to publish twenty books and numerous articles, this volume has remained his most famous and most influential work. It was immediately translated into several languages, and influential leaders in the United States, Britain, Germany, and Japan made immediate use of Mahan's writings in promoting the growth of their own navies.

Mahan wrote three additional volumes in his sea power series on naval history up to 1815, including a biography of Lord Nelson, whom he saw as the personification of sea power.

Most often remembered for advocating the use of large, heavily gunned battleships over other types of ships, stressing the importance of major fleet battles to win command of the sea, drawing attention to the sea-lanes of communication, and contributing to the growth of American overseas power, Mahan had a larger influence as well. He was the most prominent and widely read author who demonstrated the importance of historical analysis in an era of great technological change. In this, he very effectively contributed to the expansion of naval thinking beyond battle tactics and technical issues, linking naval affairs to wider national and international themes. In addition, he was the first writer to provide naval officers with a general theoretical framework for thinking about naval strategy, and directly adapted Jomini's military theories for this purpose.

Mahan was the world's most influential naval writer in the nineteenth and twentieth centuries. Recently, historians have come to measure Mahan's importance as part of a larger development and refinement of naval theory that began during the 1880s and has continued. Since Mahan's death in 1914, no comparable figure in the U.S. has combined innovative historical study with strategic

analysis. The only American naval writers who made important modifications to Mahan's theories in the twentieth century were Rear Admirals Henry E. Eccles and J.C. Wylie of the U.S. Navy. In the generation immediately following Mahan, Sir Julian Corbett and Admiral Sir Herbert Richmond in Britain, as well as Admiral Raoul Castex in France, offered important new insights for naval thinking. Later historians of the period 1660-1815 have continued to correct or to modify Mahan's historical judgements. While more recent interpretations have brought Mahan's conclusions into question, he, nevertheless, has remained an important

figure in the history of naval thought. The most recent interpretation, by Jon Sumida in 1997, stressed Mahan's view that historical study should be, "the primary agent of the advanced education for those charged with the task of directing what was technologically and bureaucratically the most complex institution of his time, and ours."

Alfred T. Mahan (1840-1914). Photo by J.E. Purdy, ca. 1904. (Courtesy Library of Congress)

the U.S. Navy tended to focus on the broader aspects of naval science, nurturing particularly the political-military aspects of the navy. Such a focus could serve neither the entire maritime community nor even some of the technical and specialized components within the navy itself. Naval architects and engineers, in particular, began to develop their own separate professional organization and to publish their own technical literature. As early as 1879, the navy had began to send young officers abroad to study. Cadet-engineers, in training to become naval architects, went to the Royal Naval College in England as well as to Glasgow University and to Paris. In 1880, the American Society of Mechanical Engineers was the first professional society formed for this group and included both civilian and naval men. Eight years later, a group of naval officers gathered at the Navy's Bureau of Steam Engineering and established the American Society of Naval Engineering, as a means to disseminate and exchange information.

Since many of the U.S. Navy's naval architects had been trained in Britain, they had become acquainted with the two main professional organizations in that country: the Institution of Engineers and the Institution of Naval Architects. Increasingly, American naval architects wanted a similar organization in the United Sates. At a dinner following the launching of the cruiser USS *Columbia* at Philadelphia in 1892, a number of naval officers discussed a plan to form such a society. However, it was not until 1893 that this plan took effect when an enlarged group, including naval constructors, marine engineers, and private shipbuilders, met in New York City and successfully established the Society of Naval Architects and Marine Engineers.

In a parallel development, also in 1893, the Massachusetts Institute of Technology began its first course in naval architecture, modeled on that of the Royal Naval College. Taking up the new methods, its classroom courses focused on mechanical drawing and classroom instruction. Among the leaders of the group who had established the Society of Naval Architects and Marine Engineers was William H. Webb, the versatile New York City ship designer and builder. Having made a fortune during his career in designing and constructing 150 ships, for sail and steam, of wood and iron, as merchantmen

and warships, Webb had already been responsible for educating one of America's greatest ship designers, Donald McKay. Long after his retirement, he established and endowed Webb's Academy and Home for Shipbuilders. Opened in 1894, it was later renamed the Webb Institute of Naval Architecture. Following the pioneering courses at the Naval Academy, MIT, and the Webb Institute, other universities began to pusue such subjects in the years leading up to World War I. Cornell, the University of Michigan, Columbia, and Lehigh each began academic programs in naval architecture.

The development of academic programs to support maritime affairs in America's universities and professional schools was one important contribution to a wider course of development that reflected the broad growth in maritime professionalization. Alongside it was the evolution of government agencies that dealt in maritime affairs. While the growth of the Navy Department had been much larger, more costly, and more complex technologically than other portions of the government's maritime activities, this same pattern of growth was also reflected in the maritime agencies that came under the control of the Treasury Department.

The Maritime Activities of the Treasury Department

In the immediate aftermath of the Civil War, the Treasury Department gradually continued its wartime trend to centralize control of cutter operations in the U.S. Revenue-Marine for law enforcement and for marine safety duties. The postwar period brought some new issues: The rise in tariffs required more cutters to control smuggling, and the new laws regulating immigration after 1862 created an additional demand for cooperation with other law-enforcement agencies. The doubling of tonnage in coastwise shipping between 1865 and 1910 created demand for improvements in the Lighthouse Establishment's aids to navigation, as did the associated growth in the size of ships and the shift from sail to steam, which created new responsibilities for the Steamboat Inspection

Although the Humane Society of Massachusetts had established volunteer lifeboat stations as early as 1807, and the Revenue Marine supervised stations on the New Jersey and New York coasts after 1848, a nationwide effort did not occur until after several shipwrecks in the winter of 1870-71. The Highland Life-Saving Station, located in an area of dangerous sand shoals along the exposed arm of Cape Cod, was one of seventy-one similar stations established in 1872 on the coasts of Cape Cod, Long Island, and New Jersey. Built in 1872 and enlarged into the form seen here in 1888, the station contained living quarters for a keeper and seven surfmen, and a boatroom for the lifesaving equipment. Surfmen were usually experienced local watermen. During the lifesaving season, from August to May, they made regular daily foot patrols along the beach for several miles, in coordination with surfmen from neighboring stations, to warn away ships standing into danger or to notify the station of a stranded vessel. During the week they performed drills with the surfboat and with the breeches-buoy and life-car methods of rescuing persons from ships stranded in heavy seas close to the beach. Surfmen were also trained to resuscitate the "apparently drowned." The men of this station were called on to rescue the crew of a wrecked vessel at least once a year. Life-saving stations were first built on the hazardous outer banks of North Carolina in 1874, on the Great Lakes and in Florida in 1875, on the West Coast in 1877, and on the Texas coast in 1882. The U.S. Life-Saving Service was established as a separate agency of the Treasury Department in 1878. By 1914, on the eve of its merger into the U.S. Coast Guard, the Life-Saving Service operated 279 stations along the coast from Maine to Washington. Photo by C.N. Taylor, 1898. (M.S.M. 78.72.2)

Service. In addition, the acquisition of Alaska opened up a huge new coastal area in which to extend all of these services and duties. From 1869 onwards, the Treasury Department began a series of bureaucratic changes to gain more efficient control of its various and separate maritime activities, including the Revenue-Marine, Steamboat Inspection Service, Lighthouse Service, and Life-Saving Service.

Among the various maritime components of the Treasury Department, the Revenue-Marine was

the largest. In 1875, Congress formally established a central authority for the Revenue-Marine Division, and the treasury secretary formally appointed Sumner I. Kimball as its chief, confirming a role he had been carrying out under the secretary's authority since 1871. Under Kimball's leadership, the Revenue-Marine moved toward a centralized, rational system of discipline for its officers and men, with improved personnel policies. Kimball also increased the service's operating effectiveness, reduced its budget, and improved its administrative efficiency.

The Lighthouse Service expanded its operations greatly after the Civil War, operating 425 light stations in 1860, 833 in 1890, and 1,662 in 1916. The Service established the first West Coast light at San Francisco, which was lit in 1854, and expanded its Pacific stations as far north as Alaska in 1895. With few harbors of refuge along its rugged 350-mile coast, Oregon posed an especial danger to mariners sailing to Portland or Seattle. To provide a warning beacon along the middle of that coast, the service built this ninety-three-foot brick tower at Yaquina Head, also known as Cape Foulweather. Just getting the building materials up the seventy-foot bluff was a feat for the increasingly professional U.S. Lighthouse Service. First lit in 1873, Yaquina Head Lighthouse remains in service today. Stereograph by J.G. Crawford, ca. 1875. (M.S.M. 87.92.4)

During his administration of the Revenue-Marine between 1871 and 1878, Kimball brought the Life-Saving Service under his direct authority, fostering professionalization in a service that up to that point had depended largely on volunteer efforts, such as the Massachusetts Humane Society. Through his efforts, Congress passed the Life-Saving Act of 1874, which established a reporting procedure for maritime accidents that would eventually provide a statistical basis to plan expansion and organization of the service's activities and for selecting appropriate sites for its stations. This Act also authorized the secretary of the treasury to award gold and silver medals for heroism in lifesaving.

Kimball went on to expand the service along the eastern seaboard to the Gulf Coast, the Great Lakes, and the Pacific Coast. In each of these regions, local watermen were hired to remain in attendance at the stations, generally from September through April, making regular patrols of the shore. Through regular practice, the surfmen maintained their skills at launching a surfboat from the beach and using the Lyle gun to set up a breeches buoy rescue line between the shore and a stranded ship. In

The low barrier islands of the Gulf Coast were a particular challenge for the Lighthouse Service. Iron screw-pile towers were developed for shoals in the Florida Keys before the Civil War, and similar structures were used along the Gulf Coast after the war. With the expansion of maritime commerce in Texas, the Brazos River Light was built in 1896. The ninety-foot tower guided traffic at the marshy mouth of the Brazos River. As depicted here after the devastating hurricane that destroyed nearby Galveston in 1900, the elevated keeper's quarters might be damaged but the tower was able to withstand severe hurricanes, as it did in 1900, 1909, 1915, and 1919. This station remained in service until a petrochemical plant was built on the site in 1967. (M.S.M. 64.882.14)

1877-78, after the loss of more than 180 lives in two wrecks on the North Carolina Outer Banks, there was a move to bring the service under the navy. Kimball, however, engineered a move that resulted in Congress creating the Life-Saving Service as a separate agency within the Treasury Department in June 1878, and he moved from his position with the Revenue-Marine to be its general superintendant until 1915.

For many years, the management of the nation's lighthouses was a separate activity under the general direction of the Treasury Department. Continuing under the direct management of the Lighthouse Board that had been established in 1852, the Lighthouse Service increased its major lights from 528 in 1870 to 1,243 in 1890, while in the same period establishing 2,500 minor lighthouse stations and virtually doubling the number of buoys from about 2,500 in 1870. The service employed new technology, placing the first gas-fueled, flashing-light buoy in service in 1881 and introducing the electric light at the Sandy Hook, New Jersey, Lighthouse in 1889. Adapting new forms of engineering and construction to differing special conditions in American waters, the U.S. Lighthouse Service followed a growing world pattern that reached a peak in the 1870s of constructing lights on offshore rocks and shoals. Among the most important of these were the construction in 1870-74 of the masonry cone built to withstand ice on Spectacle Reef in Lake Huron; the iron piles driven into the coral reefs off Florida with an eighty-foot-high open-work iron superstructure for the light and living quarters built at Fowey Rock in 1875-78 and at Alligator Reef in 1880; and the first caisson towers, filled with concrete, sunk in the sand at Duxbury Pier, Massachusetts, in 1871 and in the Chesapeake at Craighill Channel in 1873. Under very difficult conditions, the Lighthouse Service built a masonry tower on submerged St. George's Reef off the California coast in 1891.

Like the Lighthouse Service, the Steamboat Inspection Service continued its independent work, begun in the 1830s, of certifying vessels and their equipment under the Treasury Department. In the period 1867-70, this office began to publish an annual list of U.S. merchant vessels. By 1884, the laws regulating navigation had become so complex that Congress established a separate Bureau of Navigation within the Treasury Department to administer them. In a division of labor, the Bureau took on administrative and statistical duties, documentation of vessels, annual tonnage reports, while the Steamboat Inspection Service dealt with the inspection of vessels and certification of equipment as well as the examination and licensing of officers.

Treasury Department Rationalization and Reform

As the maritime world changed, the Treasury Department's administrative structure had problems in adjusting to those developments, as well as in carrying out the increasing burdens placed upon it. One of its responsibilities that cried out for reform was the Marine Hospital Service. The Treasury Department was also responsible for medical service for merchant seamen that was, in theory, paid for by contributions from wages. Because the system was ineffective, Congress reorganized it in 1870, leaving

specific arrangements for marine hospitals and general health measures in behalf of seamen to the authorities in each port, while the Marine Hospital Service officers were able to provide quarantine. Following the yellow fever epidemic of 1878, health groups all over the country demanded drastic reform in public health. But it was not until yellow fever and other bacteriological diseases again became a problem to soldiers and sailors during the Spanish-American War that both the Army and the Navy Medical Corps and the Marine Hospital Service changed dramatically. Widening its programs and responsibilities, the Marine Hospital Service was renamed the Public Health and Marine Hospital Service in 1901. In 1912, the Public Health Service began operating on a far wider scale than its origins in the maritime field.

Similarly, by the end of the 1880s the Revenue-Marine found itself with aging ships, aging officers, and no plans to provide for the growth of an officer corps. Its School of Instruction was allowed to close at a time when the country needed more activity in maritime protection and law enforcement.

Development of the U.S. Coast Guard

In 1889, in response to these new demands for regulation of American maritime activity, a Congressional bill laid plans for the U.S. Navy to take over the Revenue-Marine, placing it under its own commandant in a status similar to that of the commandant of the Marine Corps. While Congress failed to pass the bill, the debate on the subject brought about the kind of administrative reform that many in the U.S. Navy were seeking for themselves: a trained, career professional officer to head the service. In December 1889, the Secretary of the Treasury appointed the first experienced officer of the Revenue-Marine service, Captain Leonard G. Shepard, to be its chief. Nearly five years later Congress finally gave its stamp of approval for reform, passing an act that renamed the service the Revenue-Cutter Service, requiring that such appointments be continued, and adding a requirement for a similarly qualified captain of engineers. Shortly afterwards, the School of Instruction with its training ship *Chase* was reestablished and obtained a base at Arundel

maritime activities. The dramatic, worldwide growth in maritime traffic and the rapid changes in maritime technology began to create a consensus among nations that the world needed more uniformity in the practice of navigation and in aids to navigation.

One of the first considerations for navigators was the issue of time. When the new Atlantic cable telegraph line was being laid by the British ship *Great Eastern* in 1866, she received time signals by telegraph twice daily from the cable she was laying and was able to be exact about her longitude during her daily progress westward across the Atlantic. As soon as the cable was laid, the same cable was then used to compare the time, and thus the longitude differences, between the observatories at Cambridge, Massachusetts, and Greenwich, England. The American railroads, however, were a major force in creating a new international system of timekeeping at sea. In 1866, transcontinental travelers had to contend with some eighty different time standards in the United States, and some American railroad stations kept as many as six different standards for the arrival and departure of trains. In an early attempt to address this problem, the U.S. Naval Observatory in Washington had begun to issue time bulletins in 1865. In 1850 an Act of Congress had made the meridian of the Washington Observatory the American meridian for all astronomical purposes, and the Greenwich meridian the standard for nautical purposes. Thus, when Professor Charles F. Dowd of Temple Grove Ladies Seminary in Saratoga Springs, New York, first proposed a system of standard time zones, each made up of fifteen degrees of longitude, differing by one hour in time from zone to zone, he based it on the meridian of the Washington Observatory. When he first laid out his plan, eastern businessmen thought the boundaries were inconvenient, pushing the zone boundaries too far to the west. Revising his proposal, he recalculated his boundaries again, this time basing them on the maritime Greenwich meridian which moved the boundaries roughly two degrees to the eastward. Railroads all over the United States and Canada adopted Dowd's system, and on 18 November 1883 all clocks in the United States conformed, creating what one newspaper called "Horometric Harmony."

Under the pressure of railway demands, the example of the Canadian and American adoption of the Greenwich meridian for practical purposes added fuel to the fire of another issue that geographers and scientists had repeatedly discussed since 1870: the need for a world standard for longitude and time. It was hardly a new subject; every major maritime country had struggled with selecting a meridian and, as long ago as 1634, Cardinal Richelieu had called for an internationally recognized prime meridian. With the annual publication and widespread use of the British *Nautical Almanac* since 1767, many maritime nations, including the United States, had informally adopted Greenwich as the prime meridian, and the first systematic charts of the American coast, drawn by J. F. W. DesBarres in the late 1770s, also used it. These facts, in themselves, provided practical reasons for an independent America to continue using the Greenwich meridian, at least for maritime affairs, but it was not yet an established principle. In 1871, the first International Geographical Congress agreed to use the Greenwich meridian for all passage charts, but this did not apply to either coastal and harbor charts or maps of land areas, in which each country had decided to keep its national meridian.

In the mid-1870s, a Canadian railroad engineer, Sandford Fleming, became interested in the problem of clocks and time. After first espousing the idea of the twenty-four-hour clock, he moved on to develop ideas for a world-wide system of uniform time. His early ideas were developed further by international conferences at Venice in 1881 and at Rome in 1883. As a result of these preliminary conferences, Congress passed an act authorizing President Chester Arthur to call a conference on the American proposal to establish a common prime meridian for reckoning time and longitude around the world. At Washington in October 1884, delegates to the International Meridian Conference selected Greenwich as the single prime meridian, calculated longitude 180 degrees both east and west from Greenwich, established a universal solar day, making the civil, nautical, and astronomical days all begin at twelve midnight rather than the twelve noon of the nautical day, and promoted the use of the decimal system to calculate divisions of angular space. It took many years for the world's nations to accept all the Conference recommendations and to implement them into all aspects of world maritime affairs. By the time Congress formally enacted a law to this effect in 1918, confirming twenty-five years of U.S. practice, more than sixty maritime countries had formally adopted the Greenwich meridian.

International cooperation and agreement continued to have an impact on the development of American maritime affairs. In 1889, another conference, the International Maritime Conference, met in Washington, D.C., to deal with a wide variety of issues, including international "rules of the road" when ships encountered other ships, signal flag codes, and the buoyage system.

In beginning to move toward international uniformity in buoy shapes, the Conference recognized both the cardinal and lateral systems of buoyage, established that wreck buoys should be clearly distinguishable from other buoys, mandated that channel and landfall buoys should be tall and pillar shaped and that the buoys on the starboard side of a channel when entering port should be conical in shape and uniform in color. The Conference strongly recommended the color red for the right-hand conical buoys when returning to port, and black on the left or port side, but recognized the alternative use of white or striped buoys to port. Shortly afterwards, another conference meeting in Paris saw the potential in the Washington agreements and established a permanent international commission for maritime aids. Combining with a similar organization for European inland navigation, by 1898 this eventually became the Permanent International Association of Navigation Conferences (PIANC) with headquarters in Brussels. In general, these efforts to standardize navigational markers were less successful than either the efforts to standardize time or signaling at sea.

The issue of maritime signaling was an old one. In 1855, the British Board of Trade drafted the First International Code of Signals, containing 70,000 signals using eighteen flags. Most maritime nations adopted this system, which was published in 1857, but by 1887 the Board of Trade had prepared a revision and these changes were discussed in detail at the 1889 conference, where many new additions were suggested. As a result of these, a new International Code was published in 1897.

While these international agreements established a variety of new standards for American shipping, there were also internal pressures.

Domestically, Congress passed new legislation creating anchorage laws and requiring the Revenue-Marine to enforce them. In 1888, New York established regulations, and soon rules for the regulation of harbor traffic were approved in other ports. In this same period, Americans began to expand their maritime activities for pleasure, not merely for profit. The richest of the rich built themselves yachts that were larger than many a merchant ship, employing a staff for their social pleasures. While the highest strata in society were engaged in this type of activity, the more ordinary person also found pleasure and recreation afloat. In the late nineteenth and early twentieth century, many groups organized yacht clubs, and the business of pleasure became a profitable enterprise for many craftsmen. As steam surpassed sail in the commercial world, contemporary art and literature reflected a stronger strain of maritime romanticism. Joshua Slocum's world voyage and the book he wrote about it captured the imaginations of readers around the world. The sea was beginning to be seen as an arena for recreation and adventure, and this new pull toward individuality and small-boat activity began to present a problem for those concerned with maritime safety, regulation and rescue.

Maritime Labor

In the post-Civil War period, American labor faced many difficulties in adjusting to the country's rapid industrialization. The deterioration of America's seafaring skills had been evident even before the war. Perhaps the most important factor in labor difficulties on the waterfront was the creation of new opportunities in more lucrative and often less restrictive jobs in internal trades and industries. Home industries, in fact, demanded more labor than could be supplied by the existing work force. As a consequence, there was no surplus population of workers drawn to seafaring, as there had been in the first half of the nineteenth century.

At sea, the revolution in propulsion required an entirely different category of skilled and unskilled labor working in entirely new conditions. In 1890, for example, a large steamship carried as many as 170 men to tend the boilers

Joshua Slocum: The First Solo Circumnavigator

Americans have long been fascinated by the solitary struggles of a sailor alone in a small boat on the open sea. Perhaps the attraction is the idea of an independent man struggling with primordial elements, or maybe it is the more amorphous romanticism of adventure on the high seas. In either case, for the past century the round-the-world exploits of Joshua Slocum have epitomized the solo voyager. Yet Slocum was not the first American to sail a long distance alone. Among other Americans of his time, Alfred Johnson had taken a dory from Gloucester to Liverpool to celebrate the centennial of American independence. Later, in 1882-83, Bernard Gilboy sailed from San Francisco to Australia in an eighteen-foot boat.

The son of a Methodist deacon and a lighthouse-keeper's daughter, Joshua Slocum was born in 1844 and raised in Nova Scotia, where both sides of his family had been seafarers. Shipping out as a cook on a fishing vessel at the age of sixteen, he later sailed widely under the British flag in the grain and cargo trades. By the age of eighteen, he had passed the Board of Trade examination and qualified as second mate.

Attracted by the booming coastal trade at San Francisco in the mid-1860s, he became an American citizen there. Shortly thereafter he traveled north to work in the salmon fishery on the Columbia River and hunt furs in British Columbia. During this period, he sold a design for an improved boat for gillnet fishing.

In 1869, Slocum returned to sea, this time under the American flag in the coastal trade between San Francisco and Seattle. Getting his first command, the bark *Washington,* he brought her as one of the first American vessels to enter Cook Inlet in Alaska after the departure of the Russians. During a salmon fishing expedition, the ship dragged anchor and was lost, but he saved his cargo of fish. Getting a new command from the same owners, he sailed the barkentine *Constitution* from San Francisco to Hawaii and to Mexican ports. His wife, whom he had married in Australia in 1871, often accompanied him on voyages until her death in 1885. Their eldest son Victor was born on board *Constitution*. In 1874-76, Slocum commanded the *Benjamin Aymar.* When her owners decided to sell her in the Philippines, Slocum and his

little family were stranded there. Slocum organized workmen on the shore of Subic Bay to build an eighty-ton steamship for a naval architect. In payment for his services, the architect gave Slocum a ninety-ton schooner, *Pato*, which Slocum first used to carry lumber, then refitted for a successful salmon fishing expedition in the Sea of Okhotsk, bringing his cargo across the Pacific to sell profitably in Victoria, British Columbia.

Briefly coming ashore, he took up a long-standing interest in writing to serve for a time as correspondent for the *San Francisco Bee*. Back at sea in 1878, he commanded the *Amethyst*, then the full-rigged ship *Northern Light*, and finally the bark *Aquidneck.* In the last ship, he, his second wife, and two children were wrecked on a sandbar at Antonina, below São Paulo, in 1887. Penniless and stranded once again, Slocum built a thirty-five-foot open boat–or canoe, as he preferred to call it–that combined his recollections of a Cape Ann dory, the lines of an elegant Japanese sampan, and the rig of a Chinese sampan. His wife made the sails, and his son was the carpenter, ropemaker, and

Joshua Slocum (1844-1909) sails his former oyster sloop Spray *off the coast of Australia in 1896, during his single-handed voyage around the world. (M.S.M. 46.606)*

"general roustabout." Christened on 13 May 1888, the anniversary of the emancipation of Brazil's slaves, Slocum named her *Liberdade*.

In this open boat, Slocum with his wife and two children sailed 5,510 miles in an epic journey from the Bay of Paranaguá, Brazil, to Cape Roman, South Carolina. In 1890, he privately published his first book, the dramatic account of the *Voyage of the Liberdade*.

After a number of unsuccessful business ventures, Slocum returned briefly to his wife's family in Massachusetts, from whence his own Nova Scotia family had emigrated as Loyalists more than a century before. There he acquired the beached hull of an old oyster sloop at Fairhaven, across the harbor from New Bedford. Slocum completely rebuilt the thirty-four-foot, nine-inch vessel named *Spray* at a cost of $553.62.

After sailing her for a year and trying to eke out a living as a fisherman around Boston, Slocum decided to sail his stout little vessel on the first solo circumnavigation of the globe. Closely watched by the press and reported by every passing vessel, Slocum left Boston on 24 April 1895, sailed to Nova Scotia, and then crossed the Atlantic to Gibraltar, intending to pass through the Suez Canal. At Gibraltar, British naval officers warned Slocum of pirates in the Red Sea. He recrossed the Atlantic to Brazil in forty days and coasted south to the Straits of Magellan. Encountering very heavy weather there, he struggled for two months to get through the

350-mile long waterway. There Slocum saw the roughest seas he had ever been in, what he later called "the greatest sea adventure of my life."

Sailing westward, he reached the Marquesas in forty-five days. When Slocum called at Samoa, Mrs. Robert Louis Stevenson presented him with some of her late husband's books, including several volumes of sailing directions. Sailing on to Australia, he remained there for nine months, earning a good income by lecturing and charging admission to come aboard *Spray*. From Australia, he continued his journey, crossing the Indian Ocean to South Africa, where he remained to lecture for another three months at Durban and Cape Town.

From South Africa, Slocum sailed northward, calling at both Saint Helena and Ascension Islands. Off the coast of Brazil, he encountered the U.S. battleship *Oregon* as she rushed past on her famous passage from the Pacific to the Atlantic in the tense days preceding the Spanish-American War.

Sighting her off the mouth of the Amazon River, Slocum could read the signal flags *Oregon* flew: C-T-B above a Spanish flag, meaning "Are there enemy Spanish warships near?" Unaware that war had broken out, Slocum made his famous reply: "Let us keep together for mutual protection." Too far away to read his signal flags, the battleship made no reply as she sped on toward the West Indies.

Slocum completed his 46,000-

mile circumnavigation on 27 June 1898 when he entered the harbor at Newport, Rhode Island. The following year, he began to publish his account of the voyage in *Century Magazine*, and the entire story was published as *Sailing Alone Around the World* in 1900. Slocum's tale was enormously popular, earning him enough money from royalties to buy a house and settle on Martha's Vineyard. He continued to publish articles in *Century Magazine*, *McClure's*, and other popular journals while maintaining and sailing the *Spray* in local waters for the next few years. Sailing alone, he took the *Spray* on trips to the West Indies in the winters of 1905, 1907, and 1908. On 19 November 1909, Joshua Slocum departed Martha's Vineyard in the *Spray* for his winter holiday. He and *Spray* were never seen again.

A remarkable figure, Slocum simultaneously represented the last generation of American sailing-ship captains and the first generation of American small-boat sailors. Entirely self-taught, he became a popular writer whose work is still widely read a century later.

and engines. Working in four-hour watches, a large proportion of these men were coal trimmers, who did the heavy work of carrying coal from the bunkers to the boiler furnace, and then carried away the ash as the stokers fed the boilers. It was hot and dirty work in very confined conditions below decks, all made even more difficult by the noise and danger of the machinery. The rapid change in technology brought with it serious tensions between those working with the new technology and those who were trained in, or who romanticized, the skills involved in sailing ships. In general, however, the quality of seamanship, the general conditions of work at sea, and the general scale of wages improved for American seamen as steam came to dominate the seafaring of the late nineteenth century. The course of improvement, however, was not so obvious at the time and often shrouded in controversy.

During the last decades of the nineteenth century, American seamen were largely better-paid than foreign seamen, while American seamen in the coastal trades were paid better than American seamen on foreign voyages, and American seamen in steamships were paid higher than those serving in sailing vessels. Wages were a positive feature of maritime labor in those decades; but there were serious negatives. The increasing size, speed, and number of steamships created far greater dangers for seamen than had existed in the past. In 1884, for example, one-third of all shipping accidents in American waters were collisions, and in the following year five percent of the 677 collisions resulted in the total loss of a vessel. In comparing the losses of sail to those of steam vessels in the period between 1872 and 1879, one observer found that 1.4 percent more sailing ships were lost than steamships, suggesting somewhat greater safety in steamships. In terms of health and diet, the seaman's position was improving. Seamen were slowly getting more food and a greater variety of it. As steamships traveled faster, there were increasing opportunities for reprovisioning and fewer complications in the preservation of food supplies.

Labor, like other groups in society, answered in its own way to the organizational processes under way in America in the late nineteenth century. Unionization was labor's response to the incorporation movement taking place throughout society, but most conspicuously in business and industry. Some workers devoted their energies to the establishment of a national labor party, but those efforts failed in the election of 1872. During the depressions of the 1870s, 1880s, and 1890s the nation was beset by literally thousands of strikes for better wages and working conditions. Many of these agitations assumed regional and national proportions and were too often met, not with understanding but with federal or state suppression, which in turn led to the formation of more unions and alliances among unions, as well as further labor-industry estrangement.

Labor conflict was not as obvious in the maritime industries as it was in other industries, but strong resentment was clearly present. One source of open conflict was longshoremen's wages on the Atlantic and Gulf coasts. Between the years 1874 and 1886, the waterfronts of New York, Boston, and Galveston were the scenes of wildcat strikes. The Galveston affair, brought about by the refusal of the Mallory Steamship Company to meet its longshoremen's wage demands, attracted the attention of the Noble Order of the Knights of Labor, the most significant industrial union of that time. A secret fraternal organization founded in 1869 and patterned on British and European cooperative models, it had a Texas membership of more than 20,000. The Knights orchestrated a widespread boycott against the Mallory Line and the railroads that serviced its wharves. Coinciding with strikes by the union against other trans-Mississippi railroads, the Galveston boycott became part of the general strike of 1886, which for several months came close to shutting down the transportation system of the American southwest.

None of these waterfront strikes succeeded. In each instance the companies replaced the striking longshoremen with strikebreakers derisively called "scabs": Italian immigrants, greenhands, and imported Scottish laborers in New York; black longshoremen from Baltimore and New York Italians in Boston; and black longshoremen in Galveston. In the end, the previously employed longshoremen either returned at company wage levels, or were, as in the Galveston case, locked out entirely as a penalty for their affiliation with the Knights of Labor. At its zenith in the 1880s, the Knights of Labor boasted more than 700,000 members and was extremely broad in its repre-

Other than black cooks and stewards, who made up much of the membership of the 1901 Marine Cooks, Stewards, and Waiters' Union of the Atlantic and Gulf, African-American maritime laborers were excluded from waterfront and seafaring unions. However, whether organized in unions or simply by occupational affiliation, maritime laborers often cooperated in labor actions to benefit from company concessions. Sitting on a barge at the bow of an ocean steamship, these black coal passers talk about striking during maritime labor actions on the New York waterfront in June 1911. (Courtesy Library of Congress)

sentation, excluding only bankers, gamblers, lawyers, and stockholders from membership. But the public's perception of the union as unacceptably radical undermined its effectiveness. Following the failure of the Galveston boycott, when it was publicly, if unfairly, implicated in the sensational May 1886 Haymarket Riot in Chicago, membership in the Knights of Labor dropped precipitously. By 1890, the union was on the road to extinction.

Other unions developed among seamen operating on inland waters. The Maritime Engineers Beneficial Association was founded in 1875, followed by the Lake Seaman's Union in 1878, the Coast Seaman's Union in 1885, and the National Seaman's Union in 1892.

In the shipbuilding industries ashore, unions were rare outside the large cities, where unions in the early 1870s were able to secure a relatively high wage for new construction at three to four dollars per day with an eight-to-nine-hour working day. By 1882, John Roach & Sons' Chester shipyard below Philadelphia was paying highly skilled workers about fourteen dollars per week, moderately skilled workers eleven dollars a week, and unskilled workers about seven and a half dollars a week. Workers in Scotland were receiving about 44 percent less. American wage rates in the shipbuilding industry were determined largely by wage levels in other areas of engineering work, such as locomotive construction and steel construction. The U.S. Navy determined its pay for civilian yard workers by comparison to the rates in similar crafts, and

In his 1912 painting, Men of the Docks, *George Bellows focused on longshoremen on the snowy Brooklyn waterfront, overwhelmed by the looming New York skyline, the Brooklyn Bridge, and the steel bulk of a large ocean steamship. As an artist of real life, and a sometime Socialist, Bellows sought to capture these essential but otherwise overlooked laborers, and the harsh realities of their environment. Oil, 45 x 63.5 inches. (Courtesy Maier Museum of Art, Randolph-Macon Woman's College, Lynchburg, Virginia)*

adjusted them every six months. In the smaller centers of the wooden shipbuilding industry, where labor was unorganized, living costs low, and the work force relatively stable, the workday was longer and the wage levels were about 25 to 50 percent below other areas. The financial crisis of the 1870s forced a dispersion of large numbers of skilled workers, leaving few younger workers entering the shipbuilding trades. In New England, displaced workmen from Canada found jobs at low wages, but they often came into conflict with local labor. By and large, these small shipbuilding centers relied on transient labor, working on an irregular basis on particular vessels for specific periods of a few months.

Unlike British seamen after 1854, American seamen in the foreign trades went largely unprotected from abuse. For the service of providing a seaman a berth at sea, it was normal practice in foreign voyages from all American ports for boardinghouse masters and company crimps to take an advance of up to 25 percent of a seaman's wages. The 1866 New York Boarding House Act attempted to enforce decent living standards in boardinghouses, but only succeeded in reducing their numbers by nearly half. In 1872, Congress passed the Shipping Commissioner's Act, creating regional offices for a U.S. Commission of Navigation designed to act as conduits for employment. This act required seamen to sign the shipping articles that specified pay and conditions of their service in the presence of a federal commissioner and specified that each seaman be paid in person. The lawmakers thought these regulations would prevent seamen being shanghaied or otherwise forced to pay an advance on their wages to a crimp. In practice the system was not as effective as the lawmakers had hoped. Boardinghouse

owners, shipmasters, and shipowners joined to resist all reforms of the crimping system, thus allowing shipping companies to continue to obtain seamen at much lower wages than otherwise. In 1884, Congress attempted to abolish the evils of crimping through the Dingley Act, making it unlawful to pay advances of any kind. The boardinghouse owners and shippers, however, quickly persuaded Congress to amend the law in 1886, allowing advances to be paid for debts. By declaring the crimping fee a debt, any owner or master could circumvent the regulation.

Shipowners resisted further regulation by proving that American seamen received the highest overall pay in the world, ignoring the deplorable conditions under which those wages were earned and the liens placed upon wages through the crimping system. Once on board, American seamen had to work in circumstances primitive by almost any measure. Corporal punishment was common, and disobedience was treated as mutiny. Blacklisting still prevailed. Fourteen-hour days—with the normal alternating four-hour watch periods often increased by a constant work period during daylight hours—and seven-day weeks were routine for ordinary seamen. The industry's accident rate in 1900 was second only to that of coal mining, and only sharecroppers earned a more meager wage than did seamen. Long voyages and low wage levels made family life impossible. The advent of steam further worsened conditions, as the owners treated and paid workers as unskilled labor.

Appeals to justice paid poor dividends. When in 1895 Congress passed the Maguire Act, which, among other improvements, abolished imprisonment for leaving a vessel in coastwise trade, the Supreme Court, supporting lower court rulings perpetuating imprisonment, asserted that the

West Coast seamen and maritime laborers were among the first to organize themselves in unions, establishing the Coast Seamen's Union in 1885. It was reorganized as the Sailors' Union in 1891 and combined with the Great Lakes and Gulf unions to form a National Seamen's Union in 1892. Engine-room crews and cooks and stewards also organized unions. During San Francisco's great transportation strike from July to October 1901, seamen, waterfront workers, and other transportation laborers struck in opposition to company attempts to break union solidarity. Here, San Francisco seamen, most of whom worked in the coastal lumber trade, gather in front of the Sailors' Union on Steuart Street during the 1901 strike. Although the strikers resisted union-breaking efforts, true recognition of seamen's rights would not come until the 1915 La Follette Seamen's Act, but friction between unions and shipping companies would persist in the American merchant marine. (Courtesy San Francisco Maritime National Historical Park, Wyland Stanley Photographic Collection)

Gathered around the halyard used to raise or lower the main topgallant yard, the watch on the American bark Alice *suggests the conditions for mariners under sail at the end of the nineteenth century. Largely confined to long-distance runs with bulk or low-value cargoes, like* Alice's *New York-to-New Zealand route, deep-water sailors frequently spent 100 days at sea, working alternate four-hour watch periods, eating salted provisions, and at the mercy of the ship's officers, who might be tyrants or, like this vessel's officers, might be considerate of their crews when conditions permitted. (M.S.M. 96.113.1.11)*

Thirteenth Amendment, which outlawed slavery, was inapplicable to seafaring! Basing its January 1897 ruling on maritime law going back as far as 900 years before Christ, and to other long-standing international precedents, the Court declared invalid those provisions of the Maguire Act abolishing imprisonment. "Indeed," the Court declared, "seamen are treated by Congress . . . as deficient in that full and intelligent responsibility for their acts which is accredited to ordinary adults. . . . It can not be open to doubt that the provision against involuntary servitude was never intended to apply to their contracts." This was the same Supreme Court that in the 1890s declared an income tax unconstitutional, validated the use of the injunction against labor disorders, and legalized racial segregation. No laws or legal

traditions provided workers with protection against abuses by the owners of property. Law was mired in conservative precedent and had not become socially conscious.

Not until 1915 were firm steps finally taken to emancipate American seamen from their conditions of near-slavery. In that year, the La Follette Seamen's Act prohibited imprisonment for desertion in both foreign and domestic trades, made important strides in improving safety at sea, enabled seamen to receive half pay in every port worked by their vessel, increased the size of living quarters, upgraded the scale of provisions, and outlawed the payment of advance or allotment. When President Woodrow Wilson signed the bill on 4

Robert La Follette (1855-1925) was an attorney, Republican Congressman from Wisconsin, 1885-91, Wisconsin governor, and Senator, 1906-25. As a progressive governor and Senator, La Follette pressed for political and economic reforms. Despite the importance of his state's commerce on the Great Lakes, La Follette was not acting on a mandate from his constituents when he sponsored an act for the benefit of seamen in Congress. Rather, it reflected his stance against big business and his friendship with lifelong seamen's advocate Andrew Furuseth. La Follette's bill eliminated imprisonment as punishment for desertion from a vessel, abolished the payment of advances on wages, which nearly always went to the "crimps" who supplied crews, required improvements in shipboard living conditions, and established standards for the rating of able-bodied seamen. To make the bill more acceptable in Congress, La Follette added provisions to improve shipboard safety procedures for passengers and crew alike. Many shipowners opposed this effort to improve the economic bargaining position of seamen, but La Follette pushed the bill through both houses of Congress near the end of the winter session in February 1915. Although President Wilson was inclined to sign the legislation into law, the secretary of state recommended against it for political reasons. However, La Follette and Furuseth persuaded Wilson that the bill provided simple "justice" for an otherwise disenfranchised and nearly enslaved group of American laborers. Wilson signed the legislation on 4 March 1915, and the Senator from agricultural Wisconsin became a hero to American seamen. Although the Republican La Follette agreed with Wilson on many social issues, he opposed the arming of American merchant ships and the declaration of war on Germany, provisions that at least temporarily enhanced the American merchant marine. (Courtesy Library of Congress)

March 1915, he did so because "it seemed the only chance," as he expressed it, "to get something like justice to a class of workmen who have been too much neglected by our laws."

Symbolizing the racial inequality found within the maritime community, the La Follette Act answered organized labor's effort to halt the employment of lesser-paid foreign seaman, particularly Asians, by mandating that 75 percent of an American ship's crew must understand English. Earlier in the nineteenth century, blacks had found employment at sea in a variety of skilled and unskilled positions, but toward the end of the century European immigrants came to dominate both skilled and menial positions in American ships. As on shore, seagoing blacks found themselves increasingly limited to service positions such as waiters and cooks. Reflecting wider trends in American society at the turn of the century, the U.S. Navy gradually limited blacks to menial positions; in 1917 racial segregation was institutionalized in that branch

of the service, and further recruitment of blacks was discouraged.

Part of the reason for the failure to reform this practice lay in the decline in numbers of American seamen in oceangoing vessels, sinking from 135,000 in 1870 to 105,000 in 1900. At the same time, however, seamen in coastal waters made more money than those in foreign trades and those in steam vessels made relatively higher wages than those in sail.

Throughout the nineteenth century, women were increasingly found in the maritime industries. Captains' wives went to sea increasingly in this period, but, as one historian has explained, they were neither feminists nor the ideal women of the Victorian era, but rather women who were devoted to their husbands and had a highly developed sense of self. In the 1890s, the first women were licensed as steamboat pilots on the Mississippi. The U.S. Lighthouse Service also recognized women as lighthouse keepers in a

Ida Lewis,
Lighthouse Keeper
and Lifesaving Heroine

Ida Lewis (1842-1911) in her rescue boat, ca. 1900. (Courtesy Newport Historical Society)

Idawalley Zorada Lewis Wilson, better known as Miss Ida Lewis, was a lighthouse keeper who earned fame for her dramatic rescues. The daughter of the keeper of the lighthouse on Lime Rock, at the entrance to the inner harbor at Newport, Rhode Island, Ida Lewis was born in 1842. After her father suffered a paralytic stroke, Ida unofficially carried on her father's duties for many years.

She made her first rescue in about 1858, when she rowed four men to safety after their boat had capsized in Newport Harbor. In 1866 she rescued a number of individuals as well as one of financier August Belmont's prize sheep. In March 1869 she received national attention when she rescued two soldiers who were drowning after their sailboat capsized in a sudden gale. A newspaperman from the *New York Times* reported the incident, likening Ida Lewis to Grace Darling, the

famous British lighthouse-keeper's daughter from Longstone Light in the North Sea's Farne Islands, who in September 1838 had rescued the survivors of the wrecked *Forfarshire*. The report widely circulated in other papers across the United States, earning Lewis the soubriquet "the Grace Darling of America." In June 1869, the editor of *Harper's New Monthly Magazine* commented that she was "a girl in her twenty-eighth year, slender, blue-eyed, with light brown hair, frank and hearty and likely to be more famous next summer than any Newport belle." The editor went on to wonder whether it was "feminine for young women to row boats in storms," but concluded that no "donkey" would think it unfeminine in Ida Lewis to save men from drowning.

From this time on, she received national recognition. In 1869 alone, she estimated that nine thousand people visited Lime Rock Lighthouse, including such dignitaries as General William T. Sherman and Vice President Schuyler Colfax. Tourists continued to come in the years following. The people of Newport presented her with a new boat, the *Rescue,* while the coast artillery soldiers stationed at Fort Adams gave her a gold watch and chain. At the same time, she became prominent locally for her temperance work, saving "men from worse dangers than the waves."

Her rescue work continued when she saved three soldiers stranded on a reef in 1877. In 1879, the Lighthouse Service officially appointed Ida Lewis the keeper of the Lime Rock Light, seven years after her father's death and twenty years after she had first begun to perform her father's duties.

In 1881, after she rescued two soldiers who had fallen through the harbor ice as they were returning to Fort Adams, the Secretary of the Treasury awarded her the Gold Medal for Life-Saving, recognizing the most recent incident as well as the thirteen previous rescues she had performed. This medal was the highest of the two decorations that Congress had first authorized in 1874. Later, she received many other medals. In 1906, the year she made her last rescue, the Carnegie Hero Fund designated her a life beneficiary with a pension of $30 a month, and the American Cross of Honor Society awarded her its gold medal and the title, "Bravest Woman in America."

In 1892, Ida Lewis left her accustomed lighthouse duties to marry. But she found she was unhappy away from Lime Rock Light, and she left

her husband to return to carry on her duties. "The light is my child," she told a newspaper reporter, "and I know when it needs me, even if I sleep." After her death in 1911, Ida Lewis was buried in the Common Burying Ground on Newport's Farewell Street, where today passers-by can easily see the carved granite tombstone emblazoned with an anchor, crossed oars, and the epitaph: "The Grace Darling of America." The former Lime Rock Lighthouse now serves as the headquarters of the Ida Lewis Yacht Club.

few instances. Women were first allowed to serve in the U.S. Navy in 1908 with the establishment of the Navy Nurse Corps. The navy gave these women their first overseas assignments in 1910, with duty in the Philippines, Guam, Samoa, and Hawaii, and in 1913 the first Navy Nurses served at sea in the transport ships *Mayflower* and *Dolphin*.

Federal Maritime Improvements

As the federal government expanded and reorganized its agencies involved in maritime affairs, it also became involved in a number of government-sponsored activities that provided direct benefits to navigation. Important federal projects focused on improving the vast river transportation system that stretched from Pittsburgh to Montana and from St. Paul to New Orleans and created an important network that brought commodities to ports serving the coastal trade, to industries along the waterways, or for export in oceangoing ships.

Similar work, such as the early locks at Sault Ste. Marie on the Great Lakes, the Cape Cod Ship Canal, the Lake Washington Canal at Seattle, and the Houston Ship Channel were started by private commercial interests, but the government became involved as they became too difficult for local interests to maintain. The government had been involved with internal water transportation since 1820, when Congress authorized a survey to consider improvements on the Ohio and the Mississippi Rivers. This was consolidated further in the Rivers and Harbors Act of 1824, which gave the Army Corps of Engineers the responsibility for improvements at seaports and along inland waterways. By the post-Civil War period, substantial improvements had been made on the rivers that had already served to stimulate steamboat navigation. These efforts continued until competition from the railroads made them no longer viable.

Among the many projects the Army Corps of Engineers undertook was the enlargement of the Louisville and Portland Canal around the Falls of the Ohio River, beginning in 1874. This project eventually involved the construction of movable, wicket dams to maintain water levels in the

A twenty-three-foot fall in the St. Mary's River between Lake Superior and Lake Huron blocked the smooth flow of commerce between those lakes. After U.S. control of the south side of the river was confirmed by the Treaty of the Sault in 1820, efforts by individuals and the State of Michigan to build a navigation lock at Sault Ste. Marie resulted in the 350-foot State Lock, constructed between 1853 and 1855. By the 1870s this lock was too small for the bulk carriers that had begun carrying iron ore out of Lake Superior. With principal responsibility for constructing and maintaining internal waterways, the U.S. Army Corps of Engineers designed a new lock. Here, ca. 1880, Corps of Engineers personnel pose with a model of the original 1855 State Lock (left) and the new 515-foot Weitzel Lock (right), which opened in 1881. As Great Lakes bulk carriers continued to increase in size, the 800-foot Poe Lock replaced the State Lock in 1896, the 1,350-foot Davis and Sabin Locks were opened in 1914 and 1919, the 800-foot MacArthur Lock replaced the Weitzel Lock in 1943, and a new 1,200-foot Poe Lock was opened in 1968. (Courtesy Corps of Engineers' Canal Park Museum Collection, Superior, Wisconsin)

Ohio. The first of these was completed at Davis Island near Pittsburgh in 1885.

The needs of grain and timber shippers on the Upper Mississippi River drew attention to the region, and in 1867-77 the Corps of Engineers constructed the Des Moines Rapids Canal and maintained a navigable channel up to St. Paul. In 1875-79, James Eads, the steamboat builder

Another initiative was the idea for an inland waterway from Cape Cod to Florida that avoided many coastal hazards. One of its champions was the navy's leading educational reformer, Rear Admiral Stephen B. Luce. A strong advocate of federal aid for deepening and improving the Erie, Delaware and Raritan, and Chesapeake and Delaware Canals, Luce saw the inland waterways as important for logistical supply for the armed forces as well as for commercial trade.

As early as the 1680s, colonists had proposed eliminating the dangerous ocean passage around Cape Cod, Massachusetts, with a canal across the inner end of that sandy arm. A U.S. government survey plotted a route in 1825, and several private companies planned work in the 1870s and 1880s. Finally, in 1907 financier August Belmont established a syndicate to dig and operate the eight-mile canal, which opened for traffic on 29 July 1914. Its fifteen-foot depth restricted its use to smaller coastal, fishing, and recreational vessels, but a significant number of coal barges were towed through on the way to or from Boston or Portland. The U.S. government took over operation of the canal, 1918-20, and purchased it in 1928. In the 1930s, the Army Corps of Engineers widened and deepened the waterway just in time for an increase in traffic during World War II. Photo by William H. Zerbe, ca. 1916. (M.S.M. 64.551.6)

and moving force behind the first bridge across the Mississippi, succeeded with a privately financed engineering project to construct a channel through the Mississippi Delta bar, increasing the size of ships that could enter the port of New Orleans. In 1879, Congress established the Mississippi River Commission to oversee continuing river improvements and to regulate shipping. The Commission faced ongoing controversy over its policy of controlling the river and its frequent floods with higher and higher levees.

Maritime Science and Scientific Exploration

The rise of American maritime professionalism, bureaucracy, standardization, and regulation was, in many respects, the result of the impact of science and technology on American maritime activity. Maritime science brought the technological developments that called for maritime professionalism, and Americans played a direct role in furthering maritime science itself.

In the years before the Civil War, the armed services had dominated the federal government's activities in maritime science through exploration. After the war, they never fully resumed this role. Nevertheless, the U.S. Navy carried on many enterprises that had begun earlier, while new work reflected the general movement away from government sponsorship to initiatives in the private sector, demonstrating a merging of maritime affairs with wider national interests.

The Naval Observatory in Washington obtained the best astronomical telescope of its kind in 1873, and built a new building in northwest Washington in 1893. Gradually, however, the observatory turned from pioneering research to more routine activities, such as providing accurate time signals.

Unlike other countries, the United States continued to have two agencies that produced hydrographic charts. The Coast Survey published coastal charts, and the U.S. Navy's Hydrographic Office published ocean charts. In 1866, when the Hydrographic Office and the Naval Observatory were separated into two distinct agencies, the Hydrographic Office shifted from being a wide-ranging scientific enterprise, providing charts for little-known and poorly covered waters of the world, to being an office that simply prepared, published, and distributed charts, sailing directions, and nautical books related to and required in navigation, for the use of all vessels of the United States.

In 1872, the Hydrographic Office laid plans for a comprehensive survey of the Pacific, but without long-term funding this ambitious project was soon put aside. However, the navy did not give it up entirely. In 1874, The USS *Tuscarora*, commanded by Captain George Belknap, made soundings along a proposed telegraph line between the United States and Japan. In the process, Belknap experimented with new types of sounding machines and made an important contribution by recording surface and subsurface ocean temperatures. Belknap also discovered that, off Japan, the Pacific was far deeper than anyone imagined the ocean to be, finding no bottom in sounding to depths of 4,643 fathoms (more than five miles) of water.

In response to regional conflict over the impact of new fishing methods, the government entered the realm of fisheries science as well. Among the first to show serious interest was the assistant secretary of the Smithsonian and Director of the National Museum, Spencer Fullerton Baird. In the late 1860s, he was named by Congress to head a temporary commission to look into the fishery resources of the country, particularly responding to disputes between hook-and-line fishermen and net fisherman in Southern New England. Established by a joint resolution of Congress in 1871, the U.S. Fish Commission grew into an agency with its own budget. Establishing a laboratory at Woods Hole, Massachusetts, in 1885, it branched out from research issues to management of hatcheries and fish culture. In 1903 the independent commission became the Bureau of Fisheries in the Department of Commerce. Work such as Baird's was clearly related to larger trends in American life.

The interplay between pure and applied research appeared in other areas as well. In Wisconsin, Increase Lapham repeatedly attempted to interest the government in establishing a weather bureau that could provide storm warnings for the Great Lakes. Colonel Albert J. Meyer of the Army Signal Corps saw an opportunity in this, and in 1870 convinced Congress to permit military installations in states and territories across the country to make meteorological observations that could be used for weather forecasting and to provide storm warnings on the lakes and on the coasts. While the army's interest in this proposal was mainly to occupy its men with useful service when there was little military work to do, Congress saw humanitarian and economic value in the work, increasing its budget correspondingly. By 1881, when civilians joined the enterprise to do research in the newly forming branch of science called meteorology, tensions grew with the military. Finally, in 1890, Congress separated this activity from the army, creating a new agency under the Department of Agriculture, linking it to scientific work in the land-grant colleges and state agricultural offices.

The Coast Survey was close to completing its survey of the Atlantic and Pacific seaboards in the years after the Civil War. By 1867, the Coast Survey had begun a triangulation along the thirty-ninth parallel to establish a transcontinental arc that linked the survey systems on the Pacific and Atlantic coasts, as well as the land-survey work that the Geodetic Survey had undertaken across the West. In 1878, the two agencies of the Treasury Department were combined into one, with the name Coast and Geodetic Survey, to provide a complete and authoritative map for the entire country. In 1884, Congress established a joint commission to examine the organization of the Signal Service, Geological Survey, Coast and Geodetic Survey, and the U.S. Navy's Hydrographic Office. Although no organizational change resulted, this commission sparked a debate about the role of the government in this type of practical scientific activity. The failure to compartmentalize this complementary work that involved maritime and other sciences demonstrated the importance of science to each department of government and the various uses and interconnections involved. Historians of cartography have observed that the interdepartmental rivalry between the two chart-making agencies

E.W. Scripps,
Alexander Agassiz,
and the Maritime Sciences

The 234-foot iron-hulled auxiliary steamship Albatross *was launched at Wilmington, Delaware, in 1882. Built to the specifications of U.S. Commissioner of Fisheries Spencer F. Baird, the ship was equipped with a then-sophisticated seagoing laboratory and advanced equipment for collecting marine specimens, even at great depths. The* Albatross *was also the first U.S. government vessel lighted with electricity. The ship's first five years of service were spent in research efforts in support of the Atlantic fisheries. The* Albatross *was transferred to the Pacific in 1887, and Alexander Agassiz underwrote and conducted three scientific voyages aboard, beginning in 1891. The* Albatross *was decommissioned in 1921 after nearly forty years of voyaging in service to marine science. (19-N-Box 42, courtesy National Archives)*

The U.S. government was not alone in its contributions to the maritime sciences; much was accomplished through privately funded scientific research, such as that underwritten by newspaper magnate Edward Wyllis Scripps. In a half-century career, Scripps acquired control of more than thirty daily newspapers, acquiring a fortune in the process. In 1903, Scripps became interested in the University of California's program of field investigation on animal life in the Pacific. In 1891, William E. Ritter, who had just received his Harvard Ph.D., became head of the new Zoology Department at Berkeley. The following year he instituted the first in a series of field investigations into marine life on the California coast. Ten years later, these grew into more intensive investigations that required greater support from the university.

The 1901 season ended with a serious deficit, and Ritter began to seek additional funding to establish a permanent laboratory. At the same time, the U.S. government began developing the harbor at San Pedro, where Ritter had previously based his operations. Looking further to the south, he saw that San Diego provided a good location for collecting marine biological samples as well as good sources for funding such operations. Among the businessmen he encountered in 1903 was E.W. Scripps, who initially knew little about marine science but soon became the most enthusiastic advocate of Ritter's plans. In the autumn of 1903, Scripps and his half-sister, Ellen Browning Scripps, endowed the San Diego Marine Biological Association, and provided the Scripps yacht *Loma* for the association's scientific work. In 1912 the association became the Scripps Institution of Biological Research at La Jolla, and was renamed the Scripps Institution of Oceanography in 1925.

Another major figure in marine science, Alexander Agassiz, used his wealth to benefit marine science; he also cultivated his own considerable talents to make substantial marine scientific contributions. The son of Louis Agassiz, Professor of Natural History at Harvard, Alexander Agassiz was born in 1835 in Neuchâtel, Switzerland, where his father

had begun his professorial career. After spending his early years in Freiburg im Breisgau, young Agassiz joined his father in America in 1849, studied engineering and science at Harvard, and graduated in 1855. He devoted his early career to mining and became a stockholder and superintendent of the Calumet and Hecla copper mines in Michigan's upper peninsula from 1865 to 1869, acquiring a fortune from this investment of money and talent. Agassiz donated large sums to support the study of biology and took special interest in funding the Harvard Museum of Comparative Zoology, which housed his father's collections. In 1865, he and his step-mother, Elizabeth Cary Agassiz, published *Seaside Studies in Natural History,* and in 1871 he wrote *Marine Animals of Massachusetts Bay.* He spent part of each year at his private laboratory in his summer home, Castle Hill, at Newport, Rhode Island, as well as at Harvard and in Michigan.

After leaving his business career to become curator of the Museum of Comparative Zoology in 1874, he examined and classified the echinoderm collections made by HMS *Challenger* in her world-ranging oceanographic survey expedition of 1872-76. In 1877, Agassiz shifted his interest from zoological studies to deep-sea dredging for abyssal fauna. Using his experience in the mining industry, he began work at his own expense in the Gulf of Mexico, the Caribbean, and on the Atlantic coast of

the United States on three cruises during the years 1877-80 in the U.S. Coast Survey steamer *Blake.*

After leaving the curatorship at Harvard in 1885, he continued his scientific work to make a comparative study of marine fauna on both coasts of the Isthmus of Panama. For this purpose, in 1891 he was in charge of a dredging operation in the U.S. Fish Commission steamer *Albatross* on a cruise that explored deep-water areas from the west coast of Central America to the Galapagos Islands, the west coast of Mexico, and in the Gulf of California.

Completing this work, Agassiz shifted the focus of his scientific investigations to the formation of coral atolls. In 1893-94, he worked in the Bahamas and in Bermuda and moved on to examine the Great Barrier Reef in 1896, the Fiji Islands in 1897, the central Pacific islands in 1898-1900, and then moved into the Indian Ocean in 1900-02 to study the Maldives. At his death in 1910, he was recognized both as an industrial leader who supported American science and as a scientist in his own right.

probably was an impetus for innovation. By 1915, American-made charts had the reputation for being technically superior to European charts and were noted for their clarity and technical innovation.

Among the innovative ideas of the U.S. Navy's Hydrographic Office was a proposal by its chief cartographer in 1878 that a permanent international board serve as an intermediary between the various hydrographic offices in the world. Forty years later, these ideas led to the formation of the International Hydrographic Bureau in 1919-21. This international cooperation and communication had been needed for decades. As late as 1903, no fewer than eight different units of measurement were used on charts around the world, and there was a similar lack of uniformity in the representation of charted objects as well as in the format of sailing directions, light lists, and other information.

From 1866, the U.S. Navy's participation in world exploration took two separate directions. One aim was to locate the most appropriate route for an interoceanic canal in Central America, an international public work that would cut the maritime distance between the East and West Coasts by half and eliminate the stormy passage around Cape Horn. Between 1869 and 1871, army and navy expeditions surveyed several canal routes across Mexico, Honduras, Nicaragua, Panama, and Colombia. An inter-agency commission appointed by President Grant to examine the relative merits of each site decided in favor of the Nicaragua route, and others repeatedly supported this conclusion until 1902, even when the French-sponsored company of Ferdinand de Lesseps (builder of the Suez Canal) began to build a sea-level canal across Panama in 1880. When the holders of the assets to the bankrupt de Lesseps venture suddenly lowered their price for the holdings and franchises to the Panama route early in 1902, the U.S. abandoned its support for the Nicaragua plan and took over construction along the fifty-one-mile route that roughly paralleled the track of the American-financed Panama Railroad.

The other area of repeated naval exploration was the Arctic, where hopes for the discovery of a northwest passage over the top of North America still influenced theories about the untracked Arctic ice. Carried out with a combination of public and private funding, American Arctic exploration was also inspired by a search for Britain's Sir John Franklin, who had been lost in the ice with 129 men while seeking the northwest passage in 1847. In 1860-62, Captain Charles Franklin Hall made his first attempt to complete the work that Lieutenant Edward J. De Haven and Dr. Elisha Kent Kane of the U.S. Navy had begun with the first American attempts to rescue Sir John Franklin in 1850-51 and 1853-55. In 1864, Hall sailed from New London, Connecticut, with assistance from that port's experienced Arctic whalemen, on his second voyage in search of Franklin, a privately-funded attempt that lasted five years in the Arctic. After returning from this voyage, Hall called on President Grant, who so enthusiastically supported Hall's work that Congress voted $50,000 for a third expedition. Under written orders from Grant in 1871, the navy and the National Academy of Sciences ordered Hall to take command of the USS *Polaris* in order to examine Arctic geography and to reach the geographical North Pole. In August 1871, *Polaris* reached a pack-ice barrier in latitude 82° north, then the most northerly point ever reached by a vessel. Before he could make a sledge journey toward the pole the following spring, Hall died and the expedition degenerated. The *Polaris* was lost in the ice, and the survivors were rescued from boats and ice floes in the summer of 1873.

In 1879, Congress authorized sending naval officers on an Arctic voyage in the *Jeannette*, a ship purchased by James Gordon Bennett, an Arctic enthusiast and owner of the *New York Herald*. She sailed from San Francisco in a new quest for the North Pole via Alaskan waters and the Bering Sea, acquiring useful meteorological and geographical information on those coasts as she moved north. On the night of 12 June 1881, ice crushed the *Jeannette*, and the survivors dragged their three boats and equipment over the pack ice and eventually reached the Siberian coast, but became separated. In the bitter Arctic cold, only engineer George W. Melville and his boat crew survived.

In the United States, a civil engineer in the U.S. Navy, Robert E. Peary, continued the symbolic quest for the North Pole with a combination of public and private support. On his first expedi-

After the Civil War, naval exploration increasingly focused on the Arctic, either to find evidence of the lost British expedition led by Sir John Franklin or to reach the North Pole. Several of these expeditions relied on American whalemen with Arctic whaling experience and on Inuits or Eskimos to survive in that hostile climate. By far the most active Inuits in assisting U.S. northern expeditions were Ebierbing, called Joe, and his wife Tookoolito, called Hannah. After assisting New London, Connecticut, whalemen in Davis Strait in the 1850s and traveling with British whalers to England, where they met Queen Victoria, Joe and Hannah became the guides and friends of Charles F. Hall for his Arctic expeditions. In 1871 they accompanied Hall on the government-sponsored Polaris Expedition toward the North Pole, during which Hall died in northern Greenland and the Polaris was lost in the ice. Joe and Hannah helped part of the crew survive as they drifted south on an ice floe. After residing in Connecticut for several years, Joe returned to the Arctic after Hannah's death, again participating in Arctic expeditions. These wax figures of Joe and Hannah in native dress, with fishing implements in hand, were created for the 1876 Centennial Exposition in Philadelphia, the first of a number of international expositions at which U.S. government-sponsored advances in science and technology received public exposure. Stereograph by Wilson. (M.S.M. 95.76)

tion in 1891-92, he explored the Greenland Ice Cap and on his second and third expeditions in 1893-95 and 1898-1900, Peary crossed the Greenland Ice Cap and explored the northeast coast of Greenland. Moving further and further north on subsequent expeditions, on 6 April 1909 Peary became the first man acknowledged to reach the North Pole (although his claim was disputed by Frederick Cook, who announced that he had reached the Pole a year earlier).

While Peary drew public attention to the North Pole, the Norwegian Roald Amundsen was attempting to realize the four-hundred-year-old dream of finding the northwest passage. Sailing from Baffin Bay in 1903 to reach the Bering Sea over four seasons in his seventy-foot fishing boat *Gjöa,* Amundsen reached San Francisco on 19 October 1906, closing an era in maritime exploration that had begun with the voyages of Cartier, Frobisher, and Drake.

While the public perception of these voyages concentrated on the epic adventures of daring seamen seeking such symbolic goals as the North Pole, their real importance consisted in substantive and technical advances to scientific knowledge of the North American Arctic region. This expansion of scientific knowledge was part of the much wider expansion of knowledge, higher education, and concrete technological and industrial results that accompanied the participation of public and private enterprise in maritime professionalization. This scientific progress was accompanied by the attempts to improve government administration in America that touched the full range of the country's maritime activities. The dramatic growth in the maritime interconnections between government regulation, bureaucratic growth, and professionalization were responses to the central changes in science, technology, industry, and economic affairs that were clearly seen in America during the years following the Civil War.

CHAPTER 12

Expansion and Transformation of Maritime America

ROM THE LATE 1890s onwards, one could clearly recognize the transformation in America's relationship with the sea. The frontier had disappeared as the nation expanded across the continent, linking all coasts with commercial ties. As a result of its increasing emphasis on foreign relations, the United States, like other nations around the world, gained political colonies overseas. Despite the international rivalries of the time, new forms of international cooperation and innovative, practical applications in international law came to fruition. As technological changes were introduced in ships of all kinds, the nature of warfare at sea also changed, linking broad aspects of naval and merchant affairs more closely together, yet creating even greater differences between warships and merchant ships. Meanwhile, upheavals in distant nations added to the stream of immigrants who came by sea and added new layers of culture and character to the nation. And, while the serious matters of science and technology, war and commerce,

remained the central issues in American maritime affairs, Americans increasingly turned to the sea for leisure and recreation.

Seaside Recreation

As American cities grew larger and became increasingly dominated by industry, the lives of urban residents became more predictable, with both time and disposable income to expend for leisure. To avoid the heat, crowding, and diseases of summer, increasing numbers sought to escape, even for a day, to the fresh air and seemingly healthful surroundings of lake, river, and sea coast. Steamboats had provided access for decades, but after the Civil War expanding rail

Detail from The Yacht Namouna, *by Julius Stewart. (Courtesy Wadsworth Atheneum, Hartford, Connecticut. The Ella Gallup Sumner and Mary Catlin Sumner Collection Fund)*

With increased leisure time in rapidly industrializing urban America, and increased emphasis on the healthful attributes of outdoor activity, the shore became a focus for recreation after the Civil War. From Maine to the Pacific Northwest, ocean- and lakefront hotels, amusement parks, excursion boats, yacht clubs, and private homes and camps brought more Americans than ever into contact with the sea. Here, as the Atlantic surf thunders in, a well-dressed group enjoys the fresh salt air, while nearby Watch Hill Light warns coastal shipping away from this hazardous point on the route between New York and Boston. Photo by Edward H. Newbury, ca. 1900. (M.S.M. 80.41.416)

lines and, by the 1880s, electric trolley lines, provided economical mobility to ordinary citizens. For example, the Atlantic Railroad had reached the coast of New Jersey in 1853, and a resort called Atlantic City grew up around its terminus, bringing with it the tawdry and the fair. In 1871, the first oceanside boardwalk was constructed there so that visitors could enjoy the cool sea breezes. On the boardwalk, concession stands for saltwater taffy first appeared in 1883, and some of the earliest picture postcard views in America were introduced in 1893. As early as 1820 city people began to seek leisure on the ocean barrier beach at Coney Island near New York City, and a pavilion and bathhouse had been added in 1844. With increasing demand for exotic amusements at the beach, developers began to bring amusement parks to the seaside, building Steeplechase Park, Luna Park, and Dreamland Park at Coney Island between 1897 and 1905.

In other areas, steamboats took day-trippers to a variety of attractions and seaside places. Along the eastern shore of Lake Michigan, for example, at the turn of the century the North Michigan Transportation Company purchased large tracts of undeveloped and unproductive waterfront sand dunes, some of them burnt over or ravaged by logging operations. The company subdivided the tracts with lots for summer homes, laid out roads, and built courses for the newly popular sport of golf. Sending steamships from Chicago on regular runs to stop at many of the western Michigan harbors from Muskegon to Mackinac Island, the Northern Michigan Transportation Company provided resort hotels and sold inexpensive lots for summer homes to Chicago-area schoolteachers and middle-class suburbanites at places like Manistee, Onekama on Portage Lake, Frankfort near Crystal Lake, Traverse City, Glen Arbor

*Commodore Cornelius Vanderbilt had commissioned the first American steam yacht—the 270-foot North
Star—launched in 1853. By 1880, New York Yacht Club members owned twenty sizable steam yachts, and
other prosperous ports harbored these expensive vessels as well. Built in 1882, the 247-foot iron-hulled
steam yacht* Namouna *was among the grandest of the day. Owned by James Gordon Bennett, Jr., the
ostentatious editor of the* New York Herald, *the vessel carried a crew of fifty who made numerous transatlantic passages at the whim of the owner. Bennett had been a hard-sailing yachtsman since the 1850s, had
served in the Civil War aboard his own yacht, and participated in the first transatlantic yacht race in 1866.
Aboard* Namouna, *his first steam yacht, Bennett carried his guests and associates between his homes in the
U.S. and France and on tour throughout the Mediterranean. In 1890 Julius Stewart painted this view of the
yacht underway off Venice, Italy, with owner James Gordon Bennett, Jr., at left, talking to one of the many
women he entertained on board during his eighteen years of ownership. (Courtesy Wadsworth Atheneum,
Hartford, Connecticut. The Ella Gallup Sumner and Mary Catlin Sumner Collection Fund)*

near Glen Lake, and Charlevoix, where summer
colonies sprang up. On the East Coast, the richest of the New York rich went to the "Queen of
Resorts," Newport, Rhode Island, for their
seaside pleasures. There, prominent business
leaders and socialites like Mrs. Astor, Isaac
Bell, August Belmont, Edward Berwind, and
Cornelius Vanderbilt II and his brothers, all
employed some of the greatest American architects of the day—Richard Morris Hunt, Horace
Trumbauer, Charles McKim, and Stanford
White—to build "summer cottages" modeled on
such treasures as the Trianons of Versailles,
English country homes, Mansard's French
chateaux, and Italian villas. Traveling from
New York by overnight steamboat on the Fall

River Line, they lavishly entertained visiting
royalty and each other at their seaside cottages,
sailed in their opulent yachts with professional
crews, and conducted business that shaped
American industrial and financial directions.

American interest in gadgets and speed
was also evident in waterborne recreation. As early as the Civil War,
Philadelphia mechanics were racing fast, unstable sailboats on the Delaware River, while in
New York the shallow-draft sandbagger, with
its movable ballast and large sail area, was an
equally popular racing machine for working
watermen and for amateur yachtsmen. American
yacht clubs, which were established around the

In his 1874 painting, Sailboats Racing on the Delaware, *Thomas Eakins captured the popularity of sailboat racing among laborers, watermen, and the middle class in shoreside communities after the Civil War. The boat types varied from place to place: single-sail, shallow-draft catboats in Massachusetts; shallow-draft "sandbaggers," with movable sandbag ballast to counterbalance large sails, around New York, New Orleans, and West Coast ports; log canoes in Chesapeake Bay; and boats like these fifteen-foot tuckups around Philadelphia. Despite their local differences, most of the racing boats of this period were derived from working watercraft designed for fishing, oystering, or gunning, modified with extremely large sails that made for fast, exciting, unpredictable action. Through the 1870s and 1880s, tuckup racing was particularly popular on the Delaware River. On a summer Sunday or Monday, as many as sixty tuckups might race over a thirty-mile course, attracting crowds of spectators and gamblers. But by the early twentieth century, as urban waterfronts became less accessible, and as yacht-racing rules were adopted to equalize performance, much of this spirited, undisciplined competition vanished. Thereafter, sailboat racing was largely the province of yacht clubs, which sponsored formal races for clearly defined classes of boats. (Courtesy Philadelphia Museum of Art: Given by Mrs. Thomas Eakins and Miss Mary Adeline Williams)*

country after the 1870s, sponsored racing in many types of boats, some of them designed to club specifications. The America's Cup became the premier international sailing trophy after a British yacht crossed the Atlantic in 1870 to attempt to recapture the "hundred guinea cup" won in England by the yacht *America* in 1851. As a test of international yachting prowess, sailed in increasingly large and technically advanced boats with large professional crews, the America's Cup attracted wide press attention

every few years when another British or Canadian yachtsman issued a challenge. American yachtsmen successfully defended the cup twelve times between 1870 and 1903. The 1903 defender *Resolute*, designed by Nathanael Herreshoff at 143 feet in length and carrying more than one-third of an acre of sail, was the largest single-masted vessel ever built.

The 1870s had witnessed the beginning of a long-term canoe "craze." The New York Canoe

Club and the American Canoe Association provided organized structures for international competition in sail and paddle canoes. Many Americans used canoes for leisurely interludes on quiet lakes, or to "rough it" on camping trips. Other localized recreational boat types for hunting, fishing, or racing developed across the country during the last quarter of the nineteenth century.

The latest power technology also appeared in recreational craft. Large steam yachts and small steam launches both made use of the principal motive force of the nineteenth century, though a licensed engineer was required to operate these engines, no matter how small. In 1883 Frank Ofeldt invented an engine for small boats that ran on volatile naphtha, a derivative of petroleum. While the designer had made them so anyone could run the engine without a license, not everyone could afford naphtha power. A typical twenty-one-foot launch cost $750, or one and one-half times the annual wage of the workmen who built the boats. Yet, between 1885 and 1904 wealthy patrons bought some two thousand naphtha launches.

By the 1890s, the first practical gasoline-powered internal combustion engines had been developed for marine uses. Perfected as the single-cylinder "one-lunger" by 1900, and refined in powerful, multicylinder forms as the automobile industry developed through the ensuing decade, the gasoline engine offered increasing access to the water for recreational users. While one group perfected speedboats, with high-power engines and sophisticated hull designs, others developed the small outboard motor, which by 1910 offered the ultimate in convenient boating. Constantly changing and expanding technology became the norm in all areas of the maritime world, not only in yachts, but also in waterfront industries, in fishing vessels, in blue-water merchantmen, as well as in the navy.

The Expansion of the U.S. Navy, 1885-1915

During these years, a number of forces came together in American politics, economics, and

The internal combustion engine, developed in Europe and the U.S. by the 1880s, became the most influential force in the expansion of recreational boating at the end of the nineteenth century. From the 1890s through the 1910s, hundreds of small engine manufacturers met local demands for power in recreational watercraft and small fishing vessels. These boating enthusiasts demonstrate the appeal of early one-cylinder, two-cycle engines: in their simplicity they could be maintained and tinkered with by the boat owner. (Negative 3441F, © Rosenfeld Collection, Mystic Seaport Museum, Inc.)

society that remade the U.S. Navy. For a century, Congress had debated the proper role and function of the navy, and the likely security threats to the nation. Traditionally, the issue turned on arguments whether or not the U.S. Navy should go beyond protecting trade, patrolling the coasts, and controlling piracy to become something much more: a symbol of national power, providing muscle behind diplomacy and operating within the context of global politics. In the years immediately following the Civil War, the general sentiment in the country had favored a restricted role for the navy. For a number of years, even the great powers had been generally apathetic about their relative naval strength. This changed in the mid-1880s for a combination of reasons.

By 1884, the leading naval power, Britain, began to feel threatened by Russia's policy in Central Asia. Tension was growing between France and Britain over Egypt, while friction was beginning

Benjamin F. Tracy (1830-1915) served as secretary of the navy in the administration of President Benjamin Harrison, 1889-93. Born in New York State and trained as a lawyer, Tracy was serving as a district attorney when the Civil War began. He served as an officer in the Union Army and was awarded a Congressional Medal of Honor for bravery in battle. After the war he returned to his law practice and was active in New York Republican politics for many years before being named secretary of the navy, despite his lack of naval experience. With no preconceptions about the navy, Tracy read Alfred Thayer Mahan's theories on the essential role of sea power and made them the basis for his policies. "We must have armored battleships," Tracy told the president, and he requested appropriations for both Atlantic and Pacific fleets. With efficient organization and a clear purpose, Tracy pushed forward the construction of a modern, well-rounded fleet, and made important improvements in naval construction and supply facilities. (Courtesy Library of Congress)

to develop between Britain and Germany at the same time that Franco-German relations remained cordial. From this point onward, the major powers began to expand naval construction. In Britain, for example, politicians and the press noted some of this activity, along with the improved technology and naval capabilities it brought. The attention this attracted from the press created "naval scares" in 1884 and in 1888, resulting in public demand for even larger and more powerful warships. This, in turn, had a similar effect in other countries, and the naval shipbuilding rivalry spiraled on with increasing momentum.

While the United States was initially uninvolved in this rivalry, it nevertheless had an effect on American perceptions. In practical terms, the rapid changes taking place in the major navies created a technological imperative that required smaller navies to make some pretense of keeping up if they wished to retain military credibility. Even the most restrictive role for a navy required technological improvements and, with them, new designs, more money, and new ways to manage the new developments in technology. In the United States this change occurred in the midst of rapid industrial expansion and growing public support for the nation to play a larger role in international politics. The rise in sentiment for a stronger navy was also tangentially linked to other contemporary issues, including cultural movements such as Social Darwinism, militant Christianity, and the social dislocation connected with industrialization. In such a political, social, and economic environment, attempts to update the navy's equipment were subtly translated into a fundamental change in naval policy.

Thirty new vessels were added to the fleet in the mid-1880s, and in December 1889 the new secretary of the navy, Benjamin F. Tracy, called for construction of twenty armored battleships—twelve in the Atlantic and eight in the Pacific—that would be combat-ready, even in peacetime. "A war, though defensive in principle," Tracy declared, "may be conducted most effectively by being offensive in its operations." The Naval Appropriation Act, passed on 30 June 1890, provided the United States with her first modern battleships. Tracy's views reflected some of the ideas promoted by Rear Admiral

Confident that the nation's steel industry could at last support construction of large armored warships, the U.S. Navy asked Congress to appropriate funds for the first two American battleships, Texas and Maine, in 1886. Battleship number two, the USS Maine, was originally planned as an armored cruiser, but reclassified as a second-class battleship before her commissioning in 1895. The 318-foot Maine mounted her four ten-inch guns in two turrets, the forward turret offset to starboard and the after one offset to port to allow all guns to fire both fore and aft. The Maine participated in routine exercises along the Atlantic coast until January 1898, when she was ordered to Havana to protect American citizens during revolutionary rioting there. Three weeks after her arrival, on the evening of 15 February, the Maine was suddenly blasted by an explosion that killed 251 of her crew and left the ship a twisted wreck on the bottom of Havana Harbor. The U.S. blamed Spain for sinking the Maine, and Congress used the incident to militate for Cuban independence. When Spain severed relations, the U.S. imposed a naval blockade on Cuba and declared war on Spain on 25 April 1898. "Remember the Maine" was the watchword of this fifteen-week, two-ocean war. Official investigation in 1898 and 1911 concluded that the ship was sunk by a mine, but new research in 1976 showed that the explosion was probably caused by spontaneous combustion in a coal bunker. (M.S.M. 97.86.24)

Stephen B. Luce and Captain Alfred Thayer Mahan in their writings from the Naval War College concerning the critical importance of a battle fleet. Tracy was also responsible for rescuing the Naval War College from those who demanded exclusive technological training for officers at the expense of investing in broad, political-military education for senior naval officers. Through Tracy's patronage, Mahan's writings became an important voice of innovative naval thought, promoting the construction of an isthmian canal, explaining the importance of the Caribbean to the United States, forming a naval staff, and building a fleet of capital ships.

While these ideas were important, they reflected rather than created change in American naval policy. More significant were developments in the American steel industry that made possible the construction of advanced types of warships. Another factor was the reformation of the navy's shipyards and shore establishments from bastions of political patronage to merit-based employment practices.

Deep in the hold of the battleship Massachusetts, *a member of the "black gang" feeds the boilers in one of the ship's eight fire rooms. Even with a pair of efficient triple-expansion engines to turn the ship's twin screws, the coal passers had to shovel as much as twelve tons of coal per hour to produce enough steam to drive the ship at a full fifteen knots. Once the navy abandoned sail power after constructing the transitional steel "ABCD" ships, the black gang of the engine room replaced the able-bodied seamen, skilled in handling sails, as the essential driving force in naval vessels. Largely unseen—and unappreciated for the soot they produced and the labor of loading coal that they imposed on the entire crew—the engineers, firemen, electricians, machinists, wipers, trimmers, and coal passers remained in constant attendance to the ship's power plant. As foreign as these duties were in the traditional navy, their existence in the new steel navy moved the service closer to industrial labor ashore and attracted a new generation of young men who entered the navy to learn a trade. For the navy as a whole, coal became a strategic commodity and, as naval squadrons were sent to operate in distant waters, coaling stations became essential naval installations. Fleet colliers—coal delivery ships—were also introduced to refuel warships at sea. Detroit Publishing Company photo, ca. 1899. (Courtesy Library of Congress)*

At the same time, President Benjamin Harrison worked with Tracy to plan expansion of American naval bases to distant places such as Samoa, Hawaii, Haiti, and Santo Domingo. Tracy's period as Secretary (1889-1893) was a turning point for the U.S. Navy and the new directions included the creation of an American naval battle fleet designed to carry heavy guns and capable of operating offensively in distant seas, accompanied by strategic ideas and tactical doctrine to perpetuate its new role, and supported by domestic industry.

The Spanish-American War

The Spanish-American War represented a change in the general direction of American history as well as in American naval and diplomatic traditions. The United States went to war in 1898 in direct violation of the Monroe Doctrine which had declared that the United States would not interfere with existing colonies. Yet the nation intervened militarily in Spanish affairs for an unprecedented reason: the humanitarian relief of Cuba and the Philippines from what it considered Spanish brutality.

For the first time, the United States went to war for an abstract concept of morality. Through it, the United States justified its overseas expansion and its acquisition of new territory in the Caribbean and in the Pacific. America's declaration of war was sparked by the mysterious sinking of the USS *Maine* in Havana harbor on 15 February 1898, killing 253 of her 358 officers and men. For many Americans, the dramatic American naval victories that followed—at Manila Bay on 1 May 1898, and off Santiago, Cuba, on 3 July 1898—justified the modernization and expansion of the navy that had been underway for a decade and a half. Less dramatic, but equally significant, was the ability of the United States to move troops and supplies in support of these operations. The Spanish-American War transformed world opinion. Before the war, few if any countries viewed the United States as anything more than a minor regional power. American naval actions in 1898 demonstrated both the capacity and the desire to be an actor on the world stage.

Appropriated in 1888, the 340-foot protected cruiser Olympia was built at the Union Iron Works in San Francisco and commissioned in 1895. With a crew of thirty-three officers and 395 enlisted men, the USS Olympia was a modern warship, armed with eight-inch guns, rapid-fire guns, and torpedo tubes. Yet, as this photograph by Frances Benjamin Johnston shows, the crew was still organized into traditional navy messes of approximately twenty-four men, who ate on the berth deck where their hammocks were later slung. These members of the port watch (identified by the trim on the left shoulder) eat at a portable hanging table, which will be returned to its overhead position after the meal. The ship supplied each mess with basic rations of meat, hardtack, beans, potatoes, and coffee, which were supplemented by produce and condiments purchased with a mess fund comprised of a portion of each man's daily food allowance. The cook for each mess used these funds to purchase additional food in port, and both the preferences of each mess and the specialties of each mess cook were represented in the food served. But after a general mess system was instituted in the navy in 1902, the ships' cooks began to produce identical fare for the entire crew. Some of these men may have been on board the Olympia when she served as Commodore George Dewey's flagship at the Battle of Manila Bay on 1 May 1898, when the U.S. squadron destroyed the seven defending Spanish warships without suffering a single death. For this heroic action, the Olympia is maintained as a naval museum in Philadelphia. (Courtesy Library of Congress)

Postwar Naval Developments

The unwarranted expectation that future wars would be, like the war between the United States and Spain, of short duration and with low casualty rates, influenced postwar diplomacy among the world's maritime powers. With the exception of the country's maritime policy during the Civil War, when it had copied traditional British practice, the United States had traditionally opposed the right of belligerent powers to close the seas to its enemies through blockade and seizure of merchant shipping. During the Spanish-American War, the United States Navy had been extremely careful in its wartime dealings with merchant shipping in the war areas. It had limited capture to Spanish ships that were blockade-runners or ships carrying contraband directly to the enemy. Even though U.S. naval vessels captured ten British merchantmen on these grounds during the war, there was no international protest arising from it.

The USS Oregon was one of the three Indiana-class "coast" battleships authorized by Congress in 1890. In accordance with Secretary of the Navy Tracy's request for separate battle fleets on the Atlantic and the Pacific, the 348-foot Oregon was built at the Union Iron Works in San Francisco. At the time of her commissioning in 1896, the Oregon and her sisters Indiana and Massachusetts were the most heavily armed battleships in the world. The Oregon was best known for her sixty-six-day, 14,000-mile run around Cape Horn in 1898 to join the Atlantic Fleet off Cuba during the Spanish-American War. In this stern view, taken by J.S. Johnston in 1898, visitors inspect the ship's battery of six-, eight-, and thirteen-inch guns, which bombarded shore installations and Spanish cruisers during the Battle of Santiago on 3 July 1898. (M.S.M. 58.1175)

U.S. Navy's plans to develop a humanitarian Code of Naval Warfare. President McKinley declared this code a part of American law in 1900, and it remained in force until 1904, when it was withdrawn by those who feared it would restrict the United States too much in negotiations at the forthcoming Hague Peace Conference of 1907. The recent experience of the Boer War in 1899-1902 and the Russo-Japanese War in 1904-05 gave additional urgency to the issues at hand. In the end, the conference failed to establish a comprehensive and internationally agreed upon maritime code. Nevertheless, it represented groundwork for future consideration of these issues.

A decade later, in the Declaration of London (1909), the leading maritime powers agreed to a basic code that provided for an international prize court to deal with maritime disputes through judicial means. Although the United States ratified the declaration's basic provisions, a small but influential group of American admirals, including Alfred Mahan, George Dewey, and the American delegate to the conference, Charles Stockton, argued in vain that an attack from a determined enemy at sea required legal support for the exercise of stronger, not weaker, belligerent rights. Nevertheless, prevailing opinion in both Britain and America prevented either nation from following this more warlike course in their diplomatic negotiations on international law.

Although the world's largest naval power, Britain, never ratified the agreements, the United States Senate did ratify both the agreement for an international prize court and the code outlined in the Declaration of London. Such international conferences were very slowly creating the basis for restraints on naval warfare through international law and legal process. Yet, these agreements to limit naval attack on shipping had an inherent weakness. They were based on several assumptions that would not be borne out in the future: that large naval and maritime powers would be either neutral in

Sensing a trend toward greater freedom for wartime commerce, President William McKinley proposed in his Annual Message to Congress in December 1898 an international humanitarian agreement that would prevent a belligerent from capturing any private property at sea, whoever the owners. The British prime minister, Lord Salisbury, opposed the idea, and the Hague Conference of 1899 tabled the issue, but the establishment of the Permanent Court of International Arbitration did provide a means for peaceful settlement of disputes between nations.

In the meantime, Captain Charles Stockton at the Naval War College moved ahead with the

war or fight only limited wars for limited objectives, that close blockade of an enemy would remain a feasible choice in the conditions of future warfare, and that major neutral powers would aggressively defend their neutral rights in wartime.

In the years before 1914, the United States Navy continued to develop its strength and capabilities. The most dramatic demonstration of its capacity in the years between 1899 and 1917 was the round-the-world cruise of the Great White Fleet, from December 1907 to February 1909. Behind it lay President Theodore Roosevelt's devotion to expanding the navy. During his two terms of office from 1901 to 1909, Roosevelt overshadowed the six successive men that served in his cabinet as secretary of the navy, dominating the formulation of naval policy. During his first term, Roosevelt raised naval appropriations from $85 million to $118 million and procured authorization for ten first-class battleships, four armored cruisers, and seventeen other vessels. Despite rising Congressional opposition, Roosevelt was able to obtain four more battleships, but was unsuccessful in achieving his full naval construction plan. Toward the end of his term, Roosevelt reversed his views and publicly called for a halt to naval expansion, in order to avert a naval arms race after the Royal Navy launched HMS *Dreadnought* in 1906, its first all-big-gun battleship, and by far the most powerful, most heavily armored warship of the day.

As the navy was growing, it was fundamentally changing its outward appearance. Steam and steel completely replaced sailing warships. At the same time, ships developed new roles and special characteristics that reflected the new fabric of the navy. While battleships and cruisers dominated broad naval calculations, other types were not ignored. Following the lead of European navies, the U.S. Navy launched its first experimental torpedo boat in 1886. Built by the master of yacht design and maritime technology, Nathanael Herreshoff, in Bristol, Rhode Island, the ninety-four-foot *Stiletto* heralded a new class of fast and highly maneuverable ships designed to carry the recently developed self-propelled torpedo. The small torpedo-destroyer boat evolved into the U.S. Navy's larger and more seaworthy destroyer-type vessel with the USS *Bainbridge* in 1898.

Undersea warfare had been a naval dream for centuries, and American designers, beginning with David Bushnell during the American Revolution, were in the forefront of naval submarine development. Congress first authorized construction of a naval submarine in 1893. That vessel, the *Plunger*, was never completed and the navy did not obtain a successful submarine until 1900, when it purchased a boat built by John Holland at the Crescent Shipyard in Elizabeth, New Jersey, which entered service as the USS *Holland*. Holland's design used diving planes for maneuvering, and had the newly developed gasoline engine for surface power and an electric motor run off storage batteries for undersea power. It was the first truly effective naval submarine and launched the U.S. Navy's submarine service. Soon, however, Germany would surpass the U.S. in the development of submarine warfare.

The potential for naval air service was first demonstrated in 1910 (seven years after the Wright brothers introduced powered flight) when civilian pilot Eugene Ely made the first successful takeoff of an airplane from shipboard on the cruiser *Birmingham*. Two months later, in January 1911, Ely made the first aircraft landing on shipboard, engaging a rudimentary arresting system as he touched down on a temporary deck built above the stern of the armored cruiser *Pennsylvania*. Naval aviation was first expected to perform scouting and observation for conventional naval vessels, but, as with undersea warfare, the new technology would greatly alter naval strategy.

The fleet was changing in other ways as well. In 1911, the navy refitted the old protected cruiser *San Francisco* as its first vessel for the specialized work of mine warfare. A year later, Rear Admiral Bradley A. Fiske was the first to patent a means to launch a torpedo attack from an aircraft. The navy launched the tanker *Maumee* in 1915. Built to carry bunker fuel oil instead of coal for the fleet, she was the U.S. Navy's first surface ship powered by a diesel engine. In 1917, the *Maumee* pioneered underway refueling operations that heralded mobile support for the fleet, allowing the navy to begin to free itself from coaling stations, a major constraint that accompanied steam power.

The scope of innovation in maritime technology ranged from more mundane, but equally impor-

The Voyage of the Great White Fleet, 1907-1909

On 16 December 1907, President Theodore Roosevelt reviewed sixteen battleships of the U.S. Navy as they sailed from Hampton Roads, Virginia, on a round-the-world cruise. It was unprecedented for so large a number of steam-powered, steel warships to undertake so long a voyage. Despite the technical challenges, particularly the problem of providing fuel for so many ships for so long a period, President Roosevelt justified the cruise on several grounds: as a means to exercise the fleet for wartime conditions, as a way to impress the American people and stimulate popular interest in the Navy, and as a demonstration of American naval capability overseas. In particular, Roosevelt was concerned about the possibility of war with Japan following the recent racial tensions that occurred with immigrants in California. At the same time, the voyage would be a secret test of the U.S. Navy's plans to reinforce the Philippines with the fleet in the event of an attack.

Under the command of Rear Admiral Robley D. "Fighting Bob" Evans, the crisply painted white battleships *Connecticut, Georgia, Illinois, Kansas, Kearsarge, Kentucky, Louisiana, Minnesota, Missouri, Nebraska, New Jersey, Ohio, Rhode Island, Vermont, Virginia,* and *Wisconsin*—along with

smaller vessels and colliers—sailed south around Cape Horn to the West Coast of the United States. Enroute, the fleet spent Christmas at Port of Spain on Trinidad, and called at Rio de Janeiro in Brazil, Punta Arenas in Chile, Callao in Peru, and Magdalena Bay in Mexico before reaching San Francisco in May 1908.

The U.S. fleet was the largest single naval contingent to enter the Pacific Ocean up to that time, exceeding in size Admiral Rozhdestvenski's Russian Baltic Fleet that had participated in the Russo-Japanese War in 1904-05.

Admiral Evans, the navy's most senior officer and the last

naval officer on active duty to have served in the Civil War, had not been well at the outset of the cruise. As the fleet made its way around South America, he became increasingly ill. At San Francisco, Rear Admiral Charles S. Sperry succeeded him as commander in chief of the fleet and remained in charge for the rest of its voyage around the world.

The fleet remained in San Francisco until 7 July 1908, when it got underway to cross the Pacific. Among the junior officers on board were young men who, thirty-five years later, would become the most famous American admirals of the Second World War: Ensigns William F. Halsey, Raymond Spruance, and F. Kent Hewitt. The fleet sailed first to Honolulu, then headed south to New Zealand, a passage of 3,850 miles and the longest uninterrupted leg of the world cruise. Enroute, the fleet passed within sight of Tutuila in American Samoa, but, remarkably, the battleships did not refuel. Carefully conserving their coal, they all completed the passage.

At Auckland in August, New Zealanders greeted the U.S. Navy warmly during a six-day visit. Then, crossing the Tasman Sea in a winter storm, the fleet spent a month in Australian waters, calling at

---

Led by the USS Connecticut, *and maintaining 400-yard intervals as they pass in review before President Theodore Roosevelt, the sixteen battleships of the Great White Fleet steam out of Hampton Roads, Virginia, on 16 December 1907. Photo by C. E. Waterman. (M.S.M. 97.127.2)*

EXPANSION AND TRANSFORMATION OF MARITIME AMERICA

Sydney and Melbourne, and then along the southern coast to Albany. Australians welcomed the American fleet so warmly that the press reported that the British Government was uneasy about it.

From Albany, the fleet headed north, passing through the Lombok Strait, at the eastern tip of Java, then steaming across the Java Sea, through the Macassar Strait between Borneo and Sulawesi, passing within sight of Zamboanga on Mindanao, to Manila, where the fleet anchored on 2 October 1908. With a cholera epidemic spreading through the Philippines, the fleet stayed only to coal in the oppressive heat. Their work, disrupted by a typhoon, lasted eight days. Heading north for Japan, the fleet met a second typhoon, sweeping three men overboard (two of whom were rescued), causing considerable damage to the ships, and delaying the fleet's arrival at Yokohama. The Japanese greeted the Americans sailors with great courtesy that coincided with a resolution of the tensions over Japanese immigration to America and the conclusion of the Root-Takahira Agreement that solidified bilateral relations. While the visit of American sailors complemented other and separate forces that were at work and helped to warm the open relations between the two countries, military and naval leaders on both sides continued to consider each other potential threats.

Leaving Japan just as the Japanese Navy was preparing for its autumn fleet exercise against a potential naval attack from the Philippines, seven battleships of the American Fleet's Second Division called at Amoy off the Chinese coast. The Chinese welcomed the fleet with a specially built entertainment center.

The two squadrons soon reunited in Manila Bay, where the American fleet carried out its own battle practice, 14-25 November. Departing from the Philippines, the fleet shaped its course for the Strait of Malacca, passing Singapore on 6 December and going on to Colombo, Ceylon, where the fleet refueled. In this British colony, the Scottish businessman and yachting challenger for the America's Cup, Sir Thomas Lipton, presented five pounds of tea to each American officer and a pound for each enlisted man.

Leaving Ceylon just a few days before Christmas, the fleet sailed up the Red Sea to the Suez Canal, making the largest group transit in the history of the canal, passing through in three separate groups that closed the canal to all other traffic for nearly four days. After recoaling at Port Said, the fleet temporarily broke up into separate units. The First Division went to Messina to provide humanitarian assistance after the recent earthquake there; the Second Division went to Marseilles; individual ships of the Third Division called at Greek and Turkish ports; while individual ships of the Fourth Division visited North African ports.

Eventually rejoining at Gibraltar, the sixteen battleships sailed for home on 6 February 1909. Two weeks later, thousands of spectators joined President Roosevelt in greeting the fleet as it entered Hampton Roads on Washington's Birthday. In the last weeks of his administration, Roosevelt exulted that the Great White Fleet had been the first battle fleet to circumnavigate the globe. Later, he would reflect in his autobiography, "The most important service that I rendered to peace was the voyage of the battle fleet around the world."

On its return, the fleet found that the U.S. Navy had permanently changed. The cruise occurred while world politics were belligerent, and the Great White Fleet made a bold statement in that context. The cruise showed both the American public and the world community that, if necessary, the United States could respond to events in the Pacific. Beyond that, the cruise made little diplomatic impact. At home, however, the cruise and the publicity that went with it drew more public attention to the navy. More than anything else, it sparked a new and critical examination of the navy's administrative structure and its designs for new ships. Just as battleship gray now replaced whitepainted hulls, while more functional fittings supplanted gilded and ornate scrollwork, the U.S. Navy moved toward modernization, greater efficiency, and professionalism.

When the U.S. Navy first called for submarine proposals in 1888, submarine pioneer John P. Holland had been trying to interest the navy in his submarine theories for more than ten years. Holland's first naval design, the Plunger, *failed because of engine problems, but his* Holland, *purchased by the navy in 1900, was successful enough that the navy authorized the six Adder-class submarines. Equipped with a single torpedo tube, the sixty-three-foot Adder-class boats were powered by a gasoline engine on the surface and an electric motor when submerged. They could dive to 100 feet, using diving planes to overcome the reserve buoyancy that Holland designed into his boats as a safety feature. These were the first submarines equipped with periscopes, although they only provided forward visibility. The Adder-class* Porpoise, *shown here underway on the surface, was built at the Crescent Shipyard in Elizabethport, New Jersey, under contract from the Holland Torpedo Boat Company. Commissioned in 1903, the* Porpoise *carried a seven-man crew. They avoided the pioneer submariners' risks of gasoline fumes or fire on board, and the hazards of hydrogen or chlorine gas produced by the wet-cell batteries. However, on one occasion in 1904 the* Porpoise *lost its reserve buoyancy and sank to 125 feet. Only by pumping out the ballast tanks by hand was the crew able to return to the surface. The* Porpoise *was one of four U.S. Navy submarines stationed in the Philippines after 1908, serving through the First World War. Photograph by James Burton, ca. 1904. (Negative B373, © Mystic Seaport Museum, Inc., Rosenfeld Collection, Mystic, Connecticut)*

tant, naval innovations such as water-tube boilers, gyroscopes to replace the magnetic compass, a new compass card divided by degrees as well as points, electric logs to measure speed and distance, to the feat of towing the floating dry dock *Dewey* 13,089 miles from the East Coast to Olongapo in the Philippines. While some things had narrow naval applications, others had wider significance, such as the research into tuberculosis undertaken in naval hospitals. All of this work took place within the context of a nation innovating and expanding in many other ways in the new century.

Changes in American Foreign Policy

While America had entered the Spanish-American War in 1898 for humanitarian reasons, the country had to face seriously the consequences of that decision in the years following the war and to determine what responsibilities it should accept. The idea that the United States would accept colonial responsibility had not been seriously

[451]

EXPANSION AND TRANSFORMATION OF MARITIME AMERICA

Civilian pilot Eugene Ely landed his Curtiss biplane on a temporary deck on the USS Pennsylvania *on 18 January 1911, two months after demonstrating that a plane could take off from shipboard. The two demonstrations pointed out the possibility of naval aviation, something Assistant Secretary of the Navy Theodore Roosevelt had encouraged as early as 1898. The navy's first pilot, Lieutenant Theodore Ellyson, was still in training in 1911, but he proposed the arresting system used to stop Ely's plane as it landed. Hooks on the plane were designed to engage wires strung across the deck between sandbags, with a canvas barrier to stop the plane if it missed the wires. The system worked, and in more substantial form it has been the method used on aircraft carriers ever since. Copy photo by Edwin Levick. (M.S.M. 94.125.56)*

examined beforehand and was not easily accepted by all Americans afterwards. Business interests that had originally opposed the war were anxious afterwards to take commercial advantage of the situation that was offered. Church and missionary groups argued that America had a moral obligation to extend "the beneficent rule of the United States" to the former Spanish colonies. Others were concerned about the growth of French, German, or British power if the United States did not intervene to maintain a balance of power in the Pacific. As Peter Finley Dunne satirized the public's reaction to McKinley's decisions in his popular 1899 book, *Mr. Dooley in Peace and War:* "I know what I'd do if I was Mack," said Mr. Hennessy. "I'd hist a flag over th' Ph'lippeens, an' I'd take in th' whole lot iv thim." "An' yet," said Mr. Dooley, "tis not more thin two months since ye larned whether they were islands or canned goods."

Yet, Congress and a subsequent election supported President McKinley's initiative in taking on imperial responsibilities. America's acquisition of the Philippine Islands, Guam, and Hawaii was a turning point that made America's relationship with the Pacific Ocean into "a duty to the Orient" that had great significance for the country in the coming century. Most of those who supported the Philippine acquisition saw it as a link to expanding America's Asian trade.

The treaty ending the War with Spain was scarcely completed before the first crisis arose in China. In September 1899, Secretary of State John Hay delivered his "Open Door" note, asking for equality of American trade in China. Quickly, Americans found themselves drawn into the issues of the Asian mainland. Determined to maintain equal trade rights and to prevent the dismembering of China, American forces joined European powers in responding to the Boxer Rebellion in 1900. Repeatedly during the next half century, the United States was faced with opposition to its Open Door Policy. First Russia, then Japan, directly challenged the United States on these issues. As a result, the United States slowly began to expand its naval forces in Asia, including the organization of a larger and permanent U.S. Asiatic Fleet and the establishment of a regular naval patrol on the Yangtze River in 1903. American business interests attempted unsuccessfully to include maritime trade in the Philippines under the regulations that protected American domestic shipping, but they were unsuccessful and the Philippine trade remained open to international competition. Armed resistance had immediately developed to American rule in the Philippines. American naval and military forces suppressed it in 1901, but difficulties continued for many years.

The acquisition of Puerto Rico and the temporary control of Cuba led America back again to its longstanding interest in the Caribbean. As Alfred Thayer Mahan wrote in his book, *Naval Strategy*, "One thing is sure: The Caribbean Sea is the strategic key to the two great oceans, the Atlantic and the Pacific, our own chief maritime frontiers." Comparing America's relationship with the Caribbean to Britain's experience in the Mediterranean, he argued that the Caribbean was the central point of America's maritime strategy. Along with its Caribbean colonies, the United States acquired a maritime sphere of influence embracing that entire sea and giving impetus to further involvement in the region. The battleship *Oregon*'s dramatic wartime journey around Cape Horn in sixty-seven days to join the Atlantic Fleet (steaming at an average speed of twelve knots for almost 15,000 miles) gave popular credence to the idea that the United States needed to become more closely involved in the plans to build a canal between the two oceans.

The 1901 Hay-Pauncefote Treaty opened the way for the United States to build a canal of its

President Theodore Roosevelt (1858-1919) took office in 1901, following the assassination of President William McKinley. At age forty-two, this dynamic former assistant secretary of the navy, Rough Rider, governor of New York, and historian became the youngest president to that date. The author of a history of the naval War of 1812, and an advocate of Mahan's theory of sea power, Roosevelt promoted U.S. Navy growth and outreach during his administrations, 1901-09. But the cornerstone of his view of U.S. strategy was construction of a canal across the Isthmus of Panama to link the East and West Coasts and make the Caribbean a crossroads of world commerce. After the U.S. took over the French canal project in 1903 and pushed its engineering forward with modern American technology, Roosevelt decided to visit Panama in 1906 to publicize the progress. Aboard the new battleship Louisiana, he made the first trip outside the U.S. by a sitting president, spending two weeks touring the canal project. Early on a rainy November morning, as he climbed into this ninety-five-ton Bucyrus steam shovel excavating the future Pedro Miguel Locks, Roosevelt offered photographers a compelling image of American manifest destiny. Photo by Underwood and Underwood, 1906. (Courtesy Library of Congress)

own. Following the treaty, Great Britain reduced its forces on the North American and West Indies Station that had been devoted to protecting British interests and providing a stabilizing force in the region since the eighteenth century. By 1905, the Royal Navy had virtually with-

The Panama Canal

Of all the tremendous forces on land and sea, only plate tectonics and civil engineering have proved able to separate continents. The movements of the Earth's crust shifted the Americas an ocean away from Africa over the course of millions of years of upheaval. It took only decades for human labor and ingenuity to split North and South America with a navigable channel, the Panama Canal. Like the opening of the Suez Canal in 1879, which put water between the continents of Africa and Asia and joined the Mediterranean Sea with the Indian Ocean, the piercing of the Isthmus of Panama in 1914 brought a host of changes to the way people moved around on, and thought about, the sea. It marked a new epoch in American maritime history.

The construction of the Panama Canal affected the relationship between America and the sea in three general ways. First, the canal changed the flow of American commerce. It also created a third saltwater coast for the United States, along with a colony, the Canal Zone, devoted to navigation. Finally, the canal altered the way the nation planned defense, prepared for war, and treated its closest neighbors in the Caribbean.

The waterway made the world smaller for mariners and their cargoes. The distance by sea between New York and San Francisco decreased by nearly eight thousand miles, saving the trip around South America. Steamers traveling from New York to Japan or China previously headed east to the Suez Canal to get there, but now saved nearly four thousand miles via the Panama route, shortening the trip by two weeks for a vessel averaging ten knots. The West Coast became five thousand five hundred miles closer to the principal ports of Europe, Liverpool and Hamburg. Saving time and money for merchant shipping was an important reason for digging between the continents, following a long tradition of taking the shortcut across the narrowest spot in the entire American landmass.

The Spanish established a "royal road" across Panama only decades after Vasco Nunez de Balboa became the first European to cross the isthmus in 1513. The road became an important link in the maritime system that brought precious metals in the holds of galleons from Peru to Spain. The dense jungle of the region engulfed the road as the Spanish Empire declined, but in 1849 a partnership of American shipping merchants led by William H. Aspinwall reopened the land route just in time to profit from the California gold rush. In their system, a stagecoach service connected two steamship lines, one from New York to the port of Aspinwall (later Colón) constructed on the Caribbean coast, the other on the Pacific side from ancient Panama City to San Francisco. The investors then imported workers, mainly Chinese and Irish, who completed a railroad across the isthmus in 1855.

Two decades later, planning began for a canal across Central America. Several routes were proposed, the favored American one being Cornelius Vanderbilt's partial water crossing of Nicaragua, which he used to compete with Aspinwall's Panama Railroad in getting California-bound passengers from the Atlantic to the Pacific.

"An interocean canal will be the great ocean thoroughfare between our Atlantic and Pacific shores and virtually a part of the coastline of the United States," wrote President Rutherford B. Hayes in 1880.

An international congress met in 1879 to consider proposals for a Central American canal and selected the plan of the French engineer Ferdinand de Lesseps. Having successfully completed the sea-level Suez Canal in 1860-69, de Lesseps brought thousands of Jamaican laborers to the isthmus and began work in 1881 on a sea-level canal, including a nine-mile tunnel through the continental divide. De Lesseps later changed to a more economical lock-type canal, but in 1892-93 his company went bankrupt, and the courts found de Lesseps and his son Charles guilty of breach of trust in the failure.

In 1901, Great Britain renounced her rights to an isthmian canal in the Hay-Pauncefote Treaty, abrogating the Clayton-Bulwer agreement and permitting the United States to construct and control a canal that would be free and open to the ships of all nations on equal terms. By a later amendment to the agreement, Britain agreed to allow the United States to fortify the canal.

With ratification of this agreement, the United States had to choose a route for the proposed canal. The government still favored the Nicaragua route as the most promising, but then de Lesseps's successor, the New Panama Canal Company, unexpectedly lowered the asking price for its assets and franchises from $109 million to $40 million. On 28 June 1902, Congress immediately passed the Spooner Act, which stipulated two conditions for canal construction: purchase of the New Panama Canal Company for $40 million, and a grant by Colombia to perpetual control over the canal. The Act also established the Isthmian Canal Commission to control the construction of the waterway and gave it the right to purchase Nicaraguan rights if the negotiations for Panama failed.

In January 1903, diplomats from the United States and Colombia concluded the Hay-Herran Convention that provided for the United States to pay $10 million and an annual rental of $250,000 for a ninety-nine year lease, with renewal option, to a six-mile-wide canal zone. The U.S. Senate ratified the agreement, but Colombia rejected it, hoping to negotiate a higher payment after the New Panama Canal Company's charter expired the following year.

Theodore Roosevelt was deeply concerned at this turn of events and, on 2 November 1903, ordered U.S. warships to maintain the 1846 Treaty of New Granada that had granted the United States the right to maintain "free and uninterrupted transit" across the isthmus. Simultaneously, patriotic Panamanians and foreigners linked to the Panama Railroad declared the independence of their province from Colombia. The United States government immediately recognized the new country and, within two weeks, on 18 November 1903, concluded the Hay-Bunau-Varilla Treaty which granted the United States perpetual use and control of a ten-mile-wide canal zone across Panama with full sovereignty and the right to fortify it. The United States guaranteed Panama's independence, agreeing to pay $10 million dollars and, beginning nine years after ratification, to pay an additional $250,000 as an annual fee.

The U.S. Senate ratified the Treaty. Ten days later, on 4 May 1904, Lieutenant Mark Brooke of the U.S. Corps of Engineers took possession of the canal works at Panama and began work using the French equipment remaining on the site. The following year, work halted temporarily when many workmen were dying of tropical diseases and there was disagreement on whether to construct a sea-level or a lock canal.

To solve one key issue, Colonel William C. Gorgas of the U.S. Army Medical Corps developed a health initiative to reduce death from malaria and yellow fever. He instituted a successful program of drainage, spraying, and sewage systems that eventually allowed canal construction to resume safely.

In June 1906, after experts determined that they would have to cut through mountains on the western leg of the canal and that there was a twelve-foot difference in tidal ranges between the Atlantic and Pacific sides of the projected canal, President Roosevelt authorized construction to continue. The fifty-one-mile canal would run in a northwest-southeast direction from the Atlantic entrance, which was actually some twenty-seven miles west of the Pacific entrance. The plan for the canal involved five steps: (1) damming the Chagres River to make man-made Lake Gatun through which a ship channel could be dredged; (2) constructing a harbor on the Caribbean side at Colón and dredging a sea-level canal from the harbor to the dam; (3) building the Gatun Locks at the dam to raise and lower ships eighty-five feet between sea-level and the new lake; (4) excavating the nine-mile-long and

300-foot-wide Gaillard Cut from Gatun Lake through the mountains of the continental divide; and (5) building the Pedro Miguel Locks and the Miraflores Locks to lower and raise ships to a dredged channel leading to Balboa Harbor on the Pacific side. This massive project to create the largest locks, dam, and man-made hole in the world (the Gatun Locks and Dam and the Gaillard Cut), continued for twelve years. The locks were constructed between 1909 and 1913, and excavation in the Gaillard Cut proceeded to the point where water was allowed into the canal, effectively breaching the isthmus, in October 1913. Dredging of the channel continued even after the first ships transited the waterway in 1914.

The success of the undertaking depended on the migration of tens of thousands of West Indian and southern European laborers. The Republic of Panama prohibited Chinese immigration, which had helped build the Panama Railroad, and the British colonial government in Kingston restricted the Jamaican emigration that had provided labor for the French effort, because many were stranded in Panama and had to be repatriated at British expense. The third wave of immigrants to go to work in Panama, then, came mainly from Barbados, Martinique, Guadeloupe, Spain, Italy, and Greece, comprising a labor force that expanded from fewer than a thousand in 1904 to more than forty-three thousand in 1913. Even after

completion of the canal, the number of employees never dipped below ten thousand, few of them Panamanian citizens, while several thousand additional foreigners from the shores of the Caribbean and the Mediterranean lived in

Millions of cubic yards of rock and dirt were gouged out of the continental divide during construction of the Panama Canal. In this view of the Gaillard Cut in December 1912, steam shovels load dirt trains, which will haul the fill out for use in a breakwater at the Pacific end of the canal, and to construct the Gatun Dam forming Gatun Lake, which supplied water to the canal. Photo by Ernest Hallen. (185-G-3-X1, Courtesy National Archives)

the port cities at either end of the canal.

The cosmopolitan atmosphere of Colón and Panama City resulted from the mixing of people from around the Atlantic world, and from the prominent Chinese community remaining from the 1850s, who ran stores, eateries, laundries, and lotteries. Both the new port of Colón and the old port of Panama had wild "sailortown" districts as well, with 350 saloons between them, most owned by expatriate Americans and frequented by the crews of merchant and naval vessels in transit, and by the U.S. military garrison defending the waterway.

Colonel George Washington Goethals, who headed the final stages of canal construction and became first governor of the Canal Zone, claimed from experience that the lawlessness and decadence of the two cities outstripped that of Deadwood, South Dakota, during the Black Hills gold rush of 1878. In direct contrast, Goethals's orderly Canal Zone was an insulated world of enforced sobriety and order, though literally across the street from the crowded, riotous terminal cities. The Panama Canal Zone was a unique maritime colony, organized for the purpose of defense and navigation, and kept rigorously "shipshape" by the officers and engineers in charge. Canal tolls and profits from supplying coal, provisions, and repairs to passing vessels financed a lavish lifestyle for the American residents, who numbered about three thousand. They received their

wages in gold and resided rent-free in pleasant houses. Conversely, the West Indian workforce received wages in silver and lived mainly outside the zone in crowded and expensive urban quarters. Few Panamanians were employed by the canal at all, fueling local resentment of Americans, West Indians, and the Canal Zone itself.

The opening of the canal fulfilled many of the optimistic predictions about its influence on the flow of commerce. United States trade with South America doubled within three years, partly because the Panama Canal provided much faster transit between New York and the "wrong side" of South America, and between San Francisco and the East Coast. Vessels making the passage were also speeded by the fact that fouling organisms like barnacles on their hulls died in the fresh water of Gatun Lake and fell off, improving the ships' hydrodynamics. The Pacific Steam Navigation Company's *Oriana* demolished the record for a voyage from New York to the major Chilean port of Iquique soon after the canal opened, making the passage in fifteen days. In 1915, the W.R. Grace Line introduced service from the west coast of the United States to Brazil and Argentina on the east coast of South America. At the same time, the First World War disrupted navigation between South America and Europe, allowing U.S. trade, much of it by way of the Panama Canal, to take its place, and helping this nation become the world's leading exporter.

Although President Theodore Roosevelt said the canal was needed for "the commerce of the world," he believed the most important ships to use the canal would be battleships, not merchant vessels. Accepting the arguments of Admiral Alfred Thayer Mahan, Roosevelt maintained that building the canal would permit the U.S. Navy to maintain a single, unified fleet able to steam to the Atlantic or Pacific quickly to meet threats. This reasoning gained urgency after the U.S. gained outposts of empire in Puerto Rico and the Philippines in 1898, and steeled Roosevelt's determination to assist Panama in breaking away from Colombia for the sake of a canal treaty. Roosevelt subsequently took great personal interest in the canal construction, becoming the first American president to leave the country while in office when he visited the site in 1906.

Woodrow Wilson, who was president during the completion of the project, initially accepting Mahan's and Roosevelt's theory of a unified fleet dependent on the canal, and the Navy Department drew up its war plans accordingly. The Panama Canal opened two weeks before war broke out in Europe in August 1914, apparently allowing these plans to be put into operation. But before the fleet could make its first trip to the West Coast for the Panama Exposition in San Francisco, landslides closed the famous Gaillard Cut. This deep gash through the continental divide became a tourist attraction during construction

Dwarfed by the five-story iron gates of the Gatun Locks, riveting crews complete the doors. Detroit Publishing Company photo, ca. 1913. (Courtesy Library of Congress)

and was often likened to the Grand Canyon, but it proved so unstable that the canal remained impassable on and off for two years, until October 1916. In the meantime, skepticism about the viability of the canal grew in Congress, which passed an unprecedented naval construction bill providing for two fleets after all.

Nevertheless, United States defense during and between the world wars focused on the Panama Canal. Regarded as the key to the Western Hemisphere's security, the canal and its approaches through the Windward

Passage (between Cuba and Haiti) and the Mona Passage (between the Dominican Republic and Puerto Rico) were guarded by a U.S. military and naval presence that increased dramatically after the waterway opened. In accord with Mahan's naval analysis, the U.S. established naval facilities in the vicinity of the canal and its approaches: at Balboa in the Canal Zone, on the Puerto Rican island of Culebra, and at Guantánamo Bay on the southeast coast of Cuba. U.S. military forces were also deployed to control the political and economic destinies of the Caribbean republics in order to maintain order in what had become the pivotal region for national security. Strategic considerations centering on the potential German threat to Panama prompted President Wilson to order the U.S. Marines to invade and occupy Haiti

(1915-34) and the Dominican Republic (1916-24), and to purchase the Danish Virgin Islands (1917). In each case, German merchants, bankers, and shipping agents lost their share of business to Americans after the U.S. declaration of war in April 1917, when U.S. authorities sequestered German nationals to prevent them from aiding U-boats or attempting sabotage. The need to maintain authority in the Caribbean for the sake of the canal, prescribed by Mahan and perceived by naval planners even after the end of World War I, motivated the formation of a permanent naval squadron in the Caribbean, based in the Canal Zone. The Special Service Squadron was on call during the 1920s to engage in "gunboat diplomacy" where unrest broke out, and then during the 1930s to implement Franklin Roosevelt's Good Neighbor policy with "good will cruises" to the ports of Central America and the Antilles. At home in the anchorage at Balboa near the Pacific terminal of the canal, the sailors endured life aboard hot, stifling cruisers and often had bloody run-ins with the Panamanian police in the Cocoa Grove red-light district of Panama City.

The canal itself, with its vulnerable locks near both the Caribbean and Pacific entries, was defended by a regiment of infantry, a submarine base, several airfields, and an increasing number of artillery and anti-aircraft emplacements. Still, repeated "fleet problem" naval exercises demonstrated the vulnerability of the locks to air strikes, and the possibility loomed that an enemy might scuttle or blow up a ship in a lock chamber. These weaknesses became more serious with the outbreak of World War II in 1939. In order to reduce the risk, the Roosevelt administration began building a second set of locks at a distance from the Gatun, Miraflores, and Pedro Miguel Locks, to be reserved for the use of American ships. The new chambers were to be twenty-five feet wider than the original 110-foot double-flight locks in order to permit the passage of new *Montana*-class battleships and aircraft carriers fitted with anti-torpedo "blisters" on their hulls. The renewed construction on the locks and artillery positions combined to triple the labor force in the Canal Zone in six years to more than thirty-seven thousand in 1942, coming mainly from El Salvador, Costa Rica, and Jamaica. Work on the lock project halted within months after Pearl Harbor, however, as the realization set in that

The Panama Canal fostered a flourishing sea trade between the east and west coasts. In this view, on 14 December 1928, the 1919 American tanker Dean Emery *(left) rises in the Pedro Miguel Locks before passing through the canal on her way from Los Angeles to Baltimore with 9,300 tons of gasoline. Descending in the east lock is the Dollar Line steamship* President Hayes, *on the way from New York to San Francisco with cargo. Behind the* President Hayes, *the new Panama-Pacific liner* Virginia *waits for the use of the lock on her way to California. In 1928, 6,253 vessels, carrying more than 29,600,000 tons of cargo, passed through the canal. Photo by Ernest Hallen. (185-G-1108, Courtesy National Archives)*

EXPANSION AND TRANSFORMATION OF MARITIME AMERICA

the alternate route would not be ready for years. The existing route reached its all-time height of activity during the war, averaging sixteen transits daily.

As World War II went on, the size, range, and destructive power of newly developed weaponry reached enormous proportions, including ships that would not fit even the unfinished wider locks; planes that could attack (or protect) Panama from bases thousands of miles away; and bombs that could damage the fragile locks beyond repair. U.S. defense planners began to discount the importance of the waterway, recognizing both its indefensibility and the inevitability of a permanent two-fleet U.S. Navy that would never require transit. American control of the Panama Canal thus began to slip after the war.

The gradual shift in authority over the Panama Canal from the United States to the Republic of Panama started in the late 1940s, with the departure of American troops and planes from airbases on Panamanian soil outside the Canal Zone, and the transfer of long-range air defense to Trinidad. In 1955 the U.S. and Panama ratified a treaty that relinquished to the republic the right to supply ships in transit and the port facilities at the Caribbean terminal. An unratified treaty of 1967 would have replaced the Canal Zone with a bilateral administration, but opposition in the U.S. Senate, the Nixon White house, and the Omar Torrijos regime in Panama prevented an agreement for another decade. With the proliferation of "Panamax" navy and commercial ships too large for the Panama Canal locks after World War II, and with the shift to containerization, the significance of the passage to U.S. commerce declined, with less than one percent of the gross national product traveling by way of Panama. When negotiations resumed in 1977, Torrijos's threat to bomb Gatun Dam and drain the canal spurred the Carter administration to agree to surrender the Canal Zone immediately and arrange for the transition of the canal itself in 1999. Despite strenuous opposition in the U.S., the Senate ratified the treaty in 1979 by one vote over the required two-thirds majority.

The enduring importance of the isthmus to America and the sea is suggested by the invasion of Panama in 1989, however, when the Bush administration cited the security of the canal as a reason for the removal of Manuel Noriega. The Republic of Panama will gain complete control of the Panama Canal in 1999, but 150 years of close involvement between the United States and the shortest route across the continent is unlikely to end with the transition.

Eric Roorda

drawn from the Caribbean, consciously leaving the U.S. Navy to carry on Britain's earlier role. At the same time, however, Germany showed increasing interest in the region and even developed a contingency plan for war with the United States, which its naval leaders soon considered unrealistic. Nevertheless, the possibility of such a threat from Germany, Britain, or any other nation continued to influence American strategic thinking about the Caribbean throughout the period 1898 to 1917.

Construction of the Panama Canal by the United States and acquisition of the Canal Zone expanded the importance of the Caribbean as a vital part of American security interests. President Theodore Roosevelt and his administration were determined that no other naval power obtain any position that would enable it to threaten the canal or the approaches to it. Concern for the canal underlay American anxiety over Cuban insecurity and led to the Platt Amendment, which in effect made Cuba a quasi-protectorate of the United States. Under its terms the U.S. Navy leased land and established a naval and coaling base at Cuba's Guantánamo Bay in 1903 for a newly established Caribbean division of the Atlantic Fleet. In his 1906 "corollary" to the Monroe Doctrine, Theodore Roosevelt precluded any European intervention in American affairs by announcing that, "Chronic wrongdoing . . . in the Western Hemisphere . . . may force the United States . . . to the exercise of an international police power." This policy soon lead to numerous interventions by United States Navy and Marine Corps forces: into the Dominican Republic in 1905; Cuba in 1906 and again in 1912; Nicaragua in 1909, 1910, and 1912; and Honduras in 1911. American naval forces also occupied parts of Haiti from 1915 until 1933 and the Dominican Republic from 1916 to 1924. In October 1913, just seven months after a new administration had taken office in Washington, ships of the U.S. Navy were ordered to cruise off Mexico's Gulf coast, standing by to protect American lives and interests during an uprising against President Victoriano Huerta of Mexico. On 9 April 1914, a group of eight sailors in a small unarmed boat from the USS *Dolphin* went ashore at Tampico, Mexico, to obtain supplies. When the boat inadvertently entered restricted waters as it approached the landing on the Pánuco River, local Mexican government forces under General Ignacio Moreles Zaragoza seized the boat and detained it for half an hour.

An exchange of demands between the senior American naval commander and General Zaragoza led to a concentration of American naval vessels off Mexico's east coast just as the United States learned of the impending arrival of a German steamer with ammunition for Heurta's government forces. With Congressional backing, Wilson ordered the navy to seize the customhouse at Veracruz, which forestalled the landing at least for a few weeks. While the incident seemed trivial, it contributed to Huerta's eventual resignation and revealed once again the extent of American fears about the stability of its Latin American neighbors, German intervention, and their possible effects on American maritime control in the Caribbean. Two years later, when Germany was at war with the European powers, this same fear motivated the United States to purchase the Danish Virgin Islands in August 1916. The USS *Dolphin* arrived at St. Thomas on 9 April 1917, and the squadron commander assumed office as the first governor of the Virgin Islands Territory only four days after the United States joined the war against Germany.

The growth of American political and military interest in the Caribbean was also reflected in the expansion of American maritime trade and commerce in the region. American-flag sailing ships continued to trade in the region, carrying logwood from Haiti and molasses from Puerto Rico. There were even American whalers hunting off Venezuela, Haiti, and the Dominican Republic. American steamship operations grew quickly in the region. Firms such as the Mallory Line, New York and Cuba Mail Line, and the New York and Puerto Rico Line did well. In 1869, the trade in fresh bananas had begun when the schooner *Trade Wind* landed a cargo of Honduran bananas at New Orleans and showed that the green-picked fruit could properly ripen en route. In 1880, a specially-designed refrigerator steamer, *S. & J. Oteri,* added impetus to the trade. In the 1870s, a former Cape Cod fisherman, Lorenzo Dow Baker, succeeded in carrying Caribbean fruit to Boston and went on to develop a system of banana plantations on the island of Jamaica. He formed the Boston Fruit Company in the 1880s, and in 1899 that firm merged with the Central American fruit interests of Minor C. Keith to become the United Fruit Company. United Fruit became perhaps the most pervasive United States presence in Latin America, with lines connecting

Cuba, Jamaica, Colombia, Honduras, and the Canal Zone to the major East Coast and Gulf ports, and with strong economic and political influence in each of those nations.

When Charles Morse's attempt to create a coastal shipping cartel in 1906-07 failed the following year, the Morse-controlled steamship lines serving Havana, San Juan, and Santo Domingo reformed into the Atlantic, Gulf, and West Indies Steamship Lines. The new company soon expanded to dominate Caribbean commerce.

Acquisition of overseas colonies in the wake of the Spanish-American War created a dilemma for the United States: Had the peoples of these island territories automatically received all the rights of American citizens under the Constitution? In a series of decisions, called "the Insular Cases," the Supreme Court ruled in 1901 that, while Puerto Rico and the other islands had ceased to be foreign territory and that goods shipped between them and the continental United States were free from duty, annexation did not automatically confer on the islanders the full privileges of U.S. citizenship. It was the right of Congress to extend only such Constitutional privileges as it saw fit to grant in each specific case. Puerto Ricans received full citizenship in 1917, but Virgin Islanders waited until 1927.

Immigration

During the period 1880-1914 immigration to the United States became a major force in the transformation and expansion of the nation. During those thirty-five years alone, some 23,000,000 people arrived, more than half of all the immigrants ever to enter the country. Almost all of them came by sea. Although immigrants arrived at all U.S. ports, New York's Ellis Island, established in 1892, and San Francisco's Angel Island, established in 1910, were the principal centers for immigration.

As the numbers arriving from Germany slowed in this period, the persecution of Jews in Russia contributed to the large immigration from Russia and Russian Poland while large numbers also came from Austria-Hungary, the Balkans, and Italy. New and larger concentrations of foreign-born immigrants gathered in the larger cities: Poles,

Bohemians, and Hungarians in Chicago; Italians and Jews in New York; Irish and Italians in Boston. The years between 1905 and 1914 marked the zenith of the new immigration with numbers surpassing the million mark in six of those nine years. In the peak year of 1914, 73.4 percent of the new immigrants came from southern and eastern Europe while 13.4 percent came from northern and western Europe. The arrival of such large numbers of immigrants from diverse cultural backgrounds raised many social issues as they crowded into the cities, convincing some Americans that the traditional melting pot was boiling over. Political forces grew to restrict immigration, and some of these views became linked with such diverse problems as the status of blacks in the United States and the rise of the prohibition movement.

In 1885, Congress had passed an act that limited the importation of contract labor, but modified it in 1891, 1907, and 1917 with respect to skilled and domestic labor and certain professionals. In 1903, Congress authorized the inspection of immigrants at European ports of departure, approved the deportation of illegal immigrants and, for the first time, excluded anarchists and prostitutes. In 1906, the Bureau of Immigration was established to maintain statistics and records on immigration.

On the West Coast, Chinese immigration had begun in the 1850s, and Japanese immigration began in the 1880s. At first welcomed for their labor, though discriminated against socially and politically, the Chinese continued to arrive in California through the 1870s. The Pacific Mail Steamship Company provided regular service between San Francisco and China, carrying hundreds of young men anxious to find "gold mountain" in America before returning to China. But many Chinese stayed in America, performing menial labor in construction, agriculture, and service jobs and meeting increasing opposition from whites during the turbulent economic times of the 1870s and 1880s. The Chinese Exclusion Act of 1882 barred further immigration of Chinese laborers, a prohibition that was extended to almost all Chinese in 1888, renewed in 1892 and again in 1902 to remain in effect indefinitely.

Already a strong presence in the sugar plantations of Hawaii when the islands were annexed by the United States, Japanese laborers who flocked to Seattle met discrimination equal to that against the

The hundreds of thousands of European emigrants who flooded the principal arrival port of New York after the Civil War overwhelmed the immigration depot that had been established at Castle Garden in 1855. In 1890 Congress authorized a new facility on Ellis Island, near the Statue of Liberty in New York Harbor. The complex was opened in 1892, burned in 1897, and was reopened in 1900 in the form seen here. The three steamboats transported immigrants from arriving steamships to the processing depot at Ellis Island. Inside the main building, immigrants were given a medical examination to eliminate the chronically ill, interviewed to eliminate criminals and anarchists, and then assisted in purchasing transportation to their destinations in the U.S. During the height of immigration through Ellis Island, between 1905 and 1914, the facility commonly processed 30,000 immigrants per week. More than 90 percent were admitted; the 5-10 percent considered dangerously ill or undesirable were returned to Europe at the expense of the shipping companies. Ellis Island closed in 1954, after having processed twelve million immigrants during its sixty-two years of operation. Photo by A. Loeffler, 1905. (M.S.M. 85.74.1)

Chinese. Most Japanese "immigrants" were actually contract laborers, who fled the poor economic climate in Japan to find a fortune in America before returning home. Most found agricultural work, but others took service jobs, worked on the railroads, or labored in the extractive mining, lumber, and salmon-fishing industries. A Japanese and Korean Exclusion League was organized in 1905 and San Francisco sent Chinese, Japanese and Korean children to separate, segregated schools. Through Theodore Roosevelt's "Gentlemen's Agreement" with Japan in 1907-08, Japan agreed to stop the emigration of workers. Some states limited the rights of Japanese immigrants to own and lease land, eventually leading to anti-American riots and long-term antagonism between the two countries. Congress made several attempts to limit immigration through English-

language literacy tests. Finally, in 1917, Congress passed that restriction over President Woodrow Wilson's veto. It was another major step in ending the historic process by which the nation had been peopled, closing an era in American history.

Immigration had a great impact on maritime industries and on the American waterfront. While most immigrants traveled to America in foreign-flag vessels, the challenges that this great influx of people presented were a major factor in the way in which ports grew and developed to handle this human cargo. The waterfront was often the first place where some of the social issues emerged for immigrants. Jack London, in his 1905 book *Tales of the Fish Patrol*, caught some the racial and ethnic tensions that existed in the interactions among a variety of recent immigrants and other

Frances Benjamin Johnston photographed these Eastern European emigrants sitting amid the machinery on the foredeck of the Holland-America liner Amsterdam, *ca. 1902. These women and children are likely traveling to join a husband or other family member already established in the U.S. This form of "chain migration," whereby an individual came to find work and become established before sending for the rest of the family, characterized the majority of immigration after the Civil War. By the 1870s the process of European emigration to the U.S. was highly structured. The transatlantic fare, which included transportation to a major emigration port such as Hamburg or Liverpool, was relatively inexpensive for basic third-class steerage accommodations. Prospective emigrants were screened before obtaining a visa and being assigned to a steamship. For the principal European steamship lines, the increasing stream of emigrants provided a high-volume, low-cost cargo for the passage to the U.S. Older steamships like the* Amsterdam *could accommodate perhaps 800 steerage passengers. The great liners built after 1900 might carry 1,500 to 2,000. Steerage passengers such as these women and children were housed in large compartments deep in the hull, with ranks of iron bunk beds, rough mess tables, and rudimentary sanitary facilities. Law required that ample, basic food be served. When weather and seasickness permitted, the emigrants sought fresh air on deck, but unlike first- and second-class passengers who had the upper decks to themselves, steerage passengers were restricted to the foredeck. (Courtesy Library of Congress)*

Americans in San Francisco Bay. There were many social issues involving immigration in San Francisco. The temptations of the city's "Barbary Coast" were reputed to have enticed more than a thousand British sailors to desert their ships in 1900. However, the city's reputation as a sailor's wildest port-of-call largely disappeared after the Great Earthquake of 1906.

In general, maritime labor mirrored the stresses of American society as it struggled to deal with the ethnic and social issues of the time. The maritime experience, however, remained a rite of passage for nearly all immigrants in this period. The journey to America was almost always by sea. The experience of that sea passage, the manner in which ships defined what individuals could bring with them from their country of origin, and the debarkation and processing in American ports at places such as New York's

Ellis Island and San Francisco's Angel Island, were all part of an Americanization process that immigrants shared with one another. And on a larger scale, immigration as well as the entire range of American maritime affairs were being directly affected by events that were occurring in Europe between 1898 and 1917.

Neutrality in World War One

With the outbreak of the European War in 1914, the safety of commerce at sea became a major concern for the neutral United States. The conditions of naval warfare in the twentieth century made the situation starkly different from what it had been a hundred years earlier, when American shipowners profited from neutral shipping in non-contraband goods. In the new circumstances, neutrals were vulnerable. President Woodrow Wilson initially believed that it was essential for the preservation of the United States that Americans remain neutral in the European War. We must remain neutral, he said, because "The people of the United States are drawn from many nations, and chiefly from the nations now at war." The great role for the United States, he felt, was to play the part of impartial mediator: the one nation in the world that could "speak the counsels of peace and accommodation, not as a partisan, but as a friend." Wilson's actions, however, soon became more partisan than his words.

Immediately upon receipt of the news that war had broken out in Europe, Wilson sent diplomatic notes to all of the belligerent powers, asking each to agree to the limitations on naval warfare that had been outlined in the Declaration of London in 1909. Austria-Hungary and Germany readily agreed to Wilson's proposal since it gave an opportunity for large-scale trade with neutrals. France and Russia made their acceptance dependent on Britain's agreement to Wilson's proposal. Britain also accepted it, but made so many modifications and exceptions to the rules, enlarging the definitions and lists of contraband items in the 1909 Declaration, that other countries could not agree with Britain's position.

Frustrated by his inability to gain a consensus based on the Declaration of London, Wilson

From the time of the California gold rush until the Chinese Exclusion Act of 1882 severely limited further arrivals of Chinese workers in the U.S., tens of thousands of young Chinese men crossed the Pacific to find economic success in the U.S. before returning to their families in China. Some found wealth in mining or service jobs and returned to China as wealthy men; many more provided essential labor for railroad construction and agricultural development projects, but never made more than a living wage and never returned home. Excluded from U.S. citizenship, and increasingly discriminated against by European-Americans as the U.S. economy faltered after 1870, these Chinese lived a circumscribed life as perpetual foreigners in America, joined by a small number of Chinese women. Several thousand found seasonal work as fish processors in the expanding salmon canneries on the Pacific Coast. The Chinese shrimp fishermen depicted here on San Francisco Bay pursued one form of self-employment available to the Chinese. Living in small fishing villages on the bay, and using their nets to catch shrimp, smelt, herring, and other fish, they sold the dried catch in San Francisco as well as shipping it home to China. But even independent fishermen like these faced discrimination. In 1876 the Italian Fishermen's Union in San Francisco protested that the Chinese method of fishing with fine-mesh nets was wasteful of the fish stocks they all depended on. (Courtesy San Francisco Maritime National Historical Park, J.E. Dewey Photographic Collection)

Cape Verdeans and the Sea: Race, Place, and Space in the Making of an Atlantic World

Located some 280 miles off the coast of West Africa, the small archipelago that comprises the Cape Verde Islands might seem like an odd place to begin a story about race, place, and space and the sea. Although the Cape Verde Islands were among the first places in Africa that the Portuguese colonized in the mid-fifteenth century, they proved to be a major disappointment when the islands failed to repeat the earlier successes of the Portuguese in Madeira and the Azores. In fact, in the early years of settlement, the islands became the epitome of a failed sugar colony. Their only early value to the Portuguese was as a dumping ground for convicts (*degredados*) and a beachhead for Portuguese economic and commercial interest in the Senegambia region.

During the sixteenth and seventeenth centuries the Cape Verde Islands would be propelled to new economic heights when the islands become an important entrepôt for the transatlantic slave trade. But after the focus of the slave trade shifted further south to the more successful sugar plantation economy in Sao Tome, the Cape Verde Islands once again became marginalized economically and politically and remained so except for the occasional visits from vessels in search of supplies. Not until the nineteenth century did the Cape Verde Islands once again become an important part of the Atlantic world. Yet it is not Cape Verde's economic or political significance that sheds light on the islands' place within the Atlantic world but, rather, the dispersal of its most vital resource—its people—around the globe and the subsequent formation of maritime communities in Guinea Bissau, Angola, Mozambique, Brazil, Portugal, Cuba, Argentina, and most importantly the United States, which underscores the linkages between Cape Verde and the sea. The story of the Cape Verde Islands and its people is vital to American maritime history because it demonstrates, as do few other examples, the nexus between communities in Africa and the United States.

In particular the matrix of events that took place in the period from 1878 to 1921 represents one of the transforming moments in the formation of a transatlantic community. From the final abolition of slavery in Portugal's colonies in 1878 until just after World War I,

two factors exerted influence on how Cape Verdeans became important historical actors in American maritime history and the Atlantic world: mass migration and the decline of the American whaling industry.

Although examples of Cape Verdean migration to the Americas were not unheard of before the nineteenth century, during the forty-year period between 1878 and 1921 Cape Verdeans became a significant presence in New England. The height of Cape Verdean migration occurred between 1900 and 1920, when some 28,000 men and women left the islands, and 67 percent of these emigrants came to the United States. Almost all of the pioneering Cape Verdean emigrants to the U.S. came from the island of Brava as a result of connections made with visiting U.S. whaling vessels. Once this link was made, the process of chain migration followed and took Cape Verdeans from Brava to the whaling port of New Bedford, Massachusetts, and nearby maritime communities such as Boston and Providence. An important feature of the dispersal of Cape Verdeans across the Atlantic Ocean in the nineteenth and twentieth centuries was that many of the emigrants to the United States were young men who, upon their arrival in the United States, came to work in the maritime industries as whalers, longshoremen, and commercial fishermen. Like the legendary John da Lomba and Antonio Coelho, many of these men discov-

ered that the maritime world was one of the few spaces in American society that allowed these men of African descent to move beyond the often narrow boundaries of identity that so rigidly defined American social relations. Thus, the sea came to represent for many Cape Verdean men a kind of democratic space where prevailing ideas about race did not hinder access to opportunity.

Cape Verdeans took advantage of the opportunity they found in the American whaling industry to become entrepreneurs. The best indication of how Cape Verdeans responded to the opportunities they found in the United States was the development of a transatlantic system of support known as the

---

Antoine DeSant (ca. 1815-1886) was among the early Cape Verdeans who found employment on New England whaleships to escape the economic stagnation in the islands. After signing aboard a whaleship that called at the Cape Verdes about 1830, he made at least seven whaling voyages during the 1830s and 1840s from New London, Connecticut, before settling in that port as a barber and later a grocer. Throughout the nineteenth century, many other young Cape Verdean men used the American whaling industry as an avenue of opportunity, frequently settling in New England and pursuing maritime occupations while maintaining links with their Atlantic homeland. Photo by Bolles and Frisbee, ca. 1880. (M.S.M. 92.119.1)

"Brava" packet trade. The Brava packet trade was an effort by many Cape Verdean immigrants to reconnect with their homeland through regular trips back to the Cape Verde Islands. Beginning as early as 1892, Cape Verdeans pooled their resources to buy old sailing vessels, which had been made obsolete with the advent of steamship technology. They converted them into cargo and passenger ships known as packets to indicate that they sailed on a more or less fixed schedule, carrying passengers, mail, and packages. With the purchase of the sixty-four-ton fishing schooner *Nellie May*, Antonio Coelho became the first Cape Verdean packet owner. Within a short time Cape Verdean settlers in New England port cities owned a fleet of former fishing vessels, whaleships, and small merchant ships and began to make regular six-week passages on the 3,545-mile route between New Bedford and Cape Verde. The significance of this mode of transportation was not merely that it was owned and operated by Cape Verdeans in America, but that it opened up a line of communication between those who had departed and those who remained on the islands. Marilyn Halter has demonstrated that verbal greetings sent to long-separated relatives and friends, which were essential to "maintaining the bonds between those who have been separated by the distance of the ocean," formed an important part of this connection.

The Brava packet trade served to strengthen the links between Cape Verdean communities in the U.S. and on the islands. More importantly, it fueled the creation of a Cape Verdean universe that spanned from New Bedford to Brava. In this Black Atlantic world, those who were a part of the Cape Verdean community spoke creole and associated almost exclusively with other Cape Verdeans. Still, the hopes and aspirations of most Cape Verdean immigrants embodied American ideals about community. In this context, Cape Verdeans began to develop a collective identity during the first two decades of the twentieth century, and this sense of identity was informed both by their presence in America and by their participation in an Atlantic world they helped shape and define.

Dwayne E. Williams

abandoned the effort in late October 1914, urging instead that the belligerents follow the existing rules of international law. Britain moved quickly to extend the list of contraband items and to revive the doctrine of "continuous voyage" to justify the interception of vessels trading to areas susceptible to German control, including neutral Denmark, Finland, Sweden, and the Netherlands.

In July 1914, 43 percent of the world's merchant ships, totaling some 21 million tons, flew either the British flag or that of an overseas dominion. Germany's fleet was second largest, its 5.5 million tons comprising 12 percent of the world's tonnage. France, Japan, Norway, and the United States each had merchant fleets that were barely one-third the size of Germany's. Britain's maritime trade was particularly important to her at this time, as two-thirds of her food supply and many commodities essential to her industry came by sea. Moreover, Britain's worldwide empire was held together almost exclusively by maritime connections. By finding a way to restrict Britain's maritime trade, Germany could inflict considerable, perhaps even decisive, damage on its adversary. By rejecting the limitations on naval warfare outlined in the Declaration of London, the British government increased the effectiveness of its navy to counter the German threat to its merchant shipping.

When the war broke out, most officers of the Imperial German Navy were concentrating their thoughts on large battles between fleets, not an attack on trade. Even before the war, however, a few far-sighted officers realized that a decisive battle might not be possible and began to develop a different concept: a war on enemy trade. Because of the size of Britain's merchant fleet, however, it would be very difficult for Germany to mount an offensive large enough to have significant effect. Furthermore, Germany herself, with the world's third largest empire, had her own overseas vulnerabilities. Yet, if successful, such a campaign would not only deprive Britain of essential cargoes, but might also cause significant panic in the maritime community to drive up marine insurance rates to prohibitive levels, paralyzing world shipping. To counter this threat the British government had created, at the outbreak of war, a tacit partnership to share risks and losses with shipowners, agreeing to reinsure 80 percent of all war risks. Other belligerents and many neutrals, including the United States, adopted similar plans.

In the opening phase of the war, both the Royal Navy and the French Navy sought to control the German maritime threat by concentrating their own naval forces in European waters and preventing the Imperial German Navy's battle fleet from operating freely on the open seas. The British government gradually expanded the scope of its control of the sea, declaring the North Sea a military area and laying extensive minefields. In November 1914 First Lord of the Admiralty Winston Churchill threatened to strangle Germany with an economic blockade, prompting German Admiral Alfred von Tirpitz to respond: "England wants to starve us! We can play the same game. We can bottle her up and torpedo every English or allied ship which nears any harbor in Great Britain, thereby cutting off large food supplies." The following February, Germany declared the waters around the British Isles a war zone, where its submarines would torpedo enemy merchant ships on sight. Germany warned that any neutral ships entering the war zone did so at their own risk.

In contrast to his accommodating manner with British incursions on neutral rights, Wilson reacted sharply to the German announcement. "It is of course not necessary to remind the German Government," his note of protest stated, "that the sole right of a belligerent in dealing with neutral vessels on the high seas is limited to visit and search." Secretary of State William Jennings Bryan followed with a stern warning that if American lives were lost or ships destroyed, "it would be difficult for the Government of the United States to act in any other light than as an indefensible violation of neutral rights" and hold Germany entirely responsible.

In retaliation against the German declaration of unrestricted submarine warfare, the British government announced that it would seize any ship or cargo presumed to be sailing to an enemy port. With both sides employing the idea that justifiable retaliation was a sound basis on which to disregard international law, the combination of the German U-boat policy and the British economic blockade of Germany created an entirely new problem for the United States. Wilson was particularly concerned that disregard for neutral rights at sea would lead the United States into war as it had in 1812, and he did all that he could to avoid it. On one hand, he felt that it was appropriate to allow the British to continue their blockade as it followed the precedent followed during the Civil War, when the United States was the belligerent imposing a blockade and Britain the neutral. Other members of Wilson's cabinet strongly objected to the president's view, arguing that the situation was entirely different and that American support for the British policy would clearly show that the United States had taken sides in the conflict and that Germany would be entirely justified in attacking the United States as a belligerent. After failing in an attempt to negotiate an agreement between Britain and Germany over the rights of neutral commerce, Wilson finally responded to the new British policy at the end of March, a month after its declaration (in contrast to his immediate denunciation of Germany's policy). Wilson merely noted that the British actions were "subversive of the rights of neutral nations on the high seas," expecting that the British government had already considered the possibilities of such violations occurring and, "in the event they should unhappily occur, will be prepared to make full reparation for every act."

Initially, the U-boat attacks were not a serious threat to American merchant shipping, its first losses coming instead from a German surface raider and from mines in the North Sea. On 1 May 1915, however, *U-30* attacked the American tanker *Gulflight*, which had managed to get too close to a fight between a British patrol boat and the German submarine. The American ship was towed to port with three dead.

The growing number of German U-boat attacks on merchant shipping with the loss of American lives was the issue that stirred public debate and created political pressure. The most dramatic of these events was the sinking of the 30,396-ton, four-funneled Cunard liner *Lusitania* on 7 May 1915. The ship sank in only eighteen minutes with 1,201 lives lost, including 128 Americans. Among them was Alfred Vanderbilt, the heir to the Vanderbilt fortune, and Charles Frohman, America's leading theatrical producer. The ship was one of the best-known passenger ships of the time, and her sinking set off a diplomatic controversy that created a massive reaction against Germany in the United States. A week before the *Lusitania* had sailed from New York, the German ambassador to the United States, Graf von Bernstorff, had asked the State Department to warn Americans against traveling on belligerent ships. As a well-known British-flag liner, the *Lusitania* certainly fell in that category. Moreover, the widely read naval annual, *Jane's Fighting Ships*, had listed her and her sister ship, *Mauritania*, as British auxiliary cruisers in their 1914 edition, as had the official *Navy List*. Although she was not actually serving as an auxiliary cruiser or troop carrier, the British could have modified the *Lusitania* easily and quickly for that service. The ship was carrying 4,200 cases of rifle ammunition and 1,271 cases of nonexplosive fuses and empty shrapnel shells, but there is no persuasive evidence that she was carrying a large shipment of explosives or contraband weapons.

On hearing the news of the sinking, President Wilson acted quickly, directing a reluctant Secretary of State Bryan to send an official diplomatic note of protest, demanding that Germany abandon her policy of unrestricted warfare, disavow the sinking of the *Lusitania*, and make reparation for the loss of American lives. Repeating his demand that Germany be strictly accountable for such acts, Wilson insisted that "American citizens act within their indisputable rights in taking their ships and in traveling wherever their legitimate business calls them upon the high seas." In reply, the German government made a conciliatory reply, but went on, to Wilson's dissatisfaction, to contend that the *Lusitania* was armed and carrying contraband ammunition. As the exchange of diplomatic notes continued through the spring, Wilson took issue with Germany's contention that Britain's strangling blockade justified its own policy of unrestricted submarine warfare. Unwilling to risk American involvement in the war, however, Secretary of State Bryan refused to sign the formal diplomatic note conveying these views and resigned from office. His successor, Robert Lansing, did so in early June. In its reply, the German government offered to grant immunity to passenger ships that were distinguished by special markings and under the direct control of the American government.

During the first two years of his administration Wilson had taken little interest in naval affairs, ignoring proposals for improvements made by his own secretary of the navy, Josephus Daniels, and the suggestions of the admirals. Suddenly, world events forced Wilson to add other measures to achieve his goals. In addition to the sinking of the *Lusitania* were gloomy forecasts on the outcome of the European war as well as Japan's demands on

China and its seizure of Germany's Pacific islands. Without previous notice, Wilson instructed Daniels on 21 July 1915 to prepare a "wise and adequate naval program, to be proposed to Congress at the next session." As a first step, Wilson said, "we must have professional naval advice for a Navy in order to stand upon an equality with the most practicable," thus giving impetus to provide a staff for the Chief of Naval Operations, a position which Congress had only established on 3 March 1915, and which Rear Admiral William S. Benson had just assumed in May as its first occupant. On the same day, Wilson rejected the German offer of immunity for American passenger ships and declared that any further acts of this kind would be regarded "as deliberately unfriendly" to the United States.

Within ten days of the president's request to prepare plans for a "wise and adequate naval program" the navy's General Board, presided over by Admiral of the Navy George Dewey, agreed upon a dramatic departure from any earlier American naval policy: "The Navy of the United States should ultimately be equal to the most powerful maintained by any other nation in the world." With more specific instructions, they went on during the next three months to outline a practical plan of naval construction that the president could present to Congress, a plan that would take effect over a five-year period. In their official report, the General Board concluded:

> Defense from invasion is not the only function of a Navy. It must protect our seaborne commerce and drive that of the enemy from the sea. The best way to accomplish all these objectives is to find and defeat the hostile fleet or any of its detachments at a distance from our coast sufficiently great to prevent interruption of our normal course of national life. The current war has shown that a navy of the size recommended by this board in previous years can no longer be considered adequate to the defensive needs of the United States. Our present Navy is not sufficient to give due weight to the diplomatic remonstrances of the United States in peace or to enforce its policies in war.

Certainly, diplomatic remonstrances were the tool of the moment. In spite of German assurances to the contrary, it was not long before more incidents at sea created further tensions between Germany and the United States. Sixty miles northwest of the Orkney Islands, a submarine sank the steamship *Leelanaw* in July. But oddest of all was the 1,571-ton *Pass of Balmaha*, a full-rigged ship with an auxiliary motor, recently transferred from British to American registry. On 4 August 1915, she encountered the submarine *U-36* in the North Sea and surrendered to the submarine. Taken into port, the Germans armed her with two deck guns hidden under a deck cargo of timber. Returning to sea some months later with the name *Seeadler* and under the command of Kapitänleutnant Felix Graf von Luckner, she soon became the most famous of the German surface raiders. Then, on 19 August, without warning, *U-27* torpedoed and sank the 600-foot British White Star passenger liner *Arabic* off the Irish coast. Among the forty-four casualties were two Americans. In response to this, Ambassador von Bernstorff in Washington assured the Wilson administration on his own initiative that "liners will not be sunk by our submarines without warning and without safety for the lives of non–combatants, providing that the liners do not try to escape or offer resistance." The ambassador's assurances presaged a temporary resolution of the divided opinion within the German government. Shortly afterward, the Kaiser forbade the sinking of any passenger ship and, to ensure that this order was carried out, replaced Vice Admiral Bachmann with Admiral Henning von Holtzendorf. In mid-September, Holtzendorf temporarily suspended the U-boat campaign, and the German government formally apologized for the loss of American lives in the *Arabic*. For some months, Germany conducted a restricted submarine campaign, placing more emphasis on the High Seas Fleet than on submarines, but its policies for submarine operations varied from month to month, with occasional sinkings continuing to take American lives.

For Woodrow Wilson, the course of the war in Europe created a dilemma. Although the German government was clearly making some provision to safeguard neutral American-flag merchant vessels, the United States was largely dependent on foreign-flag ships to carry its overseas commerce, and it was precisely those vessels that were in jeopardy. In a speech at Cleveland in January 1916, Wilson explained:

> The United States is trying to keep up the processes of peaceful commerce while all the

world is at war and while all the world is in need of the essential things which the United States produces, and yet by an oversight, for which it is difficult to forgive ourselves, we did not provide ourselves when there was proper peace and opportunity with a mercantile marine, by means of which we could carry on the commerce of the world without the interference of the motives of other nations which might be engaged in controversy not our own.

In the light of the German Navy's attacks on merchant commerce, members of Congress began to fear that another serious incident could force the United States into the war. As they watched the trends in the president's conduct of foreign policy, several members of Wilson's own Democratic Party revolted. On 7 February 1916, Representative Jeff McLemore of Texas introduced a resolution requesting the president to advise all Americans not to travel on armed vessels. Interpreting McLemore's resolution as an attack on his presidential leadership and representing an outlook that would limit the rights of Americans to travel freely on the high seas, Wilson reacted adamantly. Two weeks later, in a meeting of party leaders at the White House, Wilson made it clear that he would not alter what he considered to be a fundamental interpretation of American rights. Repeating his views to the Senate Foreign Relations Committee a few days later, Wilson declared that he refused to "consent to any abridgement of the rights of American citizens in any respect." The following day, 25 February, Senator Thomas P. Gore of Oklahoma introduced a resolution that demanded protection for American's noncontraband trade and denied passports to Americans who wanted to travel on the armed ships of belligerent countries. During the debate on this resolution, Wilson's opponents tried to embarrass the administration by modifying Gore's original resolution into a direct challenge. They added to it a provision that specified, in the event that there were American casualties when German forces sank an armed merchant vessel, the situation "would constitute a just and sufficient cause of war between the United States and the German Empire." Faced with this political challenge to his leadership, Wilson was able to table the motions in both houses and prevent them coming to a vote.

On 24 March 1916 near Dieppe, *U-29* torpedoed without warning the unarmed French cross-channel passenger ferry *Sussex*. The ship managed to reach port, but fifty people died, half of them Americans. Regarding the attack as a violation of the pledge that Germany had given following the *Arabic* incident, Secretary of State Lansing advised Wilson to take drastic action and recommended that the United States immediately cut off diplomatic relations with Germany. Wilson resisted going to such an extreme; instead, he issued an ultimatum on 18 April 1916, demanding that Germany stop its current attacks on merchant and passenger shipping. The following day, Wilson made an address to Congress in which he repeated the substance of his note and appealed to Germany's prewar support for restraints on naval warfare, saying, "All sober-minded men must unite in hoping that the Imperial German Government, which has in other circumstances stood as the champion of all that we are now contending for in the interest of humanity, may recognize the justice of our demands and meet them in the spirit in which they are made."

Not wanting to create a dangerous confrontation with a major neutral power, Berlin responded with assurances that, from the first of May, German submarines would no longer sink merchant vessels without warning and without first securing the lives of those on board. Berlin ordered its naval commanders in the North Sea and the Atlantic to operate only in accordance with the principles of the prize regulations, following visit and search. In effect, this put a virtual halt to submarine activity in these areas. In its reply, Germany had further requested that the United States would demand and insist that the British government also observe the rules of international law, but Wilson refused. Lansing informed Berlin that the United States could not agree to "a suggestion that respect by German naval authorities for the rights of the citizens of the United States upon the high seas should in any way or in the slightest degree be made contingent upon the conduct of any other Government affecting the rights of neutrals and noncombatants. Responsibility in such matters is single, not joint; absolute, not relative." From May 1916 until the end of January 1917, Germany honored its pledge.

During this interim period, Woodrow Wilson

was engaged in promoting an important part of his broad maritime program: Building, as he said in an extemporaneous speech in St Louis, "incomparably the greatest navy in the world." The proposal that Secretary Daniels crafted to present to Congress on behalf of the Wilson administration contained a number of unusual features that some naval leaders had recently advocated and that allowed for longer-term planning and a broader concept in naval procurement. First, it moved to secure the navy's Congressional funding authorization for a period of years, instead of dealing with it on the basis of an annual budget. Secondly, it outlined a program for building a full fleet, not just one type of ship in each construction authorization bill. Finally, it proposed a program that was larger than any Congress had ever considered in the history of the Republic.

Not surprisingly, the 1916 Navy Bill ran into serious opposition, especially in the Midwest and among Southern Democrats, who reflected the old "anti-navalist" views and wanted a small navy that would clearly stay away from foreign entanglements. A combination of Republican and pro-navy Democrats were the strongest supporters of the bill. Neither Wilson's political pressure on members of the Naval Affairs Committee nor his series of public addresses in Cleveland, New York, Detroit, and St. Louis succeeded in getting the bill through Congress unscathed. On 2 June 1916, just as Congress was agreeing on a compromise naval bill that omitted any reference to building battleships, news arrived of the great sea battle between the British and German fleets that had taken place a few days earlier off Jutland. The news of the battle transformed opinion in Congress. Americans now saw clearly that the Royal Navy might not be able to stand up against the Imperial Germany Navy. Moreover, the early, detailed accounts of the battle suggested to American statesmen that not only were battleships necessary, they were superior to battle cruisers. Almost immediately, Senate leaders restored the provisions in the naval bill for battleships. At the same time, the senior Republican on the Senate Naval Affairs Committee, Massachusetts Senator Henry Cabot Lodge, declared that a five-year construction program was too slow, and amended it to a three-year plan. On 21 July 1916, exactly one year after Wilson had made his revolutionary suggestion to

Josephus Daniels, the Senate passed the bill. With the approval of the House it became law on 21 August, authorizing the construction of 156 American naval vessels: ten battleships, six battle cruisers, ten scout cruisers, fifty destroyers, sixty-eight submarines, three fuel ships, two ammunition ships, two destroyer tenders, a gunboat, a repair ship, a transport, and a hospital ship.

The Road to War

Toward the end of 1916, Germany began to explore the possibility of a negotiated peace and asked the United States to consider mediating between the warring powers. Wilson was interested in the possibility, but with the distraction of general elections in both the United States and Britain, as well as the reluctance of Germany to state her aims and the hesitancy of the Allies to put forward any terms that were favorable to the Central Powers, the peace attempt foundered. By early January 1917 German naval leaders realized that their limited U-boat campaign could at best only weaken the enemy but not bring about its defeat. Faced with a stalemate on the western front, German generals supported the idea that all-out submarine warfare might be Germany's last chance for a favorable outcome. One senior German admiral calculated that, while this policy would probably bring the United States into the war, U-boats could prevent American ships from bringing a meaningful military force to bear against Germany. On 31 January 1917 the German government advised Washington that on the following day Germany planned to renew unrestricted submarine attacks on all neutral and belligerent shipping to or from any of the Allies in a zone around Great Britain, France, Italy, and the eastern Mediterranean. In response to the German notification, Wilson announced to Congress that he had recalled the American ambassador from Berlin and had severed diplomatic relations with Germany. Resisting Secretary Lansing's recommendation to ask Congress for an immediate declaration of war, Wilson told the Congress, "if American ships and American lives should in fact be sacrificed by their [German] naval commanders in heedless contravention of the just and obvious dictates of humanity, I shall take the liberty of coming again before the Congress to ask that

Although a British blockade strangled German maritime commerce during World War I, neutral U.S. ports remained open to both British and German shipping until the U.S. declared war on Germany in April 1917. In 1916 the German commercial U-boat Deutschland *evaded the British blockade and reached the U.S. twice, in July and November, landing cargoes of chemicals and dyes in Baltimore and New London, and returning to Germany with essential war materiels: nickel, tin, silver, and crude rubber. Despite British diplomatic protest, the U.S. invoked its neutral status to permit these trading voyages, and the* Deutschland's *presence stirred both pro- and anti-German sentiment in America. One of seven commercial U-boats designed for trade under the blockade, the 213-foot* Deutschland *was later converted for German naval service. U-53 also visited the U.S. in 1916, calling at Newport, Rhode Island, before sinking several Allied ships off the American coast as a demonstration of U-boat range. Photo by George Thompson. (M.S.M. 63.1.3)*

authority . . . for the protection of our seamen and our people in the prosecution of their legitimate errands on the high seas." On the very day of Wilson's announcement, *U-53* sank the American steamship *Housatonic* off Bishop's Light, and nine days later another U-boat sank an American schooner in the Mediterranean.

At the same time, tensions between Germany and the United States increased when British naval intelligence intercepted and decoded a secret message from German Foreign Secretary Alfred Zimmermann to the German ambassador in Mexico, proposing an alliance between Mexico and Germany, and suggesting that, with German financial support, Mexico could regain her lost territory in New Mexico, Texas, and Arizona. The British government passed this intelligence on to the American ambassador in London, who reported it to the State Department in Washington, which in turn released it to the press on 1 March.

Announcement of the Zimmermann telegram gave added force to Wilson's request to Congress, made a few days earlier, that it authorize the president to arm American merchant ships "to protect our ships and our people in their legitimate and peaceful pursuits on the seas." When what Wilson dubbed a "little group of willful men" under Senator Robert La Follette filibustered the bill to death, the administration determined that it was unnecessary to have special congressional authority, as the right of arming merchant ships was already implied in statute law.

As the United States took these steps, Germany's campaign of unrestricted submarine warfare continued. For a time, it seemed as if the German Navy's predictions for submarine warfare were accurate. The figures rose sharply: In January 1917, U-boats sank 328,391 tons of Allied shipping; in February, 520,412 tons; in March, 564,497 tons; in April, a wartime peak of 860,334 tons. These figures included American casualties, bringing Wilson's policy of armed neutrality into question. On 25 February, *U-50* sank the British liner *Laconia* fifty miles northwest of Fastnet and several Americans died. On 12 March, the American steamer *Algonquin* was sunk, followed rapidly by the *Vigilancia* on 16 March, *City of Memphis* on 17 March, the tanker *Illinois* on 18 March, *Healdton* on 21 March, and *Aztec* on 1 April. In a little more than a week, sixty-three Americans lost their lives at sea.

In the last week of March, the American Ambassador in London cabled Washington a proposal that he had made several times already. "I know personally and informally that they [the British leaders] hope for the establishment of full and frank naval interchange of information and cooperation. Knowing their spirit and methods, I can not too strongly recommend that our government send here immediately an Admiral of our own who will bring our navy's plans and inquiries." Washington responded instantly by dispatching Rear Admiral William S. Sims, then serving as president of the Naval War College, and traveling with an assumed name, to England in the liner *New York*.

At an extraordinary session convened on 2 April 1917, Wilson requested that Congress declare that Germany's recent course of action was noth-

ing less than war. "It is a war against all nations," he said, ". . . Armed neutrality, it now appears, is impracticable. Because submarines are in effect outlaws when used as the German submarines have been used against merchant shipping, it is impossible to defend ships against their attacks as the law of nations has assumed." As a result of German attacks, the United States had lost a total of 216 people and twenty-one ships since the war in Europe began in 1914. Following Wilson's request, both houses of Congress acted and the president signed the proclamation of war on 6 April 1917.

Conclusion

The half-century between 1866 and 1917 saw dramatic change in American activity at sea and in America's relationship with the sea. The innovations ranged across the full scope of such activity, encompassing social and economic change as well as changes in the very fabric of our maritime world. A black smudge of coal smoke on the horizon replaced the more romantic image of a square-rigger, hull-down. It was an era that saw the development of the submarine and an entirely new type of warfare at sea that would no longer abide by the traditional restraints of international law. It was a Dark Age, in another sense, that witnessed the continuing decline of the American merchant marine's overseas trade and shipbuilding industry. It was an era that witnessed social, racial, and ethnic discrimination and the germination of additional seeds for future problems, but it was also a time of widespread growth in worldwide maritime activities, in America's inland navigation, and in the growth of maritime science and technology. The period was one marked by increased professionalization, international cooperation, and great strides in understanding the maritime environment scientifically. America's international trade was maritime trade, whether or not carried in ships under the American flag. At the same time, the dramatic growth of America's world-wide role was increasingly symbolized by the rapid changes and growth in the United States Navy. As America entered the next phase of its maritime development, it did so in a context dominated by world war.

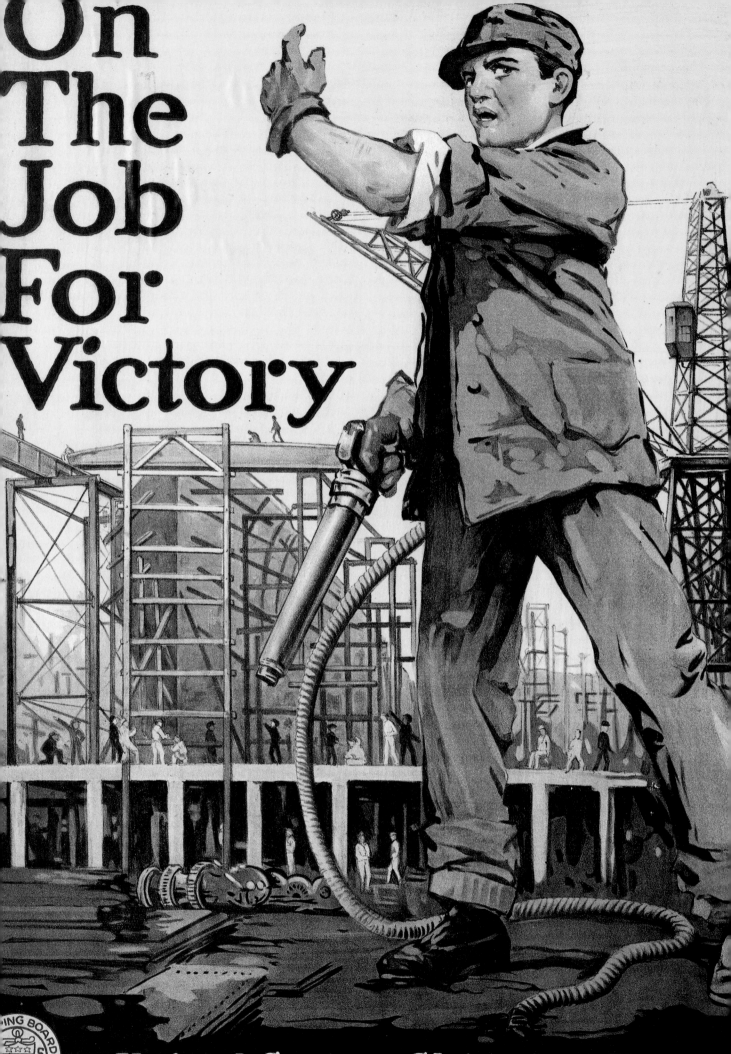

On
The
Job
For
Victory

United States Shipping Board
Emergency Fleet Corporation

CHAPTER 13

World War I

ORLD WAR I HAD AN enormous impact on America's maritime industries and enterprises. In just months, the conflict created extraordinary opportunities for growth not experienced since the 1850s. When the outbreak of hostilities in the summer of 1914 seriously disrupted traditional North Atlantic shipping networks and delivery systems, American vessels rapidly and lucratively filled the gaps. During the years of neutrality, Congress passed legislation conducive to American shipping, and once the United States declared war and mobilized its economy, the government assembled a mercantile fleet of such enormity as to alter the whole structure of international shipping. An extraordinary extension of commerce through new oceanic trading routes accompanied the wartime rise of American sea power. By the end of 1918, the United States Merchant Marine had grown from a position of insignificance to one second in ranking only to that of Great Britain. The growth was hardly limited to commercial shipping; simultaneously, the *sine qua non* of the nation's oceanic commerce, the United States Navy, received an unprecedented boost in support, securing both presidential and congressional commitments to build to a level not merely second in the world, but superior to that of all nations. Shipbuilding and shipping, both mercantile and naval, were among America's greatest wartime enterprises, and were carried on at unheard of, almost revolutionary, levels. Not least of all, the growth of the nation's naval and mercantile strength played an important part in shaping American foreign policy as the nation sought to exert its influence as a world power.

On the job for victory, the watch phrase for the U.S. Shipping Board's Emergency Fleet Corporation, is epitomized in this morale-building poster by an unidentified artist. With his pneumatic rivet gun, the shipyard riveter was the industrial hero of America's unprecedented shipbuilding effort during World War I. (M.S.M. 58.688.8; Claire White-Peterson photo)

Some of these developments had preceded the war's outbreak in Europe. A powerful navy, one complementary to the nation's growing international position, had been in the works for three decades. Most recently, Presidents Theodore Roosevelt and William Howard Taft had strongly supported extensive naval construction. Woodrow Wilson, however, viewed naval growth quite differently, and for a short period it appeared that the navy would stagnate under his administration.

At heart an antimilitarist at odds with the Mahanian theory of a world perpetually at war for control of the global marketplace, Wilson initially sought to separate himself from the saber-rattling of his presidential predecessors. He envisioned a stable and orderly world, run not by gunboat diplomacy among competing expansionist industrial powers, but rather governed by the supremacy of law and reason and the efficacy of the bargaining process. His appointment of Josephus Daniels as secretary of the navy emphasized this vision. Daniels strongly supported a policy of American neutrality, and when war broke out in late July 1914, he turned a deaf ear to the efforts of the Mahanians, the Navy League, and other big-navy advocates to substantially increase the navy's fighting capability. Daniels and Wilson saw the escalation of European war preparedness as a product of unbridled imperialistic and militaristic thinking, a mindset that had to be eliminated from the conduct of world affairs.

In the face of these strongly held views, Wilson's and Daniels's conversion in 1915 and 1916 to a policy of preparedness and to the construction of a navy "second to none" seemed quite remarkable. In retrospect, however, this dramatic change in policy reflected not a revision of Wilson's world view, but a shift in the means of attaining the end he sought so passionately–a Christian commonwealth of nations. The behavior of the belligerents in the first two years of the war, and their refusal to consent to arbitration and conform to the peace-seeking model Wilson championed, had soured the president and convinced him that only by taking an active part in the war, and by superintending the peace that followed, could America "in truth," as he expressed it, "show the way." Consequently, Wilson turned to a strong military with its implied–or apparent–capability of forcing conformity to law and reason in his effort to rid the world of instability and disorder. Once con-

vinced of the need for a strategic change, Wilson, a born crusader, committed himself to military expansion with extraordinary zeal.

When President Wilson signed the joint Congressional resolution declaring that a state of war existed between the United States and Germany on 6 April 1917, the prospect for an Allied victory looked bleak. Distancing the United States from the Allies, the resolution defined American participation in the war as an "Associated Power," not participating in the Allied war aims. Although President Wilson had failed to have the United States serve as the impartial arbiter at a peace conference in 1915-16, he wanted to cooperate with the Allies only to the extent of halting German militarism and defeating the U-boat threat. The Wilson administration was willing to commit itself to the war against the Central Powers only to the degree that it served America's own interests and contributed to achieving a stronger political position for achieving Wilson's long-range vision of international peace.

At that point in the war, U-boat successes were at their wartime peak, and the losses in Allied shipping exceeded the industrial capacity to replace them. While losses slowly declined from the April peak, they still held at the level of about 500,000 tons a month, while the projected capacity of Allied shipyards to produce new vessels was not more than 130,000 tons a month. As the German people increasingly felt the slow effects of the Allied economic blockade, German leaders felt justified in returning a harsh response to it. The U-boat campaign left the British people only a few weeks supply of grain, ten days stock of sugar, and a very serious shortage of oil. If German attacks had cut further into Britain's oil supply, the Admiralty seriously considered the possibility of ordering the Grand Fleet to operate at half speed and to cut back on antisubmarine operations. On land, the German defeat of the French Aisne and Champagne offenses created mutiny in the French army and, in Flanders, the British army was suffering huge casualties. On the eastern front, the German army's defeat of the Russian offensive in July was soon followed by the November Revolution and a separate peace for Russia at Brest-Litovsk the following year. At the end of 1917, the Germans had also defeated the Italians in the Caporetto campaign, capturing the entire area northeast of Venice. In virtually every area, the Central Powers seemed to have the upper hand.

The U.S. Navy
Goes to War

As a neutral, the United States did not have full knowledge of the military and naval situation in Europe and had made no firm plans as to how American forces might participate. While waiting to make detailed arrangements with the Allied powers, the U.S. Navy's first reaction was to use its contingency plan for war with Germany, "War Plan Black," but this plan was drafted on the idea that the German High Seas Fleet had appeared in the Caribbean and had to be defeated by the American Battle Fleet. The plan was not designed to deal with the submarine threat to merchant shipping that was actually taking place. In the Pacific, "War Plan Orange" focused on the defense and fortification of Guam as the centerpiece of American strategy in the Pacific. Despite newspaper reports that suggested that Japan, while allied by treaty to Great Britain, might actually be in league with Germany, the Wilson administration was very careful to do nothing provocative. At the same time, the United States was not optimistic about the ability of the Allies to win the war. Peering toward the future, American leaders imagined that they could easily find themselves fighting alone, facing an enemy threat on three sides, from Germany, Japan, and Mexico. In the short term, however, the naval priorities for the U. S. were to protect the coast of the United States and its possessions and to secure the safety of American cargo and passengers on the high seas.

The submarine was the greatest threat, both in European waters and in America. The appearance of *U-53*, as well as the voyage of the commercial submarine *Deutschland* to Baltimore and New London in 1916, clearly showed German capacity to cross the Atlantic and to mount a submarine offensive along the East Coast of the United States and in the Caribbean. Rumors were rife of German submarine and raider activities in the West Indies and in South American waters. In 1917, the United States Navy had no experience in antisubmarine warfare and had to depend upon what American naval men could learn from the British, but that had to await formal connections with the Royal Navy. From the outset, it was clear that the practical issues dictated that the U. S. Navy would have to act in concert with the Royal Navy in a way that

involved not only cooperation and coordination, but areas of subordination. Many American naval officers found this difficult to accept and continued to resent it long afterwards. Without exact knowledge of either the war situation or the methods and plans to combat it, the U.S. Navy's first war moves were to concentrate the U.S. Battle Fleet in the lower portion of Chesapeake Bay and to augment the patrolling activities of the Caribbean Squadron in order to protect the Panama Canal. In addition, orders were sent out to begin installing submarine nets and other obstructions to thwart an enemy attack on American ports.

From Britain's point of view in early 1917, the U.S. Navy could make the best contribution to the naval war by maintaining one squadron to attack any surface raiders that escaped the blockade in European waters, maintaining another squadron that protected Allied shipping on the east coast of South America from the River Plate to Europe, providing destroyers to operate antisubmarine patrols from a base in Ireland, providing patrols to protect the Panama Canal and to prevent Germany from developing bases in the Caribbean area, and maintaining its Asiatic Squadron on station while the Royal Navy withdrew from Asia for operations in European waters.

With the declaration of war, the U.S. Navy expanded its recruiting efforts. During the war, naval enlistment increased nearly eight-fold, from 65,777 to a high of 497,030 men and women in active and reserve service. In addition, all U.S. Coast Guardsmen and their vessels were transferred to the navy for the duration of the war. Their first war action occurred at 4:00 A.M. on 6 April 1917–the very day the transfer took place–when four Coast Guard cutters embarked 165 soldiers to assist in seizing 23 German merchant ships in New York Harbor for internment.

The first formal meeting between American and Allied naval representatives for discussions on American participation took place at Hampton Roads, Virginia, and in Washington, D.C., 10-13 April 1917. In this series of meetings, it was clear that the primary interest of the United States was to protect its own coasts and, then to serve in an adjunct role with both the Royal

Navy and the French Navy, but after detailed discussions and some initial hesitation American officials accepted the British proposals.

For the first time in its history, the United States agreed to undertake portions of specific naval responsibilities with another country, dividing up precise regions of the sea for American operations in a manner that would become much more common later in the century. In the North Atlantic, a U.S. Navy squadron was maintained from Cape Sable to longitude 5° west and then south to latitude 20° north. In the South Atlantic, the area was along the Brazilian coast between latitude 5° south to latitude 35° south and as far out as longitude 30° west. In the Pacific, the United States took responsibility for the area stretching from the border with Canada all the way south to Colombia. In the Caribbean, the U. S. Navy patrolled the Gulf of Mexico and Central America as far south as the border with Colombia and east to Jamaica and the Virgin Islands. The potential threats in the Caribbean were German submarines, surface raiders, and the Etappe vessels supplying them. Although this area never saw an important battle during the First World War, the U.S. believed that the protection of trade was of the highest importance. In the years 1917-19, more than 5,600 merchant ships passed through the Panama Canal, carrying an estimated 21,400,000 tons of cargo. Of particular importance for the Allied war effort were cargoes of oil from Mexico and nitrates from Chile that also passed through the Caribbean. On average, an estimated 800,000 tons of shipping sailed from the Caribbean every month in 1918, with nearly 20 percent of it using the Yucatan Channel between Cuba and Mexico, making that area a potential hunting ground for U-boats.

Given the range of German naval activities in 1914-15, it was necessary and prudent for the United States and the Allies to prepare against German naval threats on a worldwide basis, but the most critical situation at the moment was the battle with the submarine being fought three thousand miles away in the Eastern Atlantic. In fact, the ability of the United States to relieve the Royal Navy of responsibility in distant areas was an important contribution that allowed the British to concentrate their assets on other areas, particularly the U-boat problem. Upon it rested Britain's immediate future and the main bulwark of Allied

naval defense. This threat most concerned the American ambassador in London, Walter Hines Page. In Washington, Assistant Secretary of the Navy Franklin Roosevelt, more than others, had seen the importance of responding promptly to Page's request that Washington immediately send an American admiral to London and to support sending American destroyers.

In response, Rear Admiral William S. Sims arrived in England on 10 April and began meeting with Admiralty officials. At first, the British were reluctant to reveal the true depth of the crisis to Sims. No one in the United States had any idea of its seriousness, and the information had been withheld from the British public. Insisting on having complete information in order to work effectively with the Royal Navy, Sims was astounded to learn just how desperate the situation really was. He was deeply shocked when the First Sea Lord, Admiral Jellicoe, told him that, at that moment, the Royal Navy could see no solution to the U-boat problem.

Officials in Washington tended to discount Sims's reports as the exaggerated views of an on-scene commander who had lost the broad perspective and become overly attached to the British viewpoint. It took a long time for Sims to overcome this reaction and to convince Washington that the situation was really very urgent. At the outset, the most critical need was for destroyers, the type of ship that the British had found most useful in countering U-boats.

Responding to the plea for American naval ships in Europe, on 24 April 1917 Commander Joseph K. Taussig sailed with the six destroyers of Destroyer Division Eight from Boston for Queenstown (now Cobh), Ireland. Naval artist Bernard Gribble captured the evocative moment of their arrival on 4 May 1917 in the most famous American naval painting from the war, *The Return of the Mayflower*. When the American ships arrived at Queenstown, the Royal Navy's commander in chief on the coast of Ireland, Vice-Admiral Sir Lewis Bayly, signaled Taussig to ask when the six American ships would be ready for war service after their arduous transatlantic passage. Taussig replied in a message that the U.S. Navy's destroyermen have continued to quote as an expression of their own spirit: "We are ready now, sir, that is as soon as we finish refueling. Of course, you know how destroyers are–always wanting something

done to them. But this is war, and we are ready to make the best of things and go to sea immediately."

The Royal Navy warmly welcomed the American ships, but they were only six destroyers, and many more were needed. Sims continued to press for additional ships until, by the end of August 1917, there were 35 American destroyers at Queenstown, along with two destroyer tenders to support them. As American ships and men arrived in Europe, they fell under Admiral Sims as the Commander, U.S. Naval Forces Operating in European Waters. By mid-November 1918, the United States Navy had 368 ships in Europe, including 128 submarine chasers and 85 auxiliary ships, 70,000 men and 5,000 officers. In addition to the ships, 23 naval aviation stations–30 percent of the total number of Allied naval air stations–were established along the French Atlantic coast, the Irish coast, and in England, Flanders, and Italy, with 18,000 enlisted men and 1,300 officers.

In terms of overall Allied naval operations in European waters, the United States Navy's contribution was small, but not negligible. At the height of the American contribution to the war effort in 1918, the U.S. Navy provided 14 percent of the destroyers, 5 percent of the submarines, and 3 percent of the patrol craft in British and Eastern

The arrival of six U.S. Navy destroyers in British waters on 4 May 1917 marked a turning point in Allied naval fortunes during the war. As a symbolic commitment of U.S. naval forces, and an initial complement of U.S. Navy escort craft for the protection of supply and troop convoys, Commander Joseph Taussig's Destroyer Division Eight was more significant than its numbers would warrant. Soon after the incident, artist Bernard Gribble commemorated their arrival in his monumental painting, The Return of the Mayflower, *which depicts British fishermen saluting the American destroyermen. (Courtesy U.S. Naval Academy Museum)*

Atlantic waters. In the Mediterranean, the U.S. contributed 2 percent of the destroyers and 8 percent of the patrol craft. American naval aviators, who flew 22,000 maritime reconnaissance and combat missions in Europe, comprised nearly 25 percent of the total number of Allied naval fliers. The United States provided almost 40 percent of the coastal escorts in French coastal waters, 30 percent of the minesweeping forces in French waters, and about 30 percent of the cruisers and destroyers used to escort convoys of Allied merchant shipping on the North Atlantic.

To assist in the command of these widely spread

GEE!! I WISH I WERE A MAN

I'd JOIN The NAVY

Howard Chandler Christy. 1918

NAVAL RESERVE

OR COAST GUARD

Women Join the U.S. Navy

To challenge the manhood and pique the imagination of potential recruits, Howard Chandler Christy depicted one of his popular "Christy Girls" on this 1918 poster. A New York art teacher best known as a portraitist, Christy first received public attention in 1898, when *Scribner's* and *Leslie's Weekly* magazines used his illustrations to accompany their reports on the Spanish-American War. Later, his illustrations for *Scribner's* would feature the striking Christy Girl, who, like Charles Dana Gibson's "Gibson Girl," reflected the period ideal of young womanhood—much more independent and athletic than her Victorian mother.

In spite of what this poster implies, women in 1918 did not need to wish they were men in order to contribute to the war effort. Women had served in the Navy Nurse Corps since 1908, and on 19 March 1917—eighteen days before the U.S. entered the war—the U.S. Navy authorized the enlistment of women in the Naval Reserves on a volunteer basis. By 1 December 1918 there were 11,275 navy "yeomanettes"– officially yeoman (F), for female—as well as 305 "marinettes" in the Marine Corps. These women were generally assigned as stenographers, typists, and clerks, relieving men for field service. Navy Secretary Josephus Daniels, a proponent of women's suffrage, was proud to claim that the navy paid men and women equally for equal work. But the entire yeoman (F) force was released from service by the summer of 1919 as the navy demobilized.

Civilian women also did their part by replacing the absent men in aircraft and munitions factories and other essential industries. These new, nontraditional roles for women helped to accelerate the suffrage movement, which would culminate in 1920 when women won the right to vote in the United States.

This poster, and those prepared for the Shipping Board's Emergency Fleet Corporation, represent a large-scale contribution by American graphic artists to the war effort, like a similar poster campaign in Great Britain. In April 1917 the popular artist Charles Dana Gibson persuaded the administration of the need to improve recruiting posters, and as a result George Creel asked him to create and direct the Division of Pictorial Publicity of Creel's Committee on Public Information. Under Gibson's direction, with the assistance of F.D. Casey, art editor of *Collier's* magazine, 279 members of the Society of Illustrators created 1,438 different poster images for army and navy recruitment, the Shipping Board, the Liberty Loan committees, and the Food Administration. The artists volunteered their services, and on Friday evenings the New York artists would meet with Gibson at Keen's Chop House to discuss their work. The large, colorful products of this effort convey the Wilson administration's determination to unify the country in a patriotic undertaking. They also convey more subtle messages of changing times. Creel likened the effort to an international billboard battle, won emphatically, he asserted, by the United States.

(M.S.M. 93.135.1; Claire White-Peterson photo)

naval forces, Sims organized a headquarters in London that he divided into several subsections. Of these sections, the most unusual was the Planning Section, the first of its kind for a senior operational commander in the U.S. Navy. It was the intellectual center of the headquarters, developing plans for future operations, critiquing current methods, and studying problems of current interest. In essence, the London headquarters staff was designed to be the advanced operational headquarters of the U.S. Navy Department. Naval officials in Washington dealt directly with Sims, and Sims coordinated and directed the forty-five bases under his command as well as attending to the full range of details involved in Anglo-American naval relations.

Throughout the war, American naval leaders were frustrated by what they felt was the Royal Navy's ad hoc approach to the war and the tendency of British officers to regard the United States Navy as merely a source of men and equipment to use at their whim. The establishment of the Naval Planning Section in London was one attempt to improve this situation. For the same reason, in December 1917 the United States strongly supported the establishment of an Allied Naval Council, consisting of the various naval ministers and chiefs of naval staff who met from time to time to watch over the general conduct of the naval war and to ensure cooperation.

The most important American bases were at Brest, Queenstown, Gibraltar, Inverness, and Invergordon. Queenstown was the key base at the western approaches to the English Channel for protecting transatlantic merchant shipping to and from the United States. Brest, France, handled the arrivals and departures of most American troop transports to Europe. Gibraltar was the base for American forces convoying merchant shipping in the Mediterranean. And at Inverness and Invergordon, on the Moray Firth in eastern Scotland, were stationed the American forces devoted to the North Sea Mine Barrage. Smaller American bases included six American submarines at Berehaven that helped to guard the entrance to the Irish Sea; cross-Channel troop transport support at Southampton, England; and submarine-chaser bases at Corfu in the Adriatic and in the Azores.

American battleships under the command of Admiral Sims constituted 9 percent of the major forces with the Grand Fleet. For quite a long time, however, U.S. naval leaders in Washington had been reluctant to send their battleships to join the Grand Fleet. They objected strongly that it would require dividing the U.S. Battle Fleet, thereby violating one of the dicta of naval strategy that Mahan had long asserted. For many months, the U.S. Battle Fleet stood ready in the western Atlantic, poised to react to the appearance of the German High Seas fleet in North American waters or, if necessary, to react to the Japanese in the Pacific. It was not until November 1917 that the policy changed. With an easing in Japanese-American relations, the U.S. Navy Department felt freer to act. In the end, they reasoned that, by sending a division of battleships, American sailors could maintain their morale by active service in the war zone, obtain useful training, and also show the value of building such vessels in the future. The ships that joined were not the newest American vessels. Most modern American battleships burned fuel oil, which was unavailable in wartime Britain, so the British had requested that the U.S. send coal-burning ships. In mid-December 1917, the coal-burning American battleships *New York, Delaware, Wyoming,* and *Florida* joined the Grand Fleet at Scapa Flow to become the Grand Fleet's Sixth Battle Squadron, later to be joined by the *Texas.* The officers and men of the American battleships had many new methods to learn, and were quickly incorporated into the British system of command, control, and communication. The American battleships, like their British counterparts, saw no battle action with the German Fleet in this period, but they were an active part of the fleet and were present at Scapa Flow to receive the German Battle Fleet at the end of the war. In August 1918, the oil-burning battleships *Utah, Nevada,* and *Oklahoma* arrived at Berehaven, Ireland. Armed with fourteen-inch guns, they were poised to protect convoys from an attack by a large German surface raider or battle cruiser breaking out from the North Sea. The U.S. Navy sent a tanker and a tug to support the battleships for this duty, but no German surface raiders appeared.

One of the military challenges in World War I, both on land and at sea, was to make the fighting decisive. Often, apparently sound plans and good ideas did not work in practice, resulting in stalemate or an outright slaughter of men for no discernible gain. Typically, many Americans were

Belching coal smoke, the battleship New York *demonstrates her twenty-one-knot speed. Laid down at the New York Navy Yard in 1911 and launched in 1912, the 573-foot* New York *was commissioned in April 1914 and immediately served as flagship for the U.S. Navy fleet occupying Veracruz, Mexico. After the U.S. entered the war against Germany in 1917 the* New York *crossed the Atlantic as flagship of Battleship Division Nine, arriving at Scapa Flow in December 1917. With her ten fourteen-inch guns and crew of 1,042, the* New York *helped augment the Royal Navy fleet in the North Sea. Blockade and escort duty, and an occasional brush with a U-boat, occupied the* New York *until 21 November 1918, when the German High Seas Fleet entered the Firth of Forth to surrender to the combined British and American fleet. Photograph by Enrique Muller, ca. 1914. (M.S.M. 49.218)*

keen to find technological solutions to this problem, and a variety of inventions were suggested. In the United States, such scientific work for the navy was dealt with through two boards founded during the war. One was the Naval Consulting Board, established in July 1915 and chaired by Thomas A. Edison, which received inventions and suggestions from the general public. The other was the National Research Council, established in April 1916 under the National Academy of Sciences. A major interest of both these organizations was in submarine detection. During the war years, much work was undertaken at Nahant, Massachusetts, and New London, Connecticut, on underwater sound and hydrophone listening devices. Despite initial hopes to the contrary, passive sound receivers proved relatively inefficient.

Experiments suggested that the best hope might lie in creating a method to receive echoes from transmissions of sound underwater, but no successful working system was put into operation during the war.

Other American naval innovations included the railway battery, designed by the Navy Bureau of Ordnance, which mounted a fourteen-inch naval gun on a railroad car. The U.S. Navy sent five such mobile railway batteries to France, where they fired shells that reached far behind enemy lines in such famous battles on the western front as Verdun and the Meuse-Argonne offensive.

Another American development was the subma-

The submarine chaser was a distinctive American naval contribution during the First World War. Armed with both surface guns and depth-charge launchers, and powered with three gasoline engines, these fast patrol craft were designed to hunt U-boats in coastal waters. With major shipyards fully committed to wartime construction, the U.S. Navy settled on a 110-foot wooden design that could be built in small shipyards. Construction began in March 1917, and 440 were completed by February 1919. A total of 221 saw service in European waters, while the rest were intended for coastal deployment against U-boats in U.S. waters. Here, the unarmed SC-414 shows off her speed shortly after her launch at College Point, New York, near the end of the war. (Negative 1069F, © Rosenfeld Collection, Mystic Seaport Museum, Inc.)

rine chaser, a 110-foot vessel with a maximum speed of eighteen knots, designed to hunt U-boats and destroy them with depth charges. With the enthusiastic support of Assistant Secretary of the Navy Franklin D. Roosevelt, the U.S. Navy built 440 submarine chasers during the war, 121 of which saw service under the U.S. flag in European waters, while 100 were given to the French Navy. The remainder served on the eastern seaboard of the United States.

Franklin Roosevelt was also one of the earliest and most enthusiastic supporters of the North Sea Mine Barrage, a joint Anglo-American project using a new antenna mine developed by the U.S. Navy's Bureau of Ordnance to prevent German submarines from leaving the North Sea. Envisioned as a belt of explosives up to 35 miles wide, stretching for 250 miles across the North Sea, the Mine Barrage required a huge logistical effort to ship 56,611 of the total 70,263 mines from the United States to be laid by both American and British minelayers. Completed in the last six months of the war, it cost about $40,000,000. Naval historian Paul Halpern has described the Northern Barrage as typically American, involving "tremendous effort, great enthusiasm, much money, and considerable ingenuity directed toward implementing a huge project, bold in scale." The war ended before the U.S. Navy could implement similar plans to bottle up Austrian submarines in the Adriatic, make a barrier across the Aegean, and close the straits between Sicily and the coast of North Africa at Cape Bon. The enthusiasm lent to this difficult endeavor, which ultimately proved only minimally successful, was a natural outlet of the American tendency to put energy into projects potentially solvable through technological means.

Americans had long expected a German submarine attack in North American waters, and it finally came when *U-151* arrived on 22 May 1918 and laid mines off both Chesapeake Bay and Delaware Bay, sinking ten vessels over the next ten days in the area between Norfolk and New York. This single U-boat's activity created a massive reaction in America, including hysterical reports that U-boats were about to launch seaplanes for an air attack on New York City. In preparation for attack, New York imposed a nighttime blackout for thirteen days and even erected air-raid sirens. At sea, the U.S. Navy immediately initiated coastal convoys in the area between Rhode Island and Cape Hatteras, while aircraft and dirigibles increased their patrols in the same area. In mid-July 1918, a mine laid by *U-156* sank the largest American warship lost in the war, the armored cruiser *San Diego*, which went down just ten miles southwest of Fire Island, near the entrance to New York Bay.

Four additional German submarines crossed the Atlantic during the summer of 1918. During their patrols in American waters, U-boats sank ninety-three vessels totaling 166,907 tons, forty-five of which were American ships. German U-boats succeeded in shocking Americans by bringing the war to their very beaches, but in spite of the emotional impact the Germans did far less damage than had been earlier anticipated.

For all the enthusiasm put into its mammoth commitment, the U.S. Navy did not in the end play a dominating role in World War I. Once the United States entered the conflict in April 1917,

More than a century after Robert Fulton's experiments with submarine mines, and fifty years after their successful use during the Civil War, an extremely efficient form of mine was deployed to sink ships and submarines during World War I. The U.S. enthusiastically backed the North Sea Mine Barrage to seal off the exit from the North Sea with a 250-mile barrier comprising 70,000 mines anchored at depths of as much as 300 feet, and planned similar efforts in the Mediterranean. In this view, U.S. Navy sailors prepare to lay a group of mines. (80-G-1024926, Courtesy National Archives)

the task of aiding in the Allied war effort produced an almost immediate shift away from the capital shipbuilding program to one quite unlike that anticipated by most navalists. At the center of the controversy was the long-range policy of the Navy General Board and the first chief of naval operations, Admiral William S. Benson. Perpetuating old Mahanian principles, the admiral and the board firmly believed in the inevitability of American commercial expansion and the concomitant necessity for a powerful navy to counter the nation's more aggressive competitors in the marketplace. While Germany and Japan were seen as the most likely adversaries, these men also perceived a threat in the British navy.

Based on such perceptions, with its emphasis on competition in heavy ships, the American plan contained no provisions for countering the sub-

The **Pennsylvania-class** *battleship* **Arizona** *takes to the water on 19 June 1915, in a successful launch at the New York Navy Yard in Brooklyn. Laid down in 1913 and commissioned in 1916, the 608-foot Arizona was equipped with twelve fourteen-inch guns and 31,500-horsepower steam turbine engines that could drive her at twenty-one knots. Her crew quarters were considered especially spacious and well ventilated. Because fuel oil for her oil-fired boilers was in short supply in England, the Arizona would spend the war on U.S. coastal patrol, only crossing the Atlantic to show off American naval might in European waters after the war ended. (© Rosenfeld Collection, Mystic Seaport Museum, Inc.)*

marine war then dominating the North Atlantic, and was consequently unsuited to meet the pressing demands for shipping that arose once America entered the war in April 1917. President Wilson himself soon comprehended, through his major naval representative in London, Rear Admiral Sims, that the emergency in shipping was far more critical than anyone had realized. The overwhelming majority of the vessels lost were British. In fact, U-boats were sinking one of every four deep-sea vessels clearing British ports, and only 10 percent of those sunk were being replaced. Consequently, food stocks in Great Britain were reduced to only a few weeks' supply, and access to oil, the most critical of naval stores, was dangerously limited. The situation had deteriorated to such a degree that the British Admiralty virtually conceded its inability to counter the crisis.

Given these conditions, the critical need, as Sims pointed out, was not American battleships, but ships to counter Germany's submarine campaign against the American supply line to Europe. Sims called for the immediate suspension of big-ship construction and urged that available yards be converted to the building of antisubmarine vessels, merchant ships to convey cargoes and troops to Europe, and escort vessels to ensure their safe passage. This was a policy requiring cooperation, not competition; it called for coordination with, and even subordination to, Allied maritime needs. With some reluctance, Wilson accepted Sims's judgment over that of Benson. Construction on capital ships was suspended in May 1917 and replaced by plans for 250 destroyers and 400 subchasers. At the same time, the assembly of a massive merchant fleet was inaugurated. This decision to shift U.S. naval forces to the protection of cargoes and troops proved particularly valuable when the Bolshevik Revolution in the fall of 1917 resulted in Russia's withdrawal from the war, and German forces were transferred to the western front.

Although a few vessels were assigned to the Allied intervention in Siberia and North Russia, and others continued to support American forces occupying certain Caribbean nations, inevitably the U.S. Navy's major emphasis had shifted to the antisubmarine war being fought with Great Britain in the North Atlantic. While it seemed to take an eternity to organize and appeared to some an inadequate use of the nation's naval capability, the escort sys-

Rear Admiral William S. Sims accompanies Assistant Secretary of the Navy Franklin Delano Roosevelt in 1918. Both Sims and Roosevelt frequently differed with Navy Secretary Daniels, but the combination succeeded. William S. Sims (1858-1936) was born in Canada and graduated from the Naval Academy in 1880. Beginning his service in a sailing vessel of the "old" wooden navy, Sims became a leading gunnery expert in the "new" steel navy and a protege of President Theodore Roosevelt. Before the war he was serving as president of the U.S. Naval Institute. Sent to England in 1917, Sims was the leading proponent of the convoy system that operated so successfully despite German U-boats. He encouraged the U.S. to dispatch destroyers to assist the Allies in British waters, and then he served as commander of U.S. naval forces operating in European waters. An effective and outspoken officer, Sims retired in 1922. (Courtesy Library of Congress)

"Ship of Fools"– The SS *Oscar II*

One of the most controversial, if not bizarre, nautical undertakings of World War I was the voyage of the SS *Oscar II*, the passenger liner chartered in late 1915 by Henry Ford as part of the auto wizard's remarkable effort to stop the war. The episode was an outcome of Ford's inveterate pacifism and his sincere, but naive, belief that his legendary formulas for business success could be applied with comparable results to world affairs. Arguing that engineers like himself would "mould the political, social, industrial, and moral mass into a sound and shapely whole," Ford was convinced that the international application of his concepts of business efficiency would eradicate war and revolution and produce a world that functioned as smoothly as the engine of one of his model T's.

As one who detested conflict, Ford enthusiastically supported President Wilson's initial policy of neutrality. And he stood firm in that position even when a German submarine sank the *Lusitania* on 7 May 1915. As Ford saw it, those who had gone down with the ship had been warned not to sail on her and had foolishly assumed the risk. However, Wilson's belligerent response to the Germans distressed the Dearborn magnate, and when the president for all practical purposes tied the nation to the Allies by supporting them commercially and financially, Ford broke with Wilson and launched his own private peace campaign.

Convinced that the warring powers were incapable of reaching a truce on their own, Ford proposed to sail with other pacifists to Europe in an effort to create a commission of neutral nations that would arbitrate the conflict in a way acceptable to the belligerents. Many people thought Ford was joking, but he was dead serious, and President Wilson's dismissal of the idea fazed him not one iota. On 15 November 1915, he made his intentions public: "We're going to get the boys out of the trenches before Christmas. I've chartered a ship, and some of us are going to Europe."

The vessel Ford spoke of was the *Oscar II*, a small steamer of 750-passenger capacity chartered from the rather astonished Danish-owned Scandinavian-American Lines. A luxury ship, the *Oscar II* had been fitted out to entertain Scandinavian royalty; but was also known as one of the slowest steamers on the North Atlantic. Ford's prescription to end the war with his one-stack "Peace Ship" was remarkable, to say the least, and initial press reaction reflected that.

But the incredulity gradually shifted to criticism. Did this captain of industry think he could build world peace much as he built an automobile? Quickly, the *Oscar II* became known as the "loon ship" and the "ship of fools," its passengers "an aggregation of neurotics."

Undaunted, even by the fervid pleas of his family, Ford and a group of 141 like-minded pacifists (plus fifty-four reporters and four photographers) sailed from New York for neutral Scandinavia on 4 December 1915. The trip was a disaster from the beginning. The delegation's cohesiveness was badly rent, first by a severe storm at sea, and then by news received over the wireless of Wilson's adoption of a war-preparedness policy. In the course of the crossing, the *Oscar II* was intercepted by the British Royal Navy and detained for twenty-four hours on the charge that the ship contained contraband. Finally, Ford contracted a severe cold which intensified when the liner berthed in the sub-zero temperatures of Christiana, Norway. Rapidly losing his enthusiasm for the venture, Ford abruptly returned to the United States only one week after reaching Europe. The shaken conferees proceeded without him but were unable to achieve their goals of a mediated peace; not a single

United States declared war he abandoned his pacifism, lent his support to the president, and turned his plants to the war effort without concern for profit. Interestingly, while the overwhelming contribution of the Ford Motor Company was in its production of engines for trucks, ambulances, and airplanes, the single largest war contract let to Ford was for 112 submarine chasers, a new model called the "Eagle." Assembly-line genius though he was, Ford was unable to convert his plants rapidly enough to complete the contract, and only one such subchaser was actually commissioned before the Armistice, giving the lie to the jingle used to motivate the workers, "An Eagle a Day Keeps the Kaiser Away." Another nautical brainstorm of Ford's was his proposal for a "pee-wee" submarine powered by a Ford motor, but these one-man "mosquito" subs did not get beyond the drawing board.

Henry Ford (1863-1947) glances toward the camera as he and other peace proponents depart from New York Harbor aboard the Oscar II *in December 1915. Motivated by his hatred of "war profiteers," Ford financed the* Oscar II *voyage. The international mix of pacifists, feminists, students, educators, and journalists on board, with their lectures and discussion groups, led some to refer to the vessel as a "floating Chautauqua" after that site of progressive meetings. Frustrated by the lack of response from the warring nations, Ford soon lost interest in the mission, and once the U.S. declared war on Germany he turned his factories to military work, including the construction of submarine chasers. (From the Collections of Henry Ford Museum & Greenfield Village)*

neutral country was willing to offer its official patronage to the delegation. Months went by with deteriorating results. Ford's interest continued to wane, and the peace mission was moribund by early 1917.

Although Henry Ford had sworn earlier that no plant of his would ever be used for military purposes, when the

Secretary of the Navy Josephus Daniels decorates Seaman Ray Messanelli on board the U.S. minesweeper Heron. Daniels (1862-1948), a North Carolina newspaperman and Democratic party boss, was criticized for his lack of experience when President Wilson named him navy secretary in 1913, but he served ably throughout the Wilson administration, moving from pacifist to big-navy proponent. Many naval officers felt Daniels was too solicitous of enlisted personnel, but his course through contentious waters was notably successful. (Courtesy Library of Congress)

tem adopted by the U.S. Navy to protect American convoys of men and materials helped to challenge and then break the formidable barrier that Germany had in place when America entered the war. The deployment of American destroyers, aided by growing numbers of small American subchasers assigned to the coastal areas, assisted in taming the U-boat menace. Improved depth charges and listening devices added to the effectiveness of patrol and escort and underlined the navy's growing confidence in technological innovation. In truth, the need to combat the submarine menace produced more scientific research than any other wartime problem, and the navy, aware that a new era of warfare had arrived, was quick

to amass and coordinate the required resources.

The convoy system, when finally adopted, proved to be the final solution. The system was resisted at first by Secretary Daniels, who favored single-lane patrol coverage, and by Admiral Benson, who wanted to keep the navy's antisubmarine capabilities close to home to protect America's coasts, and who held that armed ships sailing alone would be adequate. Yet, by the end of 1917, 50 percent of all shipping was by convoy, and by war's end convoying, now routinely employed, had reduced ship losses to one-half of one percent. As Admiral Sims, always the foremost American supporter of the system, expressed it, convoying was "an unqualified success, and [one] to which the Germans devised no counter." Convoying's major attribute was its ability to reduce ship concentrations to small areas of the ocean, thereby enabling many congregations of vessels to completely escape detection; at the same time, when a convoy did attract submarines, the system offered the escort vessels the most effective means of destructive action against U-boats. In evaluating Anglo-American wartime naval cooperation, the convoying system was, the historian Michael Simpson observed, "the saviour of the whole coalition cause."

Another naval program of exceeding importance was the transportation of the American Expeditionary Force to France. At the war's outset, the navy had very few troop and cargo ships, no more than 94,000 tons total. By the war's end this branch of the navy, entitled the Cruiser and Transport Force, numbered 143 vessels, totaling 3,250,000 tons. By this means, 911,047 soldiers were ferried to France. And when even this number of ships proved insufficient to move American troops quickly to the war front, British troop carriers were engaged. British ships alone carried a million men to France. These troopships, given strong naval escort support and possessed of good speed, made voyage after voyage; by war's end only two troopships, both British and both westbound, had been sunk in this service.

While the Cruiser and Transport Force carried men to Europe, an entirely different branch, the Naval Overseas Transport Service, provided the European theater of war with supplies. At its peak, the Overseas Transport Service numbered 378 ships of 2,400,000 deadweight tons, and during the war carried 4,000,000 tons of supplies for the American Expeditionary Force and naval bases (including mines used for the North Sea Mine Barrage), 2,000,000 tons of coal, oil, and gasoline for military programs, and 350,000 tons of civilian cargoes for the United States Shipping Board. The fact that the war was concluded in 1918, two years shy of most expectations, can be laid in large part to the navy's successful employment of the antisubmarine and convoy system, the ferrying of nearly one-half of the American Expeditionary Force to France, and the successful maintenance of a supply line to the European theater.

The U.S. Shipping Board

Equally important to the American and Allied war effort were the merchant ships the navy was ordered to protect, ships to which the Wilson administration gave increasing priority. In what represented one of the greatest building projects ever conceived in the modern world, the nation's industrialists, under government contracts, set about assembling a fleet not only adequate to meet military needs, but capable of challenging Great Britain's maritime supremacy in international trade and shipping. This development represented not only a commitment to the war effort but, combined with the construction of a superior navy, was a major component of Wilson's grand strategy to strengthen America's world position by increasing its economic and military clout.

Foreign trade expansion, and a strong merchant marine to guarantee that, had been one of the central economic and philosophic planks of Wilson's candidacy for the presidency in 1912. But this desire for increased shipping capability as a means by which to secure foreign trade expansion was hardly the unique vision of the White House. With few exceptions, progressives of every political persuasion favored policies that would improve the nation's commercial competitiveness. Wilson added a world view that embodied shipping as a part of a whole. That whole concerned not only the strengthening of the domestic economy by providing outlets for its enormous surplus capacity, but envisioned America's acquisition of a favorable position in the world marketplace as a means to an even larger end—the creation of a world community based on liberal, capitalistic ideals. In essence, Wilson's hopes to create an orderly and stable world order, absent of imperialistic, militaristic, and revolutionary extremes and shaped in favor of a pro-American equilibrium, was based on the emerging power of the American political economy.

Wilson saw the post-Civil War decline of the American merchant marine as one of the major impediments to his overall objectives, and in his 1912 campaign he frequently addressed the issue. Without a great merchant marine, he argued, the United States could not take its rightful place in the world. Along with calls for tariff, banking, and business efficiency reforms,

Wilson's determination to halt the decline in the merchant marine became one of the four great planks of his political platform. To Wilson's satisfaction, tariff, banking, and business efficiency reforms were legislated very early in his presidency. The merchant marine issue was next on his agenda when it was forced abruptly and dramatically to center stage by the outbreak of World War I.

When fighting started in late July 1914, American foreign trade suffered seriously as the great bulk of the ocean's carriers, predominantly British and German ships, were withdrawn from North Atlantic service. The British vessels were diverted to critical military uses, while German ships sought refuge–many of them in American ports–from the all-powerful British navy. The crisis in shipping not only disrupted normal American oceanic trades, but also coincided with a record-breaking harvest in the States. The immediate reaction in America was panic, for on the eve of the war only 2 percent of the nation's foreign commerce was carried in American bottoms. All sectors, private as well as public, agreed that only government could move quickly enough to restore trade with Europe, trade constituting almost 80 percent of all of America's foreign commerce.

The result was the quick passage in August 1914 of a free-ships bill and a war-risk insurance measure. The former allowed for the registry under the American flag of foreign ships in foreign trade. The latter provided for governmental guarantees against losses due to war at sea, guarantees that the undercapitalized American insurance industry could not itself underwrite. Sensing the unwillingness of the private sector to take great risks without governmental backing, and wide-eyed at the prospects the war promised for capturing world markets vacated by the belligerents, Wilson and Secretary of the Treasury William Gibbs McAdoo backed a congressional bill to authorize government ownership and operation of ships. But they misjudged the tenor of the times. Their efforts ran up against extraordinary opposition–

One of just forty-four American oceangoing steamships built in 1912, the 313-foot Evelyn *steams along the New York waterfront. A. H. Bull & Company operated the* Evelyn *in their freight service between New York and Puerto Rico, which began in 1902, four years after Spain ceded Puerto Rico to the U.S. at the conclusion of the Spanish-American War. Merritt & Chapman Derrick & Wrecking Company photo. (M.S.M. 64.660.870)*

from shipowners and operators, who abhorred the plan as a form of state socialism, and from isolationists, who feared American war-zone shipping activity would compromise the nation's neutrality. When the initial shipping crisis abated in the late summer of 1914, no amount of argument would turn the opposition, and the measure was tabled for many months.

Critical to the opposition's success in defeating the plan to enhance governmental shipping capabilities was the growing realization in the private sector that American neutrality was good for American shipping. Government war-risk insurance emboldened shippers to enter the lucrative North Atlantic trade. The lack of adequate ocean tonnage was actually a boon to the owners and operators who were able to command extraordinary rates in a rapidly expanding marketplace, particularly with Allied nations. Chartering became quite active, and vessels that had been long idled in the prewar years were now at work. The free-ships bill aided greatly in this recovery; by the end of 1914 better than one-half of all American-owned vessels operating under foreign flags had been reregistered in the States. Remarkably, even with increased numbers of ships at sea, freight rates remained consistently high. For the first time in many years, American shipping was engaged at excellent profits in foreign trade. Unfazed by the government's concern that high freight rates were prejudicial to the interests of lesser-advantaged segments of the nation's export economy–agriculture, for example–and that the introduction of government ships would bring about greater equality of opportunity for those engaged in foreign trade, the private shipping sector jealously guarded its new prosperity. And its argument that prosperity in shipping would stimulate increased private maritime investment had its merits.

A good illustration of the newly invigorated interest in shipping was the creation in 1915 of the American International Corporation (AIC), which set about exporting and importing raw and manufactured products in American-built ships. A branch of the National City Bank of New York, American International's scope of activities was truly global. One of its first business transactions was to purchase, in partnership with W. R. Grace and Company, control of the Pacific Mail Steamship Company. On the verge of dissolution in 1915, Pacific Mail rebounded strongly with newly

created wartime business opportunities. The AIC now moved to form Latin American and Russian branches, acquired exclusive foreign selling rights for a number of American machine-tool builders, formed a corporation for the development of canal and railway projects in China, bought into the naval stores industry and tea importation business, began marketing sugar and construction machinery, and entered into the production and exportation of American steel. Simultaneously, in another joint venture, it purchased the New York Shipbuilding Corporation, owner of the nation's newest and largest shipyards, yards that boasted the size and the technology to build the biggest battleships, passenger liners, cargo ships, and river steamers.

The creation of the American International Corporation was a striking example of the new profitability of shipping and of its important relationship to the spectacular growth of American industry and enterprise during the years of American neutrality. It was understandable that American shipping companies considered the high profits gained during these years as only fitting after so many decades of moderate gain at best, and those companies were not pleased with any measure that would restrict their profits through government regulation or through competition in the form of government ships.

This opposition was overcome only when it became clear that the European war was far more threatening to American national interests than had been originally conceived. Within the context of the administration's preparedness program of 1915 and 1916, opposition to governmental shipping decreased steadily. As the probability of involvement in hostilities increased, it stood to reason that merchant vessels were necessary auxiliaries to the U.S. Navy. As Secretary McAdoo stressed, "A merchant marine is just as essential to the effectiveness of the Navy. . . as the guns upon the decks of our battleships!" Equally convincing in bringing the private sector around was the growing realization that an outbreak of fierce economic rivalries would likely follow the cessation of war in Europe. A "commercial war after the war" was a commonly heard prediction; nations dependent upon foreign trade, such as the United States, had best gird for that struggle by improving their transportation capabilities. Consequently, and coming from the same environment that produced the army and navy bills of June and

August 1916, the Shipping Act, signed by the President that very September, became an integral part of the nation's military and economic preparedness program.

The Shipping Act of 1916 represented a new direction of considerable significance. The act, passed for the purpose of "encouraging, developing, and creating a naval auxiliary and naval reserve," represented a clear understanding of new realities. The act also provided for the overall development of an efficient, scientifically managed foreign trade program under a new regulatory agency, the United States Shipping Board, the first ever created to oversee maritime affairs. If the private sector was unable to service trade routes critical to the nation's welfare, the Shipping Board was authorized to do so itself, with the stipulation, however, that any such lines would be vacated by the government within five years after the conclusion of war. Finally, the Shipping Act of 1916 authorized the Shipping Board to purchase, requisition, construct, and control vessels in time of national emergency. It was through this latter provision that the board sought to make its greatest wartime contribution.

The April 1917 creation of the Emergency Fleet Corporation, the shipbuilding arm of the Shipping Board, like the decision made the following month to divert naval construction to destroyers and subchasers, was a major administrative response to the crisis in shipping caused by the frightening success of Germany's submarines. The prospects that Germany would finally break the Allied blockade and starve both the war front and homefront into submission loomed large in the minds of many. The only alternative, as Wilsonians saw it, was to construct ships faster than U-boats could sink them. Efforts in this direction began with great fanfare, but soon developed serious hitches.

From the moment of its creation in September 1916, the Shipping Board experienced much difficulty in organizing its staff and setting about its business. Not until January 1917 was the board's membership finalized, and rancorously at that. This small advance was followed by a fratricidal conflict between the head of the Shipping Board, William Denman, and the head of the new Emergency Fleet Corporation, General George W. Goethals. Ostensibly a fight over wooden-ship versus steel-ship construction, the argument was also highly personal in character

U.S. Shipping Board Chairman Edward N. Hurley (right) and Emergency Fleet Corporation Director General Charles M. Schwab pose at the launch of two Emergency Fleet Corporation steamships in October 1918. Edward N. Hurley (1864-1933) rose from railroad fireman to traveling salesman to developer of the first pneumatic air drill. His Pneumatic Tool Company, organized in 1896, produced pneumatic rivet guns that revolutionized industries such as shipbuilding. A friend of Woodrow Wilson, Hurley served on the Federal Trade Commission and as part of Wilson's informal "War Cabinet." He acted as chairman of the U.S. Shipping Board from July 1917 to July 1919. Charles M. Schwab (1862-1939) was a self-taught metallurgist and expert on steel production, as well as a skilled labor negotiator, a combination that brought him the presidency of the Carnegie Steel Company in 1897. In 1901 he became the first president of U.S. Steel, then took over Bethlehem Steel and moved it into shipbuilding, amassing a large fortune in the process. Schwab served as director general of the Emergency Fleet Corporation from April to December 1918. Photo by Morris Rosenfeld. (Courtesy Library of Congress)

and was resolved only by Wilson's removal of both men in July. The president then gave full authority to Edward N. Hurley, an industrial magnate (he had pioneered in the development of riveting) and former head of the Federal Trade Commission. An acknowledged expert in the business efficiency movement and a strong advocate of increased foreign trade, Hurley salved the wounds, reorganized the effort, and began to put together the "bridge of ships" that would link America with the battlefront and sustain the fighting power of the Allies.

Hurley faced enormous obstacles, not the least of which was the situation in American shipbuilding. When Hurley took office, every shipway in the United States, of which there were 234, was occupied in construction. Of these, 70 percent were in use–or were designated for use–in naval construction, primarily of destroyers and subchasers, but the unfinished hulls of battleships and cruisers occupied quite a few of the shipways. The remainder of the nation's shipyards that were capable of building vessels in excess of 2,500 tons were tied up with contracts for foreign interests, namely, British, Norwegian, and French. To make matters worse, most contracts were for ocean liners, not cargo-carrying vessels. Taken together, the nation's yards would not be available for the Emergency Fleet Corporation's program for better than a full year.

Hurley's reaction caught the shipyards by surprise. Amidst much protest, particularly from the British, he issued an order in September 1917 commandeering all of America's merchant shipbuilding capacity. A total of 421 ships–3 million tons' worth–commissioned for private and foreign accounts, were taken into custody. The shipyards themselves were seized. Having now commandeered both the shipyards and the ships they were constructing, Hurley next requisitioned American ships already afloat, that is, all steel, oceangoing cargo and passengers ships of American registry in excess of 2,500 tons. The order covered, in sum, 657 ships. While private interests actually retained possession of their ships, both owners and vessels were put into the service and pay of the Shipping Board. By October 1917, virtually every vessel under the American flag or being built in American yards and capable of oceanic travel was pressed into war service.

While the Emergency Fleet ship-construction program was struggling to get on its feet, the Shipping Board augmented the fleet by forcing neutral maritime nations to divert their tonnage to the American and Allied cause. This was done for the most part by economic leverage. The move received strong British support. By denying neutral nations critical exports that could be secured only from the United States–for instance, foodstuffs–the Shipping Board, in conjunction with the War Trade Board and the Department of State, exerted enormous pressure on neutral nations. The British exercised their own leverage largely through their international monopoly on coal bunkers and stations. Thus, the Shipping Board acquired control of almost 2 million tons of ships, most notably 1,254,000 tons of Scandinavian steamers and sailing vessels that were placed under ninety-day charters. After often difficult and tense negotiations, another half-million tons was acquired from the Netherlands, and, by withholding much-needed steel, 150,000 tons from Japan. Additional tonnage was secured by inducing the Japanese to construct ships for the Shipping Board in exchange for steel plates. The Board also supplied steel to Chinese yards in exchange for new-built tonnage.

To this the Shipping Board added 638,000 tons of German ships laid up in American ports in August 1914 and seized by the U.S. government upon entering the war in 1917. Included among these ninety-one ships were the *Vaterland*, subsequently rechristened the *Leviathan*– at 52,117 deadweight tons the largest ship afloat–and eight other passenger liners, which were turned over to the navy for the transport of American military personnel to Europe. A few additional ships were acquired from the interned Austro-Hungarian fleet. All told, by requisition, seizure, and leverage, the Shipping Board added almost 9 million tons of vessels to American shipping. During 1917 and 1918 this fleet, aided by British ships–not the products of the trouble-ridden Emergency Fleet ship construction program– transported the American Expeditionary Force to France and kept it supplied.

That, however, was not the original plan. From the beginning, the intention was that the Emergency Fleet Corporation would build ships; fifteen million tons was the initial objective. Once this mighty armada was afloat, the argument went, it would overwhelm Germany's submarine campaign and quickly turn the tide in

The 950-foot Hamburg-America liner Vaterland *was the largest ship in the world when she arrived in New York on her maiden voyage in May 1914. She was designed to carry almost 4,000 passengers, with a crew of 1,200. At the outbreak of war in August 1914 she was interned at New York, and in April 1917 her crew damaged her engines before she was seized by the U.S. Repaired, and renamed* Leviathan, *she served as a U.S. Navy transport before reentering commercial service as the United States Lines transatlantic liner* Leviathan *in 1923. The* Leviathan *ceased service in 1934 and was scrapped in 1938. (Negative 213E, © Rosenfeld Collection, Mystic Seaport Museum, Inc.)*

favor of an Allied and American victory. But by the time the armistice was signed on 11 November 1918, the Shipping Board/Emergency Fleet effort had produced only 500,000 tons of ships, or less tonnage than that requisitioned from the Dutch. To those who assessed the costs of war, this was a great waste of resources and wealth, but these criticisms were made in hindsight, and they did not take into account the premature conclusion of the war and the extraordinary obstacles faced by the Shipping Board and Emergency Fleet Corporation as they attempted to fill expectations.

From the very beginning in late summer 1917, formidable impediments presented themselves to the quick construction of ships. Initially, the Shipping Board planned to employ existing shipyards for its building program, but, as noted above, when the nation declared war in April 1917, every yard was fully engaged. Because of the conflict between Denman and Goethals, the program was barely initiated and poorly defined when Hurley took office. Working with great energy under crisis conditions, Hurley launched his program of

acquiring existing ships through seizure, requisition, and leverage. He also moved rapidly to encourage the construction of new yards. During the war the number of shipyards constructing steel vessels in excess of 3,000 tons increased from 37 to 341. In addition, twenty-four yards built wooden vessels, while a few built experimental ships of concrete.

The most publicized of the Emergency Fleet building programs took place at the four so-called agency yards located at Bristol and Hog Island (Pennsylvania), Newark (New Jersey), and Wilmington (North Carolina). But shipyards, like ships, represent large investments in money, materials, and labor and take considerable time to build. Assembling the materials for mass production, never before attempted in shipbuilding, raised all sorts of organizational and logistical problems. The unprecedented task of constructing a shipyard on short notice was in itself a formidable one. The extremely harsh winter of 1917-18 played havoc with construction schedules and output. Then a monumental heat wave temporarily closed some yards in August 1918. A congressional investigation of alleged profiteering and mismanagement tied up thousands of administrative hours before the charges were successfully disclaimed. Serious labor unrest presented yet further obstacles. Such were the difficulties in launching an enterprise of this size and complexity that in February 1918, five months following the signing of construction contracts, the Hog Island yard, by far the largest and most sophisticated of the government operations, was only half-finished and had just laid its first keel. Ten months after America entered the war, the government's largest shipbuilding plant had yet to produce its first ship!

In time, however, the Emergency Fleet shipbuilding program extricated itself from the problems of formative organization and became one of the most proficient industries of modern times, employing with great success methods of mass production, wherein parts were prefabricated around the nation and shipped to the yards. By the summer of 1918, more than

300,000 men in 158 shipyards were constructing the greatest profusion of ships the modern world had ever seen. Prior to the war, it ordinarily took twelve to eighteen months to build a ship. Now ships were being built in twelve to eighteen weeks or less. In 1918, the New York Shipbuilding Corporation set a world record in building the 5,000-ton steel collier *Tuckahoe* in just thirty-seven days. In many shipyards, 6,000- to 8,000-ton vessels were launched at a rate of more than one a week. The Hog Island plant, with fifty shipways, became one of the great industrial wonders of the world. All told, under Emergency Fleet auspices, 533 ships–over 3 million tons–were launched in 1918, almost all of them in the last few months, which equaled total world output in any prewar year. But this was nothing compared to what had already been contracted for 1919–fully three times that tonnage. One can only imagine the magnitude of the commitment: hundreds of thousands of workers laboring across the country to extract from the earth minerals and wood products,

The 420-foot tanker Cuyamaca *is prepared for a side launch at the Pacific Marine and Construction Company yard in San Diego. The* Cuyamaca *was one of twelve experimental concrete ships built under supervision of the Concrete Ship Section of the Emergency Fleet Corporation. Launched in 1920, the* Cuyamaca *ran successfully carrying oil between the Mexican oilfields and California for several years, but the relative weight of concrete ships and high insurance rates made them uneconomical in peacetime, and all were laid up by the late 1920s. (Courtesy The Mariners' Museum, Newport News, Virginia)*

LAUNCHING ANOTHER VICTORY SHIP
UNITED STATES SHIPPING BOARD · EMERGENCY FLEET CORPORATION

Joseph Pennell's poster, Launching another Victory ship, *depicts the launch of the 253-foot bulk freighter* Lake Janet *at the Great Lakes Engineering Company yard in Ecorse, Michigan, on the Fourth of July 1918. As a patriotic gesture, the Shipping Board planned to launch 100 ships on that day; it succeeded in getting 95 vessels overboard at shipyards around the country. The* Lake Janet *was one of 99 ocean-type ships in the works at Great Lakes shipyards when the Shipping Board requisitioned the American fleet. Another 331 vessels were built on the Great Lakes for the Shipping Board, and almost all of them were given names beginning with Lake. Although they were designed for Atlantic Ocean service, the "Lakers" had to be small enough to traverse the Welland Canal, and most proved too small to be economical ocean freighters after the war. The* Lake Janet *was one of 149 Lakers sold to the Ford Motor Company for scrapping in 1927. (M.S.M. 58.688.5)*

dispatching these by rail to eighty-eight fabricating plants, and then shipping the finished products to the yards where another 300,000 workers assembled the ships. Had the war not come to such an abrupt and unforeseen end in November 1918, these ships would have poured supplies and manpower into the European war effort. As it was, few of them were launched in time to make a direct contribution. Yet it is undeniable that the Central Powers were defeated, in part, by the realization that, given the energy and enormity of American production, Germany's submarines could never prevent the United States from sending 2 million troops to France and sustaining them there for the projected duration of the war.

While this juggernaut of tonnage, ultimately some 13.5 million deadweight tons, came too late for more than minimal service during the war, it nevertheless played a significant role in the months to follow as a conveyor of American surpluses to foreign markets, including the relief of war-ravaged Europe, and as a powerful political weapon to be employed in President Wilson's effort to forge a settlement for a stable and democratic world order. In short, if the new merchant marine had come too late to assist directly in the prosecution of war, it was still able to assume a role as an agent for peace.

Wilsonian Maritime Policy

That the British were more than impressed with the Wilson administration's commitment to maritime growth is an understatement. Sir Cecil Spring Rice, the British ambassador to the United States, feared that at the war's end the United States would have "all the ships and all the gold in the world, and that the hegemony probably of the world, and certainly of the Anglo-Saxon race, [would] pass over the Atlantic." England's principal envoy fully understood the reliance of his nation on maritime power, and was deeply concerned with the rise of American competition during the war years. Others were equally concerned. Lord George Riddell, reflecting conversations with the First Sea Lord, Winston Churchill, observed that the United States resented Britain's command of the seas and had taken the opportunity to address that imbalance by building a huge merchant marine and increasing its foreign trade at the belligerents' expense. Noting England's wartime loss of large amounts of tonnage and access to markets, as well as the huge debt accumulated in the war effort, Riddell concluded that Great Britain might well annihilate itself while trying to annihilate the Germans. David Lloyd George summed up the situation in stark terms: Shipping, the prime minister said, was Great Britain's "jugular."

Such thinking expressed exactly what Woodrow Wilson, Edward Hurley, and others hoped to capitalize on. Wilson himself believed, as he expressed it to Hurley, that the American shipbuilding program had "given us a very considerable advantage over [Great Britain] in the carrying trade, and therefore in world commerce, after the struggle is over." The strategy at Paris would be to play this advantage to the hilt in order to exact from the Allies concessions that would give structure to the League of Nations concept that had become the cornerstone of Wilson's plan for an everlasting peace in "a world made safe for democracy."

Toward this end Wilson devised a three-point strategy. First, the United States would not disclose its plans for postwar uses of its rapidly expanding merchant fleet. The object was to play on Britain's fears of a government-owned American shipping fleet and to stall British plans for a return to private enterprise. To convince the British of American intentions to nationalize, Wilson ostentatiously increased the power of the Shipping Board. Second, he closed American shipyards to the construction of Allied ships and ordered the Shipping Board to withhold tonnage for Allied use until the peace treaty was signed. This was designed to hinder British, French, and Italian maritime growth and to prevent Allied orders from inhibiting continued U.S. shipping production. Third, Wilson thwarted an effort by British interests to repurchase thirty-seven steamships sold to the International Mercantile Marine in 1901, proposing instead to obtain these for U.S. use and lending strength to the notion of state control. These three stratagems underwrote the American policy, as Hurley expressed it, to "permit no arrangements for any part of shipping until there had been at least a tentative agreement on a League of Nations."

To this Hurley himself added a twofold plan to force the adoption of American shipping standards through international agreements. The first part of the plan called for the universal adoption of fair labor standards modeled on the La Follette Seamen's Act of 1915, including uniformity in wages. The second part involved adoption of an international system of uniform freight rates. As Hurley saw it, the adoption of such measures in the maritime trades would once and for all banish the unfair advantage the British and Germans had formerly enjoyed in ocean commerce. As Hurley believed, securing such agreements would forever "solve the problem of trade wars" and "would give reality and force to the 'freedom of the seas.'" Hurley, with Wilson's support, had concluded that these proposals would not only benefit American shipping but would provide a great service to the world.

It would be pleasing to say that this blend of altruism and American self-interest had a salutary effect on the outcome of the Paris deliberations. It did not. History records the Allies' staunch resistance to virtually every one of Wilson's maritime ploys. Forcing the president's hand, the Allies began releasing ships from government control for foreign trade. This put enormous pressure on the U.S. Shipping Board, which, given the restrictive covenants of the 1916 Shipping Act that limited its management

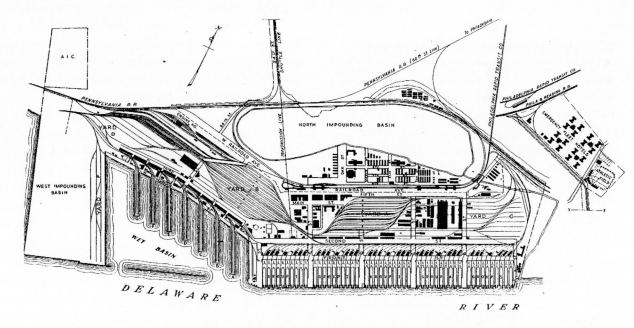

GENERAL PLAN OF HOG ISLAND SHIPYARD

SCALE-FEET
JAN 30, 1919

Hog Island

The Emergency Fleet Corporation's plant at Hog Island, Pennsylvania, was by far the largest and most impressive of the merchant ship construction operations established during World War I. Located on a swampy island on the Delaware River between Chester and Philadelphia. Hog Island served as an extraordinary representation of the nation's industrial commitment to war. By every measure, the organization and operation of the Hog Island shipyard was a wonder, a symbol of the promise of technology, organization, and social engineering in the so-called age of progressivism.

Constructed in 1917-18 by the engineering firm of Stone & Webster, the yard was organized by the American International Shipbuilding

Corporation, a branch of the J. P. Morgan banking enterprise's American International Corporation, which had been founded in 1915 and which had purchased the New York Shipbuilding Corporation, or "New York Ship," as it was known. Because New York Ship had experience in prefabrication and had demonstrated an ability to fit out ships in record time, and because the American International Corporation featured on its board some of the nation's most powerful financial and industrial magnates—men close to General Goethals, head of the Emergency Fleet Corporation— the company had been a very early recipient of wartime orders. When Edward Hurley took charge of the government's shipping operations in July 1917, he continued Goethal's commitment to New

York Ship. When the decision was made to launch an even bigger building program, involving the construction of "agency" yards on the East Coast, Hurley and the Shipping Board naturally turned to American International Shipbuilding. By the end of 1917, the Emergency Fleet Corporation had let construction contracts to the American International Shipbuilding Corporation worth over $300 million, a figure that one ranking American International officer acknowledged as "enormous and almost beyond comprehension."

The great size and complexity of the Hog Island works

(32-S-AM-36-39, Courtesy National Archives)

almost defied description. Constructed on 846 acres reclaimed from sand, bog, mud, and marsh, the yard consisted of fifty building ways and twenty-eight fitting-out piers that occupied a mile and a quarter of riverbank. Two hundred and fifty buildings were ultimately erected, including hotels, hospitals, a bank, a trade school that trained more than 11,000, a YMCA facility, twelve restaurants, and five mess halls. To accommodate the 300 carloads of materials that arrived daily, twenty locomotives hauled 465 freight cars on eighty miles of track. At the peak of operations, Hog Island had the character of a small city, with a work force of 34,049, almost all of them men. Hog Island's telephone system, with its own exchange, had the capacity for four times that population. Its sewage and water systems were as large as those of Minneapolis. Its air-compres-

sor plant, required for riveting, was the second largest in the world, inferior only to that at the Rand diamond mines in South Africa. Laid out like a military cantonment, with lettered streets and numbered buildings, this shipbuilding city possessed a constabulary of 600 army-trained guards. One hundred firefighters with motorized equipment provided additional protection.

Strong emphasis was given to health care and human welfare. Discarding the old idea that "machinery is expensive and human lives are cheap," the yard's administrators oper-

ated on the premise that "efficiency means health" and constructed the most modern hospital facilities. The concern for healthy workers extended even to meals; the yard's thirty-cent lunches of "really nourishing and well-balanced food" were prepared in "scrupulously clean" environments supervised by doctors. Shipyard morale was kept up by YMCA activities and by the encouragement of competition between Hog Island and the other agency yards.

The prize for producing the first ship went not to Hog Island, however, but to a sister

This typical Hog Island riveting gang includes the riveter, with his pneumatic gun; the holder-on, who holds the hot rivet in place; and the heater boy, who heats the rivets in a small furnace and passes them to the holder-on. By the end of 1918, Hog Island employed almost 600 riveting gangs, who averaged 242 rivets per eight-hour day. A skilled riveter earned eighty cents per hour, or as much as seventy dollars a week if working on a piecework basis. Few of these men were experienced shipwrights, but with standardized designs and an effective training program they quickly became proficient. (32-S-AM-27-1709, Courtesy National Archives)

yard in nearby Bristol, Pennsylvania, which was part of the financial empire of the Edward H. Harriman family. As the Harrimans had long vied with the House of Morgan for domination on Wall Street, the competition between Hog Island and Bristol was actually an extension of the nation's most celebrated traction and banking rivalry. Nevertheless, while Hog Island lost the honor–by slightly more than a week–of launching the first ship, its riveters were unrivaled in the speed with which they accomplished their tasks, and Hog Island's pile-driving teams won with handsome margins over teams at other yards. Eventually, the total cost for constructing the enormous yard and its multifarious facilities, and in carrying out its social engineering and promotional efforts, was $65,000,000.

In terms of organization, each group of five ways was operated as a separate yard, totaling ten such yards. In fact, each grouping represented the size of an average prewar shipyard. For the sake of speed it was determined to have fabrication plants across the country fashion and punch the plates, sections, and angles. Then, in a conscious emulation of the Ford Motor Company's production-line process, the parts were shipped to and assembled at Hog Island. Overall, a total of 3,500 American manufacturers pro-

At noontime, Front Street, along the head of the yard's fifty shipways, resembles a busy city street, with thousands of men headed for lunch, and mounted policemen on patrol to keep order. (32-S-AM-27-1721, Courtesy National Archives)

vided parts. To speed construction, a very simple prefabricated ship design was selected. The design featured rectangular midships, straight sides, round stern, and flat bottom and deck. Despite the simplicity of this design, each ship required 3,000 tons of steel, 25,000 components, and half a million rivets. Powered by up-to-date geared steam turbine engines, with oil-fired water-tube boilers, these boxy but efficient ships became known as "Hog Islanders."

The original Hog Island program called for 200 identical

400-foot cargo ships of 7,500 deadweight tons, each providing 380,000 cubic feet of cargo space. Subsequently, this order was modified to 110 cargo vessels of similar tonnage, and 70 combination cargo-troop transports of 8,000 tons. The first "Hog Islander," the freighter *Quistconck*, was launched on 5 August 1918. The name, Native American for "Hog Island," was chosen by Edith Bolling Galt Wilson, the president's wife. The *Quistconck* passed its trials on 3 November 1918, a week before the Armistice, and never saw war duty. With the war's conclusion, the shipbuilding program was radically revised, and only 12 of the troop transports were completed. In the end, all 110 cargo ships were launched, the last one in January 1921, and the shipyard was dismantled shortly thereafter.

Overall, Hog Island's performance was remarkable; by itself it could produce more ships than all the shipyards in the United Kingdom put together. The significance of the enterprise was summed up by Admiral William S. Benson, who called the Hog

Island operation "one of the greatest enterprises ever undertaken by any corporation of men in the history of the world."

Hog Island's first ship, the **Quistconck**, *lies in the wet basin, near the large bridge crane, receiving her coat of dazzle paint. The only Hog Islander completed before the Armistice, the* **Quistconck** *was the only one painted in camouflage and fitted with defensive gun tubs at bow and stern. The boxy Quistconck remained in service through the 1930s, was sold to Great Britain as a transport in 1941, and was finally scrapped in 1953. (32-S-AM-23-1332, Courtesy National Archives)*

The U.S. Navy transport USS Troy *was launched at Groton, Connecticut, in 1903 as the steamship* Minnesota. *Built for the Great Northern Railroad's Great Northern Steamship Company, the 622-foot* Minnesota *and her sister ship* Dakota *were twice as large as any other American merchant ship afloat when they were built. With vast cargo capacity and accommodations for nearly 1,500 passengers, the* Minnesota *ran between Seattle, Yokohama, and Hong Kong for eleven years before returning east for transport service in 1917. The ship's camouflage pattern was designed to distort the ship's size when viewed by a U-boat captain. The* Minnesota *was scrapped in 1923. Photo by Edwin Levick. (M.S.M. 94.125.117)*

of shipping to five years, and in light of rising pressure from the private shipping sector, had no intention of operating a massive and permanent government merchant marine in competition with free enterprise. Consequently, the Shipping Board began to seethe within from pressures to release ships, and Wilson's scheme to withhold a return to privatization until the signing of a peace treaty was fatally undermined. By Christmas 1918, Hurley had given in to British pressure and ordered the release of ships to private enterprise.

Pressures that built within the shipyards also figured in the weakening of Wilson's strategy for Paris. Even though 1,180 ships would be built by the Emergency Fleet Corporation in 1919, the justification for their completion drew immense criticism, and hundreds of additional

contracts were canceled. The result was significant unrest among the laboring force, which now faced increased competition with the return of discharged veterans. Responding to these domestic pressures, Hurley wanted to open the yards to foreign contracts, despite Wilson's order to the contrary. He did not get the president's consent. With pressures to release tonnage for competition, and with weakened resolve within the Shipping Board, Wilson was fast losing his maritime leverage at Paris.

These developments were compounded by Allied resistance to Wilson's hope to secure international agreement on the "freedom of the seas," one of his famous Fourteen Points. This proposal met fierce opposition in Paris, particularly from the British, and was eventually abandoned, one of the many compromises Wilson was forced to make to secure the preferred outlines, if not the preferred ingredients, of a League of Nations. Moreover, efforts to acquire German ships for temporary troop repatriation work were stymied for months, while the British delayed the assignment of their own ships to this service. As a result, the Shipping Board had to employ American ships in troop repatriation when Hurley would have preferred to place them in competitive foreign trade. Virtually the only success Wilson gained in the maritime strategy he took to Versailles came from his refusal to turn over interned German tonnage to the Allied shipping pool for redistribution on a *pro rata* basis to those nations that had suffered the greatest wartime shipping losses. Although the U.S. delegation hailed this as one of the great triumphs of the peace conference, it was in many ways a shallow victory if one measures Wilson's larger peace objectives against the relatively small gains achieved.

Hurley's plans to secure the international adoption of uniform freight rates and wages also met with immense resistance, so they were quickly

"Freedom of the Seas"

Of all of Woodrow Wilson's famous Fourteen Points—those concepts put forward in January 1918 by the president as axioms for a new world order—the second point, known as the "Freedom of the Seas," was believed by many to be one he held most dearly. Embodying Wilson's advocacy of the United States as the world's champion of neutral rights, and reflecting attitudes esteemed since the years of independence, it called for "Absolute freedom of navigation upon the seas, outside territorial waters, alike in peace and in war, except as the seas may be closed in whole or in part by international action for the enforcement of international covenants."

The ideal seemed to have a lot to offer. On the one hand, it appealed to Allied sympathizers who were furious at Germany's submarine warfare; on the other, it appealed to those who held Great Britain culpable for its violations of neutral rights through search and seizure of nonbelligerent ships. It was certainly a catchy term, but it was a phrase largely ambiguous and almost impossible to convert, as Secretary of State Robert Lansing bemoaned, "into concrete terms." In fact, in that it gave no recognition to the changing nature of war—that is, to the Allied need for an absolute blockade, and the

Central Powers' determination to impede Allied access to neutral supplies—it was an impracticable effort to enforce the unenforceable.

Ultimately, as defined above, "freedom of the seas" fell victim at the peace conference to fierce Allied resistance and to Wilson's abandonment of virtually all of his neutral-rights agenda in order to achieve his major objective, a League of Nations. The issue did not die altogether, however, as many Americans interpreted the ideal as more than just the neutral right of free passage in time of war, seeing it as an expression of America's traditional antagonism toward British sea power. In short, "freedom of the seas" symbolized America's refusal to accept British naval and mercantile domination of the seas. Consequently, the issue remained a contentious one

In an intentionally ironic gesture, President Woodrow Wilson twice traveled to Europe aboard the captured North German Lloyd liner George Washington to press American aims in the Paris peace negotiations. (Courtesy Library of Congress)

throughout the 1920s, and even beyond, with Americans only gradually becoming accustomed to the British Admiralty's determination to restrict neutral shipping rights during war as American naval expansion equaled and then ultimately exceeded that of Great Britain. Today, the issue itself, so vital in the early stages of this century, would have little meaning to most Americans.

tabled and then dropped. Forced to reorder his priorities by the realities of the time, Hurley found himself giving less and less attention to foreign trade competition, wage disputes in the shipyards, and accumulating surpluses in seaports, and more and more attention to providing emergency food relief to Europe. This last responsibility took on increasing importance as the American delegation in Paris viewed with alarm the disintegration of social and civil order in Russia, eastern Europe, and Germany. Provision of food to war-ravaged areas became a mainstay of American foreign policy in 1919– as a genuine humanitarian measure and as a politically pragmatic effort to introduce and maintain Western and specifically American influence in areas threatened by revolution and anarchy. The strong priority placed upon food relief forced the Shipping Board to alter its commitments accordingly.

In the end, the Wilsonian effort to employ America's new shipping prowess in world affairs left a mixed legacy. On the one hand, the prodigious growth of the American merchant marine could not be parlayed into Allied adherence to the Wilson plan for a liberal peace. Rather, it catalyzed barely submerged wartime rivalries into commercial and political animosity and strained the bargaining relationships in Paris. On the positive side, however, American aid, sent to Europe in American ships, helped shorten the war measurably, stemmed anarchy and social radicalism, and strengthened Western capitalist economies in large sections of the war-ravaged continent. Furthermore, from a purely economic standpoint, the policy served America admirably. Had the United States not built its own ships

The Maryland-class "superdreadnought" USS Colorado was authorized in the naval expansion of 1916, laid down at the New York Shipbuilding yard in 1919, and launched in 1921. With her sixteen-inch guns, oil-fired turbine engines, electric power, and twenty-one-knot speed, the 600-foot Colorado reflected President Wilson's big-navy program that challenged British naval superiority. Photo by Edwin Levick. (M.S.M. 79.53.5)

during the war and in the years immediately after, it would have been in as disadvantaged a position as it had been in 1914, possessed of huge surpluses but lacking the means to transport them. Public ownership of shipping also enabled the nation to save greatly on freight costs and brought about the establishment of permanent and lucrative trade on a worldwide basis. Constituting 22 percent of the world's oceanic fleet by 1922, the American merchant marine headed into the postwar era as a formidable national resource.

In the unfolding of events at Paris, American naval strength proved a far more effective diplomatic weapon than did Wilson's effort to leverage America's growth in merchant shipping. Although the capital-ships building program had been altered during the war to accommodate convoying and patrolling needs, Wilson's frequently voiced determination to construct a navy superior to that of Great Britain created enormous friction and brought about what Secretary of the Navy Josephus Daniels termed the "Naval Battle of Paris." In short, the cooperation that had marked Anglo-American naval relations during the war degenerated into rancorous competition at the peace conference.

Hardly had the Armistice been signed in November 1918 when Daniels and Wilson submitted to Congress a virtual duplicate of the huge naval construction bill they had submitted two years previously. Such a proposal was clearly the product of political rather than military momentum, as such a fleet could no longer be justified by wartime requirements. Understandably, the British were more than irked by this development in America. For a century, Great Britain had depended for its very existence upon its ability to service the extensive sea-lanes that linked it with its far-flung empire, and it stood to reason that a powerful navy to protect those trade routes was in every way legitimized. Considering the absence of an American empire of similar size, it was hard, if not impossible, for the British to understand the American rationale for a superior navy. London believed that America's quest for naval superiority represented nothing but a questionable effort to alter the status quo at sea. The reality of America's newly competitive merchant marine only exacerbated British alarm.

Wilson's intent to use a big-navy program as a weapon at the peace conference was made obvious by his appointment of the Anglophobic Admiral William Benson as head of the American naval contingent in Paris. Benson and Navy Secretary Daniels resisted every effort of the British to secure from the Americans a renunciation of the president's commitment to superiority on the seas, even when the British insisted they would vote against the League of Nations unless such a renunciation was forthcoming. Daniels's response was to threaten all-out competition in the building of naval ships. The American position on the disposition of the German navy also brought about discord. Whereas the British Admiralty desired the complete destruction of Germany's naval capability, Wilson and Benson wanted to leave Germany a major portion of its war fleet, hoping thus to curb continued British ambitions. The issue was ultimately resolved by the Germans themselves when they scuttled the major portion of the fleet at Scapa Flow in June 1919.

Other issues compounded the Anglo-American dissension. Great Britain's refusal to acknowledge Wilson's demand for "freedom of the seas" in both war and peace came close to wrecking the whole conference. Moreover, in addition to plans for a superior U.S. Navy, Admiral Benson now added plans for a superior merchant marine, and he linked the two programs consistently in his effort to increase America's influence in the world's carrying trades, a field of opportunity he was convinced the British were attempting to monopolize for themselves. At one point in the proceedings Benson actually concluded that war with Britain was possible, even imminent, very nearly exchanged blows with the First Lord of the British Admiralty, and counseled Daniels on the need to keep the American fleet in full war preparedness. Fortunately, Benson's concerns were given little weight by calmer minds, and a compromise was reached in April 1919 wherein the British agreed to support the League of Nations, while the Americans agreed to make no commitment on the completion of sixteen ships specified in the 1916 program but not yet in production. Wilson also agreed to abandon the new big-navy bill being framed in Congress. In contrast, then, to the efforts made by Wilson and his staff to parlay mercantile growth into diplomatic victories at Paris, the big-navy ploy seemed to produce results. Although the British in all probability would have supported the League, Wilson's naval strategy at Paris played a significant role in forcing London's hand in that direction. Some analysts, in fact, interpret the results of the naval battle at Paris as a major victory for the United States, a "turning point in the history of world sea power," as the naval historian William Braisted believed— a "landmark" in the gradual acceptance by a war-exhausted Great Britain of America's inevitable and unrestrainable progress towards naval equality.

In any event, despite the U.S. Navy's insistence upon the right to a battle fleet superior to all others, the commitment to construct such a force began to lose energy in America after the conference. In the 1920s, the Washington Naval Conference agreements on arms limitations, reached in 1922, and a new wave of antinavalism would prove a disappointing period for those whose vision of a powerful America rested upon naval omnipotence. The rise of Japan as a formidable rival in the Pacific would compound these unsettling developments. Not until the later years of the interwar period would American big-navy aspirations materialize.

The largest ship in the world
LEVIATHAN
S.S. LEVIATHA
United States Lines
managing operators for
UNITED STATES SHIPPING BOAR

CHAPTER 14

The Interwar Years

ALTHOUGH the twenty-year period from 1919 to 1939, which began with the end of one war and closed with the commencement of another, is often thought of as a single historical period, this approach is more the result of convenience than of accuracy. Certainly, from the standpoint of American maritime history, it was a period marked by two distinct phases.

The first, encompassing the final years of Woodrow Wilson's presidency, was a period of relative optimism for the American shipping industry. The early 1920s, however, forced a change in this bullish thinking—with world peace as a priority, calls for massive naval and merchant shipbuilding programs could no longer be justified. The Washington Naval Conference of 1921-22, with its treaty stipulations for naval disarmament, significantly undermined the grandiose designs of "big navy" advocates, while overbuilding by the U.S. Shipping Board and the Emergency Fleet Corporation helped bring on a serious depression in oceanic transportation. Although the nation's shipping did not seriously atrophy during the 1920s, this decade was not the most healthy for the American navy and merchant marine.

In the second phase in the mid-1930s, these trends were reversed when the breakdown of international stability and the continuation of the Great Depression created new rationales for a big navy and a big merchant marine. Coupling apprehension over growing hostilities in Europe and Asia with concern for the faltering domestic econ-

In 1923 the United States Lines could proclaim that it operated the "largest ship in the world" when the Leviathan, ex-Vaterland, *returned to transatlantic service. Despite changing economic fortunes in the interwar period, luxury sea travel flourished, and American passenger lines operated around the world. (M.S.M. 53.90; Mary Anne Stets photo)*

omy, the Roosevelt administration envisioned naval and mercantile growth, along with massive public works projects, as suitable means to achieve desired political and economic ends. Naval and merchant-marine expansion during the 1930s would have important ramifications for the nation as it weathered the economic difficulties at home and responded to the crises building abroad.

In the immediate postwar period, the U.S. Navy remained active around the world. Three of the navy's Curtiss flying boats set out in May 1919, flying via Newfoundland and the Azores to reach Lisbon, Portugal, and Plymouth, England. One of these planes completed this first transatlantic flight. In Europe, from November 1918 to September 1921, American naval forces occupied one hundred miles of the Dalmatian coastline in the Adriatic, a part of Serbia claimed by the newly established state of Yugoslavia. The United States was in the unique position of occupying the territory of one associated allied power with a naval force against the pretensions of another associated allied power, Italy. Similarly, U.S. naval forces were assigned to Turkey in January 1919 for an operation that lasted into 1924. Although the United States had not taken part in the defeat and occupation of Turkey, the last nation to make peace with the Allies, the United States became involved in this area as part of the Near East Relief Mission, to help provide humanitarian assistance and supplies of American aid to needy Armenians and Syrians. Among other duties, the U.S. Navy became involved in the transportation of 250,000 Anatolian Greeks to Greece, after the Turkish government expelled them from Asia Minor. A naval force remained in Turkish waters until tensions quieted after Constantinople (named Istanbul in 1930) was restored to Turkey and the Dardanelles was international-ized, following ratification of the 1923 Treaty of Lausanne. In China, American gunboats had been operating on the Yangtze River to protect American interests since 1903, and in December 1919 the navy formally organized them into the Yangtze Patrol.

These same years also saw both innovation and disaster. In 1922, there were several innovations in American naval aviation as the first airplanes took off and landed from the navy's newly com-missioned aircraft carrier, USS *Langley*, and the navy put lighter-than-air ships into commission, including the German-built *Los Angeles*. But the navy also experienced a series of accidents. In September 1923, seven ships of Destroyer Squadron Eleven ran aground in heavy fog off Santa Barbara, California, wrecking all the ships and killing twenty-two men. In 1925 the naval airship *Shenandoah* broke in two during a storm near Ava, Ohio, killing fourteen, and the subma-rine *S–51* sank with the loss of thirty-three after colliding with a merchant ship off Block Island. These accidents demonstrated a perceived need for improved professionalism and more refined thinking on the role of naval power. To the disap-pointment of many naval leaders, these early perceptions were quickly submerged and forgotten in another issue: the move toward naval limitations.

The Washington Naval Conference and Naval Strategy

With the armistice of 1918 and the end of German submarine warfare, a quick return to the capital-ship commitment of 1916 was naturally favored by the navalists. Battleships, the navy's maximum fighting units if judged by firepower, armament, speed, and radius, were the priority item. Accordingly, naval construction was resumed, and five battleships were completed between 1920 and 1923. Behind the navy's determination to improve the fleet's fighting capability was the notion that naval power was essential in enforcing action by the League of Nations. The refusal of the United States Senate to consent to ratification of the Treaty of Versailles, in which the League was embodied, only strengthened the navy's belief that the nation's interests would be best safeguarded by honoring the 1916 commitment to big-ship construction.

This view, however, was not shared by the American public, and support for a big navy waned as the nation concentrated on domestic and nonmilitary issues. The biggest setback to the navalists came in 1921-22. Senator William E. Borah of Idaho, a member of the Senate Foreign Affairs Committee and a key figure among the opponents of the League of Nations,

introduced a resolution whose substance became part of the Naval Appropriations Bill for 1921, requesting President Harding to call an international conference "which shall be charged with the duty of promptly entering into an understanding or agreement by which the naval expenditures and building programs of each. . . . shall be substantially reduced annually during the next five years." Following this Congressional mandate, the Harding administration, led by Secretary of State Charles Evans Hughes, pushed for international agreements to limit naval growth as a way to restrain the military buildup that had provoked World War I. Representatives of nine countries attended the Washington Naval Conference, which opened in November 1921. Over the following months, their negotiations resulted in a set of draft treaties that called for a ten-year moratorium on capital-ship construction, the scrapping of a total of almost two million tons of existing warships (of which the U.S. alone offered to scrap 845,000

"Just Men, But Mighty Important Ones!" read the caption for this photograph of the "Big Nine" at the Washington Naval Conference in November 1921. Secretary of State Charles Evans Hughes (fifth from right) hosted representatives from China, France, Italy, Great Britain, Japan, Portugal, Belgium, and the Netherlands. Besides agreeing on naval armament limitations and quotas that required the U.S., Britain, and Japan to scrap existing warships, the conference agreed on restrictions on submarine warfare, and on efforts to avoid conflict in the Pacific and to confirm China's independence. (Courtesy Library of Congress)

tons), and the establishment of a numerical ratio 5:5:3:1.67:1.67 for capital-ship tonnage among the United States, Great Britain, Japan, France, and Italy respectively. In order to secure Japan's cooperation, the United States, France, and Great Britain pledged to respect each other's

The USS Mason *(DD-191) was begun during the World War I naval construction boom and launched at the Newport News Shipbuilding and Drydock Company in March 1919. In 1922 the* Mason *was one of numerous U.S. Navy vessels decommissioned to meet the terms of the Washington Naval Treaty. After seventeen years of layup the* Mason *was recommissioned in December 1939 and in 1940 became one of fifty obsolete destroyers turned over to Great Britain in exchange for the lease of naval bases. As HMS* Broadwater *she performed North Atlantic convoy duty until she was torpedoed by a U-boat and sank south of Iceland in October 1941. Photographed in July 1920, the 314-foot* Mason *approaches her thirty-five knot speed as she displays the characteristics of these submarine killers: flush deck, four stacks, four-inch guns at bow and stern, and torpedo tubes. (Negative 4284FA, © Rosenfeld Collection, Mystic Seaport Museum, Inc.)*

rights over Pacific Island possessions and to halt military and naval construction of bases and fortifications within striking distance of that nation. For the United States, this meant Guam and the Philippines. In addition, the five nations agreed to restrict submarine operations. Three months after the conference closed in February 1922, an isolationist Congress quickly approved these propositions, along with other measures, as a set of nine treaties, with the reservation that the treaties comprised "no commitment to armed force, no alliance, no obligation to join in any defense." Congress, with strong support from the White House, continued to maintain its restraints on naval expansion. So heavy-handed were the restraints that the navy was unable to build even to allowable treaty ratios. Following approval of the treaty, construction stopped on seven battleships in February 1922, all of which had been laid down in 1919-20.

Although the Washington treaties constrained big navalism—and deeply disappointed those who believed that American security required a fleet

structured on the 1916 plan as well as fortified bases in the Pacific—those same treaties guaranteed a position of U.S. naval supremacy over Japan and, for the first time in history, parity with the British Royal Navy. The agreements also afforded opportunities for improving the existing navy, opportunities the admirals and officers were quick to grasp. For example, while cuts had been mandated in battleship construction, the treaties provided for a means of scrapping overage ships and obsolete equipment, thereby increasing overall efficiency. The treaty limitations required the navy to become more efficient in using its resources, and resulted in the development of a closer interaction of naval bureaucracy, technological innovation, and financial management. Moreover, the treaties, while curtailing construction, contained no restrictions on the improvement of services, the application of new technologies, or the engineering of new ship designs—much as the Nuclear Test Ban and Strategic Arms Limitation treaties of the 1960s and early 1970s eliminated many monster weapons, but did not prohibit—and hence, encouraged–improvements in delivery and fire-power and the development of new weapons systems. So the navy took the opportunity to increase significantly its efficiency and diversity as a fighting force. The early years of the 1920s saw the conversion from coal- to oil-fired boilers in the fleet, the installation of improved electrical power systems, refinements in gunnery, the development of vastly improved communications through radio, and the substitution of new synthetics and aluminum for heavier metals. By lessening the weights of the navy's ships, this latter development allowed for the installation of heavier defensive armament.

The failure to completely outlaw the submarine at the Washington Conference provided another opportunity for developing naval technology. The navy's improvement of its submarines ranks as one of its more significant interwar achievements. Once the problem of battery ventilation was solved, underwater target-detecting sound systems devised, and new, improved diesel engines installed, the navy was able to produce fast and durable submarines. Undersea power was important to the navy's Pacific Ocean defensive strategy, and Congress, aware of that fact, appropriated funds in the 1920s for the construction of additional submarines.

The conversion of two battle cruisers to aircraft carriers represented another naval advance in the 1920s. Naval air power, like submarines, had not been limited by the Washington treaties, and the U.S. Navy moved rapidly to add this capability to its arsenal.

The Anglo-American rivalry that had flared in Paris in 1919 did not disappear entirely in the 1920s. In the wake of the hostile atmosphere of the peace conference, American navalists feared the military capabilities of both Great Britain and Japan, each of which was seen as a threat to the United States and its possessions. Consequently, in late 1919 the Navy Department established the War Plans Division in the Office of Naval Operations, and that division quickly drafted several new war strategies. The Red Plan covered the eventuality of war with Great Britain. The old Orange Plan, formulated for war with Japan alone, was revised and updated, and a combined Red and Orange Plan was drawn up to cover the possibility of war with Great Britain *and* Japan, which were still allied by treaty. Yet another

strategy, the Green Plan, was devised to counter the remote possibility that Mexico would support an Anglo-Japanese attack.

The agreements reached at the Washington Naval Conference now prompted a reassessment of these strategies. Although hostility toward Great Britain lingered, with the termination of the Anglo-Japanese alliance and the achievement of parity with the Royal Navy, most American naval leaders dismissed Great Britain as a threat, although Britain remained an "enemy" in naval war games as a means of testing the efficiency and capabilities of the American fleet. In terms of real threats, they assigned "first importance" to Japan. Such a reordering of priorities followed easily from the navy's strong disposition to view Asia as an area of paramount importance to America. Strong believers in the myth of the China market and with the responsibility to maintain the open-door policy and to defend the Philippines, U.S. naval officers, many of whom had fought to secure an Asiatic empire for America at the turn of the century, were hardly disposed to abandon their world views. While the Washington treaties provided criteria for measuring naval security among the major naval powers, through ratios of naval force in geographical regions, their success depended on other nations following British and American naval leadership and in perpetuating the international environment of the early 1920s. Within the Asian region, for example, a balance depended on a unified and stable China acting as a counterweight to Japan. When it became increasingly clear that China was not developing in this way, most American naval officers were convinced that, given Japan's growing imperial interests in Asia, the United States and Japan were on a collision course. A large navy was therefore imperative to the nation's defense strategy. Although statesmen did not use navies in the 1920s for offensive control of the sea, the Washington treaties did not change the navy's vision of naval power; they merely confirmed and codified the earlier vision with fewer numbers of capital ships. The main American battle fleet, which had been concentrated in the Atlantic, was transferred to the Pacific in 1919; six years later, the navy held maneuvers off Hawaii, making no effort to disguise the identity of the enemy in these war games. An Asian blue-water naval strategy was also seen as a means by which to secure congressional appropriations, funds that could not be justified by a purely hemispheric defense strategy. In short, the navy came to increasingly believe in and need the Japanese threat.

The battleships and the heavy naval guns they carried remained the centerpiece of the U.S. Navy. While the U.S. Army showed the effectiveness of air attack in a widely publicized demonstration in 1921, by bombing and sinking a former German battleship (at anchor and undefended), American naval leaders were not convinced that Billy Mitchell's demonstration was similar to actual combat conditions. The Chief of Naval Operations, Admiral Edward Eberle, proclaimed, "the battleship of today, while not invulnerable to airplane attack, still possesses very efficient structural protection . . . . It can not be said, therefore, that air attack has rendered the battleship obsolete."

By 1924, members of Congress felt that the United States was falling behind in naval strength and that battleships were not the entire story. To be at strength, the navy needed cruisers, destroyers, and submarines; in particular, cruisers. Fast and heavily gunned, cruisers were designed to complement the work of the battleship by actually exercising control of the sea as commerce destroyers and blockading ships. While a number were under construction, the U.S. Navy had not commissioned a cruiser since 1908, while other countries, profiting from the recent experience of the German and British navies during the war, pushed ahead in this area. To remedy the situation, in 1924 Representative Thomas Butler of Pennsylvania introduced a bill to authorize construction of eight 10,000-ton-displacement cruisers that would bring the navy up to treaty level in this area with ships of modern design. In addition, the naval bill authorized modernization of the oldest battleships, converting them from coal to oil fuel, as well as construction of eight smaller scout cruisers and six gunboats for use in China. Congress passed the Butler Bill, effectively laying down the navy's course of ship construction for the next decade.

Congressional authorization for the plan was one thing; funding it and actually building the ships was another. Both Congress and the newly elected Republican president, Calvin Coolidge, saw the value of the bill in terms of disarmament negotiations, but were more interested in controlling government spending than in building up the U.S. Navy to treaty strength. Congress repeatedly defeated the Navy Department's attempts to fund the construction program in 1924, 1925, and 1926. In late 1926, Secretary of the Navy Curtis Wilbur asked for deficiency funds to begin the program. Congress approved this request and the navy was able to proceed with building the cruisers *Salt Lake City* and *Pensacola*, modernizing the battleships, continuing work on the 1922 authorization to convert two battle cruisers into the aircraft carriers *Saratoga* and *Lexington,* and proceeding with building the six gunboats for the Yangtze Patrol. In 1927, additional Congressional appropriations allowed the navy to begin six more cruisers.

With a view to future arms limitation negotiations, however, just as Congress was considering substantial additions to naval funding for 1928, President Coolidge asked Britain, France, Japan, and Italy to join the United States in an international conference to be held at Geneva to establish ratios on all classes of warships that had not been considered in the Washington treaties, particularly on cruisers, destroyers, and submarines. With these plans in mind, Coolidge attempted to keep American naval construction limited and unfunded, but at the same time to increase naval shipbuilding authorizations that could be cancelled after the international conference. Thus, Coolidge proceeded to try to prevent funding for the final three cruisers in the 1924 plan and, at the same time, to ask for unfunded authorization for ten new ships. Reacting to this, members of Coolidge's own Republican party organized the first major party revolt in Congress since 1910. The revolt was turned back by only two votes, but in the end Congress funded the building of the final ships in the 1924 authorization, though it refused to agree to ten more cruisers or to allow the navy to build up to parity.

The Coolidge administration's plans for naval construction were intimately tied to the issues of disarmament, but the Geneva Conference did not turn out as hoped. France and Italy declined to attend, but Coolidge decided to go ahead with a three-power conference with Britain and Japan. The course of negotiations failed to find a common ground for agreement among the three countries. Cruisers were the main area of contention, and their number was closely connected

The Birth of Naval Air Power

The addition of air power to the U.S. Navy's arsenal of weapons was likely the most important naval development of the interwar period. Even before the First World War, experimental planes had flown from and landed on decks built upon the superstructures of warships, and a flying school had been organized in Pensacola, Florida. The 1916 naval appropriations act earmarked $5 million for aviation, and following America's entry into the war the navy's air arm expanded rapidly. In 1921 a separate Bureau of Aeronautics was created under Rear Admiral William A. Moffett, whose indefatigable devotion to the cause made him the acknowledged "father of naval air." Under Moffett's administration the nation's first aircraft carrier was constructed in 1922 by converting the collier *Jupiter* into the carrier *Langley*. Three years later the navy created the new administrative position of assistant secretary of aeronautics.

None of this was accomplished easily. Opposition to the development of a naval air arm was led by proponents of the old battle-line strategy of capital ships, including the navy's first Chief of Naval Operations, Admiral William Benson, who assigned a very low priority to naval air. When he did acknowledge its potential, he talked of seaplanes, which in 1919 had made history by crossing the Atlantic. For Benson, the advantage lay in the "universal aerodromes" available to the seaplanes in contrast to the dependency of wheeled aircraft on hard-to-locate carriers. The austere budgets of the 1920s also had an impact on the debate; with the navy's allocations down a full 25 percent, there was a decided reluctance to divert scarce dollars away from battleship modernization to an as-yet-unproven and expensive air carrier wing. A diversion into lighter-than-air craft—the dirigible—consumed dollars at a time when many felt that traditional naval gun power

needed development. Ironically, the lighter-than-air program caused the death of Admiral Moffett when the dirigible *Akron* broke up during a thunderstorm.

Another deterrent was the insistence by General William "Billy" Mitchell of the Army Air Service that all aviation be incorporated into one independent unit. Mitchell's highly publicized statements—which eventually caused his court martial—and his startling live demonstration in 1921 that battleships were vulnerable to air attack and should no longer be relied upon as the ultimate sea force, created much consternation among the admirals. Relief—and validation for the navy—came in 1925 from a presidentially-appointed air policy board. Under the chairmanship of former diplomat and advisor to the Allied Maritime Transport Council in World War I, Dwight Morrow, the board dismissed Mitchell's call for consolidation and recommended retaining and

Admiral William A. Moffett (1869-1933) grew up in a merchant family in Charleston, South Carolina, and graduated from the U.S. Naval Academy in 1890. Beginning with service in outmoded steam sloops, he was a lieutenant on the protected cruiser Charleston *at Guam and Manila during the Spanish-American War. He commanded a scout cruiser at Veracruz in 1914 and then took command of the Great Lakes Naval Training Center, which he directed with efficiency as it prepared nearly one hundred thousand recruits for naval service during World War I. Postwar command of the battleship* Mississippi *was followed by appointment as first chief of the U.S. Navy's Bureau of Aeronautics in 1921. Moffett had begun to appreciate the scouting function of aircraft even before the war, and he became an especially strong and untiring advocate for naval aviation. Relying on the technical expertise of bureau officers, he pushed the interests of an independent naval flying service within the navy, in Congress, and in public and industrial forums. During his term, the navy experimented with aircraft carrier design and increasingly with offensive tactics. Moffett also favored the use of lighter-than-air ships or dirigibles for long-distance service. Admiral Moffett was encouraged by President Roosevelt's commitment to a strong and balanced navy, but he did not live to see it grow. In April 1933, Moffett was killed when the navy dirigible* Akron *crashed in a storm. The navy's dirigible program soon ended, but the naval flying service fostered by Moffett was well-established to prevail in a world war less than a decade later. Here, Admiral William Moffett surveys operations on the USS* Arkansas. *(Courtesy Library of Congress)*

strengthening naval aviation. Supportive congressional legislative action followed, setting the course for a permanent naval air arm. One important result was the launching in 1925 of the first fast carriers, the 33,000-tonners *Lexington* and *Saratoga*, built upon the hulls of uncompleted battle cruisers, and equipped with hangar space for eighty airplanes. During this period the air fleet was enlarged to roughly 1,000 planes, which ultimately would be modernized into all-metal aircraft with retractable landing gear and powerful air-cooled engines. The effectiveness of these planes as weapons of war was simultaneously enhanced by the development of torpedo and dive bombing.

Fleet maneuvers in the interwar period clearly demonstrated the significance of naval air power. The most telling of these events was the 1929 Fleet Problem IX in which the *Saratoga* eluded a strong sea, land, and air defense force and succeeded in launching a successful surprise air attack on the Panama Canal. While the use of carriers for attack purposes was gaining acceptance in most quarters, it was still debated within naval circles.

The fact that the new carriers, with top speeds from twenty-five to thirty-three knots, were significantly faster than any of the navy's pre-1922 battleships, which had limits of twenty-one knots, seems to have confounded the old-line, nonair admirals who fretted over how to meld these speedier vessels into an effective offensive force. Several maneuvers, such as Rear Admiral Harry Yarnell's successful 1932 sneak air assault on Pearl Harbor with the *Lexington* and the *Saratoga*, demonstrated again the attack capability of the navy's floating airfields, but still did not resolve the debate. Too often the tendency was to hold back the carriers as protective umbrellas for the battleships, as spotters for capital-ship gunfire, and as covers for landing forces. Never fully resolved, the controversy over the relative effectiveness of battleships versus carriers continued right up to, and even well into, the next war. High-level devotion to battleships, "the backbone of naval power," was deeply ingrained.

Still, the controversy did not deter the navy from adding flattops and carrier planes to its arsenal. The probability of war in the Pacific, in which naval capability would be the telling factor, demanded the existence of an air wing. On the war's eve the U.S. Navy possessed six fast, heavy, modern carriers, each among the world's finest, a number of smaller carriers, and thousands of aircraft. When a Japanese task force of six fast carriers put five American battleships out of action at Pearl Harbor on 7 December 1941, the significance of naval air power was made clear beyond a doubt.

The USS Langley *became the U.S. Navy's first aircraft carrier when the 1912 collier* Jupiter *was rebuilt with a flight deck bridging the hull and the pilothouse forward. Launched at the Mare Island Navy Yard in Vallejo, California, the* Jupiter *was the first U.S. Navy vessel powered by diesel engines driving electric motors, and traveling east to join the Atlantic Fleet in 1914 she was the first ship to pass through the Panama Canal from west to east. During World War I the* Jupiter *was occupied in coaling and cargo-carrying on the run to Europe. Selected for conversion to an aircraft vessel in 1919, the 542-foot ship was renamed* Langley *in 1920 and recommissioned in 1922. She spent two years on the Atlantic coast performing naval-aviation experiments and demonstrations before joining the Pacific Battle Fleet. Converted to a seaplane tender in 1937, the* Langley *was in the Philippines at the beginning of World War II and was sunk in a Japanese aerial attack off Java in February 1942. The aircraft carrier* Langley *was photographed near Gloucester, Massachusetts, in 1923. (Negative 10780F, © Rosenfeld Collection, Mystic Seaport Museum, Inc.)*

The U.S. Navy's first fast carrier, Saratoga, *passes through the Panama Canal on 7 February 1928, on her way to join the Pacific Battle Fleet. When the ship's keel was laid at the New York Shipbuilding Corporation at Camden, New Jersey, in 1920, she was planned as a battle cruiser, but to conform to limitations of the Washington treaties the vessel was converted to an aircraft carrier in 1922 and launched in 1925. Commissioned late in 1927, the 888-foot* Saratoga *was sent to the Pacific to help develop naval air tactics. During fleet exercises in 1929 she made a surprise "attack" on the Panama Canal, demonstrating the possibilities of detached fast-carrier task forces. Through the 1930s the* Saratoga *operated out of San Diego. During World War II the carrier provided air support off Guadalcanal, sustaining torpedo damage; in the Solomon, Gilbert, and Marshall Islands; in the Indian Ocean during combined operations with the British and French against Japanese installations on Java; and off Iwo Jima, where she was badly damaged in an air attack. Between battle missions the* Saratoga *was also involved in training for night flying. At the end of the war, the ship served as a troop transport, carrying nearly 30,000 servicemen back to the U.S. Outmoded by larger and more advanced carriers by this time, the* Saratoga *was sunk during atomic bomb tests at Bikini Atoll in July 1946. (183-G-948, Courtesy National Archives)*

with the range and extent of each country's merchant shipping. While Japan seemed amenable to the American proposals, there seemed to be little chance of Britain and the United States finding a mutually agreeable number of cruisers for controlling and protecting commercial traffic on the world's sea lanes, while also assuring superiority over Japan. In considering these issues, the British naval staff developed an illuminating argument that demonstrated Britain's much greater need for cruisers, while also linking naval and commercial maritime matters. Multiplying the tonnage normally at sea on defined ocean routes by the length of the route, British naval officers produced a ton-

mileage factor to analyze the needs of the three principal powers. These calculations showed, as of 1 April 1926, the following relative values:

British Empire	27,229,492,000
United States of America	12,379,311,000
Japan	3,757,721,000

In addition, these three powers owned tonnage at sea that was not on any defined ocean route in the following amounts:

British Empire	2,446,000
Japan	200,000
United States of America	153,000

While many pacifists blamed the technically oriented and inflexible American naval delegates for their failure to compromise at the conference and to agree to allow the British to have more cruisers than the U.S. Navy, American shipbuilders also contributed to the failure by hiring an effective lobbyist, William B. Shearer, to argue against disarmament in Geneva.

Nevertheless, when the French Foreign Minister, Aristide Briand, announced a proposal for the "outlawry of war," after earlier discussions with Professor James T. Shotwell of Columbia University, the Coolidge administration took up the proposal and Secretary of State Frank Kellogg began to work on a multinational treaty. By August 1928, fourteen nations had signed the treaty, and eventually 62 nations would join the pact. While all the nations agreed on the principles, they provided no means to enforce their views. Simultaneously, the Navy Department concluded that the failure of the Geneva Conference meant that the U.S. Navy must now build up to treaty strength, and it drew up a five-year plan to do so, calling for the construction of some seventy-one warships. This plan came before Congress in an election year, at the same time that the negotiations for the Kellogg-Briand Pact were taking place. A long and bitter debate took place in this context, with one faction arguing that increased armaments were the cause of war, while another suggested that the opponents were favoring "foreign interests," and a third, representing organized labor, was more interested in spreading building contracts equally between navy yards and private industry. After more than a year of debate, Congress finally passed a much-amended bill and Coolidge signed it in February 1929, only three weeks from the end of his term of office. Funding for the first year took even longer, and Coolidge signed it four days before he left the White House. In the end, the U.S. Navy began construction on fifteen new cruisers and one aircraft carrier, the USS *Ranger*.

When Coolidge left office, the U.S. Navy at sea was divided into four major components and several small groups. The main force was the U.S. Fleet, with its most important and powerful element, the Battle Fleet, based at the naval anchorage off San Pedro, California. Supporting it was the Fleet Base Force. This included three divisions of the newest battleships, cruisers,

destroyers, and the two aircraft carriers *Lexington* and *Saratoga*. The navy's submarines were commanded from the Atlantic, where the Control Force was based at New London, Connecticut. Also in the Atlantic, the Scouting Fleet had two battleship divisions with older ships, cruisers, destroyers, and the old aircraft carrier *Langley*. In addition, a small Asiatic Fleet, based in the Philippines, operated on the coast of China and in southeast Asian waters, and the Special Service Squadron operated in the Caribbean and the Gulf of Mexico. Beyond this, a small group of vessels operated in European waters.

The administration of Herbert Hoover (1929-33), coinciding with the onset of the Great Depression of 1929, proved to be the worst-case scenario for those who wanted a large navy. Combining "the most drastic cuts ever made" in naval appropriations with strict adherence to the disarmament legislation of the 1920s and a decidedly warm regard for Anglo-American amity, the Hoover administration continually frustrated efforts to increase naval firepower to treaty limits, even canceling contracts for ships for which monies had been appropriated. Hoover's appointment of Admiral William V. Pratt as Chief of Naval Operations in 1930 only compounded the frustration for advocates of a larger navy. Pratt adopted the attitude of goodwill toward Great Britain, continuing the relationship fostered by Admiral Sims in 1917-18, and sought to dampen the Anglophobia that had flared up again at the Geneva Naval Conference of 1927, and which still simmered within the navy among those who had resented British dominance over the U.S. Navy in 1917-18. They resented Pratt's open endorsement of Anglo-American amity and his ushering in of a period of cooperation in the 1930s with the idea that the problems of the world would be properly handled as long as Britain and America cooperatively dealt with them.

To add to the rancor of some disgruntled officers, Pratt had been intimately involved in the naval disarmament treaties of 1922 and 1927, agreements that navalists believed had weakened the navy's ability to fight in the Pacific. Pratt saw the Washington treaties as the logical successor to the Hague treaties of 1899 and 1907 and he opposed the idea of making contingency plans for offensive wars. While War Plan Orange, for example, envisioned an island-hopping offensive campaign across the Pacific that did not need fortified bases, Pratt curbed work on such thinking. In contrast, Pratt and Hoover called for a coastal defense system, supported by ships and aircraft sufficient only to prevent an enemy from landing on the nation's shores. Determined to avoid further naval competition, the president and the chief of naval operations endorsed the London Naval Treaty of 1930, which reiterated earlier treaty commitments to arms limitations, establishing a 10:10:6.6 ratio in heavy cruisers and a ratio of 10:10:7 in light cruisers and destroyers for Britain, the United States, and Japan, parity in submarines with 52,700 tons allowed for each nation, and extending the ban on battleship construction to 1936.

The treaty had the sharpest effect on the Royal Navy, requiring the scrapping of five battleships. This came at a time when the Royal Navy was dealing with Britain's own depression and the economic failure of important British shipbuilding firms, which seriously weakened the industrial establishment supporting the Royal Navy. This combination of factors within Britain, rather than the treaties alone, eventually allowed the U.S. Navy to surpass the Royal Navy. However, an "escalator" clause allowed Britain to resume construction if French or Italian naval construction became threatening. As a result of the treaty, the U.S. Navy needed to scrap only three battleships and delay construction on five heavy cruisers. Although American naval leaders had won approval for the treaty by promising that Hoover would use it as the basis for building up to treaty strength, there was no immediate or dramatic change for the United States. During Hoover's administration, all of the cruisers authorized in 1924 were commissioned; seven of the fifteen cruisers from the 1929 authorization were laid down and two commissioned, and the aircraft carrier *Ranger* was laid down and christened, along with a few smaller vessels.

Instead of making a dramatic move to build up a navy that might have to be scrapped, the Hoover administration decided to put what naval funds it had available into modernization programs. While doing this, Hoover sought to obtain parity through further arms-control measures, this time in the World Disarmament Conference that opened at Geneva in February 1932. In this conference, Hoover called for reducing all the world's naval armaments by one-third. Hoover's heartfelt call for disarmament fell on deaf ears, as Japan was already building up to treaty strength and the German government was already beginning to push for easing the unilateral disarmament forced on Germany in the Treaty of Versailles. Hoping to achieve financial savings, Hoover's Secretary of the Navy, Charles Francis Adams, took one step that naval officers liked, even though it never brought any savings. He reorganized the U.S. Fleet into four sections that eased the development of operating doctrine and tactics: the Battle Force, the Scouting Force, the Submarine Force, and the Base Force. As might be expected, however, Hoover's passivist strategy in foreign affairs, combined with the effects of the economic and industrial situation on the domestic front, won him the antipathy of the pro-navy historians; not since Thomas Jefferson, one bemoaned, had a president "exercised so consistent and persistent an anti-naval policy."

Such views, in reality, overstate the situation and perpetuate the belief that World War II "might have been averted by sufficient United States power afloat," as one big-navy admiral-historian wrote in 1974. Historically, this view cannot be substantiated; rather, such a view reflects fifty years of navalist lobbying, reinforced, in this case, by Cold War antagonisms and post-Vietnam frustrations. Despite the views of the critics and historical hindsight as to what was to come, the U.S. Navy's failure to maintain itself at the treaty standard during the years 1929-32 was not Hoover's fault, but the result of a number of other factors. Certainly, as a passivist, Hoover put naval armament on a low priority, but the majority of Americans supported such views at the time and called for continuing cuts to all military expenditures. In addition, the country faced a deep financial crisis as well as serious financial issues abroad over payment of war reparations and the repayment of wartime loans.

Vividly aware of the events of the previous decade, the majority of Americans looked more to diplomacy and negotiation than to armaments in their search for national security. Many shared the view that negotiating arms limitations, abolishing certain types of weapons, and decreasing the means by which one nation could attack another were directly linked to controlling the country's fiscal problems. Still, the navy remained a very expensive item in the national budget. Beyond these circumstances, the navy's leadership was split into several factions. Some held differing views toward international developments; some represented a change in outlook from one generation to the next; others wrestled with changes in steel production, new forms of propulsion, new gun and fire-control designs, changing views of ship design, the uses of radio in command and control, and the roles of submarines and aircraft, and the new threats they created. These issues raised new questions over what types of ships to build and to maintain, challenged current ideas on fleet dispositions, and even brought the rationale for the navy's existence into question. The U.S. Navy in the late 1920s and early 1930s was very much in a state of transition and had not firmly committed itself to a particular course. With no direct threat at sea, no political support for expansion, and no immediate catalyst for growth to create a clear focus, the U.S. Navy did not expand to become equal with the Royal Navy, but instead remained at the level of the world's second- or third-ranked navy.

Nevertheless, the frustration expressed over the armament limitations fixed by the politicians was a legitimate interwar naval concern. Navalists in Japan and in Great Britain railed against these same restrictions. Japanese navalists clearly resented the limitations the construction moratorium placed on their ability to develop an Asian empire and interpreted continued Anglo-American efforts to strengthen those restrictions as a thinly disguised policy of containment. Their counterparts in London agonized over the concessions given to the United States and protested that the limits set would restrict England's ability to protect its own Asian assets. In the following decade, arguments for limitations would give way to arguments against limitations, and the world's most frightening naval race would commence in response to the threats posed by the apparent ambitions of Fascist Italy and Nazi Germany, undermining the assumptions behind the Washington and London arms-control system.

The U.S. Coast Guard and Safety at Sea

With the end of the war, Secretary of the Navy Josephus Daniels was reluctant to relinquish the navy's authority over the U.S. Coast Guard, which had been transferred to its control in April 1917 after only two years of separate existence. Both Daniels and his Assistant Secretary, Franklin D. Roosevelt, wanted to bring the government's main maritime activities—the Coast Guard, Lighthouse Service, Coast and Geodetic Survey, and Army Transportation Service—under the Navy Department. The wartime experience had been a positive one for both organizations, and Coast Guard efficiency, discipline, and training had improved along naval lines. In 1919, legislation to transfer all the Coast Guard's officers, men, ships, and stations to the navy was defeated in the House of Representatives, but that was not the end of the attempt. Many Coast Guardsmen felt that they would have improved pay and conditions if they stayed in the navy, but others sided with the Coast Guard's first Commandant, Commodore Ellsworth P. Bertholf, who carried forth the original vision in establishing it as a separate service. Just on the point of retirement from service, he argued that the Coast Guard should be an emergency service that can be very important as an adjunct to the navy in time of war, but which fundamentally "exists for the particular and main purpose of performing duties which have no connection with a state of war, but which, on the contrary, are constantly necessary as peace functions." Touching a chord that resonated with public opinion on other issues, Bertholf remarked, "The Coast Guard rests on the idea of humanitarianism. The Navy rests on the idea of militarism."

In August 1919, President Wilson directed that the Coast Guard would, henceforth, operate under the Treasury Department. The proponents of unification, however, did not accept this as a final decision. Objecting to Wilson's executive order, the American Steamship Owners Association of New York, the Pacific Steamship Association, the Lake Carriers Association, the International Shipmasters Association of the Great Lakes, and several chambers of commerce at port cities, as well as senior naval officers and civilian officials, supported a revised version of Representative Campbell's bill. After much political maneuvering, the proponents of the Coast Guard were able to prevent the new bill from coming to a vote, allowing the Coast Guard to survive the most serious threat to its existence.

By 1923 the U.S. Coast Guard comprised just 206 commissioned officers, 395 warrant officers, and

3,496 enlisted men. Yet, in that same year, this small force saved a total of 2,792 people from danger, assisted vessels carrying a total of 16,253 people, seized 2,106 vessels, and removed or destroyed 46 derelicts that were hazards to navigation. During this time, the service's most dramatic and taxing work involved prohibition. To carry out these, duties, Congress voted to expand the service in 1924, transferring twenty of the navy's outdated destroyers to it and increasing the number of Coast Guard officers and men. In addition, a series of international agreements clarified the areas of patrol, confirming the three-mile limit for the United States, but allowing boarding and search within an hour's steaming of the American coast (typically about twelve miles).

The Coast Guard's work in prohibition was its most widely publicized role, but it was not its only responsibility. It participated in the International Ice Patrol that had been reestablished in 1919, and established an Oceanographic Unit in 1923, leading it into extensive operations in Greenland waters. After many years of repeated requests, Congress appropriated funds in 1929 to build expanded facilities for the Coast Guard Academy. The city of New London, Connecticut, purchased a tract of land on the Thames River and donated it to the U.S. government for this purpose. Secretary of the Treasury Andrew W. Mellon laid the cornerstone of the first building in May 1931, and the first cadets occupied the new Academy building in 1932. About the same time, the Coast Guard reorganized itself in order to achieve financial savings. Yet, even with a budget reduced by 25 percent, the newly streamlined organization had more than doubled in size since the end of the war, with 400 commissioned officers, 500 warrant officers, and 9,000 enlisted men.

The Coast Guard was challenged to keep pace with the changes taking place in American shipping. In 1931 two flying boats and a land biplane joined the Coast Guard's air fleet. In 1934, a Treasury Department reorganization transferred the Customs Service's aircraft to the Coast Guard, increasing its capabilities for maritime air patrol. As issues at sea became more complicated, Congress designated the Coast Guard in 1936 as the main federal agency for the general enforcement of all U.S. laws on the high seas and navigable waters of the United States. This act involved one of the most sweeping

grants of the federal government's police authority ever made. Moving one step further in 1939, Congress agreed with President Roosevelt's long-standing opinion and amalgamated the Lighthouse Service with the Coast Guard, beginning the full integration of federal agencies devoted to safety at sea and the prevention of marine disasters.

Government Direction of Maritime Policy

With regard to merchant shipping, the very fact that a massive commercial fleet had been authorized and built by the Wilson administration marked a major new development in American maritime history. What had formerly been an enterprise virtually monopolized by the private sector was now declared a province of the federal government. In effect, the Wilson administration had declared that the growth of commercial shipping was a prerequisite of national growth–for the greater flexibility it provided the economy; for freeing the nation from extra-national dependencies; for the expansion of foreign trade, and hence the national wealth; and as a fourth fighting arm in time of war. Thus began more than a half-century in which the government would play an increasingly directive role in the formulation of maritime policy.

The Merchant Marine Act of 1920–the Jones Act–represented the government's determination to remain a partner in the nation's shipping industry. Conceived in the wake of Anglo-American postwar maritime discord and the rise of xenophobia in this country, the act incorporated several highly discriminatory features designed, as Senator Wesley Jones, the author of the bill, expressed it, "to drive foreign shipping from our ports." Still, the new chair of the U.S. Shipping Board, the now-retired Anglophobic Admiral William Benson, complained that the act didn't go far enough to create a 100-percent all-American merchant marine. But from the beginning the discriminatory sections were either watered down or ignored, as most American shippers had no desire to engage in a commercial war and petitioned Congress accordingly, prompting

Prohibition at Sea

The ratification of the Eighteenth Amendment in 1919 and the passage of the Volstead Act enforcing Prohibition, which went into effect in January 1920, had a significant effect upon American shipping. It was a matter of record that American tourists strongly favored "wet" ships over "dry," and the U.S. Shipping Board labored for months, amid much controversy, to lessen Prohibition's impact. Its strongest fears were realized when a 1922 court decision declared that Prohibition applied to all American vessels, wherever they sailed. For four months, or until the Supreme Court finally overrode this decision, America's liner trades worldwide suffered seriously as passengers abandoned American ships for foreign vessels, which could dispense alcoholic beverages outside the three-mile limit. But a second court ruling in 1923, which restored privileges outside the limit to U.S. ships, applied also to foreign ships, forbidding them to bring liquor within U.S. territorial waters. In consequence, foreign ships had to seal their liquor stores, or jettison them at sea, before

entering U.S. ports, ending the advantage America's competitors had briefly enjoyed.

"Booze cruises," or cruises to nowhere, the primary purpose of which was to allow thirsty patrons to imbibe outside of U.S. jurisdiction, were extremely popular during the 1920s and early thirties. On Columbus Day, 1932, for example, 1,800 patrons paid thirty-five dollars each for three days on the United States Lines' SS *Leviathan*. In anticipation of over-indulgence, the company hired extra seamen whose sole responsibility was to stand the special twenty-four-hour deck watch devised to prevent drunks from falling overboard. Such extra costs, and the fact that the fares had not been fixed high enough in the first place, produced a losing venture.

Alongshore, Prohibition fostered a lively trade in illegal spirits. When Florida mariner Bill McCoy bought a used fishing vessel in 1920 and began to sit outside the three-mile limit of territorial waters, peddling his alcohol cargo to small contact boats that carried it ashore, "Rum Row"

was born. With a fleet of British-registered liquor freighters hovering off the northeast coast, fishermen, local watermen, and organized crime figures all found lucrative employment smuggling alcohol ashore in their small boats. McCoy grossed perhaps four million dollars before he was indicted in 1925, and fishermen could double their annual income in one successful evening of rum-running. Along the Canadian border, liquor smuggling flourished on the Great Lakes. At Detroit, even the smallest skiff could double as a rum runner, bringing small amounts of beer and whisky across from Windsor, Ontario.

The U.S. Coast Guard received specific instructions to interdict rum runners in 1923. As part of this effort, the three-mile territorial limit was widened to "one hour's steaming," eventually established at twelve miles. In response, fast, high-performance contact boats were built to speed back and forth, many of them powered by the big Liberty aircraft engines perfected during the war. Well-known yacht designers

After its assignment to enforce Prohibition in 1923, the U.S. Coast Guard commissioned 203 of these seventy-five-foot patrol craft to intercept the rum runners that smuggled liquor to shore from larger carriers in international waters. With a machine gun on deck and two gasoline engines to drive the vessel at eighteen miles an hour, these patrol boats were effective until even faster rumboats came along. CG-100 was photographed in September 1924. (Negative 13919F, © Rosenfeld Collection, Mystic Seaport Museum, Inc.)

drew the plans for some of these notable speedboats, and by 1930 the government was seeking advice from the same designers to improve the performance of the boats that patrolled against them.

In 1925 the Coast Guard put a fleet of 203 seventy-five-foot patrol craft into service to picket Rum Row and intercept the contact boats. Eventually this effort succeeded in breaking up

Rum Row, but the smugglers then introduced large, fast vessels that could outrun the patrol boats as they sped alcohol from Canada or the Bahamas directly into U.S. ports.

Despite numerous casualties and many captured boats during the decade-long "rum war," the flow of liquor into the U.S. was only moderately diminished. Indeed, neither the Coast Guard nor the

Treasury Department's Customs Service ever had its heart truly in the undertaking, and the task of policing thousands of miles of shoreline proved virtually impossible. At last, after thirteen contentiously dry years, the Twenty-First Amendment was ratified to repeal the Eighteenth, and on 5 December 1933 Prohibition came to an end.

Benson to remark angrily that it had been easier to run the navy than the merchant marine.

Even with the discriminatory sections set aside, the act expressed Congress's belief that governmental regulation and encouragement of shipping was necessary for the nation's welfare. While the Shipping Board was authorized to turn its fleet over to private enterprise through charter or sale, the Board was still to continue to sponsor the fleet's growth and oversee its operation. Of particular concern was support of American foreign trade. For example, the act created a groundbreaking plan of "essential trade routes" and directed the Shipping Board to operate vessels on these routes whenever private operators were unable or unwilling to do so. These lines were extensive, and the ships assigned to service them numerous. At the outset the Shipping Board earmarked 209 essential trade routes requiring 1,530 ships. Fiscally, this number was unrealistic, and it was substantially reduced over the next few years.

Still, the Shipping Board's determination to maintain essential trade routes fostered the creation of many new shipping companies in the postwar period. Several hundred such companies were capitalized, almost all of them on the expectation of purchasing cheap government ships, obtaining lucrative government charters, and securing profitable assignments in government-backed foreign trade. Large numbers of existing firms also sought to cash in on the new opportunities. One such firm was C.D. Mallory & Co., steamship operators, managers, and agents. Like many others who had obtained their first offshore shipping experience as general agents for the U.S. Shipping Board during the war, Clifford Mallory believed he could now achieve ends he had often sought but could never realize in the period prior to the war. As an operator and manager of Shipping Board tonnage, Mallory could now make use of his shipping resources on a larger scale than formerly possible, but with minimal capital investment. He could abandon the firm's previous preoccupation with the coastal trades and "go offshore," as members of his family had done successfully in the nineteenth century; and if he managed well and the government was consistent in its stated aims, he could, through purchase of government ships and services, become the owner as well as the operator of an American-flag fleet. Mallory also briefly engaged in the tramp trade. For a

As the Ford Motor Company steamship East Indian *heads south with a deckload of crated automobiles, seamen do routine work around the after deck. Launched as the* Beikoku Maru *at Uraga, Japan, in 1918, the* East Indian *was purchased by the U.S. Shipping Board and obtained by Ford as part of its fleet carrying automobiles and general cargo between the U.S., Cuba, and South America. Ford modernized the 445-foot ship in 1925 by replacing its steam engine with a diesel engine. In 1929 Ford sold more than 55,000 cars in Cuba and South America. Sailor Rupert Decker took this photo about 1928. The* East Indian *remained in service for Ford until being torpedoed off South Africa in November 1942. (M.S.M. 94.62.255)*

short period right after the war, chartering vessels from the government for tramping appealed to many shipping firms.

Three factors, however, worked against the success of American shipping in the 1920s. For one, after 1920 the Shipping Board consistently reclaimed tramps for reassignment to the liner trades it preferred. Mallory's tramp operation, fully one-half of his fleet at one time, was recalled under this policy. This trend, accompanied by a general worldwide decrease in tramping, persisted, and by 1937 American tramp shipping had disappeared. More important, no matter what inducements government provided in the way of husbanding fees and assuming other costs and charges, American ships still could not compete in foreign trade. They were older, slower, and smaller than those managed by their European and Asian competitors; their operating costs were always greater; and American statutes continued to limit the maritime industry's ability to engage in price competition. On every sea, American operators ran up against foreign lines whose costs for labor and fuel were less and whose freight conferences maintained lower rates and granted deferred rebates to shippers who employed conference line services exclusively. By law, ships under the American flag could create conferences of their own but could not join foreign-flag conferences. Moreover, American ships and companies were still forbidden to grant rebates of any kind. These difficulties were exacerbated by the onset of a serious economic decline in 1920. Beginning in midsummer of that year, cargo for the world's merchant marines became extremely scarce. By early 1921, 35 percent of the Shipping Board vessels were idle; eventually this figure would reach 70 percent. The crisis was not limited to the United States; Great Britain also suffered, and Japan possibly more. There were simply too many ships for the business. American shipbuilding suffered accordingly.

The slump in American shipping reflected basic inadequacies in United States maritime legislation. In reality, much of the enormous American fleet should have been scrapped at the war's close, but political considerations, the government's insistence on expansion of foreign trade, and an overly optimistic view of demand for ships and cargo prompted the continuation of construction for years after the cessation of hostilities, the last vessel being delivered in 1922. The availability of American ships added to an already troublesome oversupply of world tonnage and helped to increase economic distress in the maritime industries. Moreover, most of these ships were of prewar design and already obsolete; their speeds, ranging between ten and eleven knots, while barely adequate for war, were definitely inadequate for successful competition in the peacetime liner trades. In

the meantime, wages and operating expenses inflated. In addition, the Shipping Board only furthered the problem by encouraging multiple American participation in preferred routes in order to foster operational efficiency and cost-effectiveness through competition. But the tremendous slump in world shipping in the 1920s bankrupted many shipping companies and discouraged others from new initiatives.

The passage of immigration-restriction laws in the 1920s created further difficulties for American shipping. Prior to this decade, the transoceanic passenger-liner companies had depended upon a combination of cargo and steerage-class passengers to earn maximum profits. It has been estimated that between 1900 and 1924 as many as 13,500,000 persons crossed in steerage. Virtually all of these were immigrants. While the liner companies preferred to project an image of luxury and privilege, passengers in steerage outnumbered first-class travelers by as many as five to one. Although the prices they paid were a trifling compared with the costs of luxury accommodations, steerage passengers traditionally produced one-third of the shipping companies' revenues and accounted for more than half of the profits. When Congress passed immigration-restriction laws in the early 1920s, including the National Origins Act of 1924–which created quota systems and limited immigration to less than a quarter of previous annual highs–America's passenger liners experienced large losses of revenue.

It was not until 1928 that definite steps were taken to upgrade American shipping in foreign trade. In that year, subsidies to American shipping were increased. Under the provisions of the new act–the Merchant Marine Act of 1928–mail subsidies were granted for service on essential routes, and the number of subsidized routes was reduced from 209 to 45. Subsidy rates under the act were substantial, and recipients were obliged to contract for their ships with American yards. Speed and size received special consideration. Among the ships built under the act were several that matched the finest afloat, notably the sister ships *Manhattan* and *Washington* of the United States Line, 25,000-ton liners with 22.7-knot speeds that entered North Atlantic service in 1932-33. Quality vessels were added to other fleets, including those of the Matson Navigation Company, the Dollar Line, the American Export

One of the more interesting responses of the private sector to the U.S. Shipping Board's avowed goal to encourage new and improved American shipping lines and expand foreign markets in the postwar period was the Black Star Line, a product of Marcus Garvey's Universal Negro Improvement Association (UNIA), which he founded in Jamaica in 1914. Garvey moved his headquarters to New York City in 1916, launched a weekly newspaper in 1918, and established branch organizations in many American cities. Membership eventually approached one million. Then, in 1919, Garvey incorporated the Black Star Line (BSL) through public subscription. Garvey was committed to the goal of African unity, which regular shipping connections, run by blacks, could foster. In an era when blacks were discriminated against in employment and accommodations on existing lines, Garvey saw the Black Star Line as a means of establishing opportunities for communication, travel, employment, and trade between black population centers. A black shipping line, he promised his followers, "presented to every Black Man, Woman, and Child the opportunity to climb the great ladder of industrial and commercial progress." Large profits and substantial dividends were assured every person who invested in the line.

In theory a project to provide steamship transportation between the U.S., the Caribbean, and Africa, and to connect black businesses throughout the world, the Black Star Line in practice did not get beyond the Caribbean and devoted most of its energy to providing black producers and exporters a means to combat racial discrimination. To fight racism by creating "pronegroism" was his first priority; the economic enrichment of black people

his second; but Garvey's militant antiracism sabotaged the shipping business and ultimately spelled doom for the Black Star Line as economic efficiency was constantly subordinated to the use of the line's three small ships as political symbols of black consciousness. When first-year earnings were tallied, they fell short by 50 percent of matching operating costs. This unfavorable differential increased, and stock sales began to decline. A contract to purchase a better vessel from the Shipping Board was approved, but it was later rescinded by the government when the BSL could not raise the $22,500 deposit.

In 1922 Garvey was indicted on a charge of fraudulent use of the mails in the sale of BSL stock. Garvey remained free on appeal and established a new line, the Black Cross Navigation and Trading Company, which acquired a used vessel, renamed the Booker T. Washington, in 1924. After one unsuccessful voyage the new line collapsed, and Garvey was sent to prison, only to be deported by President Coolidge in 1927.

Garvey alleged that his white competitors waged a war of discrimination against him, and there was some validity to his argument. From a business perspective, however, the larger and better-established shipping firms provided services and economies the Black Star Line and successor Black Cross Company simply could not duplicate. The BSL was not alone—numerous other inexperienced firms fashioned on the golden promise of postwar gain succumbed to the same economic realities as the world edged into the dismal shipping depression of the 1920s. (Courtesy Schomburg Center for Research in Black Culture)

Until the National Origins Act of 1924 placed strict limits on Asian arrivals in the U.S., large numbers of Japanese laborers made the transpacific passage to work in the Hawaiian Islands or on the U.S. mainland. These Issei—first-generation Japanese immigrants—are prepared to land at the Angel Island Quarantine Station in San Francisco Bay, which processed Asian immigrants between 1910 and 1940. (90-G-124-519, courtesy National Archives)

Line, and the United Fruit Company. Sixty-four ships were built under the act, and another sixty-one older ships were reconstructed or raised to improved levels of performance for overseas trade. Many of these vessels benefited from significant advances in engineering: Thirteen were equipped with turbo-electric propulsion, copying recent improvements made in naval vessels, and in a radical departure the *City of New York*, operating in the South African service, was given diesel engines.

More ships would have been built, but the operators, beset by the Great Depression and the coincident collapse of trade worldwide, and sensitive to growing public criticism of the inequities and waste of the mail-subsidy program, grew reluctant to undertake new construction. As late as 1934, 220 of the 282 subsidized ships were of World War I origin. Although a number of lines fostered by the 1928 Act recorded profits, several others simply collapsed. Unfortunately, the glob-

al depression did not prevent the continuation of overbuilding elsewhere, particularly on the part of Japan, Germany, and Italy. Until the war broke out in the late 1930s, nationalistic fervor induced ship construction that only further depressed the shipping industries and added significantly to the problems prevailing at sea.

Inland Waterways and Coastal Trade

While the attention given to the nation's oceangoing fleets was substantial, the coastal and intercoastal trades continued to engage a considerable amount of tonnage. In fact, during the interwar years never less than 60 percent, and sometimes as much as 70 percent, of America's dry-cargo ships sailed the coastal and intercoastal routes. This shipping included the so-called possessional trades to Puerto Rico, Hawaii, and Alaska. Such sea services flourished as a result of the time-honored system of cabotage, the advantageous rates of water transport as compared with rail, improved port facilities, the opening of coastal and intercoastal canals, and the extensive use of these services established during World War I.

The opening of the Panama Canal just prior to the outbreak of the First World War heavily impacted intercoastal shipping; the legislation creating the canal alone had opened many new opportunities by requiring the railroads to divest themselves of any holdings in competing shipping. In the canal's first year of operation, six new American intercoastal lines were established, employing 27 ships. Twenty years later, in 1935, the cargoes and ship tonnage passing through the 50.5-mile canal had increased more than 500 percent. Some of this reflected the sharp growth in the use of tankers. Between 1914 and 1923, the U.S. tanker fleet grew by 1,400 percent. In 1923, the amount of oil shipped east from California rose dramatically by 7,392,000 tons. By 1930, when the East Texas oil fields opened, the Atlantic coast routes for tankers shifted from Mexico and the Caribbean to the Gulf of Mexico and the Middle Atlantic refineries.

World War I had put extraordinary demands upon coastal and intercoastal shipping. During the monumentally harsh winter of 1917-18, for example, a desperate coal shortage in New England was averted only by transferring the burden from the overtaxed and literally frozen railroad system to coastal deliveries by ship from the Middle Atlantic ports. National awareness of the critical importance of wartime shipping resulted in several major federal enactments. In 1918 Congress created the Inland and Coastwise Waterways Service, which, among other things, extended assistance to barge lines on the Mississippi and Warrior (Alabama) Rivers. Government assistance to towboating and barging was strengthened in 1924 by the founding of the Inland Waterways Corporation. In the following year, the government nationalized the Cape Cod Canal, purchasing it from the investors who had built it.

Although the tonnage maintained in the coastal and intercoastal trades was substantial in the 1920s and 1930s, the copious assistance meted out by the government to these fleets underlined the fact that all was not well. For many years, the railroads had been healthy competitors of coastal steaming; now new truck and auto transport developments ate further into former revenues. Improved roadways with new tunnels and bridges brought the collapse of many river and bay ferry services. The 1930s, in particular, witnessed a dramatic loss of passenger service along all coasts. When the Great Depression caused drastic declines in demand for cargo and passenger services, coastal lines that had expanded to handle offshore trade in the 1920s were driven back to their former trades by lack of opportunities, creating a glut of shipping for a diminishing amount of business.

In contrast, while the coastal trades diminished, America's inland waterways developed into one of the transportation marvels of the world. The inland-waterways system drained more than one-third of the nation through the Great Lakes and their outlets, and through the Mississippi River complex. The Great Lakes, serviced by outlets through the St. Lawrence River and the New York State Barge Canal, constituted the largest and most-traveled combination of internal seas and canalized river systems in existence. Considerable attention was given in the interwar years to upgrading the St. Lawrence River and New York State Barge Canal systems. Unfortunately, although there was

no lack of energy, these interwar efforts failed. At issue were the interests of a number of lobbies, divided principally into two camps, both of which became quite aggressive in the mid-1920s. One camp favored the nationalization and enlargement of the New York State Barge Canal between Lake Erie and the Hudson River into an "all-American ship canal." The other preferred a deep-water seaway via the St. Lawrence River. The all-American ship canal lobby combined the U.S. Navy–still reacting to its wartime experience with the British Admiralty and determined to avoid dependence on a waterway through Canada–with New York and Middle Atlantic commercial interests who saw major advantages in an outpouring of western commerce into their geographic area. Opposed were the St. Lawrence River seaway adherents: The Army Corps of Engineers, the powerful farm bloc, insurgent congressmen, and New England commercial interests who feared losing yet more commerce to the Middle Atlantic states. Costs of development favored this latter group. The Army Corps of Engineers, for example, estimated that the canalization of the St. Lawrence River for both navigation and power development would cost less than 20 percent of what it would cost to enlarge the old Erie Canal. It appeared to many, moreover, that the State of New York was trying to dump a white elephant on the federal government and then profit at the taxpayers' expense.

The obvious economy of the proposed development of the St. Lawrence Seaway, and the suitability of the St. Lawrence River as a source of hydroelectric power, gave that approach the logical advantage. But so strong was the combined power of the commercial and political interests of New York, and the patriotic appeal of improving the Erie Canal route, that the opposing views were stalemated through both the Coolidge and Hoover administrations, prompting Hoover himself to lament that "quarrels concerning water quickly get from the realm of engineering into the realm of emotion."

Even the election to the White House in 1932 of Franklin D. Roosevelt, with his record of public works projects and his favorable disposition to the development of the St. Lawrence River, did not break the logjam. Continuing opposition from Middle Atlantic commercial interests, coupled with objections from nationalistic Canadians to a St. Lawrence

Seaway, stalled negotiations throughout the decade. Not until the conclusion of World War II would these impediments be set aside, constructive negotiations undertaken, and the St. Lawrence alternative adopted.

The second unit of America's inland waterway system was the Mississippi River, with its five major trunks and numerous tributaries. The real workhorse of this system was the Ohio River, the "American Rhine," which was canalized in 1929. The Illinois River and its canals to Lake Michigan; the Missouri River to Kansas City and Sioux City; the Mississippi River to St. Paul; and the Tennessee, Cumberland, Arkansas, and Red Rivers were also major elements of the system. Over 2,000 miles of the Mississippi River system had been dredged to nine feet in depth, with another 1,600 miles improved to six feet. Although not as extensive a system as that of the Great Lakes, the Mississippi River network was probably first in importance in terms of national sentiment.

The Mississippi River and Great Lakes inland waterways systems were particularly valuable for the transportation of bulk freights of low unit value—commodities that didn't require speed and that could be handled mechanically. In the interwar period, typical cargoes were wheat, iron ore, and limestone on the Lakes; heavy iron and steel products from the Pittsburgh region down the Ohio and Mississippi to New Orleans; and wheat down the Mississippi to the same destination. Going back up the Mississippi were lumber and sugar from Louisiana and bauxite from Arkansas, as well as coffee, spices, vegetable oils, and other imported agricultural products. Gasoline from Oklahoma found its way up the Mississippi to the Great Lakes and then through the Barge and Erie Canals to outlets in New York State. The Warrior River in Alabama was a major conveyor of iron, steel, and coal from Birmingham to Mobile. Automobile parts were now moving by water from the Detroit area in both southerly and easterly directions. By 1930, the combined Mississippi River and Great Lakes internal waterway systems were carrying 227 million tons of cargo every year.

The third inland waterway network of significance was the growing intracoastal system encompassing 1,700 miles of coastline from New England to the Mexican-American border on the Gulf of Mexico, 700 miles of which had been canalized by the early 1930s. This remarkable waterway was composed of numerous legs: Boston to New York, Philadelphia, Norfolk, Beaufort, and Florida on the East Coast; thence to Mobile, New Orleans, and Corpus Christi on the Gulf of Mexico. Of these legs, save for the forty-mile constricted Delaware and Raritan Canal across New Jersey (the only stretch not twelve or more feet deep), the Boston-to-North Carolina leg had been all but completed. And in the Gulf, the canal from New Orleans to Corpus Christi near the Mexican border was well underway. The pearl of this system was unquestionably the Chesapeake and Delaware Canal, a nineteen-mile sea-level link between the head of Chesapeake Bay and the Delaware River. As part of the New Deal economic recovery program of the mid-1930s, it was significantly widened and deepened, after all of its locks were eliminated.

All told, roughly 25,000 miles of river and 2,500 to 4,000 miles of canals were in fairly good condition. While this paled in comparison with the mighty railroad network (comprising 300,000 miles of mainline track), the inland waterways were given an unusual amount of attention in the interwar period, receiving as much as $65 million annually in government support. Given that $125 million federal dollars were spent annually on the nation's roads, the government's financial commitment to the inland waterways can be seen as an acknowledgement of their considerable importance.

Technological Change Stresses the Nation's Fisheries

The red storm flag was flying its black spot the other day, above Gloucester harbor, down on Cape Ann. A midwinter gale was coming, and weeks of savage weather were overdue. Yet a dozen fishing boats at the wharves were calmly fitting out for sea. It is a way they have in old Gloucester. It is the tradition of the port never to consult the calendar. All winter long the boats go out as a matter of course.

There is a townful of people, 20,000 of them,

whose livelihood depends, in one way or another, on what comes around Eastern Point in wooden bottoms. Winter and the North Atlantic, in their ancient ominous alliance, may thunder in the kelpy caverns of the bass rocks around the point or roar on the reef of Norman's Woe nearby. Still Gloucester thinks only of the duty that lies immediately before its eyes, which is to go down to the sea in power schooners, down to the sea heaving and glistening yonder past Ten Pound Island, and do business in great waters, getting codfish for the nation's breakfast.

Only the reported population of Gloucester and the mention of power schooners (rather than sailing vessels) dates the above passage to the 1930s rather than the 1880s and shows the interwar period as it truly was, standing athwart the old and new. While these were years in which the old, romanticized notion of the interrelationship of a people and the sea still gripped the public consciousness, it was a period in which significant change took place in the fishing industry, most notably in technology.

Technology, in fact, revolutionized commercial fishing in the years between the two world wars. The most significant prewar development was the shift to powered vessels in many of the nation's fisheries. In both New England and the Pacific Northwest the steam engine had made an appearance as offshore fishing techniques changed, and the gasoline engine had also been adopted throughout the nation's fisheries. Then, after 1910, the diesel or oil engine had been perfected, providing greater economy, safety, and reliability than the gasoline engine.

By 1920, the characteristic New England off-shore fishing vessel was a schooner with an oil engine, and in the North Pacific fishing vessels had taken an even more advanced design with power. This change was highlighted on the Atlantic in 1920, when a challenge race was set up, pitting the best of the Nova Scotia fleet against the fastest Gloucester schooner. Because so many New England schooners had engines, the competitor—and winner—was the ten-year-old *Elsie*. Competition continued through the 1920s with increasingly extreme vessels, epitomized by the Canadian schooner *Bluenose*, which only emphasized that they were celebrating the myth of a sailing industry nearly gone, rather than the

reality of an industry in flux. By the time Hollywood began filming an adaptation of Rudyard Kipling's *Captains Courageous* in 1936, the producers were hard-pressed to find fishing schooners still rigged for sail.

On both coasts in the 1920s, the offshore vessels still fished with many-hooked trawl lines, set and hauled from dories carried by the "mother ship." Their catch was still prime groundfish: cod, haddock, and halibut in New England, and halibut and cod in the North Pacific. But this form of fishing, which had been preeminent for 60 years, was now challenged.

The European method of dragging a net bag, called an otter trawl, to sweep fish off the bottom, had flourished in the North Sea since the middle of the nineteenth century, but had only made occasional experimental appearances in the U.S. However, beginning in 1905, heavily capitalized English-style steel-hulled steam trawlers entered the New England offshore fishing fleet, and these in turn were superseded by both wooden- and steel-hulled vessels powered by oil engines, which were far more economical to build and operate than the bigger steam vessels. Since the otter trawl was approximately twice as productive as the trawl line in catching fish, this form of fishing became predominant by the end of the 1920s.

The increased use of the otter trawl helped bring haddock into supremacy over cod as the principal catch of the New England offshore fleet; by 1929, 250 million pounds of haddock were landed, as opposed to 120 million pounds of cod. The various flatfish known collectively as flounder also entered the market in significant quantities with use of the otter trawl.

While New England led the nation in the value of its catch, the Pacific coast and Alaska led by far in volume. Throughout the period, the most important U.S. fishery was the salmon fishery of the Pacific Northwest, particularly Alaska, which produced 500 million pounds of salmon in 1929. Whereas New England fishermen were largely private operators who sold their catch to the highest bidder, Alaska salmon fishermen worked for the canneries that processed the catch. Truly migrant laborers, the fishermen and cannery workers were shipped north in the

On all coasts, fishermen rapidly shifted to gasoline and diesel engines during the 1920s. The shift to power permitted increased use of efficient net forms of fishing and resulted in far larger annual catches. But as fish became more available in the marketplace, their natural stocks began to suffer depletion. These Gloucester, Massachusetts, fishermen clean codfish aboard a converted submarine chaser. Photo by Gordon Parks. (Negative SONJ 16583, Standard Oil (New Jersey) Co. Collection, Photographic Archives, University of Louisville)

spring to net the salmon as they returned to the rivers to spawn. A short season of dangerous, exhausting work, both on the water and in the factories, turned millions of fish into millions of cans of salmon. By fall, the workers and the canned product were on their way south again. Into the 1930s, a number of cannery companies employed old square-rigged sailing vessels for transportation, making this the last operating American fleet of square-riggers.

Canning had become the leading method of processing and marketing American fish. By volume, the second leading fish was the lowly pilchard of the California coast, 400 million pounds of which were packed as sardines in 1929. The Pacific-coast tuna fishery had also come into existence since 1910, and in the 1920s a fleet of "tuna clippers" began to fish from Southern California ports, landing several

species to be canned. Gulf-coast shrimp, as well as a large portion of the 150 million pounds of oysters harvested in the Gulf, Chesapeake Bay, New York, and Connecticut in 1929, were also canned for market. Indeed, Biloxi, Mississippi, called itself the Seafood Capital because of the volume of shrimp and oysters canned there.

Canning brought seafood into the kitchens of consumers far from the sea and long after the fish had been caught. By the late 1920s, other methods were available to do the same thing. Just as salting had been the principal method of long-term preservation through much of the nineteenth century, freezing characterized twentieth-century "fresh" fish preservation. For decades, fish processors had used cold-storage freezers to hold frozen whole fish, but in the 1920s Clarence Birdseye developed a practical quick-freezing method with his General Foods Corporation in Gloucester, Massachusetts. To appease consumers and broaden the demand for fish, processors had begun to market boneless cuts of fish called fillets in the early 1920s, and this cut of fish was ideally suited to the Birdseye process. Fresh, packaged, or frozen fillets were popularly received across the nation, and with the development of supermarket chains in the 1930s fresh fish became even more available.

Advances in communication also wrought significant interwar changes in commercial fishing. The larger powerboats were now equipped with wireless radios, carried an operator, and kept in constant touch with their owners, who, having knowledge of commercial conditions, could direct their vessels to the most lucrative markets. Radio could also be used to aid fleets in fish location. Overhead, airplanes were now being employed to do the same thing. All of these developments were as applicable to Great Lakes fishing as they were to offshore saltwater fishing.

By the late nineteenth century, several U.S. fisheries had become avenues for immigrant employment, and that trend expanded in the twentieth century. Whether it was Nova Scotia and Portuguese offshore fishermen and Italian inshore fishermen in New England, Scandinavian and Chinese fishermen and cannery workers in Alaska, or Southern European sardine and tuna fishermen in California, ethnic groups with strong fishing backgrounds dominated, or even pioneered, a number of the nation's principal fisheries. Nationwide, nearly 130,000 fishermen pursued their disparate methods by the 1930s.

The total of U.S. landings rose to 4,800,000,000 pounds by 1936, leading the world in value, but still two billion pounds less than Japanese fish landings. By this time, serious concerns over fish stocks were surfacing. The collapse of the haddock fishery on Georges Bank in the early 1930s was one symptom, as was the continuing decline in oyster production in Connecticut waters and the near-extinction of Atlantic salmon in New England rivers.

The seasonal salmon runs in the Pacific Northwest supported the nation's most productive fishery through the interwar period. In this Alaskan cannery, men and women of Eskimo, Asian, and European origins processed millions of pounds of salmon during the six-month season. (Courtesy Library of Congress)

Farther down the Atlantic Coast, the great fishery of Chesapeake Bay, while not suffering as noticeably as was New England's, was undergoing the same technological and biological transformation. Netting and seining for the most important fish—shad, alewives, and striped bass—underwent rapid modernization in this extraordinarily prolific area. In truth, with its brackish waters, many tributaries, and protection by land, Chesapeake Bay produced nine times more fish tonnage per square mile than did the legendary banks off New England. Although the U.S. Bureau of Fisheries in 1928 reported "no serious decline" in the quantities of fish available in Chesapeake Bay, this belied a growing concern for the diminishing river runs of shad, a sharp drop in striped-bass numbers, and an awareness of waste in commercial fishing, particularly in the annual destruction of literally millions of undersize fish caught in nets and seines. The fisheries on the Great Lakes had fallen dramatically by the end of the 1920s, and in the Gulf of Mexico stream spoilage, dams, and oil pollution were affecting the quality and harvesting of oysters, most notably on the Louisiana coast.

In the American Northwest, concern focused on the Columbia River, formerly the most pro-ductive fishery in the world for king, or chinook, salmon. Here the advent of commercial fishing, most notably trolling, and the constant reduction of spawning areas through industrial develop-ment and dams, and increased farming, meant

the serious depletion of salmon stocks. With increased pressure, the Alaska salmon and halibut fisheries experienced measurable declines. Inasmuch as the Alaska industry shared waters with Canada, the International Fisheries Commission framed treaties in the late 1930s for the regulation of the Pacific halibut fishery and for the rehabilitation of the Fraser River sockeye-salmon fishery. Throughout this period, technical investigations by the U.S. Fish Commission and other bodies reflected the growing need to "increase the economic value of the aquatic harvest by more complete and efficient utilization." Such developments as quick freezing, the manufacture of food by-products, and the use of fish as new sources for vitamins, occupied the interest of scientists in and out of government, and fishermen sought new species, such as the tuna on the West Coast and the deep-sea rosefish in New England.

By the eve of America's entry into World War II, it was clear that, whereas only a decade earlier reports had spoken of the nation's fisheries in terms of plenitude, ten years later stocks everywhere were under increasing pressure from over-fishing and environmental degradation. In 1939, investigators acknowledged that Pacific salmon and halibut were in danger, the shad and alewife runs in Chesapeake Bay, the supplies of shrimp and oysters in the South Atlantic and Gulf of Mexico, and the harvest of lobsters in the Gulf of Maine, were dangerously below former levels, and that major resources would have to be applied to the problem.

The Merchant Marine Act of 1936

The revelation in the early 1930s that the Shipping Act of 1928 had created a program accompanied by waste and inefficiency shook the maritime industry to its roots. No sooner had the act been passed than criticism arose over the more than liberal terms granted shippers by the Post Office and the Shipping Board. Investigations corroborated these concerns: Some companies were receiving handsome, even exorbitant, subsidies to carry a few sacks of mail; other companies had not lived up to the stipulations of their contracts; still others were rumored to have abused the system by manipulating stocks and producing fraudulent expense accounts. As the depression deepened, so did public concern. In 1932 the Hoover administration concluded that the Shipping Board would have to be stripped of its independent status. Hoover's defeat in the presidential election that year postponed that move, but in the following year President Franklin D. Roosevelt abolished the U.S. Shipping Board, transferring its functions to a newly created and streamlined Shipping Board Bureau subordinate to the secretary of commerce. In 1935 a congressional investigation of the mail contracts, chaired by Senator Hugo Black, concluded that "the subsidy system, as operated, has been a sad, miserable, and corrupting failure" and advocated the termination of all operational subsidies. It appeared to many that federal aid to shipping was in jeopardy.

While the Black Report was front-page news for several months in 1935, neither the Roosevelt administration nor the Commerce Department was prepared to adopt the extreme of abolishing subsidies. As President Roosevelt expressed it, "Government aid must be provided for American shipping to make up the differential between American and foreign shipping costs." The administration's approach was unique in that it preferred to implement an open subsidy policy in contrast to the indirect and "hidden" aids built into the legislation of the previous decade. Politically this was a remarkable development; by asking Congress to support a program of direct subsidies covering differentials in both construction and operations, the new Democratic administration was making a dramatic departure from the party's traditional adherence to free ships. In fact, the idea that an outright subsidy was at all appropriate, after years and years of resistance to the concept, was almost revolutionary.

Nevertheless, it took Congress fifteen months to reach the same conclusion, debating all that time the merits of private versus government ownership. Had tradition prevailed, aid rendered to shipping would have been minimal. But in the midst of economic depression, the logic of bolstering the economy through vigorous support for shipping steadily took hold. When the thirty-fifth draft of a bill was finally approved in both houses in June 1936, the dominant rationalization for its passage reflected the part it would play in helping to stimulate economic recovery by providing federal support for shipbuilding, shipping, and maritime labor.

The Merchant Marine Act of 1936, consciously designed by its framers to serve as a *Magna Carta* of American shipping, was a strong expression of the protectionist and nationalist attitudes shaped in the United States in response to the worldwide depression. When Secretary of State Cordell Hull observed that the British Empire "was closing up like an oyster shell," his lamentation over the inability of U.S. trade to crack the protectionist British imperial system could be applied to markets on every continent. In a recommitment to what had begun under the Wilson administration in 1916, the act of 1936 retained cabotage; mandated that a "substantial portion" of all American overseas commerce would have to be carried in American bottoms; stipulated that all federally supported ships had to be American-built and had to be manned by American crews; and required that American materials, supplies, and services had to be utilized to the greatest degree possible in the construction and operation of these ships. The Merchant Marine Act of 1936 was truly a cap-

Recreational Boating and Racing in the Interwar Years

The number of Americans engaged in yachting and recreational boating during the interwar period increased dramatically, despite the depressed economy in 1921-22 and after 1929. Since the great expansion of organized yachting and "Corinthian"–nonprofessional–boathandling in the 1870s and 1880s, every harbor, large and small, seemed to have its own yacht club, to a total of 435 in 1929. That year there were 4,750 registered U.S. and Canadian yachts, ranging from 24 feet up to the 294-foot *Savarona II*, which would be replaced in 1931 by the 408-foot *Savarona III*, the largest American yacht ever built. Overall, there were perhaps 1,500,000 pleasure boats in the U.S. in 1930.

While the majority of recreational mariners spent their time afloat in individual activities, a principal purpose of yacht clubs was organized racing. With its membership of well-known business leaders, the New York Yacht Club was the most influential club, and its annual racing cruise in New England waters was well publicized. While most racing was done in relatively sheltered waters under yacht-club auspices, ocean racing was becoming increasingly popular after World War I. The Los Angeles-to-Honolulu Transpacific Race, first held in 1906, was reestablished in 1923, the same year that the Newport-to-Bermuda Race

was inaugurated on the East Coast. Great Lakes sailors had the Chicago-Mackinac Race, begun in 1898 and reestablished in 1921. By the 1930s, periodic transatlantic races were also held, and those interested in long-distance cruising could belong to the Cruising Club of America, founded in 1924.

A great change during this period was the shift from the schooner rig to the ketch or yawl rig for larger sailing yachts, and also the shift from gaff rig to the more efficient triangular "Marconi" or Bermuda sail. Hull designs changed considerably during the period as such influential naval architects as N.G. Herreshoff, W. Starling Burgess, and Olin Stephens took an increasingly scientific approach to yacht design.

Although sport sailing was largely an activity of the wealthy, modern methods of boatbuilding allowed many of the less affluent to participate with small, relatively inexpensive craft. For decades, yacht clubs had sponsored their own fleets of identical one-design racing boats, and by the interwar period even sailors of modest means could acquire one-design, mass-produced boats, roughly twelve to twenty-five feet in length. A prototype, the Star, was designed in 1911 and its popularity was spread through a national association formed in 1922.

Later, other classes, such as the Snipe, designed in 1931, and the Comet, introduced in 1932, permitted inexpensive one-design racing on a national basis. In the latter year, avid racers even introduced winter "frostbite" racing–when ice permitted–in the northeast.

The pinnacle of all sailing races, the competition for the America's Cup, was held four times in the interwar period–1920, 1930, 1934, and 1937. Save for a scare in 1934, the Cup, emblematic of the yachting championship of the world, was defended by the New York Yacht Club with relative ease. In the 1920s the New York Yacht Club decided to move the races from Sandy Hook to Newport, Rhode Island, and to race in large sloops that conformed to the J-class measurement rule rather than in dissimilar boats equalized through handicapping. The public's interest stayed focused on the sporting efforts of the venerable Scottish tea baron, Sir Thomas Lipton, to recapture the Cup for Great Britain. Before the octogenarian Lipton finally bowed out of competition by passing away in 1931, conservative estimates placed his expenditures for five failures covering three decades at more than $10 million–this for a cup that itself cost $500. Even in the depths of the Great Depression, America's Cup competition continued. In 1936 Harold

Vanderbilt persuaded the Bath Iron Works to build his ultimate J-boat, *Ranger*, at cost as a patriotic gesture to defeat the British challenger. This last, best American J-class defender, dubbed the "super J," swept the 1937 series and established a reputation that far outlived the boat itself, which was shortly after scrapped in the war effort. America's Cup racing would not resume until 1957, when 12-meter sloops, half the size of the great Js, became the America's Cup class.

While sailboat racing attracted avid participants, and the America's Cup competition drew front-page press coverage and large spectator fleets, boating as a spectator sport was split between collegiate rowing and high-performance powerboat racing. College rowing had drawn large crowds since the 1850s, when it became the first U.S. intercollegiate sport. Harvard, Yale, Cornell, Pennsylvania, Washington, and California all produced highly competitive crews, but the rivalry that came to epitomize college rowing was that between Harvard and Yale, culminating in an annual four-mile race on the Thames River at New London, Connecticut. When Yale's eight-man crew went on to win the 1924 Olympic competition, it demonstrated the high caliber of American collegiate rowing.

If a crew race could draw tens of thousands of spectators, a powerboat race could attract hundreds of thousands; indeed, half a million people watched a race during the 1929 "Harmsworth Trophy"

*Four times between 1920 and 1937, British yachtsmen challenged the American defenders for the America's Cup, the trophy that symbolized international sailing prowess. The 1930, 1934, and 1937 series were sailed in J-class sloops, and all were won by Harold S. Vanderbilt of the New York Yacht Club. With modern Marconi (triangular) mainsails, bronze or steel hulls and aluminum fittings, and pioneering use of synthetic sailcloth, the 120- to 135-foot vessels were technological marvels of the period. Owned and sailed by wealthy industrialists during the depression, these yachts took on national significance and attracted crowds of spectators and wide press coverage during the best-of-seven racing series held off Newport, Rhode Island. The greatest and last American J boat was the 135-foot **Ranger**, built at cost by the Bath Iron Works for Vanderbilt in 1937. With her innovative hull design, she lost only two of the thirty-seven races in which she competed, then was sacrificed to the wartime demand for metal in 1941. (Negative 80434F, © Mystic Seaport Museum, Inc., Rosenfeld Collection, Mystic, Connecticut. Image acquired in honor of Franz Schneider)*

competition on the Detroit River. The automobile and the motorboat were developed almost simultaneously in the later 1890s, and both revolu-

tionized travel on their respective mediums during the first three decades of the twentieth century. Small marine engines and, by 1910, outboard motors

were cheap and readily available from dozens of local and national builders. Early, heavy marine engines began to be replaced by lighter automobile engines in racing boats by 1904, when the American Powerboat Association inaugurated the Gold Cup races as the national test of powerboat speed. In 1915 a forty-foot hydroplane named *Disturber IV*, powered by two Duesenberg engines of nearly 700 horsepower apiece, first exceeded sixty miles per hour on the water.

World War I interrupted powerboating, but the postwar period brought great changes based on wartime technology. The light, high-power aircraft engines developed during the war—especially the U.S. Liberty engine—became available for recreational use, and the 1920s became the age of speed. When the Gold Cup races excluded hydroplane hulls in 1922, the true test of speed became the British International Cup for

Motorboats—the Harmsworth Trophy—which was won by the American Gar Wood in 1920 and successfully defended in the 1920s and 1930s by Wood's *Miss Americas*. In 1932, Wood's hydroplane, *Miss America X*, reached 124 miles per hour. Although powerboat racing declined during the Depression, the introduction of the three-point hydroplane late in the 1930s set the stage for even faster speeds afloat after World War II.

The 1920s saw the real beginnings of "stock" boat production, which helped get more

Americans on the water. Rather than ordering a custom boat, one could now select a boat in the same way one selected an automobile—size, power, and price—and not coincidentally the stock-boat industry was located near the auto and engine industry in Michigan and the upper Midwest. Beginning in the early 1920s, Hacker, Dodge, Gar Wood and Chris-Craft began producing and marketing lines of standardized and fully outfitted stock boats. In certain urban areas, and particularly New York, wealthy businessmen put both stock boats and custom-designed express cruisers to work as "commuters," aboard which they could travel comfortably from their country homes to city offices in the 1920s and 1930s. Pleasureboat sales flourished through the 1920s, reaching $26,200,000 in 1929, and then plummeted with the coming of the Great Depression, dropping to just $4,800,000 in 1933.

With so many novices taking to the water in powerboats, the U.S. Power Squadrons, which had been incorporated in 1915, provided a great educational service with boating classes held in communities all over the U.S. Numerous monthly boating magazines, including *Yachting*, *Rudder*, and *Motor Boating*, also educated, amused, and informed the growing population of pleasureboat mariners.

Even the schooner fishermen of Massachusetts went racing in the interwar years. They had a long tradition of formal and informal tests of speed, sailed with a minimum of regulation. In 1920 they were challenged to compete against a representative of the expanding Nova Scotia fleet in an international series sponsored by the *Halifax* (Nova Scotia) *Herald*. An American victory in 1920 fostered the development of a number of large, fast, but essentially impractical working vessels designed to race. In reality, the series glorified sailing ability and sailing vessel design at a time when they were rapidly becoming obsolete in the face of engine power and net forms of fishing. Then the races deteriorated in wrangling as

the informal style of the fishermen clashed with the yacht-racing rules imposed during the series. Nevertheless, American and Canadian schooners competed in seven series between 1920 and 1938, and, because of widespread publicity, the unbeatable Canadian schooner *Bluenose* and the 1930 Essex-built Gloucester challenger *Gertrude L. Thebaud* came to symbolize fishing schooners for the general public. Both vessels were exhibited at the 1933 Chicago World's Fair, and the *Gertrude*

L. Thebaud became Gloucester's good-will vessel, attracting yet more attention in 1933 when, in the midst of the Great Depression, she sailed directly from the fishing grounds to the nation's capital in an effort to publicize the economically depressed state of the New England fisheries. Ironically, a symbol of affluence was used to drive home the plight of the working poor.

In the 1920s, the increasing demand for affordable pleasure boats encouraged the production of stock powerboats. Numerous firms, such as Chris-Craft, were established in the Midwest in conjunction with the automobile industry, and several automobile manufacturers experimented with boat production. The Dodge boatbuilding plant, seen here in 1930, was designed to produce 2,000 standardized runabouts a year. While the industry was crippled by the Great Depression, such standardized production has characterized recreational boats since the 1920s. (Negative 39384F, © Mystic Seaport Museum, Inc., Rosenfeld Collection, Mystic, Connecticut)

stone to a twenty-year movement to protect the nation's domestic and foreign shipping by extending the federal government's arm over maritime affairs.

Accordingly, the Merchant Marine Act of 1936 rendered substantial assistance to shipbuilding enterprises by agreeing to provide through construction subsidies the difference between building at home and abroad, thus measurably reducing the problems operators had faced in arranging for new tonnage. Construction costs for the private market were reduced further by the establishment of rules for uniformity in design. Shipowners received their support in the form of consolidated and increased subsidies designed to overcome operational differentials with foreign competitors.

The United States Maritime Commission, established by the Merchant Marine Act, had more than economic recovery as its mission, however—it reflected a growing belief that an adequate merchant marine was necessary for national defense. "Shipping," stated the Maritime Commission, "is not a business in the usual sense of the word. It is . . . an instrument of national policy, maintained at large cost to serve the needs of commerce and defense." The national defense system, it argued, could ill afford in a hostile world to wait for the private sector to respond to the new conditions. And the new Maritime Commission immediately sought to improve and expand government's authority to manage its own national fleet, which comprised, although substantially inactive, 16.5 percent of the nation's tonnage in domestic and foreign trade.

Roosevelt's appointment in 1937 of the Boston financier Joseph Kennedy as first chairman of the Maritime Commission underlined the president's belief in the importance of the commission. Kennedy and his vice chairman, Admiral Emory S. Land, a former naval chief of construction and repair, faced hard facts: in terms of world tonnage, the combined private and government American overseas fleet had fallen to fourth place, sixth in speed (ships of less than twelve knots predominated), and seventh in the age of its vessels (fully 90 percent were nearing obsolescence). Consequently, Kennedy had hardly arrived at his new office when he and Land activated the Maritime Commission's shipbuilding functions. "What's the sense of talking about an adequate or a first-class merchant marine in the face of such facts?" Kennedy asked. "For us an adequate merchant marine has to be a new merchant marine . . . . What are we going to do about it? The answer is BUILD SHIPS!—the best and most modern ships—and build them RIGHT AWAY. . . . We are going to lay the keels for new fast ships. And we are going to do it NOW."

Within two months, the first keels had been laid—speedy auxiliaries (sixteen to twenty knots) designed to accompany the navy in time of war. A ten-year, fifty-ships-per-year plan followed. Within two years, on the eve of the outbreak of war in Europe in 1939, the Maritime Commission had made substantial progress. The Commission's first contract was for a new North Atlantic liner, the 723-foot *America*, the largest commercial ship yet built in the United States. She was launched just a day before the beginning of war in Europe in 1939. Several of twelve fast tankers had been launched the same year, and the first of twenty new dry-cargo vessels had come off the ways. Still other vessels, including a series of slightly larger cargo ships and another series of freighters and combination cargo ships, were being built. Most of these ships qualified for the subsidy arrangements of the new law, which not only provided substantial twenty-year loans for up to 75 percent of cost, but also extended a differential subsidy covering as much as one-third to one-half the cost of construction. Operating subsidies had been granted to eighteen private shipping companies. The Maritime Commission had also established a new maritime training program for seafaring personnel under the auspices of the U. S. Coast Guard. A cadet system to train merchant officers accompanied it. In the prewar years, roughly 3,300 unlicensed and licensed personnel trained under these programs located at three Coast Guard stations: New York's Hoffman Island, New London's Fort Trumbull, and Alameda's Government Island in California. Finally, the Maritime Commission inaugurated the famous "Good Neighbor Fleet," which operated between New York and the east coast of South America under the house flag of the American Republics Line.

Taking great pride in the initial two years' work of the Maritime Commission, its new chairman, Admiral Land, was delighted to report to

Congress in May of 1939: "The rehabilitation of the American merchant marine is definitely under way. The long and dangerous decline. . . . has been checked, the process reversed and progress forward has begun. Prospect for the return of the American flag to a place upon seas commensurate with our country's position as a world power are the brightest in many years."

The significance of the Maritime Commission's work was not made clear for a number of years, but had not the Maritime Commission begun in 1937 to build ships for war, as well as for peace, the United States would have been sorely pressed to provide the stop-gap assistance the Allies required at the outset of war–and would have been severely handicapped in its ability to service American armed forces once the nation joined the conflict. This timely and prescient undertaking would provide the nation with just enough ships, shipyards, and experience to enable it and the Allies to weather the storm in the early stages of World War II.

The U.S. Navy Under the Roosevelt Administration

At the same time, the "big-navy" advocates got only a portion of what they believed was necessary in the 1930s; nevertheless, the support they received was of a magnitude comparable to that of the great naval expansion program of World War I. Domestic and global factors predominated in the dramatic growth of the navy in the period 1933 to 1941, and the U.S. Navy had a good friend in President Franklin D. Roosevelt.

It had not been a political whim that led Woodrow Wilson to appoint Franklin Roosevelt as Assistant Secretary of the Navy in 1913; Roosevelt was an astute student of naval history, loved the sea, and was a competent sailor. More than that, or perhaps because of all of that, Roosevelt was a big-navy man. He had been in Washington for only a month in 1913 when he affirmed his support for a "large and efficient navy." In much the same manner, twenty years later and within a week of having become chief executive in 1933, Roosevelt instructed his first Secretary of the Navy, Claude Swanson, to

announce that the fleet was to be built up to the treaty strength that previous administrations had forsaken. At the very same moment, rumors began to fly in Washington that Roosevelt was planning to revive his earlier ideas to consolidate the Coast Guard and the navy. This time, however, there was little enthusiasm for the project within either uniformed service. With the Coast Guard's new efficiency and demonstrated skills, the shipping organizations also strongly opposed such a merger. The navy, however, faced larger issues abroad.

By 1933, Japan had built her navy up to 95 percent of what the treaties permitted, while the United States was close to the same strength, having built only up to 65 percent of the greater strength that the treaty allowed. To provide for this, as well as to replace the U.S. Fleet's nearly obsolete battleships, the Chief of Naval Operations, Admiral William V. Pratt, recommended an eight-year shipbuilding and modernization program that included 119 new ships that would cost $944,363,000.

As a first step toward this goal, Congress allocated a quarter of a billion dollars of New Deal National Recovery Administration funds, designed to relieve unemployment, for the purpose of constructing thirty-two naval ships over a three-year period. This building program included light cruisers, destroyers, two aircraft carriers, and four submarines.

In 1934, Congress began to pass important supplements to this plan, well aware that Japan was rapidly reaching parity and planned to begin replacing Imperial Japanese Navy ships that became overage by 1936. Roosevelt vigorously supported Congressional initiative in the Vinson-Trammel Act of March 1934, which authorized the building of the full treaty-strength navy and the replacement of overage ships, within the limitations laid down by the Washington Treaty of 1922 and the London Naval Limitation Treaty of 1930.

Roosevelt's world view strengthened the navy's position. Hoover had questioned the validity of an aggressive policy in the Pacific. In contrast, Roosevelt, like the navy, strongly supported a perpetual presence in Asia. In 1920, for example, he had argued that America's national defense "must extend all over the Western Hemisphere,

Maritime Labor, 1917-1938

Ships may have been crucial to the nation's war effort, but they were useless without seafarers to operate them. In response to emergency wartime manpower needs in 1917, the United States Shipping Board worked out a cooperative arrangement between the nation's shipowners and maritime unions to increase the supply of American seamen. This was not easily accomplished. The history of labor-management relations in the maritime industry had traditionally been one of intense conflict and hostility, and the shipowners were loath to relinquish the prewar advantages they had acquired over labor. That the U.S. Shipping Board was able to achieve accord of any kind was quite remarkable.

Essentially, the steamship lines agreed to offer uniform salaries and war bonuses attractive enough to assure a steady supply of labor for the war's duration. It was hoped that such uniformity would help discourage job jumping and encourage work efficiency. The high wages might also lure men back to seafaring, a profession American citizens had progressively abandoned (In 1915, 90 percent of America's seamen were foreign-born). Codified in May and August of 1917, the accords became known as the "Atlantic Agreement." Similar agreements were drafted for the Pacific Coast and the Shipping Board's fleet.

The raise in salaries was substantial. On the eve of America's entry into war, the predominant wage paid able-bodied seamen was $35 per month. The 1917-18 Atlantic Agreement raised this to $60. To account for inflation, wages were increased to $75 in 1918-19 and to $85 for the last year of the accord, 1919-20. Thus, from 1917 to 1920 an able-bodied seaman's wages increased 138 percent. Similar, if not quite so large, increases were awarded firemen, mates, and engineers. Liberal overtime bonuses supplemented these substantial gains. It was a salubrious period for maritime labor, one of the most prosperous ever. "Three years of God's Free Air," is how Andrew Furuseth, the venerable leader of the International Seamen's Union, described the gains achieved as the result of war.

Furuseth, however, was realistic enough to know that these advantages could not prevail after the war. Still, the extent to which they were lost was shocking. The agreements quickly proved to be transitory, an aberration in labor-management relations, a "facade of unanimity" as one historian of the labor movement expressed it. The primary issues in postwar negotiations were high wages, the war bonuses, and labor's insistence upon union hiring preferences. When it became evident that the shipowners were determined to return to prewar conditions, labor was quick to take action. At first, the unions were successful, winning one strike in late 1918, and then another more extensive strike in 1919. But conditions were unusual in 1919. First, a short postwar period of rising freight rates brought prosperity to shipping and seemed to justify the continuation of high wages. Moreover, the fear of socialism–the "red scare"–that gripped America after the war generated fears that the maritime unions, with their international character and contacts, would be among the first American industries to be radicalized. The Shipping Board thought to avert this by acceding to union demands. No sooner had the shipping boom diminished and the red scare abated, however, than the Shipping Board, now under the leadership of the retired Admiral William S. Benson, sided with the shipowners, who maintained, with some justification, that in a failing market high wages and declining trade opportunities (much of it caused by the glut produced by the U.S. Shipping Board's massive ship-construction program) were making it difficult, if not impossible, for them to turn a profit.

Labor chose not to compromise. The showdown came in 1921, when, in the midst of a recession, unlicensed seamen refused to accept lower wages, even when presented with evidence of substantial drops in ship revenues, an increase in ship layups, and the return to the dollar's prewar purchasing power. Firemen, cooks, and engineers sympathized with the seamen. A strike ensued, completely paralyzing the Atlantic Coast. The shipowners decided to make a stand. With Admiral Benson behind them, they offered a take-it-or-leave-it wage reduction of 25 percent. The owners had the additional advantage of being able to replace the striking sailors with large numbers of nonunion men eager to take a job at virtually any price. Unable to control the easy-labor market and incapable of bankrolling the strike, the unions gave in. Industry gained more than a reduction in wages; by refusing to reemploy union members, owners also restored the open shop. Possessed of growing power and backed by the Shipping Board, companies now reduced wages drastically, even lower than those suggested by the Board. By February 1922, able-bodied seamen's wages had retreated 65 percent from wartime highs, firemen's 64 percent, first mates' 72 percent, and chief engineers' 66 percent. The maritime unions had been routed; they would not be able to regroup until the mid-1930s. A measure of the decline was the drop in union membership: in 1920 roughly 115,000 men belonged to the International Seamen's Union; in 1923 that membership stood at 16,000, and in 1929 it was considerably less. Only the hard core hung on. "Back to the abyss," was Andrew Furuseth's description of the return to prewar conditions.

The onset of the Great Depression further debilitated maritime labor. By 1930 thousands of unemployed seamen and shipworkers languished in the nation's ports. Jobs were so scarce, and the unemployed

so desperate, that men were relieved to sign on as "work-aways," performing full ship-board labor for a dollar a month, simply to get a daily bunk and a square meal. Benefit plays, charity concerts, food appeals, relief funds, and liner visitation fees did little to resolve the problem. In one three-month period the Seamen's Church Institute in New York served 679,370 free meals. Even so, in December of 1932 and again in May of 1933 the Institute was taken over by mobs of unemployed men, who were finally forcibly removed by New York's finest, the city police.

The seamen and dockworkers took their grievances to the streets. In 1934 strikes broke out on every coast. Stevedores and longshoremen struck in New Orleans, Galveston, Mobile, New York City, Seattle, San Diego, and San Francisco. Tugmen left their jobs in Toledo. In Seattle, union men sank a tug operated by strikebreakers, and in San Francisco the Embarcadero was the site of repeated altercations between maritime gangs and the police. Conspicuous among the protestors were growing numbers with socialist leanings. The communist Marine Worker's Industrial Union, for example, had a membership of 12,000 longshoremen and seamen in 1934. These developments were particularly galling to the old gladiator of labor, Andrew Furuseth. Furuseth's commitment to moderation, moralism, and idealism was shattered by

Andrew Furuseth (1854-1938) was christened Anders Andreassen by his poor farming parents in Norway. Sent to work at age eight, he received a rudimentary education before venturing to sea at age nineteen. By 1880 he had reached the West Coast and joined the numerous Scandinavian seamen who manned the coastal fleet there. For his organizing efforts among West Coast seamen he was elected secretary of the Sailors' Union of the Pacific in 1887. Four years later he retired from the sea and in 1894 became the legislative agent in Washington, D.C., for the various American seamen's unions. His lobbying efforts resulted in the landmark La Follette Seamen's Act of 1915. Furuseth served as president of the International Seamen's Union after 1908 and had close ties with Samuel Gompers's American Federation of Labor. Furuseth—shown here during the negotiations at Versailles in 1919—also maintained contact with the European seamen's unions and pushed for more universal adoption of the conditions fostered by the La Follette Act. For his untiring efforts on behalf of seamen, Furuseth was honored by sailors and government figures alike upon his death. (Courtesy Library of Congress)

the militancy and radicalism of his seafaring brethren, and he soon lost his place in the maritime labor movement to young streetfighters like Harry Bridges and Joe Curran.

By far the worst confrontations took place on the West Coast. When Pacific Coast longshoremen struck in March 1934 in an effort to achieve union recognition, they were soon joined by seamen in San Francisco. Federal efforts at conciliation failed, and a general strike ensued; clashes with city police left several dead, and virtually the entire California National Guard was activated. Sympathy strikes tied up ports on both coasts. Alarmed at the effectiveness of the strike and the damage it was doing to the nation's commerce, the Roosevelt administration introduced mediation that summer and managed to calm things. In December 1934 a major breakthrough occurred when the shipowners, under pressure from the National Labor Relations Board and the threat of another strike, agreed to recognize the International Seamen's Union (ISU) as a collective bargaining agent, acknowledged union-member employment preference, and accepted the eight-hour day in port, the three-watch system at sea, and generous wage increases. Further activism during 1935, 1936, and 1937 strengthened labor's gains, ushering in a new era in maritime labor relations. The New Deal, labor-friendly, had now extended itself to the sea and to the docks.

In the meantime, maritime labor was changing significant-

Joseph E. "Joe" Curran (1906-1981) went to sea at age sixteen and eventually earned a reputation as a troublemaker for his efforts to organize seamen. In 1935 he joined the International Seamen's Union (ISU) to make a passage from New York to California on the steamship California. Discovering that seamen's wages were higher on the West Coast, he got the crew to strike against the company and won protection from the U.S. secretary of labor. When he was blacklisted by shipping companies in 1936 he organized a nine-week strike, then rebelled against the ISU with Communist assistance, and finally established the National Maritime Union (NMU) in association with the Congress of Industrial Organizations (CIO) in 1937. Curran kept tight control on his union, which had enlisted 47,000 members within a year. He remained the most powerful figure in maritime labor into the 1950s, though his conflicts with other seafarers' unions ultimately weakened his position. In this view he confers with Captain Clifton Lastic, a black officer who commanded Liberty ships during World War II. (Courtesy National Archives)

ly within. Furuseth was near death, and the other "old line" leaders like Victor Olander and Paul Scharrenberg, were under increasing pressure from the new militants. In 1937 substantial numbers of men seceded from the ISU, the seafaring branch of the American Federation of Labor, to create a rival organization, the National Maritime Union (NMU), which, under the leadership of Joe Curran, affiliated with the newly organized and more militant Congress of Industrial Organizations (CIO). In 1937 the NMU,

often disdaining peaceful methods, won overwhelming support from seafarers on the Atlantic Coast. In response, the AFL reorganized the ISU into the Seafarers' International Union. Essentially at odds, even openly hostile to each other, the two new unions nevertheless represented the interests of more seafarers than had ever been represented before. For the first time in American history it was now possible to speak of maritime labor as an organized and powerful entity.

Admiral Emory S. Land (1879-1971), a native of Colorado, already had a master's degree from the University of Wyoming when he entered the U.S. Naval Academy in 1898. After his graduation in 1902, Land served on the Asiatic Station before taking an advanced degree in naval architecture at Massachusetts Institute of Technology. Thereafter, he served as a naval constructor, except for duty on the staff of Admiral Sims and at the American Embassy in London, 1918-21, and in the navy's Bureau of Aeronautics, 1926-28. Land acted as chief constructor and chief of the Bureau of Construction and Repair during the naval buildup, 1932-37, before retiring from the navy. He was then appointed to the U.S. Maritime Commission and acted as chairman, 1938-46, overseeing the greatest shipbuilding effort in world history. In this photograph, taken during World War II, Land displays models of the Maritime Commission's designs for a passenger ship, a standard tanker, and several standard dry-cargo ships. (U.S. Maritime Commission Photograph 1640)

must go out a thousand miles to sea, [and] must embrace the Philippines." In 1934 he reiterated this, but extended the nation's Pacific Ocean defense perimeter to "three thousand miles from the coast," or almost 1,000 miles beyond the Hawaiian Islands.

While building up the navy was a worthwhile public works project justified by hard economic times, the principal impetus for American naval rearmament was the ascendancy to power in Japan of military expansionists and their influence upon that country's mid-1930s decision to withdraw from the treaty obligations of 1921-22 and

demand naval equality with the United States and Great Britain. The Roosevelt administration fully realized that an under-strength U.S. Navy would only encourage Japanese expansion in Asia. If the renunciation of naval treaty bans meant parity for the Japanese Navy, then American interests in Asia were seriously threatened.

In 1936, the terms of the disarmament treaties expired and were not renewed. Japan and Germany embarked on extensive capital-ship building programs. Great Britain openly joined in the arms race, announcing the construction of her new *King George V* class of battleships. The United States, continuing to abide by the limitations for a brief year and a half after the expiration of the treaties, soon followed. Then war broke out on 7 July 1937 when Japan invaded China. In the course of the conflict, low-flying Japanese aircraft attacked and sank the USS *Panay*, a gunboat operating in the Yangtze River near Nanking, killing two men and wounding forty-three others. Although Japan apologized for this error and paid an indemnity, the incident caused widespread concern in the United States. Alarmed, Roosevelt called for an increase in naval tonnage that exceeded the expectations of the navy itself. In response, Congress passed a series of acts to increase the support for the navy, including the service's annual appropriations and two Naval Deficiency Acts, in 1938 and 1939. As a result of this, the navy began construction of six new battleships in the *North Carolina* and *North Dakota* classes, thirteen light cruisers, thirty-one destroyers, ten submarines, and the aircraft carrier *Essex*. In addition, Congress increased the number of naval aircraft by 3,000. With rare exceptions, all of this firepower was to be directed to the Pacific theater.

Even this building program left the U.S. Navy at a disadvantage, for while the commitment to growth was substantial, the Roosevelt administration was constrained by the country's vigorous isolationism and its aversion to the very notion of a naval race. Unsure of its position because of extreme Japanese secrecy, the United States aimed to bridge the gap between the needs of its existing fleet and the treaty limits it had failed to maintain over the years. In the meantime, the Japanese were developing a formidable fleet. As Stephen Pelz observed, while the U.S. Navy was "caught in a spiraling naval race" with Japan, it was one in which the Japanese were steadily outdistancing the United States in many categories, most notably in modernization and in number of capital ships and aircraft carriers, and of lighter craft such as submarines and destroyers.

The growing concern with Japan and Asia was balanced by the emergency in Europe. The rise of Hitler's Third Reich and the combined interests of Germany, Italy, and Japan in Latin America generated a new sensitivity to hemispheric defense and to the importance of the Atlantic Ocean. In May 1939, the U.S. Army and Navy agreed to begin planning for a unilateral American response to the threats that were simultaneously arising around the world. The result was the creation of four new two-ocean naval strategies, code-named "Rainbow," to reflect the now-complex relationship of the names of single colors that had previously been employed to denote U.S. defense policy in regard to a single nation. Rainbow Plans One and Four dealt with the defense of the Western Hemisphere out to two thousand miles off the American coast, while Rainbow Plans Two and Three dealt with wartime contingencies that might arise in coordinated wars with European powers that had colonial interests in Asia. Strategy dictated that the main naval force would remain in the Pacific, but it also recognized the growing Axis influence in South America, most notably in Brazil, that threatened the Caribbean and the Panama Canal and necessitated an American naval presence in that area. German naval potential on the Atlantic, moreover, seriously threatened American trade with South America and Europe and had to be countered with a large antisubmarine force composed of aircraft and escort and patrol vessels. In order to meet these new needs, the fleet was put in a defensive posture, even at the expense of the Philippines.

The change in overall policy was dramatic. In the twenty years since 1919 the country had come full circle, passing from attempts to reduce merchant shipbuilding, limit arms, and outlaw war in the first phase, to a second phase with dramatic growth in merchant shipbuilding, increasing naval armaments at sea, and preparations for the possibility of a war that would, once again, touch the full range of America's interests.

The U.S. Navy created a gunboat force on the Yangtze River in 1903 to protect U.S. commercial and diplomatic representatives during the internal conflict at the end of the Ch'ing Dynasty and the beginnings of the Chinese republic. Reorganized as the Yangtze Patrol in 1919, the force was strengthened to guard American ships and American residents and travelers on China's principal river after the Washington Naval Conference of 1921-22 endorsed the "open door policy" for China. The Yangtze Patrol gunboat Panay, launched at Shanghai in 1927, is shown here during trials off Woosun in August 1928. In 1937, as Japan invaded China, the Panay was stationed at Nanking to evacuate the last Americans before the Chinese capital fell to the Japanese. On 11 December 1937 the 191-foot gunboat took the Americans on board and moved upriver to escape the fighting. Although the Japanese command was informed of the Panay's presence, Japanese planes were ordered to attack all ships in the river, and on 12 December Japanese aircraft sank the Panay, with casualties. Japan paid reparations, but the incident furthered the decline of Japanese-American relations in the Pacific, presaging the outbreak of war four years later. (19-A-12457, courtesy National Archives)

Part 4

World War II and After, 1939—

CHAPTER 15

World War II

ONE WAY OF LOOKING
at World War II is to see it as three separate
wars. Studied from this perspective, the first
war took place between 1939 and 1941 and was
fought essentially between Great Britain and
Germany. American aid was instrumental in
Britain's survival during these crucial months,
and it is plausible to argue that survival alone
represented an implicit victory for Great Britain
in this phase of its dramatic struggle with
Hitler's forces. The second war, the greatest of
the three, was the conflict fought on the continent of Europe between 1941 and 1945. In its
initial stages, it was a ferocious war waged on
the Eastern Front between Germany and the
Soviet Union. Through huge and untold sacrifices of human and material resources, the
U.S.S.R. turned the tide in Europe, in the
process inflicting 75 percent of Germany's casualties. But the United States also played a significant role in this war, supplying the Allies,
defeating Hitler's submarine force, participating
in the invasion of North Africa, and spearhead-

ing the landings in Sicily, Italy, and France. The
third war within the war was that fought in the
Pacific theater between the United States and
Japan that extended from the attack on Pearl
Harbor in December 1941 to the signing of the
peace treaty in September 1945. This war was
won decisively by the United States. This chapter will focus on the second and third of these
three phases of World War II—the great war on
the European continent, with its accompanying
struggle to control the North Atlantic seaway
and launch ground invasions by sea; and the
extraordinary campaign in the Pacific, in almost
every way a war waged by and from ships.

In the autumn of 1939, war in Europe seemed
imminent, but the U.S. Navy's leaders sincerely

*Detail of heroic U.S. merchant mariners, in a
painting by Anton Otto Fischer. (Courtesy U.S.
Coast Guard Museum; Claire White-Peterson
photo)*

[551]

doubted that it would be likely for the United States to become involved in that war. Surely, they reasoned, the combined forces of the Royal Navy and the French Navy would be adequate to contain German and Italian naval forces in the Mediterranean and in the eastern North Atlantic. On the verge of the war, America's naval leaders felt secure in the tacit protection that France and Britain could give the United States; at the same time they felt the need to show a measure of naval strength at sea as a means to deter any possible conflict and to avoid being drawn into war. If there were direct dangers for the United States, the U.S. Navy's leaders saw them primarily in the Pacific, where Japan was already at war with China, and where American interests were vulnerable. In the mind of the Chief of Naval Operations, Harold R. Stark, the first consideration was sending a detachment from the U.S. Fleet, then based in California, to Pearl Harbor, Hawaii, where, he advised President Roosevelt, their presence would send a message to Japan from a "strategic, psychological standpoint." The newly established Hawaii Detachment sailed for Pearl Harbor in early October 1939 under orders "to facilitate training." This movement was the first in the chain of events that led to the large-scale buildup of the fleet at Pearl Harbor.

Although the situation in the Pacific had the highest priority, it took longer to implement American action there than it did in the Atlantic. The war in Europe moved swiftly, with German forces invading Poland in September 1939 and conquering it within twenty-nine days, partitioning its territory with the Soviet Union, which quickly overran the Baltic states and attacked Finland in November 1939. In the context of this rapid chain of events, President Roosevelt immediately proclaimed American neutrality and declared a "limited national emergency," allowing the navy to increase its strength and to recall reserve officers and men to active duty. At the same time, Roosevelt announced that the U.S. Navy would establish a neutrality patrol to keep the war away from American shores. By doing so, he intended clearly to suggest that the United States would defend itself if attacked. It already appeared as though a new U-boat war was at hand when a German submarine sank the British liner *Athenia* on the third day of the war.

While Canada immediately declared its intention to join the Allied war effort, and as the French and Dutch possessions in America were also involved, Roosevelt was concerned about safeguarding the neutrality of the remaining states in the Western Hemisphere. To this end, the United States invited all representatives of the American republics in the Congress of American States to meet at Panama. There, a month after the war in Europe had begun, the delegates drafted the Act of Panama, establishing a neutral zone that extended 300 miles off the coasts of North and South America. Giving further legitimacy to Roosevelt's neutrality patrol, the Congress of American States assigned responsibility to the U.S. Navy for patrolling this 300-mile moat. Initially organized into eight separate patrol areas, the U.S. Navy operated south from Newfoundland to the Guianas, including the Caribbean. As a further step to avoid involvement in war, Congress declared in November 1939 that the waters surrounding Great Britain were a danger zone and prohibited American-flag ships from entering those waters. At the same time, Congress modified the country's neutrality laws and allowed the United States to sell arms and ammunition to warring states, providing they paid cash and carried it in their own ships and at their own risk.

In considering defense appropriations in the Spring of 1940, the U.S. Congress increased the naval tonnage goal over the previous year and extended it to include a substantial number of aircraft, the majority of which would be assigned to the offshore "neutrality patrol," and the president ordered the recommissioning of thirty-five World War I vintage destroyers that had been laid up. Shortly afterwards, in April-June 1940 when Germany invaded Norway and Denmark, defeated France, and threatened to invade Great Britain, the U.S. realized that it could no longer assume that the Royal Navy could by itself serve as a "protective shield" in the Atlantic. To this realization was added the fear that Germany might seize the French Navy, which had fled to North African ports. In the Pacific, the continued movement of Japanese forces south added to the growing concern for American security. In the summer of 1940 the United States found itself unprepared to face a serious attack in either the Atlantic or the Pacific. By this time, the United States' highest priority was defending the Western Hemisphere. Below this, the United

States could maintain a strategic defensive to deter the Japanese in the Pacific, while moving some forces to the Atlantic where Germany presented the most active threat. One major result of this evaluation was another phase in American rearmament: The Two Ocean Navy Act, signed into law on 19 July 1940–a massive program involving $4 billion to more than double the navy by adding 200 new ships and 15,000 naval aircraft. This signaled a firm commitment to naval growth far beyond the old treaty limits. Two months later, this was accompanied by the famous "destroyers-for-bases deal" between Franklin Roosevelt and Winston Churchill, whereby the U.S. turned over fifty World War I four-stackers to the British in exchange for ninety-nine-year leases to allow the U.S. to construct military bases in Bermuda, Newfoundland, and the British West Indies.

War in the Atlantic

When Great Britain did not succumb to the German onslaught, marking in effect the Third Reich's first military setback, it was clear that the war in the Atlantic and in Europe would be an Anglo-American undertaking. The navy's plan, formulated by Chief of Naval Operations Admiral Harold Stark, called for a strong Allied offensive in the Atlantic and a defensive war in the Pacific. This approach was codified by American and British planners in March 1941 in a staff agreement, signed by naval and military representatives of both the United States and Great Britain, entitled ABC-1, in which the U.S. Navy's primary assignment was to defend the Western Hemisphere and to assist the Royal Navy, as soon as possible, in controlling the Atlantic sea-lanes and in escorting convoys of merchant vessels. The Pacific had now become a subsidiary theater. While the administration made a show of moving its capital ships from California ports to Hawaiian waters and imposed a series of economic embargoes on Japan–which in reality only strengthened Japanese rationale for expansion into South Asia–the need to "Beat Hitler First" took precedence over all other objectives.

American activity in the North Atlantic increased dramatically. The Lend-Lease Act was passed in March 1941. In April, a limited-range escort system for convoys to Britain was begun and was extended then to convoys between Canada and Iceland. On 10 April 1940, while rescuing three boatloads of survivors from a torpedoed Dutch freighter off the coast of Iceland, the USS *Niblack* (DD-424) fired depth charges at a German U-boat and became the first American warship to take action against Germany. Following Germany's seizure of Denmark and Norway in April 1940, British forces had occupied Iceland–since 1918 an independent kingdom in personal union under the Danish crown–in order to preempt German plans to secure that island as a base. Similarly, as part of the maritime defenses of the Western Hemisphere, the Danish crown colony of Greenland requested American protection in May 1940. Shortly thereafter the U.S. Coast Guard cutter *Coamache* landed American diplomatic representatives to establish an American protectorate until its government could be resumed by Denmark. In a pattern that would be repeated time and again over the next five years, this new responsibility brought the immediate need for hydrographic information, pilot books, and maritime charts of the region. By July 1941, Britain requested that the United States take over those duties. As American responsibilities spread eastward, there was an obvious need to determine a new demarcation line between the two hemispheres. In April 1941, the new commander in chief of the U.S. Atlantic Fleet, Admiral Ernest J. King, took the initiative in a fleet operation order. In a stroke reminiscent of Pope Alexander VI dividing the world between Spain and Portugal in 1493, Admiral King established a demarcation line just west of Iceland at longitude 26° west. From that meridian, the Western Hemisphere included the Azores and Greenland in the Atlantic, and stretched westward across the Americas to the International Date Line in the Pacific. In the Western Hemisphere, the United States Navy viewed the entry of any belligerent warship or aircraft as an unfriendly act.

Five weeks later, on 21 May, a German submarine sank the SS *Robin Moor* in the South Atlantic, the first American casualty in the war at sea. While two new American battleships slid down the ways in the spring of 1940, the USS *North Carolina* (BB-55) and *Washington* (BB-56), naval leaders seriously debated the feasibility of transferring upwards of one-half of the U.S. fleet to the Atlantic, creating the U.S. Atlantic Fleet

program was completed in 1943, the United States would finally achieve the goal of a navy second to none, and would use this power to overwhelm its enemies on every front.

The U.S. Navy entered World War II with certain administrative disadvantages. For one, the navy's morale had been shaken as the result of the defeat at Pearl Harbor. More importantly, the division of authority between the Chief of Naval Operations and the Commander-in-Chief of the U.S. fleet had proven inefficient. President Roosevelt could not reverse the Japanese victory, but he did remedy the leadership problem by combining the two positions into one and centering its operations in Washington, D.C. To head up this new office–which represented the greatest concentration of authority in U.S. naval history–the president appointed Admiral Ernest J. King.

King was a superb tactician who very early in the war framed the course of action that would be taken in the Pacific. He began from an almost untenable position: although obligated to a two-ocean, Europe-first strategy, King was determined not to let the Japanese consolidate their gains in the Pacific; worse, he headed a navy possessed of a one-ocean fleet, and the bulk of that was assigned to the Atlantic. The navy not only had to grapple with Japan's superior strength in the Pacific, it had to contend with German submarines in the North Atlantic and participate with British forces in the Mediterranean invasions, all under the handicap of an acute shortage of shipping.

There was a further impediment: the Americans favored a massive-thrust strategy aimed at carrying the war to the European heartland at the earliest possible moment. From the navy's perspective this would be achieved by a 1942 cross-channel invasion of France. But the British opposed this frontal strategy. Possessed of far fewer material and human resources, and ever mindful of the terrible losses in the trench warfare of World War I, they favored a plan of peripheral attack, which would be aimed at clearing the Mediterranean (the lifeline to their Middle East and Asian empires), would place strong reliance on air supremacy, would entrust the Soviet Union with the annihilation of Hitler's land forces, and would countenance an amphibious invasion of France only when Germany had been brought to a state of exhaustion.

The British-influenced decision to delay the invasion of France and embark on a peripheral campaign in the Mediterranean angered the American admirals. They not only resented the abandonment of the direct-thrust strategy–which they saw as the most expeditious way of taking the offensive against Hitler–but they were rankled over the diversion of naval resources away from the Pacific, which the navy, after suffering the humiliating defeat at Pearl Harbor, saw as its primary operational theater. The shocking rapidity of Japan's advances in the Pacific in late 1941 and early 1942 only intensified the navy's determination to regain control of that ocean. Consequently, the American naval thrust in the Pacific took on a magnitude uncharted in Allied prewar strategic planning.

Even so, the navy did not stint in its Atlantic involvement. Although the cross-channel attack the navy preferred was postponed until June of 1944, the military buildup for it, support for the interim Mediterranean landings, and the need to convoy aid to the Allies–most notably to Great Britain and the Soviet Union–necessitated control of the Atlantic Ocean. The U.S. Navy played a major part in securing that control.

The battle of the North Atlantic was one of the greatest nautical conflicts in modern history–and in retrospect, one of the pivotal events of the European war. Winston Churchill remarked that of all the campaigns of World War II, the war on the Atlantic was the one that concerned him most. The possibility that the U-boats would starve Britain into submission and deprive the Allies of a base for operations against the mainland, leaving Hitler in possession of continental Europe, seemed a distinct possibility.

For Germany the primary goal was the destruction of all vessels engaged in supplying Great Britain. The British objective was equally direct: to prevent German surface and subsurface craft from severing its lifeline. By the time of American entry into World War II, the British navy and air force had succeeded in securing the ocean against German surface warships and raiders, but the campaign against the U-boats had not fared as well. Between September 1939 and January 1942, for example, German submarines sank 4.7 million tons (1,107 ships) of

German U-boats took a devastating toll on U.S. shipping during the period 1941 to 1943. Of 590 U.S.-flag commercial vessels sunk by enemy action during World War II, 47 percent were lost in the North Atlantic and 23 percent in the Gulf and Caribbean. Until an effective coastal convoy system was developed and U.S. Navy and Coast Guard antisubmarine patrols increased–combined with improved Allied intelligence and increased shipbuilding production–the U-boats stalked shipping along the East Coast, in the Caribbean, and through the Gulf of Mexico, leaving a trail of burning ships like the one pictured here. Wallowing under a tower of oil smoke, this torpedoed U.S. tanker appears doomed. Yet, she was one of the fortunate few that were salvaged and returned to service. She is probably the four-year-old, 524-foot Pennsylvania Sun, *torpedoed 125 miles west of Key West by U-571 on 15 July 1942 while carrying 107,000 barrels of fuel oil from Port Arthur, Texas, to Belfast, Northern Ireland. Two of her forty-two-man crew and seventeen-man armed guard were killed, but the rest escaped safely. When the fire burned itself out, the crew returned the next day and got the ship to Key West. Repaired where she was launched, at Sun Shipbuilding in Chester, Pennsylvania, the* Pennsylvania Sun *later returned to service. Note the antisubmarine guns mounted at bow and stern. (U.S. Maritime Commission photo 3278)*

Allied shipping. Another million tons (391 ships) were lost to mines, most of which had been laid by submarines. Together, this constituted almost two-thirds of all Allied vessels destroyed at sea. When France fell in 1940 and the German navy was able to operate from the Bay of Biscay, the effectiveness of Admiral Karl Doenitz's U-boat campaign increased dramatically. The development of "wolf pack" operations and tanker submarines further improved Germany's long-range destructive capabilities. By war's end, German U-boats would sink a total of 197 warships and 2,828 merchantmen: 14,687,231 tons in all.

The entry of the United States into the war did not reverse the trend at first; with the navy committed to two fronts, with a paucity of ships available for antisubmarine warfare, and with Admiral King's decision to assign the bulk of what he had in the way of escorts to the convoying of troops and supplies across the Atlantic, Doenitz's U-boats ravaged unprotected merchant shipping off the Atlantic seaboard, in the Gulf of Mexico, and in the Caribbean during the first half of 1942. So effective was Hitler's undersea campaign against allied shipping between 1939 and 1943 that it has been argued that had the Nazi high command committed more extensively to submarine construction prior to the conflict, rather than to capital ships in the unsuccessful effort to challenge the British dreadnoughts, Germany might have won the war at sea, and thus the war itself.

But the Germans waited too long to put sufficient emphasis on submarine development, and in time the Allies were able to meet the threat. Immediate attention was given to the bombing of submarine pens and factories—attacking the U-boats before they reached the high seas. Admiral King's preference for a fall 1942 cross-channel attack had as one object the seizure of Hitler's submarine bases on the Bay of Biscay. But the attack did not materialize, and the campaign to meet the threat on the high seas themselves had to be intensified.

The ultimate success of this campaign can be laid to significant Anglo-American advances in radar detection and to the development of new offensive weapons. Improved shipborne and airborne radar denied U-boats the refuge of night and inclement weather; and sonar, a sound-wave device, enabled surface craft to locate submarines beneath the surface. The development of depth charges with improved range and sinking speed rendered Germany's undersea craft much more susceptible to damage. German magnetic mines were neutralized by degaussing, or demagnetizing, ships' hulls. The increased range of land-based aircraft furthered Allied antisubmarine capabilities by progressively eliminating those far-out areas in the ocean, known as "black holes," where submarines had once been safe from aerial pursuit. The attachment of new eighteen-knot escort flattops (aircraft carriers) to convoys and to aggressive hunter-killer units was yet another development in the campaign against German U-boats. Intelligence technology also played a critical part in the victory over Germany's submarines. When British cryptographers broke the U-boat Enigma key of the German high command, a major advantage was achieved.

The production of nautical charts became a criti-cal wartime activity. Under the direction of Rear Admiral Leo Otis Colbert, the Coast and Geodetic Survey expanded rapidly. Starting first preparing charts for the new bases in the West Indies and charting dangerous wrecks left by U-boats along the U.S. coast, the course of the war quickly created demands ranging from tide and current tables for wide areas of the world to very detailed charts of specific areas. In some cases, new charts had to be produced from the only information available, some of which was from surveys made years before. The production of nautical charts rose from 400,000 in 1940 to 4,000,000 in 1945, 75 percent of which were used by the U.S. Navy and the merchant service. At the same time, there was a great demand for aeronautical charts, increasing from a production of 464,000 charts in 1940 to 9,000,000 in 1945, principally for use by aviators in the U.S. Navy and Army Air Force.

The ultimate development, of course, was the production of more ships than the Germans could sink. The profusion of weapons, naval ships, and merchant vessels that poured forth from factories and shipyards in the United States helped shift the offensive away from the U-boats and to the Allies. At the height of the war on the Atlantic, from January to March of 1943, American shipyards were constructing cargo ships faster than the Germans could sink them: 1.5 million tons more per month than were lost to Axis naval and air forces. At the same time, German submarine losses began to rise precipitously as the Allied antisubmarine strategy took effect. By 1944 the rate of U-boats destroyed matched rates of production. The invasion of France in June 1944 further limited Doenitz's effectiveness by forcing him to evacuate his bases in Brittany. Indeed, German U-boats proved virtually impotent in their ability to restrict the enormous seaborne traffic from England to Normandy. For use against Allied shipping, Germany constructed 1,162 submarines; by the war's end, 941 had been sunk or had surrendered, and the battle on the Atlantic had been lost to the Anglo-American forces.

If the war in the Atlantic emphasized the necessity of antisubmarine vessels, such as escorts and destroyers, the amphibious operations launched on the beaches of North Africa, Sicily, Italy, and France, and on the myriad islands and atolls of the Pacific, depended utterly upon landing craft. Indeed, one historian has argued that the single most important naval craft in World War II was not the convoy escort vessel but the LST (landing ship tank), which became the Allies' basic vehicle carrier. Another historian has claimed the same honor for the LCVP (landing craft vehicle personnel), the much smaller steel-built vessel designed as a replacement for the wooden American prototype constructed early in the war by Andrew Higgins, a New Orleans boatbuilder. In any event, the critical importance of landing craft to the war's prosecution is indisputable. What is also indisputable is that, despite the enormous capacity of American industry–25,171 landing craft of less than fifty tons were built for the navy in 1944 alone–there were never sufficient numbers of these vessels.

The shortage of landing craft stemmed largely from the nation's need to win the war in the Atlantic against Germany *and* to produce the fighting ships required for the Pacific campaign against Japan. As the navy saw it, landing ships would be valueless unless the Atlantic was secured, and it would be folly to concentrate so heavily in Europe as to allow the Japanese to advance in the Pacific. Fighting ships were what was needed. In contrast, the U.S. Army staff insisted that the primary emphasis be placed upon the construction of landing craft, for the army's commitment to the amphibious landings planned for the European campaign depended upon the availability of these vessels. Yet, even a sufficiency of landing craft would be meaningless without the capital ships to cover the assaults on the beaches. As Admiral King could point out, sound military strategy had dictated that the Salerno invasion of September 1943 be conducted much farther up the Italian coast, but the absence of aircraft carriers limited the beachhead to the farthest range of Allied land-based planes from Sicily.

Such arguments favored the navy and a military shipbuilding program, with the result that the army in Europe never did secure its landing craft in desired numbers. In consequence, the scarcity of landing craft impacted World War II strategy in the European theater in much the same way as did the absence of carriers, the most telling example being the decision to postpone Operation Dragoon, the assault on the southern coast of France that was to have accompanied the Normandy invasion of June 1944.

In retrospect, the navy's preference for direct assault rather than a peripheral campaign proved politically prescient. The failure of the Mediterranean campaign to produce a second front formidable enough to significantly divert German forces from the Eastern Front embittered Stalin and might have contributed politically to the ensuing Cold War. The two-year delay also enabled the Soviets to overrun and hold Eastern Europe. Moreover, it provided the Germans with additional time with which to construct a defensive system along the Normandy coast. There is little evidence, however, that a cross-channel assault could have succeeded before 1944.

Still, the U.S. Navy's involvement in the amphibious invasions of North Africa, Sicily, Italy, and France was critical. Under the command of Admiral F. Kent Hewitt, the ferrying of troops and supplies to the beachheads and the bombardment of enemy coastal strongholds were the primary roles of the navy in these campaigns. In the Mediterranean, the U.S. naval force served as a junior partner to the Royal Navy. This combination proved quite effective at the November 1942 Oran and Algiers landings in the North African campaign and at three beachheads in Sicily in July 1943, where American naval gunfire helped to reduce enemy gun emplacements and break up counterattacks. Although the Anglo-American naval force erred in allowing a large number of German and Italian troops to escape from Sicily, the subsequent Allied landings at Salerno on the Italian mainland in September 1943 were accomplished with strong naval support, and the troops were able to hold on at the Anzio beachhead only because of the navy's ability to keep them supplied.

Flawed Axis naval policy, as well as Allied naval prowess, figured in the Anglo-American victories in the Mediterranean. As good fortune would have it, the Italian Navy, which might have wreaked havoc on Allied shipping in the early stages of the war, was held back on account of fuel shortages and the absence of adequate and coordinated air support. In time, Allied naval strength in the Mediterranean matched and exceeded that of Italy, countering the former

On Omaha Beach, shortly after the D-Day invasion, a rank of LSTs (landing ship tanks) unload equipment and vehicles for the U.S. Army's push inland. Barrage balloons are moored overhead to prevent a low-level German aircraft attack on the beach. Offshore, a small part of the transport fleet lies at anchor. As in the Pacific, the LSTs performed essential service in getting fighting vehicles and supplies ashore during Allied invasions in the Mediterranean and on the French coast. To bring them to the landing place, a meticulously organized support fleet sailed from numerous British ports, all under the protection of naval combat vessels. (80-G-46817, courtesy National Archives)

Italian advantage and rendering its use suicidal. The Axis failure to take the island of Malta in 1940, which seriously compromised Hitler's effort to supply General Erwin Rommel's forces in North Africa, was another critical mistake that enabled the Allies to assert their control in the Mediterranean.

In no European campaign did the navy play a more vital role than during Operation Overlord, the June 1944 invasion of France–the largest amphibious assault in history. The extent of the Normandy invasion can be measured by the number of landing craft devoted to it. Whereas the U.S. Navy contributed 102 landing craft to the invasion of French Morocco in November 1942, no fewer than 2,489 American amphibious craft took part in D-Day.

To make the immensity of the cross-channel undertaking even more graphic, the United States provided a like number of ships to the British for their own landings in Normandy. Initially, the Normandy landings were to be part of a two-pronged invasion, the second prong being an amphibious attack, Operation Dragoon, in the south of France. However, Dragoon had to be delayed for more than two months because fighting ships, merchant vessels, and landing craft were not in sufficient supply to support two simultaneous attacks.

The success of the Normandy invasion, following on from the successful experience of amphibious landings in North Africa and in the Pacific, depended heavily upon several factors. First, to prepare for Overlord, the Allies undertook

To shelter the essential supply operations on the exposed Normandy beachheads, British and American planners devised a series of artificial harbors, code-named Mulberries. The twenty-one-foot tidal rise along this coast made the undertaking particularly difficult. Floating concrete caissons were designed and built to be deployed as offshore breakwaters. Inside these, half-mile floating steel bridges led to the beach from landing platforms in deep water. To meet the army's supply needs, the Mulberries had to be completed within two weeks of D-Day. In the meantime, to provide immediate sheltered water, damaged ships were sunk to serve as breakwaters called Gooseberries. This is Gooseberry 2 off Omaha Beach, which was in position within four days of the D-Day landing. Several of the twenty-seven damaged U.S. Liberty ships and other merchant vessels deliberately sunk to form the Gooseberries are visible. This wartime marine engineering feat, completed in ten days, permitted tens of thousand of tons of supplies to follow the invading Allied forces. However, after ten days of operation the Mulberries and Gooseberries were shattered by the worst summer storm in forty years and had to be abandoned. (80-G-285154, courtesy National Archives)

the systematic preinvasion destruction by air of the German defense infrastructure: railroads, rolling stock, marshaling centers, rail hubs, and bridges of every kind. This strategy played a large part in enabling the Allies to reinforce the beachheads by sea faster than the Germans could reinforce their coastal defenses by land. A superiority in air power, moreover, would assist the Allied navies in controlling the invasion lanes.

A second factor was the decision to avoid an assault on a major seaport. The August 1942 raid on the Normandy coastal city of Dieppe, in which Canadian commandos suffered large losses, had impressed upon the Allies the impracticability of taking a port head on. While the Allies had learned this lesson, the Germans had not. Increasingly concerned that a seaport assault would be a major objective of the cross-channel invasion, they concentrated their heaviest defenses around ports, leaving the beaches less protected. With the decision to abandon the plan of taking a port, the Allies began to assemble "mulberries," artificial harbors made of disposable ships (most of which were battered Liberty ships or obsolete vessels plucked from the U.S. World War I reserve fleet), which would be towed across the channel from England and sunk off the Normandy beaches as breakwaters, with floatable concrete caissons installed as piers. In the meantime, the Allied fleets bombarded the Calais-Boulogne landing area further up the coast in a successful effort to divert German attention from Normandy.

A third factor critical to the Normandy invasion was Allied naval support. Under the command of the Royal Navy's Admiral Sir Bertram Ramsay, the Allied naval forces were organized into five task forces. Two of the five were American, commanded by Rear Admiral Allan Kirk. Naval gunfire support for the two American task forces was overpowering: three battleships, eight cruisers, numerous destroyers, and a British monitor. The remaining three naval task forces—all British—were also heavily armed. Allied naval gunfire did splendid work at Normandy. The ability of the invasion to secure a foothold in France was due in large part to the firepower provided by the combined Allied naval forces. At Omaha beach, where formidable German defenses threatened to annihilate the American attacking force, U.S. naval personnel exhibited extraordinary courage and skill in utilizing their ships' guns to overcome German gun emplacements at almost point-blank dueling range.

Naval responsibility went beyond transporting troops and providing gunfire support—although German naval and air interference was surprisingly small, some opposition by surface vessels and aircraft did occur and had to be defended against. Obstacles to landing, such as mines and beach barriers, had to be removed, and the transport of supplies and troop reinforcements and the evacuation of casualties were also carried out by the navy. Another contribution, too often ignored, was the part U.S. naval and civilian personnel played in clearing the badly damaged harbor of Cherbourg, taken in late June, thereby enabling the direct passage to France of large oceangoing supply vessels from England and the United States. Thereafter, the ability of

the Allies to overwhelm the Germans logistically would never be in doubt.

In the meantime, Operation Dragoon, postponed until sufficient landing craft could be transferred from Normandy to the Mediterranean, took place in mid-August on the beaches of the French Riviera between Cannes and Marseilles. Naval gunfire support was excellent there, and seven escort carriers provided tactical air strikes. Toulon and Marseilles were captured in late August. While naval units would later help to ferry Allied troops across the Rhine, with the successful conclusion of Dragoon and Overlord major naval operations in European waters ceased in the summer of 1944.

The War in the Pacific

The course of the war in the Pacific saw the United States make a series of strategic moves to recover after the attack on Pearl Harbor. While the actual war had some similarities with prewar contingency planning, there were a number of differences. Strategists saw five possible alternatives in looking for an avenue for counterattack on Japan: (1) through the Indian Ocean and Southeast Asia; (2) across the North Pacific through Alaska and the Aleutian Islands; (3) from the South Pacific via New Guinea and the Philippines; (4) through the central Pacific, taking key bases in the Gilbert, Marshall, and Caroline Islands, before moving into the Marianas and Formosa to a base in China from which to launch an attack on Japan; and finally, (5) in an option that did not become available until the very end of the war, an assault from northeast Asia and the Soviet Union. Not until late 1943 did the Allies see that it would not be possible to assault Japan through China. By this time, the combined chiefs of staff had developed a compromise between a southwest and a central strategy, taking advantage of American resources, and using the rapid development of fast-carrier task forces in leapfrogging and neutralizing enemy bases.

In his official report, *The U.S. Navy at War*, Admiral Ernest King treated the conflict in the Pacific as a war having four phases. The first three, from Pearl Harbor to the victory at Guadalcanal in February 1943, were essentially defensive or defensive-offensive campaigns, which denied the Japanese further gains in the Coral Sea, at Midway, and in the Solomon Islands. The last phase, which took the navy into the western Pacific in the summer of 1943, and then to within striking distance of the Japanese islands in the spring of 1945, was composed of offensive operations. Each of these phases featured naval engagements that exceeded anything previously staged on the seas. No single battle or campaign proved to be decisive, although the battle of the Philippine Sea—the "Marianas Turkey Shoot"—and the battle of Leyte Gulf, along with the American submarine campaign in the Pacific, virtually ended the Japanese naval threat.

Following Pearl Harbor, which seriously depleted American naval strength, the U.S. Navy was committed to a Germany-first strategy, pursuing a defensive posture in the Pacific. Its first action was the battle of the Java Sea in February 1942. There, despite suffering serious losses, the navy made clear its determination to halt Japanese expansion in the southern Pacific. The remarkable carrier raid upon Japan in April 1942, commanded by Admiral William Halsey and General James Doolittle, was a startling departure from the policy of holding-actions only. It represented a psychological need for retribution after the surprise attack on Hawaii rather than an effort to inflict serious damage on Japan. Another carrier engagement, the May 1942 battle of the Coral Sea, while tactically a Japanese success—the United States lost the *Lexington*, one of its precious few aircraft carriers—was actually a strategic victory for the Americans, for it checked the Japanese advance into the Pacific southeast and represented the first setback for the Japanese since the outbreak of war. This battle was noteworthy in another way: a purely aerial battle, it was the first in history in which the opposing fleets never saw each other. It was also the first of numerous battles in the Pacific theater in which carriers would figure as the principal instruments of combat.

No conflict in the Pacific documented as dramatically the significance of the fast carrier as did the battle of Midway, which occurred in June of 1942, Japan's year of reckoning. Determined to draw out and destroy the remainder of the American fleet before American industry gave

the U.S. Navy overpowering strength in the Pacific (the United States had 15 battleships, 11 carriers, 54 cruisers, 191 destroyers, and 73 submarines on the ways at the time of Pearl Harbor), the Japanese, under Admiral Isoroku Yamamoto, set out soon after the contest in the Coral Sea to take Midway Island as a way of forcing a direct confrontation. A diversionary force sent to occupy the Aleutians did not deceive the Americans who, possessing a code-breaking advantage, had deciphered Japan's true battle plan. To prevent the loss of Midway, which in Japanese hands would threaten the Hawaiian Islands and even the American West Coast, Commander-in-Chief of the Pacific Admiral Chester W. Nimitz strengthened the island's capability for land-based air power and surveillance and deployed his much less imposing force of cruisers, destroyers, and three carriers as a trap northeast of Midway under Admirals Frank J. Fletcher and Raymond Spruance.

The approaching Japanese force was detected from the air on 3 June, but Midway's land-based fighters and bombers were sadly unsuccessful in several attacks, failing to inflict any damage and losing half their numbers. In the meantime, Yamamoto's carrier planes smashed the island's defenses. Only the interdiction of Spruance's and Fletcher's carriers prevented a complete Japanese victory. In the most extraordinary event of the Pacific war, dive bombers from the *Yorktown* and the *Enterprise* caught the Japanese carrier fleet in the process of recovering its first strike on Midway and rearming and reloading for a second attack on the just-discovered American fleet. In short order three Japanese carriers were sunk, and later in the day a fourth was destroyed. Japanese air losses were especially severe—253 planes and 100 veteran pilots. Yamamoto had entered into the conflict with every expectation of destroying the American fleet with his battleships, but they had never even gotten within range. The Battle of Midway was not a contest of capital ships, but of air power; as such it certified the fast carrier as the primary weapon of the Pacific war. For the Americans, despite the loss of the *Yorktown*, it was a great victory, ranking among the greatest sea victories of all time. It was also the turning point of the Pacific conflict.

A Japanese airman captured this view of the 7 December 1941 attack on Pearl Harbor. First authorized as the site of a U.S. Navy base in 1887, even before Hawaii became a U.S. territory, this sheltered harbor one-third of the way across the Pacific was the forward base for the Pacific battle fleet. After Japan expanded its invasion of Asia in the summer of 1941 and Japanese-American relations deteriorated, the U.S prepared to defend the Philippines while the Japanese planned an attack on Manila, Hong Kong, and Singapore, as well as a surprise strike to cripple the U.S. fleet at Pearl Harbor. A Japanese carrier force set out on 26 November, and its planes began the attack just before 8:00 A.M. on Sunday, 7 December. In this view, Hickam Airfield burns in the background as the plane passes over "Battleship Row" along Ford Island. At lower left is the USS Nevada, about to get underway, only to be grounded in salvageable condition after being struck by a torpedo and bombs, with the loss of fifty men. Just aft of the Nevada is the fleet repair ship Vestal, which will escape from her berth next to the USS Arizona in damaged condition. The USS Arizona will be struck by a torpedo and eight bombs, sinking with the loss of 1,177 men. Just astern of the Vestal and Arizona, a bomb has struck the USS West Virginia, which will be hit by six torpedoes and two bombs, with the loss of 105, but will be salvaged. On her left, the USS Tennessee will survive two bomb strikes. Aft of them, the USS Oklahoma will capsize with the loss of 415 men after being struck by four torpedoes, while the USS Maryland will survive two bomb blasts. Farther to the right, the oiler Neosho has just unloaded a cargo of aviation fuel and is about to get underway successfully to avoid the bombs. At the right margin of the view is the USS California, which will be struck by two torpedoes and three bombs, sinking in salvageable condition. Although the attack was a complete surprise, and eight U.S. battleships were hit, only the Arizona and Oklahoma were so badly damaged they could not be refitted for service. They were the only U.S. battleship losses during the war. The rest returned to active duty by 1944, but by then aircraft carriers had clearly become the capital ships of the U.S. Navy. (80-G-30550, courtesy National Archives)

If fast carriers shaped success at Midway, they also were the reason for the American advance into the central and south Pacific. As the military historian Steven Ambrose pointed out, without aircraft carriers, navies were like "babies still in the womb; they were tied to the short and inelastic umbilical cord of land-based air cover." Now, with carrier air cover, navies could extend the areas over which they had influence, could "see farther and hit farther," and could "sail closer to enemy-held shorelines"–the Doolittle raid was a case in point. And, most importantly, carriers could support the amphibious landings that brought American forces closer and closer to the Japanese homeland. Without carrier air cover, Ambrose concluded, "it is doubtful that the amphibious operations in the Pacific could have been undertaken at all."

Crippled by torpedo and bomb strikes, the USS Lexington *(CV-2) heels to starboard as her crew abandons ship to board a waiting destroyer during the Battle of the Coral Sea, 8 May 1942. To prevent Japanese control of the Coral Sea, southeast of New Guinea, which would block naval communication with Australia and New Zealand, the* Lexington *and* Yorktown *moved into the area in May 1942, and their aircraft located a Japanese carrier task force. On the second day of the air battle, the* Lexington *was struck by two torpedoes and three bombs. Her crew controlled the damage but, when gasoline vapors exploded, the crew received orders to abandon ship. Soon after the crew was rescued, the American destroyer* Phelps *sank the flaming hulk with two torpedoes. Like her sister ship* Saratoga *(CV-3), the* Lexington *was built on the hull of a battle cruiser canceled to meet the limitations of the Washington Treaty. Launched in 1925, the 888-foot* Lexington *served in the Pacific through the 1930s, and was on a mission to reinforce Midway Island when the Japanese attacked Pearl Harbor. With a crew of 2,122 and eighty-one aircraft, the ship patrolled southwest of the Hawaiian Islands and launched attacks on New Britain and New Guinea before her loss during the American strategic victory in the Battle of the Coral Sea. The* Lexington *was one of five large U.S. Navy aircraft carriers lost during World War II. (80-G-7401, courtesy National Archives)*

The six-month fight for Guadalcanal Island was the initial example of a carrier-supported operation. American efforts to prevent the Japanese from retaking the island produced, in addition to three major land battles, a dozen large-scale sea battles, some of them at night among islands and shallows. Carriers, which played a critical role in providing support for the navy and the marines, took part in a series of open-sea engagements. Although both navies took large losses, the final tallies showed the United States to be the unquestioned victor. Japan's losses were severe: twenty-four ships, 900 aircraft, and more than 2,000 air crewmen. Without adequate carrier and aircraft strength, the Japanese were unable to stop the drive by the U.S. Navy and Marine Corps up the Solomons and General Douglas MacArthur's push from Papua in the west to

outflank the Japanese naval and air forces at Rabaul on New Britain. Although it took twenty hard-fought months, by March 1944 Rabaul lay in ruins, its fortifications and airfields reduced to rubble by naval air strikes and offshore bombardments. In their effort to retain New Guinea and the Solomons, the Japanese lost 4,000 planes and thousands of irreplaceable crew members. These shortages forced the Japanese to remove their remaining carriers from the South Pacific. The region had now been secured.

The fourth phase of the war in the Pacific opened with a dual thrust: as the navy drove westward into the Gilbert and Marshall Islands in the central Pacific, Douglas MacArthur drove northwest toward the Philippines. MacArthur's role in the Pacific war

The USS Essex *(CV-9) leads a carrier group through waters off the Philippines in November 1944. By the fall of 1943, such carrier groups, composed of large attack carriers like the* Essex, *smaller escort carriers like the vessel directly astern, and supporting battleships, cruisers, and destroyers, combined the offense and defense needed to control air and sea in the Pacific war. The more than thirty large attack carriers commissioned before the war's end were 872 to 888 feet in length, with crews of 3,400 men, and carried more than eighty planes. The seventy escort carriers commissioned during the war were approximately 500 feet in length, with crews of 800 to 1,000 men, and carried twenty to thirty aircraft. Many of the planes ranged along the carrier decks with wings folded are Grumman F6F Hellcat fighter planes. Introduced in 1943, they were especially effective against Japanese aircraft, as in the "Marianas Turkey Shoot" during the Battle of the Philippine Sea in June 1944. Despite their chunky appearance, they destroyed nineteen enemy aircraft for every Hellcat loss. Photo by Lieutenant William Mace. (80-G-976120, courtesy National Archives)*

had not been factored into the navy's long-planned strategy for war with Japan, and the general's success in amending War Plan Orange for his own purposes caused much interservice rancor. But the double-pronged effort had its advantages: it forced Japan to divide its resources in defending two fronts on which the United States could alternately intensify operations to cause confusion and disorder in the enemy's response. The timing was also important, for the winds of war in Europe had changed, enabling an all-out offensive in the Pacific, and American industrial capacity was at its wartime peak. The American naval forces committed to the central Pacific campaign were beneficiaries of this remarkable surge in production: nineteen carriers of assorted sizes, twelve battleships, seventeen cruisers, fifty-six destroyers, twenty-nine transports, and large numbers of landing craft supported the amphibious invasions of the Gilberts and Marianas. In the Gilberts, the invasion of Tarawa in November 1943 proved the toughest campaign. One-third of the assault troops were killed or wounded; in retrospect the Marines concluded that the island, like many others held by the Japanese, should have been bypassed. But important lessons were learned from the experience, including the need for new types of amphibious craft and for better knowledge of tidal patterns. The campaign also produced a new naval unit, the famous Underwater Demolition Program. More important, the Gilberts operation breached Japan's primary north-south defense perimeter.

The lessons learned in the Gilberts were used advantageously in the Marshalls, where the primary object, Kwajalein Island, was secured in January 1944 with only a fraction of the losses incurred at Tarawa. Eniwetok Island was the next to fall. Saipan, Guam, Tinian, Peleliu, and Ulithi in the Marianas followed. The primary sea battle for the Marianas took place to the west of these islands in the Philippine Sea in June 1944, when a Japanese carrier fleet attempted to disrupt the American invasion of Saipan. It was a futile effort. Badly outgunned, under-fueled, possessed of insufficient aircraft with inadequately trained crews, and harassed by American submarines, the Japanese effort was stopped dead in its tracks. Wave after wave of incoming Japanese carrier planes were shot down in what became known as the "Marianas Turkey Shoot." The final tally was

U. S. Submarines in the Pacific

For all the battleships and carriers in the Japanese fleet, that nation's capacity to prevail in the war was utterly dependent upon its ability to communicate with its far-flung oceanic imperium. To deny Japan the fulfillment of that objective was the U. S. Navy's primary goal. This it succeeded in doing. While Germany failed in its effort to close the Atlantic to the Allies, American submarines in the Pacific progressively impaired Japan's ability to move men and supplies, ultimately dooming that nation to defeat.

At the outset of the Pacific war, Japanese submarines took part in the Pearl Harbor attack, sank merchant vessels in the Eastern Pacific, and even shelled a Santa Barbara, California, oil refinery. But Japanese submarines had not been strategically programmed for long-range assignments and were most often reserved by the Japanese admirals for use against capital ships. Moreover, Japanese submarines did not enjoy radar, possessed primitive sonar capabilities, and became even more vulnerable when superior American cryptological and radio-range-finding devices gave the advantage to American antisubmarine warfare.

Within months after Pearl Harbor, the Japanese had lost the undersea initiative, and the

*Launch of the USS **Robalo** (SS-273) at Manitowoc, Wisconsin, 9 May 1943. One of twenty-eight U.S. Navy submarines built on fresh water at this shipbuilding port on Lake Michigan, the 311-foot Gato-class submarine passed through the Illinois River and down the Mississippi in a floating dry dock, was outfitted at New Orleans, and traveled through the Panama Canal to enter service in the Pacific. A modern diesel-electric vessel, she had diesel engines for surface running and for charging the batteries of the quiet electric motors that powered her when underwater. Stationed at Fremantle, Australia, the **Robalo** patrolled west of the Philippines and in the South China Sea, where she damaged several Japanese ships. On her fourth patrol, after sighting a Japanese battleship west of Borneo, the **Robalo** disappeared, probably sunk by a Japanese mine. She was one of fifty-two U.S. submarines lost during the war. (80-G-68535, courtesy National Archives)*

stuff that made for popular submarine war films, like *Run Silent, Run Deep* and *Destination Tokyo*, was in the works. Almost from the outset, and especially after 1942, American submarines became notably effective at intercepting Japanese shipping, penetrating to the shores of Japan itself and roaming freely in the East China Sea and shipping lanes to the south and southwest from the principal U.S. submarine bases at Pearl Harbor and at Brisbane and Perth in Australia. Beginning with 55 of its 111 submarines available for Pacific service, the U.S. added an additional 177 submarines during the course of the war.

These submariners strike a happy pose in their berths among the torpedoes, but submarine life was notably hazardous and uncomfortable. With sixty men, provisions, and torpedoes packed on board, U.S. submarines in the Pacific made patrols of six to eight weeks and more, lurking along Japanese shipping lanes, attacking Japanese warships, and performing other missions far from support. With limited communications, rudimentary living and medical facilities, and frequent exposure to enemy attack, the navy's 16,000 submariners suffered a 22-percent death rate. Even their torpedoes could be their enemy. Until the middle of the war, defective torpedoes frequently failed during attacks, and on two occasions U.S. torpedoes traveled in a circle and sank the submarines that fired them. Photo by Edward Steichen. (80-G-415497, courtesy National Archives)

One of the primary reasons for this success lay in the overextension of Japan's supply lines. While Japanese merchant shipping was sufficient at the outset of the war to link the nation with its far-flung holdings, the absence of sufficient escort vessels and a stubborn aversion to convoying placed the ocean supply line in severe jeopardy. When convoying was finally, if reluctantly, adopted in 1944, it was handled poorly. The Japanese, for example, did not get escort carriers into service until July of that year. In any event, these belated efforts would not have succeeded, as the increasing number of American sub-

marines, improved equipment, knowledge of Japanese convoy routes, and expanded experience of the American captains and crews, coupled with the navy's code-breaking skills, enabled the submarine force to zero in on Japanese shipping despite escorts, evasive tactics, and the vastness of the Pacific.

The degree to which cryptology aided the American submarine service is debated. Some analysts aver that no naval branch in the Pacific benefited more from cryptological breakthroughs. Others argue that its implementation contributed but minimally to

the success of the submarine force. There is no question that once the U.S. Navy successfully deciphered Japanese diplomatic codes in 1940 and then was able to decipher that nation's naval signals after the summer of 1942–U.S. submarines had a weapon that placed Japan's merchant and naval shipping at great disadvantage. That Admiral Chester Nimitz, the navy's Pacific commander, placed a high value on intelligence gathering, and that the Japanese persistently dismissed the possibility that their signals were being compromised, only strengthened America's hand.

This advantage compensated for certain deficiencies that might otherwise have seriously hamstrung the American effort, the most notable of which were the slow speeds of America's early-model submarines and the poor quality of the navy's torpedoes and magnetic exploders. Reports of multiple torpedo failures at close range haunted the submarine service throughout 1942 and 1943–torpedoes tended to run deeper than set for, and their exploders often detonated prematurely, or not at all. At least two torpedoes ran a full circle and sank their own submarines! Not until the middle of the war would U.S. naval ordnance, under the relentless pressure of Admiral Charles Lockwood, Jr., commander of the Pacific fleet submarine force, produce torpedoes comparable to the Japanese "long lance."

As the speed of the submarines and the performance of their hardware improved, so did their record. In October 1942, Allied submarines in the Pacific, mostly American, sank over 100,000 tons of Japanese shipping. During 1943 the monthly average exceeded that. In 1944 the tonnage sunk was double that of 1942. By the end of the war, U.S. submarines had sunk more than 1,000 Japanese merchant vessels (4.8 million deadweight tons, or 63 percent of the entire fleet), and 91, or 33 percent, of Japan's warships. American submarines were not limited to raiding Japan's

Viewed through the periscope of the USS Nautilus *(SS-168), the Japanese destroyer* Yamakaze *sinks on 25 June 1942. Like the German U-boats in the Atlantic, U.S. submarines in the Pacific were especially effective commerce raiders, destroying 1,152 Japanese merchant ships. Their undersea warfare was directed by sound and by occasional periscope glimpses of the surface like this. They in turn were hunted by aircraft and destroyers, listening for the sound of their engines and watching for periscope or torpedo tracks on the water. Launched in 1930, the* Nautilus *was one of the largest U.S. submarines active in World War II. Besides torpedoing cargo vessels and several Japanese naval vessels during her regular patrols off Japan and along supply routes, the* Nautilus *was used to land Marine rangers for assaults on several islands in the South Pacific and the Aleutians, to perform a photo-reconnaissance mission before the invasion of the Gilbert Islands, and to deliver supplies to island outposts. She survived numerous depth charge attacks. By 1945 the* Nautilus *had been superseded by the more modern wartime submarines and was inactivated and scrapped. (80-G-418331, courtesy National Archives)*

sea-lanes–they served as scouts and patrols; performed reconnaissance work; ferried troops, refugees, and VIPs; and undertook lifesaving, weather reporting, and minelaying missions.

By the end of the war in the Pacific, this minuscule branch of the navy, totaling less than 300 vessels and just 16,000 submariners, was instrumental

in severing Japan's lifeline to its military theatres of operation and cutting off access to raw materials critical to Japanese war production. The submarine service paid a high price, losing 52 boats and 22 percent of its mariners, but U.S. submarines sank 23 enemy ships for each sub lost.

315 Japanese aircraft destroyed, with a loss of only 29 American planes. The Japanese naval air arm had been dealt a crushing blow. In the meantime, U.S. submarines sank two jumbo Japanese carriers; never again would the Japanese attempt to use their carriers in an offensive maneuver. The conquest of Saipan was particularly significant because now American long-range bombers were within reach of the Japanese mainland.

The second part of the pincers movement was being carried out to the southwest. MacArthur, fulfilling his promise to return to the Philippines, landed at Leyte in October 1944. In the Pacific war's major confrontation of capital ships, the Japanese were crushed in their counterattacks in the Leyte Gulf in the same month, losing one-half of their naval combat strength. Subsequently, Admiral Halsey's carriers had a field day in attacks on Luzon, destroying 700 planes, twelve cruisers, and more than seventy transports, freighters, and tankers. Japanese efforts to transport reinforcements to the Philippines were successfully prevented by U.S. submarines and carrier planes.

Aboard the USS Essex (CV-9), the flight deck crew prepares to launch a TBM Avenger torpedo bomber, 17 February 1945, for one of the first air strikes on Japan since the Doolittle raid of April 1942. This single-engine, three-man plane became the principal carrier torpedo bomber for the navy, first serving in combat at the Battle of Midway in June 1942. With a combat radius of 225 miles, and an overall range of 1,100 miles, the planes could conduct torpedo or bomb attacks on ships, submarines, or land installations far from their carrier bases. More than 9,800 TBF and TBM models of this aircraft were produced during the war. After her launch at Newport News in 1942, the 872-foot Essex joined the Pacific fleet and saw considerable action in the central Pacific invasion, beginning in August 1943. In 1944 the Essex participated in the Battle of Leyte Gulf and actions off Manila, surviving a Kamikaze strike and several typhoons. After the February 1945 air attacks on Japanese airfields and aircraft plants she participated in the capture of Okinawa and then launched further attacks on the Japanese home islands in the last days of the war. Decommissioned after the war, the Essex would later serve during the Korean conflict and in NATO peace-keeping missions in the Atlantic and Mediterranean. Photo by Lieutenant Paul Dorsey. (80-G-469152, courtesy National Archives)

Inspired by several British designs from the mid-1930s, the PT (patrol torpedo boat) became one of the legendary U.S. Navy craft of World War II. American shipyards built 184 for Lend-Lease to Russia and Britain, and the U.S. Navy had the first experimental boats built for its own use in 1939. Based on the prototype designed by Hubert Scott-Paine of the British Power Boat Company, they were constructed of plywood and soon standardized at seventy-eight feet for the boats built by Higgins Industries in New Orleans and Huckins in Florida, and eighty feet for the boats built by the Electric Launch Company (Elco) at Bayonne, New Jersey. Specifications called for three Packard engines, a trial speed of forty knots sustained for one hour, and a cruising range of 500 miles. Carrying crews of eleven, and armed with fifty-caliber machine guns and either four torpedo tubes or two torpedo tubes and depth charges or mines, the PT boats were designed for fast attacks on surface ships, especially at night, and for reconnaissance and covert operations. Although such small wooden coastal craft might be considered obsolete in the age of aircraft, submarines, and long-range naval guns, the PTs performed exceptional service in the Mediterranean, in the Aleutians, and especially among the islands of the South Pacific, where their fast attacks and destruction of Japanese patrol and supply vessels hampered Japanese occupying forces. The U.S. Navy had ordered more than 600 PT boats by the end of the war. The eighty-foot PT-196, shown here during tests in May 1943, remained in service until October 1945 and was one of 399 PT boats built by Elco. She and her Motor Torpedo Squadron 12 won the Presidential Unit Citation for action in the New Guinea area from October 1943 to March 1944. (Lieutenant–later President–John F. Kennedy commanded a similar Elco boat, PT-109, in the South Pacific.) This boat has two torpedo tubes and four mine boxes. The fifty-caliber machine guns stand vertically under protective covers. Note the individualized paint scheme, with shark-jaw bow and camouflage topsides. (Negative 106457F, © Rosenfeld Collection, Mystic Seaport Museum, Inc.)

The final months of the war in the Pacific involved the deployment of the largest naval force and the most extensive naval logistics system in the history of warfare. By mid-August 1945, 90 percent of the U.S. Navy's vessels of submarine size or larger were in the Pacific, making a total of 1,137 combat ships, 14,847 aircraft, 2,783 large landing craft, and many thousands of smaller vessels. More than 400 bases had been established to support this force, and 152 floating drydocks were in operation at advanced bases and fleet anchorages. In getting to this point, the single most important problem in logistic support was the development

of standard advanced base units–the major naval base units were called "Lions," secondary base units called "Cubs," and a third type of unit, called "Acorns," included the personnel and materiel required to construct and operate an air base. Their organization, assembly, orderly loading on board ships in the continental United States, and the unloading, delivery, and construction of components overseas involved a complex of broad plans and fine details.

It was an immensely complicated problem of purchase, finance, transportation, and distribution that connected American industry with

On the beach at Leyte in the Philippines, U.S. Navy LSTs deliver Seabees and Marines to establish a beach-head in October 1944. The British Army's evacuation from Dunkirk in 1940 had shown the need for ocean-going ships capable of loading and unloading vehicles at the water's edge. Conceived in discussions between the British Admiralty and U.S. Navy Bureau of Ships in November 1941, the landing ship tank (LST) plans were completed in February 1942, and the first ships were floated out of their building dock in October. At 328 feet in length, with a minimum draft of less than four feet, these vessels could deliver 2,100 tons to the beach, accommodating the heaviest army battle tanks. The navy first employed them during landings on the Solomon Islands in June 1943. More than 1,000 LSTs were launched before the end of the war, and despite their ungainly appearance and hazardous duty, only 26 were sunk by enemy fire, and only 13 were lost in accidents. These three LSTs represent the wide participation of American industry in naval shipbuild-ing during the war. LST-18 was launched at Pittsburgh, Pennsylvania, in February 1943; LST-245 was launched at Evansville, Indiana, in July 1943; and LST-202 was launched at Seneca, Illinois, in March 1943. Two of these LSTs were among the 351 navy craft operated by U.S. Coast Guard crews. Absorbed into the navy as in World War I, the nearly 50,000 Coast Guardsmen served on patrol and in navy support ships, as well as in their normal rescue and security roles. As in the other services, Coast Guard women, called SPARS, took over many shoreside and clerical duties to free males for sea service. Photo by James C.W. Munde. (26-G-3544, courtesy National Archives)

Allied fighting men and women overseas. The solutions reached were reminiscent of a gigantic naval and military version of mail-order shopping firms like Sears Roebuck and Montgomery Ward, complete with catalogs for component parts to a base that could be either readily used or easily reorganized in adaptable ways. This process involved the creation of Naval Construction Battalions, manned by sailors nicknamed "Seabees," and the design of ready-made buildings. Some of their structures became widely known. Most prominent among them, perhaps, was the prefabricated "Quonset Hut," developed from a British model at Quonset Point and Davisville, Rhode Island, and used around the world.

To support the new bases, hundred of ships from

As antiaircraft gun crews begin to react, a Japanese Kamikaze comes in along the rail of the USS Missouri *(BB-63) on 11 April 1945. In the face of continuing naval defeats and the loss of much of their battleship and carrier fleets, the Japanese began to assign Kamikaze ("divine wind") pilots to attack U.S. Navy ships in 1944. Their sole mission was to crash their bomb-laden planes into Allied warships. In this case, the* Missouri *suffered only slight damage. As the last U.S. battleship completed, the* Missouri *was commissioned in June 1944 and joined a carrier task group in the western Pacific in January 1945. The carriers she protected launched the first air strikes on Japanese soil since the Doolittle raid in 1942. After providing long-range fire during the invasion of Iwo Jima, the* Missouri *protected carriers launching raids against southern Japan, then participated in the attack on Okinawa at the end of March 1945. As flagship of Admiral Halsey's Third Fleet, the* Missouri *conducted further attacks on Japan until the end of the war. (80-G-700774, courtesy National Archives)*

the navy's service squadrons were involved, shipping between the United States and advanced bases and between overseas bases. In addition, nearly a million deadweight tons of shipping controlled by the War Shipping Administration was assigned to carry naval supplies. At the height of the war effort in the Pacific, for example, 600,000 long tons per month were being shipped from the United States to support naval operating forces and for the preparation of future operations.

With the American occupation of the Philippines, the Japanese home islands were now vulnerable. In order to provide critical fighter cover for the

Integrating the U.S. Navy

Among the most significant social consequences of the Second World War was the integration of the United States armed forces, and particularly the U.S. Navy.

Black seamen had figured prominently in U.S. naval service since the American Revolution, numbering more than 10 percent of the U.S. Navy during the Civil War, and blacks were recruited in some numbers for the navy's apprentice program to create a pool of experienced American-born naval seamen through the 1880s and 1890s. However, with the spread of "Jim Crow" segregation laws throughout the South at the end of the century, the U.S. Navy position on black sailors changed. As in the merchant service, they were increasingly assigned to segregated service jobs as messmen and stewards. For the next fifty years, naval policy was based on the belief that black petty officers would not be able to command white enlisted men, and whites would not live and work in close quarters with blacks. At the same time, the navy's new training program for the expanding steam-powered battle fleet recruited white landsmen and taught them practical skills before assigning them aboard ship, making the navy more attractive to young white men.

By World War I, the U.S. Navy officially discouraged black enlistments, citing the difficulty of maintaining segre-

Aboard the USS Greer (DD 145), on convoy duty in the North Atlantic, black sailors from the steward's department and white seamen play cards in the cramped berthing area. The picture was posed in 1943, yet it makes clear the impossibility of racial segregation in an old destroyer like the Greer, with 133 men on board. Fearing that whites and blacks could not coexist on equal terms, and that white seamen would not obey black superiors, the U.S. Navy was slow to create a black officer pool and to assign black sailors to fighting ships. Ironically, black messmen were the first blacks to enter combat. At Pearl Harbor, mess attendant Dorie Miller of the battleship West Virginia assisted his wounded captain to shelter before helping fire an antiaircraft gun, for which he was awarded the Navy Cross despite hesitation within the Navy Department. Throughout the war in the Pacific, black messmen routinely served on deck in combat, even when other black sailors were restricted to noncombat vessels. (80-G-42035, courtesy National Archives)

gated quarters and working conditions on board ship, and in 1919 the navy actually stopped accepting blacks. Service positions were filled by Chinese and Filipino men until, by 1932, less than one-half of one percent of naval personnel were black.

In 1933 the navy began to recruit blacks again, in the

eventuality that war in the Pacific would limit the supply of Chinese and Filipino recruits. Naval policy favored Southern blacks, who did not have the education or independent expectations of Northern blacks. But segregation continued, and an experiment in appointing two black candidates to the U.S. Naval Academy failed. As war appeared imminent, influential blacks pressed for greater black participation in the navy, but Secretary of the Navy Frank Knox resisted.

President Franklin Roosevelt appointed a commission to review the role of blacks in the navy and, with the urging of Eleanor Roosevelt, encouraged black enlistments for political reasons. The result, beginning in June 1942, was volunteer enlistment for shoreside work, such as loading ammunition ships, or duty on small coastal craft, but not for duty on seagoing ships, except in the segregated steward's department. Later, the navy's mobile construction battalions–Seabees–accepted black volunteers, and finally in 1943 the navy instituted Selective Service draft enrollment of blacks, with the intention of reaching 10 percent black representation in the navy, equivalent to the proportion in the general population. But the war came to an end earlier than expected, and by that time black enrollment had reached only 4.8 percent.

Even with its formal effort to enlist blacks, the navy still segregated them. Black enlistees were trained at Camp Robert Smalls, a separate facility at the Great Lakes Naval Training Station, named for the black pilot who served the Union Navy in the Civil War. Beyond their continuing role as messmen on ships throughout the U.S. fleet, black enlisted men were employed in the U.S. and overseas as laborers in base companies alongshore rather than as seamen on fighting ships. Nor were blacks represented in the officer

corps. Black sailors resented their limited assignments, and white seamen resented that blacks were not equally exposed to combat. Discontent led to a number of incidents, the most famous being the "Port Chicago Mutiny" in July 1944, when black ammunition loaders refused to return to work after an explosion that killed 300 at the ammunition depot near San Francisco Bay.

Under continuing pressure to place black enlisted men on shipboard, Secretary Knox relented enough early in 1944 to assign experimental all-black enlisted crews on the destroyer escort *Mason* and submarine chaser *PC-1264*. Soon after, Knox died and Secretary of the Navy James V. Forrestal expanded black berths at sea–on support ships, not on fighting ships–but limited the proportion to 10 percent. Also under Forrestal, the navy eliminated segregated training at the Great Lakes Naval Training Station by June 1945.

In 1943 the navy instituted the V-12 program to train college-educated men as officers for the rapidly expanding service. By that time the U.S. Navy had 100,000 black enlisted men, but no black officers (Bernard Robinson, a black medical student who was commissioned in the U.S. Navy Reserve in 1942, did not begin his actual naval service until 1944). Over Knox's hesitation, Roosevelt ordered that blacks be included in the admissions testing for the V-12 program. About thirty-six black students completed this intensive training and were commissioned as officers

before the end of the war.

The journalist and diplomat Carl Rowan, a V-12 graduate, considered the program to be "instrumental not only in changing America's military, but in mobilizing this country's first groping steps to find its conscience, its heart and soul, in terms of racial and social justice." Rowan's commander on the USS *Chemung*, a tanker carrying aviation fuel for aircraft carriers in the North Atlantic, told Rowan he had not prepared the crew before Rowan's arrival on board. Rowan later said, "the skipper had shown an acute understanding of what I–and other Negroes–wanted: no special restrictions and no special favors; just the right to rise or fall on merit."

Under rising criticism, and in order to obtain some black officers even before the V-12 program graduated its first group in 1944, Secretary Knox agreed to commission ten black civilians as staff officers and to train twelve black enlisted men and commission them as line officers for field command. Sixteen black enlisted men were selected and sent to the Great Lakes Naval Training Station in January 1944 for a three-month officer training course. All sixteen completed the assignment, but just twelve were commissioned as ensigns and one as a warrant officer. Now known as the Golden Thirteen, they were commissioned in March 1944 as the first black officers in the U.S. Navy. Their assignments were routine, and none came under fire; yet as indicators that race played no role in qualifying a man for navy

The first black naval officers were commissioned at Camp Robert Smalls in March 1944. They are: (seated, left to right) Ensigns George C. Cooper, Graham E. Martin, Jesse W. Arbor, John W. Reagan, and Reginald E. Goodwin; (standing, left to right) Ensigns Dennis D. Nelson, Phillip G. Barnes, Samuel E. Barnes, Dalton L. Baugh, James E. Hair, and Frank E. Sublett, Jr., and Warrant Boatswain Charles B. Lear. Missing is Ensign William S. White. (80-G-300215, courtesy National Archives)

ones to serve as officers during World War II.

In the summer of 1945, as the war in the Pacific reached an abrupt end with the detonation of atomic bombs over Japan, Wesley A. Brown entered the U.S. Naval Academy. Four years later, as the first black graduate of Annapolis in the Academy's 104-year history, Brown represented the new era for the U.S. Navy.

Although the service still had far to go, and the postwar navy reverted to many of its prewar patterns, by the 1960s and 1970s an emphasis on equal opportunity for black seamen and officers became clear U.S. Navy policy. In fact, the navy had become more racially integrated than the society it represented.

leadership positions, they performed heroic service. Before being assigned aboard the USS *Mason*, Ensign James E. Hair commanded a mixed-race crew aboard the harbor tugboat *YTB-215*. He discovered that, "Since the crew respected me professionally, they also respected me as a man," proving the intention of the program.

Black women also sought a place in the U.S. Navy during the war. Finally, in October 1944, the navy announced that black women would be accepted in the WAVES (Women Accepted for Volunteer Emergency

Service), which had been established in 1942 to fill navy clerical positions ashore. Harriet Ida Pickens and Frances Wills became the first black women commissioned in the U.S. Navy, and the only

When Lieutenant (JG) Harriet Ida Pickens (left) and Ensign Frances Wills graduated from the Naval Reserve Midshipmen's School at Northampton, Massachusetts, in December 1944, they joined the WAVES as the first black women to serve as U.S. Navy officers. (80-G-297441, courtesy National Archives)

Framed by the elevated sixteen-inch guns, the Japanese delegation approaches the surrender table on board the USS Missouri in Tokyo Bay on 2 September 1945. Less than two months earlier, those sixteen-inch guns had bombarded military and industrial targets on the Japanese home islands, launching 2,700-pound shells from as far as twenty-three miles offshore. (80-G-700774, courtesy National Archives)

long-range bombing of Japan, the United States now targeted Iwo Jima, the Marines taking the island in a fiercely fought amphibious assault in March 1945. In the following month the Marines and the army landed on Okinawa, putting American forces only 325 miles from Japan's southern island of Kyushu. Suicidal plane attacks, which had first been used in Japan's defense of the Philippines, inflicted extensive damage on the invading American fleets, sinking several dozen small ships and damaging five carriers at Iwo Jima and causing the loss of thirty-six destroyer-size or smaller vessels and damage to 368 additional ships at Okinawa. While psychologically intimidating, these attacks, sometimes numbering 300 or more kamikaze and conventional aircraft, did not seriously disrupt operations. Roughly 2,800

enemy aircraft were shot down over Okinawa, most of them by carrier-based fighters. One final Japanese naval counterattack was thwarted when the world's largest battleship, the 70,000-ton monster *Yamato*, was sunk by carrier planes and submarines while steaming toward Okinawa on a nautical kamikaze mission, proceeding without air cover and bunkered with oil sufficient only for a one-way voyage.

The suicidal ferocity with which the Japanese garrisons defended the islands, including kamikaze planes, one-man "suicide" submarines, and fanatical banzai attacks, altered the navy's original plan to strangle Japan into submission by air and sea blockade alone. Rather, it began to prepare for a November 1945 invasion of the Japanese home islands. Fortunately, the atomic bomb attacks on Hiroshima and Nagasaki in August 1945 terminated Japanese belligerency, and this additional phase became unnecessary. In a setting befitting the navy's role in prosecuting the Pacific war, Japan's official surrender took place in Tokyo Bay on 2 September 1945 on the deck of the battleship USS *Missouri*. Thus ended World War II.

The U.S. Maritime Commission in World War II

In much the same way that the availability or absence of fighting ships determined the nature and extent of the Allied war effort, so too did the very supply of merchant shipping. This was most evident in the war's early stages, when the loss of Allied merchant vessels to air and sea attacks exceeded production; when convoy delays, slow turnarounds, roundabout routings, crew shortages, and long and hazardous voyages taxed transport severely; and when, partly because of an insufficiency of shipping, the cross-channel invasion planned for 1942 had to be postponed for almost two years. In time, however, the ships required to help turn the tide became a reality. These ships were primarily provided by the U.S. shipbuilding industry. Between 1939 and 1945, the U. S. Maritime Commission ordered 5,777 ships totaling 56.3 million deadweight tons, or almost five times the size of the nation's entire 1939 fleet. This constituted the greatest construction of ships ever undertaken. Had these ships not been produced, the war in all likelihood would have been prolonged for many months, if not years. The American wartime merchant fleet, built at a cost of almost $14,000,000,000, by a labor force that grew to more than 600,000 men and women at seventy private and governmental shipyards, constituted one of the most significant contributions made by any nation to the winning of World War II.

U.S. merchant shipping had already gone to work in support of the Allied war effort many months before Pearl Harbor. Following the outbreak of war in September 1939, the Maritime Commission sold significant numbers of its World War I reserve fleet to the British, which transaction, while helping the United States dispose of obsolete ships at reasonable prices, provided England with critically needed tonnage at a time when the survival of that nation was much in doubt. American shipping aid to the Allies increased in proportion to the growing probability of American war involvement. Following the passage of the Lend-Lease Act of March 1941, American ships brought aid not only to the British Isles, but directly to British military theaters of operation. In the last seven months of 1941, U.S. tonnage supplied British campaigns in the Middle East, Africa, the Persian Gulf, and the Indian Ocean with 48,958 vehicles, 302,698 tons of dry goods, and 814 airplanes.

The Maritime Commission also constructed vessels for the British merchant fleet, adopting a British design for an emergency eleven-knot, 10,800-deadweight-ton dry-cargo ship with reciprocating oil-fueled steam engines, designed for rapid, mass-produced welded construction. This was the famous Liberty ship. Turbine propulsion, which would have enhanced their speed significantly, was in short supply and reserved for fighting ships, so Liberties were not commercially viable vessels, serving basically as wartime expedients. The Maritime Commission ordered 260 Liberties, including 60 for the British, in early 1941.

These, and orders for other ship types, were more than doubled with the establishment of the lend-lease program in March 1941. Following Hitler's invasion of the Soviet Union in June 1941, and in reaction to enormous losses of Allied shipping to German air and sea attacks, the American building program was supplemented yet again. On the eve of Pearl Harbor, the Maritime Commission's schedule for deliveries had risen from the initial target of fifty ships per year, or roughly 500,000 deadweight tons, to 5,000,000 deadweight tons for 1942 and 7,000,000 for 1943. Directly after U.S. entry into the war, these goals were increased, and then effectively doubled. The Anglo-American decision to concentrate the merchant ship replacement and building program in the United States helped account for these augmentations in production. Factoring in the

As during World War I, women found employment in essential industries during World War II. At the Ingalls Shipyard in Pascagoula, Mississippi, Sarah Carmen Therrell, eighteen, Ruby Lee Jones, and Willhelaree King, nineteen, pose with their welding equipment. At the Kaiser shipyards near Portland, Oregon, women were employed as welders as early as April 1942, and the company began to recruit throughout the West. By mid-1943, at the height of the shipbuilding boom, women occupied as much as 65 percent of the shipyard jobs there, and comprised 21 percent of the welders. As an accommodation to the wartime labor shortage, some unions even accepted women on a contingent basis. Nevertheless, sexist and racist attitudes survived in the shipyards, and with the end of the war most women returned to more conventional roles. (U.S. Maritime Commission photo 3177)

preponderant availability of manpower and materials in the United States–and the relative safety of its shipyards from attack–President Roosevelt and Prime Minister Churchill agreed that the Maritime Commission would provide the merchant ships, while Britain would concentrate its diminished resources on the construction of fighting ships. As a result, by 1943 the United States was producing 85 percent of all Allied merchant shipping.

As it had in World War I, the production capacity of America's shipyards again proved extraordinary in World War II. Whereas in 1939 the Maritime Commission produced one ship every thirteen days, and during 1941 a ship every three and a half days, during 1943 launchings reached a record five ships *per* day. In that year alone, the nation's shipyards produced 19,210,000 deadweight tons, a quantity larger than all the tonnage delivered in the United States from 1914 through 1938. The greatest percentage of ships was built on the West Coast, predominantly at the San Francisco Bay and Columbia River yards of Henry J. Kaiser. The builder of the San Francisco Bay Bridge and the Grand Coulee, Bonneville, and Hoover Dams, Kaiser converted his construction expertise into mass production of 1,552 ships for the Maritime Commission, or fully 27 percent of all vessels constructed for the Commission between 1941 and 1945. To a lesser degree the Maritime Commission also commissioned the building of ships on the Gulf and Atlantic coasts, most notably at yards on the Delaware River and Chesapeake Bay. Even though the nation was now on a war footing, the Maritime Commission, as a public agent, was very conscious of its responsibility to maintain the private corporations to which contracts had been let, utilizing existing firms and applying the profit system to the undertaking.

While numbers of launchings increased dramatically, time spent in construction decreased. Within two years of the inauguration of the Liberty ship program, such efficiency was achieved in the assembly-line method of production that labor inputs for the construction of one ship were reduced by as much as two-thirds. Time on the ways, which initially averaged six to nine months, was down to forty days and less, and at

With a dramatic side-launch splash, the EC-2 Liberty ship Andrew Moore *is launched at the Delta Shipbuilding yard near New Orleans in October 1942. Established by the American Shipbuilding Company at the request of the Maritime Commission in 1941, the Delta yard ultimately employed 13,000 men and women, who turned out 132 Liberty ships, 32 Liberty tankers, and 24 Liberty colliers during the war. Of the more than 2,700 Liberty ships built at sixteen shipyards around the country, more than 200 were casualties of the war. The* Andrew Moore, *however, provided routine service and was ultimately scrapped in 1963. (U.S. Maritime Commission photo 2540)*

the Kaiser yards on the West Coast was about twenty days. In one extraordinary demonstration undertaken for publicity purposes, the Kaiser Permanente Metals Corp. Yard No. 2 at Richmond, California, launched the Liberty ship *Robert E. Perry* on 12 November 1942, four days and 15.5 hours after her keel was laid. She was outfitted in just three days, taking to sea 7.5 days after keel laying. In all, 2,600 Liberties entered service by the war's end.

While the bulk of the Maritime Commission's wartime ship construction was of the simple Liberty-type vessel designed for rapid building by mass-assembly method, by early 1944 the program had shifted to the construction of the new long-range design, the Victory ship, a slightly larger, but much faster (16.5 knots), rangier, and more commercially desirable turbine-driven cargo vessel. Many of these ships were taken over by the armed services for duty as troop

Even wooden shipbuilding enjoyed a revival during World War II. The Herreshoff Manufacturing Company of Bristol, Rhode Island, which was better known for America's Cup yachts and highly engineered sailing and motor craft, launched twenty-two of these wooden, 100-foot coastal cargo vessels (APc) in 1942-43. Similar to a minesweeper in design, this "Jack of all Trades" was intended for delivering military cargoes in sheltered waters. Other well-known yacht-building yards contributed PT boats, nonmagnetic wooden minesweepers, and additional support and personnel craft, sparing the use of essential steel, and providing employment for many wooden-boat builders who came out of retirement to practice their craft one more time. Painting by Duncan Gleason. (M.S.M. 55.389; Claire White-Peterson photo)

transports, provision and hospital ships, destroyer and submarine tenders, and attack cargo ships. Some were even converted into escort carriers. By war's end more than 400 Victories were in service. Another program produced roughly 700 large, fast, oceangoing tankers for both domestic and armed service use and 700 minor-type commercial vessels such as lake ore carriers, coastal cargo vessels, coastal tankers, tugs, and barges. The Maritime Commission also constructed approximately 700 craft for purely military purposes, including transports and LSTs. Yet, while the number of ships constructed by the Maritime Commission for military purposes was substantial, commercial designs made up about *77* percent of the Commission's production.

The American Merchant Marine and the War Shipping Administration

As new vessels were completed by the Maritime Commission they were transferred to the War Shipping Administration (WSA) for operational control; those required for strictly military operations were then retransferred to permanent or temporary army or navy control. In the operation of its vessels in the war effort, the WSA paralleled the Maritime Commission's commitment to strengthen private shipping firms, utilizing going concerns in order to take advantage of their equipment and experience, and to assist in preserving their organizations for postwar resumption of commercial services. At sea, all vessels came under the control of the convoy, routing, and escort divisions of the U.S. Navy and the Combined Naval Forces. At home ports, the Coast Guard, whose primary function was the protection of coastal convoys, helped to regulate merchant shipping; at ports in overseas combat areas, the vessels were most often handled by American or Allied military shore forces.

As in the First World War, purchase, requisition, and commandeering of ships served as another means of procuring needed tonnage. As World War II loomed, the army and navy independently commenced, as a preparedness measure, to purchase and charter American merchant vessels. With the outbreak of war, both service branches began to requisition tonnage, sweeping up everything that could be secured. This short free-for-all period, in which the army and navy engaged in a wasteful bidding war, lasted into January 1942, when the Maritime Commission was vested by the War Powers Acts with overall authority to procure private vessels. But the combination of ship procurement, ship operation, and shipbuilding threatened to overwhelm the Commission, and in February 1942 the War Shipping Administration was created by executive order to manage all ocean transportation not under the direct control of the military services. Although Admiral Emory Land retained overall authority over both the Maritime Commission and WSA, he and his deputy, Admiral Howard L. Vickery, now concentrated on shipbuilding, while WSA, under a second deputy, Lewis W. Douglas, an insurance executive, former congressman from Arizona, and erstwhile director of the budget under President Roosevelt, supervised the assignment and operation of ships. All privately owned vessels of any utility were soon taken over by the War Shipping Administration, including approximately 900 dry cargo vessels aggregating about 6,700,000 deadweight tons and about 440 tankers of approximately 5,200,000 deadweight tons. The WSA did not limit itself to large ships, however; vessels of virtually every kind and size deemed essential to the war effort were requisitioned, including, for example, barges, tugboats, and 700 fishing craft. The WSA also took over operational control of a number of commandeered Axis vessels.

Manning the fleet was never easy. Virtually every classification of seafarer, including fishermen, was eligible for the draft and was conscripted into the armed services. This policy contributed to an acute shortage of seamen at the outset of war, and persisted even when the armed services acknowledged the problem and released seafarers for duty in the merchant marine. A 1942 conflict between the Maritime Commission and the Coast Guard over training authority complicated matters until rationalized in favor of the Commission and WSA. Officers were also in short supply, and it was difficult to provide numbers sufficient to the needs of the rapidly expanding merchant fleet. While a good number of officers rose through the ranks on their own initiative, the Maritime Commission's Cadet Corps system was expanded of necessity from a capacity of 660 in 1938 to over 6,500 in 1943. Although a handful of women actually commanded vessels during the war, the Maritime Commission strongly resisted efforts to accept women as rank-and-file seafarers. During the course of war, 225,000 seamen and officers manned the American merchant marine. Of these, almost 6,000 died in action at sea; only the Marine Corps suffered proportionately higher casualties. Nevertheless, America's wartime merchant mariners, who maintained their civilian status

As their merchant ship sinks beneath them and the crew abandons ship, a merchant gun crew takes a parting shot at the U-boat that sank them. This painting by Anton Otto Fischer, a former seaman who served as Coast Guard artist with the rank of lieutenant commander, is based on an actual incident. Until recently, their participation was not accurately viewed as national service, but after 1942 oceangoing mariners sailed in zones of military operation and were subject to the same regulations that governed naval service. From November 1940 until the end of the war, 6,103 U.S. merchant seamen were lost; indeed, the ratio of one casualty out of every thirty-three merchant mariners exceeded the mortality rate in the U.S. Navy itself. (Courtesy U.S. Coast Guard Museum; Claire White-Peterson photo)

(unlike their British counterparts), did not receive the postwar benefits awarded members of the U.S. military service. When Congress finally awarded veteran's benefits to World War II merchant seafarers in 1988, relatively few surviving seamen qualified.

The allocation and control of the government's ships was just as significant as their construction. Once launched, the ships had to be supervised, the goal being the most efficient employment and turnaround of all ships, new or old, government or private. Some balance had to be achieved between America's outgoing military and lend-lease shipping requirements and its incoming strategic and civilian needs. The gradual, and then successful, neutralization of the submarine menace did not diminish the need for ships, as the number of Allied troops fighting abroad increased and the war fronts grew more distant from the United States. The mileage now required for transit of supplies and troops made the once-formidable 3,000-mile transatlantic passage of World War I pale in comparison. From New York, it was 5,000 miles to Murmansk, 9,000 miles to Australia via the Panama Canal, and 14,000 miles around the South African cape to the Persian Gulf. Moreover, the volume of supplies required to sustain an active fighting front was extensive: it took

seven to eight tons of supplies to sustain one soldier in Europe during World War II, and double that in the Pacific. Then, following the defeat of Germany in May 1945, the Shipping Administration had to assume the enormous burden of redeploying its ships from Europe to the Pacific.

The major responsibility of the War Shipping Administration was to meet the army's and navy's shipping requirements; at the height of the war, roughly three-quarters of the ships controlled by the Shipping Administration were allocated to army and navy cargoes (mostly army); the transport of army personnel alone during the war totaled 7,000,000 soldiers and support staff. In fact, the WSA in World War II actually relinquished control of considerably more tonnage proportionately to the service branches than had its World War I sister, the Shipping Board. But the War Shipping Administration had far greater responsibilities. Supplying a two-front war was one, of course. The shipment of lend-lease supplies to the Allies, principally Great Britain and the Soviet Union, constituted another responsibility of the first order. Great Britain's minimal domestic requirements alone exceeded 25,000,000 tons annually of imported food and supplies for its civilian population, and the Soviet Union had to be supplied via long and extremely hazardous sea-lanes. Then, as nations were liberated, their civilian populations required American support. In 1943, for example, U.S. merchant ships made 2,267 voyages to Great Britain, 328 to the Soviet Union, and 281 to other Allied nations under the lend-lease program.

A third War Shipping Administration responsibility was the importation of essential raw materials for the War Production Board. Early German submarine attacks along the U.S. Atlantic coast, in the Caribbean, and in the Gulf of Mexico had been aimed at disrupting the extensive shipment of petroleum and bauxite from South America, the latter element being a critical component of aluminum for airplanes. Manganese, tin, rubber, copper, and nitrates were additional strategic materials in short supply. Then too, the American public's craving for sugar and coffee had to be at least minimally satisfied. The exportation of materials essential to the economies of Latin America and other countries was another WSA responsibility.

The creation of a coordinated, scientifically managed, and balanced pool of ships for both war and civilian purposes was not accomplished easily. The demand for shipping from a variety of venues–military, civilian, allied–was so intense that no matter how many vessels the War Shipping Administration controlled it never seemed to possess enough to satisfy needs. This was particularly so in 1942, a period of chronic shipping shortages and a time when there was an insufficiency of ships to support an all-out, two-ocean war. Not surprisingly, the greatest challenges to WSA authority came from the U.S. service branches. It was no secret that the army and navy were not pleased with the allocation of war-

related shipping to the control of nonmilitary personnel; both service branches could point to the British decision to place maritime labor, shore and sea, under government authority in March 1941. But whereas the navy in time accustomed itself, if reluctantly, to the WSA's refusal to militarize the merchant marine, the army did not. During the 1920s and 1930s the army had built up its own overseas transportation section and did not wish to see that department duplicated or superseded by the civilian-led WSA. The army also had a very jaundiced view of the civilian labor force, with its substantial wages and limited work week. Nor was the army pleased with the prospect of having to submit to the War Shipping Administration's pooling system, in which ships could be allocated by the WSA, rather than by the generals. To the army, the WSA's concern with preserving the peacetime organization and routes of the American shipping industry, and its determination, as an instrument of the labor-friendly Roosevelt administration, to protect the recently gained rights and independence achieved by the maritime unions, bordered on the unpatriotic. Moreover, during the heated Anglo-American debate over establishing a second front, the army unabashedly sought to use U.S. shipping as a "faucet," as one general put it, to be turned off and on as necessary to force the ship-impoverished British to support American war objectives.

For its part, the War Shipping Administration accused the army of being obsessively committed to military logistics and of having developed, as a consequence, a callous indifference toward the disruptions its policies would bring to the nation's transportation industry, and to the import needs of the American and Allied civilian populations. The WSA believed, moreover, that its ability to achieve economies in ship employment

A mixed-race "checkerboard" crew relaxes during a transatlantic run on a Liberty ship. The U.S. merchant marine underwent tremendous expansion during World War II, employing 195,000 men by the end of 1944. Merchant mariners were well-trained, undergoing at least five weeks of basic training by the U.S. Maritime Service. The U.S. Merchant Marine Cadet Corps, established in 1938, the U.S. Merchant Marine Academy, established in 1941, and the state maritime academies all prepared officers for service in the world's largest merchant marine. (111-SC-180663, courtesy National Archives)

Convoying to North Russia

Much has been written about the extremely hazardous lend-lease voyages to north Russia, about the devastating attacks made on the convoys sent through those foggy, freezing Arctic waters, of the extraordinary bravery and the sacrifices made by the seamen and officers who volunteered for this often suicidal duty, and of the decision, following the near-total destruction of the famous convoy PG-17 in July 1942, to limit the service to those months when perpetual daylight did not subject the convoys to the devastations of German aircraft, long-range submarines, and fighting ships launched from occupied Norway to destroy them. With the possible exception of Malta in the Mediterranean, no theatre during World War II was more difficult to supply than the Soviet Union through its northern ports. But there was more to these convoys than heroics at sea. The organization of the Russian convoys, the logistical complexities, and the problems onshore, made the effort to aid the U.S.S.R. by this route one of the most formidable tasks of the Anglo-American war effort.

Convoys to Russia by the northern route–to the port of Murmansk and ports in the Gulf of Archangel–which had the immediate advantage over other routes of being the short-est in mileage and the closest to the Soviet military front, had commenced in August 1941, even before a special Russian Division was created in the War Shipping Administration in February 1942. Designed to carry out the mandates of the Soviet Protocols agreed upon by the Allies in late 1941, the Russian Division was granted a priority over all other programs, including the United Kingdom Import Program, and even some navy and army programs. The most immediate and greatest difficulty was finding ships for the service, a task hindered by the secrecy with which the service branches enshrouded their own well-guarded shipping pools. Consequently, for want of ships at the outset, docksides became clogged with supplies, and railroad cars carrying yet more aid for Russia were backed up hundreds of miles into the interior. In time, the WSA devised a system wherein cargo for the Russian program was assigned to interior holding and reconsignment depots. The lead time to send out a convoy was at least one month. To load a ship took approximately two weeks, with bottom cargo (steel and metals, for example) being loaded first, followed by general cargo, and then deck cargo (locomotives, rails, airplanes, etc.). Getting supplies to dock-side in the proper sequence was extremely important, as was the crewing of the ships and the guarding of supplies both at dockside and on board.

Deciding what would be loaded was often as complex as getting it to the piers, for the Soviets could choose what they wanted most at any particular time for each particular convoy. Battles ensued not only between the WSA and the Soviets over loading at American ports, but also between Soviet agencies, as the various agencies involved had their own internal struggles over who got what and when and how much. On occasion the Russians might even change priorities at dockside, or try to. But once a ship was loaded, the WSA would not make changes. Much of the early aid to northern Russia–largely munitions–was consigned to the besieged city of Leningrad. The Russians, in turn, reversed the lend-lease process by sending back items needed by the Allies, such as chrome and goose feathers.

Even before the ships were loaded, they had to be refitted to meet the brutal conditions promised by the northern seas. Cast iron or bronze propellers, which could snap or buckle in the Arctic ice, had to be replaced with steel. Concrete was poured into the

North Atlantic convoy duty, as seen from the deck of the USS Greer *(DD-145). A World War I four-stack destroyer, the* Greer *had been recommissioned in 1930 and again in 1939, joining the Navy's Neutrality Patrol in the North Atlantic in February 1940. After patrols in the Caribbean she returned to the run between Iceland and Argentia, Newfoundland, and was approaching Newfoundland on 4 September 1941 when a British plane spotted a German submarine, U-652. The plane broke off the attack, but the neutral* Greer *continued to track the U-boat. When U-652 fired two defensive torpedoes at the* Greer, *she dropped nineteen depth-charges. News of this attack led President Roosevelt to permit an undeclared naval war against Germany in the North Atlantic, until Germany declared war on the U.S. on 11 December 1941. The* Greer *continued North Atlantic and Caribbean patrol duties through April 1943 before shifting to North Africa convoy duty and ended the war as a plane guard for escort carriers. (80-G-42023, courtesy National Archives)*

bows of the ships to stiffen them against the crush of ice. Because the northern Russian ports were primitive in the way of loading and unloading equipment, deck cranes had to be installed. New heating systems sufficient to counter subzero temperatures were imperative, and on the often-correct assumption that a vessel dispatched to north Russia might be detained many months, even a year or more, and because the Russians could not, or would not, provide the necessary stores, the ships had to be stocked with supplies of fuel, food, and even fresh water sufficient to carry them over.

Most ships from the United States designated for the Murmansk or Archangel runs sailed from New York and Philadelphia. Under heavy sea guard, they were marshaled up the New England coast to Halifax, Nova Scotia, via the Cape Cod Canal. There they joined a larger convoy; on occasion Soviet ships would join a convoy.

For the most part the convoys departed Halifax for Liverpool or Glasgow, coming in north of Ireland, although some rendezvoused in Iceland before heading for Russia. Once arrived in England, the ships assigned to Russia, along with British ships similarly assigned, were then escorted up to Loch Ewe, Scotland, for a final rendezvous. At the same time the appropriate naval escort force was assembled. In short, it took months of preparation to get a convoy ready for its final departure for north Russia.

For ships fortunate enough to have survived the 2,000-mile Arctic gauntlet from Scotland to Murmansk–or about 2,500 miles to Archangel– the difficulties continued once they arrived at Murmansk or the ports in the Gulf of Archangel. Fast turnaround was paramount, as German aircraft bombed Murmansk almost daily from airfields only minutes away in Norway. But fast turnaround was often difficult, if not impossible, not merely because of constant air attack, which destroyed docksides and littered the roadway with hulks of ships, but because of logistical conditions in the Russian ports. These entrepôts were notoriously ill-equipped to handle military cargo. Murmansk had been a small fishing village until 1915, and even though it had grown rapidly in the 1930s to become the largest city above the Arctic circle, it was not a world-class port. Shore cranes and other mechanical appliances were in short supply, and those that did exist were woefully short of lifting power. On one occasion it took six weeks in Murmansk to remove a 68-ton piece of machinery from an American ship. Moreover, railway communications were inadequate–some piers were without rail connection, and the rail lines from Murmansk were periodically out of service because of German attacks. In addition, the ports in the Gulf of Archangel were ice-bound from the end of November to the end of May. Russian icebreakers were provided to keep the Archangel

ports open but were not sufficient in number to do so. On several occasions American and British ships became ice-bound and were forced to remain for many months.

Life on shore for those mariners compelled to stay in northern Russian ports was extremely arduous– "as disappointing as it was dangerous" is the way one veteran of the service described it. Entertainments ashore were nil–brothels were outlawed, and contaminated food and death-dealing bootleg liquor were common hazards. Murmansk lay in ruins from constant air attacks. The Arctic environment was oppressive; sanitation systems were virtually nonexistent; and the citizens of the northern ports appeared sullen, mirthless, and unfriendly, evidently cowed by Soviet authorities who discouraged fraternization of any kind. Allied sailors forced to stay in these ports lived a life of debilitating boredom, perpetually waiting: "waiting to go alongside a dock, waiting for an air raid, waiting to clear homeward." Once cleared, many never made it back, succumbing to the torpedo, bomb, or heavy-gauge shell they eluded on the inbound voyage. During the war, 811 merchant ships sailed for northern Russia, but only 715 returned. In the process, 2,800 Allied seamen, officers, and naval gunners gave their lives.

In time, as the Allied attack on the European mainland commenced and intensified, and as Germany withdrew its forces from Norway for continental defense, the pressure on the

north Russian convoys decreased. By this time, the bulk of the aid to Russia was going through ports in the Persian Gulf and the overland route through Iran, or through Siberia from the American Pacific Northwest. But those who were associated with the Russian aid program by way of the Arctic seas rightfully saw themselves as exceptional, members of a special fraternity that rendered aid to an ally under seafaring conditions virtually unmatched in the annals of modern warfare.

was superior to that of the service branches, citing, for example, inefficient military supply procedures attending the North African and Pacific campaigns of 1942. The WSA also had figures to prove that lay-ups under WSA management were declining markedly, that imports of nonessentials were being restricted, that loadings were virtually up to full weight capacity, and that unused space had been reduced significantly from normal peacetime averages. The WSA could likewise provide evidence that its collaboration with the British Ministry of War Transport had brought about significant shipping economies through the pooling of ships, the reassignment of routes, and the location of more efficient sources of supply. Finally, the WSA, and especially its head, Lewis Douglas, deplored the army's and the navy's hostility towards the British. As Douglas (later to become ambassador to Great Britain) saw it, Anglo-American shipping amity was absolutely critical to the successful prosecution of the war and to the development of a strong postwar North Atlantic community. Many months were absorbed in this wasteful and rancorous tug-of-war before the War Shipping Administration, with Roosevelt's support, finally achieved an upper, if not absolute, hand and control of its own fleet in early 1943.

The War Shipping Administration's concern for Anglo-American shipping cooperation laid the foundation for yet another wartime debate over the operation and disposition of American ships. The legislative mandate of the Merchant Marine Act of 1936, which governed the policy of Admiral Land and the Maritime Commission, had called for the construction of a merchant marine of international competitiveness– the British being seen as the major competitor. But the WSA under Lewis Douglas questioned whether the United States was justified in making any effort at all to supplant the British merchant navy. Douglas believed, as did the State Department and key administrators in the executive branch, that the U.S. merchant marine could not sustain itself without lavish subsidies. They also believed that, in the interests of a strong, stable international economy based on reciprocal trade, nations that depended heavily on shipping ought not to be weakened by subsidized American shipping, but rather aided and strengthened by the generous lease or sale of the vast wartime fleet being constructed in American yards. In effect, the WSA was rejecting the nationalistic philosophy underlying the 1936 shipping act and replacing it with the cooperative spirit of the Atlantic Charter of 1941, the Roosevelt-Churchill

agreement for fair play between nations allied in war and peace.

Consequently, although the debate would continue during the postwar period, the War Shipping Administration under Lewis Douglas, and later Captain Granville Conway, went to significant lengths during the war to assist Great Britain in replenishing its shipping losses and expediting its postwar maritime recovery. This included the allocation of numerous American ships to the United Kingdom Import Program, the loan of two million tons of vessels to London on bare-boat charters for the war's duration, and the formalization of Anglo-American control, in the guise of the United Maritime Authority, over all Allied shipping in order to prevent the chaotic and ruinous international competition in civil relief and rehabilitation programs that had followed decontrol in 1919. The WSA also assigned many ships to European rehabilitation programs in 1944 and 1945, contributing significantly to the stabilization and recovery of the liberated nations. Of all the American agencies engaged in war work, the WSA was likely the most vigorous and successful advocate of inter-Allied cooperation. Unlike the experience in World War I, when Anglo-American shipping competition soured postwar talks, the U.S. and British shipping agencies of World War II worked commendably to shape a harmonious nautical peace. Ultimately, the gargantuan American merchant fleet, built by the Maritime Commission and operated by the War Shipping Administration, not only provided critical logistical support for the war effort, but also helped place the economies of the Allied and liberated nations on a more solid, anticommunist footing, thereby adding a substantial degree of stability to the postwar political environment.

The construction of American fighting and merchant ships during World War II represented one of the most extraordinary undertakings in the history of warfare. From a 1930s position of inferiority, the United States had assembled in record time a navy and merchant marine in size and significance unrivaled in modern history. In both instances, naval and mercantile, the war had enabled America, in a noncompetitive manner, to displace England as "mistress of the seas." In its maritime strength the United States now reigned internationally supreme. Whether America would choose to maintain this extraordinary position in the postwar period is a subject of the concluding chapters.

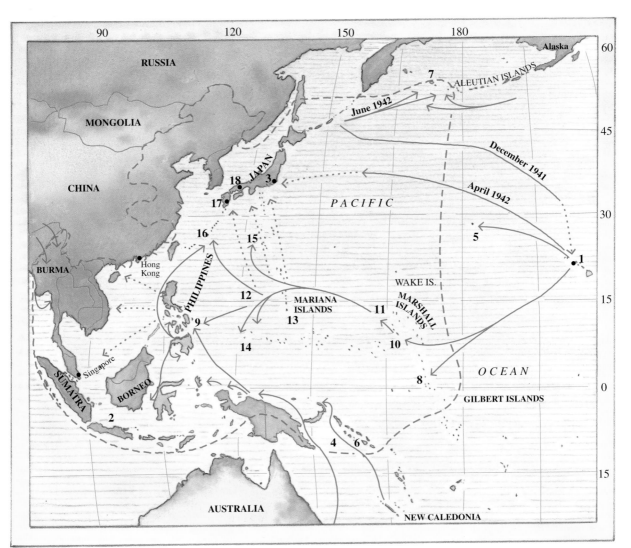

Figure 7 World War II in the Pacific

Movements

- – – – Area Under Japanese Control, August 1942
- ———— Japanese Naval Activity
- - - - - Japanese Air Strikes
- ———— Allied Naval Activity
- - - - - U.S. Air Strikes

Principal Actions

1. Pearl Harbor, Hawaii, December 1941
2. Java Sea, February-March 1942
3. Tokyo, Japan, April 1942
4. Coral Sea, May 1942
5. Midway, June 1942
6. Guadalcanal, Solomon Islands, August 1942
7. Aleutian Islands, Alaska, 1943
8. Tarawa, Gilbert Islands, November 1943
9. Leyte Gulf, 1944
10. Kwajalein, Marshall Islands, January 1944

11. Eniwetok, Marshall Islands, February 1944
12. Philippine Sea, June 1944
13. Guam, July 1944
14. Palau, September 1944
15. Iwo Jima, February-March 1945
16. Okinawa, April-June 1945
17. Nagasaki, Japan
18. Hiroshima, Japan

(Dennis O'Brien maps)

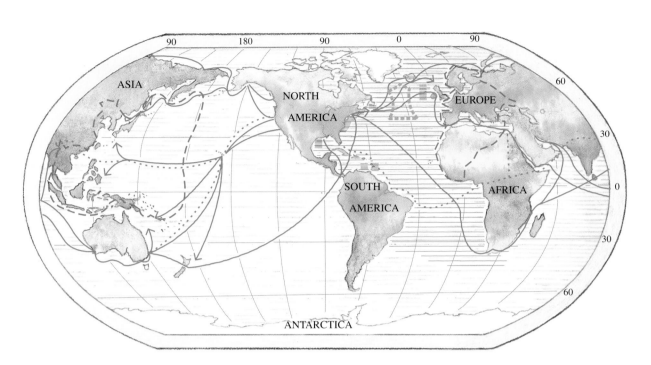

Figure 8 World War II at Sea: Convoy Routes and "The Gap"

———— Allied Supply Line

· · · · · · US Air Supply Lines

══════ Area of German
══════ Submarine Operations

≣ Areas of Heavy German
Sinking of Allied
Shipping

– – – Areas of Maximum Axis
Control (neutral nations
not shown)

▪▪▪▪▪ "The Gap" in Allied Air
Support

(Dennis O'Brien map)

CHAPTER 16

American Maritime and Naval Policy Since World War II

AT THE conclusion of World War II, the U. S. merchant marine was five times its prewar size. Totaling an enormous 58 million deadweight tons, the more than 5,000 ships that comprised the American fleet constituted 60 percent of the world's tonnage. Yet, while immediate postwar requirements, such as providing aid to the war-torn world, required a fleet of considerable size, even the most vigorous champions of American maritime growth had to concede that roughly 12 to 15 million tons would satisfy the nation's postwar needs. In this knowledge Congress deliberated not just the disposal of surplus tonnage, but, more importantly, the method of disposal. Should it shape a bill that would satisfy the Maritime Commission, the shipping industries, and maritime labor, who espoused an "America first" stance and who did not relish the thought of sharing ships with America's competitors? Or should it legislate for those, like the State Department, who held that the United States could not maintain a competitive fleet without extravagant subsidy, and who believed that American ships should be sold to the Allies to assist them in rebuilding their economies and their war-shattered merchant marines? The Merchant Ship Sales Act of 1946 in effect satisfied both positions: It sought to maintain a privately owned and operated merchant marine adequate to the needs of American commerce and defense, and in assisting America's allies it addressed the concerns of the internationalists. By pricing ships at very reasonable rates—often at less than half, or sometimes as little as one-third, of cost—the U.S. government disposed of almost 2,000 ships: 823 went to U.S. citizens, who received a preference in ship selection and were thus able to acquire the better vessels, and 1,100 went to foreign interests. Another 100 ships were chartered to U.S. citizens. The remainder were either scrapped or placed in the U. S. National Defense Reserve

Detail of the USS Seawolf *(SSN-21).*
(Courtesy Electric Boat Corporation)

The postwar U.S. merchant fleet was increasingly registered under foreign "flags of convenience." For example, the 707-foot tanker Cradle of Liberty, *launched at Newport News, Virginia, in 1954 for an oil consortium in Oklahoma, was immediately placed under Liberian registry. Lengthened more than 100 feet during a rebuild in 1974, the* Cradle of Liberty *continued to carry oil to U.S. refineries until the glut of more modern oil tankers in the 1980s caused her layup. (M.S.M. 63.33.2)*

Fleet—six anchorages located on the Atlantic, Pacific, and Gulf coasts.

The immediate effect of the Ship Sales Act was quite positive. During the early postwar period the American deep-sea merchant marine thrived on cheap ships and plenty of business. At the same time, the act helped recoup wartime expenditures and aided the restoration of many foreign fleets. By 1949 the United Kingdom, with the addition of American ships, had completely restored its tonnage to prewar levels, while the fleets of Denmark, France, and Norway had attained 90 percent of for-

mer strength. Other major beneficiaries were Greece, Italy, the Netherlands, and Panama. In effect, the United States retained its naval supremacy while accommodating the desires of the Allies to rebuild their prewar commercial fleets, trade routes, and services. The concomitant increase in trade for each enabled these nations to rapidly acquire balance of payments earnings, and was a large factor in the resuscitation of world commerce.

While the American merchant marine profited in the years immediately following the conclusion of war, continued maritime prosperity was restricted by the increasing disparities between costs of construction and operation for American ships as opposed to foreign. Moreover, given the exigencies of the Cold War, the economic and political decision to assist Germany and Japan, as well as the Allies, in the restoration of their fleets, created formidable competition for the American merchant marine. The development of "Third World" fleets in the undeveloped nations of the world further hampered American shipping. By 1950 the American fleet had dropped to 32.5 percent of world tonnage. Following the Korean War, in its efforts to forge linkages with anti-communism everywhere, the Eisenhower administration allowed U.S. allies and associates a preponderate share of the world's shipping trades. Although the U.S. Merchant Marine found itself competing with allied fleets, the procurement of shipping services from the Free World encouraged these nations to maintain remunerative economic and political ties with the United States.

This decline in the American fleet was accompanied by decline in other areas as well. Coastal and intercoastal shipping, once the bulk of the American maritime industry, was devastated by the war, and it never regained its former strength. Prewar coastal routes of significance were now replaced by truck and rail transport, and the rapid shift of home heating fuel from coal to oil, aided by the construction of inland pipelines, greatly impacted the coastal tanker trade from the Gulf of Mexico and the coal trade from the Chesapeake to the Northeast. Shipbuilding also declined as America's competitors, with significantly lower construction and labor costs, were able to increase their share of the world market.

Several other developments were bringing significant change in the nature of the American merchant marine. One development was the growing dependence of American shipping upon government cargoes. Aid to Europe in the late 1940s, the Marshall Plan being a major contributor of cargoes, became a critical component of American shipping prosperity. When this declined around 1950, the Korean War filled the gap for a short period; later, the Vietnam War did the same. Both wars required the use of the federal reserve fleet, proving the wisdom of maintaining such vessels. Both wars also underlined the fact that the major support for American shipping in the postwar period was provided by national defense policy. As the threat of conflict with the Soviet Union and Communist China continued, so did the need to provision American occupational forces situated around the world in support of the nation's alliances and containment policy. Having become highly dependent upon government programs, the shipping industry, backed strongly by the maritime unions, prevailed upon Congress to pass the Cargo Preference Act of 1954, which stipulated that not less than 50 percent of governmental cargoes be assigned to American-flag ships. Significant as it was, this act was only one of several passed to give perpetual preference to American ships in federal trade. Liner trades profited from these acts, but so did tramping. Governmental preference based on security needs became a vital underpinning of the American merchant marine. But preference implied subsidy and brought its own price, for it made a mockery of the need for ship operators to function efficiently and competitively.

A second development bringing change to the maritime industry was the wholesale transfer of American ships to foreign flags of convenience. For many years American citizens had registered their ships under foreign flags; in fact, during the period of American neutrality before World War II, the Maritime Commission, committed to aiding the Allies, had actively encouraged transfers in order to avoid the late 1930s restrictions imposed upon American shipping by Congress. After the war the practice, rather than diminishing, ballooned to extraordinary proportions, only emphasizing the problems faced by American shipping. In order to avoid higher costs of labor, taxation, and insurance in the United States, and to obtain favorable rates for loans, more and more American shipowners registered their vessels

under flags of convenience, or flags of "necessity" as they argued. Also giving impetus to such transfers was the fact that the Merchant Marine Act of 1936 limited subsidies to the liner trades. Those who sought to profit from tramping trades felt increasingly compelled to seek relief through reregistry. Between 1946 and 1950, the Maritime Commission authorized the transfer of roughly 1.5 million tons of American ships to foreign flags; much of that tonnage went to Liberia, which nation's flag-of-convenience policy was actually designed for American shippers by officials of the U.S. State Department.

Ironically, as the American merchant fleet diminished in numbers and jobs were lost for American seafarers, the maritime unions became increasingly resistant to reductions in crews and economies of manpower on U.S. ships, thereby adding to the cost differential and forcing more companies to go foreign. Competition between maritime unions in the United States further complicated matters—the intense rivalry for political power between these unions brought about wars for benefits that forced costs for the shipowners, and operational subsidies by the government, to escalate at alarming rates.

A third factor affecting American shipping was the technological revolution that swept the seas in the postwar period. The development of containerization as a substitute for break-bulk cargo handling revolutionized the sea-freight industry. Another technological change—the rapid transition in travel from sea to air—permanently changed the nature of the transoceanic passenger services. When the pride of the American liner fleet, the SS *United States*, set new records for the transatlantic passage on its inaugural runs in 1952, it was already virtually obsolete. In 1957, better than half of those persons traveling between Europe and the United States did so by airplane, and a year later this percentage jumped with the introduction of transatlantic jet aircraft. At the same time, improvements were being implemented on an international scale in the highly lucrative cruise industry, improvements American lines were not replicating.

In 1950, the state of the nation's shipping prompted the Truman administration to abolish the Maritime Commission and reestablish its functions within the Commerce Department under two agencies: the operational Maritime

U.S. efforts to compete in the postwar transatlantic passenger liner service resulted in the nation's finest liner, the SS United States. Designed by William Francis Gibbs and built by Newport News Shipbuilding, the 990-foot ship was comparatively plain in the industrial elegance of its all-metal construction and decor, but it was notably fast and efficient. Because of the sizable government subsidy invested in its construction, the ship incorporated features for military use, although it was never requisitioned for government service. It was fitted with accommodations for 913 first-class passengers, 558 cabin passengers, and 537 in tourist class. In 1952 the United States captured the blue riband for transatlantic speed by crossing in less than three and one-half days, at an average speed of thirty-five knots, several knots faster than its Cunard Line competitors Queen Elizabeth and Queen Mary. From 1952 to 1969 the ship operated between New York, Le Havre, France, and Southampton, England, maintaining an exacting schedule and carrying more than one million passengers before high labor costs and the wholesale shift to transatlantic jet airplane travel made this grandest American ocean liner obsolete. The ship was still laid up in 1997, its fate uncertain. The United States was photographed along the New York waterfront in March 1953. (Negative 135356F, © Mystic Seaport Museum, Inc., Rosenfeld Collection, Mystic, Connecticut)

Administration (MARAD), and the other regulatory and promotional Federal Maritime Board. The Eisenhower administration subsequently established a shipbuilding program that produced a fleet of thirty-five Mariners, 13,000-deadweight-ton cargo vessels capable of attaining twenty knots and suited for both commercial and wartime use. A decade later, further reorganization under the Kennedy administration resulted in the creation of the Federal Maritime Commission, which took over the regulatory functions of the Federal Maritime Board. At the same time the Merchant Marine Act of 1936 was amended to enable nonsubsidized shipowners to trade in worn-out vessels for better ships from the National Defense Reserve Fleet. Well-intended as all such programs were, they did not materially stem the decline in American shipping.

By 1970 the condition of the American merchant marine had become deplorable. The nation's tramp fleet was composed entirely, with but one exception, of ships built during World War II, and its continued existence was almost totally dependent upon the various cargo preference acts. The nation's tanker fleet was also substandard–its average 16,000-deadweight-ton carriers were grossly undersized at a time when vessels of five to ten times that capacity were coming off the ways all over the world. An aging U.S.-flag fleet was carrying just under 5 percent of U.S. foreign trade, while the share of the world's tonnage held by the United States had fallen to 6 percent. By 1970, considerably more U.S.-owned tonnage was under foreign flags than under the American. The nation's passenger liner services were also ailing; the number of travelers favoring air transport had increased to 91 percent, and those few Americans who still patronized passenger ships did so for the most part on foreign vessels, preferring the better services and lower costs they offered. With the SS *United States* laid up the previous year, only four passenger ships remained under the American flag. American President Lines terminated its trans-Pacific passenger service in 1973, and before the decade was out the other American liners were gone as well. With respect to the cruise industry, 95 percent of all passengers from American ports were now vacationing on foreign-flag ships.

All told, postwar federal aid to shipping and ship construction was enormous–some $18 billion worth between 1945 and 1970–but it failed to prevent the continued decline of America's maritime industries. As one analyst put it, with the possible exception of its container capacity, the U.S. merchant marine had become "a second-rate fleet in nearly every sense of the word." To complicate the matter, some forty-nine so-called "Third World" underdeveloped nations, including satellites of the Soviet Union, built their own merchant fleets in the years following World War II, and many of them were aggressively supporting their fleets with subsidies, preferences, and discriminations. That the Soviet Union itself had embarked upon the construction of a large, protected merchant marine prepared to operate at any cost, added another serious dimension to the crisis.

The decade of the 1970s opened with a dramatic attempt to reverse the decline. The Merchant

Marine Act of 1970 was conceived by the Nixon administration as an ambitious attempt–akin to the Manhattan Project–to upgrade and broaden the construction and operation supports first put in place by the act of 1936. In order to make the fleet more competitive, the Nixon plan budgeted $6 billion over ten years for a modernized building program geared to produce thirty ships per year. (As the size of vessels increased dramatically in the early 1970s, yearly production goals were reduced in number, and ultimately about twelve ships were launched per year between 1970 and

Launched by Newport News Shipbuilding in 1952, the Old Dominion Mariner *was the first of thirty-five Mariner-class freighters ordered by the U.S. Maritime Administration. Designed for conversion to military use in time of war, these 560-foot vessels, powered with steam turbine engines, were designed to travel at twenty knots, making them among the largest and fastest merchant ships of the day. The* Dominion Mariner *was operated by American President Lines and was renamed* President Hayes *in 1955. In 1974 the ship was sold to American Export Lines and operated as* Export Diplomat *before being chartered to the Farrell Lines and finally laid up in the U.S. reserve fleet on the James River in 1978. Made obsolete by containerization, the thirty-four-year-old ship was towed to Taiwan for scrapping in 1986. (Courtesy The Mariners' Museum, Newport News, Virginia)*

1975.) The bill also encouraged greater cost economies in construction and operation. To spur the industries to modernize their facilities and adopt standardization in production, the construction-differential subsidy (CDS) was reduced from 50 to 45 percent, with a further 2 percent reduction mandated for each year up to 1976. Although the shipbuilders were not pleased with the reduction in support, the prospect of receiving guaranteed annual contracts for construction served as a trade-off. And for the first time the CDS was not restricted to ocean liners, but applied to the construction of inland and nonliner ships as well.

Tramps and coastal carriers received additional advantages under the 1970 act, which cut them in on the government's operational-differential subsidy (ODS). In an effort to make the ODS more cost-effective, the government no longer simply paid the difference between foreign and U.S. wages for all job skills combined, but now determined differentials by a scientific comparison of wages for each and every skill. In order to control costs further, government and industry worked out agreements as to crew size before the construction of a ship even began. Overall, the 1970 act increased government subsidies, put new emphasis on efficiency and growth, and broadened aid, adding domestic and bulk operations to its once-exclusive support of the blue-water liner trades. Members of both houses of Congress passed the act by an almost unanimous vote. Such enthusiasm seemed justified. At first reckoning, U.S. shipping was aided considerably by the act, and the maritime industries began the 1970s in an optimistic mood.

Unfortunately, the Merchant Marine Act of 1970 was undermined by several factors. One was the retention of the requirement that subsidized ships be built in American yards, repaired in American yards, and crewed by American seamen, the very requirements that had first prompted shipowners to abandon the American flag. Moreover, although a number of ships were built under the act, the main line of work for the shipbuilders continued to be naval, and the shipyards were not able to keep pace with technological improvements made in Japanese, Korean, and German commercial ship construction. Consequently, American shipowners continued to favor foreign registry. When tougher environmental regulations in the 1980s imposed large penalties upon ship-

ping for maritime disasters and coastal pollution (namely oil spills), the shipowners had yet another cause to seek refuge in foreign registry. As a sign of the times, one might find in any American port an American-owned vessel built in the Netherlands, flying the Liberian flag, commanded by a German, and crewed by Filipinos.

Another factor undermining the regrowth of the American maritime industry was the disastrous shipping depression of the mid-1970s. Triggered by the Arab-Israeli War of 1973, the consequent Arab oil embargo, and skyrocketing oil prices, the depression laid up one-third of the world's tanker fleet. The crisis was exacerbated by the glut of monster tankers, 48 million tons of which had been ordered in 1968, and much of which was still coming off the ways. The depression spilled over into other trades; shipping in general came down by a half. In this environment, many nations sought to protect their shipping and shipbuilding industries through increased subsidies and protectionist policies. The United States was not remiss in this respect; in 1975 the Energy Transportation Security Act, which would have required that 20 percent of all oil imports be transported in American tankers built in American yards and manned by American seamen, was defeated only by President Gerald Ford's pocket veto. A second effort in 1979 failed under the Carter administration. Through it all, the depression in world shipping continued until the late 1980s.

Even so, the election of Ronald Reagan to the presidency in 1980 brought about dramatic changes in American maritime policy. Reflecting the new administration's strong commitment to national defense, and in particular its determination to restore U.S. maritime superiority over the Soviet Union, the federal government subordinated commercial concerns to military readiness, terminated the construction-differential policy, lifted the prohibition on foreign construction of U.S.-flag vessels, and called for a massive naval construction program of some $15 billion. The program envisioned a 600-ship fighting fleet, including auxiliary vessels, that would keep American shipyards busy for decades. Where cargo ships, tankers, and transports were to be built under the program, their designs would adhere to military specifications under Pentagon management. In effect, this program expressed the administration's belief that the

American merchant marine was best evaluated on its ability to contribute to the national defense under the control of the U.S. Navy. Unquestionably, President Reagan's policy reflected the administration's concern with the alarming increase in the capabilities of the Soviet navy and merchant marine.

President Reagan's determination to cut back all governmental expenditures except in the defense area significantly affected maritime interests. The decision to withdraw support from the American merchant marine, for example, which had the effect of throwing to U.S. competitors an even larger bulk of the world's shipping services, helped to exacerbate a rapidly growing disparity between the country's export and import trade balances, a disparity that reached $300 billion within a decade, making the United States the world's largest debtor nation. In addition, the explosion in defense spending, combined with giant tax cuts, produced the largest budget deficits in American history. The concern to address the budget imbalance through cost-cutting placed the subsidized American commercial merchant marine in a very vulnerable position.

Consequently, when studies revealed that no fewer than five cabinet-level departments and eighty federal agencies shared in regulating the maritime industries, the Shipping Act of 1984, which significantly deregulated liner shipping for carriers and shippers (mirroring similar action for civil aviation), received President Reagan's endorsement. In addition, MARAD, the federal maritime administration created in 1950, was shifted into the Department of Transportation, thus depriving shipping of much of its independence and subordinating it to the more powerful land transportation and aviation interests. The Reagan administration also announced plans to close all of the nation's merchant marine academies, with the exception of Kings Point on Long Island. Only congressional opposition prevented the proposed closures from materializing.

Also impacting maritime interests was President Reagan's decision to build a new naval auxiliary, a decision reflecting the fact that neither the commercial fleet nor the national reserve fleet met existing military requirements. Half-million-ton petroleum tankers, for example, were not viable as military transports, while the national reserve fleet was so antiquated as to be virtually useless.

Consequently, the Ready Reserve Force (RRF)–created during the Carter administration as a response to the Soviet invasion of Afghanistan and consisting of ships most useful to the military in an emergency–was beefed up dramatically. Whereas under President Carter the navy's Military Sealift Command had operated on a $40 million budget, under Reagan it was given a budget of over $1 billion. In time, another $8 billion would be allocated to purchase and modernize ships for the RRF. The logic of this move was demonstrated in 1990-91 when the Ready Reserve Force provided the ships most immediately required to supply America's response to the Iraqi invasion of Kuwait. Only when a stronghold had been secured were commercial vessels called upon.

The trend for government to favor military control and development over the commercial shipping industry seems to outline the future of American shipping. Arguments for a full-fledged U.S. Navy build-and-charter program under the Military Sealift Command have replaced support and subsidization policies established in earlier years. With the conclusion of the Cold War, a large reserve of commercial ships seems no longer necessary, and the navy, long resistant to dependence on the U.S. shipping industry and ever dubious of its "effective control" of American ships flying foreign flags, is more and more insistent upon managing its own fleet.

In implementing its policy, the government is well aware that the termination of the construction-operation subsidy has not had the disastrous effects forecast by shipowners, who now have authority to build foreign but fly the American flag. Moreover, both the Oil Pollution Act of 1990, which mandated the replacement of 147 existing tankers with ships of double-hulled construction by the year 2015, and the Cruise Ship Competitiveness Act of 1992, which permitted gambling on American cruise ships, have spurred new interest in shipbuilding and promise to keep yards busy. The lowering of U.S. labor costs and the increase of shipbuilding costs abroad in the 1990s has also aided the American ship construction industry, but whether these beneficial conditions will remain cannot be predicted.

What is certain is that the Reagan, Bush, and Clinton administrations have not been comfortable in continuing direct subsidization–under-

The characteristics of a modern oil tanker are displayed by the **American Progress**, launched by Newport News Shipbuilding in 1997 as the first tanker built in the U.S. to specifications imposed by the Oil Pollution Act of 1990. At 620 feet and 46,000 deadweight tons, the ship is smaller than the 900-1,000-foot very large (VLCC) and ultra-large (ULCC) crude carriers of the 1970s. Among the ship's safety features is double-hull construction to prevent catastrophic hull failure in case of grounding or collision. Although it appears inefficient, the bulbous bow actually increases buoyancy and produces a wave that cancels the ship's own bow wave, contributing to the vessel's speed and efficient passage through the water. The ship's control bridge and berthing spaces are all contained in the superstructure at the stern, above the efficient, slow-turning diesel engine. The first of nine similar tankers to be built at Newport News, the **American Progress** was purchased by Mobil Oil's shipping division, Mobil Shipping and Transport, joining a fleet of thirty-three tankers that carry 5 percent of the world's petroleum. (Courtesy Newport News Shipbuilding)

standably so, for the old practice of government aid no longer reflects public sentiment, a sentiment largely apathetic, if not antagonistic, to underwriting the interests of the maritime community. In this environment, even cargo preference and the venerable policy of cabotage, limiting U.S. coastal trade to U.S.-flag vessels, appear vulnerable. Although attacks on the cabotage sections of the Jones Act of 1920 were defeated in

the 1980s by a coalition of shipbuilders and the maritime unions, in the 1990s Congress and the Clinton administration took at best an apathetic approach to the protection of U.S. coastal and intercoastal trades. Congress's extraordinary decision in 1995 to terminate the House Committee on Merchant Marine and Fisheries was another portent of what the shipping industries could anticipate. Little wonder that United States shipping firms have continued to abandon the American flag, including the nation's very largest: Sea-Land and American President Lines. In 1996, another venerable company, Lykes Brothers Steamship Company, sought to avoid bankruptcy by going foreign, but failed. Shipbuilding was not excluded from these disappointing developments. When the Bush and Clinton administrations, responding to the end of the Cold War and the concern for fiscal austerity, decided to dramatically downsize the Reagan plan for a 600-ship naval fleet, U.S. shipyards understandably suffered.

For all this, the twenty-first century approached with some encouraging signs that American shipping had managed to regain a sympathetic ear. Although the Clinton administration came into power in 1993 strongly inclined to terminate all government supports for the merchant marine, including cargo preference, and renewed the Reagan proposal to close the nation's maritime academies, it responded pragmatically to industrial, labor, and military lobbying by reviving shipbuilding for U.S. Navy sealift vessels and new merchant ships. In addition, the Maritime Security Act of 1996 continued the operational subsidy program by allocating $2.1 million annually over ten years for each of forty-seven militarily useful merchant vessels. Such commitments represent only a portion of what it takes to maintain an efficient navy and merchant marine, but federal ship-construction goals promised to guarantee annually a modest flow of vessels from American yards, and support to keep some of them operating.

Nevertheless, sixty years after the passage of the historic Merchant Marine Act of 1936, the nation's maritime policy had come almost full circle. The arguments of those who maintained that subsidies and preferential treatment were required for the U.S. shipping industry to be commercially competitive were not endorsed by the many Americans whose concerns for government cost-effectiveness outweighed their belief in the national and international significance of a strong U.S.-flag merchant marine. Consequently, the shipping industry could no longer rely on Washington to provide the support customarily assigned to commercial shipping in the past.

Whether this is good for the nation is an issue of much controversy. Free trade and balanced budgets have their merits. But what if they prostrate the nation's trading capabilities? Most successful commercial nations have committed themselves to a strong merchant marine as part of their overall trade strategy. As one recent analyst observed, "a healthy merchant marine promotes successful exports, profitable trading ventures, and a national outreach to get the best available products and technology." The maintenance of a competitive merchant marine would also assist in reducing the enormous United States trade deficit. To rely heavily on foreign transport and services will not help to increase U.S. export earnings and elevate the nation from its current position as the world's leading debtor.

W hether such reasoning can overcome inward fixation on cost-cutting, deregulation, and privatization seems problematic. Without a "shipping-friendly" environment within the U.S. Congress, the return of the American merchant marine to an effective competitive level remained uncertain at the end of the twentieth century. If history can be prophecy, indications are that until the United States faces a major transportation crisis, the nation's merchant marine, which in the late 1990s constituted less than 3 percent of world tonnage and carried only 4 percent of the nation's waterborne foreign trade, is unlikely to enjoy a reversal of the continuing erosion of public support.

Towards the Twenty-First Century: The Impact of Technological Innovation

Since the end of World War II, American maritime and naval enterprise has undergone a strik-ing transformation. As in so many other aspects of human experience, technological innovation has produced fundamental changes that now are redefining traditional methods, organizational and physical structures, and human relationships. Such innovation has even redefined the nature of human work and of human interaction in the workplace; nowhere is this more apparent than in the shipping industries.

S ince ancient times a great portion of water-borne cargo had been carried in crates, barrels, boxes, bales, bags, and a variety of other forms of packaging that varied widely in size and shape. Dry-cargo "break-bulk" vessels were designed to carry such a wide assortment of objects in their holds; and while some vessel types became relatively specialized for one type of cargo, most vessels–whether in sail or steam–were configured to handle whatever form of packaging presented itself at a given moment. Thus evolved the typical modern "freighter" of the nineteenth and early twentieth centuries, with its several holds accessible from the deck through a number of large hatches. Heavy masts, booms, and deck-mounted kingposts were permanent cargo-handling fixtures aboard these vessels. Alongshore, cranes and their cargo slings also served as fairly primitive mechanical aids to the hundreds of human cargo handlers, the longshoremen and their stevedore bosses, who typically took many days either to load or to unload a freighter.

On the waterfront a traditional working culture developed among men whose labor had scarcely changed, as one of them put it, "since the days of the Phoenicians." Considerable cargo damage was unavoidable as a result of all this movement and man-handling; so was pilferage. Insurance on cargo, accordingly, was a significant portion of total shipping costs. The substantial amount of time spent alongshore in loading and unloading cargo greatly limited the earning capacity of a vessel, which typically spent far less time at sea actually transporting revenue-producing cargo than it did in port.

Then, during the early to mid-1940s, wartime necessities and war-inspired technological innovations combined to produce more efficient, nontraditional methods in waterborne transportation of the massive quantities of war materiel. From this wartime experience evolved a radically new form of cargo handling: containerization. Rather than

being placed aboard ship piece by piece, containerized cargo is packed at its point of origin in a specially designed steel box, which is essentially a truck body of standardized size, with reinforced edges so that it can be stacked on top of (or under) other such containers. Normally measuring eight feet in width by eight feet in height, these containers vary in length, but the initial design, which specified a length of twenty feet, produced the now-standard designation of a twenty-foot equivalent unit, or TEU, as the measure of cargo capacity for vessels carrying these containers. From the point of origin, the containerized items of cargo—now sealed and accompanied by appropriate documentation—would be loaded on a truck chassis and shipped over the highway system or by rail to a containerport, perhaps hundreds or even thousands of miles away; from there an ocean voyage would end at a similar containerport with comparable facilities for transporting containers—with contents presumably untouched and intact—to their final destination.

The variety of cargo carried by a traditional break-bulk ship is suggested by this glimpse into the forward hold of the Farrell Lines freighter African Endeavor *as a large crate of machinery is lowered in among the canisters, bales, and packages. Although the ship's electric deck winches permit loading and unloading under a variety of conditions, break-bulk cargo handling is slow and labor-intensive, keeping ships in port for long stretches. Launched as the* Delbrasil *at Sparrows Point, Maryland, in 1940 for the Mississippi Shipping Company of New Orleans, the 465-foot* African Endeavor *served the War Shipping Administration as the* George F. Elliot *during the war before being purchased and renamed by the Farrell Lines in 1948. In 1960 the Farrell Lines turned the twenty-year-old ship over to the Commerce Department. After a ten-year lay-up the old break-bulk freighter was scrapped in 1970. The* African Endeavor *was photographed in August 1949. (Negative 124797F, © Mystic Seaport Museum, Inc., Rosenfeld Collection, Mystic, Connecticut)*

A leading American trucking operator, Malcolm McLean, pioneered containerization in the decade after World War II. In 1956 McLean converted a tanker to hold fifty-six of the twenty-foot containers, and by October of the following year he had started East Coast-Caribbean-Gulf Coast service with a converted C-2 freighter capable of handling 226 thirty-five-foot containers. Bitter opposition from labor unions thwarted efforts to expand container service for several years, but by 1964 McLean and other shipping operators had worked out a far-reaching accommodation with representatives of the longshoremen and stevedores, which provided workers guaranteed annual incomes to compensate partially for the heavy and continuing loss of jobs through technological unemployment. Thereafter, the transformation of ocean-going American shipping, along with its cargo handling, was swift and permanent.

Containerization produced a drastic decline in port time, so that a ship could be loaded or unloaded in a matter of hours, rather than days or even weeks, whether using dockside gantry cranes or self-unloading machinery permanently mounted on the containership. In either case, the hundreds of traditional dockworkers no longer were needed; they had been replaced, in the words of one recently retired longshoreman, by "a small cadre of robotized technicians"–the handful of computer-assisted machine operators who work in relative isolation from each other while handling by mechanical means a now-invisible cargo in its standardized metal box.

The vastly greater efficiency, economy, and security (from both pilferage and damage) of cargo handling by containerization appeared to be a compelling necessity for the survival of a United States merchant marine, especially in the unsubsidized and otherwise unprotected world trade. Containerships, growing ever larger in size, speed, and carrying capacity, increasingly would be built abroad as such American shippers as Sea-Land, Matson, Lykes, and American President Lines sought to lower their costs in order to cope with the challenge of foreign fleets that now were competing with the same advanced technologies in cargo handling and transportation. Requiring huge acreage for container and truck trailer chassis storage, containership operators shifted their business away from the traditional in-town dock facilities of major ports; the result was the troubling decline of many centuries-old port cities, like Boston and New York City, as they saw their business moving to such newly created containerports as MassPort and Port Elizabeth, New Jersey.

Containerization, moreover, was only one of a number of innovations in cargo handling. An elaborate intermodal system, involving rail, highway, barge, and ocean-going transportation, developed in the United States, along with a variety of specialized vehicles designed for this system. Among waterborne vessels were the RoRo (Roll on, Roll off) ship, where a truck-mounted container could be driven on board of a stern- or

Since its introduction in the 1950s as a means of handling cargo, the standardized container has revolutionized the shipment of packaged goods. With containerships that can circle the world on schedule, with computerized tracking of cargo, and with efficient terminal facilities to speed the intermodal shift from water to road or rail transportation, a practical global economy has become possible. The Matson Line introduced containerization on the Pacific in 1958, and operates U.S. facilities in Oakland, Seattle, and Honolulu. In this photograph, the Matson containership R.J. Pfeiffer *approaches Honolulu, where the Sand Island terminal handles 400,000 containers a year. Launched by National Steel and Shipbuilding at San Diego in 1992, the 713-foot* R.J. Pfeiffer *has a capacity of 1,650 TEUs stacked in the hold and on deck. (Courtesy Matson Navigation Company)*

bow-loading ship. Similar to the RoRo, the SeaTrain type of ship had train tracks mounted in the hull so that railroad cars could be loaded and off-loaded directly. Seagoing barge carriers included the Lighter-Aboard-Ship (LASH), which employed large vessel-mounted cranes to off-load self-propelled barges (stacked in the hull of the mother ship) in those areas of the world with limited port facilities or deepwater access. Of particular importance for major inland waterways was the integrated tug or "notch" barge system, in which a single propelling unit, designed to fit

Postwar Changes in Global Trade and Shipping Patterns and Their Impact Upon American Ports of Entry

New York-New Jersey

The Port of New York-New Jersey, with its remarkably accessible and protected deep-water harbor, is the largest natural port in the United States—and one of the world's most important. Fifteen hundred square miles in size, it is fed by four rivers, contains seven bays—including the great upper bay—and enjoys an inland waterway access to New England. This great port is key to the development of an extraordinary city; for better than a century New York has reigned as the nation's trade, financial, cultural, educational, and communications capital. To this day it remains one of the wonders of the modern world.

The significance of the Port of New York-New Jersey was never clearer than during World War II, when its vast facilities were expanded further to make it the hub of America's link with the Mediterranean and European military campaigns. When the war ended, the port, with its indented shoreline and many islands, featured no less than 600 ship anchorages; 575 miles of developed waterfront; 1,822 docks, wharves, and piers; fifty floating docks; 1,100 warehouses; and numer-

ous shipyards. More than forty thousand factories lined its shores. In the immediate postwar period the port's waters swarmed with ships of every size, from the world's most elegant passenger liners and mightiest battleships to the everyday toilers: 700 tug-boats; two dozen ferries; numerous fireboats, police boats, dredges, and garbage scows; and barges and flat-boats by the hundreds. The latter, towed or pushed by tugs, were omnipresent, many of them engaged in transfer-ring railroad freight cars from one side of the harbor to the other or in carrying coal from New Jersey piers to New York City's electrical power plants. Movement of cargo took place on an immense scale—in 1945 the harbor handled 80 percent of the North Atlantic general cargo trade.

Passenger transport took place on an equally vast scale. Ferryboats carried upwards of 50 million New York-area commuters annually in the immediate postwar years, and passenger ships disgorged hundreds of thousands more. Great liners and some of the world's most glamorous cruise ships shuttled in and out of port on an almost daily basis. To add to the harbor's activity, pleasure craft, excursion

steamers, and sightseeing boats dotted its waters. And, not coincidentally, the port provided a home for no fewer than six institutions engaged in maritime education and training, including the United States Merchant Marine Academy at Kings Point, the nation's foremost academy for the preparation of officers for the merchant service.

Today the port of New York is vastly changed from the port described above. Waterborne traffic, for example, is now but a fraction of what it had been. In July and August of 1952, when the newly launched American superliner SS *United States* was setting transatlantic speed records, inbound and outbound ship movements, as noted in the *New York Times* "Shipping-Mails" column, rarely numbered less than sixty to seventy per day. Three decades later, in-and-out ship-ping had so declined that the *Times* discontinued its daily listings of harbor activity. Its last account, run on 16 April 1984, documented but three outbound sailings for that day, and one outbound for the next! Largely gone, too, are the formerly ubiquitous tugs, barges, and ferries. Most of the moorings off the Brooklyn shore are now unoccupied, and military vessels, once con-

spicuous, are difficult to find.

A scan of the waterfront also reveals significant change. Whereas much of the Manhattan shoreline was once ringed with finger piers, most of these are gone, replaced by parks, commercial districts, or high-rise condominiums. Where these piers still exist, they have been converted for use as bus depots, sanitation department garages, parking lots, or recreational facilities. Hoboken, New Jersey, that tough break-bulk cargo waterfront community immortalized in Elia Kazan's 1954 film, *On The Waterfront*, has been similarly revamped, much of its maritime environment now gentrified with fashionable bars and restaurants.

Many factors explain the remarkable changes that have occurred since World War II, technology being perhaps the most significant. A major turning point occurred in 1957, the first year that planes carried more transatlantic passengers than did ships. One by one the elegant liners were withdrawn from service; the highly subsi-

The Sea-Land container terminal at Port Elizabeth, New Jersey, represents the shift of maritime trade away from the congested New York waterfront and into shipping containers. Sea-Land was established after the pioneering experiments of its founder, trucker Malcolm McLean, to carry truck trailers on shipboard in 1956. With its early East Coast and transatlantic service, Sea-Land tied ocean shipping into the nation's expanding interstate highway system through its efficient shoreside container installations, and developed refrigerated containers as well as livestock and automobile containers. As an indication of the essential integration of land and water transportation of containers into an intermodal system, Sea-Land was purchased by the East Coast railroad corporation, CSX. (Courtesy Sea-Land; Dan Katz photo)

dized SS *United States* was retired in 1969. By 1986 only three piers for luxury ships remained on Manhattan's west side.

The American cruise ship industry, once centered in New York, had also left, moving south in order to conserve fuel and to be closer to the warm-water destinations favored by vacationers who had ready air access to such major southern departure points as Miami, Fort Lauderdale, and Puerto Rico. In the late 1970s, the New York Port Authority tried to stem the exodus by building, at great cost, a new west-side

cruise ship terminal, but the effort failed. In 1983 more than 1.5 million Americans took cruises, but New York's share of the trade was negligible; in that year only half the number of cruise passengers needed to reach the break-even point boarded in New York. Thereafter, periodic visits by Great Britain's *Queen Elizabeth II* and the continuation of cruises to Bermuda and the northeast coast would constitute New York's reminder of its former prominence as the nation's principal cruise-ship port.

The revolution in ship size and type also had much to do with diminished activity in the New York-New Jersey port area. While tonnage in and out increased from the 1960s to the 1980s, the number of ships actually using the harbor decreased because of the enormous growth in carrying capacities. One tanker of 200,000 deadweight tons, for example, now replaced twelve of the former 16,000-ton T-2 tankers common to these waters in earlier years. The same revolution took place in dry-cargo carriage, where large containerships not only carried more cargo but, by virtue of the quick turn-around afforded by increased automation, remained in port only a fraction of the time their predecessors did. The container revolution also influenced the layout of the port's waterfront. Since container operations required large storage areas that could not be provided in crowded Manhattan, and since the huge cranes required to lift the containers could not be fitted to Manhattan's aged piers, the port's cargo-handling industry shifted in the 1960s and 1970s to harbors like those of Port Elizabeth and Port Newark in New Jersey, where ample space and good rail and road connections provided more efficient operations. As a natural result of that move, there followed an outmigration of the shipping industry's corporate operations. Now such headquarters are as likely to be found in Jersey City, or even Greenwich, Connecticut, as in lower Manhattan.

The shift to the New Jersey mainland gave rise to another phenomenon—the growth of a rail-land bridge from the West Coast. By 1995, better than 50 percent of all imports into the New York-New Jersey area arrived by transcontinental container rail, thus further diminishing the volume of traffic in New York Harbor, and depriving the port authority of important revenues. Yet another significant diversion from sea transport has been effected by air competition. In recent years, international cargo moving in and out of the region by airplane has greatly increased in value, diverting billions of dollars annually from port earnings.

The shift to containerization has had some interesting peripheral impacts on port activity. In 1960, for example, nine fireboats serviced the port. Thirty-three years later these had declined to three. Although the waterpower of the boats increased over time, their numbers decreased with the decrease in risk of fire. Under the old break-bulk cargo-handling system, armies of stevedores, many of whom smoked, labored on flammable piers and in wharfside warehouses. With the introduction of containerization, these structures disappeared, and with them a great deal of the fire danger. Newer ships were also more fire-resistant; with cargoes now insulated in metal boxes, and with the need for a far-smaller work force, the container ports and vessels have far less need for fire-fighting vessels.

The decline in the number of tugs is also linked to some of the aforementioned technological developments. With fewer ships using harbor facil-

ities, fewer tugs are needed to position them for docking and departure. Moreover, steerage and power improvements have made it possible for many vessels to self-dock. And the barges and flatboats that once cluttered the port are significantly diminished in number as the city has closed its harbor-front power plants and as improved trucking and roadway systems have replaced the railroads.

The decline of New York as a shipbuilding and repair center has also been marked, with the closure of the Brooklyn Navy Yard and Brooklyn Ship Repair in the 1980s representing the most vivid example. Even fate has worked to disadvantage the city. When a new naval center scheduled for construction on Staten Island was canceled following the decision to mothball the battleship USS *Iowa*–which was damaged in a gun turret explosion in 1989–the port's hope to balance loss of trade revenue by securing major government contracts was seriously dashed. On top of economic hard times come the threats by several presidential administrations to close the port's maritime academies.

Water contamination has also handicapped the port of New York-New Jersey. When in the mid-1980s toxicity was found in Newark Bay crabs, the contaminate was traced to a Passaic River plant that had manufactured Agent Orange for military use in Vietnam. For two years dredging was forbidden until a procedure for an environmentally suitable disposal of the sediment was agreed upon. In the meantime, silt from the Passaic and Hackensack Rivers reduced Newark Bay water depths by several feet, prohibiting certain deep-draft vessels from entering the harbor. Similar difficulties beleaguered New York City's effort to utilize the container port at Howland's Hook on Staten Island.

Yet another factor that has disadvantaged the port of New York-New Jersey has been its high cost of labor. While creating efficiency of movement, reducing pilferage, and lowering insurance costs, the automation of the port actually–and ironically–resulted in a rise in labor costs. Vigorously resisted by the International Longshoremen's Association, automation was accomplished only after the association won guarantees of an annual wage–now over $34,000–for its members, whether they worked or not. The obligation to pay as many as 6,000 nonworking union members placed an unusual burden on the industry. Since the early 1960s, over $1 billion has gone into labor supports, resulting in the decision to raise assessments charged on cargo in New York. Such assessments mean that New York-New Jersey is simply an expensive place to do business.

Given all these factors, the port of New York-New Jersey has lost trade to other ports that are in a better position to take advantage of new trade patterns. By 1990, the port could no longer advertise itself as the nation's number-one harbor. Although it still

figures as a center of significant commercial activity, and although its volume and value in trade are actually larger than they have been in years previous, other ports have superseded it in rates of growth. In terms of annual freight traffic, for example, in 1994 New Orleans ranked first, with New York-New Jersey second, Houston-Galveston third, and Valdez Harbor, Alaska, fourth. In terms of dollar value, New York-New Jersey had fallen behind Los Angeles, which vaulted ahead by virtue of a ten-year growth of over 200 percent, while in the same decade New York-New Jersey rose only 10 percent. Close behind was Long Beach, with Seattle and Tacoma taking strong positions in fourth and fifth place.

The rise to prominence of the West Coast ports underlines an extraordinary shift in trade patterns. Whereas New York was once the major center for Asian commerce, that trade, with the development of excellent port facilities on the West Coast, has now bypassed the longer, costlier voyage to the East Coast, preferring instead to transship cargoes overland via rail. Larger vessel sizes, too, are a factor in this shift, as many of today's ships cannot pass through the Panama Canal. Consequently, the port of New York-New Jersey has not benefited from the tremendous boom in this nation's trade with Asia. The port's share of the East Coast trade has similarly diminished. Whereas it once served as the major port for the entire East Coast, its influence now is

increasingly confined to the Northeast, as Baltimore, Norfolk, Charleston, and Savannah–which offer lesser costs to shippers and shipowners–take a larger and larger share of the South's import and export business. Even in the Northeast, Boston is threatening New York interests.

At this writing, the port of New York-New Jersey is struggling to hold onto what it has left, and to stimulate regrowth in every way possible. While its tonnage has remained stable over the past decade, even increasing slightly, the port has not maintained its relative share in the growth of cargoes globally. The lesson learned from the loss of Asian trade has been taken to heart. If few persons anticipated the waterborne losses that New York would sustain as a result of the western rail-land bridge, many are now working to recoup some of that loss by persuading shippers from Southeast Asia to use the Suez Canal–and by fostering increased business with Latin America. Overriding all is the port's determination to retain and increase its share of European trade. Efforts to upgrade and modernize the port's terminals and transportation networks–including New York City's proposal to build a $900 million superport in Brooklyn and Staten Island, and a rail freight tunnel to New Jersey–are among the many strategies planned to reach these objectives. Whether these efforts will restore New York to its former prominence as the nation's primary distribution center are problematic, however, as trade patterns continue to shift in response to rapid changes taking place in the global economy.

While the port of New York-New Jersey feels the pinch from changes in global trade and shipping patterns, other leading U.S. ports of entry, such as Charleston, New Orleans, and Los Angeles-Long Beach, have been beneficiaries of some of the same developments.

Charleston

Charleston's rise to prominence has largely been caused by the determination of the world's ocean carriers to duplicate what the airlines, and to a certain extent the railroads, have done—concentrate on hubs, or load centers, for the most efficient and economic distribution of trade. Increasingly, the lines are designating one port for turn-around of their larger ships, while feeding other ports with smaller vessels, barges, or overland transport. This development, a global occurrence, has caused concern on every U.S. coast, but most particularly on the East Coast. For if patterns already evident materialize, the port that stands the best chance of being selected by the international shipping industry as the Atlantic Coast's southeast hub is not Baltimore, Norfolk, or Savannah, but Charleston. Unlike most of its competitors, especially Baltimore and Norfolk, which lie substantially inland, Charleston is situated virtually at seaboard, and does not incur, as do Baltimore and Norfolk, large annual costs for dredging.

Numerous transportation routes converge on Charleston, and through its excellent, virtually land-locked harbor, an extensive coastal and foreign trade takes place. The potential designation of Charleston as a load center has created much anxiety along the East Coast, to the point where shipping leaders in Baltimore and Norfolk, traditionally adversaries, have talked about cooperating, perhaps even creating an alliance of their own, to prevent their subordination to the South Carolina port.

New Orleans

Another beneficiary of recent change in international trade patterns has been New Orleans. Although the port lies 110 miles up the Mississippi River from the Gulf of Mexico, New Orleans connects with the Intracoastal Waterway, and has been for many years the major distribution hub for the lucrative trade of the Mississippi River inland waterway system, as well as being a major entrepôt for Latin American goods. In the 1980s, however, trade revenues fell in New Orleans when oil prices plummeted and as the state's energy industry foundered. As ship calls at the port declined, the city's administrators struggled to stem the tide and worried openly about the port's aging infrastructure, about its limited water depth, about trade falling to other ports along the Gulf—such as Houston, Galveston, Mobile, and Pascagoula—and even fretted over a new break-bulk terminal in Memphis, Tennessee.

Three events in 1991-92 brought New Orleans out of its lethargy. First came modernization and beautification of the city's waterfront, including hotels, a shopping mall, and a riverwalk. Second, to help pay for it, the Port Board permitted floating casinos to berth along the same waterfront. This was done despite numerous warnings that the presence of additional ships on this particularly dangerous and winding section of the bustling river would cause congestion and increase marine casualties. Declaring that gambling's rewards were worth the risk, the port authorities downplayed the warnings, but were embarrassed in 1996 when a 763-foot Hong-Kong-owned, Liberian-flagged freighter loaded with 56,000 long tons of corn lost engine power and crashed into the Riverwalk shopping mall and Riverside Hilton hotel, narrowly missing two crowded casino cruise ships, and causing tens of millions of dollars in damage.

Third, and most important, was the late 1992 signing of the North American Free Trade Agreement (NAFTA) with Canada and Mexico. President George Bush called the treaty "the first giant step" towards a free trade zone encompassing the entire Western Hemisphere, and New Orleans was at the forefront in applauding it. The increased trade with Mexico and Latin America promised to enhance New Orleans's market share and profitability, and the port hastened to accommodate the projected gains by upgrading and extending the port's infra-

With thirty major terminals for all types of cargo, the Port of Los Angeles handles more than 2,500 ship arrivals per year, representing eighty shipping lines. Pier 300 on Terminal Island opened in 1997 as the latest component of the Port of Los Angeles. Operated by American President Lines (APL), the 231-acre container facility has 4,000 feet of berthing space, with twelve fixed gantry cranes and ten mobile cranes for container handling. Successor to the Pacific Mail Steamship Company and the Dollar Steamship Line, APL was established in 1938 and began containerized shipping on the Pacific in 1961. Since the early 1980s the firm has consolidated its operations as a freight carrier in the Pacific, refined its shoreside operations, computerized its cargo tracking, and built a new fleet of 800-foot containerships. With the reduction of the federal Operating-Differential Subsidy after 1993, the new ships were built and registered overseas, and in late 1997 the firm was acquired by Neptune Orient Lines, Ltd. (Courtesy Port of Los Angeles)

structure, improvements that would be paid for in large part with anticipated casino-boat revenues. In fact, city officials predicted that commerce generated by NAFTA through lower tariffs and decreased government controls could well become the dominant pattern of American ocean trade, replacing even the East-West axis routes from Asia to Europe. In 1994-95, New Orleans ranked as the nation's busiest port, handling almost 20 percent of all general cargo exported from and imported into the United States. It was

the major handler of break-bulk cargoes, controlled the coffee market, surpassed Houston in the handling of steel and rubber, and could look forward with optimism to the rewards promised from the move towards hemispheric free trade.

Los-Angeles-Long Beach

A third trend in international commerce that has shaped the development of American ports is the tremendous growth of trade with Asia. No ports have benefited more

handsomely from this phenomenon than the neighboring ports of Los Angeles and Long Beach. Since the early 1980s, trade through the two ports has been shifting away from the western industrial nations to the more accessible markets of the Pacific Rim, where rapidly developing countries like Taiwan, South Korea, China, Indonesia, and Malaysia, as well as that region's industrial leaders—Japan, Australia, and New Zealand—have been the biggest trading partners. During the period 1983-89, when Los Angeles-Long Beach almost doubled their share of Asian commerce, the two ports, previously ranking behind Seattle, Tacoma, and Portland, vaulted to the top. Possessed of one of the largest man-made harbor complexes in the world, and spared the dredging problems of its competitor Oakland, Los Angeles-Long Beach replaced New York-New Jersey in 1984 as the nation's leading customs collection center.

Los Angeles-Long Beach has emphasized the intermodal potential of containerized shipping by linking the port complex with efficient rail and highway routes for timely distribution throughout the U.S. This land-bridge system evolved in part as a solution to the limitations of the Panama Canal, where rising toll rates and political unrest, as well as the restricted width of the canal locks, caused growing concern. Soon, more than one-third of all containerized cargo employed the oceanic intermodal overland route. In 1990, for example, Los Angeles-Long Beach commonly sent

fifteen double-stacked container trains to Chicago each week, as well as twenty-one to Kansas City, eleven to Houston, and three to Dallas, for an average of almost one container train every three hours. On this volume of trade, Los Angeles-Long Beach has catapulted into first place in the nation in terms of dollar values, and has become the busiest container complex.

Unfortunately, Los Angeles' relationship to the growing affluence of Asia, its close proximity to the huge population base of Southern California, and the extent of the port's container operations, have encouraged a lucrative trade in smuggled goods. In fact, no other entry port in the U.S. has a comparable illicit trade. The emphasis on sealed containers makes it impossible for the U.S. Customs Service to identify the true contents of the many thousands of containers in port at any moment. In 1995, roughly 1.5 million containers, carrying $140 billion worth of goods, flowed through Los Angeles-Long Beach, and customs agents were able to inspect only 3 percent of these. Prominent among export goods smuggled are stolen cars. Between 1992 and 1996, U.S. Customs seized 231 stolen cars headed for Pacific Rim countries, most of them hidden in containers. The insurance industry estimated that as many as 100,000 stolen cars were successfully smuggled to Asia during the same period. The extent to which this venerable form of illegal maritime trade is carried on through the modern facilities of Los Angeles-Long Beach illustrates the extraordinary development of U.S. trade with the Pacific Rim.

Mobile cranes like these at the new APL terminal in Los Angeles speed the loading and unloading of containers between sea and land. Although containerization put many longshoremen out of work, it has increased the speed and efficiency of cargo-handling tremendously. (Courtesy Port of Los Angeles)

snugly into the stern of a barge, could work with several cargo-carrying units, with one loading, another unloading, and still another in transit.

Such intermodal systems, as they have quickly developed in the United States in recent decades, have fulfilled the promise of unprecedented speed of delivery from point of origin to final destination. Speed at sea is only one element, and not the most important; in fact, the attempt to achieve significantly greater speeds for containerships resulted in unacceptably high costs for the greatly increased power required, as Sea-Land discovered. Its thirty-three-knot SL-7 class of 38,800-ton containerships, built in Europe and delivered in 1972, could transport a cargo of nearly 1,100 of the thirty-five- or forty-foot containers across the Atlantic in just four and a half days; but such speed required engines generating 120,000 shaft horsepower, and the operational

costs were such that within a few years the vessels were sold to the United States government for use as naval auxiliaries.

A more promising approach to significant (and reasonably economical) increase of speed at sea has produced a variety of radical departures in hull design, if not in propulsion systems as well. "Surface-effect" vessels, employing hydrofoils or air cushions, have been in general use for several decades, but their size has been limited and their normal service restricted to passenger conveyance over short distances. Unconventional single and multihull configurations also have been tested and put into initial service for seagoing cargo vessels. The general approach is to have the main, cargo- and passenger-carrying hull of the vessel ride above the water surface by being mounted on rigid struts connected to one or more slender, totally submerged hulls. The submerged hulls

When the USS Nautilus *successfully inaugurated nuclear power for ship propulsion, there was initial enthusiasm for its application in merchant as well as naval ships. Using a nuclear reactor to boil water to produce high-pressure steam for an efficient turbine engine seemed an ideal alternative to coal or oil fuel, but worldwide concern over nuclear accidents limited construction of U.S. nuclear-powered merchant ships to just one, the SS* Savannah, *launched in 1959. Named in honor of the first steam vessel to cross the ocean, and built as a combined passenger and cargo ship for the Department of Commerce, the 595-foot ship operated until 1971. The ship was deactivated after the Department of Defense decided that oil-fired engines were more cost-effective than nuclear power for cargo vessels. The* Savannah *was photographed at New York in 1964. (Negative 177984F, © Rosenfeld Collection, Mystic Seaport Museum, Inc., Mystic, Connecticut)*

would contain the propulsion system and might also employ submerged foils to provide hydrodynamic lift to the vessel. Using such a system of struts, foils (or underwater wings), and separate underwater hulls (acting like submarines by riding through the relatively calm water beneath the surface) promises greatly increased vessel stability and reduced resistance, as well as far greater speed than is possible from conventional displacement hull designs.

Greater vessel stability also may come from using a multi-hull configuration, such as a catamaran, trimaran, or quadramaran design. Even the traditional single-hull design has been greatly modified to produce far greater speeds through reducing resistance, or drag, at the stern of such a vessel. The bulbous bow also increases performance by supplying buoyancy at the bow while at the same time producing a wave that cancels the vessel's bow wave, reducing resistance and increasing speed. Coupled with a relatively new form of propulsion, the turbine-powered waterjet, such a vessel might reduce the normal time at sea by half, through nearly doubling the conventional twenty-knot speed of freighters.

Technological innovation in vessel propulsion since World War II has also fundamentally altered vessel design and use. Perhaps most widespread is the replacement of steam-generated power by diesel power for civilian applications. For major river and Great Lakes use, the diesel engine-powered carrier has almost entirely supplanted oil-fired, steam-turbine freighters.

At the same time the traditional bulk "freighters" of the Lakes have evolved into mammoth, 1,000-foot self-unloading cargo carriers measuring more than 60,000 net tons capacity and effectively limited in size only by the dimensions of the largest locks in the Lake system. Such huge vessels, equipped with twin screw propellers and lateral bow- and stern-thrusters for more precise handling in ports, possess an array of electronic gear for navigation comparable to that on the most modern oceangoing carriers.

Yet sheer size and awesome technological capability is never enough to make a Great Lakes vessel invulnerable to the winds and waves. The instantaneous foundering in early November 1975 of the "Queen of the Lakes," the *Edmund Fitzgerald,*

with the loss of all her crew and cargo, remain a constant and sobering reminder of the devastating power of the sea.

While the diesel engine has been in operation for nearly a century and widely used for small vessels in coastwise or river and harbor operations, not until well into the postwar era was diesel power seriously considered for large cargo carriers, and even then it was mostly for inland waterways. The steam-powered turbine vessel still comprises most ocean-going merchant fleets throughout the world, and is even more the accepted power system for navies. The United States Navy has made limited use of nuclear fuel, especially for submarines and aircraft carriers, but this is simply an alternative fuel source to that of conventional petroleum products; in either case, the power system is one based on steam.

The one American attempt to experiment with nuclear power for merchant vessels, SS *Savannah,* created immense problems, not the least of which was worldwide resistance by prospective port cities that feared the possibility of nuclear explosion or contamination from the presence of such a vessel. After her launch in 1959, the *Savannah* made only a few short runs before going out of service.

Also of potentially great danger, but nevertheless in general use, is a remarkably unorthodox vessel type: the LNG, or liquefied natural gas carrier. Such vessels supply major urban markets by transporting large quantities of natural gas that has been greatly compressed in volume and enclosed in large, specially reinforced spherical containers built into the hull of the LNG carrier. Such vessels require special port handling and are subject to extraordinary safety precautions, since a sudden rupture of a fully-loaded container of gas could produce an explosion comparable in potential devastation to a small nuclear bomb.

Technological innovations in vessel design also include improved screw propellers. Shipbuilding has benefited both from superior metals and protective coatings and from new vessel-construction techniques. Advances in electronics have resulted in markedly improved navigation and communications capabilities, and vessel operations are now increasingly computerized in virtually all aspects. New applications have even been found for sailpower. Especially during periods of particularly high fuel costs, experiments with fully automated sail-handling and even metal sails, housed in their own metal masts and mechanically furled and unfurled, have been made aboard ocean-going merchant vessels and cruise ships.

Automation and other forms of technological innovation produced a decline in America's dockside labor force of more than 90 percent from its immediate postwar high. The number of seafarers has also declined substantially. The large reduction in the number of American-flag vessels, especially after the early 1950s, was a major factor in the swiftly decreasing number of seagoing American workers. Later, automation and the onrush of computer-aided devices for the maritime industries resulted in still smaller crews aboard those notably fewer, if more modern and larger, vessels that replaced the increasingly obsolete wartime fleet of merchant ships.

The United States Navy, 1945-1998

During the half-century since the end of World War II, the United States Navy remained the world's largest and most technologically advanced force at sea. At the same time, those years saw remarkable change in the navy's management and direction, as well as its size, uses, and ships.

One of the most striking lessons that America's leaders learned in World War II was the need for the army, navy, and air force to work together more effectively. Since 1798, the secretary of the navy had been a separate cabinet-level department head within the executive branch. With the implementation of the National Security Act of 1947, the Navy Department, including the U.S. Marine Corps, became only one of three branches subordinate to the Department of Defense, with the secretary of the navy reduced to the position of a subcabinet-level secretariat.

Below the secretary of the navy, the senior officers in uniform are the chief of naval operations (CNO) and the commandant of the Marine Corps (CMC), who also serve as members of the Joint Chiefs of Staff. A series of Congressional

acts, beginning with the 1947 National Security Act and continuing through the 1986 Defense Reorganization Act, have reduced the CNO's command authority over the fleets at sea, while still emphasizing his role as an organizational leader. Simultaneously, Congress has transferred authority to the Department of Defense for many key administrative issues and increased the command authority of the Chairman of the Joint Chiefs of Staff and the regional commanders in chief.

While the Department of Defense was a loose federation of forces at the outset in 1947, Congress has gradually required closer and closer integration among the armed forces. In 1961, Secretary of Defense Robert McNamara imposed the Planning, Programming and Budgeting System on the Department of Defense, further reducing the Navy Department's ability to use its funds and to shape the fleet without close cooperation and compromise with the other armed services. Where once the navy could operate and develop its own logistics, do its own planning, and procure its own ships and equipment, it now does so within the context of a much larger bureaucratic organization, the Department of Defense. Today, the secretary of defense sets priorities, Congress can intervene more readily and effectively, and naval commanders report to regional commanders in chief who may be wearing the uniform of another service. These changes have increased efficiency and made the services better able to operate together, although they still have separate strategic doctrines and quite separate views of their roles, and the debate continues over the appropriate missions and roles for each service.

Once, navies could be completely understood in the context of a single nation, but since 1945, one has had to look more closely at their international context. For the United States Navy, this has been most dramatic in two areas. First, the United Nations, established at San Francisco on 24 October 1945, has had an influence on the U.S. Navy. While the methods for directly commanding military and naval forces that are outlined in the U.N. Charter have not been used, the United Nations may still order mandatory sanctions, call for cease-fire, establish peacekeeping forces, and provide other guidelines for naval operations. Since 1945, the U.S. Navy has cooperated in carrying out United Nations directives in the Korean

War in 1950-53, the Gulf War of 1990-91, and in several other incidents.

In addition, more than 150 nations participated in drafting the 1982 United Nations Convention on the Law of the Sea. One of several international agreements that affect naval action, the Law of the Sea provides clear rules limiting use of the ocean for military purposes. At the same time, it assures unencumbered access through air and sea-lanes of communication, particularly through straits and archipelagos, while recognizing the rights of coastal states to manage and protect their coasts and offshore resources.

Secondly, in the area of international institutions, the period since 1945 has seen a dramatic rise in international naval cooperation. Following the North Atlantic Treaty in April 1949, the North Atlantic Treaty Organization (NATO) established a number of regional commands. The two largest maritime powers, Great Britain and the United States, reached a compromise over the areas that their naval officers would command. In 1951, General of the Army Dwight Eisenhower became the first Supreme Allied Commander, Europe, with authority over naval forces in that area. Equivalent to him, an American officer became the Supreme Allied Commander, Atlantic, with headquarters in Norfolk, Virginia, and with a deputy from the Royal Navy. In the Mediterranean, an American admiral became the first Commander-in-Chief, Allied Forces, Southern Europe, with headquarters in Naples. In 1967, NATO further subdivided this area of responsibility, placing NATO naval forces in the Mediterranean under the command of an Italian admiral who had a Royal Navy deputy.

These NATO naval commanders focused particularly on the threat of Soviet naval forces in the period from the end of the 1960s through 1990. In doing this, the international consultative process within NATO produced a very efficient and effective structure to operate ships of different navies. Nowhere was this more dramatically evident than in the NATO Standing Naval Force, Atlantic (STANAVFOR-LANT). From its inception in 1968, it regularly cruised and exercised throughout the NATO area, with one ship from each participating nation and with its command rotating annually from naval officers of one nation to another. Over many years, this force developed practical proce-

dures for ships from different navies to work together and these became a model that regional groups in other parts of the world began to emulate. Its practical success became the basis for multinational naval operations during the Gulf War, off Haiti, and in the Adriatic in the 1990s.

During this fifty-year period, the rise of international cooperation merged with both rising Law of the Sea initiatives and with increasing trends within nations to integrate forces. These combined to create a broader perspective on international security issues, while at the same time they emphasized the increasing interdependence of naval affairs within a wide context.

Despite its relative strength on the world's oceans, the U.S. Navy declined in size during the half century following World War II. After dropping dramatically from 3,408,347 men and women in September 1945 to less than a million in 1946, the navy declined more gradually in size to reach 390,432 men and women in 1997. In the same period, the numbers of ships declined from 5,718 vessels in 1945 to 347 in 1997. During both the Korean and the Vietnam Wars, the numbers rose to about a thousand vessels, most of them built during the Second World War. By the 1970s, however, these vessels had reached the end of their useful careers and were removed from service. At this point, one of the most controversial issues concerned the optimum size of the navy. Some, such as Admiral Elmo Zumwalt, argued for a mix of large, very sophisticated and expensive ships with smaller, relatively inexpensive vessels. Admiral Zumwalt was opposed by those who preferred to concentrate on large vessels, and this controversy continued for many years. In the 1980s, the navy attempted to build a fleet of 600 ships and came very close to doing so, beginning a shipbuilding program of twenty ships a year that would last for thirty years to sustain that overall number of ships. With the end of the Cold War, however, the navy dropped 40 percent in size between 1990 and 1995, until it had been reduced to pre-World-War-II proportions.

This dramatic reduction in size reflects many fundamental changes for the navy. Some of the decrease in size stems from attempts to make military and naval forces more effective and more efficient, "doing more with less." But other factors included cuts in overall defense spending during periods of economic inflation, as well as the increased effectiveness of individual weapons and ships as a result of changes in the navy's missions and uses.

In 1945, the total national defense budget was just over $800 billion. This dropped by half to $416 billion in 1946 and by another two-thirds in 1947 to $144 billion, reaching a postwar low in 1948 with $78 billion. During the Korean War, it rose to more than $330 billion and remained in the range of $250-260 billion until the Vietnam War, when it again rose into the $300 billion range, but did not quite reach the Korean War level. In the post-Vietnam-War period, the defense budget remained at about $290 billion, declining in real terms by 39 percent from 1985 to 1996 to $246 billion. This marked a decline in total federal spending for defense from 51 percent of federal outlays in 1955, and 39 percent in 1970, to 17 percent in 1995.

In allocating its funds, the Defense Department gave the navy either the highest or the second highest amount among the three services. Although the U.S. Air Force had the largest percentage of defense expenditure in the 1950s and 1960s, during the period of greatest emphasis on nuclear weapons and strategic bombing, the navy received the most of the three services in 1948 and in 1949, and resumed the top position from the post-Vietnam-War years onward. In 1996, the navy had a budget of $75 billion, retaining the highest proportion within the overall defense budget, although budgetary and organizational pressures within the Department of Defense continued to force economy and efficiency, as well as the refinement of the navy's mission.

During most of the half century since the end of the Second World War, The U.S. Navy and all the armed services were concerned with countering the threats presented by the Soviet Union and its Warsaw Pact countries. As early as September 1945, the Joint Chiefs of Staff had identified the Soviet Union as the United States's most likely potential enemy. At first, it was unclear how the United States Navy would participate in a war with a country that was not vulnerable to naval blockade. But it soon became apparent that such a war would have to be conducted from forward bases in Japan, the Middle East, and in Europe, which would have to be supplied, sustained, and shielded by American

naval forces. This forward stance, in particular, was vulnerable to attack from submarines. Thus, the U.S. Navy was concerned about the development of the Soviet submarine force, which remained at about 300 vessels during the Cold War. Operations during World War II suggested that in a conflict conducted from forward positions it was highly advantageous to strike directly at enemy submarines and submarine bases as a means of crippling that threat. This idea of offensive strikes from forward bases against enemy naval and air bases and enemy submarines became the basis of NATO's maritime strategy for the Cold War and continued as the Soviets began to build capable surface warships in the late 1970s and 1980s.

During this same period, as the United States began to employ a foreign policy closely related to its national security policy, which combined diplomacy with military power, forward deployment of American naval forces became increasingly important. The successful use of carrier-based aircraft during the Korean War, particularly during the huge amphibious landing at Inchon in September 1950, showed the value of naval aviation, and this helped to offset some of the advantage that the navy had lost in the interservice rivalry with the Air Force, as the younger service dominated discussions on nuclear weapons.

With the commissioning of the navy's 1,046-foot-long, 56,000-ton-displacement supercarrier USS *Forrestal* (CVA-59) in 1955, the grouping of various types of warships around these ships into carrier battle groups became important features of American policy in the Mediterranean and in the Western Pacific.

At the same time, the growing fleet of nuclear submarines became an increasingly important factor in the Cold War military buildup between the U.S. and U.S.S.R. After the U.S. Navy's first nuclear-powered submarine, the *Nautilus*, made a successful passage from Pacific to Atlantic under the Arctic ice pack in 1958, the Arctic Ocean was opened to patrols by naval submarines.

In the mid-1950s, in the process of service unification, President Eisenhower shifted the country's defense priorities to nuclear deterrence based on the threat of retaliation. This "New Look" policy brought into serious question the navy's tradition-

During the undeclared war in Korea, the U.S. Navy provided sea and air support for the United Nations forces opposing North Korea. In this view, an F4U-4 Corsair from the carrier Coral Sea *overflies the anchorage off Inchon, 2 October 1950. The ships below include Military Sea Transportation Service (MSTS) freighters, tankers, a troopship, and the USS* Missouri *(lower left), the first American battleship to reach Korean waters and flagship of the U.S. Seventh Fleet. She used her sixteen-inch guns for shore bombardment missions in Korea during 1950-51 and again in 1953. (80-G-1030118, courtesy National Archives)*

al roles and missions, but it soon became apparent that not all crises would be dealt with in terms of nuclear weapons. At the same time, new guided-missile technology led to the development of highly mobile submarines that could launch intercontinental "Polaris" ballistic missiles from a wide variety of possible locations at sea. Through this approach during the administration of Admiral Arleigh Burke as Chief of Naval Operations, the navy was able to play a major role in national security policy. As a deterrent to nuclear war, the U.S. nuclear submarine force became an invulnerable, second-strike threat that guaranteed mutual assured destruction (MAD) should the Soviet Union attack the United States.

Between 1950 and 1990, the United States became involved in three major wars. All three, Korea, Vietnam, and the Gulf War, were land and air wars that had major naval and maritime components for the support of American operations. In many respects, the maritime components were crucial to the American effort, ranging from carrier operations to amphibious and riverine activity, logistic support, antisubmarine initiatives, and mine-warfare operations.

At the same time, the U.S. Navy became the "on-call" force to deal with international crises, particularly so-called "low-level" crises that did not involve the other superpower. In the 1960s, the United States was involved in crises in the Caribbean, the Mediterranean, and the Pacific as it also dealt with the Vietnam War. American leaders began to doubt the ability of the United States to sustain the great costs of being "the world's policeman," and increasingly began to look to allies and regional powers to take responsibility. In the 1970s, the United States urged such countries to provide ground forces in troubled regions, while the American contribution focused on more mobile air and naval assets.

For regional stability, and as a barrier to Soviet efforts in the oil-producing region around the Persian Gulf, the United States had depended upon Iran. This region became a major center of American attention when the shah's regime collapsed in 1979, war broke out between Iran and Iraq, and the Soviet Union invaded nearby Afghanistan. In 1980, the United States made it clear that it would not tolerate any interruption to the flow of the world's oil supply from the Persian Gulf. Placing great emphasis on naval power, the United States developed a Rapid Deployment Force–later renamed Central Command–to deal with the series of crises and wars in the Persian Gulf and Indian Ocean area that lasted for more than a decade.

Under President Ronald Reagan, the navy became the most visible element of United States defense policy. In order to maintain commitments in the Atlantic, Pacific, and Indian Oceans, as well as in the Mediterranean, Secretary of the Navy John Lehman argued publicly for the construction of a 600-ship navy to carry out the country's forward-deployment naval strategy to deal simultaneously with the Soviet Union and with potential regional crises. In the mid-1980s, the navy conducted extensive operations in such widespread locations as Lebanon, Libya, Grenada, Panama, and the Persian Gulf.

In 1989, the Navy Department reported to Congress that in the 240 crises the nation had responded to since the end of World War II, the U.S. Navy had been involved in 202 of those situations. Of those crises, the USSR had been involved in only eighteen, and only about fifteen involved major combat, with even fewer involving land or air forces. Through these situations, the U.S. Navy developed a capability for sustained, conventional deterrence that could match opposing naval forces anywhere in the world. As Chief of Naval Operations, Admiral James Watkins, described it in the 1980s, the U.S. Navy was a force designed to operate in an era of "violent peace."

Since the collapse of the Soviet Union and the end of the Cold War in 1990, the U.S. Navy has had five priorities. First is the commitment to forward deployment and preparation to fight wars and to deter conflict. Should deterrence fail, the navy is ready to dispatch joint navy and Marine Corps expeditionary forces to converge on a crisis

The aircraft carrier Forrestal *(CVA-59) was the first of the supercarriers. Launched by Newport News Shipbuilding in 1954 and commissioned on 1 October 1955, she was the first carrier laid down by the U.S. Navy since the end of World War II and the largest it had built up to that time. The first vessel specifically designed to carry jet aircraft, the 1,046-foot ship displaced 54,600 tons and had a hull width of 130 feet. The extreme width of her flight deck measured 252 feet. Too large to use the Panama Canal, the* Forrestal *also was limited to only a few dry-docks. With a crew of as many as 4,000, the ship led a carrier battle group in the Atlantic and Mediterranean, and later off Vietnam. With her huge size, the* Forrestal *provided a stable platform for aircraft takeoff and landing in the rough conditions of the Norwegian Sea and the Formosa Straits, permitting flight operations 96 percent of the time. Her four steam catapults enabled her to launch eight aircraft every sixty seconds. With these characteristics, and carrying three times as much aviation fuel as previous aircraft carriers, she could operate 100 jet aircraft from her deck. The* Forrestal *was modernized in the 1980s to extend her thirty-year life to forty-five years, but with the end of the Cold War she made a last operational deployment in 1991 and then became a pilot-training ship. In this aerial view, the* Forrestal *is shown underway in the Atlantic during the Suez Crisis of November 1956. (80-G-1002476, courtesy National Archives and Naval Historical Center)*

Begun as a conventional nuclear submarine, the George Washington *(SSBN-598) was lengthened by 130 feet during construction and launched at Groton, Connecticut, in 1959 as the world's first ballistic missile submarine. When the ship successfully launched a Polaris missile in July 1960, the United States gained the threat of mutual assured destruction in the nuclear arms race with the Soviet Union. Here, the* George Washington *lies alongside the fleet ballistic missile submarine tender* Proteus *while receiving a Polaris missile at Holy Loch, Scotland, in 1961. The U.S. Navy replenishment anchorage established at Holy Loch in 1960 was the first of several in the Atlantic and Pacific that permitted the navy to maintain the ballistic missile submarine force near the Soviet coast. (428-GX-Box 22, courtesy National Archives)*

area immediately and to strike from land, sea, and air. At sea, the navy is prepared to control selected sea areas and to maintain overall maritime supremacy. With its continuing deployment of submarines armed with ballistic missiles, the navy maintains strategic nuclear deterrence. For logistical support the navy maintains the capacity for strategic sealift to move weapons and equipment to distant areas where a regional conflict might develop and to sustain them as long as they are needed.

Just as the Cold War was ending, another crisis arose in the Persian Gulf area as Iraq invaded Kuwait. In its response to the situation, "Operation Desert Shield," the U.S. Navy moved quickly to halt Iraq from moving further and threatening Saudi Arabia, providing

the covering protection from aircraft carriers based in the Gulf of Oman and in the Red Sea as the U.S. Air Force brought in planes and the U.S. Army moved in troops. The navy brought the majority of supplies as well as Marine Corps troops from its forward positioning location at Diego Garcia Island in the Indian Ocean, and it maintained complete security for maritime transportation as allied forces built up their forces in the region. The preventive aspects of "Operation Desert Shield" changed to wartime operations in January 1991 as "Operation Desert Storm" to force Iraq's compliance with the United Nations sanctions. During this phase, the navy supported both Air Force and army operations. Upon completion of these operations, other forces withdrew, while the U.S. Navy and Marine Corps remained in the Indian Ocean to intercept contraband and serve as part of America's commitment to regional security in the Persian Gulf.

Beginning in 1993, the U.S. Navy joined NATO and Western European Union naval forces to enforce United Nations sanctions as part of an attempt to bring the warring parties in former Yugoslavia to the peace table. American warships, including surface vessels, intelligence-gathering attack submarines, and maritime air patrols were deployed to block sea commerce to and from Serbia and Montenegro, along with weapon shipments intended for all of the republics in former Yugoslavia.

In January 1994, seventeen nations joined the United States in "Operation Support Democracy," a United Nations effort to restore the democratically elected regime of

President Jean-Bertrand Aristide to power in Haiti. During this period, U.S. Marines landed in the country while naval forces maintained a coastal blockade.

Throughout these same years, the U.S. Navy and Marine Corps were involved in a variety of other activities, from supporting U.S. government efforts to halt the illicit trade in drugs, to providing security for migrants from Cuba and Haiti, to conducting relief efforts in communities struck by hurricanes and other natural disasters, to providing cooperative, bilateral training for former Communist-bloc navies in Eastern Europe through the Partnership for Peace Program.

Reflecting the broad developments in American society in the post-World War II period, and an increasing emphasis on equal opportunity and

The USS Nautilus (SSN-571) was the world's first nuclear-powered vessel. Launched by Electric Boat at Groton, Connecticut, in 1954, the 323-foot ship was "underway on nuclear power" in January 1955. The Nautilus is best known as the first ship to reach the North Pole, passing under the Arctic ice cap from Pacific to Atlantic in 1958 and demonstrating that the Arctic Ocean was navigable by nuclear submarines. Although the Nautilus was soon superseded by submarines of more efficient configuration, it continued in service through the 1970s and was converted into a museum ship at Groton, Connecticut, in the 1980s. (Courtesy Electric Boat Corporation)

The roll on-roll off (RoRo) concept was introduced during World War II with LSTs and other specialized naval craft. With the launch of the USNS Comet *(T-AKR 7) in 1957, the RoRo approach was applied to a conventional ship. The 499-foot* Comet *was designed to carry break-bulk cargo in the fore-hold and up to 700 vehicles on several decks in the after hold, which could be loaded through ramps in the stern and side in less than one day. RoRo ships remain a specialized segment of the world's merchant marine, the most prominent being the automobile carriers that deliver Asian automobiles to the United States. The* Comet *was photographed during a NATO operation off Norway in 1980. (428-GX-1179795, courtesy National Archives)*

inclusiveness, the U.S. Navy experienced many changes in the racial and ethnic backgrounds of its sailors and its leaders. In 1971, as the percentage of African Americans in the navy approached the percentage in American society, Captain Samuel L. Gravely, Jr., became the first black rear admiral. Twenty-five years later, Paul Reason became the first African American promoted to four-star admiral. As the Hispanic portion of the nation's population grew dramatically, Edward Hidalgo, who had been born in Mexico, was appointed secretary of the navy in 1979.

Women have also played increasing leadership roles in the navy in the last third of the twentieth century. In 1972, Captain Arlene B. Duerk, a nurse, became the first female rear admiral. Four years later, in July 1976, the U.S. Naval Academy admitted the first women cadets, as members of the Class of 1980. In 1978, the navy assigned nine women to duty in noncombatant ships, the first time that women in the navy had served in vessels other than hospital ships. Since

then, women pilots have flown carrier-based aircraft, although the role of women in combat remained a controversial issue in all of the military services at the end of the century.

Some social changes and innovations within the navy went very smoothly, while others raised a great deal of tension. Racial tension in the nation in the 1960s and early 1970s was reflected in the navy as well. Later, reflecting social changes within the country, some of the most controversial and difficult issues were questions of sexual harassment as men and women worked together on board ship, fraternization between officers and sailors, and homosexuality, all of which remained unresolved at the end of the century, despite sincere efforts to address them.

While men and women were changing the composition of the navy, its ships were also changing in character. Although the attack on Pearl Harbor in 1941 had clearly spelled the end of the traditional battleship era in naval affairs, battleships continued to appear on the scene from time to time in special circumstances. During the Vietnam War they returned to use their large guns in gunfire support roles, and during the Gulf War they took on an even more updated and specialized role, as vessels for launching Tomahawk guided missiles. Nevertheless, even during World War II it was clearly evident that maritime aircraft, aircraft carriers, and submarines had become the key elements of the navy, overshadowing the traditional emphasis on naval guns and surface vessels.

The fabric and equipment of naval vessels also changed. Light aluminum construction replaced steel in ship superstructures. Reinforced glass fiber (fiberglass) began to supplant wood in some smaller vessels. Nuclear power replaced diesel engines in submarines, beginning with the *Nautilus* in 1955, and in some of the largest aircraft carriers, while gas turbines replaced high-pressure steam plants in other surface ships. New types of naval vessels began to appear for the new missions the navy faced. Amphibious landing vessels, logistics support ships, and helicopter carriers appeared as smaller surface-effect vessels and mine-hunters came into service. Large nuclear-powered aircraft carriers replaced the smaller conventionally powered ships. Surface ships carrying Aegis missile systems entered the fleet as the navy moved to merge the traditional roles of

The end of the Cold War in 1990 did not end the U.S. Navy's reliance on nuclear submarines. Planned in the late 1980s, the Seawolf class of attack submarines was designed as an adaptable undersea weapons system, capable of operating against enemy submarines, surface ships, or land installations. With highly engineered sound damping that makes it the quietest submarine ever, the 353-foot Seawolf can take its 130-man crew to depths greater than 800 feet, can operate under the Arctic ice, or can perform electronic surveillance in very shallow water. Completed by the Electric Boat Corporation at Groton, Connecticut, in 1996, the Seawolf (SSN-21) was the first of three such submarines built in the 1990s. (Courtesy Electric Boat Corporation)

surface naval ships with the need to support land and air campaigns. Propeller-driven naval aircraft, which had performed so well during the Second World War, were being replaced by jet-engine aircraft even as they provided important air support during the Korean conflict in the early 1950s. Highly accurate guidance systems began to control missiles and guns for both short and long range targets. While all this was going on within the navy, sophisticated sensors, electronic data networks, and communications systems, as well as new methods for display of information, analyzing, and targeting, began to produce a revolution in military affairs. These changes, with integrated distribution of electronic data and open computer architecture, included modular components and automation that helped to reduce overall costs and manpower in all the armed services.

In the mid-1990s, a much smaller and more technologically advanced U.S. Navy and Marine

Corps dealt with diverse crises in areas such as Kuwait, Somalia, Haiti, and Bosnia, while at the same time coping with social change, rapid technological innovation, and modernization. Although the structure of international relations and the outward appearance and the size of the navy changed dramatically over the previous half century, President William J. Clinton noted that there was still continuity: "Even with all the changes in the world, some basic facts endure. . . . We are a maritime nation. . . . As long as these facts remain true, we need naval forces that can dominate the sea, project power, and protect our interests."

In the twenty-first century, the U.S. Navy will continue to reflect the fundamental dichotomy that exists between the sea and the land, the latter accepting control and the former resisting it. At the same time, continuing developments in government and private industry will bring a

In the future, the U.S. Navy may be more closely linked with the other military services. The "arsenal ship" proposed by the navy in 1996 is conceived as a twenty-first-century battleship, armed with hundreds of precision missiles carrying conventional or nuclear warheads, and operated by a small crew using advanced electronic technology. Its low profile and casemate superstructure reminiscent of a Civil War iron-clad would help make it invisible to enemy radar. This artist's rendering depicts a concept for the vessel by Lockheed-Martin, one of five competitors for the contract. (Courtesy Navy Office of Information, News Photo Division)

vast array of new technology, including remotely controlled vehicles and vessels, new weapons, and new methods of communication. None of these changes, however, can be expected to influence or alter the fundamental nature of man's continuing relationship with the sea.

The United States Coast Guard, 1945-1998

As early as 1943, Coast Guard Commandant Russell R. Waesche began to promote the Coast Guard's return to the Treasury Department after its wartime service with the U.S. Navy. In accord with long-standing

agreements to keep the services separate that had been made in 1918 and again in 1933, the transfer took place on 1 January 1946. Following full demobilization, the service was reduced to only 2,195 officers, 532 warrant officers and 15,730 enlisted men in 1947. Aside from beginning to build up the size of the force, the most urgent matter facing the postwar Coast Guard was defining its range of duties. The first question arose in 1946 with controversy over whether or not the Coast Guard would retain the licensing and inspecting duties of the Bureau of Marine Inspection and Navigation that it had assumed temporarily during the war. Congressional legislation in 1949 codified Coast Guard duties, including marine licensing and inspection, operation of loran and navigation stations, maintenance of ocean weather stations, and participation in the reactivated international ice patrol, in addition to its regular search-and-rescue role.

During these same years, the Coast Guard began to replace some of its vessels. In 1947, the service began to provide sail-training for Coast Guard Academy cadets aboard the auxiliary-powered three-masted bark *Eagle*—the former German training ship *Horst Wessel*, built in 1936 and awarded to the United States after the war. USCG *Eagle* has become a highly recognizable symbol of Coast Guard seamanship.

When the Korean War broke out in 1950, there was no declaration of war that immediately transferred the service to the Navy. Although remaining under the Treasury Department for the duration of that war and retaining their own service identity, Coast Guard units assisted the navy by assuming responsibility for port security and for providing additional ocean-station, loran, and search-and-rescue functions that were needed to support the war effort. Similarly, during the Cold War, the Coast Guard stationed ships in the Mediterranean as a means of relaying Voice of America broadcasts to Communist countries.

As technology developed, the Coast Guard began to apply it to its responsibilities. Among the prominent innovations of the late 1950s and early 1960s was the Atlantic (later Automated) Merchant Vessel Reporting System (AMVER), which facilitated search and rescue by plotting regular and routine position information. By 1962, 90 percent of American-flag vessels and more than 60 percent of foreign-flag vessels in the

North Atlantic were using the Coast Guard system. Other innovations involved navigation systems such as Omega, Loran-C, Decca, and the satellite-based global positioning systems (GPS) that would supersede radio-based technology.

When the United States became involved in the Vietnam War in 1964, Coast Guard Commandant Edwin Roland was interested in maintaining his service's military capability, and felt that the Coast Guard's role during the Korean War had been too greatly limited to an auxiliary support role. Early on in the war, when the U.S. Navy immediately needed boats to patrol inshore waters on the coast of Vietnam to interdict enemy weapons' shipments in Operation Market Time, the Coast Guard immediately provided seventeen vessels. Later, other Coast Guard forces operated on the rivers of Vietnam. In 1967, the first squadron of 311-foot Coast Guard cutters–*Barataria, Half Moon, Yakutat, Bering Strait* and *Gresham*–arrived for service in Vietnam. The Coast Guard also provided effective navigation systems for the heavy merchant shipping traffic in the region, supplied training for the Vietnamese Lighthouse Service, and maintained port security.

In the midst of its wartime service in Vietnam, the Coast Guard faced a major organizational change. In 1967, the service was transferred from the Treasury Department, where its duties had been carried out under a variety of names for 177 years, to the newly established Department of Transportation. After the end of the Vietnam War, new technology superseded the Ocean Station program. Additionally, the Coast Guard moved on to deal with the implementation of the 12-mile offshore ocean fishery zone in 1967, the adoption of 200-mile exclusive economic zones in 1977, and assignment to a long-term commitment to control illicit drug traffic and handle the flow of refugees fleeing to America by sea to escape political unrest and economic uncertainty.

Through the 1980s and 1990s, the U.S. Coast Guard refined its unique roles and missions, demonstrating that Coast Guard men and women had distinctive maritime skills. While the service had been little more than a resource pool for additional men and ships for the navy in the First World War, during the following eighty years it evolved skills that required specialized training and experience. This was formally recognized in

October 1995, when the secretary of transportation and the secretary of defense signed an agreement that clarified the Coast Guard's national defense role. Based on the expertise involved in its peace-time missions, the Coast Guard was assigned the missions of maritime interception operations, security, defense, operation of overseas ports, and environmental defense operations. Ringing the country's coastline, the Coast Guard's Maritime Defense Zones are designed to deal with potential threats to port security, harbor defense, and coastal warfare.

During "Operation Uphold Democracy" off Haiti in 1995-96, the Coast Guard demonstrated that it could conduct the same operations in foreign waters in cooperation with the navy. But the Coast Guard's role in national security was only one of its many missions at the end of the twentieth century. Search and rescue required a substantial portion of its resources. With nearly 67,000 search and rescue missions a year, the service, on a typical day in the late 1990s, saved thirteen lives and assisted 328 people. It continues to be one of the nation's primary protectors of the environment as it works to prevent and to help clean up spills of hazardous materials. With ice-breakers, navigational markers, and space-age navigation and positioning systems, it helps to keep navigable waterways clear and safe for commerce.

Enforcement of laws and treaties has always been a significant Coast Guard mission, and in the 1980s and 1990s this has involved drug interdiction. The Coast Guard's activities accounted for 25 percent of overall government seizures of cocaine and marijuana, keeping, on average, $3 billion worth of illegal drugs off American streets each year. Additionally, it worked to interdict illegal immigration, providing at the same time humanitarian service as it saved many lives while a flood of illegal immigrants from Cuba, Haiti, and China attempted to reach the United States in unseaworthy vessels. In the area of marine resource management, the Coast Guard protects the country's fish stocks by enforcing fishing regulations and by maintaining channels of communication with fishermen and oil-rig workers at sea.

The smallest of America's five armed services, the U.S. Coast Guard carried out its diverse missions in 1997 with a total of 36,492 military and 5,622

"Boat People" of Cuba and Haiti

The patron saint of Cuba is *Nuestra Señora de la Caridad del Cobre*, or "Our Copper Lady of Charity." This is the name of a statue of the Virgin Mary that three men in a boat found floating on a plank in Nipa Bay, on the northeast coast of the island, in 1620. *Caridad del Cobre* is a familiar image in Cuba, representing both the Madonna of Catholicism and Oshum, one of the "seven African powers" of the religion of Santería. Caridad del Cobre is always shown coming to the aid of three men in an open boat in heavy weather, a scene that evokes the experience of hundreds of thousands of Cubans and Haitians in recent years. Like the terrified mariners depicted in statues and medals of Caridad del Cobre, these newest maritime immigrants to the United States have been in distress on the stormy Gulf Stream, trying to reach these shores. Many drowned, died of thirst, or were killed by gasoline explosions at sea, yet the rate of attempted crossings increased until September 1994. Then U.S. immigration policy changed, eliminating all chances for future "boat people" from Cuba or Haiti to enter the country.

The Cuban and Haitian boat people who arrived in the U.S. between the early 1960s and 1994 were the last wave in four hundred years of ocean passages to this country. The scarcity of ocean transportation options and rigidity of U.S. immigration policy toward nearby islands make it unlikely that such an exodus by sea to this country will ever occur again. Though perhaps the last of the millions of boat people of all nations who emigrated before them, the Cuban and Haitian maritime migrants have the distinction of making their crossings in the smallest craft, under some of the most perilous circumstances. Though concentrated now in South Florida, New York, and New Jersey, Cuban and Haitian immigrants have resettled in all fifty states of the Union, contributing to the changing social and cultural mosaic of the nation.

One million Cuban immigrants have come to the U.S. since Fidel Castro came to power in 1959, most of them by airplane, but perhaps a quarter million by boat. The Straits of Florida are only ninety miles wide between Havana and Key West, but the Gulf Stream makes it a treacherous stretch of water. Most of the Cuban crossings took place during three events: the Camarioca boat lift of 1965, the Mariel boat lift of 1980, and the surge of departures of the early 1990s. The first boat lift occurred after Castro announced that Cubans with relatives in the U.S. could leave, if their relatives agreed to pick them up at the port of Camarioca in September 1965. The resulting exodus took place in the middle of the hurricane season, mainly aboard Florida pleasure craft, ending after 5,000 people had made the nauseating trip. The boat lift was replaced by an airlift arranged between the two countries to provide safer passage for several thousand emigrants with relatives in the U.S. every month. The airlift lasted until 1973, bringing more than a quarter million immigrants from Cuba and greatly reducing the number of boat people in the Straits of Florida.

Maritime migration from Cuba was heaviest between April and September 1980, when about 125,000 people left from the bay of Mariel, fifty miles west of Havana, in a large-scale reprise of the Camarioca boat lift. As before, Castro announced that anyone wanting to leave could be picked up at a designated port, resulting in hundreds of cabin cruisers making the trip from Florida. The "freedom flotilla" made Key West into an immigration boom town, with inflated prices for provisions and fuel, and all available vessels chartered or purchased to make the run to Mariel, returning with scores of immigrants crammed above and below deck. The fact that one thousand of the Mariel immigrants had been inmates of Cuban prisons and asylums gave the *marielistas* a bad reputation in many of the U.S. communities where they settled. The 1990 movie *Scarface* depicted the criminal career of a Mariel immigrant in Cuba and Miami, spreading the negative image of Cuban immigration and helping prepare the way for the unfavorable reception accorded the next wave of Cuban arrivals.

The flood of boat people from Cuba in the early 1990s was not the result of a boat lift allowed by the government, but of economic desperation. The end of subsidies from the Soviet Union worsened the already austere conditions of life in Cuba and prompted many residents to take their chances in a small boat or raft, especially people with relatives in the U.S. who could assist in their migration. The 1990s exodus also differed from the boat lifts because it did not take place in Florida motorboats. Instead, many left in makeshift rafts made of inner tubes, boards, and tarps, as earlier Cuban *balseros*, or rafters, had done. Others crowded into small open fishing boats. All hoped to cross the Straits of Florida before exhausting the scant amount of water they could carry. The rate of clandestine embarkations increased each year beginning in 1989, reaching a climax in August 1994, when the Cuban government suspended its efforts to stop boat people from leaving. Thousands of Cubans flocked to the beaches and ports on the northwest coast of the island to launch their floatables for

During the Camarioca boat lift of 1965, U.S. Coast Guard personnel assist Cuban refugees in the Florida Straits. (26-G-10-13-65, courtesy National Archives)

Florida. Opposition to uncontrolled Cuban immigration in that state led to a change in U.S. immigration policy on 19 August, when Cuban political refugee status was revoked. Thereafter, all Cubans intercepted at sea were taken to camps at the Guantánamo Bay Naval Base in Cuba and in the Panama Canal Zone rather than to Miami, and all Cubans who landed in Florida went to Krome Detention Center rather than to their relatives' homes. In all, 36,000 Cubans eventually completed their voyage to the U.S. during 1994. Estimates of the death toll among those taking part in the last flotilla run as high as 25 percent.

Haitian boat people started leaving in 1972, when a boat

carrying sixty-five passengers landed in Miami after an 800-mile passage. Up to 10,000 people completed the trip per year during the 1970s, reaching about 25,000 during 1980, at the same time as the Mariel boat lift in Cuba. Despite patrols by the U.S. Coast Guard to intercept and return boat people, more Haitians sailed away after the fall of the "Baby Doc" Duvalier regime in 1986, when military repression intensified. Their square-hulled sloops with patchwork sails carried the emigrants to the Bahamas and the U.S., though neither country granted them political refugee status. Cubans, on the other hand, received immigration assistance in the U.S because they were viewed as refugees from

Communism. Even Cubans committing piracy in order to make the passage were welcomed in their stolen vessels, prompting a series of bloody ferry hijackings in Havana Harbor. Haitians choosing to leave in boats faced greater obstacles, including a longer ocean passage, than did Cubans, but their numbers increased in the early 1990s as well, when the elected government of Jean-Bertrand Aristide fell to a military coup. The question of how to treat the boat people became an issue in the U.S. presidential election of 1992, after the U.S. Coast Guard ended the practice of screening those they intercepted to see if any of them qualified for political asylum. Despite the high odds that they would be stopped on the high seas and immediately returned to face reprisals, Haitians continued to embark in improvised vessels until the U.S. invasion of that country in 1994 stemmed the flow at its source.

Why have so many people ventured onto the notoriously dangerous waters of the Gulf Stream in small, overcrowded boats? This is partly because there is hardly any other way to get from Cuba or Haiti to the United States. Most transportation links between the countries, in both watercraft and aircraft, have been severed as a result of political conflict and economic distress, the same reasons that motivate people to leave their homes. In the nineteenth century, the population of Tampa and Key West, Florida, swelled with Cuban immigrants brought by the steamships of the Plant and Munson Lines, among others. Regular steamship service to Havana connected the city to New York and New Orleans as well. Later, gigantic car ferries made the short run to Key West. Service to Haiti was less frequent, but as in Cuba, Pan American Airways established another, even more convenient way to travel to the U.S. All of this ended in Cuba in 1962, when airplane flights and steamship clearances to the U.S ceased. because of worsening relations between the countries, including the Bay of Pigs invasion of April 1961, and the Cuban Missile Crisis of October 1962. The airlift prompted by the Camarioca boat lift in 1965 lasted for eight years, but most links with Cuba have been prevented by the U.S. economic embargo that has been in effect for the last thirty-five years. Airline service and commercial traffic to Haiti also ceased during the economic embargo maintained by the U.S. in the early 1990s.

Like the frightened mariners in pictures of Caridad del Cobre, three Cuban boat people drifted on the high seas in August 1994. Their little boat's engine had failed, and they were at the mercy of the Gulf Stream, which was sweeping them away from Key West to die of thirst or drown. The owner of the boat, the *Carmencita*, was a professional fisherman with brothers and sisters in Key West, whose mother back in Mariel was named Caridad, too. Like the men saved by that saint, he and his companions needed a miracle to survive, and found it in the form of a vacant fishing boat like their own, floating nearby with a working engine and a supply of fuel and water. They knew the boat, named *Analuisa*, as well as the family who owned her, neighbors from Mariel. Her nineteen passengers had been picked up by a passing cruise liner, leaving the sturdy craft behind. The lucky men in the derelict *Carmencita* made it to Key West in the *Analuisa*, joining the ranks of new immigrants to the United States rather than the untold number who have died making the attempt. The *Analuisa* then came to Mystic Seaport, joining the watercraft collection as its first immigrant vessel. The vessel represents not only the hundreds of thousands of Caribbean boat people to arrive in recent decades, but all the boat people who immigrated by sea to this country throughout its history. Among the millions of crossings these diverse boat people made, those from Cuba and Haiti have been among the most harrowing, and perhaps the last.

Eric Roorda

civilian employees, 190 aircraft, 225 cutters of more than sixty-five feet in length, and 1,400 small boats. In 1997, more than 20 percent of its budget of $3.8 billion was directed towards aids to navigation and ice operations. Almost 15 percent was spent for search and rescue, while fisheries law enforcement and drug interdiction each accounted for about 13 percent, and environmental protection and immigrant interdiction each required about 9 percent of the budget. While the U.S. Coast Guard's roles and missions are indicated by its name, in the range of its operations, the size of its ships and its fleet strength, it ranks larger than many navies in the world.

The International Order

In September 1945, fresh on the heels of victory in World War II, President Harry Truman issued two unilateral proclamations. The first asserted "jurisdiction and control" over the natural resources of the continental shelf off the U.S. coast, and the second declared that the United States had the right to establish conservation zones protecting the sea fisheries beyond the traditional three-mile territorial limit. Neither, however, impeded the traditional rights of free navigation in these zones.

Two factors led to this unilateral action. One was pressure from oil companies eager to expand offshore oil drilling on the shelf; another involved the concern that Japanese vessels might return to the Gulf of Alaska, where the two countries had argued over the salmon fishery before the war. Soon afterward, a number of Latin American states cited the American action to justify expanding not only their jurisdiction over offshore fisheries but also their claims to sovereignty out to 200 miles. The traditional three-mile limit to a coastal nation's "territorial seas" began to crumble.

Utter chaos was averted with the adoption of four conventions drawn up by the first United Nations Law of the Sea Conference (UNCLOS-1) in 1958. Most of the participating nations embraced principles pertaining to freedom of the high seas, distant-water fishing rights, and the rights enjoyed by coastal states to a contiguous twelve-mile zone off its coast and to the continental shelf beyond. The delegates were unable to agree on an article on the breadth of the territorial sea, largely because of disagreement over a nation's right to exclusive control over fisheries in a zone beyond the limits of the territorial sea.

The United Nations General Assembly convened a second conference, UNCLOS-2, to try to resolve this issue in 1960. The United States and Canada sponsored a compromise proposal for a six-mile territorial sea with a further six-mile fishing zone, but this proposal was narrowly defeated and the conference failed to reach any further conclusion. In the years that followed, cold-war tensions and the widening gulf between rich (Northern Hemisphere) and poor (Southern Hemisphere) countries prevented the United Nations from making further progress in establishing a comprehensive Law of the Sea.

Then in November 1967, Malta's idealistic ambassador to the United Nations, Arvid Pardo, astounded the international community with a speech calling for "an effective international regime over the seabed and ocean floor" beyond the zone of national jurisdiction. Calling the resources of the world's seabeds "the common heritage of mankind," Pardo sought to protect the seabeds of the world from exploitation by the industrial nations at the expense of the developing countries. Several recent developments had led him to this proposal: the fear that both the United States and the Soviet Union were about to implant nuclear missiles on the sea floor; the threat that the superpowers intended to use the seabed to dump obsolete reactors and other radioactive wastes; and technological advances that would soon make possible the recovery of mineral-rich manganese nodules from the seabed. This last possibility posed the additional threat that unregulated mining would disrupt the international markets for such minerals on which several developing nations depended for revenue. Pardo proposed that revenue from carefully regulated seabed mining should be shared by all the world's nations as a means of providing desperately needed income for those of the Third World.

Although neither the United States nor the Soviet Union wished to limit its access to seabed resources, both recognized Pardo's principle of the common heritage of mankind by supporting the UN's "Declaration of Principles Governing the Seabed" in 1970, which declared: "The exploitation of its resources shall be carried out for the benefit of mankind as a whole, . . . and taking into particular consideration the interests and needs of the developing countries." At the same time, both superpowers wanted the developing nations to accept a narrow definition of "territorial seas" to permit the widest possible arena for their blue-water navies, as well as a guarantee that submarines and other warships could pass through international straits as a matter of right. Besides, the United States claimed that nothing in the Seabed Declaration would prevent private companies from mining the seabed anyway.

In 1973, delegates met in New York City to open the Third United Nations Law of the Sea Conference (UNCLOS-3). For the next eight years, some of the world's best negotiators representing more than 150 nations met in twice-annual sessions at Caracas, Venezuela, where they adopted a consensus approach to bridge enormous ideological and economic gaps between democratic and totalitarian nations, between capitalist and socialist systems, between industrialized and developing peoples. Finally, in March 1981, the delegates met in New York for what they had unanimously agreed would be the last negotiating session. But they had not reckoned on the change in American domestic politics embodied in the new administration of President Ronald Reagan. While the bulk of the international agreement significantly protected and advanced America's maritime interests, the central issue turned on Article XI, relating to deep seabed mining. The Reagan administration recognized that this article would prevent ratification of the Law of the Sea Convention in the U.S. Senate. Many senators believed that the seabed mining provisions deterred free-market development of seabed resources, failed to guarantee a decision-making role for the United States consistent with its interests, permitted broad changes to the convention without general consent, shared benefits with national liberation movements, and required Americans to transfer privately owned technological knowledge to underdeveloped countries. Although supporters argued that the convention should be ratified on the basis that its good points outweighed its weak points, a political deadlock ensued in Congress.

However, in 1987, recognizing that the United States accepted the bulk of the Convention, the American Law Institute confirmed American policy on this point in its authoritative Restatement of the Foreign Relations Law of the United States, stating that, except in the matter of seabed-mining, the U.S. had accepted the Law of the Sea Convention "through express or tacit agreement, accompanied by consistent practice." In this way, the United States accepted the new zones that extended the sovereignty of coastal states and reduced the area of the high seas: the 12-nautical-mile territorial sea, the 24-nautical-mile contiguous zone, the 200-nautical-mile exclusive economic zone (EEZ), the legal concepts of the expanded continental shelf and archipelagic waters, as well as the legal regime for transit passage in international straits. In a proclamation issued on 27 December 1988, President Reagan formally extended the territorial seas of the United States from three to twelve nautical miles.

Following negotiations between 1986 and 1994, the United Nations General Assembly adopted a modification to the original UNCLOS-3 provision on deep seabed mining. This new agreement restructured the seabed-mining provision along free-market principles, assuring American and other firms access to seabed minerals on the basis of reasonable terms and conditions. The day after the U.N. General Assembly passed this agreement, the United States formally signed the convention on 29 July 1994, and President Clinton referred it to the Senate for ratification. Although nearly all major maritime and industrial nations had declined to ratify the original form of the Convention, it entered into force on 30 November 1994, one year after the sixtieth nation acceded to it. In the two years following adoption of the new provision on deep seabed mining, double the number of nations indicated their provisional acceptance of the treaty, pending final ratification.

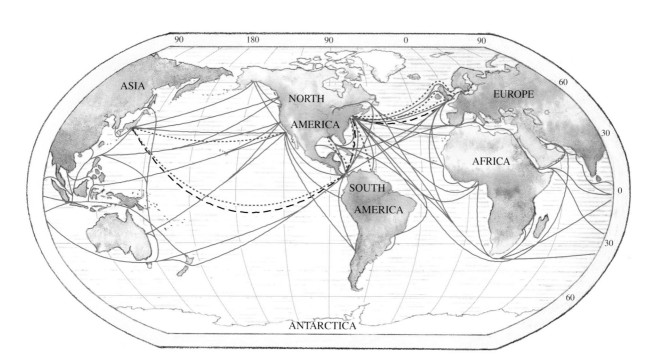

Figure 9 **Twentieth-Century World Trade Routes**

——————— Containerized Freight Routes to and from the U.S.

——————— Petroleum Routes to the U.S.

— — — Coal Routes from the U.S.

·············· Grain Routes from the U.S.

(Dennis O'Brien map)

CHAPTER 17

Americans Take to the Sea

ESPITE THE MANY changes in the patterns of American maritime activity in the last half of the twentieth century, the United States has remained a maritime nation. More than ever ours is now a global economy. Less well understood, however, is how much our nation's participation in that economy depends on maritime commerce. The value of America's foreign trade has increased fifteen-fold since 1950 in constant dollars, about half of which still goes by sea. Although down from the mid-century share of two-thirds, the value of the nation's maritime commerce is at an all-time high, again in constant dollars, and shipping remains by far the cheapest means (other than pipeline) of transporting bulk commodities over long distances. To be sure, more than 90 percent of our nation's overseas maritime commerce is carried in foreign-flag vessels, but it must be remembered that a considerable number of those ships are American-owned.

Despite the tremendous increase in volume, the pattern of traffic growth on inland waterways has been noticeably uneven. The Great Lakes system has suffered both from the competition of low-cost foreign iron ore and the exhaustion of the primary ore supply from the traditional iron ranges west of Lake Michigan and Lake Superior. Reprocessed and enriched ore in the form of pellets, or taconite, now constitutes the main iron-ore cargo for the few immense freighters still in operation. The total volume of Great Lakes traffic remains little more than that of the boom years of the later 1930s and the 1940s.

In striking contrast is the phenomenal increase of traffic on the Mississippi River system, to the

---

Ocean steamship travel shifted from transportation to recreation with the development of affordable airline travel in the 1950s. American Export Lines tried to promote its transatlantic liners Independence *and* Constitution *as the "Sunlane" to Europe, but it took a new generation of passenger ships, beginning in the 1970s, to lure Americans to sea for fun. (M.S.M. 96.142.9, Jennifer M. Stich photo)*

The first 1,000-foot ore carrier was the Stewart J. Cort, launched at Erie, Pennsylvania, in 1971. Nearly 300 feet longer than any other ore ship of the time, the Cort represented a number of innovations. The bow and stern sections were built at the Ingalls yard in Pascagoula, Mississippi, welded together, and traveled to Erie by way of the Welland Canal. There they were separated and attached to the 800-foot midship section, which was constructed of modular units. Powered by twin diesel engines, the ship was also fitted with lateral bow and stern thrusters for maneuvering. Bethlehem Steel ordered the ship to carry iron ore in the form of taconite pellets from Taconite Harbor, Minnesota, on Lake Superior, to Burns Harbor, Indiana, on Lake Michigan. Fitted with a conveyor system for self-unloading, the Cort has unloaded its entire 56,000-ton cargo in less than three hours. Operated by a crew of twenty-nine, the ship remains in service in the late-1990s. No bulk carriers have been added to the Lakes fleet since 1985. The Stewart J. Cort was photographed at Erie in 1972. (Courtesy Great Lakes Marine Historical Collection, Milwaukee Public Library)

point where in total tonnage (that is, volume not value) many of the largest ports in the United States–Port South Louisiana, Baton Rouge, New Orleans, Port of Plaquemine, and Lake Charles–are located near the mouth of the Mississippi. Moreover, other ports in the Gulf Coast region–Houston, Corpus Christi, Port

Arthur, and Texas City, Texas; Tampa, Florida; Mobile, Alabama; and Pascagoula, Mississippi–are among the nation's largest in tonnage handled. On the nation's system of coastal and inland waterways, now totaling more than 25,000 miles, the volume of traffic has doubled since 1960, and the fleet now includes some 6,000 towboats and 30,000 barges. Total cargo volume on the Mississippi now exceeds one hundred million tons annually, with well over 60 percent of all United States grain exports moving down river to the Gulf Coast. Consequently, major floods, such as occurred in 1993, have a devastating effect on the entire nation's economy as well as the business of river transportation.

Coastal commerce has also experienced an increase in traffic, especially after the opening of the trans-Alaska pipeline terminal at Valdez in 1977. The enabling legislation required that oil from the North Slope could be shipped only to ports in the "lower forty-eight," which put it under the laws regulating coastal commerce. Following the 1989 *Exxon Valdez* oil spill, the U.S. Congress passed the Oil Pollution Act of 1990, requiring that all tankers operating in U.S. coastal waters must have double-hull construction by the year 2015. The first American-built double-hull tanker, *American Progress*, entered service in 1997.

The Fisheries

President Harry Truman's unilateral declaration that the United States had the right to establish "conservation" zones protecting the fisheries beyond the traditional three-mile territorial limits along our coasts was issued in response to fears that in the postwar years Japanese fishing fleets would return to compete for what Americans considered to be "their" fish in the waters off Alaska. One result of this action came a few years later when several South American countries used the same claim to exclude American fishing vessels from the waters off their shores. These claims and counterclaims eventually led to the first Law of the Sea Conference in 1958.

In the Northwest Atlantic, on the other hand, the United States led the way to establishing the International Convention for Northwest Atlantic

The Mississippi River system remains an essential conduit for freight, much of which travels in standardized barges. Since the 1920s, the U.S. Army Corps of Engineers has turned the 640-mile stretch of the upper Mississippi between Minneapolis and St. Louis into the equivalent of a canal by constructing twenty-six dams with attached locks to maintain a minimum nine-foot depth of water for navigation. The dams have movable gates, which are opened in times of high water and closed to maintain slack-water navigation in times of low water. The locks, 110 feet wide and 600 feet long, accommodate nine standard cargo barges. Here at the new Melvin Price Lock and Dam at Alton, Illinois, north of St. Louis, the towboat Lois Ann *pushes a tow of chemical barges through the lock. Completed in 1990 to replace an earlier structure, this lock is 1,200 feet long to accommodate the long barge tows that travel between the Mississippi and Illinois River, just upstream from the lock. Built at Greenville, Mississippi, in 1974, the 131-foot* Lois Ann *is a typical shallow-draft towboat with diesel engines of 5,600 total horsepower to push fifteen-barge tows up and down the length of the Mississippi River system. (Fred Calabretta photo)*

Fisheries in 1950. For a decade or so the agreement achieved some success, but by the 1960s technology began to outstrip the ability and will for self-regulation, and the agreement broke down. Spain, the Soviet Union, and other European nations sent their fishing fleets into the northwest Atlantic to harvest the rich resources of the fishing banks off New England and Maritime Canada, and with devastating results. Modern methods, including trawlers working in conjunction with factory ships that processed the catch on site, greatly increased efficiency. Combined with the strategy of "pulse fishing"–concentrating on single species–these techniques drastically reduced populations in a few short years. To get some perspective on the growth

of fisheries in the years after World War II consider this: the total world catch increased by 25 percent during the period 1850-1950, but it then doubled in the decade from 1950 to 1960, and it doubled again to a peak yield of about 70 million metric tons by 1970.

What happened in the Georges Bank haddock fishery illustrates the point. For decades the fishermen of New England harvested a steady 20,000 to 40,000 tons of haddock per year from these grounds. By the 1930s, when motorized trawlers had almost totally replaced dory-equipped schooners, the annual catch nearly doubled to 80,000 tons,

Centered in the Middle Atlantic region and the Gulf of Mexico, the menhaden fishery underwent great changes in the decades after World War II. Since the 1870s it had been pursued as depicted here, with two oar-powered purse boats to set the purse seine around a school of menhaden on the surface, a large crew to purse and "harden" the seine by hand to concentrate the fish in a small section of the net, and a dipnet to bail the fish out of the net and into the hold of the steam-powered menhaden fishing vessel, which delivered them to the processing plant. Fishermen in this seasonal industry were largely African Americans, working as a "gang" to haul the seine by hand, often singing a chantey to coordinate the work. After World War II, aircraft were adopted to locate menhaden schools and direct the steamers—which were now largely powered by diesel engines. Motorized purse boats had been developed by the 1950s, and in the 1960s they were equipped with hydraulic power blocks to haul the seine, which reduced crew size by 50 percent. Finally, suction pumps were added to bail the fish from the net into refrigerated holds. Through the 1990s, menhaden remained in first or second place among all species caught by U.S. fishermen, with annual catches frequently topping two billion pounds. During the transitional period after World War II, the crew of the diesel-powered Promised Land *were photographed bailing fish from the seine on Long Island Sound in 1949. (Negative 124001F, © Mystic Seaport Museum, Inc., Rosenfeld Collection, Mystic, Connecticut)*

at which point haddock stocks collapsed for the first time. After this natural warning of the effects of overfishing, the population regenerated for three decades. Overfishing again took its toll, however, gradually reducing the yield to 50,000 tons a year, and then in 1965 disaster struck. A score or more of Russian factory ships appeared in these international waters to concentrate their effort on haddock. In just two years Russian and American fishermen harvested 320,000 tons of haddock, 85 percent of which consisted of two- and three-year old fish, leaving an inadequate number to renew the stock. By 1970 the catch was down to 10,000 tons and reached a low of 2,400 tons six years later. The haddock fishery had crashed.

In reaction to these and other disasters, the United States finally turned to unilateral action in the 1970s. The Magnuson Act in 1976 set up "a national program for the conservation and management" of the nation's fishery resources to prevent overfishing and to rebuild overfished stocks. The law established a 200-mile exclusive economic zone along the three American coasts, in which foreign fishing vessels could only operate with permission from the United States. Eight regional councils, with broad representation from the fishing industry, were responsible for drawing up a management plan in their respective regions that would establish total catch limits designed to achieve the "optimum yield" for each fishery, not the "maximum sustainable yield." The difference between the two is crucial to understanding why the Magnuson Act has failed. The latter is a figure determined by marine biologists to assure the ongoing sustainability of a given species. Optimum yield, on the other hand, takes into consideration the short-term economic impact of those limits on the fishing industry, and therefore permits a larger catch. There is little question that in the short run the Magnuson Act helped the American commercial fisherman. Total catch nearly doubled in the period 1977-95 to more than 10 million tons, its value increased by 20 percent in constant dollars, and the numbers of boats and people employed more than doubled in some fisheries. In the first three years the Georges Bank fleet alone increased by 30 percent to 800 vessels, and through the early 1980s New England fishing attracted investors seeking high returns, who converted the fleet to modern, steel, stern-ramp trawlers equipped with electronic fish-finding gear. This improvement in safety and efficiency came at a high cost.

As the Georges Bank fishery entered its last years, it still earned the fishermen a good return for their effort. In 1982 the fishing vessel *Odin*, a high-liner working out of New Bedford, made about thirty trips to Georges Bank, catching cod, yellowtail flounder, lemon sole, and other species totaling more than a million pounds and earning perhaps $800,000 altogether. Of that total, 40 percent went to the boatowners ($320,000), the captain took home 10 percent ($80,000), and the balance was divided among 10 or so crew members (perhaps $40,000 each). Scallopers did equally well during this period, the vessel *Montreal*, for instance, returning in February 1981 with 7,200 pounds of meats worth just over $38,000. Divided according to the above formula, the captain earned $3,800 for his ten-day effort, and each crew member nearly $2,000. No one familiar with the northeast part of Georges Bank in the dead of winter would deny that they deserved every penny of it.

But haddock, cod, and flounder populations on the 8,500-square-mile bank could not sustain the constant sweep of fishing vessels. By the early 1990s, thirteen years after implementation of the Magnuson Act, the Georges Bank fishery had crashed. A small number of vessels worked the inshore banks of the Gulf of Maine, often returning with 6,000 to 8,000 pounds of fish, mostly hake, dabs, ocean perch, and pollock, worth about $10,000. Even if a vessel could make thirty or forty five-day trips to these inshore grounds, the annual earnings would amount to little more than half the return of a decade earlier. As one fisherman with a wry sense of humor observed, "when you lose a little bit on each trip, you try to make it up on volume." All along the North Atlantic coast from Newfoundland to New York, owners defaulted on loans taken out to construct million-dollar draggers that now lay idle at their berths. Fishermen lost their billets, and processing plants laid off workers. However lucrative the policy of optimum yield had been in the short run, it ill-served both the fishermen and the once-renewable resource they depend on for their livelihoods.

The major fisheries of several other regions of the country have experienced similar crises. The industrial menhaden fishery expanded into the Gulf of Mexico and increased its efficiency after World War II by employing spotter planes to locate schools of fish, and it added motorized boats and mechanical net-hauling equipment in the 1950s, reducing the size of crews. As the principal fish meal and oil source, the menhaden fishery frequently led all U.S. fisheries in volume of catch landed. However, the industry declined by 40 percent between 1985 and 1992, leaving just a few large firms to pursue it, principally in Chesapeake Bay and Louisiana. In the late 1990s, U.S. Food and Drug Administration approval of menhaden oil as a food product suggested that this fishery would take on new significance beyond its ongoing importance in supplying poultry and hog feed.

The tuna fishery out of Pacific-Coast ports shifted from hook-and-line methods to purse seining, reaching a peak in the early 1970s. Thereafter, as the tuna fleet was restricted in the exclusive economic zones of the productive South American fishing grounds, much of it migrated halfway across the Pacific to American Samoa, at the same time cutting back in the face of expanding tuna production in the developing countries of Southeast Asia. In the 1980s, under political and economic pressure from conservationists, tuna fishermen were compelled to alter their gear to prevent the by-catch of dolphin, resulting in a

With its long coast, numerous salmon rivers, and access to the fishing grounds of the North Pacific and Bering Sea, Alaska leads the nation in fishing, both by volume and by value of fish caught. As the fishery for Alaska pollock expanded in the late 1980s, the remote ports of Dutch Harbor and Unalaska became the leading fishing ports in the U.S., followed by Kodiak. Like latter-day gold rushes, the fisheries for crab, pollock, and even salmon have gone through cycles of boom and bust, although these North Pacific resources have only recently been exposed to the pressures of intense fishing effort that resulted in severe depletion of stocks in the North Atlantic. (Courtesy Alaska Division of Tourism)

decline in U.S. tuna production. Finally, in the late 1980s the three largest U.S. tuna companies were sold to Asian interests, making this most widely consumed of all fish in the American market a truly international product, to the misfortune of U.S. fishermen.

Swordfish populations have been stressed as well. After an interlude in the 1960s when the fear of mercury concentration in swordfish curbed swordfishing for a time, the fishery has increased in scope and intensity. With the shift to the use of baited longlines for catching swordfish far at sea, swordfish stocks had fallen to two-thirds of the "optimum" yield level by the mid-1990s, and the average size of each landed fish had dropped from 266 pounds in 1965 to 84 pounds thirty years later.

The once-famous Chesapeake Bay oyster industry suffered a similar decline as pollution and the mysterious MSX organism afflicted the natural oyster beds already stressed by centuries of human harvest. In the Gulf of Mexico, a decline in oyster stocks was matched by a decline in the shrimp fishery, the result of both overfishing and human-induced changes in the ecology of the bayous where shrimp spawn. In these waters, where cultural conflict flared in the 1970s when refugee Vietnamese fishermen began shrimping, the industry has been impacted both by conservation efforts to exclude sea turtles and other species from shrimp otter trawls, and by economic pressures ashore that, for example, have replaced the shrimp canneries of Biloxi, Mississippi, with gambling casinos.

Some fisheries have fared better under the Magnuson Act, particularly those of Alaska and the Pacific Northwest, where the value of the catch rose by 30 percent in constant dollars between 1980 and 1992. In the latter year, landings at Dutch Harbor, Kodiak, Petersburg, and the other Alaska fishing ports

Fishing Women of Alaska

Leslie Leyland Fields fishes for salmon and teaches English in Kodiak, Alaska. In her book about the women who make up roughly 5 percent of Alaska's fishing population she addresses the motivations that drive those who harvest the sea.

Why, out of all the occupations and professions, choose such an extreme one? I know the reason for my choice: I married the occupation—nets, cork line, skiffs, the whole ball of web. Choosing to marry was choosing to be involved in fishing; it was that clear. For those who entered the fisheries independently, apart from relationships, the motivations usually had something to do with freedom, both economic and otherwise—controlling your own life, making your own decisions. And yet here is the twist, one of those wondrous complexities: to harness your life and occupation to earth and ocean brings a far greater dependence and helplessness. Every woman here, every fisherman, has multiple stories to tell of howling winds and tall seas breaking over her small craft, sending boat and crew desperately hobbling to shelter, an island, a cove, any kind of stay against the immeasurable forces of wind and sea. Who is really in control?

And what kind of freedom is this? The freedom to fish is not freedom from rules or laws; indeed, all levels of government circumscribe whole sets of rules around us, like a seine net encircling a school of herring. To fish does not remove all barriers, it only removes "society's," if we can use such an amorphous word. There is freedom from traditional society's expectations, but in their place comes an incredible bond, even bondage, to another set of rules equally confining. These are not only the rules that tell who, when, where, how long, how much, and in what manner fishermen can fish but also the rules each person devises simply to stay alive. And woe to those who break them.

One of the most intriguing tentacles of this story is the mythology of Alaska itself. Alaska is still wilderness, frontier—traditional male terrain overlaid with an overwhelming "mythology of maleness," of conquest, exploration, domination. Add commercial fishing and you add another layer of maleness: leadership, stoicism, instinctive knowledge of the fish and sea. Enter women. Not only women in Alaska, the frontier, but women in fishing. Not only women on deck stacking the web but women skippers yelling out orders from the wheelhouse—the world is upside down. Tradition is on its head. If I could choose one word that begins to explain some of

Leslie Leyland Fields mends a net used to catch salmon near Kodiak Island during Alaska's three-month salmon season. (Courtesy Leslie Leyland Fields; Leola Harkins photo)

this it is there in Alaska's state motto: Alaska: The Last Frontier. Do you hear it? The *last* frontier, like the Last Chance Saloon before miles of desert. There is urgency here that supersedes gender. This is the last place where man or woman can make his or her own life, where society is loose, open, like gauze, where the rules are not yet made. The Alaska myth says anyone can come here, that this is the place where ability, courage, determination, and strength bag the biggest bear, catch the most fish, win the day—all twenty-two summer hours of it.

Leslie Leyland Fields, *The Entangling Net: Alaska's Commercial Fishing Women Tell Their Lives*. Copyright 1997 by the Board of Trustees of the University of Illinois.

With the depletion of so many fish species in U.S. waters, aquaculture—the propagation of marine species in a controlled environment—seems to provide a reliable alternative source for seafood. Although shrimp, salmon, trout, and tilapia are all products of American aquaculture, the most successful effort with finfish has been the farming of catfish in artificial ponds in Alabama, Arkansas, Louisiana, and Mississippi. Since its beginnings about 1970, catfish farming has grown to comprise more than 60 percent of U.S. aquaculture production in the 1990s, with 472,000,000 pounds produced in 1996. The fish are spawned in hatcheries and released into large, manmade ponds to grow for eighteen months. They are fed a special grain mixture that floats, which makes them surface feeders and prevents the gamey flavor of bottom-feeding catfish. Like coastal seafood, the catfish are harvested with seines, as seen here, and carried live to the processing plants for distribution as fresh or frozen fillets. Aquaculture is labor-intensive, and aquaculturalists must address the maintenance of genetic diversity within the species as well as the risk of disease among a contained population, but aquaculture has become an essential maritime industry. (Courtesy Catfish Institute; Lou Manna photo)

accounted for almost 60 percent of the nation's total catch by weight and more than 40 percent by value. By the late 1980s these gains resulted in large measure from a shift from the traditional reliance on salmon, tuna, and halibut to the harvest of previously underutilized species such as Pacific cod and pollock. These species, caught by large American factory trawlers in the North Pacific, are processed as the frozen blocks of white fish used to produce the ubiquitous fried fish patties and surimi—textured fish protein marketed as "crab." Price-fixing charges levied by salmon fishermen against Alaska packing companies and Japanese buyers have added to the problems facing the Pacific fishing industry.

International demand for specialty fish products

has also led to changes. Japanese taste for sashimi—raw fish—has stressed the Atlantic yellow-fin tuna population and the previously ignored sea urchin of northern waters. Even the herring and mackerel in U.S. waters, which no longer appeal to U.S. consumers, are being caught under the terms of joint-venture arrangements whereby U.S. fishermen catch them for Russian or other foreign processors to freeze and carry home in their factory ships.

Throughout the United States the situation has left the commercial harvesters of both fin and shellfish wondering whether their particular species will be the next to crash. As lobstermen along the coast of Maine or crabbers in the Gulf smile on their way to the bank, they worry about the future. At the same time, how-ever, the crisis has led to major revisions in the way the regional management councils make decisions, and fishermen themselves are now more willing to recognize that the resources they harvest for a living are finite after all. Wholesale closures of Georges Bank in 1995 may have come too late to save the cod and haddock fish-eries, but they signal a more positive attitude toward sustainable yield as the only acceptable basis of managing a renewable resource like the nation's fisheries. Other councils have experi-mented with new and sometimes daunting regu-latory policies like limited entry or individual transferable quotas. The federal buy-back pro-gram introduced in the mid-1990s to buy unwanted fishing vessels, and natural attrition, have reduced the fishing fleets in some ports by one-third.

In some areas, particularly in the Pacific Northwest, Native-American groups have worked to retain their traditional tribal fishing rights. For example, along the Columbia River, hydroelectric dams and agricultural development in this century have altered the salmon habitat, while the commercial salmon fishery at the mouth of the river has further reduced the quantity of fish returning to native fishing sites along the river. By pressing their legal rights in court and working to reverse the degradation of the river, several tribes have revived their cultural emphasis on salmon. In a more controversial native claim, Alaska Eskimos successfully argued that their cultural traditions required the killing of several whales each year, even after U.S. commercial whaling had ceased in 1972 and the U.S. had agreed to the International Whaling Commission ban on whal-ing in 1982.

Americans have until recently been slow to adopt aquaculture as an alternative source of fish protein, with the exception of catfish farming, which has grown substantially since the 1970s in the former cotton country from Alabama across Mississippi and Louisiana. But even with the success of special feeds to raise a large volume of catfish to predictable size and quality, the prod-uct was only gradually accepted in markets out-side the South and the Mississippi Valley. Finally, with the progressive decline of natural fisheries into the 1990s, fish farming became a growth industry in other parts of the country.

Saltwater farms have experimented with the cul-tivation of trout, tilapia, salmon, and mussels, among other species, but the financial and envi-ronmental risks are great and progress is slow. The production of trout, for instance, has declined after reaching a peak in 1990, and its market value is less than one-quarter that of farm-raised catfish.

The production of Atlantic salmon, on the other hand, doubled in the decade after 1984. Overall aquaculture output in the United States also doubled in the period 1984-94 to more than 330,000 tons, worth nearly 800 million dollars. Disease, water pollution, and opposition from traditional fishermen are among the obstacles confronting the fish-farmer, yet the productivity of ocean waters can be extraordi-nary. An acre of cultivated mussel beds can produce 1,000 pounds of dry meat, compared to the 300 pounds of beef produced from an acre of pasture. Unfortunately, the American public would far rather tuck into a one-pound sirloin steak than a mess of mussel meats. Until the public demand for seafood products improves and investors are persuaded that mariculture offers a promising return, the industry faces a lackluster future. Americans still consume almost twelve times as much meat and poultry products as seafood, and the gap has been widening in the 1990s.

As the fishing industry of the lower forty-eight states declines, yet another aspect of our maritime way of life is threatened with extinc-tion. From Gloucester, Massachusetts, to San Pedro, California, along the waterfronts that once supported large fleets of fishing vessels, one now finds the sprawling floats of pleasure-boat marinas, extending far out into the channel, home to literally millions of recreational boats. Behind them rise upscale condominiums, whose residents have all but driven the port's few remaining fishing vessels from the neighborhood, along with their early-morning noises and year-round odors. Barring a miraculous recovery of stocks and the acceptance of effective manage-ment controls, the 500-year history of a prosper-ous fishery off the Atlantic coast of North America has ended, and the Pacific industry faces a serious threat as well. In the words of David Boeri, author of a study of the New England offshore fishery in the 1970s, we can "tell it goodbye, kiddo."

Rachel Carson (1907-1964) almost single-handedly made Americans aware of the natural history of the sea, and of the grave threat to the natural world posed by our increasing use of organic chemical compounds to achieve a convenient lifestyle. Though raised in an emotionally challenging family, Carson learned a love of nature and writing from her mother and received a good scientific education. Employed as a writer and editor for the U.S. Fish and Wildlife Service in a time when women were largely excluded from serious scientific endeavors, she turned her understanding of marine life and her lyrical command of language to write popular explorations of the natural world. In Under the Sea Wind *(1941) she followed waterfowl and migratory fish of the East Coast in a compelling description of their annual cycle. Her classic history of the oceans and the forces that drive them was published as* The Sea Around Us *in 1951, followed by a description of the coastal zone in* The Edge of the Sea *(1956). Carson is best known for* Silent Spring *(1962), her warning about the dire effects of unbridled technology on the natural world, particularly the unrestricted use of pesticides. Carson did not live to see how close to reality her predictions came before Americans awoke to her warnings and began to push for protective legislation. More than a generation after her death, Rachel Carson remains the leading voice in appreciation of the oceans and our relationship to them. Edwin Gray photographed Rachel Carson at Woods Hole, Massachusetts, in 1951. (Courtesy Rachel Carson History Project)*

Marine Pollution

In the years before World War II, maritime historians would have scoffed at the suggestion that water quality was a relevant part of their subject; nor would the American public have considered water pollution a matter of concern. In 1890 a Hartford, Connecticut, fish dealer admitted in a newspaper interview that the oysters he sold were frequently taken from polluted mud flats but claimed they were not adversely affected thereby. "What is the sea for?" he asked. "Didn't God make it to receive the refuse of the inhabitants of the earth? For this reason He made the water salt so as to purify the putrid matter that is poured into it." In 1923, in fact, a well-meaning American poet could seriously write of the sea that:

For ever soiled and yet for ever pure,
It draws into its depths, without a stain,
Whatever the polluted land can drain
From compost-heap and charnel ground
and sewer.

During the era in which these lines were written,

the 1920s, the nation's population averaged about 115 million people, the output of petroleum production totaled less than 2 million barrels a day, and the number of vehicles on the nation's highways averaged less than 20 million. By the 1990s, however, population had more than doubled, total crude oil production and importation had increased ninefold to almost 18 million barrels a day, and the number of vehicles had reached 200 million. In addition, the use of industrial chemicals and plastics of all sorts has grown from virtually zero in the 1920s to extraordinary totals at the end of the twentieth century. The ocean no longer "draws into its depths without a stain, whatever the polluted land can drain."

The contemporary American concern for the quality of our environment has many roots, but one of them was a marine disaster: the blowout of an oil well off the coast of Santa Barbara, California, in 1969. Accidents like the Santa Barbara blowout, the wreck of the *Amoco Cadiz* off France in 1978, or the 1989 *Exxon Valdez* grounding in Alaska, remind us of the price the marine environment pays for our having become so dependent on oil as our primary source of energy. The grounding of the

Exxon Valdez in March 1989 spilled nearly 11,000,000 gallons of crude oil into the waters of Prince William Sound, Alaska, and commanded the attention of the nation for months afterward. Within weeks the spill had heavily or moderately affected an area stretching for nearly 500 miles (the distance from Cape Cod to Chesapeake Bay or between San Francisco and San Diego) and affected more than 1,000 miles of coastline. Sea birds were killed by the tens of thousands, nearly 1,000 sea otters died, and commercial fishing was closed for much of the season throughout the region. Crisis intervention cases increased seven-fold at the mental health center in Kodiak as the port's salmon fishery was shut down all season because of the spill. Eleven thousand men and women worked on the cleanup, which cost Exxon more than one billion dollars, but damage to the company's reputation could not so easily be repaired.

As destructive as these calamities are to their immediate surroundings, they simply draw the public's attention to a condition that has been growing steadily in the years since World War II. Oil-well blowouts and tanker accidents in fact account for only a tiny fraction of the substances that pollute our coastal waters every year. It is the day-to-day waste from our industrial society that causes most of the damage: routine operation of tankers unloading their cargoes, automobile lubricants and, perhaps most damaging of all, the runoff from the chemical fertilizers, pesticides, and heavy metals that have been so heavily used in the latter half of the twentieth century. Large quantities of these pollutants sooner or later reach our coastal waters, contaminating salt marshes and deltas where so many forms of marine life spawn. Along with the 400 million tons of sediment that flows down the Mississippi River system each year comes the residue from chemical fertilizers and pesticides used to increase production on our declining farm acreage. Our industrial production is another source of marine pollution. To cite but one substance, PCBs–polychlorinated biphenyls, by-products in the manufacture of electronic equipment–have collected on the bottom of many harbors and may enter the food web as PCBs are concentrated in the tissues of marine species. Dredging navigation channels, once a routine operation, now imposes the problem of where to dump the spoils that are so heavily laden with these waste products. Until the mid-1970s, when international agreements became more effective, oil carriers routinely washed their tanks at sea, dumping the residue, which might amount to 500,000 tons of oil annually, into the world's oceans. During his ocean crossing in 1970 on the raft *Ra II*, Thor Heyerdahl reported to the United Nations that he sighted drifting clots of oil during forty-three of his fifty-seven days at sea.

Sometimes humankind contaminates the environment without the slightest knowledge of having done so. One of the most unusual forms of pollution, if it can be called that, is the introduction of new species through marine transportation.

However, the last quarter of the twentieth century has witnessed encouraging progress in the reduction of marine pollution along American shores. Passage of the Clean Water Act in 1969, the National Environmental Protection Act (NEPA) in the following year, and the Coastal Zone Management Act of 1972 have all helped to improve conditions. Since 1970 federal, state, and local governments have doubled in constant dollars the capital they have invested in sewage plants across the country, and as the federal contribution to this investment declined in the 1980s, private industry has begun to increase its share in the last decade of the century. By encouraging states to adopt more stringent restrictions on development along the water's edge, the Coastal Zone Management Act has helped reduce the rate at which we have been filling in the salt marshes on which most marine species depend as a nursery for their offspring. Yet the pressures continue to mount. Since 1970 half of the nation's single-family homes have been built in the coastal zone, according to a report from the Trust for Public Land, and by the end of the twentieth century more than three out of four Americans will be living within 50 miles of the coast. Adding to the problem are the growing numbers of people who visit the coast for a day, week, or longer for recreation and relaxation.

To cite one of the nation's most popular resorts, on a typical summer day in the early 1990s some 35,000 people could be found on the island of Nantucket, a 40 percent increase from a decade earlier, and the figure continues to expand. In the same period the number of year-round resi-

Blue Immigrants:
The Introduction of Marine Species

After sixty-four days at sea, the ship *Arbella* anchored off Cape Ann, Massachusetts, in June 1630. On board were perhaps 100,000 colonists: somewhat more than 100 men, women, and children; an assortment of livestock, plants, rats, and mice; seeds, insects, snails, and other organisms mixed in with the ship's ballast; and tens of thousands of organisms living in a rich community of marine fouling and boring organisms attached to, and burrowing in, the bottom of the hull. Today, these immigrant organisms would be recognized as part of a cosmopolitan harbor biota created by centuries of maritime commerce.

Slowly, one European marine organism after another appeared on New England's shores. Almost 400 years later, it is difficult to know exactly when each species first colonized. Indeed, so old and numerous were sailing voyages between Europe and North America—beginning in the sixteenth century, but extending back to tenth-century Norse explorations—and

so recent are our first biological investigations, few being available before the mid-nineteenth century, that it is difficult to determine exactly which species existed on America's North Atlantic shores before European contact.

Perhaps *the* most famous European colonist of New England shores is the common periwinkle, *Littorina littorea*–a species so "typical" of the Atlantic coast that many people are surprised to learn that it is not native. How the European periwinkle first arrived in North America is uncertain. Ancient populations appear to have lived in Newfoundland and other parts of eastern Canada thousands of years ago, but our modern populations seem to derive from recent introductions of the past 200 years. In the 1840s *Littorina littorea* was discovered in eastern Canada in regions already well-explored for their seashells. Whether introduced upon ballast rocks, or (as the author suspects) intentionally released to inoculate America with one of western Europe's

cheapest and most popular seafoods, we do not yet know.

Littorina moved steadily south. By the 1860s it had reached the Gulf of Maine, by the early 1870s Cape Cod, by the late 1870s Long Island Sound, and by the 1880s New Jersey. The European periwinkle quickly became one of the most dominant intertidal organisms of North America from Newfoundland to New York. Studies one hundred years later suggest that *Littorina*, coating the shores in numbers up to thousands per square yard, had a profound effect on the distribution and abundance of other animals and plants of the shore–perhaps effectively eliminating much of their favored algal food, competing with other species, affecting marsh development, providing a new shell resource for native hermit crabs, and having many, many other more subtle effects.

The green crab, *Carcinus Maenas*, was an early colonist, being introduced into Long Island Sound from Europe by the end of the eighteenth century. The green crab is also such a typical "representative" species of New England and Middle Atlantic shores it is difficult to imagine it not being here. As with the European periwinkle, one could hardly pick a potentially more successful invader, and one that could predictably cause some of the most extensive environmental change. Green crabs are omnivores (although individuals may, more or less, be specialists): they can crush or tear barnacles off rocks, they can dig for clams, they can attack and remove hermit crabs from their shells. They eat worms, algae, and organic debris. They live on exposed rocky shores and in quiet backwaters, marshes, and estuaries. They can live far up rivers where there is the slightest salt, and offshore in coastal waters. Successful invaders, of course, are typically generalists in both their food and habitat requirements, and these traits characterize not only green crabs but backyard weeds.

While ships carried the green crab–a species with great propensity to snuggle deep into old shipworm burrows–around the world (specimens were found in ports in Panama, Hawaii, and India), it is typical to find that colonists do not successfully establish everywhere they are introduced. But it is perhaps not surprising to find that the two greatest regions of successful colonization outside Europe have been the Atlantic coast of North America and the shores of eastern Australia, around Sydney. In 1990 the green

crab dramatically appeared in San Francisco Bay, where, for food, it is finding an abundant supply of clams and worms–all introduced species from Asia or New England!

By the end of the eighteenth century ships–marine-species conveyer belts–had explored most of the world, and by the mid-nineteenth century, accompanied by global events such as the California and Australia gold rushes, the world was virtually itching with shipping activity. Indeed, hundreds of ships made their way, for example, from New England, Europe, Chile, Peru, Australia, New Zealand, China, Japan, and Hawaii to San Francisco and other Pacific-Coast ports between 1849 and the early 1850s, producing, in marine biological terms, one of the greatest movements of marine organisms in the history of human endeavor! By 1853, the common New England

Since arriving in the 1980s in ships' ballast water, European zebra mussels have colonized the Great Lakes in an especially dramatic example of the introduction of marine species. Without natural predators in their new habitat, zebra mussels compete with native species for nutrients, foul marine structures, and wash ashore in tremendous numbers during storms, as shown here. (J. Leach photo)

barnacle *Balanus improvisus* had colonized the harbor of San Francisco–indeed, it was more successful than many of the human colonists that had accompanied this barnacle's parental stocks.

Ships today, however, probably do not carry the vast fouling communities they once did. Modern ship speeds, of twenty to twenty-five knots and more, sweep away many of the organisms that Sir Francis Drake carried around the world on the bottom of the *Golden Hinde* in the 1590s at four or five knots, or that a clipper ship carried round Cape Horn to California at ten or twelve knots in the 1850s. Most organisms that might survive passage through the seas at that speed are inhibited by intensely poisonous antifouling paints, although some species of seaweed have actually evolved tolerances to copper-based antifouling paints. Finally, good, rich, handsome fouling communities on vessel bottoms develop best when ships remain dockside or at anchor for weeks or months. This was typical of ship usage centuries ago, but today a containership putting into New York Harbor at 0700 is gone by 1400, which is hardly enough time for serious barnacle or weed colonization.

The bottom line, however, is not that the bottom line is clean. In 1957 the green Asian seaweed *Codium fragile tomentosoides* suddenly appeared in New York, about the same time as the launch of Sputnik, leading some to draw a natural correlation. Single *Codium* plants may grow to a meter tall and a half-meter in diameter, and in stands by the hundreds or thousands they form dense, arborescent seaweed meadows. Probably introduced as a ship fouling organism from Europe (where it had colonized by the turn of the century after an earlier introduction from Japan), *Codium*, or "Dead Man's Fingers," is now an abundant fouling species from Maine to the Middle

Atlantic region. In some places, such as Cape Cod and Long Island Sound, it is believed to have impacted local scallop fisheries.

In the early 1970s, the Asian seasquirt *Styela clava* also suddenly appeared in New England. *Styela* is typically three to six inches in length, a warty, leathery animal attached by a narrow stalk to the substrate. It is now a significant fouling organism from Massachusetts to New York. *Styela* was also likely introduced on the bottom of a ship coming from Europe, where it first appeared during the Korean War.

If we pull up a mooring in Long Island Sound today, the dominant macroscopic organisms are frequently all introduced species! Long, luxurious stands of *Codium* intermingle with the brown tubular Asian seasquirt *Styela*, and these in turn are coated with the brilliant orange colonies of another seasquirt *Botrylloides* from Southern California, released by a scientist in the 1970s. In some regions *Styela* covers almost 100 percent of the substrate, where there used to be, by local testimony, the native mussel *Mytilus*.

While ships today may carry less in the way of fouling communities on their bottoms, they remain as probably the greatest conveyers of marine life around the world—perhaps even exceeding their long historical role. Water ballast has replaced solid ballast, and modern oceangoing cargo vessels may carry thousands to millions or

even tens of millions of gallons of seawater in their ballast tanks. In this ballast (not bilge) water are all of the marine organisms found around the ship. Some cargo vessels have been found to have more than fifty species of planktonic animals and plants in their ballast tanks after only an eleven-day voyage. These modern conveyer belts, in the form of thousands of ships every day, take up ballast water in one harbor and, one to three weeks later, release the water halfway around the world. Large harbors may thus be inoculated with millions of gallons per day of foreign marine organisms—a daunting new wave of potential invasions for marine biologists to consider!

Since the opening of the St. Lawrence Seaway in 1959, even the Great Lakes have become exposed to this form of species transport as large oceangoing ships call there. As a result of ballast water release in the 1980s, the Lakes have been colonized by one of the most dramatic invasions of North America in the past 200 years: the European zebra mussel *Dreissena polymorpha*, a small bivalve mollusk with the potential to colonize two-thirds of North America's fresh (and perhaps very low brackish) water. The zebra mussel was once found only in the drainages of the Caspian and Black Seas, but it spread across the face of Western Europe during the days of canal building in the nineteenth century. The zebra mussel is a major fouling organism: literally hundreds of millions of these typically one-half-inch-long mussels can fill up water pipes and water intake bays, colonize hulls, cover pilings, marina floats, and buoys, and be washed ashore after storms as huge shell piles on previously shell-less beaches. Zebra-mussel colonization has followed rapidly across the Lakes, through the Chicago Drainage Canal, and down the Mississippi in the decade since its arrival.

The Chinese clam *Potamocorbula amurensis* appeared in the same year, 1988, in San Francisco Bay, and today occurs in densities of 10,000 and more per square meter on the floor of the bay. The Japanese crab *Hemigrapsus sanguineus* also appeared in 1988 (a good year, apparently, for North American invasions!) around Cape May, New Jersey. It will inevitably spread north to Long Island Sound and south into Delaware and Chesapeake Bays.

Three European fish appeared in the Great Lakes, one of which, the ruffle *Gymnocephalus cermuus*, does not bode well for the future of the smaller fish that it eats. And, as a sort of unintentional "trade" for the zebra mussel, the common Atlantic Coast comb jellyfish *Mnemipsis leidyi* was carried by ships to the Black Sea, where Russian oceanographers now report it to occur in hundreds of millions of tons. The comb jellyfish is a voracious consumer of zooplankton, and zooplankton stocks have declined in the Black Sea where the comb jellyfish is now abundant.

On the land, we are perhaps more used to the idea of introduced species, because we are surrounded by them in our cities and on our farms. Almost all of our abundant crops, the plants that transformed America, and which Claire Shaver Haughton has called the "Green Immigrants," have come from other continents. An empty lot in the middle of Boston, or New York, or Los Angeles may be home to weeds, earthworms, insects, spiders, nematodes, snails, and slugs—virtually all of which are native to Europe, or South America, or Asia, and were transported to America in and on the products of commerce. And so it is in our urbanized estuaries and shores and lakes as well, where human activities reaching back many centuries and actively continuing today have homogenized some of the world's coastal marine biota.

These exotic species introductions raise, of course, important questions about the future diversity of these ecosystems, in terms of the extent to which these invaders may displace or replace members of the native biota. On 29 November 1990, the U.S. Congress passed Public Law 101-646, the "Nonindigenous Aquatic Nuisance Prevention and Control Act of 1990." A section of this law established the "National Ballast Water Control Program," which, in part, calls for studies on the introduction of aquatic nuisance species by vessels.

One of these studies, the Native Biological Invasions Shipping Study, is specifically designed to characterize the amounts and sources of ballast water entering the United States, and to examine methods by which to reduce the role of ballast water as the mediator of future invasions into the U.S.

James T. Carlton

dents grew by 20 percent to 6,500. During the mid-1980s the town annually issued an average of more than 200 building permits for new dwellings, mostly summer homes. The island's main harbor accommodates almost 2,000 boats at its marinas and moorings. Despite the presence of three pump-out stations, fecal coliform concentrations often reach levels unsuitable for shellfishing and occasionally for water sports as well. The impact of such numbers of people and boats on the ecology of an island of only fifty square miles and its surrounding waters is staggering, and yet the islanders expect that growth will continue well into the twenty-first century. So too do the residents of the hundreds of communities like Nantucket that dot our shores from the State of Maine to the State of Washington. Planning for that future is a daunting prospect.

On the Waterfront

When T.S. Eliot wrote the lines "the sea is all about us / the sea is the land's edge also," he was engaged in one of humankind's greatest pleasures, looking out to sea from the vantage point of the shore. The seaside had been valued since classical times for its salubrious air, invigorating waters, and sunlit beaches. When England's Prince Regent, not yet George IV, built his extravagant pavilion at Brighton in the early nineteenth century, the seaside resort came into its own. In so doing he gave license to the social dictum that at the beach "anything goes." In their buildings, clothing, and behavior, beachgoers have ever since broken the rules that ordinarily govern conduct in polite society. This was possible because life at the beach was considered different; it was life on vacation. In this country, Newport, Rhode Island, emerged as a summer resort during the second half of the eighteenth century, but the extravagance of its "cottages" (and those in similar communities from Maine to Puget Sound) had to await the creation of a moneyed class after the Civil War.

In the closing decades of the twentieth century, wealthy Americans continue to build "trophy houses" along the nation's shoreline, and a resort mentality continues to dominate social life in these watering places. Most resorts are basically small towns or even villages, home to fishermen,

carpenters, small-business persons, and their families, who welcomed the annual arrival of "summer folk" with varying degrees of enthusiasm or regret, but who could always look forward to regaining their communities after Labor Day. But a subtle change has begun to transform these waterside towns. Increasingly, former summer residents are winterizing their houses and taking up year-round habitation. Improved highways allow many to commute to their city jobs; modern electronic systems permit others to work at home. Generous benefits and improved health have encouraged increasing numbers to retire to the shore (and to inland villages too, for that matter).

Such a change has obviously altered the livestyles of these "year-rounders," as they are coming to be called in distinction to "natives," but less apparent to outsiders are the significant ways in which the communities themselves are being transformed, as the "summer folk" no longer go home after Labor Day. Now they register to vote at town meetings, serve on committees, and bring new perspectives on old ways of doing things. They contribute to the community's cultural life, but they frequently expect increased community services, including better maintenance of the remote roads that lead to their shorefront homes.

Changes are also taking place along our nation's urban waterfronts. Wharves, warehouses, and other marine-related buildings have been abandoned during the shift from bulk-cargo handling to containerized operations, which now take place on the outskirts of traditional ports. The old port structures give way to the wrecker's ball, and in their place are built apartments and condominiums, marketplaces, aquariums, and waterfront parks. These examples of adaptive use range, both geographically and philosophically, from the reconstruction of Seattle's Fishermen's Terminal as a waterfront workplace to the conversion of Boston's Navy Yard into a residential compound. The prototype most admired by planners, and by tourists as well, is the Rouse Corporation's transformation of Baltimore's Inner Harbor into an upscale recreational center. Other projects of note include the city-run Waterman's Cooperative in Annapolis, Maryland; an extraordinary marine aquarium on the site of an old sardine cannery in Monterey, California; the Old Port Exchange area of shops, offices, and restaurants along the waterfront in Portland, Maine; and the rehabilitation of Philadelphia's riverfront by a combination of private and public groups. One factor that all of these undertakings have in common is the availability of property for reuse at low cost. But our cities are ringed with factories, railroad yards, and other industrial sites abandoned in the nation's shift away from basic small-scale manufacturing. The quality that makes waterfronts so attractive to developers is their central location, a result of the way our seaports grew out from waterfront hubs. Early streets and modern subway and bus routes still serve these centers, making them easily accessible to the public. Then too, these waterfronts offer a vista out over the harbor that attracts multitudes of people seeking visual and perhaps spiritual relief from the urban canyons that our city streets have become.

Marine Recreation

After suffering through the 1930s and converting to wartime production during the early 1940s, the boating industry rebounded after World War II. The initial challenge became to find ways to produce cheaper boats. Traditional wood construction was time-consuming and costly. Each boat was fashioned by skilled builders, thus limiting the number available and making each expensive. Aluminum, steel, and even concrete were tried as alternatives, but the real revolution arrived in the 1950s with fiber-reinforced plastic. The world's first fiberglass-cloth and polyester-resin boat was built as an experiment in 1942 by a young Ohio engineer named Ray Greene. After the war, with the chemistry and technology of this new plastic material improved by wartime experiments, including fiberglass airplane wings, fiberglass laminates began to be used in mass-production small boats. Among the pioneer builders in the U.S. before 1950 were Dyer, Cape Cod Shipbuilding, Winner Manufacturing, Gar Form, Palmer Scott, Wizard, Lunn Laminates, and Ray Greene himself.

This manufacturing method replaced craftsmen working with wood. Fiberglass boats were built by factory workers applying glass cloth and mat to a mold and soaking the lay-up with polyester

resin. While the mold was difficult to construct, once it was in place it could be used repeatedly. This was series-production, and in some cases mass-production, resulting in low-cost units. Fiberglass hulls replaced wood hulls in nearly all of American boatbuilding by 1970.

Alternative designs for both sail and powerboats also proliferated after the war. Sailing attracted a wider and younger audience with the introduction of board sailboats, such as the Alcort Sailfish and Sunfish before 1960 and the Laser after 1970, and the sailboard, which combined a surfboard hull and winglike sail, in the 1970s. The beach influence was also seen in the development of the small fiberglass and aluminum catamaran, such as the Hobie Cat, introduced in 1968. Catamarans have proven so popular that, after losing the America's Cup in conventional 12-Meter class sloops in 1983, the American challenger Dennis Conner won back the trophy in 1988 with a sixty-foot catamaran with rigid wing sails. In the 1990s, lightweight experimental catamarans with rigid wing sails have become the world's fastest sailboats, capable of sailing twice as fast as the wind.

Powerboats changed, too, with more planing hulls, like the ubiquitous Boston Whaler, driven by increasingly light and powerful outboard motors. In the 1960s, "inboard-outboard" motors combined the power of a converted automobile engine with the light propeller and drive assembly of an outboard motor. This combination, adopted for ocean powerboat racing, is used in a wide variety of powerboats, from the racy "Cigarette" boats that became popularly associated with drug-running in Florida in the 1980s, to family-sized cruisers and sportfishing boats. The most recent "powerboat," which has attained tremendous popularity in the 1990s, is the "jet ski," the maritime equivalent of a motorcycle, powered by a jet of water.

Fiberglass hulls, outboard and inboard-outboard motors, and the rising popularity of boat trailering enabled millions of Americans to get on the water. The National Association of Engine and Boat Manufacturers (now the National Marine Manufacturers Association) has estimated the number of boats in commission in America over the years. The number for 1930 was 1,500,000 and, although no further estimates were made during the 1930s, by the end of that depression

California and Hawaiian beach culture influenced the way young Americans experienced the sea, beginning in the 1960s. Hobart "Hobie" Alter brought experience as a surfer and a fascination with Hawaiian outrigger canoes to the design of the Hobie Cat, which he introduced in 1968. With its rockered fiberglass hulls, aluminum frame, trampoline deck, and wing-like sail, this catamaran sailboat was light and fast, and could be sailed right off the beach, which made it immediately attractive to many beachgoers who had never before been interested in sailing. Here, Hobie Alter demonstrates the excitement of heeling one of his fourteen-foot Hobie Cats for a wild ride in the surf. (M.S.M. 94.125, Yachting Magazine Collection)

decade the total was perhaps 1,750,000. This figure doubled by 1950 to 3,510,000, a reflection of the postwar boating boom. By 1961, industry estimates had doubled again to 7,175,000. By 1996 the projection was 15,830,000 boats in use in the United States. By the mid-1990s nearly 80 million people were involved in recreational boating. Not surprisingly, the greatest concentrations have been on the coasts. Florida and California rank high, and Michigan with its 10,000 lakes leads all the states in the number of registered boats. Since the registration and regulation of most small boats is a state function, sta-

tistics are difficult to verify, and figures for registered boats do not take into account canoes, dinghies, sailboards, and other small surfboard-like "boats." Nevertheless, it is clear that more Americans than ever before seek recreation on the water.

The explosion in recreational boating has had a profound impact on the shoreline. Boatyards and marinas have proliferated, along with manufacturers of boats, engines, sails, and equipment. It is estimated that Americans in the 1990s spend close to 20 billion dollars a year on the water.

Fun on the water has also created serious public policy issues. People driving boats often behave no differently on the water than on the highways. Summer weekends on some waterways resemble summer traffic on interstate highways. Collisions and accidents are on the rise as well as distress calls coming from people inexperienced and unprepared for the hazards and responsibilities of the sport. Recognizing the problem, many states have taken steps towards tougher law enforcement and training for boat operators, and by the late 1990s a few states had adopted mandatory operator-licensing programs.

Environmental issues have accompanied the growth of pleasure boating. The proliferation of marinas has put considerable pressure on the fragile shoreline in many boating areas. In other cases the growth of homes and businesses along the shore has infringed on the public's access to the waterfront. Recreational boating also poses a threat to wildlife. The endangered manatee in Florida faces extinction in part because of collisions with motorboats. Along the East and West Coasts, whale-watching has become an issue. Commercial whale-watching vessels have too often drawn dangerously close to whales and invaded their feeding grounds. To protect sea mammals from danger and harassment both state and federal governments have established regulations to control vessel activity near them.

Issues of waste disposal have also emerged. The concentration of recreational boaters in particular locations has often caused severe pollution. Protected waters such as mooring areas, bays, and coves have seen unacceptable levels of human pollution. Regulations requiring proper disposal of waste have been enacted since the 1970s, but enforcement is difficult. While new boats may be required to have waste-disposal systems, millions of older boats have virtually no system at all, and facilities for pumping out waste-disposal tanks aboard boats are neither numerous or convenient enough to solve the problem.

While small boats attract millions of Americans, large ships also hold an allure. As steam conquered the Atlantic, the age of the great transatlantic liner emerged. Huge vessels, each trying to make the passage in record time, carried millions of passengers. It was "the only way to cross." These vessels were often the floating equivalent of grand hotels, with elegant dining rooms and finely appointed lounges, at least for those in first class, but their purpose was transportation. Albeit large and elegant, the liners were, after all, ferries.

In the years following World War II, shipowners, facing a declining market, struggled to find new ways to use their ships. Passenger aircraft were now capable of carrying numbers of passengers across the Atlantic in a fraction of the time required for a sea voyage. Added to this new problem of a shrinking market was the continuing issue of what to do with liners during winter months, when bookings were minimal.

Britain's Cunard Line was one of the first to see an opportunity to market its luxury liners to a growing population in Europe and America whose interests were less in traveling from point to point, and more in simply enjoying the ambiance of cruising. The availability of ships for winter cruising matched nicely with the desire of travelers anxious for a winter vacation in warm climes.

Liners, however, do not necessarily make good cruise ships. Originally built to endure the harsh Atlantic, these vessels were designed to draw passengers inside. Promenades were protected and enclosed. Swimming pools were relatively small and enclosed. Outside activities were limited, and entertainment was limited. Cruise ships, whose sailing tracks were in warm water, and whose function was entertainment, had different requirements. Open decks, pools, playing courts, spas, nightclubs, and large public areas were paramount. In 1947 Cunard built its first vessel designed for the cruise trade, *Caronia*, with accommodations for 860 passengers. Cunard's venture was a success, and the number of people booking on "liners to the sun" increased.

The shift came at a time when the transatlantic passenger business was declining. Improvements in air transport spelled doom for the great passengers liners and 1958 was a pivotal year. In that year, one million people crossed the Atlantic in thirty liners, while overhead the first commercial jet flew the same route. The following year 1.5 million people flew across the Atlantic. The age of the transatlantic liner was coming to an end.

As airlines served more and more passengers, liners were shifted from Atlantic crossings to cruising. Black hulls were painted gleaming white, decks were opened, cruise directors hired, and entertainment became the focus of the voyage. For those accustomed to sailing on the classic liners, perhaps the most dramatic change on a cruise ship was the elimination of classes. Cabins, as well as other facilities, including lounges and dining rooms, which had been segregated by classes, were made available to all passengers regardless of their status. While accommodations aboard ships varied considerably, from elegant penthouses with verandas to tiny inside cabins near the waterline, once passengers left their sleeping quarters all were entitled equally to use the ship's facilities.

The largest cruise ship yet built, the Carnival Destiny *entered service for Carnival Cruise Lines in 1996. Built in Italy and registered in Panama, the 893-foot vessel is the first Panamax cruise ship, with a beam too wide to fit the Panama Canal locks. Reflecting the great popularity of Caribbean cruising, the* Carnival Destiny *accommodates more than 2,600 passengers, served by a crew of 1,000. The ship was photographed departing the modern port of Miami. (Courtesy Carnival Cruise Lines; Andy Newman photo)*

In the rush to cruising, the American merchant marine was left out. Stiff competition kept fares low so that the high costs of operation put American vessels at a serious disadvantage. European lines faced with similar challenges sought flags of convenience in an effort to keep crew and vessel costs at a minimum. The only American cruise vessels to survive were those protected by the provisions of the Jones Act. To comply with its provisions, foreign-registry cruise ships sailing from U.S. ports must stop in a foreign destination. Thus, Florida-based ships make port calls in the Bahamas, Caribbean Islands, or Cozumel, Mexico. Congress passed the Cruise Ship Competitiveness Act of 1992, which permitted gambling on U.S.-flag cruise ships, in order to give American operators an even chance.

As fleets have swelled, cruise lines have engaged in fierce competition. Some have turned to "niche marketing." Historical cruises, natural-history voyages, and other special-interest itineraries have been created to attract discrete groups. Even Disney has gotten into the act, building two large vessels, the *Disney Magic* and *Disney Wonder,* aimed at the family market.

Economies of scale have played a role as well. The Carnival Corporation has assembled a large fleet, absorbing Holland-America Line and several other cruise operators, and putting its vessels in foreign registry. Larger vessels are more economical as well. At more than 101,000 tons, the 893-foot *Carnival Destiny* is typical of this new class of vessel.

Although among the largest, the *Carnival Destiny* is only one of approximately a dozen new cruise vessels scheduled to enter service before the year 2000. Aimed at the growing American market, most of these vessels will sail from New York, from Miami or Port Canaveral, Florida, or from Los Angeles for cruises to resorts on the west coast of Mexico. By the middle of the 1990s, nearly five million Americans were booking cruises every year.

Hollywood and the Sea: American Maritime Movies

While the seafaring experience has found expression in literature and painting since America's colonial times, the twentieth century brought the sights and sounds of the sea to a mass audience through the wonder of motion pictures and the unbridled imaginations of moviemakers. A striking demonstration of cinematic achievement in the name of art, or of popular taste, was what happened to Herman Melville's great American novel, *Moby-Dick*.

Melville's literary efforts, so long slighted by readers and critics, emerged from relative obscurity during the 1920s and inspired filmmakers, along with battalions of literary critics, to interpret Melville's genius for the masses. The 1955 version of *Moby Dick*, directed by John Huston, starring Gregory Peck and Richard Basehart, and employing a screenplay substantially crafted by the science-fiction writer Ray Bradbury, still remains a hardy perennial. It persists, like many other film "classics," largely through the availability of innumerable videotape copies and frequent showings on cable television. Over many decades Melville's *Moby-Dick* has inspired a wide range of interpretations, including a futuristic rendition through one of the popu-

lar *Star Trek* films and a production in which television's second-generation *Star Trek* commander, Patrick Stewart, takes on the role of Ahab, while Gregory Peck appears in the cameo role of Father Mapple (played by Orson Welles in the 1950s version).

Even before sound came to film, a silent rendition of Herman Melville's classic mid-nineteenth-century novel had appeared, soon to be followed by an early sound version. Entitled *The Sea Beast*, and starring the wildly popular romantic stage actor, John Barrymore, this Warner Brothers' production was remarkable for its free-wheeling "improvements" over Melville's original story. As the producer, S.R. Buchman, explained, "the screen version of *Moby-Dick* exceeds the book"—not through "a profanely wanton alteration" or by "an aimless unprincipled desire for melodramatic heightening," but rather by a reworking of the plot so that Ahab could return safely to the woman he loved, "with mind restored, and with some of earth's possessions and happiness."

This Hollywood effort to remedy Melville's "infatuation with the 'relentless,'" as Mr. Buchman explained in his introduction to a 1925 edition of *Moby-Dick*, was intended as

a salutary corrective to the "horrible persecution" inflicted by the original author, who had "heartlessly cold-decked" poor Ahab. The Hollywood rendition was thus far better by providing "a kind of justice which satisfies rudimentary humaneness and compassion." Of course, this also involved, in the producer's words, "the construction of [Ahab's] early history, which shows that the loss of his leg had cost Ahab the woman he loved because an envious brother had suggested that her love for Ahab would henceforth be mere pity." That Ahab kills Moby-Dick, and that the meddlesome brother is coincidentally shanghaied aboard the whaler *Pequod* so that he can subsequently lose *his* life, suggests how far moviemakers might go in search of a happy and morally appropriate ending.

In the case of Melville's *Billy Budd*, unfinished at his death and published only after many years had elapsed, the moviemakers could hardly avoid the fact of Billy's death, so the ending was not to be happy. However, following a stark and intelligent 1949 version of *Billy Budd* on stage, written by Louis Coxe and Robert Chapman, there appeared in 1962 a closely-related Anglo-Allied film production, starring Peter Ustinov (who also served as

MGM combined popular stars Spencer Tracy, Lionel Barrymore, Mickey Rooney, and Freddie Bartholomew with scenes shot aboard actual fishing schooners to produce the 1937 interpretation of Rudyard Kipling's **Captains Courageous.**

director, scriptwriter, and producer), Robert Ryan, Melvin Douglas, and the young Terence Stamp as Billy. The film created its own message by having Ustinov's Captain Vere abandon his responsibilities of command in an act of revulsion–"I'm only a man, not fit to do the work of God or the Devil"– and immediately perish in battle. The audience, then, was to be satisfied both with a suitable act of divine retribution and an assurance that Billy Budd did not die in vain, but that his death inspired a better relationship among men and officers in the British Royal Navy.

Such presumably well-intentioned correctives to an author's original intent appeared in Hollywood's greatest success in rewriting

both history and the literature inspired by historical events: the 1780s mutiny on HMS *Bounty*. Of several movie versions of this episode, by far the most successful and memorable was the 1935 film in which Charles Laughton portrayed a crude, sadistic Captain Bligh and Clark Gable presented Fletcher Christian as heroic, mature, and a natural leader of men. Based on the enormously successful 1933 novel by Charles Nordhoff and James Norman Hall, this Oscar-winning *Mutiny on the Bounty*, as it emerged from Hollywood, managed to rewrite both novel and actual incident to the point where Bligh now commands, and wrecks, HMS *Pandora* in search of the mutineers, and the fictional character Roger Byam (played by Franchot

Tone) inspires the British naval establishment to reform itself so that the Royal Navy can rule the seas in an enlightened, humane manner. Once again, the relatively happy ending and the undeniably inspirational message are provided.

Hollywood's inspirational evocations of seafaring demonstrate, however unintentionally, how the sea breaks down parochial barriers and connects nations and cultures, so that America's experience with the sea is not confined alone to the seagoing experience of Americans. A particularly arresting example appears in the resignation speech of United States Secretary of Education William Bennett in September, 1988. As the historian and anthropologist Greg Dening relates, in his *Mr. Bligh's Bad Language: Passion, Power, and Theatre on the Bounty*, Mr. Bennett "had voiced a fear. . . that children of today are ignorant of their history. There should be more history in American schools, Mr. Bennett had been saying, but 'real history,' history that children could learn. Every American child, he was saying now on Public Radio, should know, for example, why there was a mutiny on the *Bounty*."

One may imagine, moreover, that Mr. Bennett's appreciation of the *Bounty* incident came not from the later film portrayals, such as the 1962 version, with Trevor Howard as Bligh and Marlon Brando as Christian, or 1984's notably ambiguous rendering of the *Bounty* mutiny through

Anthony Hopkins' Bligh and Mel Gibson's Christian. While far more lavish in production and, on occasion, more faithful to the historical episode, these later film portrayals failed as commercial ventures if only because their "message" was muddled and their plot resolutions unsatisfactory for a public that looked to history for useful if not inspirational lessons to guide the present.

Rudyard Kipling's short novel *Captains Courageous*, another durable classic of the sea, portrayed late-nineteenth-century American cod fishing on the Grand Banks while providing a suitably inspirational evocation of solidarity and communal obligations on board a fishing schooner from Gloucester, Massachusetts. Kipling's central character, young Harvey Cheyne, quickly casts off his selfish preoccupation and snobbish arrogance to become one of the schooner's crew and gain a remarkable level of skill and maturity in an even more remarkably brief time. When first translated into film in 1936, the story shifted to an exploration of a father (or in this instance surrogate father) and son relationship, and the point of Kipling's book largely disappeared, to be replaced by undeniably entertaining and moving portrayals by Spencer Tracy, Lionel Barrymore, and child star Freddie Bartholomew. In more recent years two made-for-television versions of *Captains Courageous* came far closer to the Kipling original and to his evocation of life under sail, but for most viewers the enduring version

would remain Hollywood's original tear-jerking epic. Somewhat more effective in conveying its message of the sea and individual maturation is the 1949 film *Down to the Sea in Ships* in which Lionel Barrymore once again is the old salt who combines with his first mate (Richard Widmark) to bring a rebellious youth (Dean Stockwell) to accept a life of duty and responsibility.

Other American maritime literary classics have fared far worse, notably Richard Henry Dana's *Two Years Before the Mast*, which emerged from Hollywood in 1946 in a virtually unrecognizable form. Starring Alan Ladd, Brian Donlevy, William Bendix, and Howard da Silva (some of the most popular film actors of the era), this version of Dana showed that moviemakers had lost neither the imaginative touch nor the artistic license that was so apparent in the 1920s creative destruction of *Moby-Dick*.

At times Hollywood produced impressive work, notably the long documentary account of *Victory at Sea*, which enjoyed the great benefit of Richard Rodgers' musical score and for many decades has been a staple of television broadcasting. The Second World War experience at sea produced dozens of films, with Atlantic convoy struggles against the German submarine menace sharing popularity with naval battles that ranged from individual submarine exploits to major fleet actions throughout the Pacific. The titles of films made during or shortly after the war indicate a fair range

of naval subject, although the drama of close quarters and undersea vulnerability may explain the predominance of submarine epics.

Such war-inspired films include: *Action in the North Atlantic* (1943), *Guadalcanal Diary* (1943), *Operation Pacific* (1951), *The Enemy Below* (1957), *Torpedo Run* (1958), *Run Silent, Run Deep* (1958), *Up Periscope* (1959), *PT 109* (1963), *In Harm's Way* (1965), and *Midway* (1976). In a lighter vein, there is "McHale's Navy" as both television series and feature film. Seagoing life and the stereotypical sailor as subjects for comedy also appear in films ranging from Popeye cartoons to Henry Fonda's 1955 portrayal of *Mr. Roberts*.

The American Civil War has received little attention beyond occasional brief re-creations of the *Monitor* and *Virginia* battle, and American naval elements of the immediate postwar era are scarcely represented beyond an occasional movie version of Jules Verne's fantasy, *20,000 Leagues Under the Sea*. The cooperation of the United States Navy has permitted Hollywood to venture with some considerable semblance of authority into the modern world of techno-thrillers, such as *The Hunt for Red October* (1990), with the ever-durable Sean Connery as the Russian submarine commander. The navy also became involved in science-fantasy, with *The Final Countdown* (1980), which plays the historical game of "what if" by transporting the modern aircraft carrier USS *Nimitz* through a time warp to the days before the 1941 attack on Pearl Harbor.

Naval action in the age of sail is relatively easier to portray than that of the machine age. The "yo-heave-ho" life has been a favorite subject for Hollywood's moviemakers, so that in his pre-Ahab days Gregory Peck could appear as the resourceful British *Captain Horatio Hornblower* (1951) of C.S. Forester's series of Naploeonic-War novels that cover the romance, brutality, and carnage of fighting sail. Among notables of the sailing age, John Paul Jones has his film biography, as have Captain Kidd and a number of other pirates. Hollywood-produced pirate movies have persisted impressively in quantity if not quality over many decades. Whether set in the past, present, or future, the swashbuckling hero or villain (be it man or woman) remains a Hollywood fixture.

Going beyond the shot-and-shell heroics of naval encounters, any sort of ship disaster has great movie-making appeal, so that the *Lusitania* has been sunk on film almost as often as the *Titanic*, with the latter vessel's catastrophic demise even managing to make it onto Broadway as a musical production. Another maritime disaster that initially found its way into song and then into television documentary is the horrifying and still-debated sinking in November, 1975 of the huge bulk carrier known as the Queen of the Great Lakes, the SS *Edmund Fitzgerald*.

Even when the vessel is not the subject, it may be the locus of dramatic conflict, as both Herman Wouk's novel and the gripping 1954 movie version of *The Caine Mutiny* demonstrate. In this light, one may compare Spencer Tracy's 1958 film portrayal and Anthony Quinn's 1990 version with Ernest Hemingway's celebrated account of *The Old Man and the Sea*. In recent years the 1842 tragedy of the *Somers* has been portrayed in a semi-documentary film, and the infamous yet ultimately inspiring episode of the revolt and trial of the African captives on the schooner *Amistad* is the subject of a full-length treatment directed by Steven Spielberg and filmed in part at the maritime centers of Newport, Rhode Island, and Mystic Seaport in Connecticut.

Other maritime films of note include the early *Down to the Sea in Ships* (1923), with the silent film star Clara Bow, as it portrays a Quaker whaling village. Elia Kazan's classic rendering of New York Port longshoremen, *On the Waterfront* (1954), starring Marlon Brando, may be compared usefully with a more recent documentary, *Longshoremen and Automation: The Changing Face of the Waterfront* (1986), which examines the impact of containerization on the traditional longshoremen's culture in San Francisco. And then, when everyone thought the shoreline was safe, if not peaceful, scary evidence to the contrary came in the form of *Jaws* (1975).

Film versions of historical vessels and seafaring episodes may impose considerably greater costs and technical difficulties than do cinematic re-creations of their land-based military counterparts, yet moviemakers recognize the durable fascination that the sea holds even for those who never venture on the water except in their imaginations. One may wonder if the next stage for such vicarious enjoyment will come through computer-based developments in virtual reality, and whether the consequent assault on many, if not all, the senses will provide more of an American seafaring experience than one expects—or desires.

Edward W. Sloan

Americans and the Sea at the End of the Twentieth century

Despite the continuing growth of America's maritime activity through the second half of the twentieth century, it no longer attracts the nation's attention as it once did. For one thing, American maritime enterprise shows little promise as an opportunity for investment or employment. The number of shipboard billets has fallen from a postwar high of more than 50,000 to less than 10,000 at century's end, and shipbuilding jobs have undergone a similar decline. Another factor is that much of today's maritime activity is virtually invisible to the American public. Containerships load and discharge their cargoes in areas far removed from downtown waterfronts and rarely remain in port for more than twenty-four hours. Oil tankers often unload at offshore terminals. No longer do the *New York Times* or other seaport newspapers give prominent play to the arrival and departure of vessels. Modern shipping has little of the romance and mystique that surrounded the sailing vessels of the nineteenth century and the steamships of the pre-World War II era. To many observers, merchant vessels are no longer so welcome a sight as they once were. Flying foreign flags and manned by foreign seamen, these vessels are seen by some as a threat to the environment; by others as an obstruction to their own use of the waterfront and coastal waters; and by still others as a grim reminder of what has been lost.

It may be too soon to suggest that the decline of fishing off our coasts will also reduce the public's awareness of maritime activities, but unless present trends are reversed, fishing vessels will, like American-flag merchant ships, gradually disappear from our waters. Fish raised by the far-less-visible aquaculture industry are even now taking the place of traditionally harvested species of seafood, and fish farms will undoubtedly continue to win an increasing share of the market. Declining stocks of striped bass, tuna, and other species sought by amateur fishermen may in time affect the popularity of sports fishing.

A third reason why Americans' awareness of maritime activities has diminished in the second half of the twentieth century is ironically due to the nation's overwhelming naval power. An unchallenged navy makes for good national defense but poor newspaper copy. Perhaps the dearth of recent naval action, except fictionally as in the nuclear submarine movies, explains the continuing popularity of television reruns featuring World War II naval action. It surely helps us understand the appeal of Patrick O'Brian's novels about the British Royal Navy during the Napoleonic era. Even though the U. S. Navy has no present opposition to its command of the world's oceans, its movements generally remain hidden from view. The advent of nuclear power and the intercontinental ballistic missile gives the nation's submarines the ability to obliterate enemy targets thousands of miles away without disclosing their own positions.

Finally, the ocean as an arena for adventure now has competition. The advent of the space age has altered the focus of the public imagination from the sea around us to the skies above. Exploration of the solar system, including manned landings on the moon, has attracted billions of dollars and thousands of scientists and engineers in the years since the launching of *Sputnik* in 1957. The box-office records set by the *Star Wars* film trilogy and the continuing appeal of the *Star Trek* television series testifies to the popularity of themes focused on space. Like sea travel, air and space travel both focus on a vessel in an alien environment. In view of the fact that space exploration has largely replaced oceanic research in the nation's attention, it is fittingly ironic that space craft have been named for such famous vessels as *Columbia, Challenger, Discovery, Atlantis,* and *Endeavour.*

Even as the American public's interest in maritime affairs has declined in recent decades, the nature of those activities has also changed. Our waters have become increasingly privatized. For centuries, while Americans acquired the interior of the continent and divided it up into their own private parcels, the nation's harbors, bays, and inland waterways remained in the public domain, easily accessible to all for commercial purposes. But this once easy come-and-go access to the waterfront, where vessel owners could load or discharge cargoes at a public wharf, build a small boat, or leave nets to dry, has virtually disappeared. In many waterside communities a similar pattern of privatizing has severely reduced public access to beaches, a situation aided in part by the "taking" rulings of some state and federal courts, which legitimize claims of private property owners. In the place of public facilities, shorefront property has been sold for hotels, condominiums, and other buildings whose purposes have little to do with use of the water.

Municipalities have also allowed privately owned marinas to extend their floats far out into public waters, where they obstruct both free navigation and an open vista from the shore. Entrepreneurs now have the privilege and profit of renting out hundreds of private moorings in harbor waters, and mariners in transit are hard-pressed to find free space for anchoring. On the other hand, these private facilities have enabled millions of Americans living at a distance from the water and able to pay the price to moor their pleasure boat at the nearest marina for weekend use. Others less well off can bring their boats to the water by trailer and launch them at a public or private ramp.

The rise of boating in the years since World War II has brought a marked shift from collective to individual maritime experiences. Until the war most Americans who traveled by water did so in large groups, whether as passengers on an eight-day ocean crossing or as excursionists on an eight-hour local outing. During the past fifty years, however, the ocean liners and coastal steamers have been replaced by literally millions of private small craft carrying at most three or four people. "Passengers" have now become "operators," and while they may wave at passing vessels their experiences remain separate, unshared with others on the same water. In social terms the motorboat has become the waterborne equivalent of the automobile.

As today's recreational boat operator takes to the water, however, he would do well to remember that if he gets into difficulty the Coast Guard will no longer automatically come to his aid, for the rescue business has to a considerable extent been turned over to private entrepreneurs. The closing of many Coast Guard stations, the automation of most lighthouses, and the removal of all lightships along our coasts, taken together, mean that no longer is there a single, resourceful organization looking out for those who go to sea. Innovative electronic gear, such as depth sounders, radar, loran, and now global-positioning-satellite

receivers, have provided the mariner with improved means of preventing disaster, and if trouble comes he does have far better means of calling for help than his predecessors. Once alerted, Coast Guard helicopters can reach the scene more quickly and rescue potential victims from danger more effectively than in the past. Nevertheless, traditionalists among the seagoing public miss the comforting notion that someone, somewhere, is watching.

Even the "seashore" experience has changed in the years since World War I. Before then, families spending a two-week vacation at the seashore usually did so as guests at one of the grand hotels, eating with other vacationers in the dining room and participating in at least some of the resort's group activities such as a fishing party or an afternoon sail. Today's seaside visitors, if they do not already own a cottage at the beach, rent one, possibly with relatives or one other family, set up housekeeping, and enjoy a much more private vacation. Only the town or state beach remains to represent the great tradition of seaside facilities truly open to the public.

Modern trends have brought marked changes in the mariner's way of life. Distinctions that once sharply separated the sailor from the landsman have almost disappeared. No longer can the mariner be dismissed as an illiterate "squarehead" and social pariah unfit for any decent employment ashore. Americans who work at sea are probably as well-educated as land-based workers; in fact, because their time at sea is strictly limited by the shortage of billets, many mariners are land-based workers for half the year. The mariner ashore is no longer confined to "sailortown" because there are no more sailortowns. When at sea, seamen are no longer consigned to a crowded "fo'c'sle" up in the vessel's bow, far removed from "officers' country" back aft. Officers and men now occupy similar quarters together in the ship's single deckhouse. Regulations governing labor conditions, from hours worked and overtime pay rates to workplace environment and safety regulations, now adhere far more closely to the standards prevalent in most shoreside employment. Perhaps no other comparable period in our nation's history has seen so many remarkable changes in the way Americans use the sea as have the five and a half decades between 1945 and the century's end.

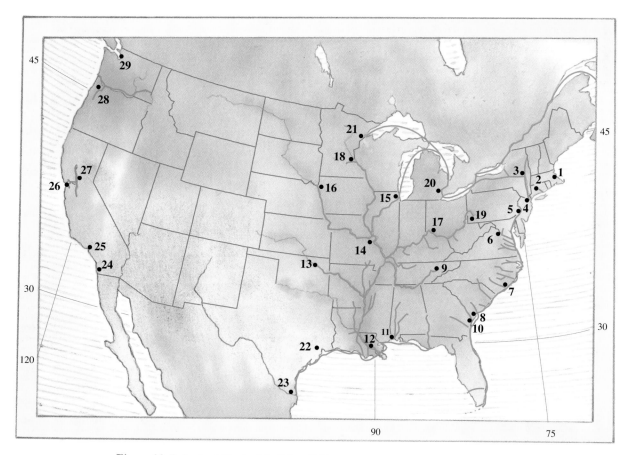

Figure 10 Principal Navigable Inland Waterways, Late Twentieth Century.

Navigable Inland Waterways (Rivers, Canals, Intra-coastal Waterways)

Principal Cities

1. Boston, Massachusetts
2. Hartford, Connecticut
3. Albany, New York
4. New York City, New York
5. Philadelphia, Pennsylvania
6. Washington, DC
7. Wilmington, North Carolina
8. Charleston, South Carolina
9. Knoxville, Tennessee
10. Savannah, Georgia
11. Mobile, Alabama
12. New Orleans, Louisiana
13. Tulsa, Oklahoma
14. St. Louis, Missouri
15. Chicago, Illinois
16. Sioux City, Iowa
17. Cincinnati, Ohio
18. Minneapolis/St. Paul, Minnesota
19. Pittsburgh, Pennsylvania
20. Detroit, Michigan
21. Duluth, Minnesota
22. Houston, Texas
23. Brownsville, Texas
24. San Diego, California
25. Los Angeles, California
26. San Francisco, California
27. Sacramento, California
28. Portland, Oregon
29. Seattle, Washington

(Dennis O'Brien map)

The Legacy of America's Maritime Past

The sea has favored North America with many gifts. First, by concealing the continent from peoples in other parts of the world (except of course from the Asians who had already crossed by land bridge during the ice age) the oceans contributed to the definition of America as a New World, an attractive sanctuary from the real or imagined oppressions of the Old. By the end of the fifteenth century, development of the vessels and navigational skills needed for deep-water voyages made possible the discovery of transatlantic sea routes favored by steady winds and currents. Settlers followed explorers in the seventeenth century as thousands of Europeans looking for a better life arrived in this "promised land." The Reverend Thomas Allen observed on the eve of the American Revolution that "our forebears left the delightful abodes of their native country and passed a raging sea that in these then solitary climes they might enjoy civil and religious liberty, and never more feel the hand of tyranny and persecution." In the course of the next two centuries some thir-

ty million more people from Europe, Africa, and Asia would reach these shores by sea, many with eager anticipation, others against their will. This paradoxical role of the Atlantic Ocean, isolating the New World from the Old as a sanctuary while at the same time providing access for the world's oppressed, guaranteed that America would become a land of immigrants. This was the nation's first and most important "gift from the sea."

At the same time, the Atlantic Ocean gave American settlers an essential lifeline back to the world they or their forebears had left behind, as well as to other colonies along the coast from Newfoundland to the West Indies. No new settlement of Europeans could exist without support from home or contact with other established colonies during its first difficult years. Maritime trade, which began as a matter of survival, in time became a means of improving the settlers' standard of living. This commerce expanded during the eighteenth and nineteenth centuries, enhanced by access through the Pacific Ocean to the continent's west coast, to

many hundreds of island archipelagoes, and to the continent of Asia itself—the fabled passage to India. As subsistence grew to improvement, so improvement came to prosperity, and in the process merchants and shipowners gradually accumulated the capital needed to establish factories, railroads, and other industrial enterprises. In time, maritime commerce provided ever-expanding markets for American manufactured goods as well as raw materials, until today the United States is both the world's most active foreign trading nation and also its most prosperous. Maritime commerce is America's second significant gift from the sea.

The role of the sea as a moat separating America from foreign powers has also made an important contribution to our national development. While an ocean does not in itself guarantee immunity from invasion, as the Revolutionary War showed, bodies of water as extensive as the Atlantic and Pacific Oceans offer considerable protection even against a strong naval power. In large part because of this geographical separation, the United States needed to spend very little on national defense during the century between 1815 and 1915, making more federal funds available for subsidizing such internal improvements as the transcontinental railroad and oceanic steamship lines. Diplomatic isolation from Europe, although never complete, was sufficient to leave the nation free to concentrate on resolving the domestic conflict over slavery. In the twentieth century, when two world wars brought enormous damage to the homelands of most of the belligerents, the mainland territories of the United States escaped virtually unscathed. For the first 350 years of its settlement by Europeans, the sea has provided the American people with an almost impervious shield. Not until the development of the intercontinental ballistic missile in the years after World War II have the oceans lost their defensive power. These oceanic moats have been an important strategic legacy to the American people.

Where the sea met the land's edge along the Atlantic coast, it gave North America yet another gift–scores of inlets, bays, and river estuaries suitable as safe harbors. Some that were near the offshore banks became fishing ports; those close to forests were shipbuilding centers; and others with access to other coastal communities or interior settlements developed into major seaports. In the history of a land whose first several generations of settlers were predominantly farmers, the

In honor of the U.S. Navy's two-hundredth anniversary, the 200-year-old USS Constitution *made a symbolic passage under sail in July 1997. (© Benjamin Mendlowitz)*

importance of seaports is not always easy to establish. Their significance to America's early history appears on several levels. First are the fishing communities whose efforts not only provided a source of food but an equally important commodity for trade throughout the Atlantic world. Second, the shipbuilding centers produced the vessels on which an independent maritime commerce depended. Without the capacity to construct vessels of their own,

Americans would have been utterly dependent on British shipowners for the carriage of exports and imports, a situation that might well have continued for decades after American political independence and would surely have impeded the economic growth of the new nation for many years.

Seaports large enough to serve as entrepôts made other, entirely different contributions to American life.

Although modest in size until the nineteenth century, they nevertheless became the nation's first cities, attracting a diverse population of artisans, shopkeepers, merchants, and professional men, most of whom had special skills. Individually, they imported, sold, or produced items needed by the vast rural population. Their workers constituted a versatile labor force, and the flow of immigrants into the seaports constantly replenished the supply of labor for projects throughout the country. Collectively, seaport dwellers comprised a market for agricultural commodities, providing farmers a means of earning a profit for their surplus produce. Through their banks and insurance companies, seaport merchants accumulated the capital that gave American

industry its start. Culturally, seaports connected the nation with the rest of the world, including other communities along the coast. Here were found our first newspapers, libraries, and colleges. Here itinerant artists, theatrical performers, dancing instructors, and architects all vied for the custom of the seaport's wealthier inhabitants. Seaports were another legacy of the sea, bringing to the American continent all the benefits as well as the drawbacks of urban life.

The enduring symbol for American maritime enterprise has been the sailing ship, and what a complex symbol it is. The design of a seagoing vessel was one of humankind's most notable achievements, combining the often contradictory attributes of stability,

Much has changed in America's relationship with the sea, but the nature of the sea itself has not changed. Winslow Homer's **The Life Line** *of 1884 still accurately symbolizes our tenuous relationship with the largest natural feature on earth. (Courtesy Philadelphia Museum of Art; George W. Elkins Collection)*

strength, capacity, economy, and speed. For Horatio Greenough, America's premier sculptor of the mid-nineteenth century, the sailing vessel was an inspiration. "Mark the majestic form of her hull as she rushes through the water," he wrote. "Observe the graceful bend of her body, the gentle transition from round to flat, the grasp of her keel, the leap of her bows, the symmetry and rich tracery of her spars and rigging, and those grand wind muscles, her sails." The sailing ship represents the most natural of all artifacts—a hull constructed of several species of timber, planks fastened with wooden treenails and caulked with cotton, deck seams payed with pitch, rigging made of hemp, and sails cut from hemp or cotton duck. And most important, it relied entirely on winds and currents to drive it across thousands of miles of the world's most severe environment—the open sea.

The symbolic meaning of the wooden sailing vessel went far beyond the maritime world. In one of the mid-nineteenth century's most popular poems, "The Building of the Ship," Henry Wadsworth Longfellow used the construction of a sailing vessel to symbolize the American union. His words may seem trite today, but every school child north of the Mason-Dixon Line on the eve of the Civil War knew them by heart:

Thou, too, sail on, O Ship of
    State!
Sail on, O Union, strong and
    great!
Humanity with all its fears,
With all the hopes of future
    years,
Is hanging breathless on thy
    fate.

No wonder that, unique among all of his artifacts, man has endowed the ship with human qualities, greeting its creation with the ceremonial bestowal of its own distinctive name. The sailing vessel, too, is an enduring part of our nation's maritime heritage.

At bottom, however, history is about people. Herein lies the greatest appeal of the maritime world as a subject for the historian. The sea offered American settlers an alternative way of life to that of the farmer—not an easier way or a more rewarding way, but a different one, as Daniel Vickers has so persuasively shown in his comparative study of fishermen and farmers. For a dispossessed son in a family without much land, or a lad bitten by the wanderlust, or simply one who had reasons of his own to leave home, going to sea was another way to live his life, or at least a part of it. Many a country boy shipped out with every intention of saving up his pay until he had enough to buy a farm, marry his girl, and settle down. It may not always have worked out that way, but the sea nevertheless seemed to offer that opportunity, at least until about the middle of the nineteenth century. The fact that life at sea was largely invisible to those who remained behind exposed it to a lot of exaggerated romanticizing, especially by writers and painters who never left the shore. But one does not have to exaggerate the stature of a full-rigged ship under sail or the dangers faced by its crew to believe that the lives of the men and women who worked at sea or dwelled along its edge deserve a place in American history. Knowledge of who went before us and how they lived and worked broadens and deepens our understanding of ourselves and our surroundings.

The central role of blacks in our maritime history should never be forgotten. The importation of Africans into

the New World directly profited hundreds of American merchants over the course of nearly two centuries. Building, outfitting, and manning slave vessels employed thousands of other Americans. Black slaves in the Caribbean raised and processed sugar into molasses, which, when made into rum by American distillers, helped purchase still more Africans into bondage. Slaveowners relied on Yankee fish, meat, and other provisions to feed their laborers. Blacks grew most of the tobacco, rice, and cotton exchanged by American merchants for the importation of cotton cloth and other manufactured goods from England and the rest of Europe. Profits earned by this trade in turn provided the capital on which was founded the American textile industry, itself largely dependent for its first half-century on slave-grown cotton. One simply cannot conceive of the Atlantic maritime world before 1860 without recognizing that enslaved Africans provided much of the labor on which it depended.

What makes the study of America and the sea so rewarding are the connections it makes between so many different aspects of our past—its regions, its produce, its people, its workplace cultures. The sea connects the lives of a broad cross-section of Americans—shipmasters, sailors, and fishermen at sea, with shipbuilders, owners, merchants, and mariners' wives at home. It joins the work of seafarers with that of farmers and factory workers.

Maritime enterprise brings the American people more closely together with those of other nations around the world. Shipboard life represents a microcosm of life itself, where hope and despair, courage and cowardice, greed and altruism, along with all the other human virtues and vices, are exposed by the never-ending struggle to bring order out of the chaos around us. For this reason, life at sea has provided countless authors, from Homer to Herman Melville, and from Joseph Conrad to Patrick O'Brian, with a special context in which to play out human dramas. It is remarkable how much maritime art, the formal ship portrait aside, also focuses on human themes. Unlike landscape paintings, in which more often than not the artist lets nature speak for itself, the seascape usually centers on the relationship between man and the sea. Copley's *Watson and the Shark*, Allston's *Rising of a Thunderstorm at Sea*, and Winslow Homer's *Life Line* are but three examples. The presence of human figures in these and other marine paintings suggests the overwhelming power of the open ocean, while the more placid sea found in the work of luminists like Fitz Hugh Lane remind us of the mariners' need for sheltered harbors. In either case, the sea has greatly enriched the work of our best writers and artists.

Literature, painting, and even theater, film, and music are all means by which our maritime past is conveyed to present and future generations, but the historian also has an important role in that mission. In earlier times the work of Carl Cutler, Arthur H. Clark, and Howard I. Chapelle stood on the shelves of many a private library. With the notable exceptions of Robert G. Albion and Samuel Eliot Morison, however, few American academic historians have considered themselves primarily maritime scholars. Nor do many of our academic institutions offer courses in the field, unlike their counterparts in Great Britain and throughout the European continent. Other than the maritime service academies, Mystic Seaport Museum is one of the few educational institutions of any sort that actually offers courses in American maritime studies. The Frank C. Munson Institute teaches graduate-level courses in maritime history and culture, and undergraduates participating in the Williams College-Mystic Seaport Maritime Studies Program can study the sea through courses in history, literature, science, and policy.

Today, several trends promise to change this state of affairs. One is the research now being undertaken by marine archaeologists at such institutions as Texas A & M University and East Carolina University. At the same time, a new generation of scholars has shed much new light on African-American seamen, the roles that women have played in the course of maritime history at sea and ashore, and the working conditions of fishermen, longshoremen, and common sailors, making up for the earlier focus on merchants and shipmasters. Finally, a number of historians, including the authors of this book, have endeavored to close the gap that has long separated the two themes of military and commercial uses of the sea. It is our hope that the present volume will further that goal as we weave naval affairs into the more inclusive field of maritime history.

The largest number of Americans are exposed to our nation's maritime past in museums, at least fifty-seven of which specialize in maritime history. Each year, hundreds of thousands of people learn about life at sea aboard the historic vessels preserved in floating condition at numerous sites around the country. The flagship of this fleet is of course the USS *Constitution*, still in commission at the Boston Navy Yard more than 200 years after its launch in 1797. Close by at Mystic Seaport lies the whaleship *Charles W. Morgan*, the oldest commercial vessel still afloat in American waters, while other examples of significant commercial and fishing vessels can be seen at South Street Seaport Museum in New York, the Chesapeake Bay Maritime Museum at St. Michaels, Maryland, the San Francisco National Maritime Historical Park, and the San Diego Maritime Museum, among others. Naval vessels abound, from the Spanish-American War cruiser *Olympia* in Philadelphia to the World War II battleships *Alabama*, *Massachusetts*, *North Carolina* and *Texas* in their respective states, the carriers *Intrepid*, *Lexington*, and *Yorktown*, and several dozen lesser warships.

Finally, one cannot fully understand maritime history without knowing about the sea itself and the life it supports. No modern writer has done more to inform Americans about the complex web of the sea than has the late Rachel Carson. Beyond her work as a skilled marine scientist, she wrote of the relationship between man and the sea in her remarkable trilogy *Under the Sea Wind*, *The Sea Around Us*, and *The Edge of the Sea*. Rachel Carson ended *The Edge of the Sea* with words that recall T.S. Eliot's "Dry Salvages":

> Now I hear the sea sounds about me; the night high tide is rising, swirling with a confused rush of waters against the rocks below my study window. . . . Hearing the rising tide, I think how it is pressing also against other shores I know—rising on a southern beach where there is no fog, but a moon edging all the waves with silver and touching the wet sands with lambent sheen, and on a still more distant shore sending its streaming currents against the moonlit pinnacles and the dark caves of the coral rock.

Then in my thoughts these shores, so different in their nature and in the inhabitants they support, are made one by the unifying touch of the sea. . . On all these shores there are echoes of past and future: of the flow of time, obliterating yet containing all that has gone before; of the sea's eternal rhythms— the tides, the beat of surf, the pressing rivers of the currents— shaping, changing, dominating; of the stream of life, flowing as inexorably as any ocean current, from past to unknown future.

The role of the sea in American affairs has constantly changed over 500 years—from a moat obscuring this continent from the Old World to a bridge for European explorers; from a defense against overseas invasion to a means of projecting American naval power around the world. Until about 1920 the oceans brought millions of immigrants to enrich our culture. More recently they have enabled Americans to export the materials of their culture to other peoples. American-flag merchant ships once plied the world's seas carrying the nation's foreign trade; now

the ships that enter and clear our ports fly almost every other flag but our own. The waters near our coasts were once a productive workplace for thousands of American fishermen; now they are becoming the playground for millions of recreational boaters and beach-goers. Through all the centuries and despite all the changes, the sea still influences the lives of Americans all across the continent and will continue to do so far into the future.

Appendix

American Maritime Museums

Many American museums contain collections relating to the nation's maritime history. The following fifty-seven members of the Council of American Maritime Museums specialize in the subject and are recommended to readers seeking further information on America's enduring relationship with the sea.

California
Maritime Museum Association of San Diego
North Harbor Drive, San Diego

Maritime Museum of Monterey
Custom House Plaza, Monterey

San Francisco Maritime National Historical Park
San Francisco

Connecticut
Connecticut River Museum
Main Street, Essex

Mystic Seaport
Mystic

U.S. Coast Guard Museum
U.S. Coast Guard Academy
Mohegan Avenue, New London

District of Columbia
Navy Museum
Washington Navy Yard

Smithsonian Institution
National Museum of American History

Georgia
Confederate Naval Historical Society
Atlanta

Hawaii
Hawaii Maritime Center
Pier 7, Honolulu

Louisiana
USS *Kidd* & Nautical Center
South River Road, Baton Rouge

Maine
Maine Maritime Museum
Washington Street, Bath
Penobscot Marine Museum
Searsport

Spring Point Museum
Southern Maine Technical College
South Portland

Maryland
Calvert Marine Museum
Solomons

Chesapeake Bay Maritime Museum
St. Michaels

Constellation Foundation, Inc.
Pier 1 Pratt Street, Baltimore

Radcliff Maritime Museum
The Maryland Historical Society
West Monument Street, Baltimore

U.S. Naval Academy Museum
U.S. Naval Academy, Annapolis

Massachusetts
Essex Shipbuilding Museum
Main Street, Essex

USS *Constitution*
Boston Naval Shipyard, Boston

USS *Constitution* Museum Foundation
Boston

Kendall Whaling Museum
Sharon

M.I.T. Museum, Hart Nautical Collection
Massachusetts Avenue, Cambridge

Nantucket Historical Association
Nantucket

New Bedford Whaling Museum
Johnny Cake Hill, New Bedford

Peabody Essex Museum
East India Square, Salem

Michigan
Michigan Maritime Museum
South Haven

New York
American Merchant Marine Museum
U.S. Merchant Marine Academy, Kings Point

Antique Boat Museum
Mary Street, Clayton

Cold Spring Harbor Whaling Museum
Main Street, Cold Spring Harbor

East End Seaport Maritime Museum
Third Street, Greenport

East Hampton Town Marine Museum
Main Street, East Hampton

Erie Canal Museum
Erie Blvd., East, Syracuse

Hudson River Maritime Museum
Rondout Landing, Kingston

Long Island Maritime Museum
West Sayville

South Street Seaport Museum
Front Street, New York

North Carolina
Graveyard of the Atlantic Museum
Hatteras Village

North Carolina Maritime Museum
Front Street, Beaufort

Ohio
Great Lakes Historical Society
Main Street, Vermilion

Oregon
Columbia River Maritime Museum
Marine Drive, Astoria

International Oceanographic Hero Foundation
Reedsport

Pennsylvania
Erie Maritime Museum
State Street, Erie

Independence Seaport Museum
Penns Landing, Philadelphia

Rhode Island
Herreshoff Marine Museum
Bristol

Museum of Yachting
Fort Adams State Park, Newport

South Carolina
Patriots Point Naval and Maritime Museum
Patriots Point, Mt. Pleasant

Texas
Texas Seaport Maritime Museum
Strand, Galveston

Vermont
Lake Champlain Maritime Museum
Basin Harbor, Vergennes

Virginia
Historic Naval Ships Association
Virginia Beach

Life-Saving Museum of Virginia
Virginia Beach

Mariners' Museum
Museum Drive, Newport News

Portsmouth Naval Shipyard Museum
High Street, Portsmouth

Washington
Center for Wooden Boats
Valley Street, Seattle

Northwest Seaport
Valley Street, Seattle

Puget Sound Maritime Historical Society
Seattle

Wisconsin
Wisconsin Maritime Museum
Maritime Drive, Manitowoc

America and the Sea
A Select Bibliography

General Works

For a more detailed bibliography of the subject of this volume see Robert G. Albion, *Naval and Maritime History: An Annotated Bibliography.* 4th ed. Mystic: Munson Institute, 1972, and Benjamin W. Labaree, *A Supplement (1971-1986) to Robert G. Albion's Naval and Maritime History: An Annotated Bibliography.* Mystic: Mystic Seaport, 1988.

Albion, Robert G. *Makers of Naval Policy, 1798-1947.* Annapolis, Maryland: Naval Institute Press, 1980.

————, et al. *New England and the Sea.* Mystic: Mystic Seaport, 1972.

————. *Sea Lanes in Wartime: The American Experience, 1775-1945,* 2nd ed. Hamden, Connecticut: Archon Books, 1968.

Baer, George W. *One Hundred Years of Sea Power: The U.S. Navy, 1890-1990.* Stanford, California: Stanford University Press, 1994.

Bass, George T. *Ships and Shipwrecks of the Americas: A History Based on Underwater Archaeology.* London: Thames and Hudson, 1988.

Bauer, K. Jack. *A Maritime History of the United States: The Role of America's Seas and Waterways.* Columbia: University of South Carolina Press, 1988.

Baughman, James P. *The Mallorys of Mystic: Six Generations in American Maritime Enterprise.* Middletown, Connecticut: Wesleyan University Press for Mystic Seaport, 1972.

Bender, Bert. *Sea-Brothers: The Tradition of American Sea Fiction from Moby-Dick to the Present.* Philadelphia: University of Pennsylvania Press, 1988.

Bess, H. David, and Martin Farris. *U.S. Maritime Policy: History and Prospects.* New York: Praeger, 1981.

Bolster, W. Jeffrey. *Black Jacks: African American Seamen in the Age of Sail.* Cambridge, Massachusetts: Harvard University Press, 1997.

Bradford, James C. *Admirals of the New Steel Navy: Makers of Naval Tradition, 1880-1930.* Annapolis, Maryland: Naval Institute Press, 1990.

————, ed. *Captains of the Old Steam Navy: Makers of the American Naval Tradition, 1840-1880.* Annapolis, Maryland: Naval Institute Press, 1986.

————, ed. *Command Under Sail: Makers of the American Naval Tradition, 1775-1850.* Annapolis, Maryland: Naval Institute Press, 1985.

————, ed. *Quarterdeck and Bridge: Two Centuries of American Naval Leaders.* Annapolis, Maryland: Naval Institute Press, 1996.

Braynard, Frank O. *Famous American Ships.* New York: Hastings House, 1956.

Brewington, Marion V. *Chesapeake Bay: A Pictorial Maritime History.* New York: Cornell Maritime Press, 1953.

Brouwer, Norman J. *International Register of Historic Ships.* 2nd ed. Peekskill, New York: Sea History Press, 1993.

Busch, Briton C. *The War Against the Seals: A History of the North American Seal Fishery.* Montreal and Kingston: McGill-Queens University Press, 1985.

————. *"Whaling Will Never Do For Me": The American Whaleman in the Nineteenth Century.* Lexington: University of Kentucky Press, 1994.

Butler, John A. *Sailing on Friday: The Perilous Voyage of America's Merchant Marine.* Washington, D.C.: Brassey's, 1997.

Canney, Donald L. *The Old Steam Navy: Frigates, Sloops, and Gunboats, 1815-1885.* Annapolis, Maryland: Naval Institute Press, 1990.

————. *The Old Steam Navy: The Ironclads, 1842-1885.* Annapolis, Maryland: Naval Institute Press, 1993.

————. *U.S. Coast Guard and Revenue Cutters, 1790-1935.* Annapolis, Maryland: Naval Institute Press, 1995.

Chapelle, Howard I. *The History of the American Sailing Navy: The Ships and Their Development.* New York: W.W. Norton, 1949.

————. *The Search for Speed Under Sail, 1700-1855.* New York: W.W. Norton, 1967.

Cogar, William B. *Dictionary of Admirals of the U.S. Navy, 1862-1918.* 2 vols. Annapolis, Maryland: Naval Institute Press, 1989, 1991.

Coletta, Paolo E. *The American Naval Heritage*. Lanham, New York: University Press of America, 1987.

———. *American Secretaries of the Navy, 1775-1972*. 2 vols. Annapolis, Maryland: Naval Institute Press, 1980.

———. *United States Navy and Marine Corps Bases*. 2 vols. Westport, Connecticut: Greenwood Publishing, 1985.

Coutau-Bégarie, Hervé. *L'Évolution de la Pensée Navale*. 6 vols. Paris: Economica, 1990-1997.

Creighton, Margaret S., and Lisa Norling, eds. *Iron Men, Wooden Women: Gender and Seafaring in the Atlantic World, 1700-1920*. Baltimore: Johns Hopkins University Press, 1996.

Deacon, Margaret. *Scientists and the Sea, 1650-1900: A Study of Marine Science*. London: Academic Press, 1971.

De La Pedraja, Rene. *The Rise and Decline of U.S. Merchant Shipping in the Twentieth Century*. New York: Twayne Publishers, 1992.

Dupree, A. Hunter. *Science in the Federal Government: A History of Policies and Activities to 1940*. Cambridge, Massachusetts: Harvard University Press, 1957.

Ellis, Richard. *Men and Whales*. New York: Alfred A. Knopf, 1991.

Evans, Stephen H. *The United States Coast Guard, 1790-1915. A Definitive History (With a Postscript 1915-1950)*. Annapolis, Maryland: Naval Institute Press, 1949.

Field, James A., Jr. *America and the Mediterranean World, 1776-1882*. Princeton, New Jersey: Princeton University Press, 1969.

Fostle, D.W. *Speedboat*. Mystic: Mystic Seaport Museum Stores, 1988.

Friedman, Norman. *U.S. Aircraft Carriers: An Illustrated Design History*. Annapolis, Maryland: Naval Institute Press, 1983.

———. *U.S. Battleships: An Illustrated Design History*. Annapolis, Maryland: Naval Institute Press, 1985.

———. *U.S. Cruisers: An Illustrated Design History*. Annapolis, Maryland: Naval Institute Press, 1984.

———. *U.S. Submarines Through 1945: An Illustrated Design History*. Annapolis, Maryland: Naval Institute Press, 1994.

Frye, John. *The Men All Singing: The Story of Menhaden Fishing*. Norfolk, Virginia: Donning, 1978.

Gibson, James R. *Otter Skins, Boston Ships, and China Goods: The Maritime Fur Trade of the Northwest Coast, 1785-1841*. Seattle: University of Washington Press, 1992.

Grossnik, Roy A. *United States Naval Aviation, 1910-1995*. Washington, D.C.: Naval Historical Center, 1997.

Guthorn, Peter J. *United States Coastal Charts*. Exton, Pennsylvania: Shillor Publishing, 1989.

Hagan, Kenneth J., ed. *In Peace and War: Interpretations of American Naval History, 1775-1978*. Westport, Connecticut: Greenwood Press, 1978.

———. *This People's Navy: The Making of American Sea Power*. New York: Free Press, 1991.

Harland, John. *Seamanship in the Age of Sail*. Annapolis, Maryland: Naval Institute Press, 1984.

Hattendorf, John B. ed., *Doing Naval History*. Newport, Rhode Island: Naval War College Press, 1995.

———, ed., *Maritime History*. 2 vols. Malabar, Florida: Krieger Publishing, 1996-97.

———, ed., *Ubi Sumus?: The State of Naval and Maritime History, 1994*.

———, and Robert S. Jordan, eds. *Maritime Strategy and the Balance of Power: Britain and America in the Twentieth Century*. London: MacMillan; New York: St. Martin's Press, 1989.

———, B. Mitchell Simpson III, and John R. Wadleigh. *Sailors and Scholars: The Centennial History of the U.S. Naval War College*. Newport, Rhode Island: Naval War College Press, 1984.

Havighurst, Walter. *The Long Ships Passing: The Story of the Great Lakes*. New York: MacMillan, 1975.

———. *Voices on the River: The Story of the Mississippi Waterways*. New York: MacMillan, 1964.

Heinl, Robert D., Jr. *Soldiers of the Sea: The U.S. Marine Corps, 1775-1962*. Annapolis, Maryland: Naval Institute Press, 1962.

Heinrich, Thomas R. *Ships for the Seven Seas: Philadelphia Shipbuilding in the Age of Industrial Capitalism*. Baltimore and London: Johns Hopkins University Press, 1997.

Herwig, Holger H. *Politics of Frustration: The United States in German Naval Planning, 1889-1941*. Boston: Little, Brown, 1976.

Hitchman, James H. *A Maritime History of the Pacific Coast, 1540-1980*. Lanham, Maryland: University Press of America, 1990.

Howarth, Stephen. *To Shining Sea: A History of the

United States Navy, 1775-1991. New York: Random House, 1991.

Howell, Colin, and Richard Twomey. *Jack Tar in History: Essays in the History of Maritime Life and Labour.* Fredericton, New Brunswick: Acadiensis Press, 1991.

Howse, Derek, and Michael Sanderson. *The Sea Chart.* Newton Abbott, UK: David and Charles, 1973.

Hutchins, John G.B. *The American Maritime Industries and Public Policy, 1789-1914.* Cambridge, Massachusetts: Harvard University Press, 1941.

Johnson, Robert E. *Far China Station. The U.S. Navy in Asian Waters, 1800-1898.* Annapolis, Maryland: Naval Institute Press, 1979.

———. *Guardians of the Sea: History of the U.S. Coast Guard, 1915 to the Present.* Annapolis, Maryland: Naval Institute Press, 1987.

———. *Thence Round Cape Horn: The Story of United States Naval Forces on Pacific Station, 1818-1923.* Annapolis, Maryland: Naval Institute Press, 1963.

Kemble, John H. *San Francisco Bay: A Pictorial Maritime History.* Cambridge, Maryland: Cornell Maritime Press, 1957.

Kennedy, Paul M. *The Rise and Fall of Great Powers: Economic Change and Military Conflict from 1500 to 2000.* New York: Random House, 1987.

Kilmarx, Robert A., ed. *America's Maritime Legacy: A History of the U.S. Merchant Marine and Shipbuilding Industry Since Colonial Times.* Boulder, Colorado: Westview Press, 1979.

King, Irving H. *The Coast Guard Under Sail: The U.S. Revenue Cutter Service, 1789-1865.* Annapolis, Maryland: Naval Institute Press, 1989.

Kochiss, John M. *Oystering from New York to Boston.* Middletown, Connecticut: Wesleyan University Press for Mystic Seaport, 1974.

Kurlansky, Mark. *Cod: A Biography of the Fish That Changed the World.* New York: Walker and Company, 1997.

Kverndal, Roald. *Seamen's Missions: Their Origin and Early Growth.* Pasadena, California: William Carey Library, 1986.

Labaree, Benjamin W., ed. *The Atlantic World of Robert G. Albion.* Middletown, Connecticut: Wesleyan University Press, 1975.

Laing, Alexander. *American Heritage History of Seafaring America.* New York: American Heritage, 1974.

———. *American Ships.* New York: American Heritage, 1971.

Long, David F. *Gold Braid and Foreign Relations: Diplomatic Activities of U.S. Naval Officers, 1798-1883.* Annapolis, Maryland: Naval Institute Press, 1988.

Love, Robert W., Jr. *The Chiefs of Naval Operations.* Annapolis, Maryland: Naval Institute Press, 1980.

———. *History of the U.S. Navy, 1775-1941.* Harrisburg, Pennsylvania: Stackpole Books, 1992.

MacLeish, William H. *The Gulf Stream: Encounter with the Blue God.* Boston: Houghton, Mifflin, 1989.

McNeill, William H. *The Pursuit of Power: Technology, Armed Force and Society since A.D. 1000.* Chicago: University of Chicago Press, 1982.

Mannix, Daniel P., and Malcolm Cowley. *Black Cargoes: A History of the Atlantic Slave Trade 1518-1865.* New York: Viking Press, 1962.

Martin, Kenneth R., and Nathan R. Lipfert. *Lobstering and the Maine Coast.* Bath: Maine Maritime Museum, 1985.

May, Ernest F., and John K. Fairbank. *America's China Trade in Historical Perspective.* Cambridge, Massachusetts: Harvard University Press, 1986.

Miller, Edward S. *War Plan Orange: The U.S. Strategy to Defeat Japan. 1897-1945.* Annapolis, Maryland: Naval Institute Press, 1991.

Modelski, George, and William R. Thompson. *Seapower in Global Politics, 1494-1993.* Seattle: University of Washington Press, 1993.

Mooney, James. L. *Dictionary of American Naval Fighting Ships.* 8 vols. Washington, D.C.: Naval Historical Center, 1959-91.

Morison, Elting E. *Admiral Sims and the Modern American Navy.* Boston: Houghton Mifflin, 1942.

———. *Men, Machines and Modern Times.* Cambridge, Massachusetts: M.I.T. Press, 1966.

Morison, Samuel Eliot. *The Maritime History of Massachusetts, 1783-1860.* Cambridge, Massachusetts: Harvard University Press, 1921.

Morris, James M. *Our Maritime Heritage: Maritime Developments and Their Impact on American Life.* Washington, D.C.: University Press of America, 1978.

Nash, John. *Seamarks: Their History and Development.* London: Stanford Maritime Press, 1985.

Noble, Dennis L. *Lighthouses & Keepers: The U.S. Lighthouse Service and its Legacy.* Annapolis, Maryland: Naval Institute Press, 1997.

O'Leary, Wayne M. *Maine Sea Fisheries: The Rise and Fall of a Native Industry, 1830-1890.* Boston:

Northeastern University Press, 1996.

Palmer, Michael. *Guardians of the Gulf: A History of America's Expanding Role in the Persian Gulf, 1833-1992*. New York: Free Press, 1992.

Paullin, Charles O. *American Voyages to the Orient, 1690-1865: An Account of Merchant and Naval Activities in China, Japan and the Various Pacific Islands*. Annapolis, Maryland: Naval Institute Press, 1971.

———. *Paullin's History of Naval Administration, 1775-1911*. Annapolis, Maryland: Naval Institute Press, 1968.

Perry, John Curtis. *Facing West: Americans and the Opening of the Pacific*. Westport, Connecticut: Praeger, 1994.

Polmar, Norman. *Aircraft Carriers: A Graphic History of Carrier Aviation and its Influence on World Events*. New York: Doubleday, 1969.

Ponko, Vincent, Jr. *Ships, Seas, and Scientists: U.S. Naval Exploration and Discovery in the Nineteenth Century*. Annapolis, Maryland: Naval Institute Press, 1974.

Pugh, Philip. *The Cost of Seapower: The Influence of Money on Naval Affairs from 1815 to the Present Day*. London: Conway Maritime Press, 1984.

Reynolds, Clark G. *Admiral John H. Towers: The Struggle for Naval Air Supremacy*. Annapolis, Maryland: Naval Institute Press, 1991.

———. *History and the Sea: Essays on Maritime Strategies*. Columbia: University of South Carolina Press, 1989.

Reynolds, Ermine S., and Kenneth R. Martin. "*A Singleness of Purpose": The Skolfields and Their Ships*. Bath: Maine Maritime Museum, 1987.

Rogers, John G. *Origins of Sea Terms*. Mystic: Mystic Seaport Museum, 1984.

Rousmaniere, John. *The Golden Pastime: A New History of Yachting*. New York: W.W. Norton, 1986.

Skaggs, Jimmy M. *The Great Guano Rush: Entrepreneurs and American Overseas Expansion*. New York: St. Martin's Griffin, 1994.

Smith, Philip C.F. *Philadelphia on the River*. Philadelphia: Philadelphia Maritime Museum, 1986.

Stein, Douglas L. *American Maritime Documents 1776-1860, Illustrated and Described*. Mystic: Mystic Seaport Museum, 1992.

Stein, Roger B. *Seascape and the American Imagination*. New York: Clarkson N. Potter, 1975.

Stephens, William P. *Traditions and Memories of American Yachting*. Brooklin, Maine: WoodenBoat, 1989.

Sweetman, Jack. *American Naval History: An Illustrated Chronology*. Annapolis, Maryland: Naval Institute Press, 1984.

Thomas, Hugh. *The Slave Trade: The Story of the Atlantic Slave Trade, 1440-1870*. New York: Simon & Schuster, 1997.

Trimble, William. *Admiral William A. Moffett: Architect of Naval Aviation*. Washington, D.C.: Smithsonian Institution Press, 1994.

Uhlig, Frank, Jr. *How Navies Fight: The U.S. Navy and its Allies*. Annapolis, Maryland: Naval Institute Press, 1994.

Vickers, Daniel F. *Farmers and Fishermen: Two Centuries of Work in Essex County, Massachusetts, 1630-1850*. Chapel Hill: University of North Carolina Press, 1994.

Webb, Robert L. *On the Northwest: Commercial Whaling in the Pacific Northwest, 1790-1967*. Vancouver: University of British Columbia Press, 1988.

Wilmerding, John. *A History of American Marine Painting*. Boston: Little, Brown, 1968.

Wood, Virginia Steele. *Live Oaking: Southern Timber for Tall Ships*. Boston: Northeastern University Press, 1981.

Part 1
Becoming America, to 1815

Allis, Frederick S. *Seafaring in Colonial Massachusetts*. Boston: Colonial Society of Massachusetts, 1980.

Andrews, Kenneth R. *Trade, Plunder, and Settlement: Maritime Enterprise and the Genesis of the British Empire, 1480-1630*. New York: Cambridge University Press, 1984.

Bailyn, Bernard. *Voyagers to the West: A Passage in the Peopling of America on the Eve of the Revolution*. New York: Alfred A. Knopf, 1986.

Bridenbaugh, Carl, and Roberta Bridenbaugh. *No Peace Beyond the Line: The English in the Caribbean, 1624-1690*. New York: Oxford University Press, 1972.

Bruchey, Stuart, ed., *The Colonial Merchant: Sources and Readings*. New York: Harper & Row, 1966.

Christie, Ian R., and Benjamin W. Labaree. *Empire or Independence, 1760-1776: A British American Dialogue on the Coming of the American Revolution*. London: Phaidon Press, and New York: W.W. Norton, 1976.

Clark, John G. *New Orleans, 1718-1812: An Economic*

History. Baton Rouge: Louisiana State University Press, 1970.

Condon, Thomas J. *New York Beginnings: The Commercial Origin of New Netherland*. New York: New York University Press, 1968.

Cressey, David. *Coming Over: Migration Communication between Europe and New England in the Seventeenth Century*. Cambridge: Cambridge University Press, 1987.

Crittenden, C.C. *The Commerce of North Carolina, 1763-1789*. New Haven: Yale University Press, 1936.

Crosby, Alfred W. *The Columbian Exchange: Biological and Cultural Consequences of 1492*. Westport, Connecticut: Greenwood Press, 1972.

Davis, Ralph. *The Rise of the Atlantic Economies*. Ithaca, New York: Cornell University Press, 1973.

Doerflinger, Thomas M. *A Vigorous Spirit of Enterprise: Merchants and Economic Development in Revolutionary Philadelphia*. Chapel Hill: University of North Carolina Press, 1986.

Dunn, Richard S. *Sugar and Slaves: The Rise of the Planter Class in the English West Indies, 1624-1713*. Chapel Hill: University of North Carolina Press, 1972.

Fowler, William M., Jr. *Jack Tars and Commodores: The American Navy, 1783-1815*. Boston: Houghton Mifflin, 1984.

———. *Rebels Under Sail: The American Navy During the Revolution*. New York: Charles Scribner's Sons, 1976.

———. *Silas Talbot, Captain of Old Ironsides*. Mystic: Mystic Seaport Museum, 1995.

Garitee, Jerome R. *The Republic's Private Navy: The American Privateering Business as Practiced by Baltimore During the War of 1812*. Middletown, Connecticut: Wesleyan University Press for Mystic Seaport, 1977.

Goldenberg, Joseph. *Shipbuilding in Colonial America*. Charlottesville: University of Virginia Press, 1976.

Kammen, Michael. *Empire and Interest: The American Colonies and the Politics of Mercantilism*. Philadelphia: J.B. Lippincott, 1970.

Klein, Herbert S. *The Middle Passage: Comparative Studies in the Atlantic Slave Trade*. Princeton, New Jersey: Princeton University Press, 1978.

Labaree, Benjamin W. *The Boston Tea Party*. New York: Oxford University Press, 1964.

Liss, Peggy K. *Atlantic Empires: The Network of Trade and Revolution, 1713-1826*. Baltimore: Johns Hopkins

University Press, 1982.

Lower, J. Arthur. *Ocean of Destiny: A Concise History of the North Pacific, 1500-1978*. Vancouver: University of British Columbia Press, 1978.

Maloney, Linda M. *The Captain from Connecticut: The Life and Naval Times of Isaac Hull*. Boston: Northeastern University Press, 1986.

Middleton, Arthur P. *Tobacco Coast: A Maritime History of Chesapeake Bay in the Colonial Era*. Newport News, Virginia: The Mariners' Museum, 1953.

Nash, Gary B. *The Urban Crucible: The Northern Seaports and the Origins of the American Revolution*. Cambridge, Massachusetts: Harvard University Press, 1986.

Papenfuse, Edward C. *In Pursuit of Profit: The Annapolis Merchants in the Era of the American Revolution, 1763-1805*. Baltimore: Johns Hopkins University Press, 1975.

Pope-Hennessy, James. *Sins of the Fathers: A Study of the Atlantic Slave Trade, 1441-1807*. New York: Alfred A. Knopf, 1968.

Price, Jacob M. *Capital and Credit in British Overseas Trade: The View from the Chesapeake*. Cambridge, Massachusetts: Harvard University Press, 1980.

Quinn, David B. *England and the Discovery of America, 1481-1620*. New York: Alfred A. Knopf, 1974.

———. *"Set Faire for Roanoke:" Voyages and Colonies, 1584-1606*. London: Allen and Unwin, 1983.

Rediker, Marcus. *Between the Devil and the Deep Blue Sea: Merchants, Seamen, Pirates, and the Anglo-American Maritime World, 1700-1750*. Cambridge: Cambridge University Press, 1987.

Reynolds, Edward. *Stand the Storm: A History of the Atlantic Slave Trade*. London: Allison & Busby, 1985.

Ritchie, Robert C. *Captain Kidd and the War Against the Pirates*. Cambridge: Harvard University Press, 1986.

Shepard, James F., and Gary M. Walton. *Shipping, Maritime Trade and the Economic Development of Colonial North America*. Cambridge: Harvard University Press, 1974.

Steele, Ian K. *The English Atlantic, 1675-1740: An Exploration of Communication and Community*. New York: Oxford University Press, 1986.

Tolles, Frederick B. *Meeting House and Counting House: The Quaker Merchants of Colonial Philadelphia, 1682-1763*. Chapel Hill: University of North Carolina Press, 1948.

Tyler, David B. *The Bay and River Delaware: A Pictorial History*. Cambridge, Maryland: Cornell Maritime Press, 1955.

Part 2
The Expanding Nation, 1815-1865

Albion, Robert G. *The Rise of New York Port, 1815-1860.* New York: Charles Scribner's Sons, 1939, 1970.

————. *Square-Riggers on Schedule: The New York Sailing Packets to England, France, and the Cotton Ports.* Princeton, New Jersey: Princeton University Press, 1938.

Bonyun, Bill and Gene. *Full Hold and Splendid Passage: America Goes to Sea, 1815-1860.* New York: Alfred A. Knopf, 1969.

Brinnin, John Malcolm. *The Sway of the Grand Saloon: A Social History of the North Atlantic.* New York: Delacorte Press, 1971.

Creighton, Margaret. *Rites and Passages: The Experience of American Whaling, 1830-1870.* New York: Cambridge University Press, 1995.

Cutler, Carl C. *Greyhounds of the Sea: The Story of the American Clipper Ship,* 3rd ed. Annapolis, Maryland: Naval Institute Press, 1984.

————. *Queens of the Western Ocean: The Story of America's Mail and Passenger Sailing Lines.* Annapolis, Maryland: Naval Institute Press, 1961.

Daggett, Kendrick P. *Fifty Years of Fortitude: The Maritime Career of Captain Jotham Blaisdell of Kennebunk, Maine, 1810-1860.* Mystic: Mystic Seaport, 1988.

Delgado, James P. *To California by Sea: A Maritime History of the California Gold Rush.* Columbia: University of South Carolina Press, 1990.

Druett, Joan, ed. *"She Was a Sister Sailor:" Mary Brewster's Whaling Journals, 1845-1851.* Mystic: Mystic Seaport, 1992.

Fowler, William M. Jr. *Under Two Flags: The American Navy in the Civil War.* New York: W.W. Norton, 1990.

Frank, Stuart M. *Herman Melville's Picture Gallery: Sources and Types of the "Pictorial" Chapters of Moby-Dick.* Fairhaven, Massachusetts: E.J. Lefkowicz, 1986.

Haites, Erik F., James Mak, and Gary M. Walton. *Western River Transportation: The Era of Early Internal Development, 1810-1860.* Baltimore: Johns Hopkins University Press, 1975.

Hatcher, Harlan, and Erich A. Walter. *A Pictorial History of the Great Lakes.* New York: Crown, 1963.

Holly, David C. *Tidewater by Steamboat: A Saga of the Chesapeake.* Baltimore: Johns Hopkins University Press, 1991.

Hunter, Louis C. *Steamboats on the Western Rivers: An Economic and Technological History.* Cambridge,

Massachusetts: Harvard University Press, 1949.

Jones, Howard. *Mutiny on the Amistad: The Saga of a Slave Revolt and its Impact on American Abolition, Law, and Diplomacy.* 2nd. ed. New York: Oxford University Press, 1997.

Kemble, John H. *The Panama Route, 1848-1869.* Berkeley: University of California Press, 1943.

Langley, Harold D. *Social Reform in the United States Navy, 1798-1862.* Urbana: University of Illinois Press, 1967.

Malley, Richard C. *Graven by the fishermen themselves: Scrimshaw in Mystic Seaport Museum.* Mystic: Mystic Seaport, 1983.

Marvel, William. *The Alabama and the Kearsarge: The Sailor's Civil War.* Chapel Hill: University of North Carolina Press, 1996.

Philbrick, Thomas. *James Fenimore Cooper and the Development of American Sea Fiction.* Cambridge, Massachusetts: Harvard University Press, 1961.

Ridgeley-Nevitt, Cedric. *American Steamships on the Atlantic.* Newark: University of Delaware Press, 1981.

Shaw, Ronald E. *Canals for a Nation: The Canal Era in the United States, 1790-1860.* Lexington: University of Kentucky Press, 1991.

Stanton, William. *The Great United States Exploring Expedition of 1838-1842.* Berkeley: University of California Press, 1975.

Tyler, David B. *Steam Conquers the Atlantic.* New York: D. Appleton-Century, 1939.

Valle, James E. *Rocks & Shoals: Order and Discipline in the Old Navy, 1800-1861.* Annapolis, Maryland: Naval Institute Press, 1980.

Wiley, Peter B. *Yankees in the Land of the Gods: Commodore Perry and the Opening of Japan.* New York: Penguin Books, 1990.

Wilmerding, John. *Fitz Hugh Lane.* New York: Praeger, 1971.

Part 3
Rise to World Power, 1865-1939

Ackerman, Edward A. *New England's Fishing Industry.* Chicago: University of Chicago Press, 1941.

Alden, John D. *The American Steel Navy: A Photographic History of the U.S. Navy from the Introduction of the Steel Hull in 1885 to the Cruise of the Great White Fleet, 1907-1909.* Annapolis, Maryland: Naval Institute Press, 1972.

Bockstoce, John R. *Whales, Ice & Men*. Seattle: University of Washington Press, 1986.

Bradford, James C., ed. *Crucible of Empire: The Spanish American War and its Aftermath*. Annapolis, Maryland: Naval Institute Press, 1993.

Braisted, William Reynolds. *The United States Navy in the Pacific, 1897-1909*. Austin: University of Texas Press, 1958.

————. *The United States Navy in the Pacific, 1909-1922*. Austin: University of Texas Press, 1971.

Brodie, Bernard. *Sea Power in the Machine Age*. Princeton, New Jersey: Princeton University Press, 1941.

Bunting, William H. *Portrait of a Port: Boston, 1852-1914*. Cambridge, Massachusetts: Belknap Press of Harvard University Press, 1971.

Challener, Richard D. *Admirals, Generals, and American Foreign Policy, 1898-1914*. Princeton, New Jersey: Princeton University Press, 1973.

Cikousky, Nicolai, Jr., and Francis Kelley. *Winslow Homer*. New Haven: Yale University Press, 1995.

Clephane, Lewis P. *History of the Naval Overseas Transportation Service in World War I*. Washington D.C.: Government Printing Office, 1969.

Cole, Bernard. *Gunboats and Marines: The United States Navy in China, 1925-1928*. Newark: University of Delaware Press, 1983.

Coogan, John W. *The United States, Britain, and Maritime Rights, 1899-1915*. Ithaca, New York: Cornell University Press, 1981.

Cooling, Benjamin Franklin. *Gray Steel and Blue Water Navy: The Formative Years of America's Military Industrial Complex, 1881-1917*. Hamden, Connecticut: Archon Press, 1979.

Department of the Navy. *United States Naval Aviation, 1910-1970*. Washington, D.C.: Department of the Navy, 1970.

Dingman, Roger. *Power in the Pacific: The Origins of Naval Arms Limitation, 1914-1922*. Chicago: University of Chicago Press, 1976.

Drake, Frederick C. *The Empire of the Seas: A Biography of Rear Admiral Robert Wilson Shufeldt, USN*. Honolulu: University of Hawaii Press, 1984.

Dunne, W.M.P. *Thomas F. McManus and the American Fishing Schooners: An Irish-American Success Story*. Mystic: Mystic Seaport Museum, 1994.

German, Andrew W. *Down on T Wharf: The Boston Fisheries as Seen Through the Photographs of Henry D.*

Fisher. Mystic: Mystic Seaport Museum, 1982.

Goldberg, Joseph P. *The Maritime Story: A Study in Labor-Management Relations*. Cambridge, Massachusetts: Harvard University Press, 1958.

Hagan, Kenneth J. *American Gunboat Diplomacy and the Old Navy, 1877-1889*. Westport, Connecticut: Greenwood Publishing, 1973.

Hall, Christopher. *Britain, America and Arms Control, 1921-37*. New York: St Martin's Press, 1987.

Halpern, Paul G. *A Naval History of World War I*. Annapolis, Maryland: Naval Institute Press, 1994.

Hattendorf, John B. *Mahan on Naval Strategy: Selections from the Writings of Rear Admiral Alfred Thayer Mahan*. Annapolis, Maryland: Naval Institute Press, 1991.

Hayes, John D., and John B. Hattendorf, eds. *The Writings of Stephen B. Luce*. Newport, Rhode Island: Naval War College Press, 1975.

Healy, David. *Gunboat Diplomacy in the Wilson Era: The U.S. Navy in Haiti, 1915-1916*. Madison: University of Wisconsin Press, 1976.

Herrick, Walter R. *The American Naval Revolution*. Baton Rouge: Louisiana State University Press, 1967.

Hurley, Edward M. *The Bridge to France*. Philadelphia: J.B. Lippincott, 1927.

Leutze, James R. *Bargaining for Supremacy: Anglo-American Naval Collaboration, 1937-1941*. Chapel Hill: University of North Carolina Press, 1977.

Karsten Peter. *The Naval Aristocracy: The Golden Age of Annapolis and the Emergence of Modern American Navalism*. New York: Free Press, 1972.

King, Irving H. *The Coast Guard Expands: New Roles, New Frontiers*. Annapolis, Maryland: Naval Institute Press, 1996.

Leavitt, John F. *Wake of the Coasters*. 2nd. ed. Mystic: Mystic Seaport, 1984.

Melhorn, Charles M. *Two-Block Fox: The Rise of the Aircraft Carrier, 1911-1929*. Annapolis, Maryland: Naval Institute Press, 1974.

Michalka, Wolfgang, ed. *Der Erste Weltkrieg: Wirkung, Wahrnemung, Analyse*. Muenchen: R. Piper GmBh & Co., 1994.

Misa, Thomas J. *A Nation of Steel: The Making of Modern America, 1865-1925*. Baltimore: Johns Hopkins University Press, 1995.

Murfett, Malcolm. *Fool-Proof Relations: The Search for Anglo-American Naval Cooperation During the Chamberlain Years, 1937-1940*. Singapore: University of Singapore

Press, 1984.

Nelson, Bruce. *Workers on the Waterfront: Seamen, Longshoremen, and Unionism in the 1930s.* Urbana: University of Illinois Press, 1990.

Noble, Dennis L. *That Others Might Live: The U.S. Life-Saving Service, 1878-1915.* Annapolis, Maryland: Naval Institute Press, 1994.

Reckner, James R. *Teddy Roosevelt's Great White Fleet.* Annapolis, Maryland: Naval Institute Press, 1988.

Reynolds, Clark G. *The Fast Carriers: The Forging of an Air Navy.* New York: McGraw-Hill, 1968.

Roskill, Stephen. *Naval Policy Between the Wars, Vol. I: The Period of Anglo-American Antagonism, 1919-1929.* New York: Walker & Company, 1968.

Safford, Jeffrey J. *Wilsonian Maritime Diplomacy, 1913-1921.* New Brunswick, New Jersey: Rutgers University Press, 1978.

Simpson, Michael. ed. *Anglo-American Naval Relations, 1917-1919.* Publications of the Navy Records Society, vol. 130. London: Scholar Press, 1991.

Sims, William S. *The Victory at Sea.* Annapolis, Maryland: Naval Institute Press, 1984.

Spector, Ronald. *Admiral of the New Navy: The Life and Career of George Dewey.* Baton Rouge: Louisiana State University Press, 1974, 1988.

Shulman, Mark Russell. *Navalism and the Emergence of American Sea Power, 1882-1893.* Annapolis, Maryland: Naval Institute Press, 1995.

Sniffen, Harold S. *Antonio Jacobsen's Painted Ships on Painted Oceans.* Newport News, Virginia: The Mariners' Museum, 1994.

Still, William N., Jr. *American Sea Power in the Old World: The United States Navy in Europe and Near Eastern Waters, 1865-1917.* Westport, Connecticut: Greenwood Publishing, 1980.

Sumida, Jon Tetsuro. *Inventing Grand Strategy: The Classic Works of Alfred Thayer Mahan Reconsidered.* Baltimore: Johns Hopkins University Press, 1997

Sweetman, Jack. *The Landing at Veracruz, 1914.* Annapolis, Maryland: Naval Institute Press, 1968.

Trask, David F. *Captains & Cabinets: Anglo-American Naval Relations, 1917-1918.* Columbia: University of Missouri Press, 1972.

————. *The War with Spain in 1898.* New York: MacMillan, 1981.

Turk, Richard W. *The Ambiguous Relationship: Theodore Roosevelt and Alfred Thayer Mahan.* Westport,

Connecticut: Greenwood Press, 1987.

U.S. Maritime Commission. *Economic Survey of the American Merchant Marine.* Washington, D.C.: Government Printing Office, 1937.

U.S. Office of Naval Records and Library. *American Ship Casualties of the World War.* Washington, D.C.: Government Printing Office, 1923.

Weintraub, Hyman. *Andrew Furuseth: Emancipator of the Seamen.* Berkeley: University of California Press, 1959.

Wheeler, Gerald E. *Admiral William Veazie Pratt, U.S. Navy: A Sailor's Life.* Washington, D.C.: Naval History Division, 1974

————. *Prelude to Pearl Harbor: The United States Navy and the Far East, 1921-1931.* Columbia: University of Missouri Press, 1963.

Williams, William J. *The Wilson Administration and the Shipbuilding Crisis of 1917: Steel Ships and Wooden Steamers.* Lewiston, New York: Edward Mellon Press, 1992.

Willoughby, Malcolm F. *Rum War at Sea.* Washington, D.C.: Government Printing Office, 1964.

Willoughby, William R. *The St. Lawrence Waterway: A Study in Politics and Diplomacy.* Madison: University of Wisconsin Press, 1961.

Yerxa, Donald A. *Admirals and Empire: The United States Navy and the Caribbean, 1898-1945.* Columbia: University of South Carolina Press, 1991.

Part 4
World War II and After, 1939-

Albion, Robert G., and Robert H. Connery. *Forrestal and the Navy.* New York: Columbia University Press, 1962.

Ballantine, Duncan S. *U.S. Naval Logistics in the Second World War.* Princeton, New Jersey: Princeton University Press, 1949.

Behrens. C.B.A. *Merchant Shipping and the Demands of War.* London: His Majesty's Stationery Office, 1955.

Benford, Harry, ed. *A Half-Century of Maritime Technology, 1943-1993.* Jersey City, New Jersey: Society of Naval Architects and Marine Engineers, 1993.

Blair, Claire J. *Silent Victory: The U.S. Submarine War Against Japan.* Philadelphia & New York: J.B. Lippincott, 1975.

Boeri, David, and James Gibson. *"Tell it Good-Bye, Kiddo:" The Decline of the New England Offshore Fishery.*

Camden, Maine: International Marine, 1976.

Bone, Kevin, ed. *The New York Waterfront: Evolution and Building Culture of the Port and Harbor.* New York: Monacelli Press, 1997.

Boog, Horst, Werner Rahn, et. al. *Der Globale Krieg: Die Ausweitung zum Weltkrieg und der Wechsel der Initiative. Das Deutsche Reich und der Zweite Weltkrieg,* vol. 6. Stuttgart: Deutsche Verlags-Anstalt, 1990.

Buckley, Christopher. *Steaming to Bamboola: The World of a Tramp Freighter.* New York: Viking, 1982.

Buell, Thomas B. *Master of Sea Power: A Biography of Admiral Ernest J. King.* Boston: Little, Brown, 1980.

———. *The Quiet Warrior: A Biography of Admiral Raymond A. Spruance.* Boston: Little, Brown, 1974.

Carlisle, Rodney S. *Sovereignty for Sale: The Origins and Evolution of the Panamanian and Liberian Flags of Convenience.* Annapolis, Maryland: Naval Institute Press, 1981.

Chowning, Larry S. *Chesapeake Legacy: Tools and Traditions.* Centreville, Maryland: Tidewater Publishers, 1995.

———. *Harvesting the Chesapeake: Tools and Traditions.* Centreville, Maryland: Tidewater Publishers, 1990.

Creswell, John. *Sea Warfare, 1939-1945.* Berkeley: University of California Press, 1967.

Davis, Vincent. *The Admiral's Lobby.* Chapel Hill: University of North Carolina Press, 1967.

———. *Postwar Defense Policy and the U.S. Navy, 1943-1946.* Chapel Hill: University of North Carolina Press, 1966.

Davidson, Joel R. *The Unsinkable Fleet: The Politics of U.S. Navy Expansion in World War II.* Annapolis, Maryland: Naval Institute Press, 1996.

Dickinson, Bob, and Andy Vladimir. *Selling the Sea: An Inside Look at the Cruise Industry.* New York: John Wiley & Sons, 1997.

Eccles, Henry E. *Military Concepts and Philosophy.* New Brunswick, New Jersey: Rutgers University Press, 1965.

Field, James A. *History of United States Naval Operations: Korea.* Washington, D.C.: Government Printing Office, 1962.

Friedman, Norman. *Desert Victory: The War for Kuwait.* Annapolis, Maryland: Naval Institute Press, 1991.

Furer, Julius Augustus. *Administration of the Navy Department in World War II.* Washington, D.C.: Government Printing Office, 1959.

Garrity-Blake, Barbara J. *The Fish Factory: Work and Meaning for Black and White Fishermen of the American Menhaden Industry.* Knoxville: University of Tennessee Press, 1994.

Hartmann Frederick H. *Naval Renaissance: The U.S. Navy in the 1980s.* Annapolis, Maryland: Naval Institute Press, 1990.

Hewlett, Richard G., and Francis Harris. *Nuclear Navy, 1946-1962.* Chicago: University of Chicago Press, 1974.

Hone, Thomas C. *Power and Change: The Administrative History of the Office of the Chief of Naval Operations, 1946-1986.* Washington, D.C.: Naval Historical Center, 1986.

Hooper, Edwin B., Dean C. Allard, and Oscar Fitzgerald. *The United States Navy and the Vietnam Conflict.* Washington, D.C.: Naval History Division, 1976.

Hoopes, Townsend, and Douglas Brinkley. *Driven Patriot: The Life and Times of James Forrestal.* New York: Alfred A. Knopf, 1992.

Howarth, Stephen. *Men of War: Great Naval Captains of World War II.* New York: St. Martin's Press, 1992.

———, and Derek Law. *The Battle of the Atlantic, 1939-1945: The 50th Anniversary Naval Conference.* Annapolis, Maryland: Naval Institute Press, 1994.

Hughes, Wayne P. *Fleet Tactics: Theory and Practice.* 2nd ed. Annapolis, Maryland: Naval Institute Press, 1998.

Jantscher, Gerald R. *Bread Upon the Waters: Federal Aids to the Maritime Industries.* Washington, D.C.: Brookings Institution, 1975.

Jordan, Robert S. *Alliance Strategy and Navies.* London: Pinter Publishers, 1990.

Junger, Sebastian. *The Perfect Storm: A True Story of Men Against the Sea.* New York: W.W. Norton, 1997.

King, Admiral Ernest J. *The U.S. Navy at War, 1941-1945.* Washington, D.C.: U.S. Navy Department, 1946.

Land, Emory S. *Winning the War with Ships: Land, Sea and Air–Mostly Land.* New York: Robert M. McBride, 1958.

Lane, Frederic. *Ships for Victory: A History of Shipbuilding under the United States Maritime Commission During World War II.* Baltimore: Johns Hopkins University Press, 1951.

Lawrence, Samuel A. *United States Merchant Shipping Policies and Politics.* Washington, D.C.: Brookings Institution, 1966.

Lehman, John F., Jr. *Command of the Seas: Building the 600 Ship Navy*. New York: Scribners, 1988.

Leighton, Richard, and Robert Coakley. *Global Logistics and Strategy, 1940-1943*. Washington, D.C.: Government Printing Office, 1970.

Love, Robert W., Jr. *History of the U.S. Navy, 1942-1991*. Harrisburg, Pennsylvania: Stackpole Books, 1992.

McClosky, William. *Fish Decks: Seafarers of the North Atlantic*. New York: Paragon House, 1990.

MacLeish, William H. *Oil and Water: The Struggle for Georges Bank*. Boston: Atlantic Monthly Press, 1985.

McPhee, John. *Looking for a Ship*. New York: Farrar, Straus and Giroux, 1990.

Marolda, Edward J., and Oscar P. Fitzgerald. *The United States Navy and the Vietnam Conflict*. Washington, D.C.: Naval Historical Center, 1986.

Matthiessen, Peter. *Men's Lives*. New York: Random House, 1986.

Meigs, Montgomery C. *Slide Rules and Submarines: American Scientists and Subsurface Warfare in World War II*. Washington, D.C.: National Defense University Press, 1990.

Milner, Marc. *North Atlantic Run: The Royal Canadian Navy and the Battle for the Convoys*. Toronto: University of Toronto Press, 1985.

Morison, Samuel Eliot. *The Two-Ocean War: A Short History of the United States Navy in the Second World War*. Boston: Little, Brown, 1963.

Mostert, Noel. *Supership*. New York: Alfred A. Knopf, 1974.

Muir, Malcolm, Jr. *Black Shoes and Blue Water: Surface Warfare in the United States Navy, 1945-1975*. Washington, D.C: Naval Historical Center, 1996.

Palmer, Michael. *On Course to Desert Storm: The U.S. Navy and the Persian Gulf*. Washington, D.C.: Naval Historical Center, 1992.

Potter, E.B. *Nimitz*. Annapolis, Maryland: Naval Institute Press, 1976.

Prados, John. *Combined Fleet Decoded: The Secret History of American Intelligence and the Japanese Navy in World War II*. New York: Random House, 1995.

Riesenberg, Felix, Jr. *Sea War: The Story of the U.S. Merchant Marine in World War II*. New York: Rinehart, 1956.

Runyon, Timothy J., and Jan Copes. *To Die Gallantly: The Battle of the Atlantic*. Boulder, Colorado: Westview Press, 1994.

Sanger, Clyde. *Ordering the Oceans: The Making of the Law of the Sea*. Toronto: University of Toronto Press, 1987.

Sokolsky, Joel J. *Seapower in the Nuclear Age: The United States Navy and NATO, 1949-1980*. Annapolis, Maryland: Naval Institute Press, 1991.

Spector, Ronald H. *Eagle Against the Sun: The American War with Japan*. New York: Free Press, 1985.

Stillwell, Paul, ed. *The Golden Thirteen: Recollections of the First Black Naval Officers*. Annapolis, Maryland: Naval Institute Press, 1993.

Syrett, David. *The Defeat of the German U-Boats*. Columbia: University of South Carolina Press, 1994.

Uhlig, Frank, ed. *Vietnam: The Naval Story*. Annapolis, Maryland: Naval Institute Press, 1986.

U.S. Naval War College. *Sound Military Decision*. Annapolis, Maryland: Naval Institute Press, 1992.

Waddington, C.H. *OR in World War 2: Operational Research against the U-Boat*. London: Elek Science, 1973.

War Shipping Administration. *The United States Merchant Marine at War*. Washington, D.C.: Government Printing Office, 1946.

Warner, William W. *Distant Water: The Fate of the North Atlantic Fisherman*. Boston, Massachusetts, 1983.

Wylie, J.C. *Military Strategy: A General Theory of Power Control*. Annapolis, Maryland: Naval Institute Press, 1989.

Zumwalt, Elmo R., Jr. *On Watch: A Memoir*. New York: Quadrangle/The New York Times Book Co., 1976.

Contributors

Text Authors

This volume has been written by the current faculty of the Frank C. Munson Institute of American Maritime Studies at Mystic Seaport, Connecticut. Established under the directorship of Harvard Professor Robert G. Albion in 1955, the Institute continues, with more than forty years of experience, to provide graduate-level, accredited courses in maritime studies during the summer months.

Benjamin W. Labaree is professor of History and Environmental Studies emeritus at Williams College. He holds an undergraduate degree from Yale University and a Ph.D. from Harvard University, and has taught in Mystic Seaport's summer Munson Institute program since 1966, acting as its director from 1974 to 1996. He was the founding director of the Williams College-Mystic Seaport Maritime Studies Program in 1977, serving until 1989, when he became director of the Center for Environmental Studies at Williams. He retired from teaching in 1992. The author of numerous books on colonial and maritime history, he is an elected member of the Massachusetts Historical Society, the American Antiquarian Society, and the Colonial Society of Massachusetts, and serves on the board of *The American Neptune* and the Newburyport Maritime Society.

William M. Fowler, Jr. is Director of the Massachusetts Historical Society. Formerly professor of History at Northeastern University, he is an authority on the early history of the U.S. Navy. He is also editor of *The New England Quarterly*, a historical review of New England life and letters; president of the New England Historic Genealogical Society; president of the Colonial Society of Massachusetts; and vice president of the USS *Constitution* Museum Foundation. For more than ten years he has been a lecturer in the Munson Institute program. A graduate of Northeastern University, Professor Fowler has an M.A. and Ph.D. from the University of Notre Dame.

Andrew W. German is Mystic Seaport's Exhibitions Research Fellow for America and the Sea and editor of *The Log of Mystic Seaport*, the Museum's quarterly. He received his undergraduate degree from Yale University, and attended the Munson Institute in 1976. The author of several books and numerous articles on American maritime history, he has served as editor in Mystic Seaport's publishing program and as lecturer in fisheries history for the Munson Institute and the Williams College-Mystic Seaport Maritime Studies Program.

John B. Hattendorf is the Ernest J. King Professor of Maritime History at the Naval War College. In 1996 he succeeded Ben Labaree as adjunct director of the Munson Institute. A Munson graduate in 1970, he took his undergraduate degree in History at Kenyon College, his master's degree at Brown University, his doctorate at the University of Oxford, and he was awarded an honorary doctor of humane letters from Kenyon College. He is the author, editor, or co-editor of more than 25 books in the field of maritime and naval history. He has been elected to the council of the International Commission on Maritime History, a vice-president of the North American Society for Oceanic History, a vice-president of the Hakluyt Society, a corresponding member of the Society for Nautical Research (UK), the Royal Swedish Academy of Naval Science, and the Académie du Var (France), a member of council of the Navy Records Society, and a Fellow of the Royal Historical Society.

Jeffrey J. Safford is emeritus professor of History at Montana State University. A Rutgers University Ph.D., he has specialized in the interrelationship between U.S. maritime policy and foreign affairs, particularly during the two twentieth-century world wars. Formerly vice president of the North American Society for Oceanic History, he is an editorial board member of the *International Journal of Maritime History*, and is a founding member of the International Maritime Economic History Association. He first lectured at the Munson Institute in 1970.

Edward W. Sloan is Charles H. Northam Professor of History at Trinity College, Hartford, Connecticut, and adjunct professor of Management with Rensselaer at Hartford. With undergraduate and graduate degrees from Yale University, he holds M.A. and Ph.D. degrees in History from Harvard University, where his major field was Maritime and Naval History. Formerly a financial and transportation analyst for a New York investment banking firm, he has lectured and served as seminar leader since 1963, and for many years was assistant director of the Munson Institute. During the summer of 1996 he was co-director, with Benjamin Labaree, of a National Endowment for the Humanities Institute on America and the Sea. Currently serving on the editorial board of the *International Journal of Maritime History*, he has a special interest in the impact of steam propulsion on the nineteenth-century maritime world, a subject on which he has written extensively.

Vignette Authors

James Carlton received a Ph.D from the University of California at Davis. A specialist in the study of introduced species, he is Director of the Williams College-Mystic Seaport Maritime Studies Program.

Margaret S. Creighton received a Ph.D. from Boston University and is associate professor of History and chair of American Cultural Studies at Bates College. She is the author of *Rites and Passages: The Experience of American Whaling, 1830-1870* (1996) and coeditor of *Iron Men, Wooden Women: Gender and Seafaring in the Atlantic World, 1700-1920* (1996).

Fred Dalzell received a Ph.D. from Harvard University and served as teaching fellow in the Williams College-Mystic Seaport Maritime Studies Program. He has a special interest in the maritime dimensions of cultural contact.

Glenn Gordinier is completing his Ph.D. at the University of Connecticut. As research associate at Mystic Seaport, he teaches in the Williams College-Mystic Seaport Maritime Studies Program.

Lisa Norling received a Ph.D. from Rutgers University and served as teaching fellow in the Williams College-Mystic Seaport Maritime Studies Program. Currently assistant professor of History at the University of Minnesota, she coedited *Iron Men, Wooden Women: Gender and Seafaring in the Atlantic World, 1700-1920* (1996) and is preparing to publish her dissertation on the roles of nineteenth-century New England maritime women.

William N. Peterson, Senior Curator at Mystic Seaport, is author of *Mystic Built: Ships and Shipyards of the Mystic, River, Connecticut, 1784-1919* (1988).

Eric Roorda received a Ph.D. from Johns Hopkins University and served as teaching fellow in the Williams College-Mystic Seaport Maritime Studies Program. A specialist in U.S-Caribbean relations, he is currently assistant professor of History at Bellarmine College and has written *The Dictator Next Door: The Good Neighbor Policy and the Trujillo Regime in the Dominican Republic 1930-1945* (1998).

Daniel Vickers received a Ph.D. from Princeton University and teaches Maritime History at Memorial University in St. John's, Newfoundland. He is the author of *Farmers and Fishermen: Two Centuries of Work in Essex County, Massachusetts, 1630-1850* (1994).

Dwayne E. Williams received a Ph.D. from the University of Minnesota and is assistant professor of History at Susquehanna University. He has made a particular study of the African diaspora and the Cape Verde Islands.

Julie Winch received a Ph.D. from Bryn Mawr College and is associate professor of History at the University of Massachusetts, Boston. The author of *Philadelphia's Black Elite* (1988), she is completing a new biography of James Forten.

Index

A

abuses of seamen, 423—425
Acts of Trade, colonial, 61—62
A.D. Vance, **342**
Adams, John, 182—185
African Americans
  freemen, 288—289
  sailors, 351
African Endeavor, 600
Agassiz, Alexander, 432—433
agriculture
  importance of after War of 1812, 237—238
  relationship with maritime commerce, 94
Alabama, **343,** 354, 366
Alaska
  purchase of, 284
  salmon fishery, 13c, 533—535, 634c
  steamship service to, 380
  women, maritime, 635
Albatross, **432**
Algiers, U.S. war with, 157
Alice, **425**
Allegrini, F., 34c
Alter, Hobie, **646**
America, **180**
American, **280**
American Coast Pilot (Blunt), 175, 177
American Progress, **598**
America's Cup, 14, 440, 537—538
Amistad, 287—288
Amsterdam, 464
Anaconda Plan, 344, 346
Andrew Moore, **579**
Andrews, Evangeline Walker, 78
Annapolis, naval academy at, 332
Antarctica, discovery of, 292c
antisubmarine warfare, 479, 489, 492—493, 567—569
Arctic exploration, 434
Arizona, **488, 564**
Army, Continental, 129—130
Arnold, Benedict, 143—145c
Articles of Confederation, 156—157
Asia
  economic lure of, 5
  immigrants from, **530**
  during 1900s, 453, 515
  U.S. trade with, 388, 605, 607—608
Atlanta, **338**
Atlantic City, 438
Atlantic Ocean
  coastline description, 19
  pirates, 57—58c
  trade routes in 1700s, 127
  transatlantic liners, 6—7, 647
  during World War II, 553—562
aviation, naval, 447, 452c, 512, 517—519

B

Bachrach, D., 404c—405c
Bahamas, **170**
Bainbridge, William, 213, 219—221
Baltick, **110**
Baltimore
  clippers, 223
  as major seaport in 1800s, **250,** 251, 256
  shipbuilding, 223—224
Bankes, T.W., 360c
Barbary corsairs, 157, 181, 191

Barbot, Jean, 91c
bark, description of, 64
Barney, Joshua, 155c
Barrelet, John J., 199c
Barres, Joseph Des, 120c, 123c, 134c
battleships, modern, 442—443, 618
Bellows, George, 423c
Bennett, James Gordon, **439**
Bennett, William James, 257c
Benson, William S., 488, 492, 509, 517, 524, 527
Bethel, **84**
bethels, establishment of, 254
Billy Budd (Melville), 649
Biloxi Bay, **60**
Bingham, George Caleb, 265c
Bjarni, Herjolfson, 30—31
Black Ball Line, 278
black seamen, 288—289, 351, 422c, 426, 574—576, **583,** 659
Black Star Line, 529
Blakeman, A. Noel, 340
blockades, Civil War, 337—342, 344—348, **361**
Blunt, Edmund M., 175, 177, **178**
boating, recreational, 537—540, 645—647, 654
Bolles, Nancy Chapman, **298**
Bonhomme Richard, 149—150, 152, **153**
Bonny, Anne, **58**
Boston
  effects of British taxation on, 113
  Knowles Riot, 85
  as major seaport in 1600s, 43—44
  as major seaport in 1700s, 70, **115, 120**
  as major seaport in 1800s, 250
  as major seaport in 1900s, **398**
  preparations for Revolutionary War, 130
Boston Light, **76**
Boston Massacre, 109, **116**
Boston Tea Party, 109, 114—119
bounty systems, 179—180, 258
Bowditch, Nathaniel, 175—179, **178**
Bowen, Ashley, 67c
Boxer, 222—223
Bradford, William, 30c
Brady, Matthew, 336c
Bratt, J.H., 399c
Brava packet trade, 468
Brazos River Light, **412**
Brewster, Mary, 291, **302**
Brock, Eliza, 298
Bry, Theodor de, 24c, 28c, 32c, 43c, 46c, 52c
buccaneers, 57—58c
Buffalo as major port in 1800s, 258
buoys, international uniformity in, 417
Burgis, William, 73c, 75c—76c
Burns, Milton J., 395c
Burton, James, 451c
Bushnell, David, 143
Butler Bill, 516
Buttersworth, James E., **11,** 12, 307c, 311c
Buttersworth, Thomas, 224c

C

Cabot, John, 29
Cabot, Sebastian, 29
cabotage, 168, 245
Cairo, **347**
Calabretta, Fred, 631c
"Calico Jack" Rackam, 58c
California, **564**

Calyo, Nicolino, 250c
Canada
　conflicts over fishing rights, 179, 259
　creation of, 366
　U.S. invasion of in 1812, 213
canals
　Cape Cod, **430**
　construction of, 244, 246—249, 256, 532
　decline of, 376—377
　Erie, 247—248, 281—282
　Panama, 434, 454—461, **520,** 530
　St. Lawrence River, 531—532
　Suez, 383—384
canning seafood, development of, 534
cannons, design of naval, 334—335
canoes
　recreational use of, 440—441
　types of Native American, **25,** 26—27, **28, 45**
Cape Breton Island, **82**
Cape Cod Canal, **430**
Cape Verdeans, 466—468
Captains Courageous, 651
Carbutt, J., 377
cargo, containerization of, 599—601, **603,** 604, 607—608
Caribbean
　British control of during 1700s, 98
　piracy in 1800s, 324
　sugar industry, 52c, 53, 98
　U.S. maritime commerce, 134, 170c, 453, 461—462
Carleton, Guy, 143—144
Carlton, James T., 643
Carnival Destiny, **648**
Carolina, settlement of, 46
Carson, Rachel, **638,** 661
Carter, Jimmy, 597
Cartier, Jacques, 36
catfish farming, 636c
Cavelier, René-Robert, 58, **59**
celestial navigation, 176
CG-100, **526**
Champion, **372**
Champlain, Lake, **144-145, 232**
Champlain, Samuel de, 38
chanteys, 319
Chapman, Conrad Wise, 357c
charity groups, marine, 174
Charleston
　attack on during Civil War, 345-346
　attack on during Revolutionary War, 146
　as major seaport in 1600/1700s, **74, 101**
　as major seaport in 1900s, 606
　privateering during War of 1812, 225-226
　slave trade, 103
Charles W. Morgan, 660
Charles W. Wetmore, 374-375
charts, nautical, 431, 434, 558
Chauncey, Isaac, 230
Chesapeake, 198—199, **229**
Chesapeake Bay
　fishing industry, 535
　geographical description of, 20
　as major seaport in 1700s, 74
　pilot schooners, 223, 243c
　tobacco industry, 45, 63c, 68, 74, 108c
Chicago, **388**
Chicago waterfront, **377**
children on whaling voyages, 291—292
China. *See also* Asia
　immigrants from, 462
　U.S. trade with, 158, 168, 283—284
Christopher Columbus, 375
churches for seamen, 254

Churchill, Winston S., **554**
Cincinnati as major port in 1800s, 257
Cinqué, Joseph, **288**
circumnavigator, first solo, 418—420
City of Paris, **382**
Civil War
　blockades, 337—342, 344—348, **361**
　commerce raiding, 357
　Confederate States Navy, 335—339, 344—349, 354, 365
　cotton industry, 355
　Great Britain's role, 339, 365—366
　impact on maritime interests, 7—9, 323—324
　shipbuilding boom, 358—359
　torpedo usage, 357c
　types of vessels, 351—353, 356
　Union Navy, 339—342, 344—348, 351
Cleawland, **64—65**
Clinton, DeWitt, 247
Clinton, William, 598
clipper ships, 223, 306, **308,** 309—310, **311**
coal
　replaced by diesel in 1900s, 447
　trade, 368—371
　use of in 1800s, 444c
coastal trade. *See also* commerce, maritime
　modern, 630
　during 1800s, 5, 245, 371
　during 1900s, 592
Coast Guard, U.S.. *See also* Navy, U.S.
　Academy, 524
　development of, 413—415
　modern role, 621, 625
　technological advancements, 620—621
　during Vietnam War, 621
　under Wilson administration, 523—524
Coast Survey, 246, 431
code, establishment of maritime, 446
codes, deciphering of, 568
cod fishing
　bounty system, 179
　drying and salting process, **24,** 33—34
　use of trawl lines, 259
Coercive Acts, 119—120
Cold War, 613
colleges, marine, 404c, 405—406, 409
Collet, John, 150c
Collins, Edward Knight, 297, 303, 307
Collins Line, 330
colonies, North American
　commercial status during 1700s, 103
　creation of seaports, 69—71, 74—75
　major exports, 74
　relationship with Great Britain, 60—63, 111, 120—121, 123, 126
　wars at sea, 83
colonization
　of North America, 36, 38—39, 42—47
　overview of, 53
　settlement dates of North America, **95**
Colorado, **380, 508**
Columbia, 158—159
Columbus, Christopher, 29
Columbus (ship), **32**
commerce, maritime. *See also* economy, U.S. maritime
　after Civil War, 381—384, 386—387
　after Revolutionary War, 7, 157—158, 166—170, 174, 179, 182, 199—202, 206
　during Civil War, 357
　coastal, 5, 245, 371, 592, 630
　during colonial America, 74, 93—94
　Latin American, 285—287
　modern, 629—630

Index

Native American trading, 27, **46**
neutral trade hazards, 194—199
Pacific, 158—163
packet lines, development of, 278—281
prior to Civil War, 245, 272
prior to Revolutionary War, 60—63, 101, 103—105, 110, 114
privateering's effects on, 84—85
regional specialization, 241—242
during Revolutionary War, 119, 132—133
during 1600s, 44, 57, 61
slave trade, 88—93
trading patterns of 1700s, 63, 68—69, **127**
during War of 1812, 228
during World War I, 480, 494—496, 524
Commerce and Labor Department, establishment of, 414—415
computerization in vessel design, 610—611
concrete ships, **499**
Coney Island, 438
Confederate States Navy, 335—339, 344—349, 354, 365
Confederation, Articles of, 156—157
Confidence, 232
Connecticut, 267
conservation, maritime
  fishing zones, 630, 632—633
  need for, 13—14
Constitution, **184**, 214—221, **405, 657**, 660
Constitution, U.S., ratification of, 166—167
containerization of cargo, 599—601, **603**, 604, 607—608
Continental Army, 129—130
Continental Association 1774, 120—123
Continental Congress, 129, 156—157
Continental Navy, 130—132, 141—142, 144—145
continental shelf, 21—22
convoys
  during World War I, 492—493
  during World War II, 568, 584—586, 589
Cook, James, 158
Coolidge, Calvin, 516
Copley, John Singleton, 107c
Cornè, Michele Felice, 171c, 175c, 180c, 184c, 193c, 214c
Cornwallis, Charles, 154, 156
Corwin, George, 49
cotton industry
  during Civil War, 355
  effects on slave trade, 185, 190
  first water-powered mill, 230
  growth in 1700s, 185
  growth in 1800s, 238, 250, 317—320
Crawford, J.G., 411c
Creighton, Margaret, 296
Crepin, Louis Phillipe, 155c
Crèvecoeur, Michel Guillaume Jean de, 102
crew racing, college, 538
crimping system, 423—424
Crispus Attucks, 116c
cruisers
  after World War I, 516, 520
  high-powered super, 351
cruise ship industry, 603, 647—648
cryptology, 568
Cuba
  immigrants from, 622—624
  U.S. trade with in 1700s, 135
Curran, Joseph, **545**
currents
  global ocean, 21—22
  Gulf Stream, 125
Currier, N., 325c
Customs Service, establishment of, 168—169
Cuyamaca, **499**
D
Dale, Richard, 190—191

Dalzell, Fred, 163
Dana, Richard Henry Jr., 304—305, 331
dangers, maritime, 78c
  collisions, 421
  due to faulty navigation, 174—175
  effects on seamen, 11, 47, 75, 77—78, 106
  for steamboats, 217
Daniels, Josephus, **492**, 508—509, 523
David Crockett, 209, **311**
Davidson, George, 160c
Davis, Charles Henry, *Nautical Almanac*, 334
D-Day, 560—562
Deane, Silas, 131
Decatur, Stephen, 213, 215—216, 231—232, **233**
Decker, Rupert, 527
de Lesseps, Ferdinand, 454—455
Depression, Great, 531, 544
DeSant, Antoine, **466**
Desert Shield, Operation, 616
Detroit as major port in 1800s, **236, 257**
Deutschland, **474**
development, waterfront, 644—645
Dewey, J.E., 465c
Diligence, **67**
discrimination. *See also* black seamen
  against black sailors, 426
  in the shipping industry, 529
ditty boxes, 294
Dobson, W.B., 224
Dodd, Robert, 136c
Dolphin, 461
Donnan, Elizabeth, 92
Dorsey, Paul, 570c
Douglass, Frederick, 288
Douglass, Robert Jr., 187c
Dowd, Charles F., 416
Down-Easters, 384—385, **386**, 390
Drake, Francis, **34**, 36, 38
drowning, prevention of, 174
dugout canoes, **25**, 26—27, **28**, 45
Dutch
  Caribbean holdings in 1600s, 53, 57
  early influence on New York, 73c
  English offensive against in 1600/1700s, 76
  Hudson River valley settlement, 45—46
duties, 111—113, 166—168
E
Eakins, Thomas, *Racing on the Delaware*, **440**
Easterly, Thomas, 258c
East India Company, 114—115, 121
East Indian, **527**
economy, U.S. maritime. *See also* commerce, maritime
  in 1700s, 56, 170, 172
  in 1800s, 238, 241—242
Elliott, William, 153c
Ellis Island, **463**
Elmina, **92**
embargoes, trade. *See also* commerce, maritime
  of 1807, 199, 201, 206—207, 211
  of 1812, 212—213, 217
Emergency Fleet Corporation, 496—498
Emmet, Elizabeth, 204c
engines. *See also* steam-powered vessels
  diesel and gasoline powered, 441, 610
  steam powered, 392
England. *See* Great Britain
Enterprise, 222—223
Equiano, Olaudah, 92
Ericsson, John, **329**
Erie Canal, 247—248, 281—282
Erik the Red, 30—31
Eskimos, early North American, 26

Essex, 195, 227, **228, 566, 570**
Evans, Robley D., 448—449
exports. *See also* cotton industry; tobacco industry
  after Civil War, 381
  after Revolutionary War, 171—172, 190, 317
  after War of 1812, 238
  prior to Revolutionary War, 103—105, 110
Exxon Valdez, 638—689

F

Fanny, **243**
farming, fish, 636c, 637
Farragut, David G., 345c, 346—348
Far West, **379**
Federalists, 166—167
Fields, Leslie Leyland, 635
Fischer, Anton Otto, 582
Fish, Preserved (person), **278**
Fisher, Henry D., 249c, 370c
fishermen
  description of New England, 48—51, 130
  economic hardships of, 52
fishing industry
  after Revolutionary War, 179
  conservation zones, 630, 632—633
  decline of, 633—634, 636—637
  development of, 13
  farming of fish, 636c, 637
  modern, 631—632, 637, 653
  New England in 1600/1700s, 47, 85—86, 122
  during 1800s, 258—259, 264—265
  scientific research, 431
  smoking fish, **24**
  technological advances, 393—395, 398—399, 533—535
  various North American coasts, 22—23
flakes, **51**
Fog Warning, **397**
food, navy, 445c
Forbes, Margaret Perkins, 208—210
Forbes, Robert Bennet, 210
Ford, Henry, 490—491
foreign trade. *See* commerce, maritime
Forrestal, **615**
Forten, James, 186—189
France
  expansion into North America, 35—36, 38, 57—59, **95**
  Louisiana Purchase, 192—193
  Normandy invasion, 560—562
  role during Revolutionary War, 146—147
  seizing U.S. neutral traders, 196
  struggle with Great Britain for North American control, 79, 82—83, 98
  Treaty of Amity and Commerce, 133—134
  U.S. quasi-war with, 182—185
Franconia, **279**
Franklin, Benjamin, 124—125
Fredricks, Charles, 329c
freemen, African Americans, 288—289
Fresnel lighthouse lens, 246
fruit trade, 384
Fulton, Robert, 203—204
fur trade, Northwest coast, 158, 160—162
Furuseth, Andrew, **544**

G

Gaillard Cut, 456—458
Gale of 1862, 260—263
Galveston boycott, 421—422
Garvey, Marcus, 529
Gelston, David, 169c
General Armstrong, 227c
General Monk, **155**
Geneva Conference, 516, 521—522
Geo. W. Wylly, **378**

Georges Bank, 259—263, 633
George Washington
  ocean liner, **507**
  submarine, **616**
Germany
  during World War I, 469—473, 479—480, 487
  during World War II, 556—557
Gerstäcker, Friedrich, 270
Gibbons v. Ogden, 245
Gibson, Charles Dana, 483
Gifford, Caroline, 300—301
Gilbert Islands, 565—566
Glasgow, 132
Gleason, Duncan, 580c
Gloucester
  fishermen of, **534**
  Gale of 1862, 262—263
  waterfront, **241**
Gold Coast, 91c, **92**
Gold Cup races, 539
gold rush, 273—274
government. *See also* Coast Guard, U.S.; Navy, U.S.
  commerce regulation after Revolutionary War, 166—170, 179, 182, 207
  commerce regulation during World War I, 495—496
  commerce regulation in 1800s, 245—246
  maritime policy in early 1900s, 524
  navigation projects, 174, 429
  regulation of steamboat industry, 268, 271
  role in maritime enterprise, 10
  shipping subsidies, 536, 595—598
grain trade, 384
Grant, U.S., 347—348
Grasse, Comte de, 154—155
Gray, Edwin, 638c
Gray, Robert, 158—160c
Great Britain. *See also* Navy, Royal
  after Revolutionary War, 170—172, 196
  after War of 1812, 239
  after World War I, 501, 508—509
  during Civil War, 339, 365—366
  control of North America in 1600/1700s, 60—62, 76, 79, 82—83, 97—98
  exploration of North America, 36, 38—39, 42, **95**
  privateer's effects on, 140
  relationship with colonies, 69, 111, 126
  during Revolutionary War, 143—146
  trade impasse in 1800s, 285—286
  U.S. dependence on in 1800s, 206, 317
  use of American ships, 312
  during War of 1812, 212—222, 231
  during World War I, 469—470, 474, 479—482, 484
Great Lakes
  commerce on, 271—272
  decline in modern commerce, 629—630c
  description of, 21
  iron mining, 370, 372—373
  steamships on, 374—375
  during War of 1812, 230
Great Republic, **11**
Great White Fleet, 448—450
Greenland, Norse Settlements of, 30—31
Greenwich meridian, 416—417
Greenwood, John, 104c, 176c
Greer, **585**
Gribble, Bernard, *The Return of the Mayflower*, 481c
Griffiths, John W., **312**
Griffon, 59c
guano fertilizer, 286c, 287
Gulf Stream, 124—125
Gulf War, Persian, 615—617
Gurnsey, J., 302c

Guy, Francis, 168c

H

haddock fishery, 631—632
Haida natives, 161—162
Haiti, 617, 622—624
Hall, Charles Franklin, 434—435c
Hall, James Norman, *Mutiny on the Bounty*, 650—651
Hallen, Ernest, 456, 459c
Hamilton, Paul, 217
Hannah, 130
Hansen, J., 243c
Harding, Warren, 513—514
Harkins, Leola, 635
Harriet, 158
Hartford, **345**
Harvey Birch, **358**
Haskins, Amos, **290**
Haven, Gilbert, 255c
Hawaii
   growth of in 1700s, 162—163
   role in world trade, 380—381
   U.S. influence on, 284
Hayes, Rutherford B., 459c
Heine, Peter B.W., 328
Hewes, Joseph, **131**
Highland Life-Saving Station, The, **410**
Hinckley, Isaac, 173c
Hobie Cats, 646c
Hog Island, 502—505
Hollard, John C., 451c
Homer, Winslow, 396—397, **658**
Hoover, Herbert, 521—522
Hopkins, Esek, 93, **104**, 131—132
Hudson, Henry, 38
Hudson River, **244**
   Dutch West India Company settlement, 45—46
   during 1700s, 72—73
   steamboat launching, 204
Huerta, Victoriano, 461
Huge, Jurgen F., 267c
Hughes, Charles Evans, **513**
Hugill, Stan, 319
Hull, Isaac, 214
hulls, design of, 609—610
humane societies, establishment of, 174
Hunley, 354, **357**
Hurley, Edward N., **496**, 497—498, 501—502, 506, 508
Hutchinson, Thomas, 115—117
hydroplanes, 539

I

ice as a preservative, 259, 265
Iceland, Norse of, 30—31
ice trade
   after Civil War, 368
   development of, 241
immigrants. *See also* colonization
   from Cape Verde Islands, 467
   from Cuba and Haiti, 622—624
   fisherman, 262—263
   passage to America, 6, **7**, 39—42, 100—101, 313—316
immigration. *See also* colonization
   after Civil War, 367
   restriction laws, 528
   during 1700s, 98, 100—101
   during 1900s, 462—465
IMM (International Mercantile Marine Corporation), 383
impressment of sailors, 196—199c
Indians. *See* Native Americans
Influence of Sea Power Upon History, The (Mahan), 407
Ingstad, Helge, 31
inland waterways
   development in early 1900s, 531

importance of, 6
improvements to after Civil War, 429—430
principal, **275, 655**
steamboats on, 266—267
insurance, marine, 173—174
International Mercantile Marine Corporation (IMM), 383
International Seamen's Union, 544—545
Iraq, Kuwait invasion of, 616
ironclad vessels, 336—337, **338**, 347, 352, **353**, 390
iron industry
   after Civil War, 386—387
   Great Lakes, 370, 372—373, 629—630c
Isherwood, Benjamin F., **349**
Iwo Jima, 577

J

J. Pierpont Morgan, **376**
Jack, **136**
Jacobsen, Antonio, 382c
Japan
   assaults on during World War II, 562—565
   immigrants from, 462—463
   increasing power before World War II, 515
   navy, 542, 546—547, 555—556
   submarines during World War II, 567
   U.S. trade with, 326c, 327—328c
Jarvis, John Wesley, 169c, 215c, 227c, 230c
Java, **219—220**, 221
Jay, John, 182
Jefferson, 161—163
Jefferson, Thomas
   Louisiana Purchase, 192—193
   trade embargo, 199, 201, 206—207, 211
   views of maritime commerce, 181—182
   war with Tripoli, 190—191
Jenkins's Ear, War of, 79, 82
Jews in America, establishment of, 62c
Jocelyn, Nathaniel, 288c
Johnson, Robert, *Nova Britannia*, 37c
Johnston, Frances Benjamin, 464c
Johnston, J.S., 446c
Johnston, William, 93
Jones, John Paul, 147—154
Jordan, Newell B., 385
Jupiter, **519**

K

Kamehameha I, 163—163
Kearsarge, **350**, 351
ketch, description of, 64
Kimball, Sumner I., 410
King, Ernest J., **555**, 556—559
King George's War, 83, 85
Kipling, Rudyard, *Captains Courageous*, 651
Knights of Labor, 421—422
Knowles Riot, 85
Knox, Frank, 575
Koko Head, **391**
Korean War, 614c

L

labor, maritime
   after Civil War, 417, 421—426, 429
   prior to World War II, 543—545
   technology's effects on, 421
Lady Washington, 158—159
La Follette Seamen's Act, 425—426
Lake Janet, **500**
Land, Emory S., 541—542
landing ship tanks (LSTs), 572c
Lane, Fitz High, 241c
Langley, **519**
La Salle, Robert Cavelier, Sieur de, 58, **59**
Lastic, Clifton, **545**
Latin American trade, 285—287

latitude, early methods for determining, 177
Launching another Victory Ship, **500**
launchings, ship, **173**, 204, 441
Law, John, 60c
Law of the Sea, 625—626
Lawrence, George, 240
laws, establishment of maritime, 446
Leach, J., 641c
Ledyard, John, 158
Leitch, Thomas, 101c
letter-of-marque vessels, 83
Leviathan, **498, 510**
Levick, Edwin, 452c, 508c
Levy, Moses, **62**
Lewis, Ida, 427—428
Lexington, **147, 565**
Leyte Gulf, Battle of, 570, 572c
Liberty, 113
Liberty ships, 578—579
Library and Naval Records, Office of, 406
licensing American merchant vessels, 167
Life Line, The (Homer), **658**
Life-Saving Service, 411—412, 414—415
life-saving stations, 410c, 411
Lighthouse Board, 246
lighthouses
    establishment of, 174
    expansion in 1800s, 246
    first American, 75, **76**
    Lime Rock, 427—428
    Yaquina Head, 411
Lighthouse Service, 411c, 412—413
Lime Rock Lighthouse, 427—428
Lindsay, David, 93
liners, transatlantic, 6—7, 647
liquefied natural gas carriers (LNG), 610
Little Brewster Island, 75, **76**
Livingston, Robert R., 193, 202—204c
Lloyd's of London, 173
LNG (liquefied natural gas carriers), 610
lobster fishery, 399
locks. *See also* inland waterways
    Great Lakes, 429c
    Mississippi River, **631**
Loeffler, A., 463
Lois Ann, **631**
Long Beach as major seaport, 607—608
longitude, early methods for determining, 177
Los-Angeles as major seaport, 607—608
Louisbourg (Cape Breton Island), **82**
Louisiana Purchase, 5, 192—193
LSTs (landing ship tanks), 572c
Luce, Stephen B., 403, **404**, 405—407, 430
lumber industry, 367—368
Lusitania, 470

M

MacArthur, Douglas, 565, 570
Mace, William, 566c
Mackenzie, Alexander Slidell, 333
mackerel fishery, 259
Macon's Bill Number Two, 211
Madison, John, 212—213, 217
Magnuson Act, 632—33, 644
Maguire Act, 424—425
Mahan, Alfred Thayer, 407—**408**
mail service, steamship, 274, 297
Maine, 443c, 444
Mallory, Clifford, 527
Mallory, Stephen, 336—337
Mallory Line, 378
Manner of Their Fishing, The (White), **25**
Marblehead, 48—51, 86

Marianas Islands, 566, 570
Marine Hospital Service, 413
Marine School Act, 406
Maritime Commission, U.S., 541—542, 577—581
Maryland, **564**
Mary Powell, **244**
Mason, **514**
Massachusetts, **444**
Matraini, N., 135c
Maury, Matthew F., *Sailing Directions,* 332, 334
Mayer, J.P., 240
Maysville, **197**
McDougall, Alexander, 374—375
McFarlane, Duncan, 359c
Mediterranean, naval attack on, 559
Melville, Herman, 313—316, 354, 649
menhaden fishery, 395, 632c
mercantilism
    colonial break with Great Britain, 132—133
    replaced by naval focus in 1900s, 8
Mercator, Gerard, 35c
merchant marine. *See also* Navy, U.S.
    after World War I, 511
    after World War II, 591—597
    prior to Civil War, 317
    during World War I, 477—478, 493—501, 508—509
    during World War II, 581—583c, 587
Merchant Marine Act of 1936, 536, 541, 587, 594
Merchant Marine Act of 1970, 595—596
merchants, success of, 202, 205—206
Merchant Ship Sales Act of 1946, 591—592
meridian, prime, 416—417
Merrick, George B., 270
mess system (food), 445c
meteorology, development of, 431
Mexico
    trade during 1800s, 287
    U.S. war with in 1800s, 325c, 326—327
Mexico, Gulf of, 20—21
Miami, **341**
Midway, Battle of, 563—564
Mine Barrage, North Sea, 486, **487**
mining, seabed, 625—626
Mississippi River
    control of after Civil War, 347—348
    description of, 20—21
    exploration of, 58—59c
    increased use of, 532, 629—630
    locks, 631c
    navigational challenges, 246
    steamboat service to, 266
Missouri, 573, **577, 614**
Missouri River, steamboat service to, 266
Mitchell, William, 517
Moby-Dick (Melville), 649
Moffett, William A., **518**
Moll, Herman, 33c
Monitor, 352, **353**
Monomoy Light, **247**
Montardier, Alexander, 197c
Moore, J.H., *The New Practical Navigator,* 175—177
Morgan Line, 378
Morris, Richard V., 190—191
movies, hollywood maritime, 649—652
Muller, Enrique, 485
Munde, James C.W., 572c
Murmansk, 586
museums, American maritime, 662—663
Mutiny on the Bounty (Nordhoff and Hall), 650—651
Myers, William C., 332c
Myrick, Eliza Mitchell, **102**
Mystic, Civil War shipbuilding boom at, 358—359

N

Namouna, **439**

Nantucket
mariner's wives of, 102
as whaling center, 86—88, 179, 181

naphtha launches, 441

Napoleon
Continental war against, 222
expansionism plans, 192—193

Nashville, 358c

Native Americans
battles against Europeans, 43c
as first American mariners, 23—27
as traders of Pacific Northwest, **46,** 161—162
tribal fishing rights, 637

Nautical Almanac (Davis), 334

Nautilus, **569, 617**

Naval Academy, 332, 404c, 405

Naval Architects and Marine Engineers, Society of, 409

Naval Institute, U.S., 405—406

Naval Intelligence, Office of, 406

Naval War College, 404c, 406

navigation
celestial, 176
early books on, 175, 179
early use of maps, 35c
improvements after Civil War, 415—417, 429

Navigation Acts, 61, 63, 76, 245

navigational aids, establishment of, 174

Navy, Japanese Imperial, 555—556

Navy, Royal. *See also* Great Britain
compared to U.S. navy, 522—523
impressment of U.S. sailors, 85, 196—199c
Normandy invasion, 562
during Revolutionary War, 143—146
during War of 1812, 212—222
during World War I, 479—482, 484

Navy, U.S.. *See also* Coast Guard, U.S.; merchant marine
after Civil War, 387—389, 403—409
after Revolutionary War, 157—158, 185
after World War I, 511—514
after World War II, 612—613
aviation service, 447, 452c, 512, 517—519, 559
during Civil War, 337—342, 344—348, 354, 356, **361,** 365
compared to Royal Navy, 522—523
establishment of, 7
expansion of, 441—442, 447—449, 542, 546—547
future of, 619—620
integration of, 575—576, **583,** 617—618
modern, 615, 618—619
prior to Civil War, 324—326, 331
reductions in, 512—514, 521—522, 598, 612—613
during Revolutionary War, 130—132, 141—142, 146, 154
141
steam power, 327—330, 349c
during Tripoli War, 190—191, **193,** 233c
United Nations influence on, 611—612
during War of 1812, 212—222
during war with Mexico, 325c
women in, 483, 618
during World War I, 473, 478—481, 484
during World War II, 553—573, 577, **588**

Negro Seamen Acts, The, 289

Neosho, 564

Neptune, 160, **383**

Nevada, **564**

New American Practical Navigator (Bowditch), 177—179

New Bedford, **87**

Newbury, Edward H., 438

New England
cotton mills, 230
fishing industry, 47, 85—86, 258—259, 264—265, 533, 535

map of in 1600s, **44**
maritime economy in 1700s, 56
during Revolutionary War, 144—146
whaling industry, 86—88, 179, 181

New England Restraining Act, 122—123

Newfoundland, 29, **51**

Newman, Andy, 648c

New Orleans
Louisiana Purchase, 192—193
as major seaport in 1800s, 194—**195,** 257, **319**
as major seaport in 1900s, 606—607

Newport, Christopher, 42

Newport (RI), 439

New Practical Navigator, The (Moore), 175—177

New York
as declining seaport in late 1900s, 602—606
as major seaport in early 1900s, **423,** 602
as major seaport in 1600s, 74
as major seaport in 1700s, 72, **73,** 74, **75,** 122—**123, 142, 168**
as major seaport in 1800s, 206, 250, 277—282, 320

New York, **485**

Nieuw Amsterdam, establishment of, 45—46

Non-Intercourse Act, 211

Nordhoff, Charles, 319, 650—651

Norling, Lisa, 302

Normandy invasion, 560—562

Norse, expansionism of, 27—31

North, Lord Frederick, 114—115

North America, discovery of, 29—32

North Michigan Transportation Company, 438

North Pole, exploration of, 434—435

North River Steam Boat, 203

North Sea Mine Barrage, 486, **487**

North Star, **439**

Northwest coast
fur trade, 158, 160—162
settlements, **27**

Norway, Greenland's dependence on, 31

Nova Britannia (Johnson), 37

nuclear submarines, 613—614, **619**

O

O'Brien, Dennis, 275

ocean liners, 6—7, 647

octants, **176,** 177

oil, whale, 34—35. *See also* whaling industry

Okinawa, 577

Oklahoma, **564**

Old Dominion Mariner, **595**

Old Ironsides. *See Constitution*

Olmsted, Frederick Law, 270

Olympia, **445**

Operation Desert Shield, 616

Operation Overlord, 560—562

Oregon, **446**

Oscar II, 490—491

Ottavicini, I., 135c

otter trawls, 533

oyster industry, 398—399, 634

P

Pacific Ocean
description of coastline, 21
fishing industry, 634, 636
maritime activity in 1800s, 282—284, 335—336c
Native Americans of Pacific Northwest, **46,** 161—162
naval presence prior to World War II, 546—547
survey of, 431
U.S. commercial presence in, 158—163
whaling industry, 181
during World War II, 562—573, 577, **588**

packets, 278—281, 309—310

Palmer, John, 138—139

Palmer, Nathaniel B., 290—291, **292**

Panama Canal, 434, 454—461, **520,** 530
Panay, **547**
Parks, Gordon, 535
Patapsco, **225**
Peale, Charles Willson, 131c
Peale, Rembrandt, 233c
Pearl Harbor, 519, 552, 555, **564**
Pearson, Richard, 152—153
Peary, Robert E., 434—435
Pelham, John, 116c
Penn, William, 46
Pennell, Joseph, *Launching another Victory Ship,* 500c
Pennsylvania, **452**
Pennsylvania, settlement of, 46—47
Pennsylvania Sun, **557**
Penobscot Bay, 144—145, **146**
Pepperrell, William, Jr., **80, 81**—82
Pepperrell, William, Sr., 81
Perry, Matthew Calbraith, **326,** 327—328c, 329
Perry, Oliver Hazard, **230**—231
Persian Gulf War, 615—617
Peterson, John E.C., 383c
Peterson, William N., 359
Philadelphia
  as major seaport in 1600s, 46—47, 71
  as major seaport in 1700s, 71, 74, **189**
Philadelphia, **183,** 191
Philippine Islands
  U.S. acquisition of, 452—453
  during World War II, 570, 572c
Phoenix, **142,** 204, **205, 369**
Pilgrims, 42
pilots, steamboat, 269
Pinckney, Charles Cotesworth, 182—183
pinnaces, 64
pirates
  female, **58**
  naval activity against, 324
  raids by, 57—58c
Pitt, William, 82—83
Plantation Act of 1764, 111—112
Plymouth colony, 42
Pocahontas, 43c
Pocock, Nicholas, 99c, 219c
Polaris Expedition, 434—435c
pollution, marine, 638—639, 644, 647
Pook's turtles, 347c
Port Act, 119
Port Blakely, **368**
Porter, David D., 228c, 348
Portsmouth (NH), **134**
Post, Charles A., 340
powerboats
  modern, 645
  racing of, 538—539
Pownall, Thomas, 73
Pratt, William V., 521—522
Preble, Edward, 191, **192**
prime meridian, adoption of, 416—417
privateering
  during Revolutionary War, 136, 140—141
  during 1700s, 83—85
  during War of 1812, 224—226
prohibition at sea, 525—526
Promised Land, **632**
PTs (patrol torpedo boats), **571**
Purdy, J.E., 408c
Puritans
  as fishermen, 47
  migration to North America, 39, 43
Q
Quebec, **155**

Queen City, **376**
Quistconck, **505**
Quonset Huts, 572
R
racing
  crew, 538
  powerboat, 538—539
  schooner, 540
  yacht, 14, 310—311, 439—440, 537—538
Racing on the Delaware (Eakins), **440**
Rackam, "Calico Jack," 58c
railroads
  effects on marine transportation, 376—378
  in New England in 1800s, 251
Rambler, **226**
Randle, C., 145c
Ranger, 149, 152
Rattlesnake, **224**
Read, Mary, **58**
Reagan, Ronald, 596—597
Reaper, **173**
recreation, maritime
  after Civil War, 417, 437—438
  boating, 537—540, 645—647, 654
  development of, 14—15, 310
  during 1900s, 645—648
Reid, Samuel, **227**
Reinagle, H., 232c
religion
  churches for seamen, 254
  role in European emigration to North America, 39
Reprisal, 146
resorts, waterfront, 644
resuscitation of drowning victims, 174
Return of the Mayflower (Gribble), **481**
Revenge, 137—139
Revenue-Cutter Service, 169, 211, 413—415
Revenue-Marine Division, 410—413
Revere, Paul, 115c—116c
Revolutionary War
  effects on commerce, 119, 132—134
  end of, 156
  France's role, 146—147
  Great Britain's role, 143—146
  New England during, 144—146
  privateering during, 136, 140—141
  U.S. Navy during, 130—132, 141—142, 146, 154
rice as major export, 74
Riddell, George, 501
Ritter, William E., 432—433
rivers. *See* Hudson River; inland waterways; Mississippi River; Missouri River; St. Lawrence River
R.J. Pfeiffer, **601**
Roach, John, 393
Roads, John, 48—51
Robalo, **567**
Rodney, George, 134—135
Rolph, Annie M., 391c
Roorda, Eric, 460, 624
Roosevelt, Franklin D., **489,** 552, **554**
Roosevelt, Theodore, 447—449, **453,** 457
Ropes, John, 136c
RoRo Ships, **618**
Rose, **142**
Rosenfeld, Morris, **496**
Roux, Antoine, 198c
Roux, Frederic, 243c
rowing, college, 538
rum-rumming, 525—526
Russell, Thomas, 255c
Russia, 584—586
S

Sailing Directions (Maury), 332, 334
sailing vessels. *See also* ships, types of
  compared to steam, 304—305, 327—328, 386
  as legacy of maritime past, 658—659
  modern, 645
  during 1800s, 371, 392
  wooden, 309—310, 312, 317, 384, 389—390
sailmakers, description of, 186—189
sailors. *See* seamen
sailortowns, 252—255
salaries, seamens', 421—424, 543—545
Salem (MA), **203**
salmon fishery
  Alaskan, 13c, 533—535
  growth after Civil War, 398
Samuel, **171**
San Francisco as major seaport in 1800s, 273—274
Santee, **405**
Saratoga, **520**
Saucy Jack, 226
Savannah, **609**
Sawyer, Herbert, 217
SC-414, **486**
Schetky, John Christian, 229c
schools, marine, 404c, 405—406, 409
schooners
  description of, 64
  types of, 368, 540
science, maritime, 430—435
Scourge, **224**
Scripps, Edward Wyllis, 432—433
Seabees, 572
Sea-Land container terminal, **603**
sealing industry, 290, 400—401
Seaman's Bride, **308**
seamen
  abuses/discipline of, 331—332c, 423—425
  benevolence societies, 252—255
  black, 288—289, 351, 422c, 426, 574—576, **583**
  colonial American, 106—109, **118**
  impressment by Royal Navy, 196—198
  typical early 1800s, 196
  view of women, 293—296
  wages, 421—424
Seamen's Protection Certificates, 198, **289**
seaports
  after Revolutionary War, 172, 202
  British tax laws effects on, 111—113
  commercial specialization of, 249—250
  growth of, 69—71, 74—75, 104—105, 172, 237
  importance of, 657—658
  largest modern, 630
  privateering's effects on, 141
  during 1600/1700s, 69—71, 74—75, 104—105, 205
  during 1800s, 237, **321**
Seawolf, **619**
segregation in U.S. Navy, 574—575
Semmes, Raphael, **343**
Serapis, 149—150, 152, **153**
Serres, Dominic, 142c
Seven Years' War, 84—85
sextants, 176c, 177
Sexton, Mark, 78c, 81c
shallops, **51,** 64
Shannon, **229**
Sheffield, Isaac, 296c
shellfish industry, 259, 264—265, 398
Shenandoah, 365
shipbuilding. *See also* ships, types of; shipyards
  after Civil War, 389—393
  after Revolutionary War, 172
  after World War I, 528

during Civil War, 358—359
colonial, 64—67
major centers, 310
during War of 1812, 228
wooden, 309—310, 312, 317, 384, 389—390
during World War I, 498—499
shipowners, economic challenges of, 172—173
Shipping Act of 1916, 496
Shipping Board, U.S.
  abolishment of, 536
  labor conflicts, 543—545
  maintenance of trade routes, 527
  role of, 496—498
shipping industry. *See* commerce, maritime
ships, launching of, **173,** 204, 441
ships, licensing of, 167
ships, types of. *See also* sailing vessels; steam-powered vessels
  battle, 85, 442—443
  clipper, 223, 306, **308,** 309—310, **311**
  colonial, **66—67**
  concrete, 499
  cruise, 603, 647—648
  ironclad, 336—337, **338,** 347, 352, 390
  modern, 609—611, 618—19, 645
  nuclear-powered, 610
  RoRo, 618
  schooners, 64, 223, 243c, 368, 540
  sloops, 64, 539c, 588c
  steel, 390, 393
  Victory, 579—580
  wooden, 309—310, 312, 317, 384, 389—390
shipwrecks, 174, **175**
shipyards
  after World War II, 596
  Hog Island, 502—505
  during World War I, 498—499
  during World War II, 579
shrimp fishery, 634
Sicily, naval attack on, 559
signals, first international code of, 417
Sims, William S., 480—481, 484, **489,** 492—493
slave coast, African, 91c, **92**
slavery
  American resistance to, 288
  effects on income distribution, 242
  importance in maritime history, 659
  promise of emancipation, 346c
slave trade
  on Cape Verde Islands, 467
  Continental Association's banning of, 121
  cotton's effects on, 185, 190
  dependence on sugar industry, 52c
  naval activity against, 324—325
  during 1600/1700s, 88—93
  during 1800s, 287
Sloan, Edward W., 652
sloops
  description of, 64
  J-class, 538c
  Star Class, 539c
Smalls, Robert, **346**
Smibert, John, 81c
Smith, James, **296,** 307c
Smith, John, 42, 44c
Smith, Thomas, **61**
Smith, Venture, 89
Smith, William, 26c
smuggling
  alcohol during 1900s, 525—526
  due to trade embargoes, 207, 211
  on Mississippi River, 223

during 1600/1700s, 68
Somers, 333
Soo Locks, 372—373
South Carolina, **198**
Soviet Union, 613, 615
Spain
  control of Caribbean in 1600s, 57
  exploration of North America, 29, 32—33, 36, 38, **95**
  trade with U.S. in 1700s, 134
Spanish-American War, 443c, 444—445
species, marine, colonization of, 640—643
sponge-gathering, 395, 398
Spooner, Libby, 300—302
Spray, **419,** 420
St. Eustatius, 134, **135**
St. Helena, **99**
St. Lawrence River, canalization of, 531—532
St. Louis
  as major port in 1800s, 257, **258**
  steamboat service to, 266
Stamp Act, 109, 112—113
Statia, 134, **135**
Steamboat Inspection Service, 413
Steam Engineering, Bureau of, **349**
steam-powered vessels. *See also* ships, types of
  Chesapeake Bay, 256
  coexistence with railroads, 378—379
  compared to sailing, 304—305, 327—328, 386, 391
  dangers for, 217
  development of, 202—205c
  engines, 392
  financing of, 268
  government regulations on, 268, 271
  Great Lakes, 373—375
  on inland waterways, 204, **265,** 266—267, **272,** 373—375, 380
  jobs on, 269—270
  modern, 610
  New England, 250—251
  oceangoing, 297, 303, 306
  regional designs of, 266—267
  during 1800s, 245, 250—251, 256, 266, 292, 297, 351, 373—375
  schooners, 368
  sinking of, **307**
  use by navy, 326—330, 349c
  whaleback, 374—375
Stebbins, Nathaniel L., 371c
steel industry, 373
steel ships, 390, 393
Steenwyck, Cornelis, **79**
Steerage, The (Stieglitz), 7c
Steers, George, 310
Steichen, Edward, 568c
Stets, Mary Anne, 281, 283c, 383c, 395c, 401c, 511c
Stevens, John, 202, 204—205c
Stewart, Julius, 439c
Stewart J. Cort, **630**
Stich, Jennifer M., 629c
Stieglitz, Alfred, *The Steerage,* 7c
Stine, Anne, 31
Stoddert, Benjamin, 184—185
stone schooners, 368
Stonington (CT), 137—138
strikes, maritime laborer, 421, 543—545
Strout, Robert Bruce, **294**
Stuart, Alexander Charles, 380c
submarine chasers, 485—486, 489
submarines
  development of, 143, 447, 451c
  man-powered Confederate, 354
  naval improvements to, 515
  nuclear, 613—614, **619**
  Robert Fulton's experiments, 204c

during World War I, 475, 479, 487
during World War II, 567—569
subsidies, government shipping, 387, 536, 541
Suez Canal, 383—384
Sugar Act, 111—113
sugar industry, **52,** 53, 88, 98
Sultana, **360**
swordfish populations, 634
T
Talbot, Silas, 184c
Tanner, Benjamin, 216c
Tariff Act, 168
taxes, maritime, 111—113, 166—168
Taylor, C.N., 410c
Taylor, Edward T., **255**
tea
  British, 114—117
  Chinese, 168
technology, advancements on maritime
  after World War II, 593
  Coast Guard, 620—621
  containerization of cargo, 599—601, **603,** 604, 607—608
  effects on laborers, 421
  fishing industry, 393—395, 398—399, 533—535
  naval, 442, 514—515, 618—619
  shipbuilding industry, 389—393
  vessel design, 609—611
  whaling/sealing industries, 400—401
  during World War I, 485—486, 492
  during World War II, 558
Tennessee, **564**
textile manufacturing, 228, 230
Thomas W. Lawson, 371
Thompson, George, 474c
Ticonderoga, 388
timekeeping, international system for, 416
tobacco industry
  Chesapeake Bay, 45, 63c, 68, 74, 108c
  during Revolutionary War, 134
Tocqueville, Alexis de, 239—240
tonnage, measurement of, 367
Tonnage Act, 167
Tontine Coffee House, **168**
torpedo boats (PTs), **571**
torpedoes
  Civil War, 357c
  development of, 337
  World War II, 569
Townshend Act, 113
Tracy, Benjamin E., 442—444
trade. *See also* commerce, maritime
  embargoes, 199, 201, 206—207, 211—213, 217
  routes, **127, 321,** 627
trawl lines, 533
Treasury Department, U.S.
  maritime activities of, 409—415
Treaty of Amity and Commerce, 133—134
Treaty of Paris, 156
Tripoli, U.S. war with, 190—191, **193,** 233c
Trowbridge, John T., 270
Tryal, **142**
Tudor, Frederic, 241
tuna fish populations, 633—634
Turtle, 143
Twain, Mark, 269—270
U
U-boats, German, 478, 480, 486—487, 492—493, 557c, 558
Ulysses, **175**
umiaks, **25**
underwater sound devices, 485
Union Navy, 339—342, 344—348, 351
unions, maritime, 421—422, 543—545

United Nations
  call for modern international order, 625—626
  influence on navy, 611—612
United States, 215, **216, 594**

V

Vaterland, **498**
Verrazano, Giovanni da, **34,** 35—36
Vestal, **564**
Vickers, Daniel, 51, 263
Victory ships, 579—580
Vietnam War, 621
Virginia, 352, **459**

W

Waddell, Anne Kirten, **70**
Waddell, John, **70**
wages, seamens', 421—424, 543—545
Wallace, James, 142c
Walters, Samuel, 279c
Wampanoag, 351
wampum, 23
War of 1812, 227
  end of, 231—233
  events leading to, 212
  naval battles, 212—223, 227, 229c
  privateering, 224—226
  shipbuilding, 228
wars. *See also* Civil War; Revolutionary War; War of 1812;
  World War I; World War II
  Algiers, 157
  Cold, 613
  Jenkins's Ear, 79, 82
  King George's, 83, 85
  Persian Gulf, 615—617
  Seven Years, 84—85
  Spanish-American, 443c, 444—445
  Tripoli, 190—191, **193,** 233c
  U.S. quasi war with France, 182—183
  U.S. with Mexico, 325c, 326—327
  Vietnam, 621
War Shipping Administration (WSA)
  during World War II, 581—584, 587
Washington, George
  as Chief of Continental Army, 129—130
  maritime commerce, 181—182
  Yorktown victory, 156
Washington Naval Conference, 513—515
Watch Hill Light, **438**
waterfronts, modern, 644—645
Waterman, C.E., 449c
waterways, inland. *See* inland waterways
Watson, Brook, **107**
weather, ocean effects on, 13
Webb Institute of Naval Architecture, 409
Welles, Gideon, 344
West Indies
  American trade with, 170—171
  during 1800s, 285—286
  sugar exports, 53
West Virginia, **564**
westward expansion, 273
whaleback steamships, 374—375
whaling industry
  after Civil War, 400—401
  after Revolutionary War, 179
  children on voyages, 291—292
  early colonial, 86—88
  hunting description, 13
  Nantucket, 86—88, 179, 181
  New Bedford, **87**
  New England, 86—88, 179, 181
  Pacific Ocean, 181
  during 1500s, 34—35
  during 1800s, 289
  technological advancements, 400—401
Whipple, Seth Arca, 372c
Whitcombe, Thomas, 147c
White, John, 25c, 28c
White-Peterson, Claire, 280c, 477, 483
Wilkes, Charles, 335, **336**
Wilkinson, John, 342
Williams, Dwayne E., 468
Williams, Eric, 93
Wilson, Woodrow
  Coast Guard policy, 523—524
  expansion of merchant marine, 493—501, 508—509, 524
  maritime policy, 478, 501, 506—509
  during World War I, 465, 469—473
winds
  Gulf Stream, 125
  primary prevailing, 21—22
Winslow, John A., **350**
Wollaston, John, 70c
women, maritime
  influence of on shipboard culture, 291—295
  integration into U.S. Navy, 483, 576, 618
  roles in maritime industries, **400,** 426—429, 635
  during wartime, 578c, 581
  as wives of mariners, 102, 298—302
Wood, William, 25
wooden shipbuilding, 309—310, 312, 317, 384, 389—390
World War I
  commerce during, 480, 494—496, 524
  convoys during, 492—493
  Germany's role, 469—473, 479—480, 487
  Great Britain's role, 469—470, 474, 479—482, 484
  merchant marine's role, 477—478, 493—501, 508—509
  shipbuilding during, 498—499
  Shipping Board, 496—498
  submarines, 475, 479, 487
  technological advancements, 485—486, 492
  U.S. Navy during, 473, 478—481, 484
  U.S. neutrality, 465, 469
  Woodrow Wilson's role, 465, 469—473
World War II
  Atlantic Ocean activities, 553—562
  convoys during, 568, 584—586, 589
  end of, 577
  Germany's role, 556—557
  Japan's role, 562—565, 567
  merchant marine's role, 581—583c, 587
  Normandy invasion, 560—562
  overview, 551
  Pacific Ocean activities, 562—573, 577, **588**
  Philippine Islands during, 570, 572c
  shipyards during, 579
  submarines, 567—569
  technological advancements, 558
  torpedoes, 569
  U.S. Navy during, 553—573, 577, **588**
  WSA (War Shipping Administration), 581—584, 587
WSA (War Shipping Administration)
  during World War II, 581—584, 587
Wyoming, **370**

Y

yacht racing, 14, 310—311, 439—440, 537—538
Yamakaze, **569**
Yamamoto, Isoroku, 563
Yaquina Head Lighthouse, **411**
Young Brutus, **243**
Young Teaser, 224

Z

Zaragoza, Ignacio Moreles, 461
Zerbe, William H., 430
Zocchi, G., 39C

AMERICA AND THE SEA